Financial Aid for Persons with Disabilities and Their Families 2018 - 2020

Fourteenth Edition

Gail A. Schlachter
R. David Weber

A Listing of Scholarships, Fellowships, Grants-in-Aid, and Other Sources of Free Money Available Primarily or Exclusively to Persons with Disabilities or Members of Their Families, Plus a Set of Six Indexes: Program Title, Sponsoring Organization, Residency, Tenability, Subject, and Deadline Date

Formerly Published as *Financial Aid for the Disabled and Their Families*

AdmitHub
Boston, Massachusetts

AdmitHub
Harvard Innovation Launch Lab
114 Western Ave.
Boston, MA 02134
(617) 575-9369
E-mail: rsp@admithub.com
Visit our web site: www.admithub.com

Manufactured in the United States of America

Contents

Foreword **5**

Introduction **7**

    Why This Directory Is Needed 7
    What's Unique about the Directory 7
    What's Excluded 8
    Sample Entry 9
    What's Updated 10
    How the Directory Is Organized 8
    How to Use the Directory 10
    Plans to Update the Directory 11
    Other Related Publications 11
    Acknowledgements 11

About the Authors **14**

**Financial Aid Programs for
Persons with Disabilities & Their Families** **15**

    Any Disability **17**
        Undergraduates 19
        Graduate Students 59
    Visual Disabilities **101**
        Undergraduates 103
        Graduate Students 135
    Hearing Disabilities **157**
        Undergraduates 159
        Graduate Students 164
    Physical/Orthopedic Disabilities **169**
        Undergraduates 171
        Graduate Students 187
    Other Disabilities/Disorders **195**
        Undergraduates 197
        Graduate Students 268
    Families of the Disabled **293**
        Undergraduates 295
        Graduate Students 371

Indexes **395**

    Program Title Index 397
    Sponsoring Organization Index 425
    Residency Index 435
    Tenability Index 443
    Subject Index 451
    Calendar Index 463

About Dr. Gail Schlachter and Reference Service Press

Dr. Gail Ann Schlachter (1943-2015), original founder of Reference Service Press, was working as a librarian in the mid-1970s when she recognized that women applying for college faced significant obstacles finding information about financial aid resources designed to help them. This challenge inspired her to publish her ground-breaking book, Directory of Financial Aids for Women, in 1977. The book's success prompted additional financial aid directories for other underserved communities, including the present volume for Hispanic Americans.

By 1985, the business had become so successful that she left her job as a publishing company executive to run her company, Reference Service Press, full-time. Over the years, the company's offerings expanded to over two dozen financial aid titles covering many different types of students—law students, business students, students studying abroad, and many more. The company's success was driven by its database of tens of thousands of financial aid programs, laboriously hand-built over the decades and kept current to exacting specifications. In 1995, Reference Service Press once again broke new ground by launching one of the first-ever searchable electronic databases of financial aid resources (initially through America Online). For more background about the founding and success of Reference Service Press, see Katina Strauch's 1997 "Against the Grain" interview with Dr. Schlachter, available at http://docs.lib.purdue.edu/cgi/viewcontent.cgi?article=2216&context=atg.

Dr. Schlachter was also a major figure in the library community for nearly five decades. She served: as reference book review editor for RQ (now Reference and User Services Quarterly) for 10 years; as president of the American Library Association's Reference and User Services Association; as editor of the Reference and User Services Association Quarterly; seven terms on the American Library Association's governing council; and as a member of the association's Executive Board at the time of her death. She was posthumously inducted into the California Library Association Hall of Fame. The University of Wisconsin School of Library and Information Studies named Dr. Schlachter an "Alumna of the Year," and she was recognized with both the Isadore Gilbert Mudge Citation and the Louis Shores/Oryx Press Award.

Dr. Schlachter will be remembered for how her financial aid directories helped thousands of students achieve their educational and professional dreams. She also will be remembered for her countless contributions to the library profession. And, as an American Library Association Executive Board resolution from June 2015 says, she will be remembered, "most importantly, for her mentorship, friendship, and infectious smile." Yet, despite her impressive lifetime of professional accomplishments, Dr. Schlachter always was most proud of her family, including her husband Stuart Hauser, her daughter Dr. Sandy Hirsh (and Jay Hirsh) and son Eric Goldman (and Lisa Goldman), and her grandchildren Hayley, Leah, Jacob, and Dina.

Introduction

WHY THIS DIRECTORY IS NEEDED

With a total population of more than 50 million, people with disabilities constitute America's largest (and fastest growing) "minority" group. Each year, billions of dollars in financial aid are set aside to assist persons with disabilities, along with members of their families. But, how can these individuals find out about the available funding?

While numerous print and online listings have been prepared to identify and describe general financial aid opportunities (those open to all segments of society), none of those resources have ever covered more than a small portion of the programs aimed primarily or exclusively at individuals with disabilities or their family members. That's why Gail A. Schlachter and R. David Weber biennially issue *Financial Aid for Persons with Disabilities and Their Families* (formerly published as *Financial Aid for the Disabled and Their Families)*, which identifies billions of dollars set aside each year specifically for members of these groups to support study, research, creative activities, travel, career development, emergencies, and much more.

WHAT'S UNIQUE ABOUT THE DIRECTORY

Financial Aid for Persons with Disabilities and Their Families is the first and only publication to identify and provide comprehensive information on the more than 1,200 programs established to provide funding to those with physical, sensory, or other disabilities, as well as to their family members. The listings in this book cover every major field of study, are sponsored by more than 600 different private and public agencies and organizations, and are open to all levels of applicants—from high school and college students to professionals, postdoctorates, and others. And, not only does *Financial Aid for Persons with Disabilities and Their Families* provide the most comprehensive coverage of available funding, it also displays the most informative program descriptions (on the average, more than twice the detail found in any other listing).

In addition to this extensive and focused coverage, the 2018-2020 edition of the directory offers several other unique features. First, all funding described here is substantial; every program offers at least $1,000, and many award $10,000 or more. Even better, all of this is "free" money; not one dollar will ever need to be repaid (provided, of course, recipients meet the program requirements). Another plus: you can take the money awarded by these funding programs to any number of locations. Unlike other financial aid directories, which often list large numbers of scholarships available only to students enrolled at one specific school, all of the entries in this book are "portable." And, many of the programs listed here have never been covered in other financial aid directories. So, even if you have searched elsewhere, you will want to look here for new leads.

Here's another advantage: unlike other funding directories, which generally follow a straight alphabetical arrangement, this one groups entries by both type of disability (e.g., hearing impairments, visual impairments) and academic level (undergraduate and graduate)—making it easy for a user to search for appropriate programs. The same convenience is offered in the indexes, where the entries are also subdivided by disability and academic level. With this unique arrangement, users with one set of characteristics (e.g., persons with hearing impairments) will be able to find all programs set aside specifically for them—and not be distracted or have to waste time sorting through descriptions of programs intended for individuals with other types of disabilities.

In fact, everything about the directory has been designed to make your search for funding as easy as possible. You can identify programs not only by recipient group and type of funding, but also by program title, sponsoring organizations, where you live, where you want to spend the money, individual subject areas, and even deadline date (so fundseekers working within specific time constraints can locate programs that are still open). Plus, you'll find all the information you need to decide if a program is a match for you: purpose, eligibility requirements, financial data, duration, special features, limitations, number awarded, and application date. You even get fax numbers, toll-free numbers, e-mail addresses, and web site locations (when available), along with complete contact information, to make your requests for applications proceed smoothly.

Reviewers have consistently praised the unique value of *Financial Aid for Persons with Disabilities and Their Families.* For example, *Disability Resources Monthly* called the directory a "must-have." *College Financial Aid* agreed and, because of its "wealth of information," gave the directory its "four-star" (highest) rating. *American Reference Books Annual* predicted that "this directory will assuredly be a major reference tool in most libraries" and labeled it "an essential purchase." The directory has been chosen as one of the "best reference books of the year" by *Library Journal* and as one of the "outstanding reference books of the year" by the New York Public Library, which commended Reference Service Press for its "excellent contribution in an area of publishing where quality is at a premium."

WHAT'S EXCLUDED

While this book is intended to be the most comprehensive source of information on funding available to persons with disabilities and members of their families, there are some types of programs we've specifically excluded from the directory:

- *Awards open equally to all segments of the population.* Only funding opportunities open primarily or exclusively to persons with disabilities, or members of their families, are covered here.

- *Programs administered by individual academic institutions solely for their own students.* The directory identifies "portable" programs—ones that can be used at any number of schools. Financial aid administered by individual schools specifically for their own students is not covered. Write directly to the schools you are considering to get information on their offerings.

- *Services,* such as training and counseling, that do not involve actual financial assistance to the disabled person. To obtain information on those benefits, check with the appropriate federal, state, local, or private social service agency in your area.

- *Nonmonetary benefits,* such as special license plates for persons with disabilities. To obtain information, check with the appropriate agency in your area.

- *Money for study or research outside the United States.* Since there are comprehensive and up-to-date directories that describe the funding available for study and research abroad, only programs that support study, research, or other activities in the United States are covered here.

- *Restrictive programs,* where the funds are generally available only to a limited geographic area (specific cities or counties only), or in limited amounts (under $1,000).

- *Money that must be repaid.* The focus here is on "free money." If a program requires repayment or charges interest, it's not listed. Now you can find out about billions of dollars in aid and know (if you meet the program requirements) that not one dollar of that will ever need to be repaid.

WHAT'S UPDATED

The preparation of each new edition of *Financial Aid for Persons with Disabilities and Their Families* involves extensive updating and revision. To insure that the information included is both reliable and current, the editors at Reference Service Press 1) reviewed and updated all relevant programs covered in the previous edition of the directory, 2) collected information on all programs open to persons with disabilities and their families that were added to Reference Service Press' funding database since the last edition of the directory, and then 3) searched extensively for new program leads in a variety of sources, including printed directories, news reports, journals, newsletters, house organs, annual reports, and sites on the Internet. Our policy is to write program descriptions only from information supplied in print or online by the sponsoring organization (no information is ever taken from secondary sources). If that information could not be found, we sent up to four letters or e-mails (followed by up to three telephone inquiries, if necessary) to those sponsors. Despite our best efforts, however, some sponsors still failed to respond and, as a result, their programs are not included in this edition of the directory.

The 2018-2020 edition of the directory completely revises and updates the earlier biennial edition. Programs that have ceased operations have been dropped. Profiles of continuing programs have been rewritten to reflect operations as of late 2017; nearly 75% of these programs reported substantive changes in their locations, requirements (particularly application deadline), or benefits since the previous edition. In addition, hundreds of new entries have been added to the program section of the directory. The resulting list describes the more than 1,200 biggest and best sources of free money available to persons with disabilities or members of their families.

HOW THE DIRECTORY IS ORGANIZED

Financial Aid for Persons with Disabilities and Their Families is divided into two separate sections: 1) a descriptive list of financial aid programs designed primarily or exclusively for persons with disabilities and their families and 2) a set of six indexes, each designed to target available funding.

Financial Aid Available to Persons with Disabilities and Their Families. The first section of the directory describes 1,201 funding opportunities aimed primarily or exclusively at persons with disabilities and members of their families. Entries in this section are grouped into the following six chapters, to make it easy to search for funding intended for members of specific disability groups (the list is based on a condensation of the disability categories established in Public Law 94-142, the Education for All Handicapped Children Act):

Any Disability: Funding for persons with any disability (programs that do not specify or restrict the type of eligible disability).

Visual Disabilities: Funding for individuals who have visual impairments (are partially sighted or blind), with or without correction.

Hearing Disabilities: Funding established specifically for individuals who have difficulty in receiving linguistic information, with or without amplification.

Physical/Orthopedic Disabilities: Funding established specifically for individuals with 1) a severe physical/orthopedic impairment caused by birth defects, diseases or disorders (e.g., multiple sclerosis), or other causes (e.g., accidents, amputations); or 2) a severe, chronic disability that was manifested before age 22 (e.g., spina bifida).

Other Disabilities/Disorders: Funding established specifically for individuals who have a communication disorder (such as stuttering or voice impairment), have a learning disability (including such conditions as brain injury and dyslexia), are emotionally disturbed, or have other chronic or acute health problems, such as cancer, tuberculosis, or hemophilia.

Families of the Disabled: Funding established specifically for the children, stepchildren, adopted children, grandchildren, parents, siblings, and other dependents or family members of persons with disabilities.

To make it easy to target available funding, each of these six chapters is then further divided into two sections for undergraduates and graduate studentss.

Within each section, entries are arranged alphabetically by program title. Some programs supply assistance to more than one specific group or supply more than one type of assistance, so those are listed in all relevant subsections. For example, since the Anne Smedinghoff Scholarship is for students who have been diagosed with cancer or have a parent or sibling with with cancer, the program is described in both the Other Disabilities/Disorders *and* Families of the Disabled chapters. Similarly, the Arizona Council of the Blind Scholarship Program is open to blind students at the undergraduate and graduate school level, so the program entry is included in both the Undergraduates *and* Graduate Students sections of the Visual Disabilities chapter.

We have designed each program profile to include information, when available, on program title, organization address, telephone number, fax and toll-free numbers, e-mail address, web site, purpose, eligibility, money awarded, duration, special features, limitations, number of awards, and application deadline (refer to the sample on page 7).

Each of the entries in the directory has been written using information provided by the sponsoring organizations (in print or online) through the end of 2017.

Indexes. To help you find the aid you need, we have constructed six indexes; these will let you access the listings by program title, sponsoring organization, residency, tenability, subject focus, and deadline date. These indexes use a word-by-word alphabetical arrangement. Note: numbers in the index refer to entry numbers, not to page numbers, in the book.

    Program Title Index. If you know the name of a particular funding program and want to find out where it is covered in the directory, use the Program Title Index. To assist you in your search, every program is listed by all its known names, former names, and abbreviations. Since one program can be listed in more than one category (e.g., a program providing assistance to persons with disabilities *and* to members of their family for either undergraduate *or* graduate study would be listed in four places), each entry number in the index has been coded to indicate both availability groups (e.g., families of the disabled) and academic level. By using this coding system, readers can easily identify the programs that match their financial needs and eligibility characteristics.

    Sponsoring Organization Index. This index provides an alphabetical listing of the 600+ organizations sponsoring financial aid programs represented in the first part of the directory. As in the Program Title Index, entry numbers have been coded to indicate both recipient group and funding type.

    Residency Index. Some programs listed in this book are restricted to persons with disabilities or their families in a particular state or region. Others are open to these individuals wherever they live. This index helps you identify programs available only to residents in your area as well as programs that have no residency requirements. To assist you further, we've also indicated the types of funding and intended recipient groups for the programs open to residents in each of the areas listed in the index.

    Tenability Index. This index identifies the geographic locations where the funding described in the directory may be used. Index entries (city, county, state, region) are arranged alphabetically and subdivided by funding type and recipient group. Use this index when you or your family members are looking for money to support research, study, or other activities in a particular geographic area.

    Subject Index. This index allows the reader to use more than 250 subject headings to access the financial aid programs designed primarily or exclusively for persons with disabilities and members of their families listed in the first part of the directory. Extensive "see" and "see also" references facilitate the search for appropriate financial aid programs.

    Calendar Index. Since most financial aid programs have specific deadline dates, some may have closed by the time you begin to look for funding. You can use the Calendar Index to determine which programs are still open. This index is arranged by recipient group and divided by funding type (e.g., scholarships, grants-in-aid) and month during which the deadline falls. Filing dates can and quite often do vary from year to year; consequently, this index should be used only as a guide for deadlines beyond 2018.

HOW TO USE THE DIRECTORY

Here are some tips to help you get the most out of the funding opportunities listed in this edition of *Financial Aid for Persons with Disabilities and Their Families.*

To Locate Funding Available to Individuals with Various Types of Disabilities. To bring programs with similar eligibility requirements together, the directory is organized into six type-of-disability chapters: Any Disability; Visual Disabilities; Hearing Disabilities; Physical/Orthopedic Disabilities; Other Disabilities/Disorders; and Families of the Disabled. If you have a disability, be sure to check not only the chapter that relates directly to you (e.g., Hearing Disabilities) but also the Disabilities in General chapter, where programs that do not specify or restrict the type of eligible disabilities are listed.

To Locate Programs for Particular Academic Level. If you are looking for programs for undergraduates or graduate students, you can browse through either of those sections in the directory without first consulting an index.

To Find Information on a Particular Financial Aid Program. If you know the name of a particular financial aid program, the type of funding offered by the program, and the intended recipients, then go directly to the appropriate category in the first section of the directory, where you will find the program profiles arranged alphabetically by title. If you are looking for a specific program and do not find it in the section you have checked, be sure to refer to the Program Title Index to see if it is covered elsewhere. To save time, always check the Program Title Index first if you know the name of a specific award but are not sure under which category it would be listed.

To Locate Programs Sponsored by a Particular Organization. The Sponsoring Organization Index makes it easy to determine groups that provide financial assistance to persons with disabilities and their families, or to identify specific financial aid programs offered by a particular organization. Each entry number in this index is coded to identify academic level and recipient group, so that you can quickly target appropriate entries.

To Browse Quickly Through the Listings. Turn to the type of funding and recipient categories that interest you and read the "Summary" paragraph in each entry. In seconds, you'll know if this is an opportunity that might apply to you. If it is, read the rest of the information in the entry to make sure you meet all of the program requirements before writing or going online for an application form. Please, save your time and energy. Don't apply if you don't qualify!

To Locate Programs Open to Residents of or Tenable in a Particular Area. The Residency Index identifies financial aid programs open to persons with disabilities or their family members who reside in a particular state, region, or country. The Tenability Index shows where the money can be spent. In both indexes, "see" and "see also" references are used liberally, to help you find the funding that's right for you, and index entries for a particular geographic area are divided by both funding type and recipient group. When using these indexes, always check the listings under the term "United States," since the programs indexed there have no geographic restrictions and can be used in any area.

To Locate Financial Aid Programs for Persons with Disabilities and Their Families in a Particular Subject Area. Turn to the Subject Index first if you are interested in identifying financial aid programs for individuals with disabilities or their family members that focus on a particular subject area. To help you target your search, the recipient group (e.g., hearing disabilities) and academic level (undergraduate and graduate student) are clearly identified. Extensive cross-references are provided.

To Locate Financial Aid Programs for Persons with Disabilities and Their Families by Deadline Date. If you are working with specific time constraints and want to weed out the financial aid programs whose filing dates you won't be able to meet, turn first to the Calendar Index and check the program references listed under the funding type, recipient group, and month of interest to you. Note: not all sponsoring organizations supplied deadline information; those programs are listed under the "Deadline not specified" entries in the index. To identify every relevant financial aid program, regardless of filing dates, read through all the entries in each of the recipient chapters (e.g., Any Disability) and funding categories that apply.

To Locate Financial Aid Programs Open to All Segments of the Population. Only programs available specifically to individuals with disabilities or their family members are listed in this publication.

However, there are thousands of other programs open equally to all segments of the population for which persons with disabilities and their families could apply. To identify those general programs, talk to your local librarian or financial aid officer.

PLANS TO UPDATE THE DIRECTORY

This volume, covering 2018-2020, is the fourteenth biennial edition of *Financial Aid for Persons with Disabilities and Their Families*. The next edition will cover the years 2020-2022 and will be released in the first half of 2020.

ACKNOWLEDGEMENTS

A debt of gratitude is owed all the organizations that contributed information to this edition of *Financial Aid for Persons with Disabilities and Their Families*. Their generous cooperation has helped to make this publication a current and comprehensive survey of awards.

SAMPLE ENTRY

(1) **[902-2Q]**

(2) **Joe Cleres Memorial Scholarships**

(3) New Outlook Pioneers
Attn: Scholarship Administrator
1801 California Street, 44th Floor
Denver, CO 80202
(800) 872-5995
E-mail: donLsage@gmail.com
Web: www.newoutlookpioneers.org

(4) **Summary** To provide financial assistance to students at all educational levels who are physically or mentally challenged.

(5) **Eligibility** This program is open to students with physical or mental disabilities who are enrolled or planning to enroll in high school, college, trade school, or graduate school. Applicants or their representatives must submit a 1-page essay describing how the student has met the challenge of his or her disability, including the severity of the disability. They may also include up to 1 page of supporting documentation, but photographs, audio or videotapes, display materials, films, or scrapbooks are not considered.

(6) **Financial data** Stipends range from $500 to $2,000. Funds are paid directly to the school for tuition support only.

(7) **Duration** 1 year.

(8) **Additional information** This program began in 1996 by Lucent Technologies as the New Outlook Scholarships for Students with Disabilities. The current name was adopted in 2005. New Outlook Pioneers is an affiliate of TelecomPioneers. Its members are employees and retirees of Lucent Technologies, Avaya Communication, and Agere.

(9) **Number awarded** Varies each year; recently, 16 were awarded: 1 at $2,000, 2 at $1,500, 3 at $1,000, 2 at $750, and 8 at $500.

(10) **Deadline** March of each year.

DEFINITION

(1) **Entry number:** Consecutive number that is given to each entry and used to identify the entry in the indexes.

(2) **Program title:** Title of scholarship, fellowship, grant-in-aid, or other source of free money described in the directory.

(3) **Sponsoring organization:** Name, address, telephone number, toll-free number, fax number, e-mail address, and/or web site (when information was supplied) for the organization sponsoring the program.

(4) **Summary:** Identifies the major program requirements; read the rest of the entry for additional detail.

(5) **Eligibility:** Describes qualifications required of applicants, application procedures, and selection process.

(6) **Financial data:** Financial details of the program, including fixed sum, average amount, or range of funds offered, expenses for which funds may and may not be applied, and cash-related benefits supplied (e.g., room and board).

(7) **Duration:** Period for which support is provided; renewal prospects.

(8) **Additional information:** Any unusual (generally nonmonetary) benefits, restrictions, or requirements associated with the program.

(9) **Number awarded:** Total number of recipients each year or other specified period.

(10) **Deadline:** The month by which applications must be submitted.

ABOUT THE AUTHORS

Dr. Gail Ann Schlachter (1943-2015) worked for more than three decades as a library manager, a library educator, and an administrator of library-related publishing companies. Among the reference books to her credit are the biennially-issued *Directory of Financial Aids for Women* and two award-winning bibliographic guides: *Minorities and Women: A Guide to Reference Literature in the Social Sciences* (which was chosen as an "outstanding reference book of the year" by *Choice)* and *Reference Sources in Library and Information Services* (which won the first Knowledge Industry Publications "Award for Library Literature"). She was the reference book review editor for *RQ* (now *Reference and User Services Quarterly)* for 10 years, was a past president of the American Library Association's Reference and User Services Association, was the editor-in-chief of the *Reference and User Services Association Quarterly,* and was serving her sixth term on the American Library Association's governing council at the time of her death. In recognition of her outstanding contributions to reference service, Dr. Schlachter was named the University of Wisconsin School of Library and Information Studies "Alumna of the Year" and was awarded both the Isadore Gilbert Mudge Citation and the Louis Shores/Oryx Press Award.

Dr. R. David Weber taught history and economics at Los Angeles Harbor College (in Wilmington, California) for many years and continues to teach history there as an emeritus professor. During his years at Harbor College, and earlier at East Los Angeles College, he directed the Honors Program and was frequently chosen the "Teacher of the Year." He has written a number of critically-acclaimed reference works, including *Dissertations in Urban History* and the three-volume *Energy Information Guide.* With Gail Schlachter, he is the author of Reference Service Press' *Directory of Financial Aid for Women* and a number of other financial aid titles, including the *College Student's Guide to Merit and Other No-Need Funding,* which was chosen as one of the "outstanding reference books of the year" by *Choice.*

Financial Aid Programs for Persons with Disabilities and Their Families

Any Disability ●

Visual Disabilities ●

Hearing Disabilities ●

Physical/Orthopedic Disabilities ●

Other Disabilities/Disorders ●

Families of the Disabled ●

Any Disability

Undergraduates   ●

Graduate Students   ●

Described here are 249 funding opportunities that do not specify or restrict the type of eligible disability. Of these, 127 are for undergraduates and 122 are for graduate students. All of this is "free" money. Not one dollar will need to be repaid (provided, of course, that recipients meet all program requirements). If you are looking for a particular program and don't find it in this section, be sure to check the Program Title Index to see if it is covered elsewhere in the directory.

Undergraduates

[1]
AAHD FREDERICK J. KRAUSE SCHOLARSHIP ON HEALTH AND DISABILITY

American Association on Health and Disability
Attn: Scholarship Committee
110 North Washington Street, Suite 328-J
Rockville, MD 20850
(301) 545-6140, ext. 206   Fax: (301) 545-6144
E-mail: scholarship@aahd.us
Web: www.aahd.us/initiatives/scholarship-program

Summary To provide financial assistance to undergraduate and graduate students who have a disability, especially those studying a field related to health and disability.

Eligibility This program is open to high school graduates who have a documented disability and are enrolled in an accredited 4-year college or university as a full-time undergraduate (sophomore or higher) or full- or part-time graduate student. Preference is given to students working on a degree in public health, disability studies, health promotion, audiology, special education, or other field related to health and disability. Along with their application, they must submit a 2-page personal statement that includes a personal history, educational and career goals, extracurricular activities, and reasons why they should be selected to receive this scholarship. U.S. citizenship or permanent resident status is required.

Financial data Stipends range up to $1,000.

Duration 1 year.

Additional data This program began in 2009.

Number awarded 3 each year.

Deadline November of each year.

[2]
AAPA PAST PRESIDENTS SCHOLARSHIP

American Academy of Physician Assistants
Attn: Physician Assistant Foundation
2318 Mill Road, Suite 1300
Alexandria, VA 22314-6868
(571) 319-4510   E-mail: pafoundation@aapa.org
Web: www.pa-foundation.org

Summary To provide financial assistance to student members of the American Academy of Physician Assistants (AAPA) who demonstrate community service leadership.

Eligibility This program is open to AAPA student members who have completed at least 1 semester of an accredited physician assistant program. Applicants must be able to demonstrate service leadership through their physician assistant program or through a community health organization or project.

Financial data The stipend is $1,000.

Duration 1 year; nonrenewable.

Number awarded 1 each year.

Deadline May of each year.

[3]
ACADEMY OF SPECIAL DREAMS FOUNDATION COLLEGE SCHOLARSHIP FUND

Academy of Special Dreams Foundation
115 West California Boulevard, Suite 326
Pasadena, CA 91105
E-mail: specialacademy@gmail.com
Web: www.specialacademy.org/scholarship

Summary To provide financial assistance to college students who have a disability and are majoring in a field of art.

Eligibility This program is open to students who have a disability and are enrolled or planning to enroll full or part time at a college, university, trade school, art school, or other art degree program. Applicants must be majoring or planning to major in any field of art (e.g., design, painting, drawing, photography, sculpture, video, animation). They must be lawful residents of the United States. Along with their application, they must submit 1) a statement from their physician or other medical provider describing their disability; 2) a portfolio of at least 5 images; and 3) a personal statement describing their commitment to art.

Financial data Stipends are $1,000, $500, or $250.

Duration 1 year.

Number awarded Varies each year; recently, 3 were awarded.

Deadline Applications may be submitted at any time.

[4]
ACCESS TECHNOLOGY SCHOLARSHIP

California Association for Postsecondary Education
  and Disability
Attn: Scholarships
10073 Valley View Street, Suite 242
Cypress, CA 90630
(562) 397-2810   Fax: (866) 577-3387
E-mail: caped38@gmail.com
Web: www.caped.io/scholarships/scholarship-application

Summary To provide funding to undergraduate and graduate students in California who have a disability and use assistive technology.

Eligibility This program is open to students at public and private colleges and universities in California who have a physical, mental, or learning disability. Applicants must be using assistive technology hardware or software to access their college courses. Undergraduates must have completed at least 6 semester credits and have a GPA of 2.5 or higher. Graduate students must have completed at least 3 semester units and have a GPA of 3.0 or higher. Along with their application, they must submit 1) a 250-word essay describing their progress towards meeting their educational and/or vocational goals; 2) a 500-word essay on how they manage their disability; and 3) a 750-word description of the assistive technology hardware and/or software they are using to access their course materials. They must also submit a letter of recommendation from a faculty person, verification of disability, and unofficial transcripts.

Financial data The grant is $1,000.

Duration 1 year.
Number awarded 1 or 2 each year.
Deadline August of each year.

[5]
ACXIOM DIVERSITY SCHOLARSHIP PROGRAM

Acxiom Corporation
601 East Third Street
P.O. Box 8190
Little Rock, AR 72203-8190
(501) 342-1000   Toll Free: (877) 314-2049
E-mail: Candice.Davis@acxiom.com
Web: www.acxiom.com/about-acxiom/careers

Summary To provide financial assistance and possible work experience to upper-division and graduate students who are members of a diverse population that historically has been underrepresented in the information technology work force.

Eligibility This program is open to juniors, seniors, and graduate students who are working full time on a degree in a field of information technology, including computer science, computer information systems, management information systems, information quality, information systems, engineering, mathematics, statistics, or related areas of study. Women, veterans, minorities, and individuals with disabilities are encouraged to apply. Applicants must have a GPA of 3.0 or higher. Along with their application, they must submit a 500-word essay describing how the scholarship will help them achieve their academic, professional, and personal goals. Selection is based on academic achievement, relationship of field of study to information technology, and relationship of areas of professional interest to the sponsor's business needs.

Financial data The stipend is $5,000 per year.

Duration 1 year; may be renewed 1 additional year, provided the recipient remains enrolled full time, maintains a GPA of 3.0 or higher, and (if offered an internship) continues to meet internship expectations.

Additional data Recipients may be offered an internship (fall, spring, summer, year-round) at 1 of the sponsor's offices in Austin (Texas), Conway (Arkansas), Downers Grove (Illinois), Little Rock (Arkansas), Nashville (Tennessee), New York (New York), or Redwood City (California).

Number awarded Up to 5 each year.
Deadline December of each year.

[6]
AHIMA FOUNDATION DIVERSITY SCHOLARSHIPS

American Health Information Management Association
Attn: AHIMA Foundation
233 North Michigan Avenue, 21st Floor
Chicago, IL 60601-5809
(312) 233-1131   Fax: (312) 233-1537
E-mail: info@ahimafoundation.org
Web: www.ahimafoundation.org

Summary To provide financial assistance to members of the American Health Information Management Association (AHIMA) who are interested in working on an undergraduate or graduate degree in health information management (HIM) or health information technology (HIT) and who will contribute to diversity in the profession.

Eligibility This program is open to AHIMA members who are enrolled at least half time in an accredited program. Applicants must be working on a degree in HIM or HIT at the associate, bachelor's, post-baccalaureate, master's, or doctoral level. They must have a GPA of 3.5 or higher and at least 6 credit hours remaining after the date of the award. To qualify for this support, applicants must demonstrate how they will contribute to diversity in the health information management profession; diversity is defined as differences in race, ethnicity, nationality, gender, sexual orientation, socioeconomic status, age, physical capabilities, or religious beliefs. Along with their application, they must submit essays on assigned topics related to their involvement in the HIM profession. Selection is based on the clarity and completeness of thought in the essays; cumulative GPA; volunteer, work, and/or leadership experience; honors, awards, or recognitions; commitment to the HIM profession; and references.

Financial data Stipends are $1,000 for associate degree students, $1,500 for bachelor's degree or post-baccalaureate certificate students, $2,000 for master's degree students, or $2,500 for doctoral degree students.

Duration 1 year.

Additional data This program includes the Ester May Sherard Scholarship.

Number awarded 1 or more each year.
Deadline September of each year.

[7]
AHIMA VETERANS SCHOLARSHIP

American Health Information Management Association
Attn: AHIMA Foundation
233 North Michigan Avenue, 21st Floor
Chicago, IL 60601-5809
(312) 233-1131   Fax: (312) 233-1537
E-mail: info@ahimafoundation.org
Web: www.ahimafoundation.org

Summary To provide financial assistance to veterans and spouses of veterans and active-duty service personnel who are interested in working on an undergraduate or graduate degree in health information management (HIM) or health information technology (HIT).

Eligibility This program is open to 1) veterans of the armed forces, including Army, Navy, Air Force, Marine Corps, Coast Guard, Reserves, and National Guard; and 2) spouses and surviving spouses of servicemembers, including active-duty military, retirees, veterans, and wounded warriors. Applicants must be working full time on a degree in HIM or HIT at the associate, bachelor's, post-baccalaureate, master's, or doctoral level. They must have at least 6 credit hours remaining after the date of the award. Along with their application, they must submit an essay of 250 to 400 words on their educational and career ambitions, record of military service, record of personal achievement, community service, desire to serve others and make a positive community impact, and leadership potential. In the selection process, preference is given to 1) physically wounded or disabled veterans; 2) surviving spouses; and 3) those who served in a combat tour of duty.

Financial data Stipends are $1,000 for associate degree students, $1,500 for bachelor's degree or post-baccalaureate certificate students, $2,000 for master's degree students, or $2,500 for doctoral degree students.

Duration 1 year.

Additional data Effective in 2018, this program includes the John Kloss Memorial Veteran Scholarship and other scholarships supported by Nuance Communications and the Walter Reed Society.

Number awarded 4 each year.

Deadline September of each year.

[8]
ALLSTATE FOUNDATION/VHSL ACHIEVEMENT AWARDS

Virginia High School League
1642 State Farm Boulevard
Charlottesville, VA 22911
(434) 977-8475   Fax: (434) 977-5943
E-mail: info@vhsl.org
Web: www.vhsl.org/about/scholarships

Summary To provide financial assistance to high school seniors who have participated in activities of the Virginia High School League (VHSL) and plan to attend college in any state.

Eligibility This program is open to seniors graduating from high schools that are members of the VHSL and planning to attend a college or university in any state. Applicants must have participated in 1 or more VHSL athletic activities (baseball, basketball, cheer, cross country, field hockey, football, golf, gymnastics, lacrosse, soccer, softball, swimming, tennis, indoor and outdoor track, volleyball, wrestling) and/or academic activities (student publications, creative writing, drama, forensics, film festival, debate, scholastic bowl). They must have a GPA of 3.0 or higher. Each school may nominate up to 4 students: 1 female athlete, 1 male athlete, 1 academic participant, and 1 courageous achievement candidate. The courageous achievement category is reserved for students who have overcome serious obstacles to make significant contributions to athletic and/or academic activities. The obstacles may include a serious illness, injury, or disability; a challenging social or home situation; or another extraordinary situation where the student has displayed tremendous courage against overwhelming odds. Along with their application, students must submit a 500-word essay describing how extracurricular activities have enhanced their educational experience. Candidates are judged separately in the 6 VHSL enrollment groups (1A-6A). Selection is based on the essay; involvement in other school-sponsored activities; involvement in activities outside of school; and 2 letters of support.

Financial data The stipend is $1,500.

Duration 1 year.

Additional data This program, which began in 1992, is currently supported by the Allstate Foundation. The courageous achievement category, designated the Andrew Mullins Courageous Achievement Award, was added in 2002.

Number awarded 19 each year. For each of the 6 groups (A, AA, and AAA), 1 female athlete, 1 male athlete, and 1 academic participant are selected. In addition, 1 courageous achievement candidate is selected statewide.

Deadline March of each year.

[9]
ALYSSA MCCROSKEY MEMORIAL SCHOLARSHIP

California Association for Postsecondary Education and Disability
Attn: Scholarships
10073 Valley View Street, Suite 242
Cypress, CA 90630
(562) 397-2810   Fax: (866) 577-3387
E-mail: caped38@gmail.com
Web: www.caped.io/scholarships/scholarship-application

Summary To provide financial assistance to undergraduate and graduate students in California who have a disability and have attempted to help other students regain their mental health.

Eligibility This program is open to students at public and private colleges and universities in California who have a physical, mental, or learning disability. Applicants must be "making a positive difference" in the lives of other students who are struggling to maintain or regain their mental health. Undergraduates must have completed at least 6 semester credits and have a GPA of 2.5 or higher. Graduate students must have completed at least 3 semester units and have a GPA of 3.0 or higher. Along with their application, they must submit 1) a 250-word essay describing their progress towards meeting their educational and/or vocational goals; 2) a 500-word essay on how they manage their disabiity; and 3) a 750-word essay on how they are making a positive difference in the lives of students with mental health conditions. They must also submit a letter of recommendation from a faculty person, verification of disability, and unofficial transcripts.

Financial data The stipend is $1,000.

Duration 1 year.

Number awarded 1 each year.

Deadline August of each year.

[10]
AMERICAN BUS ASSOCIATION YELLOW RIBBON SCHOLARSHIP

American Bus Association
Attn: ABA Foundation
111 K Street, N.E., Ninth Floor
Washington, DC 20002
(202) 842-1645   Toll Free: (800) 283-2877
Fax: (202) 842-0850   E-mail: abainfo@buses.org
Web: www.buses.org

Summary   To provide financial assistance for college or graduate school to people with disabilities, veterans, and children of wounded veterans who are preparing for a career in the transportation, travel, and tourism industry.

Eligibility   This program is open to U.S. and Canadian citizens and permanent residents who are enrolled as an undergraduate or graduate student in a program related to the transportation, travel, and tourism industry. Applicants must 1) have a physical or sensory disability; 2) be a veteran of the U.S. or Canadian military; or 3) be a child or a wounded U.S. or Canadian military veteran. They must have a GPA of 3.0 or higher.

Financial data   The stipend is $2,500.

Duration   1 or more each year.

Deadline   April of each year.

[11]
AMS FRESHMAN UNDERGRADUATE SCHOLARSHIPS

American Meteorological Society
Attn: Development and Student Program Manager
45 Beacon Street
Boston, MA 02108-3693
(617) 227-2426, ext. 3907   Fax: (617) 742-8718
E-mail: dFernandez@ametsoc.org
Web: www.ametsoc.org

Summary   To provide financial assistance to high school seniors planning to attend college to prepare for a career in the atmospheric or related oceanic or hydrologic sciences.

Eligibility   This program is open to high school seniors entering their freshman year of college to work on a bachelor's degree in the atmospheric or related oceanic or hydrologic sciences. Applicants must be U.S. citizens or permanent residents planning to enroll full time. Along with their application, they must submit a 500-word essay on how they believe their college education, and what they learn in the atmospheric and related sciences, will help them to serve society during their professional career. Selection is based on performance in high school, including academic records, recommendations, scores from a national examination, and the essay. Financial need is not considered. The sponsor specifically encourages applications from women, minorities, and students with disabilities who are traditionally underrepresented in the atmospheric and related oceanic sciences.

Financial data   The stipend is $2,500 per academic year.

Duration   1 year; may be renewed for the second year of college study.

Number awarded   Varies each year; recently, 11 were awarded.

Deadline   January of each year.

[12]
AMS SENIOR NAMED SCHOLARSHIPS

American Meteorological Society
Attn: Development and Student Program Manager
45 Beacon Street
Boston, MA 02108-3693
(617) 227-2426, ext. 3907   Fax: (617) 742-8718
E-mail: dFernandez@ametsoc.org
Web: www.ametsoc.org

Summary   To provide financial assistance to college seniors majoring in the atmospheric sciences.

Eligibility   This program is open to full-time students entering their final year of undergraduate study and majoring in the atmospheric or related sciences. Applicants must be U.S. citizens or permanent residents enrolled at a U.S. institution and have a cumulative GPA of 3.25 or higher. Along with their application, they must submit 200-word essays on 1) their most important attributes and achievements that qualify them for this scholarship; and 2) their career goals in the atmospheric or related sciences. Financial need is considered in the selection process. The sponsor specifically encourages applications from women, minorities, and students with disabilities who are traditionally underrepresented in the atmospheric and related sciences.

Financial data   Stipends range from $2,000 to $10,000.

Duration   1 year.

Additional data   All scholarships awarded through this program are named after individuals who have assisted the sponsor in various ways.

Number awarded   Approximately 20 each year.

Deadline   January of each year.

[13]
AUGER & AUGER DISABLED SCHOLAR AWARD

Auger & Auger Attorneys at Law
Attn: Scholarship
717 South Torrence Street, Suite 101
Charlotte, NC 28294
(704) 364-3361   Toll Free: (855) 971-1114
Fax: (704) 365-0326
Web: www.augerlaw.com/disabled-scholar-award

Summary   To provide financial assistance for college to students who have a disability.

Eligibility   This program is open to graduating high school seniors and current undergraduate students. Applicants must have a documented disability and a GPA of 2.8 or higher. Along with their application, they must submit an essay of 500 to 1,000 words on 1 of the following topics: 1) a time in their life when they have overcome their disability to do something extraordinary; or 2) what they have learned from living with their disability. Selection is based on the essay and academic merit.

Financial data   The stipend is $1,000.

Duration   1 year.

Additional data   This program began in 2014.

Number awarded 2 each year: 1 in fall and 1 in spring.

Deadline July of each year for fall; November of each year for spring.

[14]
BETTY BACON MEMORIAL SCHOLARSHIP

California Association for Postsecondary Education and Disability
Attn: Scholarships
10073 Valley View Street, Suite 242
Cypress, CA 90630
(562) 397-2810   Fax: (866) 577-3387
E-mail: caped38@gmail.com
Web: www.caped.io/scholarships/scholarship-application

Summary To provide financial assistance to undergraduate and graduate students in California who have a disability.

Eligibility This program is open to students at public and private 4-year colleges and universities in California who have a physical, mental, or learning disability. Undergraduates must have completed at least 6 semester credits and have a GPA of 2.5 or higher. Graduate students must have completed at least 3 semester units and have a GPA of 3.0 or higher. Along with their application, they must submit 1) a 250-word essay describing their progress towards meeting their educational and/or vocational goals; and 2) a 500-word essay on how they manage their disabiity. They must also submit a letter of recommendation from a faculty person, verification of disability, and unofficial transcripts.

Financial data The stipend is $1,000.

Duration 1 year.

Number awarded 1 each year.

Deadline August of each year.

[15]
BLANDY EXPERIMENTAL FARM RESEARCH EXPERIENCES FOR UNDERGRADUATES PROGRAM

University of Virginia
Attn: Blandy Experimental Farm
400 Blandy Farm Lane
Boyce, VA 22620
(540) 837-1758, ext. 292   Fax: (540) 837-1523
E-mail: blandy@virginia.edu
Web: sites.google.com/site/blandyreu

Summary To provide an opportunity for undergraduates to conduct ecological and evolutionary research during the summer at the Blandy Experimental Farm in Clarke County, Virginia.

Eligibility This program is open to undergraduate students interested in ecological and evolutionary biology. Applicants must submit a proposal for a research project at the farm under the mentorship of a professional staff member. Current research interests of the staff include plant reproductive ecology, aquatic community ecology, biological invasions, plant population biology, conservation biology, pollination, and plant succession. Interested students should submit, along with their application, a cur-

rent transcript, 2 letters of recommendation, a statement describing how this program would contribute to their education and career goals, and the names of the mentors whose research areas interest them. They must be U.S. citizens or permanent residents. Applications are especially encouraged from underrepresented minorities, persons with disabilities, and women.

Financial data Students receive a $5,775 stipend, an additional meal budget, free housing, and a modest budget for supplies and travel.

Duration 11 weeks, from late May through mid-August.

Additional data This program, established in 1993, receives funding support from the Research Experiences for Undergraduates (REU) program of the National Science Foundation.

Number awarded 10 each year.

Deadline February of each year.

[16]
BMO CAPITAL MARKETS LIME CONNECT EQUITY THROUGH EDUCATION SCHOLARSHIPS FOR STUDENTS WITH DISABILITIES

Lime Connect, Inc.
590 Madison Avenue, 21st Floor
New York, NY 10022
(212) 521-4469   Fax: (212) 521-4099
E-mail: info@limeconnect.com
Web: www.limeconnect.com

Summary To provide financial assistance to students with disabilities working on a bachelor's or graduate degree in a business or technical field at a college or university in Canada or the United States.

Eligibility This program is open to undergraduate and graduate students at 4-year colleges and universities in the United States or Canada who have a disability. International students with disabilities enrolled at universities in the United States or Canada are also eligible. Applicants must be working full time on a degree in a business, engineering, mathematics, physics, statistics, or a related field. Along with their application, they must submit an essay on their career goals and why they believe they should be selected to receive this scholarship. Preference is given to students preparing for a career in financial services with a focus on capital markets. Financial need is not considered in the selection process.

Financial data The stipend is $10,000 for students at U.S. universities or $C5,000 for students at Canadian universities.

Duration 1 year.

Additional data This program is jointly sponsored by BMO Capital Markets and Lime Connect, an organization founded in 2006 to promote employment of people with disabilities. BMO Capital Markets established its Equity Through Education program in 2005 and in 2011 invited Lime Connect to administer a component of the program for students with disabilities.

Number awarded   Varies each year; recently, 11 were awarded.
Deadline   December each year.

[17]
BUCKFIRE & BUCKFIRE DISABILITY SCHOLARSHIP

Buckfire & Buckfire, P.C.
Attn: Scholarships
29000 Inkster Road, Suite 150
Southfield, MI 48034
(248) 595-7544   Toll Free: (888) 797-8787
Fax: (248) 569-6737   E-mail: info@buckfirelaw.com
Web: www.buckfirelaw.com/library/scholarships.cfm

Summary   To provide financial assistance for college to students who have a disability.
Eligibility   This program is open to U.S. citizens who have a disability, including (but not limited to) physical disabilities, medical conditions, mental and psychiatric conditions, speech and language, learning disabilities, behavioral conditions, and other conditions. Applicants must have completed at least 1 semester at an accredited college or university and have a GPA of 3.0 or higher. Selection is based on academic achievement and an essay on how they are working to overcome adversity caused by their disability and what they have learned from the experience.
Financial data   The stipend is $1,000.
Duration   1 year.
Additional data   This program began in 2014.
Number awarded   1 each year.
Deadline   March of each year.

[18]
"BUSINESS PLAN" SCHOLARSHIP FOR STUDENTS WITH DISABILITIES

Fit Small Business
Attn: Scholarship
315 Madison Avenue, 24th Floor
New York, NY 10017
(212) 555-3434
E-mail: mprosser@fitsmallbusiness.com
Web: www.fitsmallbusiness.com

Summary   To recognize and reward, with scholarships, undergraduate and graduate students who have a disability and submit outstanding essays about writing a business plan.
Eligibility   This competition is open to undergraduate and graduate students who have a documented disability; qualifying disabilities include, but are not limited to, physical disabilities, medical conditions, mental and psychiatric conditions, speech and language, learning disabilities, behavioral conditions, and all other disabling conditions. Applicants must submit an essay of 500 to 1,000 words on what they learned from writing a business plan. They are not asked to submit the actual plan; instead, they should focus on what they learned about researching for the business plan, what they learned about the specific industry during researching the business plan, what they learned

about the key assumptions upon which the plan depended, why they no longer thought the business was viable after writing the plan, and how and why the business plan changed during the process of getting feedback. Selection is based on originality, writing style, and quality of ideas.
Financial data   The award is a $1,000 scholarship.
Duration   The competition is held twice each year.
Additional data   This program began in 2014.
Number awarded   2 each year: 1 in fall and 1 in spring.
Deadline   October of each year for fall; March of each year for spring.

[19]
CALIFORNIA-HAWAII ELKS MAJOR PROJECT UNDERGRADUATE SCHOLARSHIP PROGRAM FOR STUDENTS WITH DISABILITIES

California-Hawaii Elks Association
Attn: Scholarship Committee
5450 East Lamona Avenue
Fresno, CA 93727-2224
(559) 255-4531   Fax: (559) 456-2659
E-mail: chea@chea-elks.org
Web: www.chea-elks.org/youth-activities/scholarships

Summary   To provide financial assistance to residents of California and Hawaii who have a disability and are interested in attending college in any state.
Eligibility   This program is open to residents of California or Hawaii who have a physical impairment, neurological impairment, visual impairment, hearing impairment, and/or speech/language disorder. Applicants must be a senior in high school, be a high school graduate, or have passed the GED test. They must be planning to attend a college, university, community college, or vocational school in any state. U.S. citizenship is required. Selection is based on financial need, GPA, severity of disability, seriousness of purpose, and depth of character. Applications are available from an Elks Lodge in California or Hawaii; students must first request an interview with the lodge's scholarship chairman, secretary, or Exalted Ruler.
Financial data   The stipend is $3,000 per year for 4-year colleges or universities or $1,000 for community colleges and vocational schools.
Duration   1 year; may be renewed for up to 3 additional years or until completion of an undergraduate degree, whichever occurs first.
Number awarded   20 to 50 each year.
Deadline   March of each year.

[20]
CAPED EXCELLENCE SCHOLARSHIP

California Association for Postsecondary Education
   and Disability
Attn: Scholarships
10073 Valley View Street, Suite 242
Cypress, CA 90630
(562) 397-2810   Fax: (866) 577-3387
E-mail: caped38@gmail.com
Web: www.caped.io/scholarships/scholarship-application

Summary To provide financial assistance to undergraduate and graduate students in California who have a disability and can demonstrate academic achievement and involvement in community and campus activities.

Eligibility This program is open to students at public and private colleges and universities in California who have a physical, mental, or learning disability. Undergraduates must have completed at least 6 semester credits and have a GPA of 2.5 or higher. Graduate students must have completed at least 3 semester units and have a GPA of 3.0 or higher. Applicants must submit 1) a 250-word essay describing their progress towards meeting their educational and/or vocational goals; 2) a 500-word essay on how they manage their disabiity; and 3) a 750-word description of how their campus and/or community involvement supports their academic achievement. They must also submit a letter of recommendation from a faculty person, verification of disability, and unofficial transcripts. This award is presented to the applicant who demonstrates the highest level of academic achievement and involvement in community and campus life.

Financial data The stipend is $1,500.

Duration 1 year.

Number awarded 1 each year.

Deadline August of each year.

[21]
CAPED MEMORIAL SCHOLARSHIP

California Association for Postsecondary Education
  and Disability
Attn: Scholarships
10073 Valley View Street, Suite 242
Cypress, CA 90630
(562) 397-2810   Fax: (866) 577-3387
E-mail: caped38@gmail.com
Web: www.caped.io/scholarships/scholarship-application

Summary To provide financial assistance to undergraduate and graduate students in California who have a disability.

Eligibility This program is open to students at public and private colleges and universities in California who have a physical, mental, or learning disability. Undergraduates must have completed at least 6 semester credits and have a GPA of 2.5 or higher. Graduate students must have completed at least 3 semester units and have a GPA of 3.0 or higher. Applicants must submit 1) a 250-word essay describing their progress towards meeting their educational and/or vocational goals; and 2) a 500-word essay on how they manage their disabiity. They must also submit a letter of recommendation from a faculty person, verification of disability, and unofficial transcripts.

Financial data The stipend is $1,000.

Duration 1 year.

Number awarded 1 each year.

Deadline August of each year.

[22]
CARVER SCHOLARS PROGRAM

Roy J. Carver Charitable Trust
202 Iowa Avenue
Muscatine, IA 52761-3733
(563) 263-4010   Fax: (563) 263-1547
E-mail: info@carvertrust.org
Web: www.carvertrust.org/index.php?page=scholars

Summary To provide financial assistance to students in Iowa who are attending college despite having to overcome significant obstacles.

Eligibility This program is open to students attending the 3 public universities in Iowa, the 22 participating private 4-year colleges and universities in the state, or a community college in Iowa and planning to transfer to 1 of those 4-year institutions. Applicants must be sophomores seeking support for their junior year. They must present evidence of unusual social and/or other barriers to attending college full time; examples include, but are not limited to, students who 1) are from 1-parent families; 2) are attending college while working full time; 3) have social, mental, or physical disabilities; or 4) have families to support. They must have graduated from a high school in Iowa or have been residents of the state for at least 5 consecutive years immediately prior to applying, be full-time students, have at least a 2.8 GPA, be U.S. citizens, and submit a financial profile indicating insufficient personal, family, and institutional resources to pay full-time college tuition. A particular goal of the program is to assist students "who fall between the cracks of other financial aid programs." Applications must be submitted to the financial aid office at the Iowa college or university the applicant attends.

Financial data Stipends generally average $5,200 at public universities or $7,600 at private colleges in Iowa.

Duration 1 year; may be renewed 1 additional year.

Additional data This program began in 1988.

Number awarded Varies each year; since the program's establishment, it has awarded more than 3,900 scholarships worth more than $21 million.

Deadline March of each year.

[23]
CATHERINE T. MURRAY MEMORIAL SCHOLARSHIP

Ocean State Center for Independent Living
Attn: Office Manager
1944 Warwick Avenue
Warwick, RI 02889
(401) 738-1013, ext. 10   Toll Free: (866) 857-1161
Fax: (401) 738-1083   TDD: (401) 244-7792
E-mail: cmckenna@oscil.org
Web: www.oscil.org/scholarship.html

Summary To provide financial assistance to residents of Rhode Island who have a disability and are interested in attending college in any state.

Eligibility This program is open to residents of Rhode Island who have a significant disability. Applicants must be enrolled or planning to enroll in an academic, trade, or vocational educational program in any state and/or to acquire assistive or adaptive equipment or devices to access such an educational opportunity. Along with their application, they must submit a 1-page essay describing their career goals and plans. Selection is based on that essay, merit, and financial need.

Financial data The stipend is $1,000.

Duration 1 year.

Additional data This program began in 1995.

Number awarded 1 each year.

Deadline March of each year.

[24]
CFA INSTITUTE 11 SEPTEMBER MEMORIAL SCHOLARSHIP

CFA Institute
Attn: Research Foundation
915 East High Street
P.O. Box 2082
Charlottesville, VA 22902-2082
(434) 951-5499   Toll Free: (800) 247-8132
Fax: (434) 951-5240   E-mail: rf@cfainstitute.org
Web: www.cfainstitute.org

Summary To provide financial assistance to individuals and their families who were disabled or killed in the September 11, 2001 terrorist attacks and who wish to major in business-related fields in college.

Eligibility This program is open to residents of any state or country who either 1) were permanently disabled in the attacks of September 11, 2001; or 2) are the spouses, domestic partners, or children of anyone killed or permanently disabled in the attacks. Applicants must be working full or part time on an undergraduate degree in finance, economics, accounting, or business ethics. Selection is based on demonstrated leadership and good citizenship, academic record, and financial need.

Financial data Stipends range up to $25,000 per year, depending on the need of the recipient.

Duration 1 year; renewable up to 4 additional years.

Additional data The CFA (Chartered Financial Analyst) Institute was formerly the Association for Investment Management and Research (AIMR). It lost at least 56 of its members and CFA candidates in the terrorist attacks of 11 September. This program is managed by Scholarship Management Services, a division of Scholarship America.

Number awarded Varies each year; recently, 12 were awarded.

Deadline May of each year.

[25]
CHICAGO INJURY CENTER'S ANNUAL SCHOLARSHIP FUND FOR DISABLED VETERANS

Chicago Injury Center
308 West Erie Street, Suite 300b
Chicago, IL 60654
(312) 818-4450   E-mail: pearlrosemail@gmail.com
Web: www.chicagoinjurycenter.com

Summary To provide financial assistance for college to disabled veterans.

Eligibility This program is open to honorably discharged veterans who have a disability. Applicants must be enrolled or planning to enroll as an undergraduate or graduate student at an accredited college, university, community college, or trade school. They must have a GPA of 2.5 or higher. Along with their application, they must submit a brief biography and a 500-word essay on 1) the hurdles they have had to overcome as a veteran with a disability and how it has prepared them to face the challenges of their particular course of study; and 2) how they believe the military and their road to recovery has helped prepare them for the challenges that they will face as a student.

Financial data Stipends are $1,000, $500, or $250.

Duration 1 year.

Additional data This program began in 2015.

Number awarded 1 at $1,000, 1 at $500, and 2 at $250 each year.

Deadline May of each year.

[26]
CHIEF MASTER SERGEANT OF THE AIR FORCE SCHOLARSHIP PROGRAM

Air Force Sergeants Association
Attn: Membership and Field Relations
5211 Auth Road
Suitland, MD 20746
(301) 899-3500   Toll Free: (800) 638-0594
Fax: (301) 899-8136   E-mail: staff@hqafsa.org
Web: www.hqafsa.org/scholarships.html

Summary To provide financial assistance for college to the dependent children of enlisted Air Force personnel.

Eligibility This program is open to the unmarried children (including stepchildren and legally adopted children) of enlisted active-duty, retired, or veteran members of the U.S. Air Force, Air National Guard, or Air Force Reserves. Applicants must be attending or planning to attend an accredited academic institution. They must have an unweighted GPA of 3.5 or higher. Along with their application, they must submit 1) a paragraph on their life objectives and what they plan to do with the education they receive; and 2) an essay on the most urgent problem facing society today. High school seniors must also submit a transcript of all high school grades and a record of their SAT or ACT scores. Selection is based on academic record, character, leadership skills, writing ability, versatility, and potential for success. Financial need is not a consideration. A unique aspect of these scholarships is that applicants may supply additional information regarding circumstances that entitle them to special consideration; examples of such circumstances include student disabilities, financial hardships, parent disabled and unable to work, parent missing in action/killed in action/prisoner of war, or other unusual extenuating circumstances.

Financial data Stipends range from $1,000 to $3,500; funds may be used for tuition, room and board, fees, books, supplies, and transportation.

Duration 1 year; may be renewed if the recipient maintains full-time enrollment.

Additional data The Air Force Sergeants Association administers this program on behalf of the Airmen Memorial Foundation. It was established in 1987 and named in honor of CMSAF Richard D. Kisling, the late third Chief Master Sergeant of the Air Force. In 1997, following the deaths of CMSAF's (Retired) Andrews and Harlow, it was given its current name. The highest-ranked applicant receives the Paul W. Airey Memorial Scholarship, sponsored by GEICO Insurance.

Number awarded Varies each year; recently, 11 worth $16,500 were awarded: 1 at $3,500, 1 at $2,500, 1 at $2,000, 1 at $1,500, and 7 at $1,000. Since this program began, it has awarded more than 270 scholarships valued at more than $383,580.

Deadline March of each year.

[27]
CHRISTIAN A. HERTER MEMORIAL SCHOLARSHIP

Massachusetts Office of Student Financial Assistance
454 Broadway, Suite 200
Revere, MA 02151
(617) 391-6070   Fax: (617) 727-0667
E-mail: osfa@osfa.mass.edu
Web: www.mass.edu/osfa/programs/herter.asp

Summary To provide financial assistance to Massachusetts high school students who have overcome major adversities and plan to attend college in any state.

Eligibility This program is open to residents of Massachusetts who are attending a secondary school in grades 10-11, have a cumulative GPA of 2.5 or higher, and are planning to work full time on an undergraduate degree at an accredited institution in the United States. Applicants must be able to demonstrate 1) difficult personal circumstances in their lives (e.g., physical or mental abuse, catastrophic illness) or other personal obstacles or hardships of a societal, geographic, mental, or physical nature; 2) high financial need; and 3) strong academic promise to continue their education beyond high school at a college or university. They must be nominated by their school or a public agency. U.S. citizenship or permanent resident status is required.

Financial data Awards cover up to 50% of the student's unmet financial need.

Duration 4 years.

Additional data This program began in 1972.

Number awarded 25 each year.

Deadline February of each year.

[28]
COLLABORATIVE RESEARCH EXPERIENCES FOR UNDERGRADUATES

Computing Research Association
1828 L Street, N.W., Suite 800
Washington, DC 20036-4632
(202) 234-2111   Fax: (202) 667-1066
E-mail: creu@cra.org
Web: www.cra.org/cra-w/creu

Summary To provide funding to underrepresented undergraduate students who are interested in conducting a research project in computer science or engineering.

Eligibility This program is open to teams of 2 or 4 undergraduates who have completed 2 years of study, including at least 4 courses in computer science or computer engineering, at a college or university in the United States. Applicants must be interested in conducting a research project directly related to computer science or computer engineering. They must apply jointly with 1 or 2 sponsoring faculty members. Teams consisting of underrepresented groups (women, African Americans, Mexican-Americans, American Indians, Alaska Natives, Native Hawaiians, Pacific Islanders, mainland Puerto Ricans, individuals who identify as part of the LGBTQI community, and persons with disabilities) are especially encouraged to apply; teams may also include students from non-underrepresented groups, but financial support is available only to underrepresented students. U.S. citizenship or permanent resident status is required.

Financial data The program provides a stipend of $3,000 for the academic year. Students who wish to participate in an optional summer extension receive an additional stipend of $4,000. Additional funding up to $1,500 per team may be available for purchase of supporting materials and/or travel to conferences to present the work.

Duration 1 academic year plus an optional summer extension.

Additional data This program is sponsored by the Computing Research Association's Committee on the Status of Women in Computing Research (CRA-W) and the Coalition to Diversify Computing (CDC) in cooperation with the National Science Foundation.

Number awarded Varies each year; recently, 14 teams of students received support from this program.

Deadline May of each year.

[29]
COURAGE KENNY REHABILITATION INSTITUTE SCHOLARSHIP FOR PEOPLE WITH DISABILITIES

Allina Health System
Courage Kenny Rehabilitation Institute
Attn: Vocational Services Department
3915 Golden Valley Road
Minneapolis, MN 55422
(612) 775-2570
E-mail: ckrivocationalservices@allina.com
Web: www.allinahealth.org

Summary To provide financial assistance to Minnesota residents who have a disability and are interested in attending college in any state.

Eligibility This program is open to U.S. citizens who are residents of Minnesota or have received services from Courage Kenny Rehabilitation Institute. Applicants must have a sensory impairment or physical disability and a desire to gain technical expertise beyond high school. They must be attending or planning to attend a college or technical school in any state. Along with their application, they must submit a concise essay that reflects their educational aspirations, career goals, and how a scholarship will help meet their needs. Selection is based on that essay, employment history, honors and awards, leadership experience, and financial need. Graduation ranking is not considered.

Financial data The stipend is $1,000.

Duration 1 year.

Additional data The Courage Kenny Rehabilitation Institute was established in 2013 when Courage Center merged with the Sister Kenny Rehabilitation Institute and became part of Allina Health.

Number awarded 1 or more each year.

Deadline May of each year.

[30]
CYNTHIA RUTH RUSSELL SCHOLARSHIP

Kansas Masonic Foundation, Inc.
Attn: Director of Development and Programs
2909 S.W. Maupin Lane
Topeka, KS 66614-5335
(785) 357-7646 Fax: (785) 357-7406
E-mail: Dave@kansasmasonic.foundation
Web: www.kansasmasonic.foundation

Summary To provide financial assistance to Kansas residents who have a disability and are attending a college or university in the state.

Eligibility This program is open to residents of Kansas who have a medically-approved disability. Applicants must be attending or planning to attend 1 of 7 public institutions of higher education in the state as a full-time undergraduate or graduate student. Along with their application, they must submit a description of their disability, documentation of the disability from a doctor, transcripts, and documentation of financial need.

Financial data The stipend is $5,000.

Duration 1 year.

Number awarded 1 or more each year.

Deadline March of each year.

[31]
DEFENSE INTELLIGENCE AGENCY UNDERGRADUATE TRAINING ASSISTANCE PROGRAM

Defense Intelligence Agency
Attn: Human Resources, HCH-4
200 MacDill Boulevard, Building 6000
Bolling AFB, DC 20340-5100
(202) 231-2736 Fax: (202) 231-4889
TDD: (202) 231-5002 E-mail: staffing@dia.mil
Web: www.dia.mil

Summary To provide loans-for-service and work experience to high school seniors and lower-division students interested in majoring in specified fields and working for the U.S. Defense Intelligence Agency (DIA).

Eligibility This program is open to graduating high school seniors and college freshmen and sophomores interested in working full time on a baccalaureate degree in 1 of the following fields in college: biology, chemistry, computer science, engineering, foreign area studies, human resources, intelligence analysis, international relations, microbiology, pharmacology, physics, political science, or toxicology. High school seniors must have a GPA of 2.75 or higher and either 1) an SAT combined critical reading and mathematics score of 1000 or higher plus 500 or higher on the writing portion or 2) an ACT score of 21 or higher. College freshmen and sophomores must have a GPA of 3.0 or higher. All applicants must be able to demonstrate financial need (household income ceiling of $70,000 for a family of 4 or $80,000 for a family of 5 or more) and leadership abilities through extracurricular activities, civic involvement, volunteer work, or part-time employment. Students and all members of their immediate family must be U.S. citizens. Minorities, women, and persons with disabilities are strongly encouraged to apply.

Financial data Students accepted into this program receive tuition (up to $18,000 per year) at an accredited college or university selected by the student and endorsed by the sponsor; reimbursement for books and needed supplies; an annual salary to cover college room and board expenses and for summer employment; and a position at the sponsoring agency after graduation. Recipients must work for DIA after college graduation for at least 1 and a half times the length of study. For participants who leave DIA earlier than scheduled, the agency arranges for payments to reimburse DIA for the total cost of education (including the employee's pay and allowances).

Duration 4 years, provided the recipient maintains a GPA of 2.75 during the freshman year and 3.0 or higher in subsequent semesters.

Additional data Recipients are provided a challenging summer internship and guaranteed a job at the agency in their field of study upon graduation.

Number awarded Only a few are awarded each year.

Deadline October of each year.

[32]
DEXTER G. JOHNSON EDUCATIONAL AND BENEVOLENT TRUST GRANTS

Dexter G. Johnson Educational and Benevolent Trust
Attn: Betty Crews
P.O. Box 26663
Oklahoma City, OK 73126-0663
(405) 232-3340   Fax: (405) 232-3340

Summary   To provide financial assistance for vocational training, audiological evaluations, corrective surgery, speech therapy, or medical devices to the children of residents of Oklahoma who have disabilities.

Eligibility   Residents of Oklahoma with disabilities are eligible to apply for this program for their children if they need financial assistance for vocational training, audiological evaluations, corrective surgery, speech therapy, or orthopedic or hearing aid devices.

Financial data   Grants range from $70 to $2,500.

Number awarded   Varies; approximately 10 each year.

Deadline   Applications may be submitted at any time.

[33]
DISABILITY AWARENESS SCHOLARSHIP

United States Military VA Loan
200 112th Avenue N.E., Suite 310
Bellevue, WA 98004
Toll Free: (888) 851-7871   Fax: (425) 454-7547
E-mail: scholarship@MilitaryVALoan.com
Web: www.militaryvaloan.com

Summary   To recognize and reward, with college scholarships, high school seniors and current college and graduate students (disabled or not) who submit outstanding essays about overcoming disability.

Eligibility   This program is open to anyone older than 17 years of age who either has not yet begun college or is currently enrolled full time as an undergraduate or graduate student at a college or other institution of higher education. Applicants are not required to have a disability themselves, but they must submit an essay of 500 to 1,000 words on how they or someone they know overcame disability to do something great. They must have a GPA of 3.0 or higher.

Financial data   The stipend is $1,000.

Duration   1 year.

Number awarded   1 each year.

Deadline   January of each year.

[34]
DISABLED PERSON NATIONAL SCHOLARSHIP COMPETITION

Disabled Person, Inc.
P.O. Box 230636
Encinitas, CA 92023-0636
(760) 420-1269   E-mail: info@disabledperson.com
Web: www.disabledperson.com/scholarships/15

Summary   To recognize and reward, with college scholarships, undergraduate and graduate students who have a disability and submit outstanding essays on an assigned topic.

Eligibility   This competition is open to U.S. citizens who have a disability and are enrolled as full-time undergraduate or graduate students at a college or university in the United States. High school seniors and part-time students are not eligible. Applicants must submit an essay, up to 750 words in length, on a topic that changes annually; recently, students were asked to write on the impact on their community of the new regulations of the Office of Federal Contract Compliance concerning the hiring of people with disabilities for federal contractors.

Financial data   The award is a $1,000 scholarship.

Duration   The competition is held annually.

Number awarded   2 each year: 1 in the fall and 1 in the spring.

Deadline   October of each year for fall; April of each year for spring.

[35]
DISABLED STUDENTS PURSUING A CAREER IN LAW SCHOLARSHIP

Friedl Richardson Trial Lawyers
Attn: Scholarship Coordinator
19840 North Cave Creek Road
Phoenix, AZ 85024
(602) 553-2220   E-mail: randy@friedlrichardson.com
Web: www.friedlrichardson.com

Summary   To provide financial assistance for college to students who have a disability and are interested in preparing for a career in the law.

Eligibility   This program is open to students who have a disability and are enrolled or planning to enroll at a college or university in any state. Applicants must be interested in preparing for a career in the law. They must be U.S. citizens and have a GPA of 2.8 or higher. Along with their application, they must submit an essay or video explaining why they are an excellent candidate for this scholarship.

Financial data   The stipend is $1,000.

Duration   1 year.

Number awarded   1 each year.

Deadline   July of each year.

[36]
DISTRIBUTED RESEARCH EXPERIENCES FOR UNDERGRADUATES

Computing Research Association
1828 L Street, N.W., Suite 800
Washington, DC 20036-4632
(202) 234-2111   Fax: (202) 667-1066
E-mail: dreu@cra.org
Web: www.cra.org/cra-w/dreu

Summary   To provide an opportunity for underrepresented undergraduate students to work on a summer research project in computer science or engineering.

Eligibility   This program is open to members of underrepresented groups (women, Hispanics, African Americans, American Indians, students with disabilities) who are entering their junior or senior year of college. Applicants must be interested in conducting a summer research project directly related to computer science or computer engineering under the mentorship of a faculty member at the mentor's home university. They must be U.S. citizens or permanent residents. Selection is based on the student's potential for success in graduate school, the extent of the student's experience and skills, the student's potential gain from the experience, and the potential that the student's participation will advance the goals of the program.

Financial data Students receive a stipend of $7,000 plus relocation travel assistance up to $500 if appropriate.

Duration 10 weeks during the summer.

Additional data This program began in 1994 as the Distributed Mentor Project (DMP) by the Computing Research Association's Committee on the Status of Women in Computing Research (CRA-W). In 2007, the Coalition to Diversify Computing (CDC) became a cosponsor of the program and in 2009 it was given its current name. From the beginning, funding has been provided by the National Science Foundation.

Number awarded Varies each year; recently, 46 students were selected to participate in this program.

Deadline February of each year.

[37]
DIVERSITY IN PSYCHOLOGY AND LAW RESEARCH AWARD

American Psychological Association
Attn: Division 41 (American Psychology-Law Society)
c/o Kathy Gaskey, Administrative Officer
P.O. Box 11488
Southport, NC 28461-3936
(910) 933-4018　　　　　　　　Fax: (910) 933-4018
E-mail: apls@ec.rr.com
Web: www.apadivisions.org

Summary To provide funding to student members of the American Psychology-Law Society (AP-LS) who are interested in conducting a research project related to diversity.

Eligibility This program is open to undergraduate and graduate student members of AP-LS who are interested in conducting research on issues related to psychology, law, multiculturalism, and/or diversity (e.g., research pertaining to psycholegal issues on race, gender, culture, sexual orientation). Students from underrepresented groups are strongly encouraged to apply; underrepresented groups include, but are not limited to: racial and ethnic minorities; first-generation college students; lesbian, gay, bisexual, and transgender students; and students with physical disabilities. Applicants must submit a project description that includes a statement of the research problem, the project's likely impact on the field of psychology and law broadly, methodology, budget, and an overview of relevant literature. Selection is based on the impact of the project on diversity and multiculturalism and the expected completion within the allocated time.

Financial data The grant is $1,000.

Duration The project must be completed within 1 year.

Number awarded Up to 5 each year.

Deadline December of each year.

[38]
EDWARD T. AND MARY A. CONROY MEMORIAL SCHOLARSHIP PROGRAM

Maryland Higher Education Commission
Attn: Office of Student Financial Assistance
6 North Liberty Street, Ground Suite
Baltimore, MD 21201
(410) 767-3301　　　　　　　Toll Free: (800) 974-0203
Fax: (410) 332-0250　　　　　　TDD: (800) 735-2258
E-mail: osfamail.mhec@maryland.gov
Web: www.mhec.state.md.us

Summary To provide financial assistance for college or graduate school in Maryland to children and spouses of victims of the September 11, 2001 terrorist attacks and specified categories of veterans, public safety employees, and their children or spouses.

Eligibility This program is open to entering and continuing undergraduate and graduate students in the following categories: 1) children and surviving spouses of victims of the September 11, 2001 terrorist attacks who died in the World Trade Center in New York City, in the Pentagon in Virginia, or on United Airlines Flight 93 in Pennsylvania; 2) veterans who have, as a direct result of military service, a disability of 25% or greater and have exhausted or are no longer eligible for federal veterans' educational benefits; 3) children and unremarried surviving spouses of armed forces members whose death or 100% disability was directly caused by military service; 4) POW/MIA veterans of the Vietnam Conflict and their children; 5) state or local public safety officers or volunteers who became 100% disabled in the line of duty; 6) children and unremarried surviving spouses of state or local public safety employees or volunteers who died or became 100% disabled in the line of duty. and 7) children and unremarried surviving spouses or a school employee who, as a result of an act of violence, either died in the line of duty or sustained an injury that rendered the school employee 100% disabled. The parent, spouse, veteran, POW, public safety officer or volunteer, or school employee must have been a resident of Maryland at the time of death or when declared disabled. Applicants must be planning to enroll at a 2- or 4-year Maryland college or university as a full-time or part-time degree-seeking undergraduate or graduate student or attend a private career school. Financial need is not considered.

Financial data The amount of the award is equal to tuition and fees at a Maryland postsecondary institution, to a maximum of $10,182. The total amount of all Maryland scholarship awards from all sources may not exceed the cost of attendance or $19,000, whichever is less.

Duration Up to 5 years of full-time study or 8 years of part-time study.

Number awarded Varies each year.

Deadline July of each year.

[39]
EXELON SCHOLARSHIPS

Society of Women Engineers
Attn: Scholarship Selection Committee
203 North LaSalle Street, Suite 1675
Chicago, IL 60601-1269
(312) 596-5223   Toll Free: (877) SWE-INFO
Fax: (312) 644-8557   E-mail: scholarships@swe.org
Web: societyofwomenengineers.swe.org

Summary To provide financial assistance to women who will be entering their freshman, sophomore, or junior year and are interested in studying engineering or computer science.

Eligibility This program is open to women who are enrolling full time in their freshman, sophomore, or junior year at an ABET-accredited 4-year college or university. Preference is given to students at Bradley University, Illinois Institute of Technology, University of Illinois at Chicago, University of Illinois at Urbana-Champaign, University of Maryland-Baltimore County, University of Maryland at College Park, Morgan State University, Pennsylvania State University, or Purdue University. Applicants must be planning to major in computer science or computer, electrical, or mechanical engineering. U.S. citizenship is required. Preference is given to members of groups underrepresented in engineering and computer science, including ethnic and racial minorities, persons with disabilities, and veterans. Selection is based on merit.

Financial data The stipend is $1,000.

Duration 1 year.

Additional data This program is sponsored by Exelon Corporation, parent of ComEd and PECO, the electric utilities for northern Illinois and southeastern Pennsylvania, respectively.

Number awarded 5 each year.

Deadline May of each year for entering freshmen; February of each year for continuing sophomores and juniors.

[40]
FAMILIES OF FREEDOM SCHOLARSHIP FUND

Scholarship America
Attn: Scholarship Management Services
One Scholarship Way
P.O. Box 297
St. Peter, MN 56082
(507) 931-1682   Toll Free: (877) 862-0136
Fax: (507) 931-9168
E-mail: info@familiesoffreedom.org
Web: www.familiesoffreedom.org

Summary To provide college scholarships to financially-needy individuals and the families of individuals who were victims of the terrorist attacks on September 11, 2001.

Eligibility This program is open to the individuals who were disabled as a result of the terrorist attacks on September 11, 2001 and to the relatives of those individuals who were killed or permanently disabled during the attacks. Primarily, the fund will benefit dependents (including spouses and children) of the following groups: airplane crew and passengers; World Trade Center workers and visitors; Pentagon workers and visitors; and rescue workers, including firefighters, emergency medical personnel, and law enforcement personnel. Applicants must be enrolled or planning to enroll in an accredited 2- or 4-year college, university, or vocational/technical school in the United States. They must be able to demonstrate financial need. In addition, all students who can demonstrate financial need are eligible.

Financial data Stipends range from $1,000 to $28,000 per year, depending upon the need of the recipient. Recently, awards averaged $14,553 per academic year. Funds are distributed annually, in 2 equal installments. Checks are made payable jointly to the student and the student's school.

Duration 1 year; may be renewed.

Additional data This program was established on September 17, 2001. The fundraising goal of $100 million was reached on September 4, 2002. The fund will operate until December 31, 2030.

Number awarded Varies each year; recently, 827 students received nearly $13 million in assistance. Since the program began, it has awarded $135 million to 3,100 students.

Deadline Full-time students must apply by May of each year; other students must submit their applications by the end of the term.

[41]
FLEETWOOD MEMORIAL FOUNDATION RETRAINING FOR FIREFIGHTERS OR PEACE OFFICERS

Fleetwood Memorial Foundation
c/o North Texas Community Foundation
306 West Seventh Street, Suite 1045
Fort Worth, TX 76102
(817) 877-0702   Fax: (817) 632-8711
E-mail: rmoore@northtexascf.org
Web: www.fleetwoodmemorial.org/form.php

Summary To provide financial assistance to injured law enforcement or fire protection personnel in Texas who are interested in retraining for a new career.

Eligibility This program is open to certified Texas law enforcement or fire protection personnel who have been injured in the performance of their duties so they are unable to return to their previous job. Applicants must be interested in enrolling at a state or county institute of higher education in Texas to obtain training for a new career.

Financial data Grants are designed to pay for books and tuition. Funds are disbursed for the hours passed the previous semester. No payment is provided for non-grade point hours. Room and board may be supported if funding is available.

Duration These are 1-time grants.

Number awarded Since its inception in 1974, the foundation has provided more than 500 grants to qualified recipients, totaling nearly $4.0 million.

Deadline Applications may be submitted at any time.

[42]
FLORA MARIE JENKINS MEMORIAL DISABILITY SCHOLARSHIP

Marc Whitehead & Associates, Attorneys at Law, LLP
5300 Memorial Drive, Suite 725
Houston, TX 77007
(713) 228-8888   Toll Free: (800) 562-9830
Fax: (713) 225-0940
Web: www.disabilitydenials.com/disability-scholarship

Summary To provide financial assistance for college to students with disabilities.

Eligibility This program is open to U.S. citizens and permanent residents who have a documented disability. Applicants must be enrolled or accepted for enrollment as an undergraduate at a 2- or 4-year college or university. Along with their application, they must submit an essay of 700 to 1,500 words on the impact their disability has had on their life and how it will influence them in the future. Selection is based primarily on the originality, merit, and substantive quality of the essay.

Financial data The stipend is $5,000.

Duration 1 year.

Number awarded 1 each year.

Deadline April of each year.

[43]
GENERATION GOOGLE SCHOLARSHIPS FOR HIGH SCHOOL SENIORS

Google Inc.
Attn: Scholarships
1600 Amphitheatre Parkway
Mountain View, CA 94043-8303
(650) 253-0000   Fax: (650) 253-0001
E-mail: generationgoogle@google.com
Web: www.google.com

Summary To provide financial assistance to members of underrepresented groups planning to work on a bachelor's degree in a computer-related field.

Eligibility This program is open to high school seniors planning to enroll full time at a college or university in the United States or Canada. Applicants must be members of a group underrepresented in computer science: African Americans, Hispanics, American Indians, Filipinos/Native Hawaiians/Pacific Islanders, women, or people with a disability. They must be interested in working on a bachelor's degree in computer science, computer engineering, or a closely-related field. Selection is based on academic achievement, leadership, and passion for computer science and technology.

Financial data The stipend is $10,000 per year for U.S. students or $C5,000 for Canadian students.

Duration 1 year; may be renewed for up to 3 additional years or until graduation, whichever comes first.

Additional data Recipients are required to attend Google's Computer Science Summer Institute at Mountain View, California, Seattle, Washington, or Cambridge, Massachusetts in the summer.

Number awarded Varies each year.

Deadline February of each year.

[44]
GOOGLE LIME SCHOLARSHIPS FOR STUDENTS WITH DISABILITIES

Lime Connect, Inc.
590 Madison Avenue, 21st Floor
New York, NY 10022
(212) 521-4469   Fax: (212) 521-4099
E-mail: info@limeconnect.com
Web: www.limeconnect.com

Summary To provide financial assistance to students with disabilities working on a bachelor's or graduate degree in a computer-related field at a college or university in Canada or the United States.

Eligibility This program is open to students at colleges and universities in the United States or Canada who have a disability and are enrolled in any year of undergraduate or graduate study. International students with disabilities enrolled at universities in the United States or Canada are also eligible. Applicants must be working full time on a degree in computer science, computer engineering, or a closely-related technical field. Along with their application, they must submit 3 essays that demonstrate their "passion for computer science." Financial need is not considered in the selection process.

Financial data The stipend is $10,000 for students at U.S. universities or $C5,000 for students at Canadian universities.

Duration 1 year.

Additional data This program is jointly sponsored by Google and Lime Connect, an organization founded in 2006 to promote employment of people with disabilities.

Number awarded Varies each year; recently, 12 were awarded.

Deadline November of each year.

[45]
GOVERNOR'S COALITION FOR YOUTH WITH DISABILITIES SCHOLARSHIPS

Governor's Coalition for Youth with Disabilities
c/o Department of Rehabilitation Services
Bureau of Rehabilitation Services
55 Farmington Avenue, 12th Floor
Hartford, CT 06105
(860) 424-4844   Toll Free: (800) 537-2549
Fax: (860) 424-4850
E-mail: DORS.BRS.ContactUs@ct.gov
Web: www.ct.gov/brs/cwp/view.asp?A=3890&Q=472714

Summary To provide financial assistance for college to Connecticut residents who have a disability.

Eligibility This program is open to seniors graduating from high schools in Connecticut who have a disability. Applicants must be planning to attend a college or university in any state. Along with their application, they must submit personal statements on their intended major or specific occupational skill they are seeking, a description of their disability and how it has impacted their life experiences, and how they will use what they have learned from those experiences.

Financial data A stipend is awarded (amount not specified).

Duration 1 year.

Additional data This program began in 1994 with support from the governor of Connecticut and many business, labor organization, and individual donors in the state.

Number awarded Varies each year; recently, 18 of these scholarships, with a value of $30,950, were awarded.

Deadline December of each year.

[46]
HARRY GREGG FOUNDATION GRANTS

Harry Gregg Foundation
Attn: Grants Administrator
One Verney Drive
Greenfield, NH 03047
(603) 547-3311, ext. 1490
Toll Free: (800) 394-3311, ext. 1490 (within NH)
Fax: (603) 547-6212
E-mail: hgf@crotchedmountain.org
Web: www.crotchedmountain.org

Summary To provide financial assistance for vocational or college education, assistive technology, or other purposes to children and adults in New Hampshire who have physical, emotional, or intellectual disabilities.

Eligibility This program is open to New Hampshire residents of all ages who have physical, intellectual, learning, cognitive, developmental, or emotional disabilities. Funds may be requested for broad purposes but must specifically benefit the applicant. Examples of acceptable purposes include, but are not limited to: the costs of non-reimbursed medical or therapy treatments; specialty equipment, services, or supplies; modifications to living area, workplace, or vehicle; respite services for the recipient or care givers; costs of attending a special camp or recreational activities; vocational or academic classes; or specialized driver evaluation and training. Selection is based on demonstrated need for a product of service, the applicant's financial circumstances, and the ability of the foundation to help improve the quality of life of a grant recipient.

Financial data Most grants range up to $1,200.

Duration Recipients may receive a maximum of 4 grants (no more than 2 in any year).

Additional data This foundation was established in 1989. If a request is not funded, applicants may reapply 6 months later for the same or a different purpose.

Number awarded Nearly 150 each year. Since this foundation was established, it has awarded more than 7,000 grants worth more than $2.5 million.

Deadline March, June, September, or December of each year.

[47]
HONDA SWE SCHOLARSHIPS

Society of Women Engineers
Attn: Scholarship Selection Committee
203 North LaSalle Street, Suite 1675
Chicago, IL 60601-1269
(312) 596-5223   Toll Free: (877) SWE-INFO
Fax: (312) 644-8557   E-mail: scholarships@swe.org
Web: societyofwomenengineers.swe.org

Summary To provide financial assistance to undergraduate women from designated states, especially members of underrepresented groups, who are majoring in designated engineering specialties.

Eligibility This program is open to SWE members who are entering their junior or senior year at a 4-year ABET-accredited college or university. Preference is given to members of underrepresented ethnic or racial groups, candidates with disabilities, and veterans. Applicants must be U.S. citizens working full time on a degree in automotive engineering, chemical engineering, computer science, electrical engineering, engineering technology, manufacturing engineering, materials science and engineering, or mechanical engineering. They must be residents of or attending college in Illinois, Indiana, Michigan, Ohio, Pennsylvania, or Wisconsin. Financial need is considered in the selection process.

Financial data The stipend is $1,000.

Duration 1 year.

Additional data This program is sponsored by American Honda Motor Company.

Number awarded 5 each year.

Deadline February of each year.

[48]
HORATIO ALGER NATIONAL CAREER AND TECHNICAL SCHOLARSHIP PROGRAM

Horatio Alger Association of Distinguished Americans, Inc.
99 Canal Center Plaza, Suite 320
Alexandria, VA 22314
(703) 684-9444   Toll Free: (844) HAA-4200
Fax: (703) 548-3822
E-mail: scholarships@horatioalger.org
Web: scholars.horatioalger.org

Summary To provide financial assistance to high school seniors and recent graduates who have overcome adversity and plan to engage in career or technical training.

Eligibility This program is open to high school seniors and graduates who are younger than 30 years of age. Applicants must be planning to enroll at a nonprofit post-secondary institution in any state to complete a career or technical program. They must be U.S. citizens, be able to demonstrate critical financial need (must qualify for a federal Pell Grant), have a record of involvement in community service activities, and have displayed perseverance in overcoming adversity. Examples of adversity include having been in foster care or a ward of the state; having been homeless; experiencing the death, incarceration, or abandonment of a parent or guardian; living in a household where alcohol or drugs are or were abused; having a physical or mental disability or serious illness; or suffering from physical or mental abuse.

Financial data The stipend is $2,500.

Duration 1 year.

Additional data This program began in 1984.

Number awarded 510 each year.

Deadline Applications for the first round must be submitted by May of each year. Applications are also accepted in additional rounds in June and July.

[49]
HORATIO ALGER NATIONAL SCHOLARSHIP PROGRAM

Horatio Alger Association of Distinguished Americans, Inc.
99 Canal Center Plaza, Suite 320
Alexandria, VA 22314
(703) 684-9444   Toll Free: (844) HAA-4200
Fax: (703) 548-3822
E-mail: scholarships@horatioalger.org
Web: scholars.horatioalger.org

Summary To provide financial assistance for college to high school seniors who have overcome adversity.

Eligibility This program is open to seniors at high schools in all 50 states, the District of Columbia, and Puerto Rico. Applicants must be planning to enroll at a college in any state to work on a bachelor's degree (they may begin at a 2-year college and then transfer to a 4-year institution). They must be U.S. citizens, be able to demonstrate critical financial need ($55,000 or less adjusted gross income per family), have a GPA 2.0 or higher, have a record of involvement in co-curricular and community activities, and have displayed integrity and perseverance in overcoming adversity. Examples of adversity include having been in foster care or a ward of the state; having been homeless; experiencing the death, incarceration, or abandonment of a parent or guardian; living in a household where alcohol or drugs are or were abused; having a physical or mental disability or serious illness; or suffering from physical or mental abuse.

Financial data The stipend is $22,000.

Duration 4 years.

Additional data This program began in 1984.

Number awarded 106 each year.

Deadline October of each year.

[50]
INCIGHT SCHOLARSHIPS

Incight Education
Attn: Scholarship Coordinator
111 S.W. Columbia Street, Suite 1170
Portland, OR 97201
(971) 244-0305   Fax: (971) 244-0304
E-mail: scholarship@incight.org
Web: www.incighteducation.org/scholarship

Summary To provide financial assistance to residents of California, Oregon, and Washington who have a disability or impairment and are interested in attending college in any state.

Eligibility This program is open to residents of California, Oregon, and Washington who have a documented disability or impairment, including a physical, cognitive, or learning disability. Applicants must be entering or attending a college, university, community college, or trade school in any state as a full-time undergraduate or graduate student. They must be able to demonstrate outstanding community involvement and motivation to attend postsecondary education in order to further their ability to contribute to society. Financial need and academic merit are not considered in the selection process.

Financial data Stipends range from $500 to $1,500 per year.

Duration 1 year; may be renewed up to 3 additional years.

Number awarded Up to 100 each year.

Deadline March of each year.

[51]
IOWA VETERANS TRUST FUND ASSISTANCE

Iowa Department of Veterans Affairs
Attn: Trust Fund and Grants Administrator
Camp Dodge, Building 3465
7105 N.W. 70th Avenue
Johnston, IA 50131-1824
(515) 727-3443   Toll Free: (800) VET-IOWA
Fax: (515) 727-3713   E-mail: missy.miller@iowa.gov
Web: www.va.iowa.gov/benefits

Summary To provide funding to veterans in Iowa who need assistance for various educational, medical, or personal expenses.

Eligibility This program is open veterans in Iowa who have a household income at or below 200% of the federal poverty guideline and less than $15,000 in liquid assets. Applicants must need funding for 1) travel expenses for wounded veterans or visiting spouses, directly related to follow-up medical care; 2) job training or college tuition assistance; 3) unemployment assistance during a period of unemployment due to prolonged physical or mental condition or disability resulting from military service; 4) dental, vision, hearing, and prescription drug assistance; 5) durable equipment to allow veterans to remain in their home or to fully utilize their home; 6) individual or family counseling and substance abuse programs; 7) ambulance and emergency room services for veterans who are trauma patients; 8) emergency housing repair, emergency transitional housing assistance, and emergency vehicle repair; and/or 9) expenses related to established a minor child is a dependent of a deceased veteran.

Financial data Maximum assistance for each category of need is 1) travel expenses of $25 per day, to a maximum of $1,000; 2) job training or college tuition to $3,000; 3) unemployment assistance of $500 per month, to a maximum of $3,000 in a year or $6,000 in a lifetime; 4) dental care of $2,500, vision care of $500, hearing care of $1,500, and prescription drugs of $1,500; 5) durable equipment to a lifetime maximum of $2,500; 6) counseling to a maximum of $5,000 per family in a 12-month period, $2,500 for individual veteran counseling services; or $3,500 for individual veteran substance abuse treatment and counseling combined; 7) ambulance and emergency room services to $5,000; 8) housing repair to $3,000, transitional housing to $1,000, or vehicle repair to $2,500; and/or 9) minor child expenses to $2,500.

Duration Assistance is provided until the maximum amount in each category has been reached.

Number awarded Varies each year.

Deadline Applications may be submitted at any time.

[52]
JAY KAPLAN MEMORIAL SCHOLARSHIP

Vermont Student Assistance Corporation
Attn: Scholarship Programs
10 East Allen Street
P.O. Box 2000
Winooski, VT 05404-2601
(802) 654-3798   Toll Free: (888) 253-4819
Fax: (802) 654-3765 TDD: (800) 281-3341 (within VT)
E-mail: info@vsac.org
Web: www.vsac.org

Summary To provide financial assistance to residents of Vermont, especially those with disabilities, who are interested in working on a degree in science or finance at a college in any state.

Eligibility This program is open to residents of Vermont who are attending or planning to attend a college or university in any state. Applicants must be seeking training or education related to science or finance. Preference is given to students who have a documented disability (must submit school 504 or IEP plan). Along with their application, they must submit a 250-word essay on their interest in and commitment to the career or program of study they have chosen to pursue; their short- and long-term academic, career, and/or employment goals; their financial need; the impact that their participation in community service has had on their life; and what they believe distinguishes their application from others that may be submitted. Selection is based on that essay, a letter of recommendation, and financial need.

Financial data The stipend is $2,000.

Duration 1 year; nonrenewable.

Additional data The Jay Kaplan Retirement Education Fund, Inc. established this program in 2011.

Number awarded 2 each year.

Deadline March of each year.

[53]
JEAN B. CRYOR MEMORIAL SCHOLARSHIP PROGRAM

Maryland Higher Education Commission
Attn: Office of Student Financial Assistance
6 North Liberty Street, Ground Suite
Baltimore, MD 21201
(410) 767-3301   Toll Free: (800) 974-0203
Fax: (410) 332-0250   TDD: (800) 735-2258
E-mail: osfamail.mhec@maryland.gov
Web: www.mhec.state.md.us

Summary To provide financial assistance for college or graduate school in Maryland to children and spouses of victims of the September 11, 2001 terrorist attacks and specified categories of veterans, public safety employees, and their children or spouses.

Eligibility This program is open to entering and continuing undergraduate and graduate students in the following categories: 1) children and surviving spouses of victims of the September 11, 2001 terrorist attacks who died in the World Trade Center in New York City, in the Pentagon in Virginia, or on United Airlines Flight 93 in Pennsylvania; 2) veterans who have, as a direct result of military service, a disability of 25% or greater and have exhausted or are no longer eligible for federal veterans' educational benefits; 3) children and unremarried surviving spouses of armed forces members whose death or 100% disability was directly caused by military service; 4) POW/MIA veterans of the Vietnam Conflict and their children; 5) state or local public safety officers or volunteers who became 100% disabled in the line of duty; 6) children and unremarried surviving spouses of state or local public safety employees or volunteers who died or became 100% disabled in the line of duty. and 7) children and unremarried surviving spouses or a school employee who, as a result of an act of violence, either died in the line of duty or sustained an injury that rendered the school employee 100% disabled. The parent, spouse, veteran, POW, public safety officer or volunteer, or school employee must have been a resident of Maryland at the time of death or when declared disabled. Applicants must be planning to enroll at a 2- or 4-year Maryland college or university as a full-time or part-time degree-seeking undergraduate or graduate student or attend a private career school. Financial need is not considered.

Financial data The amount of the award is equal to tuition and fees at a Maryland postsecondary institution, to a maximum of $10,182. The total amount of all Maryland scholarship awards from all sources may not exceed the cost of attendance or $19,000, whichever is less.

Duration Up to 5 years of full-time study or 8 years of part-time study.

Number awarded Varies each year.

Deadline July of each year.

[54]
JEAN KENNEDY SMITH PLAYWRITING AWARD

John F. Kennedy Center for the Performing Arts
Education Department
Attn: Kennedy Center American College Theater
 Festival
2700 F Street, N.W.
Washington, DC 20566
(202) 416-8864   Fax: (202) 416-8860
E-mail: ghenry@kennedy-center.org
Web: web.kennedy-center.org

Summary To recognize and reward the student authors of plays on the theme of disability.

Eligibility Students at any accredited junior or senior college in the United States are eligible to compete, provided their college agrees to participate in the Kennedy Center American College Theater Festival (KCACTF). Undergraduate students must be carrying at least 6 semester hours, graduate students must be enrolled in at least 3 semester hours, and continuing part-time students must be enrolled in a regular degree or certificate program. This award is presented to the best student-written script that explores the human experience of living with a disability.

Financial data The winning playwright receives a cash award of $1,000, active membership in the Dramatists Guild, Inc., and a fellowship providing transportation, housing, and per diem to attend a prestigious playwriting program.

Duration The award is presented annually.

Additional data This award, first presented in 1999, is part of the Michael Kanin Playwriting Awards Program. The Dramatists Guild, Inc. and VSA arts participate in the selection of the winning script. The sponsoring college or university must pay a registration fee of $275 for each production.

Number awarded 1 each year.

Deadline November of each year.

[55]
JOE CLERES MEMORIAL SCHOLARSHIPS

New Outlook Pioneers
Attn: Scholarship Administrator
1801 California Street, 44th Floor
Denver, CO 80202
Toll Free: (800) 872-5995
E-mail: donLsage@gmail.com
Web: www.newoutlookpioneers.org

Summary To provide financial assistance to students at all educational levels who are physically or mentally challenged.

Eligibility This program is open to students with physical or mental disabilities who are enrolled or planning to enroll in high school, college, trade school, or graduate school. Applicants or their representatives must submit a 1-page essay describing how the student has met the challenge of his or her disability, including the severity of the disability. They may also include up to 1 page of sup-

porting documentation, but photographs, audio or video-tapes, display materials, films, or scrapbooks are not considered.

Financial data Stipends range from $500 to $2,000. Funds are paid directly to the school for tuition support only.

Duration 1 year.

Additional data This program began in 1996 by Lucent Technologies as the New Outlook Scholarships for Students with Disabilities. The current name was adopted in 2005. New Outlook Pioneers is an affiliate of TelecomPioneers. Its members are employees and retirees of Lucent Technologies, Avaya Communication, and Agere.

Number awarded Varies each year; recently, 16 were awarded: 1 at $2,000, 2 at $1,500, 3 at $1,000, 2 at $750, and 8 at $500.

Deadline March of each year.

[56]
JOYCE WALSH JUNIOR DISABILITY AWARDS

National Federation of Music Clubs
1646 West Smith Valley Road
Greenwood, IN 46142
(317) 882-4003   Fax: (317) 882-4019
E-mail: info@nfmc-music.org
Web: www.nfmc-music.org

Summary To recognize and reward, with financial assistance for further study, young instrumentalists and vocalists with disabilities who are members of the National Federation of Music Clubs (NFMC).

Eligibility This program is open to musicians (instrumentalists or vocalists) who are between 12 and 18 years of age, U.S. citizens, and junior members of the federation. Applicants must submit 1) a letter from a medical doctor stating the nature and duration of a mental or physical disability; 2) a CD or DVD, up to 10 minutes in length, of their performance of 2 selections from contrasting style periods; and 3) a letter of recommendation from a teacher, tutor, or clergyman. Financial need is not considered in the selection process.

Financial data The awards are $2,000 for first place and $1,500 for second place. In addition, regional awards are $700. All awards must be used for musical study.

Duration The awards are presented annually.

Additional data These awards are funded by the T-Shirt Project Endowment. There is a $10 entry fee.

Number awarded 7 each year: 1 first-place award, 1 second-place award, and 5 regional awards (1 in each of the 5 NFMC regions).

Deadline February of each year.

[57]
KAISER PERMANENTE COLORADO DIVERSITY SCHOLARSHIP PROGRAM

Kaiser Permanente
Attn: Office of Diversity and Inclusion
2500 South Havana Street
Aurora, CO 80014
Toll Free: (877) 457-4772
E-mail: co-diversitydevelopment@kp.org
Web: app.smarterselect.com

Summary To provide financial assistance to Colorado residents who come from diverse backgrounds and are interested in working on an undergraduate or graduate degree in a health care field at a public college in the state.

Eligibility This program is open to all residents of Colorado, including those who identify as 1 or more of the following: African American, Asian Pacific, Native American, Latino, lesbian, gay, bisexual, transgender, intersex, U.S. veteran, and/or a person with a disability. Applicants must be enrolled or planning to enroll full time at a publicly-funded college, university, or technical school in Colorado as 1) a graduating high school senior with a GPA of 2.7 or higher; 2) a GED recipient with a GED score of 520 or higher; 3) an undergraduate student; or 4) a graduate or doctoral student. They must be preparing for a career in health care (e.g., athletic training, audiology, cardiovascular perfusion technology, clinical medical assisting, cytotechnology, dental assisting, dental hygiene, diagnostic medicine, dietetics, emergency medical technology, medicine, nursing, occupational therapy, pharmacy, phlebotomy, physical therapy, physician assistant, radiology, respiratory therapy, social work, sports medicine, surgical technology). Selection is based on academic achievement, character qualities, community outreach and volunteering, and financial need. Along wit their application, they must submit 300-word essays on the following topics: 1) their exposure to other cultures; 2) issues that challenge health care today; and 3) the social responsibilities of a health care provider.

Financial data Stipends range from $1,400 to $2,600 per year.

Duration 1 year; may be renewed.

Number awarded Varies each year; recently, 24 were awarded.

Deadline February of each year.

[58]
KAISER PERMANENTE NORTHWEST HEALTH CARE CAREER SCHOLARSHIPS

Kaiser Permanente Northwest
Attn: Community Health Careers Coordinator
500 N.E. Multnomah Street, Suite 100
Portland, OR 97232
(503) 813-4478   E-mail: kpnwscholarship@gmail.com
Web: www.kpnwscholarship.scholarsapply.org/Awards

Summary To provide financial assistance to seniors at designated high schools in Oregon and southwestern Washington who plan to attend college in any state to prepare for a career as a health care professional.

Eligibility This program is open to seniors graduating from 106 approved high schools in Oregon and 26 in southwestern Washington. Applicants must be planning to enroll full time at a college or university in any state to prepare for a career as a medical or dental health care professional. They must have a GPA of 2.5 or higher. Proof of U.S. citizenship or permanent resident status is not required; undocumented students and those with Deferred Action for Childhood Arrival (DACA) status are eligible. Preference is given to students who 1) can demonstrate financial need; 2) are the first member of their family to attend college; 3) speak English plus a second language fluently; 4) are a member of a diverse population, including an ethnic or racial group underrepresented in the health professions (Black or African American, Hispanic or Latino, Native American, Asian or Pacific Islander), LGBTQ, and those with a disability; 5) engage in organized health and wellness activities at school and/or school-based health center activities; or 6) regularly volunteer or work in a public health setting such as a free clinic or health education organization.

Financial data Most stipends are $2,000 per year. Some awards are for $10,000 or $5,000 ($5,000 or $2,500 per year).

Duration 1 year (the freshman year of college) for the $2,000 awards or 2 years (the freshmen and sophomore years) for the $10,000 and $5,000 students; recipients may apply for 1 additional year (the junior year of college) of funding at $2,000.

Additional data This program began in 2008.

Number awarded At least 1 at each of the 132 approved high schools plus 24 to former recipients entering their junior year of college.

Deadline January of each year.

[59]
KAMEHAMEHA SCHOOLS CLASS OF 1972 SCHOLARSHIP

Pauahi Foundation
Attn: Scholarships
567 South King Street, Suite 160
Honolulu, HI 96813-3036
(808) 534-3966   Fax: (808) 534-3890
E-mail: scholarships@pauahi.org
Web: www.pauahi.org/scholarships

Summary To provide financial assistance to residents of any state, especially Native Hawaiians, who have faced challenging situations and are interested in attending college or graduate school.

Eligibility This program is open to undergraduate and graduate students from any state whose lives have been impacted by challenging situations (e.g., death of a significant family member, domestic violence, sexual abuse, poverty, major health problems). Applicants must be attending or planning to attend a 2- or 4-year college, university, or vocation/technical school in any state. They must be able to demonstrate financial need, a GPA of 2.8 or higher, and the potential to be successfully enriched by an educational opportunity. Along with their application, they must submit a letter of recommendation from a social service agency or counselor citing their challenging and extraordinary life circumstances and how they would benefit from this scholarship. Preference is given to Native Hawaiians (descendants of the aboriginal inhabitants of the Hawaiian Islands prior to 1778).

Financial data   The stipend is $1,000.

Duration   1 year.

Additional data   This program was established by the Kamehameha Schools class of 1972 to provide assistance to all students of Hawaiian descent.

Number awarded   2 each year.

Deadline   February of each year.

[60]
KELLY LAW TEAM DISABLED VETERAN SCHOLARSHIP

Kelly Law Team
1 East Washington Street, Suite 500
Phoenix, AZ 85004
(602) 283-4122
E-mail: mike@jkphoenixpersonalinjuryattorney.com
Web: www.jkphoenixpersonalinjuryattorney.com

Summary   To provide financial assistance to veterans who have a disability and are interested in attending college.

Eligibility   This program is open to veterans who have a disability rating of 30% or higher. Applicants must be enrolled or planning to enroll at a college, university, junior college, or trade or vocational school. Along with their application, they must submit a 100-word statement of their educational goals. They may also submit, at their discretion, a 1,000-word essay on the effect their military service has had on their life.

Financial data   The stipend is $1,000. Funds are paid directly to the recipient's college.

Duration   1 year.

Number awarded   1 each year.

Deadline   February.

[61]
KIM AND HAROLD LOUIE FAMILY FOUNDATION SCHOLARSHIPS

Kim and Harold Louie Family Foundation
1325 Howard Avenue, Suite 949
Burlingame, CA 94010
(650) 491-3434   Fax: (650) 490-3153
E-mail: louiefoundation@gmail.com
Web: www.louiefamilyfoundation.org

Summary   To provide financial assistance for college to high school seniors who have faced special challenges in completing their education.

Eligibility   This program is open to graduating high school seniors who plan to enroll either full time or at least substantial part time at an accredited college, university, or vocational program in any state. Applicants must be able to demonstrate outstanding personal achievements, academic merit, leadership qualities, and/or community service. They must have a GPA of 3.5 or higher and an

SAT score of at least 1800 (out of 2400) or 1200 (out of 1600) or an ACT score of at least 25. Special consideration is given to students who have a demonstrated financial need, whose parents did not attend college, who have a documented disability, or whose parents are U.S. veterans or currently in the U.S. military. Along with their application, they must submit 2 essays of 500 words each on assigned topics that change annually.

Financial data   Stipends vary each year; recently, they averaged approximately $3,000.

Duration   1 year.

Number awarded   Varies each year; recently, 33 were awarded. The foundation expects to award $100,000 in scholarships each year.

Deadline   March of each year.

[62]
KRISTIN CAPERTON INSPIRATION AWARD

United States Academic Decathlon
P.O. Box 4351
Mankato, MN 56002
(712) 326-9589   Fax: (712) 366-3701
E-mail: awards@usad.org
Web: www.usad.org

Summary   To recognize and reward participants in the United States Academic Decathlon (USAD) competition who have overcome disabilities or other significant obstacles.

Eligibility   Coaches of teams participating in the USAD may nominate any of the student members of their team for this award. Nominees must have overcome significant obstacles, such as disabilities, in order to have participated in the Decathlon. Letters of nomination must indicated 1) the special circumstances that have made the nominee more challenging, more dificult, and more noteworthy than those of other competitors; and 2) the role of the nominee on the Academic Decathlon team. Selection is based on courage, determination, and dedication.

Financial data   The award is a $1,500 scholarship.

Duration   The award is presented annually.

Number awarded   1 each year.

Deadline   Nominations must be submitted by March of each year.

[63]
LOREEN ARBUS FOCUS ON DISABILITY SCHOLARSHIP

Academy of Television Arts & Sciences Foundation
Attn: Education Department
5220 Lankershim Boulevard
North Hollywood, CA 91601-3109
(818) 754-2820   Fax: (818) 761-ATAS
E-mail: ctasupport@televisionacademy.com
Web: www.emmys.com/foundation/programs/cta

Summary   To recognize and reward outstanding college student videos that have a focus on disability.

Eligibility   This award is available to undergraduate and graduate students currently enrolled at a college, university, or community college. U.S. citizenship is not required, but all applicants must be enrolled at schools in the United States. All entries must have been produced for school-related classes, groups, or projects. This award is presented to the entry that best 1) sheds light on people with disabilities by having a main character with a disability; 2) helps emerging artists within this community gain recognition; or 3) increases visibility for artists with disabilities.

Financial data The award is a $10,000 scholarship.

Duration The award is presented annually.

Additional data This program is sponsored by the Loreen Arbus Foundation.

Number awarded 1 each year.

Deadline January of each year.

[64]
MARINE CORPS LEAGUE SCHOLARSHIPS

Marine Corps League
Attn: Scholarship Committee
3619 Jefferson Davis Highway, Suite 115
Stafford, VA 22554
(703) 207-9588   Toll Free: (800) MCL-1775
Fax: (703) 207-0047   E-mail: mcl@mcleague.org
Web: www.mclnational.org

Summary To provide college aid to students whose parents served in the Marines and to members of the Marine Corps League or Marine Corps League Auxiliary.

Eligibility This program is open to 1) children of Marines who were killed in action; 2) spouses, children, grandchildren, great-grandchildren, and stepchildren of active Marine Corps League and/or Auxiliary members; and 3) members of the Marine Corps League and/or Marine Corps League. Applicants must be seeking further education and training as a full-time student and be recommended by the commandant of an active chartered detachment of the Marine Corps League or the president of an active chartered unit of the Auxiliary. They must have a GPA of 3.0 or higher. Financial need is not considered in the selection process.

Financial data A stipend is awarded (amount not specified). Funds are paid directly to the recipient.

Duration 1 year; may be renewed up to 3 additional years upon reapplication.

Number awarded Varies, depending upon the amount of funds available each year.

Deadline July of each year.

[65]
MARYLAND COMMUNITY COLLEGE TUITION WAIVER FOR STUDENTS WITH DISABILITIES

Maryland Higher Education Commission
Attn: Office of Student Financial Assistance
6 North Liberty Street, Ground Suite
Baltimore, MD 21201
(410) 767-3301   Toll Free: (800) 974-0203
Fax: (410) 332-0250   TDD: (800) 735-2258
E-mail: osfamail.mhec@maryland.gov
Web: www.mhec.state.md.us

Summary To provide financial assistance to residents of Maryland who have a disability and plan to attend a community college in the state.

Eligibility This program is open to Maryland residents who have a disability and are receiving Supplemental Security Income (SSI) or Social Security Disability Insurance (SSDI) benefits. Applicants must be taking or planning to take credit classes at a community college in the state; non-credit courses do not qualify. They must complete and submit a FAFSA.

Financial data Recipients are exempt from paying tuition and mandatory fees at community colleges in Maryland for up to 12 credits per semester if they are taking classes as part of a degree or certificate program designed to lead to employment or for up to 6 credits if they are enrolled in a community college for any other reason.

Duration 1 semester; may be renewed.

Additional data This waiver was first available in 2012.

Number awarded Varies each year.

Deadline February of each year.

[66]
MASSACHUSETTS REHABILITATION COMMISSION OR COMMISSION FOR THE BLIND TUITION WAIVER PROGRAM

Massachusetts Office of Student Financial Assistance
454 Broadway, Suite 200
Revere, MA 02151
(617) 391-6070   Fax: (617) 727-0667
E-mail: osfa@osfa.mass.edu
Web: www.mass.edu/osfa/programs/categorical.asp

Summary To provide financial assistance for college to Massachusetts residents who are clients of specified disability agencies in the state.

Eligibility Applicants for this assistance must be certified as clients by the Massachusetts Rehabilitation Commission or Commission for the Blind. They must have been permanent residents of Massachusetts for at least 1 year, must be U.S. citizens or permanent residents, and may not be in default on any federal student loan.

Financial data Eligible clients are exempt from any tuition payments for an undergraduate degree or certificate program at public colleges or universities in Massachusetts.

Duration Up to 4 academic years, for a total of 130 semester hours.

Additional data Recipients may enroll either part or full time in a Massachusetts publicly-supported institution.

Number awarded Varies each year.

Deadline Deadline not specified.

[67]
MAYS MISSION SCHOLARSHIPS

Mays Mission for the Handicapped, Inc.
Attn: Scholarship Program
604 Colonial Drive
Heber Springs, AR 72545
(501) 362-7526   Toll Free: (888) 503-7955
Fax: (501) 362-7529   E-mail: info@maysmission.org
Web: www.maysmission.org/programs.html

Summary To provide financial assistance to college students with significant physical and/or mental disabilities.

Eligibility This program is open to U.S. residents with significant physical and/or mental disabilities. Applicants must be working full time on a baccalaureate degree at a 4-year college or university. They must have a score of 18 or higher on the ACT or 870 or higher on the SAT. Along with their application, they must submit a short biography that includes their goals, aspirations, and accomplishments along with a brief description of how they have overcome their disability.

Financial data A stipend is awarded (amount not specified).

Duration 1 year; may be renewed, provided the recipient remains enrolled full time with a GPA of 2.3 or higher.

Number awarded 7 scholars are supported at a time.

Deadline June of each year.

[68]
MICHIGAN ELKS ASSOCIATION GOLD KEY SCHOLARSHIP PROGRAM

Michigan Elks Association
c/o Kevin Quinn, Charitable Grant Fund Executive
  Director
2413 Longmeadow N.W.
Grand Rapids, MI 49504
(616) 791-6379   E-mail: grmielk@gmail.com
Web: www.mielks.org/program/gold.html

Summary To provide financial assistance to "special needs" students in Michigan who plan to attend college in any state.

Eligibility This program is open to "special needs" students who are Michigan residents. For the purposes of this program, "special needs" students are defined as those who are physically or mentally challenged. Applicants must be high school seniors and planning to attend an accredited college, university, trade school, or vocational school in any state. They must submit a statement on the nature and degree of their "special needs;" the school they have chosen to attend and why; their educational and career goals; how they anticipate financing school; the special equipment, devices, and/or supportive services they require; and their extracurricular activities, interests, and/or hobbies. Other required submissions include high school transcripts, a 200-word letter from their parent describing the family financial situation and the student's need for assistance, 3 letters of recommendation, and verification of "special needs" from a doctor. Sponsorship by a local Elks lodge is required.

Financial data The stipend is $2,000 per year.

Duration 1 year; may be renewed up to 3 additional years.

Number awarded Varies each year; recently, 22 were awarded.

Deadline The sponsoring lodge must forward the application to the district commissioner by December of each year.

[69]
MICROSOFT DISABILITY SCHOLARSHIP

Seattle Foundation
Attn: Scholarship Administrator
1200 Fifth Avenue, Suite 1300
Seattle, WA 98101-3151
(206) 515-2119   Fax: (206) 622-7673
E-mail: scholarships@seattlefoundation.org
Web: www.seattlefoundation.org

Summary To provide funding to high school seniors in Washington who have a disability and plan to major in designated fields at a college in any state.

Eligibility This program is open to seniors graduating from high schools in Washington who have a disability, including visual, hearing, mobility, cognitive, speech, or other. Applicants must be planning to enroll full or half time at a 2- or 4-year college, university, or vocational/technical school in any state. They must have a GPA of 3.0 or higher and be able to demonstrate financial need. Their proposed major must be business administration, computer science, computer information systems, engineering, law, or a related field. Along with their application, they must submit 1) a 500-word essay on how they plan to be engaged in the technology industry or technology law or policy in their career; 2) a 500-word essay on their vision of how Microsoft can innovate its future devices and services solutions to creatively and successfully support those living with disabilities in the workplace and in daily life to reach their potential; and 3) a 250-word essay on their financial need. U.S. citizenship is not required.

Financial data The stipend is $5,000. Funds are paid directly to the recipient's college or university.

Duration 1 year.

Additional data This program is sponsored by the Microsoft disAbility Employee Resource Group.

Number awarded 1 to 3 each year.

Deadline April of each year.

[70]
MINNESOTA HOCKEY DISABLED GRANT PROGRAM

Minnesota Hockey
Attn: Scholarship Committee
317 Washington Street
St. Paul, MN 55102
(651) 602-5727   Fax: (651) 222-1055
E-mail: info@minnesotahockey.org
Web: www.minnesotahockey.org

Summary To provide financial assistance to residents of Minnesota who have participated in Minnesota Disabled Hockey and wish to attend college or other personal growth and development activities.

Eligibility This program is open to residents of Minnesota who have participated in a Disabled Hockey program of an affiliate association of Minnesota Hockey. Applicants must be planning to attend a postsecondary institution or engage in other personal growth and development activities. As part of their application, they must include information on how they plan to use the scholarship, the number of years they have played disabled hockey, participation in community activity or volunteer work during the past 4 years, extracurricular activities, and hobbies and interests. They must also submit a letter on why they are applying for the scholarship, their contributions to their team or organization, and the significance of hockey in their personal development. Financial need is not considered in the selection process.

Financial data The stipend is $1,000. Funds are sent directly to the recipient's postsecondary institution or personal growth and development program.

Duration 1 year.

Number awarded 1 or more each year.

Deadline March of each year.

[71]
MINNESOTA SOCIAL SERVICE ASSOCIATION DIVERSITY SCHOLARSHIP

Minnesota Social Service Association
Attn: Director of Member Services
125 Charles Avenue
St. Paul, MN 55103
(651) 789-4328   Fax: (651) 224-6540
E-mail: tmarchio@mnssa.org
Web: ww.mnssa.org

Summary To provide financial assistance to students from a diverse background who are enrolled in an undergraduate program in the health and human services field at a college in the upper Midwest.

Eligibility This program is open to residents of any state entering their junior or senior year at a college or university in Iowa, Minnesota, North Dakota, South Dakota, or Wisconsin. Applicants must be working full time on a degree in the health and human services field and have a GPA of 3.0 or higher. They must be from a diverse background, which may be along the dimensions of race, ethnicity, gender, sexual orientation, socioeconomic status, age, physical ability, religion, or other ideology. Financial need is considered in the selection process.

Financial data The stipend is $1,000.

Duration 1 year.

Number awarded 1 each year.

Deadline May of each year.

[72]
MISSOURI PUBLIC SERVICE OFFICER OR EMPLOYEE'S CHILD SURVIVOR GRANT PROGRAM

Missouri Department of Higher Education
Attn: Student Financial Assistance
205 Jefferson Street
P.O. Box 1469
Jefferson City, MO 65102-1469
(573) 751-2361   Toll Free: (800) 473-6757
Fax: (573) 751-6635   E-mail: info@dhe.mo.gov
Web: www.dhe.mo.gov

Summary To provide financial assistance to disabled public safety officers in Missouri and the spouses and children of disabled or deceased officers who are interested in attending college in the state.

Eligibility This program is open to residents of Missouri who are 1) public safety officers who were permanently and totally disabled in the line of duty; 2) spouses of public safety officers who were killed or permanently and totally disabled in the line of duty; or 3) children of Missouri public safety officers or Department of Transportation employees who were killed or permanently and totally disabled while engaged in the construction or maintenance of highways, roads, and bridges. Applicants must be Missouri residents enrolled or accepted for enrollment as a full-time undergraduate student at a participating Missouri college or university; children must be younger than 24 years of age. Students working on a degree or certificate in theology or divinity are not eligible. U.S. citizenship or permanent resident status is required.

Financial data The maximum annual grant is the lesser of 1) the actual tuition charged at the school where the recipient is enrolled; or 2) the amount of tuition charged to a Missouri undergraduate resident enrolled full time in the same class level and in the same academic major as a student at the University of Missouri at Columbia.

Duration 1 year; may be renewed.

Additional data Public safety officers include firefighters, police officers, capitol police officers, parole officers, probation officers, state correctional employees, water safety officers, conservation officers, park rangers, and highway patrolmen.

Number awarded Varies each year; recently, 11 students received $47,045 in support from this program.

Deadline There is no application deadline, but early submission of the completed application is encouraged.

[73]
MOBILITY SCOOTERS DIRECT SCHOLARSHIP PROGRAM

Mobility Scooters Direct.com
4135 Dr. Martin Luther King Jr. Boulevard, Suite D21
Fort Myers, FL 33916
(754) 263-7850
E-mail: afatalo@mobilityscootersdirect.com
Web: www.mobilityscootersdirect.com/scholarship

Summary To provide financial assistance through a random drawing to undergraduate and graduate students who have a disability.
Eligibility This program is open to students who have a disability and are currently enrolled at a college or university. Undergraduates must be enrolled in at least 6 credit hours and have completed at least 40 credit hours. Graduate students must be enrolled in at least 3 credit hours and have completed at least 10 credit hours. All applicants must have a GPA of 3.0 or higher, a declared major, and a record of involvement on campus or in the community. Along with their application, they must submit a letter of recommendation and a 500-word essay on their aspirations and goals as a student, including why they feel they should be chosen to receive this scholarship. The recipient is selected randomly from among qualified entries.
Financial data The stipend is $1,200.
Duration 1 year.
Number awarded 1 each year.
Deadline December of each year.

[74]
MUSICIANS WITH SPECIAL NEEDS SCHOLARSHIP

Sigma Alpha Iota Philanthropies, Inc.
One Tunnel Road
Asheville, NC 28805
(828) 251-0606   Fax: (828) 251-0644
E-mail: nh@sai-national.org
Web: app.smarterselect.com

Summary To provide financial assistance for college or graduate school to members of Sigma Alpha Iota (an organization of women musicians) who have a disability and are working on a degree in music.
Eligibility This program is open to members of the organization who either 1) have a sensory or physical impairment and are enrolled in a graduate or undergraduate degree program in music; or 2) are preparing to become a music teacher or therapist for people with disabilities. Performance majors must submit a 15-minute DVD of their work; non-performance majors must submit evidence of work in their area of specialization, such as composition, musicology, or research.
Financial data The stipend is $1,500.
Duration 1 year.
Number awarded 1 each year.
Deadline March of each year.

[75]
NATIONAL INSTITUTES OF HEALTH UNDERGRADUATE SCHOLARSHIP PROGRAM

National Institutes of Health
Attn: Office of Intramural Training and Education
2 Center Drive
Building 2, Room 2E24
Bethesda, MD 20892-0230
(301) 594-2222   Fax: (301) 594-9606
TDD: (888) 352-3001   E-mail: ugsp@nih.gov
Web: www.training.nih.gov/programs/ugsp

Summary To provide loans-for-service for undergraduate education in the life sciences to students from disadvantaged backgrounds.
Eligibility This program is open to U.S. citizens, nationals, and permanent residents who are enrolled or accepted for enrollment as full-time students at accredited 4-year institutions of higher education and committed to careers in biomedical, behavioral, and social science health-related research. Applicants must come from a family that meets federal standards of low income, currently defined as a family with an annual income below $23,540 for a 1-person family, ranging to below $81,780 for families of 8 or more. They must have a GPA of 3.3 or higher or be in the top 5% of their class. Selection is based on commitment to a career in biomedical, behavioral, or social science health-related research as an employee of the National Institutes of Health (NIH); academic achievements; recommendations and evaluations of skills, abilities, and goals; and relevant extracurricular activities. Applicants are ranked according to the following priorities: first, juniors and seniors who have completed 2 years of undergraduate course work including 4 core science courses in biology, chemistry, physics, and calculus; second, other undergraduates who have completed those 4 core science courses; third, freshmen and sophomores at accredited undergraduate institutions; and fourth, high school seniors who have been accepted for enrollment as full-time students at accredited undergraduate institutions. The sponsor especially encourages applications from underrepresented minorities, women, and individuals with disabilities.
Financial data Stipends are available up to $20,000 per year, to be used for tuition, educational expenses (such as books and lab fees), and qualified living expenses while attending a college or university. Recipients incur a service obligation to work as an employee of the NIH in Bethesda, Maryland for 10 consecutive weeks (during the summer) during the sponsored year and, upon graduation, for 52 weeks for each academic year of scholarship support. The NIH 52-week employment obligation may be deferred if the recipient goes to graduate or medical school.
Duration 1 year; may be renewed for up to 3 additional years.
Number awarded 15 each year.
Deadline March of each year.

[76]
NATIONAL PRESS CLUB SCHOLARSHIP FOR JOURNALISM DIVERSITY

National Press Club
Attn: Executive Director's Office
529 14th Street, N.W., 13th Floor
Washington, DC 20045
(202) 662-7599
Web: www.press.org/about/scholarships/diversity

Summary To provide funding to high school seniors who are planning to major in journalism in college and who will bring diversity to the field.

Eligibility This program is open to high school seniors who have been accepted to college and plan to prepare for a career in journalism. Applicants must submit 1) a 500-word essay explaining how they would add diversity to U.S. journalism; 2) up to 5 work samples demonstrating an ongoing interest in journalism through work on a high school newspaper or other media; 3) letters of recommendation from 3 people; 4) a copy of their high school transcript; 5) documentation of financial need; 6) a letter of acceptance from the college or university of their choice; and 7) a brief description of how they have pursued journalism in high school.

Financial data The stipend is $2,000 for the first year and $2,500 for each subsequent year. The program also provides an additional $500 book stipend, designated the Ellen Masin Persina Scholarship, for the first year.

Duration 4 years.

Additional data The program began in 1990.

Number awarded 1 each year.

Deadline February of each year.

[77]
NATIONAL SPACE GRANT COLLEGE AND FELLOWSHIP PROGRAM

National Aeronautics and Space Administration
Attn: Office of Education
300 E Street, S.W.
Mail Suite 6M35
Washington, DC 20546-0001
(202) 358-1069   Fax: (202) 358-7097
E-mail: aleksandra.korobov@nasa.gov
Web: www.nasa.gov

Summary To provide financial assistance to undergraduate and graduate students interested in preparing for a career in a space-related field.

Eligibility This program is open to undergraduate and graduate students at colleges and universities that participate in the National Space Grant program of the U.S. National Aeronautics and Space Administration (NASA) through their state consortium. Applicants must be interested in a program of study and/or research in a field of science, technology, engineering, or mathematics (STEM) related to space. A specific goal of the program is to recruit and train U.S. citizens, especially underrepresented minorities, women, and persons with disabilities, for careers in aerospace science and technology. Financial need is not considered in the selection process.

Financial data Each consortium establishes the terms of the fellowship program in its state.

Additional data NASA established the Space Grant program in 1989. It operates through 52 consortia in each state, the District of Columbia, and Puerto Rico. Each consortium includes selected colleges and universities in that state as well as other affiliates from industry, museums, science centers, and state and local agencies.

Number awarded Varies each year.

Deadline Each consortium sets its own deadlines.

[78]
NAVY SEAL FOUNDATION SCHOLARSHIPS

Navy Seal Foundation
Attn: Chief Financial Officer
1619 D Street, Building 5326
Virginia Beach, VA 23459
(757) 363-7490   Fax: (757) 363-7491
E-mail: info@navysealfoundation.org
Web: www.navysealfoundation.org

Summary To provide financial assistance for college or graduate school to Naval Special Warfare (NSW) personnel and their families.

Eligibility This program is open to active-duty Navy SEALS, Special Warfare Combatant-craft Crewmen (SWCC), and military personnel assigned to other NSW commands. Their dependent children and spouses are also eligible. Applicants must be entering or continuing full or part-time students working on an associate or bachelor's degree. Active-duty and spouses, but not dependent children, may also work on a graduate degree. Selection is based on GPA, SAT scores, class ranking, extracurricular activities, volunteer community involvement, leadership positions held, military service record, and employment (as appropriate).

Financial data Stipends are $15,000, $7,500, or $5,000 per year.

Duration 1 year; may be renewed.

Number awarded Varies each year; recently, the Navy Seal Foundation awarded 16 scholarships for all of its programs: 3 for 4 years at $15,000 per year to high school seniors and graduates, 3 for 1 year at $7,500 to high school seniors and graduates, 3 for 1 year at $15,000 to current college students, 3 for 1 year at $7,500 to current college students, and 4 for 1 year at $5,000 to spouses.

Deadline February of each year.

[79]
NBCFAE NATIONAL SCHOLARSHIP PROGRAM

National Black Coalition of Federal Aviation Employees
c/o Phyllis Seaward, National Education, Recruitment, and Training Chair
FAA Employee Relations Division
800 Independence Avenue, S.W.
Washington, DC 20591
(202) 276-4891
E-mail: nationalnbcfaescholarship@nbcfaeinfo.org
Web: nbcfae.clubexpress.com

Summary To provide financial assistance to undergraduate students, especially those from underrepresented groups, who are interested in preparing for a career in a field related to aviation.

Eligibility This program is open to entering and continuing full-time undergraduate students preparing for a career in aviation, science, or technology. Applicants must be U.S. citizens and have a GPA of 2.5 or higher. The program encourages applications from women, minorities, and people with disabilities. Selection is based on academic achievement, leadership, community involvement, and financial need.

Financial data   The stipend is $1,000.
Duration   1 year.
Additional data   This program began in 2005.
Number awarded   Up to 8 each year: 8 in each of the sponsor's regions.
Deadline   May of each year.

[80]
NBCUNIVERSAL TONY COELHO MEDIA SCHOLARSHIPS

American Association of People with Disabilities
Attn: Scholarships
2013 H Street, N.W., Fifth Floor
Washington, DC 20006
(202) 521-4316   Toll Free: (800) 840-8844
E-mail: scholarship@aapd.com
Web: www.aapd.com

Summary   To provide financial assistance to undergraduate and graduate students who have a disability and are working on a degree in communication or other media-related field.

Eligibility   This program is open to students who have any kind of disability and are 1) second-year associate degree students; 2) undergraduate sophomores, juniors, or seniors; or 3) graduate students. Applicants must be working on a degree in communication or other media-related field. Along with their application, they must submit essays of 300 to 350 words each on 1) what disability means to them; and 2) how their degree will affect the disability community. Selection is based on demonstrated leadership characteristics, connection between their degree and the disability community, engagement within the communications and/or media fields, difficulty of course work, success in course work, and character.

Financial data   The stipend is $5,625.
Duration   1 year.
Additional data   This program began in 2013 with support from NBCUniversal.
Number awarded   8 each year.
Deadline   June of each year.

[81]
NCCPA ENDOWED SCHOLARSHIPS

American Academy of Physician Assistants
Attn: Physician Assistant Foundation
2318 Mill Road, Suite 1300
Alexandria, VA 22314-6868
(571) 319-4510   E-mail: pafoundation@aapa.org
Web: www.pa-foundation.org

Summary   To provide financial assistance to student members of the American Academy of Physician Assistants (AAPA) who are underrepresented minorities or economically and/or educationally disadvantaged.

Eligibility   This program is open to AAPA student members who have completed at least 1 semester of an accredited physician assistant program. Applicants must qualify as 1) an underrepresented minority (American Indian, Alaska Native, Black or African American, Hispanic or Latino, Native Hawaiian or other Pacific Islander,

or Asian); 2) economically disadvantaged (with income below a specified level); or 3) educationally disadvantaged (from a high school with low SAT scores, from a school district in which less than half of graduates go on to college, has a diagnosed physical or mental impairment, English is not their primary language, the first member of their family to attend college).

Financial data   The stipend is $2,000.
Duration   1 year; nonrenewable.
Additional data   This program is sponsored by the National Commission on Certification of Physician Assistants (NCCPA).
Number awarded   2 each year.
Deadline   May of each year.

[82]
NEUROSCIENCE SCHOLARS PROGRAM

Society for Neuroscience
Attn: Neuroscience Scholars Program
1121 14th Street, N.W., Suite 1010
Washington, DC 20005
(202) 962-4000   Fax: (202) 962-4941
E-mail: nsp@sfn.org
Web: www.sfn.org

Summary   To provide funding to underrepresented students in neuroscience who are interested in participating in activities of the Society for Neuroscience (SfN).

Eligibility   This program is open to undergraduate and graduate students and postdoctoral fellows in neuroscience who are interested in attending the society's annual meeting and participating in other activities related to the field. Applicants must be from a group recognized as underrepresented in the biomedical, behavioral, clinical, and social sciences, defined as Blacks or African Americans, Hispanics or Latinos, American Indians or Alaska Natives, Native Hawaiians and other Pacific Islanders, and individuals with disabilities. U.S. citizenship or permanent resident status is required. Selection is based on academic excellence, research interests, experience, and a 500-word essay on professional goals and what they hope to gain from the fellowship.

Financial data   Participants selected as fellows receive a mentoring team to discuss the fellow's research, career plans, and overall experience; complimentary SfN membership; a travel award to attend the SfN annual meeting each fall; and an annual stipend of $1,500 to support allowed professional development activities.
Duration   Support is provided over a 2-year period.
Additional data   Funding for this program is provided by the National Institute of Neurological Disorders and Stroke.
Number awarded   15 fellows are selected each year.
Deadline   June of each year.

[83]
NEW JERSEY STATE ELKS SPECIAL CHILDREN'S SCHOLARSHIP

New Jersey State Elks
c/o Special Children's Committee
665 Rahway Avenue
P.O. Box 1596
Woodbridge, NJ 07095-1596
(732) 326-1300   E-mail: info@njelks.org
Web: www.njelks.org

Summary To provide financial assistance to high school seniors in New Jersey (girls and boys are judged separately) who have a disability and plan to attend college in any state.

Eligibility This program is open to seniors graduating from high schools in New Jersey who have a disability. Applicants must be planning to attend a college or university in any state. Along with their application, they must submit a brief statement of their ultimate goal, including their particular purpose in the planned education sought and their career goal. Selection is based on academic standing, general worthiness, and financial need. Boys and girls are judged separately.

Financial data The stipend is $2,500 per year. Funds are paid directly to the recipient's college or university.

Duration 4 years.

Number awarded 2 each year: 1 to a boy and 1 to a girl.

Deadline April of each year.

[84]
NEW YORK MILITARY ENHANCED RECOGNITION INCENTIVE AND TRIBUTE (MERIT) SCHOLARSHIPS

New York State Higher Education Services Corporation
Attn: Student Information
99 Washington Avenue
Albany, NY 12255
(518) 473-1574   Toll Free: (888) NYS-HESC
Fax: (518) 473-3749   TDD: (800) 445-5234
E-mail: scholarships@hesc.com
Web: www.hesc.ny.gov

Summary To provide financial assistance to disabled veterans and the family members of deceased or disabled veterans who are residents of New York and interested in attending college in the state.

Eligibility This program is open to New York residents who served in the armed forces of the United States or state organized militia at any time on or after August 2, 1990 and became severely and permanently disabled as a result of injury or illness suffered or incurred in a combat theater or combat zone or during military training operations in preparation for duty in a combat theater or combat zone of operations. Also eligible are the children, spouses, or financial dependents of members of the armed forces of the United States or state organized militia who at any time after August 2, 1990 1) died, became severely and permanently disabled as a result of injury or illness suffered or incurred, or are classified as missing in action in a combat theater or combat zone of operations; 2) died as a result of injuries incurred in those designated areas; or 3) died or became severely and permanently disabled as a result of injury or illness suffered or incurred during military training operations in preparation for duty in a combat theater or combat zone of operations. Applicants must be attending or accepted at an approved program of study as full-time undergraduates at a public college or university or private institution in New York.

Financial data At public colleges and universities, this program provides payment of actual tuition and mandatory educational fees; actual room and board charged to students living on campus or an allowance for room and board for commuter students; and allowances for books, supplies, and transportation. At private institutions, the award is equal to the amount charged at the State University of New York (SUNY) for 4-year tuition and average mandatory fees (or the student's actual tuition and fees, whichever is less) plus allowances for room, board, books, supplies, and transportation. Recently, maximum awards were $23,045 for students living on campus or $15,125 for commuter students.

Duration This program is available for 4 years of full-time undergraduate study (or 5 years in an approved 5-year bachelor's degree program).

Additional data This program was previously known as the New York State Military Service Recognition Scholarships (MSRS).

Number awarded Varies each year; recently, 93 students received more than $1.3 million from is program.

Deadline April of each year.

[85]
NEW YORK STATE WORLD TRADE CENTER MEMORIAL SCHOLARSHIPS

New York State Higher Education Services Corporation
Attn: Student Information
99 Washington Avenue
Albany, NY 12255
(518) 473-1574   Toll Free: (888) NYS-HESC
Fax: (518) 473-3749   TDD: (800) 445-5234
E-mail: scholarships@hesc.com
Web: www.hesc.ny.gov

Summary To provide financial assistance to undergraduates in New York who are survivors or victims of the terrorist attacks on September 11, 2001 or their relatives.

Eligibility This program is open to 1) the children, spouses, and financial dependents of deceased or severely and permanently disabled victims of the September 11, 2001 terrorist attacks or the subsequent rescue and recovery operations; and 2) survivors of the terrorist attacks who are severely and permanently disabled as a result of injuries sustained in the attacks or the subsequent rescue and recovery operations. Applicants must be attending or accepted at an approved program of study as full-time undergraduates at a public college or university or private institution in New York.

Financial data At public colleges and universities, this program provides payment of actual tuition and mandatory educational fees; actual room and board charged to students living on campus or an allowance for room and board for commuter students; and allowances for books, supplies, and transportation. At private institutions, the award is equal to the amount charged at the State University of New York (SUNY) for 4-year tuition and average mandatory fees (or the student's actual tuition and fees, whichever is less) plus allowances for room, board, books, supplies, and transportation. Recently, maximum awards were $23,045 for students living on campus or $15,125 for commuter students.

Duration This program is available for 4 years of full-time undergraduate study (or 5 years in an approved 5-year bachelor's degree program).

Number awarded Varies each year; recently, 807 students received more than $13.3 in support from this program.

Deadline April of each year.

[86]
NJUA EXCELLENCE IN DIVERSITY SCHOLARSHIP

New Jersey Utilities Association
50 West State Street, Suite 1117
Trenton, NJ 08608
(609) 392-1000   Fax: (609) 396-4231
E-mail: info@njua.com
Web: www.njua.com

Summary To provide financial assistance to minority, female, and disabled high school seniors in New Jersey interested in attending college in the state.

Eligibility This program is open to seniors graduating from high schools in New Jersey who are women, minorities (Black or African American, Hispanic or Latino, American Indian or Alaska Native, Asian, Native Hawaiian or Pacific Islander, or 2 or more races), or persons with disabilities. Applicants must be planning to work on a bachelor's degree at a college or university in the state. Along with their application, they must submit a 500-word essay explaining their career ambition and why they have chosen that career. Children of employees of any New Jersey Utilities Association-member company are ineligible. Selection is based on overall academic excellence and demonstrated financial need. U.S. citizenship or permanent resident status is required.

Financial data The stipend is $1,500 per year. Funds are paid to the recipient's college or university.

Duration 4 years.

Number awarded 2 each year.

Deadline April of each year.

[87]
OKLAHOMA GOODWILL INDUSTRIES ABILITIES SCHOLARSHIP

Oklahoma City Community Foundation
Attn: Scholarship Coordinator
1000 North Broadway
P.O. Box 1146
Oklahoma City, OK 73101-1146
(405) 606-2907   Fax: (405) 235-5612
E-mail: w.minter@occf.org
Web: occf.academicworks.com/opportunities/1841

Summary To provide financial assistance to high school seniors in Oklahoma who have a disability and plan to attend college in any state.

Eligibility This program is open to seniors graduating from high schools in Oklahoma who have a disability as defined by the Americans with Disabilities Act (ADA). Applicants must be planning to attend a public college or technology center in any state. They must have a GPA of 3.0 or higher. Along with their application, they must submit 2 reflection papers on 1) why their disability does not define who they are; and 2) their academic and future goals. Selection is based on those statements, academic record, leadership and participation in school or community activities, work experience, unusual personal or family circumstances, and financial need. U.S. citizenship is required.

Financial data The stipend is $1,000.

Duration 1 year.

Additional data This program was established in 2006 by Oklahoma Goodwill Industries.

Number awarded 1 or more each year.

Deadline May of each year.

[88]
OTTO SUSSMAN TRUST GRANTS

Otto Sussman Trust
30 Jericho Executive Plaza, Suite 200W
Jericho, NY 11753-1028
(202) 965-5450

Summary To provide financial assistance to residents of selected states who are attending college or graduate school in any state and experiencing financial need because of special circumstances, such as illness or injury.

Eligibility This program is open to residents of New York, New Jersey, Oklahoma, or Pennsylvania who are currently enrolled as full-time juniors, seniors, or graduate students at a college or university in any state. Applicants must be experiencing extreme special circumstances, such as unemployment, death of a parent, or medical expenses not covered by insurance. They must have a GPA of 3.0 or higher.

Financial data The amount awarded varies, depending upon the needs of the recipient, but generally varies from $5,000 to $10,000.

Duration This is a 1-time grant.

Number awarded Varies each year.

Deadline July of each year.

[89]
PA FOUNDATION SCHOLARSHIPS

American Academy of Physician Assistants
Attn: Physician Assistant Foundation
2318 Mill Road, Suite 1300
Alexandria, VA 22314-6868
(571) 319-4510   E-mail: pafoundation@aapa.org
Web: www.pa-foundation.org

Summary To provide financial assistance to student members of the American Academy of Physician Assistants (AAPA).

Eligibility This program is open to AAPA student members who have completed at least 1 semester of an accredited physician assistant program. Applicants must be in good academic standing.

Financial data The stipend is $1,000.

Duration 1 year; nonrenewable.

Number awarded 9 each year.

Deadline May of each year.

[90]
PCMA EDUCATION FOUNDATION DIVERSITY SCHOLARSHIP

Professional Convention Management Association
Attn: PCMA Education Foundation
35 East Wacker Drive, Suite 500
Chicago, IL 60601
(312) 423-7262   Toll Free: (877) 827-7262
Fax: (312) 423-7222   E-mail: foundation@pcma.org
Web: www.pcma.org/scholarships/diversity-student

Summary To provide financial assistance to student members of the Professional Convention Management Association (PCMA) who are from underrepresented groups and are majoring in a field related to the meetings or hospitality industry.

Eligibility This program is open to PCMA members who are currently enrolled in at least 6 credit hours with a major directly related to the meetings or hospitality industry. Applicants must be students traditionally underrepresented in the industry, including (but not limited to) those identifying by a certain race, sex, color, religion, creed, sexual orientation, gender identity or expression, or disability, as well as those with a history of overcoming adversity. They must have a GPA of 2.75 or higher. Along with their application, they must submit a 750-word essay that details how they became interested in the meetings and events industry and a short paragraph describing the potential impact receiving this scholarship would have for them. Selection is based on that essay, academic record, meetings industry experience, and a letter of recommendation.

Financial data The stipend is $2,500.

Duration 1 year.

Number awarded 1 each year.

Deadline March of each year.

[91]
PENNSYLVANIA ASSOCIATION OF MEDICAL SUPPLIERS SCHOLARSHIP

Pennsylvania Association of Medical Suppliers
1820 Linglestown Road
Harrisburg, PA 17110
(717) 909-1958   Fax: (717) 388-8446
E-mail: Kelly@pamsonline.org
Web: www.pamsonline.org

Summary To provide financial assistance to high school seniors in Pennsylvania and Delaware who use home medical equipment and services to overcome a physical challenge and are interested in attending college in any state.

Eligibility This program is open to seniors graduating from high school in Pennsylvania and Delaware who are planning to enroll in a postsecondary educational program in any state. Applicants must have been successful in their educational pursuits while overcoming physical challenges with the help of home medical equipment and services (e.g., wheelchairs, respiratory devices). Along with their application, they must submit a short essay that describes their experiences with home medical equipment and how it helps them pursue higher education.

Financial data The stipend is $1,000.

Duration 1 year.

Number awarded 1 each year.

Deadline April of each year.

[92]
P.O. PISTILLI SCHOLARSHIPS

Design Automation Conference
c/o Andrew B. Kahng, Scholarship Director
University of California at San Diego-Jacobs School of Engineering
Jacobs Hall, EBU3B, Rpp, 2134
9500 Gilman Drive
La Jolla, CA 92093-0404
(858) 822-4884   Fax: (858) 534-7029
E-mail: abk@cs.ucsd.edu
Web: www.dac.com

Summary To provide financial assistance to female, minority, or disabled high school seniors who are interested in preparing for a career in computer science or electrical engineering.

Eligibility This program is open to graduating high school seniors who are members of underrepresented groups: women, African Americans, Hispanics, Native Americans, and students with disabilities. Applicants must be interested in preparing for a career in electrical engineering, computer engineering, or computer science. They must have at least a 3.0 GPA, have demonstrated high achievements in math and science courses, have demonstrated involvement in activities associated with the underrepresented group they represent, and be able to demonstrate significant financial need. U.S. citizenship is not required, but applicants must be U.S. residents when they apply and must plan to attend an accredited U.S. college or university. Along with their application, they must submit 3 letters of recommendation, official transcripts, ACT/SAT and/or PSAT scores, a personal statement outlining future goals and why they think they should receive this scholarship, and documentation of financial need.

Financial data   Stipends are $4,000 per year. Awards are paid each year in 2 equal installments.

Duration   1 year; may be renewed up to 4 additional years.

Additional data   This program is funded by the Design Automation Conference of the Association for Computing Machinery's Special Interest Group on Design Automation.

Number awarded   2 to 7 each year.

Deadline   January of each year.

[93]
PORAC SCHOLARSHIPS

Peace Officers Research Association of California
Attn: Peace Officers Research and Education
  Foundation
4010 Truxel Road
Sacramento, CA 95834-3725
(916) 928-3777   Toll Free: (800) 937-6722
Fax: (916) 928-3760   E-mail: scholarships@porac.org
Web: www.porac.org

Summary   To provide financial assistance to relatives of members of the Peace Officers Research Association of California (PORAC) and to members who are medically retired.

Eligibility   This program is open to residents of California and Nevada who are 1) family members of law enforcement officers who have died in the line of duty; 2) dependents whose parent or legal guardian is an active PORAC member; 3) spouses and dependents of deceased PORAC members; and 4) PORAC members who have medically retired. Applicants must be enrolled or planning to enroll full-time at a college or university in any state. They may be interested in scholastic or vocational study, but they are encouraged to consider law enforcement as a career. Along with their application, they must submit a 1-page essay on "My goals, present and future: why I am applying for this scholarship and its importance to me." Selection is based on the essay, academic achievement (GPA of 2.0 or higher for dependents), school activities, community service, and financial need.

Financial data   The stipend is $1,500.

Duration   1 year.

Number awarded   Varies each year; recently, 25 were awarded.

Deadline   March of each year.

[94]
POWERING EDUCATION SCHOLARSHIPS

Alpha One
127 Main Street
South Portland, ME 04106
(207) 767-2189   Toll Free: (800) 640-7200
Fax: (207) 799-8346   E-mail: mardi@alphaonenow.org
Web: www.alphaonenow.com

Summary   To provide financial assistance to undergraduate and graduate students in Maine who have disabilities.

Eligibility   This program is open to high school seniors, undergraduates, and graduate students at schools in Maine. Applicants must have a disability. They must have a "B" average or equivalent GPA. Along with their application, they must submit a personal essay of 500 to 1,000 words on how their disability has helped shape their view of the world and themselves as a person, a letter of recommendation, and current transcripts.

Financial data   The stipend is $2,000. Funds are paid directly to the recipient's institution after completion of the first semester, provided the student earns a GPA of 2.5 or higher.

Duration   1 year.

Number awarded   3 each year.

Deadline   March of each year.

[95]
REHABGYM SCHOLARSHIP

Vermont Student Assistance Corporation
Attn: Scholarship Programs
10 East Allen Street
P.O. Box 2000
Winooski, VT 05404-2601
(802) 654-3798   Toll Free: (888) 253-4819
Fax: (802) 654-3765   TDD: (800) 281-3341 (within VT)
E-mail: info@vsac.org
Web: www.vsac.org

Summary   To provide financial assistance to residents of Vermont who have undergone a significant physical challenge and plan to attend college in any state.

Eligibility   This scholarship is available to residents of Vermont who are attending or planning to attend a college or university in any state. Applicants must be able to demonstrate that they have undergone a significant physical challenge or illness and have met the challenge with courage and perseverance. Along with their application, they must submit a 250-word essay on their interest in and commitment to the career or program of study they have chosen to pursue; their short- and long-term academic, career, and/or employment goals; their financial need; the impact that their participation in community service has had on their life; and what they believe distinguishes their application from others that may be submitted. Selection is based on that essay and financial need.

Financial data   The stipend is $1,000.

Duration   1 year.

Additional data   This program began in 2006.

Number awarded   1 each year.

Deadline   March of each year.

[96]
REHABMART.COM SCHOLARSHIP FUND

Rehabmart, LLC
1367 Sydneys Pass
Watkinsville, GA 30677-8393
(706) 213-1144   Toll Free: (800) 827-8283
Fax: (888) 507-7326
E-mail: assistance@rehabmart.com
Web: www.rehabmart.com/scholarship

Summary To provide financial assistance to students with disabilities and those who are majoring in health science or special education.

Eligibility This program is open to students who are enrolled or planning to enroll at a 2- or 4-year college, university, or technical college. Applicants must be 1) a student with a disability; 2) enrolling as a health sciences student; or 3) majoring in special needs education. Along with their application, they must submit a personal biography and an essay on the medical device, technology, or therapeutic technique they believe has made the biggest difference in the life (or will make in the future) of an adult or child with a disability. There are no requirements for the length of the biography or essay, but only those of at least 250 words are typically considered for winning a scholarship. In the selection process, higher priority is given to biographies that include education goals, extracurricular activities, and other interests that help explain who the student is and what they are about. Priority is also given to essays that provide a clear explanation of the device, technology, or technique and how it would make a significant impact on the life of an adult or child with a disability.

Financial data Stipends range from $250 to $2,500.
Duration 1 year.
Additional data This program began in 2016.
Number awarded 15 each year; a total of $25,000 is available for this program each year.
Deadline May or October of each year.

[97]
RJT CRIMINAL DEFENSE DISABLED VETERAN SCHOLARSHIP

RJT Criminal Defense Attorney
2820 Camino Del Rio South, Suite 110
San Diego, CA 92108
(619) 577-0868
E-mail: mike@sandiegocriminallawyerrt.com
Web: www.sandiegocriminallawyerrt.com

Summary To provide financial assistance for college to veterans who have a disability rating.

Eligibility This program is open to veterans of the U.S. armed forces who have a disability rating of 30% or higher. Applicants must be enrolled or planning to enroll at a college, university, community college, or trade school. Along with their application, they must submit 1) a short statement on their educational goals; and 2) an essay up to 1,000 words in length on how their military service has affected their life.

Financial data The stipend is $1,000.
Duration 1 year.

Number awarded 1 each year.
Deadline February of each year.

[98]
ROBERT DOLE SCHOLARSHIP FOR DISABLED STUDENTS

United Negro College Fund
Attn: Scholarships and Grants Department
1805 Seventh Street, N.W.
Washington, DC 20001
(202) 810-0258   Toll Free: (800) 331-2244
E-mail: scholarships@uncf.org
Web: www.scholarships.uncf.org

Summary To provide financial assistance to underrepresented minority college who have a disability and are enrolled at colleges and universities that are members of the United Negro College Fund (UNCF).

Eligibility This program is open to African Americans/Blacks, American Indians, Native Alaskans, Asian Pacific Islander Americans, and Hispanic Americans who have a physical or mental disability. Applicants must be enrolled at UNCF institutions. They must have a GPA of 2.5 or higher. Along with their application, they must submit a 500-word essay on the challenges of their disability, how they have achieved their educational goals, and how they have assisted others who may have a disability.

Financial data The stipend is $3,500.
Duration 1 year.
Number awarded Varies each year.
Deadline October of each year.

[99]
RUNWAY OF DREAMS SCHOLARSHIP

Springboard Foundation
14 Glenbrook Drive
Mendham, NJ 07945-2306
(973) 813-7260, ext. 302   Fax: (973) 813-7261
E-mail: info@thespringboardfoundation.org
Web: www.thespringboardfoundation.org

Summary To provide financial assistance to college students who have a disability and are majoring in a field related to fashion.

Eligibility This program is open to students enrolled full time at a 4-year college or university with a major in fashion design, fashion merchandising and buying, fashion production and management, fashion technology, clothing and textile studies, visual presentation and styling, fashion journalism and publishing, or fashion marketing, public relations, or advertising. Applicants must have a documented disability that is protected under the Americans with Disabilities Act and/or the Rehabilitation Act of 1973. They must have completed at least 24 credits and have a GPA of 3.0 or higher. Along with their application, they must submit a list of extracurricular activities (e.g., sports, volunteer activities, part-time jobs) and a statement of 150 to 300 words describing their career objectives and why this scholarship is important to furthering those objectives.

Financial data The stipend is $2,500.
Duration 1 year.

Additional data The Runway of Dreams Foundation provides funding for this program. Recipients are required to serve as a spokesperson for the sponsor, as by participating in an in-person or virtual foundation event, appearing on the foundation website, or other forms of collateral and promotion.

Number awarded 1 each year.

Deadline June of each year.

[100]
SAULT TRIBE SPECIAL NEEDS SCHOLARSHIPS

Sault Tribe of Chippewa Indians
Attn: Higher Education Department
523 Ashmun Street
Sault Ste. Marie, MI 49783
(906) 635-6050, ext. 26312   Toll Free: (800) 793-0660
Fax: (906) 635-7785
E-mail: BMacArthur@saulttribe.net
Web: www.saulttribe.com

Summary To provide financial assistance for education at any level to members of the Sault Tribe of Chippewa Indians who have a disability.

Eligibility This program is open to members of the Sault Tribe who have a documented physical or emotional disability. Applicants must be enrolled in an educational program at any level. Along with their application, they must submit a letter from themselves or a parent describing the proposed use of the funds and an itemized list of the expected costs.

Financial data The stipend is $1,000.

Duration 1 year.

Number awarded 4 each year: 2 for students under 18 years of age and 2 for students 18 years of age or older.

Deadline May of each year.

[101]
SENTINELS OF FREEDOM SCHOLARSHIPS

Sentinels of Freedom
2303 Camino Ramon, Suite 270
P.O. Box 1316
San Ramon, CA 94583
(925) 380-6342   Fax: (925) 867-1078
E-mail: info@sentinelsoffreedom.org
Web: www.sentinelsoffreedom.org

Summary To provide assistance to veterans and current military personnel who became disabled as a result of injuries sustained in the line of duty on or after September 11, 2001.

Eligibility This program is open to members of the U.S. armed forces (active, Guard, or Reserves) who have received or will receive an honorable discharge. Applicants must be rated as 50% or more disabled as a result of service-related events, including combat-related injuries, training accidents, or non-physical injuries, sustained after September 11, 2001. They must be enrolled or planning to enroll full time at a college, university, or vocational school. Selection is based on motivation and drive to reach personal, educational, and career goals.

Financial data Assistance is available for the following needs: housing subsidies (paid directly to the housing provider), training and employment opportunities, career and networking assistance, or financial and personal mentorship.

Duration Assistance may be provided for up to 4 years.

Additional data The first assistance granted by this program was awarded in 2004.

Number awarded Varies each year. Since the program was established, it has supported more than 200 current and former servicemembers.

Deadline May of each year for fall; October of each year for spring.

[102]
SOUTH DAKOTA REDUCED TUITION FOR VETERANS

South Dakota Board of Regents
Attn: Scholarship Committee
306 East Capitol Avenue, Suite 200
Pierre, SD 57501-2545
(605) 773-3455   Fax: (605) 773-5320
E-mail: info@sdbor.edu
Web: www.sdbor.edu

Summary To provide free tuition at South Dakota public colleges and universities to certain veterans.

Eligibility This program is open to current residents of South Dakota who have been discharged from the military forces of the United States under honorable conditions. Applicants must meet 1 of the following criteria: 1) served on active duty at any time between August 2, 1990 and March 3, 1991; 2) received an Armed Forces Expeditionary Medal, Southwest Asia Service Medal, or other U.S. campaign or service medal for participation in combat operations against hostile forces outside the boundaries of the United States: or 3) have a service-connected disability rating of at least 10%. They may not be eligible for any other educational assistance from the U.S. government. Qualifying veterans must apply for this benefit within 20 years after the date proclaimed for the cessation of hostilities or within 6 years from and after the date of their discharge from military service, whichever is later. They must be attending or planning to attend a South Dakota state-supported institution of higher education or state-supported technical or vocational school.

Financial data Eligible veterans receive a waiver of tuition. The waiver applies only to tuition, not fees.

Duration Eligible veterans are entitled to receive 1 month of tuition waiver for each month of qualifying service, from a minimum of 1 year to a maximum of 4 years.

Number awarded Varies each year.

Deadline Deadline not specified.

[103]
SPRINGBOARD FOUNDATION DOW SCHOLARSHIPS

Springboard Foundation
14 Glenbrook Drive
Mendham, NJ 07945-2306
(973) 813-7260, ext. 302   Fax: (973) 813-7261
E-mail: info@thespringboardfoundation.org
Web: www.thespringboardfoundation.org/apply-new

Summary To provide financial assistance to college students who have a disability.

Eligibility This program is open to students enrolled full time at a 4-year college or university in either Texas or Midland, Michigan. Applicants must have a documented disability that is protected under the Americans with Disabilities Act and/or the Rehabilitation Act of 1973. They must have completed at least 24 credits and have a GPA of 3.0 or higher. Along with their application, they must submit a list of extracurricular activities (e.g., sports, volunteer activities, part-time jobs) and a statement of 150 to 300 words describing their career objectives and why this scholarship is important to furthering those objectives.

Financial data The stipend is $2,500.

Duration 1 year.

Additional data This program is sponsored by Dow Chemical Company. Recipients are required to serve as a spokesperson for the sponsor, as by participating in an in-person or virtual foundation event, appearing on the foundation website, or other forms of collateral and promotion.

Number awarded 2 each year: 1 to a student in Texas and 1 in Midland, Michigan.

Deadline June of each year.

[104]
SPRINGBOARD FOUNDATION SCHOLARSHIPS

Springboard Foundation
14 Glenbrook Drive
Mendham, NJ 07945-2306
(973) 813-7260, ext. 302   Fax: (973) 813-7261
E-mail: info@thespringboardfoundation.org
Web: www.thespringboardfoundation.org/apply-new

Summary To provide financial assistance to college students who have a disability.

Eligibility This program is open to students enrolled full time at a 4-year college or university. Applicants must have a documented disability that is protected under the Americans with Disabilities Act and/or the Rehabilitation Act of 1973. They must have completed at least 24 credits and have a GPA of 3.0 or higher. Along with their application, they must submit a list of extracurricular activities (e.g., sports, volunteer activities, part-time jobs) and a statement of 150 to 300 words describing their career objectives and why this scholarship is important to furthering those objectives.

Financial data The stipend is $2,500 or $1,500.

Duration 1 year.

Additional data The $2,500 scholarships are sponsored by Colgate-Palmolive. Recipients are required to serve as a spokesperson for the sponsor, as by participat-

ing in an in-person or virtual foundation event, appearing on the foundation website, or other forms of collateral and promotion.

Number awarded Varies each year; recently, 3 at $2,500 and 5 and $1,500 were awarded.

Deadline June of each year.

[105]
SPRINGBOARD FOUNDATION STEM SCHOLARSHIPS

Springboard Foundation
14 Glenbrook Drive
Mendham, NJ 07945-2306
(973) 813-7260, ext. 302   Fax: (973) 813-7261
E-mail: info@thespringboardfoundation.org
Web: www.thespringboardfoundation.org/apply-new

Summary To provide financial assistance to college students who have a disability and are majoring in a field of science, technology, engineering, or mathematics (STEM).

Eligibility This program is open to students enrolled full time at a 4-year college or university with a STEM major. Applicants must have a documented disability that is protected under the Americans with Disabilities Act and/or the Rehabilitation Act of 1973. They must have completed at least 24 credits and have a GPA of 3.0 or higher. Along with their application, they must submit a list of extracurricular activities (e.g., sports, volunteer activities, part-time jobs) and a statement of 150 to 300 words describing their career objectives and why this scholarship is important to furthering those objectives.

Financial data The stipend is $2,500.

Duration 1 year.

Additional data Oracle provides funding for this program. Recipients are required to serve as a spokesperson for the sponsor, as by participating in an in-person or virtual foundation event, appearing on the foundation website, or other forms of collateral and promotion.

Number awarded 2 each year.

Deadline June of each year.

[106]
STATE VOCATIONAL REHABILITATION SERVICES PROGRAM

Department of Education
Office of Special Education and Rehabilitative Services
Attn: Rehabilitation Services Administration
400 Maryland Avenue, S.W., Room 5014
Washington, DC 20202-2800
(202) 245-7325   Fax: (202) 245-7590
E-mail: Carol.Dobak@ed.gov
Web: www2.ed.gov/programs/rsabvrs/index.html

Summary To provide financial assistance to individuals with disabilities for undergraduate or graduate study pursued as part of their program of vocational rehabilitation.

Eligibility To be eligible for vocational rehabilitation services, an individual must 1) have a physical or mental impairment that is a substantial impediment to employment; 2) be able to benefit in terms of employment from vocational rehabilitation services; and 3) require vocational rehabilitation services to prepare for, enter, engage in, or retain gainful employment. Priority is given to applicants with the most significant disabilities. Persons accepted for vocational rehabilitation develop an Individualized Written Rehabilitation Program (IWRP) in consultation with a counselor for the vocational rehabilitation agency in the state in which they live. The IWRP may include a program of postsecondary education, if the disabled person and counselor agree that such a program will fulfill the goals of vocational rehabilitation. In most cases, the IWRP will provide for postsecondary education only to a level at which the disabled person will become employable, but that may include graduate education if the approved occupation requires an advanced degree as a minimum condition of entry. Students accepted to a program of postsecondary education as part of their IWRP must apply for all available federal, state, and private financial aid.

Financial data   Funding for this program is provided by the federal government through grants to state vocational rehabilitation agencies. Grants under the basic support program currently total more than $3.1 billion per year. States must supplement federal funding with matching funds of 21.3%. Persons who are accepted for vocational rehabilitation by the appropriate state agency receive financial assistance based on the cost of their education and other funds available to them, including their own or family contribution and other sources of financial aid. Allowable costs in most states include tuition, fees, books, supplies, room, board, transportation, personal expenses, child care, and expenses related to disability (special equipment, readers, attendants, interpreters, or note takers).

Duration   Assistance is provided until the disabled person achieves an educational level necessary for employment as provided in the IWRP.

Additional data   Information on this program is available only from state vocational rehabilitation agencies.

Number awarded   Varies each year; recently, more than 1.2 million people (of whom more than 80% have significant disabilities) were participating in this program.

Deadline   Deadline not specified.

[107]
STEVE FASTEAU PAST PRESIDENTS' SCHOLARSHIP

California Association for Postsecondary Education
  and Disability
Attn: Scholarships
10073 Valley View Street, Suite 242
Cypress, CA 90630
(562) 397-2810   Fax: (866) 577-3387
E-mail: caped38@gmail.com
Web: www.caped.io/scholarships/scholarship-application

Summary   To provide financial assistance to undergraduate and graduate students in California who have a disability and have demonstrated outstanding leadership.

Eligibility   This program is open to students at public and private colleges and universities in California who have a physical, mental, or learning disability. Applicants must have high academic achievement and have shown leadership and dedication to the advancement of students with disabilities in postsecondary education. Undergraduates must have completed at least 6 semester credits and have a GPA of 2.5 or higher. Graduate students must have completed at least 3 semester units and have a GPA of 3.0 or higher. Along with their application, they must submit 1) a 250-word essay describing their progress towards meeting their educational and/or vocational goals; 2) a 500-word essay on how they manage their disabiity; and 3) a 750-word essay on howthey have demonstrated leadership skills and dedication to the advancement of educational opportunities for students with disabilities in the postsecondary education setting They must also submit a letter of recommendation from a faculty person, verification of disability, and unofficial transcripts.

Financial data   The stipend is $2,500.

Duration   1 year.

Number awarded   1 each year.

Deadline   August of each year.

[108]
STUDENTS WITH DISABILITIES ENDOWED SCHOLARSHIPS HONORING ELIZABETH DALEY JEFFORDS

Vermont Student Assistance Corporation
Attn: Scholarship Programs
10 East Allen Street
P.O. Box 2000
Winooski, VT 05404-2601
(802) 654-3798   Toll Free: (888) 253-4819
Fax: (802) 654-3765 TDD: (800) 281-3341 (within VT)
E-mail: info@vsac.org
Web: www.vsac.org

Summary   To provide financial assistance to high school seniors with disabilities in Vermont who are interested in enrolling at a college in any state.

Eligibility   This program is open to graduating high school seniors in Vermont who have a documented disability. Applicants must be planning to attend a college or university in any state. Along with their application, they must submit documentation of their disability (school 504 or IEP plan) and a 250-word essay on their interest in and commitment to the career or program of study they have chosen to pursue; their short- and long-term academic, career, and/or employment goals; their financial need; the impact that their participation in community service has had on their life; and what they believe distinguishes their application from others that may be submitted. Selection is based on that essay, a letter of recommendation, a personal interview, and financial need.

Financial data   The stipend is $1,500.

Duration   1 year; nonrenewable.

Additional data   Former Senator James M. Jeffords established this program in 2006 to honor his wife.

Number awarded   1 or more each year.

Deadline   March of each year.

[109]
SUMMIT DISABILITY LAW GROUP SCHOLARSHIP PROGRAM

Summit Disability Law Group
11693 South 700 East, Suite 120
Draper, UT 84020
(801) 845-0056
Web: www.summitdisabilitylawgroup.com

Summary To provide financial assistance to students who have a disability and are interested in attending college in any state.

Eligibility This program is open to students who have a physician-documented disability and are enrolled or planning to enroll at a college or university in any state. Applicants must have a GPA of 3.5 or higher. Along with their application, they must submit a 500-word essay explaining how their disability affects them in the education setting.

Financial data The stipend is $1,000.

Duration 1 year.

Number awarded 1 each year.

Deadline July of each year.

[110]
SUPREME EMBLEM CLUB OF THE UNITED STATES OF AMERICA GRANT-IN-AID AWARDS

Supreme Emblem Club of the United States of America
c/o PSP Billie Lee, Scholarship Awards
1901 Whitaker Drive
Fremont, OH 43420
Web: www.emblemclub.org/html/program.html

Summary To provide financial aid for college to members or the children of members of the Supreme Emblem Club of the United States of America who have a physically challenging condition.

Eligibility This program is open to high school graduates or those already in college. Applicants must be sponsored by the Emblem Club in which the student or the student's mother or grandmother is a member. They must be serious about continuing their education but, because of a physically challenging situation, are unable to meet the high criteria applied to the Emblem Club's Scholarship Program.

Financial data The amount awarded varies each year. Funds must be used for tuition, books, or fees.

Duration 1 year.

Additional data The sponsoring Emblem Club must be a current contributor to the regular scholarship fund for the applicant to be considered for an award.

Number awarded Varies each year.

Deadline March of each year.

[111]
SWIM WITH MIKE

University of Southern California
3501 Watt Way
Heritage Hall
MC 0602
Los Angeles, CA 90089-0602
(213) 740-4155   Fax: (213) 740-1306
E-mail: swimwithmike@gmail.com
Web: www.swimwithmike.org

Summary To provide financial assistance for college or graduate school to physically challenged athletes.

Eligibility This program is open to athletes who participated in organized competitive youth, high school, or collegiate athletics and subsequently have sustained a life-changing accident or illness (e.g., paralysis, blindness, cancer, amputation, head injuries). Applicants must meet the admission standards of a 4-year or graduate-level institution of higher learning. Along with their application, they must submit a personal statement with an emphasis on their athletic history and experience and their educational goals, 3 letters of recommendation, verification of disability, and documentation of financial need.

Financial data Stipends depend on the need of the recipient.

Duration 1 year; may be renewed, provided the recipient.

Additional data This program began in 1981 at the University of Southern California to assist All-American swimmer Mike Nyeholt, who was paralyzed in a motorcycle accident. Since its establishment, it has provided more than $18 million in assistance to 199 athletes at 97 universities throughout the country. Recipients are expected to participate in Swim with Mike activities and to support the organization both during and after college.

Number awarded Varies each year; recently, 51 athletes received $985,000 in scholarships.

Deadline April of each year.

[112]
TEXAS 4-H AND YOUTH DEVELOPMENT COURAGEOUS HEART SCHOLARSHIPS

Texas 4-H and Youth Development Program
Attn: Extension 4-H and Youth Development Specialist
Texas A&M University
4180 Highway 6
College Station, TX 77845
(979) 845-1212   Fax: (979) 845-6495
E-mail: texas4h@ag.tamu.edu
Web: texas4-h.tamu.edu/scholarships

Summary To provide financial assistance to high school seniors who have been active in Texas 4-H activities in spite of unforeseen obstacles related to their medical/health, family, and/or educational situation.

Eligibility This program is open to graduating seniors at high schools in Texas who have been actively participating in 4-H during the current year and at least 2 of the 3 previous years and plan to attend a college, university, or accredited technical school in the state. Applicants must be able to demonstrate that they have overcome extreme obstacles related to medical, family, and/or education circumstances. They must have taken and passed all necessary standardized tests for graduation and admittance to the college or university of their choice. Along with their application, they must submit a detailed narrative of the obstacles they have overcome or are in the process of overcoming, including how long they have been dealing with the obstacle, the person or persons who have helped them through their situation, and how 4-H has played a positive role in overcoming their obstacle; the narrative should include details about such family situations as care of family members, medical problems, learning disabilities, or family financial burdens. Selection is based on that narrative (25%), 4-H experience and narratives (28%), letters of recommendation (15%), financial need (12%), and a personal interview. U.S. citizenship is required.

Financial data   The stipend is $5,000.

Duration   1 year.

Number awarded   1 or more each year.

Deadline   Students submit their applications to their county extension office, which must forward them to the district extension office by February of each year.

[113]
TEXAS EXEMPTION FOR PEACE OFFICERS DISABLED IN THE LINE OF DUTY

Texas Higher Education Coordinating Board
Attn: Grants and Special Programs
1200 East Anderson Lane
P.O. Box 12788
Austin, TX 78711-2788
(512) 427-6340   Toll Free: (800) 242-3062
Fax: (512) 427-6420
E-mail: grantinfo@thecb.state.tx.us
Web: www.collegeforalltexans.com

Summary   To provide educational assistance at public colleges in the state to disabled Texas peace officers.

Eligibility   This program is open to Texas residents who are permanently disabled as a result of an injury suffered as a peace officer and are unable to continue employment as a peace officer because of the disability. Applicants must be planning to attend a publicly-supported college or university in Texas as an undergraduate student.

Financial data   Eligible students are exempted from the payment of all dues, fees, and tuition charges at publicly-supported colleges and universities in Texas.

Duration   Up to 12 semesters.

Additional data   For more information, students should contact the admission office at the institution they plan to attend.

Number awarded   Varies each year; recently, 12 of these exemptions, worth $112,057, were awarded.

Deadline   Deadline not specified.

[114]
TEXAS MUTUAL SCHOLARSHIP PROGRAM

Texas Mutual Insurance Company
Attn: Office of the President
6210 East Highway 290
Austin, TX 78723-1098
(512) 224-3820   Toll Free: (800) 859-5995, ext. 3820
Fax: (512) 224-3889   TDD: (800) 853-5339
E-mail: information@texasmutual.com
Web: www.texasmutual.com/workers/scholarship.shtm

Summary   To provide financial assistance for college to workers and their families covered by workers' compensation insurance in Texas.

Eligibility   This program is open to 1) employees who qualify for lifetime income benefits as a result of injuries suffered on the job as covered by the Texas Workers' Compensation Act; 2) unmarried children and spouses of injured workers; and 3) unmarried children and unremarried spouses of employees who died as a result of a work-related injury. The employee's company must have been a Texas Mutual Insurance Company policyholder at the time of the accident. Children must be between 16 and 25 years of age. Surviving spouses must still be eligible for workers' compensation benefits. Financial need is considered in the selection process.

Financial data   Scholarships are intended to cover normal undergraduate, technical, or vocational school tuition and fees, to a maximum of $6,000 per semester. Those funds are paid directly to the college or vocational school. The cost of course-related books and fees are also reimbursed, up to a maximum of $500 per semester. Those funds are paid directly to the student.

Duration   1 year; may be renewed if the recipient remains enrolled full time and maintains a GPA of 2.5 or higher.

Number awarded   Varies each year.

Deadline   Applications may be submitted at any time.

[115]
THE FELDMAN LAW FIRM DISABLED VETERAN SCHOLARSHIP

The Feldman Law Firm, PLLC
1 East Washington Street, Suite 500
Phoenix, AZ 85004
(602) 540-7887
E-mail: mike@afphoenixcriminalattorney.com
Web: www.afphoenixcriminalattorney.com

Summary   To provide financial assistance to veterans who have a disability and are interested in attending college.

Eligibility   This program is open to veterans who have a disability rating of 30% or higher. Applicants must be enrolled or planning to enroll at a college, university, junior college, or vocational school. Along with their application, they must submit a 125-word statement of their educational goals. They may also submit, at their discretion, an 850-word essay on how their military service has made an impact on their life.

Financial data The stipend is $1,000. Funds are paid directly to the recipient's college.

Duration 1 year.

Number awarded 1 each year.

Deadline November.

[116]
TROY BARBOZA EDUCATIONAL FUND SCHOLARSHIP

Hawai'i Community Foundation
Attn: Scholarship Department
827 Fort Street Mall
Honolulu, HI 96813
(808) 566-5570   Toll Free: (888) 731-3863
Fax: (808) 521-6286
E-mail: scholarships@hcf-hawaii.org
Web: hcf.scholarships.ngwebsolutions.com

Summary To provide financial assistance to disabled public employees in Hawaii or their dependents who plan to attend college in any state.

Eligibility This program is open to 1) disabled public employees in Hawaii who were injured in the line of duty; 2) dependents or other immediate family members of public employees in Hawaii who were disabled or killed in the line of duty; and 3) private citizens in Hawaii who have performed a heroic act for the protection and welfare of others. The public employee must work or have worked in a job where lives are risked for the protection and safety of others. The injury must have left the employee incapacitated or incapable or continuing in his or her profession. For private citizens, the heroic act must have occurred after October 21, 1986. Applicants must submit a short statement describing their course of study, career goals, outstanding attributes, talents, community service, family circumstances, and any other relevant information. Financial need is considered in the selection process.

Financial data The amount awarded varies, depending upon the needs of the recipient and the funds available; recently, the average value of the scholarships awarded by the foundation was $2,800.

Duration 1 year; scholarships for employees and their dependents may be renewed; scholarships for private citizens who have performed a heroic act are nonrenewable.

Additional data This program began in 1991.

Number awarded 1 or more each year.

Deadline February of each year.

[117]
U'ILANI STENDER SCHOLARSHIP

Pauahi Foundation
Attn: Scholarships
567 South King Street, Suite 160
Honolulu, HI 96813-3036
(808) 534-3966   Fax: (808) 534-3890
E-mail: scholarships@pauahi.org
Web: www.pauahi.org/scholarships

Summary To provide financial assistance to residents of any state, especially Native Hawaiians, who have faced challenging situations and are interested in attending college or graduate school.

Eligibility This program is open to undergraduate and graduate students from any state whose lives have been impacted by challenging situations (e.g., death of a significant family member, domestic violence, sexual abuse, poverty, major health problems). Applicants must be attending or planning to attend a 2- or 4-year college, university, or vocation/technical school; graduate school; or a private, independent school designed to accommodate their special circumstances. They must be able to demonstrate financial need and the motivation and desire to succeed in an educational program. Along with their application, they must submit 1) an essay demonstrating a clear and realistic plan to pursue their career objectives; and 2) a letter of recommendation from a social service agency, counselor, or teacher citing their challenging or special life circumstances and how they would benefit from this scholarship. Preference is given to Native Hawaiians (descendants of the aboriginal inhabitants of the Hawaiian Islands prior to 1778), orphans, and indigent applicants.

Financial data The stipend is $1,700.

Duration 1 year.

Number awarded 4 each year.

Deadline February of each year.

[118]
UTAH ELKS ASSOCIATION SPECIAL NEEDS STUDENT SCHOLARSHIP AWARD

Utah Elks Association
c/o Linda Gaines, Scholarship Chair
Provo Lodge 849
632 East 220 North
Pleasant Grove, UT 84062-2825
(801) 796-6069   Fax: (801) 373-6071
E-mail: lginutah@gmail.com
Web: www.elksinutah.org

Summary To provide financial assistance for college to high school seniors in Utah who have a disability or other special need.

Eligibility This program is open to seniors graduating from high schools in Utah who have a special need, such as a disability. Applicants must submit 1) a supporting letter from a doctor or professional person stating the nature of the special need; and 2) a 500-word essay on their career and life goals and their plan to achieve those. Selection is based on that essay, academic achievement, community service, honors and awards, leadership, and financial need. U.S. citizenship is required.

Financial data A stipend is awarded (amount not specified).

Duration 1 year.

Number awarded Varies each year, depending upon the funds available.

Deadline January of each year.

[119]
VIRGIN ISLANDS EXCEPTIONAL CHILDREN GRANTS

Virgin Islands Board of Education
60B, 61, and 62 Dronningens Gade
P.O. Box 11900
St. Thomas, VI 00801
(340) 774-4546   Fax: (340) 774-3384
E-mail: stt@myviboe.com
Web: www.myviboe.com/exceptional-children

Summary To provide financial assistance to residents of the Virgin Islands who have a disability and need to attend school on the mainland.

Eligibility This program is open to school-age residents of the Virgin Islands who have a physical or mental disability. Applicants must be able to demonstrate that they need educational training not available in the territory.

Financial data The stipend is $2,000 per year.

Duration 1 year; may be renewed up to 3 additional years.

Additional data This program is offered as part of the Special Legislative Grants of the Virgin Islands Board of Education.

Number awarded Varies each year.

Deadline May of each year.

[120]
VOCATIONAL REHABILITATION AND EMPLOYMENT SERVICE PROGRAM

Department of Veterans Affairs
Attn: Veterans Benefits Administration
Vocational Rehabilitation and Employment Service
810 Vermont Avenue, N.W.
Washington, DC 20420
(202) 418-4343   Toll Free: (800) 827-1000
Web: www.benefits.va.gov/vocrehab/index.asp

Summary To provide funding to veterans with service-connected disabilities who need assistance to find employment or, if seriously disabled, to live independently.

Eligibility This program is open to veterans who have a service-connected disability of at least 10% or a memorandum rating of 20% or more from the Department of Veterans Affairs (VA). They must qualify for services provided by the Vocational Rehabilitation and Employment Service Program that include assistance finding and keeping a job, including the use of special employer incentives and job accommodations; on-the-job training, apprenticeships, and unpaid work experiences; postsecondary training at a college, vocational, technical, or business school; supportive rehabilitation services such as case management, counseling, and medical referrals; independent living services for veterans unable to work due to the severity of their disabilities.

Financial data While in training and for 2 months after, eligible disabled veterans may receive subsistence allowances in addition to their disability compensation or retirement pay. For most training programs, the current full-time monthly rate is $605.44 with no dependents, $751 with 1 dependent, $885 with 2 dependents, and $64.50 for each additional dependent; proportional rates apply for less than full-time training.

Duration Veterans remain eligible for these services up to 12 years from either the date of separation from active military service or the date the veteran was first notified by VA of a service-connected disability rating (whichever came later).

Number awarded Varies each year.

Deadline Applications are accepted at any time.

[121]
VSA EMERGING YOUNG ARTISTS PROGRAM

John F. Kennedy Center for the Performing Arts
Attn: Department of VSA and Accessibility
2700 F Street, N.W.
Washington, DC 20566
(202) 416-8898   Toll Free: (800) 444-1324
Fax: (202) 416-4840   TDD: (202) 416-8728
E-mail: vsainfo@kennedy-center.org
Web: education.kennedy-center.org

Summary To recognize and reward emerging visual artists who have a disability.

Eligibility This competition is open to visual artists between 16 and 25 years of age who have a disability. Applicants must submit samples of their work along with a brief essay on a theme that changes annually examines the vital creative spark behind their work. Their essays should describe the force that drives their artistic interest and informs the path they take each day as they move toward their future.

Financial data Awards are $20,000 for the grand award, $10,000 for the first award, $6,000 for the second award, and $2,000 for each award of excellence.

Duration The competition is held annually.

Additional data This competition, first held in 2003, is sponsored by VSA and the Volkswagen Group of America. VSA was established in 1974 as the National Committee-Arts for the Handicapped. In 1985 its name was changed to Very Special Arts and in 2010 to VSA. In 2011, it merged with the Kennedy Center's Office on Accessibility to become the Department of VSA and Accessibility at the John F. Kennedy Center for the Performing Arts. The art work is displayed at the S. Dillon Ripley Center of the Smithsonian Institution in the fall of each year.

Number awarded 15 each year: 1 grand award, 1 first award, 1 second award, and 12 awards of excellence.

Deadline June of each year.

[122]
VSA INTERNATIONAL YOUNG SOLOISTS AWARD

John F. Kennedy Center for the Performing Arts
Attn: Department of VSA and Accessibility
2700 F Street, N.W.
Washington, DC 20566
(202) 416-8898   Toll Free: (800) 444-1324
Fax: (202) 416-4840   TDD: (202) 416-8728
E-mail: vsainfo@kennedy-center.org
Web: education.kennedy-center.org

Summary To recognize and reward young musicians from any country who are physically or mentally challenged.

Eligibility This competition is open to musicians (instrumental or vocal) between 14 and 25 years of age who have a disability. Musical ensembles of 2 to 5 performers are also eligible if at least 1 member has a disability and all members are between 14 and 25 years of age. Applicants must be either 1) U.S. citizens or permanent residents; or 2) citizens of other countries living in the United States (as on a student visa). They may be performers in any type of music, including, but not limited to, rock, alt rock, pop, indie, classical, country, folk, jazz, R&B/blues, hip hop, rap, Latin, and world. Along with their application, they must submit recordings of 3 musical selections (audio or video) and a 1-page personal narrative that describes why they should be selected to receive this award. Tapes are evaluated on the basis of technique, tone, intonation, rhythm, and interpretation.

Financial data The award is $2,000. Funds must be used to assist the recipients' music career.

Duration The competition is held annually.

Additional data The sponsor was established in 1974 as the National Committee-Arts for the Handicapped. In 1985 its name was changed to Very Special Arts and in 2010 to VSA. In 2011, it merged with the Kennedy Center's Office on Accessibility to become the Department of VSA and Accessibility at the John F. Kennedy Center for the Performing Arts.

Number awarded 4 each year.

Deadline January of each year.

[123]
WBM DISABLED VETERANS SCHOLARSHIP

Whitfield, Bryson & Mason LLP
1205 Fourth Avenue North
Nashville, TN 37208
(615) 921-6500
Web: www.nashvillepersonalinjurylawyerwbm.com

Summary To provide financial assistance to veterans who have a disability and are interested in attending college.

Eligibility This program is open to veterans who have a disability rating of 30% or higher. Applicants must be enrolled or planning to enroll at a 4-year college or university. They may submit, at their discretion, an 800-word essay about how their military service has changed their life.

Financial data The stipend is $1,000. Funds are paid directly to the recipient's college.

Duration 1 year.

Number awarded 2 each year.

Deadline January of each year.

[124]
WELLS FARGO SCHOLARSHIP PROGRAM FOR PEOPLE WITH DISABILITIES

Scholarship America
Attn: Scholarship Management Services
One Scholarship Way
P.O. Box 297
St. Peter, MN 56082
(507) 931-1682   Toll Free: (844) 402-0357
Fax: (507) 931-9168
E-mail: pwdscholarships@scholarshipamerica.org
Web: www.scholarsapply.org/pwdscholarship

Summary To provide financial assistance for college to high school seniors and current undergraduates who have a disability.

Eligibility This program is open to high school seniors and graduates who are enrolled or planning to enroll full or half time at an accredited 2- or 4-year college or university in any state. Applicants must have an identified disability that impacts 1 or more major life activity. They must have a GPA of 3.0 or higher. Along with their application, they must submit an essay on the life experiences that have shaped who they are today. Selection is based on that essay, academic record, demonstrated leadership and participation in school and community activities, honors, work experience, a statement of goals and aspirations, an outside appraisal, and financial need.

Financial data The stipend is $2,500 per year for full-time students or $1,250 per year for half-time students.

Duration 1 year; scholarships may be renewed up to 3 additional years by full-time students or up to 7 additional years by half-time students or until completion of a bachelor's degree, whichever occurs first. Renewal depends on the recipient's maintaining satisfactory academic progress and a cumulative GPA of 2.5 or higher.

Additional data This program, established in 2017, is sponsored by Wells Fargo.

Number awarded Varies each year.

Deadline Applications must be submitted by January of each year or until 700 applications have been received, whichever occurs first.

[125]
WISCONSIN TALENT INCENTIVE PROGRAM (TIP) GRANTS

Wisconsin Higher Educational Aids Board
131 West Wilson Street, Suite 902
P.O. Box 7885
Madison, WI 53707-7885
(608) 266-2206   Fax: (608) 267-2808
E-mail: cassie.weisensel@wi.gov
Web: www.heab.state.wi.us/programs.html

Summary To provide financial assistance for college to needy and educationally disadvantaged students in Wisconsin.

Eligibility This program is open to residents of Wisconsin entering a college or university in the state who meet the requirements of both financial need and educational disadvantage. Financial need qualifications include 1) family contribution (a dependent student whose expected parent contribution is $200 or less or an independent student whose maximum academic year contribution is $200 or less); 2) Temporary Assistance to Needy Families (TANF) or Wisconsin Works (W2) benefits (a dependent student whose family is receiving TANF or W2 benefits or an independent student who is receiving TANF or W2 benefits); or 3) unemployment (a dependent student whose parents are ineligible for unemployment compensation and have no current income from employment, or an independent student and spouse, if married, who are ineligible for unemployment compensation and have no current income from employment). Educational disadvantage qualifications include students who are 1) enrolled in a special academic support program due to insufficient academic preparation; 2) a first-generation college student (neither parent graduated from a 4-year college or university); 3) disabled according to the Department of Workforce Development, the Division of Vocational Rehabilitation, or a Wisconsin college or university that uses the Americans with Disabilities Act definition; 4) currently or formerly incarcerated in a correctional institution; or 5) from an environmental or academic background that deters the pursuit of educational plans. Students already in college are not eligible.

Financial data   Stipends range up to $1,800 per year.

Duration   1 year; may be renewed up to 4 additional years, provided the recipient continues to be a Wisconsin resident enrolled at least half time in a degree or certificate program, makes satisfactory academic progress, demonstrates financial need, and remains enrolled continuously from semester to semester and from year to year. If recipients withdraw from school or cease to attend classes for any reason (other than medical necessity), they may not reapply.

Number awarded   Varies each year.

Deadline   Deadline not specified.

[126]
WSAJ PAST PRESIDENTS' SCHOLARSHIP

Washington State Association for Justice
1809 Seventh Avenue, Suite 1500
Seattle, WA 98101-1328
(206) 464-1011   Fax: (206) 464-0703
E-mail: anita@washingtonjustice.org
Web: www.washingtonjustice.org

Summary   To provide financial assistance to Washington high school seniors who have a disability or have been a victim of injury and plan to attend college in any state.

Eligibility   This program is open to seniors graduating from high schools in Washington who are planning to work on a bachelor's degree at an institution of higher education in any state. Applicants must be able to demonstrate 1) financial need; 2) a history of achievement despite having been a victim of injury or overcoming a disability, handicap, or similar challenge; 3) a record of serving others; and 4) a commitment to apply their education toward helping people in need or protecting the rights of injured persons.

Financial data   The stipend is $7,500. Funds are paid directly to the recipient's chosen institution of higher learning to be used for tuition, room, board, and fees.

Duration   1 year.

Additional data   This fund was established in 1991 when the sponsor's name was the Washington State Trial Lawyers Association.

Number awarded   1 each year.

Deadline   March of each year.

[127]
WSI SCHOLARSHIPS

Workforce Safety & Insurance
1600 East Century Avenue, Suite 1
P.O. Box 5585
Bismarck, ND 58506-5585
Toll Free: (800) 777-5033   Fax: (888) 786-8695
TDD: (800) 366-6888   E-mail: ndwsi@nd.gov
Web: www.workforcesafety.com

Summary   To provide financial assistance for college to injured workers and the families of workers who became disabled or died in work-related accidents in North Dakota.

Eligibility   This program is open to 1) workers in North Dakota who have suffered an injury compensable by the state's Workforce Safety & Insurance (WSI); 2) spouses and children of catastrophically injured workers; and 3) surviving spouses and children of workers killed in a catastrophic injury. Applicants must be attending or planning to attend an accredited college, university, or technical school in any state. Injured workers must be able to demonstrate that a scholarship would be beneficial and appropriate upon successful completion of a rehabilitation program.

Financial data   The maximum stipend is $10,000 per year.

Duration   1 year; may be renewed up to 4 additional years.

Additional data   This program began in 1997. The sponsoring company was formerly North Dakota Workers Compensation.

Number awarded   Varies each year.

Deadline   Deadline not specified.

Graduate Students

[128]
AAHD FREDERICK J. KRAUSE SCHOLARSHIP ON HEALTH AND DISABILITY

American Association on Health and Disability
Attn: Scholarship Committee
110 North Washington Street, Suite 328-J
Rockville, MD 20850
(301) 545-6140, ext. 206   Fax: (301) 545-6144
E-mail: scholarship@aahd.us
Web: www.aahd.us/initiatives/scholarship-program

Summary To provide financial assistance to undergraduate and graduate students who have a disability, especially those studying a field related to health and disability.

Eligibility This program is open to high school graduates who have a documented disability and are enrolled in an accredited 4-year college or university as a full-time undergraduate (sophomore or higher) or full- or part-time graduate student. Preference is given to students working on a degree in public health, disability studies, health promotion, audiology, special education, or other field related to health and disability. Along with their application, they must submit a 2-page personal statement that includes a personal history, educational and career goals, extracurricular activities, and reasons why they should be selected to receive this scholarship. U.S. citizenship or permanent resident status is required.

Financial data Stipends range up to $1,000.

Duration 1 year.

Additional data This program began in 2009.

Number awarded 3 each year.

Deadline November of each year.

[129]
AAPA PAST PRESIDENTS SCHOLARSHIP

American Academy of Physician Assistants
Attn: Physician Assistant Foundation
2318 Mill Road, Suite 1300
Alexandria, VA 22314-6868
(571) 319-4510   E-mail: pafoundation@aapa.org
Web: www.pa-foundation.org

Summary To provide financial assistance to student members of the American Academy of Physician Assistants (AAPA) who demonstrate community service leadership.

Eligibility This program is open to AAPA student members who have completed at least 1 semester of an accredited physician assistant program. Applicants must be able to demonstrate service leadership through their physician assistant program or through a community health organization or project.

Financial data The stipend is $1,000.

Duration 1 year; nonrenewable.

Number awarded 1 each year.

Deadline May of each year.

[130]
ACADEMIC LIBRARY ASSOCIATION OF OHIO DIVERSITY SCHOLARSHIP

Academic Library Association of Ohio
c/o Eileen Theodore-Shusta, Diversity Committee
  Chair
Ohio University
Library Administrative Services
422 Alden
30 Park Place
Athens, OH 45701
(740) 593-2989   E-mail: theodore@ohio.edu
Web: www.alaoweb.org

Summary To provide financial assistance to residents of Ohio who are working on a master's degree in library science at a school in any state and will contribute to diversity in the profession.

Eligibility This program is open to residents of Ohio who are enrolled or entering an ALA-accredited program for a master's degree in library science, either on campus or via distance education. Applicants must be able to demonstrate how they will contribute to diversity in the profession, including (but not limited to) race or ethnicity, sexual orientation, life experience, physical ability, and a sense of commitment to those and other diversity issues. Along with their application, they must submit 1) a list of participation in honor societies or professional organizations, awards, scholarships, prizes, honors, or class offices; 2) a list of their community, civic, organizational, or volunteer experiences; and 3) an essay on their understanding of and commitment to diversity in libraries, including how they, as library school students and future professionals, might address the issue.

Financial data The stipend is $1,500.

Duration 1 year.

Number awarded 2 each year.

Deadline March of each year.

[131]
ACCESS TECHNOLOGY SCHOLARSHIP

California Association for Postsecondary Education
  and Disability
Attn: Scholarships
10073 Valley View Street, Suite 242
Cypress, CA 90630
(562) 397-2810   Fax: (866) 577-3387
E-mail: caped38@gmail.com
Web: www.caped.io/scholarships/scholarship-application

Summary To provide funding to undergraduate and graduate students in California who have a disability and use assistive technology.

Eligibility This program is open to students at public and private colleges and universities in California who have a physical, mental, or learning disability. Applicants must be using assistive technology hardware or software to access their college courses. Undergraduates must have completed at least 6 semester credits and have a GPA of 2.5 or higher. Graduate students must have completed at least 3 semester units and have a GPA of 3.0 or higher. Along with their application, they must submit 1) a 250-word essay describing their progress towards meeting their educational and/or vocational goals; 2) a 500-word essay on how they manage their disabiity; and 3) a 750-word description of the assistive technology hardware and/or software they are using to access their course materials. They must also submit a letter of recommendation from a faculty person, verification of disability, and unofficial transcripts.

Financial data The grant is $1,000.

Duration 1 year.

Number awarded 1 or 2 each year.

Deadline August of each year.

[132]
ACXIOM DIVERSITY SCHOLARSHIP PROGRAM

Acxiom Corporation
601 East Third Street
P.O. Box 8190
Little Rock, AR 72203-8190
(501) 342-1000   Toll Free: (877) 314-2049
E-mail: Candice.Davis@acxiom.com
Web: www.acxiom.com/about-acxiom/careers

Summary To provide financial assistance and possible work experience to upper-division and graduate students who are members of a diverse population that historically has been underrepresented in the information technology work force.

Eligibility This program is open to juniors, seniors, and graduate students who are working full time on a degree in a field of information technology, including computer science, computer information systems, management information systems, information quality, information systems, engineering, mathematics, statistics, or related areas of study. Women, veterans, minorities, and individuals with disabilities are encouraged to apply. Applicants must have a GPA of 3.0 or higher. Along with their application, they must submit a 500-word essay describing how the scholarship will help them achieve their academic, professional, and personal goals. Selection is based on academic achievement, relationship of field of study to information technology, and relationship of areas of professional interest to the sponsor's business needs.

Financial data The stipend is $5,000 per year.

Duration 1 year; may be renewed 1 additional year, provided the recipient remains enrolled full time, maintains a GPA of 3.0 or higher, and (if offered an internship) continues to meet internship expectations.

Additional data Recipients may be offered an internship (fall, spring, summer, year-round) at 1 of the sponsor's offices in Austin (Texas), Conway (Arkansas), Downers Grove (Illinois), Little Rock (Arkansas), Nashville (Tennessee), New York (New York), or Redwood City (California).

Number awarded Up to 5 each year.

Deadline December of each year.

[133]
AFRL/DAGSI OHIO STUDENT-FACULTY RESEARCH FELLOWSHIP PROGRAM

Dayton Area Graduate Studies Institute
3155 Research Boulevard, Suite 205
Kettering, OH 45420
(937) 781-4001   Fax: (937) 781-4005
E-mail: kelam@dagsi.org
Web: www.dagsi.org/pages/osrfp_proinforeq.html

Summary To provide funding to faculty and graduate students from any state who are enrolled at universities in Ohio that participate in the Dayton Area Graduate Studies Institute (DAGSI) and are interested in conducting research in aerospace technologies of interest to the U.S. Air Force.

Eligibility This program is open to research teams of full-time graduate students and faculty at 18 designated Ohio universities that participate in DAGSI. Applicants must be interested in conducting research that will utilize the facilities of the Air Force Research Laboratory (AFRL) at Wright-Patterson Air Force Base. All 4 directorates at the AFRL (sensors, materials and manufacturing, human effectiveness, and aerospace systems) participate in this program. Applications from Ph.D. candidates must be developed and written largely by the student, with support, guidance, and input as necessary from the faculty partner. For master's projects, the proposal can be developed and written jointly by the faculty member and the student. All participants (faculty and student) must be U.S. citizens. Underrepresented minorities, women, and persons with disabilities are strongly urged to apply.

Financial data Grants provide stipends of $23,500 for students who have a master's degree and are working on a Ph.D. or $18,500 for students who have a bachelor's degree and are working on a master's; student's tuition for 1 academic year; a faculty stipend of $11,000; student and faculty allowances of $3,000 each for program-related travel or other approved expenses; and overhead at a maximum off-campus rate of 26% of student and faculty stipends and miscellaneous allowances. The maximum DAGSI contribution is $51,000 for Ph.D. programs or $43,500 for master's programs; a cost-share commitment equal to one-third of the DAGSI contribution must be provided by the university, industry, AFRL, or other allowable government source.

Duration 1 year; master's awards are nonrenewable but Ph.D. awards may be renewed for 2 additional years. Students are expected to spend 8 consecutive weeks conducting research at AFRL and faculty members are expected to spend at least 3 weeks over the year conducting research at AFRL.

Additional data DAGSI was established in 1994 as a consortium of graduate engineering schools at the University of Dayton, Wright State University, and the Air Force Institute of Technology. The Ohio State University and the University of Cincinnati joined as affiliated members in 1996 and Miami University and Ohio University joined as associate members in 2001. Students from the following universities are also eligible to participate in this program: University of Akron, Bowling Green State University, Central State University, Cleveland State University, Kent State University, Shawnee State University, University of Toledo, Youngstown State University, Medical College of Ohio, Northeastern Ohio Universities College of Medicine, and Case Western Reserve University.

Number awarded At least 10 each year.

Deadline January of each year.

[134]
AGING RESEARCH DISSERTATION AWARDS TO INCREASE DIVERSITY

National Institute on Aging
Attn: Office of Extramural Affairs
7201 Wisconsin Avenue, Suite 2C-218
Bethesda, MD 20814
(301) 402-4158   Fax: (301) 402-2945
TDD: (301) 451-0088   E-mail: hunterc@nia.nih.gov
Web: www.grants.nih.gov

Summary To provide financial assistance to doctoral candidates from underrepresented groups who wish to conduct research on aging.

Eligibility This program is open to doctoral candidates conducting research on a dissertation with an aging-related focus, including the basic biology of aging; chronic, disabling, and degenerative diseases of aging, with a particular focus on Alzheimer's Disease; multiple morbidities; individual behavioral and social changes with aging; caregiving; longevity; and the consequences for society of an aging population. Applicants must be 1) members of an ethnic or racial group underrepresented in biomedical or behavioral research (Blacks or African Americans, Hispanics or Latinos, American Indians, Alaska Natives, Native Hawaiians, and other Pacific Islanders); 2) individuals with disabilities; or 3) individuals from socially, culturally, economically, or educationally disadvantaged backgrounds that have inhibited their ability to prepare for a career in health-related research. They must be U.S. citizens, nationals, or permanent residents.

Financial data Grants provide $23,376 per year for stipend and up to $20,000 for additional expenses. No funds may be used to pay for tuition or fees associated with completion of doctoral studies. The institution may receive up to 8% of direct costs as facilities and administrative costs per year.

Duration Up to 2 years.

Number awarded Up to 5 each year.

Deadline Applications must be submitted by February, June, or October of each year.

[135]
AHIMA FOUNDATION DIVERSITY SCHOLARSHIPS

American Health Information Management Association
Attn: AHIMA Foundation
233 North Michigan Avenue, 21st Floor
Chicago, IL 60601-5809
(312) 233-1131   Fax: (312) 233-1537
E-mail: info@ahimafoundation.org
Web: www.ahimafoundation.org

Summary To provide financial assistance to members of the American Health Information Management Association (AHIMA) who are interested in working on an undergraduate or graduate degree in health information management (HIM) or health information technology (HIT) and who will contribute to diversity in the profession.

Eligibility This program is open to AHIMA members who are enrolled at least half time in an accredited program. Applicants must be working on a degree in HIM or HIT at the associate, bachelor's, post-baccalaureate, master's, or doctoral level. They must have a GPA of 3.5 or higher and at least 6 credit hours remaining after the date of the award. To qualify for this support, applicants must demonstrate how they will contribute to diversity in the health information management profession; diversity is defined as differences in race, ethnicity, nationality, gender, sexual orientation, socioeconomic status, age, physical capabilities, or religious beliefs. Along with their application, they must submit essays on assigned topics related to their involvement in the HIM profession. Selection is based on the clarity and completeness of thought in the essays; cumulative GPA; volunteer, work, and/or leadership experience; honors, awards, or recognitions; commitment to the HIM profession; and references.

Financial data Stipends are $1,000 for associate degree students, $1,500 for bachelor's degree or post-baccalaureate certificate students, $2,000 for master's degree students, or $2,500 for doctoral degree students.

Duration 1 year.

Additional data This program includes the Ester May Sherard Scholarship.

Number awarded 1 or more each year.

Deadline September of each year.

[136]
AHIMA VETERANS SCHOLARSHIP

American Health Information Management Association
Attn: AHIMA Foundation
233 North Michigan Avenue, 21st Floor
Chicago, IL 60601-5809
(312) 233-1131   Fax: (312) 233-1537
E-mail: info@ahimafoundation.org
Web: www.ahimafoundation.org

Summary To provide financial assistance to veterans and spouses of veterans and active-duty service personnel who are interested in working on an undergraduate or graduate degree in health information management (HIM) or health information technology (HIT).

Eligibility This program is open to 1) veterans of the armed forces, including Army, Navy, Air Force, Marine Corps, Coast Guard, Reserves, and National Guard; and 2) spouses and surviving spouses of servicemembers, including active-duty military, retirees, veterans, and wounded warriors. Applicants must be working full time on a degree in HIM or HIT at the associate, bachelor's, post-baccalaureate, master's, or doctoral level. They must have at least 6 credit hours remaining after the date of the award. Along with their application, they must submit an essay of 250 to 400 words on their educational and career ambitions, record of military service, record of personal achievement, community service, desire to serve others and make a positive community impact, and leadership potential. In the selection process, preference is given to 1) physically wounded or disabled veterans; 2) surviving spouses; and 3) those who served in a combat tour of duty.

Financial data Stipends are $1,000 for associate degree students, $1,500 for bachelor's degree or post-baccalaureate certificate students, $2,000 for master's degree students, or $2,500 for doctoral degree students.

Duration 1 year.

Additional data Effective in 2018, this program includes the John Kloss Memorial Veteran Scholarship and other scholarships supported by Nuance Communications and the Walter Reed Society.

Number awarded 4 each year.

Deadline September of each year.

[137]
ALA CENTURY SCHOLARSHIP

American Library Association
Attn: Association of Specialized and Cooperative
  Library Agencies
50 East Huron Street
Chicago, IL 60611-2795
(312) 280-4395   Toll Free: (800) 545-2433, ext. 4395
Fax: (312) 280-5273   TDD: (888) 814-7692
E-mail: ascla@ala.org
Web: www.ala.org/ascla/asclaawards/asclacentury

Summary To provide financial assistance to library science students with disabilities.

Eligibility This program is open to students with disabilities who have been admitted to an ALA-accredited library school to work on a master's or doctoral degree. Applicants must submit medical documentation of their disability or disabilities and a description of the services and/or accommodations they require for their studies. U.S. or Canadian citizenship is required. Selection is based on academic excellence, leadership, professional goals, and financial need.

Financial data The stipend is $2,500; funds are to be used for services or accommodations not provided by law or by the university.

Duration 1 year.

Additional data This scholarship was first offered in 2000.

Number awarded 1 or more each year.

Deadline February of each year.

[138]
ALYSSA MCCROSKEY MEMORIAL SCHOLARSHIP

California Association for Postsecondary Education
  and Disability
Attn: Scholarships
10073 Valley View Street, Suite 242
Cypress, CA 90630
(562) 397-2810   Fax: (866) 577-3387
E-mail: caped38@gmail.com
Web: www.caped.io/scholarships/scholarship-application

Summary To provide financial assistance to undergraduate and graduate students in California who have a disability and have attempted to help other students regain their mental health.

Eligibility This program is open to students at public and private colleges and universities in California who have a physical, mental, or learning disability. Applicants must be "making a positive difference" in the lives of other students who are struggling to maintain or regain their mental health. Undergraduates must have completed at least 6 semester credits and have a GPA of 2.5 or higher. Graduate students must have completed at least 3 semester units and have a GPA of 3.0 or higher. Along with their application, they must submit 1) a 250-word essay describing their progress towards meeting their educational and/or vocational goals; 2) a 500-word essay on how they manage their disabiity; and 3) a 750-word essay on how they are making a positive difference in the lives of students with mental health conditions. They must also submit a letter of recommendation from a faculty person, verification of disability, and unofficial transcripts.

Financial data The stipend is $1,000.

Duration 1 year.

Number awarded 1 each year.

Deadline August of each year.

[139]
AMERICAN BUS ASSOCIATION YELLOW RIBBON SCHOLARSHIP

American Bus Association
Attn: ABA Foundation
111 K Street, N.E., Ninth Floor
Washington, DC 20002
(202) 842-1645   Toll Free: (800) 283-2877
Fax: (202) 842-0850   E-mail: abainfo@buses.org
Web: www.buses.org

Summary To provide financial assistance for college or graduate school to people with disabilities, veterans, and children of wounded veterans who are preparing for a career in the transportation, travel, and tourism industry.

Eligibility This program is open to U.S. and Canadian citizens and permanent residents who are enrolled as an undergraduate or graduate student in a program related to the transportation, travel, and tourism industry. Applicants must 1) have a physical or sensory disability; 2) be a veteran of the U.S. or Canadian military; or 3) be a child or a wounded U.S. or Canadian military veteran. They must have a GPA of 3.0 or higher.

Financial data   The stipend is $2,500.
Duration   1 or more each year.
Deadline   April of each year.

[140]
AMERICAN EPILEPSY SOCIETY PREDOCTORAL RESEARCH FELLOWSHIPS

American Epilepsy Society
135 South LaSalle Street, Suite 2850
Chicago, IL 60603
(312) 883-3800   Fax: (312) 896-5784
E-mail: info@aesnet.org
Web: www.aesnet.org

Summary   To provide funding to doctoral candidates who are interested in conducting dissertation research related to epilepsy.

Eligibility   This program is open full-time doctoral students conducting dissertation research with an epilepsy-related theme under the guidance of a mentor with expertise in epilepsy research. Applicants must have a defined research plan and access to institutional resources to conduct the proposed project. Selection is based on the applicant's potential and commitment to develop as an independent and productive epilepsy researcher, academic record, and research experience; the mentor's research qualifications; the research training plan; and the quality of the research facilities, resources, and training opportunities. Applications are especially encouraged from women, members of minority groups, and people with disabilities. U.S. citizenship is not required, but all research must be conducted in the United States.

Financial data   Grants range up $30,000, including $29,000 as stipend and $1,000 for travel support and complimentary registration to attend the sponsor's annual meeting.

Duration   1 year; nonrenewable.

Additional data   In addition to the funding provided by the American Epilepsy Society, support is available from the TESS Research Foundation for applications focused on epilepsy due to SLC13A5 mutations; the LGS Foundation for applications focused on Lennox-Gastaut-Syndrome; the PCDH19 Alliance for applications focused on epilepsy due to PCDH19 mutations; the Dravet Syndrome Foundation for applications focused on Dravet Syndrome; Wishes for Elliott for applications focused on epilepsy due to SCN8A mutations; and the TS Alliance for applications focused on epilepsy associated with tuberous sclerosis complex (TSC).

Number awarded   Varies each year.

Deadline   Letters of intent must be submitted by October of each year; final proposals are due in January.

[141]
AMERICAN SPEECH-LANGUAGE-HEARING FOUNDATION SCHOLARSHIP FOR STUDENTS WITH A DISABILITY

American Speech-Language-Hearing Foundation
Attn: Programs Administrator
2200 Research Boulevard
Rockville, MD 20850-3289
(301) 296-8703   Toll Free: (800) 498-2071, ext. 8703
Fax: (301) 296-8567
E-mail: foundationprograms@asha.org
Web: www.ashfoundation.org

Summary   To provide financial assistance to persons with disabilities who are interested in studying communication sciences or related programs in graduate school.

Eligibility   This program is open to full-time graduate students who are enrolled in communication sciences and disorders programs, with preference given to students who have a disability. Applicants must submit an essay, up to 5 pages in length, on a topic that relates to the future of leadership in the discipline. They must also submit brief statements on the major classification that best describes their impairment and the limitations that their disability has posed. Selection is based on academic promise and outstanding academic achievement.

Financial data   The stipend is $5,000. Funds must be used for educational support (e.g., tuition, books, school-related living expenses), not for personal or conference travel.

Duration   1 year.

Additional data   This program is supported by the Leslie Londer Fund.

Number awarded   1 each year.

Deadline   May of each year.

[142]
AMNH GRADUATE STUDENT FELLOWSHIP PROGRAM

American Museum of Natural History
Attn: Richard Gilder Graduate School
Central Park West at 79th Street
New York, NY 10024-5192
(212) 769-5055   E-mail: Fellowships-rggs@amnh.org
Web: www.amnh.org

Summary   To provide financial assistance to doctoral students in selected programs at designated universities who are interested in utilizing the resources of the American Museum of Natural History in their training and research program.

Eligibility   This program is open to doctoral students in scientific disciplines practiced at the museum. The applicant's university exercises educational jurisdiction over the program and awards the degree; the museum curator serves as a graduate adviser, co-major professor, or major professor. Both U.S. citizens and noncitizens are eligible to apply. Candidates for a master's degree are not eligible. The museum encourages women, minorities, persons with disabilities, and Vietnam Era and disabled veterans to apply.

Financial data Fellowships provide a stipend and health insurance.

Duration 1 year; may be renewed up to 4 additional years.

Additional data The cooperating universities (and their relevant programs) are Columbia University, in astronomy, earth and planetary sciences (including paleontology), and evolutionary, ecological, and environmental biology; Cornell University in entomology; the Graduate Center of City University of New York in earth and planetary sciences (including paleontology), and evolutionary biology; New York University in molecular biology; and Stony Brook University in astronomy and astrophysics. Students must apply simultaneously to the museum and to 1 of the cooperating universities.

Number awarded Varies each year.

Deadline December of each year.

[143]
AMS GRADUATE FELLOWSHIPS

American Meteorological Society
Attn: Development and Student Program Manager
45 Beacon Street
Boston, MA 02108-3693
(617) 227-2426, ext. 3907   Fax: (617) 742-8718
E-mail: dFernandez@ametsoc.org
Web: www.ametsoc.org

Summary To encourage students entering their first year of graduate school to work on an advanced degree in the atmospheric and related oceanic and hydrologic sciences.

Eligibility This program is open to students entering their first year of graduate study and planning to work on an advanced degree in the atmospheric or related oceanic or hydrologic sciences. Applicants must be U.S. citizens or permanent residents and have a GPA of 3.25 or higher. Along with their application, they must submit 200-word essays on 1) their most important achievements that qualify them for this scholarship; and 2) their career goals in the atmospheric or related sciences. Selection is based on academic record as an undergraduate. The sponsor specifically encourages applications from women, minorities, and students with disabilities who are traditionally underrepresented in the atmospheric and related sciences.

Financial data The stipend is $25,000 per academic year.

Duration 9 months.

Additional data This program was initiated in 1991. It is funded by high-technology firms and government agencies.

Number awarded Varies each year; recently, 6 were awarded.

Deadline January of each year.

[144]
APAGS DISABILITIES GRANT PROGRAM

American Psychological Association
Attn: American Psychological Association of Graduate Students
750 First Street, N.E.
Washington, DC 20002-4242
(202) 336-6014   Fax: (202) 336-5694
E-mail: apags@apa.org
Web: www.apa.org/about/awards/apags-disabilities.aspx

Summary To provide funding to graduate students who are members of the American Psychological Association of Graduate Students (APAGS) and wish to develop a project that promotes training and educational experiences in disability issues.

Eligibility This program is open to members of APAGS who are enrolled at least half time in a master's or doctoral program at an accredited university. Applicants must be interested in developing a project that promotes training and educational experiences in practice or services for persons with disabilities or the recruitment, retention, and training of individuals with disabilities. Examples include, but are not limited to, workshops, conferences, speaker series, mentorship programs, and the development of student organizations with a focus on disability issues.

Financial data The grant is $1,000.

Duration The grant is presented annually.

Additional data This grant was first awarded in 2009.

Number awarded 1 each year.

Deadline November of each year.

[145]
ARNOLD & PORTER KAYE SCHOLER DIVERSITY SCHOLARSHIP

Arnold & Porter Kaye Scholer LLP
Attn: Manager of Attorney Recruiting
601 Massachusetts Avenue, N.W.
Washington, DC 20001
(202) 942-5000   Fax: (202) 942-5999
E-mail: recruitingdc@apks.com
Web: www.apks.com

Summary To provide financial assistance to law students who contribute to the diversity of their law school and the legal profession.

Eligibility This program is open to students enrolled in the first year at an ABA-accredited law school who contribute to the diverse background of the law school body, demonstrate strong academic achievement, and demonstrate an interest in promoting diversity in the legal profession. The sponsor defines diversity to include qualified minorities, women, individuals with disabilities, protected veterans, and LGBT individuals. Applicants must submit a resume, official law transcript, and a personal statement that describes their personal background and the importance of diversity in their life and the legal profession. They may also submit information on their financial need, but that is not required.

Financial data The stipend is $10,000; funds are paid directly to the law school to help finance the second year.

Duration 1 year.
Number awarded 1 or more each year.
Deadline March of each year.

[146]
ASP GRADUATE STUDENT VISITOR PROGRAM

National Center for Atmospheric Research
Attn: Advanced Study Program
3090 Center Green Drive
P.O. Box 3000
Boulder, CO 80307-3000
(303) 497-1328   Fax: (303) 497-1646
E-mail: paulad@ucar.edu
Web: www.asp.ucar.edu/graduate/graduate_visitor.php

Summary To provide an opportunity for graduate students to conduct research at the National Center for Atmospheric Research (NCAR) in Boulder, Colorado under the supervision of a staff member.

Eligibility This program is open to advanced M.S. and Ph.D. students in the atmospheric and related sciences, engineering, and scientific computing. Interdisciplinary studies utilizing the NCAR resources in climate, weather, and related disciplines are also welcome. Applicants should consult with an NCAR staff member who will agree to serve as a host for the research project. Students may not apply directly for this program; the application must be submitted by the NCAR staff member in collaboration with the student's thesis adviser. Selection is based on 1) the programmatic fit and need to visit NCAR as part of the thesis or final project work; and 2) the commitment to student mentoring by the NCAR host and the student's adviser. The program encourages applications from members of groups historically underrepresented in the atmospheric and related sciences, including Blacks or African Americans, Hispanics or Latinos, American Indians and Alaska Natives, women, first-generation college students, LGBT students, and students with disabilities.

Financial data Support is limited to travel expenses for the student and a per diem allowance of $2,000 per month. Travel expenses are also supported for the student's thesis adviser for visits up to 2 weeks. The student's university must provide all support for the student's salary and benefits.

Duration Visits may extend from a few months to a year, but most are 3 to 6 months.

Additional data NCAR is operated by the University Corporation for Atmospheric Research (a consortium of more than 100 North American universities and research institutes) and sponsored by the National Science Foundation. This program was established in 2006.

Number awarded Varies each year; recently, 24 students received support from this program.

Deadline October of each year.

[147]
BASIC PSYCHOLOGICAL SCIENCE RESEARCH GRANT

American Psychological Association
Attn: American Psychological Association of Graduate Students
750 First Street, N.E.
Washington, DC 20002-4242
(202) 336-6014   E-mail: apags@apa.org
Web: www.apa.org/about/awards/apags-science.aspx

Summary To provide funding to members of the American Psychological Association of Graduate Students (APAGS) who are interested in conducting graduate research in psychological science, including those dealing specifically with diversity issues.

Eligibility This program is open to members of the association who are enrolled at least half time in a psychology or neuroscience graduate program at an accredited university. Applicants must be interested in conducting thesis, dissertation, or other research in psychological science. Along with their application, they must submit a curriculum vitae, letter of recommendation, and 3-page research proposal. The program includes grants specifically reserved for research focused on diversity, defined to include issues of age, sexual orientation, physical disability, socioeconomic status, race/ethnicity, workplace role/position, religious and spiritual orientation, and work/family concerns. Applicants for diversity grants must also submit a 250-word statement that explains 1) how this research applies to one or more areas of diversity; and 2) how the overall merit and broader implications of this study contribute to our psychological understanding of diversity.

Financial data The stipend is $1,000.

Duration 1 year.

Additional data These grants were first awarded in 2009; the diversity component began in 2014.

Number awarded Approximately 12 each year, of which up to 3 are reserved for researchers specifically focusing on diversity issues.

Deadline November of each year.

[148]
BAY AREA MINORITY LAW STUDENT SCHOLARSHIPS

Bar Association of San Francisco
Attn: Diversity Pipeline Programs Manager
301 Battery Street, Third Floor
San Francisco, CA 94111-3203
(415) 782-8914   Fax: (415) 477-2388
E-mail: emcgriff@sfbar.org
Web: www.sfbar.org

Summary To provide financial assistance to underrepresented students from any state who are interested in attending law school in northern California.

Eligibility This program is open to underrepresented students (women, racial and ethnic minorities, students with disabilities, LGBT students) who accept offers of admission from designated law schools in northern California. Applicants must submit a 500-word essay on obstacles they have overcome in pursuing their education and the qualities and talents they would bring to the legal profession. Financial need is considered in the selection process.

Financial data The stipend is $10,000 per year.
Duration 3 years.
Additional data This program began in 1998. Since then, more than $1.7 million in scholarships have been awarded to 93 students. The designated law schools are the Berkeley School of Law at the University of California, University of California at Davis School of Law, Golden Gate University School of Law, Hastings College of the Law at the University of California, McGeorge School of Law of University of the Pacific, University of San Francisco School of Law, Santa Clara University School of Law, and Stanford Law School.
Number awarded Varies each year; recently, 4 were awarded.
Deadline April of each year.

[149]
BB&K FIRST YEAR LAW STUDENT DIVERSITY FELLOWSHIP/SCHOLARSHIP PROGRAM

Best Best & Krieger LLP
Attn: Recruiting and Professional Development
  Manager
3390 University Avenue, Fifth Floor
P.O. Box 1028
Riverside, CA 92502
(951) 686-1450   Fax: (951) 686-3083
E-mail: daneal.bailey@bbklaw.com
Web: www.bbklaw.com

Summary To provide financial assistance and work experience at designated offices of Best Best & Krieger (BB&K) in California to students at law schools who will contribute to the diversity of the firm.
Eligibility This program is open to full-time first-year students at ABA-accredited law schools. Applicants must be a member of a diverse group (including ethnic, gender, physical disability, and/or sexual orientation), be making a meaningful contribution to the diversity of the law school student body, and be likely to make similar impacts in the legal community upon entering the practice of law. They must have been invited to a summer associate position with the firm and be committed to practice law after graduation in the area where that associateship will be performed. Along with their application, they must submit law school and undergraduate transcripts, a current resume, a legal writing sample that has not been edited by an attorney, and personal statements describing 1) why they should be considered for this program; and 2) how they will contribute to diversity in their community.
Financial data The stipend is $7,500.
Duration The selected student must complete a paid summer associate position in a participating office of BB&K, must be invited and must return to BB&K the following summer. Funds are paid following completion of the student's second summer with the firm.

Additional data Participating BB&K offices are located in Ontario, Riverside, and Irvine.
Number awarded 1 each year.
Deadline January of each year.

[150]
BETTY BACON MEMORIAL SCHOLARSHIP

California Association for Postsecondary Education
  and Disability
Attn: Scholarships
10073 Valley View Street, Suite 242
Cypress, CA 90630
(562) 397-2810   Fax: (866) 577-3387
E-mail: caped38@gmail.com
Web: www.caped.io/scholarships/scholarship-application

Summary To provide financial assistance to undergraduate and graduate students in California who have a disability.
Eligibility This program is open to students at public and private 4-year colleges and universities in California who have a physical, mental, or learning disability. Undergraduates must have completed at least 6 semester credits and have a GPA of 2.5 or higher. Graduate students must have completed at least 3 semester units and have a GPA of 3.0 or higher. Along with their application, they must submit 1) a 250-word essay describing their progress towards meeting their educational and/or vocational goals; and 2) a 500-word essay on how they manage their disabiity. They must also submit a letter of recommendation from a faculty person, verification of disability, and unofficial transcripts.
Financial data The stipend is $1,000.
Duration 1 year.
Number awarded 1 each year.
Deadline August of each year.

[151]
BIUNNO SCHOLARSHIP FOR LAW STUDENTS WITH DISABILITIES

Essex County Bar Association
Attn: Committee on the Rights of Persons with
  Disabilities
Historic Courthouse, Room B-01
470 Dr. Martin Luther King, Jr. Boulevard
Newark, NJ 07102
(973) 622-6207   Fax: (973) 622-4341
E-mail: info@EssexBar.com
Web: www.EssexBar.com

Summary To provide financial assistance to students with disabilities from New Jersey who are interested in attending a law school in any state.
Eligibility Applicants must be able to demonstrate a present and permanent physical or mental disability that substantially limits 1 or more of the major life activities (medical documentation is required); be residents of New Jersey, with preference given to Essex County residents; be attending or accepted at a law school in any state; and have earned a GPA of 3.0 or higher as an undergraduate student (if an incoming law student) or in law school. Pri-

ority is given to applicants who are planning a career in the field of advocacy for persons with disabilities. Intent may be demonstrated by completion of a course in disability law, work in a disability or disability-related clinic, or prior job experience in an advocacy field or with a public interest organization. Students who can demonstrate financial need receive priority.

Financial data Stipends range from $3,000 to $6,000. Funds are paid directly to the recipient's school or to a company providing equipment for the disabled student.

Duration 1 year.

Number awarded 1 or more each year.

Deadline May of each year.

[152]
BMO CAPITAL MARKETS LIME CONNECT EQUITY THROUGH EDUCATION SCHOLARSHIPS FOR STUDENTS WITH DISABILITIES

Lime Connect, Inc.
590 Madison Avenue, 21st Floor
New York, NY 10022
(212) 521-4469   Fax: (212) 521-4099
E-mail: info@limeconnect.com
Web: www.limeconnect.com

Summary To provide financial assistance to students with disabilities working on a bachelor's or graduate degree in a business or technical field at a college or university in Canada or the United States.

Eligibility This program is open to undergraduate and graduate students at 4-year colleges and universities in the United States or Canada who have a disability. International students with disabilities enrolled at universities in the United States or Canada are also eligible. Applicants must be working full time on a degree in a business, engineering, mathematics, physics, statistics, or a related field. Along with their application, they must submit an essay on their career goals and why they believe they should be selected to receive this scholarship. Preference is given to students preparing for a career in financial services with a focus on capital markets. Financial need is not considered in the selection process.

Financial data The stipend is $10,000 for students at U.S. universities or $C5,000 for students at Canadian universities.

Duration 1 year.

Additional data This program is jointly sponsored by BMO Capital Markets and Lime Connect, an organization founded in 2006 to promote employment of people with disabilities. BMO Capital Markets established its Equity Through Education program in 2005 and in 2011 invited Lime Connect to administer a component of the program for students with disabilities.

Number awarded Varies each year; recently, 11 were awarded.

Deadline December each year.

[153]
BRADLEY ANNUAL DIVERSITY SCHOLARSHIP

Bradley Arant Boult Cummings LLP
Attn: Recruiting Manager
One Federal Place
1819 Fifth Avenue North
Birmingham, AL 35203-2119
(205) 521-8000   Fax: (205) 488-6445
E-mail: vkranzusch@babc.com
Web: www.bradley.com

Summary To provide financial assistance and summer work experience to law students who are members of groups traditionally underrepresented in the legal profession.

Eligibility This program is open to students currently enrolled in the first or second year of at ABA-accredited law schools. Applicants must reflect the diversity of the legal marketplace and be from a group traditionally underrepresented in the legal profession based on their age, ancestry, gender, color, national origin, disability, place of birth, religion, sexual orientation, or veteran status. They must be interested in a summer clerkship at 1 of the sponsoring firm's offices. Along with their application, they must submit a 750-word essay on the importance of diversity in the legal profession and the ways in which their receipt of the scholarship would further the sponsor's desire to improve diversity in the legal profession. Selection is based on that essay, academic qualifications, involvement in community activities, significant work and personal achievements, and financial need.

Financial data The stipend is $10,000 for a second-year student or $5,000 for a first-year student. A salary (amount not specified) is paid for the summer clerkship.

Duration 1 summer and 1 academic year.

Additional data The firm's law offices are located in Birmingham, Charlotte, Houston, Huntsville, Jackson, Montgomery, Nashville, Tampa, and Washington, D.C.

Number awarded 2 each year: 1 to a first-year student and 1 to a second-year student.

Deadline March of each year.

[154]
"BUSINESS PLAN" SCHOLARSHIP FOR STUDENTS WITH DISABILITIES

Fit Small Business
Attn: Scholarship
315 Madison Avenue, 24th Floor
New York, NY 10017
(212) 555-3434
E-mail: mprosser@fitsmallbusiness.com
Web: www.fitsmallbusiness.com

Summary To recognize and reward, with scholarships, undergraduate and graduate students who have a disability and submit outstanding essays about writing a business plan.

Eligibility This competition is open to undergraduate and graduate students who have a documented disability; qualifying disabilities include, but are not limited to, physical disabilities, medical conditions, mental and psychiatric conditions, speech and language, learning disabilities, behavioral conditions, and all other disabling conditions. Applicants must submit an essay of 500 to 1,000 words on what they learned from writing a business plan. They are not asked to submit the actual plan; instead, they should focus on what they learned about researching for the business plan, what they learned about the specific industry during researching the business plan, what they learned about the key assumptions upon which the plan depended, why they no longer thought the business was viable after writing the plan, and how and why the business plan changed during the process of getting feedback. Selection is based on originality, writing style, and quality of ideas.

Financial data The award is a $1,000 scholarship.
Duration The competition is held twice each year.
Additional data This program began in 2014.
Number awarded 2 each year: 1 in fall and 1 in spring.
Deadline October of each year for fall; March of each year for spring.

[155]
CAPED EXCELLENCE SCHOLARSHIP

California Association for Postsecondary Education and Disability
Attn: Scholarships
10073 Valley View Street, Suite 242
Cypress, CA 90630
(562) 397-2810   Fax: (866) 577-3387
E-mail: caped38@gmail.com
Web: www.caped.io/scholarships/scholarship-application

Summary To provide financial assistance to undergraduate and graduate students in California who have a disability and can demonstrate academic achievement and involvement in community and campus activities.
Eligibility This program is open to students at public and private colleges and universities in California who have a physical, mental, or learning disability. Undergraduates must have completed at least 6 semester credits and have a GPA of 2.5 or higher. Graduate students must have completed at least 3 semester units and have a GPA of 3.0 or higher. Applicants must submit 1) a 250-word essay describing their progress towards meeting their educational and/or vocational goals; 2) a 500-word essay on how they manage their disabiity; and 3) a 750-word description of how their campus and/or community involvement supports their academic achievement. They must also submit a letter of recommendation from a faculty person, verification of disability, and unofficial transcripts. This award is presented to the applicant who demonstrates the highest level of academic achievement and involvement in community and campus life.
Financial data The stipend is $1,500.
Duration 1 year.
Number awarded 1 each year.
Deadline August of each year.

[156]
CAPED MEMORIAL SCHOLARSHIP

California Association for Postsecondary Education and Disability
Attn: Scholarships
10073 Valley View Street, Suite 242
Cypress, CA 90630
(562) 397-2810   Fax: (866) 577-3387
E-mail: caped38@gmail.com
Web: www.caped.io/scholarships/scholarship-application

Summary To provide financial assistance to undergraduate and graduate students in California who have a disability.
Eligibility This program is open to students at public and private colleges and universities in California who have a physical, mental, or learning disability. Undergraduates must have completed at least 6 semester credits and have a GPA of 2.5 or higher. Graduate students must have completed at least 3 semester units and have a GPA of 3.0 or higher. Applicants must submit 1) a 250-word essay describing their progress towards meeting their educational and/or vocational goals; and 2) a 500-word essay on how they manage their disabiity. They must also submit a letter of recommendation from a faculty person, verification of disability, and unofficial transcripts.
Financial data The stipend is $1,000.
Duration 1 year.
Number awarded 1 each year.
Deadline August of each year.

[157]
CHICAGO INJURY CENTER'S ANNUAL SCHOLARSHIP FUND FOR DISABLED VETERANS

Chicago Injury Center
308 West Erie Street, Suite 300b
Chicago, IL 60654
(312) 818-4450   E-mail: pearlrosemail@gmail.com
Web: www.chicagoinjurycenter.com

Summary To provide financial assistance for college to disabled veterans.
Eligibility This program is open to honorably discharged veterans who have a disability. Applicants must be enrolled or planning to enroll as an undergraduate or graduate student at an accredited college, university, community college, or trade school. They must have a GPA of 2.5 or higher. Along with their application, they must submit a brief biography and a 500-word essay on 1) the hurdles they have had to overcome as a veteran with a disability and how it has prepared them to face the challenges of their particular course of study; and 2) how they believe the military and their road to recovery has helped prepare them for the challenges that they will face as a student.
Financial data Stipends are $1,000, $500, or $250.
Duration 1 year.
Additional data This program began in 2015.

Number awarded 1 at $1,000, 1 at $500, and 2 at $250 each year.

Deadline May of each year.

[158]
CIA GRADUATE SCHOLARSHIP PROGRAM

Central Intelligence Agency
Attn: Human Resource Management
Recruitment and Retention Center, 4B14-034 DD1
Washington, DC 20505
(703) 371-2107
Web: www.cia.gov

Summary To provide scholarship/loans and work experience to graduate students who are interested in employment with the Central Intelligence Agency (CIA).

Eligibility This program is open to U.S. citizens entering their first or second year of full-time graduate work. Applicants must have a GPA of 3.0 or higher, be able to demonstrate financial need (household income of $70,000 or less for a family of 4 or $80,000 or less for a family of 5 or more), and be able to meet the same employment standards as permanent employees of the CIA. Selection is based on academic excellence, relevant practical or job experience in field of interest, proficiency in a foreign language, demonstrated leadership qualities, and genuine interest in contributing to CIA's mission.

Financial data The stipend ranges up to $18,000 per year for tuition, fees, books, and supplies. For summer employment, scholars are provided a salary ($19.12 to $22.96 per hour) and an optional benefits package (health, dental, and vision insurance, life insurance, and retirement) They must agree to continue employment with the CIA after college graduation for a period 1.5 times the length of their college support.

Duration 1 year; may be renewed, provided the recipient remains enrolled full time and maintains a GPA of 3.0 or higher.

Additional data Prior to graduation, students must work at a CIA facility in the Washington, D.C. area for at least 60 to 90 days. The agency pays the cost of transportation between school and the Washington D.C. area and provides a housing allowance. After completing that tour, students must still have at least 1 year of full-time classes prior to graduation.

Number awarded Varies each year.

Deadline August of each year.

[159]
COOLEY DIVERSITY FELLOWSHIP PROGRAM

Cooley LLP
Attn: Diversity and Inclusion Manager
1299 Pennsylvania Avenue, N.W., Suite 700
Washington, DC 20004
(202) 842-7800   Fax: (202) 842-7899
E-mail: diversityfellowship@cooley.com
Web: www.cooley.com/diversityfellowship

Summary To provide financial assistance and work experience to law students who are committed to promoting diversity in their community and are interested in summer associateships and employment at an office of Cooley LLP.

Eligibility This program is open to students enrolled full time at an ABA-accredited law school and planning to graduate 2 years after applying. Applicants must submit a 3-page personal statement describing their demonstrated commitment to promoting diversity (e.g., ethnicity, gender, physical disability, and/or sexual orientation) in their community. They must be interested in a summer associateship. Selection is based on undergraduate and law school academic performance, personal achievements, leadership abilities, community service, and demonstrated commitment to promoting diversity and inclusion.

Financial data The award includes a stipend of $10,000 after completing a summer associateship after the first year of law school, another stipend of $10,000 after completing another summer associateship after the second year of law school, and another stipend of $10,000 after graduating from law school and joining the firm as a full-time associate.

Duration 3 years.

Additional data Summer associates may work in any of the firm's offices in California (Los Angeles, Palo Alto, San Diego, or San Francisco), Colorado (Broomfield), Massachusetts (Boston), New York (New York), Virginia (Reston), Washington (Seattle), or Washington, D.C.

Number awarded 1 or more each year.

Deadline January of each year.

[160]
CYNTHIA RUTH RUSSELL SCHOLARSHIP

Kansas Masonic Foundation, Inc.
Attn: Director of Development and Programs
2909 S.W. Maupin Lane
Topeka, KS 66614-5335
(785) 357-7646   Fax: (785) 357-7406
E-mail: Dave@kansasmasonic.foundation
Web: www.kansasmasonic.foundation

Summary To provide financial assistance to Kansas residents who have a disability and are attending a college or university in the state.

Eligibility This program is open to residents of Kansas who have a medically-approved disability. Applicants must be attending or planning to attend 1 of 7 public institutions of higher education in the state as a full-time undergraduate or graduate student. Along with their application, they must submit a description of their disability, documentation of the disability from a doctor, transcripts, and documentation of financial need.

Financial data The stipend is $5,000.

Duration 1 year.

Number awarded 1 or more each year.

Deadline March of each year.

[161]
DEBORAH J. BROYLES DIVERSE SCHOLARS PROGRAM

Reed Smith LLP
Attn: U.S. Legal Recruiting Manager
225 Fifth Avenue
Pittsburgh, PA 15222
(412) 288-3131   Fax: (412) 288-3063
E-mail: DiverseScholars@reedsmith.com
Web: careers.reedsmith.com

Summary To provide financial assistance and summer work experience to law students who are committed to diversity.

Eligibility This program is open to students who are completing their first year of law school and are authorized to work in the United States. Applicants must be able to demonstrate a record of academic excellence and a commitment to diversity and inclusion. The sponsor defines diversity to include race, ancestry, religion, color, sex, age, national origin, sexual orientation, gender identity and/or expression, disability, and veteran's status. Along with their application, they must submit a 750-word personal statement on why they believe it is important to strive for diversity and inclusion in the legal profession.

Financial data The stipend is $20,000. Recipients are also offered a summer associate position at their choice of the firm's U.S. offices after completion of their second year of law school (in Chicago, Houston, Los Angeles, New York, Philadelphia, Pittsburgh, Princeton, San Francisco, or Washington, D.C.).

Duration 1 year (the second year of law school).

Additional data The firm established this program in 2008 as part of its commitment to promote diversity in the legal profession. The program was renamed in 2016 to honor the firm's outstanding female African American partner.

Number awarded 2 each year.

Deadline July of each year.

[162]
DISABILITY AWARENESS SCHOLARSHIP

United States Military VA Loan
200 112th Avenue N.E., Suite 310
Bellevue, WA 98004
Toll Free: (888) 851-7871   Fax: (425) 454-7547
E-mail: scholarship@MilitaryVALoan.com
Web: www.militaryvaloan.com

Summary To recognize and reward, with college scholarships, high school seniors and current college and graduate students (disabled or not) who submit outstanding essays about overcoming disability.

Eligibility This program is open to anyone older than 17 years of age who either has not yet begun college or is currently enrolled full time as an undergraduate or graduate student at a college or other institution of higher education. Applicants are not required to have a disability themselves, but they must submit an essay of 500 to 1,000 words on how they or someone they know over-

came disability to do something great. They must have a GPA of 3.0 or higher.

Financial data The stipend is $1,000.

Duration 1 year.

Number awarded 1 each year.

Deadline January of each year.

[163]
DISABLED PERSON NATIONAL SCHOLARSHIP COMPETITION

Disabled Person, Inc.
P.O. Box 230636
Encinitas, CA 92023-0636
(760) 420-1269   E-mail: info@disabledperson.com
Web: www.disabledperson.com/scholarships/15

Summary To recognize and reward, with college scholarships, undergraduate and graduate students who have a disability and submit outstanding essays on an assigned topic.

Eligibility This competition is open to U.S. citizens who have a disability and are enrolled as full-time undergraduate or graduate students at a college or university in the United States. High school seniors and part-time students are not eligible. Applicants must submit an essay, up to 750 words in length, on a topic that changes annually; recently, students were asked to write on the impact on their community of the new regulations of the Office of Federal Contract Compliance concerning the hiring of people with disabilities for federal contractors.

Financial data The award is a $1,000 scholarship.

Duration The competition is held annually.

Number awarded 2 each year: 1 in the fall and 1 in the spring.

Deadline October of each year for fall; April of each year for spring.

[164]
DIVERSITY BAR PREPARATION SCHOLARSHIP

Washington State Association for Justice
1809 Seventh Avenue, Suite 1500
Seattle, WA 98101-1328
(206) 464-1011   Fax: (206) 464-0703
E-mail: sara@washingtonjustice.org
Web: www.washingtonjustice.org

Summary To provide funding to residents of Washington who will increase the diversity of the legal profession and are planning to take a bar review course.

Eligibility This program is open to residents of Washington who are graduating from law school or are currently employed as law clerks. Applicants must belong to a group underrepresented in the practice of law because of historical discrimination based on disability, gender, race, ethnicity, religion, sexual orientation, gender identity, or gender expression. Along with their application, they must submit 1) a resume that includes past work experience along with any achievements, honors, clubs, association, community activities, or hobbies; and 2) a 2-page essay on why they would like to be considered for this scholarship, especially their ideal law practice and how that fits into the mission of the Washington State Association for Justice (WSAJ). Selection is based on demonstrated interest and intent to practice in the plaintiff's bar, financial need, academic achievements, extracurricular and community activities, and life experiences.

Financial data The stipend provides up to full payment of tuition for a bar review course.

Duration This is a 1-time grant.

Number awarded 1 or more each year.

Deadline January of each year.

[165]
DIVERSITY IN PSYCHOLOGY AND LAW RESEARCH AWARD

American Psychological Association
Attn: Division 41 (American Psychology-Law Society)
c/o Kathy Gaskey, Administrative Officer
P.O. Box 11488
Southport, NC 28461-3936
(910) 933-4018   Fax: (910) 933-4018
E-mail: apls@ec.rr.com
Web: www.apadivisions.org

Summary To provide funding to student members of the American Psychology-Law Society (AP-LS) who are interested in conducting a research project related to diversity.

Eligibility This program is open to undergraduate and graduate student members of AP-LS who are interested in conducting research on issues related to psychology, law, multiculturalism, and/or diversity (e.g., research pertaining to psycholegal issues on race, gender, culture, sexual orientation). Students from underrepresented groups are strongly encouraged to apply; underrepresented groups include, but are not limited to: racial and ethnic minorities; first-generation college students; lesbian, gay, bisexual, and transgender students; and students with physical disabilities. Applicants must submit a project description that includes a statement of the research problem, the project's likely impact on the field of psychology and law broadly, methodology, budget, and an overview of relevant literature. Selection is based on the impact of the project on diversity and multiculturalism and the expected completion within the allocated time.

Financial data The grant is $1,000.

Duration The project must be completed within 1 year.

Number awarded Up to 5 each year.

Deadline December of each year.

[166]
DONALD W. BANNER DIVERSITY SCHOLARSHIP

Banner & Witcoff, Ltd.
Attn: Christopher Hummel
1100 13th Street, N.W., Suite 1200
Washington, DC 20005-4051
(202) 824-3000   Fax: (202) 824-3001
E-mail: chummel@bannerwitcoff.com
Web: www.bannerwitcoff.com/about/diversity

Summary To provide financial assistance to law students who come from groups historically underrepresented in intellectual property law.

Eligibility This program is open to students enrolled in the first or second year of a J.D. program at an ABA-accredited law school in the United States. Applicants must come from a group historically underrepresented in intellectual property law; that underrepresentation may be the result of race, sex, ethnicity, sexual orientation, disability, education, culture, religion, age, or socioeconomic background. Selection is based on academic merit, commitment to the pursuit of a career in intellectual property law, written communication skills, oral communication skills (determined through an interview), leadership qualities, and community involvement.

Financial data The stipend is $5,000 per year.

Duration 1 year (the second or third year of law school); students who accept and successfully complete the firm's summer associate program may receive an additional $5,000 for a subsequent semester of law school.

Number awarded 1 each year.

Deadline October of each year.

[167]
DRUG ABUSE DISSERTATION RESEARCH

National Institute on Drug Abuse
Attn: Division of Clinical Neuroscience and Behavioral
   Research
6101 Executive Boulevard, Suite 3154
Bethesda, MD 20892-9593
(301) 443-3207   Fax: (301) 443-6814
E-mail: aklinwm@mail.nih.gov
Web: www.grants.nih.gov

Summary To provide financial assistance to doctoral candidates interested in conducting dissertation research on drug abuse treatment and health services.

Eligibility This program is open to doctoral candidates who are conducting dissertation research in a field of the behavioral, biomedical, or social sciences related to drug abuse treatment, including research in epidemiology, prevention, treatment, services, and women and sex/gender differences. Students working on an M.D., D.O., D.D.S., or similar professional degree are not eligible. Applicants must be U.S. citizens, nationals, or permanent residents and must have completed all requirements for the doctoral degree except the dissertation. Special attention is paid to recruiting members of racial and ethnic groups underrepresented in the biomedical and behavioral sciences (African Americans, Hispanic Americans, Native Americans, Alaskan Natives, and Pacific Islanders), persons with disabilities, and individuals from disadvantaged backgrounds.

Financial data The maximum grant is $50,000 per year, including support for the recipient's salary (up to $21,180 per year), research assistant's salary and direct research project expenses. Funding may not be used for tuition, alterations or renovations, faculty salary, contracting costs, or space rental. The recipient's institution may receive facilities and administrative costs of up to 8% of total direct costs.

Duration　Up to 2 years; may be extended for 1 additional year.

Number awarded　Varies each year, depending on the availability of funds.

Deadline　February, June, or October of each year.

[168]
EDWARD T. AND MARY A. CONROY MEMORIAL SCHOLARSHIP PROGRAM

Maryland Higher Education Commission
Attn: Office of Student Financial Assistance
6 North Liberty Street, Ground Suite
Baltimore, MD 21201
(410) 767-3301　　　　　　Toll Free: (800) 974-0203
Fax: (410) 332-0250　　　　TDD: (800) 735-2258
E-mail: osfamail.mhec@maryland.gov
Web: www.mhec.state.md.us

Summary　To provide financial assistance for college or graduate school in Maryland to children and spouses of victims of the September 11, 2001 terrorist attacks and specified categories of veterans, public safety employees, and their children or spouses.

Eligibility　This program is open to entering and continuing undergraduate and graduate students in the following categories: 1) children and surviving spouses of victims of the September 11, 2001 terrorist attacks who died in the World Trade Center in New York City, in the Pentagon in Virginia, or on United Airlines Flight 93 in Pennsylvania; 2) veterans who have, as a direct result of military service, a disability of 25% or greater and have exhausted or are no longer eligible for federal veterans' educational benefits; 3) children and unremarried surviving spouses of armed forces members whose death or 100% disability was directly caused by military service; 4) POW/MIA veterans of the Vietnam Conflict and their children; 5) state or local public safety officers or volunteers who became 100% disabled in the line of duty; 6) children and unremarried surviving spouses of state or local public safety employees or volunteers who died or became 100% disabled in the line of duty. and 7) children and unremarried surviving spouses or a school employee who, as a result of an act of violence, either died in the line of duty or sustained an injury that rendered the school employee 100% disabled. The parent, spouse, veteran, POW, public safety officer or volunteer, or school employee must have been a resident of Maryland at the time of death or when declared disabled. Applicants must be planning to enroll at a 2- or 4-year Maryland college or university as a full-time or part-time degree-seeking undergraduate or graduate student or attend a private career school. Financial need is not considered.

Financial data　The amount of the award is equal to tuition and fees at a Maryland postsecondary institution, to a maximum of $10,182. The total amount of all Maryland scholarship awards from all sources may not exceed the cost of attendance or $19,000, whichever is less.

Duration　Up to 5 years of full-time study or 8 years of part-time study.

Number awarded　Varies each year.

Deadline　July of each year.

[169]
FAEGRE BAKER DANIELS DIVERSITY AND INCLUSION FELLOWSHIPS

Faegre Baker Daniels
Attn: Diversity and Pro Bono Coordinator
300 North Meridian Street, Suite 2700
Indianapolis, IN 46204
(317) 237-8298　　　　　　Fax: (317) 237-1000
E-mail: brita.horvath@faegrebd.com
Web: www.faegrebd.com/fellowship

Summary　To provide financial assistance and summer work experience to students from diverse backgrounds entering the second year of law school.

Eligibility　This program is open to residents of any state who are entering their second year at an accredited law school. Applicants must reflect diversity, defined to mean that they come from varied ethnic, racial, cultural, and lifestyle backgrounds, as well as those with disabilities or unique viewpoints. They must also be interested in a place in the sponsor's associate program during the summer between their second and third year of law school. Along with their application, they must submit a 2-page personal statement describing how or why they will contribute meaningfully to diversity and inclusion at the sponsoring firm and/or in the legal profession.

Financial data　The stipend is $10,000.

Duration　1 year.

Additional data　This law firm was formerly Baker & Daniels LLP. Recipients of these fellowships may elect to conduct their associateship at offices in Boulder, Chicago, Denver, Des Moines, Fort Wayne, Indianapolis, Minneapolis, Silicon Valley (East Palo Alto), South Bend, and Washington, D.C.

Number awarded　3 each year.

Deadline　September of each year.

[170]
FINNEGAN DIVERSITY SCHOLARSHIP

Finnegan, Henderson, Farabow, Garrett & Dunner, LLP
Attn: Attorney Recruitment Manager
901 New York Avenue, N.W.
Washington, DC 20001-4413
(202) 408-4034　　　　　　Fax: (202) 408-4400
E-mail: diversityscholarship@finnegan.com
Web: www.finnegan.com

Summary　To provide financial assistance and work experience to law students from diverse groups who are interested in a career in intellectual property law.

Eligibility　This program is open to law students who have demonstrated a commitment to a career in intellectual property law and are currently enrolled either as a first-year full-time student or second-year part-time student. Applicants must contribute to enhancing diversity; the sponsor defines diversity broadly, and has considered members of racial, ethnic, disabled, and sexual orientation groups that have been historically underrepresented in the legal profession. They must have earned an undergraduate degree in life sciences, chemistry, engineering, or computer science, or have substantial prior trademark experience. Selection is based on academic performance at the undergraduate, graduate (if applicable), and law school level; relevant work experience; community service; leadership skills; and special accomplishments.

Financial data The stipend is $15,000 per year.

Duration 1 year; may be renewed 1 additional year as long as the recipient completes a summer associateship with the sponsor and maintains of GPA of 3.0 or higher.

Additional data The sponsor, the world's largest intellectual property law firm, established this scholarship in 2003. Summer associateships are available at its offices in Washington, D.C., Atlanta, Boston, Palo Alto, or Reston.

Number awarded 1 each year.

Deadline January of each year.

[171]
FISH & RICHARDSON DIVERSITY FELLOWSHIP PROGRAM

Fish & Richardson P.C.
Recruiting Department
Attn: Fellowship Program
12390 El Camino Real
San Diego, CA 92130
(858) 678-5070   Fax: (858) 678-5099
E-mail: diversity@fr.com
Web: www.fr.com/about/diversity

Summary To provide financial assistance for law school to students who will contribute to diversity in the legal profession.

Eligibility This program is open to students enrolled in the first year at a law school anywhere in the country. Applicants must be African American/Black, American Indian/Alaskan Native, Hispanic/Latino, Native Hawaiian/Pacific Islander, Asian, person with disabilities, military veteran, or openly GLBT. Along with their application, they must submit a 500-word essay describing their background, what led them to the legal field, their interest in the sponsoring law firm, and what they could contribute to its practice and the profession. They must also indicate their first 3 choices of an office of the firm where they are interested in a summer associate clerkship.

Financial data The stipend is $10,000, of which $5,000 is paid after completion of their first-year summer clerkship with the firm and an additional $5,000 is paid after the student receives and accepts an associate offer with the firm after completion of a second-year summer clerkship.

Duration 1 year; may be extended for a second year.

Additional data Recipients are also offered a paid associate clerkship during the summer following their first and second year of law school at an office of the firm in the location of their choice in Atlanta, Austin, Boston, Dallas, Delaware, Houston, New York, San Diego, Silicon Valley, Twin Cities, or Washington, D.C. This program began in 2005.

Number awarded 1 or more each year.

Deadline January of each year.

[172]
GAIUS CHARLES BOLIN DISSERTATION AND POST-MFA FELLOWSHIPS

Williams College
Attn: Dean of the Faculty
880 Main Street
Hopkins Hall, Third Floor
P.O. Box 141
Williamstown, MA 01267
(413) 597-4351   Fax: (413) 597-3553
E-mail: gburda@williams.edu
Web: faculty.williams.edu

Summary To provide financial assistance to members of underrepresented groups who are interested in teaching courses at Williams College while working on their doctoral dissertation or building their post-M.F.A. professional portfolio.

Eligibility This program is open to members of underrepresented groups, including ethnic minorities, first-generation college students, women in predominantly male fields, and scholars with disabilities. Applicants must be 1) doctoral candidates in any field who have completed all work for a Ph.D. except for the dissertation; or 2) artists who completed an M.F.A. degree within the past 2 years and are building their professional portfolio. They must be willing to teach a course at Williams College. Along with their application, they must submit a full curriculum vitae, a graduate school transcript, 3 letters of recommendation, a copy of their dissertation prospectus or samples of their artistic work, and a description of their teaching interests within a department or program at Williams College. U.S. citizenship or permanent resident status is required.

Financial data Fellows receive $50,000 for the academic year, plus housing assistance, office space, computer and library privileges, and a research allowance of up to $4,000.

Duration 2 years.

Additional data Bolin fellows are assigned a faculty adviser in the appropriate department. This program was established in 1985. Fellows are expected to teach a 1-semester course each year. They must be in residence at Williams College for the duration of the fellowship.

Number awarded 2 each year.

Deadline November of each year.

[173]
GEOGRAPHY AND SPATIAL SCIENCES DOCTORAL DISSERTATION RESEARCH IMPROVEMENT AWARDS

National Science Foundation
Directorate for Social, Behavioral, and Economic Sciences
Attn: Geography and Spatial Sciences Program
4201 Wilson Boulevard
Arlington, VA 22230
(703) 292-7301   TDD: (800) 281-8749
E-mail: tbaerwal@nsf.gov
Web: www.nsf.gov

Summary To provide funding for dissertation research to doctoral candidates in geography and spatial sciences.

Eligibility This program is open to doctoral candidates at U.S. universities in fields related to geography and spatial sciences who are conducting dissertation research. Applicants are encouraged to propose plans for research about the nature, causes, and consequences of human activity and natural environmental processes across a range of scales. Proposals should offer promise of contributing to scholarship by enhancing geographical knowledge, concepts, theories, methods, and their application to societal problems and concerns. In the selection process, the sponsor values the advancement of scientific knowledge and activities that contribute to societally relevant outcomes, such as full participation of women, persons with disabilities, and underrepresented minorities in science, technology, engineering, or mathematics (STEM).

Financial data Grants are $18,000, including both direct and indirect costs. Funds may be used only for research and related costs; support is not provided for a stipend or salary for the student or for tuition.

Duration 1 year.

Number awarded 25 to 35 each year.

Deadline Applications may be submitted at any time.

[174]
GEOLOGICAL SOCIETY OF AMERICA GRADUATE STUDENT RESEARCH GRANTS

Geological Society of America
Attn: Program Officer-Grants, Awards and Recognition
3300 Penrose Place
P.O. Box 9140
Boulder, CO 80301-9140
(303) 357-1060   Toll Free: (888) 443-4472, ext. 1060
Fax: (303) 357-1070   E-mail: awards@geosociety.org
Web: www.geosociety.org/grants/gradgrants.htm

Summary To provide funding to graduate student members of the Geological Society of America (GSA) interested in conducting research at universities in the United States, Canada, Mexico, or Central America.

Eligibility This program is open to GSA members working on a master's or doctoral degree at a university in the United States, Canada, Mexico, or Central America. Applicants must be interested in conducting geological research. Minorities, women, and persons with disabilities are strongly encouraged to apply. Selection is based on the scientific merits of the proposal, the capability of the investigator, and the reasonableness of the budget.

Financial data Grants range up to $2,500 and recently averaged $1,851. Funds can be used for the cost of travel, room and board in the field, services of a technician or field assistant, funding of chemical and isotope analyses, or other expenses directly related to the fulfillment of the research contract. Support is not provided for the purchase of ordinary field equipment, for maintenance of the families of the grantees and their assistants, as reimbursement for work already accomplished, for institutional overhead, for adviser participation, or for tuition costs.

Duration 1 year.

Additional data In addition to general grants, GSA awards a number of specialized grants.

Number awarded Varies each year; recently, the society awarded nearly 400 grants worth more than $723,000 through this and all of its specialized programs.

Deadline January of each year.

[175]
GOOGLE LIME SCHOLARSHIPS FOR STUDENTS WITH DISABILITIES

Lime Connect, Inc.
590 Madison Avenue, 21st Floor
New York, NY 10022
(212) 521-4469   Fax: (212) 521-4099
E-mail: info@limeconnect.com
Web: www.limeconnect.com

Summary To provide financial assistance to students with disabilities working on a bachelor's or graduate degree in a computer-related field at a college or university in Canada or the United States.

Eligibility This program is open to students at colleges and universities in the United States or Canada who have a disability and are enrolled in any year of undergraduate or graduate study. International students with disabilities enrolled at universities in the United States or Canada are also eligible. Applicants must be working full time on a degree in computer science, computer engineering, or a closely-related technical field. Along with their application, they must submit 3 essays that demonstrate their "passion for computer science." Financial need is not considered in the selection process.

Financial data The stipend is $10,000 for students at U.S. universities or $C5,000 for students at Canadian universities.

Duration 1 year.

Additional data This program is jointly sponsored by Google and Lime Connect, an organization founded in 2006 to promote employment of people with disabilities.

Number awarded Varies each year; recently, 12 were awarded.

Deadline November of each year.

[176]
GORMAN-METZ SCHOLARSHIP

Brookhaven National Laboratory
Attn: Diversity Office, Human Resources Division
Building 400B
P.O. Box 5000
Upton, New York 11973-5000
(631) 344-2703   Fax: (631) 344-5305
E-mail: palmore@bnl.gov
Web: www.bnl.gov/diversity/programs.asp

Summary To provide financial assistance to graduate students with disabilities who are working on a degree in a field of science, engineering, or mathematics.

Eligibility This program focuses on the children of current or retired employees of Brookhaven Science Associates, but it is also available to students who have a disability and are enrolled or entering a graduate degree program. Undergraduates may apply, but they are considered only in years when no graduate students qualify. Preference is given to studies in science, engineering, or mathematics. Applicants must submit an essay on the objectives of their planned education program and their long-range professional goals. Selection is based on academic records, references, career goals, and other factors deemed appropriate; financial need is not considered.

Financial data The stipend is $5,000.

Duration 1 year; nonrenewable.

Additional data This program began in 1997.

Number awarded 1 each year.

Deadline March of each year.

[177]
GRADUATE FELLOWSHIP IN THE HISTORY OF SCIENCE

American Geophysical Union
Attn: History of Geophysics
2000 Florida Avenue, N.W.
Washington, DC 20009-1277
(202) 777-7522   Toll Free: (800) 966-2481
Fax: (202) 328-0566
E-mail: HistoryofGeophysics@agu.org
Web: education.agu.org

Summary To provide funding to doctoral candidates conducting dissertation research in the history of geophysics.

Eligibility This program is open to doctoral candidates at U.S. institutions who have passed all preliminary examinations. Applicants must be completing a dissertation in the history of the geophysical sciences, including topics related to atmospheric sciences, biogeosciences, geodesy, geomagnetism and paleomagnetism, hydrology, ocean sciences, planetary sciences, seismology, space physics, aeronomy, tectonophysics, volcanology, geochemistry, and petrology. They must submit a cover letter with a curriculum vitae, undergraduate and graduate transcripts, a 10-page description of the dissertation topic and proposed research plan, and 3 letters of recommendation. U.S. citizenship or permanent resident status is required. Applications are encouraged from women, minorities, and

students with disabilities who are traditionally underrepresented in the geophysical sciences.

Financial data The grant is $5,000; funds are to be used to assist with the costs of travel to obtain archival or research materials.

Duration 1 year.

Number awarded 1 each year.

Deadline September of each year.

[178]
GRADUATE RESEARCH FELLOWSHIP PROGRAM OF THE NATIONAL SCIENCE FOUNDATION

National Science Foundation
Directorate for Education and Human Resources
Attn: Division of Graduate Education
4201 Wilson Boulevard, Room 875S
Arlington, VA 22230
(703) 331-3542   Toll Free: (866) NSF-GRFP
Fax: (703) 292-9048   E-mail: info@nsfgrfp.org
Web: www.nsf.gov

Summary To provide financial assistance to graduate students interested in working on a master's or doctoral degree in fields supported by the National Science Foundation (NSF).

Eligibility This program is open to U.S. citizens, nationals, and permanent residents who wish to work on research-based master's or doctoral degrees in a field of science, technology, engineering, or mathematics (STEM) supported by NSF (including astronomy, chemistry, computer and information sciences and engineering, geosciences, engineering, life sciences, materials research, mathematical sciences, physics, psychology, social sciences, or STEM education and learning). Other work in medical, dental, law, public health, or practice-oriented professional degree programs, or in joint science-professional degree programs, such as M.D./Ph.D. and J.D./Ph.D. programs, is not eligible. Applications normally should be submitted during the senior year in college or in the first year of graduate study; eligibility is limited to those who have completed no more than 12 months of graduate study since completion of a baccalaureate degree. Applicants who have already earned an advanced degree in science, engineering, or medicine (including an M.D., D.D.S., or D.V.M.) are ineligible. Selection is based on 1) intellectual merit of the proposed activity: strength of the academic record, proposed plan of research, previous research experience, references, appropriateness of the choice of institution; and 2) broader impacts of the proposed activity: full participation of women, persons with disabilities, and underrepresented minorities in science, technology, engineering, and mathematics (STEM); improved STEM education and educator development at any level; increased public scientific literacy and public engagement with science and technology; improved well-being of individuals in society; development of a diverse, globally competitive STEM workforce; increased partnerships between academia, industry, and others; improved national security; increased economic competitiveness of the US; and enhanced infrastructure for research and education.

Financial data The stipend is $34,000 per year; an additional $12,000 cost-of-education allowance is provided to the recipient's institution.

Duration Up to 3 years, usable over a 5-year period.

Number awarded Approximately 2,000 each year.

Deadline October of each year.

[179]
GRADUATE STUDENT FELLOWSHIPS AT FDA

National Science Foundation
Directorate for Engineering
Attn: Division of Chemical, Bioengineering,
  Environmental, and Transport Systems
4201 Wilson Boulevard, Room 565S
Arlington, VA 22230
(703) 292-7942   Fax: (703) 292-9098
TDD: (800) 281-8749   E-mail: lesterow@nsf.gov
Web: www.nsf.gov

Summary To provide an opportunity for graduate students to conduct research at an intramural laboratory of the U.S. Food and Drug Administration (FDA).

Eligibility This program is open to graduate students (preferably Ph.D. students) in science, engineering, and mathematics fields of interest to the National Science Foundation (NSF). Applicants must be U.S. citizens, nationals, or permanent residents. They must be proposing a program of full- or part-time work at an FDA intramural laboratory in an area related to their research, conducted under the guidance of an academic adviser and an FDA mentor. The program encourages applications from all citizens, including women and men, underrepresented minorities, and persons with disabilities.

Financial data Graduate students may receive stipends $2,100 per month, plus transportation expenses. The faculty adviser may receive 10% of the total award for research-related expenses, excluding equipment. The academic institution receives an allowance of 15% of total direct costs for administrative expenses. The total award may be up to $35,000 for a fellowship for a single student. FDA provides office space, research facilities, research costs in the form of expendable and minor equipment purchases in the host laboratory, and the time of its research staff.

Duration 1 to 4 semesters.

Additional data This program is also offered by the NSF Directorate for Computer and Information Science and Engineering.

Number awarded A total of 3 to 10 grants for all FDA programs is awarded each year; total funding is approximately $500,000.

Deadline March of each year.

[180]
HAROLD H. WILKE SCHOLARSHIP

United Church of Christ
Attn: Associate Director, Grant and Scholarship
  Administration
700 Prospect Avenue East
Cleveland, OH 44115-1100
(216) 736-2166   Toll Free: (866) 822-8224, ext. 2166
Fax: (216) 736-3783   E-mail: scholarships@ucc.org
Web: www.ucc.org/wilke.scholarship

Summary To provide financial assistance to members of United Church of Christ (UCC) congregations who have a disability or are involved with persons with disabilities and are preparing for ministry.

Eligibility This program is open to members of UCC congregations who have been members for at least 1 year and either have a disability or are directly involved in ministry to persons with disabilities. Applicants must be enrolled at an ATS-accredited seminary as preparation for authorized ministry in the UCC. They must have a GPA of 3.0 or higher.

Financial data A stipend is awarded (amount not specified).

Duration 1 year.

Additional data This scholarship was established in 1981.

Number awarded 1 or more each year.

Deadline February of each year.

[181]
HARTER SECREST & EMERY LLP DIVERSITY SCHOLARSHIP

Harter Secrest & Emery LLP
Attn: Legal Recruiter
1600 Bausch & Lomb Place
Rochester, NY 14604-2711
(585) 231-1414   Fax: (585) 232-2152
E-mail: cgordon@hselaw.com
Web: www.hselawcareers.com/law-student/diversity

Summary To provide financial assistance and summer work experience in Rochester, New York to law students from any state who will contribute to the diversity of the legal profession.

Eligibility This program is open to students who are currently enrolled full time in their first year at an ABA-accredited law school. Students who are members of populations historically underrepresented in the legal profession are encouraged to apply. They must also be interested in a summer associateship at the sponsoring law firm's main office in Rochester, New York. The firm defines diversity to include women, minorities, persons with disabilities, and/or persons of differing sexual orientations and gender identities. Selection is based on academic record, interest and capacity for a successful career during the remainder of law school and in the legal profession, and contribution to the diversity of the student body at law school. A disclosure of financial circumstances is not required, but a demonstrated need for financial assistance may be taken into consideration. The finalists are invited to an interview.

Financial data The stipend for the academic year is $7,500, paid directly to the student's law school. The salary for the summer associateship is the same as for all associates of the firm.

Duration The summer associateship is for 12 weeks following the first year of law school. The academic stipend is for the second year.

Additional data This program began in 2005 for students at Cornell University Law School. In 2008, it was expanded to students at all ABA-accredited law schools.

Number awarded 1 each year.

Deadline January of each year.

[182]
HAZEL D. COLE FELLOWSHIP

University of Washington
Attn: Stroum Center for Jewish Studies
Henry M. Jackson School of International Studies
Thomson Hall
Box 353650
Seattle, WA 98195-3650
(206) 543-0138   Fax: (206) 685-0668
E-mail: jewishst@uw.edu
Web: www.jewishstudies.washington.edu

Summary To provide funding to pre- and postdoctoral scholars in Jewish studies who are interested in conducting research at the University of Washington.

Eligibility This program is open to postdoctoral scholars who completed their Ph.D. within the past 3 years and to doctoral candidates working on a dissertation. Applicants must be interested in conducting research in a field of Jewish studies while in residence at the University of Washington for the tenure of their fellowship. They may be from any American or foreign university. Along with their application, they must submit a current curriculum vitae, a description of their scholarly interests and their proposed research project, a proposal for a course they would like to teach (including a prospective syllabus), 2 letters of recommendation, and an academic writing sample. The program encourages applications from women, minorities, individuals with disabilities, and covered veterans.

Financial data The fellowship provides a stipend of $50,000 plus benefits.

Duration 1 year.

Additional data The fellow also offers an undergraduate seminar or lecture course and makes a public presentation.

Number awarded 1 each year.

Deadline October of each year.

[183]
HEALTH POLICY RESEARCH SCHOLARS

Robert Wood Johnson Foundation
50 College Road East
Princeton, NJ 08540-6614
Toll Free: (877) 843-RWJF   E-mail: mail@rwjf.org
Web: www.rwjf.org

Summary To provide funding to doctoral students from diverse backgrounds interested in working on a degree related to health policy.

Eligibility This program is open to full-time doctoral students in the first or second year of their program. Applicants must be from underrepresented populations or disadvantaged backgrounds (e.g., first-generation college students, individuals from lower socioeconomic backgrounds, members of racial and ethnic groups underrepresented in doctoral programs, people with disabilities). They must be working on a degree in a field related to health policy, such as urban planning, political science, economics, ethnography, education, social work, or sociology; the program is not intended for students working on a clinical doctorate without a research focus. Prior experience or knowledge in health policy is neither required nor expected.

Financial data The stipend is $30,000 per year. Scholars are also eligible for $10,000 research grants if their dissertation is related to health policy.

Duration Up to 4 years. Participants may continue in the program without the annual stipend for a fifth year or until they complete their doctoral program, whichever occurs first.

Number awarded Up to 50 each year.

Deadline March of each year.

[184]
HELEN SEITZ SCHOLARSHIP

United Methodist Foundation of Indiana
8401 Fishers Center Drive
Fishers, IN 46038-2318
(317) 788-7879   Toll Free: (877) 391-8811
Fax: (317) 788-0089
E-mail: foundation@UMFIndiana.org
Web: www.umfindiana.org/endowments

Summary To provide financial assistance to students from Indiana who are preparing for a career in Christian education and are attending a seminary in any state that is approved by the United Methodist Church (UMC).

Eligibility This program is open to students of Christian education who are certified by a District Committee of the Indiana Conference of the UMC. Applicants must be enrolled full time at an approved seminary in any state. They must be seeking ordination as a deacon or elder. Along with their application, they must submit documentation of financial need and a statement of their vocational goals.

Financial data Stipends are awarded at the rate of $100 per credit hour (per semester) and $200 per projected decade of service remaining (per semester).

Duration 1 year; may be renewed.

Number awarded 1 or more each year.

Deadline May of each year for fall semester; October of each year for spring semester.

[185]
HENRY P. DAVID GRANTS FOR RESEARCH AND INTERNATIONAL TRAVEL IN HUMAN REPRODUCTIVE BEHAVIOR AND POPULATION STUDIES

American Psychological Foundation
750 First Street, N.E.
Washington, DC 20002-4242
(202) 336-5843   Fax: (202) 336-5812
E-mail: foundation@apa.org
Web: www.apa.org/apf/funding/david.aspx

Summary To provide funding to young psychologists who are interested in conducting research on reproductive behavior.

Eligibility This program is open to doctoral students in psychology working on a dissertation and young psychologists who have no more than 10 years of postgraduate experience. Applicants must be interested in conducting research on human reproductive behavior or an area related to population concerns. Along with their application, they must submit a current curriculum vitae, 2 letters of recommendation, and an essay of 1 to 2 pages on their interest in human reproductive behavior or in population studies. The sponsor encourages applications from individuals who represent diversity in race, ethnicity, gender, age, disability, and sexual orientation.

Financial data The grant is $1,500.

Duration The grant is presented annually.

Additional data Every third year (2017, 1020), the program also provides support for a non-U.S. reproductive health/population science professional to travel to and participate in the Psychosocial Workshop, held in conjunction with the Population Association of America annual meeting.

Number awarded 2 in the years when the program offers support to a non-U.S. professional to travel to the United States; 1 in other years.

Deadline November of each year.

[186]
INCIGHT SCHOLARSHIPS

Incight Education
Attn: Scholarship Coordinator
111 S.W. Columbia Street, Suite 1170
Portland, OR 97201
(971) 244-0305   Fax: (971) 244-0304
E-mail: scholarship@incight.org
Web: www.incighteducation.org/scholarship

Summary To provide financial assistance to residents of California, Oregon, and Washington who have a disability or impairment and are interested in attending college in any state.

Eligibility This program is open to residents of California, Oregon, and Washington who have a documented disability or impairment, including a physical, cognitive, or learning disability. Applicants must be entering or attending a college, university, community college, or trade school in any state as a full-time undergraduate or graduate student. They must be able to demonstrate outstanding community involvement and motivation to attend postsecondary education in order to further their ability to contribute to society. Financial need and academic merit are not considered in the selection process.

Financial data Stipends range from $500 to $1,500 per year.

Duration 1 year; may be renewed up to 3 additional years.

Number awarded Up to 100 each year.

Deadline March of each year.

[187]
IRELL & MANELLA DIVERSITY SCHOLARSHIP AWARD

Irell & Manella LLP)
Attn: Manager of Recruiting and Development
1800 Avenue of the Stars, Suite 900
Los Angeles, CA 90067-4276
(310) 277-1010   Fax: (310) 203-7199
E-mail: egondwe@irell.com
Web: www.irell.com/about-diversity.html

Summary To provide financial assistance to students who have completed their first year of law school, meet the sponsor's criteria for diversity, and are interested in a summer associateship in southern California.

Eligibility This program is open to students who have completed their first year of full-time study at an ABA-accredited law school. Applicants must meet the sponsor's criteria for diversity, which includes (but is not limited to) racial and ethnic minorities; women; gay, lesbian, bisexual, or transgender (GLBT) individuals; persons with disabilities; and/or applicants from a disadvantaged socioeconomic background. Along with their application, they must submit a 500-word personal statement describing their academic and leadership achievements and commitment to diversity and inclusion. Selection is based on academic achievement, writing and interpersonal skills, demonstrated leadership ability, commitment to diversity, and commitment to contributing to the legal profession.

Financial data The stipend is $15,000.

Duration 1 year of academic study and 10 weeks of summer associate work.

Additional data This program began in 2015. Applicants may indicate their preference for an associateship at the firm's offices in Century City (Los Angeles) or Newport Beach.

Number awarded 2 each year.

Deadline September of each year.

[188]
JEAN B. CRYOR MEMORIAL SCHOLARSHIP PROGRAM

Maryland Higher Education Commission
Attn: Office of Student Financial Assistance
6 North Liberty Street, Ground Suite
Baltimore, MD 21201
(410) 767-3301   Toll Free: (800) 974-0203
Fax: (410) 332-0250   TDD: (800) 735-2258
E-mail: osfamail.mhec@maryland.gov
Web: www.mhec.state.md.us

Summary To provide financial assistance for college or graduate school in Maryland to children and spouses of victims of the September 11, 2001 terrorist attacks and specified categories of veterans, public safety employees, and their children or spouses.

Eligibility This program is open to entering and continuing undergraduate and graduate students in the following categories: 1) children and surviving spouses of victims of the September 11, 2001 terrorist attacks who died in the World Trade Center in New York City, in the Pentagon in Virginia, or on United Airlines Flight 93 in Pennsylvania; 2) veterans who have, as a direct result of military service, a disability of 25% or greater and have exhausted or are no longer eligible for federal veterans' educational benefits; 3) children and unremarried surviving spouses of armed forces members whose death or 100% disability was directly caused by military service; 4) POW/MIA veterans of the Vietnam Conflict and their children; 5) state or local public safety officers or volunteers who became 100% disabled in the line of duty; 6) children and unremarried surviving spouses of state or local public safety employees or volunteers who died or became 100% disabled in the line of duty. and 7) children and unremarried surviving spouses or a school employee who, as a result of an act of violence, either died in the line of duty or sustained an injury that rendered the school employee 100% disabled. The parent, spouse, veteran, POW, public safety officer or volunteer, or school employee must have been a resident of Maryland at the time of death or when declared disabled. Applicants must be planning to enroll at a 2- or 4-year Maryland college or university as a full-time or part-time degree-seeking undergraduate or graduate student or attend a private career school. Financial need is not considered.

Financial data The amount of the award is equal to tuition and fees at a Maryland postsecondary institution, to a maximum of $10,182. The total amount of all Maryland scholarship awards from all sources may not exceed the cost of attendance or $19,000, whichever is less.

Duration Up to 5 years of full-time study or 8 years of part-time study.

Number awarded Varies each year.

Deadline July of each year.

[189]
JEAN KENNEDY SMITH PLAYWRITING AWARD

John F. Kennedy Center for the Performing Arts
Education Department
Attn: Kennedy Center American College Theater Festival
2700 F Street, N.W.
Washington, DC 20566
(202) 416-8864   Fax: (202) 416-8860
E-mail: ghenry@kennedy-center.org
Web: web.kennedy-center.org

Summary To recognize and reward the student authors of plays on the theme of disability.

Eligibility Students at any accredited junior or senior college in the United States are eligible to compete, provided their college agrees to participate in the Kennedy Center American College Theater Festival (KCACTF). Undergraduate students must be carrying at least 6 semester hours, graduate students must be enrolled in at least 3 semester hours, and continuing part-time students must be enrolled in a regular degree or certificate program. This award is presented to the best student-written script that explores the human experience of living with a disability.

Financial data The winning playwright receives a cash award of $1,000, active membership in the Dramatists Guild, Inc., and a fellowship providing transportation, housing, and per diem to attend a prestigious playwriting program.

Duration The award is presented annually.

Additional data This award, first presented in 1999, is part of the Michael Kanin Playwriting Awards Program. The Dramatists Guild, Inc. and VSA arts participate in the selection of the winning script. The sponsoring college or university must pay a registration fee of $275 for each production.

Number awarded 1 each year.

Deadline November of each year.

[190]
JOE CLERES MEMORIAL SCHOLARSHIPS

New Outlook Pioneers
Attn: Scholarship Administrator
1801 California Street, 44th Floor
Denver, CO 80202
Toll Free: (800) 872-5995
E-mail: donLsage@gmail.com
Web: www.newoutlookpioneers.org

Summary To provide financial assistance to students at all educational levels who are physically or mentally challenged.

Eligibility This program is open to students with physical or mental disabilities who are enrolled or planning to enroll in high school, college, trade school, or graduate school. Applicants or their representatives must submit a 1-page essay describing how the student has met the challenge of his or her disability, including the severity of the disability. They may also include up to 1 page of supporting documentation, but photographs, audio or video-tapes, display materials, films, or scrapbooks are not considered.

Financial data Stipends range from $500 to $2,000. Funds are paid directly to the school for tuition support only.

Duration 1 year.

Additional data This program began in 1996 by Lucent Technologies as the New Outlook Scholarships for Students with Disabilities. The current name was adopted in 2005. New Outlook Pioneers is an affiliate of TelecomPioneers. Its members are employees and retirees of Lucent Technologies, Avaya Communication, and Agere.

Number awarded Varies each year; recently, 16 were awarded: 1 at $2,000, 2 at $1,500, 3 at $1,000, 2 at $750, and 8 at $500.

Deadline March of each year.

[191]
JOHN C. DANFORTH CENTER ON RELIGION AND POLITICS DISSERTATION COMPLETION FELLOWSHIP

Washington University
Attn: John C. Danforth Center on Religion and Politics
118 Umrath Hall
Campus Box 1066
One Brookings Drive
St. Louis, MO 63130
(314) 935-9545   Fax: (314) 935-5755
E-mail: rap@wustl.edu
Web: rap.wustl.edu/dissertation-completion-fellowship

Summary To provide financial assistance to graduate students who are interested in completing their dissertation while in residence at the John C. Danforth Center on Religion and Politics of Washington University in St. Louis.

Eligibility This program is open to graduate students currently enrolled in a doctoral program in religion, politics, history, American studies, anthropology, gender and sexuality, or a related field. Applicants must be working on a dissertation that is centrally concerned with historical or contemporary topics in the religious and political experience of the United States. They must have received approval for the dissertation prospectus from their home institutions, satisfied all other requirements for doctoral candidacy, and be prepared to complete their dissertation before the conclusion of the fellowship. Members of underrepresented groups are encouraged to apply.

Financial data Fellows receive a stipend of $28,000 and a limited allowance for relocation expenses.

Duration 1 year; nonrenewable.

Number awarded Up to 2 each year.

Deadline January of each year.

[192]
JOSEPH B. GITTLER AWARD OF THE AMERICAN PSYCHOLOGICAL FOUNDATION

American Psychological Foundation
750 First Street, N.E.
Washington, DC 20002-4242
(202) 336-5843   Fax: (202) 336-5812
E-mail: foundation@apa.org
Web: www.apa.org/apf/funding/gittler.aspx

Summary To recognize and reward scholars in psychology who have made outstanding contributions to the philosophical foundations of the discipline.

Eligibility This award is available to psychologists who have an Ed.D., Psy.D., or Ph.D. degree and who are making and will continue to make scholarly contributions to the philosophical foundations of psychological knowledge. Self-nominations are welcome. Selection is based on conformance with stated program goals and magnitude of contributions. The sponsor encourages nominations of individuals who represent diversity in race, ethnicity, gender, age, disability, and sexual orientation.

Financial data The award is $7,500.

Duration The award is presented annually.

Additional data This award was first presented in 2008.

Number awarded 1 each year.

Deadline Nominations must be submitted by May of each year.

[193]
KAISER PERMANENTE COLORADO DIVERSITY SCHOLARSHIP PROGRAM

Kaiser Permanente
Attn: Office of Diversity and Inclusion
2500 South Havana Street
Aurora, CO 80014
Toll Free: (877) 457-4772
E-mail: co-diversitydevelopment@kp.org
Web: app.smarterselect.com

Summary To provide financial assistance to Colorado residents who come from diverse backgrounds and are interested in working on an undergraduate or graduate degree in a health care field at a public college in the state.

Eligibility This program is open to all residents of Colorado, including those who identify as 1 or more of the following: African American, Asian Pacific, Native American, Latino, lesbian, gay, bisexual, transgender, intersex, U.S. veteran, and/or a person with a disability. Applicants must be enrolled or planning to enroll full time at a publicly-funded college, university, or technical school in Colorado as 1) a graduating high school senior with a GPA of 2.7 or higher; 2) a GED recipient with a GED score of 520 or higher; 3) an undergraduate student; or 4) a graduate or doctoral student. They must be preparing for a career in health care (e.g., athletic training, audiology, cardiovascular perfusion technology, clinical medical assisting, cytotechnology, dental assisting, dental hygiene, diagnostic medicine, dietetics, emergency medical technology, medicine, nursing, occupational therapy, pharmacy, phlebotomy, physical therapy, physician assistant, radiology, respiratory therapy, social work, sports medicine, surgical technology). Selection is based on academic achievement, character qualities, community outreach and volunteering, and financial need. Along wit their application, they must submit 300-word essays on the following topics: 1) their exposure to other cultures; 2) issues that challenge health care today; and 3) the social responsibilities of a health care provider.

Financial data Stipends range from $1,400 to $2,600 per year.

Duration 1 year; may be renewed.

Number awarded Varies each year; recently, 24 were awarded.

Deadline February of each year.

[194]
KAMEHAMEHA SCHOOLS CLASS OF 1972 SCHOLARSHIP

Pauahi Foundation
Attn: Scholarships
567 South King Street, Suite 160
Honolulu, HI 96813-3036
(808) 534-3966   Fax: (808) 534-3890
E-mail: scholarships@pauahi.org
Web: www.pauahi.org/scholarships

Summary To provide financial assistance to residents of any state, especially Native Hawaiians, who have faced challenging situations and are interested in attending college or graduate school.

Eligibility This program is open to undergraduate and graduate students from any state whose lives have been impacted by challenging situations (e.g., death of a significant family member, domestic violence, sexual abuse, poverty, major health problems). Applicants must be attending or planning to attend a 2- or 4-year college, university, or vocation/technical school in any state. They must be able to demonstrate financial need, a GPA of 2.8 or higher, and the potential to be successfully enriched by an educational opportunity. Along with their application, they must submit a letter of recommendation from a social service agency or counselor citing their challenging and extraordinary life circumstances and how they would benefit from this scholarship. Preference is given to Native Hawaiians (descendants of the aboriginal inhabitants of the Hawaiian Islands prior to 1778).

Financial data The stipend is $1,000.

Duration 1 year.

Additional data This program was established by the Kamehameha Schools class of 1972 to provide assistance to all students of Hawaiian descent.

Number awarded 2 each year.

Deadline February of each year.

[195]
KEKER, VAN NEST & PETERS DIVERSITY SCHOLARSHIP

Keker, Van Nest & Peters LLP
Attn: Director of Attorney Recruiting and Professional Development
633 Battery Street, Fourth Floor
San Francisco, CA 94111-1809
(415) 773-6649   E-mail: RecruitingInfo@keker.com
Web: www.keker.com

Summary To provide financial assistance to students at designated law schools in the San Francisco Bay area who will contribute to diversity of litigators in the area.

Eligibility This program is open to full-time first- and second-year students at the University of California Berkeley School of Law, Hastings College of the Law, or Stanford Law School. Applicants must be students of color; members of the lesbian, gay, bisexual, transgender, and queer (LGBTQ) community; disabled; or otherwise able to contribute to the diversity of litigators in the Bay area. Selection is based on academic record, demonstrated interest in complex litigation, employment history, background, the extent to which the applicant would contribute to diversity, clinical or other non-academic legal experience, community service, and commitment to remaining in the Bay area after graduation. Applicants may request to have financial need considered in the selection process, but it is not required.

Financial data The sponsor allocates $75,000 for this program each year and distributes it among the recipients according to their number and quality.

Duration 1 year.

Number awarded Up to 3 each year.

Deadline April of each year.

[196]
KING & SPALDING DIVERSITY FELLOWSHIP PROGRAM

King & Spalding, LLP
Attn: Associate Director of Human Resources and Diversity
1180 Peachtree Street
Atlanta, GA 30309
(404) 572-4643   Fax: (404) 572-5100
E-mail: cabney@kslaw.com
Web: www.kslaw.com

Summary To provide financial assistance and summer work experience at U.S. offices of King & Spalding to law students who will contribute to the diversity of the legal community.

Eligibility This program is open to second-year law students who 1) come from a minority ethnic or racial group (American Indian/Alaskan Native, Asian American/Pacific Islander, Black/African American, Hispanic, or multiracial); 2) are a member of the gay, lesbian, bisexual, or transgender (GLBT) community; or 3) have a disability. Applicants must receive an offer of a clerkship at a U.S. office of King & Spalding during their second-year summer. Along with their application, they must submit a 500-

word personal statement that describes their talents, qualities, and experiences and how they would contribute to the diversity of the firm.

Financial data Fellows receive a stipend of $10,000 for their second year of law school and a paid summer associate clerkship at a U.S. office of the firm during the following summer.

Duration 1 year.

Additional data The firm's U.S. offices are located in Atlanta, Austin, Charlotte, Houston, Los Angeles, New York, San Francisco, Silicon Valley, and Washington.

Number awarded Up to 4 each year.

Deadline August of each year.

[197]
K&L GATES DIVERSITY FELLOWSHIP

K&L Gates LLP
Attn: Legal Recruitment and Development Assistant
925 Fourth Avenue, Suite 2900
Seattle, WA 98104-1158
(206) 370-5760   E-mail: tia.chang@klgates.com
Web: www.klgates.com/aboutus/diversity

Summary To provide financial assistance and summer work experience in Seattle to law students from any state who come from diverse backgrounds.

Eligibility This program is open to first-year students at ABA-accredited law schools in the United States. Applicants must identify with 1 of the firm's affinity groups at the firmwide and local office levels, including those for women lawyers; lesbian, gay, bisexual and transgender (LGBT), and allies lawyers; lawyers of color; working parents; veterans; and lawyers with disabilities. Along with their application, they must submit a 500-word personal statement describing the contribution they would make to the legal profession in general and the sponsoring firm in particular.

Financial data Fellows receive a paid associateship with the Seattle office of the sponsoring firm during the summer following their first year of law school and an academic scholarship of $10,000 for their second year of law school.

Duration 1 year.

Number awarded 1 each year.

Deadline January of each year.

[198]
LAW AND SOCIAL SCIENCES DOCTORAL DISSERTATION RESEARCH IMPROVEMENT GRANTS

National Science Foundation
Attn: Directorate for Social, Behavioral, and Economic
  Sciences
Division of Social and Economic Sciences
4201 Wilson Boulevard, Room 995N
Arlington, VA 22230
(703) 292-7023   Fax: (703) 292-9083
TDD: (800) 281-8749   E-mail: hsilvers@nsf.gov
Web: www.nsf.gov

Summary To provide funding for dissertation research to doctoral candidates in fields related to law and social sciences.

Eligibility This program is open to doctoral candidates who have passed their qualifying examinations, completed all course work required for the degree, and had their dissertation topic approved. Fields of study including crime, violence, and punishment; economic issues; governance; legal decision making; legal mobilization and conceptions of justice; and litigation and the legal profession. Applicants must submit a project description that includes the scientific significance of the work, its relationship to other current research, and the design of the project in sufficient detail to permit evaluation. In the selection process, consideration is given to the project's broader impact of contributing to societally relevant outcomes, including full participation of women, persons with disabilities, and underrepresented minorities in science, technology, engineering, and mathematics (STEM).

Financial data Grants range up to $20,000. Funds may be used only for costs directly associated with the conduct of dissertation research.

Duration Up to 12 months.

Number awarded Varies each year.

Deadline January of each year.

[199]
LOREEN ARBUS FOCUS ON DISABILITY SCHOLARSHIP

Academy of Television Arts & Sciences Foundation
Attn: Education Department
5220 Lankershim Boulevard
North Hollywood, CA 91601-3109
(818) 754-2820   Fax: (818) 761-ATAS
E-mail: ctasupport@televisionacademy.com
Web: www.emmys.com/foundation/programs/cta

Summary To recognize and reward outstanding college student videos that have a focus on disability.

Eligibility This award is available to undergraduate and graduate students currently enrolled at a college, university, or community college. U.S. citizenship is not required, but all applicants must be enrolled at schools in the United States. All entries must have been produced for school-related classes, groups, or projects. This award is presented to the entry that best 1) sheds light on people with disabilities by having a main character with a disability; 2) helps emerging artists within this community gain recognition; or 3) increases visibility for artists with disabilities.

Financial data The award is a $10,000 scholarship.

Duration The award is presented annually.

Additional data This program is sponsored by the Loreen Arbus Foundation.

Number awarded 1 each year.

Deadline January of each year.

[200]
MARK T. BANNER SCHOLARSHIP FOR LAW STUDENTS

Richard Linn American Inn of Court
c/o Amy Ziegler, Scholarship Chair
Green Burns & Crain
300 South Wacker Drive, Suite 2500
Chicago, IL 60606
(312) 987-2926   Fax: (312) 360-9315
E-mail: marktbannerscholarship@linninn.org
Web: www.linninn.org/Pages/scholarship.shtml

Summary To provide financial assistance to law students who are members of a group historically underrepresented in intellectual property law.

Eligibility This program is open to students at ABA-accredited law schools in the United States who are members of groups historically underrepresented (by race, sex, ethnicity, sexual orientation, or disability) in intellectual property law. Applicants must submit a 3-page statement on how ethics, civility, and professionalism have been their focus; how diversity has impacted them; and their commitment to a career in intellectual property law. Selection is based on academic merit; written and oral communication skills; leadership qualities; community involvement; commitment, qualities and actions toward ethics, civility and professionalism; and commitment to a career in IP law.

Financial data The stipend is $5,000.

Duration 1 year.

Number awarded 1 each year.

Deadline November of each year.

[201]
MATHEMATICA SUMMER FELLOWSHIPS

Mathematica Policy Research, Inc.
Attn: Human Resources
600 Alexander Park
P.O. Box 2393
Princeton, NJ 08543-2393
(609) 799-3535   Fax: (609) 799-0005
E-mail: humanresources@mathematica-mpr.com
Web: www.mathematica-mpr.com

Summary To provide an opportunity for graduate students in social policy fields to work on an independent summer research project at an office of Mathematica Policy Research, Inc.

Eligibility This program is open to students enrolled in a master's or Ph.D. program in public policy or a social science. Applicants must be interested in conducting independent research on a policy issue of relevance to the economic and social problems of minority groups or individuals with disabilities. They are placed with a mentor in 1 of the following divisions: health research, human services research, or survey research. The proposed research must relate to the work of Mathematica, but fellows do not work on Mathematica projects. Qualified minority students and students with disabilities are encouraged to apply.

Financial data The stipend is $10,000. Fellows also receive $500 for project-related expenses.

Duration 3 months during the summer.

Additional data Mathematica offices are located in Ann Arbor (Michigan), Cambridge (Massachusetts), Chicago (Illinois), Oakland (California), Princeton (New Jersey), and Washington, D.C. Fellows may indicate their choice of location, but they are assigned to the office where the work of the research staff meshes best with their topic and interests.

Number awarded Up to 5 each year.

Deadline March of each year.

[202]
MCGUIREWOODS DIVERSITY SCHOLARSHIP PROGRAM

McGuireWoods LLP
Attn: Attorney Recruiting Manager
1750 Tysons Boulevard, Suite 1800
Tysons Corner, VA 22102
(703) 712-5000   Fax: (703) 712-5261
E-mail: jdunton@mcguirewoods.com
Web: www.mcguirewoods.com/Our-Firm/Diversity.aspx

Summary To provide financial assistance to law students who come from various groups that are traditionally underrepresented in law schools and the legal profession.

Eligibility This program is open to first-year law students who are committed to contributing to and supporting diversity within the legal profession. The sponsor defines diversity to include considerations of age, sex, gender identity, race, ethnicity, national origin, disability, religion, sexual orientation, marital status, and veteran status, as well as educational and professional backgrounds. It also considers other factors, such as whether a student is the first family member to attend college, from an economically disadvantaged family, a past or present member of the military, or demonstrating a strong commitment to promoting diversity in their graduate school, law school, and community. Selection is based on law school and undergraduate academic performance, personal achievements, involvement in community activities and diversity-related student organizations, and a personal statement explaining their commitment to diversity in the legal profession.

Financial data The stipend is $5,000.

Duration 1 year.

Number awarded Up to 8 each year.

Deadline May of each year.

[203]
MENTAL HEALTH RESEARCH DISSERTATION GRANT TO INCREASE WORKFORCE DIVERSITY

National Institute of Mental Health
Attn: Division of Extramural Activities
6001 Executive Boulevard, Room 6138
Bethesda, MD 20892-9609
(301) 443-3534   Fax: (301) 443-4720
TDD: (301) 451-0088   E-mail: armstrda@mail.nih.gov
Web: www.grants.nih.gov

Summary To provide research funding to doctoral candidates from underrepresented groups planning to prepare for a research career in any area relevant to mental health and/or mental disorders.

Eligibility This program is open to doctoral candidates conducting dissertation research in a field related to mental health and/or mental disorders at a university, college, or professional school with an accredited doctoral degree granting program. Applicants must be 1) members of an ethnic or racial group that has been determined by the National Science Foundation to be underrepresented in health-related sciences (i.e., African Americans, Hispanic Americans, Alaska Natives, American Indians, Native Hawaiians, and other Pacific Islanders); 2) individuals with disabilities; or 3) individuals from socially, culturally, economically, or educationally disadvantaged backgrounds that have inhibited their ability to prepare for a career in health-related research. They must be U.S. citizens, nationals, or permanent residents.

Financial data The stipend is $23,376. An additional grant up to $15,000 is provided for additional research expenses, fringe benefits (including health insurance), travel to scientific meetings, and research costs of the dissertation. Facilities and administrative costs are limited to 8% of modified total direct costs.

Duration Up to 2 years; nonrenewable.

Number awarded Varies each year.

Deadline Applications must be submitted by February, June, or October of each year.

[204]
MILDRED COLODNY DIVERSITY SCHOLARSHIP FOR GRADUATE STUDY IN HISTORIC PRESERVATION

National Trust for Historic Preservation
Attn: Scholarship Coordinator
2600 Virginia Avenue, N.W., Suite 1000
Washington, DC 20037
(202) 588-6124   Toll Free: (800) 944-NTHP, ext. 6124
Fax: (202) 588-6038   E-mail: dfield@savingplaces.org
Web: forum.savingplaces.org

Summary To provide financial assistance for study, conference attendance, and summer work experience to graduate students interested in working on a degree in a field related to historic preservation.

Eligibility This program is open to students in their final year of undergraduate study intending to enroll in a graduate program in historic preservation and graduate students enrolled in or intending to enroll in historic preservation programs; these programs may be in a department of history, architecture, American studies, urban planning, museum studies, or a related field with a primary emphasis on historic preservation. The program of study must be at a U.S. college, university, or other institution and students must be eligible to work in the United States. Applications are especially encouraged from people who will contribute to diversity in the field of historic preservation. The sponsor defines diversity to include people of all races, creeds, genders, ages, sexual orientations, religions, physical characteristics and abilities, veteran status, and economic or social backgrounds. Selection is

based on financial need, undergraduate academic performance, promise shown for future achievement, commitment to working in preservation in the United States following graduation, and potential to help increase diversity within the preservation movement.

Financial data The program provides a stipend of up to $15,000 that covers graduate school tuition, a summer internship with the sponsor following the student's first year of study, and the student's attendance at a National Preservation Conference.

Duration 1 year; nonrenewable.

Additional data Internships may be completed at the sponsor's Washington, D.C. office or 1 of its historic museum sites.

Number awarded 1 each year.

Deadline February of each year.

[205]
MOBILITY SCOOTERS DIRECT SCHOLARSHIP PROGRAM

Mobility Scooters Direct.com
4135 Dr. Martin Luther King Jr. Boulevard, Suite D21
Fort Myers, FL 33916
(754) 263-7850
E-mail: afatalo@mobilityscootersdirect.com
Web: www.mobilityscootersdirect.com/scholarship

Summary To provide financial assistance through a random drawing to undergraduate and graduate students who have a disability.

Eligibility This program is open to students who have a disability and are currently enrolled at a college or university. Undergraduates must be enrolled in at least 6 credit hours and have completed at least 40 credit hours. Graduate students must be enrolled in at least 3 credit hours and have completed at least 10 credit hours. All applicants must have a GPA of 3.0 or higher, a declared major, and a record of involvement on campus or in the community. Along with their application, they must submit a letter of recommendation and a 500-word essay on their aspirations and goals as a student, including why they feel they should be chosen to receive this scholarship. The recipient is selected randomly from among qualified entries.

Financial data The stipend is $1,200.

Duration 1 year.

Number awarded 1 each year.

Deadline December of each year.

[206]
MUSICIANS WITH SPECIAL NEEDS SCHOLARSHIP

Sigma Alpha Iota Philanthropies, Inc.
One Tunnel Road
Asheville, NC 28805
(828) 251-0606   Fax: (828) 251-0644
E-mail: nh@sai-national.org
Web: app.smarterselect.com

Summary To provide financial assistance for college or graduate school to members of Sigma Alpha Iota (an organization of women musicians) who have a disability and are working on a degree in music.

Eligibility This program is open to members of the organization who either 1) have a sensory or physical impairment and are enrolled in a graduate or undergraduate degree program in music; or 2) are preparing to become a music teacher or therapist for people with disabilities. Performance majors must submit a 15-minute DVD of their work; non-performance majors must submit evidence of work in their area of specialization, such as composition, musicology, or research.

Financial data The stipend is $1,500.

Duration 1 year.

Number awarded 1 each year.

Deadline March of each year.

[207]
NASA EDUCATION AERONAUTICS SCHOLARSHIP AND ADVANCED STEM TRAINING AND RESEARCH FELLOWSHIP

National Aeronautics and Space Administration
Attn: National Scholarship Deputy Program Manager
Office of Education and Public Outreach
Ames Research Center
Moffett Field, CA 94035
(650) 604-6958   E-mail: elizabeth.a.cartier@nasa.gov
Web: nspires.nasaprs.com

Summary To provide financial assistance to members of underrepresented groups interested in working on a graduate degree in fields of science, technology, engineering, and mathematics (STEM) of interest to the U.S. National Aeronautics and Space Administration (NASA).

Eligibility This program (identified as AS&ASTAR) is open to students who have a bachelor's degree and have historically been underrepresented in NASA-related fields (women, minorities, persons with disabilities, and veterans). Applicants must be working on a research-based master's or doctoral degree in a NASA-related field of STEM, including chemistry, computer and information science and engineering, geosciences (e.g., geophysics, hydrology, oceanography, paleontology, planetary science), engineering (e.g., aeronautical, aerospace, biomedical, chemical, civil, computer, electrical, electronic, environmental, industrial, materials, mechanical, nuclear, ocean, optical, systems), life sciences (e.g., biochemistry, cell biology, environmental biology, genetics, neurosciences, physiology), materials research, mathematical sciences, or physics and astronomy). They must arrange with a researcher at a NASA Center to serve as a technical adviser in collaboration with the student's faculty adviser. Research must be conducted at a NASA Center as a team project involving the student, the faculty adviser, and the NASA technical adviser. In the selection process, consideration is given to the proposed use of NASA facilities, content, and people. Applications must include a plan for a Center-Based Research Experience (CBRE) to be conducted during the summer at the NASA facility. Students must be U.S. citizens and have a GPA of 3.0 or higher.

Financial data Grants provide a stipend of $25,000 for master's degree students or $30,000 for doctoral candidates, $10,000 for tuition offset and fees, $8,000 as a CBRE allowance, $1,000 as a health insurance allowance, $4,500 as a faculty adviser allowance, and $1,500 as a fellow professional development allowance.

Duration 1 year; may be renewed up to 2 additional years.

Additional data The participating NASA facilities are Ames Research Center (Moffett Field, California), Armstrong Flight Research Center (Edwards, California), Glenn Research Center (Cleveland, Ohio), Goddard Space Flight Center (Greenbelt, Maryland), Jet Propulsion Laboratory (Pasadena, California), Johnson Space Center (Houston, Texas), Kennedy Space Center (Kennedy Space Center, Florida), Langley Research Center (Hampton, Virginia), Marshall Space Flight Center (Marshall Space Flight Center, Alabama), and Stennis Space Center (Stennis Space Center, Mississippi).

Number awarded At least 13 each year.

Deadline June of each year.

[208]
NATIONAL SPACE GRANT COLLEGE AND FELLOWSHIP PROGRAM

National Aeronautics and Space Administration
Attn: Office of Education
300 E Street, S.W.
Mail Suite 6M35
Washington, DC 20546-0001
(202) 358-1069   Fax: (202) 358-7097
E-mail: aleksandra.korobov@nasa.gov
Web: www.nasa.gov

Summary To provide financial assistance to undergraduate and graduate students interested in preparing for a career in a space-related field.

Eligibility This program is open to undergraduate and graduate students at colleges and universities that participate in the National Space Grant program of the U.S. National Aeronautics and Space Administration (NASA) through their state consortium. Applicants must be interested in a program of study and/or research in a field of science, technology, engineering, or mathematics (STEM) related to space. A specific goal of the program is to recruit and train U.S. citizens, especially underrepresented minorities, women, and persons with disabilities, for careers in aerospace science and technology. Financial need is not considered in the selection process.

Financial data Each consortium establishes the terms of the fellowship program in its state.

Additional data NASA established the Space Grant program in 1989. It operates through 52 consortia in each state, the District of Columbia, and Puerto Rico. Each consortium includes selected colleges and universities in that state as well as other affiliates from industry, museums, science centers, and state and local agencies.

Number awarded Varies each year.

Deadline Each consortium sets its own deadlines.

[209]
NAVY SEAL FOUNDATION SCHOLARSHIPS

Navy Seal Foundation
Attn: Chief Financial Officer
1619 D Street, Building 5326
Virginia Beach, VA 23459
(757) 363-7490   Fax: (757) 363-7491
E-mail: info@navysealfoundation.org
Web: www.navysealfoundation.org

Summary   To provide financial assistance for college or graduate school to Naval Special Warfare (NSW) personnel and their families.

Eligibility   This program is open to active-duty Navy SEALS, Special Warfare Combatant-craft Crewmen (SWCC), and military personnel assigned to other NSW commands. Their dependent children and spouses are also eligible. Applicants must be entering or continuing full or part-time students working on an associate or bachelor's degree. Active-duty and spouses, but not dependent children, may also work on a graduate degree. Selection is based on GPA, SAT scores, class ranking, extracurricular activities, volunteer community involvement, leadership positions held, military service record, and employment (as appropriate).

Financial data   Stipends are $15,000, $7,500, or $5,000 per year.

Duration   1 year; may be renewed.

Number awarded   Varies each year; recently, the Navy Seal Foundation awarded 16 scholarships for all of its programs: 3 for 4 years at $15,000 per year to high school seniors and graduates, 3 for 1 year at $7,500 to high school seniors and graduates, 3 for 1 year at $15,000 to current college students, 3 for 1 year at $7,500 to current college students, and 4 for 1 year at $5,000 to spouses.

Deadline   February of each year.

[210]
NBCUNIVERSAL TONY COELHO MEDIA SCHOLARSHIPS

American Association of People with Disabilities
Attn: Scholarships
2013 H Street, N.W., Fifth Floor
Washington, DC 20006
(202) 521-4316   Toll Free: (800) 840-8844
E-mail: scholarship@aapd.com
Web: www.aapd.com

Summary   To provide financial assistance to undergraduate and graduate students who have a disability and are working on a degree in communication or other media-related field.

Eligibility   This program is open to students who have any kind of disability and are 1) second-year associate degree students; 2) undergraduate sophomores, juniors, or seniors; or 3) graduate students. Applicants must be working on a degree in communication or other media-related field. Along with their application, they must submit essays of 300 to 350 words each on 1) what disability means to them; and 2) how their degree will affect the disability community. Selection is based on demonstrated leadership characteristics, connection between their degree and the disability community, engagement within the communications and/or media fields, difficulty of course work, success in course work, and character.

Financial data   The stipend is $5,625.

Duration   1 year.

Additional data   This program began in 2013 with support from NBCUniversal.

Number awarded   8 each year.

Deadline   June of each year.

[211]
NCCPA ENDOWED SCHOLARSHIPS

American Academy of Physician Assistants
Attn: Physician Assistant Foundation
2318 Mill Road, Suite 1300
Alexandria, VA 22314-6868
(571) 319-4510   E-mail: pafoundation@aapa.org
Web: www.pa-foundation.org

Summary   To provide financial assistance to student members of the American Academy of Physician Assistants (AAPA) who are underrepresented minorities or economically and/or educationally disadvantaged.

Eligibility   This program is open to AAPA student members who have completed at least 1 semester of an accredited physician assistant program. Applicants must qualify as 1) an underrepresented minority (American Indian, Alaska Native, Black or African American, Hispanic or Latino, Native Hawaiian or other Pacific Islander, or Asian); 2) economically disadvantaged (with income below a specified level); or 3) educationally disadvantaged (from a high school with low SAT scores, from a school district in which less than half of graduates go on to college, has a diagnosed physical or mental impairment, English is not their primary language, the first member of their family to attend college).

Financial data   The stipend is $2,000.

Duration   1 year; nonrenewable.

Additional data   This program is sponsored by the National Commission on Certification of Physician Assistants (NCCPA).

Number awarded   2 each year.

Deadline   May of each year.

[212]
NEUROSCIENCE SCHOLARS PROGRAM

Society for Neuroscience
Attn: Neuroscience Scholars Program
1121 14th Street, N.W., Suite 1010
Washington, DC 20005
(202) 962-4000   Fax: (202) 962-4941
E-mail: nsp@sfn.org
Web: www.sfn.org

Summary   To provide funding to underrepresented students in neuroscience who are interested in participating in activities of the Society for Neuroscience (SfN).

Eligibility   This program is open to undergraduate and graduate students and postdoctoral fellows in neuroscience who are interested in attending the society's annual meeting and participating in other activities related to the field. Applicants must be from a group recognized as underrepresented in the biomedical, behavioral, clinical, and social sciences, defined as Blacks or African Americans, Hispanics or Latinos, American Indians or Alaska Natives, Native Hawaiians and other Pacific Islanders, and individuals with disabilities. U.S. citizenship or permanent resident status is required. Selection is based on academic excellence, research interests, experience, and a 500-word essay on professional goals and what they hope to gain from the fellowship.

Financial data Participants selected as fellows receive a mentoring team to discuss the fellow's research, career plans, and overall experience; complimentary SfN membership; a travel award to attend the SfN annual meeting each fall; and an annual stipend of $1,500 to support allowed professional development activities.

Duration Support is provided over a 2-year period.

Additional data Funding for this program is provided by the National Institute of Neurological Disorders and Stroke.

Number awarded 15 fellows are selected each year.

Deadline June of each year.

[213]
OREGON STATE BAR SCHOLARSHIPS

Oregon State Bar
Attn: Diversity and Inclusion Department
16037 S.W. Upper Boones Ferry Road
P.O. Box 231935
Tigard, OR 97281-1935
(503) 620-0222
Toll Free: (800) 452-8260, ext. 338 (within OR)
Fax: (503) 684-1366   TDD: (503) 684-7416
E-mail: cling@osbar.org
Web: www.osbar.org/diversity/programs.html#scholar

Summary To provide financial assistance to entering and continuing students from any state enrolled at law schools in Oregon, especially those who will help the Oregon State Bar achieve its diversity and inclusion objectives.

Eligibility This program is open to students entering or continuing at 1 of the law schools in Oregon (Willamette, University of Oregon, and Lewis and Clark). Preference is given to students who will contribute to the Oregon State Bar's diversity and inclusion program, defined to include age, culture, disability, ethnicity, gender and gender identity or expression, geographic location, national origin, race, religion, sex, sexual orientation, and socio-economic status. Along with their application, they must submit a 500-word personal statement on either 1) how their status as a person of diversity has influenced their decision to become a lawyer and how will it influence them throughout their legal professional career; or 2) a challenge they have faced, how they met the challenge, and how that experience will affect the decisions they will make as a legal professional. They must also submit a sample of their legal writing. Selection is based on the personal statement (35%), legal writing ability (25%), academic achievement

(15%), work experience and honors (10%), and financial need (15%).

Financial data The stipend is $2,000 per year. Funds are credited to the recipient's law school tuition account.

Duration 1 year; recipients may reapply.

Number awarded 10 each year.

Deadline March of each year.

[214]
OTTO SUSSMAN TRUST GRANTS

Otto Sussman Trust
30 Jericho Executive Plaza, Suite 200W
Jericho, NY 11753-1028
(202) 965-5450

Summary To provide financial assistance to residents of selected states who are attending college or graduate school in any state and experiencing financial need because of special circumstances, such as illness or injury.

Eligibility This program is open to residents of New York, New Jersey, Oklahoma, or Pennsylvania who are currently enrolled as full-time juniors, seniors, or graduate students at a college or university in any state. Applicants must be experiencing extreme special circumstances, such as unemployment, death of a parent, or medical expenses not covered by insurance. They must have a GPA of 3.0 or higher.

Financial data The amount awarded varies, depending upon the needs of the recipient, but generally varies from $5,000 to $10,000.

Duration This is a 1-time grant.

Number awarded Varies each year.

Deadline July of each year.

[215]
PA FOUNDATION SCHOLARSHIPS

American Academy of Physician Assistants
Attn: Physician Assistant Foundation
2318 Mill Road, Suite 1300
Alexandria, VA 22314-6868
(571) 319-4510   E-mail: pafoundation@aapa.org
Web: www.pa-foundation.org

Summary To provide financial assistance to student members of the American Academy of Physician Assistants (AAPA).

Eligibility This program is open to AAPA student members who have completed at least 1 semester of an accredited physician assistant program. Applicants must be in good academic standing.

Financial data The stipend is $1,000.

Duration 1 year; nonrenewable.

Number awarded 9 each year.

Deadline May of each year.

[216]
PERKINS COIE DIVERSITY STUDENT FELLOWSHIPS

Perkins Coie LLP
Attn: Chief Diversity Officer
131 South Dearborn Street, Suite 1700
Chicago, IL 60603-5559
(312) 324-8593   Fax: (312) 324-9400
E-mail: diversity@perkinscoie.com
Web: www.perkinscoie.com

Summary To provide financial assistance to law students who reflect the diversity of communities in the country.

Eligibility This program is open to students enrolled in the first year of a J.D. program at an ABA-accredited law school. Applicants must contribute meaningfully to the diversity of the law school student body and the legal profession. Diversity is defined broadly to include members of racial, ethnic, disabled, and sexual orientation minority groups, as well as those who may be the first person in their family to pursue higher education. Applicants must submit a 1-page personal statement that describes their unique personal history, a legal writing sample, a current resume, and undergraduate and law school transcripts. They are not required to disclose their financial circumstances, but a demonstrated need for financial assistance may be taken into consideration.

Financial data The stipend is $7,500.

Duration 1 year.

Additional data Fellows are also offered a summer associateship at their choice of the firm's offices in Chicago, Madison, Phoenix, Portland, San Francisco, Seattle, or Washington, D.C.

Number awarded Varies each year; recently, 7 were awarded.

Deadline January of each year.

[217]
POSTDOCTORAL RESEARCH FELLOWSHIPS IN BIOLOGY

National Science Foundation
Directorate for Biological Sciences
Attn: Division of Biological Infrastructure
4201 Wilson Boulevard, Room 615N
Arlington, VA 22230
(703) 292-2299   Fax: (703) 292-9063
TDD: (800) 281-8749   E-mail: bio-dbi-prfb@nsf.gov
Web: www.nsf.gov

Summary To provide funding for research and training in specified areas related to biology to junior doctoral-level scientists at sites in the United States or abroad.

Eligibility This program is open to citizens, nationals, and permanent residents of the United States who are graduate students completing a Ph.D. or who have earned the degree no earlier than 12 months preceding the deadline date. Applicants must be interested in a program of research and training in any of 3 competitive areas: 1) Broadening Participation of Groups Underrepresented in Biology, designed to increase the diversity of scientists by providing support for research and training to biologists with disabilities and underrepresented minority (Native American, Native Pacific Islander, Alaskan Native, African American, and Hispanic) biologists; 2) Research Using Biological Collections, to address key questions in biology and potentially develop applications that extend biology to physical, mathematical, engineering, and social sciences by the use of biological research collections in museums and archives in the United States and abroad; and 3) National Plant Genome Initiative (NPGI) Postdoctoral Research Fellowships, for postdoctoral training in plant improvement and associated sciences such as physiology and pathology, quantitative genetics, or computational biology. They must identify a sponsor at a host institution who will serve as a mentor for their training program.

Financial data Grants are $69,000 per year, including $54,000 as a stipend for the fellow and $15,000 as a fellowship allowance that is intended to cover direct research expenses, facilities and other institutional resources, and fringe benefits. An extra allowance of $10,000 is provided to fellows who go overseas.

Duration Fellowships are 24 to 36 months for Broadening Participation, 24 months for Research Using Biological Collections, or 36 months for NPGI Postdoctoral Research Fellowships.

Number awarded Approximately 40 each year in each competitive area.

Deadline October of each year.

[218]
POWERING EDUCATION SCHOLARSHIPS

Alpha One
127 Main Street
South Portland, ME 04106
(207) 767-2189   Toll Free: (800) 640-7200
Fax: (207) 799-8346 E-mail: mardi@alphaonenow.org
Web: www.alphaonenow.com

Summary To provide financial assistance to undergraduate and graduate students in Maine who have disabilities.

Eligibility This program is open to high school seniors, undergraduates, and graduate students at schools in Maine. Applicants must have a disability. They must have a "B" average or equivalent GPA. Along with their application, they must submit a personal essay of 500 to 1,000 words on how their disability has helped shape their view of the world and themselves as a person, a letter of recommendation, and current transcripts.

Financial data The stipend is $2,000. Funds are paid directly to the recipient's institution after completion of the first semester, provided the student earns a GPA of 2.5 or higher.

Duration 1 year.

Number awarded 3 each year.

Deadline March of each year.

[219]
PROSKAUER SILVER SCHOLAR PROGRAM

Proskauer Rose LLP
Attn: Diversity and Inclusion Officer
Eleven Times Square
New York, NY 10036-8299
(212) 969-5042   Fax: (212) 969-2900
E-mail: silverscholar@proskauer.com
Web: www.proskauer.com/diversity/silverscholar

Summary To provide financial assistance and work experience to law students who are members of historically underrepresented groups in the legal profession and are interested in a summer associateship and a permanent position with the sponsoring law firm.

Eligibility This program is open to students currently enrolled full time in the first or second year at an ABA-accredited law school. Applicants must be members of racial and/or ethnic minority groups, be differently abled, or be from disadvantaged socioeconomic backgrounds. They must be U.S. citizens or authorized to work in the United States. First-year students must accept an offer to participate in the summer associate program, successfully complete that program in the following summer, return for at least 2 weeks during the summer after their second year of law school, and receive and accept an offer to join the firm; second-year students must accept an offer to participate in the summer associate program, successfully complete that program in the following summer, and receive and accept an offer to join the firm. Along with their application, they must a legal writing sample and a 500-word personal statement that addresses why diversity is important to them, how they have been a leader and advanced diversity in their community, and how diversity can be improved in the legal profession.

Financial data The stipend is $30,000, paid in installments.

Duration 1 year of academic study and 1 or 2 summers as a summer associate.

Additional data Summer associateships are available at the firm's offices in Los Angeles and New York.

Number awarded 1 each year.

Deadline January of each year for first-year students; August of each year for second-year students.

[220]
RALPH KARSTEDT SCHOLARSHIP

United Methodist Foundation of Indiana
8401 Fishers Center Drive
Fishers, IN 46038-2318
(317) 788-7879   Toll Free: (877) 391-8811
Fax: (317) 788-0089
E-mail: foundation@UMFIndiana.org
Web: www.umfindiana.org/endowments

Summary To provide financial assistance to ministerial students from Indiana who have a disability and are attending a seminary in any state that is approved by the United Methodist Church (UMC).

Eligibility This program is open to candidates for ordination who have a disability and are certified by a District Committee of the Indiana Conference of the UMC. Applicants must be enrolled full time at an approved seminary in any state. They must be seeking ordination as a deacon or elder. Along with their application, they must submit documentation of financial need and a statement of their vocational goals.

Financial data Stipends are awarded at the rate of $100 per credit hour (per semester) and $200 per projected decade of service remaining (per semester).

Duration 1 year; may be renewed.

Number awarded 1 or more each year.

Deadline May of each year for fall semester; October of each year for spring semester.

[221]
RAMSEY COUNTY BAR FOUNDATION LAW STUDENT SCHOLARSHIP

Ramsey County Bar Foundation
Attn: Diversity Committee
332 Minnesota Street, Suite W-710
St. Paul, MN 55101
(651) 222-0846   Fax: (651) 223-8344
E-mail: Cheryl@ramseybar.org
Web: www.ramseybar.org/foundation

Summary To provide financial assistance to members of groups traditionally underrepresented in the legal profession who are attending law school in Minnesota.

Eligibility This program is open to residents of any state who are currently enrolled at a Minnesota law school. Applicants must be a member of a group traditionally underrepresented in the legal profession, including race, sex, ethnicity, sexual orientation, or disability. They must contribute meaningfully to diversity in their community, have a record of academic or professional achievement, and display leadership qualities through past work experience, community involvement, or student activities.

Financial data The stipend ranges up to $6,000.

Duration 1 year.

Number awarded Varies each year; recently, 7 were awarded.

Deadline February of each year.

[222]
REED SMITH/BNY MELLON DIVERSITY FELLOWSHIP PROGRAM

Reed Smith LLP
Attn: John L. Scott
599 Lexington Avenue, 22nd Floor
New York, NY 10022
(212) 505-6099   Fax: (212) 521-5450
E-mail: JLScott@reedsmith.com

Summary To provide financial assistance and summer work experience in New York to law students who are committed to diversity.

Eligibility This program is open to students who are completing their first year of law school and are authorized to work in the United States. Applicants must be able to demonstrate a record of academic scholarship, dedication to community service and/or leadership, and an understanding of the importance of diversity and inclusion in the legal profession. The sponsor defines diversity to include race, ancestry, religion, color, sex, age, national origin, sexual orientation, gender identity and/or expression, disability, and veteran's status. They must be interested in a summer associate program at the New York offices of the sponsoring law firm and at BNY Mellon. Along with their application, they must submit a personal statement on the ways in which they consider themselves to be a "diverse" individual and how their life experiences as a diverse individual have impacted their academic and work experiences, have influenced their career choices, and will have in shaping or influencing their legal career.

Financial data The program provides a summer associate salary and a stipend of $5,000 for the recipient's second year of law school.

Duration 10 weeks during the summer (5 weeks at the law firm's New York office and 5 weeks at BNY Mellon's New York office) and 1 year of academic study.

Number awarded 1 each year.

Deadline February of each year.

[223]
REED SMITH/KAISER PERMANENTE 1L DIVERSITY FELLOWSHIP PROGRAM

Reed Smith LLP
Attn: Manager of Legal Recruiting
101 Second Street, Suite 1800
San Francisco, CA 94195
(415) 543-8700   Fax: (415) 391-8269
E-mail: jsisco@reedsmith.com

Summary To provide financial assistance and summer work experience in the San Francisco Bay area to law students who are committed to diversity.

Eligibility This program is open to students who are completing their first year of law school and are authorized to work in the United States. Applicants must be able to demonstrate a record of academic scholarship, dedication to community service and/or leadership, and an understanding of the importance of diversity and inclusion in the legal profession. The sponsor defines diversity to include race, ancestry, religion, color, sex, age, national origin, sexual orientation, gender identity and/or expression, disability, and veteran's status. They must be interested in a summer associate program at the sponsor's San Francisco office and the Oakland office of Kaiser Permanent Foundation Health Plan, Inc. Along with their application, they must submit a personal statement on the ways in which they consider themselves to be a "diverse" individual and how their life experiences as a diverse individual have impacted their academic and work experiences, have influenced their career choices, and will have in shaping or influencing their legal career.

Financial data The program provides a summer associate salary and a stipend of $5,000 for the recipient's second year of law school.

Duration 10 weeks during the summer (7 weeks at the law firm's San Francisco office and 3 weeks at Kaiser's Oakland office) and 1 year of academic study.

Additional data The firm established this program in 2008 as part of its commitment to promote diversity in the legal profession.

Number awarded 1 each year.

Deadline March of each year.

[224]
REED SMITH/MCKESSON 1L DIVERSITY FELLOWSHIP PROGRAM

Reed Smith LLP
Attn: Legal Recruiting Coordinator
101 Second Street, Suite 1800
San Francisco, CA 94195
(415) 543-8700   Fax: (415) 391-8269
E-mail: ahathaway@reedsmith.com

Summary To provide financial assistance and summer work experience in San Francisco to law students who are committed to diversity.

Eligibility This program is open to students who are completing their first year of law school and are authorized to work in the United States. Applicants must be able to demonstrate a record of academic scholarship; demonstrated commitment to pro bono work, community service, and/or leadership; and an understanding of the importance of diversity and inclusion in the legal profession. The sponsor defines diversity to include race, ancestry, religion, color, sex, age, national origin, sexual orientation, gender identity and/or expression, disability, and veteran's status. They must be interested in a summer associate program at the San Francisco offices of the sponsoring law firm and McKesson. Along with their application, they must submit a personal statement on the ways in which they consider themselves to be a "diverse" individual and how their life experiences as a diverse individual have influenced or shaped their experiences within the legal community and their commitment to diversity and inclusion in the legal profession.

Financial data The program provides a summer associate salary of $15,000 per month and a stipend of $5,000 for the recipient's second year of law school.

Duration 10 weeks during the summer (7 weeks at the law firm's San Francisco office and 3 weeks at McKesson) and 1 year of academic study.

Number awarded 1 each year.

Deadline January of each year.

[225]
ROBERT A. DANNELS MEMORIAL SCHOLARSHIP

American Nuclear Society
Attn: Scholarship Coordinator
555 North Kensington Avenue
La Grange Park, IL 60526-5535
(708) 352-6611   Toll Free: (800) 323-3044
Fax: (708) 352-0499   E-mail: outreach@ans.org
Web: www.ans.org/honors/scholarships/dannels

Summary To provide financial assistance to disabled or other students who are interested in working on a graduate degree in nuclear science or engineering.

Eligibility This program is open to full-time graduate students in programs leading to an advanced degree in nuclear science, nuclear engineering, or other nuclear-related field at an accredited institution in the United States. Applicants must be members of the American Nuclear Society (ANS) and sponsored by the faculty adviser of an ANS student chapter or an individual ANS member, but they may be citizens of any country. Selection is based on academic achievement. Students with disabilities are particularly encouraged to apply.

Financial data The stipend is $3,500.

Duration 1 year; nonrenewable.

Additional data This program is offered by the Mathematics and Computation Division (M&CD) of the ANS.

Number awarded 1 each year.

Deadline January of each year.

[226]
RUTH L. KIRSCHSTEIN NATIONAL RESEARCH SERVICE AWARD FOR INDIVIDUAL PREDOCTORAL FELLOWS IN NURSING RESEARCH

National Institute of Nursing Research
Attn: Extramural Research Training Program Director
6701 Democracy Boulevard, Room 710
Bethesda, MD 20892-4870
(301) 496-9558   Fax: (301) 480-8260
TDD: (301) 451-0088   E-mail: banksdh@mail.nih.gov
Web: www.grants.nih.gov

Summary To provide financial aid to registered nurses who are pursuing doctoral study in a field relevant to the work of the National Institute of Nursing Research (NINR).

Eligibility This program is open to registered nurses who are enrolled or accepted for enrollment full time in a Ph.D. or equivalent doctoral degree program (but not a health professional degree such as M.D., D.O., D.D.S., or D.V.M.). Applicants must be sponsored by a domestic for-profit or nonprofit, public or private institution, such as a university, college, hospital, or laboratory. Members of underrepresented racial and ethnic groups and individuals with disabilities are especially encouraged to apply. Only U.S. citizens, nationals, and permanent residents are eligible.

Financial data The fellowship provides an annual stipend of $23,376, a tuition and fee allowance (60% of costs up to $16,000 or 60% of costs up to $21,000 for dual degrees), and an institutional allowance of $4,200 for travel to scientific meetings and for laboratory and other training expenses.

Duration Up to 5 years.

Number awarded Varies each year, depending on the availability of funds.

Deadline April, August, or December of each year.

[227]
RUTH L. KIRSCHSTEIN NATIONAL RESEARCH SERVICE AWARD INDIVIDUAL PREDOCTORAL MD/PHD OR OTHER DUAL-DEGREE FELLOWSHIP

National Institutes of Health
Office of Extramural Research
Attn: Grants Information
6705 Rockledge Drive, Suite 4090
Bethesda, MD 20892-7983
(301) 435-0714   Fax: (301) 480-0525
TDD: (301) 451-5936   E-mail: grantsinfo@nih.gov
Web: grants.nih.gov

Summary To provide financial assistance to students working on a combined M.D./Ph.D. or other dual doctoral degree and preparing for a career in biomedical and behavioral research.

Eligibility This program is open to students enrolled in an accredited M.D./Ph.D. or other dual-degree program (e.g., D.O./Ph.D., D.D.S./Ph.D, Au.D.,Ph.D., D.V.M./Ph.D.) and planning a career as a physician/scientist or other clinician/scientist. Applicants in M.D./Ph.D. programs must have entered the program no more than 48 months prior to applying and must have identified a research project and sponsor. Applicants in other dual-degree programs may have entered at any time but they must have identified a research project and sponsor. Members of under-represented racial and ethnic groups and individuals with disabilities are especially encouraged to apply. Only U.S. citizens, nationals, and permanent residents are eligible.

Financial data The fellowship provides an annual stipend of $22,920, a tuition and fee allowance (60% of costs up to $21,000), and an institutional allowance of $4,200 (or $3,100 at federal and for-profit institutions) for travel to scientific meetings, health insurance, and laboratory and other training expenses.

Duration Up to 6 years.

Additional data These fellowships are offered by most components of the National Institutes of Health (NIH).

Number awarded Varies each year.

Deadline April, August, or December of each year.

[228]
RUTH L. KIRSCHSTEIN NATIONAL RESEARCH SERVICE AWARDS FOR INDIVIDUAL PREDOCTORAL FELLOWS

National Institutes of Health
Office of Extramural Research
Attn: Grants Information
6705 Rockledge Drive, Suite 4090
Bethesda, MD 20892-7983
(301) 435-0714   Fax: (301) 480-0525
TDD: (301) 451-5936   E-mail: grantsinfo@od.nih.gov
Web: grants.nih.gov

Summary To provide financial assistance for dissertation research in the United States or any other country to doctoral candidates preparing for a career in biomedical or behavioral science.

Eligibility This program is open to students enrolled in a Ph.D. or equivalent research degree program in the biomedical, behavioral, health, or clinical sciences. Students in health professional degree programs (e.g., M.D., D.O., D.D.S., D.V.M.) or dual-degree programs are not eligible. Applicants must be at the dissertation research stage of their doctoral program at a public or private institution of higher education (especially a Hispanic Serving Institution, Historically Black College or University, Tribal College or University, Alaska Native and Native Hawaiian Serving Institution, or Asian American Native American Pacific Islander Serving Institution). They may select a foreign institution if they can demonstrate why the facilities, the sponsor, or other aspects of the proposed experience are more appropriate than training in a domestic setting. Members of underrepresented racial and ethnic groups and individuals with disabilities are especially encouraged to apply. They must be U.S. citizens, nationals, or permanent residents.

Financial data The fellowship provides an annual stipend of $23,376, a tuition and fee allowance (60% of costs up to $16,000), and an institutional allowance of $4,200 (or $3,100 at federal and for-profit institutions) for travel to scientific meetings, health insurance, and laboratory and other training expenses.

Duration Up to 5 years, although most are for 2 or 3 years.

Additional data These fellowships are offered by most components of the National Institutes of Health (NIH).

Number awarded Varies each year.

Deadline April, August, or December of each year.

[229]
RUTH L. KIRSCHSTEIN NATIONAL RESEARCH SERVICE AWARDS FOR INDIVIDUAL PREDOCTORAL FELLOWSHIPS TO PROMOTE DIVERSITY IN HEALTH-RELATED RESEARCH

National Institutes of Health
Office of Extramural Research
Attn: Grants Information
6705 Rockledge Drive, Suite 4090
Bethesda, MD 20892-7983
(301) 435-0714   Fax: (301) 480-0525
TDD: (301) 451-5936   E-mail: grantsinfo@nih.gov
Web: www.grants.nih.gov

Summary To provide financial assistance to students from underrepresented groups interested in working on a doctoral degree and preparing for a career in biomedical and behavioral research.

Eligibility This program is open to students enrolled or accepted for enrollment in a Ph.D. or equivalent research degree program; a formally combined M.D./Ph.D. program; or other combined professional doctoral/research Ph.D. program in the biomedical, behavioral, or clinical sciences. Students in health professional degree programs (e.g., M.D., D.O., D.D.S., D.V.M.) are not eligible. Applicants must be 1) members of an ethnic or racial group underrepresented in biomedical or behavioral research; 2) individuals with disabilities; or 3) individuals

from socially, culturally, economically, or educationally disadvantaged backgrounds that have inhibited their ability to prepare for a career in health-related research. They must be U.S. citizens, nationals, or permanent residents.

Financial data The fellowship provides an annual stipend of $23,376, a tuition and fee allowance (60% of costs up to $16,000 or 60% of costs up to $21,000 for dual degrees), and an institutional allowance of $4,200 ($3,100 at for-profit and federal institutions) for travel to scientific meetings, health insurance, and laboratory and other training expenses.

Duration Up to 5 years for Ph.D. students or up to 6 years for M.D./Ph.D. or other combined research degree programs.

Additional data These fellowships are offered by most components of the National Institutes of Health (NIH). Contact the NIH for a list of names and telephone numbers of responsible officers at each component.

Number awarded Varies each year.

Deadline April, August, or December of each year.

[230]
RUTH L. KIRSCHSTEIN NATIONAL RESEARCH SERVICE AWARDS (NRSA) FELLOWSHIPS FOR STUDENTS AT INSTITUTIONS WITH NIH-FUNDED INSTITUTIONAL PREDOCTORAL DUAL-DEGREE TRAINING PROGRAMS

National Institutes of Health
Office of Extramural Research
Attn: Grants Information
6705 Rockledge Drive, Suite 4090
Bethesda, MD 20892-7983
(301) 435-0714   Fax: (301) 480-0525
TDD: (301) 451-5936   E-mail: grantsinfo@od.nih.gov
Web: grants.nih.gov

Summary To provide financial assistance in the United States or any other country to students engaged in predoctoral dual-degree research and clinical training programs in health-related fields.

Eligibility This program is open to students enrolled in a formally combined dual-degree program (e.g., M.D./Ph.D., D.O./Ph.D., D.D.S./Ph.D., Au.D./Ph.D., D.V.M./Ph.D.). Applicants must be entering the research or clinical stage of their doctoral program at a public or private institution of higher education (especially a Hispanic Serving Institution, Historically Black College or University, Tribal College or University, Alaska Native and Native Hawaiian Serving Institution, or Asian American Native American Pacific Islander Serving Institution). The institution must have received funding from the National Institutes of Health (NIH) for its dual-degree program. Applicants may select a foreign institution if they can demonstrate why the facilities, the sponsor, or other aspects of the proposed experience are more appropriate than training in a domestic setting. Members of underrepresented racial and ethnic groups and individuals with disabilities are especially encouraged to apply. They must be U.S. citizens, nationals, or permanent residents.

Financial data The fellowship provides an annual stipend of $23,376, a tuition and fee allowance (60% of costs up to $21,000), and an institutional allowance of $4,200 (or $3,100 at federal and for-profit institutions) for travel to scientific meetings, health insurance, and laboratory and other training expenses.

Duration Up to 6 years.

Additional data These fellowships are offered by most components of the National Institutes of Health (NIH).

Number awarded Varies each year.

Deadline April, August, or December of each year.

[231]
SARASOTA COUNTY BAR ASSOCIATION RICHARD R. GARLAND DIVERSITY SCHOLARSHIP

Community Foundation of Sarasota County
Attn: Manager, Scholarships and Special Initiatives
2635 Fruitville Road
Sarasota, FL 34237
(941) 556-7150   Fax: (941) 952-1951
E-mail: scholarships@cfsarasota.org
Web: www.cfsarasota.org

Summary To provide financial assistance and work experience in Sarasota County, Florida to law students from any state who will add to the diversity of the legal profession.

Eligibility This program is open to first- through third-year law students of traditionally underrepresented backgrounds (e.g., race, color, religion, national origin, ethnicity, age, gender, sexual orientation, physical disability, socioeconomic background). Applicants must be interested in practicing law after graduation and in obtaining summer placement in private law firms or government agencies in Sarasota County. They may be attending law school in any state but they should have or have had family, school, or community ties to the county. Along with their application, they must submit a 250-word essay describing how their particular background would help the Sarasota County Bar Association achieve its goal of making the local legal community more diverse.

Financial data Students receive a salary for their summer employment and a stipend of $5,000, sent directly to their law school, upon completion of their employment.

Duration 1 summer for employment and 1 year for law school enrollment.

Additional data This program is sponsored by the Sarasota County Bar Association.

Number awarded 1 or more each year.

Deadline January of each year.

[232]
SAULT TRIBE SPECIAL NEEDS SCHOLARSHIPS

Sault Tribe of Chippewa Indians
Attn: Higher Education Department
523 Ashmun Street
Sault Ste. Marie, MI 49783
(906) 635-6050, ext. 26312   Toll Free: (800) 793-0660
Fax: (906) 635-7785
E-mail: BMacArthur@saulttribe.net
Web: www.saulttribe.com

Summary To provide financial assistance for education at any level to members of the Sault Tribe of Chippewa Indians who have a disability.

Eligibility This program is open to members of the Sault Tribe who have a documented physical or emotional disability. Applicants must be enrolled in an educational program at any level. Along with their application, they must submit a letter from themselves or a parent describing the proposed use of the funds and an itemized list of the expected costs.

Financial data The stipend is $1,000.

Duration 1 year.

Number awarded 4 each year: 2 for students under 18 years of age and 2 for students 18 years of age or older.

Deadline May of each year.

[233]
SCHWABE, WILLIAMSON & WYATT SUMMER ASSOCIATE DIVERSITY SCHOLARSHIP

Schwabe, Williamson & Wyatt, Attorneys at Law
Attn: Recruiting Manager
1211 S.W. Fifth Avenue, Suite 1900
Portland, OR 97204
(503) 796-2436   Fax: (503) 796-2900
E-mail: wcase@schwabe.com
Web: www.schwabe.com/careers-associates

Summary To provide financial assistance and summer work experience in Portland, Oregon or Seattle, Washington to law students who will bring to the legal profession differences related to race, gender, ethnicity, religion, disability, and sexual orientation.

Eligibility This program is open to first-year students working on a J.D. degree at an ABA-accredited law school. Applicants must 1) contribute to the diversity of the law school student body and the legal community; 2) possess a record of academic achievement, capacity, and leadership as an undergraduate and in law school that indicates promise for a successful career in the legal profession; and 3) demonstrate a commitment to practice law in the Pacific Northwest upon completion of law school. They must be interested in a paid summer associateship at the sponsoring law firm's office in Portland, Oregon or Seattle, Washington. Along with their application, they must submit a resume, undergraduate and law school transcripts, a legal writing sample, and a 1- to 2-page personal statement explaining their interest in the scholarship and how they will contribute to diversity in the legal community.

Financial data The program provides a paid summer associateship during the summer following completion of the first year of law school and an academic scholarship of $7,500 to help pay tuition and other expenses during the recipient's second year of law school.

Duration 1 year.

Number awarded 1 each year.

Deadline January of each year.

[234]
SCIENCE GRADUATE STUDENT GRANT FUND

Foundation for Science and Disability, Inc.
c/o Richard Mankin, Grants Committee Chair
USDA-ARS-CMAVE
1700 S.W. 23rd Drive
Gainesville, FL 32608
(352) 374-5774   Fax: (352) 374-5804
E-mail: rmankin1@ufl.edu
Web: www.stemd.org

Summary To provide supplemental grants to students with disabilities who are interested in working on a graduate degree in a science-related field.

Eligibility This program is open to 1) college seniors who have a disability and have been accepted to a graduate or professional school in the sciences; and 2) graduate science students who have a disability. Applicants must be U.S. citizens interested in working on a degree in an area of engineering, mathematics, medicine, science, or technology. Along with their application, they must submit an essay (about 250 words) describing professional goals and objectives, as well as the specific purpose for which the grant would be used. Selection is based on financial need, sincerity of purpose, and scholarship and/or research ability.

Financial data The grant is $1,000. Funds may be used for an assistive device or instrument, as financial support to work with a professor on an individual research project, or for some other special need.

Duration The award is granted annually.

Additional data The Foundation for Science and Disability, Inc. is an affiliate society of the American Association for the Advancement of Science.

Number awarded 1 or more each year.

Deadline November of each year.

[235]
SIDLEY DIVERSITY AND INCLUSION SCHOLARSHIP

Sidley Austin LLP
Attn: Scholarships
One South Dearborn Street
Chicago, IL 60603
(312) 853-7000   Fax: (312) 853-7036
E-mail: scholarship@sidley.com
Web: www.sidleycareers.com

Summary To provide financial assistance and work experience to law students who come from a diverse background.

Eligibility The program is open to students entering their second year of law school; preference is given to students at schools where the sponsor conducts on-campus interviews or participates in a resume collection. Applicants must have a demonstrated ability to contribute meaningfully to the diversity of the law school and/or legal profession, including racial or ethnic diversity, sexual orientation or gender identity, disability, veteran status, and/or other areas underrepresented or otherwise important to diversity in the legal profession. Along with their application, they must submit a 500-word essay that includes a description of their academic and personal strengths; exceptional contributions, through community service or otherwise, to the cause of diversity; and/or how they have overcome adversity, such as a personal or family history of educational or socioeconomic disadvantage, and have demonstrated the tenacity and talent to excel in the legal profession. Selection is based on academic achievement and leadership qualities.

Financial data The stipend is $20,000.

Duration 1 year.

Additional data This program began in 2011. Recipients are expected to participate in the sponsor's summer associate program following their second year of law school. They must apply separately for the associate position. The firm has offices in Boston, Chicago, Dallas, Houston, Los Angeles, New York, Palo Alto, San Francisco, and Washington, D.C.

Number awarded Up to 15 each year.

Deadline September of each year.

[236]
STATE VOCATIONAL REHABILITATION SERVICES PROGRAM

Department of Education
Office of Special Education and Rehabilitative Services
Attn: Rehabilitation Services Administration
400 Maryland Avenue, S.W., Room 5014
Washington, DC 20202-2800
(202) 245-7325   Fax: (202) 245-7590
E-mail: Carol.Dobak@ed.gov
Web: www2.ed.gov/programs/rsabvrs/index.html

Summary To provide financial assistance to individuals with disabilities for undergraduate or graduate study pursued as part of their program of vocational rehabilitation.

Eligibility To be eligible for vocational rehabilitation services, an individual must 1) have a physical or mental impairment that is a substantial impediment to employment; 2) be able to benefit in terms of employment from vocational rehabilitation services; and 3) require vocational rehabilitation services to prepare for, enter, engage in, or retain gainful employment. Priority is given to applicants with the most significant disabilities. Persons accepted for vocational rehabilitation develop an Individualized Written Rehabilitation Program (IWRP) in consultation with a counselor for the vocational rehabilitation agency in the state in which they live. The IWRP may include a program of postsecondary education, if the disabled person and counselor agree that such a program will fulfill the goals of vocational rehabilitation. In most cases, the IWRP will provide for postsecondary education only to a level at which the disabled person will become employable, but that may include graduate education if the approved occupation requires an advanced degree as a minimum condition of entry. Students accepted to a program of postsecondary education as part of their IWRP must apply for all available federal, state, and private financial aid.

Financial data Funding for this program is provided by the federal government through grants to state vocational rehabilitation agencies. Grants under the basic support program currently total more than $3.1 billion per year. States must supplement federal funding with matching funds of 21.3%. Persons who are accepted for vocational rehabilitation by the appropriate state agency receive financial assistance based on the cost of their education and other funds available to them, including their own or family contribution and other sources of financial aid. Allowable costs in most states include tuition, fees, books, supplies, room, board, transportation, personal expenses, child care, and expenses related to disability (special equipment, readers, attendants, interpreters, or note takers).

Duration Assistance is provided until the disabled person achieves an educational level necessary for employment as provided in the IWRP.

Additional data Information on this program is available only from state vocational rehabilitation agencies.

Number awarded Varies each year; recently, more than 1.2 million people (of whom more than 80% have significant disabilities) were participating in this program.

Deadline Deadline not specified.

[237]
STEVE FASTEAU PAST PRESIDENTS' SCHOLARSHIP

California Association for Postsecondary Education
and Disability
Attn: Scholarships
10073 Valley View Street, Suite 242
Cypress, CA 90630
(562) 397-2810   Fax: (866) 577-3387
E-mail: caped38@gmail.com
Web: www.caped.io/scholarships/scholarship-application

Summary To provide financial assistance to undergraduate and graduate students in California who have a disability and have demonstrated outstanding leadership.

Eligibility This program is open to students at public and private colleges and universities in California who have a physical, mental, or learning disability. Applicants must have high academic achievement and have shown leadership and dedication to the advancement of students with disabilities in postsecondary education. Undergraduates must have completed at least 6 semester credits and have a GPA of 2.5 or higher. Graduate students must have completed at least 3 semester units and have a GPA of 3.0 or higher. Along with their application, they must submit 1) a 250-word essay describing their progress towards meeting their educational and/or vocational goals; 2) a 500-

word essay on how they manage their disability; and 3) a 750-word essay on how they have demonstrated leadership skills and dedication to the advancement of educational opportunities for students with disabilities in the postsecondary education setting They must also submit a letter of recommendation from a faculty person, verification of disability, and unofficial transcripts.

Financial data The stipend is $2,500.

Duration 1 year.

Number awarded 1 each year.

Deadline August of each year.

[238]
STOEL RIVES FIRST-YEAR DIVERSITY FELLOWSHIPS

Stoel Rives LLP
Attn: Senior Lawyer Recruiting Manager
760 S.W. Ninth Avenue, Suite 3000
Portland, OR 97205
(503) 224-3380   Fax: (503) 220-2480
E-mail: dorianna.phillips@stoel.com
Web: www.stoel.com/diversity.aspx?Show=2805

Summary To provide financial assistance for law school and work experience to law students who bring diversity to the profession and are interested in a summer associate position with designated offices of Stoel Rives.

Eligibility This program is open to first-year law students who contribute to the diversity of the student body at their law school and who will contribute to the diversity of the legal community. The first defines diversity to include differing life experiences, cultures, and backgrounds, as well as gender, race, national origin, religion, sexual orientation, gender identity, disability, marital status, and age. Applicants must be willing to accept a summer associate position at Stoel Rives offices in Portland, Salt Lake City, or Seattle. Selection is based on academic excellence, leadership ability, personal and professional accomplishments, commitment to community service, commitment to living in Portland, Salt Lake City, or Seattle, and meaningful contribution to the diversity of the legal community.

Financial data The program provides a stipend of $7,500 to help defray expenses of law school and a salaried summer associate position.

Duration 1 year.

Additional data This program began in 2004.

Number awarded At least 2 each year.

Deadline January of each year.

[239]
SWIM WITH MIKE

University of Southern California
3501 Watt Way
Heritage Hall
MC 0602
Los Angeles, CA 90089-0602
(213) 740-4155   Fax: (213) 740-1306
E-mail: swimwithmike@gmail.com
Web: www.swimwithmike.org

Summary To provide financial assistance for college or graduate school to physically challenged athletes.

Eligibility This program is open to athletes who participated in organized competitive youth, high school, or collegiate athletics and subsequently have sustained a life-changing accident or illness (e.g., paralysis, blindness, cancer, amputation, head injuries). Applicants must meet the admission standards of a 4-year or graduate-level institution of higher learning. Along with their application, they must submit a personal statement with an emphasis on their athletic history and experience and their educational goals, 3 letters of recommendation, verification of disability, and documentation of financial need.

Financial data Stipends depend on the need of the recipient.

Duration 1 year; may be renewed, provided the recipient.

Additional data This program began in 1981 at the University of Southern California to assist All-American swimmer Mike Nyeholt, who was paralyzed in a motorcycle accident. Since its establishment, it has provided more than $18 million in assistance to 199 athletes at 97 universities throughout the country. Recipients are expected to participate in Swim with Mike activities and to support the organization both during and after college.

Number awarded Varies each year; recently, 51 athletes received $985,000 in scholarships.

Deadline April of each year.

[240]
TEXAS YOUNG LAWYERS ASSOCIATION DIVERSITY SCHOLARSHIP PROGRAM

Texas Young Lawyers Association
Attn: Diversity Committee
1414 Colorado, Fourth Floor
P.O. Box 12487
Austin, TX 78711-2487
(512) 427-1529   Toll Free: (800) 204-2222, ext. 1529
Fax: (512) 427-4117   E-mail: btrevino@texasbar.com
Web: www.tyla.org

Summary To provide financial assistance to residents of any state who are from diverse groups attending law school in Texas.

Eligibility This program is open to members of recognized diverse groups, including diversity based on gender, national origin, race, ethnicity, sexual orientation, gender identity, disability, socioeconomic status, and geography. Applicants must be attending an ABA-accredited law school in Texas. Along with their application, they must submit brief essays on 1) their experience with diversity and their commitment to bring diversity to the legal profession; 2) why they believe diversity is important to the practice of law; and 3) what the Texas Young Lawyers Association and the State Bar of Texas can do to promote and support diversity in the legal profession. Selection is based on those essays, academic performance, demonstrated commitment to diversity, letters of recommendation, and financial need.

Financial data The stipend ranges from $1,500 to $5,000.

Duration 1 year.

Number awarded At least 9 each year: at least 1 at each accredited law school in Texas.

Deadline October of each year.

[241]
THE HONORABLE JOEL K. ASARCH ELDER LAW AND SPECIAL NEEDS SECTION SCHOLARSHIP

The New York Bar Foundation
One Elk Street
Albany, NY 12207
(518) 487-5651   Fax: (518) 487-5699
E-mail: moclair@tnybf.org
Web: www.tnybf.org/fellandschol

Summary To provide financial assistance to law students in New York, especially those with a disability, who have an interest in elder law.

Eligibility This program is open to students in the second or third year at law schools in New York. Applicants must be actively participating in an elder law clinic at their law school or have performed other substantial efforts that demonstrate interest in the legal rights of the elderly or the practice of elder law. They must have a GPA of 2.5 or higher. Preference is given to students who 1) demonstrate a present and permanent physical or mental disability that substantially limits 1 or more of the major life activities of the individual; or 2) can demonstrate financial need. Selection is based on demonstrated interest in elder law; academic record; recommendations; an essay on their interest in elder law; and maturity, integrity and professionalism.

Financial data The stipend is $2,500.

Duration 1 year.

Additional data This program began in 2009 as the Elder Law Scholarship, sponsored by the Elder Law and Special Needs Section of the New York State Bar Association.

Number awarded 1 each year.

Deadline November of each year.

[242]
THE REV. VIRGINIA KREYER SCHOLARSHIP

United Church of Christ
Attn: Associate Director, Grant and Scholarship
  Administration
700 Prospect Avenue East
Cleveland, OH 44115-1100
(216) 736-2166   Toll Free: (866) 822-8224, ext. 2166
Fax: (216) 736-3783   E-mail: scholarships@ucc.org
Web: www.ucc.org/kreyer_scholarship

Summary To provide financial assistance to members of United Church of Christ (UCC) congregations who have a disability and are preparing for ministry.

Eligibility This program is open to members of UCC congregations who have been members for at least 1 year and have a disability. Applicants must be preparing for authorized ministry in the UCC through seminary training, a UCC regional lay ministry program of study, and/or an association/conference committee on ministry mentoring program of study. They must have a GPA of 3.0 or higher.

Financial data A stipend is awarded (amount not specified). Funds may be used to help defray the cost of tuition, assistive devices, specialized software, hardware, specialized services, specialized assistants, transportation, and adapted vehicles.

Duration 1 year.

Additional data This scholarship was established in 2010 and first awarded in 2015.

Number awarded 1 or more each year.

Deadline February of each year.

[243]
U'ILANI STENDER SCHOLARSHIP

Pauahi Foundation
Attn: Scholarships
567 South King Street, Suite 160
Honolulu, HI 96813-3036
(808) 534-3966   Fax: (808) 534-3890
E-mail: scholarships@pauahi.org
Web: www.pauahi.org/scholarships

Summary To provide financial assistance to residents of any state, especially Native Hawaiians, who have faced challenging situations and are interested in attending college or graduate school.

Eligibility This program is open to undergraduate and graduate students from any state whose lives have been impacted by challenging situations (e.g., death of a significant family member, domestic violence, sexual abuse, poverty, major health problems). Applicants must be attending or planning to attend a 2- or 4-year college, university, or vocation/technical school; graduate school; or a private, independent school designed to accommodate their special circumstances. They must be able to demonstrate financial need and the motivation and desire to succeed in an educational program. Along with their application, they must submit 1) an essay demonstrating a clear and realistic plan to pursue their career objectives; and 2) a letter of recommendation from a social service agency, counselor, or teacher citing their challenging or special life circumstances and how they would benefit from this scholarship. Preference is given to Native Hawaiians (descendants of the aboriginal inhabitants of the Hawaiian Islands prior to 1778), orphans, and indigent applicants.

Financial data The stipend is $1,700.

Duration 1 year.

Number awarded 4 each year.

Deadline February of each year.

[244]
VOCATIONAL REHABILITATION AND EMPLOYMENT SERVICE PROGRAM

Department of Veterans Affairs
Attn: Veterans Benefits Administration
Vocational Rehabilitation and Employment Service
810 Vermont Avenue, N.W.
Washington, DC 20420
(202) 418-4343   Toll Free: (800) 827-1000
Web: www.benefits.va.gov/vocrehab/index.asp

Summary To provide funding to veterans with service-connected disabilities who need assistance to find employment or, if seriously disabled, to live independently.

Eligibility This program is open to veterans who have a service-connected disability of at least 10% or a memorandum rating of 20% or more from the Department of Veterans Affairs (VA). They must qualify for services provided by the Vocational Rehabilitation and Employment Service Program that include assistance finding and keeping a job, including the use of special employer incentives and job accommodations; on-the-job training, apprenticeships, and unpaid work experiences; postsecondary training at a college, vocational, technical, or business school; supportive rehabilitation services such as case management, counseling, and medical referrals; independent living services for veterans unable to work due to the severity of their disabilities.

Financial data While in training and for 2 months after, eligible disabled veterans may receive subsistence allowances in addition to their disability compensation or retirement pay. For most training programs, the current full-time monthly rate is $605.44 with no dependents, $751 with 1 dependent, $885 with 2 dependents, and $64.50 for each additional dependent; proportional rates apply for less than full-time training.

Duration Veterans remain eligible for these services up to 12 years from either the date of separation from active military service or the date the veteran was first notified by VA of a service-connected disability rating (whichever came later).

Number awarded Varies each year.

Deadline Applications are accepted at any time.

[245]
VSA EMERGING YOUNG ARTISTS PROGRAM

John F. Kennedy Center for the Performing Arts
Attn: Department of VSA and Accessibility
2700 F Street, N.W.
Washington, DC 20566
(202) 416-8898   Toll Free: (800) 444-1324
Fax: (202) 416-4840   TDD: (202) 416-8728
E-mail: vsainfo@kennedy-center.org
Web: education.kennedy-center.org

Summary To recognize and reward emerging visual artists who have a disability.

Eligibility This competition is open to visual artists between 16 and 25 years of age who have a disability. Applicants must submit samples of their work along with a brief essay on a theme that changes annually examines the vital creative spark behind their work. Their essays should describe the force that drives their artistic interest and informs the path they take each day as they move toward their future.

Financial data Awards are $20,000 for the grand award, $10,000 for the first award, $6,000 for the second award, and $2,000 for each award of excellence.

Duration The competition is held annually.

Additional data This competition, first held in 2003, is sponsored by VSA and the Volkswagen Group of America. VSA was established in 1974 as the National Committee-Arts for the Handicapped. In 1985 its name was changed to Very Special Arts and in 2010 to VSA. In 2011, it merged with the Kennedy Center's Office on Accessibility to become the Department of VSA and Accessibility at the John F. Kennedy Center for the Performing Arts. The art work is displayed at the S. Dillon Ripley Center of the Smithsonian Institution in the fall of each year.

Number awarded 15 each year: 1 grand award, 1 first award, 1 second award, and 12 awards of excellence.

Deadline June of each year.

[246]
VSA INTERNATIONAL YOUNG SOLOISTS AWARD

John F. Kennedy Center for the Performing Arts
Attn: Department of VSA and Accessibility
2700 F Street, N.W.
Washington, DC 20566
(202) 416-8898   Toll Free: (800) 444-1324
Fax: (202) 416-4840   TDD: (202) 416-8728
E-mail: vsainfo@kennedy-center.org
Web: education.kennedy-center.org

Summary To recognize and reward young musicians from any country who are physically or mentally challenged.

Eligibility This competition is open to musicians (instrumental or vocal) between 14 and 25 years of age who have a disability. Musical ensembles of 2 to 5 performers are also eligible if at least 1 member has a disability and all members are between 14 and 25 years of age. Applicants must be either 1) U.S. citizens or permanent residents; or 2) citizens of other countries living in the United States (as on a student visa). They may be performers in any type of music, including, but not limited to, rock, alt rock, pop, indie, classical, country, folk, jazz, R&B/blues, hip hop, rap, Latin, and world. Along with their application, they must submit recordings of 3 musical selections (audio or video) and a 1-page personal narrative that describes why they should be selected to receive this award. Tapes are evaluated on the basis of technique, tone, intonation, rhythm, and interpretation.

Financial data The award is $2,000. Funds must be used to assist the recipients' music career.

Duration The competition is held annually.

Additional data The sponsor was established in 1974 as the National Committee-Arts for the Handicapped. In 1985 its name was changed to Very Special Arts and in 2010 to VSA. In 2011, it merged with the Kennedy Cen-

ter's Office on Accessibility to become the Department of VSA and Accessibility at the John F. Kennedy Center for the Performing Arts.

Number awarded 4 each year.

Deadline January of each year.

[247]
WILLIAM REECE SMITH, JR. DIVERSITY SCHOLARSHIPS

Carlton Fields Jorden Burt
Attn: Nancy Faggianelli, Chief Diversity Officer
Corporate Center Three at International Plaza
4221 West Boy Scout Boulevard, Suite 1000
Tampa, FL 33607-5780
(813) 229-4321   Toll Free: (888) 223-9191
Fax: (813) 229-4133
E-mail: nfaggianelli@carltonfields.com
Web: www.carltonfields.com/diversity

Summary To provide financial assistance and work experience at Carlton Fields Jorden Burt to law students who come from a diverse background.

Eligibility This program is open to students completing their first year at an ABA-accredited law school who come from a diverse background, including ethnicity, race, gender, sexual orientation, culture, or disabilities. Applicants must be interested in a summer associateship at the sponsoring firm's law offices in Miami, Orlando, Tampa, or West Palm Beach. They must be able to demonstrate a record of achievement that holds great promise for a successful legal career, a high level of work intensity, a desire to practice law in a highly focused but collegial setting, demonstrated leadership ability, excellent writing and interpersonal skills, and academic achievement.

Financial data The program provides a stipend of $5,000 for law school and a paid summer associateship (salary not specified).

Duration 1 year.

Additional data This program began in 2011.

Number awarded 2 each year.

Deadline February of each year.

[248]
WINSTON & STRAWN DIVERSITY SCHOLARSHIP PROGRAM

Winston & Strawn LLP
Attn: Amanda Sommerfeld, Diversity Committee Chair
333 South Grand Avenue, 38th Floor
Los Angeles, CA 90071-1543
(213) 615-1724   Fax: (213) 615-1750
E-mail: asommerfeld@winston.com
Web: www.winston.com

Summary To provide financial assistance to diverse law students who are interested in practicing in a city in which Winston & Strawn LLP has an office.

Eligibility This program is open to second-year law students who represent the varied experiences of different races, ethnic groups, genders, sexual orientation, ages, religions, national origins and disabilities. Applicants must submit a resume, law school transcript, and 500-word personal statement. Selection is based on 1) interest in practicing law after graduation in a large law firm in a city in which Winston & Strawn has an office (currently, Charlotte, Chicago, Dallas, Houston, Los Angeles, New York, San Francisco, and Washington, D.C.); 2) law school and undergraduate record, including academic achievements and involvement in extracurricular activities; 3) demonstrated leadership skills; 4) and interpersonal skills.

Financial data The stipend is $10,000.

Duration 1 year (the third year of law school).

Additional data This program began in 2004.

Number awarded 3 each year.

Deadline September of each year.

[249]
WRITING COMPETITION TO PROMOTE DIVERSITY IN LAW SCHOOLS AND IN THE LEGAL PROFESSION

Law School Admission Council
Attn: Office of Diversity Initiatives
662 Penn Street
P.O. Box 40
Newtown, PA 18940-0040
(215) 968-1338   TDD: (215) 968-1169
E-mail: DiversityOffice@lsac.org
Web: www.lsac.org

Summary To recognize and reward law students who submit outstanding essays on what law schools can do to promote diversity.

Eligibility This competition is open to J.D. candidates in each year of study at law schools in the United States and Canada that are members of the Law School Admission Council (LSAC). Applicants must submit articles, up to 20 pages in length, on the techniques, resources and strategies law schools can utilize to recruit and retain students of color, students living with a disability, LGBTQ students, and other students who are from groups underrepresented in law schools and the legal profession. Selection is based on research and use of relevant sources and authorities; quality and clarity of legal analysis, persuasion, and writing; understanding, interpretations, and conclusions regarding diversity and the implications of diversity in this context; and compliance with all competition procedures.

Financial data The prize is $5,000.

Duration The prize is awarded annually.

Number awarded 3 each year: 1 to a student in each year of law school.

Deadline April of each year.

Visual Disabilities

Undergraduates ●

Graduate Students ●

Described here are 191 funding opportunities available to individuals who have visual impairments (are partially sighted or blind), with or without correction. Of these, 121 are for undergraduates and 70 are for graduate students. All of this is "free" money. Not one dollar will need to be repaid (provided, of course, that recipients meet all program requirements). If you are looking for a particular program and don't find it in this section, be sure to check the Program Title Index to see if it is covered elsewhere in the directory.

Undergraduates

[250]
ACB STUDENTS BRENDA DILLON MEMORIAL SCHOLARSHIP

American Council of the Blind
Attn: Coordinator, Scholarship Program
6300 Shingle Creek Parkway, Suite 195
Brooklyn Center, MN 55430-2136
(612) 332-3242   Toll Free: (800) 424-8666
E-mail: deetheien@acbes.org
Web: www.acb.org/scholarship

Summary To provide financial assistance for college to students who are blind.

Eligibility This program is open to undergraduate students in any field of study who are blind. Applicants must submit verification of legal blindness in both eyes; SAT or ACT scores; information on extracurricular activities (including involvement in the American Council of the Blind); employment record; and a 500-word autobiographical sketch that includes their personal goals, strengths, weaknesses, hobbies, honors, achievements, and reasons for choice of field or courses of study. A cumulative GPA of 3.3 or higher is generally required. Financial need is not considered in the selection process.

Financial data The stipend is at least $1,500.

Duration 1 year.

Additional data Scholarship winners are expected to be present at the council's annual conference; the council will cover all reasonable expenses connected with convention attendance.

Number awarded 1 each year.

Deadline February of each year.

[251]
ADRIENNE ASCH MEMORIAL SCHOLARSHIP

National Federation of the Blind
Attn: Scholarship Committee
200 East Wells Street
Baltimore, MD 21230
(410) 659-9314, ext. 2415   Fax: (410) 685-5653
E-mail: scholarships@nfb.org
Web: www.nfb.org/scholarships

Summary To provide financial assistance to entering or continuing undergraduate and graduate blind students.

Eligibility This program is open to legally blind students who are working on or planning to work full time on an undergraduate or graduate degree. Along with their application, they must submit transcripts, standardized test scores, proof of legal blindness, 2 letters of recommendation, and a letter of endorsement from their National Federation of the Blind state president or designee. Selection is based on academic excellence, service to the community, and financial need.

Financial data The stipend is $3,000.

Duration 1 year; recipients may resubmit applications up to 2 additional years.

Additional data Scholarships are awarded at the federation convention in July. Recipients must attend the convention at federation expense; that funding is in addition to the scholarship grant.

Number awarded 1 each year.

Deadline March of each year.

[252]
ALFRED CAMP MEMORIAL SCHOLARSHIP

Georgia Council of the Blind
c/o Debbie Williams, Scholarship Committee Chair
1477 Nebo Road
Dallas, GA 30157
(770) 595-1007
E-mail: williamsdebk@wmconnect.com
Web: www.georgiacounciloftheblind.org

Summary To provide financial assistance students in Georgia who plan to attend college or graduate school in any state and are either legally blind or have legally blind parents.

Eligibility This program is open to residents of Georgia who are either 1) legally blind students; or 2) sighted students financially dependent on legally blind parents. Applicants must be enrolled or accepted for enrollment at a vocational/technical school, a 2- or 4-year college, or a master's or doctoral program in any state. All fields of study are eligible. Selection is based on academic transcripts, 2 letters of recommendation, a 1-page typed statement of the applicant's educational goals, an audio cassette recording of the applicant reading the goals statement, extracurricular activities, and financial need.

Financial data Stipends up to $1,000 per year are available.

Duration 1 year; recipients may reapply.

Additional data This program began in 1988.

Number awarded 1 or more each year.

Deadline June of each year.

[253]
ALLEN-SPRINKLE MEMORIAL GIFT

National Federation of the Blind of West Virginia
c/o Mary Ann Saunders, Scholarship Committee Chair
101 Eighth Avenue, Apartment 511
Huntington, WV 25701
(304) 697-1434   E-mail: saunders@wvdsl.net
Web: www.nfbwv.org

Summary To provide financial assistance to legally blind residents of West Virginia who are interested in attending college or graduate school in any state.

Eligibility This program is open to legally blind residents of Virginia who are graduating high school seniors, undergraduates, or graduate students. Applicants must be enrolled or planning to enroll full time at an accredited college, university, postsecondary vocational institute, or graduate school in any state. Along with their application, they must submit 2 letters of recommendation, transcripts, verification of blindness, and a personal letter that includes the kinds of things that interest them, their goals and aspirations, and how this scholarship would help them. Selection is based on academic excellence, community service, and financial need.

Financial data The stipend is $1,000.

Duration 1 year.

Additional data The winner is expected to attend the annual convention of the National Federation of the Blind of West Virginia.

Number awarded 1 each year.

Deadline June of each year.

[254]
AMERICAN COUNCIL OF THE BLIND OF MINNESOTA SCHOLARSHIPS

American Council of the Blind of Minnesota
Attn: Scholarship Committee Chair
P.O. Box 19091
Minneapolis, MN 55419
(612) 824-2131   Toll Free: (866) YAY-ACBM
E-mail: juliettesilvers@gmail.com
Web: www.acb.org/minnesota/Scholarship.html

Summary To provide financial assistance to blind and visually-impaired residents of Minnesota who are interested in attending college or graduate school in any state.

Eligibility This program is open to residents of Minnesota who are blind or visually-impaired. Applicants may be either high school seniors entering their first year of postsecondary study or students in their second year or above of undergraduate or graduate study in any state. Along with their application, they must submit 2 essays of 500 words each on 1) a situation in which they solved a problem or broke down a blindness-related barrier in order to meet an academic requirement; and 2) a pair of instances in which they would or have advocated for their own needs or the needs of others. Selection is based on those essays, extracurricular activities, transcripts, and letters of recommendation.

Financial data The stipend is $1,000.

Duration 1 year.

Number awarded 2 each year: 1 to a high school senior entering college and 1 to a student already enrolled in a postsecondary educational program.

Deadline June of each year.

[255]
AMERICAN COUNCIL OF THE BLIND OF OREGON SCHOLARSHIPS

American Council of the Blind
Attn: Coordinator, Scholarship Program
6300 Shingle Creek Parkway, Suite 195
Brooklyn Center, MN 55430-2136
(612) 332-3242   Toll Free: (800) 424-8666
E-mail: deetheien@acbes.org
Web: www.acb.org/scholarship

Summary To provide financial assistance for college to blind students, especially those from Oregon.

Eligibility This program is open to legally blind students who are entering or attending college. Preference is given to residents of Oregon, but if no students from that state apply, residents of other states are considered. Applicants must submit verification of legal blindness in both eyes; SAT or ACT scores; information on extracurricular activities (including involvement in the American Council of the Blind); employment record; and a 500-word autobiographical sketch that includes their personal goals, strengths, weaknesses, hobbies, honors, achievements, and reasons for choice of field or courses of study. A cumulative GPA of 3.3 or higher is generally required. Financial need is not considered in the selection process.

Financial data The stipend is $2,500.

Duration 1 year.

Additional data Funding for this scholarship is provided by the American Council of the Blind of Oregon, formerly the Oregon Council of the Blind. Scholarship winners are expected to be present at the council's annual conference; the council will cover all reasonable expenses connected with convention attendance.

Number awarded 1 or 2 each year.

Deadline February of each year.

[256]
AMERICAN COUNCIL OF THE BLIND OF TEXAS SCHOLARSHIPS

American Council of the Blind of Texas
c/o Cynthia Julun, Scholarship Committee Chair
7390 Pindo Circle, Apartment 218
Beaumont, TX 77708
(409) 924-9803   E-mail: cjulun@sbcglobal.net
Web: www.acbtexas.org

Summary To provide financial assistance to blind and visually-impaired residents of Texas who are interested in attending college in any state.

Eligibility This program is open to residents of Texas who can document legal or total blindness. Applicants must be enrolled or planning to enroll at a college, university, or trade/vocational school in any state. They must have a GPA of 3.0 or higher. Along with their application, they must submit documentation of blindness, transcripts, a copy of their acceptance letter (if not yet attending college), letters of recommendation, and a 1- to 2-page autobiography, including information on their family, hobbies, activities, community service, and educational and career goals. Selection is based on career goals, academic achievement, and letters of recommendation.

Financial data Stipends range from $250 to $1,000 per year. Funds may be used for any educational purpose, including tuition, books, housing, and transportation.

Duration 1 year; recipients may reapply.

Additional data This program includes the Carolyn Garrett Scholarship, the Randy and Viola Greene Scholarship, and the Durward K. McDaniel Scholarship.

Number awarded Varies each year; recently, 3 were awarded.

Deadline July of each year.

[257]
ARIZONA COUNCIL OF THE BLIND SCHOLARSHIP PROGRAM

Arizona Council of the Blind
Attn: Scholarship Committee
16845 North 29th Avenue, Suite 139
Phoenix, AZ 85053
(602) 285-0269   E-mail: scholarship@azcb.org
Web: www.acb.org/arizona

Summary To provide financial assistance for undergraduate or graduate studies to legally blind Arizona residents.

Eligibility This program is limited to Arizona residents. Applicants must be legally blind and enrolled or planning to enroll in vocational, technical, graduate, or professional training programs beyond the high school level. Along with their application, they must submit a 2-page autobiographical sketch that includes their personal goals, strengths, weaknesses, hobbies, honors, achievements, proposed course of study, why they have chosen that, and how obtaining a scholarship would help their educational experience. Selection is based on that sketch, GPA, test scores (ACT, SAT, GRE, GMAT, LSAT, etc.), work experience, and extracurricular activities. Unless extenuating circumstances exist, a 3.25 GPA is required.

Financial data The stipend is $1,000.

Duration 1 year; recipients may reapply.

Number awarded 2 each year.

Deadline April of each year.

[258]
ARKANSAS COUNCIL OF THE BLIND SCHOLARSHIPS

Arkansas Council of the Blind
c/o Dewayne Hodges, President
710 Cones Road
Hot Springs, AR 71901
(501) 520-1382
Web: www.arkansasacb.org/Our-Purpose.html

Summary To provide financial assistance to blind residents of Arkansas who are interested in attending college in any state.

Eligibility This program is open to residents of Arkansas who are blind. Applicants must be attending or planning to attend a college or university in any state.

Financial data The stipend is $1,000.

Duration 1 year.

Number awarded Up to 3 each year.

Deadline March of each year.

[259]
ARNOLD SADLER MEMORIAL SCHOLARSHIP

American Council of the Blind
Attn: Coordinator, Scholarship Program
6300 Shingle Creek Parkway, Suite 195
Brooklyn Center, MN 55430-2136
(612) 332-3242   Toll Free: (800) 424-8666
E-mail: deetheien@acbes.org
Web: www.acb.org/scholarship

Summary To provide financial assistance to undergraduate or graduate students who are blind and are interested in studying in a field of service to persons with disabilities.

Eligibility This program is open to undergraduate and graduate students in rehabilitation, education, law, or other fields of service to persons with disabilities. Applicants must be legally blind in both eyes. Along with their application, they must submit verification of legal blindness in both eyes; SAT, ACT, GRE, or similar scores; information on extracurricular activities (including involvement in the American Council of the Blind); employment record; and a 500-word autobiographical sketch that includes their personal goals, strengths, weaknesses, hobbies, honors, achievements, and reasons for choice of field or courses of study. A cumulative GPA of 3.3 or higher is generally required. Financial need is not considered in the selection process.

Financial data The stipend is $1,500.

Duration 1 year.

Additional data This scholarship is funded by the Arnold Sadler Memorial Scholarship Fund. Scholarship winners are expected to be present at the council's annual conference; the council will cover all reasonable expenses connected with convention attendance.

Number awarded 1 each year.

Deadline February of each year.

[260]
ASHLEY K. FRITZ MEMORIAL "HUMANITARIAN" SCHOLARSHIP

The See the Future Fund
Attn: Thomas Theune, Founder and Chair
P.O. Box 63022
Colorado Springs, CO 80962-3022
(719) 471-3200   Fax: (719) 471-3210
E-mail: twtheune@comcast.net
Web: www.seethefuture.org

Summary To provide financial assistance to blind or visually-impaired residents of Colorado who demonstrate exceptional humanitarian abilities and are interested in attending college or graduate school in any state.

Eligibility This program is open to residents of Colorado who meet standards of blindness or visual impairment. Applicants must be enrolled full time at a postsecondary program in any state as 1) a freshman entering an academic program; 2) a sophomore, junior, or senior in an academic program; 3) a graduate student in an academic program; or 4) a student in a vocational/technical school or community college. This award is reserved for an applicant who demonstrates exceptional humanitarian and leadership abilities.

Financial data The stipend is $1,000. Funds are paid directly to the recipient's institution to be used for tuition, fees, books, room, and board.

Duration 1 year.

Number awarded 1 each year.

Deadline February of each year.

[261]
BAY STATE COUNCIL OF THE BLIND SCHOLARSHIP

American Council of the Blind
Attn: Coordinator, Scholarship Program
6300 Shingle Creek Parkway, Suite 195
Brooklyn Center, MN 55430-2136
(612) 332-3242   Toll Free: (800) 424-8666
E-mail: deetheien@acbes.org
Web: www.acb.org/scholarship

Summary To provide financial assistance for college to blind students from Massachusetts.

Eligibility This program is open to legally blind students who are residents of Massachusetts or attending college in the state. Applicants must submit verification of legal blindness in both eyes; SAT or ACT scores; information on extracurricular activities (including involvement in the American Council of the Blind); employment record; and a 500-word autobiographical sketch that includes their personal goals, strengths, weaknesses, hobbies, honors, achievements, and reasons for choice of field or courses of study. A cumulative GPA of 3.3 or higher is generally required. Financial need is not considered in the selection process.

Financial data The stipend is $1,000.

Duration 1 year.

Additional data This scholarship is sponsored by the Bay State Council of the Blind, an affiliate of the American Council of the Blind. Scholarship winners are expected to be present at the council's annual conference; the council will cover all reasonable expenses connected with convention attendance.

Number awarded 1 each year.

Deadline February of each year.

[262]
BETTY J. NICELEY MEMORIAL SCHOLARSHIP

National Federation of the Blind of Kentucky
c/o Lora Felty Stephens, Scholarship Committee Chair
1127 Sharon Court
Ashland, KY 41101
(606) 324-3394   E-mail: scholarships@nfbofky.org
Web: www.nfbofky.org/kscholar.php

Summary To provide financial assistance to blind students who use Braille and either reside or attend college in Kentucky.

Eligibility This program is open to students who are legally blind or visually-impaired and/or eligible for services from the Kentucky Office for the Blind. Applicants must be 1) residents of Kentucky enrolled or planning to

enroll full or part time at a college or university in any state; or 2) residents of other states attending or accepted at a college or university in Kentucky. They must be able to read Braille and demonstrate how they find it an essential part of their daily life. Along with their application, they must submit a 500-character description of their educational goals, and a 2,000-character explanation of how the scholarship will help them achieve their academic and career goals and how they would like to be involved in the National Federation of the Blind of Kentucky.

Financial data The stipend is $1,000.

Duration 1 year.

Additional data Finalists are required to attend and participate in the annual convention of the National Federation of the Blind of Kentucky; travel, hotel accommodations, registration fees, and banquet tickets are provided.

Number awarded 1 each year.

Deadline July of each year.

[263]
BEVERLY PROWS MEMORIAL SCHOLARSHIP

National Federation of the Blind of Washington
Attn: Scholarship Chair
P.O. Box 2516
Seattle, WA 98111
(425) 823-6380   E-mail: president@nfbw.org
Web: www.nfbw.org/scholarships.html

Summary To provide financial assistance for undergraduate or graduate study in any state to blind students in Washington.

Eligibility This program is open to legally blind residents of Washington state who are working on or planning to work on a full-time college or graduate degree at a school in any state. Applicants must submit a list of honors and awards they have received, information on their community service involvement, high school and/or college transcripts, and 3 letters of reference.

Financial data The stipend is $3,000.

Duration 1 year; recipients may reapply.

Additional data This program began in 1991. Winners must attend the state convention of the National Federation of the Blind of Washington to accept the award; convention expenses are covered.

Number awarded 1 each year.

Deadline August of each year.

[264]
BILL TOMLIN SCHOLARSHIP AWARD

Association for Education and Rehabilitation of the
  Blind and Visually Impaired-Arkansas Chapter
c/o Debbie Adams, Awards Committee Chair
4207 Park Avenue
Hot Springs, AR 71901
E-mail: debeadams@yahoo.com
Web: ar.aerbvi.org/awards.htm

Summary To provide financial assistance to blind and visually-impaired residents of Arkansas interested in attending college in any state.

Eligibility This program is open to residents of Arkansas who are blind or visually-impaired and enrolled or planning to enroll in a postsecondary educational or vocational training program in any state. Applicants must submit an autobiography of 1 to 2 pages that includes their personal goals, perceived strengths and needs, hobbies, honors, extracurricular activities, and achievements. Selection is based on that autobiography, 2 letters of recommendation, and transcripts.

Financial data The stipend is $1,000. Funds may be used for the purchase of textbooks, specialized materials, or adaptive equipment.

Duration 1 year.

Number awarded 1 or more each year.

Deadline April of each year.

[265]
BROTHER JAMES KEARNEY SCHOLARSHIP FOR THE BLIND

Lavelle Fund for the Blind, Inc.
Attn: Scholarship Program Coordinator
307 West 38th Street, Suite 1905
New York, NY 10018
(212) 668-9801   Fax: (212) 668-9803
E-mail: jdulitz@lavellefund.org
Web: www.lavellefund.org

Summary To provide financial assistance to blind residents of the New York tri-state region who are attending designated colleges in the New York City area.

Eligibility This program is open to residents of Connecticut, New Jersey, and New York who are legally blind or severely visually-impaired. Residents of Pennsylvania who attend either of the schools for the blind in Philadelphia (Overbrook School for the Blind or St. Lucy Day School for Children with Visual Impairments) are also eligible. Applicants must be working on or planning to work full time on an undergraduate or graduate degree at 1 of 11 designated colleges and universities in the New York City area. They must be able to demonstrate financial need.

Financial data Stipends provide for payment of tuition, fees, room, board, and books, to a maximum of $15,000.

Duration 1 year; may be renewed up to 3 additional years.

Additional data This program was formerly named the Lavelle Fund for the Blind Scholarships. The 11 participating institutions are Canisius College (Buffalo, New York), Dominican College (Orangeburg, New York), Fordham University (Bronx, New York), LeMoyne College (Syracuse, New York), Manhattanville College (Purchase, New York), Marist College (Poughkeepsie, New York), Marymount Manhattan College (New York, New York), Molloy College (Rockville Centre, New York), Seton Hall University (South Orange, New Jersey), St. John's University (Jamaica, New York), and St. Thomas Aquinas College (Sparkill, New York).

Number awarded Varies each year.

Deadline June of each year.

[266]
BYRD BRYANT SCHOLARSHIP PROGRAM

Alabama Council of the Blind
Attn: Scholarship Committee Chair
276 Inglenook Lane
Sylacauga, AL 35151
(256) 375-5667   E-mail: alabama.acb@gmail.com
Web: www.alacb.org/byrd-bryant-scholarship

Summary To provide financial assistance to blind residents of Alabama who are interested in attending college in any state.

Eligibility This program is open to residents of Alabama who are legally blind. Applicants must be enrolled or planning to enroll full time at a college, university, or technical school in any state. They must have a GPA of 3.0 or higher. Along with their application, they must submit a 500-word essay on their vocational objectives and the outlook for employment in their area of choice.

Financial data The stipend is $1,000.

Duration 1 year.

Number awarded 1 or more each year.

Deadline April of each year.

[267]
CALIFORNIA COUNCIL OF THE BLIND SCHOLARSHIPS

California Council of the Blind
Attn: Executive Office
1303 J Street, Suite 400
Sacramento, CA 95814-2900
(916) 441-2100   Toll Free: (800) 221-6359 (within CA)
Fax: (916) 441-2188   E-mail: ccotb@ccbnet.org
Web: www.ccbnet.org/scholar.htm

Summary To provide financial assistance for undergraduate or graduate study in any state to blind people in California.

Eligibility Applicants must be legally blind residents of California who are enrolled or planning to enroll full time at an accredited college or university at either the undergraduate or graduate level. The school may be in any state. Along with their application, they must submit a 200-word statement on their purpose in undertaking college work and their vocational goals. Selection is based on academic achievement and financial need.

Financial data The amount of the assistance depends on the availability of funds and the needs of the applicant.

Duration 1 year; may be renewed. For graduate students, support is limited to 2 years of work for a master's degree or 3 years for a Ph.D.

Number awarded Varies each year.

Deadline May of each year.

[268]
CARL J. MEGEL SPECIAL EDUCATION SCHOLARSHIP

Illinois Federation of Teachers
500 Oakmont Lane
P.O. Box 390
Westmont, IL 60559
(630) 468-4080   Fax: (630) 468-4089
Web: www.ift.org/your-benefits/scholarships

Summary To provide financial assistance to children of members of the Illinois Federation of Teachers (IFT) who have been enrolled in special education and are interested in attending college in any state.

Eligibility This program is open to graduating high school seniors who are children of currently-employed active members of the IFT or of deceased members who were in good standing at the time of their death. Applicants must be enrolled in a special education school, class, or program for students with autism, cognitive disability, deaf-blindness, deafness, emotional disability, hearing impairment, multiple disabilities, orthopedic impairment, other health impairment, specific learning disability, speech or language impairment, traumatic brain injury, or visual impairment. Along with their application, they must submit an essay describing how any obstacles and/or achievements that you have encountered in your life have helped shape your decision to complete a post-secondary education.

Financial data The stipend is $1,000.

Duration 1 year.

Number awarded 1 each year.

Deadline February of each year.

[269]
CHARLES AND BETTY ALLEN SCHOLARSHIP

National Federation of the Blind of Kentucky
c/o Lora Felty Stephens, Scholarship Committee Chair
1127 Sharon Court
Ashland, KY 41101
(606) 324-3394   E-mail: scholarships@nfbofky.org
Web: www.nfbofky.org/kscholar.php

Summary To provide financial assistance to blind students who are residents of Kentucky and interested in attending college in any state.

Eligibility This program is open to students who are legally blind or visually-impaired and/or eligible for services from the Kentucky Office for the Blind. Applicants must be residents of Kentucky enrolled or planning to enroll full time at a college or university in any state. They must have a GPA of 3.0 or higher and be recommended by a fellow member of the National Federation of the Blind (NFB) of Kentucky. Along with their application, they must submit a 500-character description of their educational goals, and a 2,000-character explanation of how the scholarship will help them achieve their academic and career goals and how they would like to be involved in the NFB of Kentucky. Preference is given to totally blind students.

Financial data The stipend is $1,000.

Duration 1 year.

Additional data Finalists are required to attend and participate in the annual convention of the National Federation of the Blind of Kentucky; travel, hotel accommodations, registration fees, and banquet tickets are provided.

Number awarded 1 each year.

Deadline July of each year.

[270]
CHARLES AND MELVA T. OWEN MEMORIAL SCHOLARSHIPS

National Federation of the Blind
Attn: Scholarship Committee
200 East Wells Street
Baltimore, MD 21230
(410) 659-9314, ext. 2415   Fax: (410) 685-5653
E-mail: scholarships@nfb.org
Web: www.nfb.org/scholarships

Summary To provide financial assistance to entering or continuing undergraduate or graduate students who are blind.

Eligibility This program is open to legally blind students who are working on or planning to work full time on an undergraduate or graduate degree. Scholarships, however, are not awarded for the study of religion or solely to further general or cultural education; the academic program should be directed towards attaining financial independence. Along with their application, they must submit transcripts, standardized test scores, proof of legal blindness, 2 letters of recommendation, and a letter of endorsement from their National Federation of the Blind state president or designee. Selection is based on academic excellence, service to the community, and financial need.

Financial data Stipends are $10,000, $5,000, or $3,000.

Duration 1 year; recipients may resubmit applications up to 2 additional years.

Additional data Scholarships are awarded at the federation convention in July. Recipients must attend the convention at federation expense; that funding is in addition to the scholarship grant.

Number awarded 2 each year: 1 at $10,000 and 1 at $3,000.

Deadline March of each year.

[271]
CHICAGO LIGHTHOUSE SCHOLARSHIPS

Chicago Lighthouse for People Who Are Blind or Visually Impaired
Attn: Scholarship Coordinator
1850 West Roosevelt Road
Chicago, IL 60608-1298
(312) 666-1331, ext. 3655   Fax: (312) 243-8539
TDD: (312) 666-8874
E-mail: maureen.reid@chicagolighthouse.org
Web: www.chicagolighthouse.org

Summary To provide financial assistance to blind or visually-impaired college and graduate students from Illinois.

Eligibility This program is open to undergraduate and graduate students who are legally blind, totally blind, visually-impaired, or multi-disabled and either residents of Illinois or attending college in that state. Undergraduate and graduate students must have a GPA of 3.0 or higher; vocational students must have a GPA of 2.5 or higher. Applicants must submit essays of 1 to 2 pages about 1) their economic need and how they plan to use the scholarship if they receive it; and 2) their visual impairment, their background, their educational and career goals, and how this scholarship will help achieve those goals. Selection is based on academic achievement, career goal, extracurricular activities, character, and personal and family financial need.

Financial data Stipends range from $1,000 to $5,000; funds may be used for tuition, technology (such as computers and software), readers, books and classroom materials, housing, transportation, or other approved educational items.

Duration 1 year; may be renewed up to 3 additional years.

Additional data This program began in 2004.

Number awarded Varies each year; recently, 38 of these scholarships, with a value of more than $76,000, were awarded.

Deadline March of each year.

[272]
DALE M. SCHOETTLER SCHOLARSHIP FOR VISUALLY IMPAIRED STUDENTS

California State University
CSU Foundation
Attn: Director, Foundation Programs and Services
401 Golden Shore, Sixth Floor
Long Beach, CA 90802-4210
(562) 951-4509   E-mail: amoore@calstate.edu
Web: www.calstate.edu/Foundation/Scholarship.shtml

Summary To provide financial assistance to undergraduate and graduate students with visual impairments at campuses of the California State University (CSU) system.

Eligibility This program is open to full-time undergraduate and graduate students enrolled at CSU campuses who have been declared visually-impaired or legally blind. Applicants must have a cumulative GPA of 2.8 or higher.

Financial data The stipend is $6,500.

Duration 1 year.

Number awarded 42 each year.

Deadline May of each year.

[273]
DAVID NEWMEYER SCHOLARSHIP

American Council of the Blind of Ohio
Attn: Scholarship Committee
3805 North High Street, Suite 305
Columbus, OH 43214
(614) 221-6688 Toll Free: (800) 835-2226 (within OH)
E-mail: acbo.scholarships@gmail.com
Web: www.acbohio.org

Summary To provide financial assistance to entering or continuing Ohio undergraduate students who are blind.

Eligibility This program is open to 1) residents of Ohio who are high school seniors or current college students; and 2) students at colleges and universities in Ohio. Applicants must be legally blind and working on or planning to work on an undergraduate degree in any field. Along with their application, they must submit transcripts (must have a GPA of 3.0 or higher), a certificate of legal blindness, and an essay of 250 to 500 words on their career objectives, future plans, personal goals, other academic or personal qualities, and why they believe they are qualified to receive this scholarship. Financial need is not the sole factor considered in the selection process.

Financial data The stipend is $2,000 per year.

Duration 1 year; recipients may reapply.

Additional data Winners are required to attend the Saturday workshops at the sponsor's annual convention; a stipend for meals and workshops is provided.

Number awarded 1 each year.

Deadline July of each year.

[274]
DELTA GAMMA FOUNDATION FLORENCE MARGARET HARVEY MEMORIAL SCHOLARSHIP

American Foundation for the Blind
Attn: Scholarship Coordinator
1108 Third Avenue, Suite 200
Huntington, WV 25701
(304) 710-3034   Toll Free: (800) AFB-LINE
Fax: (646) 478-9260   E-mail: apreece@afb.net
Web: www.afb.org/scholarships.asp

Summary To provide financial assistance to blind undergraduate and graduate students who wish to study in the field of rehabilitation and/or education of the blind.

Eligibility This program is open to legally blind juniors, seniors, or graduate students. U.S. citizenship is required. Applicants must be studying in the field of rehabilitation and/or education of visually-impaired and blind persons. Along with their application, they must submit 200-word essays on 1) their past and recent achievements and accomplishments; 2) their intended field of study and why they have chosen it; and 3) the role their visual impairment has played in shaping their life. Financial need is considered in the selection process.

Financial data The stipend is $1,000.

Duration 1 year.

Additional data This scholarship is supported by the Delta Gamma Foundation and administered by the American Foundation for the Blind.

Number awarded 1 each year.

Deadline April of each year.

[275]
DUANE BUCKLEY MEMORIAL SCHOLARSHIP

American Council of the Blind
Attn: Coordinator, Scholarship Program
6300 Shingle Creek Parkway, Suite 195
Brooklyn Center, MN 55430-2136
(612) 332-3242   Toll Free: (800) 424-8666
E-mail: deetheien@acbes.org
Web: www.acb.org/scholarship

Summary To provide financial assistance for college to blind high school seniors who have overcome challenges.

Eligibility This program is open to graduating high school seniors who are legally blind in both eyes and have overcome extraordinary challenges. Applicants must submit verification of legal blindness in both eyes; SAT or ACT scores; information on extracurricular activities (including involvement in the American Council of the Blind); employment record; and a 500-word autobiographical sketch that includes their personal goals, strengths, weaknesses, hobbies, honors, achievements, and reasons for choice of field or courses of study. A cumulative GPA of 3.3 or higher is generally required. Financial need is not considered in the selection process.

Financial data The stipend is $1,000.

Duration 1 year.

Additional data The scholarship winner is expected to be present at the council's annual national convention; the council will cover all reasonable costs connected with convention attendance.

Number awarded 1 each year.

Deadline February of each year.

[276]
ECCLESTON-CALLAHAN SCHOLARSHIPS

Central Florida Foundation
Attn: Eccleston-Callahan Memorial Fund
800 North Magnolia Avenue, Suite 1200
Orlando, FL 32803
(407) 872-3050   Fax: (407) 425-2990
E-mail: info@cffound.org
Web: www.cffound.org/receive/scholarships

Summary To provide financial assistance to students with disabilities enrolled at specified Florida colleges and universities.

Eligibility This program is open to students at designated colleges and universities in Florida who have a physical disability (blindness, mobility impairment, or deafness). Applicants must be enrolled full time, have a GPA of 3.0 or higher, be younger than 21 years of age, and be able to demonstrate financial need.

Financial data The stipend is $1,000 per year.

Duration 1 year; may be renewed.

Additional data The participating institutions are the University of Florida, the University of Central Florida, Florida A&M University, Florida State University, Valencia Community College, Seminole Community College, and Orlando Tech.

Number awarded Varies each year.

Deadline June of each year.

[277]
EMERSON FOULKE MEMORIAL SCHOLARSHIP

National Federation of the Blind of Kentucky
c/o Lora Felty Stephens, Scholarship Committee Chair
1127 Sharon Court
Ashland, KY 41101
(606) 324-3394   E-mail: scholarships@nfbofky.org
Web: www.nfbofky.org/kscholar.php

Summary To provide financial assistance for college to blind students from Kentucky who are majoring in fields related to aspects of perception.

Eligibility This program is open to students who are legally blind or visually-impaired and/or eligible for services from the Kentucky Office for the Blind. Applicants must be 1) residents of Kentucky enrolled or planning to enroll full or part time at a college or university in any state; or 2) residents of other states attending or accepted at a college or university in Kentucky. They must be interested in working on a degree in psychology, science, research, technology, or general education. Along with their application, they must submit a 500-character description of their educational goals, and a 2,000-character explanation of how the scholarship will help them achieve their academic and career goals and how they would like to be involved in the National Federation of the Blind of Kentucky.

Financial data The stipend is $1,000.

Duration 1 year.

Additional data Finalists are required to attend and participate in the annual convention of the National Federation of the Blind of Kentucky; travel, hotel accommodations, registration fees, and banquet tickets are provided.

Number awarded 1 each year.

Deadline July of each year.

[278]
EMIL A. HONKA SCHOLARSHIPS

Montana Association for the Blind
7 West Sixth Street, Suite E
P.O. Box 465
Helena, MT 59624
(406) 442-9411   Fax: (406) 442-1612
E-mail: lglueckert@milp.us
Web: www.mtblind.org/programs.htm

Summary To provide financial assistance to blind residents of Montana who are attending college or graduate school in any state.

Eligibility This program is open to residents of Montana who are blind or have a prognosis of serious vision loss and are working on an undergraduate or graduate degree in any field at a college or university in any state. Preference is given to applicants who have completed 12 or more college credits and have a GPA of 2.5 or higher. Selection is based primarily on financial need.

Financial data The stipend is $1,000 per year.

Duration 1 year; recipients may reapply.

Additional data Recipients must attend the annual convention of the sponsoring organization to accept their award; expenses to attend the convention are reimbursed.

Number awarded Up to 2 each year.

Deadline March of each year.

[279]
EMMA SKOGEN SCHOLARSHIP

North Dakota Association of the Blind
c/o Tracy Wicken, Scholarship Committee Chair
733 Dawn Circle
Grand Forks, ND 58203
(701) 772-7669   E-mail: trwicken@nd.gov
Web: www.ndab.org

Summary To provide financial assistance for vocational school to blind students in North Dakota.

Eligibility This program is open to North Dakota residents who are blind or visually-impaired and attending a vocational or trade school. Applicants must provide information on what they plan to study, where, and when; their long-term career goals; and their financial need. Selection is based on clarity of study plan, long-term career goals, GPA, letter of recommendation, extracurricular involvements, and financial need.

Financial data The stipend is $1,000.

Duration 1 year.

Additional data This program began in 2004.

Number awarded 1 each year.

Deadline March of each year.

[280]
ESTHER V. TAYLOR SCHOLARSHIPS

Kansas Association for the Blind and Visually Impaired
712 South Kansas Avenue, Suite 410
Topeka, KS 66603
(785) 235-8990   Toll Free: (800) 799-1499 (within KS)
Fax: (785) 233-2539   E-mail: kabvi@att.net
Web: www.kabvi.com/Scholarship%20Form.html

Summary To provide financial assistance to residents of Kansas who are blind or visually-impaired and interested in attending college in any state.

Eligibility This program is open to blind and visually-impaired residents of Kansas who are attending or planning to attend a college, university, or technical school in any state. Applicants must submit an autobiographical sketch that includes their goals, strengths, weaknesses, hobbies, honors, extracurricular activities, and achievements. Financial need is considered in the selection process.

Financial data The stipend is $1,000.

Duration 1 year.

Number awarded 2 each year.

Deadline April of each year.

[281]
E.U. AND GENE PARKER SCHOLARSHIP

National Federation of the Blind
Attn: Scholarship Committee
200 East Wells Street
Baltimore, MD 21230
(410) 659-9314, ext. 2415   Fax: (410) 685-5653
E-mail: scholarships@nfb.org
Web: www.nfb.org/scholarships

Summary To provide financial assistance to entering or continuing undergraduate and graduate blind students who have supported the work of the National Federation of the Blind (NFB).

Eligibility This program is open to legally blind students who are working on or planning to work full time on an undergraduate or graduate degree. Applicants must be able to demonstrate strong support for the NFB's work. Along with their application, they must submit transcripts, standardized test scores, proof of legal blindness, 2 letters of recommendation, and a letter of endorsement from their NFB state president or designee. Selection is based on academic excellence, service to the community, and financial need.

Financial data The stipend is $3,000.

Duration 1 year; recipients may resubmit applications up to 2 additional years.

Additional data Scholarships are awarded at the federation convention in July. Recipients must attend the convention at federation expense; that funding is in addition to the scholarship grant.

Number awarded 1 each year.

Deadline March of each year.

[282]
EUNICE FIORITO MEMORIAL SCHOLARSHIP

American Council of the Blind
Attn: Coordinator, Scholarship Program
6300 Shingle Creek Parkway, Suite 195
Brooklyn Center, MN 55430-2136
(612) 332-3242   Toll Free: (800) 424-8666
E-mail: deetheien@acbes.org
Web: www.acb.org/scholarship

Summary To provide financial assistance to undergraduate or graduate students who are blind and are interested in studying in a field of advocacy or service for persons with disabilities.

Eligibility This program is open to undergraduate and graduate students in rehabilitation, education, law, or other fields of service or advocacy for persons with disabilities. Applicants must be legally blind in both eyes. Along with their application, they must submit verification of legal blindness in both eyes; SAT, ACT, GRE, or similar scores; information on extracurricular activities (including involvement in the American Council of the Blind); employment record; and a 500-word autobiographical sketch that includes their personal goals, strengths, weaknesses, hobbies, honors, achievements, and reasons for choice of field or courses of study. A cumulative GPA of 3.3 or higher is generally required. Financial need is not considered in the selection process. Preference is given to students with little or no vision.

Financial data The stipend is $2,000.

Duration 1 year.

Additional data The scholarship winner is expected to be present at the council's annual national convention; the council will cover all reasonable costs connected with convention attendance.

Number awarded 1 each year.

Deadline February of each year.

[283]
FLORIDA COUNCIL OF CITIZENS WITH LOW VISION SCHOLARSHIP

Florida Council of Citizens with Low Vision
c/o Leslie Spoone
3924 Lake Mirage Boulevard
Orlando, FL 32817
(407) 678-4163   E-mail: lesliespoone@cfl.rr.com

Summary To provide financial assistance to residents of Florida who have low vision and are interested in attending college in any state.

Eligibility This program is open to Florida residents who are enrolled or accepted for enrollment at a college, university, or trade school in any state. Applicants must be legally blind; preference is given to students with low vision. They must have a GPA of 3.0 or higher and be working to increase advancement potential in their chosen field. Selection is based on academic excellence, a narrative statement on their vocational objectives and outlook for employment in their chosen field, work experience, extracurricular activities, and 2 letters of recommendation.

Financial data The stipend is $1,000.

Duration 1 year.

Number awarded 1 each year.

Deadline March of each year.

[284]
FLOYD CALLWARD MEMORIAL SCHOLARSHIP

National Federation of the Blind of New Hampshire
c/o Andrew Harmon, Scholarship Chair
5 Central Square, Apartment 609
Keene, NH 03431
(603) 992-4053   E-mail: nfbnh.scholars@gmail.com

Summary To provide financial assistance to blind students in New Hampshire who are interested in working on an undergraduate or graduate degree at a school in any state.

Eligibility This program is open to legally blind and totally blind residents of New Hampshire who are attending or planning to attend college or graduate school in any state. Applicants may be attending college immediately after high school, returning to college at a later age, attending graduate or professional school, or enrolled in postsecondary vocational training. Blind non-residents who are attending school in New Hampshire are also eligible. Along with their application, they must submit 1) a brief essay about themselves, including their activities, interests, hobbies, personal goals, what they have done to deal with situations involving their blindness, and how the scholarship will help them; 2) 2 letters of recommendation; 3) high school and/or college transcripts; and 4) proof of legal blindness. Financial need is not considered.

Financial data The stipend is $1,000. The funds may be used to purchase education-related equipment or services or to defray the costs of tuition, board, and other school fees.

Duration 1 year.

Additional data This program began in 1990.

Number awarded 1 or more each year.

Deadline January of each year.

[285]
FLOYD QUALLS MEMORIAL SCHOLARSHIPS

American Council of the Blind
Attn: Coordinator, Scholarship Program
6300 Shingle Creek Parkway, Suite 195
Brooklyn Center, MN 55430-2136
(612) 332-3242   Toll Free: (800) 424-8666
E-mail: deetheien@acbes.org
Web: www.acb.org/scholarship

Summary To provide financial assistance to entering and continuing undergraduate and graduate students who are blind.

Eligibility This program is open to legally blind students in 4 categories: entering freshmen in academic programs, undergraduates (sophomores, juniors, and seniors) in academic programs, graduate students in academic programs, and vocational school students or students working on an associate's degree from a community college. Applicants must submit verification of legal blindness in both eyes; SAT, ACT, GRE, or similar scores; information on extracurricular activities (including involvement in the American Council of the Blind); employment record; and a 500-word autobiographical sketch that includes their personal goals, strengths, weaknesses, hobbies, honors, achievements, and reasons for choice of field or courses of study. A cumulative GPA of 3.3 or higher is generally required. Financial need is not considered in the selection process.

Financial data The stipend is $2,500.

Duration 1 year.

Additional data Scholarship winners are expected to be present at the council's annual conference; the council will cover all reasonable expenses connected with convention attendance.

Number awarded At least 4 each year: 1 in each of the 4 categories.

Deadline February of each year.

[286]
FLOYD R. CARGILL SCHOLARSHIP

Illinois Council of the Blind
Attn: Office Manager
522 East Monroe, Suite 200
P.O. Box 1336
Springfield, IL 62705-1336
(217) 523-4967   Fax: (217) 523-4302
E-mail: icb@icbonline.org
Web: www.icbonline.org/scholarship-application

Summary To provide financial assistance to blind and visually-impaired residents of Illinois who are interested in attending college in any state.

Eligibility This program is open to graduating high school seniors and full-time undergraduate or graduate students at colleges and universities in any state who are blind or visually-impaired residents of Illinois. Applicants must be U.S. citizens and have a GPA of 3.5 or higher. Along with their application, they must submit a 2-page autobiographical sketch that includes their personal goals, strengths, weaknesses, hobbies, honors, and achievements.

Financial data The stipend is $1,000.

Duration 1 year.

Number awarded 1 or more each year.

Deadline July of each year.

[287]
FRED SCHEIGERT SCHOLARSHIPS

Council of Citizens with Low Vision International
c/o American Council of the Blind
2200 Wilson Boulevard, Suite 650
Arlington, VA 22201
(202) 467-5081   Toll Free: (800) 733-2258
Fax: (703) 465-5085   E-mail: scholarship@cclvi.org
Web: www.cclvi.org/Scholarship/scholarship.html

Summary To provide financial assistance to entering and continuing undergraduate and graduate students with low vision.

Eligibility This program is open to full-time undergraduate and graduate students who have been certified by an ophthalmologist as having low vision. Applicants may be entering freshmen, undergraduates, or graduate students. They must have a GPA of 3.2 or higher and a record of involvement in their school and/or local community. Along with their application, they must submit 200-word essays on 1) what influenced their interest in their identified academic/vocational discipline; 2) their work experience and extracurricular activities; 3) any honors, awards, or citations received; and 4) how they plan to use the scholarship monies.

Financial data The stipend is $3,000.

Duration 1 year.

Number awarded 3 each year: 1 each to an entering freshman, undergraduate, and graduate student.

Deadline July of each year.

[288]
FRIENDS IN ART SCHOLARSHIP

Friends in Art
c/o Harvey Miller
196 East French Broad Street
Brevard, NC 28712-3410
E-mail: hhmiller@citcom.net
Web: www.friendsinart.com/scholarship.htm

Summary To provide financial assistance to blind students who are majoring or planning to major in fields related to the arts.

Eligibility This program is open to blind and visually-impaired high school seniors and college students who are majoring or planning to major in music, art, drama, or creative writing. Music students must submit a tape with their performance of a fast piece and a slow piece; art students must submit 10 slides of their work; drama students must submit a tape with a dramatic presentation and a comic presentation; creative writing students must submit examples of their work. Selection is based on achievement, talent, and excellence in the arts.

Financial data The stipend is $1,500.

Duration 1 year.

Additional data This program began in 1999.

Number awarded 1 each year.

Deadline April of each year.

[289]
FRIENDS OF FRESHMAN SCHOLARSHIP

American Council of the Blind of Ohio
Attn: Scholarship Committee
3805 North High Street, Suite 305
Columbus, OH 43214
(614) 221-6688   Toll Free: (800) 835-2226 (within OH)
E-mail: acbo.scholarships@gmail.com
Web: www.acbohio.org

Summary To provide financial assistance to entering college freshmen from Ohio who are blind.

Eligibility This program is open to residents of Ohio who are entering freshmen at colleges and universities in any state. Applicants must be legally blind and planning to work on an undergraduate degree in any field. Along with their application, they must submit transcripts (must have a GPA of 3.0 or higher), a certificate of legal blindness, and an essay of 250 to 500 words on their career objectives, future plans, personal goals, other academic or personal qualities, and why they believe they are qualified to receive this scholarship. Financial need is not the sole factor considered in the selection process.

Financial data The stipend is $1,000.

Duration 1 year.

Additional data Winners are required to attend the Saturday workshops at the sponsor's annual convention; a stipend for meals and workshops is provided.

Number awarded 1 each year.

Deadline July of each year.

[290]
GAYLE M. KRAUSE-EDWARDS SCHOLARSHIP

Florida Council of the Blind
c/o Sheila Young, Education and Leadership
 Committee Chair
2304 Amherst Avenue
Orlando, FL 32804
(407) 425-9200   E-mail: sheilayoung125@att.net
Web: www.fcb.org/node/871

Summary To provide financial assistance to blind residents of Florida who are attending college in any state and can demonstrate outstanding academic and leadership achievements.

Eligibility This program is open to blind residents of Florida who have completed at least 1 semester at a college or university in any state. Applicants must have a GPA of 3.2 or higher and be able to demonstrate outstanding academic and leadership achievements. They must be enrolled full time. Along with their application, they must submit a narrative statement on their vocational objectives and outlook for employment in their chosen field. Financial need is not considered in the selection process.

Financial data The stipend is $1,500.

Duration 1 year.

Number awarded 1 each year.

Deadline March of each year.

[291]
HANK HOFSTETTER OPPORTUNITY GRANTS

American Council of the Blind of Indiana
c/o James R. Durst
Indiana School for the Blind and Visually Impaired
7725 North College Avenue
Indianapolis, IN 46240
Web: www.acb-indiana.org/3/miscellaneous8.htm

Summary To provide financial assistance to Indiana residents who are blind and need materials or equipment to continue their education or meet other goals.

Eligibility This fund is open to certified legally blind Indiana residents who are unable to obtain funding through other means. Applicants must need funding for an activity, materials, and/or equipment that will enhance their educational, entrepreneurial, or vocational aims. Along with their application, they must submit a 1-page statement on why they should be considered for a grant, a list of other options or sources that have already been tried, and a reference letter.

Financial data The amount awarded varies, depending upon the needs of the recipient. A total of $1,000 is available annually.

Duration These are 1-time grants.

Number awarded 1 each year.

Deadline Requests may be submitted at any time but should be received at least 90 days prior to the need.

[292]
HARRY LUDWIG MEMORIAL SCHOLARSHIP

Oregon Office of Student Access and Completion
Attn: Scholarship Processing Coordinator
1500 Valley River Drive, Suite 100
Eugene, OR 97401-2146
(541) 687-7422   Toll Free: (800) 452-8807, ext. 7422
Fax: (541) 687-7414   TDD: (800) 735-2900
E-mail: cheryl.a.connolly@state.or.us
Web: app.oregonstudentaid.gov/Catalog/Default.aspx

Summary To provide financial assistance to residents of Oregon who are visually-impaired and are interested in attending college or graduate school in the state.

Eligibility This program is open to residents of Oregon who are visually-impaired (have residual acuity of 20/70 or less in the better eye with correction, or their visual field is restricted to 20 degrees or less in the better eye). Applicants must be enrolled or planning to enroll as full-time undergraduate or graduate students at a college or university in Oregon.

Financial data Stipends for scholarships offered by the Oregon Office of Student Access and Completion (OSAC) range from $1,000 to $10,000 but recently averaged $4,368.

Duration 1 year.

Additional data This program is administered by the OSAC with funds provided by the Oregon Community Foundation.

Number awarded Varies each year; recently, 7 were awarded.

Deadline February of each year.

[293]
HAWAII ASSOCIATION OF THE BLIND SCHOLARSHIP

Hawaii Association of the Blind
Attn: Scholarship Committee
225 Liliuokalani Avenue, Number 5D
Honolulu, HI 96815
(808) 521-1402   E-mail: sixsense@gmail.com
Web: www.acb.org/hawaii/scholarship.htm

Summary To provide financial assistance to blind residents of Hawaii who plan to attend college in any state.

Eligibility This program is open to Hawaii residents who meet the legal definition of blindness or visual impairment. Applicants must be members of the American Council of the Blind but may not be members of any other national organization for the blind. They must submit high school and/or college transcripts, 2 letters of reference, and a 2-page letter describing their educational goals.

Financial data Stipends are at least $500 per semester ($1,000 per year).

Duration 1 year.

Number awarded 1 or more each year.

Deadline May of each year for fall semester; November of each year for spring semester.

[294]
HAZEL TEN BROEK MEMORIAL SCHOLARSHIP

National Federation of the Blind of Washington
Attn: Scholarship Chair
P.O. Box 2516
Seattle, WA 98111
(425) 823-6380   E-mail: president@nfbw.org
Web: www.nfbw.org/scholarships.html

Summary To provide financial assistance for undergraduate or graduate study in any state to blind students in Washington.

Eligibility This program is open to legally blind residents of Washington state who are working on or planning to work on a full-time college or graduate degree at a school in any state. Applicants must submit a list of honors and awards they have received, information on their community service involvement, high school and/or college transcripts, and 3 letters of reference.

Financial data The stipend is $2,000.

Duration 1 year.

Additional data This program began in 1996. Winners must attend the state convention of the National Federation of the Blind of Washington to accept the award; convention expenses are covered.

Number awarded 1 each year.

Deadline August of each year.

[295]
JAMES DOYLE CASE MEMORIAL SCHOLARSHIPS

Mississippi Council of the Blind
c/o Randy Thompson, Scholarship Committee
107 Chalet Strasse
Brandon, MS 39042-2082
(601) 956-7906   E-mail: bonnieg06@comcast.net
Web: www.mscouncioftheblind.org/node/3

Summary To provide financial assistance to legally blind residents of Mississippi and their children who plan to attend college or graduate school in any state.

Eligibility This program is open to residents of Mississippi who are legally blind or the children of at least 1 legally blind parent. Applicants must be enrolled full time or accepted for enrollment in an undergraduate, graduate, or vocational/technical program in any state and have a GPA of 3.0 or higher. Along with their application, they must submit a 2-page autobiographical sketch, transcripts, standardized test scores (ACT or SAT for undergraduates; GRE, MCAT, LSAT, etc. for graduate students), 2 letters of recommendation, proof of acceptance from a postsecondary school, and verification of blindness of the qualifying person (applicant or parent).

Financial data The stipend is $1,500 per year.

Duration 4 years.

Number awarded 2 each year.

Deadline February of each year.

[296]
JAMES F. NELSON, JR. SCHOLARSHIPS

National Federation of the Blind of Virginia
c/o Sarah Patnaude, Scholarship Committee Chair
13905 Turtle Hill Road
Midlothian, VA 23112-4103
(804) 591-6153   E-mail: patnaude.sarah@yahoo.com
Web: www.nfbv.org/category/students

Summary To provide financial assistance for college to blind students from Virginia.

Eligibility This program is open to legally blind students who are either residents of Virginia or enrolled full time at a college or university in the state. Applicants may be graduating high school seniors or current college students. Along with their application, they must submit 250-word essays on 1) their most notable quality; 2) their attitude about blindness; 3) how they have demonstrated leadership ability; 4) what the selection committee needs to know about them; and 5) the 2 questions they most want to ask the scholarship committee and why. Selection is based on academic excellence, community service, and leadership potential.

Financial data The stipend is $1,500.

Duration 1 year.

Number awarded Up to 3 each year.

Deadline September of each year.

[297]
JAMES R. OLSEN MEMORIAL SCHOLARSHIP

American Council of the Blind
Attn: Coordinator, Scholarship Program
6300 Shingle Creek Parkway, Suite 195
Brooklyn Center, MN 55430-2136
(612) 332-3242   Toll Free: (800) 424-8666
E-mail: deetheien@acbes.org
Web: www.acb.org/scholarship

Summary To provide financial assistance to outstanding blind college students.

Eligibility This program is open to legally blind students enrolling or continuing in an undergraduate program. Applicants must submit verification of legal blindness in both eyes; SAT or ACT scores; information on extracurricular activities (including involvement in the American Council of the Blind); employment record; and a 500-word autobiographical sketch that includes their personal goals, strengths, weaknesses, hobbies, honors, achievements, and reasons for choice of field or courses of study. A cumulative GPA of 3.3 or higher is generally required. Financial need is not considered in the selection process.

Financial data The stipend is $2,500.

Duration 1 year.

Additional data The scholarship winner is expected to be present at the council's annual national convention; the council will cover all reasonable costs connected with convention attendance.

Number awarded 1 each year.

Deadline February of each year.

[298]
JENNICA FERGUSON MEMORIAL SCHOLARSHIP OF OHIO

National Federation of the Blind of Ohio
c/o Deborah Kendrick, Scholarship Committee Chair
2514 Hackberry Street
Cincinnati, OH 45206
(513) 673-4474   E-mail: dkkendrick@earthlink.net
Web: www.nfbohio.org/new

Summary To provide financial assistance to blind residents of Ohio who are interested in working on an undergraduate or graduate degree at a school in any state.

Eligibility This program is open to residents of Ohio who are legally blind. Applicants must be attending or planning to attend an accredited institution of higher education in any state as a full-time undergraduate or graduate student. Along with their application, they must submit 2 letters of recommendation, current transcripts, a letter about themselves that includes how they have dealt with their blindness and their hopes and dreams, and a letter from an officer of the National Federation of the Blind of Ohio indicating that they have discussed their scholarship application with that officer. Selection is based on academic excellence, community service, and financial need.

Financial data The stipend is $1,500.

Duration 1 year.

Number awarded 1 each year.

Deadline May of each year.

[299]
JOHN HEBNER MEMORIAL SCHOLARSHIP

American Council of the Blind
Attn: Coordinator, Scholarship Program
6300 Shingle Creek Parkway, Suite 195
Brooklyn Center, MN 55430-2136
(612) 332-3242   Toll Free: (800) 424-8666
E-mail: deetheien@acbes.org
Web: www.acb.org/scholarship

Summary To provide financial assistance for college to blind or visually-impaired students who are also employed full time.

Eligibility This program is open to blind or visually-impaired students who are employed full time. Applicants must submit verification of legal blindness in both eyes; SAT or ACT scores; information on extracurricular activities (including involvement in the American Council of the Blind); employment record; and a 500-word autobiographical sketch that includes their personal goals, strengths, weaknesses, hobbies, honors, achievements, and reasons for choice of field or courses of study. A cumulative GPA of 3.3 or higher is generally required. Financial need is not considered in the selection process.

Financial data The stipend is at least $1,000.

Duration 1 year.

Number awarded 1 each year.

Deadline February of each year.

[300]
JOHN T. MCCRAW SCHOLARSHIPS

National Federation of the Blind of Maryland
c/o Scholarship Committee Chair
30 Haddington Road
Lutherville, MD 21093
E-mail: Jesse.hartle63@gmail.com
Web: www.nfbmd.org/scholarship

Summary To provide financial assistance for college to blind students from Maryland.

Eligibility This program is open to legally blind students who are residents of Maryland or enrolled full time at a university, 2- or 4-year college, or vocational/technical school in the state. Applicants must be able to demonstrate academic achievement and community involvement. Along with their application, they must submit 2 letters of recommendation, a current transcript, and a statement that describes the honors they have received, what they have done to deal with situations involving their blindness, what they are like as a person, their goals and aspirations, and how this scholarship will help them.

Financial data The stipend is either $2,000 or $1,500.

Duration 1 year; recipients may reapply.

Additional data A special scholarship may be awarded to former McCraw Scholarship recipients. To apply for this special scholarship, former recipients must still meet all of the requirements for the scholarship program and submit a new application. Recipients must attend the sponsor's annual convention; financial assistance to attend the convention may be provided if the recipient needs and requests it (this is in addition to the scholarship grant).

Number awarded 2 each year: 1 at $2,000 and 1 at $1,500.

Deadline April of each year.

[301]
JOSEPH ROEDER SCHOLARSHIP

National Industries for the Blind
Attn: Learning and Development Manager
1310 Braddock Place
Alexandria, VA 22314-1691
(703) 310-0500   Fax: (703) 310-0494
E-mail: kgallagher@nib.org
Web: www.nib.org/resources/grants-and-scholarships

Summary To provide financial assistance to blind undergraduate and graduate students who working on a degree in a business-related field.

Eligibility This program is open to students who are blind and enrolled in college or graduate school. Applicants must be working on a degree in a field related to business. Along with their application, they must submit an essay of 200 to 500 words on their career history and future career goals.

Financial data The stipend is $2,500.

Duration 1 year.

Additional data This program began in 2012.

Number awarded 1 each year.

Deadline May of each year.

[302]
KELLIE CANNON MEMORIAL SCHOLARSHIP

American Council of the Blind
Attn: Coordinator, Scholarship Program
6300 Shingle Creek Parkway, Suite 195
Brooklyn Center, MN 55430-2136
(612) 332-3242   Toll Free: (800) 424-8666
E-mail: deetheien@acbes.org
Web: www.acb.org/scholarship

Summary To provide financial assistance to students who are blind and interested in preparing for a career in the computer field.

Eligibility This program is open to high school seniors, high school graduates, and college students who are blind and interested in majoring in computer information systems or data processing. Applicants must submit verification of legal blindness in both eyes; SAT or ACT scores; information on extracurricular activities (including involvement in the American Council of the Blind); employment record; and a 500-word autobiographical sketch that includes their personal goals, strengths, weaknesses, hobbies, honors, achievements, and reasons for choice of field or courses of study. A cumulative GPA of 3.3 or higher is generally required. Financial need is not considered in the selection process, but the severity of the applicant's visual impairment and his/her study methods are taken into account.

Financial data The stipend is $1,000.

Duration 1 year.

Additional data This program is sponsored by Blind Information Technology Specialists (BITS), Inc., a special interest affiliate of the American Council of the Blind. The scholarship winner is expected to be present at the council's annual national convention; the council will cover all reasonable costs connected with convention attendance.

Number awarded 1 each year.

Deadline February of each year.

[303]
KENNETH JERNIGAN SCHOLARSHIP

National Federation of the Blind
Attn: Scholarship Committee
200 East Wells Street
Baltimore, MD 21230
(410) 659-9314, ext. 2415   Fax: (410) 685-5653
E-mail: scholarships@nfb.org
Web: www.nfb.org/scholarships

Summary To provide financial assistance to entering or continuing undergraduate and graduate blind students.

Eligibility This program is open to legally blind students who are working on or planning to work full time on an undergraduate or graduate degree. Along with their application, they must submit transcripts, standardized test scores, proof of legal blindness, 2 letters of recommendation, and a letter of endorsement from their National Federation of the Blind state president or designee. Selection is based on academic excellence, service to the community, and financial need.

Financial data The stipend is $12,000.

Duration 1 year; recipients may resubmit applications up to 2 additional years.

Additional data Scholarships are awarded at the federation convention in July. Recipients must attend the convention at federation expense; that funding is in addition to the scholarship grant. This scholarship is given by the American Action Fund for Blind Children and Adults, a nonprofit organization that assists blind people.

Number awarded 1 each year.

Deadline March of each year.

[304]
KENNETH TIEDE MEMORIAL SCHOLARSHIPS

National Federation of the Blind of Kansas
c/o Dianne Hemphill, Scholarship Chair
600 North Bel Rue Street
Derby, KS 67037-7300
(316) 201-1323   E-mail: diannehemphill@cox.net
Web: www.nfbks.org/conventions/scholarships.shtml

Summary To provide financial assistance for college to blind students from Kansas.

Eligibility This program is open to legally blind undergraduate and graduate students who are residents of Kansas or attending or planning to attend a college, university, or technical school in the state. Applicants must have a GPA of 2.5 or higher. They must be able to attend the state convention of the National Federation of the Blind of Kansas. Selection is based on academic excellence, community service, and financial need.

Financial data The stipend is $1,000.

Duration 1 year.

Number awarded Up to 3 each year.

Deadline June of each year.

[305]
LANCASTER SCHOLARSHIP

VisionCorps Foundation
244 North Queen Street
Lancaster, PA 17603
(717) 291-5951   E-mail: info@visioncorps.net
Web: www.visioncorps.net/Content/scholarships.asp

Summary To provide financial assistance to Pennsylvania residents who are legally blind veterans and interested in working on a degree at any level at a college in any state.

Eligibility This program is open to veterans who are residents of Pennsylvania and legally blind. Applicants must be attending or planning to attend an institution of higher education at any level in any state. Along with their application, they must submit a brief description of their career goal. Financial need is considered in the selection process.

Financial data The stipend is $1,000 per year.

Duration 1 year; may be renewed up to 3 additional years.

Additional data This sponsor was formerly the Susquehanna Foundation for the Blind.

Number awarded 1 or more each year.

Deadline January of each year.

[306]
LARRY STREETER MEMORIAL SCHOLARSHIP

National Federation of the Blind
Attn: Scholarship Committee
200 East Wells Street
Baltimore, MD 21230
(410) 659-9314, ext. 2415   Fax: (410) 685-5653
E-mail: scholarships@nfb.org
Web: www.nfb.org/scholarships

Summary To provide financial assistance to blind students working on an undergraduate or graduate degree in any field.

Eligibility This program is open to legally blind students who are working on or planning to work full time on an undergraduate or graduate degree in any field. Applicants must be attempting to "elevate their quality of life, equipping them to be active, productive participants in their family, community, and the workplace." Along with their application, they must submit transcripts, standardized test scores, proof of legal blindness, 2 letters of recommendation, and a letter of endorsement from their National Federation of the Blind state president or designee. Selection is based on academic excellence, service to the community, and financial need.

Financial data The stipend is $5,000.

Duration 1 year; recipients may resubmit applications up to 2 additional years.

Additional data This program began in 2011. Scholarships are awarded at the federation convention in July. Recipients must attend the convention at federation expense; that funding is in addition to the scholarship grant.

Number awarded 1 each year.

Deadline March of each year.

[307]
LIGHTHOUSE GUILD COLLEGE-BOUND SCHOLARSHIPS

Lighthouse Guild
Attn: Director Special Programs
250 West 64th Street
New York, NY 10023
(212) 769-7801   Toll Free: (800) 284-4422
Fax: (212) 769-6266
E-mail: scholars@lighthouseguild.org
Web: www.lighthouseguild.org

Summary To provide financial assistance to legally blind high school seniors who plan to attend college in any state.

Eligibility This program is open to high school seniors who are legally blind and U.S. citizens. Applicants must be planning to attend an accredited college or university in any state. Along with their application, they must submit transcripts, SAT and/or ACT scores, 3 letters of recommendation and 500-word essays on 1) their educational and personal goals; and 2) the influence of an outstanding

teacher on their education and/or personal development. Selection is based on academic and personal achievements; financial need is not considered.

Financial data The stipend is $10,000.

Duration 1 year; nonrenewable.

Additional data This sponsor was established in 2014 as the result of a merger of Lighthouse International and the Jewish Guild for the Blind.

Number awarded 20 each year.

Deadline March of each year.

[308]
LILLIAN GORELL SCHOLARSHIP FUND

Pittsburgh Foundation
Attn: Scholarship Coordinator
Five PPG Place, Suite 250
Pittsburgh, PA 15222-5414
(412) 391-5122   Fax: (412) 391-7259
E-mail: turnerd@pghfdn.org
Web: www.pittsburghfoundation.org/node/1655

Summary To provide financial assistance to entering or continuing undergraduate and graduate students, especially those who are blind or studying the arts.

Eligibility This program is open to all applicants, but preference is given to blind students and to those working on a degree in the arts. Applicants must be enrolled or planning to enroll at a college or university in any state. Along with their application, they must submit 1) a brief essay explaining their educational goals; 2) official transcripts; and 3) a statement of the amount they need and the purpose for which the award will be used.

Financial data A stipend is awarded (amount not specified). Funds are intended to be used for maintenance, supplies, instructions, tuition, room, board, and any other expenses related to attending an educational institution.

Duration 1 year; recipients may reapply until completion of their educational program.

Number awarded 1 or more each year.

Deadline April of each year.

[309]
LILLIAN S. EDELSTEIN SCHOLARSHIP FOR THE BLIND

National Federation of the Blind
Attn: Scholarship Committee
200 East Wells Street
Baltimore, MD 21230
(410) 659-9314, ext. 2415   Fax: (410) 685-5653
E-mail: scholarships@nfb.org
Web: www.nfb.org/scholarships

Summary To provide financial assistance to entering or continuing undergraduate and graduate blind students.

Eligibility This program is open to legally blind students who are working on or planning to work full time on an undergraduate or graduate degree. Along with their application, they must submit transcripts, standardized test scores, proof of legal blindness, 2 letters of recommendation, and a letter of endorsement from their National Federation of the Blind state president or designee. Selection is based on academic excellence, service to the community, and financial need.

Financial data The stipend is $3,000.

Duration 1 year; recipients may resubmit applications up to 2 additional years.

Additional data Scholarships are awarded at the federation convention in July. Recipients must attend the convention at federation expense; that funding is in addition to the scholarship grant.

Number awarded 1 each year.

Deadline March of each year.

[310]
MARY P. OENSLAGER SCHOLASTIC ACHIEVEMENT AWARDS

Learning Ally
Attn: National Achievement Awards
20 Roszel Road
Princeton, NJ 08540
(609) 520-8084   Toll Free: (800) 221-4792
Fax: (609) 987-8116   E-mail: naa@LearningAlly.org
Web: www.learningally.org/NAA/Application-SAA.aspx

Summary To recognize and reward the outstanding academic achievements of blind college seniors and graduate students.

Eligibility To be eligible for this award, candidates must 1) be blind or visually-impaired; 2) have received, or will receive, a bachelor's, master's, or doctoral degree from a 4-year accredited college or university in the United States or its territories during the year the award is given; and 3) have been registered members of Learning Ally for at least 1 year. Selection is based on academic excellence, leadership, and service to others.

Financial data Top winners receive $6,000 each and special honors winners $2,000 each.

Duration The awards are presented annually.

Additional data These awards are named for the founder of the program who established it in 1959 and endowed it with a gift of $1 million in 1990. Learning Ally was formerly named Recording for the Blind and Dyslexic.

Number awarded 6 each year: 3 top winners and 3 special honors winners.

Deadline April of each year.

[311]
MASSACHUSETTS REHABILITATION COMMISSION OR COMMISSION FOR THE BLIND TUITION WAIVER PROGRAM

Massachusetts Office of Student Financial Assistance
454 Broadway, Suite 200
Revere, MA 02151
(617) 391-6070   Fax: (617) 727-0667
E-mail: osfa@osfa.mass.edu
Web: www.mass.edu/osfa/programs/categorical.asp

Summary To provide financial assistance for college to Massachusetts residents who are clients of specified disability agencies in the state.

Eligibility Applicants for this assistance must be certified as clients by the Massachusetts Rehabilitation Commission or Commission for the Blind. They must have been permanent residents of Massachusetts for at least 1 year, must be U.S. citizens or permanent residents, and may not be in default on any federal student loan.

Financial data Eligible clients are exempt from any tuition payments for an undergraduate degree or certificate program at public colleges or universities in Massachusetts.

Duration Up to 4 academic years, for a total of 130 semester hours.

Additional data Recipients may enroll either part or full time in a Massachusetts publicly-supported institution.

Number awarded Varies each year.

Deadline Deadline not specified.

[312]
MAX EDELMAN SCHOLARSHIP

American Council of the Blind of Ohio
Attn: Scholarship Committee
3805 North High Street, Suite 305
Columbus, OH 43214
(614) 221-6688   Toll Free: (800) 835-2226 (within OH)
E-mail: acbo.scholarships@gmail.com
Web: www.acbohio.org

Summary To provide financial assistance to entering or continuing undergraduate students in Ohio who are blind.

Eligibility This program is open to 1) residents of Ohio who are high school seniors or current college students; and 2) students at colleges and universities in Ohio. Applicants must be legally blind and working on or planning to work on an undergraduate degree in any field. Along with their application, they must submit transcripts (must have a GPA of 3.0 or higher), a certificate of legal blindness, and an essay of 250 to 500 words on their career objectives, future plans, personal goals, other academic or personal qualities, and why they believe they are qualified to receive this scholarship. Financial need is not the only factor considered in the selection process.

Financial data The stipend is $2,000 per year.

Duration 1 year; recipients may reapply.

Additional data Winners are required to attend the Saturday workshops at the sponsor's annual convention; a stipend for meals and workshops is provided.

Number awarded 1 each year.

Deadline July of each year.

[313]
MCGREGOR SCHOLARSHIP PROGRAM

Iowa Educational Services for the Blind and Visually Impaired
Attn: Director of Human Resources
1002 G Avenue
Vinton, IA 52349
(319) 472-5221, ext. 1226
Toll Free: (800) 645-4579 (within IA)
Fax: (319) 472-5174
E-mail: jruegg@iowa-braille.k12.ia.us
Web: www.iowa-braille.k12.ia.us

Summary To provide financial assistance for college to Iowa residents who are blind.

Eligibility This program is open to residents of Iowa who became blind or visually-impaired prior to reaching the age of 21. Applicants must be graduating high school seniors, high school graduates, or GED recipients who are within 8 years of high school graduation or receipt of the GED. They must be enrolled or planning to enroll full time at an accredited college, university, or vocational school in any state and have a GPA of 2.5 or higher. Along with their application, they must submit an autobiographical sketch (from 300 to 500 words) that includes a statement of their goals and how this scholarship will help them achieve those goals.

Financial data The stipend is $2,500 per year.

Duration 1 year; may be renewed if the recipient maintains a GPA of 2.5 or higher.

Additional data This sponsor was previously named the Iowa Braille School.

Number awarded Varies each year; recently, 7 were awarded.

Deadline April of each year.

[314]
MICHAEL J. MCGOWAN LEADERSHIP SCHOLARSHIP

National Organization for Albinism and
    Hypopigmentation
Attn: Scholarship Committee
P.O. Box 959
East Hampstead, NH 03826-0959
(603) 887-2310   Toll Free: (800) 473-2310
Fax: (800) 648-2310
E-mail: scholarship@albinism.org
Web: www.albinism.org

Summary To provide financial assistance to undergraduate students with albinism.

Eligibility This program is open to students with albinism who are enrolled or planning to enroll in an undergraduate program at an institution of higher education in the United States or Canada. Applicants must submit a 500-word essay on their leadership potential, extracurricular involvement, academic achievement, educational background, and vocational goals; an eye report documenting a diagnosis of albinism; at least 2 letters of recommendation; an academic transcript (including SAT/ACT scores, if applicable); and a letter of acceptance of proof of enrollment from an institution of higher learning.

Financial data The stipend is $3,000.

Duration 1 year.

Additional data This program began in 2008. Albinism is a condition that frequently leads to vision difficulties.

Number awarded 1 each year.

Deadline April of each year.

[315]
MISSOURI COUNCIL OF THE BLIND SCHOLARSHIPS

Missouri Council of the Blind
Attn: Scholarship Program
5453 Chippewa Street
St. Louis, MO 63109-1635
(314) 832-7172   Toll Free: (800) 342-5632 (within MO)
Fax: (314) 832-7796   E-mail: aa@moblind.org
Web: www.missouricounciloftheblind.org

Summary To provide financial assistance for college or graduate school to blind students in Missouri.

Eligibility This program is open to Missouri residents who are high school or college graduates, legally blind, and in good academic standing. Applicants must be working on or planning to work on an undergraduate or graduate degree. They should have a specific goal in mind and that goal should be realistically within reach.

Financial data A stipend is awarded (amount not specified).

Duration 1 year; may be renewed if the recipient maintains a GPA of 2.0 or higher.

Number awarded Varies each year; recently, 14 were awarded.

Deadline April of each year.

[316]
MISSOURI REHABILITATION SERVICES FOR THE BLIND

Missouri Department of Social Services
Attn: Family Support Division
615 Howerton Court
P.O. Box 2320
Jefferson City, MO 65102-2320
(573) 751-4249   Toll Free: (800) 592-6004
Fax: (573) 751-4984   TDD: (800) 735-2966
Web: www.dss.mo.gov/fsd/rsb

Summary To provide support to blind and visually-impaired residents of Missouri who are engaged in rehabilitation training, including enrollment at a college or university.

Eligibility This program is open to residents of Missouri who qualify as visually-impaired, ranging from those who cannot read regular print to those who are totally blind. Applicants must be engaged in a program of vocational rehabilitation, including full-time enrollment at a college or university in Missouri or another state.

Financial data A range of support services are available. For college and university students, that includes transportation; housing and maintenance (up to the cost of double occupancy dormitory charges at the University of Missouri at Columbia); books, equipment, tools, and supplies; reader service; and interpreter service for deaf-blind persons.

Duration Qualified blind people are eligible for this assistance as long as they are attending college.

Number awarded Varies each year.

Deadline Deadline not specified.

[317]
MOUSE HOLE SCHOLARSHIPS

Blind Mice, Inc.
16810 Pinemoor Way
Houston, TX 77058
(713) 893-7277   E-mail: blindmicemart@att.net
Web: www.blindmicemegamall.com

Summary To provide financial assistance for college to blind students and the children of blind parents.

Eligibility This program is open to visually-impaired students and to sighted students who have visually-impaired parents. Applicants must be high school seniors or graduates who have never been enrolled in college. Along with their application, they must submit an essay, between 4 and 15 pages in length, on a topic that changes annually; recently, students were asked to imagine that they are attending their tenth high school reunion and to think back over their life since they graduated from high school. Essays are judged on originality, creativity, grammar, spelling, and the judge's overall impression of the applicant.

Financial data Stipends are $2,000 for the winner and $1,000 for the first runner-up.

Duration 1 year.

Additional data This program began in 2003. The winner receives the Antonia M. Derks Memorial Scholarship and the first runner-up receives the Kelsey Campbell Memorial Scholarship.

Number awarded 2 each year. Since the program began, it has awarded more than $28,350 in scholarships.

Deadline May of each year.

[318]
NATIONAL FEDERATION OF THE BLIND OF CALIFORNIA SCHOLARSHIPS

National Federation of the Blind of California
c/o Mary Willows, President
3934 Kern Court
Pleasanton, CA 94588
(925) 462-8575   E-mail: mwillows@sbcglobal.net
Web: sixdots.org/resources

Summary To provide financial assistance to blind residents of California interested in attending college or graduate school in any state.

Eligibility This program is open to residents of California who are legally blind. Applicants must be enrolled or planning to enroll as a full-time student in an undergraduate or graduate degree program in any state. They must have a GPA of 3.0 or higher. Along with their application, they must submit a 500-word statement on the educational and career goals they wish to achieve with the assistance of this scholarship, their involvement in the blindness community, the alternative techniques they use to do their school work (e.g., Braille, large print, recording, adapted computer), and any rehabilitation services they are receiving.

Financial data Stipends are $2,000 or $1,500.

Duration 1 year.

Additional data This program includes the following named awards: the Gerald Drake Memorial Scholarship, the LaVyrl "Pinky" Johnson Memorial Scholarship, the Julie Landucci Scholarship, and the Lawrence "Muzzy" Marcelino Memorial Scholarship.

Number awarded Varies each year; recently, 2 at $1,500 and 1 at $2,000 were awarded.

Deadline September of each year.

[319]
NATIONAL FEDERATION OF THE BLIND OF COLORADO SCHOLARSHIP

National Federation of the Blind of Colorado
Attn: Scholarship Committee Chair
2233 West Shepperd Avenue
Littleton, CO 80120-2038
(303) 507-6291   E-mail: rascal.angel2@gmail.com
Web: www.nfbco.org

Summary To provide financial assistance to legally blind residents of Colorado who are interested in attending college in any state.

Eligibility This program is open to legally blind residents of Colorado who are enrolled or planning to enroll full time at a college or university in any state (except for 1 scholarship reserved for an applicant who is employed full time and studying part time). Applicants must submit 2 letters of recommendation, current transcripts, a personal letter that describes their best qualities, and a letter from a state officer of the National Federation of the Blind of Colorado indicating that they have discussed their scholarship application with that officer. Selection is based on academic excellence, service to the community, and financial need.

Financial data The stipend ranges from $800 to $6,000.

Duration 1 year; recipients may reapply.

Number awarded Varies each year; a total of $15,000 is available for this program annually.

Deadline April of each year.

[320]
NATIONAL FEDERATION OF THE BLIND OF CONNECTICUT SCHOLARSHIPS

National Federation of the Blind of Connecticut
477 Connecticut Boulevard, Suite 217
East Hartford, CT 06108
(860) 289-1971   E-mail: info@nfbct.org
Web: www.nfbct.org/html/schinfo.htm

Summary To provide financial assistance for college or graduate school to blind students from Connecticut.

Eligibility This program is open to full-time undergraduate and graduate students who are legally blind. Applicants must be residents of Connecticut or attending school in the state. Along with their application, they must submit 2 letters of recommendation, academic transcripts, a description of their career goals and how this scholarship might help them achieve those, and a letter from a state officer of the National Federation of the Blind of Connecticut confirming that they have discussed their application with him or her. Selection is based on academic excellence, service to the community, and financial need.

Financial data Stipends range from $3,000 to $5,000.

Duration 1 year.

Additional data This program consists of the following named awards: the C. Rodney Demarest Memorial Scholarship ($3,000), the Howard E. May Memorial Scholarship ($5,000), the Jonathan May Memorial Scholarship ($4,000), and the Mary Main Memorial Scholarship ($3,000). The latter 3 programs are supported by the John A. Coccomo, Sr. Foundation. Recipients are expected to attend the annual convention of the National Federation of the Blind of Connecticut.

Number awarded 4 each year.

Deadline September of each year.

[321]
NATIONAL FEDERATION OF THE BLIND OF IDAHO SCHOLARSHIPS

National Federation of the Blind of Idaho
c/o Dana Ard, President
1320 East Washington Street
Boise, ID 83712
(208) 345-3906   E-mail: scholarship@nfbidaho.org
Web: www.nfbidaho.org/?s=scholarship

Summary To provide financial assistance to blind residents of Idaho who are interested in attending college in any state.

Eligibility This program is open to blind residents of Idaho who are enrolled or planning to enroll full time at a college or university in any state. Applicants must submit a 700-word essay about themselves, including their most notable qualities, their attitude about blindness, and examples of their demonstrated leadership. Selection is based on academic achievement, community service, and financial need.

Financial data Stipends range from $1,000 to $2,500.

Duration 1 year.

Number awarded 3 each year.

Deadline March of each year.

[322]
NATIONAL FEDERATION OF THE BLIND OF ILLINOIS SCHOLARSHIPS

National Federation of the Blind of Illinois
c/o Deborah Kent Stein, Scholarship Committee Chair
5817 North Nina Avenue
Chicago, IL 60631
(773) 203-1394   E-mail: dkent5817@att.net
Web: www.nfbofillinois.org/?page_id=97

Summary To provide financial assistance for college or graduate school to blind students in Illinois.

Eligibility This program is open to legally blind full-time undergraduate and graduate students. Applicants must be residents of Illinois or attending a college or university in the state. Along with their application, they must submit a personal essay that describes their strengths, achievements, and aspirations; what is important to them; who they hope to become; if a particular person or experience

has changed their life; how their blindness has affected them; and how they handle blindness at school, on the job, and in interpersonal relationships. Selection is based on academic excellence and service to the community.

Financial data Stipends $2,000 or $1,500 per year.

Duration 1 year; recipients may reapply.

Additional data This program includes the Peter Grunwald Scholarship.

Number awarded 3 each year: 1 at $2,000 and 2 at $1,500.

Deadline March of each year.

[323]
NATIONAL FEDERATION OF THE BLIND OF KENTUCKY SCHOLARSHIPS

National Federation of the Blind of Kentucky
c/o Lora Felty Stephens, Scholarship Committee Chair
1127 Sharon Court
Ashland, KY 41101
(606) 324-3394   E-mail: scholarships@nfbofky.org
Web: www.nfbofky.org/kscholar.php

Summary To provide financial assistance for college to blind students from Kentucky.

Eligibility This program is open to students who are legally blind or visually-impaired and/or eligible for services from the Kentucky Office for the Blind. Applicants must be 1) residents of Kentucky enrolled or planning to enroll full or part time at a college or university in any state; or 2) residents of other states attending or accepted at a college or university in Kentucky. Along with their application, they must submit a 500-character description of their educational goals, and a 2,000-character explanation of how the scholarship will help them achieve their academic and career goals and how they would like to be involved in the National Federation of the Blind of Kentucky.

Financial data Stipends are $500 or $1,000.

Duration 1 year.

Additional data Finalists are required to attend and participate in the annual convention of the National Federation of the Blind of Kentucky; travel, hotel accommodations, registration fees, and banquet tickets are provided.

Number awarded 1 or 2 each year.

Deadline July of each year.

[324]
NATIONAL FEDERATION OF THE BLIND OF LOUISIANA SCHOLARSHIPS

National Federation of the Blind of Louisiana
c/o Eric Guillory, Scholarship Committee Chair
Louisiana Center for the Blind
101 South Trenton Street
Ruston, LA 71270
(318) 251-2891   Toll Free: (800) 234-4166 (within LA)
Fax: (318) 251-0109 E-mail: eguillory@lcb-ruston.com
Web: www.nfbla.org/scholarships

Summary To provide financial assistance to blind residents of Louisiana who are interested in attending college in any state.

Eligibility This program is open to residents of Louisiana who are legally blind. Applicants must be enrolled or planning to enroll in a full-time postsecondary program of study or training at an accredited college, university, or trade/technical school in any state. Along with their application, they must submit a letter that provides general background information, a brief description of their educational and employment goals, details of noteworthy accomplishments, a concise summary of alternative techniques they have used to become a successful blind student, and how the scholarship would benefit them. Selection is based on academic excellence, leadership ability, service to the community, and financial need.

Financial data Stipends range from $750 to $1,500 per year.

Duration 1 year; recipients may reapply.

Additional data Recipients must attend the annual convention of the National Federation of the Blind of Louisiana. Convention expenses are covered.

Number awarded Varies each year: recently, 1 at $1,500, 2 at $1,000, and 1 at $750 were awarded.

Deadline March of each year.

[325]
NATIONAL FEDERATION OF THE BLIND OF MASSACHUSETTS SCHOLARSHIPS

National Federation of the Blind of Massachusetts
c/o Amy Ruell, President
9 Quail Run
Hingham, MA 02043
(617) 752-1116   E-mail: aruell@comcast.net
Web: www.nfbma.org/students

Summary To provide financial assistance for college or graduate school to blind students from Massachusetts.

Eligibility This program is open to legally blind students who are entering or enrolled at a postsecondary educational institution on a full-time basis. Applicants must be residents of Massachusetts or attending school in the Commonwealth. Along with their application, they must provide information on the high school, college, or graduate program they have attended; their high school or undergraduate GPA; a list of honors and awards they have received; and essays on their career goal and plan for the future, how blindness has affected their life so far, how they see it affecting their future, and their involvement in blindness organizations. Financial need is not considered in the selection process.

Financial data The stipend is $1,000.

Duration 1 year.

Additional data Finalists must attend the annual convention of the National Federation of the Blind of Massachusetts.

Number awarded Up to 3 each year.

Deadline December of each year.

[326]
NATIONAL FEDERATION OF THE BLIND OF MINNESOTA SCHOLARSHIP

National Federation of the Blind of Minnesota
Attn: Lori Anderson, Scholarship Committee
100 East 22nd Street
Minneapolis, MN 55404
(612) 270-4381
E-mail: Scholarships.nfbmn@gmail.com
Web: members.tcq.net/nfbmn/students/scholarship.htm

Summary To provide financial assistance to blind residents of Minnesota who are interested in attending college in the state.

Eligibility This program is open to residents of Minnesota who are blind or visually-impaired. Applicants must be attending or planning to attend a college, university, or technical school in the state. Along with their application, they must submit a personal letter on their goals and academic and community activities, official transcripts, and 2 letters of recommendation. Selection is based on scholastic excellence and community and campus service.

Financial data The stipend is $1,500 or $1,000.

Duration 1 year.

Additional data The recipient must attend the national convention of the National Federation of the Blind; all expenses are paid.

Number awarded 2 each year: 1 at $1,500 and 1 at $1,000.

Deadline April of each year.

[327]
NATIONAL FEDERATION OF THE BLIND OF MISSISSIPPI SCHOLARSHIPS

National Federation of the Blind of Mississippi
c/o Necy Spratt, Scholarship Committee
2006 Nelle Street
Tupelo, MS 38801-3232
(662) 844-9332   E-mail: nicetygirl@comcast.net
Web: www.nfbofmississippi.org/scholarships.html

Summary To provide financial assistance to blind residents of Mississippi who are interested in attending college in any state.

Eligibility This program is open to residents of Mississippi who are legally blind and attending or planning to attend a college or university in any state. Applicants must submit their SAT or ACT scores, a list of honors and awards, information on their community service, and a personal letter about themselves that conveys their best qualities. Selection is based on academic excellence, community service, and financial need.

Financial data A stipend is awarded (amount not specified).

Duration 1 year.

Number awarded 1 or more each year.

Deadline February of each year.

[328]
NATIONAL FEDERATION OF THE BLIND OF NEBRASKA SCHOLARSHIP

National Federation of the Blind of Nebraska
c/o Shane Buresh, Scholarship Committee Chair
411 North 75th Street
Lincoln, NE 68505
(402) 465-5468   E-mail: scholarship@ne.nfb.org
Web: www.ne.nfb.org/scholarship-form

Summary To provide financial assistance to blind residents of Nebraska who plan to attend college in any state.

Eligibility This program is open to residents of Nebraska who are blind and attending or planning to attend a postsecondary institution in any state. Applicants must submit a letter that describes their educational plans, vocational goals, and awards. Their letter should also explain how they deal with situations involving their blindness and how the scholarship will help them.

Financial data The maximum stipend is $1,000.

Duration 1 year.

Number awarded 5 each year: the National Federation of the Blind of Nebraska awards 1 scholarship at $1,000 and other scholarships are presented by its Lincoln and Omaha chapters and by the Nebraska Association of Blind Students.

Deadline September of each year.

[329]
NATIONAL FEDERATION OF THE BLIND OF NEW JERSEY SCHOLARSHIPS

National Federation of the Blind of New Jersey
c/o Jerilyn Higgins, Scholarship Chair
2 Old Farm Road
Verona, NJ 07044-1726
(973) 239-8874   Toll Free: (866) 632-1940
E-mail: jdhiggins3@verizon.net
Web: www.nfbnj.org/scholarships.php

Summary To provide financial assistance to entering and continuing undergraduate and graduate students from New Jersey who are blind.

Eligibility This program is open to legally blind students who are working on or planning to work full time on an undergraduate or graduate degree. Applicants must be residents of New Jersey or attending school in the state. Along with their application, they must submit a personal letter, 2 letters of recommendation, transcripts, and a letter of endorsement from an officer of the National Federation of the Blind of New Jersey. Selection is based on academic excellence, service to the community, and financial need.

Financial data A stipend is awarded (amount not specified).

Duration 1 year.

Number awarded Varies each year; recently, 2 were awarded.

Deadline March of each year.

[330]
NATIONAL FEDERATION OF THE BLIND OF NEW YORK SCHOLARSHIPS

National Federation of the Blind of New York State, Inc.
Attn: Catherine Mendez, Scholarship Committee Chair
P.O. Box 205666 Sunset Station
Brooklyn, NY 11220
(718) 567-7821   Fax: (718) 765-1843
E-mail: scholarships@nfbny.org
Web: www.nfbny.org/scholarships

Summary To provide financial assistance to blind residents of New York who are interested in attending college or graduate school in any state.

Eligibility This program is open to residents of New York who are legally blind. Applicants must be entering or enrolled in a degree program at the undergraduate, graduate, or postgraduate level at a school in any state. Along with their application, they must submit a 500-word essay explaining their goals, attitudes, and approach to living with blindness.

Financial data A stipend is awarded (amount not specified).

Duration 1 year.

Additional data This program includes the following named awards: the Gisela Distal Memorial Scholarship and the Maryanne Swaton Memorial Scholarship.

Number awarded At least 3 each year.

Deadline September of each year.

[331]
NATIONAL FEDERATION OF THE BLIND OF OHIO SCHOLARSHIPS

National Federation of the Blind of Ohio
c/o Deborah Kendrick, Scholarship Committee Chair
2514 Hackberry Street
Cincinnati, OH 45206
(513) 673-4474   E-mail: dkkendrick@earthlink.net
Web: www.nfbohio.org/new

Summary To provide financial assistance to blind residents of Ohio who are interested in working on an undergraduate or graduate degree at a school in any state.

Eligibility This program is open to residents of Ohio who are legally blind. Applicants must be attending or planning to attend an accredited institution of higher education as a full-time undergraduate or graduate student. Along with their application, they must submit 2 letters of recommendation, current transcripts, a letter about themselves that includes how they have dealt with their blindness and their hopes and dreams, and a letter from an officer of the National Federation of the Blind of Ohio indicating that they have discussed their scholarship application with that officer. Selection is based on academic excellence, community service, and financial need.

Financial data The stipend is $1,000.

Duration 1 year.

Additional data This program includes the Robert Eschbach Scholarship and the Barbara E. Fohl Memorial Scholarship.

Number awarded   2 each year.
Deadline   May of each year.

[332]
NATIONAL FEDERATION OF THE BLIND OF OREGON SCHOLARSHIPS

National Federation of the Blind of Oregon
c/o Carla McQuillan, President
5005 Main Street
Springfield, OR 97478
(541) 653-9153   E-mail: president@nfb-oregon.org
Web: www.nfb-oregon.org

Summary   To provide financial assistance for college or graduate school to blind residents of Oregon.

Eligibility   This program is open to blind residents of Oregon who are working on or planning to work on an undergraduate or graduate degree at a college or university in the state. Applicants must be enrolled full time or enrolled part time and working full time. Along with the application, they must submit a personal letter that includes what they consider their best qualities and the techniques and approaches they practice concerning their blindness. Selection is based on academic excellence, community service, and financial need.

Financial data   Stipends range from $2,000 to $5,000 per year.

Duration   1 year; recipients may apply for the Len Hannon Scholarship as an additional year of support at the same value as their original scholarship.

Number awarded   5 each year: 1 at $5,000, 2 at $3,000, and 2 at $2,000.

Deadline   June of each year.

[333]
NATIONAL FEDERATION OF THE BLIND OF PENNSYLVANIA SCHOLARSHIPS

National Federation of the Blind of Pennsylvania
Attn: Scholarship Committee
42 South 15th Street, Suite 222
Philadelphia, PA 19102
(215) 988-0888   E-mail: zrb5030@psu.edu
Web: www.nfbp.org/students

Summary   To provide financial assistance to blind residents of Pennsylvania who are interested in attending college in any state.

Eligibility   This program is open to residents of Pennsylvania who are legally blind. Applicants must be enrolled or planning to enroll full time at a college or university in any state. Along with their application, they must submit a personal letter about themselves, especially the techniques and approaches they use to overcome blindness. Selection is based on academic excellence, community service, and financial need.

Financial data   The stipend is $1,000.

Duration   1 year.

Number awarded   2 each year.

Deadline   August of each year.

[334]
NATIONAL FEDERATION OF THE BLIND OF SOUTH CAROLINA SCHOLARSHIPS

National Federation of the Blind of South Carolina
c/o Shannon Cook, Scholarship Committee Chair
2446 Harrison Road
Columbia, SC 29204
(803) 254-0222   E-mail: cookcafe@sc.rr.com
Web: www.nfbofsc.org/scholarships

Summary   To provide financial assistance for college to legally blind students from South Carolina.

Eligibility   This program is open to legally blind undergraduates who are residents of South Carolina or attending a college or university in the state. Applicants must submit 2 letters of recommendation, a current transcript, ACT and/or SAT test scores (high school seniors only), and a 250-word personal letter explaining their reasons for applying for a scholarship and how it will assist them to achieve a professional goal. Selection is based on academic excellence, community service, and participation in the National Federation of the Blind.

Financial data   A stipend is awarded (amount not specified).

Duration   1 year.

Additional data   Winners are required to attend the annual convention of the National Federation of the Blind of South Carolina at the federation's expense.

Number awarded   1 or more each year.

Deadline   July of each year.

[335]
NATIONAL FEDERATION OF THE BLIND OF TEXAS MERIT SCHOLARSHIPS

National Federation of the Blind of Texas
Attn: Scholarship Committee
1600 East Highway 6, Suite 215
Alvin, TX 77511
(281) 968-7733   Fax: (281) 809-4860
E-mail: scholarships@nfbtx.org
Web: www.nfbtx.org/scholarships.php

Summary   To provide financial assistance to blind residents of Texas who are interested in attending college in any state.

Eligibility   This program is open to blind residents of Texas who are enrolled or planning to enroll full time at a college or university in any state. Applicants must submit proof of legal blindness, a current transcript, a 2-page personal letter, and 2 letters of recommendation. Selection is based on academic excellence, community service, and financial need.

Financial data   Stipends are $1,500 or $1,000 per year.

Duration   1 year; recipients may reapply.

Additional data   This program includes 1 scholarship sponsored by the Houston chapter of the National Federation of the Blind of Texas.

Number awarded   3 each year: 1 at $1,500 and 2 at $1,000.

Deadline   June of each year.

[336]
NATIONAL FEDERATION OF THE BLIND SCHOLARSHIPS

National Federation of the Blind
Attn: Scholarship Committee
200 East Wells Street
Baltimore, MD 21230
(410) 659-9314, ext. 2415 Fax: (410) 685-5653
E-mail: scholarships@nfb.org
Web: www.nfb.org/scholarships

Summary To provide financial assistance for college or graduate school to blind students.

Eligibility This program is open to legally blind students who are working on or planning to work on an undergraduate or graduate degree. In general, full-time enrollment is required, although 1 scholarship may be awarded to a part-time student who is working full time. Along with their application, they must submit transcripts, standardized test scores, proof of legal blindness, 2 letters of recommendation, and a letter of endorsement from their National Federation of the Blind state president or designee. Selection is based on academic excellence, service to the community, and financial need.

Financial data Stipends are $5,000 or $3,000.

Duration 1 year; recipients may resubmit applications up to 2 additional years.

Additional data Scholarships are awarded at the federation convention in July. Recipients must attend the convention at federation expense; that funding is in addition to the scholarship grant.

Number awarded 20 each year: 3 at $5,000 and 17 at $3,000.

Deadline March of each year.

[337]
NEW JERSEY COMMISSION FOR THE BLIND AND VISUALLY IMPAIRED COLLEGE SERVICES

New Jersey Commission for the Blind and Visually
Impaired
Attn: Coordinator of Vocational Rehabilitation and
Transition Services
153 Halsey Street, Sixth Floor
P.O. Box 47017
Newark, NJ 07101-8004
(973) 648-3660 Toll Free: (877) 685-8878
E-mail: Amanda.gerson@dhs.state.nj.us
Web: www.state.nj.us

Summary To provide financial assistance to clients of the New Jersey Commission for the Blind and Visually Impaired (NJCBVI) who are interested in attending college in the state.

Eligibility This program is open to residents of New Jersey who have been determined eligible for vocational rehabilitation services through the NJCBVI. Applicants must be interested in attending an accredited college or university in the state in a program that is consistent with the employment goal listed on their Individualized Plan for Employment (IPE) and approved by the Commission.

They must have been accepted into an accredited college or university in the state as a full-time undergraduate or graduate student.

Financial data For tuition and fees, undergraduates receive up to $5,210 per semester and graduate students receive up to $614 per credit. All students also receive $5,064 per semester for room and board, $350 per semester for books and supplies, up to $150 per month for public transportation or 31 cents per mile for car travel, $40 per month for Internet service, a personal maintenance allowance that depends on financial need, and reader service up to $125 per month for undergraduates or $200 per month for graduate students.

Duration 1 semester; may be renewed until completion of a degree, provided the recipient remains enrolled full time, makes satisfactory progress toward degree completion, and maintains a GPA of 2.0 or higher as an undergraduate or 3.0 or higher as a graduate student.

Number awarded Varies each year.

Deadline Deadline not specified.

[338]
NFBCT-COCCOMO QUARTERLY GRANTS

National Federation of the Blind of Connecticut
Attn: Quarterly Grant Committee
477 Connecticut Boulevard, Suite 217
East Hartford, CT 06108
(860) 289-1971 E-mail: info@nfbct.org
Web: www.nfbct.org/html/coccomo.htm

Summary To provide financial assistance to blind people in Connecticut interested in a program of training, employment, independent living, or technological advancement.

Eligibility This assistance is available to residents of Connecticut who meet the state's definition of legal blindness. Applicants must be seeking support for activities in the areas of training, employment, independent living, or technological advancement. A wide range of requests are considered, including a talking watch, a computer system, a note taker (such as a Braille Note or Braille Lite), payment assistance for postsecondary part-time course work, or even a new suit for the sake of maximizing impressions on job interviews. Along with their application, they must submit a statement about themselves, their goals, and how the requested product or service will enhance their daily life and/or career aspirations.

Financial data Grants depend on the nature of the request.

Duration These are 1-time grants. Recipients are eligible for a second grant 2 years after receiving the first grant.

Additional data This program is supported by the John A. Coccomo, Sr. Foundation and administered by the National Federation of the Blind of Connecticut (NFBCT).

Number awarded Varies each year.

Deadline February, May, August, or November of each year.

[339]
NORA WEBB-MCKINNEY SCHOLARSHIP

American Council of the Blind of Ohio
Attn: Scholarship Committee
3805 North High Street, Suite 305
Columbus, OH 43214
(614) 221-6688 Toll Free: (800) 835-2226 (within OH)
E-mail: acbo.scholarships@gmail.com
Web: www.acbohio.org

Summary To provide financial assistance to Ohio students who are interested in working on an undergraduate or graduate degree involving service to blind people.

Eligibility This program is open to 1) residents of Ohio who are high school seniors or current undergraduate or graduate students; and 2) undergraduate and graduate students from any state enrolled at colleges and universities in Ohio. Applicants must be interested in working on or planning to work on a degree in a field related to blindness (e.g., special education, rehabilitation, teaching or counseling, orientation and mobility, or a concentration on programs serving people who are blind). They may be blind or sighted. Along with their application, they must submit transcripts (must have a GPA of 3.0 or higher) and an essay of 250 to 500 words on their career objectives, future plans, personal goals, other academic or personal qualities, and why they believe they are qualified to receive this scholarship. Financial need is not the sole factor considered in the selection process.

Financial data The stipend is $2,000 per year.

Duration 1 year; recipients may reapply.

Additional data Winners are required to attend the Saturday workshops at the sponsor's annual convention; a stipend for meals and workshops is provided.

Number awarded 1 each year.

Deadline July of each year.

[340]
NORMA SHECTER MEMORIAL SCHOLARSHIP

American Council of the Blind
Attn: Coordinator, Scholarship Program
6300 Shingle Creek Parkway, Suite 195
Brooklyn Center, MN 55430-2136
(612) 332-3242 Toll Free: (800) 424-8666
E-mail: deetheien@acbes.org
Web: www.acb.org/scholarship

Summary To provide financial assistance for college to students who are blind.

Eligibility This program is open to undergraduate students in any field of study who are blind. Applicants must submit verification of legal blindness in both eyes; SAT or ACT scores; information on extracurricular activities (including involvement in the American Council of the Blind); employment record; and a 500-word autobiographical sketch that includes their personal goals, strengths, weaknesses, hobbies, honors, achievements, and reasons for choice of field or courses of study. A cumulative GPA of 3.3 or higher is generally required. Financial need is not considered in the selection process.

Financial data The stipend is at least $1,500.

Duration 1 year.

Additional data Scholarship winners are expected to be present at the council's annual conference; the council will cover all reasonable expenses connected with convention attendance.

Number awarded 1 each year.

Deadline February of each year.

[341]
NORTH CAROLINA COUNCIL OF THE BLIND SCHOLARSHIP

North Carolina Council of the Blind
2429 New Orleans Street
Greensboro, NC 27406
Toll Free: (800) 344-7113 (within NC)
E-mail: nccb2020@gmail.com
Web: www.nccounciloftheblind.org/Topics.html

Summary To provide financial assistance to blind and visually-impaired North Carolina residents who are interested in attending college in any state.

Eligibility This program is open to blind and visually-impaired residents of North Carolina who are high school seniors or students currently enrolled at a college or vocational school in any state. Applicants must submit 2 reference letters, a transcript of courses completed, and a brief biographical statement that includes their educational background, financial need, and other pertinent information about themselves.

Financial data The stipend is $1,500.

Duration 1 year.

Number awarded Up to 4 each year.

Deadline March of each year.

[342]
NORTH DAKOTA ASSOCIATION OF THE BLIND SCHOLARSHIPS

North Dakota Association of the Blind
c/o Tracy Wicken, Scholarship Committee Chair
733 Dawn Circle
Grand Forks, ND 58203
(701) 772-7669 E-mail: trwicken@nd.gov
Web: www.ndab.org

Summary To provide financial assistance to blind students in North Dakota who are interested in attending college or graduate school in any state.

Eligibility This program is open to North Dakota residents who have a visual impairment that cannot be corrected with prescription glasses and are attending an institution of higher education in any state. They may be entering freshmen, undergraduates, or graduate students. Applicants for the $2,000 scholarship must be full-time students and have a GPA of 2.5 or higher; applicants for the $1,000 scholarships may be part-time students. Along with their application, they must submit 2 letters of recommendation, transcripts, a family financial aid statement, and a 500-word essay that describes their extracurricular activities and hobbies, how the scholarship will help them, their goals and aspirations, and what they have done to deal with situations involving their vision loss. Selection is based on academic excellence, financial need, and service to the community.

Financial data Stipends are $2,000 or $1,000.

Duration 1 year.

Additional data This program began in 1990.

Number awarded 3 each year: 1 at $2,000 and 2 at $1,000.

Deadline March of each year.

[343]
ORACLE SCHOLARSHIP FOR EXCELLENCE IN COMPUTER SCIENCE

National Federation of the Blind
Attn: Scholarship Committee
200 East Wells Street
Baltimore, MD 21230
(410) 659-9314, ext. 2415   Fax: (410) 685-5653
E-mail: scholarships@nfb.org
Web: www.nfb.org/scholarships

Summary To provide financial assistance to entering or continuing undergraduate and graduate blind students who are interested in working on a degree in a field related to computer science.

Eligibility This program is open to legally blind students who are working on or planning to work full time on an undergraduate or graduate degree in computer science, computer engineering, user experience, or a related field. Along with their application, they must submit transcripts, standardized test scores, proof of legal blindness, 2 letters of recommendation, and a letter of endorsement from their National Federation of the Blind state president or designee. Selection is based on academic excellence, service to the community, and financial need.

Financial data The stipend is $8,000.

Duration 1 year; recipients may resubmit applications up to 2 additional years.

Additional data This program is sponsored by Oracle Corporation. Scholarships are awarded at the federation convention in July. Recipients must attend the convention at federation expense; that funding is in addition to the scholarship grant.

Number awarded 1 each year.

Deadline March of each year.

[344]
ORACLE SCHOLARSHIP FOR EXCELLENCE IN STEM

National Federation of the Blind
Attn: Scholarship Committee
200 East Wells Street
Baltimore, MD 21230
(410) 659-9314, ext. 2415   Fax: (410) 685-5653
E-mail: scholarships@nfb.org
Web: www.nfb.org/scholarships

Summary To provide financial assistance to entering or continuing undergraduate and graduate blind students who are interested in working on a degree in a field of science, technology, engineering, and mathematics (STEM).

Eligibility This program is open to legally blind students who are working on or planning to work full time on an undergraduate or graduate degree in a field of STEM. Along with their application, they must submit transcripts, standardized test scores, proof of legal blindness, 2 letters of recommendation, and a letter of endorsement from their National Federation of the Blind state president or designee. Selection is based on academic excellence, service to the community, and financial need.

Financial data The stipend is $8,000.

Duration 1 year; recipients may resubmit applications up to 2 additional years.

Additional data This program is sponsored by Oracle Corporation. Scholarships are awarded at the federation convention in July. Recipients must attend the convention at federation expense; that funding is in addition to the scholarship grant.

Number awarded 1 each year.

Deadline March of each year.

[345]
PAUL AND ELLEN RUCKES SCHOLARSHIP

American Foundation for the Blind
Attn: Scholarship Coordinator
1108 Third Avenue, Suite 200
Huntington, WV 25701
(304) 710-3034   Toll Free: (800) AFB-LINE
Fax: (646) 478-9260   E-mail: apreece@afb.net
Web: www.afb.org/scholarships.asp

Summary To provide financial assistance to legally blind students who wish to work on a graduate or undergraduate degree in engineering or computer, physical, or life sciences.

Eligibility This program is open to legally blind undergraduate or graduate students who are U.S. citizens working or planning to work full time on a degree in engineering or the computer, physical, or life sciences. Along with their application, they must submit 200-word essays on 1) their past and recent achievements and accomplishments; 2) their intended field of study and why they have chosen it; and 3) the role their visual impairment has played in shaping their life. Financial need is considered in the selection process.

Financial data The stipend is $2,000.

Duration 1 year.

Number awarded 2 each year.

Deadline April of each year.

[346]
PEARSON AWARD

National Federation of the Blind
Attn: Scholarship Committee
200 East Wells Street
Baltimore, MD 21230
(410) 659-9314, ext. 2415   Fax: (410) 685-5653
E-mail: scholarships@nfb.org
Web: www.nfb.org/scholarships

Summary To provide financial assistance to entering or continuing undergraduate and graduate blind students.

Eligibility This program is open to legally blind students who are working on or planning to work full time on an undergraduate or graduate degree. Along with their application, they must submit transcripts, standardized test scores, proof of legal blindness, 2 letters of recommendation, and a letter of endorsement from their National Federation of the Blind state president or designee. Selection is based on academic excellence, service to the community, and financial need.

Financial data The stipend is $3,000.

Duration 1 year; recipients may resubmit applications up to 2 additional years.

Additional data Scholarships are awarded at the federation convention in July. Recipients must attend the convention at federation expense; that funding is in addition to the scholarship grant.

Number awarded 1 each year.

Deadline March of each year.

[347]
POULSON FAMILY SCHOLARSHIPS

Utah Council of the Blind
Attn: Leslie Gertsch, Executive Director
P.O. Box 1415
Bountiful, UT 84011-1415
(801) 299-0670   Toll Free: (800) 273-4569
Fax: (801) 292-6046   E-mail: ucb.board@gmail.com
Web: www.utahcounciloftheblind.org/scholarships.html

Summary To provide financial assistance to members of the Utah Council of the Blind (UCB) who plan to attend college or graduate school in the state.

Eligibility This program is open to UCB members who are entering or enrolled as an undergraduate or graduate student at a college or university in Utah. Applicants must be blind or visually-impaired. Selection is based on GPA, test scores (SAT or ACT for entering or continuing freshmen; GRE, GMAT, LSAT, etc. for continuing graduate students), work experience, and extracurricular activities.

Financial data The stipend is at least $1,000.

Duration 1 year; may be renewed.

Number awarded Varies each year; recently, 5 were awarded.

Deadline April of each year.

[348]
RED ROSE SCHOLARSHIP

VisionCorps Foundation
244 North Queen Street
Lancaster, PA 17603
(717) 291-5951   E-mail: info@visioncorps.net
Web: www.visioncorps.net/Content/scholarships.asp

Summary To provide financial assistance to legally blind Pennsylvania residents who are interested in working on an undergraduate degree at a college in any state.

Eligibility This program is open to residents of Pennsylvania who are legally blind. Applicants must be high school seniors or graduates planning to attend a 2- or 4-year college or university in any state. Along with their application, they must submit a brief description of their career goal. Financial need is considered in the selection process.

Financial data The stipend is $1,500 per year.

Duration 2 years; may be renewed another 2 years by students at 4-year institutions.

Additional data This sponsor was formerly the Susquehanna Foundation for the Blind.

Number awarded 1 or more each year.

Deadline January of each year.

[349]
R.L. GILLETTE, GLADYS C. ANDERSON, AND KAREN D. CARSEL MEMORIAL SCHOLARSHIP

American Foundation for the Blind
Attn: Scholarship Coordinator
1108 Third Avenue, Suite 200
Huntington, WV 25701
(304) 710-3034   Toll Free: (800) AFB-LINE
Fax: (646) 478-9260   E-mail: apreece@afb.net
Web: www.afb.org/scholarships.asp

Summary To provide financial assistance to legally blind undergraduate women who are studying literature or music.

Eligibility This program is open to women who are legally blind, U.S. citizens, and enrolled full time in a 4-year baccalaureate degree program in music. Along with their application, they must submit 200-word essays on 1) their past and recent achievements and accomplishments; 2) their intended field of study and why they have chosen it; and 3) the role their visual impairment has played in shaping their life. They must also submit a sample performance tape or CD (not to exceed 30 minutes) or a creative writing sample. Financial need is considered in the selection process.

Financial data The stipend is $3,500.

Duration 1 academic year.

Additional data Until 2017, this program consisted of 3 separate scholarships.

Number awarded 1 each year.

Deadline April of each year.

[350]
ROBERT AND HAZEL STALEY MEMORIAL SCHOLARSHIP

National Federation of the Blind of North Carolina
c/o Alan Chase
1217 Manassas Court, Unit C
Raleigh, NC 27609
(910) 612-2220   E-mail: aachase1@gmail.com
Web: www.nfbofnc.org

Summary To provide financial assistance to undergraduate and graduate students from North Carolina who are blind and interested in attending college in any state.

Eligibility This program is open to legally blind residents of North Carolina who are attending or planning to attend a college or university in any state. Applicants must be working on or planning to work on an undergraduate or graduate degree. Along with their application, they must submit 2 letters of recommendation, a current transcript, and a letter of introduction about themselves that includes their likes and dislikes, how their blindness has affected them, the honors and awards they have received, and their school and extracurricular activities. Selection is based on academic excellence and service to the community.

Financial data The stipend is $1,500. Funds may be used for the purchase of equipment, reader services, transportation, or other services or materials necessary to accomplish the recipient's educational objectives. They are not intended to offset support provided by state or federal agencies.

Duration 1 year.

Additional data Recipients must attend the annual convention of the National Federation of the Blind of North Carolina, at federation expense, where they receive their awards.

Number awarded Up to 2 each year.

Deadline June of each year.

[351]
ROSS N. AND PATRICIA PANGERE FOUNDATION SCHOLARSHIPS

American Council of the Blind
Attn: Coordinator, Scholarship Program
6300 Shingle Creek Parkway, Suite 195
Brooklyn Center, MN 55430-2136
(612) 332-3242   Toll Free: (800) 424-8666
E-mail: deetheien@acbes.org
Web: www.acb.org/scholarship

Summary To provide financial assistance to blind students working on an undergraduate or graduate degree in business.

Eligibility This program is open to undergraduate and graduate students working on a degree in business. Applicants must submit verification of legal blindness in both eyes; SAT, ACT, GMAT, or similar scores; information on extracurricular activities (including involvement in the American Council of the Blind); employment record; and a 500-word autobiographical sketch that includes their personal goals, strengths, weaknesses, hobbies, honors, achievements, and reasons for choice of field or courses of study. A cumulative GPA of 3.3 or higher is generally required. Financial need is not considered in the selection process.

Financial data The stipend is $2,500.

Duration 1 year.

Additional data This program is funded by the Ross N. and Patricia Pangere Foundation. The scholarship winner is expected to be present at the council's annual national convention; the council will cover all reasonable costs connected with convention attendance.

Number awarded 2 or 3 each year.

Deadline February of each year.

[352]
RUDOLPH DILLMAN MEMORIAL SCHOLARSHIP

American Foundation for the Blind
Attn: Scholarship Coordinator
1108 Third Avenue, Suite 200
Huntington, WV 25701
(304) 710-3034   Toll Free: (800) AFB-LINE
Fax: (646) 478-9260   E-mail: apreece@afb.net
Web: www.afb.org/scholarships.asp

Summary To provide financial assistance to legally blind undergraduate or graduate students studying in the field of rehabilitation and/or education of visually-impaired and blind persons.

Eligibility This program is open to legally blind U.S. citizens who have been accepted to an accredited undergraduate or graduate training program within the broad field of rehabilitation and/or education of blind and visually-impaired persons. Along with their application, they must submit 200-word essays on 1) their past and recent achievements and accomplishments; 2) their intended field of study and why they have chosen it; and 3) the role their visual impairment has played in shaping their life.

Financial data The stipend is $2,500 per year.

Duration 1 academic year; previous recipients may not reapply.

Number awarded 4 each year.

Deadline April of each year.

[353]
SALEM FOUNDATION ANGEL AND MARIE SOLIE SCHOLARSHIP

Oregon Office of Student Access and Completion
Attn: Scholarship Processing Coordinator
1500 Valley River Drive, Suite 100
Eugene, OR 97401-2146
(541) 687-7422   Toll Free: (800) 452-8807, ext. 7422
Fax: (541) 687-7414   TDD: (800) 735-2900
E-mail: cheryl.a.connolly@state.or.us
Web: app.oregonstudentaid.gov/Catalog/Default.aspx

Summary To provide financial assistance to residents of Oregon who are visually-impaired and are interested in attending college in the state.

Eligibility This program is open to residents of Oregon who are visually-impaired (have residual acuity of 20/70 or less in the better eye with correction, or their visual field is restricted to 20 degrees or less in the better eye). Applicants must be enrolled or planning to enroll as full-time undergraduate students at a 4-year college or university in Oregon. They must be U.S. citizens.

Financial data Stipends for scholarships offered by the Oregon Office of Student Access and Completion (OSAC) range from $1,000 to $10,000 but recently averaged $4,368.

Duration 1 year.

Number awarded Varies each year.

Deadline February of each year.

[354]
SEE THE FUTURE FUND SCHOLARSHIPS

The See the Future Fund
Attn: Thomas Theune, Founder and Chair
P.O. Box 63022
Colorado Springs, CO 80962-3022
(719) 471-3200   Fax: (719) 471-3210
E-mail: twtheune@comcast.net
Web: www.seethefuture.org

Summary To provide financial assistance to blind or visually-impaired residents of Colorado who are interested in attending college or graduate school in any state.

Eligibility This program is open to residents of Colorado who meet standards of blindness or visual impairment. Applicants must be enrolled full time at a postsecondary program in any state as 1) a freshman entering an academic program; 2) a sophomore, junior, or senior in an academic program; 3) a graduate student in an academic program; or 4) a student in a vocational/technical school or community college. Selection is based on academic achievement, school and community service, and financial need.

Financial data Stipends are $3,000, $2,500, or $2,000 per year. Funds are paid directly to the recipient's institution to be used for tuition, fees, books, room, and board.

Duration Up to 4 years.

Additional data This program began in 1998.

Number awarded Varies each year; recently, the program offered 1 scholarship at $3,000 per year for 4 years, 1 at $2,500 per year for 4 years, 1 at $2,000 per year for 4 years, and 3 at $2,000 per year for 2 years.

Deadline February of each year.

[355]
SOUTH DAKOTA REDUCED TUITION FOR VISUAL IMPAIRMENT

South Dakota Board of Regents
Attn: Scholarship Committee
306 East Capitol Avenue, Suite 200
Pierre, SD 57501-2545
(605) 773-3455   Fax: (605) 773-5320
E-mail: info@sdbor.edu
Web: www.sdbor.edu

Summary To provide waiver of tuition and fees to residents of South Dakota who have a visual impairment and are interested in attending college or graduate school in the state.

Eligibility This program is open to visually-impaired residents of South Dakota who can meet the entrance requirements for admission to a postsecondary educational institution (including graduate school and medical school) under the supervision of the state board of regents. For purposes of the program, "visual impairment" means that the person cannot, with use of correcting glasses, see sufficiently well to perform ordinary activities for which eyesight is essential. This program does not extend to visually-impaired persons who are entitled to receive tuition and fee support from the state's department of vocational rehabilitation.

Financial data Qualified applicants receive a total waiver of standard tuition and fees.

Duration Benefits are provided until the recipient has earned 225 semester hours of credit or the equivalent.

Additional data Applicants should contact the financial aid director at the South Dakota college or university they plan to attend, not the sponsor. The exemption from charges does not apply if a course is repeated because of unsatisfactory performance within the student's control.

Number awarded Varies each year.

Deadline Deadline not specified.

[356]
SPECIAL PEOPLE GIFTS OF LOVE PROGRAM

Italian Catholic Federation
8393 Capwell Drive, Suite 110
Oakland, CA 94621
(510) 633-9058   Toll Free: (888) ICF-1924
Fax: (510) 633-9758   E-mail: info@icf.org
Web: www.icf.org/charity

Summary To provide funding to individuals who have a disability and desire additional training or instruction.

Eligibility This program is open to 1) individuals who have a disability and desire formal training or instruction in a particular vocation, academic, athletic, or artistic field; 2) qualified instructors on behalf of an individual with a disability who exhibits a particular skill to be developed and who desires formal instruction or training; or 3) adults with custodial responsibility for, and on behalf of, an individual with a disability who exhibits a particular skill to be developed and who desires formal instruction or training. The program defines disability to include ADD/ADHD, amputee, autism, cerebral palsy, emotional disturbances, hearing impairments or deafness, mental retardation, multiple sclerosis, muscular dystrophy, orthopedic impairments, specific learning disabilities, speech and language impairments, spina bifida, spinal cord injury, traumatic brain injury, visual impairments and blindness, or other health impairments that require special education or related services. Applicants must submit an essay on how they intend to use the grant funds to assist them with their disability or to achieve the goals of the program. Financial need is considered in the selection process.

Financial data A stipend is awarded (amount not specified). Funds are not intended to support tuition.

Duration These are 1-time grants.

Number awarded Varies each year.

Deadline Deadline not specified.

[357]
TAER STUDENT WITH A VISUAL IMPAIRMENT SCHOLARSHIP

Texas Association for Education and Rehabilitation of the Blind and Visually Impaired
c/o Mary Shore
Texas School for the Blind and Visually Impaired
1100 West 45th Street
Austin, TX 78756
(512) 206-9156   E-mail: shorem@tsbvi.edu
Web: www.txaer.org/scholarships—awards.html

Summary To provide financial assistance to residents of Texas who have a visual impairment and are interested in attending college in any state.

Eligibility This program is open to residents of Texas who have a visual impairment and are enrolled or planning to enroll at a college or university in any state. Applicants must be able to demonstrate financial need. Along with their application, they must submit a letter regarding the goal of their education.

Financial data The stipend is $1,000.

Duration 1 year.

Number awarded 1 or 2 each year.

Deadline February of each year.

[358]
TERESA BLESSING SCHOLARSHIP

Florida Council of the Blind
c/o Sheila Young, Education and Leadership Committee Chair
2304 Amherst Avenue
Orlando, FL 32804
(407) 425-9200   E-mail: sheilayoung125@att.net
Web: www.fcb.org/node/871

Summary To provide financial assistance to blind residents of Florida who are attending college in any state.

Eligibility This program is open to blind residents of Florida who have completed at least 1 semester at a college or university in any state. Applicants must have a GPA of 3.0 or higher and be enrolled full time. Along with their application, they must submit a narrative statement on their vocational objectives and outlook for employment in their chosen field. Financial need is not considered in the selection process.

Financial data The stipend is $1,000.

Duration 1 year.

Number awarded 1 each year.

Deadline March of each year.

[359]
TEXAS BLIND/DEAF STUDENT EXEMPTION PROGRAM

Texas Higher Education Coordinating Board
Attn: Grants and Special Programs
1200 East Anderson Lane
P.O. Box 12788
Austin, TX 78711-2788
(512) 427-6340   Toll Free: (800) 242-3062
Fax: (512) 427-6420
E-mail: grantinfo@thecb.state.tx.us
Web: www.collegeforalltexans.com

Summary To provide a tuition exemption at Texas public colleges to undergraduate or graduate blind and/or deaf residents of the state.

Eligibility This program is open to Texas residents who can present certification from the Department of Assistive and Rehabilitative Services of their deafness or blindness. Applicants must present to the registrar of a public college or university in Texas a copy of their high school transcript, a letter of recommendation, proof that they have met all admission requirements, and a statement of purpose that indicates the certificate, degree program, or professional enhancement that they intend to pursue.

Financial data Eligible students are exempted from the payment of all dues, fees, and tuition charges at publicly-supported colleges and universities in Texas.

Duration Up to 8 semesters, provided the recipient maintains a GPA of 2.0 or higher as an undergraduate or 3.0 or higher as a graduate student.

Number awarded Varies each year; recently, 3,493 students received $11,469,863 in support through this program.

Deadline Deadline not specified.

[360]
THEODORE R. AND VIVIAN M. JOHNSON SCHOLARSHIP PROGRAM

State University System of Florida
Attn: Board of Governors
325 West Gaines Street
Tallahassee, FL 32399-0400
(850) 245-0466   Fax: (850) 245-9685
E-mail: info@flbog.org
Web: www.flbog.edu

Summary To provide financial assistance to Florida undergraduate students who have disabilities.

Eligibility This program is open to students with disabilities enrolled or planning to enroll at a State University System of Florida institution. Applicants must be able to verify the nature and/or extent of their disability, which may be in 1 or more of the following classifications: attention deficit disorder (ADD); attention deficit hyperactivity disorder (ADHD); autism spectrum disorder; blind or low vision; deaf or hard of hearing; orthopedic disability; psychological, emotional, or behavioral disability; speech/language impairment; specific learning disability; traumatic brain injury; or other health disabilities. They must have a GPA of 2.0 or higher and be able to document financial need.

Along with their application, they must submit a 1-page personal statement on their achievements, activities, career goals, and the effects of their disability(ies).

Financial data The stipend depends on the availability of funds.

Duration 1 year; may be renewed up to 5 additional years, provided the recipient maintains a GPA of 2.0 or higher and enrolls in at least 18 credits each academic year.

Additional data This program is administered by the equal opportunity program at each of the 12 State University System of Florida 4-year institutions. Contact that office for further information. Funding is provided by the Theodore R. and Vivian M. Johnson Foundation, with matching funding from the Florida Legislature.

Number awarded Several each year.

Deadline April of each year.

[361]
TIMOTHY TURPIN SCHOLARSHIP

Florida Council of the Blind
c/o Sheila Young, Education and Leadership
 Committee Chair
2304 Amherst Avenue
Orlando, FL 32804
(407) 425-9200   E-mail: sheilayoung125@att.net
Web: www.fcb.org/node/871

Summary To provide financial assistance to blind high school seniors in Florida who plan to attend college in any state to study a field that will increase advancement potential in their chosen field.

Eligibility This program is open to seniors graduating from high schools in Florida who are legally blind and planning to enroll full time at a college or university in any state. Applicants must have a GPA of 3.0 or higher. They must intend to work on a degree that will increase advancement potential in their chosen field. Along with their application, they must submit a narrative statement on their vocational objectives and outlook for employment in their chosen field. Financial need is not considered in the selection process.

Financial data The stipend is $1,000.

Duration 1 year.

Number awarded 1 each year.

Deadline March of each year.

[362]
VISIONCORPS FOUNDATION FOR THE BLIND TRUSTEES' SCHOLARSHIP

VisionCorps Foundation
244 North Queen Street
Lancaster, PA 17603
(717) 291-5951   E-mail: info@visioncorps.net
Web: www.visioncorps.net/Content/scholarships.asp

Summary To provide financial assistance to legally blind Pennsylvania residents who are interested in working on an undergraduate or graduate degree or other academic program at a school in any state.

Eligibility This program is open to residents of Pennsylvania who are legally blind. Applicants must be working on an undergraduate or graduate degree or other specialized program intended to generate upward mobility in employment. Along with their application, they must submit a brief description of their career goal. Financial need is considered in the selection process.

Financial data A stipend is awarded (amount not specified).

Duration 1 year.

Additional data This sponsor was formerly the Susquehanna Foundation for the Blind.

Number awarded 1 or more each year.

Deadline January of each year.

[363]
VISUAL AID VOLUNTEERS OF FLORIDA SCHOLARSHIPS

Visual Aid Volunteers of Florida
c/o Mariann Witengier, Scholarship Committee
2900 Harriet Drive
Orlando, FL 32812
(321) 512-5624   E-mail: mizzwit@gmail.com
Web: www.vavf.org/vavf-scholarship

Summary To provide financial assistance to blind residents of Florida who are interested in attending college.

Eligibility This program is open to seniors graduating from high schools in Florida who are blind and planning to attend college in any state. As part of their application, students must submit a statement of career goals, a list of extracurricular activities, 3 letters of recommendation, and a short paper (1 print page or 2 Braille pages) about themselves and how this scholarship will make a difference to them.

Financial data The stipend is $2,000 for the first year and $1,000 in subsequent years.

Duration 1 year; may be renewed.

Number awarded Varies each year; recently, 4 new scholarships and 2 renewals were awarded.

Deadline March of each year.

[364]
WASHINGTON COUNCIL OF THE BLIND SCHOLARSHIPS

Washington Council of the Blind
c/o Tim McCorcle, Scholarship Committee Chair
2253 N.E. 54th Street
Seattle, WA 98105-3213
Toll Free: (206) 522-5850
E-mail: t.mccorcle@comcast.net
Web: www.wcbinfo.org/scholarships

Summary To provide financial aid to blind students in Washington who plan to attend college or graduate school in any state.

Eligibility This program is open to blind residents of Washington state who are enrolled or planning to enroll at an accredited college, university, vocational school, or graduate school in any state. Applicants must submit a 1,000-word statement of their reasons for applying for this scholarship and how it will assist them to achieve their goals. The statement should include a brief description of their background, education, work experience, economic status, strengths, weaknesses, and personal goals for the next 5 to 10 years. Interviews are required.

Financial data The stipend ranges from $1,000 to $4,000.

Duration 1 year.

Number awarded Varies each year; recently, 9, worth $17,500, were awarded.

Deadline August of each year.

[365]
WHITE CANE SCHOLARSHIP

Lions of Michigan
Attn: Scholarship Committee
5730 Executive Drive
Lansing, MI 48911
(517) 887-6640   Fax: (517) 887-6642
E-mail: lions@lionsofmi.com
Web: lionsofmi.com

Summary To provide financial assistance to residents of Michigan who are legally blind and interested in attending college in any state.

Eligibility This program is open to residents of Michigan who are legally blind and attending or planning to attend an accredited trade or business school, college, or university in any state. Applicants must have a GPA of 2.5 or higher. They must be U.S. citizens. Along with their application, they must submit an essay explaining why they need this scholarship.

Financial data The stipend is $3,000.

Duration 1 year.

Number awarded 3 each year.

Deadline December of each year.

[366]
WILLIAM AND DOROTHY FERRELL SCHOLARSHIP

Association for Education and Rehabilitation of the
  Blind and Visually Impaired
Attn: Scholarship Committee
1703 North Beauregard Street, Suite 440
Alexandria, VA 22311-1717
(703) 671-4500, ext. 201   Toll Free: (877) 492-2708
Fax: (703) 671-6391   E-mail: scholarships@aerbvi.org
Web: www.aerbvi.org/resources/aer-scholarships

Summary To provide financial assistance to blind undergraduate and graduate students who wish to study for a career in service to blind and visually-impaired people.

Eligibility Applicants for this award must be legally blind (have a visual acuity of 20/200 or less in the best-corrected eye and/or a visual field of 20 degrees of less). They must be preparing for a career in service to blind and visually-impaired people (special education, orientation and mobility, rehabilitation training, etc.). Along with their application, they must submit an autobiographical sketch that includes information on their vocational goals, work or

volunteer experiences, outside activities including the extent to which they play a leadership role, and other details about their objectives. Financial need is not considered in the selection process.

Financial data The stipend is $1,000.

Number awarded 2 every other year.

Deadline March of even-numbered years.

[367]
WILLIAM G. COREY MEMORIAL SCHOLARSHIP

American Council of the Blind
Attn: Coordinator, Scholarship Program
6300 Shingle Creek Parkway, Suite 195
Brooklyn Center, MN 55430-2136
(612) 332-3242   Toll Free: (800) 424-8666
E-mail: deetheien@acbes.org
Web: www.acb.org/scholarship

Summary To provide financial assistance for college to blind undergraduate and graduate students from Pennsylvania.

Eligibility This program is open to legally blind undergraduate and graduate students who are residents of Pennsylvania or attending college in the state. Applicants must submit verification of legal blindness in both eyes; SAT, ACT, GRE, or similar scores; information on extracurricular activities (including involvement in the American Council of the Blind); employment record; and a 500-word autobiographical sketch that includes their personal goals, strengths, weaknesses, hobbies, honors, achievements, and reasons for choice of field or courses of study. A cumulative GPA of 3.3 or higher is generally required. Financial need is not considered in the selection process.

Financial data The stipend is $1,500.

Duration 1 year.

Additional data Scholarship winners are expected to be present at the council's annual conference; the council will cover all reasonable expenses connected with convention attendance.

Number awarded 1 each year.

Deadline February of each year.

[368]
WISCONSIN COUNCIL OF THE BLIND AND VISUALLY IMPAIRED SCHOLARSHIPS

Wisconsin Council of the Blind and Visually Impaired
Attn: Scholarship Committee
754 Williamson Street
Madison, WI 53703-3546
(608) 255-1166   Toll Free: (800) 783-5213
Fax: (608) 255-3301   E-mail: info@wcblind.org
Web: www.wcblind.org

Summary To provide financial assistance to blind students from Wisconsin who are planning to attend college in the state.

Eligibility This program is open to legally blind residents of Wisconsin who are enrolled or entering college or vocational school in the state full or part time. Applicants must have a GPA of 3.0 or higher. Along with their application, they must submit documentation of GPA, a statement of their vocational goal, a list of extracurricular activities, a brief essay on how they see themselves becoming involved with the sponsor, a description of their visual impairment and how it impacts their life, and a 400-word description of a special attribute or accomplishment that sets them apart. Financial need is not considered in the selection process.

Financial data The stipend is $2,000.

Duration 1 year.

Number awarded 10 each year.

Deadline March of each year.

[369]
WISCONSIN HEARING AND VISUALLY HANDICAPPED STUDENT GRANT PROGRAM

Wisconsin Higher Educational Aids Board
131 West Wilson Street, Suite 902
P.O. Box 7885
Madison, WI 53707-7885
(608) 266-0888   Fax: (608) 267-2808
E-mail: cindy.cooley@wi.gov
Web: www.heab.state.wi.us/programs.html

Summary To provide financial support for undergraduate study to Wisconsin residents who are legally deaf or blind.

Eligibility This program is open to Wisconsin residents who can submit evidence of a severe or profound hearing or visual impairment certified by a medical examiner. Applicants must be enrolled at least half time at a branch of the University of Wisconsin, a technical college in the state, a Wisconsin independent college or university, a tribal college in the state, or an institution out of state that specializes in the training of deaf, hard of hearing, or visually handicapped students or that offers a program of study not offered by a Wisconsin institution. Financial need is considered in the selection process.

Financial data Grants range from $250 to $1,800 per academic year.

Duration 1 year; may be renewed up to 4 additional years.

Number awarded Varies each year.

Deadline Deadline not specified.

[370]
WYCB SCHOLARSHIP

Wyoming Council of the Blind
c/o Linda Johnson
308 North Gilbert Street
Powell, WY 82435
Web: www.wycb.info/scholarship

Summary To provide financial assistance to blind residents of Wyoming who are interested in attending college or graduate school in any state.

Eligibility This program is open to residents of Wyoming who are legally blind or visually-impaired. Applicants must be entering or enrolled at a vocational training program, college, university, community college, or graduate school in any state and have a GPA of 2.0 or higher. Along

with their application, they must submit a 2-page autobiographical sketch that includes 1) how they will use this scholarship and how it will it impact their educational experience; 2) their short and long-term educational and work goals; and 3) their personal and academic achievements, work experience, hobbies, and any other information they think would be helpful. Financial need is not considered in the selection process. Leading candidates are interviewed.

Financial data The stipend is $1,500.

Duration 1 year.

Number awarded 1 each year.

Deadline March of each year.

Graduate Students

[371]
ADRIENNE ASCH MEMORIAL SCHOLARSHIP

National Federation of the Blind
Attn: Scholarship Committee
200 East Wells Street
Baltimore, MD 21230
(410) 659-9314, ext. 2415   Fax: (410) 685-5653
E-mail: scholarships@nfb.org
Web: www.nfb.org/scholarships

Summary To provide financial assistance to entering or continuing undergraduate and graduate blind students.

Eligibility This program is open to legally blind students who are working on or planning to work full time on an undergraduate or graduate degree. Along with their application, they must submit transcripts, standardized test scores, proof of legal blindness, 2 letters of recommendation, and a letter of endorsement from their National Federation of the Blind state president or designee. Selection is based on academic excellence, service to the community, and financial need.

Financial data The stipend is $3,000.

Duration 1 year; recipients may resubmit applications up to 2 additional years.

Additional data Scholarships are awarded at the federation convention in July. Recipients must attend the convention at federation expense; that funding is in addition to the scholarship grant.

Number awarded 1 each year.

Deadline March of each year.

[372]
ALFRED CAMP MEMORIAL SCHOLARSHIP

Georgia Council of the Blind
c/o Debbie Williams, Scholarship Committee Chair
1477 Nebo Road
Dallas, GA 30157
(770) 595-1007
E-mail: williamsdebk@wmconnect.com
Web: www.georgiacounciloftheblind.org

Summary To provide financial assistance students in Georgia who plan to attend college or graduate school in any state and are either legally blind or have legally blind parents.

Eligibility This program is open to residents of Georgia who are either 1) legally blind students; or 2) sighted students financially dependent on legally blind parents. Applicants must be enrolled or accepted for enrollment at a vocational/technical school, a 2- or 4-year college, or a master's or doctoral program in any state. All fields of study are eligible. Selection is based on academic transcripts, 2 letters of recommendation, a 1-page typed statement of the applicant's educational goals, an audio cassette recording of the applicant reading the goals statement, extracurricular activities, and financial need.

Financial data Stipends up to $1,000 per year are available.

Duration 1 year; recipients may reapply.

Additional data This program began in 1988.

Number awarded 1 or more each year.

Deadline June of each year.

[373]
ALLEN-SPRINKLE MEMORIAL GIFT

National Federation of the Blind of West Virginia
c/o Mary Ann Saunders, Scholarship Committee Chair
101 Eighth Avenue, Apartment 511
Huntington, WV 25701
(304) 697-1434　　　　E-mail: saunders@wvdsl.net
Web: www.nfbwv.org

Summary To provide financial assistance to legally blind residents of West Virginia who are interested in attending college or graduate school in any state.

Eligibility This program is open to legally blind residents of Virginia who are graduating high school seniors, undergraduates, or graduate students. Applicants must be enrolled or planning to enroll full time at an accredited college, university, postsecondary vocational institute, or graduate school in any state. Along with their application, they must submit 2 letters of recommendation, transcripts, verification of blindness, and a personal letter that includes the kinds of things that interest them, their goals and aspirations, and how this scholarship would help them. Selection is based on academic excellence, community service, and financial need.

Financial data The stipend is $1,000.

Duration 1 year.

Additional data The winner is expected to attend the annual convention of the National Federation of the Blind of West Virginia.

Number awarded 1 each year.

Deadline June of each year.

[374]
ALMA MURPHEY MEMORIAL SCHOLARSHIP

American Council of the Blind
Attn: Coordinator, Scholarship Program
6300 Shingle Creek Parkway, Suite 195
Brooklyn Center, MN 55430-2136
(612) 332-3242　　　　　　Toll Free: (800) 424-8666
E-mail: deetheien@acbes.org
Web: www.acb.org/scholarship

Summary To provide financial assistance for graduate education to students who are blind.

Eligibility This program is open to graduate students in any field of study who are blind and use Braille. Applicants must submit verification of legal blindness in both eyes; GRE or similar scores; information on extracurricular activities (including involvement in the American Council of the Blind); employment record; and a 500-word autobiographical sketch that includes their personal goals, strengths, weaknesses, hobbies, honors, achievements, and reasons for choice of field or courses of study. A cumulative GPA of 3.3 or higher is generally required. Financial need is not considered in the selection process.

Financial data The stipend is $1,500.

Duration 1 year.

Additional data Funding for this scholarship is provided by the Braille Revival League of Missouri, an affiliate of the American Council of the Blind. Scholarship winners are expected to be present at the council's annual conference; the council will cover all reasonable expenses connected with convention attendance.

Number awarded 1 each year.

Deadline February of each year.

[375]
AMERICAN COUNCIL OF THE BLIND OF MINNESOTA SCHOLARSHIPS

American Council of the Blind of Minnesota
Attn: Scholarship Committee Chair
P.O. Box 19091
Minneapolis, MN 55419
(612) 824-2131　　　　　　Toll Free: (866) YAY-ACBM
E-mail: juliettesilvers@gmail.com
Web: www.acb.org/minnesota/Scholarship.html

Summary To provide financial assistance to blind and visually-impaired residents of Minnesota who are interested in attending college or graduate school in any state.

Eligibility This program is open to residents of Minnesota who are blind or visually-impaired. Applicants may be either high school seniors entering their first year of postsecondary study or students in their second year or above of undergraduate or graduate study in any state. Along with their application, they must submit 2 essays of 500 words each on 1) a situation in which they solved a problem or broke down a blindness-related barrier in order to meet an academic requirement; and 2) a pair of instances in which they would or have advocated for their own needs or the needs of others. Selection is based on those essays, extracurricular activities, transcripts, and letters of recommendation.

Financial data The stipend is $1,000.

Duration 1 year.

Number awarded 2 each year: 1 to a high school senior entering college and 1 to a student already enrolled in a postsecondary educational program.

Deadline June of each year.

[376]
ARIZONA COUNCIL OF THE BLIND SCHOLARSHIP PROGRAM

Arizona Council of the Blind
Attn: Scholarship Committee
16845 North 29th Avenue, Suite 139
Phoenix, AZ 85053
(602) 285-0269   E-mail: scholarship@azcb.org
Web: www.acb.org/arizona

Summary To provide financial assistance for undergraduate or graduate studies to legally blind Arizona residents.

Eligibility This program is limited to Arizona residents. Applicants must be legally blind and enrolled or planning to enroll in vocational, technical, graduate, or professional training programs beyond the high school level. Along with their application, they must submit a 2-page autobiographical sketch that includes their personal goals, strengths, weaknesses, hobbies, honors, achievements, proposed course of study, why they have chosen that, and how obtaining a scholarship would help their educational experience. Selection is based on that sketch, GPA, test scores (ACT, SAT, GRE, GMAT, LSAT, etc.), work experience, and extracurricular activities. Unless extenuating circumstances exist, a 3.25 GPA is required.

Financial data The stipend is $1,000.

Duration 1 year; recipients may reapply.

Number awarded 2 each year.

Deadline April of each year.

[377]
ARNOLD SADLER MEMORIAL SCHOLARSHIP

American Council of the Blind
Attn: Coordinator, Scholarship Program
6300 Shingle Creek Parkway, Suite 195
Brooklyn Center, MN 55430-2136
(612) 332-3242   Toll Free: (800) 424-8666
E-mail: deetheien@acbes.org
Web: www.acb.org/scholarship

Summary To provide financial assistance to undergraduate or graduate students who are blind and are interested in studying in a field of service to persons with disabilities.

Eligibility This program is open to undergraduate and graduate students in rehabilitation, education, law, or other fields of service to persons with disabilities. Applicants must be legally blind in both eyes. Along with their application, they must submit verification of legal blindness in both eyes; SAT, ACT, GRE, or similar scores; infor-

mation on extracurricular activities (including involvement in the American Council of the Blind); employment record; and a 500-word autobiographical sketch that includes their personal goals, strengths, weaknesses, hobbies, honors, achievements, and reasons for choice of field or courses of study. A cumulative GPA of 3.3 or higher is generally required. Financial need is not considered in the selection process.

Financial data The stipend is $1,500.

Duration 1 year.

Additional data This scholarship is funded by the Arnold Sadler Memorial Scholarship Fund. Scholarship winners are expected to be present at the council's annual conference; the council will cover all reasonable expenses connected with convention attendance.

Number awarded 1 each year.

Deadline February of each year.

[378]
ASHLEY K. FRITZ MEMORIAL "HUMANITARIAN" SCHOLARSHIP

The See the Future Fund
Attn: Thomas Theune, Founder and Chair
P.O. Box 63022
Colorado Springs, CO 80962-3022
(719) 471-3200   Fax: (719) 471-3210
E-mail: twtheune@comcast.net
Web: www.seethefuture.org

Summary To provide financial assistance to blind or visually-impaired residents of Colorado who demonstrate exceptional humanitarian abilities and are interested in attending college or graduate school in any state.

Eligibility This program is open to residents of Colorado who meet standards of blindness or visual impairment. Applicants must be enrolled full time at a postsecondary program in any state as 1) a freshman entering an academic program; 2) a sophomore, junior, or senior in an academic program; 3) a graduate student in an academic program; or 4) a student in a vocational/technical school or community college. This award is reserved for an applicant who demonstrates exceptional humanitarian and leadership abilities.

Financial data The stipend is $1,000. Funds are paid directly to the recipient's institution to be used for tuition, fees, books, room, and board.

Duration 1 year.

Number awarded 1 each year.

Deadline February of each year.

[379]
BEVERLY PROWS MEMORIAL SCHOLARSHIP

National Federation of the Blind of Washington
Attn: Scholarship Chair
P.O. Box 2516
Seattle, WA 98111
(425) 823-6380   E-mail: president@nfbw.org
Web: www.nfbw.org/scholarships.html

Summary To provide financial assistance for undergraduate or graduate study in any state to blind students in Washington.

Eligibility This program is open to legally blind residents of Washington state who are working on or planning to work on a full-time college or graduate degree at a school in any state. Applicants must submit a list of honors and awards they have received, information on their community service involvement, high school and/or college transcripts, and 3 letters of reference.

Financial data The stipend is $3,000.

Duration 1 year; recipients may reapply.

Additional data This program began in 1991. Winners must attend the state convention of the National Federation of the Blind of Washington to accept the award; convention expenses are covered.

Number awarded 1 each year.

Deadline August of each year.

[380]
BROTHER JAMES KEARNEY SCHOLARSHIP FOR THE BLIND

Lavelle Fund for the Blind, Inc.
Attn: Scholarship Program Coordinator
307 West 38th Street, Suite 1905
New York, NY 10018
(212) 668-9801   Fax: (212) 668-9803
E-mail: jdulitz@lavellefund.org
Web: www.lavellefund.org

Summary To provide financial assistance to blind residents of the New York tri-state region who are attending designated colleges in the New York City area.

Eligibility This program is open to residents of Connecticut, New Jersey, and New York who are legally blind or severely visually-impaired. Residents of Pennsylvania who attend either of the schools for the blind in Philadelphia (Overbrook School for the Blind or St. Lucy Day School for Children with Visual Impairments) are also eligible. Applicants must be working on or planning to work full time on an undergraduate or graduate degree at 1 of 11 designated colleges and universities in the New York City area. They must be able to demonstrate financial need.

Financial data Stipends provide for payment of tuition, fees, room, board, and books, to a maximum of $15,000.

Duration 1 year; may be renewed up to 3 additional years.

Additional data This program was formerly named the Lavelle Fund for the Blind Scholarships. The 11 participating institutions are Canisius College (Buffalo, New York), Dominican College (Orangeburg, New York), Fordham University (Bronx, New York), LeMoyne College (Syracuse, New York), Manhattanville College (Purchase, New York), Marist College (Poughkeepsie, New York), Marymount Manhattan College (New York, New York), Molloy College (Rockville Centre, New York), Seton Hall University (South Orange, New Jersey), St. John's University (Jamaica, New York), and St. Thomas Aquinas College (Sparkill, New York).

Number awarded Varies each year.

Deadline June of each year.

[381]
CALIFORNIA COUNCIL OF THE BLIND SCHOLARSHIPS

California Council of the Blind
Attn: Executive Office
1303 J Street, Suite 400
Sacramento, CA 95814-2900
(916) 441-2100   Toll Free: (800) 221-6359 (within CA)
Fax: (916) 441-2188   E-mail: ccotb@ccbnet.org
Web: www.ccbnet.org/scholar.htm

Summary To provide financial assistance for undergraduate or graduate study in any state to blind people in California.

Eligibility Applicants must be legally blind residents of California who are enrolled or planning to enroll full time at an accredited college or university at either the undergraduate or graduate level. The school may be in any state. Along with their application, they must submit a 200-word statement on their purpose in undertaking college work and their vocational goals. Selection is based on academic achievement and financial need.

Financial data The amount of the assistance depends on the availability of funds and the needs of the applicant.

Duration 1 year; may be renewed. For graduate students, support is limited to 2 years of work for a master's degree or 3 years for a Ph.D.

Number awarded Varies each year.

Deadline May of each year.

[382]
CHARLES AND MELVA T. OWEN MEMORIAL SCHOLARSHIPS

National Federation of the Blind
Attn: Scholarship Committee
200 East Wells Street
Baltimore, MD 21230
(410) 659-9314, ext. 2415   Fax: (410) 685-5653
E-mail: scholarships@nfb.org
Web: www.nfb.org/scholarships

Summary To provide financial assistance to entering or continuing undergraduate or graduate students who are blind.

Eligibility This program is open to legally blind students who are working on or planning to work full time on an undergraduate or graduate degree. Scholarships, however, are not awarded for the study of religion or solely to further general or cultural education; the academic program should be directed towards attaining financial independence. Along with their application, they must submit transcripts, standardized test scores, proof of legal blindness, 2 letters of recommendation, and a letter of endorsement from their National Federation of the Blind state president or designee. Selection is based on academic excellence, service to the community, and financial need.

Financial data Stipends are $10,000, $5,000, or $3,000.

Duration 1 year; recipients may resubmit applications up to 2 additional years.

Additional data Scholarships are awarded at the federation convention in July. Recipients must attend the convention at federation expense; that funding is in addition to the scholarship grant.

Number awarded 2 each year: 1 at $10,000 and 1 at $3,000.

Deadline March of each year.

[383]
CHICAGO LIGHTHOUSE SCHOLARSHIPS

Chicago Lighthouse for People Who Are Blind or
    Visually Impaired
Attn: Scholarship Coordinator
1850 West Roosevelt Road
Chicago, IL 60608-1298
(312) 666-1331, ext. 3655   Fax: (312) 243-8539
TDD: (312) 666-8874
E-mail: maureen.reid@chicagolighthouse.org
Web: www.chicagolighthouse.org

Summary To provide financial assistance to blind or visually-impaired college and graduate students from Illinois.

Eligibility This program is open to undergraduate and graduate students who are legally blind, totally blind, visually-impaired, or multi-disabled and either residents of Illinois or attending college in that state. Undergraduate and graduate students must have a GPA of 3.0 or higher; vocational students must have a GPA of 2.5 or higher. Applicants must submit essays of 1 to 2 pages about 1) their economic need and how they plan to use the scholarship if they receive it; and 2) their visual impairment, their background, their educational and career goals, and how this scholarship will help achieve those goals. Selection is based on academic achievement, career goal, extracurricular activities, character, and personal and family financial need.

Financial data Stipends range from $1,000 to $5,000; funds may be used for tuition, technology (such as computers and software), readers, books and classroom materials, housing, transportation, or other approved educational items.

Duration 1 year; may be renewed up to 3 additional years.

Additional data This program began in 2004.

Number awarded Varies each year; recently, 38 of these scholarships, with a value of more than $76,000, were awarded.

Deadline March of each year.

[384]
CMMS DESHAE LOTT MINISTRIES SCHOLARSHIPS

CMMS Deshae Lott Ministries Inc.
Attn: Outreach Selection Committee
P.O. Box 9232
Bossier City, LA 71113-9232
E-mail: deshaelott@hotmail.com
Web: www.deshae.org/index.html

Summary To provide financial assistance to students who have serious physical disabilities and are working on a graduate degree in any field.

Eligibility This program is open to graduate students who have a serious physical disability and are working on a degree in any field. To qualify as having a serious physical disability, they must require complete assistance from human beings and/or major complex durable medical equipment to perform at least 3 of 13 defined daily life functions such as bathing and personal hygiene, dressing and grooming, preparing and administering medications, performing routine medical procedures, transportation, seeing, or hearing. Along with their application, they must submit a 1-page essay on how they see the work they are doing toward their degree as benefiting the human spirit and how they see their academic training relating to their avocation. U.S. citizenship is required.

Financial data Stipends are $2,000 or $1,500.

Duration 1 year.

Additional data This program was established in 2007 by Deshae E. Lott, Ph.D. who has limb girdle muscular dystrophy. It receives assistance from ministers of the Christian Metaphysicians and Mystics Society (CMMS).

Number awarded Up to 4 each year.

Deadline June of each year.

[385]
DALE M. SCHOETTLER SCHOLARSHIP FOR VISUALLY IMPAIRED STUDENTS

California State University
CSU Foundation
Attn: Director, Foundation Programs and Services
401 Golden Shore, Sixth Floor
Long Beach, CA 90802-4210
(562) 951-4509   E-mail: amoore@calstate.edu
Web: www.calstate.edu/Foundation/Scholarship.shtml

Summary To provide financial assistance to undergraduate and graduate students with visual impairments at campuses of the California State University (CSU) system.

Eligibility This program is open to full-time undergraduate and graduate students enrolled at CSU campuses who have been declared visually-impaired or legally blind. Applicants must have a cumulative GPA of 2.8 or higher.

Financial data The stipend is $6,500.

Duration 1 year.

Number awarded 42 each year.

Deadline May of each year.

[386]
DELTA GAMMA FOUNDATION FLORENCE MARGARET HARVEY MEMORIAL SCHOLARSHIP

American Foundation for the Blind
Attn: Scholarship Coordinator
1108 Third Avenue, Suite 200
Huntington, WV 25701
(304) 710-3034   Toll Free: (800) AFB-LINE
Fax: (646) 478-9260   E-mail: apreece@afb.net
Web: www.afb.org/scholarships.asp

Summary To provide financial assistance to blind undergraduate and graduate students who wish to study in the field of rehabilitation and/or education of the blind.

Eligibility This program is open to legally blind juniors, seniors, or graduate students. U.S. citizenship is required. Applicants must be studying in the field of rehabilitation and/or education of visually-impaired and blind persons. Along with their application, they must submit 200-word essays on 1) their past and recent achievements and accomplishments; 2) their intended field of study and why they have chosen it; and 3) the role their visual impairment has played in shaping their life. Financial need is considered in the selection process.

Financial data The stipend is $1,000.

Duration 1 year.

Additional data This scholarship is supported by the Delta Gamma Foundation and administered by the American Foundation for the Blind.

Number awarded 1 each year.

Deadline April of each year.

[387]
EMIL A. HONKA SCHOLARSHIPS

Montana Association for the Blind
7 West Sixth Street, Suite E
P.O. Box 465
Helena, MT 59624
(406) 442-9411   Fax: (406) 442-1612
E-mail: lglueckert@milp.us
Web: www.mtblind.org/programs.htm

Summary To provide financial assistance to blind residents of Montana who are attending college or graduate school in any state.

Eligibility This program is open to residents of Montana who are blind or have a prognosis of serious vision loss and are working on an undergraduate or graduate degree in any field at a college or university in any state. Preference is given to applicants who have completed 12 or more college credits and have a GPA of 2.5 or higher. Selection is based primarily on financial need.

Financial data The stipend is $1,000 per year.

Duration 1 year; recipients may reapply.

Additional data Recipients must attend the annual convention of the sponsoring organization to accept their award; expenses to attend the convention are reimbursed.

Number awarded Up to 2 each year.

Deadline March of each year.

[388]
E.U. AND GENE PARKER SCHOLARSHIP

National Federation of the Blind
Attn: Scholarship Committee
200 East Wells Street
Baltimore, MD 21230
(410) 659-9314, ext. 2415   Fax: (410) 685-5653
E-mail: scholarships@nfb.org
Web: www.nfb.org/scholarships

Summary To provide financial assistance to entering or continuing undergraduate and graduate blind students who have supported the work of the National Federation of the Blind (NFB).

Eligibility This program is open to legally blind students who are working on or planning to work full time on an undergraduate or graduate degree. Applicants must be able to demonstrate strong support for the NFB's work. Along with their application, they must submit transcripts, standardized test scores, proof of legal blindness, 2 letters of recommendation, and a letter of endorsement from their NFB state president or designee. Selection is based on academic excellence, service to the community, and financial need.

Financial data The stipend is $3,000.

Duration 1 year; recipients may resubmit applications up to 2 additional years.

Additional data Scholarships are awarded at the federation convention in July. Recipients must attend the convention at federation expense; that funding is in addition to the scholarship grant.

Number awarded 1 each year.

Deadline March of each year.

[389]
EUNICE FIORITO MEMORIAL SCHOLARSHIP

American Council of the Blind
Attn: Coordinator, Scholarship Program
6300 Shingle Creek Parkway, Suite 195
Brooklyn Center, MN 55430-2136
(612) 332-3242   Toll Free: (800) 424-8666
E-mail: deetheien@acbes.org
Web: www.acb.org/scholarship

Summary To provide financial assistance to undergraduate or graduate students who are blind and are interested in studying in a field of advocacy or service for persons with disabilities.

Eligibility This program is open to undergraduate and graduate students in rehabilitation, education, law, or other fields of service or advocacy for persons with disabilities. Applicants must be legally blind in both eyes. Along with their application, they must submit verification of legal blindness in both eyes; SAT, ACT, GRE, or similar scores; information on extracurricular activities (including involvement in the American Council of the Blind); employment record; and a 500-word autobiographical sketch that includes their personal goals, strengths, weaknesses, hobbies, honors, achievements, and reasons for choice of field or courses of study. A cumulative GPA of 3.3 or higher is generally required. Financial need is not considered in the selection process. Preference is given to students with little or no vision.

Financial data The stipend is $2,000.

Duration 1 year.

Additional data The scholarship winner is expected to be present at the council's annual national convention; the council will cover all reasonable costs connected with convention attendance.

Number awarded 1 each year.

Deadline February of each year.

[390]
FLOYD CALLWARD MEMORIAL SCHOLARSHIP

National Federation of the Blind of New Hampshire
c/o Andrew Harmon, Scholarship Chair
5 Central Square, Apartment 609
Keene, NH 03431
(603) 992-4053   E-mail: nfbnh.scholars@gmail.com

Summary To provide financial assistance to blind students in New Hampshire who are interested in working on an undergraduate or graduate degree at a school in any state.

Eligibility This program is open to legally blind and totally blind residents of New Hampshire who are attending or planning to attend college or graduate school in any state. Applicants may be attending college immediately after high school, returning to college at a later age, attending graduate or professional school, or enrolled in postsecondary vocational training. Blind non-residents who are attending school in New Hampshire are also eligible. Along with their application, they must submit 1) a brief essay about themselves, including their activities, interests, hobbies, personal goals, what they have done to deal with situations involving their blindness, and how the scholarship will help them; 2) 2 letters of recommendation; 3) high school and/or college transcripts; and 4) proof of legal blindness. Financial need is not considered.

Financial data The stipend is $1,000. The funds may be used to purchase education-related equipment or services or to defray the costs of tuition, board, and other school fees.

Duration 1 year.

Additional data This program began in 1990.

Number awarded 1 or more each year.

Deadline January of each year.

[391]
FLOYD QUALLS MEMORIAL SCHOLARSHIPS

American Council of the Blind
Attn: Coordinator, Scholarship Program
6300 Shingle Creek Parkway, Suite 195
Brooklyn Center, MN 55430-2136
(612) 332-3242   Toll Free: (800) 424-8666
E-mail: deetheien@acbes.org
Web: www.acb.org/scholarship

Summary To provide financial assistance to entering and continuing undergraduate and graduate students who are blind.

Eligibility This program is open to legally blind students in 4 categories: entering freshmen in academic programs, undergraduates (sophomores, juniors, and seniors) in academic programs, graduate students in academic programs, and vocational school students or students working on an associate's degree from a community college. Applicants must submit verification of legal blindness in both eyes; SAT, ACT, GRE, or similar scores; information on extracurricular activities (including involvement in the American Council of the Blind); employment record; and a 500-word autobiographical sketch that includes their personal goals, strengths, weaknesses, hobbies, honors, achievements, and reasons for choice of field or courses of study. A cumulative GPA of 3.3 or higher is generally required. Financial need is not considered in the selection process.

Financial data The stipend is $2,500.

Duration 1 year.

Additional data Scholarship winners are expected to be present at the council's annual conference; the council will cover all reasonable expenses connected with convention attendance.

Number awarded At least 4 each year: 1 in each of the 4 categories.

Deadline February of each year.

[392]
FLOYD R. CARGILL SCHOLARSHIP

Illinois Council of the Blind
Attn: Office Manager
522 East Monroe, Suite 200
P.O. Box 1336
Springfield, IL 62705-1336
(217) 523-4967   Fax: (217) 523-4302
E-mail: icb@icbonline.org
Web: www.icbonline.org/scholarship-application

Summary To provide financial assistance to blind and visually-impaired residents of Illinois who are interested in attending college in any state.

Eligibility This program is open to graduating high school seniors and full-time undergraduate or graduate students at colleges and universities in any state who are blind or visually-impaired residents of Illinois. Applicants must be U.S. citizens and have a GPA of 3.5 or higher. Along with their application, they must submit a 2-page autobiographical sketch that includes their personal goals, strengths, weaknesses, hobbies, honors, and achievements.

Financial data The stipend is $1,000.

Duration 1 year.

Number awarded 1 or more each year.

Deadline July of each year.

[393]
FRED SCHEIGERT SCHOLARSHIPS

Council of Citizens with Low Vision International
c/o American Council of the Blind
2200 Wilson Boulevard, Suite 650
Arlington, VA 22201
(202) 467-5081   Toll Free: (800) 733-2258
Fax: (703) 465-5085   E-mail: scholarship@cclvi.org
Web: www.cclvi.org/Scholarship/scholarship.html

Summary To provide financial assistance to entering and continuing undergraduate and graduate students with low vision.

Eligibility This program is open to full-time undergraduate and graduate students who have been certified by an ophthalmologist as having low vision. Applicants may be entering freshmen, undergraduates, or graduate students. They must have a GPA of 3.2 or higher and a record of involvement in their school and/or local community. Along with their application, they must submit 200-word essays on 1) what influenced their interest in their identified academic/vocational discipline; 2) their work experience and extracurricular activities; 3) any honors, awards, or citations received; and 4) how they plan to use the scholarship monies.

Financial data The stipend is $3,000.

Duration 1 year.

Number awarded 3 each year: 1 each to an entering freshman, undergraduate, and graduate student.

Deadline July of each year.

[394]
HARRY LUDWIG MEMORIAL SCHOLARSHIP

Oregon Office of Student Access and Completion
Attn: Scholarship Processing Coordinator
1500 Valley River Drive, Suite 100
Eugene, OR 97401-2146
(541) 687-7422   Toll Free: (800) 452-8807, ext. 7422
Fax: (541) 687-7414   TDD: (800) 735-2900
E-mail: cheryl.a.connolly@state.or.us
Web: app.oregonstudentaid.gov/Catalog/Default.aspx

Summary To provide financial assistance to residents of Oregon who are visually-impaired and are interested in attending college or graduate school in the state.

Eligibility This program is open to residents of Oregon who are visually-impaired (have residual acuity of 20/70 or less in the better eye with correction, or their visual field is restricted to 20 degrees or less in the better eye). Applicants must be enrolled or planning to enroll as full-time undergraduate or graduate students at a college or university in Oregon.

Financial data Stipends for scholarships offered by the Oregon Office of Student Access and Completion (OSAC) range from $1,000 to $10,000 but recently averaged $4,368.

Duration 1 year.

Additional data This program is administered by the OSAC with funds provided by the Oregon Community Foundation.

Number awarded Varies each year; recently, 7 were awarded.

Deadline February of each year.

[395]
HAZEL TEN BROEK MEMORIAL SCHOLARSHIP

National Federation of the Blind of Washington
Attn: Scholarship Chair
P.O. Box 2516
Seattle, WA 98111
(425) 823-6380   E-mail: president@nfbw.org
Web: www.nfbw.org/scholarships.html

Summary To provide financial assistance for undergraduate or graduate study in any state to blind students in Washington.

Eligibility This program is open to legally blind residents of Washington state who are working on or planning to work on a full-time college or graduate degree at a school in any state. Applicants must submit a list of honors and awards they have received, information on their community service involvement, high school and/or college transcripts, and 3 letters of reference.

Financial data The stipend is $2,000.

Duration 1 year.

Additional data This program began in 1996. Winners must attend the state convention of the National Federation of the Blind of Washington to accept the award; convention expenses are covered.

Number awarded 1 each year.

Deadline August of each year.

[396]
HOLLY ELLIOTT AND LAUREL GLASS SCHOLARSHIP ENDOWMENT

United Methodist Higher Education Foundation
Attn: Scholarships Administrator
60 Music Square East, Suite 350
P.O. Box 340005
Nashville, TN 37203-0005
(615) 649-3990   Toll Free: (800) 811-8110
Fax: (615) 649-3980
E-mail: umhefscholarships@umhef.org
Web: www.umhef.org

Summary To provide financial assistance to students at United Methodist seminaries who are deaf or deaf-blind.

Eligibility This program is open to students enrolled full time at United Methodist theological schools who are culturally deaf, orally deaf, deafened, late deafened, deaf-blind, or hard of hearing. Applicants must have a GPA of 3.0 or higher and be preparing for specialized ministries in the church, including (but not limited to) those wishing to become ordained. They must have been active, full members of a United Methodist Church for at least 1 year prior to applying. Financial need and U.S. citizenship or permanent resident status are required.

Financial data The stipend is at least $1,000 per year.

Duration 1 year; nonrenewable.

Additional data This program began in 2004.

Number awarded 1 each year.
Deadline February of each year.

[397]
JAMES DOYLE CASE MEMORIAL SCHOLARSHIPS

Mississippi Council of the Blind
c/o Randy Thompson, Scholarship Committee
107 Chalet Strasse
Brandon, MS 39042-2082
(601) 956-7906   E-mail: bonnieg06@comcast.net
Web: www.mscounciloftheblind.org/node/3

Summary To provide financial assistance to legally blind residents of Mississippi and their children who plan to attend college or graduate school in any state.

Eligibility This program is open to residents of Mississippi who are legally blind or the children of at least 1 legally blind parent. Applicants must be enrolled full time or accepted for enrollment in an undergraduate, graduate, or vocational/technical program in any state and have a GPA of 3.0 or higher. Along with their application, they must submit a 2-page autobiographical sketch, transcripts, standardized test scores (ACT or SAT for undergraduates; GRE, MCAT, LSAT, etc. for graduate students), 2 letters of recommendation, proof of acceptance from a postsecondary school, and verification of blindness of the qualifying person (applicant or parent).

Financial data The stipend is $1,500 per year.
Duration 4 years.
Number awarded 2 each year.
Deadline February of each year.

[398]
JENNICA FERGUSON MEMORIAL SCHOLARSHIP OF OHIO

National Federation of the Blind of Ohio
c/o Deborah Kendrick, Scholarship Committee Chair
2514 Hackberry Street
Cincinnati, OH 45206
(513) 673-4474   E-mail: dkkendrick@earthlink.net
Web: www.nfbohio.org/new

Summary To provide financial assistance to blind residents of Ohio who are interested in working on an undergraduate or graduate degree at a school in any state.

Eligibility This program is open to residents of Ohio who are legally blind. Applicants must be attending or planning to attend an accredited institution of higher education in any state as a full-time undergraduate or graduate student. Along with their application, they must submit 2 letters of recommendation, current transcripts, a letter about themselves that includes how they have dealt with their blindness and their hopes and dreams, and a letter from an officer of the National Federation of the Blind of Ohio indicating that they have discussed their scholarship application with that officer. Selection is based on academic excellence, community service, and financial need.

Financial data The stipend is $1,500.
Duration 1 year.

Number awarded 1 each year.
Deadline May of each year.

[399]
JOANN FISCHER SCHOLARSHIP

American Council of the Blind of Ohio
Attn: Scholarship Committee
3805 North High Street, Suite 305
Columbus, OH 43214
(614) 221-6688 Toll Free: (800) 835-2226 (within OH)
E-mail: acbo.scholarships@gmail.com
Web: www.acbohio.org

Summary To provide financial assistance to Ohio graduate students who are blind and working on a degree in any field.

Eligibility This program is open to 1) residents of Ohio who are currently enrolled as graduate students; and 2) graduate students at colleges and universities in Ohio. Applicants must be legally blind and working on or planning to work on a degree in any field. Along with their application, they must submit transcripts (must have a GPA of 3.0 or higher), a certificate of legal blindness, and an essay of 250 to 500 words on their career objectives, future plans, personal goals, other academic or personal qualities, and why they believe they are qualified to receive this scholarship. Financial need is not the sole factor considered in the selection process.

Financial data The stipend is $2,500 per year.
Duration 1 year; recipients may reapply.

Additional data Winners are required to attend the Saturday workshops at the sponsor's annual convention; a stipend for meals and workshops is provided.

Number awarded 1 each year.
Deadline July of each year.

[400]
JOSEPH ROEDER SCHOLARSHIP

National Industries for the Blind
Attn: Learning and Development Manager
1310 Braddock Place
Alexandria, VA 22314-1691
(703) 310-0500   Fax: (703) 310-0494
E-mail: kgallagher@nib.org
Web: www.nib.org/resources/grants-and-scholarships

Summary To provide financial assistance to blind undergraduate and graduate students who working on a degree in a business-related field.

Eligibility This program is open to students who are blind and enrolled in college or graduate school. Applicants must be working on a degree in a field related to business. Along with their application, they must submit an essay of 200 to 500 words on their career history and future career goals.

Financial data The stipend is $2,500.
Duration 1 year.
Additional data This program began in 2012.
Number awarded 1 each year.
Deadline May of each year.

[401]
KENNETH JERNIGAN SCHOLARSHIP

National Federation of the Blind
Attn: Scholarship Committee
200 East Wells Street
Baltimore, MD 21230
(410) 659-9314, ext. 2415   Fax: (410) 685-5653
E-mail: scholarships@nfb.org
Web: www.nfb.org/scholarships

Summary   To provide financial assistance to entering or continuing undergraduate and graduate blind students.

Eligibility   This program is open to legally blind students who are working on or planning to work full time on an undergraduate or graduate degree. Along with their application, they must submit transcripts, standardized test scores, proof of legal blindness, 2 letters of recommendation, and a letter of endorsement from their National Federation of the Blind state president or designee. Selection is based on academic excellence, service to the community, and financial need.

Financial data   The stipend is $12,000.

Duration   1 year; recipients may resubmit applications up to 2 additional years.

Additional data   Scholarships are awarded at the federation convention in July. Recipients must attend the convention at federation expense; that funding is in addition to the scholarship grant. This scholarship is given by the American Action Fund for Blind Children and Adults, a nonprofit organization that assists blind people.

Number awarded   1 each year.

Deadline   March of each year.

[402]
KENNETH TIEDE MEMORIAL SCHOLARSHIPS

National Federation of the Blind of Kansas
c/o Dianne Hemphill, Scholarship Chair
600 North Bel Rue Street
Derby, KS 67037-7300
(316) 201-1323   E-mail: diannehemphill@cox.net
Web: www.nfbks.org/conventions/scholarships.shtml

Summary   To provide financial assistance for college to blind students from Kansas.

Eligibility   This program is open to legally blind undergraduate and graduate students who are residents of Kansas or attending or planning to attend a college, university, or technical school in the state. Applicants must have a GPA of 2.5 or higher. They must be able to attend the state convention of the National Federation of the Blind of Kansas. Selection is based on academic excellence, community service, and financial need.

Financial data   The stipend is $1,000.

Duration   1 year.

Number awarded   Up to 3 each year.

Deadline   June of each year.

[403]
LANCASTER SCHOLARSHIP

VisionCorps Foundation
244 North Queen Street
Lancaster, PA 17603
(717) 291-5951   E-mail: info@visioncorps.net
Web: www.visioncorps.net/Content/scholarships.asp

Summary   To provide financial assistance to Pennsylvania residents who are legally blind veterans and interested in working on a degree at any level at a college in any state.

Eligibility   This program is open to veterans who are residents of Pennsylvania and legally blind. Applicants must be attending or planning to attend an institution of higher education at any level in any state. Along with their application, they must submit a brief description of their career goal. Financial need is considered in the selection process.

Financial data   The stipend is $1,000 per year.

Duration   1 year; may be renewed up to 3 additional years.

Additional data   This sponsor was formerly the Susquehanna Foundation for the Blind.

Number awarded   1 or more each year.

Deadline   January of each year.

[404]
LARRY STREETER MEMORIAL SCHOLARSHIP

National Federation of the Blind
Attn: Scholarship Committee
200 East Wells Street
Baltimore, MD 21230
(410) 659-9314, ext. 2415   Fax: (410) 685-5653
E-mail: scholarships@nfb.org
Web: www.nfb.org/scholarships

Summary   To provide financial assistance to blind students working on an undergraduate or graduate degree in any field.

Eligibility   This program is open to legally blind students who are working on or planning to work full time on an undergraduate or graduate degree in any field. Applicants must be attempting to "elevate their quality of life, equipping them to be active, productive participants in their family, community, and the workplace." Along with their application, they must submit transcripts, standardized test scores, proof of legal blindness, 2 letters of recommendation, and a letter of endorsement from their National Federation of the Blind state president or designee. Selection is based on academic excellence, service to the community, and financial need.

Financial data   The stipend is $5,000.

Duration   1 year; recipients may resubmit applications up to 2 additional years.

Additional data   This program began in 2011. Scholarships are awarded at the federation convention in July. Recipients must attend the convention at federation expense; that funding is in addition to the scholarship grant.

Number awarded 1 each year.
Deadline March of each year.

[405]
LIGHTHOUSE GUILD GRADUATE SCHOOL SCHOLARSHIP

Lighthouse Guild
Attn: Director Special Programs
250 West 64th Street
New York, NY 10023
(212) 769-7801   Toll Free: (800) 284-4422
Fax: (212) 769-6266
E-mail: scholars@lighthouseguild.org
Web: www.lighthouseguild.org

Summary To provide financial assistance to legally blind students who are working on a graduate degree at a university in any state.

Eligibility This program is open to graduate students who are legally blind and U.S. citizens. Applicants must be enrolled or planning to enroll at an accredited college or university in any state. Along with their application, they must submit transcripts, 3 letters of recommendation and a 500-word essay on their educational and personal goals. Selection is based on academic and personal achievements; financial need is not considered.

Financial data The stipend is $10,000.

Duration 1 year; nonrenewable.

Additional data This sponsor was established in 2014 as the result of a merger of Lighthouse International and the Jewish Guild for the Blind.

Number awarded 1 or more each year.

Deadline March of each year.

[406]
LILLIAN GORELL SCHOLARSHIP FUND

Pittsburgh Foundation
Attn: Scholarship Coordinator
Five PPG Place, Suite 250
Pittsburgh, PA 15222-5414
(412) 391-5122   Fax: (412) 391-7259
E-mail: turnerd@pghfdn.org
Web: www.pittsburghfoundation.org/node/1655

Summary To provide financial assistance to entering or continuing undergraduate and graduate students, especially those who are blind or studying the arts.

Eligibility This program is open to all applicants, but preference is given to blind students and to those working on a degree in the arts. Applicants must be enrolled or planning to enroll at a college or university in any state. Along with their application, they must submit 1) a brief essay explaining their educational goals; 2) official transcripts; and 3) a statement of the amount they need and the purpose for which the award will be used.

Financial data A stipend is awarded (amount not specified). Funds are intended to be used for maintenance, supplies, instructions, tuition, room, board, and any other expenses related to attending an educational institution.

Duration 1 year; recipients may reapply until completion of their educational program.

Number awarded 1 or more each year.
Deadline April of each year.

[407]
LILLIAN S. EDELSTEIN SCHOLARSHIP FOR THE BLIND

National Federation of the Blind
Attn: Scholarship Committee
200 East Wells Street
Baltimore, MD 21230
(410) 659-9314, ext. 2415   Fax: (410) 685-5653
E-mail: scholarships@nfb.org
Web: www.nfb.org/scholarships

Summary To provide financial assistance to entering or continuing undergraduate and graduate blind students.

Eligibility This program is open to legally blind students who are working on or planning to work full time on an undergraduate or graduate degree. Along with their application, they must submit transcripts, standardized test scores, proof of legal blindness, 2 letters of recommendation, and a letter of endorsement from their National Federation of the Blind state president or designee. Selection is based on academic excellence, service to the community, and financial need.

Financial data The stipend is $3,000.

Duration 1 year; recipients may resubmit applications up to 2 additional years.

Additional data Scholarships are awarded at the federation convention in July. Recipients must attend the convention at federation expense; that funding is in addition to the scholarship grant.

Number awarded 1 each year.

Deadline March of each year.

[408]
LINWOOD WALKER SCHOLARSHIP

American Council of the Blind of Ohio
Attn: Scholarship Committee
3805 North High Street, Suite 305
Columbus, OH 43214
(614) 221-6688   Toll Free: (800) 835-2226 (within OH)
E-mail: acbo.scholarships@gmail.com
Web: www.acbohio.org

Summary To provide financial assistance to blind Ohio graduate students in service-related fields.

Eligibility This program is open to 1) residents of Ohio who are currently enrolled as graduate students; and 2) graduate students at colleges and universities in Ohio. Applicants must be legally blind and working on or planning to work on a degree in a service-related field (e.g., teaching, health care, public administration). Along with their application, they must submit transcripts (must have a GPA of 3.0 or higher), a certificate of legal blindness, and an essay of 250 to 500 words on their career objectives, future plans, personal goals, other academic or personal qualities, and why they believe they are qualified to receive this scholarship. Financial need is not the sole factor considered in the selection process.

Financial data The stipend is $2,500 per year.

Duration 1 year; recipients may reapply.

Additional data Winners are required to attend the Saturday workshops at the sponsor's annual convention; a stipend for meals and workshops is provided.

Number awarded 1 each year.

Deadline July of each year.

[409]
MARY P. OENSLAGER SCHOLASTIC ACHIEVEMENT AWARDS

Learning Ally
Attn: National Achievement Awards
20 Roszel Road
Princeton, NJ 08540
(609) 520-8084   Toll Free: (800) 221-4792
Fax: (609) 987-8116   E-mail: naa@LearningAlly.org
Web: www.learningally.org/NAA/Application-SAA.aspx

Summary To recognize and reward the outstanding academic achievements of blind college seniors and graduate students.

Eligibility To be eligible for this award, candidates must 1) be blind or visually-impaired; 2) have received, or will receive, a bachelor's, master's, or doctoral degree from a 4-year accredited college or university in the United States or its territories during the year the award is given; and 3) have been registered members of Learning Ally for at least 1 year. Selection is based on academic excellence, leadership, and service to others.

Financial data Top winners receive $6,000 each and special honors winners $2,000 each.

Duration The awards are presented annually.

Additional data These awards are named for the founder of the program who established it in 1959 and endowed it with a gift of $1 million in 1990. Learning Ally was formerly named Recording for the Blind and Dyslexic.

Number awarded 6 each year: 3 top winners and 3 special honors winners.

Deadline April of each year.

[410]
MISSOURI COUNCIL OF THE BLIND SCHOLARSHIPS

Missouri Council of the Blind
Attn: Scholarship Program
5453 Chippewa Street
St. Louis, MO 63109-1635
(314) 832-7172 Toll Free: (800) 342-5632 (within MO)
Fax: (314) 832-7796   E-mail: aa@moblind.org
Web: www.missouricounciloftheblind.org

Summary To provide financial assistance for college or graduate school to blind students in Missouri.

Eligibility This program is open to Missouri residents who are high school or college graduates, legally blind, and in good academic standing. Applicants must be working on or planning to work on an undergraduate or graduate degree. They should have a specific goal in mind and that goal should be realistically within reach.

Financial data A stipend is awarded (amount not specified).

Duration 1 year; may be renewed if the recipient maintains a GPA of 2.0 or higher.

Number awarded Varies each year; recently, 14 were awarded.

Deadline April of each year.

[411]
NATIONAL FEDERATION OF THE BLIND OF CALIFORNIA SCHOLARSHIPS

National Federation of the Blind of California
c/o Mary Willows, President
3934 Kern Court
Pleasanton, CA 94588
(925) 462-8575   E-mail: mwillows@sbcglobal.net
Web: sixdots.org/resources

Summary To provide financial assistance to blind residents of California interested in attending college or graduate school in any state.

Eligibility This program is open to residents of California who are legally blind. Applicants must be enrolled or planning to enroll as a full-time student in an undergraduate or graduate degree program in any state. They must have a GPA of 3.0 or higher. Along with their application, they must submit a 500-word statement on the educational and career goals they wish to achieve with the assistance of this scholarship, their involvement in the blindness community, the alternative techniques they use to do their school work (e.g., Braille, large print, recording, adapted computer), and any rehabilitation services they are receiving.

Financial data Stipends are $2,000 or $1,500.

Duration 1 year.

Additional data This program includes the following named awards: the Gerald Drake Memorial Scholarship, the LaVyrl "Pinky" Johnson Memorial Scholarship, the Julie Landucci Scholarship, and the Lawrence "Muzzy" Marcelino Memorial Scholarship.

Number awarded Varies each year; recently, 2 at $1,500 and 1 at $2,000 were awarded.

Deadline September of each year.

[412]
NATIONAL FEDERATION OF THE BLIND OF CONNECTICUT SCHOLARSHIPS

National Federation of the Blind of Connecticut
477 Connecticut Boulevard, Suite 217
East Hartford, CT 06108
(860) 289-1971   E-mail: info@nfbct.org
Web: www.nfbct.org/html/schinfo.htm

Summary To provide financial assistance for college or graduate school to blind students from Connecticut.

Eligibility This program is open to full-time undergraduate and graduate students who are legally blind. Applicants must be residents of Connecticut or attending school in the state. Along with their application, they must submit 2 letters of recommendation, academic transcripts, a description of their career goals and how this scholarship might help them achieve those, and a letter from a state officer of the National Federation of the Blind of Connecticut confirming that they have discussed their application with him or her. Selection is based on academic excellence, service to the community, and financial need.

Financial data Stipends range from $3,000 to $5,000.

Duration 1 year.

Additional data This program consists of the following named awards: the C. Rodney Demarest Memorial Scholarship ($3,000), the Howard E. May Memorial Scholarship ($5,000), the Jonathan May Memorial Scholarship ($4,000), and the Mary Main Memorial Scholarship ($3,000). The latter 3 programs are supported by the John A. Coccomo, Sr. Foundation. Recipients are expected to attend the annual convention of the National Federation of the Blind of Connecticut.

Number awarded 4 each year.

Deadline September of each year.

[413]
NATIONAL FEDERATION OF THE BLIND OF ILLINOIS SCHOLARSHIPS

National Federation of the Blind of Illinois
c/o Deborah Kent Stein, Scholarship Committee Chair
5817 North Nina Avenue
Chicago, IL 60631
(773) 203-1394   E-mail: dkent5817@att.net
Web: www.nfbofillinois.org/?page_id=97

Summary To provide financial assistance for college or graduate school to blind students in Illinois.

Eligibility This program is open to legally blind full-time undergraduate and graduate students. Applicants must be residents of Illinois or attending a college or university in the state. Along with their application, they must submit a personal essay that describes their strengths, achievements, and aspirations; what is important to them; who they hope to become; if a particular person or experience has changed their life; how their blindness has affected them; and how they handle blindness at school, on the job, and in interpersonal relationships. Selection is based on academic excellence and service to the community.

Financial data Stipends $2,000 or $1,500 per year.

Duration 1 year; recipients may reapply.

Additional data This program includes the Peter Grunwald Scholarship.

Number awarded 3 each year: 1 at $2,000 and 2 at $1,500.

Deadline March of each year.

[414]
NATIONAL FEDERATION OF THE BLIND OF MASSACHUSETTS SCHOLARSHIPS

National Federation of the Blind of Massachusetts
c/o Amy Ruell, President
9 Quail Run
Hingham, MA 02043
(617) 752-1116   E-mail: aruell@comcast.net
Web: www.nfbma.org/students

Summary To provide financial assistance for college or graduate school to blind students from Massachusetts.

Eligibility This program is open to legally blind students who are entering or enrolled at a postsecondary educational institution on a full-time basis. Applicants must be residents of Massachusetts or attending school in the Commonwealth. Along with their application, they must provide information on the high school, college, or graduate program they have attended; their high school or undergraduate GPA; a list of honors and awards they have received; and essays on their career goal and plan for the future, how blindness has affected their life so far, how they see it affecting their future, and their involvement in blindness organizations. Financial need is not considered in the selection process.

Financial data The stipend is $1,000.

Duration 1 year.

Additional data Finalists must attend the annual convention of the National Federation of the Blind of Massachusetts.

Number awarded Up to 3 each year.

Deadline December of each year.

[415]
NATIONAL FEDERATION OF THE BLIND OF NEW JERSEY SCHOLARSHIPS

National Federation of the Blind of New Jersey
c/o Jerilyn Higgins, Scholarship Chair
2 Old Farm Road
Verona, NJ 07044-1726
(973) 239-8874   Toll Free: (866) 632-1940
E-mail: jdhiggins3@verizon.net
Web: www.nfbnj.org/scholarships.php

Summary To provide financial assistance to entering and continuing undergraduate and graduate students from New Jersey who are blind.

Eligibility This program is open to legally blind students who are working on or planning to work full time on an undergraduate or graduate degree. Applicants must be residents of New Jersey or attending school in the state. Along with their application, they must submit a personal letter, 2 letters of recommendation, transcripts, and a letter of endorsement from an officer of the National Federation of the Blind of New Jersey. Selection is based on academic excellence, service to the community, and financial need.

Financial data A stipend is awarded (amount not specified).

Duration 1 year.

Number awarded Varies each year; recently, 2 were awarded.

Deadline March of each year.

[416]
NATIONAL FEDERATION OF THE BLIND OF NEW YORK SCHOLARSHIPS

National Federation of the Blind of New York State, Inc.
Attn: Catherine Mendez, Scholarship Committee Chair
P.O. Box 205666 Sunset Station
Brooklyn, NY 11220
(718) 567-7821   Fax: (718) 765-1843
E-mail: scholarships@nfbny.org
Web: www.nfbny.org/scholarships

Summary To provide financial assistance to blind residents of New York who are interested in attending college or graduate school in any state.

Eligibility This program is open to residents of New York who are legally blind. Applicants must be entering or enrolled in a degree program at the undergraduate, graduate, or postgraduate level at a school in any state. Along with their application, they must submit a 500-word essay explaining their goals, attitudes, and approach to living with blindness.

Financial data A stipend is awarded (amount not specified).

Duration 1 year.

Additional data This program includes the following named awards: the Gisela Distal Memorial Scholarship and the Maryanne Swaton Memorial Scholarship.

Number awarded At least 3 each year.

Deadline September of each year.

[417]
NATIONAL FEDERATION OF THE BLIND OF OHIO SCHOLARSHIPS

National Federation of the Blind of Ohio
c/o Deborah Kendrick, Scholarship Committee Chair
2514 Hackberry Street
Cincinnati, OH 45206
(513) 673-4474   E-mail: dkkendrick@earthlink.net
Web: www.nfbohio.org/new

Summary To provide financial assistance to blind residents of Ohio who are interested in working on an undergraduate or graduate degree at a school in any state.

Eligibility This program is open to residents of Ohio who are legally blind. Applicants must be attending or planning to attend an accredited institution of higher education as a full-time undergraduate or graduate student. Along with their application, they must submit 2 letters of recommendation, current transcripts, a letter about themselves that includes how they have dealt with their blindness and their hopes and dreams, and a letter from an officer of the National Federation of the Blind of Ohio indicating that they have discussed their scholarship application with that officer. Selection is based on academic excellence, community service, and financial need.

Financial data The stipend is $1,000.

Duration 1 year.

Additional data This program includes the Robert Eschbach Scholarship and the Barbara E. Fohl Memorial Scholarship.

Number awarded 2 each year.
Deadline May of each year.

[418]
NATIONAL FEDERATION OF THE BLIND OF OREGON SCHOLARSHIPS

National Federation of the Blind of Oregon
c/o Carla McQuillan, President
5005 Main Street
Springfield, OR 97478
(541) 653-9153   E-mail: president@nfb-oregon.org
Web: www.nfb-oregon.org

Summary To provide financial assistance for college or graduate school to blind residents of Oregon.

Eligibility This program is open to blind residents of Oregon who are working on or planning to work on an undergraduate or graduate degree at a college or university in the state. Applicants must be enrolled full time or enrolled part time and working full time. Along with the application, they must submit a personal letter that includes what they consider their best qualities and the techniques and approaches they practice concerning their blindness. Selection is based on academic excellence, community service, and financial need.

Financial data Stipends range from $2,000 to $5,000 per year.

Duration 1 year; recipients may apply for the Len Hannon Scholarship as an additional year of support at the same value as their original scholarship.

Number awarded 5 each year: 1 at $5,000, 2 at $3,000, and 2 at $2,000.

Deadline June of each year.

[419]
NATIONAL FEDERATION OF THE BLIND SCHOLARSHIPS

National Federation of the Blind
Attn: Scholarship Committee
200 East Wells Street
Baltimore, MD 21230
(410) 659-9314, ext. 2415   Fax: (410) 685-5653
E-mail: scholarships@nfb.org
Web: www.nfb.org/scholarships

Summary To provide financial assistance for college or graduate school to blind students.

Eligibility This program is open to legally blind students who are working on or planning to work on an undergraduate or graduate degree. In general, full-time enrollment is required, although 1 scholarship may be awarded to a part-time student who is working full time. Along with their application, they must submit transcripts, standardized test scores, proof of legal blindness, 2 letters of recommendation, and a letter of endorsement from their National Federation of the Blind state president or designee. Selection is based on academic excellence, service to the community, and financial need.

Financial data Stipends are $5,000 or $3,000.

Duration 1 year; recipients may resubmit applications up to 2 additional years.

Additional data Scholarships are awarded at the federation convention in July. Recipients must attend the convention at federation expense; that funding is in addition to the scholarship grant.

Number awarded 20 each year: 3 at $5,000 and 17 at $3,000.

Deadline March of each year.

[420]
NEW JERSEY COMMISSION FOR THE BLIND AND VISUALLY IMPAIRED COLLEGE SERVICES

New Jersey Commission for the Blind and Visually Impaired
Attn: Coordinator of Vocational Rehabilitation and Transition Services
153 Halsey Street, Sixth Floor
P.O. Box 47017
Newark, NJ 07101-8004
(973) 648-3660   Toll Free: (877) 685-8878
E-mail: Amanda.gerson@dhs.state.nj.us
Web: www.state.nj.us

Summary To provide financial assistance to clients of the New Jersey Commission for the Blind and Visually Impaired (NJCBVI) who are interested in attending college in the state.

Eligibility This program is open to residents of New Jersey who have been determined eligible for vocational rehabilitation services through the NJCBVI. Applicants must be interested in attending an accredited college or university in the state in a program that is consistent with the employment goal listed on their Individualized Plan for Employment (IPE) and approved by the Commission. They must have been accepted into an accredited college or university in the state as a full-time undergraduate or graduate student.

Financial data For tuition and fees, undergraduates receive up to $5,210 per semester and graduate students receive up to $614 per credit. All students also receive $5,064 per semester for room and board, $350 per semester for books and supplies, up to $150 per month for public transportation or 31 cents per mile for car travel, $40 per month for Internet service, a personal maintenance allowance that depends on financial need, and reader service up to $125 per month for undergraduates or $200 per month for graduate students.

Duration 1 semester; may be renewed until completion of a degree, provided the recipient remains enrolled full time, makes satisfactory progress toward degree completion, and maintains a GPA of 2.0 or higher as an undergraduate or 3.0 or higher as a graduate student.

Number awarded Varies each year.

Deadline Deadline not specified.

[421]
NORA WEBB-MCKINNEY SCHOLARSHIP

American Council of the Blind of Ohio
Attn: Scholarship Committee
3805 North High Street, Suite 305
Columbus, OH 43214
(614) 221-6688   Toll Free: (800) 835-2226 (within OH)
E-mail: acbo.scholarships@gmail.com
Web: www.acbohio.org

Summary To provide financial assistance to Ohio students who are interested in working on an undergraduate or graduate degree involving service to blind people.

Eligibility This program is open to 1) residents of Ohio who are high school seniors or current undergraduate or graduate students; and 2) undergraduate and graduate students from any state enrolled at colleges and universities in Ohio. Applicants must be interested in working on or planning to work on a degree in a field related to blindness (e.g., special education, rehabilitation, teaching or counseling, orientation and mobility, or a concentration on programs serving people who are blind). They may be blind or sighted. Along with their application, they must submit transcripts (must have a GPA of 3.0 or higher) and an essay of 250 to 500 words on their career objectives, future plans, personal goals, other academic or personal qualities, and why they believe they are qualified to receive this scholarship. Financial need is not the sole factor considered in the selection process.

Financial data The stipend is $2,000 per year.

Duration 1 year; recipients may reapply.

Additional data Winners are required to attend the Saturday workshops at the sponsor's annual convention; a stipend for meals and workshops is provided.

Number awarded 1 each year.

Deadline July of each year.

[422]
NORTH DAKOTA ASSOCIATION OF THE BLIND SCHOLARSHIPS

North Dakota Association of the Blind
c/o Tracy Wicken, Scholarship Committee Chair
733 Dawn Circle
Grand Forks, ND 58203
(701) 772-7669   E-mail: trwicken@nd.gov
Web: www.ndab.org

Summary To provide financial assistance to blind students in North Dakota who are interested in attending college or graduate school in any state.

Eligibility This program is open to North Dakota residents who have a visual impairment that cannot be corrected with prescription glasses and are attending an institution of higher education in any state. They may be entering freshmen, undergraduates, or graduate students. Applicants for the $2,000 scholarship must be full-time students and have a GPA of 2.5 or higher; applicants for the $1,000 scholarships may be part-time students. Along with their application, they must submit 2 letters of recommendation, transcripts, a family financial aid statement, and a 500-word essay that describes their extracurricular

activities and hobbies, how the scholarship will help them, their goals and aspirations, and what they have done to deal with situations involving their vision loss. Selection is based on academic excellence, financial need, and service to the community.
Financial data   Stipends are $2,000 or $1,000.
Duration   1 year.
Additional data   This program began in 1990.
Number awarded   3 each year: 1 at $2,000 and 2 at $1,000.
Deadline   March of each year.

[423]
ORACLE SCHOLARSHIP FOR EXCELLENCE IN COMPUTER SCIENCE

National Federation of the Blind
Attn: Scholarship Committee
200 East Wells Street
Baltimore, MD 21230
(410) 659-9314, ext. 2415   Fax: (410) 685-5653
E-mail: scholarships@nfb.org
Web: www.nfb.org/scholarships

Summary   To provide financial assistance to entering or continuing undergraduate and graduate blind students who are interested in working on a degree in a field related to computer science.
Eligibility   This program is open to legally blind students who are working on or planning to work full time on an undergraduate or graduate degree in computer science, computer engineering, user experience, or a related field. Along with their application, they must submit transcripts, standardized test scores, proof of legal blindness, 2 letters of recommendation, and a letter of endorsement from their National Federation of the Blind state president or designee. Selection is based on academic excellence, service to the community, and financial need.
Financial data   The stipend is $8,000.
Duration   1 year; recipients may resubmit applications up to 2 additional years.
Additional data   This program is sponsored by Oracle Corporation. Scholarships are awarded at the federation convention in July. Recipients must attend the convention at federation expense; that funding is in addition to the scholarship grant.
Number awarded   1 each year.
Deadline   March of each year.

[424]
ORACLE SCHOLARSHIP FOR EXCELLENCE IN STEM

National Federation of the Blind
Attn: Scholarship Committee
200 East Wells Street
Baltimore, MD 21230
(410) 659-9314, ext. 2415   Fax: (410) 685-5653
E-mail: scholarships@nfb.org
Web: www.nfb.org/scholarships

Summary   To provide financial assistance to entering or continuing undergraduate and graduate blind students

who are interested in working on a degree in a field of science, technology, engineering, and mathematics (STEM).
Eligibility   This program is open to legally blind students who are working on or planning to work full time on an undergraduate or graduate degree in a field of STEM. Along with their application, they must submit transcripts, standardized test scores, proof of legal blindness, 2 letters of recommendation, and a letter of endorsement from their National Federation of the Blind state president or designee. Selection is based on academic excellence, service to the community, and financial need.
Financial data   The stipend is $8,000.
Duration   1 year; recipients may resubmit applications up to 2 additional years.
Additional data   This program is sponsored by Oracle Corporation. Scholarships are awarded at the federation convention in July. Recipients must attend the convention at federation expense; that funding is in addition to the scholarship grant.
Number awarded   1 each year.
Deadline   March of each year.

[425]
PAUL AND ELLEN RUCKES SCHOLARSHIP

American Foundation for the Blind
Attn: Scholarship Coordinator
1108 Third Avenue, Suite 200
Huntington, WV 25701
(304) 710-3034   Toll Free: (800) AFB-LINE
Fax: (646) 478-9260   E-mail: apreece@afb.net
Web: www.afb.org/scholarships.asp

Summary   To provide financial assistance to legally blind students who wish to work on a graduate or undergraduate degree in engineering or computer, physical, or life sciences.
Eligibility   This program is open to legally blind undergraduate or graduate students who are U.S. citizens working or planning to work full time on a degree in engineering or the computer, physical, or life sciences. Along with their application, they must submit 200-word essays on 1) their past and recent achievements and accomplishments; 2) their intended field of study and why they have chosen it; and 3) the role their visual impairment has played in shaping their life. Financial need is considered in the selection process.
Financial data   The stipend is $2,000.
Duration   1 year.
Number awarded   2 each year.
Deadline   April of each year.

[426]
PEARSON AWARD

National Federation of the Blind
Attn: Scholarship Committee
200 East Wells Street
Baltimore, MD 21230
(410) 659-9314, ext. 2415   Fax: (410) 685-5653
E-mail: scholarships@nfb.org
Web: www.nfb.org/scholarships

Summary To provide financial assistance to entering or continuing undergraduate and graduate blind students.
Eligibility This program is open to legally blind students who are working on or planning to work full time on an undergraduate or graduate degree. Along with their application, they must submit transcripts, standardized test scores, proof of legal blindness, 2 letters of recommendation, and a letter of endorsement from their National Federation of the Blind state president or designee. Selection is based on academic excellence, service to the community, and financial need.

Financial data The stipend is $3,000.

Duration 1 year; recipients may resubmit applications up to 2 additional years.

Additional data Scholarships are awarded at the federation convention in July. Recipients must attend the convention at federation expense; that funding is in addition to the scholarship grant.

Number awarded 1 each year.

Deadline March of each year.

[427]
POULSON FAMILY SCHOLARSHIPS

Utah Council of the Blind
Attn: Leslie Gertsch, Executive Director
P.O. Box 1415
Bountiful, UT 84011-1415
(801) 299-0670　　　　　Toll Free: (800) 273-4569
Fax: (801) 292-6046　　E-mail: ucb.board@gmail.com
Web: www.utahcounciloftheblind.org/scholarships.html

Summary To provide financial assistance to members of the Utah Council of the Blind (UCB) who plan to attend college or graduate school in the state.
Eligibility This program is open to UCB members who are entering or enrolled as an undergraduate or graduate student at a college or university in Utah. Applicants must be blind or visually-impaired. Selection is based on GPA, test scores (SAT or ACT for entering or continuing freshmen; GRE, GMAT, LSAT, etc. for continuing graduate students), work experience, and extracurricular activities.

Financial data The stipend is at least $1,000.

Duration 1 year; may be renewed.

Number awarded Varies each year; recently, 5 were awarded.

Deadline April of each year.

[428]
ROBERT AND HAZEL STALEY MEMORIAL SCHOLARSHIP

National Federation of the Blind of North Carolina
c/o Alan Chase
1217 Manassas Court, Unit C
Raleigh, NC 27609
(910) 612-2220　　　　E-mail: aachase1@gmail.com
Web: www.nfbofnc.org

Summary To provide financial assistance to undergraduate and graduate students from North Carolina who are blind and interested in attending college in any state.
Eligibility This program is open to legally blind residents of North Carolina who are attending or planning to attend a college or university in any state. Applicants must be working on or planning to work on an undergraduate or graduate degree. Along with their application, they must submit 2 letters of recommendation, a current transcript, and a letter of introduction about themselves that includes their likes and dislikes, how their blindness has affected them, the honors and awards they have received, and their school and extracurricular activities. Selection is based on academic excellence and service to the community.

Financial data The stipend is $1,500. Funds may be used for the purchase of equipment, reader services, transportation, or other services or materials necessary to accomplish the recipient's educational objectives. They are not intended to offset support provided by state or federal agencies.

Duration 1 year.

Additional data Recipients must attend the annual convention of the National Federation of the Blind of North Carolina, at federation expense, where they receive their awards.

Number awarded Up to 2 each year.

Deadline June of each year.

[429]
ROSS N. AND PATRICIA PANGERE FOUNDATION SCHOLARSHIPS

American Council of the Blind
Attn: Coordinator, Scholarship Program
6300 Shingle Creek Parkway, Suite 195
Brooklyn Center, MN 55430-2136
(612) 332-3242　　　　　Toll Free: (800) 424-8666
E-mail: deetheien@acbes.org
Web: www.acb.org/scholarship

Summary To provide financial assistance to blind students working on an undergraduate or graduate degree in business.
Eligibility This program is open to undergraduate and graduate students working on a degree in business. Applicants must submit verification of legal blindness in both eyes; SAT, ACT, GMAT, or similar scores; information on extracurricular activities (including involvement in the American Council of the Blind); employment record; and a 500-word autobiographical sketch that includes their personal goals, strengths, weaknesses, hobbies, honors, achievements, and reasons for choice of field or courses of study. A cumulative GPA of 3.3 or higher is generally required. Financial need is not considered in the selection process.

Financial data The stipend is $2,500.

Duration 1 year.

Additional data This program is funded by the Ross N. and Patricia Pangere Foundation. The scholarship winner is expected to be present at the council's annual national convention; the council will cover all reasonable costs connected with convention attendance.

Number awarded   2 or 3 each year.
Deadline   February of each year.

[430]
ROY JOHNSON SCHOLARSHIPS

Michigan Department of Licensing and Regulatory
  Affairs
Attn: Bureau of Services for Blind Persons
201 North Washington Square
P.O. Box 30652
Lansing, MI 48909
(517) 373-2062   Toll Free: (800) 292-4200
Fax: (517) 335-5140   TDD: (517) 373-4025
Web: www.michigan.gov

Summary   To provide tuition assistance to residents of
any state who are blind and interested in working on a
graduate degree at a college in Michigan.

Eligibility   This program is open to blind people (regardless of sex, race, color, religion, or age) who have received
a bachelor's degree from an accredited college or university in the United States. Applicants must be working on or
planning to work on a graduate degree at an institution in
Michigan. Both college seniors and currently-enrolled
graduate students are eligible. Factors considered in the
selection process include financial need, scholastic
record, college recommendations, and applicant's plans
for graduate education.

Financial data   Stipends range from $250 to $1,000.
Funds may be used to cover tuition, room and board, or
reader services.

Duration   1 year.

Additional data   Funds must be used to pursue graduate studies at an accredited college in Michigan.

Number awarded   Varies each year; recently, 13 were
awarded.

Deadline   May of each year.

[431]
RUDOLPH DILLMAN MEMORIAL
SCHOLARSHIP

American Foundation for the Blind
Attn: Scholarship Coordinator
1108 Third Avenue, Suite 200
Huntington, WV 25701
(304) 710-3034   Toll Free: (800) AFB-LINE
Fax: (646) 478-9260   E-mail: apreece@afb.net
Web: www.afb.org/scholarships.asp

Summary   To provide financial assistance to legally
blind undergraduate or graduate students studying in the
field of rehabilitation and/or education of visually-impaired
and blind persons.

Eligibility   This program is open to legally blind U.S. citizens who have been accepted to an accredited undergraduate or graduate training program within the broad
field of rehabilitation and/or education of blind and visually-impaired persons. Along with their application, they
must submit 200-word essays on 1) their past and recent
achievements and accomplishments; 2) their intended

field of study and why they have chosen it; and 3) the role
their visual impairment has played in shaping their life.

Financial data   The stipend is $2,500 per year.

Duration   1 academic year; previous recipients may not
reapply.

Number awarded   4 each year.

Deadline   April of each year.

[432]
SEE THE FUTURE FUND SCHOLARSHIPS

The See the Future Fund
Attn: Thomas Theune, Founder and Chair
P.O. Box 63022
Colorado Springs, CO 80962-3022
(719) 471-3200   Fax: (719) 471-3210
E-mail: twtheune@comcast.net
Web: www.seethefuture.org

Summary   To provide financial assistance to blind or
visually-impaired residents of Colorado who are interested
in attending college or graduate school in any state.

Eligibility   This program is open to residents of Colorado who meet standards of blindness or visual impairment. Applicants must be enrolled full time at a postsecondary program in any state as 1) a freshman entering an
academic program; 2) a sophomore, junior, or senior in an
academic program; 3) a graduate student in an academic
program; or 4) a student in a vocational/technical school
or community college. Selection is based on academic
achievement, school and community service, and financial need.

Financial data   Stipends are $3,000, $2,500, or $2,000
per year. Funds are paid directly to the recipient's institution to be used for tuition, fees, books, room, and board.

Duration   Up to 4 years.

Additional data   This program began in 1998.

Number awarded   Varies each year; recently, the program offered 1 scholarship at $3,000 per year for 4 years,
1 at $2,500 per year for 4 years, 1 at $2,000 per year for 4
years, and 3 at $2,000 per year for 2 years.

Deadline   February of each year.

[433]
SOUTH DAKOTA REDUCED TUITION FOR
VISUAL IMPAIRMENT

South Dakota Board of Regents
Attn: Scholarship Committee
306 East Capitol Avenue, Suite 200
Pierre, SD 57501-2545
(605) 773-3455   Fax: (605) 773-5320
E-mail: info@sdbor.edu
Web: www.sdbor.edu

Summary   To provide waiver of tuition and fees to residents of South Dakota who have a visual impairment and
are interested in attending college or graduate school in
the state.

Eligibility   This program is open to visually-impaired
residents of South Dakota who can meet the entrance
requirements for admission to a postsecondary educational institution (including graduate school and medical

school) under the supervision of the state board of regents. For purposes of the program, "visual impairment" means that the person cannot, with use of correcting glasses, see sufficiently well to perform ordinary activities for which eyesight is essential. This program does not extend to visually-impaired persons who are entitled to receive tuition and fee support from the state's department of vocational rehabilitation.

Financial data Qualified applicants receive a total waiver of standard tuition and fees.

Duration Benefits are provided until the recipient has earned 225 semester hours of credit or the equivalent.

Additional data Applicants should contact the financial aid director at the South Dakota college or university they plan to attend, not the sponsor. The exemption from charges does not apply if a course is repeated because of unsatisfactory performance within the student's control.

Number awarded Varies each year.

Deadline Deadline not specified.

[434]
SUSQUEHANNA POST-GRADUATE SCHOLARSHIP

VisionCorps Foundation
244 North Queen Street
Lancaster, PA 17603
(717) 291-5951   E-mail: info@visioncorps.net
Web: www.visioncorps.net/Content/scholarships.asp

Summary To provide financial assistance to legally blind Pennsylvania residents who are interested in working on a graduate degree at a school in any state to prepare for a career in rehabilitation services for people who are blind.

Eligibility This program is open to residents of Pennsylvania who are legally blind. Applicants must be interested in working on a graduate degree in a professional field serving people who are blind (e.g., rehabilitation teaching, orientation and mobility instruction, teacher of the visually-impaired). Along with their application, they must submit a brief description of their career goal. Financial need is considered in the selection process.

Financial data The stipend is $3,000 per year.

Duration 2 years.

Additional data This sponsor was formerly the Susquehanna Foundation for the Blind.

Number awarded 1 or more each year.

Deadline January of each year.

[435]
TEXAS BLIND/DEAF STUDENT EXEMPTION PROGRAM

Texas Higher Education Coordinating Board
Attn: Grants and Special Programs
1200 East Anderson Lane
P.O. Box 12788
Austin, TX 78711-2788
(512) 427-6340   Toll Free: (800) 242-3062
Fax: (512) 427-6420
E-mail: grantinfo@thecb.state.tx.us
Web: www.collegeforalltexans.com

Summary To provide a tuition exemption at Texas public colleges to undergraduate or graduate blind and/or deaf residents of the state.

Eligibility This program is open to Texas residents who can present certification from the Department of Assistive and Rehabilitative Services of their deafness or blindness. Applicants must present to the registrar of a public college or university in Texas a copy of their high school transcript, a letter of recommendation, proof that they have met all admission requirements, and a statement of purpose that indicates the certificate, degree program, or professional enhancement that they intend to pursue.

Financial data Eligible students are exempted from the payment of all dues, fees, and tuition charges at publicly-supported colleges and universities in Texas.

Duration Up to 8 semesters, provided the recipient maintains a GPA of 2.0 or higher as an undergraduate or 3.0 or higher as a graduate student.

Number awarded Varies each year; recently, 3,493 students received $11,469,863 in support through this program.

Deadline Deadline not specified.

[436]
VISIONCORPS FOUNDATION FOR THE BLIND TRUSTEES' SCHOLARSHIP

VisionCorps Foundation
244 North Queen Street
Lancaster, PA 17603
(717) 291-5951   E-mail: info@visioncorps.net
Web: www.visioncorps.net/Content/scholarships.asp

Summary To provide financial assistance to legally blind Pennsylvania residents who are interested in working on an undergraduate or graduate degree or other academic program at a school in any state.

Eligibility This program is open to residents of Pennsylvania who are legally blind. Applicants must be working on an undergraduate or graduate degree or other specialized program intended to generate upward mobility in employment. Along with their application, they must submit a brief description of their career goal. Financial need is considered in the selection process.

Financial data A stipend is awarded (amount not specified).

Duration 1 year.

Additional data This sponsor was formerly the Susquehanna Foundation for the Blind.

Number awarded   1 or more each year.
Deadline   January of each year.

[437]
WASHINGTON COUNCIL OF THE BLIND SCHOLARSHIPS

Washington Council of the Blind
c/o Tim McCorcle, Scholarship Committee Chair
2253 N.E. 54th Street
Seattle, WA 98105-3213
Toll Free: (206) 522-5850
E-mail: t.mccorcle@comcast.net
Web: www.wcbinfo.org/scholarships

Summary   To provide financial aid to blind students in Washington who plan to attend college or graduate school in any state.

Eligibility   This program is open to blind residents of Washington state who are enrolled or planning to enroll at an accredited college, university, vocational school, or graduate school in any state. Applicants must submit a 1,000-word statement of their reasons for applying for this scholarship and how it will assist them to achieve their goals. The statement should include a brief description of their background, education, work experience, economic status, strengths, weaknesses, and personal goals for the next 5 to 10 years. Interviews are required.

Financial data   The stipend ranges from $1,000 to $4,000.

Duration   1 year.

Number awarded   Varies each year; recently, 9, worth $17,500, were awarded.

Deadline   August of each year.

[438]
WILLIAM AND DOROTHY FERRELL SCHOLARSHIP

Association for Education and Rehabilitation of the
  Blind and Visually Impaired
Attn: Scholarship Committee
1703 North Beauregard Street, Suite 440
Alexandria, VA 22311-1717
(703) 671-4500, ext. 201   Toll Free: (877) 492-2708
Fax: (703) 671-6391   E-mail: scholarships@aerbvi.org
Web: www.aerbvi.org/resources/aer-scholarships

Summary   To provide financial assistance to blind undergraduate and graduate students who wish to study for a career in service to blind and visually-impaired people.

Eligibility   Applicants for this award must be legally blind (have a visual acuity of 20/200 or less in the best-corrected eye and/or a visual field of 20 degrees of less). They must be preparing for a career in service to blind and visually-impaired people (special education, orientation and mobility, rehabilitation training, etc.). Along with their application, they must submit an autobiographical sketch that includes information on their vocational goals, work or volunteer experiences, outside activities including the extent to which they play a leadership role, and other

details about their objectives. Financial need is not considered in the selection process.

Financial data   The stipend is $1,000.

Number awarded   2 every other year.

Deadline   March of even-numbered years.

[439]
WILLIAM G. COREY MEMORIAL SCHOLARSHIP

American Council of the Blind
Attn: Coordinator, Scholarship Program
6300 Shingle Creek Parkway, Suite 195
Brooklyn Center, MN 55430-2136
(612) 332-3242   Toll Free: (800) 424-8666
E-mail: deetheien@acbes.org
Web: www.acb.org/scholarship

Summary   To provide financial assistance for college to blind undergraduate and graduate students from Pennsylvania.

Eligibility   This program is open to legally blind undergraduate and graduate students who are residents of Pennsylvania or attending college in the state. Applicants must submit verification of legal blindness in both eyes; SAT, ACT, GRE, or similar scores; information on extracurricular activities (including involvement in the American Council of the Blind); employment record; and a 500-word autobiographical sketch that includes their personal goals, strengths, weaknesses, hobbies, honors, achievements, and reasons for choice of field or courses of study. A cumulative GPA of 3.3 or higher is generally required. Financial need is not considered in the selection process.

Financial data   The stipend is $1,500.

Duration   1 year.

Additional data   Scholarship winners are expected to be present at the council's annual conference; the council will cover all reasonable expenses connected with convention attendance.

Number awarded   1 each year.

Deadline   February of each year.

[440]
WYCB SCHOLARSHIP

Wyoming Council of the Blind
c/o Linda Johnson
308 North Gilbert Street
Powell, WY 82435
Web: www.wycb.info/scholarship

Summary   To provide financial assistance to blind residents of Wyoming who are interested in attending college or graduate school in any state.

Eligibility   This program is open to residents of Wyoming who are legally blind or visually-impaired. Applicants must be entering or enrolled at a vocational training program, college, university, community college, or graduate school in any state and have a GPA of 2.0 or higher. Along with their application, they must submit a 2-page autobiographical sketch that includes 1) how they will use this scholarship and how it will it impact their educational experience; 2) their short and long-term educational and work goals; and 3) their personal and academic achievements, work experience, hobbies, and any other information they think would be helpful. Financial need is not considered in the selection process. Leading candidates are interviewed.

Financial data   The stipend is $1,500.

Duration   1 year.

Number awarded   1 each year.

Deadline   March of each year.

Hearing Disabilities

Undergraduates ●

Graduate Students ●

Described here are 30 funding opportunities available to individuals who have difficulty in receiving linguistic information, with or without amplification. Of these, 17 are for undergraduates and 13 are for graduate students. All of this is "free" money. Not one dollar will need to be repaid (provided, of course, that recipients meet all program requirements). If you are looking for a particular program and don't find it in this section, be sure to check the Program Title Index to see if it is covered elsewhere in the directory.

Undergraduates

[441]
ALEXANDER GRAHAM BELL COLLEGE SCHOLARSHIP AWARDS PROGRAM

Alexander Graham Bell Association for the Deaf and
  Hard of Hearing
Attn: College Scholarship Program
3417 Volta Place, N.W.
Washington, DC 20007-2778
(202) 337-5220   Fax: (202) 337-8314
TDD: (202) 337-5221   E-mail: financialaid@agbell.org
Web: www.agbell.org/Document.aspx?id=266

Summary   To provide financial assistance to undergraduate and graduate students with moderate to profound hearing loss.

Eligibility   This program is open to full-time undergraduate students who have been diagnosed with a moderate to profound bilateral hearing loss prior to their fourth birthday (hearing loss averages 60dB or greater in the better ear in the speech frequencies of 500, 1000, and 2000 Hz). Applicants must be committed to using listening and spoken language as their primary mode of communication. They must be accepted or enrolled at a mainstream college or university as a full-time undergraduate or graduate student and have a GPA of 3.25 or higher. Along with their application, they must submit a 1-page essay on 1 of the following topics: 1) if they could invent or improve upon a product, what it would be and why; 2) if they could change 1 thing to improve society on a local or global level, what it would be and why; or 3) their goals, how or why they became their goals, and the impact they hope to have over the course of their life. Financial need is not considered in the selection process.

Financial data   Stipends range from $2,500 to $10,000 per year.

Duration   1 year; may be renewed 1 additional year.

Additional data   This program includes the following named awards: the Allie Raney Hunt Scholarship, the Bennion Family Scholarship, the Deaf and Hard of Hearing Section Scholarship Fund, the Elsie M. Bell Grosvenor Scholarship Awards, the Federation of Jewish Women's Organization Scholarship, the Herbert P. Feibelman, Jr. Scholarship, the Ladies' Auxiliary National Rural Letter Carriers Scholarship, the Louis DiCarlo Scholarship, the Lucille B. Abt Scholarships, the Robert H. Weitbrecht Scholarship, the Samuel M. and Gertrude G. Levy Scholarship Fund, the Volta Scholarship Fund, and the Walter W. and Thelma C. Hissey College Scholarships.

Number awarded   Varies each year; recently, 20 were awarded.

Deadline   February of each year.

[442]
ANDERS TJELLSTROM SCHOLARSHIPS

Cochlear Americas
Attn: Scholarships
13059 East Peakview Avenue
Centennial, CO 80111
(303) 790-9010   Toll Free: (800) 483-3123
Fax: (303) 790-1157
E-mail: Customer@Cochlear.com
Web: www.cochlear.com

Summary   To provide financial assistance for college to students who have a Baha device.

Eligibility   This program is open to graduating high school seniors, current university students, and older students who have been accepted into a university course. Applicants must have a Baha device (developed by Dr. Anders Tjellström to restore hearing to deaf students). They must have a GPA of 2.5 or higher. Along with their application, they must submit a 1,000-word personal statement on their academic aspirations and other interests, including why they chose their proposed area of study, their postgraduate aspirations, why they wish to receive this scholarship, and how their Cochlear technology has impacted their life. Selection is based on academic achievement and demonstrated commitment to the ideals of leadership and humanity.

Financial data   The stipend is $2,000 per year.

Duration   1 year; may be renewed up to 3 additional years, provided the recipient maintains a GPA of 2.5 or higher.

Additional data   This program began in 2012.

Number awarded   Varies each year; recently, 3 were awarded.

Deadline   September of each year.

[443]
ARTS AND SCIENCES AWARDS

Alexander Graham Bell Association for the Deaf and
  Hard of Hearing
Attn: Financial Aid Coordinator
3417 Volta Place, N.W.
Washington, DC 20007-2778
(202) 337-5220   Fax: (202) 337-8314
TDD: (202) 337-5221   E-mail: financialaid@agbell.org
Web: www.agbell.org/ArtsSciencesAward

Summary   To provide financial aid to hearing-impaired students who are participating in extracurricular activities in arts and sciences.

Eligibility   This program is open to residents of the United States or Canada who have been diagnosed prior to their fourth birthday as having a moderate to profound bilateral hearing loss and who use spoken language as their primary form of communication. They must be between 6 and 19 years of age and enrolled in an art or science program as an extracurricular activity during afterschool time, summer, or weekends. Programs can be offered through museums, nature centers, art or music centers, zoological parks, space and science camps, dance and theater studios, martial arts studios, or any other program with a focus on the arts or sciences. Recreational summer camps, sports camps or sports, and travel and study abroad programs that do not have an explicit arts or science focus are not eligible. Membership in the Alexander Graham Bell Association is not required, but preference is given to members.

Financial data Recently, awards ranged from $100 to $2,000.

Duration 1 year; may be renewed upon reapplication.

Number awarded Varies each year; recently, 38 students received a total of $29,000 in these awards.

Deadline April of each year.

[444]
CARL J. MEGEL SPECIAL EDUCATION SCHOLARSHIP

Illinois Federation of Teachers
500 Oakmont Lane
P.O. Box 390
Westmont, IL 60559
(630) 468-4080   Fax: (630) 468-4089
Web: www.ift.org/your-benefits/scholarships

Summary To provide financial assistance to children of members of the Illinois Federation of Teachers (IFT) who have been enrolled in special education and are interested in attending college in any state.

Eligibility This program is open to graduating high school seniors who are children of currently-employed active members of the IFT or of deceased members who were in good standing at the time of their death. Applicants must be enrolled in a special education school, class, or program for students with autism, cognitive disability, deaf-blindness, deafness, emotional disability, hearing impairment, multiple disabilities, orthopedic impairment, other health impairment, specific learning disability, speech or language impairment, traumatic brain injury, or visual impairment. Along with their application, they must submit an essay describing how any obstacles and/or achievements that you have encountered in your life have helped shape your decision to complete a postsecondary education.

Financial data The stipend is $1,000.

Duration 1 year.

Number awarded 1 each year.

Deadline February of each year.

[445]
CAROLINE KARK AWARD FOR DEAF STUDENTS

New York State Grange
100 Grange Place
Cortland, NY 13045
(607) 756-7553   Fax: (607) 756-7757
E-mail: nysgrange@nysgrange.org
Web: www.nysgrange.org/educationalassistance.html

Summary To provide financial assistance to members of the Grange in New York who are deaf and attending college in any state.

Eligibility This program is open to members of the New York State Grange who are currently enrolled at a college in any state. Applicants must be deaf.

Financial data A stipend is awarded (amount not specified).

Duration 1 year; nonrenewable.

Number awarded 1 or more each year.

Deadline April of each year.

[446]
ECCLESTON-CALLAHAN SCHOLARSHIPS

Central Florida Foundation
Attn: Eccleston-Callahan Memorial Fund
800 North Magnolia Avenue, Suite 1200
Orlando, FL 32803
(407) 872-3050   Fax: (407) 425-2990
E-mail: info@cffound.org
Web: www.cffound.org/receive/scholarships

Summary To provide financial assistance to students with disabilities enrolled at specified Florida colleges and universities.

Eligibility This program is open to students at designated colleges and universities in Florida who have a physical disability (blindness, mobility impairment, or deafness). Applicants must be enrolled full time, have a GPA of 3.0 or higher, be younger than 21 years of age, and be able to demonstrate financial need.

Financial data The stipend is $1,000 per year.

Duration 1 year; may be renewed.

Additional data The participating institutions are the University of Florida, the University of Central Florida, Florida A&M University, Florida State University, Valencia Community College, Seminole Community College, and Orlando Tech.

Number awarded Varies each year.

Deadline June of each year.

[447]
GRAEME CLARK SCHOLARSHIPS

Cochlear Americas
Attn: Scholarships
13059 East Peakview Avenue
Centennial, CO 80111
(303) 790-9010   Toll Free: (800) 483-3123
Fax: (303) 790-1157
E-mail: Customer@Cochlear.com
Web: www.cochlear.com

Summary To provide financial assistance for college to students who have received a Nucleus Cochlear Implant.

Eligibility This program is open to graduating high school seniors, current university students, and older students who have been accepted into a university course. Applicants must have received a Nucleus Cochlear Implant. They must have a GPA of 2.5 or higher. Along with their application, they must submit a 1,000-word personal statement on their academic aspirations and other interests, including why they chose their proposed area of study, their postgraduate aspirations, why they wish to receive this scholarship, and how their Cochlear technology has impacted their life. Selection is based on academic achievement and demonstrated commitment to the ideals of leadership and humanity.

Financial data The stipend is $2,000 per year.

Duration 1 year; may be renewed up to 3 additional years, provided the recipient maintains a GPA of 2.5 or higher.

Additional data This program began in 2002.

Number awarded Varies each year; recently, 5 were awarded.

Deadline September of each year.

[448]
J. PARIS MOSLEY SCHOLARSHIP

Cleveland Foundation
Attn: Scholarship Processing
1422 Euclid Avenue, Suite 1300
Cleveland, OH 44115-2001
(216) 861-3810   Fax: (216) 861-1729
E-mail: TCFscholarships@clevefdn.org
Web: www.clevelandfoundation.org

Summary To provide financial assistance for college to high school seniors in any state who are deaf or whose primary caregivers are deaf.

Eligibility This program is open to high school seniors in any state who are deaf or hard of hearing or have a relative living in their household who is deaf or hard of hearing. Applicants must be planning to attend a college, university, vocational school, or other postsecondary program in any state. They must use some form of sign language, have a GPA of 2.5 or higher, and be able to demonstrate financial need. Preference is given to students of African American, Latino American, or Native American descent.

Financial data The stipend ranges from $500 to $1,000.

Duration 1 year.

Number awarded 1 or more each year.

Deadline March of each year.

[449]
LOUISE TUMARKIN ZAZOVE SCHOLARSHIPS

Louise Tumarkin Zazove Foundation
c/o Barbara D. Reed, Treasurer
2903 Craig Road
Ann Arbor, MI 48103
E-mail: philip@ltzfoundation.org
Web: www.ltzfoundation.org/scholarships.php

Summary To provide financial assistance for college to people with hearing loss.

Eligibility This program is open to U.S. citizens and permanent residents who have a significant bilateral hearing loss. Applicants must be enrolled or planning to enroll as an undergraduate student at a college or university in any state. Along with their application, they must submit a transcript of high school and/or college grades, 3 letters of recommendation, documentation of the severity of the hearing loss, information on any special circumstances by or about the family, and documentation of financial need.

Financial data A stipend is awarded (amount not specified). Funds are paid directly to schools.

Duration 1 year; may be renewed up to 3 additional years, provided the recipient continues to do well in school and demonstrate financial need.

Additional data This program began in 2003.

Number awarded Varies each year; since the program was established, it has awarded 35 scholarships.

Deadline May of each year.

[450]
OPTIMIST INTERNATIONAL COMMUNICATION CONTEST FOR THE DEAF AND HARD OF HEARING

Optimist International
Attn: Programs Department
4494 Lindell Boulevard
St. Louis, MO 63108
(314) 371-6000   Toll Free: (800) 500-8130, ext. 235
Fax: (314) 371-6006   E-mail: programs@optimist.org
Web: www.optimist.org/e/member/scholarships2.cfm

Summary To recognize and reward, with college scholarships, outstanding presentations made by hearing-impaired high school students.

Eligibility This program is open to young people up to and including grade 12 in the United States and Canada, to CEGEP in Québec, and to grade 13 in the Caribbean. Applicants must be identified by a qualified audiologist as deaf or hard of hearing with a hearing loss of 40 decibels or more. They are invited to make a presentation (using oral communication, sign language, or a combination of both) from 4 to 5 minutes on a topic that changes annually; a recent topic was "What the World Gains from Optimism." Competition is first conducted at the level of individual clubs, with winners advancing to zone and then district competitions. Selection is based on material organization (40 points), delivery and presentation (30 points), and overall effectiveness (30 points).

Financial data Each district winner receives a $2,500 college scholarship, payable to an educational institution of the recipient's choice, subject to the approval of Optimist International.

Duration The competition is held annually.

Additional data Entry information is available only from local Optimist Clubs.

Number awarded Nearly 300 Optimist International clubs participate in this program each year. Each participating district offers 1 scholarship; some districts may offer a second award with separate competitions for signing and oral competitors, or for male and female entrants.

Deadline Each club sets its own deadline. Districts must submit materials to the national office by June of each year.

[451]
SCHOLARSHIP TRUST FOR THE HEARING IMPAIRED

Travelers Protective Association of America
Attn: TPA Scholarship Trust for the Hearing Impaired
2041 Exchange Drive
St. Charles, MO 63303-5987
(636) 724-2227   Toll Free: (877) 872-2638
Fax: (636) 724-2457   E-mail: vsedodo@tpahq.org
Web: www.tpahq.org/scholarshiptrust/apply

Summary To provide assistance to deaf and hearing-impaired persons interested in obtaining additional education, mechanical devices, specialized medical treatment, or other treatments.

Eligibility This assistance is available to U.S. residents who are deaf or hearing-impaired. Applicants must be able to demonstrate that they need assistance in obtaining mechanical devices, medical or specialized education, speech classes, note takers, interpreters, or other areas of need that are directly related to hearing impairment.

Financial data Grants typically range from $100 to $1,000.

Duration 1 year; recipients may reapply.

Additional data This fund was established in 1975.

Number awarded Varies each year; since the trust was established, it has distributed more than $2 million to more than 5,000 recipients.

Deadline March, June, September, or December of each year.

[452]
SERTOMA SCHOLARSHIPS FOR HARD OF HEARING OR DEAF STUDENTS

Sertoma International
Attn: Scholarships
1912 East Meyer Boulevard
Kansas City, MO 64132-1174
(816) 333-8300, ext. 214   Fax: (816) 333-4320
TDD: (816) 333-8300
E-mail: infosertoma@sertomahq.org
Web: www.sertoma.org/what-we-do/scholarships

Summary To provide financial assistance for college to hearing-impaired students.

Eligibility This program is open to students who have a minimum 40dB bilateral hearing loss and are interested in working full time on a bachelor's degree at a 4-year college or university in the United States. Students working on a graduate degree, community college degree, associate degree, or vocational program degree are ineligible. Applicants must have a GPA of 3.2 or higher. Along with their application, they must submit a personal statement of 300 to 500 words on how this scholarship will help them achieve their goals. U.S. citizenship is required. Selection is based on academic achievement, honors and awards received, community volunteer activities, interscholastic activities, extracurricular activities, and 2 letters of recommendation.

Financial data The stipend is $1,000 per year.

Duration 1 year; may be renewed up to 4 times.

Additional data Sertoma, which stands for SERvice TO MAnkind, is a volunteer service organization with 25,000 members in 800 clubs across North America. Funding for this program is provided by Oticon, Inc. and the Sertoma Foundation.

Number awarded Varies each year; recently, 50 were awarded.

Deadline April of each year.

[453]
SPECIAL PEOPLE GIFTS OF LOVE PROGRAM

Italian Catholic Federation
8393 Capwell Drive, Suite 110
Oakland, CA 94621
(510) 633-9058   Toll Free: (888) ICF-1924
Fax: (510) 633-9758   E-mail: info@icf.org
Web: www.icf.org/charity

Summary To provide funding to individuals who have a disability and desire additional training or instruction.

Eligibility This program is open to 1) individuals who have a disability and desire formal training or instruction in a particular vocation, academic, athletic, or artistic field; 2) qualified instructors on behalf of an individual with a disability who exhibits a particular skill to be developed and who desires formal instruction or training; or 3) adults with custodial responsibility for, and on behalf of, an individual with a disability who exhibits a particular skill to be developed and who desires formal instruction or training. The program defines disability to include ADD/ADHD, amputee, autism, cerebral palsy, emotional disturbances, hearing impairments or deafness, mental retardation, multiple sclerosis, muscular dystrophy, orthopedic impairments, specific learning disabilities, speech and language impairments, spina bifida, spinal cord injury, traumatic brain injury, visual impairments and blindness, or other health impairments that require special education or related services. Applicants must submit an essay on how they intend to use the grant funds to assist them with their disability or to achieve the goals of the program. Financial need is considered in the selection process.

Financial data A stipend is awarded (amount not specified). Funds are not intended to support tuition.

Duration These are 1-time grants.

Number awarded Varies each year.

Deadline Deadline not specified.

[454]
TEXAS BLIND/DEAF STUDENT EXEMPTION PROGRAM

Texas Higher Education Coordinating Board
Attn: Grants and Special Programs
1200 East Anderson Lane
P.O. Box 12788
Austin, TX 78711-2788
(512) 427-6340   Toll Free: (800) 242-3062
Fax: (512) 427-6420
E-mail: grantinfo@thecb.state.tx.us
Web: www.collegeforalltexans.com

Summary To provide a tuition exemption at Texas public colleges to undergraduate or graduate blind and/or deaf residents of the state.

Eligibility This program is open to Texas residents who can present certification from the Department of Assistive and Rehabilitative Services of their deafness or blindness. Applicants must present to the registrar of a public college or university in Texas a copy of their high school transcript, a letter of recommendation, proof that they have met all admission requirements, and a statement of purpose that indicates the certificate, degree program, or professional enhancement that they intend to pursue.

Financial data Eligible students are exempted from the payment of all dues, fees, and tuition charges at publicly-supported colleges and universities in Texas.

Duration Up to 8 semesters, provided the recipient maintains a GPA of 2.0 or higher as an undergraduate or 3.0 or higher as a graduate student.

Number awarded Varies each year; recently, 3,493 students received $11,469,863 in support through this program.

Deadline Deadline not specified.

[455]
THEODORE R. AND VIVIAN M. JOHNSON SCHOLARSHIP PROGRAM

State University System of Florida
Attn: Board of Governors
325 West Gaines Street
Tallahassee, FL 32399-0400
(850) 245-0466   Fax: (850) 245-9685
E-mail: info@flbog.org
Web: www.flbog.edu

Summary To provide financial assistance to Florida undergraduate students who have disabilities.

Eligibility This program is open to students with disabilities enrolled or planning to enroll at a State University System of Florida institution. Applicants must be able to verify the nature and/or extent of their disability, which may be in 1 or more of the following classifications: attention deficit disorder (ADD); attention deficit hyperactivity disorder (ADHD); autism spectrum disorder; blind or low vision; deaf or hard of hearing; orthopedic disability; psychological, emotional, or behavioral disability; speech/language impairment; specific learning disability; traumatic brain injury; or other health disabilities. They must have a GPA of 2.0 or higher and be able to document financial need. Along with their application, they must submit a 1-page personal statement on their achievements, activities, career goals, and the effects of their disability(ies).

Financial data The stipend depends on the availability of funds.

Duration 1 year; may be renewed up to 5 additional years, provided the recipient maintains a GPA of 2.0 or higher and enrolls in at least 18 credits each academic year.

Additional data This program is administered by the equal opportunity program at each of the 12 State University System of Florida 4-year institutions. Contact that office for further information. Funding is provided by the Theodore R. and Vivian M. Johnson Foundation, with matching funding from the Florida Legislature.

Number awarded Several each year.

Deadline April of each year.

[456]
VIRGINIA COBB SCHOLARSHIP

The Charity League, Inc.
Attn: Scholarship Committee
P.O. Box 530233
Birmingham, AL 35253-0233
(205) 876-3830   E-mail: epmilne8@gmail.com
Web: www.thecharityleague.org/scholarships

Summary To provide financial assistance to high school seniors in Alabama who have a speech or hearing impairment and are interested in attending college in any state.

Eligibility This program is open to seniors graduating from high schools in Alabama and planning to enroll at a college or university in any state. Applicants must have a speech or hearing impairment. Along with their application, they must submit an essay of 1 to 2 pages about themselves, their achievements, and their goals.

Financial data The stipend ranges from $500 to $2,000.

Duration 1 year.

Additional data This program began in 2002.

Number awarded 1 each year.

Deadline May of each year.

[457]
WISCONSIN HEARING AND VISUALLY HANDICAPPED STUDENT GRANT PROGRAM

Wisconsin Higher Educational Aids Board
131 West Wilson Street, Suite 902
P.O. Box 7885
Madison, WI 53707-7885
(608) 266-0888   Fax: (608) 267-2808
E-mail: cindy.cooley@wi.gov
Web: www.heab.state.wi.us/programs.html

Summary To provide financial support for undergraduate study to Wisconsin residents who are legally deaf or blind.

Eligibility This program is open to Wisconsin residents who can submit evidence of a severe or profound hearing or visual impairment certified by a medical examiner. Applicants must be enrolled at least half time at a branch of the University of Wisconsin, a technical college in the state, a Wisconsin independent college or university, a tribal college in the state, or an institution out of state that specializes in the training of deaf, hard of hearing, or visually handicapped students or that offers a program of study not offered by a Wisconsin institution. Financial need is considered in the selection process.

Financial data Grants range from $250 to $1,800 per academic year.

Duration 1 year; may be renewed up to 4 additional years.

Number awarded Varies each year.
Deadline Deadline not specified.

Graduate Students

[458]
ALAN B., '32, AND FLORENCE B., '35, CRAMMATTE FELLOWSHIP

Gallaudet University Alumni Association
Attn: Graduate Fellowship Fund Committee
Peikoff Alumni House
Gallaudet University
800 Florida Avenue, N.E.
Washington, DC 20002-3695
(202) 651-5060   Fax: (202) 651-5062
TDD: (202) 651-5060
E-mail: alumni.relations@gallaudet.edu
Web: www.gallaudet.edu

Summary To provide financial assistance to deaf students who wish to work on a graduate degree in a field related to business at universities for people who hear normally.

Eligibility This program is open to deaf and hard of hearing graduates of Gallaudet University or other accredited academic institutions who have been accepted for graduate study in a business-related field at colleges or universities for people who hear normally. Applicants must be working full time on a doctorate or other terminal degree. Financial need is considered in the selection process.

Financial data The amount awarded varies, depending upon the needs of the recipient and the availability of funds.

Duration 1 year; may be renewed.

Additional data This fund is 1 of 12 designated funds included in the Graduate Fellowship Fund of the Gallaudet University Alumni Association.

Number awarded Up to 1 each year.

Deadline April of each year.

[459]
ALEXANDER GRAHAM BELL COLLEGE SCHOLARSHIP AWARDS PROGRAM

Alexander Graham Bell Association for the Deaf and Hard of Hearing
Attn: College Scholarship Program
3417 Volta Place, N.W.
Washington, DC 20007-2778
(202) 337-5220   Fax: (202) 337-8314
TDD: (202) 337-5221 E-mail: financialaid@agbell.org
Web: www.agbell.org/Document.aspx?id=266

Summary To provide financial assistance to undergraduate and graduate students with moderate to profound hearing loss.

Eligibility This program is open to full-time undergraduate students who have been diagnosed with a moderate to profound bilateral hearing loss prior to their fourth birthday (hearing loss averages 60dB or greater in the better ear in the speech frequencies of 500, 1000, and 2000 Hz). Applicants must be committed to using listening and spoken language as their primary mode of communication. They must be accepted or enrolled at a mainstream college or university as a full-time undergraduate or graduate student and have a GPA of 3.25 or higher. Along with their application, they must submit a 1-page essay on 1 of the following topics: 1) if they could invent or improve upon a product, what it would be and why; 2) if they could change 1 thing to improve society on a local or global level, what it would be and why; or 3) their goals, how or why they became their goals, and the impact they hope to have over the course of their life. Financial need is not considered in the selection process.

Financial data Stipends range from $2,500 to $10,000 per year.

Duration 1 year; may be renewed 1 additional year.

Additional data This program includes the following named awards: the Allie Raney Hunt Scholarship, the Bennion Family Scholarship, the Deaf and Hard of Hearing Section Scholarship Fund, the Elsie M. Bell Grosvenor Scholarship Awards, the Federation of Jewish Women's Organization Scholarship, the Herbert P. Feibelman, Jr. Scholarship, the Ladies' Auxiliary National Rural Letter Carriers Scholarship, the Louis DiCarlo Scholarship, the Lucille B. Abt Scholarships, the Robert H. Weitbrecht Scholarship, the Samuel M. and Gertrude G. Levy Scholarship Fund, the Volta Scholarship Fund, and the Walter W. and Thelma C. Hissey College Scholarships.

Number awarded Varies each year; recently, 20 were awarded.

Deadline February of each year.

[460]
ALPHA SIGMA PI FRATERNITY FELLOWSHIP

Gallaudet University Alumni Association
Attn: Graduate Fellowship Fund Committee
Peikoff Alumni House
Gallaudet University
800 Florida Avenue, N.E.
Washington, DC 20002-3695
(202) 651-5060   Fax: (202) 651-5062
TDD: (202) 651-5060
E-mail: alumni.relations@gallaudet.edu
Web: www.gallaudet.edu

Summary To provide financial assistance to deaf students who wish to work on a doctoral degree at universities for people who hear normally.

Eligibility This program is open to deaf and hard of hearing graduates of Gallaudet University or other accredited colleges or universities who have been accepted for graduate study at academic institutions for people who hear normally. Applicants must be working full time on a doctorate or other terminal degree. Preference is given to alumni members of Alpha Sigma Pi Fraternity. Financial need is considered in the selection process.

Financial data The amount awarded varies, depending upon the needs of the recipient and the availability of funds.

Duration 1 year; may be renewed.

Additional data This program began in 1999 as 1 of 12 designated funds within the Graduate Fellowship Fund of the Gallaudet University Alumni Association.

Number awarded Up to 1 each year.

Deadline April of each year.

[461]
CMMS DESHAE LOTT MINISTRIES SCHOLARSHIPS

CMMS Deshae Lott Ministries Inc.
Attn: Outreach Selection Committee
P.O. Box 9232
Bossier City, LA 71113-9232
E-mail: deshaelott@hotmail.com
Web: www.deshae.org/index.html

Summary To provide financial assistance to students who have serious physical disabilities and are working on a graduate degree in any field.

Eligibility This program is open to graduate students who have a serious physical disability and are working on a degree in any field. To qualify as having a serious physical disability, they must require complete assistance from human beings and/or major complex durable medical equipment to perform at least 3 of 13 defined daily life functions such as bathing and personal hygiene, dressing and grooming, preparing and administering medications, performing routine medical procedures, transportation, seeing, or hearing. Along with their application, they must submit a 1-page essay on how they see the work they are doing toward their degree as benefiting the human spirit and how they see their academic training relating to their avocation. U.S. citizenship is required.

Financial data Stipends are $2,000 or $1,500.

Duration 1 year.

Additional data This program was established in 2007 by Deshae E. Lott, Ph.D. who has limb girdle muscular dystrophy. It receives assistance from ministers of the Christian Metaphysicians and Mystics Society (CMMS).

Number awarded Up to 4 each year.

Deadline June of each year.

[462]
DORIS BALLANCE ORMAN, '25, FELLOWSHIP

Gallaudet University Alumni Association
Attn: Graduate Fellowship Fund Committee
Peikoff Alumni House
Gallaudet University
800 Florida Avenue, N.E.
Washington, DC 20002-3695
(202) 651-5060   Fax: (202) 651-5062
TDD: (202) 651-5060
E-mail: alumni.relations@gallaudet.edu
Web: www.gallaudet.edu

Summary To provide financial assistance to deaf women who wish to work on a graduate degree at universities for people who hear normally.

Eligibility This program is open to deaf or hard of hearing women graduates of Gallaudet University or other accredited academic institutions who have been accepted for graduate study at colleges or universities for people who hear normally. Applicants must be working full time on a doctorate or other terminal degree. They must have a particular interest in the arts, the humanities, or community leadership. Financial need is considered in the selection process.

Financial data The amount awarded varies, depending upon the needs of the recipient and the availability of funds.

Duration 1 year; may be renewed.

Additional data This program is 1 of 12 designated funds within the Graduate Fellowship Fund of the Gallaudet University Alumni Association.

Number awarded Up to 1 each year.

Deadline April of each year.

[463]
GALLAUDET UNIVERSITY ALUMNI ASSOCIATION GRADUATE FELLOWSHIP FUND

Gallaudet University Alumni Association
Attn: Graduate Fellowship Fund Committee
Peikoff Alumni House
Gallaudet University
800 Florida Avenue, N.E.
Washington, DC 20002-3695
(202) 651-5060   Fax: (202) 651-5062
TDD: (202) 651-5060
E-mail: alumni.relations@gallaudet.edu
Web: www.gallaudet.edu

Summary To provide financial assistance to deaf students who wish to work on a graduate degree at universities for people who hear normally.

Eligibility This program is open to deaf and hard of hearing graduates of Gallaudet University or other accredited academic institutions who have been accepted for graduate study at colleges or universities for people who hear normally. Applicants must be working full time on a doctoral or other terminal degree. Financial need is considered in the selection process.

Financial data The amount awarded varies, depending upon the number of qualified candidates applying for assistance, the availability of funds, and the needs of individual applicants.

Duration 1 year; may be renewed.

Additional data This program includes the following named fellowships: the Boyce R. Williams, '32; Fellowship; the David Peikoff, '29 Fellowship; the James N. Orman, '23, Fellowship; the John A. Trundle, 1885, Fellowship; the Old Dominion Foundation Fellowship; the Waldo T., '49 and Jean Kelsch, '51, Cordano Fellowship; and the I. King Jordan, '70 Fellowship. Recipients must carry a full-time semester load.

Number awarded Varies each year.
Deadline April of each year.

[464]
GEORGE H. NOFER SCHOLARSHIP

Alexander Graham Bell Association for the Deaf and
Hard of Hearing
Attn: College Scholarship Program
3417 Volta Place, N.W.
Washington, DC 20007-2778
(202) 337-5220   Fax: (202) 337-8314
TDD: (202) 337-5221   E-mail: financialaid@agbell.org
Web: www.agbell.org/NoferScholarship

Summary To provide financial assistance to graduate
students in public policy or law who have moderate to profound hearing loss.

Eligibility This program is open to 1) graduate students
working on a master's or doctoral degree in public policy;
and 2) students accepted at an accredited law school.
Applicants must have been diagnosed with a moderate to
profound bilateral hearing loss prior to their fourth birthday
and be committed to using spoken language as their primary mode of communication. They must be accepted or
enrolled at a mainstream college or university as a full-
time student and have an undergraduate GPA of 3.0 or
higher. Along with their application, they must submit a 2-
page essay discussing their career goals, including extracurricular activity involvement, financial situation, their use
of listening and spoken language, and the impact on them
of hearing loss. Financial need is considered in the selection process.

Financial data The stipend is $5,000 per year.

Duration 1 year; may be renewed 2 additional years if
the recipient maintains a GPA of 3.0 or higher.

Number awarded Up to 3 each year.

Deadline April of each year.

[465]
HENRY SYLE MEMORIAL FELLOWSHIP FOR SEMINARY STUDIES

Gallaudet University Alumni Association
Attn: Graduate Fellowship Fund Committee
Peikoff Alumni House
Gallaudet University
800 Florida Avenue, N.E.
Washington, DC 20002-3695
(202) 651-5060   Fax: (202) 651-5062
TDD: (202) 651-5060
E-mail: alumni.relations@gallaudet.edu
Web: www.gallaudet.edu

Summary To provide financial assistance to deaf students who wish to pursue seminary studies at universities
for people who hear normally.

Eligibility This program is open to deaf and hard of
hearing graduates of Gallaudet University or other accredited academic institutions who have been accepted for
graduate seminary study at colleges or universities for
people who hear normally. Applicants must be working full

time on a theological doctoral or other terminal degree.
Financial need is considered in the selection process.

Financial data The amount awarded varies, depending
upon the needs of the recipient and the availability of
funds.

Duration 1 year; may be renewed.

Additional data This fund was established in 1990 as 1
of 12 designated funds within the Graduate Fellowship
Fund of the Gallaudet University Alumni Association.

Number awarded 1 each year.

Deadline April of each year.

[466]
HOLLY ELLIOTT AND LAUREL GLASS SCHOLARSHIP ENDOWMENT

United Methodist Higher Education Foundation
Attn: Scholarships Administrator
60 Music Square East, Suite 350
P.O. Box 340005
Nashville, TN 37203-0005
(615) 649-3990   Toll Free: (800) 811-8110
Fax: (615) 649-3980
E-mail: umhefscholarships@umhef.org
Web: www.umhef.org

Summary To provide financial assistance to students at
United Methodist seminaries who are deaf or deaf-blind.

Eligibility This program is open to students enrolled full
time at United Methodist theological schools who are culturally deaf, orally deaf, deafened, late deafened, deaf-
blind, or hard of hearing. Applicants must have a GPA of
3.0 or higher and be preparing for specialized ministries in
the church, including (but not limited to) those wishing to
become ordained. They must have been active, full members of a United Methodist Church for at least 1 year prior
to applying. Financial need and U.S. citizenship or permanent resident status are required.

Financial data The stipend is at least $1,000 per year.

Duration 1 year; nonrenewable.

Additional data This program began in 2004.

Number awarded 1 each year.

Deadline February of each year.

[467]
IADES FELLOWSHIP AWARD

International Alumnae of Delta Epsilon Sorority
c/o Virginia Borggaard
2453 Bear Den Road
Frederick, MD 21701-9321
Fax: (301) 663-3231   TDD: (301) 663-9235
E-mail: vborggaard@juno.com
Web: www.iades1957.org/scholarships

Summary To provide financial assistance to deaf
women who are working on a doctoral degree.

Eligibility This program is open to deaf women who
have completed 12 or more units in a doctoral-level program and have a GPA of 3.0 or more. They need not be
members of Delta Epsilon. Along with their application,
they must submit official transcripts, a recent copy of their
audiogram, and 2 letters of recommendation.

Financial data The stipend is $2,000.
Duration 1 year.
Number awarded 1 or more each year.
Deadline September of each year.

[468]
JOHN C. DANFORTH CENTER ON RELIGION AND POLITICS DISSERTATION COMPLETION FELLOWSHIP

Washington University
Attn: John C. Danforth Center on Religion and Politics
118 Umrath Hall
Campus Box 1066
One Brookings Drive
St. Louis, MO 63130
(314) 935-9545   Fax: (314) 935-5755
E-mail: rap@wustl.edu
Web: rap.wustl.edu/dissertation-completion-fellowship

Summary To provide financial assistance to graduate students who are interested in completing their dissertation while in residence at the John C. Danforth Center on Religion and Politics of Washington University in St. Louis.

Eligibility This program is open to graduate students currently enrolled in a doctoral program in religion, politics, history, American studies, anthropology, gender and sexuality, or a related field. Applicants must be working on a dissertation that is centrally concerned with historical or contemporary topics in the religious and political experience of the United States. They must have received approval for the dissertation prospectus from their home institutions, satisfied all other requirements for doctoral candidacy, and be prepared to complete their dissertation before the conclusion of the fellowship. Members of underrepresented groups are encouraged to apply.

Financial data Fellows receive a stipend of $28,000 and a limited allowance for relocation expenses.

Duration 1 year; nonrenewable.
Number awarded Up to 2 each year.
Deadline January of each year.

[469]
REGINA OLSON HUGHES, '18, FELLOWSHIP

Gallaudet University Alumni Association
Attn: Graduate Fellowship Fund Committee
Peikoff Alumni House
Gallaudet University
800 Florida Avenue, N.E.
Washington, DC 20002-3695
(202) 651-5060   Fax: (202) 651-5062
TDD: (202) 651-5060
E-mail: alumni.relations@gallaudet.edu
Web: www.gallaudet.edu/gff_info.xml

Summary To provide financial assistance to deaf students who wish to work on a graduate degree in fine arts at universities for people who hear normally.

Eligibility This program is open to deaf and hard of hearing graduates of Gallaudet University or other accredited academic institutions who have been accepted for graduate study in fine arts at colleges or universities for

people who hear normally. Applicants must be working full time on a doctoral or other terminal degree. Financial need is considered in the selection process.

Financial data The amount awarded varies, depending upon the needs of the recipient and the availability of funds.

Duration 1 year; may be renewed.

Additional data This program, established in 1995, is 1 of 12 designated funds within the Graduate Fellowship Fund of the Gallaudet University Alumni Association.

Number awarded Up to 1 each year.
Deadline April of each year.

[470]
TEXAS BLIND/DEAF STUDENT EXEMPTION PROGRAM

Texas Higher Education Coordinating Board
Attn: Grants and Special Programs
1200 East Anderson Lane
P.O. Box 12788
Austin, TX 78711-2788
(512) 427-6340   Toll Free: (800) 242-3062
Fax: (512) 427-6420
E-mail: grantinfo@thecb.state.tx.us
Web: www.collegeforalltexans.com

Summary To provide a tuition exemption at Texas public colleges to undergraduate or graduate blind and/or deaf residents of the state.

Eligibility This program is open to Texas residents who can present certification from the Department of Assistive and Rehabilitative Services of their deafness or blindness. Applicants must present to the registrar of a public college or university in Texas a copy of their high school transcript, a letter of recommendation, proof that they have met all admission requirements, and a statement of purpose that indicates the certificate, degree program, or professional enhancement that they intend to pursue.

Financial data Eligible students are exempted from the payment of all dues, fees, and tuition charges at publicly-supported colleges and universities in Texas.

Duration Up to 8 semesters, provided the recipient maintains a GPA of 2.0 or higher as an undergraduate or 3.0 or higher as a graduate student.

Number awarded Varies each year; recently, 3,493 students received $11,469,863 in support through this program.

Deadline Deadline not specified.

Physical/Orthopedic Disabilities

Undergraduates ●

Graduate Students ●

Described here are 83 funding opportunities available to individuals with 1) a severe physical/orthopedic impairment caused by birth defects (e.g., absence of an extremity), diseases or disorders (e.g., multiple sclerosis), or other causes (e.g., accidents, amputations), or 2) a severe, chronic disability that was manifested before age 22 (for example, spina bifida and cerebral palsy). In all, 60 are for undergraduates and 23 are for graduate students. All of this is "free" money. Not one dollar will need to be repaid (provided, of course, that recipients meet all program requirements). If you are looking for a particular program and don't find it in this section, be sure to check the Program Title Index to see if it is covered elsewhere in the directory.

Undergraduates

[471]
180 MEDICAL SCHOLARSHIPS

180 Medical
Attn: Scholarship Committee
8516 N.W. Expressway
Oklahoma City, OK 73162
Toll Free: (877) 688-2729   Fax: (888) 718-0633
E-mail: scholarships@180medical.com
Web: www.180medical.com/scholarships

Summary To provide financial assistance for college to students who have spinal cord injuries, spina bifida, or transverse myelitis.

Eligibility This program is open to U.S. citizens who are enrolled or planning to enroll full time at a 2- or 4-year college or university as an undergraduate or graduate student. Applicants must be under a doctor's care for spina bifida, a spinal cord injury, and ostomy (ileostomy, colostomy, or urostomy), neurogenic bladder, or transverse myelitis. Along with their application, they must submit 1) a physician's note documenting the diagnosis; 2) an official transcript; 3) a list of significant awards or honors they have received during school for academic or extracurricular activities; 4) a list of extracurricular, sports, community, employment, or other activities; and 5) a 750-word essay on how their medical condition has affected their life and their goals for the future.

Financial data The stipend is $1,000.

Duration 1 year.

Number awarded 7 each year.

Deadline May of each year.

[472]
ABC MEDICAL SCHOLARSHIP PROGRAM

ABC Home Medical Supply Inc.
15 East Uwchlan Avenue, Suite 430
Exton, PA 19341
(866) 897-8588   Fax: (877) 785-7396
E-mail: info@abc-med.com
Web: www.abc-med.com/scholarships

Summary To recognize and reward, including with college scholarships, participants in adaptive sports.

Eligibility This program is open to athletes who have physical disabilities and participate in adaptive sports. Awards are presented in 3 categories: 1) adaptive sports, in which awards are presented in age groups (junior, college, adult) and awarded on the basis of good sportsmanship, respect for themselves and others, and leadership characteristics on their adaptive sports team; 2) scholar athlete, for individuals in need of financial assistance for college tuition; and 3) making a difference, for individuals who are trying to improve their lives or the lives of others around them. Applicants must submit a short essay in which they answer questions about what they would use the funds for if they were to win this award, how it would

help them to accomplish their goals, and what adaptive sports mean to them.

Financial data Award amounts vary.

Duration These are 1-time awards.

Number awarded Varies each year.

Deadline March or September of each year.

[473]
ABLE FLIGHT CAREER TRAINING SCHOLARSHIPS

Able Flight, Inc.
Attn: Scholarships
91 Oak Leaf Lane
Chapel Hill, NC 27516
(919) 942-4699   E-mail: info@ableflight.org
Web: www.ableflight.org/scholarships

Summary To provide financial assistance to people who have a physical disability and wish to attend college or technical school to prepare for a career in aviation.

Eligibility This program is open to U.S. citizens who use wheelchairs because of spinal cord injury, have congenital birth defects, have lost limbs, or have other physical disabilities. Applicants must be interested in enrolling in a program of career training at a facility selected and approved by the sponsor. They must be working on 1) an FAA-issued Repairman Certificate (Light Sport Aircraft) with Maintenance Rating; 2) an FAA Dispatcher License; or 3) an academic degree related to an aviation career (e.g., aviation management, air traffic control). Along with their application, they must submit an essay of 300 to 500 words describing how they feel this scholarship will change their life and a statement from their attending physician describing the nature of their disability and the effects of the disability upon their level of physical activity.

Financial data Scholarships cover course fees, testing fees, and travel and lodging as required.

Duration Most training programs for FAA licenses last 23 to 25 days. The length of academic degree programs is determined by the sponsor on an individual basis.

Number awarded Varies each year.

Deadline Applications may be submitted at any time.

[474]
ACCESS PATH TO PSYCHOLOGY AND LAW EXPERIENCE (APPLE) PROGRAM

American Psychological Association
Attn: Division 41 (American Psychology-Law Society)
c/o Jorge Varela, Minority Affairs Committee Co-Chair
Sam Houston State University
Department of Psychology and Philosophy
Box 2447
Huntsville, TX 77341
(936) 294-4161   E-mail: jgv002@shsu.edu
Web: www.apadivisions.org

Summary To provide an opportunity for undergraduate students from underrepresented groups to gain research and other experience to prepare them for graduate work in psychology and law.

Eligibility This program is open to undergraduate students who are members of underrepresented groups, including, but are not limited to, racial and ethnic minorities; first-generation college students; lesbian, gay, bisexual, and transgender students; and students with physical disabilities. Applicants must be interested in participating in a program in which they work on research for approximately 10 hours per week; participate in GRE classes and/or other development opportunities; attend a conference of the American Psychology-Law Society (AP-LS); submit a proposal to present their research at an AP-LS conference or in the Division 41 program of an American Psychological Association (APA) conference; submit a summary of their research experience to the AP-LS Minority Affairs Committee chair within 1 month of its completion; and correspond with a secondary mentor from the Minority Affairs Committee to participate in the ongoing assessment of this program. Selection is based on the quality of the proposed research and mentoring experience and the potential for the student to become a successful graduate student.

Financial data Grants range up to $3,000, including a stipend of $1,200 per semester or $800 per quarter or summer, $100 for research expenses, and up to $500 to attend the AP-LS conference.

Duration Up to 1 year.

Number awarded 6 each year.

Deadline November of each year.

[475]
AMERIGLIDE ACHIEVER SCHOLARSHIP

AmeriGlide, Inc.
3901A Commerce Park Drive
Raleigh, NC 27610
Toll Free: (800) 790-1635   Fax: (800) 791-6524
E-mail: scholarship@ameriglide.com
Web: www.ameriglide.com/Scholarship

Summary To provide financial assistance to undergraduate and graduate students who use a wheelchair.

Eligibility This program is open to full-time undergraduate and graduate students at 2- and 4-year colleges and universities who use a manual or electric wheelchair or mobility scooter. Applicants must have completed at least 1 year of college and have a GPA of 3.0 or higher. They must be legal residents of the United States or have a valid student visa. Along with their application, they must submit a 500-word essay on topics that change annually; recently, students were invited to write on their career and life goals.

Financial data The stipend is $2,500.

Duration 1 year.

Additional data This program began in 2008.

Number awarded 1 each year.

Deadline May of each year.

[476]
ANNE M. FASSETT SCHOLARSHIP

Southwest Florida Community Foundation
8771 College Parkway, Building 2, Suite 201
Fort Myers, FL 33919
(239) 274-5900   Fax: (239) 274-5930
E-mail: scholarships@floridacommunity.com
Web: www.floridacommunity.com

Summary To provide financial assistance to students who use a wheelchair and either reside in selected counties in Florida or attend a public college in that state.

Eligibility This program is open to 1) seniors graduating from high schools in Charlotte, Collier, Glades, Henry, or Lee County, Florida; and 2) residents of any state currently enrolled or planning to enroll at a Florida state college, community college, or technical school. Applicants must have a physical disability and use a wheelchair. They must be able to demonstrate financial need.

Financial data A stipend is awarded (amount not specified).

Duration 1 year.

Number awarded 1 each year.

Deadline February of each year.

[477]
ARIZONA HISPANIC CHAMBER OF COMMERCE SCHOLARSHIP

Arizona Community Foundation
Attn: Director of Scholarships
2201 East Camelback Road, Suite 405B
Phoenix, AZ 85016
(602) 381-1400   Toll Free: (800) 222-8221
Fax: (602) 381-1575
E-mail: scholarship@azfoundation.org
Web: azfoundation.academicworks.com

Summary To provide financial assistance to upper-division students of Hispanic heritage working on a bachelor's degree in business at a college in Arizona.

Eligibility This program is open to students entering their junior or senior year in a business degree program at an accredited college or university in Arizona. Applicants must have at least 1 parent of Hispanic heritage. They must be enrolled full time and have a GPA of 3.0 or higher. Preference is given to applicants who have a recognized physical disability or are dependents of or employees of a company that is a member of the Arizona Hispanic Chamber of Commerce.

Financial data The stipend is $5,000 per year.

Duration 1 year; may be renewed 1 additional year.

Additional data This program is sponsored by the Arizona Hispanic Chamber of Commerce. Recipients are paired with a mentor from the chamber.

Number awarded Varies each year.

Deadline April of each year.

[478]
ASSE DIVERSITY COMMITTEE UNDERGRADUATE SCHOLARSHIP

American Society of Safety Engineers
Attn: ASSE Foundation
Scholarship Award Program
520 North Northwest Highway
Park Ridge, IL 60068-2538
(847) 699-2929   Fax: (847) 296-3769
E-mail: assefoundation@asse.org
Web: foundation.asse.org/scholarships-and-grants

Summary To provide financial assistance to upper-division students who come from diverse groups and are working on a degree related to occupational safety.

Eligibility This program is open to students who are working on an undergraduate degree in occupational safety, health, environment, industrial hygiene, occupational health nursing, or a closely-related field (e.g., industrial or environmental engineering). Applicants must be full-time students who have completed at least 60 semester hours and have a GPA of 3.0 or higher. A goal of this program is to support individuals regardless of race, ethnicity, gender, religion, personal beliefs, age, sexual orientation, physical challenges, geographic location, university, or specific area of study. U.S. citizenship is not required. Membership in the American Society of Safety Engineers (ASSE) is not required, but preference is given to members.

Financial data The stipend is $1,000 per year.

Duration 1 year; recipients may reapply.

Number awarded 1 each year.

Deadline November of each year.

[479]
BOBBY DODD MEMORIAL SCHOLARSHIP FOR OUTSTANDING COMMUNITY SERVICE

Georgia District Civitan Foundation, Inc.
c/o Louise Crapps, Scholarship Committee Chair
2454 Monterey Drive, N.E.
Marietta, GA 30068-3050
(770) 971-1833   E-mail: louisecrapps@bellsouth.net
Web: www.georgiacivitan.org/html/foundation.html

Summary To provide financial assistance to high school seniors in Georgia who are physically challenged, have an outstanding record of community service, and plan to attend college in any state.

Eligibility This program is open to physically-challenged seniors graduating from high schools in Georgia and planning to attend an accredited college or university in any state. Membership in Civitan International is not required, but Junior Civitan Club members are encouraged to apply. Interested students must submit a 500-word essay on their community activities and how those experiences have prepared them for life. In the selection process, academic achievement and financial need are considered, but the overwhelming factor is community service involvement.

Financial data The winner receives $1,200 and the runner-up receives $800. Funds are paid directly to the student.

Duration 1 year.

Number awarded 2 each year.

Deadline January of each year.

[480]
BOBBY JONES OPEN SCHOLARSHIPS

American Syringomyelia & Chiari Alliance Project, Inc.
P.O. Box 1586
Longview, TX 75606-1586
(903) 236-7079   Toll Free: (800) ASAP-282
Fax: (903) 757-7456   E-mail: info@ASAP.org
Web: www.asap.org

Summary To provide financial assistance for college or graduate school to members of the American Syringomyelia & Chiari Alliance Project (ASAP) and their children.

Eligibility This program is open to students entering or enrolled in college or graduate school who have syringomeylia (SM) and/or Chiari Malformation (CM) or whose parent is affected by SM and/or CM. Applicants or parents must have been ASAP members for at least 6 months. They may be of any age. Along with their application, they must submit 4 essays on assigned topics related to their experience with SM and/or CM. Selection is based on those essay and financial need.

Financial data Stipends are $1,000 for full-time students or $500 for part-time students. Recipients may reapply, but they may receive only a total of $4,000 in support from this program.

Duration 1 year.

Additional data This program is funded by the Bobby Jones Open, an annual golf tournament in which participation is restricted to golfers named Bobby Jones (e.g., Robert Jones, Roberta Jones). The tournament began in 1979 and since 1990 has raised money for activities of the ASAP.

Number awarded Varies each year; a total of $5,000 is available for this program annually.

Deadline May of each year.

[481]
BRYON RIESCH SCHOLARSHIPS

Bryon Riesch Paralysis Foundation
P.O. Box 1388
Waukesha, WI 53187-1388
(262) 547-2083   E-mail: info@brpf.org
Web: www.brpf.org/scholarship-application

Summary To provide financial assistance to undergraduate and graduate students who have a neurological disability or the children of people with such a disability.

Eligibility This program is open to students entering or enrolled at a 2- or 4-year college or university as an undergraduate or graduate student. Applicants must have a neurological disability or be the child of a person with such a disability. First priority is given to individuals suffering from a direct spinal cord injury or disease resulting in paralysis such as spinal tumors, strokes, or aneurysms affecting the spinal cord, or spina bifida. Other diseases and disorders that qualify include multiple sclerosis, traumatic brain injuries, Parkinson's, and cerebral palsy. Priority is also given to residents of Wisconsin. Applicants must have a GPA of 2.5 or higher in high school or college. Along with their application, they must submit a 200-word essay on why they deserve the scholarship, a statement of their 5- and 10-year goals, and a list of work experience. Financial need is not considered in the selection process.

Financial data   The stipend is $2,000.

Duration   1 year; may be renewed.

Number awarded   Varies each semester; recently, 7 were awarded for the fall semester and 5 for the spring semester.

Deadline   June of each year for fall semester; December of each year for spring semester.

[482]
BUILDING RURAL INITIATIVE FOR DISABLED THROUGH GROUP EFFORT (B.R.I.D.G.E.) ENDOWMENT FUND SCHOLARSHIPS

National FFA Organization
Attn: Scholarship Office
6060 FFA Drive
P.O. Box 68960
Indianapolis, IN 46268-0960
(317) 802-4419   Fax: (317) 802-5419
E-mail: scholarships@ffa.org
Web: www.ffa.org/participate/scholarships

Summary   To provide financial assistance to FFA members who have disabilities and are interested in studying agriculture in college.

Eligibility   This program is open to members with physical disabilities who are graduating high school seniors planning to enroll full time in college. Applicants must be interested in working on a 2- or 4-year degree in agriculture. Selection is based on academic achievement, FFA involvement, community service, and leadership skills. U.S. citizenship is required.

Financial data   The stipend is $5,000.

Duration   1 year; nonrenewable.

Additional data   This program is supported by the Dr. Scholl Foundation, Outdoor Advertising Association of America, and numerous individuals.

Number awarded   1 each year.

Deadline   January of each year.

[483]
CARL J. MEGEL SPECIAL EDUCATION SCHOLARSHIP

Illinois Federation of Teachers
500 Oakmont Lane
P.O. Box 390
Westmont, IL 60559
(630) 468-4080   Fax: (630) 468-4089
Web: www.ift.org/your-benefits/scholarships

Summary   To provide financial assistance to children of members of the Illinois Federation of Teachers (IFT) who

have been enrolled in special education and are interested in attending college in any state.

Eligibility   This program is open to graduating high school seniors who are children of currently-employed active members of the IFT or of deceased members who were in good standing at the time of their death. Applicants must be enrolled in a special education school, class, or program for students with autism, cognitive disability, deaf-blindness, deafness, emotional disability, hearing impairment, multiple disabilities, orthopedic impairment, other health impairment, specific learning disability, speech or language impairment, traumatic brain injury, or visual impairment. Along with their application, they must submit an essay describing how any obstacles and/or achievements that you have encountered in your life have helped shape your decision to complete a post-secondary education.

Financial data   The stipend is $1,000.

Duration   1 year.

Number awarded   1 each year.

Deadline   February of each year.

[484]
CHASA EDUCATIONAL SCHOLARSHIPS

Children's Hemiplegia and Stroke Association
4101 West Green Oaks, Suite 305
PMB 149
Arlington, TX 76016
E-mail: info437@chasa.org
Web: chasa.org/we-can-help/college-scholarships

Summary   To provide financial assistance for college to students affected by hemiparesis, hemiplegia, or pediatric stroke.

Eligibility   This program is open to people who are 25 years of age or younger. Applicants must have been affected by childhood hemiparesis or hemiplegia or by pediatric stroke with onset of condition prior to 18 years of age. They must be attending or planning to attend a college, university, or vocational school to work on a degree or certification. Along with their application, they must submit an essay on the goals they have set for their future and the experience that they feel has prepared them the most for attaining those goals.

Financial data   Stipends range up to $3,000 per year.

Duration   1 year; may be renewed up to 3 additional years.

Additional data   This program began in 2000. It includes the Megan Chesney Scholarship Fund, established in 2007.

Number awarded   Varies each year; recently, 14 were awarded.

Deadline   August of each year.

[485]
CHILDREN'S BRITTLE BONE FOUNDATION AND OI FOUNDATION IMPACT GRANT PROGRAM

Children's Brittle Bone Foundation
Attn: Impact Grant Program
7701 95th Street
Pleasant Prairie, WI 53158
(773) 263-2223   Fax: (262) 947-0724
E-mail: impactgrants@oif.org
Web: www.cbbf.org/impact-grants

Summary To provide funding for education or other personal needs to people who have osteogenesis imperfecta (OI).

Eligibility This program is open to people who have OI and are seeking funding for equipment or services that will improve their quality of life. Examples of acceptable requests include education-related items such as tuition assistance at the preschool to postdoctoral level; prescribed exercise therapy equipment for physical or occupational therapy; orthotics, braces, and walkers; manual or electric wheelchairs or scooters; adaptive technology such as computers or hearing aids; dental intervention; vehicle modifications such as lifts or pedal extensions or vehicle purchases; travel reimbursement to receive specialized care; outdoor ramps that provide access to a home; or accessibility aides such as reachers, shower chairs, or kitchen carts.

Financial data Recently, grants ranged from $396 to $20,000 and averaged nearly $5,500.

Duration Funds must be used within 12 months.

Additional data This program is provided jointly by the Children's Brittle Bone Foundation and the Osteogenesis Imperfecta (OI) Foundation.

Number awarded Varies each year; recently, 17 were awarded.

Deadline February of each year.

[486]
CHRISTINA SKOSKI, M.D., SCHOLARSHIP

Amputee Coalition
Attn: Programs and Services Coordinator
9303 Center Street, Suite 100
Manassas, VA 20110
(703) 330-1699, ext. 7102   Toll Free: (888) 267-5669
TDD: (865) 525-4512
E-mail: dan@amputee-coalition.org
Web: www.amputee-coalition.org

Summary To provide financial assistance for college to high school seniors who have a congenital limb difference or an amputation.

Eligibility This program is open to graduating high school seniors who have a congenital limb difference or an amputation. Applicants must be planning to enroll full time in college in the fall after graduation. They must have a GPA of 3.5 or higher and minimum scores of 1980 on the SAT or 28 on the ACT. Either the student or a parent or guardian must be a registered Friend of the Amputee Coalition.

Financial data The stipend is $1,000.
Duration 1 year; nonrenewable.
Additional data This program began in 2010.
Number awarded 1 each year.
Deadline April of each year.

[487]
COL CARL F. BASWELL COMBAT WOUNDED ENGINEER SCHOLARSHIP

Army Engineer Association
Attn: Director Washington DC Operations
P.O. Box 30260
Alexandria, VA 22310-8260
(703) 428-7084   Fax: (703) 428-6043
E-mail: xd@armyengineer.com
Web: www.armyengineer.com/scholarships.htm

Summary To provide financial assistance for college to U.S. Army Engineers who were wounded in combat in Iraq or Afghanistan.

Eligibility This program is open to U.S. Army Engineers who were wounded in combat and received a Purple Heart during Operation Iraqi Freedom or Operation Enduring Freedom. Applicants must be working on or planning to work on an associate, bachelor's, or master's degree at an accredited college or university. Selection is based primarily on financial need, although potential for academic success and personal references are also considered.

Financial data The stipend is $2,500.
Duration 1 year.
Additional data This program began in 2010.
Number awarded 1 each year.
Deadline June of each year.

[488]
DUNHAM-KERLEY SCHOLARSHIP

Pride Foundation
Attn: Educational Programs Director
2014 East Madison Street, Suite 300
Seattle, WA 98122
(206) 323-3318   Toll Free: (800) 735-7287
Fax: (206) 323-1017
E-mail: scholarships@pridefoundation.org
Web: www.pridefoundation.org

Summary To provide financial assistance to residents of the Northwest who are lesbian, gay, bisexual, transgender, or queer (LGBTQ) or a straight ally, have physical disabilities and/or financial neee, and are interested in attending college in any state.

Eligibility This program is open to residents of Alaska, Idaho, Montana, Oregon, or Washington who self-identify as LGBTQ or a straight ally. Applicants must be attending or planning to attend college in any state. They must have physical disabilities or demonstrated financial need. Selection is based on demonstrated commitment to social justice and LGBTQ concerns, leadership in their communities, the ability to be academically and personally successful, and (to some extent) financial need.

Financial data Recently, the average stipend for all scholarships awarded by the foundation was approximately $4,160. Funds are paid directly to the recipient's school.

Duration   1 year; recipients may reapply.

Additional data   This program began in 2013.

Number awarded   1 each year. Since it began offering scholarships in 1993, the foundation has awarded a total of more than $4.0 million to more than 1,500 recipients.

Deadline   January of each year.

[489]
EAGA SCHOLARSHIP FUND

Eastern Amputee Golf Association
Attn: Lind Buck, Secretary
2015 Amherst Drive
Bethlehem, PA 18015-5606
(610) 867-9295   Fax: (610) 867-9295
E-mail: lindajean18015@aolc.com
Web: www.eagagolf.org/scholarships.html

Summary   To provide financial assistance for college to members of the Eastern Amputee Golf Association (EAGA) and their families.

Eligibility   This program is open to students who are residents of and/or currently enrolled or accepted for enrollment at a college or university in designated eastern states (Connecticut, Delaware, District of Columbia, Maine, Maryland, Massachusetts, New Hampshire, New Jersey, New York, Pennsylvania, Rhode Island, Vermont, Virginia, or West Virginia). Applicants must be amputee members of the association (those who have experienced the loss of 1 or more extremities at a major joint due to amputation or birth defect) or members of their families. Financial need is considered in the selection process.

Financial data   The stipend is $1,000.

Duration   1 year; may be renewed if the recipient maintains a GPA of 2.0 or higher and continues to demonstrate financial need.

Additional data   The EAGA was incorporated in 1987. It welcomes 2 types of members: amputee members and associate members (non-amputees who are interested in the organization and support its work but are not eligible for these scholarships). This program includes the following named scholarships: the Paul DesChamps Scholarship Award, the Tom Reed Scholarship, the Ray Froncillo Scholarship, the Howard Taylor Scholarship, the Paul Liemkuehler Memorial Scholarship, the Buffalo Amputee Golf Classic Scholarship Award, and the Lehigh Valley Amputee Support Group Scholarship Award.

Number awarded   Varies each year; recently, 20 were awarded.

Deadline   June of each year.

[490]
EASTER SEALS SOUTH CAROLINA
EDUCATIONAL SCHOLARSHIPS

Easter Seals South Carolina
Attn: Scholarship Program
3020 Farrow Road
P.O. Box 5715
Columbia, SC 29250
(803) 627-3857   Fax: (803) 356-6902
E-mail: mgriffin@sc.easterseals.com
Web: www.easterseals.com

Summary   To provide financial assistance for college or graduate school to South Carolina students who have a mobility impairment.

Eligibility   This program is open to South Carolina residents and students attending a college or university in the state who have a significant and medically certified mobility impairment. Applicants must be enrolled or planning to enroll in an undergraduate or graduate program. They must be able to demonstrate financial need. Preference is given to students carrying at least 9 credit hours and making satisfactory academic progress toward graduation.

Financial data   The maximum stipend is $1,000.

Duration   1 year; may be renewed.

Additional data   This program began in 1985.

Number awarded   1 or more each year.

Deadline   June of each year.

[491]
ECCLESTON-CALLAHAN SCHOLARSHIPS

Central Florida Foundation
Attn: Eccleston-Callahan Memorial Fund
800 North Magnolia Avenue, Suite 1200
Orlando, FL 32803
(407) 872-3050   Fax: (407) 425-2990
E-mail: info@cffound.org
Web: www.cffound.org/receive/scholarships

Summary   To provide financial assistance to students with disabilities enrolled at specified Florida colleges and universities.

Eligibility   This program is open to students at designated colleges and universities in Florida who have a physical disability (blindness, mobility impairment, or deafness). Applicants must be enrolled full time, have a GPA of 3.0 or higher, be younger than 21 years of age, and be able to demonstrate financial need.

Financial data   The stipend is $1,000 per year.

Duration   1 year; may be renewed.

Additional data   The participating institutions are the University of Florida, the University of Central Florida, Florida A&M University, Florida State University, Valencia Community College, Seminole Community College, and Orlando Tech.

Number awarded   Varies each year.

Deadline   June of each year.

[492]
ELAINE CHAPIN FUND SCHOLARSHIPS

Elaine Chapin Fund
1440 Heritage Landing, Suite 109
St. Charles, MO 63303
E-mail: elainechapinfund@gmail.com
Web: sites.google.com/site/theelainechapinfund

Summary To provide financial assistance for college to people who have multiple sclerosis (MS) and their families.

Eligibility This program is open to people whose lives have been affected by MS, either directly or as a family member. Applicants must be enrolled or planning to enroll as full-time undergraduates at an accredited 2- or 4-year college, university, or vocational/technical school in the United States. They must be U.S. citizens. Along with their application, they must submit a short essay on the impact of MS on their life. Selection is based on that essay, academic standing, and financial need.

Financial data The stipend is $1,000.

Duration 1 year.

Additional data This program is administered through the Gateway Area Chapter of the National Multiple Sclerosis Society.

Number awarded Varies each year; recently, 9 were awarded.

Deadline April of each year.

[493]
EXTREMITY SCHOLARSHIP PROGRAM

The Limb Preservation Foundation
Attn: Executive Director
1721 East 19th Avenue, Suite 106
Denver, CO 80218
(303) 429-0688   Fax: (303) 487-3667
E-mail: khill@limbpreservation.org
Web: limbpreservation.org

Summary To provide financial assistance to residents of designated Rocky Mountain states who are patients or survivors of diseases of the extremities and interested in attending college or graduate school in any state.

Eligibility This program is open to residents of the Rocky Mountain region (Arizona, Colorado, Idaho, Kansas, Montana, Nebraska, New Mexico, Utah, and Wyoming) who are enrolled or planning to enroll at a college, university, vocational school, or graduate school in any state. Applicants must be patients or survivors who have battled or are battling a limb-threatening condition due to trauma, tumor, or infection. Along with their application, they must submit an essay of 500 to 1,000 words on 1 of the following topics: 1) the advice they would give to another person who is going through a similar limb-threatening experience; 2) their career aspirations; or 3) an important personal relationship and how it has influenced them during their experience with limb tumor, trauma, or infection. Selection is based on that essay, letters of recommendation, and financial need.

Financial data The stipend is $2,500 per year. Funds are paid directly to the recipient's institution.

Duration 4 years, provided the recipient maintains a GPA of 2.25 or higher.

Number awarded Varies each year; recently, 7 were awarded.

Deadline September of each year for fall semester; May of each year for spring semester.

[494]
FCPA HIGH SCHOOL SCHOLARSHIP

Florida Cleft Palate-Craniofacial Association, Inc.
Attn: Scholarship Committee
6300 Sagewood Drive, Suite H255
Park City, UT 84098
(435) 602-1329   Fax: (435) 487-2011
E-mail: info@floridacleft.org
Web: www.floridacleft.org/fcpa-hs-scholarship

Summary To provide financial assistance to high school seniors in Florida who have a craniofacial anomaly and plan to attend college in any state.

Eligibility This program is open to seniors graduating from high schools in Florida who have a cleft lip or palate or other craniofacial anomaly. Applicants must be planning to attend a college or university in any state. They must be nominated by a member of the Florida Cleft Palate-Craniofacial Association (FCPA). Along with their application, they must submit a 125-word essay on their educational goals and past or current community service activities.

Financial data The stipend is $1,000.

Duration 1 year; nonrenewable.

Number awarded 1 each year.

Deadline March of each year.

[495]
GOLDEN CORRAL SCHOLARSHIP FUND

National Multiple Sclerosis Society-Greater Carolinas
   Chapter
3101 Industrial Drive, Suite 210
Raleigh, NC 27609
(919) 834-0678   Toll Free: (800) 344-4867
Fax: (704) 527-0406   E-mail: nct@nmss.org
Web: www.nationalmssociety.org

Summary To provide financial assistance to high school seniors and graduates from South Carolina and North Carolina who have multiple sclerosis (MS) or have a parent with MS and who are planning to attend college in any state.

Eligibility This program is open to graduating high school seniors, recent graduates, and GED recipients from South Carolina and North Carolina who have MS or a parent who has MS. Applicants must be planning to enroll as a first-time student at a 2- or 4-year college, university, or vocational/technical school in the United States on at least a half-time basis. Along with their application, they must submit an essay on the impact MS has had on their lives. Selection is based on that essay, academic record, leadership and participation in school or community activities, work experience, goals and aspirations, an outside appraisal, special circumstances, and financial need. U.S. citizenship or permanent resident status is required.

Financial data Stipends range up to $3,000.

Duration 1 year.

Additional data This program, which operates jointly with the Central North Carolina chapter, receives support from the Golden Corral Corporation.

Number awarded Varies each year; recently, 50 were awarded.

Deadline January of each year.

[496]
HANSEN INJURY LAW FIRM SCHOLARSHIP

Hansen Injury Law Firm
6126 West State Street, Suite 200
Boise, ID 83703
(208) 505-9456
Web: www.hanseninjurylawfirm.com/scholarships

Summary To provide financial assistance to residents of any state who have been injured in an accident and are interested in attending college.

Eligibility This program is open to residents of any state who are enrolled to planning to enroll at a college or university. Applicants must have been negatively impacted by a car crash, bicycle accident, or other events leading to personal injuries. They must have a GPA of 3.5 or higher. Along with their application, they must submit a 500-word essay explaining how their accident affects them in an educational setting.

Financial data The stipend is $1,000. Funds are disbursed to the academic institution of their choice.

Duration 1 year.

Number awarded 1 each year.

Deadline July of each year.

[497]
INNOVATION IN MOTION SCHOLARSHIP

SpinLife.com LLC
Attn: Scholarship Department
330 West Spring Street, Suite 303
Columbus, OH 43215
(614) 564-1400   Toll Free: (800) 850-0335
Fax: (614) 564-1401
E-mail: collegescholarships@spinlife.com
Web: www.spinlife.com/scholarship

Summary To provide financial assistance to college students who use a wheelchair.

Eligibility This program is open to students over 17 years of age who are currently enrolled at an accredited 4-year educational institution and use a manual or power wheelchair. Applicants must have a GPA of 3.0 or higher. They may not have been subject to any disciplinary action by any educational, law enforcement, or other agency. Along with their application, they must submit an essay on a topic that changes annually; recently, students were asked to write about what "life in motion" means to them. Financial need is not considered in the selection process. U.S. legal residency or a valid student visa are required.

Financial data Awards are a $1,000 scholarship and a $500 gift card for a product of the sponsor.

Duration 1 year; nonrenewable.

Number awarded 2 each year: 1 scholarship and 1 gift card.

Deadline June of each year.

[498]
ISBA SCHOLARSHIPS

Illinois Spina Bifida Association
2211 North Oak Park Avenue
Chicago, IL 60707
(773) 444-0305   Fax: (773) 444-0327
E-mail: info@i-sba.org
Web: www.i-sba.org/programs

Summary To provide financial assistance to adult residents of Illinois who have spina bifida and are interested in attending college or graduate school in any state.

Eligibility This program is open to adult residents of Illinois who have spina bifida. Applicants must be enrolled or planning to enroll at a 2- or 4-year college or university, online courses, technical or trade school, or other continuing education program in any state as an undergraduate or graduate student. Along with their application, they must submit essays of 250 to 500 words on 1) the accomplishments or contributions (school, extracurricular, community, or Illinois Spina Bifida Association) they have made of which they are most proud; and 2) their career goals and the reasons for selecting those. Selection is based on those essays, transcripts, and letters of recommendation.

Financial data Stipends range up to $2,000.

Duration 1 year.

Additional data Recipients are expected to volunteer with the Illinois Spina Bifida Association at least once during the following year.

Number awarded Varies each year; recently, 8 were awarded.

Deadline June of each year.

[499]
JEAN DRISCOLL "DREAM BIG" AWARD

Spina Bifida Association of Greater New England
Attn: Executive Director
219 East Main Street, Suite 100B
Milford, MA 01757
(508) 482-5300   Toll Free: (888) 479-1900
Fax: (508) 482-5301
E-mail: edugan@SBAGreaterNE.org
Web: www.sbagreaterne.org

Summary To provide funding for educational, developmental, or assistive programs to residents of New England who have spina bifida.

Eligibility This program is open to residents of New England who are 14 years of age or older and have spina bifida. Applicants must be seeking funding for educational, developmental, or assistive programs that will enable them to achieve their goals despite limitations imposed by spina bifida. Eligible degree programs include associate, technical, bachelor's, and graduate. Along with their application, they must submit a personal statement, at least 2 paragraphs in length, describing their goals in life and their determination to "dream big;" the statement should include future educational pursuits or examples of camps or training courses taken to assist them in achieving their dreams.

Financial data   The stipend is $1,000.

Duration   The award is granted annually.

Number awarded   1 each year.

Deadline   May of each year.

[500]
JOHN E. MAYFIELD ABLE SCHOLARSHIP

Community Foundation of Middle Tennessee
Attn: Scholarship Coordinator
3833 Cleghorn Avenue, Suite 400
Nashville, TN 37215-2519
(615) 321-4939, ext. 116   Toll Free: (888) 540-5200
Fax: (615) 327-2746   E-mail: pcole@cfmt.org
Web: www.cfmt.org

Summary   To provide financial assistance to high school seniors in Tennessee who have participated as a wheelchair athlete in programs of Athletes Building Life Experiences (ABLE) and plan to attend college in any state.

Eligibility   This program is open to seniors graduating from high schools in Tennessee who plan to enroll full time at a college or university in any state. Applicants must have participated in wheelchair athletic activities of the ABLE program. Along with their application, they must submit an essay describing their educational plans and how those plans will help them reach their career goals. Financial need is considered in the selection process.

Financial data   Stipends range from $500 to $2,500 per year. Funds are paid to the recipient's school and must be used for tuition, fees, books, supplies, room, board, or miscellaneous expenses.

Duration   1 year.

Additional data   This program began in 2002.

Number awarded   1 or more each year.

Deadline   March of each year.

[501]
JOHN LEPPING MEMORIAL SCHOLARSHIP

Lep Foundation for Youth Education
Attn: Scholarship Selection Committee
9 Whispering Spring Drive
Millstone Township, NJ 08510
E-mail: lepfoundation@aol.com
Web: www.lepfoundation.org/applications

Summary   To provide financial assistance to high school seniors in New Jersey, New York, or Pennsylvania who have a physical disability or psychological handicap and plan to attend college in any state.

Eligibility   This program is open to seniors graduating from high schools in New Jersey, New York, or Pennsylvania and planning to enroll at a college, university, community college, or vocational school in any state. Applicants must have a disability, including (but not limited to) physical disabilities (e.g., spinal cord injury, loss of limb, birth defects, Lyme disease) or psychological handicaps (e.g., autism, cerebral palsy, post-traumatic stress). Along with

their application, they must submit a brief statement of their career goals and ambitions for the future and a 500-word essay on why they feel they are the best candidate for this award. Financial need is considered in the selection process.

Financial data   The stipend is $5,000. Funds are paid directly to the recipient's school.

Duration   1 year.

Number awarded   At least 4 each year.

Deadline   April of each year.

[502]
JUMPSTART MS SCHOLARSHIP

National Multiple Sclerosis Society-Upper Midwest Chapter
Attn: Jumpstart MS Scholarship Program
200 12th Avenue South
Minneapolis, MN 55415
(612) 335-7937   Toll Free: (800) 582-5296
Fax: (612) 335-7997 E-mail: krista.harding@nmss.org
Web: www.nationalmssociety.org

Summary   To provide financial assistance to high school freshmen from Iowa, Minnesota, and North and South Dakota who have multiple sclerosis (MS) or have a parent with MS and are planning to attend college in any state.

Eligibility   This program is open to students currently enrolled as freshmen at high schools in Iowa, Minnesota, North Dakota, and South Dakota who have MS or a parent who has MS. Applicants must be planning to enroll at a 2- or 4-year college, university, or vocational/technical school in the United States after they graduate from high school. Along with their application, they must submit an 850-word essay on the impact MS has had on their lives. Selection is based on that essay, academic record, leadership and participation in school or community activities, goals and aspirations, and special circumstances (such as financial need).

Financial data   The stipend is $1,500.

Duration   1 year.

Additional data   This program is sponsored by Best Buy.

Number awarded   1 each year.

Deadline   February of each year.

[503]
JUSTWALKERS.COM MOBILITY SCHOLARSHIP PROGRAM

Just Health Shops
Attn: JustWalkers.com
11840 West Market Place, Suite H
Fulton, MD 20759
Toll Free: (800) 998-7750   Fax: (301) 776-0716
E-mail: scholarship@justwalkers.com
Web: www.justwalkers.com

Summary   To provide financial assistance to undergraduate and graduate students who use a mobility device.

Eligibility   This program is open to legal U.S. residents and students with valid visas who are entering or enrolled in an undergraduate or graduate program. Applicants must use a wheelchair, power scooter, crutches, rollator, or other mobility device on a regular basis. They must have a GPA of 3.0 or higher. Along with their application, they must submit a 600-word essay describing a time when they faced a major obstacle, what they did, and what the experience taught them. Selection is based on merit and creative storytelling.

Financial data   The stipend is $1,000. Funds are sent directly to the recipient's college or university.

Duration   1 year.

Number awarded   1 each year.

Deadline   June of each year.

[504]
KRISTOFER ROBINSON SCHOLARSHIP

Communities Foundation of Texas
Attn: Scholarship Department
5500 Caruth Haven Lane
Dallas, TX 75225-8146
(214) 750-4222   Fax: (214) 750-4210
E-mail: scholarships@cftexas.org
Web: cftexas.academicworks.com/opportunities/680

Summary   To provide financial assistance to residents of Texas who are paraplegic or quadriplegic and plan to attend school at any level in the state.

Eligibility   This program is open to paraplegic and quadriplegic residents of Texas who are enrolled or planning to enroll in a public or private elementary school, junior school, high school, technical school, college, university, or graduate school in the state. Applicants must be able to demonstrate financial need to continue their education. Along with their application, they must submit transcripts, information on their current or planned college, and their academic major.

Financial data   A stipend is awarded (amount not specified).

Duration   1 year; may be renewed up to 3 additional years.

Number awarded   Up to 4 each year.

Deadline   April of each year.

[505]
LISA JONES MEMORIAL SCHOLARSHIP

Spina Bifida Association of Indiana
P.O. Box 19814
Indianapolis, IN 46219-0814
(317) 592-1630   E-mail: sbainoffice@sbain.org
Web: www.sbain.org

Summary   To provide financial assistance to residents of Indiana who have spina bifida and are interested in attending college in any state.

Eligibility   This program is open to residents of Indiana who have spina bifida. Applicants must be enrolled or planning to enroll at a college, junior college, or approved trade, vocational, or business school in any state. They are not required to be members of the Spina Bifida Association of Indiana (SBAIN), but they must join if granted a scholarship. Along with their application, they must submit an essay on how they have shown determination, perse-

verance, and independence in their life. Financial need is not considered in the selection process.

Financial data   A stipend is awarded (amount not specified).

Duration   1 semester; recipients may reapply.

Number awarded   2 each year.

Deadline   April of each year.

[506]
LITTLE PEOPLE OF AMERICA SCHOLARSHIPS

Little People of America, Inc.
Attn: Vice President of Programs
250 El Camino Real, Suite 218
Tustin, CA 92780
(714) 368-3689   Toll Free: (888) LPA-2001
Fax: (714) 368-3367   E-mail: info@lpaonline.org
Web: www.lpaonline.org

Summary   To provide financial assistance for college or graduate school to members of the Little People of America (LPA), to their families, and (in limited cases) to others.

Eligibility   This program is open to members of LPA (limited to people who, for medical reasons, are 4 feet 10 inches or under in height). Applicants must be high school seniors or students attending college, vocational school, or graduate school. Along with their application, they must submit a 500-word personal statement that explains their reasons for applying for a scholarship, their plans for the future, how they intend to be of service to LPA after graduation, and any other relevant information about themselves, their family, their background, and their educational achievements. Financial need is also considered in the selection process. Scholarships are awarded in the following priority order: 1) members of LPA who have a medically diagnosed form of dwarfism; 2) immediate family members of dwarfs who are also paid members of LPA; and 3) people with dwarfism who are not members of LPA.

Financial data   Stipends range from $250 to $1,000.

Duration   1 year; awards are limited to 2 for undergraduate study and 1 for graduate study.

Number awarded   Varies; generally between 5 and 10 each year.

Deadline   April of each year.

[507]
MAHO & PRENTICE SCHOLARSHIP

Maho & Prentice, LLP
Attn: Collegiate Scholarship
629 State Street, Suite 217
Santa Barbara, CA 93101
(805) 962-1930   Fax: (805) 456-2141
Web: www.maho-prentice.com/Law-Scholarships.shtml

Summary   To provide financial assistance to high school seniors and current college students who have suffered an injury.

Eligibility   This program is open to graduating high school seniors and students already enrolled at a college or university in any state. Applicants must submit a 300-word essay on how an injury has affected their life.

Financial data The stipend is $1,000.
Duration 1 year.
Number awarded 1 each year.
Deadline May of each year.

[508]
MATTHEW DEBONO MEMORIAL SCHOLARSHIP FUND

Aplastic Anemia & MDS International Foundation, Inc.
Attn: Scholarship Program
4330 East West Highway, Suite 230
Bethesda, MD 20814
(301) 279-7202, ext. 111   Toll Free: (800) 747-2820
Fax: (301) 279-7205   E-mail: help@aamds.org
Web: www.aamds.org

Summary To provide financial assistance for undergraduate or graduate study in any field to students who have a bone marrow failure disease.

Eligibility This program is open to high school seniors or graduates who plan to enroll and current full- and part-time undergraduate and graduate students at 2- or 4-year colleges, universities, or vocational/technical schools. Applicants must have a medical diagnosis of aplastic anemia, myelodysplastic syndromes (MDS), paroxysmal nocturnal hemoglobinuria (PNH), or a related bone marrow failure disease. They must be 35 years of age or younger. Selection is based on academic record, essays on their goals and ambitions and the impact of the disease, demonstrated leadership, participation in school and community activities, work experience, overall quality of the application, and financial need.

Financial data Stipends range from $1,000 to $2,000.
Duration 1 year; nonrenewable.
Additional data The family of Matthew Debono established this program more than 25 years ago and re-established it with the current sponsor in 2011.
Number awarded Varies each year; recently, 14 were awarded.
Deadline March of each year.

[509]
MID AMERICA CHAPTER MS SOCIETY SCHOLARSHIP PROGRAM

National Multiple Sclerosis Society-Mid America
  Chapter
Attn: Scholarship Program
7611 State Line Road, Suite 100
Kansas City, MO 64114
(816) 448-2180   Toll Free: (800) 344-4867
Fax: (816) 361-2369   E-mail: jean.long@nmss.org
Web: www.nationalmssociety.org

Summary To provide financial assistance to high school seniors and graduates from the Midwest region who have multiple sclerosis (MS) or have a parent with MS and are planning to attend college in any state.

Eligibility This program is open to graduating high school seniors, recent graduates, and GED recipients from Kansas, western Missouri, Nebraska, or Pottawattamie County, Iowa who have MS or a parent who has MS.

Applicants must be planning to enroll as a first-time student at a 2- or 4-year college, university, or vocational/technical school in the United States on at least a half-time basis. Along with their application, they must submit an essay on the impact MS has had on their lives. Selection is based on that essay, academic record, leadership and participation in school or community activities, work experience, goals and aspirations, an outside appraisal, special circumstances, and financial need. U.S. citizenship or permanent resident status is required.

Financial data The stipend is $1,000.
Duration 1 year.
Number awarded Varies each year; recently, 7 were awarded.
Deadline January of each year.

[510]
NAGA EDUCATIONAL SCHOLARSHIP GRANT

National Amputee Golf Association
Attn: Executive Director
701 Orkney Court
Smyrna, TN 37167-6395
(615) 967-4555   E-mail: info@nagagolf.org
Web: www.nagagolf.org

Summary To provide financial assistance for college to members of the National Amputee Golf Association (NAGA) and their dependents.

Eligibility This program is open to amputee members in good standing in the association and their dependents. Applicants must submit information on their scholastic background (GPA in high school and college, courses of study); type of amputation and cause (if applicable), a cover letter describing their plans for the future; and documentation of financial need. They need not be competitive golfers. Selection is based on academic record, financial need, involvement in extracurricular or community activities, and area of study.

Financial data The stipend for a 4-year bachelor's degree program is $1,000 per year. The stipend for a 2-year technical or associate degree is $500 per year.
Duration Up to 4 years, provided the recipient maintains at least half-time enrollment and a GPA of 3.0 or higher and continues to demonstrate financial need.
Number awarded 1 or more each year.
Deadline June of each year.

[511]
NATIONAL MS SOCIETY SCHOLARSHIP PROGRAM

National Multiple Sclerosis Society
Attn: Scholarship Fund
900 South Broadway, Suite 200
Denver, CO 80209
(303) 698-6100, ext. 15259   E-mail: nmss@act.org
Web: www.nationalmssociety.org

Summary To provide financial assistance for college to students who have Multiple Sclerosis (MS) or are the children of people with MS.

Eligibility This program is open to 1) high school seniors who have MS and will be attending an accredited postsecondary school for the first time; 2) high school seniors who are the children of parents with MS and will be attending an accredited postsecondary school for the first time; 3) high school (or GED) graduates of any age who have MS and will be attending an accredited postsecondary school for the first time; and 4) high school (or GED) graduates of any age who have a parent with MS and will be attending an accredited postgraduate school for the first time. Applicants must be U.S. citizens or permanent residents who plan to enroll for at least 6 credit hours per semester in an undergraduate course of study at an accredited 2- or 4-year college, university, or vocational/technical school in the United States or its territories to work on a degree, license, or certificate. Along with their application, they must submit a 1-page personal statement on the impact MS has had on their life. Selection is based on that statement, academic record, leadership and participation in school or community activities, work experience, goals and aspirations, an outside appraisal, special circumstances, and financial need.

Financial data Stipends range from $1,000 to $3,000 per year.

Duration 1 year; may be renewed.

Additional data This program, which began in 2003, is managed by ACT Scholarship and Recognition Services.

Number awarded Varies each year; recently, 815 were awarded.

Deadline January of each year.

[512]
PVA EDUCATIONAL SCHOLARSHIP PROGRAM

Paralyzed Veterans of America
Attn: Communications and Membership Department
801 18th Street, N.W.
Washington, DC 20006-3517
(202) 416-7776   Toll Free: (800) 424-8200, ext. 776
Fax: (202) 416-1250   TDD: (202) 416-7622
E-mail: christih@pva.org
Web: www.pva.org

Summary To provide financial assistance for college to members of the Paralyzed Veterans of America (PVA) and their families.

Eligibility This program is open to PVA members, spouses of members, and unmarried dependent children of members under 24 years of age. Applicants must be attending or planning to attend an accredited U.S. college or university as a full- or part-time student. They must be U.S. citizens. Along with their application, they must submit a personal statement explaining why they wish to further their education, short- and long-term academic goals, how this will meet their career objectives, and how it will affect the PVA membership. Selection is based on that statement, academic records, letters of recommendation, and extracurricular and community activities.

Financial data The stipend is $1,000.

Duration 1 year.

Additional data This program began in 1986.

Number awarded Varies each year; recently 20 were awarded. Since this program was established, it has awarded more than $300,000 in scholarships.

Deadline June of each year.

[513]
SBWIS EDUCATIONAL SCHOLARSHIP IN MEMORY OF MARY ANN POTTS

Spina Bifida Wisconsin, Ltd.
Attn: Scholarship Fund
830 North 109th Street, Suite 6
Wauwatosa, WI 53226
(414) 607-9061   Fax: (414) 607-9602
E-mail: sbwis@sbwis.org
Web: www.sbwis.org/services

Summary To provide financial assistance to residents of Wisconsin who have spina bifida and are interested in attending college or graduate school in any state.

Eligibility This program is open to residents of Wisconsin of any age who have spina bifida. Applicants must be enrolled or planning to enroll at a college, graduate school, trade school, or specialized educational training program in any state. Along with their application, they must submit a personal statement explaining their goals and what they want to accomplish with the education or training they will receive. There is no age limitation. Selection is based on that statement, academic record, community service, work history, and leadership.

Financial data A stipend is awarded (amount not specified); funds are paid directly to the recipient's institution to be used for payment of tuition, books, room and board, and specialized equipment needs.

Duration 1 year; recipients may reapply.

Additional data This program began in 1996.

Number awarded A limited number are awarded each year.

Deadline August of each year.

[514]
SCOTT DECKER, M.D., MEMORIAL SCHOLARSHIP

Amputee Coalition
Attn: Programs and Services Coordinator
9303 Center Street, Suite 100
Manassas, VA 20110
(703) 330-1699, ext. 7102   Toll Free: (888) 267-5669
TDD: (865) 525-4512
E-mail: dan@amputee-coalition.org
Web: www.amputee-coalition.org

Summary To provide financial assistance for college to high school seniors who have an acquired or congenital limb loss.

Eligibility This program is open to graduating high school seniors, recent high school graduates, adults returning to school, and current full-time college students, including military veterans and active-duty military personnel. Applicants must have an acquired or congenital limb loss. They must have a GPA of 3.0 or higher and minimum scores in the 60th percentile on the SAT or ACT. Preference is given to residents of Maryland, although non-Maryland applicants are also eligible.

Financial data   The stipend is $1,000.

Duration   1 year; nonrenewable.

Additional data   This program began in 2015.

Number awarded   4 each year.

Deadline   April of each year.

[515]
SILVER CROSS SCHOLARSHIP

Silver Cross
1005 Skyview Drive, Suite 104
Burlington, ON L7P 5B1
Canada
Toll Free: (800) 572-9310   Fax: (905) 335-1612
E-mail: dbaker@silvercross.com
Web: www.silvercross.com/scholarship.html

Summary   To provide financial assistance for college to students who use mobility equipment.

Eligibility   This program is open to students enrolled or planning to enroll full time at a college or university in the United States or Canada. Applicants must use mobility equipment (e.g., power wheelchair, manual wheelchair, mobility scooter). Along with their application, they must submit an essay on a topic that changes annually but relates to mobility disorders; recently, students were asked to identify the strategies they use that could help other younger students overcome barriers to success (physical or otherwise) in education or day-to-day life.

Financial data   The stipend is $1,500.

Duration   1 year.

Number awarded   1 each year.

Deadline   December of each year.

[516]
SONORAN SPINE FOUNDATION SCHOLARSHIP

Sonoran Spine Research and Education Foundation
c/o ASU Foundation
Donor Relations and Scholarship Coordinator
300 East University Drive, Fifth Floor
P.O. Box 2260
Tempe, AZ 85280-2260
(480) 965-9720   E-mail: Monica.Peterson@asu.edu
Web: www.spineresearch.org

Summary   To provide financial assistance to residents of Arizona enrolled at designated universities in the state who have a diagnosed spinal deformity.

Eligibility   This program is open to residents or Arizona who are enrolled as full-time undergraduate or graduate students at Arizona State University, Northern Arizona University, or the University of Arizona. Applicants must have a diagnosed spinal deformity (e.g., scoliosis, kyphosis). Along with their application, they must submit an essay of 1 to 2 pages describing their medical history regarding their spinal deformity, how they have overcome obstacles in their life presented by that condition, and how this scholarship will assist in achieving their educational and career goals. Selection is based on that essay,

involvement in community and/or school activities, and financial need.

Financial data   The stipend is $1,000.

Duration   1 year.

Additional data   This program began in 2000.

Number awarded   1 or more each year.

Deadline   May of each year.

[517]
SPECIAL PEOPLE GIFTS OF LOVE PROGRAM

Italian Catholic Federation
8393 Capwell Drive, Suite 110
Oakland, CA 94621
(510) 633-9058   Toll Free: (888) ICF-1924
Fax: (510) 633-9758   E-mail: info@icf.org
Web: www.icf.org/charity

Summary   To provide funding to individuals who have a disability and desire additional training or instruction.

Eligibility   This program is open to 1) individuals who have a disability and desire formal training or instruction in a particular vocation, academic, athletic, or artistic field; 2) qualified instructors on behalf of an individual with a disability who exhibits a particular skill to be developed and who desires formal instruction or training; or 3) adults with custodial responsibility for, and on behalf of, an individual with a disability who exhibits a particular skill to be developed and who desires formal instruction or training. The program defines disability to include ADD/ADHD, amputee, autism, cerebral palsy, emotional disturbances, hearing impairments or deafness, mental retardation, multiple sclerosis, muscular dystrophy, orthopedic impairments, specific learning disabilities, speech and language impairments, spina bifida, spinal cord injury, traumatic brain injury, visual impairments and blindness, or other health impairments that require special education or related services. Applicants must submit an essay on how they intend to use the grant funds to assist them with their disability or to achieve the goals of the program. Financial need is considered in the selection process.

Financial data   A stipend is awarded (amount not specified). Funds are not intended to support tuition.

Duration   These are 1-time grants.

Number awarded   Varies each year.

Deadline   Deadline not specified.

[518]
SPINA BIFIDA ASSOCIATION OF ALABAMA ADVANCED EDUCATION SCHOLARSHIP PROGRAM

Spina Bifida Association of Alabama
Attn: Scholarship Committee
P.O. Box 35
Gadsden, AL 35902
(256) 617-1414   E-mail: info@sbaofal.org
Web: www.sbaofal.org/prog_services.html

Summary   To provide financial assistance to Alabama residents who have spina bifida and are interested in working on an undergraduate or graduate degree at a school in any state.

Eligibility This program is open to entering or continuing undergraduate and graduate students at colleges and universities in any state who have spina bifida. Applicants must reside in Alabama and have been residents of that state for at least 2 consecutive years. They must graduate from high school with a GPA of 2.0 or higher. Along with their application, they must submit 1) an essay on their educational and career goals, aspects of their background and character relevant to their likelihood of academic success, and other factors they wish to have considered, all in relationship to spina bifida; 2) verification of disability, signed by a physician; and 3) transcripts of grades for high school and other educational levels.

Financial data The stipend is $1,000 per year; funds are sent directly to the recipient's institution of higher education.

Duration 1 year; may be renewed up to 3 additional years for undergraduates, up to 1 additional years for graduate students, or up to 2 additional years for students in postgraduate school, law school, or medical school. Renewal depends on the recipient's maintaining a GPA of 2.25 or higher each semester.

Number awarded Up to 4 each year.

Deadline May of each year.

[519]
SPINA BIFIDA ASSOCIATION OF CONNECTICUT SCHOLARSHIP FUND

Spina Bifida Association of Connecticut, Inc.
Attn: Scholarship Committee
P.O. Box 2545
Hartford, CT 06146-2545
Web: sbacct.tripod.com/SBAC.org___Programs.htm

Summary To provide financial assistance to residents of Connecticut who have spina bifida and are interested in attending college in any state.

Eligibility This program is open to residents of Connecticut who have spina bifida and are attending or planning to attend a college, university, trade school, vocational institution, or business school in any state. Applicants must submit an essay (2 to 3 pages) on their educational goals; reasons for selecting those goals; outstanding accomplishments or contributions made through school, extracurricular, religious group, or Spina Bifida Association of Connecticut (SBAC) member activities; and community and volunteer work. Selection is based on academic record, other efforts shown in school, involvement in the community, leadership qualities, commitment to personal goals, and work history.

Financial data The stipend is $1,000. Funds are paid directly to the recipient's school.

Duration 1 year.

Number awarded 1 or more each year.

Deadline May of each year.

[520]
SPINA BIFIDA ASSOCIATION OF NORTH TEXAS SCHOLARSHIP

Spina Bifida Association of North Texas
Attn: Scholarship Program
801 Avenue H East, Suite 101
Arlington, TX 76011
(972) 238-8755 E-mail: information@spinabifidant.org
Web: www.spinabifidant.org

Summary To provide financial assistance to residents of Texas who were born with spina bifida and are interested in attending college in any state.

Eligibility This program is open to residents of Texas who were born with spina bifida. Applicants must be enrolled in or accepted into a college, junior college, or approved trade school in any state. Along with their application, they must submit a personal statement describing their goals in life, future educational pursuits, and anything else they wish the selection committee to know about them. Selection is based on that statement, academic record, community service, work history, leadership, and financial need.

Financial data A stipend is awarded (amount not specified); funds are paid directly to the recipient to be used for payment of tuition, books, room and board, and specialized equipment needs.

Duration 1 year; may be renewed.

Number awarded Varies each year; recently, 4 were awarded.

Deadline March of each year.

[521]
SPINA BIFIDA COALITION OF CINCINNATI POSTSECONDARY EDUCATION SCHOLARSHIP

Spina Bifida Coalition of Cincinnati
644 Linn Street, Suite 635
Cincinnati, OH 45203
(513) 923-1378   Fax: (513) 381-0525
E-mail: sbccincy@sbccincy.org
Web: www.sbccincy.org/support/scholarships

Summary To provide financial assistance to residents of the service area of the Spina Bifida Coalition of Cincinnati (SBCC) who have spina bifida and are interested in postsecondary education in any state.

Eligibility This program is open to residents of Ohio, southeastern Indiana, and northern Kentucky who have spina bifida. Applicants must be interested in participating in a program of postsecondary education in any state. Along with their application, they must submit an essay on why they have chosen their college and their field of study.

Financial data The stipend ranges from $500 to $2,000.

Duration 1 year; may be renewed, up to a lifetime maximum of $2,000.

Number awarded Varies each year.

Deadline June of each year.

[522]
THE BENNETT CLAYTON FOUNDATION SCHOLARSHIP PROGRAM

The Bennett Clayton Foundation
36910 County Road 15
St. Peter, MN 56082
(507) 327-4114   E-mail: bcfforoi@aol.com
Web: www.bcfforoi.org/BCF%20Scholarship.htm

Summary   To provide financial assistance to residents of designated states who have Osteogenesis Imperfecta (OI) and are interested in attending college in any state.

Eligibility   This program is open to residents of Iowa, Minnesota, North Dakota, South Dakota, or Wisconsin who have OI. Applicants must be high school seniors or current undergraduates enrolled full time at a 2- or 4-year college, university, or vocational/technical school in any state. Along with their application, they must submit a personal statement on the impact OI has had on their life. Selection is based on that statement, academic record, demonstrated leadership and participation in school and community activities, honors, work experience, a statement of goals and aspirations, unusual personal or family circumstances, and an outside appraisal; financial need is not considered.

Financial data   The stipend is $3,000. Checks are mailed to the student's home made payable to the educational institution of the recipient.

Duration   1 year; may be renewed up to 3 additional years or until completion of a bachelor's degree, whichever occurs first.

Additional data   This program is administered by Scholarship Management Services, a division of Scholarship America.

Number awarded   1 or more each year.

Deadline   February of each year.

[523]
THE DREAM INSTITUTE HEAP SCHOLAR AWARD SCHOLARSHIPS

The DREAM Institute
Attn: High Education Assistance Program (HEAP)
P.O. Box 52785
Tulsa, OK 74152-0785
(918) 660-3408   E-mail: dream@dreaminstitute.org
Web: www.dreaminstitute.org/Programs.htm

Summary   To provide financial assistance to residents of Oklahoma who have a physical and/or learning disability and are interested in attending college in the state.

Eligibility   This program is open to residents of Oklahoma who have been diagnosed with a physical and/or learning disability. Applicants must be enrolled or planning to enroll full time at a 2- or 4-year college or university in the state. They must have a GPA of 2.0 or higher and be able to demonstrate financial need. Along with their application, they must submit a personal statement of 4 to 8 pages on their professional and career goals, how their program or degree will help them achieve those goals, any special services and/or accommodations they received and the self-advocacy skills they used to acquire those services and/or accommodations, their family background and how their family has impacted their future educational plans, their biggest life challenge and how they dealt with it, how this program will impact their continuing education, the impact of their disability on their educational goals, how their disability has impacted their academic performance, the process that they use to attain their short- and long-run goals, and whom they admire the most and why.

Financial data   The stipend depends on the need of the recipient. Funds are available to help pay for tuition, fees, books, and dormitory fees.

Duration   1 year; may be renewed up to 3 additional years.

Additional data   Scholars are invited to participate in an orientation workshop designed to equip them with the information they will require as a college student with a disability. They also qualify for special tutoring. The sponsor's name stands for Disability-Resources-Educational Advocacy-Motivation.

Number awarded   Varies each year; recently, 3 new and 10 renewal scholarships were awarded.

Deadline   April of each year.

[524]
THE SHOOT FOR THE FUTURE SCHOLARSHIP FUND

Community Foundation of Middle Tennessee
Attn: Scholarship Coordinator
3833 Cleghorn Avenue, Suite 400
Nashville, TN 37215-2519
(615) 321-4939, ext. 116   Toll Free: (888) 540-5200
Fax: (615) 327-2746   E-mail: pcole@cfmt.org
Web: www.cfmt.org

Summary   To provide financial assistance to college students from Tennessee who have spinal cord injuries.

Eligibility   This program is open to individuals who have spinal cord injuries but have overcome obstacles while displaying enthusiasm and perseverance. Applicants must be residents of Tennessee attending or planning to attend a 2- or 4-year college or university in any state or residents of other states attending college in Tennessee. Financial need is considered in the selection process.

Financial data   Stipends range from $500 to $2,500 per year. Funds are paid to the recipient's school and must be used for tuition, fees, books, supplies, room, board, or miscellaneous expenses.

Duration   1 year; may be renewed.

Additional data   This program began in 2014.

Number awarded   1 or more each year.

Deadline   March of each year.

[525]
THEODORE R. AND VIVIAN M. JOHNSON SCHOLARSHIP PROGRAM

State University System of Florida
Attn: Board of Governors
325 West Gaines Street
Tallahassee, FL 32399-0400
(850) 245-0466   Fax: (850) 245-9685
E-mail: info@flbog.org
Web: www.flbog.edu

Summary To provide financial assistance to Florida undergraduate students who have disabilities.

Eligibility This program is open to students with disabilities enrolled or planning to enroll at a State University System of Florida institution. Applicants must be able to verify the nature and/or extent of their disability, which may be in 1 or more of the following classifications: attention deficit disorder (ADD); attention deficit hyperactivity disorder (ADHD); autism spectrum disorder; blind or low vision; deaf or hard of hearing; orthopedic disability; psychological, emotional, or behavioral disability; speech/language impairment; specific learning disability; traumatic brain injury; or other health disabilities. They must have a GPA of 2.0 or higher and be able to document financial need. Along with their application, they must submit a 1-page personal statement on their achievements, activities, career goals, and the effects of their disability(ies).

Financial data The stipend depends on the availability of funds.

Duration 1 year; may be renewed up to 5 additional years, provided the recipient maintains a GPA of 2.0 or higher and enrolls in at least 18 credits each academic year.

Additional data This program is administered by the equal opportunity program at each of the 12 State University System of Florida 4-year institutions. Contact that office for further information. Funding is provided by the Theodore R. and Vivian M. Johnson Foundation, with matching funding from the Florida Legislature.

Number awarded Several each year.

Deadline April of each year.

[526]
TUITION WAIVER FOR DISABLED CHILDREN OF KENTUCKY VETERANS

Kentucky Department of Veterans Affairs
Attn: Tuition Waiver Coordinator
321 West Main Street, Suite 390
Louisville, KY 40202
(502) 595-4447   Toll Free: (800) 928-4012 (within KY)
Fax: (502) 595-3369
Web: www.veterans.ky.gov

Summary To provide financial assistance for college to the children of Kentucky veterans who have a disability related to their parent's military service.

Eligibility This program is open to the children of veterans who have acquired a disability as a direct result of their parent's military service. The disability must have been designated by the U.S. Department of Veterans Affairs as compensable (currently defined as spina bifida). The veteran parent must 1) have served on active duty with the U.S. armed forces or in the National Guard or Reserve component on state active duty, active duty for training, or inactive duty training; and 2) be (or if deceased have been) a resident of Kentucky. Applicants must have been admitted to a state-supported university, college, or vocational training institute in Kentucky.

Financial data Eligible children are exempt from payment of tuition at state-supported institutions of higher education in Kentucky.

Duration There are no age or time limits on the waiver.

Number awarded Varies each year.

Deadline Deadline not specified.

[527]
USOC 2002 OLYMPIC AND PARALYMPIC WINTER GAMES LEGACY SCHOLARSHIPS

United States Olympic Committee
Sport Performance
Attn: Legacy Scholarship
One Olympic Plaza
Colorado Springs, CO 80909-5760
(719) 632-5551   Toll Free: (800) 933-4473
Fax: (719) 578-4654
Web: www.teamusa.org

Summary To provide financial assistance for college to athletes who either participated in the 2002 Winter Olympics or Paralympics or are currently attending college in Utah.

Eligibility This program is open to 1) 2002 Olympians and Paralympians who are currently attending college; 2) current athletes who are training and attending college in Utah; and 3) retired Olympians/Paralympians who are attending college in Utah. Applicants must submit an essay of 1 to 2 pages on why they deserve this scholarship, including their plans as those related to their education, career objectives, and long-term goals. Selection is based on competitive status, previous receipt of scholarships, and financial need.

Financial data A stipend is awarded (amount not specified). Funds are available for tuition, fees, books, and room and board only.

Duration 1 year; may be renewed.

Additional data This program was established following the 2002 Winter Olympics in Salt Lake City.

Number awarded Varies each year.

Deadline April or October of each year.

[528]
USOC ATHLETE TUITION GRANT PROGRAM

United States Olympic Committee
Attn: Athlete Support Department
One Olympic Plaza
Colorado Springs, CO 80909-5760
(719) 632-5551   Toll Free: (800) 933-4473
Fax: (719) 578-4654
Web: www.teamusa.org

Summary To provide financial assistance to athletes who are currently in training for the Olympics or Paralympics and enrolled in college.

Eligibility This program is open to athletes who have demonstrated competitive excellence in important international competitions. Applicants must have been accepted to receive Elite Athlete Health Insurance and/or Direct Athlete Support from the United States Olympic Committee (USOC) and be endorsed by the National Governing Body (NGB) for their particular sport. They must be enrolled at an accredited college or university. Also eligible are retired athletes who participated in the Olympics Games, Paralympic Games, or Pan American Games within the past 4 years; athletes with disabilities who are members of the current U.S. Paralympics Elite or National Team; and retired Paralympians who competed in a Paralympic Games within the past 5 years. Priority is given to applicants who have a current top 8 World Championships placement or world ranking. Financial need is considered in the selection process.

Financial data A stipend is awarded (amount not specified). Funds may be used for tuition and mandatory fees only; books, parking fees, and room and board costs are not covered.

Duration 1 year; may be renewed. Retired athletes are only eligible for 1 grant.

Number awarded Varies each year.

Deadline April, July, or October of each year.

[529]
VALIANT SCHOLARSHIP

Illinois Spina Bifida Association
2211 North Oak Park Avenue
Chicago, IL 60707
(773) 444-0305   Fax: (773) 444-0327
E-mail: info@i-sba.org
Web: www.i-sba.org/programs

Summary To provide financial assistance to residents of Illinois who have spina bifida and are interested in attending college or graduate school in any state.

Eligibility This program is open to residents of Illinois who have spina bifida. Applicants must be enrolled or planning to enroll at a 2- or 4-year college or university in any state. Along with their application, they must submit personal statements on 1) how they can impact the future of younger children with spina bifida; and 2) how they have displayed leadership, impacted the less fortunate, and made a difference.

Financial data Stipends range up to $2,000.

Duration 1 year.

Additional data Recipients are expected to volunteer with the Illinois Spina Bifida Association at least once during the following year.

Number awarded 1 each year.

Deadline June of each year.

[530]
YE NOTORIOUS KREWE OF THE PEG LEG PIRATE SCHOLARSHIPS

Ye Notorious Krewe of the Peg Leg Pirate, Inc.
P.O. Box 1854
Ruskin, LA 33575-1854
Web: www.peglegpirate.org

Summary To provide financial assistance for college or graduate school to amputees and their families.

Eligibility This program is open to amputees, families of amputees, and organizations that work with amputees. Applicants must be attending or planning to attend an accredited college, university, community college, vocational/technical school, or graduate school. They must have a GPA of 3.5 or higher. Along with their application, they must submit 2 recommendations, transcripts, documentation of financial need, and a 300-word essay describing their future goals.

Financial data Stipends vary but recently have averaged $1,150. Funds are paid directly to the recipient's institution.

Duration 1 year.

Additional data This program began in 2008.

Number awarded Varies each year; recently 4 were awarded.

Deadline March of each year.

Graduate Students

[531]
180 MEDICAL SCHOLARSHIPS

180 Medical
Attn: Scholarship Committee
8516 N.W. Expressway
Oklahoma City, OK 73162
Toll Free: (877) 688-2729   Fax: (888) 718-0633
E-mail: scholarships@180medical.com
Web: www.180medical.com/scholarships

Summary To provide financial assistance for college to students who have spinal cord injuries, spina bifida, or transverse myelitis.

Eligibility This program is open to U.S. citizens who are enrolled or planning to enroll full time at a 2- or 4-year college or university as an undergraduate or graduate student. Applicants must be under a doctor's care for spina bifida, a spinal cord injury, and ostomy (ileostomy, colostomy, or urostomy), neurogenic bladder, or transverse myelitis. Along with their application, they must submit 1) a physician's note documenting the diagnosis; 2) an official transcript; 3) a list of significant awards or honors they have received during school for academic or extracurricular activities; 4) a list of extracurricular, sports, community, employment, or other activities; and 5) a 750-word essay on how their medical condition has affected their life and their goals for the future.

Financial data   The stipend is $1,000.

Duration   1 year.

Number awarded   7 each year.

Deadline   May of each year.

[532]
AMERIGLIDE ACHIEVER SCHOLARSHIP

AmeriGlide, Inc.
3901A Commerce Park Drive
Raleigh, NC 27610
Toll Free: (800) 790-1635   Fax: (800) 791-6524
E-mail: scholarship@ameriglide.com
Web: www.ameriglide.com/Scholarship

Summary   To provide financial assistance to undergraduate and graduate students who use a wheelchair.

Eligibility   This program is open to full-time undergraduate and graduate students at 2- and 4-year colleges and universities who use a manual or electric wheelchair or mobility scooter. Applicants must have completed at least 1 year of college and have a GPA of 3.0 or higher. They must be legal residents of the United States or have a valid student visa. Along with their application, they must submit a 500-word essay on topics that change annually; recently, students were invited to write on their career and life goals.

Financial data   The stipend is $2,500.

Duration   1 year.

Additional data   This program began in 2008.

Number awarded   1 each year.

Deadline   May of each year.

[533]
ASSE DIVERSITY COMMITTEE GRADUATE SCHOLARSHIP

American Society of Safety Engineers
Attn: ASSE Foundation
Scholarship Award Program
520 North Northwest Highway
Park Ridge, IL 60068-2538
(847) 699-2929   Fax: (847) 296-3769
E-mail: assefoundation@asse.org
Web: foundation.asse.org/scholarships-and-grants

Summary   To provide financial assistance to graduate students who come from diverse groups and are working on a degree related to occupational safety.

Eligibility   This program is open to students who are working on a graduate degree in occupational safety, health, environment, industrial hygiene, occupational health nursing, or a closely-related field (e.g., industrial or environmental engineering). Applicants must be full- or part-time students who have completed at least 9 semester hours and have a GPA of 3.5 or higher. A goal of this program is to support individuals regardless of race, ethnicity, gender, religion, personal beliefs, age, sexual orientation, physical challenges, geographic location, university, or specific area of study. U.S. citizenship is not required. Membership in the American Society of Safety

Engineers (ASSE) is not required, but preference is given to members.

Financial data   The stipend is $1,000 per year.

Duration   1 year; recipients may reapply.

Number awarded   1 each year.

Deadline   November of each year.

[534]
BOBBY JONES OPEN SCHOLARSHIPS

American Syringomyelia & Chiari Alliance Project, Inc.
P.O. Box 1586
Longview, TX 75606-1586
(903) 236-7079   Toll Free: (800) ASAP-282
Fax: (903) 757-7456   E-mail: info@ASAP.org
Web: www.asap.org

Summary   To provide financial assistance for college or graduate school to members of the American Syringomyelia & Chiari Alliance Project (ASAP) and their children.

Eligibility   This program is open to students entering or enrolled in college or graduate school who have syringomeylia (SM) and/or Chiari Malformation (CM) or whose parent is affected by SM and/or CM. Applicants or parents must have been ASAP members for at least 6 months. They may be of any age. Along with their application, they must submit 4 essays on assigned topics related to their experience with SM and/or CM. Selection is based on those essay and financial need.

Financial data   Stipends are $1,000 for full-time students or $500 for part-time students. Recipients may reapply, but they may receive only a total of $4,000 in support from this program.

Duration   1 year.

Additional data   This program is funded by the Bobby Jones Open, an annual golf tournament in which participation is restricted to golfers named Bobby Jones (e.g., Robert Jones, Roberta Jones). The tournament began in 1979 and since 1990 has raised money for activities of the ASAP.

Number awarded   Varies each year; a total of $5,000 is available for this program annually.

Deadline   May of each year.

[535]
BRYON RIESCH SCHOLARSHIPS

Bryon Riesch Paralysis Foundation
P.O. Box 1388
Waukesha, WI 53187-1388
(262) 547-2083   E-mail: info@brpf.org
Web: www.brpf.org/scholarship-application

Summary   To provide financial assistance to undergraduate and graduate students who have a neurological disability or the children of people with such a disability.

Eligibility   This program is open to students entering or enrolled at a 2- or 4-year college or university as an undergraduate or graduate student. Applicants must have a neurological disability or be the child of a person with such a disability. First priority is given to individuals suffering from a direct spinal cord injury or disease resulting in paralysis such as spinal tumors, strokes, or aneurysms affecting the spinal cord, or spina bifida. Other diseases and disorders that qualify include multiple sclerosis, traumatic brain injuries, Parkinson's, and cerebral palsy. Priority is also given to residents of Wisconsin. Applicants must have a GPA of 2.5 or higher in high school or college. Along with their application, they must submit a 200-word essay on why they deserve the scholarship, a statement of their 5- and 10-year goals, and a list of work experience. Financial need is not considered in the selection process.

Financial data The stipend is $2,000.

Duration 1 year; may be renewed.

Number awarded Varies each semester; recently, 7 were awarded for the fall semester and 5 for the spring semester.

Deadline June of each year for fall semester; December of each year for spring semester.

[536]
CHILDREN'S BRITTLE BONE FOUNDATION AND OI FOUNDATION IMPACT GRANT PROGRAM

Children's Brittle Bone Foundation
Attn: Impact Grant Program
7701 95th Street
Pleasant Prairie, WI 53158
(773) 263-2223   Fax: (262) 947-0724
E-mail: impactgrants@oif.org
Web: www.cbbf.org/impact-grants

Summary To provide funding for education or other personal needs to people who have osteogenesis imperfecta (OI).

Eligibility This program is open to people who have OI and are seeking funding for equipment or services that will improve their quality of life. Examples of acceptable requests include education-related items such as tuition assistance at the preschool to postdoctoral level; prescribed exercise therapy equipment for physical or occupational therapy; orthotics, braces, and walkers; manual or electric wheelchairs or scooters; adaptive technology such as computers or hearing aids; dental intervention; vehicle modifications such as lifts or pedal extensions or vehicle purchases; travel reimbursement to receive specialized care; outdoor ramps that provide access to a home; or accessibility aides such as reachers, shower chairs, or kitchen carts.

Financial data Recently, grants ranged from $396 to $20,000 and averaged nearly $5,500.

Duration Funds must be used within 12 months.

Additional data This program is provided jointly by the Children's Brittle Bone Foundation and the Osteogenesis Imperfecta (OI) Foundation.

Number awarded Varies each year; recently, 17 were awarded.

Deadline February of each year.

[537]
CMMS DESHAE LOTT MINISTRIES SCHOLARSHIPS

CMMS Deshae Lott Ministries Inc.
Attn: Outreach Selection Committee
P.O. Box 9232
Bossier City, LA 71113-9232
E-mail: deshaelott@hotmail.com
Web: www.deshae.org/index.html

Summary To provide financial assistance to students who have serious physical disabilities and are working on a graduate degree in any field.

Eligibility This program is open to graduate students who have a serious physical disability and are working on a degree in any field. To qualify as having a serious physical disability, they must require complete assistance from human beings and/or major complex durable medical equipment to perform at least 3 of 13 defined daily life functions such as bathing and personal hygiene, dressing and grooming, preparing and administering medications, performing routine medical procedures, transportation, seeing, or hearing. Along with their application, they must submit a 1-page essay on how they see the work they are doing toward their degree as benefiting the human spirit and how they see their academic training relating to their avocation. U.S. citizenship is required.

Financial data Stipends are $2,000 or $1,500.

Duration 1 year.

Additional data This program was established in 2007 by Deshae E. Lott, Ph.D. who has limb girdle muscular dystrophy. It receives assistance from ministers of the Christian Metaphysicians and Mystics Society (CMMS).

Number awarded Up to 4 each year.

Deadline June of each year.

[538]
COL CARL F. BASWELL COMBAT WOUNDED ENGINEER SCHOLARSHIP

Army Engineer Association
Attn: Director Washington DC Operations
P.O. Box 30260
Alexandria, VA 22310-8260
(703) 428-7084   Fax: (703) 428-6043
E-mail: xd@armyengineer.com
Web: www.armyengineer.com/scholarships.htm

Summary To provide financial assistance for college to U.S. Army Engineers who were wounded in combat in Iraq or Afghanistan.

Eligibility This program is open to U.S. Army Engineers who were wounded in combat and received a Purple Heart during Operation Iraqi Freedom or Operation Enduring Freedom. Applicants must be working on or planning to work on an associate, bachelor's, or master's degree at an accredited college or university. Selection is based primarily on financial need, although potential for academic success and personal references are also considered.

Financial data The stipend is $2,500.

Duration 1 year.

Additional data This program began in 2010.

Number awarded 1 each year.
Deadline June of each year.

[539]
DISABLED LAW STUDENT SCHOLARSHIP

Hermann Law Group
560 White Plains Road, Suite 630
Tarrytown, NY 10591
(914) 286-3030   Toll Free: (888) 491-9087
E-mail: info@nymetrodisability.com
Web: www.nymetrodisability.com

Summary To provide financial assistance to law students who have a personal physical or mental disability.

Eligibility This program is open to students currently enrolled at a law school in the United State. Applicants must have a personal physical or mental disability. Along with their application, they must submit an essay of 1,000 to 1,500 words on how they have worked to succeed despite the disability.

Financial data The stipend is $1,000.

Duration 1 year.

Number awarded 1 each year.

Deadline August of each year.

[540]
EASTER SEALS SOUTH CAROLINA EDUCATIONAL SCHOLARSHIPS

Easter Seals South Carolina
Attn: Scholarship Program
3020 Farrow Road
P.O. Box 5715
Columbia, SC 29250
(803) 627-3857   Fax: (803) 356-6902
E-mail: mgriffin@sc.easterseals.com
Web: www.easterseals.com

Summary To provide financial assistance for college or graduate school to South Carolina students who have a mobility impairment.

Eligibility This program is open to South Carolina residents and students attending a college or university in the state who have a significant and medically certified mobility impairment. Applicants must be enrolled or planning to enroll in an undergraduate or graduate program. They must be able to demonstrate financial need. Preference is given to students carrying at least 9 credit hours and making satisfactory academic progress toward graduation.

Financial data The maximum stipend is $1,000.

Duration 1 year; may be renewed.

Additional data This program began in 1985.

Number awarded 1 or more each year.

Deadline June of each year.

[541]
ELLIOTT G. HEARD JR. MEMORIAL SCHOLARSHIP

Elliott G. Heard Jr. Memorial Scholarship Committee
P.O. Box 214
Mullica Hill, NJ 08062
(609) 202-0061   Fax: (703) 903-3690
E-mail: yhbautista@yahoo.com

Summary To provide financial assistance to students enrolled or planning to enroll at an accredited law school.

Eligibility This program is open to college seniors who have been accepted to an accredited law school and students currently enrolled in law school who are not in their final semester. Applicants must be U.S. citizens. Along with their application, they must submit a 500-word essay describing why they should be considered for this scholarship and why they decided on a career in the law. Minorities, women, and the physically challenged are especially encouraged to apply. Finalists are invited to an interview. Selection is based on academic achievement, community service, leadership, citizenship, and financial need.

Financial data The stipend is $1,000.

Duration 1 year; nonrenewable.

Additional data This program is named after the first African American jurist in Gloucester County, New Jersey.

Number awarded 2 each year.

Deadline October of each year.

[542]
EXTREMITY SCHOLARSHIP PROGRAM

The Limb Preservation Foundation
Attn: Executive Director
1721 East 19th Avenue, Suite 106
Denver, CO 80218
(303) 429-0688   Fax: (303) 487-3667
E-mail: khill@limbpreservation.org
Web: limbpreservation.org

Summary To provide financial assistance to residents of designated Rocky Mountain states who are patients or survivors of diseases of the extremities and interested in attending college or graduate school in any state.

Eligibility This program is open to residents of the Rocky Mountain region (Arizona, Colorado, Idaho, Kansas, Montana, Nebraska, New Mexico, Utah, and Wyoming) who are enrolled or planning to enroll at a college, university, vocational school, or graduate school in any state. Applicants must be patients or survivors who have battled or are battling a limb-threatening condition due to trauma, tumor, or infection. Along with their application, they must submit an essay of 500 to 1,000 words on 1 of the following topics: 1) the advice they would give to another person who is going through a similar limb-threatening experience; 2) their career aspirations; or 3) an important personal relationship and how it has influenced them during their experience with limb tumor, trauma, or infection. Selection is based on that essay, letters of recommendation, and financial need.

Financial data The stipend is $2,500 per year. Funds are paid directly to the recipient's institution.

Duration 4 years, provided the recipient maintains a GPA of 2.25 or higher.

Number awarded Varies each year; recently, 7 were awarded.

Deadline September of each year for fall semester; May of each year for spring semester.

[543]
ISBA SCHOLARSHIPS

Illinois Spina Bifida Association
2211 North Oak Park Avenue
Chicago, IL 60707
(773) 444-0305   Fax: (773) 444-0327
E-mail: info@i-sba.org
Web: www.i-sba.org/programs

Summary To provide financial assistance to adult residents of Illinois who have spina bifida and are interested in attending college or graduate school in any state.

Eligibility This program is open to adult residents of Illinois who have spina bifida. Applicants must be enrolled or planning to enroll at a 2- or 4-year college or university, online courses, technical or trade school, or other continuing education program in any state as an undergraduate or graduate student. Along with their application, they must submit essays of 250 to 500 words on 1) the accomplishments or contributions (school, extracurricular, community, or Illinois Spina Bifida Association) they have made of which they are most proud; and 2) their career goals and the reasons for selecting those. Selection is based on those essays, transcripts, and letters of recommendation.

Financial data Stipends range up to $2,000.

Duration 1 year.

Additional data Recipients are expected to volunteer with the Illinois Spina Bifida Association at least once during the following year.

Number awarded Varies each year; recently, 8 were awarded.

Deadline June of each year.

[544]
JEAN DRISCOLL "DREAM BIG" AWARD

Spina Bifida Association of Greater New England
Attn: Executive Director
219 East Main Street, Suite 100B
Milford, MA 01757
(508) 482-5300   Toll Free: (888) 479-1900
Fax: (508) 482-5301
E-mail: edugan@SBAGreaterNE.org
Web: www.sbagreaterne.org

Summary To provide funding for educational, developmental, or assistive programs to residents of New England who have spina bifida.

Eligibility This program is open to residents of New England who are 14 years of age or older and have spina bifida. Applicants must be seeking funding for educational, developmental, or assistive programs that will enable them to achieve their goals despite limitations imposed by spina bifida. Eligible degree programs include associate,

technical, bachelor's, and graduate. Along with their application, they must submit a personal statement, at least 2 paragraphs in length, describing their goals in life and their determination to "dream big;" the statement should include future educational pursuits or examples of camps or training courses taken to assist them in achieving their dreams.

Financial data The stipend is $1,000.

Duration The award is granted annually.

Number awarded 1 each year.

Deadline May of each year.

[545]
JUSTWALKERS.COM MOBILITY SCHOLARSHIP PROGRAM

Just Health Shops
Attn: JustWalkers.com
11840 West Market Place, Suite H
Fulton, MD 20759
Toll Free: (800) 998-7750   Fax: (301) 776-0716
E-mail: scholarship@justwalkers.com
Web: www.justwalkers.com

Summary To provide financial assistance to undergraduate and graduate students who use a mobility device.

Eligibility This program is open to legal U.S. residents and students with valid visas who are entering or enrolled in an undergraduate or graduate program. Applicants must use a wheelchair, power scooter, crutches, rollator, or other mobility device on a regular basis. They must have a GPA of 3.0 or higher. Along with their application, they must submit a 600-word essay describing a time when they faced a major obstacle, what they did, and what the experience taught them. Selection is based on merit and creative storytelling.

Financial data The stipend is $1,000. Funds are sent directly to the recipient's college or university.

Duration 1 year.

Number awarded 1 each year.

Deadline June of each year.

[546]
KRISTOFER ROBINSON SCHOLARSHIP

Communities Foundation of Texas
Attn: Scholarship Department
5500 Caruth Haven Lane
Dallas, TX 75225-8146
(214) 750-4222   Fax: (214) 750-4210
E-mail: scholarships@cftexas.org
Web: cftexas.academicworks.com/opportunities/680

Summary To provide financial assistance to residents of Texas who are paraplegic or quadriplegic and plan to attend school at any level in the state.

Eligibility This program is open to paraplegic and quadriplegic residents of Texas who are enrolled or planning to enroll in a public or private elementary school, junior school, high school, technical school, college, university, or graduate school in the state. Applicants must be able to demonstrate financial need to continue their education. Along with their application, they must submit transcripts, information on their current or planned college, and their academic major.

Financial data   A stipend is awarded (amount not specified).

Duration   1 year; may be renewed up to 3 additional years.

Number awarded   Up to 4 each year.

Deadline   April of each year.

[547]
LITTLE PEOPLE OF AMERICA SCHOLARSHIPS

Little People of America, Inc.
Attn: Vice President of Programs
250 El Camino Real, Suite 218
Tustin, CA 92780
(714) 368-3689   Toll Free: (888) LPA-2001
Fax: (714) 368-3367   E-mail: info@lpaonline.org
Web: www.lpaonline.org

Summary   To provide financial assistance for college or graduate school to members of the Little People of America (LPA), to their families, and (in limited cases) to others.

Eligibility   This program is open to members of LPA (limited to people who, for medical reasons, are 4 feet 10 inches or under in height). Applicants must be high school seniors or students attending college, vocational school, or graduate school. Along with their application, they must submit a 500-word personal statement that explains their reasons for applying for a scholarship, their plans for the future, how they intend to be of service to LPA after graduation, and any other relevant information about themselves, their family, their background, and their educational achievements. Financial need is also considered in the selection process. Scholarships are awarded in the following priority order: 1) members of LPA who have a medically diagnosed form of dwarfism; 2) immediate family members of dwarfs who are also paid members of LPA; and 3) people with dwarfism who are not members of LPA.

Financial data   Stipends range from $250 to $1,000.

Duration   1 year; awards are limited to 2 for undergraduate study and 1 for graduate study.

Number awarded   Varies; generally between 5 and 10 each year.

Deadline   April of each year.

[548]
MATTHEW DEBONO MEMORIAL SCHOLARSHIP FUND

Aplastic Anemia & MDS International Foundation, Inc.
Attn: Scholarship Program
4330 East West Highway, Suite 230
Bethesda, MD 20814
(301) 279-7202, ext. 111   Toll Free: (800) 747-2820
Fax: (301) 279-7205   E-mail: help@aamds.org
Web: www.aamds.org

Summary   To provide financial assistance for undergraduate or graduate study in any field to students who have a bone marrow failure disease.

Eligibility   This program is open to high school seniors or graduates who plan to enroll and current full- and part-time undergraduate and graduate students at 2- or 4-year colleges, universities, or vocational/technical schools. Applicants must have a medical diagnosis of aplastic anemia, myelodysplastic syndromes (MDS), paroxysmal nocturnal hemoglobinuria (PNH), or a related bone marrow failure disease. They must be 35 years of age or younger. Selection is based on academic record, essays on their goals and ambitions and the impact of the disease, demonstrated leadership, participation in school and community activities, work experience, overall quality of the application, and financial need.

Financial data   Stipends range from $1,000 to $2,000.

Duration   1 year; nonrenewable.

Additional data   The family of Matthew Debono established this program more than 25 years ago and re-established it with the current sponsor in 2011.

Number awarded   Varies each year; recently, 14 were awarded.

Deadline   March of each year.

[549]
PATRICK JURIS SCHOLARSHIP

Spina Bifida Association of Illinois
2211 North Oak Park Avenue
Chicago, IL 60707
(773) 444-0305   Fax: (773) 444-0327
E-mail: info@i-sba.org
Web: www.patrickjurisscholarshipfund.org

Summary   To provide financial assistance to residents of Illinois who have spina bifida and are working on an undergraduate or graduate degree in a field of service to others at a graduate school in any state.

Eligibility   This program is open to residents of Illinois who have spina bifida. Applicants must be enrolled at a college or university in any state and working on an undergraduate or graduate degree in a field that will prepare them for a career in service to others. Along with their application, they must submit a personal statement on how they plan to advocate for others in need.

Financial data   The stipend is $2,000.

Duration   1 year.

Additional data   This program began in 2012. Recipients are expected to volunteer with the Spina Bifida Association of Illinois at least once during the following year.

Number awarded   1 each year.

Deadline   June of each year.

[550]
SBWIS EDUCATIONAL SCHOLARSHIP IN MEMORY OF MARY ANN POTTS

Spina Bifida Wisconsin, Ltd.
Attn: Scholarship Fund
830 North 109th Street, Suite 6
Wauwatosa, WI 53226
(414) 607-9061   Fax: (414) 607-9602
E-mail: sbwis@sbwis.org
Web: www.sbwis.org/services

Summary To provide financial assistance to residents of Wisconsin who have spina bifida and are interested in attending college or graduate school in any state.

Eligibility This program is open to residents of Wisconsin of any age who have spina bifida. Applicants must be enrolled or planning to enroll at a college, graduate school, trade school, or specialized educational training program in any state. Along with their application, they must submit a personal statement explaining their goals and what they want to accomplish with the education or training they will receive. There is no age limitation. Selection is based on that statement, academic record, community service, work history, and leadership.

Financial data A stipend is awarded (amount not specified); funds are paid directly to the recipient's institution to be used for payment of tuition, books, room and board, and specialized equipment needs.

Duration 1 year; recipients may reapply.

Additional data This program began in 1996.

Number awarded A limited number are awarded each year.

Deadline August of each year.

[551]
SONORAN SPINE FOUNDATION SCHOLARSHIP

Sonoran Spine Research and Education Foundation
c/o ASU Foundation
Donor Relations and Scholarship Coordinator
300 East University Drive, Fifth Floor
P.O. Box 2260
Tempe, AZ 85280-2260
(480) 965-9720   E-mail: Monica.Peterson@asu.edu
Web: www.spineresearch.org

Summary To provide financial assistance to residents of Arizona enrolled at designated universities in the state who have a diagnosed spinal deformity.

Eligibility This program is open to residents or Arizona who are enrolled as full-time undergraduate or graduate students at Arizona State University, Northern Arizona University, or the University of Arizona. Applicants must have a diagnosed spinal deformity (e.g., scoliosis, kyphosis). Along with their application, they must submit an essay of 1 to 2 pages describing their medical history regarding their spinal deformity, how they have overcome obstacles in their life presented by that condition, and how this scholarship will assist in achieving their educational and career goals. Selection is based on that essay, involvement in community and/or school activities, and financial need.

Financial data The stipend is $1,000.

Duration 1 year.

Additional data This program began in 2000.

Number awarded 1 or more each year.

Deadline May of each year.

[552]
SPINA BIFIDA ASSOCIATION OF ALABAMA ADVANCED EDUCATION SCHOLARSHIP PROGRAM

Spina Bifida Association of Alabama
Attn: Scholarship Committee
P.O. Box 35
Gadsden, AL 35902
(256) 617-1414   E-mail: info@sbaofal.org
Web: www.sbaofal.org/prog_services.html

Summary To provide financial assistance to Alabama residents who have spina bifida and are interested in working on an undergraduate or graduate degree at a school in any state.

Eligibility This program is open to entering or continuing undergraduate and graduate students at colleges and universities in any state who have spina bifida. Applicants must reside in Alabama and have been residents of that state for at least 2 consecutive years. They must graduate from high school with a GPA of 2.0 or higher. Along with their application, they must submit 1) an essay on their educational and career goals, aspects of their background and character relevant to their likelihood of academic success, and other factors they wish to have considered, all in relationship to spina bifida; 2) verification of disability, signed by a physician; and 3) transcripts of grades for high school and other educational levels.

Financial data The stipend is $1,000 per year; funds are sent directly to the recipient's institution of higher education.

Duration 1 year; may be renewed up to 3 additional years for undergraduates, up to 1 additional years for graduate students, or up to 2 additional years for students in postgraduate school, law school, or medical school. Renewal depends on the recipient's maintaining a GPA of 2.25 or higher each semester.

Number awarded Up to 4 each year.

Deadline May of each year.

[553]
YE NOTORIOUS KREWE OF THE PEG LEG PIRATE SCHOLARSHIPS

Ye Notorious Krewe of the Peg Leg Pirate, Inc.
P.O. Box 1854
Ruskin, LA 33575-1854
Web: www.peglegpirate.org

Summary To provide financial assistance for college or graduate school to amputees and their families.

Eligibility This program is open to amputees, families of amputees, and organizations that work with amputees. Applicants must be attending or planning to attend an accredited college, university, community college, vocational/technical school, or graduate school. They must have a GPA of 3.5 or higher. Along with their application, they must submit 2 recommendations, transcripts, documentation of financial need, and a 300-word essay describing their future goals.

Financial data Stipends vary but recently have averaged $1,150. Funds are paid directly to the recipient's institution.

Duration 1 year.

Additional data This program began in 2008.

Number awarded Varies each year; recently 4 were awarded.

Deadline March of each year.

Other Disabilities/ Disorders

Undergraduates   ●

Graduate Students   ●

Described here are 335 funding opportunities available to individuals who have a communication disorder (such as stuttering or voice impairment), have a learning disability (including such conditions as brain injury and dyslexia), are emotionally disturbed, or have other chronic or acute health problems, such as cancer or hemophilia. Of these, 256 are for undergraduates and 79 are for graduate students. All of this is "free" money. Not one dollar will need to be repaid (provided, of course, that recipients meet all program requirements). If you are looking for a particular program and don't find it in this section, be sure to check the Program Title Index to see if it is covered elsewhere in the directory.

Undergraduates

[554]
A. RICHARD GROSSMAN COLLEGE SCHOLARSHIP FUND

Dr. Richard Grossman Community Foundation
1464 Hidden Valley Road
Thousand Oaks, CA 91361
(805) 497-7380　　　　E-mail: infodrgcf@gmail.com
Web: www.drgcf.org/?page_id=1279

Summary　To provide financial assistance for college to students who are burn survivors or children of first responders.

Eligibility　This program is open to burn survivors and children of first responders who are graduating high school seniors, GED recipients, or students currently enrolled at a college or university. Applicants must submit 1-page essays on at least 1 of the following topics: 1) why they think they are a deserving recipient of this scholarship; 2) how their degree or certificate will contribute to their life and future goals; 3) if a burn survivor, how their burn injury has influenced and impacted their life and the person they are today; and 4) the individual whom they consider their hero, heroine, or role model.

Financial data　The stipend is $2,500 per year.

Duration　1 year; may be renewed up to 4 additional years, provided the recipient maintains a GPA of 2.0 or higher.

Additional data　This program was formerly offered by the Circle of Care Burn Foundation.

Number awarded　Varies each year; recently, 2 new and 2 renewal scholarships were awarded.

Deadline　June of each year.

[555]
ABBVIE CF SCHOLARSHIPS

AbbVie Inc.
Attn: AbbVie CF Scholarship Program
1 North Waukegan Road
North Chicago, IL 60064
Toll Free: (800) 255-5162
E-mail: info@AbbVieCFScholarship.com
Web: www.abbviecfscholarship.com

Summary　To provide financial assistance for college or graduate school to students with cystic fibrosis (CF).

Eligibility　This program is open to high school seniors, vocational school students, college students, and graduate students with CF. U.S. citizenship is required. Applicants must submit 1) a creative presentation (e.g., a written work, piece of art, craft, collage, photograph) on what sets them apart from their peers, what inspires them to live life to the fullest, or anything else that they think makes them unique; 2) a photograph; and 3) a 250-word essay on a topic that changes annually. Selection is based on the essay, the creative presentation, academic record, and extracurricular activities. Information on all winners is posted on the sponsor's web site to allow the public to select a Thriving Undergraduate Student and a Thriving Graduate Student.

Financial data　The stipend is $2,500. The Thriving Students receive an additional award (recently, $20,500 for a total award of $23,000 to honor the program's 23rd year).

Duration　1 year.

Additional data　This program started in 1992 and was previously sponsored by Solvay Pharmaceuticals, Inc. with the name SolvayCARES Scholarships and subsequently by Abbott Laboratories with the name CFCareForward Scholarships. The current name and sponsorship began in 2011. Winners also receive a 1-year supply of nutritional drinks and vitamins. The essay, creative presentations, and photograph of all recipients who agree to be considered are posted online so patients, families, friends, physicians, the CF community, and the general public can vote to select the Thriving Students.

Number awarded　40 each year: 30 undergraduates and 10 graduate students; of those, 1 is designated the Thriving Undergraduate Student and 1 the Thriving Graduate Student.

Deadline　May of each year.

[556]
ABBVIE IMMUNOLOGY SCHOLARSHIP

Scholarship America
Attn: Scholarship Management Services
One Scholarship Way
P.O. Box 297
St. Peter, MN 56082
(507) 931-1682　　　　Toll Free: (800) 537-4180
Fax: (507) 931-9168
E-mail: AbbVieImmunology@scholarshipamerica.org
Web: www.scholarsapply.org

Summary　To provide financial assistance for college or graduate school to students who have designated inflammatory diseases.

Eligibility　This program is open to U.S. citizens and permanent residents who are enrolled or planning to enroll full or part time in an undergraduate or graduate program at an accredited 2- or 4-year college, university, or vocational/technical school. Applicants must have been diagnosed with 1 of the following inflammatory diseases: ankylosing spondylitis (AS), Crohn's disease (CD), hidradenitis suppurativa (HS), juvenile idiopathic arthritis (JIA), psoriasis (Ps), psoriatic arthritis (PsA), rheumatoid arthritis (RA), ulcerative colitis (UC), or uveitis (UV). Along with their application, they must submit an essay on 1 of the following topics: 1) the advice they would give to another student who have the same disease they have and are entering high school or college; 2) how their diagnosis has changed their outlook and helped turn challenges or difficult tasks into opportunities; or 3) what they have learned about themselves during their journey living with their disease. Selection is based on the essay, academic excellence, community involvement, and ability to serve as a positive role model in the immunology community.

Financial data The stipend is $5,000 for students working on an associate degree or $15,000 for students working on a bachelor's, master's, or doctoral degree.

Duration 1 year; nonrenewable.

Additional data This program began in 2016 with funding from AbbVie Inc.

Number awarded Varies each year; recently, 45 were awarded.

Deadline January of each year.

[557]
ACHIEVEMENT SCHOLARSHIP FOR STUDENTS WITH A HISTORY OF CHRONIC ILLNESS FUND

Delaware Community Foundation
Attn: Director of Finance
100 West Tenth Street, Suite 115
P.O. Box 1636
Wilmington, DE 19899-1636
(302) 571-8004   Fax: (302) 571-1553
E-mail: jdarling@delcf.org
Web: www.delcf.org/scholarships

Summary To provide financial assistance to Delaware residents who have experienced a chronic illness and are interested in attending college in any state.

Eligibility This program is open to students and former students of Delaware schools who have experienced a health-related issue, not necessarily a chronic illness, that has lasted 6 months or longer and has impaired their ability to pursue their education. Applicants must be interested in pursuing academic or vocational education at an institution in any state. Priority is given to students of the First State School (presently part of the Red Clay School District) and any of its branches. Preference may be given to students with the greatest financial need.

Financial data The program provides tuition assistance at academic or vocational qualified institutions of higher education in Delaware or other states.

Duration 1 year; recipients may reapply.

Additional data This program was formerly named the Youth Opportunity Scholarships.

Number awarded 1 or more each year.

Deadline March of each year.

[558]
ALLEGRA FORD THOMAS SCHOLARSHIP

National Center for Learning Disabilities
Attn: Scholarship
32 Laight Street, Second Floor
New York, NY 10013-2152
(212) 545-7510   Toll Free: (888) 575-7373
Fax: (212) 545-9665   E-mail: afscholarship@ncld.org
Web: www.ncld.org/scholarships-and-awards

Summary To provide financial assistance to high school seniors who have a learning disability and plan to attend a community college or vocational training program.

Eligibility This program is open to high school seniors who have a documented learning disability and plan to attend a 2-year community college, vocational/technical training program, or specialized program for students with learning disabilities. Applicants must 1) articulate their challenges and recognize the need for self-advocacy; 2) be committed to postsecondary academic study or career training and have begun to set realistic career goals; 3) participate in school and community activities; 4) have demonstrated perseverance and commitment to achieving personal goals; and 5) be able to demonstrate financial need. U.S. citizenship is required.

Financial data The stipend is $2,500.

Duration 1 year; nonrenewable.

Additional data This program began in 2002 as the Anne Ford Scholarship. In 2009, it was expanded with support from Allegra Ford (Anne's daughter) and named the Anne Ford and Allegra Ford Scholarships. Effective in 2012, the program was separated into 2 separate scholarships and in 2013 the Allegra Ford Scholarship became the Allegra Ford Thomas Scholarship.

Number awarded 1 each year.

Deadline November of each year.

[559]
ANDRE SOBEL AWARD

André Sobel River of Life Foundation
Attn: Awards
8581 Santa Monica Boulevard, Suite 80
P.O. Box 361640
Los Angeles, CA 90036
(310) 276-7111   Fax: (310) 276-0244
E-mail: asware@andreriveroflife.org
Web: www.andreriveroflife.org/participate

Summary To recognize and reward young survivors of life-threatening illnesses who submit outstanding essays on their illness.

Eligibility This competition is open to survivors of life-threatening illnesses between 12 and 21 years of age. Applicants are allowed to define themselves as a survivor; no medical definition or certain amount of time is required. They must submit an essay, up to 1,500 words in length, on a topic that changes annually but relates to their illness.

Financial data First prize is $5,000. Other cash prizes are awarded to second- and third-place winners.

Duration The competition is held annually.

Additional data These awards were first presented in 2000.

Number awarded 3 cash prizes are awarded each year.

Deadline January of each year.

[560]
ANDREW CRAIG MEMORIAL SCHOLARSHIP

PKU Organization of Illinois
P.O. Box 102
Palatine, IL 60078-0102
(630) 344-9758   E-mail: pkuillinois@gmail.com
Web: www.pkuil.org

Summary To provide financial assistance to Illinois residents who have been diagnosed with phenylketonuria (PKU) and are interested in attending college in any state.

Eligibility This program is open to residents of Illinois who have been diagnosed with PKU or an allied disorder. Applicants must be enrolled or planning to enroll at an accredited college, university, or vocational school in any state. Along with their application, they must submit a short essay about themselves, their experiences with PKU or allied disorder, and their future aspirations.

Financial data The stipend is $2,000 per year.

Duration 1 year; recipients may reapply but not in successive years.

Additional data This program began in 1997.

Number awarded 5 each year.

Deadline August of each year.

[561]
ANNE AND MATT HARBISON SCHOLARSHIP

P. Buckley Moss Society
74 Poplar Grove Lane
Mathews, VA 23109
(540) 932-1728   Toll Free: (800) 430-1320
E-mail: society@mosssociety.org
Web: www.mosssociety.org/page.php?id=30

Summary To provide financial assistance for college to high school seniors with language-related learning disabilities.

Eligibility Eligible to be nominated for this scholarship are high school seniors with language-related learning disabilities. Nominations must be submitted by a member of the P. Buckley Moss Society. The nomination packet must include verification of a language-related learning disability from a counselor or case manager, a high school transcript, 2 letters of recommendation, and 4 essays by the nominees (on themselves; their learning disability and its effect on their lives; their extracurricular, community, work, and church accomplishments; and their plans for next year).

Financial data The stipend is $1,500. Funds are paid to the recipient's college or university.

Duration 1 year; may be renewed for up to 3 additional years.

Additional data This program began in 1998.

Number awarded 1 each year.

Deadline March of each year.

[562]
ANNE FORD SCHOLARSHIP

National Center for Learning Disabilities
Attn: Scholarship
32 Laight Street, Second Floor
New York, NY 10013-2152
(212) 545-7510   Toll Free: (888) 575-7373
Fax: (212) 545-9665   E-mail: afscholarship@ncld.org
Web: www.ncld.org/scholarships-and-awards

Summary To provide financial assistance to high school seniors who have a learning disability and plan to attend a 4-year college or university.

Eligibility This program is open to high school seniors who have a documented learning disability and plan to work full time on a bachelor's degree at a 4-year college or

university. Applicants must have a GPA of 3.0 or higher and be able to demonstrate financial need. They must 1) articulate their challenges and recognize the importance of self-advocacy; 2) be committed to completing a 4-year college degree and have begun to set realistic career goals; 3) participate in school and community activities; 4) have demonstrated academic achievements consistent with college and career goals; 5) plan to contribute to society in ways that increase opportunities for other individuals with learning disabilities; and 6) excel as a role model and spokesperson for others who struggle with learning disabilities. U.S. citizenship is required.

Financial data The stipend is $2,500 per year.

Duration 4 years.

Additional data This program began in 2002 as the Anne Ford Scholarship. In 2009, it was expanded with support from Allegra Ford (Anne's daughter) and named the Anne Ford and Allegra Ford Scholarships. Effective in 2012, the program was separated into 2 separate scholarships.

Number awarded 1 or 2 each year.

Deadline November of each year.

[563]
ANNE SMEDINGHOFF MEMORIAL SCHOLARSHIP

Ulman Cancer Fund for Young Adults
Attn: Scholarship Committee
921 East Fort Avenue, Suite 325
Baltimore, MD 21230
(410) 964-0202   Toll Free: (888) 393-FUND
Fax: (888) 964-0402
E-mail: scholarship@ulmanfund.org
Web: www.ulmanfund.org/scholarships

Summary To provide financial assistance for college or graduate school to students who have been diagnosed with cancer or have or have lost a family member with cancer.

Eligibility This program is open to students who 1) have been diagnosed with cancer; 2) have a parent or sibling living with cancer; or 3) have lost a parent or sibling to cancer. Applicants must be attending, or planning to attend, a college or university in any state to work on an undergraduate, graduate, or professional degree. They should demonstrate the qualities of the program's namesake-adventurous, upbeat, vivacious, and with a strong desire to make a difference in the lives of others. The first diagnosis of cancer (whether of the applicant, a parent, or sibling) must have occurred after the applicant was 15 years of age. Along with their application, they must submit a 500-word essay or 3-minute video on either 1) a letter that they would have liked to receive during their cancer experience; or 2) what they would tell the young adults who participate in the sponsor's summer-long drive to support the organization about being a young adult impacted by cancer. U.S. citizenship or permanent resident status is required.

Financial data The stipend is $2,500. Funds are paid directly to the educational institution.

Duration 1 year.

Additional data This program, which began in 2013, is funded by the 4K for Cancer, an organization of college students who ride bicycles across the country every summer and raise funds for cancer. Recipients are obligated to organize and run a bone marrow registry drive with the support of Delete Blood Cancer and There Goes My Hero.

Number awarded 1 each year.

Deadline March of each year.

[564]
ANNUAL BREAST CANCER SURVIVOR SCHOLARSHIP

Nikko Cosmetic Surgery Center
1001 West Loop S, Suite 813
Houston, TX 77027
(713) 960-1311   E-mail: michael@drnikko.com
Web: www.drnikko.com

Summary To provide financial assistance for college to breast cancer survivors.

Eligibility This program is open to U.S. citizens who are breast cancer survivors. Applicants must be enrolled or planning to enroll at a college, university, community college, or trade school in any state. Along with their application, they must submit 1) a 100-page essay about their educational goals; and 2) an essay of 650 to 1,000 words on how being diagnosed with breast cancer has affected their life.

Financial data The stipend is $1,000.

Duration 1 year.

Number awarded 2 each year.

Deadline September of each year.

[565]
AR-CEC EXCEPTIONAL STUDENT SCHOLARSHIP

Arkansas Council for Exceptional Children
c/o Gwen Neal, Scholarship Chair
Arkansas State University
School of Teacher Education and Leadership
P.O. Box 1450
State University, AR 72467
(870) 972-2678   E-mail: gneal@astate.edu
Web: cec.k12.ar.us/scholarships.html

Summary To provide financial assistance to high school seniors in Arkansas who have a disability and plan to attend college in any state.

Eligibility This program is open to seniors graduating from high schools in Arkansas who have an identified disability as defined by IDEA. Applicants must be planning to enter a college, university, or technical school in any state. Selection is based on the completed application (1-3 points), letters of recommendation (2-4 points), transcripts (1-3 points), and a 500-word autobiographical statement that includes a statement of need or importance of the scholarship in the accomplishment of their educational objectives (1-10 points).

Financial data The stipend is $1,500.

Duration 1 year.

Number awarded 1 each year.

Deadline May of each year.

[566]
AUTISM DELAWARE ADULTS WITH AUTISM SCHOLARSHIP

Autism Delaware
Attn: Scholarship Chair
924 Old Harmony Road, Suite 201
Newark, DE 19713
(302) 224-6020   Fax: (302) 224-6017
E-mail: delautism@delautism.org
Web: www.delautism.org

Summary To provide financial assistance to adult residents of Delaware who have an autism spectrum disorder and are interested in attending college in any state.

Eligibility This program is open to adult residents of Delaware who have completed high school or earned a GED and have been accepted into a college, university, community college, trade school, or vocational training program. Applicants must submit evidence that they have an autism spectrum disorder and that they possess the capacity to complete a postsecondary program. Along with their application, they must submit a cover letter describing why they are pursuing their particular plan of study and their plans for employment once they complete the program, a current resume, transcripts, an explanation of their support system and how it ensures the successful completion of a postsecondary program, and letters of support.

Financial data The stipend is at least $1,000.

Duration 1 year.

Number awarded 1 or more each year.

Deadline March of each year.

[567]
AVONTE OQUENDO MEMORIAL SCHOLARSHIP FOR AUTISM

The Perecman Firm, P.L.L.C.
250 West 57th Street, Suite 401
New York, NY 10107
(212) 577-9325
Web: www.perecman.com

Summary To provide financial assistance for college or graduate school to people diagnosed with autism and their families.

Eligibility This program is open students currently enrolled or accepted at an accredited college or university as an undergraduate or graduate students. Applicants or a close family member must have been diagnosed with a form of autism, including Asperger syndrome. Along with their application, they must submit an essay of 500 to 1,000 words on 1 of the following topics: 1) a time that they have had to overcome an obstacle as a person with autism that other people would not have had to face; 2) how their family member's autism has affected them and how they have adapted to help them; and 3) what they feel is the biggest obstacle holding people with autism back today. Selection is based on the essay and transcripts.

Financial data The stipend is $1,000.
Duration 1 year.
Number awarded 1 each year.
Deadline July of each year.

[568]
BAER REINTEGRATION SCHOLARSHIPS

The Center for Reintegration, Inc.
347 West 37th Street
New York, NY 10018
(212) 957-5090   Fax: (212) 974-0228
E-mail: baerscholarships@reintegration.com
Web: www.reintegration.com/scholarship-program

Summary To provide financial assistance to undergraduate and graduate students diagnosed with schizophrenia.

Eligibility This program is open to U.S. citizens diagnosed with bipolar disorder, schizophrenia, or schizoaffective disorder. Applicants must be receiving medical treatment for the disease and be actively involved in rehabilitative or reintegrative efforts. They must be interested in pursuing postsecondary education, including trade or vocational school programs, high school equivalency programs, associate degrees, bachelor's degrees, or graduate programs. Along with their application, they must submit an essay on their career goal and their rationale for choosing that goal; how this course of study will help them achieve their career goal; how their illness has impacted their ability to succeed in school, maintain employment, or establish relationships; steps they have taken to prepare for pursuit of this education; rationale for the specific school chosen; and their plans to continue treatment while pursuing an education. Selection is based on the quality of the essay, academic success, 3 references, thoughtfulness and appropriateness of academic and vocational/career goals, rehabilitation involvement, success in dealing with the disease, recent volunteer and/or vocational experience, and completion of application requirements.

Financial data The amount awarded varies, depending upon the specific needs of the recipient. Funds may be used to pay for tuition and related expenses, such as textbooks and laboratory fees.

Duration 1 year; may be renewed.

Additional data This program began in 2015 as the successor to the Lilly Reintegration Scholarships. It is supported by the Sidney R. Baer, Jr. Foundation.

Number awarded Varies each year; generally, 70 to 120 of these scholarships (including renewals) are awarded annually.

Deadline January of each year.

[569]
BEF GENERAL ACADEMIC SCHOLARSHIPS

Boomer Esiason Foundation
c/o Chris McEwan
483 Tenth Avenue, Suite 300
New York, NY 10018
(646) 292-7939   Fax: (646) 292-7945
E-mail: cmcewan@esiason.org
Web: www.esiason.org

Summary To provide financial assistance to undergraduate and graduate students who have cystic fibrosis (CF).

Eligibility This program is open to CF patients who are working on an undergraduate or graduate degree. Applicants must submit a letter from their doctor confirming the diagnosis of CF and a list of daily medications, information on financial need, a detailed breakdown of tuition costs from their academic institution, transcripts, and a 2-page essay on 1) their postgraduation goals; and 2) the importance of compliance with CF therapies and what they practice on a daily basis to stay healthy. Selection is based on academic ability, character, leadership potential, service to the community, and financial need. Finalists are interviewed by telephone.

Financial data Stipends range from $500 to $2,500. Funds are paid directly to the academic institution to assist in covering the cost of tuition and fees.

Duration 1 year; nonrenewable.

Additional data Recipients must be willing to participate in the sponsor's CF Ambassador Program by speaking once a year at a designated CF event to help educate the general public about CF.

Number awarded 10 to 15 each year.

Deadline March, June, September, or December of each year.

[570]
BERNER SCHOLARSHIP FOR STUDENTS WITH EPILEPSY

Epilepsy Foundation of Greater Chicago
Attn: Jeff Moore, Individual Gift Officer
17 North State Street, Suite 650
Chicago, IL 60602
(312) 939-8622   Toll Free: (800) 273-6027
E-mail: jmoore@epilepsychicago.org
Web: www.epilepsychicago.org

Summary To provide financial assistance to residents of Illinois who have epilepsy and are enrolled or entering college or graduate school in any state.

Eligibility This program is open to residents of Illinois who have a diagnosis of epilepsy. Applicants must be enrolled or planning to enroll as full-time undergraduate or graduate students at a college or university in any state. Along with their application, they must submit a 1- to 2-page essay describing their community and leadership activities, books they've read recently, how they anticipate using their college education, and any other activities they think might be significant. Selection is based on academic accomplishment, community partnership and leadership, and financial need.

Financial data The stipend is $10,000 per year, including a grant of $5,000 and an interest-free loan of $5,000. The loan must be repaid within 7 years.

Duration 1 year; may be renewed up to 3 additional years.

Number awarded 1 each year.

Deadline April of each year.

[571]
BETH CAREW MEMORIAL SCHOLARSHIPS

Colburn-Keenan Foundation, Inc.
31 Moody Road
P.O. Box 811
Enfield, CT 06083-0811
Toll Free: (800) 966-2431   Fax: (888) 345-0259
E-mail: admin@colkeen.org
Web: www.colkeen.org/?page_id=123

Summary To provide financial assistance for college to students who have a bleeding disorder.

Eligibility This program is open to high school seniors and college freshmen, sophomores, and juniors who have hemophilia, von Willebrand's Disease, or a related inherited bleeding disorder. Applicants must be attending or planning to attend an accredited 2- or 4-year college or university in the United States as a full-time student. They must be able to demonstrate participation in volunteer activities specifically within the bleeding disorders community.

Financial data Stipends range from $3,000 to $6,000 per year.

Duration 1 year; recipients may reapply.

Additional data This program was established by AHF, Inc. in 2002 to honor Beth Carew, who died in 1994 as 1 of the very few women to have hemophilia A. Following the deaths of Donald Colburn and Kathy Ann Keenan, founders of AHF, the Colburn-Keenan Foundation was established; in 2007, it assumed responsibility for administering this program.

Number awarded Up to 20 each year.

Deadline April of each year.

[572]
BEYOND THE CURE AMBASSADOR SCHOLARSHIP PROGRAM

National Children's Cancer Society
Attn: Scholarships
500 North Broadway, Suite 1850
St. Louis, MO 63102
(314) 241-1600   Toll Free: (800) 532-6459
Fax: (314) 241-1996   E-mail: pgabris@thenccs.org
Web: www.thenccs.org/scholarship

Summary To provide financial assistance for college to childhood cancer survivors.

Eligibility This program is open to childhood cancer survivors currently younger than 25 years of age who were diagnosed with cancer or a high grade or anaplastic brain tumor before the age of 18. Applicants must be enrolled or planning to enroll full time at an accredited college, university, or vocational/technical school. They must

have a GPA of 2.5 or higher. Along with their application, they must submit a 2-page essay on how being diagnosed with cancer at a young age has impacted their life and future goals. Selection is based on that essay, GPA, medical history, commitment to community service, and financial need. U.S. citizenship is required.

Financial data Stipends range up to $3,500. Funds are disbursed directly to the recipient's institution.

Duration 1 year; may be renewed up to 3 additional years, provided the recipient remains enrolled full time, maintains an overall GPA of 2.5 or higher, and completes 15 hours of volunteer work with the sponsoring organization.

Additional data This program began in 2008.

Number awarded 40 each year.

Deadline March of each year.

[573]
BIAWA EASTERN WASHINGTON STUDENT SCHOLARSHIP

The Brain Injury Alliance of Washington
Attn: Scholarships
316 Broadway, Suite 305
P.O. Box 3044
Seattle, WA 98114
(206) 467-4807   Toll Free: (877) 982-4292
E-mail: jennak@biawa.org
Web: www.biawa.org/scholarship.php

Summary To provide financial assistance for college in eastern Washington to survivors of brain injury who are residents of the state.

Eligibility This program is open to residents of Washington who are survivors of brain injury. Applicants must be graduating high school seniors or undergraduates enrolled full or part time at a college or university in eastern Washington.

Financial data The stipend is $1,000. Funds are paid directly to the institution.

Duration 1 year; nonrenewable.

Number awarded 1 each year.

Deadline August of each year.

[574]
BIORX/HEMOPHILIA OF NORTH CAROLINA EDUCATIONAL SCHOLARSHIPS

BioRx, LLC
Attn: Hemophilia Services
7167 East Kemper Road
Cincinnati, OH 45249
Toll Free: (866) 442-4679   Fax: (919) 319-0016
E-mail: cbarnes@biorx.net
Web: www.biorxhemophilia.com

Summary To provide financial assistance for college to people with hemophilia, their caregivers, and their families.

Eligibility This program is open to caregivers of children or adults affected with bleeding disorders, people who have been diagnosed with a bleeding disorder, and siblings and parents of people diagnosed with bleeding disorders. Residents of all states are eligible. Applicants must be enrolled or planning to enroll at an accredited college, university, or certified training program. Along with their application, they must submit an essay of 1 to 2 pages describing their occupational goals and objectives in life and how their or their family's experiences with bleeding disorders have affected their choices. Preference is given to applicants who are studying or planning to study a health care-related field. Selection is primarily based on merit, although financial need may be considered as well.

Financial data The stipend ranges from $500 to $3,000.

Duration 1 year.

Additional data This program, established in 2004, is sponsored by BioRx and administered by Hemophilia of North Carolina (although no preference is given to residents of North Carolina.

Number awarded 4 each year, of which at least 1 of which is reserved for an applicant studying in a health-related field.

Deadline April of each year.

[575]
BLEEDING AND CLOTTING DISORDERS INSTITUTE SCHOLARSHIP FUND

Community Foundation of Central Illinois
Attn: Program Manager
3625 North Sheridan Road
Peoria, IL 61604
(309) 674-8730　　　　　Fax: (309) 674-8754
E-mail: jessica@communityfoundationci.org
Web: www.communityfoundationci.org

Summary To provide financial assistance to students who have a bleeding or clotting disorder, live in the service area of the Bleeding and Clotting Disorders Institute (BCDI) in Illinois, and are interested in attending college in any state.

Eligibility This program is open to residents of the BCDI service area (all of Illinois outside of the Chicago area) who are diagnosed with a congenital or acquired chronic bleeding disorder or a congenital clotting disorder. Applicants must be enrolled or planning to enroll full time at an accredited trade/vocational school, junior college, or 4-year college or university in any state. They must have a GPA of 2.5 or higher. Along with their application, they must submit a 250-word essay on how receiving this scholarship will help them to meet their career goals. Selection is based on the essay and demonstrated desire to succeed.

Financial data The stipend is $1,500. Funds are disbursed directly to the recipient's school to be used to cover the cost of tuition, books, and required fees.

Duration 1 year.

Additional data This program is supported by the BCDI.

Number awarded A limited number are awarded each year.

Deadline March of each year.

[576]
BMW HOPE ENDOWMENT SCHOLARSHIP

Epsilon Sigma Alpha International
Attn: ESA Foundation
363 West Drake Road
Fort Collins, CO 80526
(970) 223-2824　　　　　Fax: (970) 223-4456
E-mail: esainfo@epsilonsigmaalpha.org
Web: www.epsilonsigmaalpha.org

Summary To provide financial assistance for college to students who have epilepsy.

Eligibility This program is open to students who have epilepsy. Applicants must be 1) graduating high school seniors with a GPA of 3.0 or higher or with minimum scores of 22 on the ACT or 1030 on the combined critical reading and mathematics SAT; 2) enrolled in college with a GPA of 3.0 or higher; 3) enrolled at a technical school or returning to school after an absence for retraining of job skills or obtaining a degree; or 4) engaged in online study through an accredited college, university, or vocational school. They may be attending or planning to attend an accredited school anywhere in the United States and major in any field. Along with their application, they must submit a letter from a physician verifying that they have epilepsy. Selection is based on service and leadership (40 points), financial need (40 points), and scholastic ability (10 points). A $5 processing fee is required.

Financial data The stipend is $1,000.

Duration 1 year; may be renewed.

Additional data Epsilon Sigma Alpha (ESA) is a women's service organization, but scholarships are available to both men and women. This program began in 2009. Completed applications must be submitted to the ESA state counselor who then verifies the information before forwarding them to the scholarship director.

Number awarded 1 each year.

Deadline January of each year.

[577]
BONNIE STRANGIO EDUCATION SCHOLARSHIP

Boomer Esiason Foundation
c/o Chris McEwan
483 Tenth Avenue, Suite 300
New York, NY 10018
(646) 292-7939　　　　　Fax: (646) 292-7945
E-mail: cmcewan@esiason.org
Web: www.esiason.org

Summary To provide financial assistance to undergraduate and graduate students who have cystic fibrosis (CF) and a demonstrated commitment to the prevention and cure of the disease.

Eligibility This program is open to CF patients who are working on an undergraduate or graduate degree. Applicants must be able to demonstrate exemplary service and commitment to the prevention and cure of CF. Along with their application, they must submit a letter from their doctor confirming the diagnosis of CF and a list of daily medications, information on financial need, a detailed breakdown of tuition costs from their academic institution, transcripts, and a 2-page essay on 1) their postgraduation goals; and 2) the importance of compliance with CF therapies and what they practice on a daily basis to stay healthy. Selection is based on academic ability, character, leadership potential, service to the community, and financial need. Finalists are interviewed by telephone.

Financial data The stipend ranges from $500 to $1,000. Funds are paid directly to the academic institution to assist in covering the cost of tuition and fees.

Duration 1 year; nonrenewable.

Additional data This program began in 2005.

Number awarded 1 each year.

Deadline June of each year.

[578]
BOOK COLEMAN, FOSTER DOW AND IRMA DOW SCHOLARSHIPS

United Cerebral Palsy Association of Greater Indiana
Attn: Scholarship Program
8020 Zionsville Road
Indianapolis, IN 46268
(317) 871-4032   E-mail: kelley@ucpaindy.org
Web: www.ucpaindy.org/scholarships

Summary To provide financial assistance to high school seniors in Indiana who have cerebral palsy and plan to attend college in any state.

Eligibility This program is open to seniors graduating from high schools in Indiana who have cerebral palsy. Applicants must be planning to attend a recognized educational or training institution in any state. Along with their application, they must submit a brief essay on their career goals. Selection is based on that essay, academic excellence, community participation and contribution, extracurricular involvement, and recommendations.

Financial data The stipend is $2,000. Funds are paid directly to the recipient's institution.

Duration 1 year.

Additional data The Book-Coleman Scholarship began in 1994; the Foster Dow and Irma Dow Scholarships were added in 2006.

Number awarded At least 3 each year.

Deadline March of each year.

[579]
BRADLEY D. GENDRON MEMORIAL SCHOLARSHIP

Diabetes Scholars Foundation
310 Busse Highway, Suite 256
Park Ridge, IL 60068
(312) 215-9861   Fax: (847) 991-8739
E-mail: m.podjasek@diabetesscholars.org
Web: www.diabetesscholars.org/college-scholarship

Summary To provide financial assistance to high school seniors from Colorado who have diabetes and plan to attend college in any state.

Eligibility This program is open to seniors graduating from high schools in Colorado who have Type 1 diabetes

and plan to attend an accredited 4-year university, college, or trade/technical school in any state. Applicants must be able to demonstrate active involvement in the diabetes community, academic accomplishment, participation in community and/or extracurricular activities, and successful management of the challenges of living with diabetes. Financial need is not considered in the selection process. U.S. citizenship or permanent resident status is required.

Financial data The stipend is $1,000.

Duration 1 year.

Number awarded 1 each year.

Deadline April of each year.

[580]
BRADLEY KRUEGER SCHOLARSHIP

Bleeding Disorders Alliance Illinois
Attn: Program Coordinator
210 South DesPlaines Street
Chicago, IL 60661-5500
(312) 427-1495   Fax: (312) 427-1602
E-mail: ahii@bdai.org
Web: www.bdai.org/support/assistance/scholarships

Summary To provide financial assistance for attendance at a college in any state to residents of Illinois who have a bleeding disorder and their families.

Eligibility This program is open to residents of Illinois who have a bleeding disorder and their spouses, parents, siblings, and children; people who are carriers of the disease are also eligible. Applicants must be attending or planning to attend a postsecondary institution, including a trade school, in any state. Along with their application, they must submit essays on their goals for furthering their education, the steps they have taken to meet those goals, how this scholarship will help them achieve those goals, what it means to them to live with hemophilia, and what they consider their responsibility to the bleeding disorders community. Financial need is not considered in the selection process.

Financial data Stipends range up to $5,000. Funds are paid directly to the educational institution to be used for payment of tuition, room and board, books, and supplies (including computer equipment).

Duration 1 year.

Additional data Bleeding Disorders Alliance Illinois was formerly the Hemophilia Foundation of Illinois.

Number awarded 1 or more each year.

Deadline June of each year.

[581]
BRESSMAN LAW TRAUMATIC BRAIN INJURY SCHOLARSHIP

Bressman Law
Attn: David Bressman
5186 Blazer Parkway
Dublin, OH 43017
(614) 538-1116   Toll Free: (877) 538-1116
Fax: (614) 761-8399
Web: www.bressmanlaw.com/Scholarship

Summary To provide financial assistance for college to students who have suffered a traumatic brain injury.

Eligibility This program is open to high school seniors and current undergraduates who have suffered a traumatic brain injury. Applicants must have a GPA in high school or college of 3.0 or higher. Along with their application, they must submit proof of legal residency in the United States, documentation of their diagnosis from a qualified medical professional, transcripts, and an essay of 1 to 3 pages about their struggle with a traumatic brain injury, how they received the injury, how their life has changed since, the issues they have encountered, and how they have overcome those.

Financial data The stipend is $1,000.

Duration 1 year.

Additional data This program began in 2015.

Number awarded 1 each year.

Deadline January of each year.

[582]
BRIAN MORDEN MEMORIAL SCHOLARSHIP

Brian Morden Foundation
2809 Columbia Drive
Altoona, PA 16602
E-mail: brianmordenfoundation@gmail.com
Web: www.brianmordenfoundation.org/scholarship.htm

Summary To provide financial assistance to students, including cancer survivors, who are interested in studying computer science, medicine, or music in college.

Eligibility This program is open to U.S. citizens who, by summer of the year they apply, will have graduated from high school. Applicants must be majoring or planning to major in computer-related fields, medicine, or music. They are not required to be cancer survivors, but cancer survivors are asked to share information on their treatment and to explain how their cancer experience has affected their life. All applicants are asked to submit 5 other brief statements on assigned topics. Selection is based on those statements, GPA, extracurricular activities, awards and honors, and their plan of study.

Financial data The stipend is at least $1,000.

Duration 1 year.

Additional data This program honors Brian Morden, who died of cancer in 2003 when he was 19 years of age.

Number awarded 2 or 3 each year.

Deadline March of each year.

[583]
BRYON RIESCH SCHOLARSHIPS

Bryon Riesch Paralysis Foundation
P.O. Box 1388
Waukesha, WI 53187-1388
(262) 547-2083   E-mail: info@brpf.org
Web: www.brpf.org/scholarship-application

Summary To provide financial assistance to undergraduate and graduate students who have a neurological disability or the children of people with such a disability.

Eligibility This program is open to students entering or enrolled at a 2- or 4-year college or university as an under-

graduate or graduate student. Applicants must have a neurological disability or be the child of a person with such a disability. First priority is given to individuals suffering from a direct spinal cord injury or disease resulting in paralysis such as spinal tumors, strokes, or aneurysms affecting the spinal cord, or spina bifida. Other diseases and disorders that qualify include multiple sclerosis, traumatic brain injuries, Parkinson's, and cerebral palsy. Priority is also given to residents of Wisconsin. Applicants must have a GPA of 2.5 or higher in high school or college. Along with their application, they must submit a 200-word essay on why they deserve the scholarship, a statement of their 5- and 10-year goals, and a list of work experience. Financial need is not considered in the selection process.

Financial data The stipend is $2,000.

Duration 1 year; may be renewed.

Number awarded Varies each semester; recently, 7 were awarded for the fall semester and 5 for the spring semester.

Deadline June of each year for fall semester; December of each year for spring semester.

[584]
CALVIN DAWSON MEMORIAL SCHOLARSHIP

Hemophilia Foundation of Greater Florida
1350 Orange Avenue, Suite 227
Winter Park, FL 32789
(407) 629-0000   Toll Free: (800) 293-6527
Fax: (407) 629-9600
E-mail: HFGF@hemophiliaflorida.org
Web: www.hemophiliaflorida.org/scholarships.html

Summary To provide financial assistance to residents of Florida who have a bleeding disorder and are interested in attending college in any state.

Eligibility This program is open to residents of Florida who have hemophilia or other related hereditary bleeding disorder. Applicants may be graduating high school seniors or students already enrolled at a college, technical or trade school, or other certification program in any state. Along with their application, they must submit a brief essay on their occupational objectives and goals in life. Selection is based on that essay, merit, community service, and financial need.

Financial data Stipends range up to $1,000. Funds are paid directly to the recipient's college.

Duration 1 year.

Number awarded Varies each year; recently, 4 were awarded.

Deadline April of each year.

[585]
CANCER FOR COLLEGE CAROLINA SCHOLARSHIPS

Cancer for College
981 Park Center Drive
Vista, CA 92081
(760) 599-5096
E-mail: applications@cancerforcollege.org
Web: www.cancerforcollege.org/application.html

Summary To provide financial assistance to undergraduate and graduate students from North and South Carolina who are cancer patients or survivors.
Eligibility This program is open to undergraduate and graduate students who are originally from or currently attending or entering accredited colleges, universities, community colleges, or trade schools in North or South Carolina. Applicants must be a cancer patient or survivor. Along with their application, they must submit transcripts, verification of their cancer diagnosis, 2 letters of recommendation, and information on their financial situation.
Financial data Stipends range from $1,000 to $5,000.
Duration 1 year.
Number awarded Varies each year; recently, 7 were awarded.
Deadline January of each year.

[586]
CANCER FOR COLLEGE PACIFIC NORTHWEST SCHOLARSHIPS

Cancer for College
981 Park Center Drive
Vista, CA 92081
(760) 599-5096
E-mail: applications@cancerforcollege.org
Web: www.cancerforcollege.org/application.html

Summary To provide financial assistance to undergraduate and graduate students from the Pacific Northwest who are cancer patients or survivors.
Eligibility This program is open to undergraduate and graduate students who are originally from or current attending accredited colleges, universities, community colleges, or trade schools in Idaho, Montana, Oregon, or Washington. Applicants must be a cancer patient or survivor. Along with their application, they must submit transcripts, verification of their cancer diagnosis, 2 letters of recommendation, and information on their financial situation.
Financial data Stipends range from $1,000 to $5,000.
Duration 1 year.
Additional data This program includes the Henry Streuli Scholarship.
Number awarded Varies each year; recently, 6 were awarded.
Deadline January of each year.

[587]
CANCER FOR COLLEGE SCHOLARSHIPS

Cancer for College
981 Park Center Drive
Vista, CA 92081
(760) 599-5096
E-mail: applications@cancerforcollege.org
Web: www.cancerforcollege.org/application.html

Summary To provide financial assistance to undergraduate and graduate students who are cancer patients or survivors.
Eligibility This program is open to undergraduate and graduate students enrolled or planning to enroll at accredited colleges, universities, community colleges, or trade schools in the United States and Puerto Rico. Applicants must be a cancer patient or survivor. Along with their application, they must submit transcripts, verification of their cancer diagnosis, 2 letters of recommendation, and information on their financial situation. Preference is given to residents of California and students attending college in southern California.
Financial data Stipends range from $1,000 to $5,000 per year.
Duration 1 year; some of the $1,000 scholarships (designated as Perpetual Scholarships) may be renewed up to 3 additional years.
Additional data This program began in 1993. Perpetual Scholarship recipients must be willing to attend regional events associated with the program and be available for interviews and/or media coverage.
Number awarded Varies each year; recently, 20 general and 1 perpetual scholarship were awarded.
Deadline January of each year.

[588]
CANCER SURVIVORS' SCHOLARSHIP

Cancer Survivors' Fund
P.O. Box 792
Missouri City, TX 77459
(281) 437-7142   Fax: (281) 596-7244
E-mail: csf@cancersurvivorsfund.org
Web: www.cancersurvivorsfund.org

Summary To provide financial assistance for college to students who have had cancer.
Eligibility This program is open to students who are enrolled in or accepted for enrollment in an accredited undergraduate school. Applicants must be a cancer survivor or currently diagnosed with cancer; they do not have to be receiving treatment to qualify. They must submit an essay, from 500 to 1,200 words in length, on how their experience with cancer has impacted their life values and career goals. Selection is based on the applicant's personal hardship and financial need.
Financial data A stipend is awarded (amount not specified).
Duration 1 year.
Additional data Recipients must agree to do volunteer work to use their cancer experience to help other young cancer patients and survivors cope with a life-threatening or life-altering event.
Number awarded Varies each year; recently, 41 were awarded.
Deadline March of each year for fall semester; October of each year for spring semester.

[589]
CANCER UNWRAPPED TEEN WRITING CONTEST

Cancer Pathways
1400 Broadway
Seattle, WA 98122-3809
(206) 709-1400   Fax: (866) 200-2383
E-mail: info@cancerpathways.org
Web: www.cancerpathways.org/cancer-unwrapped

Summary To recognize and reward high school students in Washington who submit outstanding essays related to their experience with cancer.

Eligibility This competition is open to students enrolled in grades 9-12 at high schools in Washington. Applicants must have been affected by cancer, either through a personal diagnosis or that of a family member or friend. They must submit an essay of 500 to 2,000 words about their experience of dealing with cancer.

Financial data The prize is $1,000.

Duration The competition is held annually.

Additional data This competition was established in 2006 by Gilda's Club Seattle. The name was "It's Always Something" Writing Contest; it offered the Guy Robichaud Prizes and the Kai Leamer Prizes. The organization adopted its current name in 2016.

Number awarded Varies each year; recently, 15 were awarded.

Deadline March of each year.

[590]
CANDICE'S SICKLE CELL ANEMIA FUND SCHOLARSHIPS

Candice's Sickle Cell Anemia Fund, Inc.
Attn: Candice Young-Deler
P.O. Box 672237
Bronx, NY 10467-0237
(646) 436-0477   E-mail: cscfinc@gmail.com
Web: www.candicessicklecellfund.org/scholarships

Summary To provide financial assistance for college to students from the tri-state area of Connecticut, New Jersey, and New York who have sickle cell disease.

Eligibility This program is open to college students who have sickle cell disease and live or attend school in the tri-state area. Applicants must submit a 250-word essay on how sickle cell disease has affected their life and education, their educational goals, how they expect to achieve those, and a person in their lives who has been instrumental to help them persevere. They must also commit to at least 5 hours of service to an activity of the sponsor during the year of their award.

Financial data The stipend is $1,500.

Duration 1 year.

Additional data These scholarships were first awarded in 2001.

Number awarded 3 each year.

Deadline April of each year.

[591]
CARL J. MEGEL SPECIAL EDUCATION SCHOLARSHIP

Illinois Federation of Teachers
500 Oakmont Lane
P.O. Box 390
Westmont, IL 60559
(630) 468-4080   Fax: (630) 468-4089
Web: www.ift.org/your-benefits/scholarships

Summary To provide financial assistance to children of members of the Illinois Federation of Teachers (IFT) who have been enrolled in special education and are interested in attending college in any state.

Eligibility This program is open to graduating high school seniors who are children of currently-employed active members of the IFT or of deceased members who were in good standing at the time of their death. Applicants must be enrolled in a special education school, class, or program for students with autism, cognitive disability, deaf-blindness, deafness, emotional disability, hearing impairment, multiple disabilities, orthopedic impairment, other health impairment, specific learning disability, speech or language impairment, traumatic brain injury, or visual impairment. Along with their application, they must submit an essay describing how any obstacles and/or achievements that you have encountered in your life have helped shape your decision to complete a post-secondary education.

Financial data The stipend is $1,000.

Duration 1 year.

Number awarded 1 each year.

Deadline February of each year.

[592]
CFSF STANDARD SCHOLARSHIPS

Cystic Fibrosis Scholarship Foundation
1555 Sherman Avenue, Suite 116
Evanston, IL 60201
(847) 328-0127   Fax: (847) 328-4525
E-mail: mkbcfsf@aol.com
Web: www.cfscholarship.org/scholarships

Summary To provide financial assistance to undergraduate students who have cystic fibrosis (CF).

Eligibility This program is open to students enrolled or planning to enroll in college (either a 2- or 4-year program) or vocational school. Applicants must have CF. Along with their application, they must submit an essay on a topic that changes annually; recently, students were asked to write about a person from the 20th century. Selection is based on academic achievement, leadership, and financial need.

Financial data Most stipends are $1,000 per year, although some designated awards range up to $2,500. Funds are sent directly to the student's institution to be used for tuition, books, room, and board.

Duration 1 year; some awards may be renewed up to 3 additional years.

Additional data These scholarships were first awarded for 2002. The program includes the Kevin Tidwell Memorial Scholarship of $2,500 per year for 4 years, the Glen

Parsons Memorial Scholarship of $2,500 per year for 4 years, the Tim and Ritch Dangel Memorial Scholarship of $2,000 per year for 4 years, and the Michael Geddes Memorial Scholarships, 2 awarded at $2,000 per year for 2 years.

Number awarded   Varies each year; recently, 42 were awarded, including 16 renewable awards, 21 single-year awards, and the 5 named awards.

Deadline   March of each year.

[593]
CHALIK & CHALIK SURVIVOR'S SCHOLARSHIP

Chalik & Chalik Law Offices
Attn: Jason Chalik
10063 N.W. First Court
Plantation, FL 33324
(954) 858-5751   Toll Free: (855) 529-0269
E-mail: media@chaliklaw.com
Web: www.chaliklaw.com

Summary   To provide financial assistance for college or law school to students who have survived a serious medical diagnosis.

Eligibility   This program is open to U.S. citizens and others authorized to work in the United States who have been accepted or are attending a university or law school. Applicants must submit an essay of 1 to 3 pages describing how their experience with cancer or other serious disease has influenced their choice to obtain a higher education. They must have an undergraduate GPA of 3.0 or higher.

Financial data   The stipend is $1,000. Funds are sent directly to the recipient's institution to be used only for tuition.

Duration   1 year.

Additional data   This program began in 2015.

Deadline   January of each year.

[594]
CHEF ALAIN ROBY CULINARY SCHOLARSHIP

Diabetes Scholars Foundation
310 Busse Highway, Suite 256
Park Ridge, IL 60068
(312) 215-9861   Fax: (847) 991-8739
E-mail: m.podjasek@diabetesscholars.org
Web: www.diabetesscholars.org/college-scholarship

Summary   To provide financial assistance to high school seniors from Illinois who have diabetes and plan to major in culinary arts in college.

Eligibility   This program is open to seniors graduating from high schools in Illinois who have Type 1 diabetes and plan to attend an accredited university, college, or trade/technical school in any state. Applicants must be planning to work on an associate or bachelor's degree in culinary arts. They must be able to demonstrate active involvement in the diabetes community, academic accomplishment, participation in community and/or extracurricular activities, and successful management of the challenges of living with diabetes. Financial need is not considered in the

selection process. U.S. citizenship or permanent resident status is required.

Financial data   The stipend is $5,000.

Duration   1 year.

Number awarded   1 each year.

Deadline   April of each year.

[595]
COLLEGE ACCESS AND SUCCESS SCHOLARSHIP

California Association for Postsecondary Education
  and Disability
Attn: Scholarships
10073 Valley View Street, Suite 242
Cypress, CA 90630
(562) 397-2810   Fax: (866) 577-3387
E-mail: caped38@gmail.com
Web: www.caped.io/scholarships/scholarship-application

Summary   To provide financial assistance to undergraduate and graduate students in California who have an intellectual disability or are on the autism spectrum.

Eligibility   This program is open to students at public and private colleges and universities in California who have an intellectual disability or are on the autism spectrum. Undergraduates must have completed at least 6 semester credits and have a GPA of 2.5 or higher. Graduate students must have completed at least 3 semester units and have a GPA of 3.0 or higher. Applicants must submit 1) a 250-word essay describing their progress towards meeting their educational and/or vocational goals; 2) a 500-word essay on how they manage their disabiity; and 3) a 750-word essay on how the skills and tools they develop in college will support their career goals. They must also submit a letter of recommendation from a faculty person, verification of disability, and unofficial transcripts.

Financial data   The stipend is $1,000.

Duration   1 year.

Number awarded   1 each year.

Deadline   August of each year.

[596]
COLORADO CHAPTER NHF ACADEMIC SCHOLARSHIP PROGRAM

National Hemophilia Foundation-Colorado Chapter
Attn: Academic Scholarship Program
1385 South Colorado Boulevard, Suite 610
Denver, CO 80222
(720) 545-0755   E-mail: info@cohemo.org
Web: www.cohemo.org

Summary   To provide financial assistance to residents of Colorado who have a bleeding disorder or are relatives of a person with a bleeding disorder and are interested in attending college in any state.

Eligibility   This program is open to residents of Colorado who are 1) persons with hemophilia or a related inherited bleeding disorder; 2) parents of a minor child with a bleeding disorder; 3) siblings of a person with a bleeding disorder; and 4) immediate family members of persons who died because of complications of a bleeding disorder. Applicants must be enrolled or planning to enroll at a college, university, or trade school in any state. Selection is based on academic merit, employment status, narrative and reference letters, impact of the bleeding disorder on educational activities, and financial need.

Financial data The stipend is $2,500. Funds must be used for tuition, room, board, and related educational expenses.

Duration 1 year; nonrenewable.

Number awarded 1 each year.

Deadline April of each year.

[597]
COMPREHENSIVE BLEEDING DISORDERS CENTER SCHOLARSHIP FUND

Community Foundation of Central Illinois
Attn: Program Manager
3625 North Sheridan Road
Peoria, IL 61604
(309) 674-8730   Fax: (309) 674-8754
E-mail: jessica@communityfoundationci.org
Web: www.communityfoundationci.org

Summary To provide financial assistance to students who have a bleeding disorder, live in the service area of the Comprehensive Bleeding Disorders Center (CBDC) in Illinois, and are interested in attending college in any state.

Eligibility This program is open to residents of the CBDC service area (all of Illinois outside of Chicago) who are diagnosed with a congenital or acquired chronic bleeding disorder or a congenital clotting disorder and have attended any hemophilia treatment center's comprehensive clinic during the past year. Applicants must be enrolled or planning to enroll full or part time at an accredited trade/vocational school, junior college, or 4-year college or university in any state. They must have a GPA of 2.5 or higher. Selection is based on their motivation to accomplish their educational and career goals, potential for scholarship, citizenship, and leadership; financial need is considered only if other factors are equal.

Financial data The stipend is $1,500. Funds are disbursed directly to the recipient's school to be used to cover the cost of tuition, books, and required fees.

Duration 1 year.

Additional data This program is supported by the CBDC.

Number awarded 3 each year.

Deadline March of each year.

[598]
COUEY MEMORIAL EDUCATIONAL SCHOLARSHIP

Georgia Transplant Foundation
Attn: Scholarship Program
2201 Macy Drive
Roswell, GA 30076
(770) 457-3796   Fax: (770) 457-7916
E-mail: gtf@gatransplant.org
Web: www.gatransplant.org

Summary To provide financial assistance to residents of Georgia who are transplant recipients or siblings of recipients and interested in attending college in any state.

Eligibility This program is open to residents of Georgia who are entering or continuing at an accredited institution of higher learning in any state. Applicants must be an organ transplant recipient or the sibling of a recipient. Along with their application, they must submit a 3-page personal statement on their career objectives, how this scholarship will help them attain their goals, and how transplantation has affected their life. Selection is based on that statement, transcripts, high school exit examination scores, ACT/SAT scores, 3 letters of reference, and financial need.

Financial data The stipend is $1,000 per year.

Duration 1 year; may be renewed up to 3 additional years.

Number awarded 1 each year.

Deadline April of each year.

[599]
CRISTIN ANN BAMBINO MEMORIAL SCHOLARSHIP

New York Schools Insurance Reciprocal
Attn: Executive Director
333 Earle Ovington Boulevard, Suite 1030
Uniondale, NY 11553-3624
(516) 640-3053   Toll Free: (800) 476-9747
Web: nysir.org/category/scholarships

Summary To provide financial assistance to special education seniors graduating from high schools that subscribe to the New York Schools Insurance Reciprocal (NYSIR) who plan to attend college in any state.

Eligibility This program is open to seniors graduating from NYSIR-subscriber high schools who have been enrolled in special education and have worked through special challenges to complete high school. Applicants must be planning to attend a college or university in any state. Along with their application, they must submit a 650-word essay on their accomplishments, how they overcame their challenges, how they can serve as a role model for other young people with special challenges, and what they plan to study in college. Financial need is not considered in the selection process.

Financial data The first-place winner receives a $5,000 scholarship, second-place a $4,000 scholarship and regional winners $3,000 scholarships.

Duration 1 year.

Number awarded 9 each year: 1 first-place, 1 second-place, and 7 regional scholarships.
Deadline March of each year.

[600]
CULPEPPER EXUM SCHOLARSHIP FOR PEOPLE WITH KIDNEY DISEASE

National Kidney Foundation Serving Western Missouri,
  Kansas and Oklahoma
Attn: Scholarship Program
6405 Metcalf Avenue, Suite 204
Overland Park, KS 66202-4086
(913) 262-1551, ext. 473   Toll Free: (800) 444-8113
Fax: (913) 722-4841   E-mail: nkfswmo@kidney.org
Web: www.kidney.org

Summary To provide financial assistance to residents of Kansas and western Missouri who are dialysis or transplant patients and interested in attending college in any state.
Eligibility This program is open to residents of Kansas and western Missouri who are attending or planning to attend a college or university in any state. Applicants must be dialysis or transplant patients. Along with their application, they must submit brief essays on their educational plans and goals and how receipt of this scholarship would help them achieve those goals. Financial need is considered in the selection process.
Financial data The stipend is $1,000. Funds are paid directly to the recipient's institution.
Duration 1 year.
Number awarded 2 each year: 1 to a resident of Kansas and 1 to a resident of western Missouri.
Deadline May of each year.

[601]
CURE CANCER SUPPORT SCHOLARSHIP

Lep Foundation for Youth Education
Attn: Scholarship Selection Committee
9 Whispering Spring Drive
Millstone Township, NJ 08510
E-mail: lepfoundation@aol.com
Web: www.lepfoundation.org/applications

Summary To provide financial assistance to high school seniors and current college students in any state who have cancer.
Eligibility This program is open to residents of any state who are enrolled or planning to enroll at a college, university, community college, or vocational school. Applicants must have cancer, diagnosed in childhood, and documented financial need because of the burdens imposed on them and their families because of the disease and related treatments. Along with their application, they must submit 1) a brief statement on their diagnosis and the challenges they and their families faced because of the disease and its treatments, including their career goals and ambitions; and 2) a 500-word essay on why they feel they are the best candidate for this award.
Financial data The stipend is $5,000. Funds are paid directly to the recipient's school.

Duration 1 year.
Additional data This program began in 2016 as a collaboration between CURE Media Group and the Lep Foundation for Youth Education.
Number awarded Varies each year; recently, 5 were awarded.
Deadline May of each year.

[602]
DAKOTA PEQUENO MEMORIAL SCHOLARSHIP

Epilepsy Foundation of Michigan
Attn: Development Director
25200 Telegraph Road, Suite 110
Southfield, MI 48033
(248) 351-7979, ext. 1217   Toll Free: (800) 377-6226
Fax: (248) 351-2101
E-mail: info@epilepsymichigan.org
Web: www.epilepsymichigan.org/page.php?id=223

Summary To provide financial assistance to high school seniors and graduates in Michigan who have epilepsy and are planning to attend college in any state.
Eligibility This program is open to high school seniors and graduates between 17 and 25 years of age in Michigan who have a diagnosis of epilepsy or a seizure disorder. Applicants must be planning to enroll at a postsecondary academic or vocational program in any state. Along with their application, they must submit a brief essay about their experience dealing with epilepsy. Selection is based on that essay, how the applicant has faced challenges due to epilepsy, career goals, recommendations, and community involvement; financial need is not considered.
Financial data The stipend is $1,000.
Duration 1 year.
Additional data This program began in 2009.
Number awarded 1 or 2 each year.
Deadline March of each year.

[603]
DALY "PERFECT MATCH" SCHOLARSHIP

Georgia Transplant Foundation
Attn: Scholarship Program
2201 Macy Drive
Roswell, GA 30076
(770) 457-3796   Fax: (770) 457-7916
E-mail: gtf@gatransplant.org
Web: www.gatransplant.org

Summary To provide financial assistance to residents of Georgia who are transplant recipients or dependents or siblings of recipients and interested in attending college in any state.
Eligibility This program is open to residents of Georgia who are entering or continuing at an accredited institution of higher learning in any state. Applicants must be an organ transplant recipient or the dependent or sibling of a recipient. Along with their application, they must submit a 3-page personal statement on their career objectives, how this scholarship will help them attain their goals, and how

transplantation has affected their life. Selection is based on that statement, transcripts, high school exit examination scores, ACT/SAT scores, 3 letters of reference, and financial need.

Financial data The stipend is $1,000 per year.

Duration 1 year; may be renewed up to 3 additional years.

Number awarded 1 each year.

Deadline April of each year.

[604]
DEANNA LYNN POTTS SCHOLARSHIP

Cystinosis Foundation
Attn: Scholarship Committee
58 Miramonte Drive
Moraga, CA 94556
Toll Free: (888) 631-1588
Web: www.cystinosis.com/Scholarship

Summary To provide financial assistance for college to students who have cystinosis.

Eligibility This program is open to high school seniors and graduates who have had to postpone entry into college but who have now been accepted at an accredited college, university, or vocational school. Applicants must have cystinosis. Along with their application, they must submit a 500-word essay about a person who played a vital role in their life. Selection is based on that essay (40 points), transcripts (20 points), and letters of recommendation (20 points).

Financial data The stipend is $1,000. Funds are paid directly to the educational institution to be applied to tuition, room, and board.

Duration 1 year.

Number awarded 1 each year.

Deadline March of each year.

[605]
DEAR JACK SCHOLARSHIP

Cancer for College
981 Park Center Drive
Vista, CA 92081
(760) 599-5096
E-mail: applications@cancerforcollege.org
Web: www.cancerforcollege.org/application.html

Summary To provide financial assistance to undergraduate and graduate students who are cancer patients or survivors and working on or planning to work a degree in music.

Eligibility This program is open to undergraduate and graduate students who are entering or currently enrolled at accredited colleges, universities, community colleges, or trade schools in any state. Applicants must be working on a degree in music and able to express how they plan to prepare for a career in music. They must be a cancer patient or survivor. Along with their application, they must submit transcripts, verification of their cancer diagnosis, 2 letters of recommendation, and information on their financial situation.

Financial data The stipend ranges from $1,000 to $5,000.

Duration 1 year.

Number awarded 1 each year.

Deadline January of each year.

[606]
DELUCA, RICCIUTI & KONIECZKA MENTAL HEALTH SCHOLARSHIP

DeLuca, Ricciuti & Konieczka
Attn: Anthony DeLuca
225 Ross Street, Fourth Floor
Pittsburgh, PA 15219
(412) 281-6869   Fax: (412) 281-1350
E-mail: drkattorneys@gmail.com
Web: www.drkattorneys.com/scholarship

Summary To provide financial assistance to undergraduate and graduate students who have struggled with mental health issues.

Eligibility This program is open to students enrolled or accepted at a college, university, technical school, or graduate school in the United States. Applicants must have struggled with mental health issues but found a way to manage and overcome those issues. They must have a GPA of 3.0 or higher and be willing to share their story with the general public. Along with their application, they must submit an essay of 1 to 3 pages about their life with mental health issues, the struggles they have encountered, and how they have overcome those.

Financial data The stipend is $1,000.

Duration 1 year.

Number awarded 1 each year.

Deadline July of each year.

[607]
DIABETES, INCORPORATED COLLEGE SCHOLARSHIP

Diabetes, Incorporated
Attn: Executive Director
P.O. Box 9368
Rapid City, SD 57709-9368
(605) 341-1273   Fax: (605) 342-5887
E-mail: diabetesinc@qwestoffice.net
Web: www.diabetesincorporated.org/Scholarship.html

Summary To provide financial assistance to high school seniors and current college students who have or have a family member who has diabetes and is a member of Diabetes, Incorporated.

Eligibility This program is open to graduating high school seniors and students who are continuing their education beyond high school. Applicants must have diabetes or have a family member who has diabetes. In either case, they must have a relative who is a current member of Diabetes, Incorporated. Along with their application, they must submit a 100-word essay on how their life has been affected by diabetes. Selection is based on that essay, GPA and SAT/ACT score, honors and awards, and community contribution. Preference is given to previous participants in the sponsor's Kamp for Kids.

Financial data The stipend is $1,000 per year. Funds are paid directly to the educational institution.

Duration 1 year; recipients may reapply.

Additional data This program includes the following named awards: the Kris Sanders Scholarship, the Micah Jerde Scholarship, and the Daniel Silvernail Scholarship.

Number awarded Varies each year; recently, 11 were awarded.

Deadline April of each year.

[608]
DIALYSIS SCHOLARSHIP FOUNDATION

Dialysis Scholarship Foundation, Inc.
P.O. Box 372278
Denver, CO 80237
E-mail: Inquiry@DialysisScholarshipFund.org
Web: www.dialysisscholarshipfund.org/index.html

Summary To provide financial assistance for college or graduate school to dialysis patients who are awaiting a kidney transplant.

Eligibility This program is open to students entering or enrolled in college or graduate school and undergoing dialysis until they are able to undergo a kidney transplant. Applicants must submit brief statements on their future educational plans, why they are interested in this scholarship, and any special skills and qualifications they have acquired from employment, volunteer work, or other activities.

Financial data A stipend is awarded (amount not specified).

Duration 1 year; may be renewed, provided the recipient maintains a GPA of 3.0 or higher with satisfactory attendance.

Additional data This program began in 2012.

Number awarded Varies each year; recently, 11 were awarded.

Deadline Deadline not specified.

[609]
DIANE AND PETER CHRISTODOULOU MEMORIAL SCHOLARSHIP

Community Foundation of the Ozarks
Attn: Scholarship Coordinator
421 East Trafficway
P.O. Box 8960
Springfield, MO 65801-8960
(417) 864-6199   Toll Free: (888) 266-6815
Fax: (417) 864-8344   E-mail: bhersh@cfozarks.org
Web: www.cfozarks.org

Summary To provide financial assistance to high school seniors in Missouri who have learning disabilities and are interested in attending college in any state.

Eligibility This program is open to seniors graduating from high schools in Missouri who have learning disabilities but can meet entrance requirements for a postsecondary institution in any state. Applicants must submit an essay describing why they want to receive this scholarship, the course of study or major field of interest they plan to follow, and proposed occupation or profession, and any

other abilities they have. Selection is based on the student's strengths, the nature of the student's learning disability, the student's non-academic activities and interests, a measure of the student's motivation, and the student's potential for success in college (as measured by class rank, cumulative GPA, and SAT or ACT scores). In case of a tie, preference is given to members of the Learning Disabilities Association of Missouri and their families and to applicants who can demonstrate financial need.

Financial data The stipend is $1,000.

Duration 1 year.

Additional data This program was formerly administered by the Learning Disabilities Association of Missouri as the Diane Christodoulou Memorial Scholarship.

Number awarded 2 each year.

Deadline March of each year.

[610]
DICK GRIFFITHS MEMORIAL SCHOLARSHIP

California Association for Postsecondary Education
  and Disability
Attn: Scholarships
10073 Valley View Street, Suite 242
Cypress, CA 90630
(562) 397-2810   Fax: (866) 577-3387
E-mail: caped38@gmail.com
Web: www.caped.io/scholarships/scholarship-application

Summary To provide financial assistance to undergraduate and graduate students in California who have a learning disability, especially involving mathematics.

Eligibility This program is open to students at public and private colleges and universities in California who have a learning disability and are especially challenged in mathematics. Undergraduates must have completed at least 6 semester credits and have a GPA of 2.5 or higher. Graduate students must have completed at least 3 semester units and have a GPA of 3.0 or higher. Applicants must submit 1) a 250-word essay describing their progress towards meeting their educational and/or vocational goals; 2) a 500-word essay on how they manage their disabiity; and 3) a 750-word essay on the strategies they have used to overcome their mathematics challenges. They must also submit a letter of recommendation from a faculty person, verification of disability, and unofficial transcripts.

Financial data The stipend is $1,000.

Duration 1 year.

Number awarded 1 each year.

Deadline August of each year.

[611]
DOLLARS 4 TIC SCHOLARS TOURETTE SYNDROME SCHOLARSHIP

Kelsey B. Diamantis TS Scholarship Family
  Foundation, Inc.
21801 Little Bear Lane
Boca Raton, FL 33428
(561) 487-9526   E-mail: info@dollars4ticscholars.org
Web: www.dollars4ticscholars.org

Summary To provide financial assistance for college to students who have Tourette Syndrome (TS).

Eligibility This program is open to undergraduate and graduate students with TS who are enrolled or planning to enroll at a college or university. Applicants must have a GPA of 2.5 or higher. They must submit a letter from their doctor confirming the diagnosis of TS, documentation of financial need, 3 letters of recommendation, and transcripts.

Financial data The stipend is $1,000.

Duration 1 year.

Additional data This program began in 2015.

Number awarded 1 or more each year.

Deadline April of each year.

[612]
DONNA T. DARRIEN MEMORIAL SCHOLARSHIP

Donna T. Darrien Memorial Foundation for Sickle Cell, Inc.
P.O. Box 3331
Newark, NJ 07103
(973) 282-1997   E-mail: dtdsicklecell@hotmail.com
Web: www.dtdsicklecell.org/scholarship-information

Summary To provide financial assistance to residents of New Jersey who have or whose parents have sickle cell disease and are interested in attending college in any state.

Eligibility This program is open to residents of New Jersey who are able to document a diagnosis of sickle cell disease or are the children of parents with the disease. Applicants must be enrolled or planning to enroll at an accredited college, university, or vocational/technical school in any state and have a GPA of 2.0 or higher. Along with their application, they must submit a 1,000-word essay on how they face their challenges, their educational plans, and their career objectives. Financial need is not considered in the selection process.

Financial data A stipend is awarded (amount not specified).

Duration 1 year; recipients may reapply.

Additional data This program began in 2001.

Number awarded 1 or more each year.

Deadline April of each year.

[613]
DOREEN MCMULLAN MCCARTHY MEMORIAL ACADEMIC SCHOLARSHIP FOR WOMEN WITH BLEEDING DISORDERS

National Hemophilia Foundation
Attn: Victory for Women Program
7 Penn Plaza
370 Seventh Avenue, Suite 1204
New York, NY 10001
(212) 328-3700   Toll Free: (800) 42-HANDI, ext. 2
Fax: (212) 328-3777   E-mail: sroger@hemophilia.org
Web: www.hemophilia.org

Summary To provide financial assistance for college or graduate school to women who have a bleeding disorder.

Eligibility This program is open to women who are entering or already enrolled in an undergraduate or graduate program at a university, college, or accredited vocational school. Applicants must have von Willebrand Disease, hemophilia or other clotting factor deficiency, platelet disorder, or carrier status. Along with their application, they must submit a 250-word essay that describes how their education and future career plans will benefit others in the bleeding disorders community. Selection is based on that essay, achievements, and community service to the bleeding disorders community.

Financial data The stipend is $2,500.

Duration 1 year.

Additional data The program, known also as V4W, was established in 2005 as the Project Red Flag Academic Scholarship for Women with Bleeding and later named the Victory for Women Academic Scholarship for Women with Bleeding Disorders.

Number awarded 1 each year.

Deadline March of each year.

[614]
DOTTIE R. WALKER SCHOLARSHIP

Learning & Education About Disabilities
Attn: LEAD Foundation
415 North Tejon Street
P.O. Box 38895
Colorado Springs, CO 80937
(719) 209-8888 E-mail: leadfoundationco@gmail.com
Web: www.leadcolorado.org/programs/scholarships

Summary To provide financial assistance to residents of Colorado who have a learning disability and are interested in attending college in any state.

Eligibility This program is open to Colorado residents who have a documented, specific learning disability or AD/HD (e.g., dyslexia, perceptual, or communicative disabilities). Applicants must be working on or planning to work on a postsecondary degree at a college or university in any state. They must have a GPA of 2.8 or higher. Preference is given to applicants who have faced the challenges of having a learning disability, understand the importance of advocacy and self-knowledge in overcoming those challenges, and are willing to serve as role models for other students with learning disabilities.

Financial data The stipend is $1,000.

Duration 1 year; nonrenewable.

Additional data This program was formerly named the LEAD Foundation Community Scholarship.

Number awarded 1 each year.

Deadline March of each year.

[615]
DOUG HITESHEW MEMORIAL SCHOLARSHIP PROGRAM

Hemophilia Foundation of Maryland
Attn: Executive Director
13 Class Court, Suite 200
Parkville, MD 21234
(410) 661-2307   Toll Free: (800) 964-3131
Fax: (410) 661-2308   E-mail: miller8043@comcast.net
Web: www.hfmonline.webs.com/scholarship-info

Summary To provide financial assistance to residents of Maryland and students attending college in the state who have hemophilia or von Willebrand Disease or are immediate family of such people.

Eligibility This program is open to students who have hemophilia or von Willebrand Disease and their siblings, children, or parents. Applicants must be 1) Maryland residents who are entering or attending a community college, junior college, 4-year college, university, or vocational school in any state; or 2) students who have attended a Maryland school for at least 1 year. Along with their application, they must submit 1-page essays on 1) their career goals; and 2) their previous participation with the Hemophilia Foundation of Maryland or another chapter and how they plan to contribute to the chapter in the future. Selection is based on those essays, academic goals, transcripts of current academic work, volunteer work, and letters of recommendation.

Financial data Stipends are $2,500, $1,000, or $500.

Duration 1 year.

Additional data This program began in 2010.

Number awarded Varies each year; recently, 9 were awarded: 3 at $2,500 each to students who live or attend school in Maryland and have a bleeding disorder, 3 at $1,000 each to siblings or children of persons who live in Maryland and have a bleeding disorder, and 3 at $500 each to parents of children who live in Maryland and have a bleeding disorder.

Deadline April of each year.

[616]
DUGDALE/VAN EYS SCHOLARSHIP AWARD

Tennessee Hemophilia and Bleeding Disorders
  Foundation
Attn: Scholarship Committee
1819 Ward Drive, Suite 102
Murfreesboro, TN 37129
(615) 900-1486   Toll Free: (888) 703-3269
Fax: (615) 900-1487   E-mail: mail@thbdf.org
Web: www.thbdf.org

Summary To provide financial assistance for college to students with hemophilia or their family members in Tennessee.

Eligibility This program is open to college-bound high school seniors, college students, and technical school students who have a bleeding disorder and are receiving treatment in Tennessee. Their children, spouses, and guardians are also eligible. Applicants must have a GPA of 2.5 or higher and be enrolled or planning to enroll full time.

They must submit a 500-word essay on their life goals, a resume, 3 letters of recommendation, proof of enrollment, and documentation of community service of at least 10 hours per semester. Financial need is considered in the selection process.

Financial data Stipends range from $500 to $2,000.

Duration 1 year; recipients may reapply.

Number awarded Varies each year; recently, 6 were awarded: 1 at $2,000, 1 at $1,500, 1 at $1,000, and 3 at $500.

Deadline March of each year.

[617]
EDUCATION ADVANTAGE COMMUNITY COLLEGE OR TECHNICAL SCHOLARSHIP

Baxalta Incorporated
c/o Scholarship America
Scholarship Management Services
P.O. Box 297
One Scholarship Way
St. Peter, MN 56082
Toll Free: (877) 544-3018
E-mail: baxalta@scholarshipamerica.org
Web: www.baxaltahematology.com

Summary To provide financial assistance to people who have hemophilia and are interested in working on an associate degree or technical certificate.

Eligibility This program is open to people who have hemophilia A or B, including those with inhibitors or von Willebrand's Disease. Applicants must be enrolled or planning to enroll part or full time at a community college, junior college, trade or vocational school, or other eligible program. They may be of any age. Along with their application, they must submit a 500-word personal statement that covers their career goals and educational objectives, how hemophilia or von Willebrand's Disease has impacted their life, their plans for the future, and a volunteer activity of which they're proud and why it made a difference. U.S. citizenship or permanent resident status is required.

Financial data The stipend is $1,000 per year.

Duration 1 year; may be renewed 1 additional year, provided the recipient maintains satisfactory academic performance and provides proof of an annual visit to a comprehensive clinic.

Additional data Baxter Healthcare Corporation began this program began 2010. The current sponsor spun off from Baxter in 2015.

Number awarded Varies each year; recently, 3 were awarded.

Deadline April of each year.

[618]
EDUCATION ADVANTAGE UNIVERSITY SCHOLARSHIP

Baxalta Incorporated
c/o Scholarship America
Scholarship Management Services
One Scholarship Way
P.O. Box 297
St. Peter, MN 56082
Toll Free: (877) 544-3018
E-mail: baxalta@scholarshipamerica.org
Web: www.baxaltahematology.com

Summary To provide financial assistance to people who have hemophilia and are interested in working on a bachelor's degree.

Eligibility This program is open to people who have hemophilia A or B, including those with inhibitors or von Willebrand's Disease. Applicants must be enrolled or planning to enroll full time at a 4-year college or university. Along with their application, they must submit a 500-word personal statement that covers their career goals and educational objectives, how hemophilia or von Willebrand's Disease has impacted their life, their plans for the future, and a volunteer activity of which they're proud and why it made a difference. U.S. citizenship or permanent resident status is required.

Financial data The stipend is $7,000 per year.

Duration 1 year; may be renewed up to 3 additional years or until a bachelor's degree is earned, provided the recipient remains enrolled full time, maintains satisfactory academic performance, and provides proof of an annual visit to a comprehensive clinic.

Additional data Baxter Healthcare Corporation began this program began 2010. The current sponsor spun off from Baxter in 2015.

Number awarded Varies each year; recently, 16 were awarded.

Deadline April of each year.

[619]
EDUCATION IS POWER SCHOLARSHIPS

MedProRx, Inc.
Attn: Scholarship Coordinator
140 Northway Court
Raleigh, NC 27615-4916
Toll Free: (866) 571-3100
E-mail: educationispower@medprorx.com
Web: www.medprorx.com

Summary To provide financial assistance for college to people with a bleeding disorder.

Eligibility This program is open to residents of the United States who are living with hemophilia or von Willebrand Disease. Applicants must be entering or attending a community college, junior college, 4-year college, university, or vocational school. They must be able to demonstrate a record of community involvement and/or volunteer work. Along with their application, they must submit a 250-word essay on 1 of the following: 1) their dreams and aspirations; 2) what they are most passionate about; 3) how

living with a bleeding disorder has affected their life; or 4) what they would change if they had the power to change something in the world.

Financial data Stipends range from $500 to $2,500.

Duration 1 year.

Additional data This program began in 2006.

Number awarded At least 20 each year. Since this program began, it has awarded 454 scholarships with a value of $445,000.

Deadline May of each year.

[620]
ELAM BAER AND JANIS CLAY EDUCATIONAL SCHOLARSHIP

Epilepsy Foundation of Minnesota
Attn: Scholarships
1600 University Avenue West, Suite 300
St. Paul, MN 55104
(651) 287-2312   Toll Free: (800) 779-0777, ext. 2312
Fax: (651) 287-2325   E-mail: dwhite@efmn.org
Web: www.epilepsyfoundationmn.org

Summary To provide financial assistance to residents of Minnesota and eastern North Dakota who have epilepsy and are interested in attending college in any state.

Eligibility This program is open to graduating high school seniors and high school graduates who live in Minnesota or eastern North Dakota. Applicants must have a diagnosis of epilepsy or other seizure disorder. They must have been accepted at a postsecondary academic or vocational program. Along with their application, they must submit a 250-word essay on something of direct personal importance to them as a person with epilepsy. Selection is based on how the applicant has faced challenges due to epilepsy, career goals, achievements, involvement with the Epilepsy Foundation of Minnesota and or the community, and letters of recommendation; financial need is not considered.

Financial data The stipend is $1,000.

Duration 1 year.

Additional data These scholarships were first awarded in 2006.

Number awarded 10 each year.

Deadline March of each year.

[621]
ELIZABETH LULU SCHOLARSHIP

Elizabeth Lulu Scholarship Foundation
11293 Patom Drive
Culver City, CA 90230
Fax: (323) 763-5858
E-mail: elizabethluluscholarship@gmail.com
Web: www.lizzielulu.org/apply-for-the-scholarship

Summary To provide financial assistance for college to high school seniors who have cystic fibrosis.

Eligibility This program is open to graduating high school seniors who have cystic fibrosis and plans to attend a college or university. Applicants must submit academic information (GPA, SAT and/or ACT scores), a list of extracurricular activities, a letter from their doctor or social worker confirming their cystic fibrosis diagnosis and prognosis, information on financial need, a 1-page essay on their future goals and aspirations, and a 1-paragraph statement on what they have accomplished in spite of cystic fibrosis.

Financial data   The stipend is $1,000.

Duration   1 year.

Additional data   This program began in 2007.

Number awarded   2 each year.

Deadline   April of each year.

[622]
ELIZABETH NASH FOUNDATION SCHOLARSHIP PROGRAM

Elizabeth Nash Foundation
P.O. Box 1260
Los Gatos, CA 95031-1260
E-mail: scholarships@elizabethnashfoundation.org
Web: www.elizabethnashfoundation.org

Summary   To provide financial assistance for college or graduate school to individuals with cystic fibrosis (CF).

Eligibility   This program is open to undergraduate and graduate students who have CF. Applicants must be able to demonstrate clear academic goals and a commitment to participate in activities outside the classroom. U.S. citizenship is required. Selection is based on academic record, character, demonstrated leadership, service to CF-related causes and the broader community, and financial need.

Financial data   Stipends range from $1,000 to $2,500. Funds are paid directly to the academic institution to be applied to tuition and fees.

Duration   1 year; recipients may reapply.

Additional data   This program began in 2005. Recipients must agree to support the program by speaking at a local event or writing an article for publication by the foundation.

Number awarded   Varies each year; recently, 16 were awarded. Since the program was established, it has awarded more than 115 scholarships.

Deadline   April of each year.

[623]
EPILEPSY FOUNDATION NEW ENGLAND SCHOLARSHIPS

Epilepsy Foundation New England
Attn: Director of Community Engagement and
 Education
335 Main Street, Unit 8
Wilmington, MA 01887
(617) 506-6041   Fax: (617) 506-6047
E-mail: swelby@epilepsynewengland.org
Web: www.epilepsynewengland.org

Summary   To provide financial assistance to residents of Massachusetts, Rhode Island, New Hampshire, and Maine who have epilepsy and are interested in attending college or graduate school in any state.

Eligibility   This program is open to residents of Massachusetts, Rhode Island, New Hampshire, or Maine who have been diagnosed with epilepsy (seizure disorder). Applicants must be accepted or enrolled in a postsecondary educational or vocational program in any state as an undergraduate or graduate student. Along with their application, they must submit an essay (up to 220 words in length) on their academic and career goals and how having epilepsy has affected or influenced those goals and their work towards achieving them.

Financial data   The stipend is $2,500.

Duration   1 year; may be renewed.

Additional data   This program includes the Richard Bonasera Scholarships and the Leslie G. Brody and Amy Seeherman Scholarships.

Number awarded   At least 4 each year.

Deadline   February of each year.

[624]
EPILEPSY FOUNDATION OF NEW JERSEY SCHOLARSHIP PROGRAM

Epilepsy Foundation of New Jersey
Attn: Scholarship Program
1 AAA Drive, Suite 203
Trenton, NJ 08691
Toll Free: (800) 336-5843   Fax: (609) 392-5621
TDD: (800) 852-7899   E-mail: aracioppi@efnj.com
Web: www.efnj.com/what-we-offer/programs

Summary   To provide financial assistance to high school seniors in New Jersey who have epilepsy and are planning to attend college in any state.

Eligibility   This program is open to seniors graduating from high schools in New Jersey who have epilepsy. Applicants must be planning to attend a college or university in any state. Along with their application, they must submit a brief personal statement explaining their academic and career goals. Selection is based on academic achievement, participation in activities, and financial need.

Financial data   The stipend is $1,000 per year. Funds are paid directly to the recipient.

Duration   1 year.

Number awarded   At least 3 each year.

Deadline   April of each year.

[625]
ERIC DELSON MEMORIAL SCHOLARSHIP

CVS Caremark
c/o Scholarship America
Scholarship Management Services
One Scholarship Way
P.O. Box 297
St. Peter, MN 56082
(507) 931-1682
Web: www.cvsspecialty.com

Summary   To provide financial assistance for high school, college, or graduate school to students with a bleeding disorder.

Eligibility   This program is open to students diagnosed with a bleeding disorder who are 1) high school seniors, high school graduates or equivalent (GED), college students, or graduate students currently enrolled or planning to enroll full time at an accredited 2- or 4-year college, university, or vocational/technical school; or 2) students entering grades 7-12 at a private secondary school in the United States. Selection is based on academic record, demonstrated leadership and participation in school and community activities, work experience, a statement of educational and career goals, unusual personal or family circumstances, and an outside appraisal.

Financial data The stipend is $2,500 for college students or $1,500 for high school students. Funds are paid in 2 equal installments directly to the recipient.

Duration 1 year; may be renewed for up to 3 additional years, provided the recipient maintains a GPA of 2.5 or higher for the freshman year and 3.0 or higher for subsequent years.

Number awarded 4 each year: 3 for college students and 1 for a high school student.

Deadline June of each year.

[626]
ERIC DOSTIE MEMORIAL COLLEGE SCHOLARSHIP

NuFACTOR Specialty Pharmacy
Attn: Scholarship Administrator
41093 County Center Drive, Suite B
Temecula, CA 92591
(951) 296-2516   Toll Free: (800) 323-6832, ext. 1300
Fax: (855) 270-7347   E-mail: info@kelleycom.com
Web: www.nufactor.com

Summary To provide financial assistance for college to students with hemophilia or members of their families.

Eligibility This program is open to 1) students with hemophilia or a related bleeding disorder; or 2) members of their families. Applicants must be U.S. citizens and enrolled or planning to enroll full time at an accredited 2- or 4-year college or university. They must have a GPA of 2.5 or higher. Along with their application, they must submit an essay on how their education will be used to serve humankind and to encourage self-improvement and enrichment. Selection is based on academic achievement, community service, and financial need.

Financial data The stipend is $1,000.

Duration 1 year.

Number awarded 10 each year.

Deadline February of each year.

[627]
ERIC MARDER SCHOLARSHIP

Eric Marder Scholarship Fund
Attn: Scholarship Committee
1912 Rolling Green Circle
Sarasota, FL 34240
E-mail: annie3907@verizon.net
Web: www.ericsfund.org/about.html

Summary To provide financial assistance to undergraduates with a primary immune deficiency disease.

Eligibility This program is open to U.S. citizens entering or attending college or technical training school who have a primary immune deficiency disease. Applicants must submit a 500-word autobiographical essay, 2 letters of recommendation, a family financial statement, and a letter of verification from their immunologist. Financial need is the main factor considered in selecting the recipients and the size of the award.

Financial data Stipends range from $750 to $2,000; funds are paid directly to the student.

Duration 1 year; may be renewed.

Additional data This program began in 1986 as a program of the Immune Deficiency Foundation. It became a separate foundation in 2015.

Number awarded Varies each year.

Deadline April of each year.

[628]
ERIC MARTINEZ MEMORIAL SCHOLARSHIP FOR AN INDIVIDUAL WITH DOWN SYNDROME

United Parent Support for Down Syndrome
Attn: UPS for DownS Memorial Scholarship Program
1070 South Roselle Road
Schaumburg, IL 60193
(847) 895-2100   E-mail: embarrett@upsfordowns.org
Web: www.upsfordowns.org/support/Scholarships.aspx

Summary To provide financial assistance to individuals who have Down syndrome and are interested in obtaining education beyond high school.

Eligibility This program is open to individuals who have Down syndrome and are interested in a program of educational or job training opportunities beyond high school. Applicants must be interested in educational opportunities that may include, but are not limited to, college, community college, trade school, vocational school, job training, or adult continuing education. Along with their application, they must submit a 1-page essay on 1) their accomplishments, community involvement, and future career plans; and 2) how receipt of the scholarship will help them achieve their personal goals. Other factors considered in the selection process may be transcripts, records of community service, employment history, records of extracurricular activities, independent living skills, a statement of how the applicant educates others on the needs of those with disabilities, and a record of assistive technology used and how it has impacted the applicant or others. U.S. citizenship is required.

Financial data The stipend is $2,500. Funds are sent directly to the institution or service provider.

Duration Funds may be used over multiple years or in multiple programs, but must be used within a 3-year period.

Number awarded 1 each year.

Deadline May of each year.

[629]
ERIN TRUJEQUE MEMORIAL SCHOLARSHIPS

Children's Cancer Fund of New Mexico
112 14th Street S.W.
Albuquerque, NM 87102
(505) 243-3618   Fax: (505) 243-1490
E-mail: ccfnm@ccfnm.org
Web: www.ccfnm.org/ccfnm/scholarships

Summary To provide financial assistance to high school seniors in New Mexico who have been treated for childhood cancer and plan to attend college in any state.

Eligibility This program is open to seniors graduating from high schools in New Mexico who have been diagnosed or treated for childhood cancer at a pediatric oncology treatment facility in the state. Applicants must be planning to enroll full or part time at an institution of higher education in any state. Along with their application, they must submit a short essay about how they have overcome their experiences with childhood cancer and how their goals for the future have been affected by that experience.

Financial data Stipends depend on the availability of funds; recently, they averaged nearly $3,500.

Duration Students may receive support for only 2 academic terms (fall, spring, or summer) each year. They may receive awards for a total of 8 semesters of undergraduate study or 4 semesters of graduate study.

Additional data Recipients must complete at least 12 hours of volunteer service for the sponsor before funds are disbursed.

Number awarded Varies each year; recently, 28 of these scholarships, with a value of $97,300, were awarded.

Deadline March of each year for academic year; October of each year for spring or summer.

[630]
EXERCISE FOR LIFE ATHLETIC SCHOLARSHIPS

Boomer Esiason Foundation
c/o Chris McEwan
483 Tenth Avenue, Suite 300
New York, NY 10018
(646) 292-7939   Fax: (646) 292-7945
E-mail: cmcewan@esiason.org
Web: www.esiason.org

Summary To provide financial assistance to high school seniors and college undergraduates who have been involved in athletics and who have cystic fibrosis (CF).

Eligibility This program is open to CF patients who are college-bound high school seniors or students already enrolled as undergraduates. Applicants must have been involved in athletics. They should be jogging on a regular basis and training for a 1.5 mile run. Along with their application, they must submit a letter from their doctor confirming the diagnosis of CF and a list of daily medications, information on financial need, a detailed breakdown of tuition costs from their academic institution, a completed running log, transcripts, and a 2-page essay on 1) their postgraduation goals; and 2) the importance of compli-

ance with CF therapies and what they practice on a daily basis to stay healthy. Selection is based on academic ability, athletic ability, character, leadership potential, service to the community, financial need, and daily compliance to CF therapy. Male and female students compete separately.

Financial data The stipend is $10,000. Funds are paid directly to the academic institution to assist in covering the cost of tuition and fees.

Duration 1 year; nonrenewable.

Number awarded 4 each year: 2 to high school seniors (1 male and 1 female) and 2 to college students (1 male and 1 female).

Deadline June of each year.

[631]
EXPECT MIRACLES FOUNDATION SCHOLARSHIP

Expect Miracles Foundation
6 Quail Run
Hingham, MA 02043
(617) 391-9235
E-mail: info@expectmiraclesfoundation.org
Web: www.expectmiraclesfoundation.org

Summary To provide financial assistance to students from New England and the greater New York area who have been diagnosed with cancer and are interested in attending college in any state.

Eligibility This program is open to U.S. citizens and permanent residents who have been diagnosed, either previously or currently, with cancer. Applicants must be high school seniors or college freshman, sophomores, or juniors who have been treated for cancer at a facility in New England or the greater New York area. They must be enrolled or planning to enroll at an accredited 4-year college or university in any state. Along with their application, they must submit a 500-word essay on how their cancer diagnosis has changed them and why this scholarship is important to them. Financial need is considered in the selection process.

Financial data The stipend is $7,500 per year.

Duration 1 year; recipients may reapply.

Number awarded 1 or more each year.

Deadline April of each year.

[632]
FLICKER OF HOPE SCHOLARSHIPS

Flicker of Hope Foundation
Attn: Scholarship Committee
8624 Janet Lane
Vienna, VA 22180
(703) 698-1626   Fax: (703) 698-6225
E-mail: info@flickerofhope.org
Web: flickerofhope.org/scholarship

Summary To provide financial assistance for college to burn survivors.

Eligibility This program is open to high school seniors and graduates who are burn survivors and enrolled or planning to enroll in college. Applicants must submit a

500-word essay describing the circumstances of how they were burned, how that injury has affected their life, and the benefits to be derived from their planned course of study. Selection is based on severity of burn injury, academic performance, community service, and financial need.

Financial data Stipends average $3,000. Funds are paid directly to the postsecondary institution.

Duration 1 year.

Additional data This program began in 2003.

Number awarded Varies each year; since the program began, it has awarded $180,000 in scholarships to 60 students.

Deadline June of each year.

[633]
FRANK SELENY SCHOLARSHIPS

Hawaii Children's Cancer Foundation
1814 Liliha Street
Honolulu, HI 96817
(808) 528-5161 Toll Free: (866) 443-HCCF (within HI)
Fax: (808) 521-4689   E-mail: info@hccf.org
Web: www.hccf.org/family-support

Summary To provide financial assistance to residents of Hawaii who have had cancer and are interested in attending college in any state.

Eligibility This program is open to residents of Hawaii who were diagnosed with cancer before 18 years of age. Applicants must have been accepted into a college or vocational training program in any state.

Financial data The stipend is $1,000.

Duration 1 year.

Additional data This foundation was established in 1991.

Number awarded 2 each year.

Deadline Deadline not specified.

[634]
GALAXY SCHOLARSHIPS

Pediatric Brain Tumor Foundation of the United States
Attn: Family Support Program Manager
302 Ridgefield Court
Asheville, NC 28806
(828) 665-6891, ext. 306   Toll Free: (800) 253-6530
Fax: (828) 665-6894   E-mail: info@curethekids.org
Web: www.curethekids.org

Summary To provide financial assistance for college to high school seniors who are survivors of a brain or spinal cord tumor.

Eligibility This program is open to high school seniors and recent graduates who have been diagnosed at or before age 19 with a primary malignant or non-malignant central nervous system brain and/or spinal cord tumor. Applicants must be planning to enroll at an accredited community college or undergraduate school. They must agree to participate in the sponsor's volunteer program. Along with their application, they must submit an essay, proof of tumor diagnosis, GPA, intent to register for college, high school transcripts, and recommendations.

Financial data The stipend is $1,500 per year.

Duration 1 year; may be renewed 1 additional year for students working on an associate degree or 3 additional years for students working on a bachelor's degree.

Additional data This program, which began in 2013, receives funding from individual donors.

Number awarded Varies each year; recently, 4 were awarded.

Deadline March of each year.

[635]
GASPARI SCIENCE SCHOLARSHIP

Diabetes Scholars Foundation
310 Busse Highway, Suite 256
Park Ridge, IL 60068
(312) 215-9861   Fax: (847) 991-8739
E-mail: m.podjasek@diabetesscholars.org
Web: www.diabetesscholars.org/college-scholarship

Summary To provide financial assistance to high school seniors who have diabetes and plan to major in science in college.

Eligibility This program is open to graduating high school seniors who have Type 1 diabetes and plan to attend an accredited 4-year university, college, or trade/technical school in any state. Applicants must be planning to major in science. They must be able to demonstrate active involvement in the diabetes community, academic accomplishment, participation in community and/or extracurricular activities, and successful management of the challenges of living with diabetes. Financial need is not considered in the selection process. U.S. citizenship or permanent resident status is required.

Financial data The stipend is $1,000.

Duration 1 year.

Number awarded 1 each year.

Deadline April of each year.

[636]
GEMM LEARNING'S LIVING WITH DYSLEXIA SCHOLARSHIP

Gemm Learning
877 Post Road East, Suite 2
Westport, CT 06880
Toll Free: (877) 914-4366
E-mail: scholarships@gemmlearning.com
Web: www.gemmlearning.com/scholarships.php

Summary To recognize and reward, with college scholarships, students who submit outstanding essays on their dyslexia.

Eligibility This competition is open to students who have dyslexia and are attending or planning to attend college. Applicants must submit an essay of 300 to 500 words on what it has been like to live with dyslexia. Selection is based entirely on the essay.

Financial data The award is a $1,000 scholarship.

Duration The competition is held semiannually.

Additional data This program began in 2013.

Number awarded   2 each year: 1 for fall semester and 1 for spring semester.
Deadline   June of each year for fall semester; November of each year for spring semester.

[637]
GEORGE AND LINDA PRICE SCHOLARSHIP
Hemophilia Association of the Capital Area
8136 Old Keene Mill Road, Suite A312
Springfield, VA 22152
(703) 352-7641   Fax: (540) 427-6589
E-mail: admin@hacacares.org
Web: www.hacacares.org

Summary   To provide financial assistance to individuals with bleeding disorders and their families who are members of the Hemophilia Association of the Capital Area (HACA) and interested in attending college or graduate school in any state.

Eligibility   This program is open to residents of northern Virginia, Montgomery and Prince George's County in Maryland, and Washington, D.C. who have a bleeding disorder and their siblings and parents. Applicants must be members of HACA. They must be 1) high school seniors or graduates who have not yet attended college; 2) full-time freshmen, sophomores, or juniors at a college, university, or vocational/technical school in any state; or 3) college seniors planning to attend graduate school and students already enrolled at a graduate school in any state. Along with their application, they must submit a 500-word essay on what they have done to contribute to the bleeding disorders community and how they plan to contribute to that community in the future. Financial need is not considered in the selection process.

Financial data   The stipend is $2,500.
Duration   1 year; recipients may reapply.
Number awarded   2 each year.
Deadline   May of each year.

[638]
GEORGIA CHAPTER OF THE INTERNATIONAL TRANSPLANT NURSES SOCIETY SCHOLARSHIP
Georgia Transplant Foundation
Attn: Scholarship Program
2201 Macy Drive
Roswell, GA 30076
(770) 457-3796   Fax: (770) 457-7916
E-mail: gtf@gatransplant.org
Web: www.gatransplant.org

Summary   To provide financial assistance to residents of Georgia who are transplant recipients or their siblings or dependents and interested in attending college in any state to work on a degree in health care.

Eligibility   This program is open to residents of Georgia who are entering or continuing at an accredited institution of higher learning in any state to work on a degree in health care. Applicants must be an organ transplant recipient, a dependent of a recipient, a parent of a recipient, a living donor, or the sibling of a recipient (both the sibling

and the recipient must be under 22 years of age). Along with their application, they must submit a 3-page personal statement on their career objectives, how this scholarship will help them attain their goals, and how transplantation has affected their life. Selection is based on that statement, transcripts, high school exit examination scores, ACT/SAT scores, 3 letters of reference, and financial need.

Financial data   The stipend is $1,000.
Duration   1 year; nonrenewable.
Additional data   This program is sponsored by the Georgia Chapter of the International Transplant Nurses Society.
Number awarded   1 each year.
Deadline   April of each year.

[639]
GERTRUDE DAWSON SCHOLARSHIP
Metropolitan Seattle Sickle Cell Task Force
P.O. Box 20194
Seattle, WA 98102
(253) 226-5578   E-mail: info@msscf.org
Web: www.mssctf.org/blog/scholarships-and-internships

Summary   To provide financial assistance to residents of Washington who have sickle cell disease and are attending college in the state.

Eligibility   This program is open to residents of Washington who are currently enrolled at a college, university, or trade/technical school in the state. Applicants must have sickle cell disease. They must have a GPA of 2.5 or higher and be able to demonstrate financial need. Along with their application, they must submit a 1,000-word essay on the impact of sickle cell disease on their lives or on society. U.S. citizenship or permanent resident status is required.

Financial data   The stipend is $5,000. Funds are disbursed directly to the recipient's institution.
Duration   1 year.
Number awarded   1 or more each year.
Deadline   June of each year.

[640]
GREAT LAKES HEMOPHILIA FOUNDATION EDUCATION SCHOLARSHIPS
Great Lakes Hemophilia Foundation
Attn: Program Services Committee
638 North 18th Street, Suite 108
Milwaukee, WI 53233
(414) 937-6782   Toll Free: (888) 797-GLHF
Fax: (414) 257-1225   E-mail: kkoppen@glhf.org
Web: www.glhf.org/what-we-do/scholarships

Summary   To provide financial assistance to Wisconsin residents who have a bleeding disorder (and their families) and are interested in attending college in any state.

Eligibility   This program is open to members of the bleeding disorder community in Wisconsin. Applicants must be attending or planning to attend college, vocational school, technical school, or a certification program in any state. Along with their application, they must submit an essay of 500 to 750 words on their educational and career goals, what they have done to work toward achieving those goals, how the education or training program in which they are enrolled will help them meet their goals, what they consider the most significant challenges associated with living with a bleeding disorder, the opportunities or benefits have those challenges provided them, and how they plan on contributing back to the bleeding disorders community. First priority is given to people affected by bleeding disorders, then to parents of young children with bleeding disorders, and then to spouses of individuals with bleeding disorders. If sufficient funds are available, consideration may be given to siblings and other family members of individuals with a bleeding disorder. Financial need is considered in the selection process.

Financial data Stipends range up to $3,000.

Duration 1 year.

Number awarded Varies each year; recently, 3 were awarded.

Deadline April of each year.

[641]
GUNNAR ESIASON OWN IT SCHOLARSHIP

Boomer Esiason Foundation
c/o Chris McEwan
483 Tenth Avenue, Suite 300
New York, NY 10018
(646) 292-7939   Fax: (646) 292-7945
E-mail: cmcewan@esiason.org
Web: www.esiason.org

Summary To provide financial assistance to high school seniors, undergraduates, and graduate students who have cystic fibrosis (CF) and a resolve to OWN the disease.

Eligibility This program is open to CF patients who are high school seniors or students already working on an undergraduate or graduate degree. Applicants must be able to demonstrate a will to learn and achieve, despite having CF. Along with their application, they must submit 1) a letter from their doctor confirming the diagnosis of CF; 2) information on financial need with a detailed breakdown of tuition costs from their academic institution; 3) transcripts from high school, college, and/or graduate school; 4) a short essay (up to 350 words) on how they think the Boomer Esiason Foundation impacts the CF community; 5) a long essay (more than 350 words) on how they OWN their CF; and 6) a letter of 200 to 350 words from a friend about them and how they OWN their CF.

Financial data The stipend ranges from $1,000 to $5,000. Funds are paid directly to the academic institution to assist in covering the cost of tuition and fees.

Duration 1 year; nonrenewable.

Additional data This program began in 2016.

Number awarded 1 each year.

Deadline September of each year.

[642]
GUTHRIE-KOCH PKU SCHOLARSHIP

National PKU News
6869 Woodlawn Avenue, N.E., Suite 116
Seattle, WA 98115-5469
(206) 525-8140   Fax: (206) 525-5023
E-mail: sarah@pkunews.org
Web: www.pkunews.org/guthrie-koch-scholarship

Summary To provide financial assistance for college to students with phenylketonuria (PKU).

Eligibility This program is open to college-age people from any country who have PKU and are on the required diet. Applicants must be accepted as an undergraduate at an accredited college or technical school before the scholarship is awarded, but they may apply before acceptance is confirmed. Along with their application, they must submit a statement that includes why they are applying for the scholarship, educational objectives and career plans, school and community activities, honors and awards, work history, current diet and how they cope with it on a daily basis, overall experience with PKU, attitudes toward the PKU diet now and in the past, and the influence PKU has had on their life. Selection is based on that statement, academic record, educational and career goals, extracurricular activities, volunteer work, and letters of recommendation. Financial need is considered but is not required; students can be awarded a scholarship without having significant financial need.

Financial data Stipends range from $500 to $3,500.

Duration 1 year.

Additional data This program began in 1998 as the Robert Guthrie PKU Scholarship to honor Dr. Robert Guthrie, who had died in 1995. After the death of Dr. Richard Koch in 2011, the name was changed to recognize his contributions to research on PKU.

Number awarded Varies each year; recently, 8 were awarded.

Deadline February of each year.

[643]
HARVEY SIMON MEMORIAL SCHOLARSHIP

The Simon Cancer Foundation
P.O. Box 25093
Tamarac, FL 33320
(954) 288-8455   E-mail: thescf@gmail.com
Web: www.thescf.org/Scholarships.html

Summary To provide financial assistance to cancer patients and survivors who are currently attending college.

Eligibility This program is open to cancer patients and survivors who are currently enrolled at a 4-year college or university. Applicants must have a GPA of 3.0 or higher and a record of strong leadership and community service. Along with their application, they must submit a 1,000-word essay on how their experience with cancer has driven them to help others. Selection is based on that essay (20%), GPA (30%), leadership (30%), and participation in extracurricular activities (20%).

Financial data The stipend is $1,000.

Duration 1 year; nonrenewable.

Number awarded   Varies each year; recently, 5 were awarded.

Deadline   January of each year.

[644]
HAWKINS SPIZMAN KILGO, LLC CHILDHOOD CANCER AWARENESS SCHOLARSHIP

Hawkins Spizman Kilgo, LLC
1535 Mount Vernon Road, Suite 200
Atlanta, GA 30338
(770) 685-6400   Fax: (770) 685-6403
E-mail: info@hawkinsduilaw.com
Web: www.hawkinsduilaw.com

Summary   To provide financial assistance to undergraduate and graduate students who are survivors of childhood cancer or loved ones of survivors.

Eligibility   This program is open to students currently enrolled or accepted for enrollment as an undergraduate or graduate student at an accredited college or university in any state. Applicants must be a survivor or childhood cancer or a loved one who has been directly affected by childhood cancer. They must have a GPA of 2.8 or higher. Along with their application, they must submit an essay of 500 to 1,000 words on 1 of the following: 1) how childhood cancer affected them; 2) how cancer has influenced their dreams and career goals; or 3) what they would say to a young person who has just been diagnosed with cancer to help them prepare for their future.

Financial data   The stipend is $1,000.

Duration   1 year.

Number awarded   1 each year.

Deadline   July of each year.

[645]
HEATHER BURNS MEMORIAL SCHOLARSHIPS

Heather Burns Memorial Scholarship Fund
1159 North Detroit Avenue
Tulsa, OK 74106
(918) 582-1515   E-mail: info@hbmsf.org
Web: www.hbmsf.org/home.html

Summary   To provide financial assistance for college to high school seniors in Oklahoma who have sickle cell anemia disease or other life-threatening disease.

Eligibility   This program is open to seniors graduating from high schools in Oklahoma who have been accepted to a college, university, or other school of higher learning in any state. Applicants must have been diagnosed with sickle cell anemia disease or other life-threatening disease (e.g., lupus, diabetes). They must have a high school GPA of 2.5 or higher. Along with their application, they must submit a current high school transcript, SAT/ACT scores, proof of U.S. citizenship or permanent residency, 3 letters of reference, and a 500-word essay describing their goals for college, their personal and professional ambitions, why they deserve to receive this scholarship, and any special hardships or financial needs.

Financial data   A stipend is awarded (amount not specified).

Duration   1 year.

Additional data   This program began in 2010.

Number awarded   Several each year.

Deadline   September of each year.

[646]
HEMOPHILIA ASSOCIATION OF NEW JERSEY SCHOLARSHIPS

Hemophilia Association of New Jersey
Attn: Scholarship Committee
197 Route 18 South, Suite 206 North
East Brunswick, NJ 08816
(732) 249-6000   Fax: (732) 249-7999
E-mail: hemnj@comcast.net
Web: www.hanj.org/scholar.html

Summary   To provide financial assistance to New Jersey residents who have a bleeding disorder and are interested in attending college or graduate school in any state.

Eligibility   This program is open to New Jersey residents who have a bleeding disorder (Hemophilia A or B, von Willebrand Disease, or a similar blood coagulation disorder). Applicants must be attending or planning to attend an accredited college or university in any state as an undergraduate or graduate student. They must have at least a 2.5 GPA, have been actively involved in extracurricular activities, and be able to demonstrate financial need. Along with their application, they must submit a family financial profile, official transcripts, and a brief essay (up to 2 pages) on how they meet the eligibility criteria. Membership in the Hemophilia Association of New Jersey is required.

Financial data   The stipend is $1,500 per year for undergraduates or $2,000 per year for graduate students.

Duration   1 year; undergraduate scholarships may be renewed for up to 3 additional years and graduate scholarships may be renewed 1 additional year.

Additional data   The undergraduate scholarships include the Robert and Dennis Kelly Memorial Scholarship. The graduate scholarship is designated the Paul D. Amitrani Scholarship.

Number awarded   5 each year: 4 undergraduate scholarships and 1 graduate fellowship.

Deadline   April of each year.

[647]
HEMOPHILIA FEDERATION OF AMERICA EDUCATIONAL SCHOLARSHIPS

Hemophilia Federation of America
Attn: Scholarship Committee
820 First Street, N.E., Suite 720
Washington, DC 20002
(202) 675-6984   Toll Free: (800) 230-9797
Fax: (202) 675-6983
E-mail: scholarship@hemophiliafed.org
Web: www.hemophiliafed.org

Summary   To provide financial assistance for college to students who have a blood clotting disorder.

Eligibility   This program is open to high school seniors and current college students who have a blood clotting disorder. Applicants must be attending or planning to attend an accredited 2- or 4-year college, university, or trade school in the United States. Along with their application, they must submit a 1-page essay on their goals and aspirations and how the blood clotting community has played a part in their lives. Financial need is also considered in the selection process.

Financial data The stipend is $2,000 per year.

Duration 1 year; may be renewed.

Number awarded 2 each year.

Deadline April of each year.

[648]
HEMOPHILIA FEDERATION OF AMERICA MEDICAL/HEALTHCARE SERVICES EDUCATIONAL SCHOLARSHIP

Hemophilia Federation of America
Attn: Scholarship Committee
820 First Street, N.E., Suite 720
Washington, DC 20002
(202) 675-6984   Toll Free: (800) 230-9797
Fax: (202) 675-6983
E-mail: scholarship@hemophiliafed.org
Web: www.hemophiliafed.org

Summary To provide financial assistance to undergraduate and graduate students who have a bleeding disorder and are working on a degree in a medical or health-related field.

Eligibility This program is open to undergraduate and graduate students who have a bleeding disorder. Applicants must be preparing for a career in medicine or a health-related field. Along with their application, they must submit an essay of 1 to 2 pages on why they chose to study in their field and why they think it is the right path for them. Financial need is considered in the selection process.

Financial data The grant is $4,000.

Duration 1 year.

Number awarded 1 each year.

Deadline April of each year.

[649]
HEMOPHILIA FOUNDATION OF MICHIGAN ACADEMIC SCHOLARSHIPS

Hemophilia Foundation of Michigan
Attn: Outreach and Community Education Manager
1921 West Michigan Avenue
Ypsilanti, MI 48197
(734) 544-0015   Toll Free: (800) 482-3041
Fax: (734) 544-0095   E-mail: lclothier@hfmich.org
Web: www.hfmich.org/?module=Page&sID=scholarships

Summary To provide financial assistance to Michigan residents with hemophilia and their families who are interested in attending college in any state.

Eligibility This program is open to high school seniors, high school graduates, and currently-enrolled college students who are Michigan residents and have hemophilia or another bleeding disorder. Family members of people with bleeding disorders and family members of people who

have died from the complications of a bleeding disorder are also eligible. Applicants must submit a 300-word statement on their educational and career goals, the role that the bleeding disorder has played in influencing those goals, and how receiving the scholarship will help them to meet those goals. Selection is based on that statement, academic merit, employment status, reference letters, financial need, and the impact of bleeding disorder on educational activities.

Financial data The stipend is $2,500.

Duration 1 year; recipients may reapply.

Number awarded 2 each year.

Deadline March of each year.

[650]
HEMOPHILIA FOUNDATION OF MINNESOTA/ DAKOTAS SCHOLARSHIPS

Hemophilia Foundation of Minnesota/Dakotas
Attn: Scholarship Program
750 South Plaza Drive, Suite 207
Mendota Heights, MN 55120-1505
(651) 406-8655   Toll Free: (800) 994-HFMD
Fax: (651) 406-8656
E-mail: hemophiliafound@visi.com
Web: www.hfmd.org/resources/scholarships

Summary To provide financial assistance to residents of Minnesota, North Dakota, and South Dakota who have a bleeding disorder and are interested in attending college in any state.

Eligibility This program is open to residents of Minnesota, North Dakota, and South Dakota who have an inherited bleeding disorder and/or are patients at a hemophilia treatment center in those states. Applicants must be participating in programs and services of the Hemophilia Foundation of Minnesota/Dakotas. They must be attending or planning to attend a college or university in any state. Financial need is considered in the selection process.

Financial data The stipend is $1,000. Funds are paid to the academic institution.

Duration 1 year.

Number awarded 10 each year.

Deadline May of each year.

[651]
HEMOPHILIA OF INDIANA JUDY MOORE MEMORIAL SCHOLARSHIP

Hemophilia of Indiana
Attn: Community Outreach Coordinator
6910 North Shadeland Avenue, Suite 140
Indianapolis, IN 46220
(317) 570-0039   Toll Free: (800) 241-2873
Fax: (317) 570-0058
Web: www.hemophiliaofindiana.org

Summary To provide financial assistance to residents of Indiana who have a bleeding disorder and are interested in attending college or graduate school in any state.

Eligibility This program is open to residents of Indiana who have been diagnosed with a bleeding disorder, including (but not limited to) von Willebrand's disease, hemophilia A, or hemophilia B. Applications must be enrolled, or planning to enroll as an undergraduate or graduate student at a college, university, junior college, or vocational school in any state. Selection is based on academic standing, an essay, and recommendations.

Financial data A stipend is awarded (amount not specified).

Duration 1 year.

Number awarded 1 or more each year.

Deadline Deadline not specified.

[652]
HEMOPHILIA OF IOWA SCHOLARSHIPS

Hemophilia of Iowa, Inc.
Attn: Scholarship Committee
6300 Rockwell Drive, N.E., Suite 104
Cedar Rapids, IA 52402-7220
Toll Free: (319) 393-4007
E-mail: hoi_director@hemophiliaofiowa.com
Web: www.hemophiliaofiowa.org/scholarships.html

Summary To provide financial assistance to members of Hemophilia of Iowa who are interested in attending college in any state.

Eligibility This program is open to members of the sponsoring organization who either have hemophilia (or a related bleeding disorder) or are the immediate family member (caregiver, sibling, child) of someone who has hemophilia or a related bleeding disorder. Applicants may be graduating high school seniors or students currently enrolled at an accredited college, university, or trade school in any state. Along with their application, they must submit brief statements on 1) their short- and long-range career plans; and 2) their personal background related to the bleeding disorder community. Selection is based on personal qualities and community service. Applicants who have a record of outstanding support for the mission of Hemophilia of Iowa are considered for supplemental funding provided by the John Heisner Scholarship and the Dude Cremer Scholarship.

Financial data The stipend is $1,000 for students with a bleeding disorder or $750 for family members. Applicants selected for the supplemental funding provided by the named scholarships receive an additional $500.

Duration 1 semester; recipients may reapply.

Number awarded Varies each year; recently, 20 were awarded.

Deadline April of each year.

[653]
HSC ACADEMIC SCHOLARSHIP PROGRAM

Hemophilia of South Carolina
Attn: Academic Scholarship Awards Program
439 Congaree Road, Suite 5
Greenville, SC 29607
(864) 350-9941   Fax: (864) 244-8287
E-mail: Info@hemophiliasc.org
Web: www.hemophiliasc.org/services

Summary To provide financial assistance to residents of South Carolina who are affiliated with the bleeding disorders community and interested in attending college in any state.

Eligibility This program is open to residents of South Carolina who are persons with a bleeding disorder or children, siblings, parents, or spouses of someone with a bleeding disorder. Applicants must be enrolled or planning to enroll at an accredited college, university, or vocational/ technical school in any state. Along with their application, they must submit transcripts that include SAT scores; a summary about themselves that includes a statement of their goals for the future, volunteer work, awards, and organizations to which they belong; and an essay on the impact that hemophilia has had on them and their family. Selection is based on that essay, academic merit, leadership qualities, reference letters, and financial need.

Financial data The stipend ranges from $500 to $1,500. Funds are paid directly to the recipient's school.

Duration 1 year.

Number awarded Up to 5 each year.

Deadline May of each year.

[654]
HUEY AND ANGELINA WILSON NONTRADITIONAL SCHOLARSHIPS

Louisiana Hemophilia Foundation
Attn: Scholarship Committee
3636 South Sherwood Forest Boulevard, Suite 390
Baton Rouge, LA 70816-5211
(225) 291-1675   Toll Free: (800) 749-1680
Fax: (225) 291-1679   E-mail: contact@lahemo.org
Web: www.lahemo.org/services/scholarships

Summary To provide financial assistance for college in the state to Louisiana residents who are nontraditional students and a hemophilia patient or the parent of a patient.

Eligibility This program is open to residents of Louisiana who are a hemophilia patient or the parent of a patient. Applicants must be enrolled or planning to enroll at a Louisiana college or university as a nontraditional student. Along with their application, they must submit a 250-word essay on why they should receive this scholarship.

Financial data The stipend is $1,000 per semester.

Duration 1 semester. Recipients may reapply if they remain enrolled full time, have a GPA of 2.75 or higher, and provide 8 hours of community service to the sponsoring organization.

Number awarded Varies each semester; the foundation first awards scholarships to traditional students; if funds remain, it may award scholarships to qualified nontraditional students.

Deadline June of each year for fall semester; December of each year for spring semester.

[655]
HUEY AND ANGELINA WILSON TRADITIONAL SCHOLARSHIPS

Louisiana Hemophilia Foundation
Attn: Scholarship Committee
3636 South Sherwood Forest Boulevard, Suite 390
Baton Rouge, LA 70816-5211
(225) 291-1675   Toll Free: (800) 749-1680
Fax: (225) 291-1679   E-mail: contact@lahemo.org
Web: www.lahemo.org/services/scholarships

Summary To provide financial assistance to Louisiana residents who have hemophilia or another bleeding disorder and are interested in attending college in the state.

Eligibility This program is open to residents of Louisiana who have hemophilia or another bleeding disorder. Applicants must be enrolled or planning to enroll at an accredited Louisiana college or university as an undergraduate student. They must have completed a high school curriculum to qualify for the TOPS program. Along with their application, they must submit a 250-word essay on why they should receive this scholarship.

Financial data The stipend is $1,000 per semester.

Duration 1 semester. Recipients may reapply if they provide 8 hours of community service to the sponsoring organization each semester.

Number awarded Up to 15 each semester.

Deadline June of each year for fall semester; December of each year for spring semester.

[656]
HYDROCEPHALUS ASSOCIATION SCHOLARSHIPS

Hydrocephalus Association
4340 East West Highway, Suite 905
Bethesda, MD 20814
(301) 202-3811   Toll Free: (888) 598-3789, ext. 22
Fax: (301) 202-3813
E-mail: scholarship@hydroassoc.com
Web: www.hydroassoc.org/scholarships

Summary To provide financial assistance for college or graduate school to young adults with hydrocephalus.

Eligibility This program is open to individuals between the ages of 17 and 30 who have hydrocephalus. The scholarship must be used for an educational purpose, including, but not limited to, a 4-year or junior college, a high school postgraduate year to prepare for college, a technical or trade school, an accredited employment training program, or a graduate program. Applicants may be in the process of applying to a program or university or already enrolled. They must include essays on their hobbies, interests, and activities; their educational and career goals; how having hydrocephalus has impacted their life; how they would help others with hydrocephalus; and how the scholarship will help them. Financial need is not considered in the selection process.

Financial data The stipend is $1,000. Funds may be used for tuition, books, housing, or any other educationally-related expense.

Duration 1 year; nonrenewable.

Additional data This program includes 5 named scholarships: the Gerald Schwartz Fudge Scholarship, established in 1994, the Morris L. and Rebecca Ziskind Memorial Scholarship, established in 2001, the Anthony Abbene Scholarship, established in 2002, the Justin Scot Alston Memorial Scholarship, established in 2004, and the Mario J. Tocco Hydrocephalus Foundation Scholarship, established in 2007.

Number awarded Varies each year; recently, 8 were awarded.

Deadline April of each year.

[657]
ICEC DR. LESLIE P. GRAHAM SCHOLARSHIP

Illinois Council for Exceptional Children
c/o Jeanette Ortery, Scholarship Co-Chair
18 Field Point Road
Montgomery, IL 60538
(630) 892-8429   E-mail: 01Jortery@gmail.com
Web: illinoiscec.org/iced-dr-leslie-p-graham-scholarship

Summary To provide financial assistance to high school seniors in Illinois who have a disability and plan to attend college in the state.

Eligibility This program is open to seniors graduating from high schools in Illinois who plan to enter a college, university, or trade or technical school in the state. Applicants must have a verified disability (copy of IEP must be submitted) and a GPA of 2.5 or higher. They must be able to demonstrate financial need.

Financial data A stipend is awarded (amount not specified).

Duration 1 year.

Number awarded 1 or more each year.

Deadline March of each year.

[658]
INDIANA DONOR NETWORK FOUNDATION SCHOLARSHIP

Indiana Donor Network, Inc.
Attn: Foundation/Care Council
3760 Guion Road
Indianapolis, IN 46222-1618
(317) 685-0389   Toll Free: (888) 275-4676
E-mail: info@INDonorNetwork.org
Web: www.indianadonornetwork.org

Summary To provide financial assistance to residents of Indiana who have been involved in organ or tissue donation and are interested in attending college in any state.

Eligibility This program is open to family members of Indiana organ and tissue donors as well as living organ donors, transplant recipients, people waiting for organs, and their families. Applicants must be enrolled or planning to enroll full or part time at a college, university, or technical school in any state. They must have a GPA of 2.0 or higher. There are no age limitations and nontraditional students are encouraged to apply. Along with their application, they must submit a 2- to 5-page essay on their career goals, experience with organ or tissue donation and/or transplantation, and personal goals.

Financial data   A stipend is awarded (amount not specified).

Duration   1 year; nonrenewable.

Number awarded   Varies each year.

Deadline   March of each year.

[659]
INDIANA DONOR NETWORK SCHOLARSHIPS

Indiana Donor Network
Attn: Foundation
3760 Guion Road
Indianapolis, IN 46222-1618
(317) 685-0389   Toll Free: (888) 275-4676
E-mail: info@INDonorNetwork.org
Web: www.indianadonornetwork.org

Summary   To provide financial assistance for college attendance in any state to Indiana residents who are organ, tissue, or eye transplant donors, recipients, candidates, or their families.

Eligibility   This program is open to Indiana residents who are organ, tissue, or eye transplant donors, recipients, candidates, or relatives (including spouses, parents, children, grandchildren, siblings, aunts, uncles, nieces, nephews, and cousins). Applicants must be high school seniors or students already attending a college or technical school in any state on a full- or part-time basis. They must have a GPA of 2.0 or higher; high school seniors must be in the top 50% of their class. Along with their application, they must submit a 1,500-word essay describing their career goals, experience with organ or tissue donation and/or transplantation, and personal goals. Financial need is considered in the selection process.

Financial data   Recently, stipends were $3,000, $2,000, or $1,000.

Duration   1 year; nonrenewable.

Additional data   This organization was formerly named the Indiana Organ Procurement Organization (IOPO).

Number awarded   Varies each year; recently, 3 were awarded: 1 at $3,000, 1 at $2,000, and 1 at $1,000.

Deadline   March of each year.

[660]
ISABELLE CHRISTENSON MEMORIAL SCHOLARSHIP

Izzie's Gifts of Hope Foundation
c/o Center for Organ Recovery and Education
204 Sigma Drive
RIDC Park
Pittsburgh, PA 15238
(724) 591-6009   E-mail: izziesgifts@gmail.com
Web: www.izziesgifts.org/scholarships.php

Summary   To provide financial assistance for college to organ transplant candidates, donors, recipients, and their families.

Eligibility   This program is open to organ transplant candidates, recipients, donor family members, and immediate family members of a transplant candidate or recipi-

ent. Applicants must be attending or planning to attend a college, university, or trade/technical school. Along with their application, they must submit an explanation of how donation/transplantation has influenced their life; an explanation of what they have done or what you will do to promote organ, tissue and cornea donation; a description of any community service in which they have taken part; a statement on their educational and career goals; and 2 letters of recommendation.

Financial data   A stipend is awarded (amount not specified).

Duration   1 year; nonrenewable.

Additional data   This program awarded its first scholarship in 2010.

Number awarded   Varies each year; recently, 7 were awarded.

Deadline   March of each year.

[661]
JABEZ LEGACY SCHOLARSHIP

Pride Foundation
Attn: Educational Programs Director
2014 East Madison Street, Suite 300
Seattle, WA 98122
(206) 323-3318   Toll Free: (800) 735-7287
Fax: (206) 323-1017
E-mail: scholarships@pridefoundation.org
Web: www.pridefoundation.org

Summary   To provide financial assistance to lesbian, gay, bisexual, transgender, and queer (LGBTQ) residents of Washington who have faced barriers and are interested in attending college in any state.

Eligibility   This program is open to residents of Washington who identify as LGBTQ. Applicants must be attending or planning to attend college in any state to work on an undergraduate degree in any field. They must have faced significant barriers to their pursuit of education, such as learning disabilities or lack of family or financial support. Selection is based on demonstrated commitment to social justice and LGBTQ concerns, leadership in their communities, the ability to be academically and personally successful, and (to some extent) financial need.

Financial data   Recently, the average stipend for all scholarships awarded by the foundation was approximately $4,160. Funds are paid directly to the recipient's school.

Duration   1 year; recipients may reapply.

Additional data   This program began in 2013.

Number awarded   1 each year. Since it began offering scholarships in 1993, the foundation has awarded a total of more than $4.0 million to more than 1,500 recipients.

Deadline   January of each year.

[662]
JACKIE SPELLMAN SCHOLARSHIPS

Jackie Spellman Scholarship Foundation
935 Eldridge Road
Box 200
Sugar Land, TX 77478
Toll Free: (888) 553-JSSF
E-mail: jackiespellmanfoundation@gmail.com
Web: www.jackiespellmanbenefit.org/scholarship.shtml

Summary To provide financial assistance for college or graduate school to students who have or whose family member has leukemia or lymphoma.

Eligibility This program is open to high school seniors, community college and 4-year university students, and graduate students who are leukemia or lymphoma survivors, patients, and/or children, siblings, or parents of leukemia or lymphoma patients. Applicants must be U.S. citizens and enrolled or planning to enroll full time. They must have a GPA of 3.0 or higher and be able to demonstrate financial need. Along with their application, they must submit transcripts; SAT and/or ACT test scores; documentation of financial need; a letter describing any special circumstances that have impacted their academic performance, community service, or leadership activities (if relevant); and an essay of 600 to 800 words describing how leukemia or lymphoma has affected their life, their future plans and desired career path, and how this scholarship will impact them. Students majoring in health or nursing-related majors may receive priority.

Financial data Stipends range from $1,000 to $5,000.

Duration 1 year.

Number awarded Approximately 15 each year.

Deadline April of each year.

[663]
JACOB N. SHANBERGE, M.D. MEMORIAL SCHOLARSHIP

Great Lakes Hemophilia Foundation
Attn: Program Services Committee
638 North 18th Street, Suite 108
Milwaukee, WI 53233
(414) 937-6782   Toll Free: (888) 797-GLHF
Fax: (414) 257-1225   E-mail: kkoppen@glhf.org
Web: www.glhf.org/what-we-do/scholarships

Summary To provide financial assistance to Wisconsin residents who have a bleeding disorder (and their families) and are interested in attending college in any state.

Eligibility This program is open to members of the bleeding disorder community in Wisconsin. Applicants must be attending or planning to attend college, vocational school, technical school, or a certification program in any state to prepare for a career in science or medicine. Along with their application, they must submit an essay of 500 to 750 words on their educational and career goals, what they have done to work toward achieving those goals, how the education or training program in which they are enrolled will help them meet their goals, what they consider the most significant challenges associated with living with a bleeding disorder, the opportunities or benefits have

those challenges provided them, and how they plan on contributing back to the bleeding disorders community. First priority is given to people affected by bleeding disorders, then to parents of young children with bleeding disorders, and then to spouses of individuals with bleeding disorders. If sufficient funds are available, consideration may be given to siblings and other family members of individuals with a bleeding disorder. Financial need is considered in the selection process.

Financial data Stipends range up to $3,000.

Duration 1 year.

Number awarded 1 each year.

Deadline April of each year.

[664]
JAMES AND PATRICIA SOOD SCHOLARSHIP

Ulman Cancer Fund for Young Adults
Attn: Scholarship Committee
921 East Fort Avenue, Suite 325
Baltimore, MD 21230
(410) 964-0202   Toll Free: (888) 393-FUND
Fax: (888) 964-0402
E-mail: scholarship@ulmanfund.org
Web: www.ulmanfund.org/scholarships

Summary To provide financial assistance to students who have been diagnosed with cancer or have or have lost a family member with cancer and are interested in working on an undergraduate or graduate degree in education.

Eligibility This program is open to students who 1) have been diagnosed with cancer; 2) have a parent or sibling living with cancer; or 3) have lost a parent or sibling to cancer. Applicants must be attending, or planning to attend, a college or university in any state to work on an undergraduate or graduate degree in education. The first diagnosis of cancer (whether of the applicant, a parent, or sibling) must have occurred after the applicant was 15 years of age. Along with their application, they must submit a 500-word essay or 3-minute video on either 1) a letter that they would have liked to receive during their cancer experience; or 2) what they would tell the young adults who participate in the sponsor's summer-long drive to support the organization about being a young adult impacted by cancer. U.S. citizenship or permanent resident status is required.

Financial data The stipend is $2,500. Funds are paid directly to the educational institution.

Duration 1 year.

Additional data Recipients are obligated to organize and run a bone marrow registry drive with the support of Delete Blood Cancer and There Goes My Hero.

Number awarded 1 each year.

Deadline March of each year.

[665]
JAMES HAMILTON MEMORIAL SCHOLARSHIP

Sangre de Oro, Inc.
6301 Fourth Street, N.W., Suite 6
Albuquerque, NM 87107
(505) 341-9321   E-mail: sdo@sandredeoro.org
Web: www.sangredeoro.org

Summary To provide financial assistance to residents of New Mexico who have hemophilia and are interested in attending college in any state.

Eligibility This program is open to residents of New Mexico who have hemophilia and are U.S. citizens or eligible non-citizens. Applicants must be enrolled or accepted for enrollment as a regular student working on a degree or certificate in an eligible program in any state. They must be able to demonstrate financial need and evidence of application for at least 2 other sources of financial aid. A personal interview is required.

Financial data A stipend is awarded (amount not specified).

Duration 1 year; may be renewed, provided the recipient maintains a GPA of 2.5 or higher.

Number awarded 1 or more each year.

Deadline July of each year for fall semester; November of each year for spring semester.

[666]
JAMIE L. ROBERTS MEMORIAL SCHOLARSHIP

Ulman Cancer Fund for Young Adults
Attn: Scholarship Committee
921 East Fort Avenue, Suite 325
Baltimore, MD 21230
(410) 964-0202   Toll Free: (888) 393-FUND
Fax: (888) 964-0402
E-mail: scholarship@ulmanfund.org
Web: www.ulmanfund.org/scholarships

Summary To provide financial assistance for college or graduate school to students who have been diagnosed with cancer or have or have lost a family member with cancer.

Eligibility This program is open to students who 1) have been diagnosed with cancer; 2) have a parent or sibling living with cancer; or 3) have lost a parent or sibling to cancer. Applicants must be attending, or planning to attend, a college or university in any state to work on an undergraduate, graduate, or professional degree. They should demonstrate the qualities of the program's namesake-an infectious positive attitude, love of adventure, and ability to inspire others to achieve higher goals. The first diagnosis of cancer (whether of the applicant, a parent, or sibling) must have occurred after the applicant was 15 years of age. Along with their application, they must submit a 500-word essay or 3-minute video on either 1) a letter that they would have liked to receive during their cancer experience; or 2) what they would tell the young adults who participate in the sponsor's summer-long drive to support the organization about being a young adult

impacted by cancer. U.S. citizenship or permanent resident status is required.

Financial data The stipend is $2,500. Funds are paid directly to the educational institution.

Duration 1 year.

Additional data This program, which began in 2014, is funded by the 4K for Cancer, an organization of college students who ride bicycles across the country every summer and raise funds for cancer. Recipients are obligated to organize and run a bone marrow registry drive with the support of Delete Blood Cancer and There Goes My Hero.

Number awarded 6 each year.

Deadline March of each year.

[667]
JASON ACKERMAN MEMORIAL SCHOLARSHIPS

Jason Ackerman Foundation
Attn: Executive Director
18761 Hillstone Drive
Odessa, FL 33556
(813) 91-JASON
E-mail: info@jasonackermanfoundation.org
Web: www.becauseofjason.org/programs

Summary To provide financial assistance to residents of Florida who have survived a serious illness and are interested in attending college in the state.

Eligibility This program is open to residents of Florida who are enrolled or planning to enroll at a public college, university, community college, or vocational/technical school in the state. Applicants must have survived a tragic circumstance due to illness or otherwise before the age of 21. They must have a GPA of 2.5 or higher. Awards are presented to applicants who demonstrate the greatest financial need and the greatest desire to be a positive influence in the community.

Financial data A stipend is awarded (amount not specified).

Duration 1 year; may be renewed, provided the recipient maintains a GPA of 2.5 or higher and completes at least 20 hours of community service.

Additional data This program began in 2011.

Number awarded 1 or more each year.

Deadline May of each year.

[668]
JAY CUTLER ATHLETIC SCHOLARSHIPS

Diabetes Scholars Foundation
310 Busse Highway, Suite 256
Park Ridge, IL 60068
(312) 215-9861   Fax: (847) 991-8739
E-mail: m.podjasek@diabetesscholars.org
Web: www.diabetesscholars.org/college-scholarship

Summary To provide financial assistance for college to high school seniors who have diabetes and plan to participate in sports.

Eligibility This program is open to graduating high school seniors who have Type 1 diabetes and plan to attend an accredited 4-year university, college, or trade/

technical school in any state. Applicants must be planning to play a competitive sport in college. They must be able to demonstrate active involvement in the diabetes community, academic accomplishment, participation in community and/or extracurricular activities, and successful management of the challenges of living with diabetes. Financial need is not considered in the selection process. U.S. citizenship or permanent resident status is required.

Financial data   The stipend is $5,000.

Duration   1 year.

Number awarded   5 each year.

Deadline   April of each year.

[669]
JAY FRANKE SCHOLARSHIP

Diabetes Scholars Foundation
310 Busse Highway, Suite 256
Park Ridge, IL 60068
(312) 215-9861   Fax: (847) 991-8739
E-mail: m.podjasek@diabetesscholars.org
Web: www.diabetesscholars.org/college-scholarship

Summary   To provide financial assistance to high school seniors who have diabetes and plan to major in the arts in college.

Eligibility   This program is open to graduating high school seniors who have Type 1 diabetes and plan to attend an accredited 4-year university, college, or trade/technical school in any state. Applicants must be planning to major in the arts (e.g., music, theater, dance). They must be able to demonstrate active involvement in the diabetes community, academic accomplishment, participation in community and/or extracurricular activities, and successful management of the challenges of living with diabetes. Financial need is not considered in the selection process. U.S. citizenship or permanent resident status is required.

Financial data   The stipend is $5,000.

Duration   1 year.

Number awarded   2 each year.

Deadline   April of each year.

[670]
JC RUNYON FOUNDATION SCHOLARSHIPS

JC Runyon Foundation
P.O. Box 383251
Germantown, TN 38183-3251
(901) 969-3115
E-mail: nshaheen@jcrunyonfoundation.org
Web: jcrunyonfoundation.org/application-process

Summary   To provide financial assistance for college to persons of any age who have struggled with substance abuse and/or mental illness.

Eligibility   This program is open to students who are entering or continuing undergraduates at an accredited college, university, or trade school. Applicants must have completed at least 1 inpatient stay at an accredited psychiatric facility, substance abuse center, or similar behavioral health treatment center. There are no age restrictions or specific time frame between high school graduation and

college. Along with their application, they must submit 1) an essay of any length on their journey through substance abuse and/or mental illness, including their future plans, personal history of treatment, leadership potential, and how this funding will help them achieve their goals; 2) letters of recommendation from a guidance counselor, teacher, school administrator, therapist/psychiatrist/psychologist, physician, or other qualified person; and 3) academic record, including GPA and SAT/ACT scores.

Financial data   The stipend is $3,000.

Duration   1 year.

Number awarded   1 or more each year.

Deadline   May of each year.

[671]
JEFFREY P. MEYER MEMORIAL SCHOLARSHIP

Ulman Cancer Fund for Young Adults
Attn: Scholarship Committee
921 East Fort Avenue, Suite 325
Baltimore, MD 21230
(410) 964-0202   Toll Free: (888) 393-FUND
Fax: (888) 964-0402
E-mail: scholarship@ulmanfund.org
Web: www.ulmanfund.org/scholarships

Summary   To provide financial assistance for college or graduate school to young adults who have cancer or are cancer survivors.

Eligibility   This program is open to students who are between 18 and 25 years of age and have battled cancer or are currently undergoing active treatment. The first diagnosis of cancer must have occurred after they were 15 years of age. Applicants must be attending or planning to attend a 2- or 4-year college or university to work on an undergraduate or graduate degree. They must be U.S. citizens or permanent residents. Along with their application, they must submit a 500-word essay or 3-minute video on either 1) a letter that they would have liked to receive during their cancer experience; or 2) what they would tell the young adults who participate in the sponsor's summer-long drive to support the organization about being a young adult impacted by cancer. In the selection process, preference is given to applicants who embody the words of the program's namesake to "stay positive, stay realistic, and have the courage to take control of your life."

Financial data   The stipend is $2,500. Funds are paid directly to the educational institution.

Duration   1 year.

Additional data   Recipients are obligated to organize and run a bone marrow registry drive with the support of Delete Blood Cancer and There Goes My Hero.

Number awarded   1 each year.

Deadline   March of each year.

[672]
JERRY CAHILL YOU CANNOT FAIL SCHOLARSHIPS

Boomer Esiason Foundation
c/o Chris McEwan
483 Tenth Avenue, Suite 300
New York, NY 10018
(646) 292-7939   Fax: (646) 292-7945
E-mail: cmcewan@esiason.org
Web: www.esiason.org

Summary To provide financial assistance for college to undergraduate students who have been involved in athletics and who have cystic fibrosis (CF).

Eligibility This program is open to CF patients who have completed at least 1 semester of undergraduate course work. Applicants must be student-athletes who "don't let the disease get in their way of living lives filled with purpose, passion, optimism, and courage." Along with their application, they must submit a letter from their doctor confirming the diagnosis of CF and a list of daily medications, information on financial need, a detailed breakdown of tuition costs from their academic institution, transcripts, and a 2-page essay on 1) their postgraduation goals; and 2) the importance of compliance with CF therapies and what they practice on a daily basis to stay healthy. Selection is based on academic ability, athletic ability, character, leadership potential, service to the community, financial need, and daily compliance to CF therapy. Male and female students compete separately.

Financial data The stipend is $5,000. Funds are paid directly to the academic institution to assist in covering the cost of tuition and fees.

Duration 1 year; nonrenewable.

Additional data This program began in 2013.

Number awarded 2 each year: 1 to a male and 1 to a female.

Deadline April of each year.

[673]
JESSICA BETH SCHWARTZ MEMORIAL SCHOLARSHIP

Gift of Life Donor Program
Attn: Volunteer Liaison
401 North Third Street
Philadelphia, PA 19123-4101
(215) 557-8090, ext. 1138
Toll Free: (800) DONORS-1
E-mail: kantczak@donors1.org
Web: www.donors1.org/patient/resources/jessiesday

Summary To provide financial assistance to transplant recipients who live in the service area of the Gift of Life Donor Program and are interested in attending college in any state.

Eligibility This program is open to recipients of solid organ transplants who live in the eastern half of Pennsylvania, southern New Jersey, or Delaware. Applicants must be younger than 25 years of age and either graduating high school seniors or students currently enrolled at a 2- or 4-year college, university, or trade/technical school in any state. Along with their application, they must submit 1) a 200-word essay describing an educational initiative to promote organ and tissue donation and transplantation awareness in high school or college students; 2) a 500-word personal statement describing their transplant story and extracurricular and/or volunteer activities; 3) letters of reference; and 4) a current transcript. Financial need is not considered in the selection process.

Financial data The stipend is $2,500.

Duration 1 year.

Number awarded Up to 4 each year.

Deadline April of each year.

[674]
JILL M. BALBONI MEMORIAL SCHOLARSHIPS

Cystic Fibrosis Scholarship Foundation
1555 Sherman Avenue, Suite 116
Evanston, IL 60201
(847) 328-0127   Fax: (847) 328-4525
E-mail: mkbcfsf@aol.com
Web: www.cfscholarship.org/scholarships

Summary To provide financial assistance for college to high school seniors who have cystic fibrosis (CF).

Eligibility This program is open to high school seniors who have CF and are planning to enroll in college (either a 2- or 4-year program) or vocational school. Applicants must have a GPA of 3.2 or higher and scores of at least 1750 on the SAT or 25 on the ACT. The must have a record of giving back to their community through volunteer work, speaking engagements, club and organization participation, or other activities. Along with their application, they must submit a 500-word essay on how they exemplify the spirit of the program's namesake, using concrete examples to show their enthusiasm for life and their "can do" attitude. Selection is based on academic achievement, leadership, and financial need.

Financial data The stipend is $1,250 per year.

Duration 4 years, provided the recipient remains enrolled full time and maintains a GPA of 3.0 or higher.

Additional data This program began in 2014.

Number awarded 2 each year.

Deadline March of each year.

[675]
JILL WEAVER STARKMAN SCHOLARSHIP

Ulman Cancer Fund for Young Adults
Attn: Scholarship Committee
921 East Fort Avenue, Suite 325
Baltimore, MD 21230
(410) 964-0202   Toll Free: (888) 393-FUND
Fax: (888) 964-0402
E-mail: scholarship@ulmanfund.org
Web: www.ulmanfund.org/scholarships

Summary To provide financial assistance for college or graduate school to students who have been diagnosed with cancer or have or have lost a family member with cancer.

Eligibility This program is open to students who 1) have been diagnosed with cancer; 2) have a parent or sibling living with cancer; or 3) have lost a parent or sibling to cancer. Applicants must be attending, or planning to attend, a college or university in any state to work on an undergraduate, graduate, or professional degree. They should demonstrate the qualities of the program's namesake-the spirit of adventure and compassion and skill for communicating with humans and animals alike. The first diagnosis of cancer (whether of the applicant, a parent, or sibling) must have occurred after the applicant was 15 years of age. Along with their application, they must submit a 500-word essay or 3-minute video on either 1) a letter that they would have liked to receive during their cancer experience; or 2) what they would tell the young adults who participate in the sponsor's summer-long drive to support the organization about being a young adult impacted by cancer. U.S. citizenship or permanent resident status is required.

Financial data The stipend is $2,500. Funds are paid directly to the educational institution.

Duration 1 year.

Additional data This program began in 2012. Recipients are obligated to organize and run a bone marrow registry drive with the support of Delete Blood Cancer and There Goes My Hero.

Number awarded 1 each year.

Deadline March of each year.

[676]
JIM DAVIES SCHOLARSHIPS

Epilepsy Foundation of Greater Chicago
Attn: Mary Jo Perlongo, Scholarship Committee
17 North State Street, Suite 650
Chicago, IL 60602
(312) 939-8622   Toll Free: (800) 273-6027
E-mail: mperlongo@epilepsychicago.org
Web: www.epilepsychicago.org

Summary To provide financial assistance to residents of Illinois who have epilepsy and are entering college in any state.

Eligibility This program is open to residents of Illinois who have a diagnosis of epilepsy. Applicants must be planning to enroll as full-time freshmen at a college or vocational/technical school in any state. Along with their application, they must submit an essay up to 220 words in length about their academic or career goals and how having epilepsy has affected or influenced their work towards those goals. Selection is based on that essay, academic merit, how well the applicant meets the scholarship's vision, letters of recommendation, achievement and/or community service, and financial need.

Financial data The stipend is $1,000.

Duration 1 year.

Number awarded Varies each year; recently, 3 were awarded.

Deadline May of each year.

[677]
JOE HOLIBAUGH MEMORIAL SCHOLARSHIP

Matrix Health Group
Attn: Memorial Scholarship Program
2202 Brownstone Court
Champaign, IL 61822
(217) 840-1033
E-mail: maria.vetter@matrixhealthgroup.com
Web: www.factorsupportnetwork.com

Summary To provide financial assistance for college to people who have a bleeding disorder.

Eligibility This program is open to graduating male and female high school seniors and students currently enrolled full time at an accredited college, university, or technical school who have hemophilia, von Willebrand's disease, or other bleeding disorder. Applicants must have a GPA of 2.0 or higher for their senior year in high school or their current year in college. Along with their application, they must submit transcripts, ACT or SAT test scores, 2 letters of recommendation, information on their work and school activities, and an essay of 300 to 400 words on 1 of the following topics: 1) the experiences that have influenced their decision to pursue their educational goals or career choice; 2) how they feel their life has been influenced by having a bleeding disorder; or 3) their biggest challenge in having a bleeding disorder and how they have or are working through it. Selection is based on that essay, academic merit, and reference letters.

Financial data The stipend is $1,000.

Duration 1 year.

Additional data This program began in 2013.

Number awarded 2 each year.

Deadline July of each year.

[678]
JOHN BULLER SCHOLARSHIP

Greater Houston Community Foundation
Attn: Scholarships Assistant
5120 Woodway Drive, Suite 6000
Houston, TX 77056
(713) 333-2236   Fax: (713) 333-2220
E-mail: jlauver@ghcf.org
Web: www.ghcfscholar.org

Summary To provide financial assistance to residents of Texas who have cystic fibrosis and are interested in attending college or graduate school in the state.

Eligibility This program is open to Texas residents who have cystic fibrosis. Applicants must be enrolled or planning to enroll as an undergraduate or graduate student at an accredited 2- or 4-year college or university in Texas. Along with their application, they must submit transcripts and information on their extracurricular activities, work experience, community service, and other activities. Financial need is considered in the selection process. U.S. citizenship is required.

Financial data The stipend is $1,000 per year.

Duration 1 year; may be renewed up to 3 additional years.

Additional data This program began in 1997.

Number awarded   1 or more each year.
Deadline   March of each year.

[679]
JOHN DUVALL MEMORIAL SCHOLARSHIP

Ulman Cancer Fund for Young Adults
Attn: Scholarship Committee
921 East Fort Avenue, Suite 325
Baltimore, MD 21230
(410) 964-0202   Toll Free: (888) 393-FUND
Fax: (888) 964-0402
E-mail: scholarship@ulmanfund.org
Web: www.ulmanfund.org/scholarships

Summary   To provide financial assistance to students who have been diagnosed with cancer or have or have lost a family member with cancer and are interested in attending designated universities.
Eligibility   This program is open to students who 1) have been diagnosed with cancer; 2) have a parent or sibling living with cancer; or 3) have lost a parent or sibling to cancer. Applicants must be working on or planning to work on an undergraduate, graduate, or professional degree at the University of Maryland, Towson University, Elon University, or the Savannah College of Art and Design. They must be able to demonstrate financial need. The first diagnosis of cancer (whether of the applicant, a parent, or sibling) must have occurred after the applicant was 15 years of age. Along with their application, they must submit a 500-word essay or 3-minute video on either 1) a letter that they would have liked to receive during their cancer experience; or 2) what they would tell the young adults who participate in the sponsor's summer-long drive to support the organization about being a young adult impacted by cancer. U.S. citizenship or permanent resident status is required.
Financial data   The stipend is $2,500. Funds are paid directly to the educational institution.
Duration   1 year.
Additional data   Recipients are obligated to organize and run a bone marrow registry drive with the support of Delete Blood Cancer and There Goes My Hero.
Number awarded   1 each year.
Deadline   March of each year.

[680]
JOHN FOY & ASSOCIATES STRONG ARM LEUKEMIA SCHOLARSHIP

John Foy & Associates
3343 Peachtree Road, Suite 350
Atlanta, GA 30326
(404) 982-4326
Web: www.johnfoy.com

Summary   To provide financial assistance to undergraduate and graduate students and their loved ones who have been affected by leukemia.
Eligibility   This program is open to entering college freshmen, undergraduates, and graduate students at accredited colleges and universities in any state. Applicants or a loved one must have been affected by leuke-

mia. Along with their application, they must submit an essay of 500 to 1,000 words on 1 of the following: 1) how living with their or their loves one's leukemia has affected their education; 2) the adjustments they have made as a student to accommodate their or a loved one's leukemia; or 3) an obstacle that people with leukemia face that they want the general public to know about.
Financial data   The stipend is $1,000.
Duration   1 year.
Number awarded   1 each year.
Deadline   December of each year.

[681]
JOHN HANLEY MEMORIAL SCHOLARSHIP AWARD

Ulman Cancer Fund for Young Adults
Attn: Scholarship Committee
921 East Fort Avenue, Suite 325
Baltimore, MD 21230
(410) 964-0202   Toll Free: (888) 393-FUND
Fax: (888) 964-0402
E-mail: scholarship@ulmanfund.org
Web: www.ulmanfund.org/scholarships

Summary   To provide financial assistance for college or graduate school to young adults who have cancer or are cancer survivors.
Eligibility   This program is open to students who are between 18 and 25 years of age and have battled cancer or are currently undergoing active treatment. The first diagnosis of cancer must have occurred after they were 15 years of age. Applicants must be attending or planning to attend a 2- or 4-year college or university to work on an undergraduate or graduate degree. They must be U.S. citizens or permanent residents. Along with their application, they must submit a 500-word essay or 3-minute video on either 1) a letter that they would have liked to receive during their cancer experience; or 2) what they would tell the young adults who participate in the sponsor's summer-long drive to support the organization about being a young adult impacted by cancer. In the selection process, consideration is given to their leadership abilities and commitment to their community.
Financial data   The stipend is $2,500. Funds are paid directly to the educational institution.
Duration   1 year.
Additional data   Recipients are obligated to organize and run a bone marrow registry drive with the support of Delete Blood Cancer and There Goes My Hero.
Number awarded   5 each year.
Deadline   March of each year.

[682]
JOHN LEPPING MEMORIAL SCHOLARSHIP

Lep Foundation for Youth Education
Attn: Scholarship Selection Committee
9 Whispering Spring Drive
Millstone Township, NJ 08510
E-mail: lepfoundation@aol.com
Web: www.lepfoundation.org/applications

Summary To provide financial assistance to high school seniors in New Jersey, New York, or Pennsylvania who have a physical disability or psychological handicap and plan to attend college in any state.

Eligibility This program is open to seniors graduating from high schools in New Jersey, New York, or Pennsylvania and planning to enroll at a college, university, community college, or vocational school in any state. Applicants must have a disability, including (but not limited to) physical disabilities (e.g., spinal cord injury, loss of limb, birth defects, Lyme disease) or psychological handicaps (e.g., autism, cerebral palsy, post-traumatic stress). Along with their application, they must submit a brief statement of their career goals and ambitions for the future and a 500-word essay on why they feel they are the best candidate for this award. Financial need is considered in the selection process.

Financial data The stipend is $5,000. Funds are paid directly to the recipient's school.

Duration 1 year.

Number awarded At least 4 each year.

Deadline April of each year.

[683]
JOHN, LYNNE, AND NICOLE BELLI MEMORIAL ENDOWMENT FUND

Georgia Firefighters Burn Foundation
Attn: Program Director
2575 Chantilly Drive
Atlanta, GA 30324
(404) 320-6223   Fax: (404) 320-6190
E-mail: ddillard@gfbf.org
Web: www.gfbf.org/survivor-services/belli

Summary To provide financial assistance to burn survivors in Georgia who are interested in attending college in any state.

Eligibility This program is open to residents of Georgia who are burn survivors and have spent time in a burn unit. Applicants must be between 16 and 26 years of age and attending of planning to attend an accredited college, university, or technical college in any state. Along with their application, they must submit essays on the following 3 topics: 1) how their burn injury has influenced and impacted their life and who they are today; 2) how they will benefit from their college education and how it will contribute to their life after graduation; and 3) why they think they are a deserving scholarship recipient. Selection is based on personal achievement and character.

Financial data The stipend is $2,500 per year.

Duration 1 year; may be renewed up to 3 additional years.

Number awarded 1 or 2 each year.

Deadline March of each year for spring; September of each year for fall.

[684]
JOHN YOUTSEY MEMORIAL SCHOLARSHIP FUND

Hemophilia of Georgia
8800 Roswell Road, Suite 170
Atlanta, GA 30350-1844
(770) 518-8272   Fax: (770) 518-3310
E-mail: mail@hog.org
Web: www.hog.org/programs/page/scholarships

Summary To provide financial assistance to residents of Georgia who have a bleeding disorder or have lost a parent because of the disorder and are interested in attending college in any state.

Eligibility This program is open to residents of Georgia who 1) have hemophilia, von Willebrand Disease, or other inherited bleeding disorder; or 2) are children whose parent died as a result of complications from a bleeding disorder. Applicants or their deceased parents must be or have been clients of Hemophilia of Georgia. They may be graduating high school seniors or students currently enrolled at an accredited college, university, vocational/technical school, or professional degree program in any state. Selection is based on academic record, financial need, and personal goals.

Financial data A stipend is awarded (amount not specified).

Duration 1 year.

Additional data Recipients must provide at least 12 hours of volunteer service with Hemophilia of Georgia.

Number awarded Varies each year. Since this program was established, it has awarded more than 400 scholarship with a value greater than $1,000,000.

Deadline April of each year.

[685]
JOSEPH JAMES MORELLI SCHOLARSHIP FUND

Park City Community Foundation
Attn: Community Impact Director
1960 Sidewinder Drive, Suite 103
P.O. Box 681499
Park City, UT 84068
(435) 731-4250   Fax: (435) 214-7489
E-mail: ollie@parkcitycf.org
Web: www.parkcitycf.org/morelli

Summary To provide financial assistance to residents of any state who have a documented learning disability and are interested in studying a field of science, technology, engineering, or mathematics (STEM) in college.

Eligibility This program is open to graduating high school seniors and current college students. Applicants must have a documented learning disability, such as dyslexia. They must be preparing for a career in a field of STEM. Along with their application, they must submit documentation of their learning disability and brief statements on the challenges they have faced in pursuing their education, why they deserve this scholarship, how they will use this opportunity to better their future, and why they are interested in preparing for a career in a STEM-related field.

Financial data Stipends range from $500 to $2,500 per year.

Duration 1 year; recipients may reapply.

Number awarded Varies each year; recently, 19 were awarded.

Deadline March of each year.

[686]
JOSH GORDY EDUCATIONAL SCHOLARSHIP

National Hemophilia Foundation
Attn: NHF/HANDI
7 Penn Plaza
370 Seventh Avenue, Suite 1204
New York, NY 10001
(212) 328-3700   Toll Free: (800) 42-HANDI, ext. 2
Fax: (212) 328-3777   E-mail: handi@hemophilia.org
Web: www.hemophilia.org

Summary To provide financial assistance for college to students with hemophilia.

Eligibility This program is open to individuals who have hemophilia A or B. Applicants must be entering or attending an accredited 2- or 4-year undergraduate institution.

Financial data The stipend is $1,000.

Duration 1 year.

Number awarded 3 each year.

Deadline August of each year.

[687]
JOSH SMITH MEMORIAL SCHOLARSHIP

Diabetes Scholars Foundation
310 Busse Highway, Suite 256
Park Ridge, IL 60068
(312) 215-9861   Fax: (847) 991-8739
E-mail: m.podjasek@diabetesscholars.org
Web: www.diabetesscholars.org/college-scholarship

Summary To provide financial assistance to high school seniors from Ohio who have diabetes and plan to attend college in any state.

Eligibility This program is open to seniors graduating from high schools in Ohio who have Type 1 diabetes and plan to attend an accredited 4-year university, college, or trade/technical school in any state. Applicants must be able to demonstrate active involvement in the diabetes community, academic accomplishment, participation in community and/or extracurricular activities, and successful management of the challenges of living with diabetes. Financial need is not considered in the selection process. U.S. citizenship or permanent resident status is required.

Financial data The stipend is $1,000.

Duration 1 year.

Number awarded 1 each year.

Deadline April of each year.

[688]
JOSHUA GOMES MEMORIAL SCHOLARSHIP

Joshua Gomes Memorial Scholarship Fund
45767 McKenzie Highway
Vida, OR 97488
(541) 896-3023   E-mail: Info@joshuagomes.org
Web: www.joshuagomes.org

Summary To provide financial assistance for college or graduate school to students who have AIDS or are HIV positive.

Eligibility This program is open to full-time undergraduate and graduate students accepted or enrolled at a college or university in the United States. Applicants must have AIDS or be HIV positive. Along with their application, they must submit a 500-word essay that explains their hopes, plans, and goals for the future; how their schooling will help lay a path to fulfilling those; what motivates them to pursue higher education; what subjects they plan to study; and what led them to that path of study. Selection is based on merit and financial need.

Financial data The stipend is $1,000.

Duration 1 year; recipients may reapply.

Additional data This program began in 2005.

Number awarded 1 or more each year.

Deadline July of each year.

[689]
JUSTNEBULIZERS.COM RESPIRATORY CARE SCHOLARSHIP

Just Health Shops
Attn: JustNebulizers.com
11840 West Market Place, Suite H
Fulton, MD 20759
Toll Free: (800) 998-7750   Fax: (301) 776-0716
E-mail: scholarship@justnebulizers.com
Web: www.justnebulizers.com

Summary To recognize and reward, with scholarships, undergraduate and graduate students who have a respiratory condition and submit outstanding videos about their condition.

Eligibility This program is open to legal U.S. residents who are enrolled in an undergraduate or graduate program. Applicants must have a respiratory condition. Instead of an application, they must submit a 3-minute video on 1) how living with a respiratory condition has molded who they are; and 2) the advice they would give to others in their situation. Selection is based on thoughtfulness in answering the questions and creativity of presenting the answers.

Financial data The award is a $1,000 scholarship. Funds are sent directly to the recipient's college or university.

Duration 1 year.

Number awarded 1 each year.

Deadline December of each year.

[690]
KARL POHRT TRIBUTE AWARD

Scholarship America
Attn: Scholarship Management Services
One Scholarship Way
P.O. Box 297
St. Peter, MN 56082
(507) 931-1682   Toll Free: (800) 537-4180
Fax: (507) 931-9168
E-mail: bincfoundation@scholarshipamerica.org
Web: www.scholarsapply.org/binc

Summary To provide financial assistance to nontraditional students and those with learning disabilities who have an affiliation with an independent bookstore and are interested in attending college or graduate school in any state.

Eligibility This program is open to high school seniors and graduates who are enrolled to planning to enroll full or part time in an undergraduate or graduate program at an accredited 2- or 4-year college, university, or vocational/technical school. Applicants must have overcome learning adversity or be a nontraditional student. They must be affiliated with an independent bookstore. Selection is based on academic record, participation and leadership in school and community activities, and financial need.

Financial data The stipend is $5,000.

Duration 1 year; recipients may reapply.

Additional data This program is sponsored by the Book Industry Charitable Foundation (BINC).

Number awarded 1 each year.

Deadline March of each year.

[691]
KATIE MACDONALD MEMORIAL SCHOLARSHIPS FOR INDIVIDUALS WITH DOWN SYNDROME

United Parent Support for Down Syndrome
Attn: UPS for DownS Memorial Scholarship Program
1070 South Roselle Road
Schaumburg, IL 60193
(847) 895-2100   E-mail: embarrett@upsfordowns.org
Web: www.upsfordowns.org/support/Scholarships.aspx

Summary To provide financial assistance to individuals who have Down syndrome and are interested in obtaining education beyond high school.

Eligibility This program is open to individuals who have Down syndrome and are interested in a program of educational or job training opportunities beyond high school. Applicants must be interested in educational opportunities that may include, but are not limited to, college, community college, trade school, vocational school, job training, or adult continuing education. Along with their application, they must submit a 1-page essay on 1) their accomplishments, community involvement, and future career plans; and 2) how receipt of the scholarship will help them achieve their personal goals. Other factors considered in the selection process may be transcripts, records of community service, employment history, records of extracurricular activities, independent living skills, a statement of

how the applicant educates others on the needs of those with disabilities, and a record of assistive technology used and how it has impacted the applicant or others. U.S. citizenship is required.

Financial data The stipend is $2,500. Funds are sent directly to the institution or service provider.

Duration Funds may be used over multiple years or in multiple programs, but must be used within a 3-year period.

Number awarded 2 each year.

Deadline May of each year.

[692]
KATZ & PHILLIPS BEATING HEART DISEASE SCHOLARSHIP

Katz & Phillips, P.A.
509 West Colonial Drive
Orlando, FL 32804
(321) 332-6864   Fax: (321) 422-3457
Web: www.orlandocriminalteam.com/giving-back

Summary To provide financial assistance to college students who have personally faced heart disease or have seen loved ones deal with the illness.

Eligibility This program is open to students who have been accepted or are enrolled at a college or university in any state. Applicants must be suffering from heart disease, have overcome heart disease, or be providing care and support for a family member with heart disease. They must have a GPA of 2.8 or higher. Along with their application, they must submit an essay of 500-1,000 words on their choice of 3 essay topics that deal with heart disease.

Financial data The stipend is $1,000.

Duration 1 year.

Number awarded 1 each year.

Deadline July of each year.

[693]
KELLY LAW TEAM AUTISM/ASD SCHOLARSHIP

Kelly Law Team
1 East Washington Street, Suite 500
Phoenix, AZ 85004
(602) 283-4122
E-mail: mike@jkphoenixpersonalinjuryattorney.com
Web: www.jkphoenixpersonalinjuryattorney.com

Summary To provide financial assistance to individuals who have been diagnosed with autism spectrum disorder (ASD) and are interested in attending college.

Eligibility This program is open to U.S. citizens who have been diagnosed with ASD. Applicants must be enrolled or planning to enroll at a college, university, junior college, or trade or vocational school. Along with their application, they must submit a 100-word statement on how the scholarship will assist in achieving their educational goals. They may also submit, at their discretion, a 1,000-word essay on how autism has affected their education.

Financial data The stipend is $1,000. Funds are paid directly to the recipient's college.

Duration 1 year.
Number awarded 1 each year.
Deadline February.

[694]
KELLY LAW TEAM DOWN SYNDROME SCHOLARSHIPS

Kelly Law Team
1 East Washington Street, Suite 500
Phoenix, AZ 85004
(602) 283-4122
E-mail: mike@jkphoenixpersonalinjuryattorney.com
Web: www.jkphoenixpersonalinjuryattorney.com

Summary To provide financial assistance to individuals who have been diagnosed with Down Syndrome and are interested in attending college.

Eligibility This program is open to U.S. citizens who have been diagnosed with Down Syndrome. Applicants must be enrolled or planning to enroll at a college, trade school, community college, secondary school, or tutoring. Along with their application, they must submit a 100-word statement on what the scholarship will do for them. They may also submit, at their discretion, an essay of 650 to 1,000 words on how Down Syndrome has affected them in terms of their education.

Financial data The stipend is $1,000. Funds are paid directly to the recipient's school.

Duration 1 year.
Number awarded 2 each year.
Deadline November.

[695]
KERMIT B. NASH ACADEMIC SCHOLARSHIP

Sickle Cell Disease Association of America
Attn: Scholarship Committee
3700 Kopppers Street
Baltimore, MD 21227
(410) 528-1555   Toll Free: (800) 421-8453
Fax: (410) 528-1495
E-mail: scdaa@sicklecelldisease.org
Web: www.sicklecelldisease.org

Summary To provide financial assistance for college to graduating high school seniors who have sickle cell disease and are members of the Sickle Cell Disease Association of America (SCDAA).

Eligibility This program is open to graduating high school seniors who are SCDAA members and have sickle cell disease (not just the trait). Applicants must have a GPA of 3.0 or higher and be U.S. citizens or permanent residents planning to attend an accredited 4-year college or university as a full-time student. They must submit a personal essay, up to 1,000 words, on an aspect of the impact of the disease on their lives or on society. Selection is based on GPA, general academic achievement and promise, SAT scores, leadership and community service, severity of academic challenges and obstacles posed by sickle cell disease, and the quality of their essay.

Financial data The stipend is $5,000 per year.

Duration Up to 4 years, provided the recipient maintains a GPA of 2.5 or higher.

Additional data The Sickle Cell Disease Association of America (SCDAA) was formerly the National Association for Sickle Cell Disease. It established this program in 1999.

Number awarded 1 each year.
Deadline May of each year.

[696]
KEVIN CHILD SCHOLARSHIP

National Hemophilia Foundation
Attn: NHF/HANDI
7 Penn Plaza
370 Seventh Avenue, Suite 1204
New York, NY 10001
(212) 328-3700   Toll Free: (800) 42-HANDI, ext. 2
Fax: (212) 328-3777   E-mail: handi@hemophilia.org
Web: www.hemophilia.org

Summary To provide financial assistance for college or graduate school to students with hemophilia.

Eligibility This program is open to high school seniors entering their first year of undergraduate study as well as those currently enrolled in college or graduate school. Applicants must have hemophilia A or B. Along with their application, they must submit a 1-page essay on their occupational objectives and goals in life and how the educational program they have planned will meet those objectives. Selection is based on that essay, academic performance, and participation in school and community activities.

Financial data The stipend is $1,000.
Duration 1 year.
Additional data The program was established in 1989.
Number awarded 1 each year.
Deadline June of each year.

[697]
KIDNEY TRANSPLANT/DIALYSIS ASSOCIATION SCHOLARSHIP PROGRAM

Kidney Transplant/Dialysis Association, Inc.
Attn: Scholarship Committee
P.O. Box 51362 GMF
Boston, MA 02205-1362
(781) 641-4000   E-mail: Business@ktda.org
Web: www.ktda.org/scholarship.html

Summary To provide financial assistance to residents of New England who are kidney patients or donors or members of their families and interested in attending college in any state.

Eligibility This program is open to residents of New England who are kidney patients, kidney donors, or members of a patient's immediate family. Applicants must be interested in continuing their education beyond high school. Along with their application, they must submit 2 letters of recommendation, transcripts, and a 500-word essay on how kidney disease has impacted their family. Selection is based on academic merit and financial need.

Financial data Stipends range from $500 to $1,000.

Duration 1 year.

Number awarded Varies each year; recently, 2 were awarded.

Deadline January of each year.

[698]
KYLE R. NOBLE MEMORIAL SCHOLARSHIP

The Oley Foundation
c/o Albany Medical Center
43 New Scotland Avenue, MC-28
Albany, NY 12208-3478
(518) 262-5079　　　　　Toll Free: (800) 776-OLEY
Fax: (518) 262-5528
E-mail: andreaguidi.oley@gmail.com
Web: www.oley.org/page/KyleNobleScholarship

Summary To provide financial assistance to students who depend on home enteral nutrition (HEN) or home parenteral nutrition (HPN) for their primary nutritional needs.

Eligibility This program is open to undergraduate, graduate, and vocational students who have a medical diagnosis of a digestive disorder (ranging from cancer to Crohn's Disease) that requires HEN and/or HPN to meet their primary nutritional needs. Applicants must submit a personal essay of 1 to 3 pages describing how they have 1) overcome obstacles and challenges posed by HEN and/or HPN; and 2) inspired others to live life to the fullest. They must submit letters from 1) a member of their health care team describing their circumstances and need for HEN and/or HPN; and 2) a teacher or adviser supporting their pursuit of their educational goals.

Financial data The stipend is $2,000 per academic year.

Duration 1 year; recipients may reapply.

Additional data This program began in 2007.

Number awarded 1 each year.

Deadline March of each year.

[699]
LARRY DEAN DAVIS SCHOLARSHIP FUND

Pediatric Brain Tumor Foundation-Georgia Chapter
Attn: Scholarship Committee
6065 Roswell Road, N.E., Suite 505
Atlanta, GA 30328-4015
(404) 252-4107　　　　　Fax: (404) 252-4108
E-mail: gachapter@curethekids.org
Web: www.curethekids.org

Summary To provide financial assistance to residents of Georgia who have had a brain or spinal cord tumor and are interested in attending college in any state.

Eligibility This program is open to Georgia residents who are survivors of a pediatric brain or spinal cord tumor. Applicants must be entering or continuing in an advanced educational setting (college, university, vocational school, or other setting) in any state. Along with their application, they must submit 1) a 500-word essay about their brain or spinal cord tumor experience, including surgery and/or treatment; 2) a 500-word biographical sketch about themselves and their future aspirations; and 3) a 250-word description of their financial need.

Financial data The stipend is $2,500.

Duration 1 year; nonrenewable.

Additional data This program began in 2002.

Number awarded Up to 2 each year.

Deadline April of each year.

[700]
LARRY SMOCK SCHOLARSHIP

National Kidney Foundation of Indiana, Inc.
Attn: Program Coordinator
911 East 86th Street, Suite 100
Indianapolis, IN 46204-1848
(317) 722-5640　　　　　Toll Free: (800) 382-9971
Fax: (317) 722-5650　　E-mail: nkfi@kidneyindiana.org
Web: www.kidney.org/offices/nkf-indiana

Summary To provide financial assistance to kidney patients in Indiana who are interested in pursuing higher education in an academic or monitored occupational setting in any state.

Eligibility This program is open to Indiana residents who have at least a high school diploma or its equivalent and who have received a kidney transplant or are on dialysis. Applicants must be interested in attending college, trade school, or vocational school in any state to work on an academic or occupational degree. Finalists are interviewed. Financial need is considered in the selection process.

Financial data A stipend is awarded (amount not specified). Funds are paid directly to the recipient's school.

Duration 1 year; may be renewed.

Additional data This fund was established in 1992.

Number awarded Several each year.

Deadline March of each year.

[701]
LEARNING DISABILITIES ASSOCIATION OF IOWA SCHOLARSHIPS

Learning Disabilities Association of Iowa
Attn: Scholarship Chair
5665 Greendale Road, Suite D
Johnston, IA 50131
(515) 280-8558　　　　　Toll Free: (888) 690-LDAI
Fax: (515) 243-1902　　E-mail: cjpaup@wccta.net
Web: www.ldaiowa.org/projects/scholarships

Summary To provide financial assistance to high school seniors in Iowa who have a learning disability and are interested in attending college in any state.

Eligibility This program is open to students with learning disabilities who are graduating from high schools in Iowa. Applicants must be planning to enroll in a 2- or 4-year college or in vocational training at a school in any state. The membership-based scholarship is reserved for a student who is 1) a member of the Learning Disabilities Association (LDA); 2) the child of an LDA member; or 3) recommended by a current LDA member. At-large scholarships are awarded to other eligible applicants, but preference is given to students who meet the membership criteria. Along with their application, they must submit an essay about themselves, including their extracurricular and community achievements, most significant accomplishments, volunteer and paid jobs, methods of financing their education, and accommodations that have been beneficial to them and will help them succeed in their postsecondary education.

Financial data   The stipend is $1,000.

Duration   1 year.

Number awarded   3 each year: 1 membership-based scholarship and 2 at-large scholarships.

Deadline   March of each year.

[702]
LEONARD FAMILY ENTREPRENEURIAL SPIRIT SCHOLARSHIP

Cancer for College
981 Park Center Drive
Vista, CA 92081
(760) 599-5096
E-mail: applications@cancerforcollege.org
Web: www.cancerforcollege.org/application.html

Summary   To provide financial assistance to undergraduate and graduate students who are cancer patients or survivors and interested in preparing for a career in the food service industry.

Eligibility   This program is open to undergraduate and graduate students who are entering or currently enrolled at accredited colleges, universities, community colleges, or trade schools in any state. Applicants must be preparing for a career in the food service industry and planning to own or operate a restaurant. They must be a cancer patient or survivor. Along with their application, they must submit transcripts, verification of their cancer diagnosis, 2 letters of recommendation, and information on their financial situation.

Financial data   The stipend ranges from $1,000 to $5,000.

Duration   1 year.

Number awarded   1 or 2 each year.

Deadline   January of each year.

[703]
LHF SCHOLARSHIPS

Louisiana Hemophilia Foundation
Attn: Scholarship Committee
3636 South Sherwood Forest Boulevard, Suite 390
Baton Rouge, LA 70816-5211
(225) 291-1675   Toll Free: (800) 749-1680
Fax: (225) 291-1679   E-mail: contact@lahemo.org
Web: www.lahemo.org/services/scholarships

Summary   To provide financial assistance to Louisiana residents who have hemophilia or other bleeding disorder and are interested in attending college in any state.

Eligibility   This program is open to residents of Louisiana who have hemophilia or other bleeding disorder. Applicants must be enrolled or planning to enroll at a college, university, or trade school in any state. Along with their application, they must submit a 250-word essay on why they should receive this scholarship.

Financial data   The stipend is $500 per semester.

Duration   1 semester. Recipients may reapply if they remain enrolled full time, have a GPA of 2.5 or higher, and provide 8 hours of community service to the sponsoring organization.

Number awarded   Up to 4 each semester.

Deadline   June of each year for fall semester; December of each year for spring semester.

[704]
LILLIAN JEANETTE CRAIG MEMORIAL SCHOLARSHIP

University of Idaho 4-H Youth Development
Attn: Shana Codr, 4-H Program Specialist
Forney 206
875 Perimeter Drive, MS 3015
Moscow, ID 83844-3015
(208) 885-6321   E-mail: scodr@uidaho.edu
Web: www.uidaho.edu

Summary   To provide financial assistance for college to members of 4-H in Idaho who are childhood cancer survivors or the sibling of someone who has had childhood cancer.

Eligibility   This program is open to residents of Idaho who have been involved with 4-H and are graduating high school seniors or current college students. Applicants must be a childhood cancer survivor or the sibling of someone who has or has had childhood cancer. If a sibling, the applicant must have lived in the same household and been between 4 and 18 years of age when the sibling was diagnosed and treated. They may be enrolled or planning to enroll at a college, university, or vocational institution in any state; preference is given to students at academic institutions in Idaho.

Financial data   The stipend is $1,000.

Duration   1 year.

Number awarded   1 or more each year.

Deadline   November of each year.

[705]
LILLY DIABETES TOMORROW'S LEADERS SCHOLARSHIPS

Diabetes Scholars Foundation
310 Busse Highway, Suite 256
Park Ridge, IL 60068
(312) 215-9861   Fax: (847) 991-8739
E-mail: m.podjasek@diabetesscholars.org
Web: www.diabetesscholars.org/college-scholarship

Summary   To provide financial assistance for college to high school seniors who have diabetes.

Eligibility   This program is open to graduating high school seniors who have Type 1 diabetes and plan to attend an accredited 4-year university, college, or trade/technical school in any state. Applicants must be able to demonstrate active involvement in the diabetes community, academic accomplishment, participation in community and/or extracurricular activities, and successful management of the challenges of living with diabetes. Financial need is not considered in the selection process. U.S. citizenship or permanent resident status is required.

Financial data   Stipends are $5,000, $4,000, or $3,00.
Duration   1 year.
Additional data   This program is sponsored by Lilly USA.
Number awarded   21 each year: 11 at $5,000, 5 at $4,000, and 5 at $3,000.
Deadline   April of each year.

[706]
LISA HANSEN-YARUSSI SCHOLARSHIP FOR WESTERN WASHINGTON

The Brain Injury Alliance of Washington
Attn: Scholarships
316 Broadway, Suite 305
P.O. Box 3044
Seattle, WA 98114
(206) 467-4807   Toll Free: (877) 982-4292
E-mail: jennak@biawa.org
Web: www.biawa.org/scholarship.php

Summary   To provide financial assistance for college in western Washington to survivors of brain injury who are residents of the state.
Eligibility   This program is open to residents of Washington who are survivors of brain injury. Applicants must be graduating high school seniors or undergraduates enrolled full or part time at a college or university in western Washington.
Financial data   The stipend is $1,000. Funds are paid directly to the institution.
Duration   1 year; nonrenewable.
Number awarded   1 each year.
Deadline   August of each year.

[707]
LISA HIGGINS HUSSMAN SCHOLARSHIP

Organization for Autism Research
Attn: Scholarship
2000 North 14th Street, Suite 240
Arlington, VA 22201
(703) 243-9710
E-mail: scholarship@researchautism.org
Web: www.researchautism.org

Summary   To provide financial assistance for college to individuals with severe autism.
Eligibility   This program is open to individuals with an established severe autism diagnosis who are attending or planning to attend an accredited 2- or 4-year college or university, vocational/technical school, or cooperative life skills program. Applicants normally attend programs that assist in skill-building, job-readiness, and other transition-related skills. Along with their application, they must submit a 1,000-word autobiographical essay that includes their reasons for applying for this scholarship; students whose communication skills are limited may include a letter from a parent or guardian. Selection is based on originality of content, challenges overcome, future aspirations, the importance of the chosen field of study, and how the scholarship will help achieve academic, career, and personal goals.

Financial data   The stipend is $3,000.
Duration   1 year; nonrenewable.
Additional data   This program began in 2013 with support from the Lisa Higgins Hussman Foundation.
Number awarded   Varies each year; recently, 15 were awarded.
Deadline   April of each year.

[708]
LISA HIGGINS-HUSSMAN FOUNDATION SCHOLARSHIP

Ulman Cancer Fund for Young Adults
Attn: Scholarship Committee
921 East Fort Avenue, Suite 325
Baltimore, MD 21230
(410) 964-0202   Toll Free: (888) 393-FUND
Fax: (888) 964-0402
E-mail: scholarship@ulmanfund.org
Web: www.ulmanfund.org/scholarships

Summary   To provide financial assistance for college or graduate school to students from Washington, D.C., Maryland, or Virginia who have been diagnosed with cancer or have or have lost a family member with cancer.
Eligibility   This program is open to students who 1) have been diagnosed with cancer; 2) have a parent, sibling, or guardian living with cancer; or 3) have lost a parent, sibling, or guardian to cancer. Applicants must be residents of Washington, D.C., Maryland, or Virginia. They must be between 15 and 35 years of age and attending, or planning to attend, a 2- or 4-year college, university, or vocational program in any state to work on an undergraduate or graduate degree. The first diagnosis of cancer (whether of the applicant, a parent, a sibling, or a guardian) must have occurred after the applicant was 15 years of age. Along with their application, they must submit a 500-word essay or 3-minute video on either 1) a letter that they would have liked to receive during their cancer experience; or 2) what they would tell the young adults who participate in the sponsor's summer-long drive to support the organization about being a young adult impacted by cancer. U.S. citizenship or permanent resident status is required.
Financial data   The stipend is $2,500. Funds are paid directly to the educational institution.
Duration   1 year.
Additional data   Recipients are obligated to organize and run a bone marrow registry drive with the support of Delete Blood Cancer and There Goes My Hero.
Number awarded   1 each year.
Deadline   March of each year.

[709]
LIVING BREATH FOUNDATION SCHOLARSHIPS

Living Breath Foundation
2031 Marsala Circle
Monterey, CA 93940
(831) 392-5283
E-mail: LivingBreathFoundation@gmail.com
Web: www.thelivingbreathfoundation.com/aid.html

Summary To provide financial assistance to residents of California and Arizona who have cystic fibrosis and are interested in attending college or graduate school in any state.

Eligibility This program is open to U.S. citizens who are residents of California or Arizona. Applicants have cystic fibrosis and be graduating high school seniors or undergraduate or graduate students continuing their education at a 2- or 4-year college, university, or trade school in any state. They must submit an essay on how continuing their education will benefit their future. Selection is based on academic record, leadership, community service, and financial need.

Financial data The stipend ranges from $1,000 to $5,000. Funds are disbursed directly to the student to assist in payment of tuition, books, or the expenses of going to school while having cystic fibrosis (e.g., private rooms, food, rooms with running water, bathrooms, parking).

Duration 1 year.

Additional data This foundation was established in 2008.

Number awarded 1 or more each year.

Deadline March of each year.

[710]
LOIS ROTHSCHILD MEMORIAL SCHOLARSHIP

International Dyslexia Association-Southwest Branch
Attn: Scholarship Committee
3915 Carlisle NE
Albuquerque, NM 87107
(505) 255-8234   E-mail: info@southwestida.org
Web: southwestida.org

Summary To provide financial assistance to high school seniors in New Mexico and El Paso, Texas who have dyslexia and are interested in attending college in New Mexico.

Eligibility This program is open to seniors graduating from high schools in New Mexico and El Paso who have been diagnosed with dyslexia. Applicants must qualify for a higher education "Bridge to Lottery" scholarship in New Mexico. They must have a current Individual Educational Program (IEP) and a GPA of 2.5 or higher. Selection is based on academic performance in relation to the severity of the specific learning disability, letters of recommendation, personal goals, and financial need.

Financial data The stipend is $1,000. Funds are paid directly to the recipient's college or university.

Duration 1 year.

Number awarded 1 each year.

Deadline March of each year.

[711]
LOS ANGELES DUI ATTORNEY DIABETES SCHOLARSHIP

Los Angeles DUI Attorney
20700 Ventura Boulevard, Suite 301A
Woodland Hills, CA 91364
(818) 794-1023
Web: www.losangelesduiattorney.com

Summary To provide financial assistance to people who have diabetes and are enrolled or planning to enroll at a college or graduate school in any state.

Eligibility This program is open to people who have been diagnosed with any type of diabetes. Applicants must be enrolled or planning to enroll as an undergraduate or graduate student at an accredited college or university. They must have a GPA of 3.0 or higher. Along with their application, they must submit an essay of 500 to 1,000 words on 1 of the following topics: 1) a way that diabetes has shaped or changed your plans in life; 2) something that they think would make the biggest difference is how our society treats diabetes; or 3) a piece of advice that they would give themselves if they could go back to the time when they first learned they had diabetes.

Financial data The stipend is $1,000.

Duration 1 year.

Additional data This program began in 2016.

Number awarded 1 year.

Deadline June of each year.

[712]
LYMAN FISHER SCHOLARSHIPS

Virginia Hemophilia Foundation
410 North Ridge Road, Suite 215
Richmond, VA 23228
Toll Free: (800) 266-8438   Fax: (800) 266-8438
E-mail: info@vahemophilia.org
Web: www.vahemophilia.org

Summary To provide financial assistance to people from Virginia who have participated in activities of the Virginia Hemophilia Foundation (VHF) and are interested in attending college.

Eligibility This program is open to members of the bleeding disorder community and their families who are attending or planning to attend college. Applicants must have a record of prior participation with VHF and be a resident of Virginia or planning to attend college in Virginia. Along with their application, they must submit a brief biographical sketch of themselves that includes their interests, hobbies, vocational and educational goals, volunteer and community involvement, and work or internship experience; a description of their previous participation with VHF and how they plan to contribute to the organization and support other persons with inherited bleeding disorders; a detailed statement of financial need; a 1-page essay on their career goals; another 1-page essay on a topic of their choice; and 3 letters of recommendation.

Financial data The stipend is $2,000.
Duration 1 year.
Number awarded 2 each year.
Deadline April of each year.

[713]
MACDONALD WOOD BURN SURVIVOR EDUCATIONAL SCHOLARSHIP PROGRAM

Arizona Burn Foundation
Attn: Scholarship Request
1432 North Seventh Street
Phoenix, AZ 85006
(602) 230-2041   Fax: (602) 230-2157
Web: 1734-4593.el-alt.com

Summary To provide financial assistance to Arizona residents who are burn injury survivors and interested in attending college in any states.

Eligibility This program is open to residents of Arizona who have survived a serious burn injury that required grafting or surgery during hospitalization. Applicants must be 17 years of age or older and enrolled or planning to enroll in an undergraduate degree, diploma, or certificate program in any state. Selection is based on ability to achieve academically, recommendations, and financial need.

Financial data The stipend is $1,500 per semester or quarter. Funds are paid directly to the educational institution.

Duration 1 semester or quarter; may be renewed, provided the recipient maintains a GPA of 2.5 or higher and volunteers for at least 1 Arizona Burn Foundation event each semester or quarter.

Number awarded Varies each year.

Deadline Applications may be submitted at any time, but they must be received at least 1 month before the start of the semester or quarter in which the student plans to enroll.

[714]
MALLORY SMITH LEGACY SCHOLARSHIP

Georgia Transplant Foundation
Attn: Scholarship Program
2201 Macy Drive
Roswell, GA 30076
(770) 457-3796   Fax: (770) 457-7916
E-mail: gtf@gatransplant.org
Web: www.gatransplant.org

Summary To provide financial assistance to residents of Georgia who are transplant recipients or dependents of recipients and interested in attending college in any state.

Eligibility This program is open to residents of Georgia who are entering or continuing at an accredited institution of higher learning in any state. Applicants must be an organ transplant recipient or the dependent of a recipient. Along with their application, they must submit a 3-page personal statement on their career objectives, how this scholarship will help them attain their goals, and how transplantation has affected their life. Selection is based on that statement, transcripts, high school exit examina-

tion scores, ACT/SAT scores, 3 letters of reference, and financial need.

Financial data The stipend is $1,000 per year.

Duration 1 year; may be renewed up to 3 additional years.

Number awarded 1 each year.

Deadline April of each year.

[715]
MARCENA LOZANO DONATE LIFE SCHOLARSHIP FUND

Marcena Lozano Donate Life Scholarship Fund
  Committee
15 Winston Road
Buffalo, NY 14216
E-mail: admin@marcenasmiracles.com
Web: www.marcenasmiracles.com

Summary To provide financial assistance to residents of New York and Pennsylvania who have received an organ transplant and are interested in attending college in any state.

Eligibility This program is open to organ transplant recipients who reside in New York or Pennsylvania. Applicants must be enrolled or planning to enroll at an accredited college, university, or trade/technical school in any state. Along with their application, they must submit a personal statement on their educational objectives and future life goals. Selection is based primarily on financial need.

Financial data Stipends range from $1,000 to $3,000.

Duration 1 year; may be renewed.

Number awarded Several each year.

Deadline July of each year for fall; November of each year for spring.

[716]
MARCO CAMASTRA SCHOLARSHIP AWARD

Learning Disabilities Association of North Carolina
1854A Hendersonville Road, Suite 239
Asheville, NC 28803-2467
E-mail: support@ldanc.org
Web: www.ldanc.org/services

Summary To provide financial assistance to high school seniors in North Carolina who have a learning disability and are interested in attending college in any state.

Eligibility This program is open to seniors graduating from high schools in North Carolina who have been diagnosed as having a learning disability or attention disorder. Applicants must be planning to attend a college, university, community college, or technical school in any state. They must be able to demonstrate that they have participated in school activities (e.g., sports, music, art, drama), persisted in academics, participated in community or church activities, and shown sensitivity to the needs or feelings of others. Along with their application, they must submit a short essay about their learning disability and how they feel they have adapted in order to succeed in school and/or life in general. Financial need is not considered in the selection process.

Financial data The stipend is $1,000.

Duration 1 year.
Number awarded 1 each year.
Deadline March of each year.

[717]
MARION HUBER LEARNING THROUGH LISTENING AWARDS

Learning Ally
Attn: National Achievement Awards
20 Roszel Road
Princeton, NJ 08540
(609) 520-8084   Toll Free: (800) 221-4792
Fax: (609) 987-8116   E-mail: naa@LearningAlly.org
Web: www.learningally.org/NAA/Application-LTL.aspx

Summary To provide financial assistance to outstanding high school students with learning disabilities who plan to continue their education.

Eligibility This program is open to seniors graduating from public or private high schools in the United States or its territories who have a specific learning disability (visual impairment or physical disability alone does not satisfy this requirement). Applicants must be planning to continue their education at a 2- or 4-year college or vocational school. They must have been registered members of Learning Ally for at least 1 year. Selection is based on academic excellence, leadership, and service to others.

Financial data Stipends are $6,000 or $2,000.

Duration 1 year.

Additional data This program began in 1991. Learning Ally was formerly named Recording for the Blind and Dyslexic.

Number awarded 6 each year: 3 at $6,000 and 3 at $2,000.

Deadline April of each year.

[718]
MARK COATS MEMORIAL SCHOLARSHIP

Matrix Health Group
Attn: Memorial Scholarship Program
2202 Brownstone Court
Champaign, IL 61822
(217) 840-1033
E-mail: maria.vetter@matrixhealthgroup.com
Web: www.factorsupportnetwork.com

Summary To provide financial assistance for college to people who have a bleeding disorder and members of their immediate family.

Eligibility This program is open to graduating male and female high school seniors and students currently enrolled full time at an accredited college, university, or technical school. Applicants must have hemophilia, von Willebrand's disease, or other bleeding disorder or be an immediate family member of a person with a bleeding disorder. Applicants must have a GPA of 2.0 or higher for their senior year in high school or their current year in college. Along with their application, they must submit transcripts, ACT or SAT test scores, 2 letters of recommendation, information on their work and school activities, and an essay of 300 to 400 words on 1 of the following topics: 1)

the experiences that have influenced their decision to pursue their educational goals or career choice; 2) how they feel their life has been influenced by having a bleeding disorder or by having a bleeding disorder in their family; or 3) their biggest challenge in having a bleeding disorder and how they have or are working through it. Selection is based on that essay, academic merit, and reference letters.

Financial data The stipend is $1,000.

Duration 1 year.

Additional data This program is supported by Homecare for the Cure and administered by Matrix Health Group.

Number awarded 1 each year.

Deadline July of each year.

[719]
MARY BARTON FREEMAN SCHOLARSHIPS

Ulman Cancer Fund for Young Adults
Attn: Scholarship Committee
921 East Fort Avenue, Suite 325
Baltimore, MD 21230
(410) 964-0202   Toll Free: (888) 393-FUND
Fax: (888) 964-0402
E-mail: scholarship@ulmanfund.org
Web: www.ulmanfund.org/scholarships

Summary To provide financial assistance for college or graduate school to students who have been diagnosed with cancer or have or have lost a family member with cancer.

Eligibility This program is open to students who 1) have been diagnosed with cancer; 2) have a parent or sibling living with cancer; or 3) have lost a parent or sibling to cancer. Applicants must be attending, or planning to attend, a college or university in any state to work on an undergraduate, graduate, or professional degree. They must be working on career or higher eduction goals. The first diagnosis of cancer (whether of the applicant, a parent, or sibling) must have occurred after the applicant was 15 years of age. Along with their application, they must submit a 500-word essay or 3-minute video on either 1) a letter that they would have liked to receive during their cancer experience; or 2) what they would tell the young adults who participate in the sponsor's summer-long drive to support the organization about being a young adult impacted by cancer. U.S. citizenship or permanent resident status is required.

Financial data The stipend is $2,500. Funds are paid directly to the educational institution.

Duration 1 year.

Additional data Recipients are obligated to organize and run a bone marrow registry drive with the support of Delete Blood Cancer and There Goes My Hero.

Number awarded 5 each year.

Deadline March of each year.

[720]
MARY BRENNAN AWARD

National Kidney Foundation of Michigan, Inc.
1169 Oak Valley Drive
Ann Arbor, MI 48108-9674
(734) 222-9800   Toll Free: (800) 482-1455 (within MI)
Fax: (734) 222-9801
E-mail: cnichols-jackson@nkfm.org
Web: www.nkfm.org

Summary To provide financial assistance to residents of Michigan who are on dialysis and are interested in continuing their education at a school in any state.

Eligibility This program is open to Michigan residents who are on dialysis. Applicants must be enrolled or planning to enroll full or part time at an accredited 2- or 4-year college, university, or vocational/technical school in any state. They must have a GPA of 2.0 or higher. Selection is based on past academic performance, potential to succeed in chosen academic program, participation and leadership in school and community activities, work experience, honors, awards, educational and career goals, unusual personal or family circumstances, and financial need.

Financial data The stipend is $1,000. Funds are paid directly to the recipient's educational institution.

Duration 1 year.

Number awarded 1 each year.

Deadline April of each year.

[721]
MATTHEW SIRAVO EPILEPSY SCHOLARSHIP AWARD

Epilepsy Foundation New England
Attn: Director of Community Engagement and
   Education
335 Main Street, Unit 8
Wilmington, MA 01887
(617) 506-6041   Fax: (617) 506-6047
E-mail: swelby@epilepsynewengland.org
Web: www.epilepsynewengland.org

Summary To provide financial assistance to high school seniors in Rhode Island who have epilepsy and are interested in attending college in any state.

Eligibility This program is open to seniors graduating from high schools in Rhode Island who are under a doctor's care for epilepsy. Applicants must be accepted or applying to a college or institute of higher education in any state. They must have performed activities beyond the classroom or in the community.

Financial data The stipend is $1,000.

Duration 1 year.

Additional data This program began as the Matty Fund in 2003. It partnered with Epilepsy Foundation New England in 2017.

Number awarded 1 each year.

Deadline March of each year.

[722]
MCEC FOUNDATION FOR EXCEPTIONAL CHILDREN SCHOLARSHIP PROGRAM

Michigan Council for Exceptional Children
Attn: MCEC Foundation for Exceptional Children
527 Grand Street
Portage, MI 49024
(269) 366-4673   Fax: (269) 365-9578
Web: www.michigancec.org

Summary To provide financial assistance to students who have been enrolled in special education in Michigan and wish to attend college in the state.

Eligibility This program is open to residents of Michigan who have been enrolled in special education or Section 504 public services but will be exiting from that program because they either are graduating from high school or have reached 26 years of age. Applicants must be planning to enroll at a postsecondary institution in Michigan. Along with their application, they must submit an essay, up to 2 pages if written or 5 minutes if recorded, that covers their career goals, how further education will help them advance those goals, and volunteer community service activities and/or experiences that demonstrate leadership skills. Financial need is considered in the selection process.

Financial data The stipend is $1,500. Funds may be used to support tuition, transportation, special equipment, or tutoring.

Duration 1 year.

Additional data This program began in 2001.

Number awarded Varies each year; recently, 14 were awarded.

Deadline May of each year.

[723]
MEG JEFFREY MEMORIAL SCHOLARSHIP

Georgia Transplant Foundation
Attn: Scholarship Program
2201 Macy Drive
Roswell, GA 30076
(770) 457-3796   Fax: (770) 457-7916
E-mail: gtf@gatransplant.org
Web: www.gatransplant.org

Summary To provide financial assistance to residents of Georgia who are transplant recipients and interested in attending college in any state.

Eligibility This program is open to residents of Georgia who are entering or continuing at an accredited institution of higher learning in any state. Applicants must be an organ transplant recipient. Along with their application, they must submit a 3-page personal statement on their career objectives, how this scholarship will help them attain their goals, and how transplantation has affected their life. Selection is based on that statement, transcripts, high school exit examination scores, ACT/SAT scores, 3 letters of reference, and financial need.

Financial data The stipend is $1,000 per year.

Duration 1 year; may be renewed up to 3 additional years.

Number awarded 1 each year.
Deadline April of each year.

[724]
MESOTHELIOMA CANCER ALLIANCE SCHOLARSHIP

Mesothelioma Cancer Alliance
c/o Early, Lucarelli, Sweeney, Meisenkothen
360 Lexington Avenue, 20th Floor
New York, NY 10017
(212) 968-2233   Toll Free: (800) 336-0086
Fax: (212) 986-2255
Web: www.mesothelioma.com/scholarship

Summary To provide financial assistance to undergraduate and graduate students who have had cancer or whose family member has had cancer.

Eligibility This program is open to U.S. citizens enrolled or planning to enroll full time at a 2- or 4-year college or university as an undergraduate or graduate student. Applicants must have battled cancer at any point in their lives (not limited to mesothelioma) or have a parent, sibling, immediate family member, or close friend who has battled or is currently fighting cancer. They must have a GPA of 3.0 or higher. Along with their application, they must submit an essay of 500 to 1,500 words or a video up to 5 minutes in length on how cancer has affected their life, how they overcame that strong adversity, how cancer has affected their outlook on their life and personal or career goals, how that adversity shaped who they are today, what the scholarship would mean to them, and why it is important. Selection is based on the positive impact they have on those around them, strength in the face of adversity, commitment to academic excellence, and financial need.

Financial data The stipend is $4,000.
Duration 1 year.
Number awarded 2 each year: 1 in fall and 1 in spring.
Deadline March of each year for fall semester; November of each year for spring semester.

[725]
MICHAEL A. COREA MEMORIAL SCHOLARSHIP

Transplant Recipients International Organization-
  Greater Cleveland Chapter
Attn: Scholarship Committee
P.O. Box 93163
Cleveland, OH 44101-5163
(440) 473-8979   E-mail: triocleveland@hotmail.com
Web: www.triocleveland.org/Scholarship_Program.html

Summary To provide financial assistance to residents of Ohio who are transplant candidates, recipients, or donors and interested in attending college in any state.

Eligibility This program is open to Ohio residents who are incoming college freshmen, continuing college students, or adults returning to college and attending or planning to attend a college, university, or trade/technical institution in any state. Applicants must be organ or tissue transplant candidates, recipients, or living donors. They must have a cumulative GPA of 2.5 or higher and be able to demonstrate financial need. Along with their application, they must submit a 300-word statement of educational goals and objectives, a statement (250 to 300 words in length) describing how transplantation influences their life, and 3 letters of recommendation.

Financial data The stipend is $1,000. Funds are disbursed directly to the recipient's institution.
Duration 1 year; nonrenewable.
Additional data This program began in 2009.
Number awarded At least 1 each year.
Deadline September of each year.

[726]
MICHAEL A. HUNTER MEMORIAL SCHOLARSHIP

Orange County Community Foundation
Attn: Scholarship Officer
4041 MacArthur Boulevard, Suite 510
Newport Beach, CA 92660
(949) 553-4202, ext. 246   Fax: (949) 553-4211
E-mail: mabril@oc-cf.org
Web: oc-cf.academicworks.com/opportunities/1568

Summary To provide financial assistance for college to leukemia and lymphoma patients and the children of non-surviving leukemia and lymphoma patients.

Eligibility This program is open to graduating high school seniors, community college students, and 4-year university students nationwide. Applicants must be leukemia or lymphoma patients and/or the children of non-surviving leukemia or lymphoma patients who are enrolled or planning to enroll full time. They must have a GPA of 3.0 or higher and be able to document financial need. Along with their application, they must submit a 600-word essay on hoe leukemia or lymphoma has affected their life.

Financial data Stipends range from $2,000 to $3,000.
Duration 1 year.
Number awarded 2 each year.
Deadline March of each year.

[727]
MICHAEL BENDIX SUTTON SCHOLARSHIPS

Michael Bendix Sutton Foundation
c/o Marion B. Sutton
300 Maritime Avenue
White Plains, NY 10601-3459

Summary To provide financial assistance to people with hemophilia who are pre-law students.

Eligibility This program is open to pre-law students who have hemophilia.

Financial data The stipend is $2,000.
Duration 1 year.
Number awarded 2 each year.
Deadline March of each year.

[728]
MICHAEL CALKINS MEMORIAL SCHOLARSHIP

Georgia Transplant Foundation
Attn: Scholarship Program
2201 Macy Drive
Roswell, GA 30076
(770) 457-3796   Fax: (770) 457-7916
E-mail: gtf@gatransplant.org
Web: www.gatransplant.org

Summary To provide financial assistance to residents of Georgia who are transplant recipients or dependents or siblings of recipients and interested in attending college in any state.

Eligibility This program is open to residents of Georgia who are entering or continuing at an accredited institution of higher learning in any state. Applicants must be an organ transplant recipient or the dependent or sibling of a recipient. Along with their application, they must submit a 3-page personal statement on their career objectives, how this scholarship will help them attain their goals, and how transplantation has affected their life. Selection is based on that statement, transcripts, high school exit examination scores, ACT/SAT scores, 3 letters of reference, and financial need.

Financial data The stipend is $1,000 per year.

Duration 1 year; may be renewed up to 3 additional years.

Number awarded 1 each year.

Deadline April of each year.

[729]
MICHAEL YASICK ADHD SCHOLARSHIP

Shire US Inc.
Attn: ADHD Scholarship Program
300 Shire Way
Lexington, MA 02421
(617) 349-0200   E-mail: mcabrey@shire.com
Web: www.shireadhdscholarship.com

Summary To provide financial assistance for college to students who have attention deficit/hyperactivity disorder (ADHD).

Eligibility This program is open to legal residents of the United States who have been diagnosed with ADHD and are enrolled or accepted in an undergraduate program at an accredited 2- or 4-year college, university, or trade/vocational/technical school. Applicants must be under the care of a licensed health professional, although they are not required to be taking medication or to have a specific future or ongoing plan of management for treatment of their ADHD. Along with their application, they must submit a 500-word essay on how ADHD has impacted their life, the challenges they have faced, and how they managed them or what you are doing to manage them. Selection is based on that essay (50%), letters of recommendation (20%), a 100-word statement on how having an ADHD coach will help them transition to higher education (15%), and a list of community, volunteer, and extracurricular activities (15%).

Financial data The stipend is $2,000. Funds are paid directly to the recipient's institution.

Duration 1 year; nonrenewable.

Additional data This program, established in 2011, also provides scholarship recipients with a year of ADHD coaching services from the Edge Foundation. It was previously named simply the Shire ADHD Scholarship Program.

Number awarded Varies each year; recently, 55 were awarded.

Deadline March of each year.

[730]
MIKE HYLTON SCHOLARSHIP

Matrix Health Group
Attn: Memorial Scholarship Program
2202 Brownstone Court
Champaign, IL 61822
(217) 840-1033
E-mail: maria.vetter@matrixhealthgroup.com
Web: www.factorsupportnetwork.com

Summary To provide financial assistance for college to men who have a bleeding disorder and members of their immediate family.

Eligibility This program is open to graduating male high school seniors and students currently enrolled full time at an accredited college, university, or technical school. Applicants must have hemophilia, von Willebrand's disease or other bleeding disorder or be an immediate family member of a person with a bleeding disorder. They must have a GPA of 2.0 or higher for their senior year in high school or their current year in college. Along with their application, they must submit transcripts, ACT or SAT test scores, 2 letters of recommendation, information on their work and school activities, and an essay of 300 to 400 words on 1 of the following topics: 1) the experiences that have influenced their decision to pursue their educational goals or career choice; 2) how they feel their life has been influenced by having a bleeding disorder or by having a bleeding disorder in their family; or 3) their biggest challenge in having a bleeding disorder and how they have or are working through it. Selection is based on that essay, academic merit, and reference letters.

Financial data The stipend is $1,000.

Duration 1 year.

Additional data This program is supported by Factor Support Network Pharmacy and administered by Matrix Health Group.

Number awarded 1 each year.

Deadline July of each year.

[731]
MILLIE GONZALEZ MEMORIAL SCHOLARSHIPS

Matrix Health Group
Attn: Memorial Scholarship Program
2202 Brownstone Court
Champaign, IL 61822
(217) 840-1033
E-mail: maria.vetter@matrixhealthgroup.com
Web: www.factorsupportnetwork.com

Summary To provide financial assistance for college to women who have a bleeding disorder.

Eligibility This program is open to graduating female high school seniors and students currently enrolled full time at an accredited college, university, or technical school. Applicants must have von Willebrand's disease or other bleeding disorder. They must have a GPA of 2.0 or higher for their senior year in high school or their current year in college. Along with their application, they must submit transcripts, ACT or SAT test scores, 2 letters of recommendation, information on their work and school activities, and an essay of 300 to 400 words on 1 of the following topics: 1) the experiences that have influenced their decision to pursue their educational goals or career choice; 2) how they feel their life has been influenced by having a bleeding disorder; or 3) their biggest challenge in having a bleeding disorder and how they have or are working through it. Selection is based on that essay, academic merit, and reference letters.

Financial data The stipend is $1,000.

Duration 1 year.

Additional data This program is supported by Factor Support Network Pharmacy and administered by Matrix Health Group.

Number awarded 1 each year.

Deadline July of each year.

[732]
MISSY AND ANGELA WOOLSEY EDUCATION AWARD

Pennsylvania Cystic Fibrosis Inc.
P.O. Box 29
Mifflinburg, PA 17844
Fax: (570) 374-2612   E-mail: bobderr@ptd.net
Web: www.pacfi.org/woolsey.html

Summary To provide financial assistance to residents of Pennsylvania who have cystic fibrosis and are interested in attending college in any state.

Eligibility This program is open to residents of Pennsylvania who have a doctor's diagnosis of cystic fibrosis. Applicants must be enrolled or planning to enroll at a college, university, trade school, or other institution of higher learning in any state. They must submit information about their financial need, high school and/or college transcripts, and an essay of 300 to 500 words about themselves, their ambitions, and their educational goals.

Financial data The stipend depends on the availability of funds.

Duration 1 year.

Number awarded 1 or more when funds are available.

Deadline Applications may be submitted at any time.

[733]
NATE SLACK SCHOLARSHIP

HF Healthcare
Attn: Scholarship
411 North Lombard Street, Suite B
Oxnard, CA 93030
Toll Free: (866) 981-1171   Fax: (805) 981-1121
E-mail: scholarship@hfhealthcare.com
Web: www.hfhealthcare.com/scholarship

Summary To provide financial assistance for college to students who have hemophilia or a related bleeding disorder and their immediate family.

Eligibility This program is open to U.S. residents who have hemophilia or a related bleeding disorder or are the immediate family member of a person with hemophilia or a related bleeding disorder. Applicants must be enrolled or planning to enroll at an accredited college, university, community college, or trade school. Along with their application, they must submit a 500-word essay the covers their experience living with hemophilia or a related bleeding disorder, their current educational goals, and what they plan to do after they complete those.

Financial data The stipend is $1,000.

Duration 1 year.

Number awarded 2 each year.

Deadline May of each year.

[734]
NATIONAL KIDNEY FOUNDATION OF UTAH AND IDAHO EDUCATIONAL SCHOLARSHIP PROGRAM

National Kidney Foundation of Utah and Idaho
3707 North Canyon Road, Suite 1D
Provo, UT 84604-4585
(801) 226-5111   Toll Free: (800) 869-5277
Fax: (801) 226-8278   E-mail: nkfu@kidneyut.org
Web: www.kidneyut.org/ps-educational-scholarship.php

Summary To provide financial assistance for college to kidney patients in Utah and Idaho.

Eligibility This program is open to residents of Utah and Idaho who are kidney transplant recipients or dialysis patients. Applicants must be attending or planning to attend a college or university in Utah, Wyoming, or Idaho.

Financial data A stipend is awarded (amount not specified).

Duration 1 year.

Number awarded Varies each year; recently, 23 were awarded.

Deadline Deadline not specified.

[735]
NCCF SURVIVOR SCHOLARSHIP PROGRAM

National Collegiate Cancer Foundation
Attn: Scholarship Committee
4858 Battery Lane, Suite 216
Bethesda, MD 20814
(240) 515-6262   E-mail: info@collegiatecancer.org
Web: www.collegiatecancer.org/scholarships

Summary To provide financial assistance for college or graduate school to cancer survivors.

Eligibility This program is open to students between 18 and 35 years of age who are cancer survivors or currently undergoing treatment for cancer. Applicants must be enrolled or planning to enroll at a college or university to work on a certificate or an associate, bachelor's, master's, or doctoral degree. Along with their application, they must submit a 1,000-word essay on 1 of 4 assigned topics related to their experiences with cancer and college. Selection is based on the essay, letters of recommendation, displaying a "Will Win" attitude, overall story of cancer survivorship, commitment to education, and financial need. U.S. citizenship or permanent resident status is required.

Financial data The stipend is $1,000.

Duration 1 year.

Number awarded Varies each year; recently, 39 were awarded.

Deadline May of each year.

[736]
NEBRASKA CHAPTER NHF POST-SECONDARY SCHOLARSHIPS

National Hemophilia Foundation-Nebraska Chapter
Attn: Scholarship Selection Committee
215 Centennial Mall South, Suite 512
Lincoln, NE 68508
(402) 742-5663   Fax: (402) 742-5677
E-mail: office@nebraskanhf.org
Web: www.nebraskanhf.org

Summary To provide financial assistance for attendance at a college in any state to high school seniors in Nebraska who have a bleeding disorder, are relatives of a person with a bleeding disorder, or are a carrier of a defective gene related to a bleeding disorder.

Eligibility This program is open to seniors graduating from high schools in Nebraska who plan to attend a college or university in any state. Applicants must have a bleeding disorder, be an immediately family member of a person with a bleeding disorder, or be the carrier of a defective gene related to a bleeding disorder. Along with their application, they must submit a brief statement on how a bleeding disorder influences their family life and a 250-word essay on their purpose and motivation for pursuing a postsecondary educational degree. Selection is based on that statement and essay, academic promise in their major field, and financial need. Preference is given to members of the Nebraska Chapter of the National Hemophilia Foundation (NHF).

Financial data The stipend ranges from $500 to $1,000 per academic term ($1,000 to $2,000 per year).

Duration 1 year.

Number awarded 1 or more each year.

Deadline June of each year.

[737]
NEW DAY EDUCATION AND REHABILITATION AWARD

Kidney & Urology Foundation of America
Attn: Program Director
63 West Main Street, Suite G
Freehold, NJ 07728
(732) 866-4444   Toll Free: (800) 633-6628
E-mail: info@kidneyurology.org
Web: www.kidneyurology.org

Summary To provide financial assistance for educational or rehabilitation activities to adults who have been diagnosed with kidney or urologic disease.

Eligibility This program is open to adults at least 25 years of age who must have been diagnosed with kidney or urologic disease. Applicants must be seeking funding to complete a degree, obtain a professional certification, learn a new job skill, change careers, or engage in physical rehabilitation. Along with their application, they must submit essays of 250 to 650 words on 1) their medical history, including their illness and how kidney disease has impacted their life, educational, or rehabilitation goals; 2) their educational background, their extracurricular activities and personal interests, any other family members attending college, any family circumstances or personal experiences that may set them apart from other applicants, and financial need; and 3) how they contribute or plan to contribute to the renal or transplant communities. Selection is based on evidence of prior achievements, motivation to accomplish stated goals, and financial need. Priority is given to applicants from the sponsoring organization's participating partner centers.

Financial data The stipend is $1,000 per year.

Duration 1 year; may be renewed up to 3 additional years.

Number awarded 1 or more each year.

Deadline May of each year.

[738]
NEW JERSEY ME/CFS ASSOCIATION HIGH SCHOOL SCHOLARSHIP

New Jersey ME/CFS Association, Inc.
Attn: Scholarship Committee Chair
P.O. Box 477
Florham Park, NJ 07932
(732) 646-0619   Toll Free: (888) 835-3677
E-mail: njmecfsa@njmecfsa.org
Web: www.njmecfsa.org/scholarships

Summary To provide financial assistance to high school seniors in New Jersey who have Chronic Fatigue Syndrome (CFS), also known as Myalgic Encephalomyelitis (ME), and plan to attend college in any state.

Eligibility This program is open to seniors graduating from high schools in New Jersey and planning to enroll full or part time at a 2- or 4-year college, university, or technical school in any state. Applicants must have been diagnosed with ME/CFS. They must have a GPA of 2.0 or higher. Recent high school graduates who had to delay continuing their education because of ME/CFS are also eligible. Along with their application, they must submit a 350-word essay on what they see as their goal for higher education or career direction and how having ME/CFS has influenced their choice. Selection is based on the sincerity of that essay, merit, and financial need.

Financial data The stipend is $1,000.

Duration 1 year.

Additional data This program began in 1999.

Number awarded 1 each year.

Deadline April of each year.

[739]
NEW JERSEY SHARING NETWORK SCHOLARSHIPS

New Jersey Sharing Network Foundation
Attn: Scholarship Committee
691 Central Avenue
New Providence, NJ 07974
(908) 516-5400   Toll Free: (800) 742-7365
Fax: (908) 516-5501
E-mail: info@njsharingnetwork.org
Web: www.njsharingnetwork.org/scholarship

Summary To provide financial assistance to high school seniors in New Jersey who are organ transplant recipients or donors (or their family or friends) and interested in attending college in any state.

Eligibility This program is open to seniors graduating from high schools in New Jersey and planning to attend a college or university in any state. Applicants must have been a donor awareness advocate or have been personally affected by or is a family member of someone personally affected by organ and tissue donation and transplantation (i.e., organ and/or tissue donor, living donor, transplant recipient, waiting for a transplant, or died waiting for a transplant). Along with their application, they must submit an essay on what donation has meant in their life, their knowledge of donation, and their active participation in awareness events.

Financial data The stipend is $5,000; funds are paid directly to the school.

Duration 1 year.

Additional data This program includes the Betsy Niles Scholarship and the Missy's Miracle Scholarship.

Number awarded Varies each year; recently, 4 were awarded.

Deadline April of each year.

[740]
NHF NEVADA SCHOLARSHIPS

National Hemophilia Foundation-Nevada Chapter
Attn: Academic Scholarship Program
7473 West Lake Mead Boulevard, Suite 100
Las Vegas, NV 89128
(702) 564-4368   Fax: (702) 446-8134
E-mail: nevada@hemophilia.org
Web: hfnvorg.presencehost.net

Summary To provide financial assistance to residents of Nevada who have a bleeding disorder and are interested in attending college in any state.

Eligibility This program is open to residents of Nevada who have an inherited bleeding disorder. Applicants must be enrolled or planning to enroll at a college, university, or trade school in any state. Along with their application, they must submit 300-word essays on 1) their educational and career goals; and 2) the impact that this scholarship would have on their education. Selection is based on those essays, academic merit, leadership qualities, reference letters, impact of the bleeding disorder on educational activities, and financial need.

Financial data Stipends range from $250 to $1,000.

Duration 1 year.

Number awarded Varies each year.

Deadline March of each year.

[741]
NJCEC SCHOLARSHIP PROGRAM

New Jersey Council for Exceptional Children
c/o Barry Schwartz, Awards Chair
17 Rossmore Terrace
Livingston, NJ 07039
(973) 533-0420   E-mail: bms17@verizon.net
Web: www.njcec.org

Summary To provide financial assistance to high school seniors in New Jersey who have a disability and plan to attend college in any state.

Eligibility This program is open to seniors graduating from high schools in New Jersey who have a diagnosed disability and are eligible for special education. Applicants must be planning to enroll at a 2- or 4-year college, university, technical school, or other recognized program in any state. Along with their application, they must submit a statement from their child study team indicating a recognized disability, 2 letters of recommendation, and a 150-word essay on why they are applying for this scholarship.

Financial data Stipends range from $500 to $2,000.

Duration 1 year.

Number awarded Several each year.

Deadline February of each year.

[742]
NJCTS YOUTH SCHOLARSHIP PROGRAM

New Jersey Center for Tourette Syndrome, Inc.
Attn: Project Coordinator
50 Division Street, Suite 205
Somerville, NJ 08876
(908) 575-7350　　　　　　Fax: (908) 575-8699
E-mail: kteabo@njcts.org
Web: www.njcts.org/programs/awards-scholarships

Summary　To provide financial assistance to high school seniors in New Jersey who have Tourette Syndrome and plan to attend college in any state.

Eligibility　This program is open to seniors graduating from high schools in New Jersey who plan to enroll full or part time at a college or trade school in any state. Applicants must have been diagnosed with Tourette Syndrome. Along with their application, they must submit an essay of 1 to 2 pages describing how Tourette Syndrome has played a part in their life; they may also submit a CD, cassette, DVD, or video of about 5 minutes in length displaying their talent in music, art, sports, or other field. Selection is based on academic achievement, community involvement, and accomplishments as an individual living with Tourette Syndrome.

Financial data　The stipend is $1,000.

Duration　1 year.

Additional data　This program began in 2004.

Number awarded　Varies each year; recently, 13 were awarded.

Deadline　April of each year.

[743]
NOVO NORDISK DONNELLY AWARDS

World Team Tennis, Inc.
Attn: Novo Nordisk Donnelly Awards
2204 Larkdale Drive
Glenview, IL 60025
(212) 586-3444, ext. 120　　　Fax: (212) 586-6277
E-mail: dstone@wtt.com
Web: www.wtt.com/pages/novo-nordisk-donnelly-awards

Summary　To recognize and reward young tennis players who have diabetes.

Eligibility　This program is open to scholar/athletes between 14 and 21 years of age who play tennis competitively either on a school team or as a ranked tournament player and have type I diabetes. Applicants must submit a 500-word essay on the significance of diabetes in their lives. Selection is based on values, commitment, sportsmanship, community involvement, and financial need.

Financial data　Awards are $7,500 for winners or $3,000 for regional finalists; funds may be used for education, tennis development, and/or medical care.

Duration　The nonrenewable awards are presented annually.

Additional data　This program was established in 1998 by the Billie Jean King Foundation in cooperation with the American Diabetes Association. It includes 2 scholarships named after sisters, Diane Donnelly Stone and Tracey Donnelly Maltby, who have had diabetes since childhood and have played tennis competitively. Novo Nordisk sponsors the program.

Number awarded　10 each year: 2 winners and 8 regional finalists.

Deadline　March of each year.

[744]
NOVO NORDISK SCHOLARSHIPS

Diabetes Scholars Foundation
310 Busse Highway, Suite 256
Park Ridge, IL 60068
(312) 215-9861　　　　　　Fax: (847) 991-8739
E-mail: m.podjasek@diabetesscholars.org
Web: www.diabetesscholars.org/college-scholarship

Summary　To provide financial assistance for college to high school seniors who have diabetes.

Eligibility　This program is open to graduating high school seniors who have Type 1 diabetes and plan to attend an accredited 4-year university, college, or trade/technical school in any state. Applicants must be able to demonstrate active involvement in the diabetes community, academic accomplishment, participation in community and/or extracurricular activities, and successful management of the challenges of living with diabetes. Financial need is not considered in the selection process. U.S. citizenship or permanent resident status is required.

Financial data　The stipend is $5,000.

Duration　1 year.

Additional data　This program is sponsored by Novo Nordisk.

Number awarded　4 each year.

Deadline　April of each year.

[745]
NOVOSECURE SCHOLARSHIP PROGRAM

Novo Nordisk Inc.
Attn: NovoSecure
800 Scudders Mill Road
Plainsboro, NJ 08536
Toll Free: (844) NOVOSEC
Web: www.mynovosecure.com

Summary　To provide financial assistance for college to adults who either have a bleeding disorder or are caregivers to people with those disorders.

Eligibility　This program is open to adults over 23 years of age currently enrolled in college or vocational school. Applicants must have hemophilia with an inhibitor or factor VII deficiency or be a primary caregiver to a person with hemophilia. They must be working on a certificate or associate or bachelor's degree to get more training to help improve their career or transition to a new field.

Financial data　Stipends $4,000 for students at 4-year colleges and universities and $2,500 for students at community colleges or vocational schools. Funds are paid directly to the university or institution.

Duration　1 year.

Additional data　This program is administered by Scholarship Managers Inc., (877) 668-6777.

Number awarded   5 each year for university and college students and 10 each year for community college and vocational school students.
Deadline   June of each year.

[746]
OLIVIA M. MARQUART SCHOLARSHIP
Ulman Cancer Fund for Young Adults
Attn: Scholarship Committee
921 East Fort Avenue, Suite 325
Baltimore, MD 21230
(410) 964-0202   Toll Free: (888) 393-FUND
Fax: (888) 964-0402
E-mail: scholarship@ulmanfund.org
Web: www.ulmanfund.org/scholarships

Summary   To provide financial assistance for college or graduate school to residents of Pennsylvania who have cancer or are cancer survivors and are interested in studying education.
Eligibility   This program is open to residents of Pennsylvania who have battled cancer or are currently undergoing active treatment. The first diagnosis of cancer must have occurred after they were 15 years of age. Applicants must be attending or planning to attend a 2- or 4-year college or university in any state to work on an undergraduate or graduate degree in education. They must be U.S. citizens. Along with their application, they must submit a 500-word essay or 3-minute video on either 1) a letter that they would have liked to receive during their cancer experience; or 2) what they would tell the young adults who participate in the sponsor's summer-long drive to support the organization about being a young adult impacted by cancer. Financial need is considered in the selection process.
Financial data   The stipend is $2,500. Funds are paid directly to the educational institution.
Duration   1 year.
Additional data   Recipients are obligated to organize and run a bone marrow registry drive with the support of Delete Blood Cancer and There Goes My Hero.
Number awarded   1 each year.
Deadline   March of each year.

[747]
O'NEILL TABANI ENRICHMENT FUND
National Down Syndrome Society
Attn: Information and Referral Specialist
666 Broadway, Eighth Floor
New York, NY 10012-2317
(212) 460-9330   Toll Free: (800) 221-4602
Fax: (212) 979-2873   E-mail: otef@ndss.org
Web: www.ndss.org

Summary   To provide financial assistance to students who have Down syndrome and wish to obtain postsecondary or other additional education.
Eligibility   This program is open to young adults who are 18 years of age or older and have Down syndrome. Applicants must be interested in participating in an postsecondary education program or enrichment courses to gain employment and other important life skills contribut-

ing to their independence. Along with their application, they must submit a 1-page essay on themselves and their interests.
Financial data   Stipends range up to $5,000 per year. Funds must be used to pay for tuition or other educational expenses at a college, educational institution, learning center, or employment training program.
Duration   1 year; nonrenewable.
Additional data   This program, formerly named the Joshua O'Neill and Zeshan Tabani Enrichment Fund, began in 2005.
Number awarded   Varies each year; recently, 18 were awarded. Since the program began, it has awarded 112 scholarships.
Deadline   March of each year.

[748]
P. BUCKLEY MOSS ENDOWED SCHOLARSHIP
P. Buckley Moss Foundation for Children's Education
108 South Wayne Avenue
Waynesboro, VA 22980
(540) 932-1728   Fax: (540) 941-8865
E-mail: foundation@mossfoundation.org
Web: www.mossfoundation.org

Summary   To provide financial assistance to high school seniors with language-related learning disabilities who plan to study visual arts in college.
Eligibility   Eligible to be nominated for this scholarship are high school seniors with language-related learning disabilities and visual arts talent. Nominations must be submitted by a member of the P. Buckley Moss Society. Nominees must be planning to attend a 4-year college or university or a 2-year community college and prepare for a career in a visual art field. The nomination packets must include evidence of financial need, verification of a language-related learning disability from a counselor or case manager, a high school transcript, 2 letters of recommendation, and 3 essays by the nominees: 1) 3 words that best describe themselves and examples of those qualities; 2) their learning disability, how it has challenged them, specific strategies they have used to cope, and its effect on their lives; and 3) where they intend to go to school and why, how they plan to use their artistic talent, and what they see themselves doing with their art in 10 years.
Financial data   The stipend is $1,000. Funds are paid to the recipient's college or university.
Duration   1 year; may be renewed for up to 3 additional years.
Additional data   This program began in 2007.
Number awarded   1 each year.
Deadline   March of each year.

[749]
PATIENT ADVOCATE FOUNDATION SCHOLARSHIPS FOR SURVIVORS

Patient Advocate Foundation
Attn: Scholarship Coordinator
421 Butler Farm Road
Hampton, VA 23669
(757) 952-1370   Toll Free: (800) 532-5274
Fax: (757) 873-8999
E-mail: events@patientadvocate.org
Web: www.patientadvocate.org/help.php?p=69

Summary To provide financial assistance for college or graduate school to students seeking to initiate or complete a course of study that has been interrupted or delayed by a diagnosis of cancer or other life threatening disease.

Eligibility This program is open to legal residents of the United States under 25 years of age who are working full time on a bachelor's degree or on an associate degree in preparation for transfer to a 4-year program. Applicants must have been diagnosed with and/or been actively treated for cancer or other chronic or life threatening disease within the past 5 years. Along with their application, they must submit a 1,000-word essay on how their diagnosis has impacted their life and future goals. Financial need is also considered in the selection process.

Financial data The stipend is $3,000 per year. Funds are paid directly to the college or university to help cover tuition and other fee costs. The cost of books is not included.

Duration 1 year; may be renewed up to 3 additional years, provided the recipient remains enrolled full time, maintains a GPA of 3.0 or higher, and performs 20 hours of community service.

Number awarded Varies each year; recently, 12 new scholarships were awarded. Since the program was established, it has awarded 71 scholarships worth more than $436,000.

Deadline February of each year.

[750]
PEDIATRIC BRAIN TUMOR FOUNDATION COLLEGE SCHOLARSHIP PROGRAM

Pediatric Brain Tumor Foundation of the United States
Attn: Family Support Program Manager
302 Ridgefield Court
Asheville, NC 28806
(828) 665-6891, ext. 306
Toll Free: (800) 253-6530, ext. 306
Fax: (828) 665-6894   E-mail: info@curethekids.org
Web: www.curethekids.org

Summary To provide financial assistance to survivors of a brain or spinal cord tumor who are entering or enrolled in college.

Eligibility This program is open to high school seniors and current college students who have been diagnosed at or before age 19 with a primary malignant or non-malignant central nervous system brain and/or spinal cord tumor. Applicants must be enrolled or planning to enroll at an accredited community college or undergraduate

school. They must submit an essay, proof of tumor diagnosis, GPA, transcripts, and recommendations.

Financial data The stipend is $1,000.

Duration 1 year; nonrenewable.

Additional data This program, which began in 2002, receives funding from the *Cycle World* Joseph C. Parkhurst Education Fund.

Number awarded Varies each year; recently, 53 were awarded. Since the program began, it has awarded more than 1,500 scholarships worth $1.7 million.

Deadline March of each year.

[751]
PEGGY SHERRELL MEMORIAL SCHOLARSHIP

Epilepsy Foundation of Kentuckiana
Attn: Director of Education
Kosair Charities Centre
982 Eastern Parkway
Louisville, KY 40217-1566
(502) 637-4440, ext. 14   Toll Free: (866) 275-1078
Fax: (502) 637-4442
Web: www.efky.org/scholarship-applications.html

Summary To provide financial assistance to nontraditional students in Kentucky and southern Indiana who have epilepsy and are interested in attending college in any state.

Eligibility This program is open to residents of Kentucky (except Boone, Campbell, Grant, and Kenton counties) or southern Indiana (Clark, Floyd, and Harrison counties) who have epilepsy or another seizure disorder and are under a physician's care. Applicants be adult learners entering college for the first time or nontraditional students returning to college to complete their degree or certification. Along with their application, they must submit 400-word essays on 1) their struggle to overcome adversity because of their epilepsy and seizures; and 2) their plans for their future educational and professional endeavors. Financial need is also considered in the selection process.

Financial data The stipend is $1,000.

Duration 1 year.

Additional data This program began in 2011.

Number awarded 1 each year.

Deadline May of each year.

[752]
PERLITA LIWANAG MEMORIAL SCHOLARSHIP

Ulman Cancer Fund for Young Adults
Attn: Scholarship Committee
921 East Fort Avenue, Suite 325
Baltimore, MD 21230
(410) 964-0202   Toll Free: (888) 393-FUND
Fax: (888) 964-0402
E-mail: scholarship@ulmanfund.org
Web: www.ulmanfund.org/scholarships

Summary To provide financial assistance for college or graduate school to students from the Washington, D.C. metropolitan area who have been diagnosed with cancer or have or have lost a family member with cancer.

Eligibility This program is open to students who 1) have been diagnosed with cancer; 2) have a parent, sibling, or guardian living with cancer; or 3) have lost a parent, sibling, or guardian to cancer. Applicants must be residents of Washington, D.C., Maryland, or northern Virginia. They must be 35 years of age or younger and attending, or planning to attend, a 2- or 4-year college, university, or vocational program in any state to work on an undergraduate or graduate degree. The first diagnosis of cancer (whether of the applicant, a parent, a sibling, or a guardian) must have occurred after the applicant was 15 years of age. Along with their application, they must submit a 500-word essay or 3-minute video on either 1) a letter that they would have liked to receive during their cancer experience; or 2) what they would tell the young adults who participate in the sponsor's summer-long drive to support the organization about being a young adult impacted by cancer. U.S. citizenship or permanent resident status is required.

Financial data The stipend is $2,500. Funds are paid directly to the educational institution.

Duration 1 year.

Additional data This program began in 2011. Recipients are obligated to organize and run a bone marrow registry drive with the support of Delete Blood Cancer and There Goes My Hero.

Number awarded 1 each year.

Deadline March of each year.

[753]
PETER AND BRUCE BIDSTRUP SCHOLARSHIP FUND

National Kidney Foundation of Arizona
Attn: Patient Services Director
360 East Coronado Road, Suite 180
Phoenix, AZ 85018
(602) 840-1644   Fax: (602) 840-2360
E-mail: glennas@azkidney.org
Web: www.azkidney.org/scholarships

Summary To provide financial assistance for college to kidney patients in Arizona.

Eligibility This program is open to students in Arizona who are undergoing dialysis treatment or have received kidney transplants. Applicants must be attending or planning to attend a college, community college, or technical school in Arizona. Financial need is considered in the selection process.

Financial data This scholarship pays the tuition fees at schools in Arizona.

Additional data This scholarship fund was established in 1985 to honor Peter and Bruce Bidstrup, who did not survive kidney disease. Its selection committee is chaired by their mother, Carol Bidstrup.

Number awarded Varies each year.

Deadline Deadline not specified.

[754]
PINK BANDANA SCHOLARSHIPS

Pink Bandana
Attn: Scholarships
P.O. Box 83282
Lincoln, NE 68501
(402) 560-1578 E-mail: scholarship@pinkbandana.org
Web: pinkbandana.org/scholarship

Summary To provide financial assistance for college in any state to high school seniors in Nebraska who have battled breast cancer or have a family member who has battled cancer.

Eligibility This program is open to seniors graduating from high schools in Nebraska and planning to enroll full time at a college, university, or community college in any state. Applicants must have battled breast cancer or have a sibling, guardian, or biological parent who has battled breast cancer within the past 10 years. Along with their application, they must submit a list of extracurricular activities, information on the member of their family who has battled breast cancer, an essay on how the battle against breast cancer has affected them and their family, and information on their financial situation.

Financial data The total stipend is $4,000, paid in increments of $1,000 per year for students at 4-year colleges and university or $2,000 per year for students at 2-year colleges.

Duration Up to 4 years for students at 4-year colleges and universities or up to students at 2-year colleges.

Number awarded 1 or more each year.

Deadline March of each year.

[755]
RALPH G. NORMAN SCHOLARSHIPS

Learning Disabilities Association of Arkansas
P.O. Box 23514
Little Rock, AR 72221
(501) 666-8777   E-mail: info@ldarkansas.org
Web: www.ldarkansas.org/norman.cfm

Summary To provide financial assistance for college to residents of Arkansas who have a learning disability.

Eligibility This program is open to Arkansas residents who have a learning disability but are ineligible for Social Security Disability (SSD) or Supplemental Security Income (SSI). Applicants must be graduating high school seniors, current college students, or GED recipients. Along with their application, they must submit documentation of their disability, transcripts of all high school and/or college courses, 2 letters of recommendation, and a 1,000-word essay about how their disability has impacted their life and about their future educational and career goals.

Financial data The stipend is $2,500.

Duration 1 year.

Number awarded 1 or more each year.

Deadline March of each year.

[756]
READY WHEN YOU ARE PROGRAM

Aaron Bonner Foundation
2400 Sixth Street, N.W.
MSC 590042
Washington, DC 20059
(202) 770-5437
E-mail: info@aaronbonnerfoundation.org
Web: www.aaronbonnerfoundation.org/scholarships.html

Summary To provide financial assistance to college students who are cancer patients or survivors.

Eligibility This program is open to students currently enrolled at a university or community college in any state. Applicants must be cancer patients or survivors. Selection is based on personal hardship and financial need.

Financial data A stipend is awarded (amount not specified).

Duration 1 year; recipients may reapply.

Number awarded Varies each year.

Deadline Deadline not specified.

[757]
RIMINGTON TROPHY SCHOLARSHIP

Boomer Esiason Foundation
c/o Chris McEwan
483 Tenth Avenue, Suite 300
New York, NY 10018
(646) 292-7939   Fax: (646) 292-7945
E-mail: cmcewan@esiason.org
Web: www.esiason.org

Summary To provide financial assistance to undergraduate and graduate students who have cystic fibrosis (CF).

Eligibility This program is open to CF patients who are working on an undergraduate or graduate degree. Applicants must submit a letter from their doctor confirming the diagnosis of CF and a list of daily medications, information on financial need, a detailed breakdown of tuition costs from their academic institution, transcripts, and a 2-page essay on 1) their postgraduation goals; and 2) the importance of compliance with CF therapies and what they practice on a daily basis to stay healthy. Selection is based on academic ability, character, leadership potential, service to the community, financial need, and daily compliance to CF therapy.

Financial data The stipend ranges from $1,000 to $2,000. Funds are paid directly to the academic institution to assist in covering the cost of tuition and fees.

Duration 1 year; nonrenewable.

Additional data This program began in 2012 in association with the Rimington Trophy, a college football award named in honor of Dave Rimington, a former player for the University of Nebraska and the president of the Boomer Esiason Foundation.

Number awarded 1 each year.

Deadline June of each year.

[758]
RISE SCHOLARSHIPS

Rise Scholarship Foundation, Inc.
Attn: Awards Selection Committee
P.O. Box 422417
Atlanta, GA 30342
E-mail: risescholarshipfoundation@gmail.com
Web: risescholarshipfoundation.org

Summary To provide financial assistance for college to high school seniors who have a learning disability.

Eligibility This program is open to graduating high school seniors who have a documented learning disability (a diagnosis of ADHD or ADD alone does not qualify) or autism spectrum disability diagnosis. Applicants must be planning to enroll in at least 2 or more core classes each semester at an accredited college or university. They must have a GPA of 2.5 or higher. Along with their application, they must submit a high school transcript, documentation of a learning disability (e.g., an I.E.P. and/or 504 plan), letters of recommendation, and an original expressive essay or piece of art (e.g., poem, drawing) that they have created and that describes how having their learning difference has affected them. Financial need is not considered in the selection process. U.S. citizenship is required.

Financial data The stipend is $2,500 for scholarship winners or $500 for honorable mention.

Duration 1 year.

Additional data The Rise Scholarship Foundation (which stands for Rewarding Individual Success in Education) was established in 2010.

Number awarded Varies each year; recently, 6 scholarship winners, including 1 for a student with autism, and 14 honorable mentions, including 4 for students with autism, were selected.

Deadline February of each year.

[759]
RJT CRIMINAL DEFENSE AUTISM SCHOLARSHIP

RJT Criminal Defense Attorney
2820 Camino Del Rio South, Suite 110
San Diego, CA 92108
(619) 577-0868
E-mail: mike@sandiegocriminallawyerrt.com
Web: www.sandiegocriminallawyerrt.com

Summary To provide financial assistance for college to people who have been diagnosed with autism.

Eligibility This program is open to U.S. citizens who have been diagnosed with autism, also known as Autism Spectrum Disorder (ASD). Applicants must be enrolled or planning to enroll at a college, university, community college, or trade school. Along with their application, they must submit 1) a 125-word statement on their educational goals; and 2) an essay up to 800 words in length on the impact autism has had on their education.

Financial data The stipend is $1,000.

Duration 1 year.

Number awarded 1 each year.

Deadline February of each year.

[760]
RMHBDA EDUCATION SCHOLARSHIP

Rocky Mountain Hemophilia and Bleeding Disorder
  Association
Attn: Executive Director
1627 West Main Street, Suite 142
Bozeman, MT 59715
(406) 586-4050   Fax: (406) 586-4050
E-mail: brad.rhmbda@gmail.com
Web: www.rmhbda.org/html/financialAssistance.html

Summary To provide financial assistance to residents of Montana and Wyoming who have a bleeding disorder or are relatives of a person with a bleeding disorder and are interested in attending college in any state.

Eligibility This program is open to residents of Montana or Wyoming who have or have a family member with an inherited bleeding disorder. Applicants must be entering or attending a 2- or 4-year undergraduate institution in any state; that includes graduating high school seniors, current undergraduate students, and adults seeking undergraduate studies later in life. They must have been involved with the Rocky Mountain Hemophilia and Bleeding Disorder Association (RMHBDA) at some point and in some capacity. Selection is based on GPA, extracurricular activities, success in various activities, volunteerism in general, volunteerism in the bleeding disorder community.

Financial data The stipend is $1,000 per year. Funds are disbursed directly to the student.

Duration 1 year; recipients may reapply.

Number awarded 1 or more each year.

Deadline May of each year.

[761]
ROBYN'S WAY SCHOLARSHIP

Oklahoma City Community Foundation
Attn: Scholarship Coordinator
1000 North Broadway
P.O. Box 1146
Oklahoma City, OK 73101-1146
(405) 606-2907   Fax: (405) 235-5612
E-mail: w.minter@occf.org
Web: occf.academicworks.com/opportunities/2209

Summary To provide financial assistance for college in any state to high school seniors in Oklahoma who come from a single parent home or from a family impacted by cancer.

Eligibility This program is open to seniors graduating from high schools in Oklahoma who are the child of a single parent or come from a family that has been impacted by cancer. Applicants must be planning to enroll at an accredited 2- or 4-year college or university in any state. Preference is given to students who 1) have been treated for cancer; 2) are a cancer survivor; 3) have lost a parent to cancer; or 4) have volunteered or are actively volunteering for a cancer related organization and/or events. Along with their application, they must submit documentation of financial need and brief essays on how cancer has impacted and affected their education and a summary of their volunteer history with cancer related organizations and/or events.

Financial data The stipend is $2,000.

Duration 1 year; nonrenewable.

Additional data This program began in 2017.

Number awarded 1 or more each year.

Deadline February of each year.

[762]
R.O.C.K. COLLEGE SCHOLARSHIP PROGRAM

American Cancer Society-Florida Division
3709 West Jetton Avenue
Tampa, FL 33629-5146
(813) 349-4405
Toll Free: (800) 444-1410, ext. 4405 (within FL)
Fax: (813) 254-5857   E-mail: susan.lee@cancer.org
Web: acsflnr.ejoinme.org/ROCK

Summary To provide financial assistance to students in Florida who have been diagnosed with cancer and are interested in attending college in any state.

Eligibility This program is open to Florida residents who have been diagnosed with cancer before the age of 21, are under 21 at the time of application, are high school seniors or graduates, and have been accepted to an accredited 2- or 4-year college, university, or vocational/ technical school in Florida. Applicants must submit a completed application form, 3 letters of recommendation (including 1 from a physician), their financial aid form, an official transcript, their SAT and/or ACT test scores, and a 500-word essay on their journey as a cancer survivor, goals, ambitions, and how this scholarship will help them achieve academic success. Selection is based on financial need, academic record, leadership ability, and community service.

Financial data Stipends provide up to $2,700 per year for tuition plus $300 per year for textbooks.

Duration 1 year; may be renewed to a maximum of 130 semester hours over 5 years, whichever comes first.

Additional data These scholarships were first awarded in 1992 as part of the Florida division's Reaching Out to Cancer Kids (R.O.C.K.) program. Recipients are expected to complete at least 10 hours of American Cancer Society community service annually.

Number awarded Varies each year; recently, 154 were awarded.

Deadline April of each year.

[763]
RON NIEDERMAN SCHOLARSHIP

Matrix Health Group
Attn: Memorial Scholarship Program
2202 Brownstone Court
Champaign, IL 61822
(217) 840-1033
E-mail: maria.vetter@matrixhealthgroup.com
Web: www.factorsupportnetwork.com

Summary To provide financial assistance for college to men who have a bleeding disorder and members of their immediate family.

Eligibility This program is open to graduating male high school seniors and students currently enrolled full time at an accredited college, university, or technical school. Applicants must have hemophilia, von Willebrand's disease or other bleeding disorder or be an immediate family member of a person with a bleeding disorder. They must have a GPA of 2.0 or higher for their senior year in high school or their current year in college. Along with their application, they must submit transcripts, ACT or SAT test scores, 2 letters of recommendation, information on their work and school activities, and an essay of 300 to 400 words on 1 of the following topics: 1) the experiences that have influenced their decision to pursue their educational goals or career choice; 2) how they feel their life has been influenced by having a bleeding disorder or by having a bleeding disorder in their family; or 3) their biggest challenge in having a bleeding disorder and how they have or are working through it. Selection is based on that essay, academic merit, and reference letters.

Financial data The stipend is $1,000.

Duration 1 year.

Additional data This program is supported by Factor Support Network Pharmacy and administered by Matrix Health Group.

Number awarded 1 each year.

Deadline July of each year.

[764]
ROSEMARY QUIGLEY MEMORIAL SCHOLARSHIP

Boomer Esiason Foundation
c/o Chris McEwan
483 Tenth Avenue, Suite 300
New York, NY 10018
(646) 292-7939   Fax: (646) 292-7945
E-mail: cmcewan@esiason.org
Web: www.esiason.org

Summary To provide financial assistance to undergraduate and graduate students who have cystic fibrosis (CF) and a demonstrated commitment to living life to the fullest.

Eligibility This program is open to CF patients who are working on an undergraduate or graduate degree. Applicants must be able to demonstrate a clear sense of life goals and a commitment to living life to the fullest, despite having CF. Along with their application, they must submit a letter from their doctor confirming the diagnosis of CF and a list of daily medications, information on financial need, a detailed breakdown of tuition costs from their academic institution, transcripts, and a 2-page essay on 1) their postgraduation goals; and 2) the importance of compliance with CF therapies and what they practice on a daily basis to stay healthy. Selection is based on academic ability, character, leadership potential, service to the community, and financial need. Finalists are interviewed by telephone.

Financial data The stipend ranges from $500 to $2,000. Funds are paid directly to the academic institution to assist in covering the cost of tuition and fees.

Duration 1 year; nonrenewable.

Number awarded 1 each year.

Deadline June of each year.

[765]
ROSS SKELTON SCHOLARSHIP

Cancer for College
981 Park Center Drive
Vista, CA 92081
(760) 599-5096
E-mail: applications@cancerforcollege.org
Web: www.cancerforcollege.org/application.html

Summary To provide financial assistance to undergraduate and graduate students from North and South Carolina who are cancer patients or survivors and working on or planning to work on a degree in engineering.

Eligibility This program is open to undergraduate and graduate students in engineering who are originally from or currently attending or entering accredited colleges, universities, community colleges, or trade schools in North or South Carolina. Applicants must be a cancer patient or survivor. Along with their application, they must submit transcripts, verification of their cancer diagnosis, 2 letters of recommendation, and information on their financial situation.

Financial data The stipend ranges from $1,000 to $5,000.

Duration 1 year.

Number awarded 1 each year.

Deadline January of each year.

[766]
RUBY'S RAINBOW SCHOLARSHIPS

Ruby's Rainbow
P.O. Box 153095
Austin, TX 78715
(512) 879-7801   E-mail: liz@rubysrainbow.org
Web: www.rubysrainbow.org/apply-now

Summary To provide financial assistance to postsecondary students who have Down syndrome.

Eligibility This program is open to students who are at least 18 years of age and have Down syndrome. Applicants must be interested in attending a class or program that will enhance their life through employment, independent living or life skills, or interests in other areas. Along with their application, they must submit 2 letters of recommendation, a high school transcript or equivalent, and a 100-word essay on an assigned topic.

Financial data The stipend is $5,000 or $3,000 per year.

Duration 1 year; recipients may not reapply in the following year, but they may do so in the year after that.

Additional data The $5,000 scholarships are designated the Maudie's Scholarship Award, the Warriors for Walt Scholarship Award, and the Austin Board of Realtors Foundation Scholarship Award. Other named scholarships include the Laura Lee Scholarship Award, the Wil Can Fly Scholarship Award, the Lovrin Baxter Scholarship Award, the Arehart Family Scholarship Award, the Sully Drake Family and Friends Scholarship Award, the Greg

Cummings Scholarship Award, the LPV Scholarship Award, and the PCSI Scholarship Award.

Number awarded Varies each year; recently, 3 at $5,000 and 32 at $3,000 were awarded.

Deadline July of each year.

[767]
SACKS FOR CF SCHOLARSHIPS

Boomer Esiason Foundation
c/o Chris McEwan
483 Tenth Avenue, Suite 300
New York, NY 10018
(646) 292-7939　　　　　Fax: (646) 292-7945
E-mail: cmcewan@esiason.org
Web: www.esiason.org

Summary To provide financial assistance to undergraduate and graduate students who have cystic fibrosis (CF).

Eligibility This program is open to CF patients who are working on an undergraduate or graduate degree. Applicants must submit a letter from their doctor confirming the diagnosis of CF and a list of daily medications, information on financial need, a detailed breakdown of tuition costs from their academic institution, transcripts, and a 2-page essay on 1) their postgraduation goals; and 2) the importance of compliance with CF therapies and what they practice on a daily basis to stay healthy. Selection is based on academic ability, character, leadership potential, service to the community, financial need, and adherence to daily CF therapy.

Financial data The stipend ranges from $3,000 to $10,000. Funds are paid directly to the academic institution to assist in covering the cost of tuition and fees.

Duration 1 year; nonrenewable.

Additional data This program is funded by AbbVie Inc., a corporate sponsor which donates $1,000 to the foundation each time a quarterback is sacked on NFL Monday Night Football games.

Number awarded 30 each year.

Deadline January of each year.

[768]
SARA ELIZABETH STUBBLEFIELD FOUNDATION SCHOLARSHIP

Sara Elizabeth Stubblefield Foundation
c/o Matthew Flanigan
Black, Hedin, Ballard, McDonald, P.C.
108 South Ninth Street
P.O. Box 4007
Mt. Vernon, IL 62864
(618) 242-3310　　　　　Fax: (618) 242-3735
Web: www.epilepsychicago.org

Summary To provide financial assistance to high school seniors in Illinois who have epilepsy and plan to attend college in any state.

Eligibility This program is open to seniors graduating from high schools in Illinois who have epilepsy and are under a physician's care for the disease. Applicants must be planning to enroll at a college or vocational/technical school in any state. Along with their application, they must

submit 250-word essays on 1) something of direct personal importance to them as a person living with epilepsy; and 2) their plans for their future educational and personal endeavors. Financial need is also considered in the selection process.

Financial data The stipend is $2,000 per year.

Duration 1 year; recipients may reapply.

Additional data This program began in 2011.

Number awarded 1 each year.

Deadline April of each year.

[769]
SATOLA FAMILY SCHOLARSHIP

Ulman Cancer Fund for Young Adults
Attn: Scholarship Committee
921 East Fort Avenue, Suite 325
Baltimore, MD 21230
(410) 964-0202　　　　　Toll Free: (888) 393-FUND
Fax: (888) 964-0402
E-mail: scholarship@ulmanfund.org
Web: www.ulmanfund.org/scholarships

Summary To provide financial assistance for college or graduate school to students who have been diagnosed with cancer or have or have lost a family member with cancer.

Eligibility This program is open to students who 1) have been diagnosed with cancer; 2) have a parent or sibling living with cancer; or 3) have lost a parent or sibling to cancer. Applicants must be attending, or planning to attend, a college or university in any state to work on an undergraduate, graduate, or professional degree. They should be able to demonstrate courage, spirit, and determination. The first diagnosis of cancer (whether of the applicant, a parent, or sibling) must have occurred after the applicant was 15 years of age. Along with their application, they must submit a 500-word essay or 3-minute video on either 1) a letter that they would have liked to receive during their cancer experience; or 2) what they would tell the young adults who participate in the sponsor's summer-long drive to support the organization about being a young adult impacted by cancer. U.S. citizenship is required.

Financial data The stipend is $2,500. Funds are paid directly to the educational institution.

Duration 1 year.

Additional data This program began in 2009. Recipients are obligated to organize and run a bone marrow registry drive with the support of Delete Blood Cancer and There Goes My Hero.

Number awarded 1 each year.

Deadline March of each year.

[770]
SCHOLARSHIP OF THE ARTS

Boomer Esiason Foundation
c/o Chris McEwan
483 Tenth Avenue, Suite 300
New York, NY 10018
(646) 292-7939   Fax: (646) 292-7945
E-mail: cmcewan@esiason.org
Web: www.esiason.org

Summary   To provide financial assistance to undergraduate and graduate students who have cystic fibrosis (CF) and are working on a degree in the arts.

Eligibility   This program is open to CF patients who are working on an undergraduate or graduate degree in the arts. Applicants must submit a sample of their work (video, painting, sketching, sculpture), a letter from their doctor confirming the diagnosis of CF and a list of daily medications, information on financial need, a detailed breakdown of tuition costs from their academic institution, transcripts, and a 2-page essay on 1) their postgraduation goals; and 2) the importance of compliance with CF therapies and what they practice on a daily basis to stay healthy. Selection is based on academic ability, character, leadership potential, service to the community, and financial need.

Financial data   Stipends range from $500 to $1,000. Funds are paid directly to the academic institution to assist in covering the cost of tuition and fees.

Duration   1 year; nonrenewable.

Number awarded   1 each year.

Deadline   May of each year.

[771]
SCHOLARSHIPS FOR VETERANS WITH POST-TRAUMATIC STRESS DISORDER

RJT Criminal Defense Attorney
2820 Camino Del Rio South, Suite 110
San Diego, CA 92108
(619) 577-0868
E-mail: mike@sandiegocriminallawyerrt.com
Web: www.sandiegocriminallawyerrt.com

Summary   To provide financial assistance for college to veterans who have Post-Traumatic Stress Disorder (PTSD).

Eligibility   This program is open to veterans of the U.S. armed forces who have been diagnosed with PTSD. Applicants must be enrolled or planning to enroll at a college, university, community college, or trade school. Along with their application, they must submit 1) a 100-word statement on their educational plans; and 2) an essay of 650 to 1,000 words on how PTSD has affected their life.

Financial data   The stipend is $1,000.

Duration   1 year.

Number awarded   2 each year.

Deadline   November of each year.

[772]
SCHWALLIE FAMILY SCHOLARSHIPS

Organization for Autism Research
Attn: Scholarship
2000 North 14th Street, Suite 240
Arlington, VA 22201
(703) 243-9710
E-mail: scholarship@researchautism.org
Web: www.researchautism.org

Summary   To provide financial assistance for college to individuals with autism.

Eligibility   This program is open to individuals with an established autism DSM-IV or DSM-V diagnosis who are attending or planning to attend an accredited 2- or 4-year college or university, vocational/technical school, or cooperative life skills program. Applicants must be enrolled full time and be working toward certification or accreditation in a particular field. Along with their application, they must submit a 1,000-word autobiographical essay that includes their reasons for applying for this scholarship. Selection is based on originality of content, challenges overcome, future aspirations, the importance of the chosen field of study, and how the scholarship will help achieve academic, career, and personal goals.

Financial data   The stipend is $3,000.

Duration   1 year; nonrenewable.

Additional data   This program began in 2008.

Number awarded   Varies each year; recently, 20 were awarded. Since the program was established, it has awarded $584,500 in scholarships to 191 students.

Deadline   April of each year.

[773]
SCOTT DELGADILLO SCHOLARSHIP

Friends of Scott Foundation
Attn: Scholarship Fund
6977 Navajo Road, Number 168
San Diego, CA 92119
(619) 993-2917   E-mail: info@friendsofscott.org
Web: www.friendsofscott.org/scholarship.aspx

Summary   To provide financial assistance for college or graduate school to childhood cancer survivors from California.

Eligibility   This program is open to California residents who are survivors of childhood cancer or patients currently receiving treatment. Applicants must be attending or planning to attend a technical school, vocational school, junior college, or 4-year college or university as an undergraduate or graduate student in any state. Along with their application, they must submit a 500-word essay on how their experience with cancer has impacted their life. Selection is based on financial need and personal hardship.

Financial data   The stipend is $1,000.

Duration   1 year.

Number awarded   Varies each year; recently, 2 were awarded.

Deadline   August of each year.

[774]
SHANNON O'DANIEL MEMORIAL SCHOLARSHIP

Epilepsy Foundation of Kentuckiana
Attn: Director of Education
Kosair Charities Centre
982 Eastern Parkway
Louisville, KY 40217-1566
(502) 637-4440, ext. 14   Toll Free: (866) 275-1078
Fax: (502) 637-4442
Web: www.efky.org/scholarship-applications.html

Summary To provide financial assistance to high school seniors in Kentucky and southern Indiana who have epilepsy and are interested in attending college in any state.

Eligibility This program is open to seniors graduating from high schools in Kentucky (except Boone, Campbell, Grant, and Kenton counties) or southern Indiana (Clark, Floyd, and Harrison counties) who have epilepsy or another seizure disorder and are under a physician's care. Applicants be planning to attend a college or university in any state. Along with their application, they must 400-word essays on 1) their struggle to overcome adversity because of their epilepsy and seizures; and 2) their plans for their future educational and professional endeavors. Financial need is also considered in the selection process.

Financial data The stipend is $1,000.

Duration 1 year.

Additional data This program began in 2001.

Number awarded 1 each year.

Deadline May of each year.

[775]
SHIRE ACES SCHOLARSHIP FOR RARE DISEASES

Shire US Inc.
c/o Scholarship Managers
P.O. Box 2810
Cherry Hill, NJ 08034
(856) 616-9311
E-mail: scholarshipmanagers@scholarshipmanagers.com
Web: www.shireaces.com

Summary To provide financial assistance to college students who have 1 of several designated rare diseases.

Eligibility This program is open to high school graduates and GED recipients who have 1 of the following rare diseases: Acute neuromyelitis optica, Alagille syndrome, CMV in transplant patients, Eosinophilic esophagitis (EoE), Fabry disease, Focal segmental glomerulosclerosis, Friedreich's ataxia, Gaucher disease, Hereditary angioedema, Hunter syndrome (MPS II), Hypoparathyroidism Metachromatic leukodystrophy (MLD), Paroxysmal nocturnal hemoglobinuria (PNH), Primary biliary cirrhosis, primary sclerosing cholangitis, progressive familial intrahepatic cholestatis, or Short bowel syndrome. Applicants must be enrolled or planning to enroll as an undergraduate or vocational student at an educational institution in the United States. They must be U.S. citizens or permanent residents.

Financial data The stipend is $5,000 per year.

Duration 1 year; may be renewed up to 3 additional years, provided the recipient remains in good academic standing.

Additional data This program, which began in 2012, stands for the Award for Collegiate Education from Shire (ACES).

Number awarded 3 each year.

Deadline February of each year.

[776]
SNOWDROP FOUNDATION SCHOLARSHIPS

Snowdrop Foundation
Attn: Executive Director
7155 Old Katy Road
Houston, TX 77070
(713) 232-9051 E-mail: trish@snowdropfoundation.org
Web: www.snowdropfoundation.org

Summary To provide financial assistance for college or graduate school to students who have been diagnosed with cancer.

Eligibility This program is open to students entering or attending college or graduate school. Applicants must have been diagnosed with cancer before the age of 21. Along with their application, they must submit a 250-word description of themselves; a 250-word description of their family situation; information on financial need; a letter from their attending physician verifying their medical history and current medical situation; and an essay of 500 to 1,000 words on how their experience with cancer has impacted their life values and career goals.

Financial data Recently, stipends averaged nearly $3,000.

Duration 1 year.

Number awarded Varies each year; recently, 75 of these scholarships, with a value of $220,000, were awarded.

Deadline April of each year.

[777]
SOOZIE COURTER HEMOPHILIA SCHOLARSHIP PROGRAM

Pfizer Inc.
Attn: Hemophilia Scholarship Program
235 East 42nd Street
New York, NY 10017
Toll Free: (844) 202-9344
Web: www.hemophiliavillage.com

Summary To provide financial assistance for college or graduate school in any field to persons with hemophilia.

Eligibility This program is open to persons with hemophilia (A or B) who are high school seniors, have a GED, or are currently attending an accredited college, university, junior college, vocational school, or graduate school. Along with their application, they must submit a 2-page essay on 1 of the following topics: 1) how hemophilia has affected their school life and how they have overcome those challenges; 2) the advice they would give to a child with hemophilia who is beginning school; or 3) the time in history they would travel back to if they could and why. Financial need is not considered in the selection process.

Financial data The stipends are $2,500 for undergraduate students or $4,000 for graduate students.

Duration 1 year.

Additional data This program began in 1998 and given its current name in 2000.

Number awarded 17 each year: 12 to undergraduates and 5 to graduate students.

Deadline July of each year.

[778]
SPECIAL PEOPLE GIFTS OF LOVE PROGRAM

Italian Catholic Federation
8393 Capwell Drive, Suite 110
Oakland, CA 94621
(510) 633-9058   Toll Free: (888) ICF-1924
Fax: (510) 633-9758   E-mail: info@icf.org
Web: www.icf.org/charity

Summary To provide funding to individuals who have a disability and desire additional training or instruction.

Eligibility This program is open to 1) individuals who have a disability and desire formal training or instruction in a particular vocation, academic, athletic, or artistic field; 2) qualified instructors on behalf of an individual with a disability who exhibits a particular skill to be developed and who desires formal instruction or training; or 3) adults with custodial responsibility for, and on behalf of, an individual with a disability who exhibits a particular skill to be developed and who desires formal instruction or training. The program defines disability to include ADD/ADHD, amputee, autism, cerebral palsy, emotional disturbances, hearing impairments or deafness, mental retardation, multiple sclerosis, muscular dystrophy, orthopedic impairments, specific learning disabilities, speech and language impairments, spina bifida, spinal cord injury, traumatic brain injury, visual impairments and blindness, or other health impairments that require special education or related services. Applicants must submit an essay on how they intend to use the grant funds to assist them with their disability or to achieve the goals of the program. Financial need is considered in the selection process.

Financial data A stipend is awarded (amount not specified). Funds are not intended to support tuition.

Duration These are 1-time grants.

Number awarded Varies each year.

Deadline Deadline not specified.

[779]
SPECTRUM SCHOLARSHIP

Spectrum Scholarship Program
Attn: Director
P.O. Box 227
Beals, ME 04611
E-mail: director@spectrumscholarshipprogram.org
Web: www.spectrumscholarshipprogram.org/apply

Summary To provide financial assistance to high school seniors in Maine who have been diagnosed with an Autism Spectrum Disorder (ASO).

Eligibility This program is open to seniors graduating from high schools in Maine who have been diagnosed with an ASO. Applicants must be planning to enroll at a post-secondary school in any state. Along with their application, they must submit an essay describing what they would like the world to know about life and learning on the spectrum of autism.

Financial data The stipend is $1,000.

Duration 1 year; nonrenewable.

Number awarded 1 each year.

Deadline April of each year.

[780]
STEPHEN T. MARCHELLO SCHOLARSHIPS

Stephen T. Marchello Scholarship Foundation
1170 East Long Place
Centennial, CO 80122
(303) 886-5018   E-mail: stmfoundation@hotmail.com
Web: www.stmfoundation.org

Summary To provide financial assistance to residents of Colorado and Montana who have survived childhood cancer and are interested in attending college in any state.

Eligibility This program is open to high school seniors who either live in or were treated for cancer in Colorado or Montana. Applicants must be working on or planning to work on an undergraduate degree at a school in any state. They must submit essays on 2 topics: 1) their academic and professional goals, why they have chosen those goals, and how this scholarship will help them obtain their goals; and 2) how being a cancer survivor has developed their character and the advice they would give to someone else going through cancer. In addition to those 2 essays, selection is based on high school GPA; SAT or ACT scores; information provided by the doctor, clinic, or hospital where they were treated; and 2 letters of reference.

Financial data Stipends range up to $2,000 per year.

Duration 1 year; may be renewed.

Additional data This foundation was established by the family of Stephen T. Marchello, who died of cancer in 1999. It awarded its first scholarship in 2000.

Number awarded Varies each year; recently, 12 were awarded.

Deadline March of each year.

[781]
STEPHEN'S SOLDIERS CANCER SURVIVORS' SCHOLARSHIP

Stephen's Soldiers Foundation
28580 Orchard Lake Road, Suite 150
Farmington, MI 48334
Toll Free: (866) 218-9930   Fax: (866) 706-0680
E-mail: info@stephenssoldiers.org
Web: www.stephenssoldiers.org/scholarships.html

Summary To provide financial assistance to high school seniors in Michigan who are or have been fighting cancer and are interested in attending college in any state.

Eligibility This program is open to seniors graduating from high schools in Michigan and planning to enroll at an accredited college or university in any state. Applicants must be a cancer survivor or currently diagnosed with cancer, although they are not required to be receiving treatment currently. They must be U.S. citizens or permanent residents and be able to document at least 15 volunteer hours with a cancer-related organization. Along with their application, they must submit a 3-minute video on how their experience with cancer has impacted their life values and career goals. Selection is based primarily on the contents of those videos.

Financial data   The stipend is $2,500.

Duration   1 year.

Additional data   This program is sponsored by Producers Choice Network.

Number awarded   3 each year.

Deadline   February of each year.

[782]
SURVIVORVISION TEXTBOOK SCHOLARSHIP PROGRAM

SurvivorVision
Attn: Textbook Program Chair
P.O. Box 5037
Woodridge, IL 60517
(630) 359-5172   E-mail: survivorvision@comcast.net
Web: www.survivorvision.org/are-you-eligible.html

Summary   To provide funding for purchase of textbooks to undergraduate and graduate students who are patients or survivors of childhood cancer.

Eligibility   This program is open to students currently enrolled at a college, university, community college, trade school, or graduate school. Applicants must be receiving or have received treatment for cancer that was diagnosed before they were 18 years of age. Along with their application, they must submit 1) a 500-word essay on how their cancer experience has affected their educational, personal, and/or life goals; 2) a 300-word essay on how a higher education will help them achieve those goals; and 3) a 300-word essay on any other information they want to share with the sponsor.

Financial data   Awards in the form of reimbursement for the purchase of textbooks range up to $1,000 per year.

Duration   1 year; may be renewed up to 4 additional years for a lifetime maximum of $5,000.

Number awarded   35 to 40 each year.

Deadline   May of each year.

[783]
SUSAN BUNCH MEMORIAL SCHOLARSHIP

California Association for Postsecondary Education
  and Disability
Attn: Scholarships
10073 Valley View Street, Suite 242
Cypress, CA 90630
(562) 397-2810   Fax: (866) 577-3387
E-mail: caped38@gmail.com
Web: www.caped.io/scholarships/scholarship-application

Summary   To provide financial assistance to undergraduate and graduate students in California who have a learning disability.

Eligibility   This program is open to students at public and private colleges and universities in California who have a learning disability. Undergraduates must have completed at least 6 semester credits and have a GPA of 2.5 or higher. Graduate students must have completed at least 3 semester units and have a GPA of 3.0 or higher. Applicants must submit 1) a 250-word essay describing their progress towards meeting their educational and/or vocational goals; 2) a 500-word essay on how they manage their disabiity; and 3) a 750-word essay on the the knowledge they would impart to incoming college students with a learning disability in an effort to enhance their success or college experience. They must also submit a letter of recommendation from a faculty person, verification of disability, and unofficial transcripts.

Financial data   The stipend is $1,000.

Duration   1 year.

Number awarded   1 each year.

Deadline   August of each year.

[784]
SUSANNA DELAURENTIS MEMORIAL SCHOLARSHIPS

Susanna DeLaurentis Charitable Foundation
7616 Mountain Avenue
Elkins Park, PA 19027
(215) 635-9405   Fax: (215) 635-9406
E-mail: info@thesusannafoundation.org
Web: www.thesusannafoundation.org/scholarships

Summary   To provide financial assistance for college to high school seniors who have serious medical difficulties.

Eligibility   This program is open to graduating high school seniors who contend with a chronic disease or other serious challenge to physical or mental health. Applicants must be planning to enroll at a college or university. Along with their application, they must submit a brief statement describing their health condition, how they have managed to excel in spite of the condition, and their plans for advanced education after high school. They should also submit information about their academic standing (GPA, ACT and/or SAT scores, class rank) and their participation in extracurricular or community activities. Financial need is not considered in the selection process.

Financial data   The stipend is $1,000.

Duration   1 year.

Additional data   This foundation was established in 1999 to honor Susanna DeLaurentis, who died from neuroblastoma, a form of cancer of the nervous system, when she was 10 years of age. Her sister died of cystic fibrosis on her 29th birthday.

Number awarded   Varies each year; recently, 12 were awarded.

Deadline   April of each year.

[785]
SWIDA COLLEGE SCHOLARSHIP

International Dyslexia Association-Southwest Branch
Attn: Scholarship Committee
3915 Carlisle NE
Albuquerque, NM 87107
(505) 255-8234   E-mail: info@southwestida.org
Web: southwestida.org

Summary To provide financial assistance to residents of New Mexico and El Paso, Texas who have dyslexia and are interested in working on an undergraduate or graduate degree at a college in any state.

Eligibility This program is open to residents of New Mexico and El Paso who have been diagnosed with dyslexia. Applicants must be working full time on an associate, bachelor's, or master's degree in any field at a 2- or 4-year college or university in any state. Selection is based on academic performance in relation to the severity of the specific learning disability, personal and professional goals, and financial need.

Financial data The stipend is $2,000. Funds are paid directly to the recipient's college or university.

Duration 1 year.

Number awarded 1 each year.

Deadline March of each year.

[786]
TEENS TAKE CHARGE SCHOLARSHIPS

Hydrocephalus Association
4340 East West Highway, Suite 905
Bethesda, MD 20814
(301) 202-3811   Toll Free: (888) 598-3789, ext. 22
Fax: (301) 202-3813
E-mail: scholarship@hydroassoc.com
Web: www.hydroassoc.org/scholarships

Summary To provide financial assistance for college or graduate school to young adults with hydrocephalus.

Eligibility This program is open to individuals between the ages of 17 and 30 who have hydrocephalus. The scholarship must be used for an educational purpose, including, but not limited to, a 4-year or junior college, a high school postgraduate year to prepare for college, a technical or trade school, an accredited employment training program, or a graduate program. Applicants may be in the process of applying to a program or university or already enrolled. They must include essays on their hobbies, interests, and activities; their educational and career goals; how having hydrocephalus has impacted their life; how they would help others with hydrocephalus; and how the scholarship will help them. Financial need is not considered in the selection process.

Financial data The stipend is $1,000. Funds may be used for tuition, books, housing, or any other educationally-related expense.

Duration 1 year; nonrenewable.

Additional data This program began in 2010.

Number awarded 5 year.

Deadline April of each year.

[787]
TENNESSEE STEP UP SCHOLARSHIPS

Tennessee Student Assistance Corporation
Parkway Towers
404 James Robertson Parkway, Suite 1510
Nashville, TN 37243-0820
(615) 741-1346   Toll Free: (800) 342-1663
Fax: (615) 741-6101   E-mail: TSAC.Aidinfo@tn.gov
Web: www.tn.gov

Summary To provide financial assistance to residents of Tennessee who have intellectual disabilities and are interested in attending designated universities in the state.

Eligibility This program is open to Tennessee residents who are completing or have completed high school in accordance with the requirements of their Individualized Education Program (IEP) as a student with intellectual disabilities. Applicants must receive a high school diploma or certificate, a special education diploma, a transition certificate, or an IEP certificate. They must enroll in an individualized program of study that includes academic, career development and exploration, and independent living skills at an eligible Tennessee university within 16 months after completing high school. Financial need is considered in the selection process.

Financial data The stipend is $3,500 per year.

Duration Up to 4 years, provided the recipient makes satisfactory academic progress in the individualized program of study.

Additional data This program began in 2013. The eligible institutions are University of Memphis, University of Tennessee, Lipscomb University, Union University, and Vanderbilt University.

Number awarded Varies each year; recently, 98 students received $339,000 in support through this program.

Deadline August of each year for fall semester; January of each year for spring semester; April of each year for summer term.

[788]
TERRILL FOUNDATION MILITARY SCHOLARSHIP

Terrill Foundation, Inc.
P.O. Box 8057
Louisville, KY 40257
E-mail: terrill.foundation@gmail.com
Web: www.terrillfoundation.org

Summary To provide financial assistance for college to military personnel who have sustained a brain injury.

Eligibility This program is open to military personnel who have sustained a brain injury. Applicants must be interested in attending a 2- or 4-year college, university, or vocational institute. They are not required to enroll full time; they may use the funding to take as little as a single class. Along with their application, they must submit brief essays on 1) their experience with neurologic disease or brain injury; and 2) why they should receive funding from the Terrill Foundation.

Financial data   A stipend is awarded (amount not specified). Funds are paid directly to the recipient's educational institution.
Duration   1 year.
Additional data   This program began in 2013.
Number awarded   1 each year.
Deadline   March of each year.

[789]
TERRILL FOUNDATION STUDENT SCHOLARSHIP

Terrill Foundation, Inc.
P.O. Box 8057
Louisville, KY 40257
E-mail: terrill.foundation@gmail.com
Web: www.terrillfoundation.org

Summary   To provide financial assistance for college to high school seniors who have been affected by brain disorders.
Eligibility   This program is open to graduating high school seniors who plan to continue their education a 2- or 4-year college, university, or vocational institute. Applicants must have been affected by brain injuries, brain tumors, or other neurologic diseases. Along with their application, they must submit brief essays on 1) their experience with neurologic disease or brain injury; and 2) why they should receive funding from the Terrill Foundation. In the selection process, grades are not a determining factor, but students must show a capacity for success in their chosen field.
Financial data   A stipend is awarded (amount not specified). Funds are paid directly to the recipient's educational institution.
Duration   1 year.
Additional data   This program began in 2009.
Number awarded   1 each year.
Deadline   March of each year.

[790]
THE DREAM INSTITUTE HEAP SCHOLAR AWARD SCHOLARSHIPS

The DREAM Institute
Attn: High Education Assistance Program (HEAP)
P.O. Box 52785
Tulsa, OK 74152-0785
(918) 660-3408   E-mail: dream@dreaminstitute.org
Web: www.dreaminstitute.org/Programs.htm

Summary   To provide financial assistance to residents of Oklahoma who have a physical and/or learning disability and are interested in attending college in the state.
Eligibility   This program is open to residents of Oklahoma who have been diagnosed with a physical and/or learning disability. Applicants must be enrolled or planning to enroll full time at a 2- or 4-year college or university in the state. They must have a GPA of 2.0 or higher and be able to demonstrate financial need. Along with their application, they must submit a personal statement of 4 to 8 pages on their professional and career goals, how their program or degree will help them achieve those goals, any

special services and/or accommodations they received and the self-advocacy skills they used to acquire those services and/or accommodations, their family background and how their family has impacted their future educational plans, their biggest life challenge and how they dealt with it, how this program will impact their continuing education, the impact of their disability on their educational goals, how their disability has impacted their academic performance, the process that they use to attain their short- and long-run goals, and whom they admire the most and why.
Financial data   The stipend depends on the need of the recipient. Funds are available to help pay for tuition, fees, books, and dormitory fees.
Duration   1 year; may be renewed up to 3 additional years.
Additional data   Scholars are invited to participate in an orientation workshop designed to equip them with the information they will require as a college student with a disability. They also qualify for special tutoring. The sponsor's name stands for Disability-Resources-Educational-Advocacy-Motivation.
Number awarded   Varies each year; recently, 3 new and 10 renewal scholarships were awarded.
Deadline   April of each year.

[791]
THE FELDMAN LAW FIRM AUTISM SCHOLARSHIP

The Feldman Law Firm, PLLC
1 East Washington Street, Suite 500
Phoenix, AZ 85004
(602) 540-7887
E-mail: mike@afphoenixcriminalattorney.com
Web: www.afphoenixcriminalattorney.com

Summary   To provide financial assistance to individuals who have been diagnosed with autism spectrum disorder (ASD) and are interested in attending college.
Eligibility   This program is open to individual who have been diagnosed with ASD. Applicants must be enrolled or planning to enroll at a college, university, junior college, or vocational school. Along with their application, they must submit a 100-word statement on their educational goals. They may also submit, at their discretion, an 850-word essay on how ASD has affected their education.
Financial data   The stipend is $1,000. Funds are paid directly to the recipient's college.
Duration   1 year.
Number awarded   1 each year.
Deadline   February.

[792]
THE ORION FUND GRANTS

The Orion Fund
P.O. Box 11518
Piedmont, CA 94611
(510) 482-2226   E-mail: theorionfund@gmail.com
Web: www.theorionfund.org/grants.php

Summary To provide financial assistance to California college and graduate students who have a serious illness or injury.

Eligibility This program is open to undergraduate and graduate students at colleges and universities in California who are younger than 30 years of age and have a serious medical condition that affects their ability to stay in school. Applicants must submit a personal statement describing the purpose of the grant and providing justification for the request, a letter of support from a campus administrator or a medical provider, unofficial transcripts, and information on financial resources.

Financial data Stipends range from $500 to $5,000. Funds may be used for medical expenses, medical technology, educational costs, and living expenses.

Duration 1 year.

Additional data This program began in 2004.

Number awarded Varies each year; since the program began, it has awarded 131 grants: 3 at $5,000, 8 at $4,000, 11 at $3,000, 7 at $2,500, 22 at $2,000, 9 at $1,500, 29 at $1,000, and 42 at $500.

Deadline February of each year.

[793]
THEODORE R. AND VIVIAN M. JOHNSON SCHOLARSHIP PROGRAM

State University System of Florida
Attn: Board of Governors
325 West Gaines Street
Tallahassee, FL 32399-0400
(850) 245-0466 Fax: (850) 245-9685
E-mail: info@flbog.org
Web: www.flbog.edu

Summary To provide financial assistance to Florida undergraduate students who have disabilities.

Eligibility This program is open to students with disabilities enrolled or planning to enroll at a State University System of Florida institution. Applicants must be able to verify the nature and/or extent of their disability, which may be in 1 or more of the following classifications: attention deficit disorder (ADD); attention deficit hyperactivity disorder (ADHD); autism spectrum disorder; blind or low vision; deaf or hard of hearing; orthopedic disability; psychological, emotional, or behavioral disability; speech/language impairment; specific learning disability; traumatic brain injury; or other health disabilities. They must have a GPA of 2.0 or higher and be able to document financial need. Along with their application, they must submit a 1-page personal statement on their achievements, activities, career goals, and the effects of their disability(ies).

Financial data The stipend depends on the availability of funds.

Duration 1 year; may be renewed up to 5 additional years, provided the recipient maintains a GPA of 2.0 or higher and enrolls in at least 18 credits each academic year.

Additional data This program is administered by the equal opportunity program at each of the 12 State University System of Florida 4-year institutions. Contact that office for further information. Funding is provided by the Theodore R. and Vivian M. Johnson Foundation, with matching funding from the Florida Legislature.

Number awarded Several each year.

Deadline April of each year.

[794]
THOMAS F. SMITH RECIPIENT SCHOLARSHIP

Georgia Transplant Foundation
Attn: Scholarship Program
2201 Macy Drive
Roswell, GA 30076
(770) 457-3796 Fax: (770) 457-7916
E-mail: gtf@gatransplant.org
Web: www.gatransplant.org

Summary To provide financial assistance to residents of Georgia who are transplant recipients and interested in attending college in any state.

Eligibility This program is open to residents of Georgia who are entering or continuing at an accredited institution of higher learning in any state. Applicants must be an organ transplant recipient. Along with their application, they must submit a 3-page personal statement on their career objectives, how this scholarship will help them attain their goals, and how transplantation has affected their life. Selection is based on that statement, transcripts, high school exit examination scores, ACT/SAT scores, 3 letters of reference, and financial need.

Financial data The stipend is $1,000 per year.

Duration 1 year; may be renewed up to 3 additional years.

Number awarded 1 each year.

Deadline April of each year.

[795]
THOMAS J. SEEFRED TRUST SCHOLARSHIPS

Thomas J. Seefred Trust
3551 Leffingwell Road
Canfield, OH 44406
(330) 540-3551 E-mail: info@seefredtrust.org
Web: www.seefredtrust.org

Summary To provide financial assistance to residents of Ohio who have juvenile diabetes and are currently enrolled at a college or university in any state.

Eligibility This program is open to students between 18 and 25 years of age who have been diagnosed with juvenile diabetes and are working full time on a bachelor's degree at an accredited college or university in any state. Applicants must be residents of Ohio; preference is given to residents of Columbiana, Mahoning, and Trumbull counties. Along with their application, they must submit a 500-word personal essay describing the impact juvenile diabetes has had on them and why they feel they should receive this scholarship. Selection is based on that essay, academic promise, recommendations, and financial need.

Financial data The stipend is $3,000.

Duration 1 year.

Additional data This program began in 2005.

Number awarded 1 or more each year.
Deadline March of each year.

[796]
TIM KENNEDY MEMORIAL SCHOLARSHIP

Matrix Health Group
Attn: Memorial Scholarship Program
2202 Brownstone Court
Champaign, IL 61822
(217) 840-1033
E-mail: maria.vetter@matrixhealthgroup.com
Web: www.factorsupportnetwork.com

Summary To provide financial assistance for college to men who have hemophilia.

Eligibility This program is open to graduating male high school seniors and students currently enrolled full time at an accredited college, university, or technical school who have hemophilia. Applicants must have a GPA of 2.0 or higher for their senior year in high school or their current year in college. Along with their application, they must submit transcripts, ACT or SAT test scores, 2 letters of recommendation, information on their work and school activities, and an essay of 300 to 400 words on 1 of the following topics: 1) the experiences that have influenced their decision to pursue their educational goals or career choice; 2) how they feel their life has been influenced by having a bleeding disorder; or 3) their biggest challenge in having a bleeding disorder and how they have or are working through it. Selection is based on that essay, academic merit, and reference letters.

Financial data The stipend is $1,000.

Duration 1 year.

Additional data This program began in 2013.

Number awarded 2 each year.

Deadline July of each year.

[797]
TRIO SCHOLARSHIP PROGRAM

Transplant Recipients International Organization, Inc.
Attn: Scholarship Committee
2100 M Street, N.W., Suite 170-353
Washington, DC 20037-1233
(202) 293-0980   Toll Free: (800) TRIO-386
E-mail: info@trioweb.org
Web: www.trioweb.org/resources/trio-scholarships.html

Summary To provide financial assistance for college to members of the Transplant Recipients International Organization (TRIO) and their families.

Eligibility This program is open to TRIO members and their immediate family who are solid organ or bone marrow candidates, recipients, donors, or their immediate family members. Applicants must be attending or planning to attend an accredited college, university, or trade/technical certificate program. They must have a cumulative GPA of 2.5 or higher and be able to demonstrate financial need. Along with their application, they must submit a 500-word essay on their personal history and educational and career ambitions and a statement on how transplantation has affected their life.

Financial data The stipend is $1,000.
Duration 1 year; nonrenewable.
Number awarded Varies each year; recently, 4 were awarded. Since the program was established 20 years ago, it has awarded 125 scholarships.
Deadline June of each year.

[798]
TYPE 1 FOR 67 YEARS SCHOLARSHIPS

Diabetes Scholars Foundation
310 Busse Highway, Suite 256
Park Ridge, IL 60068
(312) 215-9861   Fax: (847) 991-8739
E-mail: m.podjasek@diabetesscholars.org
Web: www.diabetesscholars.org/college-scholarship

Summary To provide financial assistance for college to high school seniors who have diabetes.

Eligibility This program is open to graduating high school seniors who have Type 1 diabetes and plan to attend an accredited 4-year university, college, or trade/technical school in any state. Applicants must be able to demonstrate active involvement in the diabetes community, academic accomplishment, participation in community and/or extracurricular activities, and successful management of the challenges of living with diabetes. Financial need is not considered in the selection process. U.S. citizenship or permanent resident status is required.

Financial data The stipend is $5,000.

Duration 1 year.

Number awarded 3 each year.

Deadline April of each year.

[799]
UCB FAMILY EPILEPSY SCHOLARSHIP PROGRAM

UCB, Inc.
Family Scholarship Program
c/o Summit Medical Communications
1421 East Broad Street, Suite 340
Fuquay-Varina, NC 27526
Toll Free: (866) 825-1920   Fax: (919) 567-7591
E-mail: ucbepilepsyscholarship@summitmedcomm.com
Web: www.ucbepilepsyscholarship.com

Summary To provide financial assistance for college or graduate school to epilepsy patients and their family members and caregivers.

Eligibility This program is open to epilepsy patients and their family members and caregivers. Applicants must be working on or planning to work on an undergraduate or graduate degree at an institution of higher education in the United States. They must be able to demonstrate academic achievement, a record of participation in activities outside of school, and service as a role model. Along with their application, they must submit a 1-page essay explaining why they should be selected for the scholarship, how epilepsy has impacted their life either as a patient or as a family member or caregiver, and how they will benefit from the scholarship. U.S. citizenship or permanent resident status is required.

Financial data The stipend is $5,000.

Duration 1 year; nonrenewable.

Additional data This program, previously known as the Keppra Family Epilepsy Scholarship Program, was established in 2004.

Number awarded 30 each year. Since this program was established, it has awarded $1,700,000 to more than 340 students.

Deadline April of each year.

[800]
UTAH HEMOPHILIA FOUNDATION SCHOLARSHIPS

Utah Hemophilia Foundation
772 East 3300 South, Suite 210
Salt Lake City, UT 84106
(801) 484-0325   Toll Free: (877) 463-6893
Fax: (801) 746-2488
E-mail: western@hemophiliautah.org
Web: www.hemophiliautah.org/resources.php

Summary To provide financial assistance to members of the bleeding disorders community served by the Utah Hemophilia Foundation (UHF) who are interested in attending college in any state.

Eligibility This program is open to members of the bleeding disorders community served by UHF and/or the Intermountain Hemophilia and Thrombosis Center in Salt Lake City, including those who have a bleeding disorder, their spouses, siblings, children, and parents. Applicants must be enrolled or planning to enroll at a college, university, trade school, or technical program in any state. Preference is given to applicants must directly affected by a bleeding disorder, those involved with UHF activities, those without other scholarships or financial assistance, and residents of Utah.

Financial data Stipends range from $100 to $1,500.

Duration 1 year.

Additional data This program includes awards designated as Robert Price Memorial Scholarships.

Number awarded Varies each year.

Deadline May of each year.

[801]
VARUN BHASKARAN (WAS) SCHOLARSHIP PROGRAM

Immune Deficiency Foundation
Attn: Scholarship Program
110 West Road, Suite 300
Towson, MD 21204
(410) 321-6647   Toll Free: (800) 296-4433
Fax: (410) 321-9165 E-mail: info@primaryimmune.org
Web: www.primaryimmune.org

Summary To provide financial assistance to undergraduate and graduate students who are living with Wiskott-Aldrich Syndrome (WAS).

Eligibility This program is open to students entering or attending college or graduate school who are living with WAS. Applicants must submit an autobiographical essay, 2 letters of recommendation, a family financial statement, and a letter of verification from their immunologist. Financial need is the main factor considered in selecting the recipients and the size of the award.

Financial data Stipends range from $750 to $2,000, depending on the recipient's financial need.

Duration 1 year; may be renewed.

Additional data This program began in 2011.

Number awarded Varies each year.

Deadline March of each year.

[802]
VERA YIP MEMORIAL SCHOLARSHIP

Ulman Cancer Fund for Young Adults
Attn: Scholarship Committee
921 East Fort Avenue, Suite 325
Baltimore, MD 21230
(410) 964-0202   Toll Free: (888) 393-FUND
Fax: (888) 964-0402
E-mail: scholarship@ulmanfund.org
Web: www.ulmanfund.org/scholarships

Summary To provide financial assistance for college or graduate school to students from any state who have been diagnosed with cancer or have or have lost a family member with cancer.

Eligibility This program is open to U.S. citizens and permanent residents between 15 and 35 years of age from any state. Applicants must 1) have been diagnosed with cancer and currently in relapse or active treatment; 2) have a parent or guardian living with cancer; or 3) have lost a parent or guardian to cancer. The student, parent, or guardian must have been first diagnosed with cancer after the applicant was 15 years of age. Along with their application, they must submit a 500-word essay or 3-minute video on either 1) a letter that they would have liked to receive during their cancer experience; or 2) what they would tell the young adults who participate in the sponsor's summer-long drive to support the organization about being a young adult impacted by cancer. U.S. citizenship or permanent resident status is required. This award is presented to the applicant who best demonstrates the qualities of Vera Yip of courage, determination, motivation, and dedication.

Financial data The stipend is $2,500. Funds are paid directly to the educational institution.

Duration 1 year; nonrenewable.

Additional data Recipients are obligated to organize and run a bone marrow registry drive with the support of Delete Blood Cancer and There Goes My Hero.

Number awarded 1 each year.

Deadline March of each year.

[803]
VINCENT STEFANO SCHOLARSHIP AWARD

Kidney & Urology Foundation of America
Attn: Program Director
63 West Main Street, Suite G
Freehold, NJ 07728
(732) 866-4444   Toll Free: (800) 633-6628
E-mail: info@kidneyurology.org
Web: www.kidneyurology.org

Summary To provide financial assistance for college to patients who have been diagnosed with kidney disease.

Eligibility This program is open to young adults between 17 and 25 years of age who are attending or planning to attend college. Applicants must have been diagnosed with kidney disease. Along with their application, they must submit essays of 250 to 650 words on 1) their medical history, including their illness and how kidney disease has impacted their life goals; 2) their educational background, their extracurricular activities and personal interests, any other family members attending college, any family circumstances or personal experiences that may set them apart from other applicants, and financial need; and 3) how they contribute or plan to contribute to the renal or transplant communities. Selection is based on achievements, commitment to working on a college degree, and financial need. Priority is given to applicants from the sponsoring organization's participating partner centers.

Financial data The stipend is $2,000 per year. Funds are paid directly to the recipient's institution.

Duration 1 year; may be renewed up to 3 additional years.

Additional data This program began in 2011.

Number awarded 1 or more each year.

Deadline May of each year.

[804]
VIRGINIA COBB SCHOLARSHIP

The Charity League, Inc.
Attn: Scholarship Committee
P.O. Box 530233
Birmingham, AL 35253-0233
(205) 876-3830   E-mail: epmilne8@gmail.com
Web: www.thecharityleague.org/scholarships

Summary To provide financial assistance to high school seniors in Alabama who have a speech or hearing impairment and are interested in attending college in any state.

Eligibility This program is open to seniors graduating from high schools in Alabama and planning to enroll at a college or university in any state. Applicants must have a speech or hearing impairment. Along with their application, they must submit an essay of 1 to 2 pages about themselves, their achievements, and their goals.

Financial data The stipend ranges from $500 to $2,000.

Duration 1 year.

Additional data This program began in 2002.

Number awarded 1 each year.

Deadline May of each year.

[805]
VITTORIA DIANA RICARDO SCHOLARSHIP

Ulman Cancer Fund for Young Adults
Attn: Scholarship Committee
921 East Fort Avenue, Suite 325
Baltimore, MD 21230
(410) 964-0202   Toll Free: (888) 393-FUND
Fax: (888) 964-0402
E-mail: scholarship@ulmanfund.org
Web: www.ulmanfund.org/scholarships

Summary To provide financial assistance for college or graduate school to students who have been diagnosed with cancer or have or have lost a family member with cancer.

Eligibility This program is open to students who 1) have been diagnosed with cancer; 2) have a parent or sibling living with cancer; or 3) have lost a parent or sibling to cancer. Applicants must be attending, or planning to attend, a 4-year college or university in any state to work on an undergraduate, graduate, or professional degree. They must have a GPA of 3.0 or higher in high school or college and be able to demonstrate financial need. The first diagnosis of cancer (whether of the applicant, a parent, or sibling) must have occurred after the applicant was 15 years of age. Along with their application, they must submit a 500-word essay or 3-minute video on either 1) a letter that they would have liked to receive during their cancer experience; or 2) what they would tell the young adults who participate in the sponsor's summer-long drive to support the organization about being a young adult impacted by cancer. U.S. citizenship or permanent resident status is required.

Financial data The stipend is $2,500. Funds are paid directly to the educational institution.

Duration 1 year.

Additional data Recipients are obligated to organize and run a bone marrow registry drive with the support of Delete Blood Cancer and There Goes My Hero.

Number awarded 1 each year.

Deadline March of each year.

[806]
WBDN EDUCATIONAL SCHOLARSHIP

Wisconsin Bleeding Disorders Network
W237S9730 Par Avenue
Big Bend, WI 53103
(608) 359-9103   E-mail: MyWBDN@gmail.com
Web: www.mywbdn.org/scholarships

Summary To provide financial assistance to residents of Wisconsin who have a connection to the bleeding community and are interested in attending college in any state.

Eligibility This program is open to residents of Wisconsin who have an inherited bleeding disorder, are the child of a parent with a bleeding disorder, or are the parent of a child with a bleeding disorder. Applicants must be attending or planning to attend a college or university in any state. They may be full-time traditional students or part-time nontraditional students.

Financial data   A stipend is awarded (amount not specified).

Duration   1 year.

Number awarded   Varies each year; recently, 3 were awarded.

Deadline   March of each year.

[807]
WINTERHOFF ARTHRITIS SCHOLARSHIP

Arthritis Foundation
Attn: Juvenile Arhtritis
1330 West Peachtree Street, Suite 100
Atlanta, GA 30309-2904
(404) 965-7727   Toll Free: (800) 283-7800
E-mail: jziegler@arthritis.org
Web: www.kidsgetarthritistoo.org/resources/scholarships

Summary   To provide financial assistance to college students who have a rheumatic disease.

Eligibility   This program is open to students enrolled or planning to enroll full time in an accredited undergraduate program, graduate program, or medical school in any state. Applicants must have doctor-diagnosed arthritis or related rheumatic disease and a GPA of 2.5 or higher. They must be willing to be involved with the Arthritis Foundation as an advocate, fundraiser, participant, volunteer, and/or supporter.

Financial data   The stipend is $5,000 per year. Funds may be utilized only for tuition, books, and supplies.

Duration   1 year; may be renewed up to 3 additional years, provided the recipient remains enrolled full time.

Additional data   This program began in 2010 in the Pacific Southwest region, and became nationwide in 2017.

Number awarded   Varies each year; recently, 4 new and 4 renewal scholarships were awarded.

Deadline   March of each year.

[808]
WOODY AND LOUISE REED BRIDGE TO LIFE SURVIVOR SCHOLARSHIP

Alisa Ann Ruch Burn Foundation
Attn: Scholarship
50 North Hill Avenue, Suite 305
Pasadena, CA 91106
(818) 848-0223   Toll Free: (800) 242-BURN
Fax: (818) 848-0296   E-mail: jshare@aarbf.org
Web: www.aarbf.org

Summary   To provide financial assistance for college or graduate school to burn survivors from California.

Eligibility   This program is open to California residents between 17 and 25 years of age who have been involved in the burn survivor community, as a Champ Camp counselor or camper, by participating in a burn support group or overnight recreational event of the Alisa Ann Ruch Burn Foundation (AARBF), or through leadership and volunteerism in another California burn foundation. Applicants must be enrolled or planning to enroll at a 2- or 4-year college, university, or trade/vocational school in any state as an undergraduate or graduate student. They must have a GPA of 2.5 or higher. Along with their application, they must submit brief essays on their major and why they chose that field, their educational and career goals, and why they participate in survivor programs. Selection is based on educational achievement and financial need.

Financial data   The stipend is $2,000 per year. Funds are disbursed directly to the financial institution.

Duration   1 year; recipients may reapply.

Number awarded   2 each year.

Deadline   June of each year.

[809]
WOZUMI FAMILY SCHOLARSHIP

Pride Foundation
Attn: Educational Programs Director
2014 East Madison Street, Suite 300
Seattle, WA 98122
(206) 323-3318   Toll Free: (800) 735-7287
Fax: (206) 323-1017
E-mail: scholarships@pridefoundation.org
Web: www.pridefoundation.org

Summary   To provide financial assistance for college to residents of the Northwest who are HIV positive and/or focusing on the treatment and/or eradication of the HIV virus.

Eligibility   This program is open to residents of Alaska, Idaho, Montana, Oregon, or Washington who attending or planning to attend a college, university, or vocational school in any state. Applicants must be goal-oriented, HIV positive, and/or focusing on the treatment and/or eradication of the HIV virus. Preference is given to students who are self-identified as lesbian, gay, bisexual, transgender or queer (LGBTQ), members of LGBTQ families, or allies who have been strongly supportive of the LGBTQ community. Selection is based on demonstrated commitment to social justice and LGBTQ concerns, leadership in their communities, the ability to be academically and personally successful, and (to some extent) financial need.

Financial data   Recently, the average stipend for all scholarships awarded by the foundation was approximately $4,160. Funds are paid directly to the recipient's school.

Duration   1 year; recipients may reapply.

Additional data   This program was formerly named the James and Colin Lee Wozumi Scholarship.

Number awarded   1 each year. Since it began offering scholarships in 1993, the foundation has awarded a total of more than $4.0 million to more than 1,500 recipients.

Deadline   January of each year.

Graduate Students

[810]
ABBVIE CF SCHOLARSHIPS

AbbVie Inc.
Attn: AbbVie CF Scholarship Program
1 North Waukegan Road
North Chicago, IL 60064
Toll Free: (800) 255-5162
E-mail: info@AbbVieCFScholarship.com
Web: www.abbviecfcholarship.com

Summary   To provide financial assistance for college or graduate school to students with cystic fibrosis (CF).

Eligibility   This program is open to high school seniors, vocational school students, college students, and graduate students with CF. U.S. citizenship is required. Applicants must submit 1) a creative presentation (e.g., a written work, piece of art, craft, collage, photograph) on what sets them apart from their peers, what inspires them to live life to the fullest, or anything else that they think makes them unique; 2) a photograph; and 3) a 250-word essay on a topic that changes annually. Selection is based on the essay, the creative presentation, academic record, and extracurricular activities. Information on all winners is posted on the sponsor's web site to allow the public to select a Thriving Undergraduate Student and a Thriving Graduate Student.

Financial data   The stipend is $2,500. The Thriving Students receive an additional award (recently, $20,500 for a total award of $23,000 to honor the program's 23rd year).

Duration   1 year.

Additional data   This program started in 1992 and was previously sponsored by Solvay Pharmaceuticals, Inc. with the name SolvayCARES Scholarships and subsequently by Abbott Laboratories with the name CFCareForward Scholarships. The current name and sponsorship began in 2011. Winners also receive a 1-year supply of nutritional drinks and vitamins. The essay, creative presentations, and photograph of all recipients who agree to be considered are posted online so patients, families, friends, physicians, the CF community, and the general public can vote to select the Thriving Students.

Number awarded   40 each year: 30 undergraduates and 10 graduate students; of those, 1 is designated the Thriving Undergraduate Student and 1 the Thriving Graduate Student.

Deadline   May of each year.

[811]
ABBVIE IMMUNOLOGY SCHOLARSHIP

Scholarship America
Attn: Scholarship Management Services
One Scholarship Way
P.O. Box 297
St. Peter, MN 56082
(507) 931-1682   Toll Free: (800) 537-4180
Fax: (507) 931-9168
E-mail: AbbVieImmunology@scholarshipamerica.org
Web: www.scholarsapply.org

Summary   To provide financial assistance for college or graduate school to students who have designated inflammatory diseases.

Eligibility   This program is open to U.S. citizens and permanent residents who are enrolled or planning to enroll full or part time in an undergraduate or graduate program at an accredited 2- or 4-year college, university, or vocational/technical school. Applicants must have been diagnosed with 1 of the following inflammatory diseases: ankylosing spondylitis (AS), Crohn's disease (CD), hidradenitis suppurativa (HS), juvenile idiopathic arthritis (JIA), psoriasis (Ps), psoriatic arthritis (PsA), rheumatoid arthritis (RA), ulcerative colitis (UC), or uveitis (UV). Along with their application, they must submit an essay on 1 of the following topics: 1) the advice they would give to another student who have the same disease they have and are entering high school or college; 2) how their diagnosis has changed their outlook and helped turn challenges or difficult tasks into opportunities; or 3) what they have learned about themselves during their journey living with their disease. Selection is based on the essay, academic excellence, community involvement, and ability to serve as a positive role model in the immunology community.

Financial data   The stipend is $5,000 for students working on an associate degree or $15,000 for students working on a bachelor's, master's, or doctoral degree.

Duration   1 year; nonrenewable.

Additional data   This program began in 2016 with funding from AbbVie Inc.

Number awarded   Varies each year; recently, 45 were awarded.

Deadline   January of each year.

[812]
ANNE SMEDINGHOFF MEMORIAL SCHOLARSHIP

Ulman Cancer Fund for Young Adults
Attn: Scholarship Committee
921 East Fort Avenue, Suite 325
Baltimore, MD 21230
(410) 964-0202   Toll Free: (888) 393-FUND
Fax: (888) 964-0402
E-mail: scholarship@ulmanfund.org
Web: www.ulmanfund.org/scholarships

Summary   To provide financial assistance for college or graduate school to students who have been diagnosed with cancer or have or have lost a family member with cancer.

Eligibility This program is open to students who 1) have been diagnosed with cancer; 2) have a parent or sibling living with cancer; or 3) have lost a parent or sibling to cancer. Applicants must be attending, or planning to attend, a college or university in any state to work on an undergraduate, graduate, or professional degree. They should demonstrate the qualities of the program's namesake-adventurous, upbeat, vivacious, and with a strong desire to make a difference in the lives of others. The first diagnosis of cancer (whether of the applicant, a parent, or sibling) must have occurred after the applicant was 15 years of age. Along with their application, they must submit a 500-word essay or 3-minute video on either 1) a letter that they would have liked to receive during their cancer experience; or 2) what they would tell the young adults who participate in the sponsor's summer-long drive to support the organization about being a young adult impacted by cancer. U.S. citizenship or permanent resident status is required.

Financial data The stipend is $2,500. Funds are paid directly to the educational institution.

Duration 1 year.

Additional data This program, which began in 2013, is funded by the 4K for Cancer, an organization of college students who ride bicycles across the country every summer and raise funds for cancer. Recipients are obligated to organize and run a bone marrow registry drive with the support of Delete Blood Cancer and There Goes My Hero.

Number awarded 1 each year.

Deadline March of each year.

[813]
ASHLEY ROSE HONORARY DIABETES LAW STUDENT SCHOLARSHIP

Katz & Phillips, P.A.
509 West Colonial Drive
Orlando, FL 32804
(321) 332-6864   Fax: (321) 422-3457
Web: www.orlandocriminalteam.com/giving-back

Summary To provide financial assistance to law students who have type 1 diabetes.

Eligibility This program is open to students entering or enrolled at a law school who have type 1 diabetes. Applicants must have a GPA of 2.8 or higher. Applicants must submit an essay on 1 of the following questions: 1) how living with type 1 diabetes has affected their education; 2) how they have overcome a particular challenge associated with having type 1 diabetes; or 3) how a famous individual with type 1 diabetes inspired them to succeed. Their essay must conclude with a paragraph on how the scholarship will help them.

Financial data The stipend is $1,000.

Duration 1 year.

Additional data This program began in 2014 to honor Ashley Rose Katz, the daughter of the sponsoring firm's founding partner, who was diagnosed with diabetes at the age of 18 months.

Number awarded 1 each year.

Deadline September of each year.

[814]
AVONTE OQUENDO MEMORIAL SCHOLARSHIP FOR AUTISM

The Perecman Firm, P.L.L.C.
250 West 57th Street, Suite 401
New York, NY 10107
(212) 577-9325
Web: www.perecman.com

Summary To provide financial assistance for college or graduate school to people diagnosed with autism and their families.

Eligibility This program is open students currently enrolled or accepted at an accredited college or university as an undergraduate or graduate students. Applicants or a close family member must have been diagnosed with a form of autism, including Asperger syndrome. Along with their application, they must submit an essay of 500 to 1,000 words on 1 of the following topics: 1) a time that they have had to overcome an obstacle as a person with autism that other people would not have had to face; 2) how their family member's autism has affected them and how they have adapted to help them; and 3) what they feel is the biggest obstacle holding people with autism back today. Selection is based on the essay and transcripts.

Financial data The stipend is $1,000.

Duration 1 year.

Number awarded 1 each year.

Deadline July of each year.

[815]
BAER REINTEGRATION SCHOLARSHIPS

The Center for Reintegration, Inc.
347 West 37th Street
New York, NY 10018
(212) 957-5090   Fax: (212) 974-0228
E-mail: baerscholarships@reintegration.com
Web: www.reintegration.com/scholarship-program

Summary To provide financial assistance to undergraduate and graduate students diagnosed with schizophrenia.

Eligibility This program is open to U.S. citizens diagnosed with bipolar disorder, schizophrenia, or schizoaffective disorder. Applicants must be receiving medical treatment for the disease and be actively involved in rehabilitative or reintegrative efforts. They must be interested in pursuing postsecondary education, including trade or vocational school programs, high school equivalency programs, associate degrees, bachelor's degrees, or graduate programs. Along with their application, they must submit an essay on their career goal and their rationale for choosing that goal; how this course of study will help them achieve their career goal; how their illness has impacted their ability to succeed in school, maintain employment, or establish relationships; steps they have taken to prepare for pursuit of this education; rationale for the specific school chosen; and their plans to continue treatment while pursuing an education. Selection is based on the quality of the essay, academic success, 3 references, thoughtfulness and appropriateness of academic and vocational/

career goals, rehabilitation involvement, success in dealing with the disease, recent volunteer and/or vocational experience, and completion of application requirements.

Financial data The amount awarded varies, depending upon the specific needs of the recipient. Funds may be used to pay for tuition and related expenses, such as textbooks and laboratory fees.

Duration 1 year; may be renewed.

Additional data This program began in 2015 as the successor to the Lilly Reintegration Scholarships. It is supported by the Sidney R. Baer, Jr. Foundation.

Number awarded Varies each year; generally, 70 to 120 of these scholarships (including renewals) are awarded annually.

Deadline January of each year.

[816]
BEF GENERAL ACADEMIC SCHOLARSHIPS

Boomer Esiason Foundation
c/o Chris McEwan
483 Tenth Avenue, Suite 300
New York, NY 10018
(646) 292-7939   Fax: (646) 292-7945
E-mail: cmcewan@esiason.org
Web: www.esiason.org

Summary To provide financial assistance to undergraduate and graduate students who have cystic fibrosis (CF).

Eligibility This program is open to CF patients who are working on an undergraduate or graduate degree. Applicants must submit a letter from their doctor confirming the diagnosis of CF and a list of daily medications, information on financial need, a detailed breakdown of tuition costs from their academic institution, transcripts, and a 2-page essay on 1) their postgraduation goals; and 2) the importance of compliance with CF therapies and what they practice on a daily basis to stay healthy. Selection is based on academic ability, character, leadership potential, service to the community, and financial need. Finalists are interviewed by telephone.

Financial data Stipends range from $500 to $2,500. Funds are paid directly to the academic institution to assist in covering the cost of tuition and fees.

Duration 1 year; nonrenewable.

Additional data Recipients must be willing to participate in the sponsor's CF Ambassador Program by speaking once a year at a designated CF event to help educate the general public about CF.

Number awarded 10 to 15 each year.

Deadline March, June, September, or December of each year.

[817]
BERNER SCHOLARSHIP FOR STUDENTS WITH EPILEPSY

Epilepsy Foundation of Greater Chicago
Attn: Jeff Moore, Individual Gift Officer
17 North State Street, Suite 650
Chicago, IL 60602
(312) 939-8622   Toll Free: (800) 273-6027
E-mail: jmoore@epilepsychicago.org
Web: www.epilepsychicago.org

Summary To provide financial assistance to residents of Illinois who have epilepsy and are enrolled or entering college or graduate school in any state.

Eligibility This program is open to residents of Illinois who have a diagnosis of epilepsy. Applicants must be enrolled or planning to enroll as full-time undergraduate or graduate students at a college or university in any state. Along with their application, they must submit a 1- to 2-page essay describing their community and leadership activities, books they've read recently, how they anticipate using their college education, and any other activities they think might be significant. Selection is based on academic accomplishment, community partnership and leadership, and financial need.

Financial data The stipend is $10,000 per year, including a grant of $5,000 and an interest-free loan of $5,000. The loan must be repaid within 7 years.

Duration 1 year; may be renewed up to 3 additional years.

Number awarded 1 each year.

Deadline April of each year.

[818]
BOARD OF YOUNG ADULT ADVISORS SCHOLARSHIP

Ulman Cancer Fund for Young Adults
Attn: Scholarship Committee
921 East Fort Avenue, Suite 325
Baltimore, MD 21230
(410) 964-0202   Toll Free: (888) 393-FUND
Fax: (888) 964-0402
E-mail: scholarship@ulmanfund.org
Web: www.ulmanfund.org

Summary To provide financial assistance for graduate school to young adults from the Baltimore/Washington, D.C. area who have been diagnosed with cancer or have or have lost a family member with cancer.

Eligibility This program is open to students who 1) have been diagnosed with cancer; 2) have a parent or sibling living with cancer; or 3) have lost a parent or sibling to cancer. Applicants must be residents of the Baltimore/Washington, D.C. area. They must be 35 years of age or younger and attending, or planning to attend, a college or university in any state to work on a graduate or professional degree. The first diagnosis of cancer (whether of the applicant, a parent, or sibling) must have occurred after the applicant was 15 years of age. Along with their application, they must submit a 500-word essay or 3-minute video on either 1) a letter that they would have liked to receive during their cancer experience; or 2) what they would tell the young adults who participate in the sponsor's summer-long drive to support the organization about being a young adult impacted by cancer. U.S. citizenship or permanent resident status is required.

Financial data The stipend is $2,500. Funds are paid directly to the educational institution.

Duration 1 year.

Additional data This program began in 2012. Recipients are obligated to organize and run a bone marrow registry drive with the support of Delete Blood Cancer and There Goes My Hero.

Number awarded 1 each year.

Deadline March of each year.

[819]
BONNIE STRANGIO EDUCATION SCHOLARSHIP

Boomer Esiason Foundation
c/o Chris McEwan
483 Tenth Avenue, Suite 300
New York, NY 10018
(646) 292-7939   Fax: (646) 292-7945
E-mail: cmcewan@esiason.org
Web: www.esiason.org

Summary To provide financial assistance to undergraduate and graduate students who have cystic fibrosis (CF) and a demonstrated commitment to the prevention and cure of the disease.

Eligibility This program is open to CF patients who are working on an undergraduate or graduate degree. Applicants must be able to demonstrate exemplary service and commitment to the prevention and cure of CF. Along with their application, they must submit a letter from their doctor confirming the diagnosis of CF and a list of daily medications, information on financial need, a detailed breakdown of tuition costs from their academic institution, transcripts, and a 2-page essay on 1) their postgraduation goals; and 2) the importance of compliance with CF therapies and what they practice on a daily basis to stay healthy. Selection is based on academic ability, character, leadership potential, service to the community, and financial need. Finalists are interviewed by telephone.

Financial data The stipend ranges from $500 to $1,000. Funds are paid directly to the academic institution to assist in covering the cost of tuition and fees.

Duration 1 year; nonrenewable.

Additional data This program began in 2005.

Number awarded 1 each year.

Deadline June of each year.

[820]
BRYON RIESCH SCHOLARSHIPS

Bryon Riesch Paralysis Foundation
P.O. Box 1388
Waukesha, WI 53187-1388
(262) 547-2083   E-mail: info@brpf.org
Web: www.brpf.org/scholarship-application

Summary To provide financial assistance to undergraduate and graduate students who have a neurological disability or the children of people with such a disability.

Eligibility This program is open to students entering or enrolled at a 2- or 4-year college or university as an undergraduate or graduate student. Applicants must have a neurological disability or be the child of a person with such a disability. First priority is given to individuals suffering from a direct spinal cord injury or disease resulting in paralysis such as spinal tumors, strokes, or aneurysms affecting the spinal cord, or spina bifida. Other diseases and disorders that qualify include multiple sclerosis, traumatic brain injuries, Parkinson's, and cerebral palsy. Priority is also given to residents of Wisconsin. Applicants must have a GPA of 2.5 or higher in high school or college. Along with their application, they must submit a 200-word essay on why they deserve the scholarship, a statement of their 5- and 10-year goals, and a list of work experience. Financial need is not considered in the selection process.

Financial data The stipend is $2,000.

Duration 1 year; may be renewed.

Number awarded Varies each semester; recently, 7 were awarded for the fall semester and 5 for the spring semester.

Deadline June of each year for fall semester; December of each year for spring semester.

[821]
CANCER FOR COLLEGE CAROLINA SCHOLARSHIPS

Cancer for College
981 Park Center Drive
Vista, CA 92081
(760) 599-5096
E-mail: applications@cancerforcollege.org
Web: www.cancerforcollege.org/application.html

Summary To provide financial assistance to undergraduate and graduate students from North and South Carolina who are cancer patients or survivors.

Eligibility This program is open to undergraduate and graduate students who are originally from or currently attending or entering accredited colleges, universities, community colleges, or trade schools in North or South Carolina. Applicants must be a cancer patient or survivor. Along with their application, they must submit transcripts, verification of their cancer diagnosis, 2 letters of recommendation, and information on their financial situation.

Financial data Stipends range from $1,000 to $5,000.

Duration 1 year.

Number awarded Varies each year; recently, 7 were awarded.

Deadline January of each year.

[822]
CANCER FOR COLLEGE PACIFIC NORTHWEST SCHOLARSHIPS

Cancer for College
981 Park Center Drive
Vista, CA 92081
(760) 599-5096
E-mail: applications@cancerforcollege.org
Web: www.cancerforcollege.org/application.html

Summary To provide financial assistance to undergraduate and graduate students from the Pacific Northwest who are cancer patients or survivors.

Eligibility This program is open to undergraduate and graduate students who are originally from or current attending accredited colleges, universities, community colleges, or trade schools in Idaho, Montana, Oregon, or Washington. Applicants must be a cancer patient or survivor. Along with their application, they must submit transcripts, verification of their cancer diagnosis, 2 letters of recommendation, and information on their financial situation.

Financial data Stipends range from $1,000 to $5,000.

Duration 1 year.

Additional data This program includes the Henry Streuli Scholarship.

Number awarded Varies each year; recently, 6 were awarded.

Deadline January of each year.

[823]
CANCER FOR COLLEGE SCHOLARSHIPS

Cancer for College
981 Park Center Drive
Vista, CA 92081
(760) 599-5096
E-mail: applications@cancerforcollege.org
Web: www.cancerforcollege.org/application.html

Summary To provide financial assistance to undergraduate and graduate students who are cancer patients or survivors.

Eligibility This program is open to undergraduate and graduate students enrolled or planning to enroll at accredited colleges, universities, community colleges, or trade schools in the United States and Puerto Rico. Applicants must be a cancer patient or survivor. Along with their application, they must submit transcripts, verification of their cancer diagnosis, 2 letters of recommendation, and information on their financial situation. Preference is given to residents of California and students attending college in southern California.

Financial data Stipends range from $1,000 to $5,000 per year.

Duration 1 year; some of the $1,000 scholarships (designated as Perpetual Scholarships) may be renewed up to 3 additional years.

Additional data This program began in 1993. Perpetual Scholarship recipients must be willing to attend regional events associated with the program and be available for interviews and/or media coverage.

Number awarded Varies each year; recently, 20 general and 1 perpetual scholarship were awarded.

Deadline January of each year.

[824]
CHALIK & CHALIK SURVIVOR'S SCHOLARSHIP

Chalik & Chalik Law Offices
Attn: Jason Chalik
10063 N.W. First Court
Plantation, FL 33324
(954) 858-5751   Toll Free: (855) 529-0269
E-mail: media@chaliklaw.com
Web: www.chaliklaw.com

Summary To provide financial assistance for college or law school to students who have survived a serious medical diagnosis.

Eligibility This program is open to U.S. citizens and others authorized to work in the United States who have been accepted or are attending a university or law school. Applicants must submit an essay of 1 to 3 pages describing how their experience with cancer or other serious disease has influenced their choice to obtain a higher education. They must have an undergraduate GPA of 3.0 or higher.

Financial data The stipend is $1,000. Funds are sent directly to the recipient's institution to be used only for tuition.

Duration 1 year.

Additional data This program began in 2015.

Deadline January of each year.

[825]
COLLEGE ACCESS AND SUCCESS SCHOLARSHIP

California Association for Postsecondary Education
   and Disability
Attn: Scholarships
10073 Valley View Street, Suite 242
Cypress, CA 90630
(562) 397-2810   Fax: (866) 577-3387
E-mail: caped38@gmail.com
Web: www.caped.io/scholarships/scholarship-application

Summary To provide financial assistance to undergraduate and graduate students in California who have an intellectual disability or are on the autism spectrum.

Eligibility This program is open to students at public and private colleges and universities in California who have an intellectual disability or are on the autism spectrum. Undergraduates must have completed at least 6 semester credits and have a GPA of 2.5 or higher. Graduate students must have completed at least 3 semester units and have a GPA of 3.0 or higher. Applicants must submit 1) a 250-word essay describing their progress towards meeting their educational and/or vocational goals; 2) a 500-word essay on how they manage their disability; and 3) a 750-word essay on how the skills and tools they develop in college will support their career goals. They must also submit a letter of recommendation from a faculty person, verification of disability, and unofficial transcripts.

Financial data The stipend is $1,000.

Duration 1 year.

Number awarded 1 each year.

Deadline August of each year.

[826]
COOLEY'S ANEMIA FOUNDATION/ APOPHARMA DISTINGUISHED SCHOLAR AWARD

Cooley's Anemia Foundation, Inc.
Attn: Scholarship Committee
330 Seventh Avenue, Suite 900
New York, NY 10001
(212) 279-8090   Toll Free: (800) 522-7222
Fax: (212) 279-5999
E-mail: scholarship@cooleysanemia.org
Web: www.thalassemia.org

Summary To provide financial assistance to doctoral students who have Cooley's anemia (thalassemia) and are preparing for a career in the biomedical sciences.

Eligibility This program is open to U.S. citizens who have a clinically significant form of thalassemia. Applicants must be enrolled full time in a doctoral program in biomedical sciences, including medicine, pharmacy, nursing, or basic sciences. Selection is based primarily on academic achievement.

Financial data The stipend is $20,000 per year.

Duration 1 year; recipients may reapply for 1 additional year of support.

Additional data This program is funded by ApoPharma Inc.

Number awarded 1 each year.

Deadline September of each year.

[827]
DEAR JACK SCHOLARSHIP

Cancer for College
981 Park Center Drive
Vista, CA 92081
(760) 599-5096
E-mail: applications@cancerforcollege.org
Web: www.cancerforcollege.org/application.html

Summary To provide financial assistance to undergraduate and graduate students who are cancer patients or survivors and working on or planning to work a degree in music.

Eligibility This program is open to undergraduate and graduate students who are entering or currently enrolled at accredited colleges, universities, community colleges, or trade schools in any state. Applicants must be working on a degree in music and able to express how they plan to prepare for a career in music. They must be a cancer patient or survivor. Along with their application, they must submit transcripts, verification of their cancer diagnosis, 2 letters of recommendation, and information on their financial situation.

Financial data The stipend ranges from $1,000 to $5,000.

Duration 1 year.

Number awarded 1 each year.

Deadline January of each year.

[828]
DELUCA, RICCIUTI & KONIECZKA MENTAL HEALTH SCHOLARSHIP

DeLuca, Ricciuti & Konieczka
Attn: Anthony DeLuca
225 Ross Street, Fourth Floor
Pittsburgh, PA 15219
(412) 281-6869   Fax: (412) 281-1350
E-mail: drkattorneys@gmail.com
Web: www.drkattorneys.com/scholarship

Summary To provide financial assistance to undergraduate and graduate students who have struggled with mental health issues.

Eligibility This program is open to students enrolled or accepted at a college, university, technical school, or graduate school in the United States. Applicants must have struggled with mental health issues but found a way to manage and overcome those issues. They must have a GPA of 3.0 or higher and be willing to share their story with the general public. Along with their application, they must submit an essay of 1 to 3 pages about their life with mental health issues, the struggles they have encountered, and how they have overcome those.

Financial data The stipend is $1,000.

Duration 1 year.

Number awarded 1 each year.

Deadline July of each year.

[829]
DIALYSIS SCHOLARSHIP FOUNDATION

Dialysis Scholarship Foundation, Inc.
P.O. Box 372278
Denver, CO 80237
E-mail: Inquiry@DialysisScholarshipFund.org
Web: www.dialysisscholarshipfund.org/index.html

Summary To provide financial assistance for college or graduate school to dialysis patients who are awaiting a kidney transplant.

Eligibility This program is open to students entering or enrolled in college or graduate school and undergoing dialysis until they are able to undergo a kidney transplant. Applicants must submit brief statements on their future educational plans, why they are interested in this scholarship, and any special skills and qualifications they have acquired from employment, volunteer work, or other activities.

Financial data A stipend is awarded (amount not specified).

Duration 1 year; may be renewed, provided the recipient maintains a GPA of 3.0 or higher with satisfactory attendance.

Additional data This program began in 2012.

Number awarded Varies each year; recently, 11 were awarded.

Deadline Deadline not specified.

[830]
DICK GRIFFITHS MEMORIAL SCHOLARSHIP

California Association for Postsecondary Education
  and Disability
Attn: Scholarships
10073 Valley View Street, Suite 242
Cypress, CA 90630
(562) 397-2810   Fax: (866) 577-3387
E-mail: caped38@gmail.com
Web: www.caped.io/scholarships/scholarship-application

Summary To provide financial assistance to undergraduate and graduate students in California who have a learning disability, especially involving mathematics.

Eligibility This program is open to students at public and private colleges and universities in California who have a learning disability and are especially challenged in mathematics. Undergraduates must have completed at least 6 semester credits and have a GPA of 2.5 or higher. Graduate students must have completed at least 3 semester units and have a GPA of 3.0 or higher. Applicants must submit 1) a 250-word essay describing their progress towards meeting their educational and/or vocational goals; 2) a 500-word essay on how they manage their disabiity; and 3) a 750-word essay on the strategies they have used to overcome their mathematics challenges. They must also submit a letter of recommendation from a faculty person, verification of disability, and unofficial transcripts.

Financial data The stipend is $1,000.

Duration 1 year.

Number awarded 1 each year.

Deadline August of each year.

[831]
DISABLED LAW STUDENT SCHOLARSHIP

Hermann Law Group
560 White Plains Road, Suite 630
Tarrytown, NY 10591
(914) 286-3030   Toll Free: (888) 491-9087
E-mail: info@nymetrodisability.com
Web: www.nymetrodisability.com

Summary To provide financial assistance to law students who have a personal physical or mental disability.

Eligibility This program is open to students currently enrolled at a law school in the United State. Applicants must have a personal physical or mental disability. Along with their application, they must submit an essay of 1,000 to 1,500 words on how they have worked to succeed despite the disability.

Financial data The stipend is $1,000.

Duration 1 year.

Number awarded 1 each year.

Deadline August of each year.

[832]
DOLLARS 4 TIC SCHOLARS TOURETTE SYNDROME SCHOLARSHIP

Kelsey B. Diamantis TS Scholarship Family
  Foundation, Inc.
21801 Little Bear Lane
Boca Raton, FL 33428
(561) 487-9526   E-mail: info@dollars4ticscholars.org
Web: www.dollars4ticscholars.org

Summary To provide financial assistance for college to students who have Tourette Syndrome (TS).

Eligibility This program is open to undergraduate and graduate students with TS who are enrolled or planning to enroll at a college or university. Applicants must have a GPA of 2.5 or higher. They must submit a letter from their doctor confirming the diagnosis of TS, documentation of financial need, 3 letters of recommendation, and transcripts.

Financial data The stipend is $1,000.

Duration 1 year.

Additional data This program began in 2015.

Number awarded 1 or more each year.

Deadline April of each year.

[833]
DOREEN MCMULLAN MCCARTHY MEMORIAL ACADEMIC SCHOLARSHIP FOR WOMEN WITH BLEEDING DISORDERS

National Hemophilia Foundation
Attn: Victory for Women Program
7 Penn Plaza
370 Seventh Avenue, Suite 1204
New York, NY 10001
(212) 328-3700   Toll Free: (800) 42-HANDI, ext. 2
Fax: (212) 328-3777   E-mail: sroger@hemophilia.org
Web: www.hemophilia.org

Summary To provide financial assistance for college or graduate school to women who have a bleeding disorder.

Eligibility This program is open to women who are entering or already enrolled in an undergraduate or graduate program at a university, college, or accredited vocational school. Applicants must have von Willebrand Disease, hemophilia or other clotting factor deficiency, platelet disorder, or carrier status. Along with their application, they must submit a 250-word essay that describes how their education and future career plans will benefit others in the bleeding disorders community. Selection is based on that essay, achievements, and community service to the bleeding disorders community.

Financial data The stipend is $2,500.

Duration 1 year.

Additional data The program, known also as V4W, was established in 2005 as the Project Red Flag Academic Scholarship for Women with Bleeding and later named the Victory for Women Academic Scholarship for Women with Bleeding Disorders.

Number awarded 1 each year.

Deadline March of each year.

[834]
ELIZABETH NASH FOUNDATION SCHOLARSHIP PROGRAM

Elizabeth Nash Foundation
P.O. Box 1260
Los Gatos, CA 95031-1260
E-mail: scholarships@elizabethnashfoundation.org
Web: www.elizabethnashfoundation.org

Summary To provide financial assistance for college or graduate school to individuals with cystic fibrosis (CF).

Eligibility This program is open to undergraduate and graduate students who have CF. Applicants must be able to demonstrate clear academic goals and a commitment to participate in activities outside the classroom. U.S. citizenship is required. Selection is based on academic record, character, demonstrated leadership, service to CF-related causes and the broader community, and financial need.

Financial data Stipends range from $1,000 to $2,500. Funds are paid directly to the academic institution to be applied to tuition and fees.

Duration 1 year; recipients may reapply.

Additional data This program began in 2005. Recipients must agree to support the program by speaking at a local event or writing an article for publication by the foundation.

Number awarded Varies each year; recently, 16 were awarded. Since the program was established, it has awarded more than 115 scholarships.

Deadline April of each year.

[835]
EPILEPSY FOUNDATION NEW ENGLAND SCHOLARSHIPS

Epilepsy Foundation New England
Attn: Director of Community Engagement and
  Education
335 Main Street, Unit 8
Wilmington, MA 01887
(617) 506-6041   Fax: (617) 506-6047
E-mail: swelby@epilepsynewengland.org
Web: www.epilepsynewengland.org

Summary To provide financial assistance to residents of Massachusetts, Rhode Island, New Hampshire, and Maine who have epilepsy and are interested in attending college or graduate school in any state.

Eligibility This program is open to residents of Massachusetts, Rhode Island, New Hampshire, or Maine who have been diagnosed with epilepsy (seizure disorder). Applicants must be accepted or enrolled in a postsecondary educational or vocational program in any state as an undergraduate or graduate student. Along with their application, they must submit an essay (up to 220 words in length) on their academic and career goals and how having epilepsy has affected or influenced those goals and their work towards achieving them.

Financial data The stipend is $2,500.

Duration 1 year; may be renewed.

Additional data This program includes the Richard Bonasera Scholarships and the Leslie G. Brody and Amy Seeherman Scholarships.

Number awarded At least 4 each year.

Deadline February of each year.

[836]
ERIC DELSON MEMORIAL SCHOLARSHIP

CVS Caremark
c/o Scholarship America
Scholarship Management Services
One Scholarship Way
P.O. Box 297
St. Peter, MN 56082
(507) 931-1682
Web: www.cvsspecialty.com

Summary To provide financial assistance for high school, college, or graduate school to students with a bleeding disorder.

Eligibility This program is open to students diagnosed with a bleeding disorder who are 1) high school seniors, high school graduates or equivalent (GED), college students, or graduate students currently enrolled or planning to enroll full time at an accredited 2- or 4-year college, university, or vocational/technical school; or 2) students entering grades 7-12 at a private secondary school in the United States. Selection is based on academic record, demonstrated leadership and participation in school and community activities, work experience, a statement of educational and career goals, unusual personal or family circumstances, and an outside appraisal.

Financial data The stipend is $2,500 for college students or $1,500 for high school students. Funds are paid in 2 equal installments directly to the recipient.

Duration 1 year; may be renewed for up to 3 additional years, provided the recipient maintains a GPA of 2.5 or higher for the freshman year and 3.0 or higher for subsequent years.

Number awarded 4 each year: 3 for college students and 1 for a high school student.

Deadline June of each year.

[837]
GEORGE AND LINDA PRICE SCHOLARSHIP

Hemophilia Association of the Capital Area
8136 Old Keene Mill Road, Suite A312
Springfield, VA 22152
(703) 352-7641   Fax: (540) 427-6589
E-mail: admin@hacacares.org
Web: www.hacacares.org

Summary To provide financial assistance to individuals with bleeding disorders and their families who are members of the Hemophilia Association of the Capital Area (HACA) and interested in attending college or graduate school in any state.

Eligibility This program is open to residents of northern Virginia, Montgomery and Prince George's County in Maryland, and Washington, D.C. who have a bleeding disorder and their siblings and parents. Applicants must be members of HACA. They must be 1) high school seniors or graduates who have not yet attended college; 2) full-time freshmen, sophomores, or juniors at a college, university, or vocational/technical school in any state; or 3) college seniors planning to attend graduate school and students already enrolled at a graduate school in any state. Along with their application, they must submit a 500-word essay on what they have done to contribute to the bleeding disorders community and how they plan to contribute to that community in the future. Financial need is not considered in the selection process.

Financial data   The stipend is $2,500.

Duration   1 year; recipients may reapply.

Number awarded   2 each year.

Deadline   May of each year.

[838]
GUNNAR ESIASON OWN IT SCHOLARSHIP

Boomer Esiason Foundation
c/o Chris McEwan
483 Tenth Avenue, Suite 300
New York, NY 10018
(646) 292-7939   Fax: (646) 292-7945
E-mail: cmcewan@esiason.org
Web: www.esiason.org

Summary   To provide financial assistance to high school seniors, undergraduates, and graduate students who have cystic fibrosis (CF) and a resolve to OWN the disease.

Eligibility   This program is open to CF patients who are high school seniors or students already working on an undergraduate or graduate degree. Applicants must be able to demonstrate a will to learn and achieve, despite having CF. Along with their application, they must submit 1) a letter from their doctor confirming the diagnosis of CF; 2) information on financial need with a detailed breakdown of tuition costs from their academic institution; 3) transcripts from high school, college, and/or graduate school; 4) a short essay (up to 350 words) on how they think the Boomer Esiason Foundation impacts the CF community; 5) a long essay (more than 350 words) on how they OWN their CF; and 6) a letter of 200 to 350 words from a friend about them and how they OWN their CF.

Financial data   The stipend ranges from $1,000 to $5,000. Funds are paid directly to the academic institution to assist in covering the cost of tuition and fees.

Duration   1 year; nonrenewable.

Additional data   This program began in 2016.

Number awarded   1 each year.

Deadline   September of each year.

[839]
HAWKINS SPIZMAN KILGO, LLC CHILDHOOD CANCER AWARENESS SCHOLARSHIP

Hawkins Spizman Kilgo, LLC
1535 Mount Vernon Road, Suite 200
Atlanta, GA 30338
(770) 685-6400   Fax: (770) 685-6403
E-mail: info@hawkinsduilaw.com
Web: www.hawkinsduilaw.com

Summary   To provide financial assistance to undergraduate and graduate students who are survivors of childhood cancer or loved ones of survivors.

Eligibility   This program is open to students currently enrolled or accepted for enrollment as an undergraduate or graduate student at an accredited college or university in any state. Applicants must be a survivor or childhood cancer or a loved one who has been directly affected by childhood cancer. They must have a GPA of 2.8 or higher. Along with their application, they must submit an essay of 500 to 1,000 words on 1 of the following: 1) how childhood cancer affected them; 2) how cancer has influenced their dreams and career goals; or 3) what they would say to a young person who has just been diagnosed with cancer to help them prepare for their future.

Financial data   The stipend is $1,000.

Duration   1 year.

Number awarded   1 each year.

Deadline   July of each year.

[840]
HEMOPHILIA ASSOCIATION OF NEW JERSEY SCHOLARSHIPS

Hemophilia Association of New Jersey
Attn: Scholarship Committee
197 Route 18 South, Suite 206 North
East Brunswick, NJ 08816
(732) 249-6000   Fax: (732) 249-7999
E-mail: hemnj@comcast.net
Web: www.hanj.org/scholar.html

Summary   To provide financial assistance to New Jersey residents who have a bleeding disorder and are interested in attending college or graduate school in any state.

Eligibility   This program is open to New Jersey residents who have a bleeding disorder (Hemophilia A or B, von Willebrand Disease, or a similar blood coagulation disorder). Applicants must be attending or planning to attend an accredited college or university in any state as an undergraduate or graduate student. They must have at least a 2.5 GPA, have been actively involved in extracurricular activities, and be able to demonstrate financial need. Along with their application, they must submit a family financial profile, official transcripts, and a brief essay (up to 2 pages) on how they meet the eligibility criteria. Membership in the Hemophilia Association of New Jersey is required.

Financial data   The stipend is $1,500 per year for undergraduates or $2,000 per year for graduate students.

Duration 1 year; undergraduate scholarships may be renewed for up to 3 additional years and graduate scholarships may be renewed 1 additional year.

Additional data The undergraduate scholarships include the Robert and Dennis Kelly Memorial Scholarship. The graduate scholarship is designated the Paul D. Amitrani Scholarship.

Number awarded 5 each year: 4 undergraduate scholarships and 1 graduate fellowship.

Deadline April of each year.

[841]
HEMOPHILIA FEDERATION OF AMERICA MEDICAL/HEALTHCARE SERVICES EDUCATIONAL SCHOLARSHIP

Hemophilia Federation of America
Attn: Scholarship Committee
820 First Street, N.E., Suite 720
Washington, DC 20002
(202) 675-6984   Toll Free: (800) 230-9797
Fax: (202) 675-6983
E-mail: scholarship@hemophiliafed.org
Web: www.hemophiliafed.org

Summary To provide financial assistance to undergraduate and graduate students who have a bleeding disorder and are working on a degree in a medical or health-related field.

Eligibility This program is open to undergraduate and graduate students who have a bleeding disorder. Applicants must be preparing for a career in medicine or a health-related field. Along with their application, they must submit an essay of 1 to 2 pages on why they chose to study in their field and why they think it is the right path for them. Financial need is considered in the selection process.

Financial data The grant is $4,000.

Duration 1 year.

Number awarded 1 each year.

Deadline April of each year.

[842]
HEMOPHILIA OF INDIANA JUDY MOORE MEMORIAL SCHOLARSHIP

Hemophilia of Indiana
Attn: Community Outreach Coordinator
6910 North Shadeland Avenue, Suite 140
Indianapolis, IN 46220
(317) 570-0039   Toll Free: (800) 241-2873
Fax: (317) 570-0058
Web: www.hemophiliaofindiana.org

Summary To provide financial assistance to residents of Indiana who have a bleeding disorder and are interested in attending college or graduate school in any state.

Eligibility This program is open to residents of Indiana who have been diagnosed with a bleeding disorder, including (but not limited to) von Willebrand's disease, hemophilia A, or hemophilia B. Applications must be enrolled, or planning to enroll as an undergraduate or graduate student at a college, university, junior college, or vocational school in any state. Selection is based on academic standing, an essay, and recommendations.

Financial data A stipend is awarded (amount not specified).

Duration 1 year.

Number awarded 1 or more each year.

Deadline Deadline not specified.

[843]
HYDROCEPHALUS ASSOCIATION SCHOLARSHIPS

Hydrocephalus Association
4340 East West Highway, Suite 905
Bethesda, MD 20814
(301) 202-3811   Toll Free: (888) 598-3789, ext. 22
Fax: (301) 202-3813
E-mail: scholarship@hydroassoc.com
Web: www.hydroassoc.org/scholarships

Summary To provide financial assistance for college or graduate school to young adults with hydrocephalus.

Eligibility This program is open to individuals between the ages of 17 and 30 who have hydrocephalus. The scholarship must be used for an educational purpose, including, but not limited to, a 4-year or junior college, a high school postgraduate year to prepare for college, a technical or trade school, an accredited employment training program, or a graduate program. Applicants may be in the process of applying to a program or university or already enrolled. They must include essays on their hobbies, interests, and activities; their educational and career goals; how having hydrocephalus has impacted their life; how they would help others with hydrocephalus; and how the scholarship will help them. Financial need is not considered in the selection process.

Financial data The stipend is $1,000. Funds may be used for tuition, books, housing, or any other educationally-related expense.

Duration 1 year; nonrenewable.

Additional data This program includes 5 named scholarships: the Gerald Schwartz Fudge Scholarship, established in 1994, the Morris L. and Rebecca Ziskind Memorial Scholarship, established in 2001, the Anthony Abbene Scholarship, established in 2002, the Justin Scot Alston Memorial Scholarship, established in 2004, and the Mario J. Tocco Hydrocephalus Foundation Scholarship, established in 2007.

Number awarded Varies each year; recently, 8 were awarded.

Deadline April of each year.

[844]
JACKIE SPELLMAN SCHOLARSHIPS

Jackie Spellman Scholarship Foundation
935 Eldridge Road
Box 200
Sugar Land, TX 77478
Toll Free: (888) 553-JSSF
E-mail: jackiespellmanfoundation@gmail.com
Web: www.jackiespellmanbenefit.org/scholarship.shtml

Summary To provide financial assistance for college or graduate school to students who have or whose family member has leukemia or lymphoma.

Eligibility This program is open to high school seniors, community college and 4-year university students, and graduate students who are leukemia or lymphoma survivors, patients, and/or children, siblings, or parents of leukemia or lymphoma patients. Applicants must be U.S. citizens and enrolled or planning to enroll full time. They must have a GPA of 3.0 or higher and be able to demonstrate financial need. Along with their application, they must submit transcripts; SAT and/or ACT test scores; documentation of financial need; a letter describing any special circumstances that have impacted their academic performance, community service, or leadership activities (if relevant); and an essay of 600 to 800 words describing how leukemia or lymphoma has affected their life, their future plans and desired career path, and how this scholarship will impact them. Students majoring in health or nursing-related majors may receive priority.

Financial data Stipends range from $1,000 to $5,000.

Duration 1 year.

Number awarded Approximately 15 each year.

Deadline April of each year.

[845]
JAMES AND PATRICIA SOOD SCHOLARSHIP

Ulman Cancer Fund for Young Adults
Attn: Scholarship Committee
921 East Fort Avenue, Suite 325
Baltimore, MD 21230
(410) 964-0202   Toll Free: (888) 393-FUND
Fax: (888) 964-0402
E-mail: scholarship@ulmanfund.org
Web: www.ulmanfund.org/scholarships

Summary To provide financial assistance to students who have been diagnosed with cancer or have or have lost a family member with cancer and are interested in working on an undergraduate or graduate degree in education.

Eligibility This program is open to students who 1) have been diagnosed with cancer; 2) have a parent or sibling living with cancer; or 3) have lost a parent or sibling to cancer. Applicants must be attending, or planning to attend, a college or university in any state to work on an undergraduate or graduate degree in education. The first diagnosis of cancer (whether of the applicant, a parent, or sibling) must have occurred after the applicant was 15 years of age. Along with their application, they must submit a 500-word essay or 3-minute video on either 1) a letter that they would have liked to receive during their cancer experience; or 2) what they would tell the young adults who participate in the sponsor's summer-long drive to support the organization about being a young adult impacted by cancer. U.S. citizenship or permanent resident status is required.

Financial data The stipend is $2,500. Funds are paid directly to the educational institution.

Duration 1 year.

Additional data Recipients are obligated to organize and run a bone marrow registry drive with the support of Delete Blood Cancer and There Goes My Hero.

Number awarded 1 each year.

Deadline March of each year.

[846]
JAMIE L. ROBERTS MEMORIAL SCHOLARSHIP

Ulman Cancer Fund for Young Adults
Attn: Scholarship Committee
921 East Fort Avenue, Suite 325
Baltimore, MD 21230
(410) 964-0202   Toll Free: (888) 393-FUND
Fax: (888) 964-0402
E-mail: scholarship@ulmanfund.org
Web: www.ulmanfund.org/scholarships

Summary To provide financial assistance for college or graduate school to students who have been diagnosed with cancer or have or have lost a family member with cancer.

Eligibility This program is open to students who 1) have been diagnosed with cancer; 2) have a parent or sibling living with cancer; or 3) have lost a parent or sibling to cancer. Applicants must be attending, or planning to attend, a college or university in any state to work on an undergraduate, graduate, or professional degree. They should demonstrate the qualities of the program's namesake-an infectious positive attitude, love of adventure, and ability to inspire others to achieve higher goals. The first diagnosis of cancer (whether of the applicant, a parent, or sibling) must have occurred after the applicant was 15 years of age. Along with their application, they must submit a 500-word essay or 3-minute video on either 1) a letter that they would have liked to receive during their cancer experience; or 2) what they would tell the young adults who participate in the sponsor's summer-long drive to support the organization about being a young adult impacted by cancer. U.S. citizenship or permanent resident status is required.

Financial data The stipend is $2,500. Funds are paid directly to the educational institution.

Duration 1 year.

Additional data This program, which began in 2014, is funded by the 4K for Cancer, an organization of college students who ride bicycles across the country every summer and raise funds for cancer. Recipients are obligated to organize and run a bone marrow registry drive with the support of Delete Blood Cancer and There Goes My Hero.

Number awarded 6 each year.

Deadline March of each year.

[847]
JEFFREY P. MEYER MEMORIAL SCHOLARSHIP

Ulman Cancer Fund for Young Adults
Attn: Scholarship Committee
921 East Fort Avenue, Suite 325
Baltimore, MD 21230
(410) 964-0202   Toll Free: (888) 393-FUND
Fax: (888) 964-0402
E-mail: scholarship@ulmanfund.org
Web: www.ulmanfund.org/scholarships

Summary To provide financial assistance for college or graduate school to young adults who have cancer or are cancer survivors.

Eligibility This program is open to students who are between 18 and 25 years of age and have battled cancer or are currently undergoing active treatment. The first diagnosis of cancer must have occurred after they were 15 years of age. Applicants must be attending or planning to attend a 2- or 4-year college or university to work on an undergraduate or graduate degree. They must be U.S. citizens or permanent residents. Along with their application, they must submit a 500-word essay or 3-minute video on either 1) a letter that they would have liked to receive during their cancer experience; or 2) what they would tell the young adults who participate in the sponsor's summer-long drive to support the organization about being a young adult impacted by cancer. In the selection process, preference is given to applicants who embody the words of the program's namesake to "stay positive, stay realistic, and have the courage to take control of your life."

Financial data The stipend is $2,500. Funds are paid directly to the educational institution.

Duration 1 year.

Additional data Recipients are obligated to organize and run a bone marrow registry drive with the support of Delete Blood Cancer and There Goes My Hero.

Number awarded 1 each year.

Deadline March of each year.

[848]
JILL WEAVER STARKMAN SCHOLARSHIP

Ulman Cancer Fund for Young Adults
Attn: Scholarship Committee
921 East Fort Avenue, Suite 325
Baltimore, MD 21230
(410) 964-0202   Toll Free: (888) 393-FUND
Fax: (888) 964-0402
E-mail: scholarship@ulmanfund.org
Web: www.ulmanfund.org/scholarships

Summary To provide financial assistance for college or graduate school to students who have been diagnosed with cancer or have or have lost a family member with cancer.

Eligibility This program is open to students who 1) have been diagnosed with cancer; 2) have a parent or sibling living with cancer; or 3) have lost a parent or sibling to cancer. Applicants must be attending, or planning to attend, a college or university in any state to work on an undergraduate, graduate, or professional degree. They should demonstrate the qualities of the program's namesake-the spirit of adventure and compassion and skill for communicating with humans and animals alike. The first diagnosis of cancer (whether of the applicant, a parent, or sibling) must have occurred after the applicant was 15 years of age. Along with their application, they must submit a 500-word essay or 3-minute video on either 1) a letter that they would have liked to receive during their cancer experience; or 2) what they would tell the young adults who participate in the sponsor's summer-long drive to support the organization about being a young adult impacted by cancer. U.S. citizenship or permanent resident status is required.

Financial data The stipend is $2,500. Funds are paid directly to the educational institution.

Duration 1 year.

Additional data This program began in 2012. Recipients are obligated to organize and run a bone marrow registry drive with the support of Delete Blood Cancer and There Goes My Hero.

Number awarded 1 each year.

Deadline March of each year.

[849]
JOHN BULLER SCHOLARSHIP

Greater Houston Community Foundation
Attn: Scholarships Assistant
5120 Woodway Drive, Suite 6000
Houston, TX 77056
(713) 333-2236   Fax: (713) 333-2220
E-mail: jlauver@ghcf.org
Web: www.ghcfscholar.org

Summary To provide financial assistance to residents of Texas who have cystic fibrosis and are interested in attending college or graduate school in the state.

Eligibility This program is open to Texas residents who have cystic fibrosis. Applicants must be enrolled or planning to enroll as an undergraduate or graduate student at an accredited 2- or 4-year college or university in Texas. Along with their application, they must submit transcripts and information on their extracurricular activities, work experience, community service, and other activities. Financial need is considered in the selection process. U.S. citizenship is required.

Financial data The stipend is $1,000 per year.

Duration 1 year; may be renewed up to 3 additional years.

Additional data This program began in 1997.

Number awarded 1 or more each year.

Deadline March of each year.

[850]
JOHN DUVALL MEMORIAL SCHOLARSHIP

Ulman Cancer Fund for Young Adults
Attn: Scholarship Committee
921 East Fort Avenue, Suite 325
Baltimore, MD 21230
(410) 964-0202   Toll Free: (888) 393-FUND
Fax: (888) 964-0402
E-mail: scholarship@ulmanfund.org
Web: www.ulmanfund.org/scholarships

Summary To provide financial assistance to students who have been diagnosed with cancer or have or have lost a family member with cancer and are interested in attending designated universities.

Eligibility This program is open to students who 1) have been diagnosed with cancer; 2) have a parent or sibling living with cancer; or 3) have lost a parent or sibling to cancer. Applicants must be working on or planning to work on an undergraduate, graduate, or professional degree at the University of Maryland, Towson University, Elon University, or the Savannah College of Art and Design. They must be able to demonstrate financial need. The first diagnosis of cancer (whether of the applicant, a parent, or sibling) must have occurred after the applicant was 15 years of age. Along with their application, they must submit a 500-word essay or 3-minute video on either 1) a letter that they would have liked to receive during their cancer experience; or 2) what they would tell the young adults who participate in the sponsor's summer-long drive to support the organization about being a young adult impacted by cancer. U.S. citizenship or permanent resident status is required.

Financial data The stipend is $2,500. Funds are paid directly to the educational institution.

Duration 1 year.

Additional data Recipients are obligated to organize and run a bone marrow registry drive with the support of Delete Blood Cancer and There Goes My Hero.

Number awarded 1 each year.

Deadline March of each year.

[851]
JOHN FOY & ASSOCIATES STRONG ARM LEUKEMIA SCHOLARSHIP

John Foy & Associates
3343 Peachtree Road, Suite 350
Atlanta, GA 30326
(404) 982-4326
Web: www.johnfoy.com

Summary To provide financial assistance to undergraduate and graduate students and their loved ones who have been affected by leukemia.

Eligibility This program is open to entering college freshmen, undergraduates, and graduate students at accredited colleges and universities in any state. Applicants or a loved one must have been affected by leukemia. Along with their application, they must submit an essay of 500 to 1,000 words on 1 of the following: 1) how living with their or their loves one's leukemia has affected their education; 2) the adjustments they have made as a student to accommodate their or a loved one's leukemia; or 3) an obstacle that people with leukemia face that they want the general public to know about.

Financial data The stipend is $1,000.

Duration 1 year.

Number awarded 1 each year.

Deadline December of each year.

[852]
JOHN HANLEY MEMORIAL SCHOLARSHIP AWARD

Ulman Cancer Fund for Young Adults
Attn: Scholarship Committee
921 East Fort Avenue, Suite 325
Baltimore, MD 21230
(410) 964-0202   Toll Free: (888) 393-FUND
Fax: (888) 964-0402
E-mail: scholarship@ulmanfund.org
Web: www.ulmanfund.org/scholarships

Summary To provide financial assistance for college or graduate school to young adults who have cancer or are cancer survivors.

Eligibility This program is open to students who are between 18 and 25 years of age and have battled cancer or are currently undergoing active treatment. The first diagnosis of cancer must have occurred after they were 15 years of age. Applicants must be attending or planning to attend a 2- or 4-year college or university to work on an undergraduate or graduate degree. They must be U.S. citizens or permanent residents. Along with their application, they must submit a 500-word essay or 3-minute video on either 1) a letter that they would have liked to receive during their cancer experience; or 2) what they would tell the young adults who participate in the sponsor's summer-long drive to support the organization about being a young adult impacted by cancer. In the selection process, consideration is given to their leadership abilities and commitment to their community.

Financial data The stipend is $2,500. Funds are paid directly to the educational institution.

Duration 1 year.

Additional data Recipients are obligated to organize and run a bone marrow registry drive with the support of Delete Blood Cancer and There Goes My Hero.

Number awarded 5 each year.

Deadline March of each year.

[853]
JOSHUA GOMES MEMORIAL SCHOLARSHIP

Joshua Gomes Memorial Scholarship Fund
45767 McKenzie Highway
Vida, OR 97488
(541) 896-3023   E-mail: Info@joshuagomes.org
Web: www.joshuagomes.org

Summary To provide financial assistance for college or graduate school to students who have AIDS or are HIV positive.

Eligibility This program is open to full-time undergraduate and graduate students accepted or enrolled at a college or university in the United States. Applicants must have AIDS or be HIV positive. Along with their application, they must submit a 500-word essay that explains their hopes, plans, and goals for the future; how their schooling will help lay a path to fulfilling those; what motivates them to pursue higher education; what subjects they plan to study; and what led them to that path of study. Selection is based on merit and financial need.

Financial data The stipend is $1,000.

Duration 1 year; recipients may reapply.

Additional data This program began in 2005.

Number awarded 1 or more each year.

Deadline July of each year.

[854]
JUSTNEBULIZERS.COM RESPIRATORY CARE SCHOLARSHIP

Just Health Shops
Attn: JustNebulizers.com
11840 West Market Place, Suite H
Fulton, MD 20759
Toll Free: (800) 998-7750   Fax: (301) 776-0716
E-mail: scholarship@justnebulizers.com
Web: www.justnebulizers.com

Summary To recognize and reward, with scholarships, undergraduate and graduate students who have a respiratory condition and submit outstanding videos about their condition.

Eligibility This program is open to legal U.S. residents who are enrolled in an undergraduate or graduate program. Applicants must have a respiratory condition. Instead of an application, they must submit a 3-minute video on 1) how living with a respiratory condition has molded who they are; and 2) the advice they would give to others in their situation. Selection is based on thoughtfulness in answering the questions and creativity of presenting the answers.

Financial data The award is a $1,000 scholarship. Funds are sent directly to the recipient's college or university.

Duration 1 year.

Number awarded 1 each year.

Deadline December of each year.

[855]
KARL POHRT TRIBUTE AWARD

Scholarship America
Attn: Scholarship Management Services
One Scholarship Way
P.O. Box 297
St. Peter, MN 56082
(507) 931-1682   Toll Free: (800) 537-4180
Fax: (507) 931-9168
E-mail: bincfoundation@scholarshipamerica.org
Web: www.scholarsapply.org/binc

Summary To provide financial assistance to nontraditional students and those with learning disabilities who

have an affiliation with an independent bookstore and are interested in attending college or graduate school in any state.

Eligibility This program is open to high school seniors and graduates who are enrolled to planning to enroll full or part time in an undergraduate or graduate program at an accredited 2- or 4-year college, university, or vocational/technical school. Applicants must have overcome learning adversity or be a nontraditional student. They must be affiliated with an independent bookstore. Selection is based on academic record, participation and leadership in school and community activities, and financial need.

Financial data The stipend is $5,000.

Duration 1 year; recipients may reapply.

Additional data This program is sponsored by the Book Industry Charitable Foundation (BINC).

Number awarded 1 each year.

Deadline March of each year.

[856]
KEVIN CHILD SCHOLARSHIP

National Hemophilia Foundation
Attn: NHF/HANDI
7 Penn Plaza
370 Seventh Avenue, Suite 1204
New York, NY 10001
(212) 328-3700   Toll Free: (800) 42-HANDI, ext. 2
Fax: (212) 328-3777   E-mail: handi@hemophilia.org
Web: www.hemophilia.org

Summary To provide financial assistance for college or graduate school to students with hemophilia.

Eligibility This program is open to high school seniors entering their first year of undergraduate study as well as those currently enrolled in college or graduate school. Applicants must have hemophilia A or B. Along with their application, they must submit a 1-page essay on their occupational objectives and goals in life and how the educational program they have planned will meet those objectives. Selection is based on that essay, academic performance, and participation in school and community activities.

Financial data The stipend is $1,000.

Duration 1 year.

Additional data The program was established in 1989.

Number awarded 1 each year.

Deadline June of each year.

[857]
KYLE R. NOBLE MEMORIAL SCHOLARSHIP

The Oley Foundation
c/o Albany Medical Center
43 New Scotland Avenue, MC-28
Albany, NY 12208-3478
(518) 262-5079   Toll Free: (800) 776-OLEY
Fax: (518) 262-5528
E-mail: andreaguidi.oley@gmail.com
Web: www.oley.org/page/KyleNobleScholarship

Summary To provide financial assistance to students who depend on home enteral nutrition (HEN) or home parenteral nutrition (HPN) for their primary nutritional needs.
Eligibility This program is open to undergraduate, graduate, and vocational students who have a medical diagnosis of a digestive disorder (ranging from cancer to Crohn's Disease) that requires HEN and/or HPN to meet their primary nutritional needs. Applicants must submit a personal essay of 1 to 3 pages describing how they have 1) overcome obstacles and challenges posed by HEN and/or HPN; and 2) inspired others to live life to the fullest. They must submit letters from 1) a member of their health care team describing their circumstances and need for HEN and/or HPN; and 2) a teacher or adviser supporting their pursuit of their educational goals.
Financial data The stipend is $2,000 per academic year.
Duration 1 year; recipients may reapply.
Additional data This program began in 2007.
Number awarded 1 each year.
Deadline March of each year.

[858]
LEONARD FAMILY ENTREPRENEURIAL SPIRIT SCHOLARSHIP

Cancer for College
981 Park Center Drive
Vista, CA 92081
(760) 599-5096
E-mail: applications@cancerforcollege.org
Web: www.cancerforcollege.org/application.html

Summary To provide financial assistance to undergraduate and graduate students who are cancer patients or survivors and interested in preparing for a career in the food service industry.
Eligibility This program is open to undergraduate and graduate students who are entering or currently enrolled at accredited colleges, universities, community colleges, or trade schools in any state. Applicants must be preparing for a career in the food service industry and planning to own or operate a restaurant. They must be a cancer patient or survivor. Along with their application, they must submit transcripts, verification of their cancer diagnosis, 2 letters of recommendation, and information on their financial situation.
Financial data The stipend ranges from $1,000 to $5,000.
Duration 1 year.
Number awarded 1 or 2 each year.
Deadline January of each year.

[859]
LEUKEMIA & LYMPHOMA LAW SCHOOL SCHOLARSHIP

Law Office of Renkin & Associates
Attn: Paula Renkin
320 Encinitas Boulevard
Encinitas, CA 92024
(619) 299-7100   Toll Free: (888) 837-3564
E-mail: Paula@renkinlaw.com
Web: www.renkinlaw.com

Summary To provide financial assistance to law students whose lives have been affected by leukemia or lymphoma, either in themselves or a member of their family.
Eligibility This program is open to U.S. citizens older than 18 years of age who are current or entering students at accredited law schools in the United States. Applicants must have been affected by or dealing with issues related to leukemia or lymphoma, either in themselves or a family member. They must have a GPA of 3.0 or higher from undergraduate or current law school work. Along with their application, they must submit an essay of 1 to 2 pages describing how their life has been impacted by leukemia or lymphoma.
Financial data The stipend is $1,000.
Duration 1 year.
Additional data This program began in 2015.
Number awarded 1 each year.
Deadline July of each year.

[860]
LISA HIGGINS-HUSSMAN FOUNDATION SCHOLARSHIP

Ulman Cancer Fund for Young Adults
Attn: Scholarship Committee
921 East Fort Avenue, Suite 325
Baltimore, MD 21230
(410) 964-0202   Toll Free: (888) 393-FUND
Fax: (888) 964-0402
E-mail: scholarship@ulmanfund.org
Web: www.ulmanfund.org/scholarships

Summary To provide financial assistance for college or graduate school to students from Washington, D.C., Maryland, or Virginia who have been diagnosed with cancer or have or have lost a family member with cancer.
Eligibility This program is open to students who 1) have been diagnosed with cancer; 2) have a parent, sibling, or guardian living with cancer; or 3) have lost a parent, sibling, or guardian to cancer. Applicants must be residents of Washington, D.C., Maryland, or Virginia. They must be between 15 and 35 years of age and attending, or planning to attend, a 2- or 4-year college, university, or vocational program in any state to work on an undergraduate or graduate degree. The first diagnosis of cancer (whether of the applicant, a parent, a sibling, or a guardian) must have occurred after the applicant was 15 years of age. Along with their application, they must submit a 500-word essay or 3-minute video on either 1) a letter that they would have liked to receive during their cancer experience; or 2) what they would tell the young adults who

participate in the sponsor's summer-long drive to support the organization about being a young adult impacted by cancer. U.S. citizenship or permanent resident status is required.

Financial data The stipend is $2,500. Funds are paid directly to the educational institution.

Duration 1 year.

Additional data Recipients are obligated to organize and run a bone marrow registry drive with the support of Delete Blood Cancer and There Goes My Hero.

Number awarded 1 each year.

Deadline March of each year.

[861]
LIVING BREATH FOUNDATION SCHOLARSHIPS

Living Breath Foundation
2031 Marsala Circle
Monterey, CA 93940
(831) 392-5283
E-mail: LivingBreathFoundation@gmail.com
Web: www.thelivingbreathfoundation.com/aid.html

Summary To provide financial assistance to residents of California and Arizona who have cystic fibrosis and are interested in attending college or graduate school in any state.

Eligibility This program is open to U.S. citizens who are residents of California or Arizona. Applicants have cystic fibrosis and be graduating high school seniors or undergraduate or graduate students continuing their education at a 2- or 4-year college, university, or trade school in any state. They must submit an essay on how continuing their education will benefit their future. Selection is based on academic record, leadership, community service, and financial need.

Financial data The stipend ranges from $1,000 to $5,000. Funds are disbursed directly to the student to assist in payment of tuition, books, or the expenses of going to school while having cystic fibrosis (e.g., private rooms, food, rooms with running water, bathrooms, parking).

Duration 1 year.

Additional data This foundation was established in 2008.

Number awarded 1 or more each year.

Deadline March of each year.

[862]
LOS ANGELES DUI ATTORNEY DIABETES SCHOLARSHIP

Los Angeles DUI Attorney
20700 Ventura Boulevard, Suite 301A
Woodland Hills, CA 91364
(818) 794-1023
Web: www.losangelesduiattorney.com

Summary To provide financial assistance to people who have diabetes and are enrolled or planning to enroll at a college or graduate school in any state.

Eligibility This program is open to people who have been diagnosed with any type of diabetes. Applicants must be enrolled or planning to enroll as an undergraduate or graduate student at an accredited college or university. They must have a GPA of 3.0 or higher. Along with their application, they must submit an essay of 500 to 1,000 words on 1 of the following topics: 1) a way that diabetes has shaped or changed your plans in life; 2) something that they think would make the biggest difference is how our society treats diabetes; or 3) a piece of advice that they would give themselves if they could go back to the time when they first learned they had diabetes.

Financial data The stipend is $1,000.

Duration 1 year.

Additional data This program began in 2016.

Number awarded 1 year.

Deadline June of each year.

[863]
MARY BARTON FREEMAN SCHOLARSHIPS

Ulman Cancer Fund for Young Adults
Attn: Scholarship Committee
921 East Fort Avenue, Suite 325
Baltimore, MD 21230
(410) 964-0202   Toll Free: (888) 393-FUND
Fax: (888) 964-0402
E-mail: scholarship@ulmanfund.org
Web: www.ulmanfund.org/scholarships

Summary To provide financial assistance for college or graduate school to students who have been diagnosed with cancer or have or have lost a family member with cancer.

Eligibility This program is open to students who 1) have been diagnosed with cancer; 2) have a parent or sibling living with cancer; or 3) have lost a parent or sibling to cancer. Applicants must be attending, or planning to attend, a college or university in any state to work on an undergraduate, graduate, or professional degree. They must be working on career or higher eduction goals. The first diagnosis of cancer (whether of the applicant, a parent, or sibling) must have occurred after the applicant was 15 years of age. Along with their application, they must submit a 500-word essay or 3-minute video on either 1) a letter that they would have liked to receive during their cancer experience; or 2) what they would tell the young adults who participate in the sponsor's summer-long drive to support the organization about being a young adult impacted by cancer. U.S. citizenship or permanent resident status is required.

Financial data The stipend is $2,500. Funds are paid directly to the educational institution.

Duration 1 year.

Additional data Recipients are obligated to organize and run a bone marrow registry drive with the support of Delete Blood Cancer and There Goes My Hero.

Number awarded 5 each year.

Deadline March of each year.

[864]
MESOTHELIOMA CANCER ALLIANCE SCHOLARSHIP

Mesothelioma Cancer Alliance
c/o Early, Lucarelli, Sweeney, Meisenkothen
360 Lexington Avenue, 20th Floor
New York, NY 10017
(212) 968-2233   Toll Free: (800) 336-0086
Fax: (212) 986-2255
Web: www.mesothelioma.com/scholarship

Summary To provide financial assistance to undergraduate and graduate students who have had cancer or whose family member has had cancer.

Eligibility This program is open to U.S. citizens enrolled or planning to enroll full time at a 2- or 4-year college or university as an undergraduate or graduate student. Applicants must have battled cancer at any point in their lives (not limited to mesothelioma) or have a parent, sibling, immediate family member, or close friend who has battled or is currently fighting cancer. They must have a GPA of 3.0 or higher. Along with their application, they must submit an essay of 500 to 1,500 words or a video up to 5 minutes in length on how cancer has affected their life, how they overcame that strong adversity, how cancer has affected their outlook on their life and personal or career goals, how that adversity shaped who they are today, what the scholarship would mean to them, and why it is important. Selection is based on the positive impact they have on those around them, strength in the face of adversity, commitment to academic excellence, and financial need.

Financial data The stipend is $4,000.

Duration 1 year.

Number awarded 2 each year: 1 in fall and 1 in spring.

Deadline March of each year for fall semester; November of each year for spring semester.

[865]
NCCF SURVIVOR SCHOLARSHIP PROGRAM

National Collegiate Cancer Foundation
Attn: Scholarship Committee
4858 Battery Lane, Suite 216
Bethesda, MD 20814
(240) 515-6262   E-mail: info@collegiatecancer.org
Web: www.collegiatecancer.org/scholarships

Summary To provide financial assistance for college or graduate school to cancer survivors.

Eligibility This program is open to students between 18 and 35 years of age who are cancer survivors or currently undergoing treatment for cancer. Applicants must be enrolled or planning to enroll at a college or university to work on a certificate or an associate, bachelor's, master's, or doctoral degree. Along with their application, they must submit a 1,000-word essay on 1 of 4 assigned topics related to their experiences with cancer and college. Selection is based on the essay, letters of recommendation, displaying a "Will Win" attitude, overall story of cancer survivorship, commitment to education, and financial need. U.S. citizenship or permanent resident status is required.

Financial data The stipend is $1,000.

Duration 1 year.

Number awarded Varies each year; recently, 39 were awarded.

Deadline May of each year.

[866]
OLIVIA M. MARQUART SCHOLARSHIP

Ulman Cancer Fund for Young Adults
Attn: Scholarship Committee
921 East Fort Avenue, Suite 325
Baltimore, MD 21230
(410) 964-0202   Toll Free: (888) 393-FUND
Fax: (888) 964-0402
E-mail: scholarship@ulmanfund.org
Web: www.ulmanfund.org/scholarships

Summary To provide financial assistance for college or graduate school to residents of Pennsylvania who have cancer or are cancer survivors and are interested in studying education.

Eligibility This program is open to residents of Pennsylvania who have battled cancer or are currently undergoing active treatment. The first diagnosis of cancer must have occurred after they were 15 years of age. Applicants must be attending or planning to attend a 2- or 4-year college or university in any state to work on an undergraduate or graduate degree in education. They must be U.S. citizens. Along with their application, they must submit a 500-word essay or 3-minute video on either 1) a letter that they would have liked to receive during their cancer experience; or 2) what they would tell the young adults who participate in the sponsor's summer-long drive to support the organization about being a young adult impacted by cancer. Financial need is considered in the selection process.

Financial data The stipend is $2,500. Funds are paid directly to the educational institution.

Duration 1 year.

Additional data Recipients are obligated to organize and run a bone marrow registry drive with the support of Delete Blood Cancer and There Goes My Hero.

Number awarded 1 each year.

Deadline March of each year.

[867]
PERLITA LIWANAG MEMORIAL SCHOLARSHIP

Ulman Cancer Fund for Young Adults
Attn: Scholarship Committee
921 East Fort Avenue, Suite 325
Baltimore, MD 21230
(410) 964-0202   Toll Free: (888) 393-FUND
Fax: (888) 964-0402
E-mail: scholarship@ulmanfund.org
Web: www.ulmanfund.org/scholarships

Summary To provide financial assistance for college or graduate school to students from the Washington, D.C. metropolitan area who have been diagnosed with cancer or have or have lost a family member with cancer.

Eligibility This program is open to students who 1) have been diagnosed with cancer; 2) have a parent, sibling, or guardian living with cancer; or 3) have lost a parent, sibling, or guardian to cancer. Applicants must be residents of Washington, D.C., Maryland, or northern Virginia. They must be 35 years of age or younger and attending, or planning to attend, a 2- or 4-year college, university, or vocational program in any state to work on an undergraduate or graduate degree. The first diagnosis of cancer (whether of the applicant, a parent, a sibling, or a guardian) must have occurred after the applicant was 15 years of age. Along with their application, they must submit a 500-word essay or 3-minute video on either 1) a letter that they would have liked to receive during their cancer experience; or 2) what they would tell the young adults who participate in the sponsor's summer-long drive to support the organization about being a young adult impacted by cancer. U.S. citizenship or permanent resident status is required.

Financial data The stipend is $2,500. Funds are paid directly to the educational institution.

Duration 1 year.

Additional data This program began in 2011. Recipients are obligated to organize and run a bone marrow registry drive with the support of Delete Blood Cancer and There Goes My Hero.

Number awarded 1 each year.

Deadline March of each year.

[868]
RIMINGTON TROPHY SCHOLARSHIP

Boomer Esiason Foundation
c/o Chris McEwan
483 Tenth Avenue, Suite 300
New York, NY 10018
(646) 292-7939   Fax: (646) 292-7945
E-mail: cmcewan@esiason.org
Web: www.esiason.org

Summary To provide financial assistance to undergraduate and graduate students who have cystic fibrosis (CF).

Eligibility This program is open to CF patients who are working on an undergraduate or graduate degree. Applicants must submit a letter from their doctor confirming the diagnosis of CF and a list of daily medications, information on financial need, a detailed breakdown of tuition costs from their academic institution, transcripts, and a 2-page essay on 1) their postgraduation goals; and 2) the importance of compliance with CF therapies and what they practice on a daily basis to stay healthy. Selection is based on academic ability, character, leadership potential, service to the community, financial need, and daily compliance to CF therapy.

Financial data The stipend ranges from $1,000 to $2,000. Funds are paid directly to the academic institution to assist in covering the cost of tuition and fees.

Duration 1 year; nonrenewable.

Additional data This program began in 2012 in association with the Rimington Trophy, a college football award named in honor of Dave Rimington, a former player for the

University of Nebraska and the president of the Boomer Esiason Foundation.

Number awarded 1 each year.

Deadline June of each year.

[869]
ROSEMARY QUIGLEY MEMORIAL SCHOLARSHIP

Boomer Esiason Foundation
c/o Chris McEwan
483 Tenth Avenue, Suite 300
New York, NY 10018
(646) 292-7939   Fax: (646) 292-7945
E-mail: cmcewan@esiason.org
Web: www.esiason.org

Summary To provide financial assistance to undergraduate and graduate students who have cystic fibrosis (CF) and a demonstrated commitment to living life to the fullest.

Eligibility This program is open to CF patients who are working on an undergraduate or graduate degree. Applicants must be able to demonstrate a clear sense of life goals and a commitment to living life to the fullest, despite having CF. Along with their application, they must submit a letter from their doctor confirming the diagnosis of CF and a list of daily medications, information on financial need, a detailed breakdown of tuition costs from their academic institution, transcripts, and a 2-page essay on 1) their postgraduation goals; and 2) the importance of compliance with CF therapies and what they practice on a daily basis to stay healthy. Selection is based on academic ability, character, leadership potential, service to the community, and financial need. Finalists are interviewed by telephone.

Financial data The stipend ranges from $500 to $2,000. Funds are paid directly to the academic institution to assist in covering the cost of tuition and fees.

Duration 1 year; nonrenewable.

Number awarded 1 each year.

Deadline June of each year.

[870]
ROSS SKELTON SCHOLARSHIP

Cancer for College
981 Park Center Drive
Vista, CA 92081
(760) 599-5096
E-mail: applications@cancerforcollege.org
Web: www.cancerforcollege.org/application.html

Summary To provide financial assistance to undergraduate and graduate students from North and South Carolina who are cancer patients or survivors and working on or planning to work on a degree in engineering.

Eligibility This program is open to undergraduate and graduate students in engineering who are originally from or currently attending or entering accredited colleges, universities, community colleges, or trade schools in North or South Carolina. Applicants must be a cancer patient or survivor. Along with their application, they must submit transcripts, verification of their cancer diagnosis, 2 letters of recommendation, and information on their financial situation.

Financial data The stipend ranges from $1,000 to $5,000.

Duration 1 year.

Number awarded 1 each year.

Deadline January of each year.

[871]
SACKS FOR CF SCHOLARSHIPS

Boomer Esiason Foundation
c/o Chris McEwan
483 Tenth Avenue, Suite 300
New York, NY 10018
(646) 292-7939   Fax: (646) 292-7945
E-mail: cmcewan@esiason.org
Web: www.esiason.org

Summary To provide financial assistance to undergraduate and graduate students who have cystic fibrosis (CF).

Eligibility This program is open to CF patients who are working on an undergraduate or graduate degree. Applicants must submit a letter from their doctor confirming the diagnosis of CF and a list of daily medications, information on financial need, a detailed breakdown of tuition costs from their academic institution, transcripts, and a 2-page essay on 1) their postgraduation goals; and 2) the importance of compliance with CF therapies and what they practice on a daily basis to stay healthy. Selection is based on academic ability, character, leadership potential, service to the community, financial need, and adherence to daily CF therapy.

Financial data The stipend ranges from $3,000 to $10,000. Funds are paid directly to the academic institution to assist in covering the cost of tuition and fees.

Duration 1 year; nonrenewable.

Additional data This program is funded by AbbVie Inc., a corporate sponsor which donates $1,000 to the foundation each time a quarterback is sacked on NFL Monday Night Football games.

Number awarded 30 each year.

Deadline January of each year.

[872]
SAMFUND GRANTS

The SAMFund for Young Adult Survivors of Cancer
89 South Street, Suite LL02
Boston, MA 02211
(617) 938-3484   Fax: (866) 496-8070
E-mail: grants@thesamfund.org
Web: www.thesamfund.org/get-help/grants

Summary To provide funding to young adult cancer survivors who need assistance for the transition to post-treatment life.

Eligibility This program is open to cancer survivors between 21 and 39 years of age who 1) have completed planned treatment with no evidence of disease; 2) are 1 year following the completion of planned treatment with stable disease; or 3) are in remission and on long-term hormonal therapy. Applicants must be able to demonstrate a need for funding for such purposes as graduate (but not undergraduate) tuition and loans, car and health insurance premiums, rent, utilities, family-building expenses, gym memberships, transportation costs, or current and residual medical bills. U.S. citizenship or permanent resident status is required.

Financial data Grant amounts vary but typically range from $1,500 to $2,000.

Duration These are 1-time grants.

Additional data This program, which stands for Surviving and Moving Forward, was established in 2003.

Number awarded Varies each year; since the program was established, it has awarded grants with a total value of more than $1,750,000.

Deadline June of each year.

[873]
SATOLA FAMILY SCHOLARSHIP

Ulman Cancer Fund for Young Adults
Attn: Scholarship Committee
921 East Fort Avenue, Suite 325
Baltimore, MD 21230
(410) 964-0202   Toll Free: (888) 393-FUND
Fax: (888) 964-0402
E-mail: scholarship@ulmanfund.org
Web: www.ulmanfund.org/scholarships

Summary To provide financial assistance for college or graduate school to students who have been diagnosed with cancer or have or have lost a family member with cancer.

Eligibility This program is open to students who 1) have been diagnosed with cancer; 2) have a parent or sibling living with cancer; or 3) have lost a parent or sibling to cancer. Applicants must be attending, or planning to attend, a college or university in any state to work on an undergraduate, graduate, or professional degree. They should be able to demonstrate courage, spirit, and determination. The first diagnosis of cancer (whether of the applicant, a parent, or sibling) must have occurred after the applicant was 15 years of age. Along with their application, they must submit a 500-word essay or 3-minute video on either 1) a letter that they would have liked to receive during their cancer experience; or 2) what they would tell the young adults who participate in the sponsor's summer-long drive to support the organization about being a young adult impacted by cancer. U.S. citizenship is required.

Financial data The stipend is $2,500. Funds are paid directly to the educational institution.

Duration 1 year.

Additional data This program began in 2009. Recipients are obligated to organize and run a bone marrow registry drive with the support of Delete Blood Cancer and There Goes My Hero.

Number awarded 1 each year.

Deadline March of each year.

[874]
SCHOLARSHIP OF THE ARTS

Boomer Esiason Foundation
c/o Chris McEwan
483 Tenth Avenue, Suite 300
New York, NY 10018
(646) 292-7939   Fax: (646) 292-7945
E-mail: cmcewan@esiason.org
Web: www.esiason.org

Summary To provide financial assistance to undergraduate and graduate students who have cystic fibrosis (CF) and are working on a degree in the arts.

Eligibility This program is open to CF patients who are working on an undergraduate or graduate degree in the arts. Applicants must submit a sample of their work (video, painting, sketching, sculpture), a letter from their doctor confirming the diagnosis of CF and a list of daily medications, information on financial need, a detailed breakdown of tuition costs from their academic institution, transcripts, and a 2-page essay on 1) their postgraduation goals; and 2) the importance of compliance with CF therapies and what they practice on a daily basis to stay healthy. Selection is based on academic ability, character, leadership potential, service to the community, and financial need.

Financial data Stipends range from $500 to $1,000. Funds are paid directly to the academic institution to assist in covering the cost of tuition and fees.

Duration 1 year; nonrenewable.

Number awarded 1 each year.

Deadline May of each year.

[875]
SCOTT DELGADILLO SCHOLARSHIP

Friends of Scott Foundation
Attn: Scholarship Fund
6977 Navajo Road, Number 168
San Diego, CA 92119
(619) 993-2917   E-mail: info@friendsofscott.org
Web: www.friendsofscott.org/scholarship.aspx

Summary To provide financial assistance for college or graduate school to childhood cancer survivors from California.

Eligibility This program is open to California residents who are survivors of childhood cancer or patients currently receiving treatment. Applicants must be attending or planning to attend a technical school, vocational school, junior college, or 4-year college or university as an undergraduate or graduate student in any state. Along with their application, they must submit a 500-word essay on how their experience with cancer has impacted their life. Selection is based on financial need and personal hardship.

Financial data The stipend is $1,000.

Duration 1 year.

Number awarded Varies each year; recently, 2 were awarded.

Deadline August of each year.

[876]
SNOWDROP FOUNDATION SCHOLARSHIPS

Snowdrop Foundation
Attn: Executive Director
7155 Old Katy Road
Houston, TX 77070
(713) 232-9051 E-mail: trish@snowdropfoundation.org
Web: www.snowdropfoundation.org

Summary To provide financial assistance for college or graduate school to students who have been diagnosed with cancer.

Eligibility This program is open to students entering or attending college or graduate school. Applicants must have been diagnosed with cancer before the age of 21. Along with their application, they must submit a 250-word description of themselves; a 250-word description of their family situation; information on financial need; a letter from their attending physician verifying their medical history and current medical situation; and an essay of 500 to 1,000 words on how their experience with cancer has impacted their life values and career goals.

Financial data Recently, stipends averaged nearly $3,000.

Duration 1 year.

Number awarded Varies each year; recently, 75 of these scholarships, with a value of $220,000, were awarded.

Deadline April of each year.

[877]
SOOZIE COURTER HEMOPHILIA SCHOLARSHIP PROGRAM

Pfizer Inc.
Attn: Hemophilia Scholarship Program
235 East 42nd Street
New York, NY 10017
Toll Free: (844) 202-9344
Web: www.hemophiliavillage.com

Summary To provide financial assistance for college or graduate school in any field to persons with hemophilia.

Eligibility This program is open to persons with hemophilia (A or B) who are high school seniors, have a GED, or are currently attending an accredited college, university, junior college, vocational school, or graduate school. Along with their application, they must submit a 2-page essay on 1 of the following topics: 1) how hemophilia has affected their school life and how they have overcome those challenges; 2) the advice they would give to a child with hemophilia who is beginning school; or 3) the time in history they would travel back to if they could and why. Financial need is not considered in the selection process.

Financial data The stipends are $2,500 for undergraduate students or $4,000 for graduate students.

Duration 1 year.

Additional data This program began in 1998 and given its current name in 2000.

Number awarded 17 each year: 12 to undergraduates and 5 to graduate students.

Deadline July of each year.

[878]
SURVIVORVISION TEXTBOOK SCHOLARSHIP PROGRAM

SurvivorVision
Attn: Textbook Program Chair
P.O. Box 5037
Woodridge, IL 60517
(630) 359-5172   E-mail: survivorvision@comcast.net
Web: www.survivorvision.org/are-you-eligible.html

Summary To provide funding for purchase of textbooks to undergraduate and graduate students who are patients or survivors of childhood cancer.

Eligibility This program is open to students currently enrolled at a college, university, community college, trade school, or graduate school. Applicants must be receiving or have received treatment for cancer that was diagnosed before they were 18 years of age. Along with their application, they must submit 1) a 500-word essay on how their cancer experience has affected their educational, personal, and/or life goals; 2) a 300-word essay on how a higher education will help them achieve those goals; and 3) a 300-word essay on any other information they want to share with the sponsor.

Financial data Awards in the form of reimbursement for the purchase of textbooks range up to $1,000 per year.

Duration 1 year; may be renewed up to 4 additional years for a lifetime maximum of $5,000.

Number awarded 35 to 40 each year.

Deadline May of each year.

[879]
SUSAN BUNCH MEMORIAL SCHOLARSHIP

California Association for Postsecondary Education
  and Disability
Attn: Scholarships
10073 Valley View Street, Suite 242
Cypress, CA 90630
(562) 397-2810   Fax: (866) 577-3387
E-mail: caped38@gmail.com
Web: www.caped.io/scholarships/scholarship-application

Summary To provide financial assistance to undergraduate and graduate students in California who have a learning disability.

Eligibility This program is open to students at public and private colleges and universities in California who have a learning disability. Undergraduates must have completed at least 6 semester credits and have a GPA of 2.5 or higher. Graduate students must have completed at least 3 semester units and have a GPA of 3.0 or higher. Applicants must submit 1) a 250-word essay describing their progress towards meeting their educational and/or vocational goals; 2) a 500-word essay on how they manage their disabiity; and 3) a 750-word essay on the the knowledge they would impart to incoming college students with a learning disability in an effort to enhance their success or college experience. They must also submit a letter of recommendation from a faculty person, verification of disability, and unofficial transcripts.

Financial data The stipend is $1,000.

Duration 1 year.

Number awarded 1 each year.

Deadline August of each year.

[880]
SWIDA COLLEGE SCHOLARSHIP

International Dyslexia Association-Southwest Branch
Attn: Scholarship Committee
3915 Carlisle NE
Albuquerque, NM 87107
(505) 255-8234   E-mail: info@southwestida.org
Web: southwestida.org

Summary To provide financial assistance to residents of New Mexico and El Paso, Texas who have dyslexia and are interested in working on an undergraduate or graduate degree at a college in any state.

Eligibility This program is open to residents of New Mexico and El Paso who have been diagnosed with dyslexia. Applicants must be working full time on an associate, bachelor's, or master's degree in any field at a 2- or 4-year college or university in any state. Selection is based on academic performance in relation to the severity of the specific learning disability, personal and professional goals, and financial need.

Financial data The stipend is $2,000. Funds are paid directly to the recipient's college or university.

Duration 1 year.

Number awarded 1 each year.

Deadline March of each year.

[881]
TEENS TAKE CHARGE SCHOLARSHIPS

Hydrocephalus Association
4340 East West Highway, Suite 905
Bethesda, MD 20814
(301) 202-3811   Toll Free: (888) 598-3789, ext. 22
Fax: (301) 202-3813
E-mail: scholarship@hydroassoc.com
Web: www.hydroassoc.org/scholarships

Summary To provide financial assistance for college or graduate school to young adults with hydrocephalus.

Eligibility This program is open to individuals between the ages of 17 and 30 who have hydrocephalus. The scholarship must be used for an educational purpose, including, but not limited to, a 4-year or junior college, a high school postgraduate year to prepare for college, a technical or trade school, an accredited employment training program, or a graduate program. Applicants may be in the process of applying to a program or university or already enrolled. They must include essays on their hobbies, interests, and activities; their educational and career goals; how having hydrocephalus has impacted their life; how they would help others with hydrocephalus; and how the scholarship will help them. Financial need is not considered in the selection process.

Financial data The stipend is $1,000. Funds may be used for tuition, books, housing, or any other educationally-related expense.

Duration 1 year; nonrenewable.

Additional data This program began in 2010.
Number awarded 5 year.
Deadline April of each year.

[882]
THE ORION FUND GRANTS

The Orion Fund
P.O. Box 11518
Piedmont, CA 94611
(510) 482-2226   E-mail: theorionfund@gmail.com
Web: www.theorionfund.org/grants.php

Summary To provide financial assistance to California college and graduate students who have a serious illness or injury.

Eligibility This program is open to undergraduate and graduate students at colleges and universities in California who are younger than 30 years of age and have a serious medical condition that affects their ability to stay in school. Applicants must submit a personal statement describing the purpose of the grant and providing justification for the request, a letter of support from a campus administrator or a medical provider, unofficial transcripts, and information on financial resources.

Financial data Stipends range from $500 to $5,000. Funds may be used for medical expenses, medical technology, educational costs, and living expenses.

Duration 1 year.

Additional data This program began in 2004.

Number awarded Varies each year; since the program began, it has awarded 131 grants: 3 at $5,000, 8 at $4,000, 11 at $3,000, 7 at $2,500, 22 at $2,000, 9 at $1,500, 29 at $1,000, and 42 at $500.

Deadline February of each year.

[883]
UCB FAMILY EPILEPSY SCHOLARSHIP PROGRAM

UCB, Inc.
Family Scholarship Program
c/o Summit Medical Communications
1421 East Broad Street, Suite 340
Fuquay-Varina, NC 27526
Toll Free: (866) 825-1920   Fax: (919) 567-7591
E-mail: ucbepilepsyscholarship@summitmedcomm.
  com
Web: www.ucbepilepsyscholarship.com

Summary To provide financial assistance for college or graduate school to epilepsy patients and their family members and caregivers.

Eligibility This program is open to epilepsy patients and their family members and caregivers. Applicants must be working on or planning to work on an undergraduate or graduate degree at an institution of higher education in the United States. They must be able to demonstrate academic achievement, a record of participation in activities outside of school, and service as a role model. Along with their application, they must submit a 1-page essay explaining why they should be selected for the scholarship, how epilepsy has impacted their life either as a patient or as a family member or caregiver, and how they will benefit from the scholarship. U.S. citizenship or permanent resident status is required.

Financial data The stipend is $5,000.

Duration 1 year; nonrenewable.

Additional data This program, previously known as the Keppra Family Epilepsy Scholarship Program, was established in 2004.

Number awarded 30 each year. Since this program was established, it has awarded $1,700,000 to more than 340 students.

Deadline April of each year.

[884]
VARUN BHASKARAN (WAS) SCHOLARSHIP PROGRAM

Immune Deficiency Foundation
Attn: Scholarship Program
110 West Road, Suite 300
Towson, MD 21204
(410) 321-6647   Toll Free: (800) 296-4433
Fax: (410) 321-9165 E-mail: info@primaryimmune.org
Web: www.primaryimmune.org

Summary To provide financial assistance to undergraduate and graduate students who are living with Wiskott-Aldrich Syndrome (WAS).

Eligibility This program is open to students entering or attending college or graduate school who are living with WAS. Applicants must submit an autobiographical essay, 2 letters of recommendation, a family financial statement, and a letter of verification from their immunologist. Financial need is the main factor considered in selecting the recipients and the size of the award.

Financial data Stipends range from $750 to $2,000, depending on the recipient's financial need.

Duration 1 year; may be renewed.

Additional data This program began in 2011.

Number awarded Varies each year.

Deadline March of each year.

[885]
VERA YIP MEMORIAL SCHOLARSHIP

Ulman Cancer Fund for Young Adults
Attn: Scholarship Committee
921 East Fort Avenue, Suite 325
Baltimore, MD 21230
(410) 964-0202   Toll Free: (888) 393-FUND
Fax: (888) 964-0402
E-mail: scholarship@ulmanfund.org
Web: www.ulmanfund.org/scholarships

Summary To provide financial assistance for college or graduate school to students from any state who have been diagnosed with cancer or have or have lost a family member with cancer.

Eligibility This program is open to U.S. citizens and permanent residents between 15 and 35 years of age from any state. Applicants must 1) have been diagnosed with cancer and currently in relapse or active treatment; 2) have a parent or guardian living with cancer; or 3) have lost a parent or guardian to cancer. The student, parent, or guardian must have been first diagnosed with cancer after the applicant was 15 years of age. Along with their application, they must submit a 500-word essay or 3-minute video on either 1) a letter that they would have liked to receive during their cancer experience; or 2) what they would tell the young adults who participate in the sponsor's summer-long drive to support the organization about being a young adult impacted by cancer. U.S. citizenship or permanent resident status is required. This award is presented to the applicant who best demonstrates the qualities of Vera Yip of courage, determination, motivation, and dedication.

Financial data The stipend is $2,500. Funds are paid directly to the educational institution.

Duration 1 year; nonrenewable.

Additional data Recipients are obligated to organize and run a bone marrow registry drive with the support of Delete Blood Cancer and There Goes My Hero.

Number awarded 1 each year.

Deadline March of each year.

[886]
VITTORIA DIANA RICARDO SCHOLARSHIP

Ulman Cancer Fund for Young Adults
Attn: Scholarship Committee
921 East Fort Avenue, Suite 325
Baltimore, MD 21230
(410) 964-0202   Toll Free: (888) 393-FUND
Fax: (888) 964-0402
E-mail: scholarship@ulmanfund.org
Web: www.ulmanfund.org/scholarships

Summary To provide financial assistance for college or graduate school to students who have been diagnosed with cancer or have or have lost a family member with cancer.

Eligibility This program is open to students who 1) have been diagnosed with cancer; 2) have a parent or sibling living with cancer; or 3) have lost a parent or sibling to cancer. Applicants must be attending, or planning to attend, a 4-year college or university in any state to work on an undergraduate, graduate, or professional degree. They must have a GPA of 3.0 or higher in high school or college and be able to demonstrate financial need. The first diagnosis of cancer (whether of the applicant, a parent, or sibling) must have occurred after the applicant was 15 years of age. Along with their application, they must submit a 500-word essay or 3-minute video on either 1) a letter that they would have liked to receive during their cancer experience; or 2) what they would tell the young adults who participate in the sponsor's summer-long drive to support the organization about being a young adult impacted by cancer. U.S. citizenship or permanent resident status is required.

Financial data The stipend is $2,500. Funds are paid directly to the educational institution.

Duration 1 year.

Additional data Recipients are obligated to organize and run a bone marrow registry drive with the support of Delete Blood Cancer and There Goes My Hero.

Number awarded 1 each year.

Deadline March of each year.

[887]
WINTERHOFF ARTHRITIS SCHOLARSHIP

Arthritis Foundation
Attn: Juvenile Arhtritis
1330 West Peachtree Street, Suite 100
Atlanta, GA 30309-2904
(404) 965-7727   Toll Free: (800) 283-7800
E-mail: jziegler@arthritis.org
Web: www.kidsgetarthritistoo.org/resources/scholarships

Summary To provide financial assistance to college students who have a rheumatic disease.

Eligibility This program is open to students enrolled or planning to enroll full time in an accredited undergraduate program, graduate program, or medical school in any state. Applicants must have doctor-diagnosed arthritis or related rheumatic disease and a GPA of 2.5 or higher. They must be willing to be involved with the Arthritis Foundation as an advocate, fundraiser, participant, volunteer, and/or supporter.

Financial data The stipend is $5,000 per year. Funds may be utilized only for tuition, books, and supplies.

Duration 1 year; may be renewed up to 3 additional years, provided the recipient remains enrolled full time.

Additional data This program began in 2010 in the Pacific Southwest region, and became nationwide in 2017.

Number awarded Varies each year; recently, 4 new and 4 renewal scholarships were awarded.

Deadline March of each year.

[888]
WOODY AND LOUISE REED BRIDGE TO LIFE SURVIVOR SCHOLARSHIP

Alisa Ann Ruch Burn Foundation
Attn: Scholarship
50 North Hill Avenue, Suite 305
Pasadena, CA 91106
(818) 848-0223   Toll Free: (800) 242-BURN
Fax: (818) 848-0296   E-mail: jshare@aarbf.org
Web: www.aarbf.org

Summary To provide financial assistance for college or graduate school to burn survivors from California.

Eligibility This program is open to California residents between 17 and 25 years of age who have been involved in the burn survivor community, as a Champ Camp counselor or camper, by participating in a burn support group or overnight recreational event of the Alisa Ann Ruch Burn Foundation (AARBF), or through leadership and volunteerism in another California burn foundation. Applicants must be enrolled or planning to enroll at a 2- or 4-year college, university, or trade/vocational school in any state as an undergraduate or graduate student. They must have a GPA of 2.5 or higher. Along with their application, they must submit brief essays on their major and why they chose that field, their educational and career goals, and why they participate in survivor programs. Selection is based on educational achievement and financial need.

Financial data The stipend is $2,000 per year. Funds are disbursed directly to the financial institution.

Duration 1 year; recipients may reapply.

Number awarded 2 each year.

Deadline June of each year.

Families of the Disabled

Undergraduates ●

Graduate Students ●

Described here are 313 funding opportunities open to the children, stepchildren, adopted children, grandchildren, parents, siblings, or other dependents or family members of persons with disabilities. Of these, 249 are for undergraduates and 64 are for graduate students. All of this is "free" money. Not one dollar will need to be repaid (provided, of course, that recipients meet all program requirements). If you are looking for a particular program and don't find it in this section, be sure to check the Program Title Index to see if it is covered elsewhere in the directory.

Undergraduates

[889]
AFA TEENS FOR ALZHEIMER'S AWARENESS COLLEGE SCHOLARSHIP ESSAY COMPETITION

Alzheimer's Foundation of America
Attn: AFA Teens
322 Eighth Avenue, Seventh Floor
New York, NY 10001
Toll Free: (866) 232-8484   E-mail: info@alzfdn.org
Web: www.alzfdn.org/young-leaders-of-afa/afa-teens

Summary To recognize and reward, with college scholarships, high school seniors who submit outstanding essays on the impact of Alzheimer's Disease on their life.

Eligibility The competition is open to seniors currently enrolled at a public, independent, parochial, military, home-school, or other high school in the United States. Applicants must be planning to enter an accredited 4-year college or university within 12 months. They must submit an essay of 1,200 to 1,500 words on 1) how Alzheimer's Disease has changed or impacted their life; and 2) what they have learned about themselves, their family, and/or their community in the face of coping with Alzheimer's Disease. They must also submit a 200-word autobiography, a high school transcript, and documentation of U.S. citizenship or permanent resident status. Financial need is not considered in the selection process.

Financial data Awards, in the form of college scholarships, are $5,000 for the winner, $3,500 for the first runner-up, $1,500 for each second runner-up, $1,000 for each third runner-up, $750 for teach fourth runner-up, and $500 for each honorable mention.

Duration The awards are presented annually.

Number awarded Varies each year; recently, 24 were awarded: 1 winner, 1 first runner-up, 2 second runners-up, 2 third runners-up, 10 fourth runners-up, and 8 honorable mentions.

Deadline February of each year.

[890]
AFAS MERIT SCHOLARSHIPS

Air Force Aid Society
Attn: Education Assistance Department
241 18th Street South, Suite 202
Arlington, VA 22202-3409
(703) 972-2647   Toll Free: (866) 896-5637
Fax: (703) 972-2646   E-mail: ed@afas-hq.org
Web: www.afas.org/how-we-help/afas-merit-scholarship

Summary To provide merit-based financial assistance for college to dependents of active-duty, retired, disabled, or deceased Air Force personnel who demonstrate outstanding academic achievement.

Eligibility This program is open to dependent children of Air Force personnel who are active duty, Title 10 Reservists on extended active duty, Title 32 Guard per-forming full-time active-duty service, retired due to length of active-duty service or disability, or deceased while on active duty or in retired status. Applicants must be entering their freshman year as full-time undergraduate students at an accredited college, university, or trade/vocational school. Selection is based on cumulative GPA, SAT/ACT scores, transcripts, extracurricular activities, volunteer and/or work experience, a resume, and an essay on a specified topic.

Financial data The stipend is $5,000.

Duration 1 year.

Number awarded 10 each year.

Deadline March of each year.

[891]
AIR LINE PILOTS ASSOCIATION SCHOLARSHIP PROGRAM

Air Line Pilots Association
Attn: Yvonne Willits
1625 Massachusetts Avenue, N.W., Suite 800
Washington, DC 20036
(703) 689-2270   E-mail: Yvonne.Willits@alpa.org
Web: www.alpa.org

Summary To provide financial assistance for college to the children of disabled or deceased members of the Air Line Pilots Association.

Eligibility This program is open to children of medically retired, long-term disabled, or deceased members of the Air Line Pilots Association. Although the program envisions selection of students enrolling as college freshman, eligible individuals who are already enrolled in college may also apply. Selection is based on a number of factors, including academic record and financial need.

Financial data The stipend is $3,000 per year.

Duration 1 year; may be renewed up to 3 additional years, provided the student maintains a GPA of 3.0 or higher.

Number awarded 1 each year.

Deadline March of each year.

[892]
ALABAMA G.I. DEPENDENTS' SCHOLARSHIP PROGRAM

Alabama Department of Veterans Affairs
770 Washington Avenue, Suite 470
Montgomery, AL 36102-1509
(334) 242-5077   Fax: (334) 242-5102
Web: www.va.state.al.us/gi_dep_scholarship.aspx

Summary To provide educational benefits to the dependents of disabled, deceased, and other Alabama veterans.

Eligibility This program is open to children, spouses, and unremarried widow(er)s of veterans who are currently rated as 20% or more service-connected disabled or were so rated at time of death, were a former prisoner of war, have been declared missing in action, died as the result of a service-connected disability, or died while on active military duty in the line of duty. The veteran must have been a permanent civilian resident of Alabama for at least 1 year prior to entering active military service and served honorably for at least 90 days during wartime (or less, in case of death or service-connected disability). Veterans who were not Alabama residents at the time of entering active military service may also qualify if they have a 100% disability and were permanent residents of Alabama for at least 5 years prior to filing the application for this program or prior to death, if deceased. Children and stepchildren must be under the age of 26, but spouses and widow(er)s may be of any age. Spouses cease to be eligible if they become divorced from the qualifying veteran. Widow(er)s cease to be eligible if they remarry.

Financial data Eligible dependents may attend any state-supported Alabama institution of higher learning or enroll in a prescribed course of study at any Alabama state-supported trade school without payment of any tuition, book fees, or laboratory charges.

Duration This is an entitlement program for 5 years of full-time undergraduate or graduate study or part-time equivalent for all qualifying children and for spouses and unremarried widow(er)s who veteran spouse is or was rated 100% disabled or meets other qualifying requirements. Spouses and unremarried widow(er)s whose veteran spouse is or was rated between 20% and 90% disabled may attend only 3 standard academic years.

Additional data Benefits for children, spouses, and unremarried widow(er)s are available in addition to federal government benefits. Assistance is not provided for non-credit courses, placement testing, GED preparation, continuing educational courses, pre-technical courses, or state board examinations.

Number awarded Varies each year.

Deadline Applications may be submitted at any time.

[893]
ALABAMA SCHOLARSHIPS FOR DEPENDENTS OF BLIND PARENTS

Alabama Department of Rehabilitation Services
Attn: Coordinator of Blind Services
21 Arnold Street
Talladega, AL 35160
(256) 761-6825   Toll Free: (800) 441-7607
TDD: (800) 499-1816
E-mail: dana.barber@rehab.alabama.gov
Web: www.rehab.alabama.gov

Summary To provide financial assistance for college to students whose blind parents are residents of Alabama.

Eligibility Eligible to apply are seniors or recent graduates of Alabama high schools whose family head of household is blind and whose annual family income is limited (based on federal poverty guidelines). Applicants must 1) have been permanent residents of Alabama for at least 5 years; 2) apply within 2 years after graduation from high school; and 3) be under 23 years of age.

Financial data Eligible students receive free tuition, waiver of fees, and necessary textbooks at any Alabama state-supported postsecondary institution.

Duration Up to 36 months at an institution of higher education, or for the period required to complete a course of study at a trade school.

Additional data Recipients must complete their course of study within 5 years (unless interrupted by military service), but at least prior to the age of 30.

Number awarded Varies each year.

Deadline Deadline not specified.

[894]
ALBERT M. BECKER MEMORIAL YOUTH SCHOLARSHIP

New York American Legion Press Association
Attn: Scholarship Chair
P.O. Box 424
Sanborn, NY 14132
E-mail: jackbutton@hotmail.com
Web: nyalpa.webs.com/pubslinksannualevents.htm

Summary To provide financial assistance to residents of New York who have a connection with veterans and are interested in careers in communications.

Eligibility This program is open to New York residents younger than 23 years of age who are 1) members of the American Legion, American Legion Auxiliary, or Sons of the American Legion; 2) children or grandchildren of members of those organizations; 3) children of a 50% or more disabled veteran; 4) children of a currently-serving member of the National Guard or military Reserves; or 4) children of a deceased veteran. Applicants must be enrolled or planning to enroll full time at an accredited college, university, or trade school in any school to work on a degree in communications (including public relations, journalism, reprographics, newspaper design or management, web page design, video design, social media communications, photojournalism, American history, political science, public communications, or other field of study related to the goals of the sponsor or the American Legion family). Along with their application, they must submit a 500-word essay on their field of study, the reasons for choosing their field of study, and their goals upon completion of study. Financial need and class standing are not considered. U.S. citizenship is required.

Financial data The stipend is $1,000.

Duration 1 year.

Number awarded 1 each year.

Deadline April of each year.

[895]
ALFRED CAMP MEMORIAL SCHOLARSHIP

Georgia Council of the Blind
c/o Debbie Williams, Scholarship Committee Chair
1477 Nebo Road
Dallas, GA 30157
(770) 595-1007
E-mail: williamsdebk@wmconnect.com
Web: www.georgiacounciloftheblind.org

Summary To provide financial assistance students in Georgia who plan to attend college or graduate school in any state and are either legally blind or have legally blind parents.

Eligibility This program is open to residents of Georgia who are either 1) legally blind students; or 2) sighted students financially dependent on legally blind parents. Applicants must be enrolled or accepted for enrollment at a vocational/technical school, a 2- or 4-year college, or a master's or doctoral program in any state. All fields of study are eligible. Selection is based on academic transcripts, 2 letters of recommendation, a 1-page typed statement of the applicant's educational goals, an audio cassette recording of the applicant reading the goals statement, extracurricular activities, and financial need.

Financial data Stipends up to $1,000 per year are available.

Duration 1 year; recipients may reapply.

Additional data This program began in 1988.

Number awarded 1 or more each year.

Deadline June of each year.

[896]
ALL IN FOR SKIN SCHOLARSHIP

Greater Kansas City Community Foundation
Attn: Scholarship Coordinator
1055 Broadway Boulevard, Suite 130
Kansas City, MO 64105-1595
(816) 842-0944   Fax: (816) 842-8079
E-mail: scholarships@growyourgiving.org
Web: www.growyourgiving.org

Summary To provide financial assistance to residents of Kansas and Missouri who have lost a parent due to melanoma cancer and are interested in attending college in any state.

Eligibility This program is open to graduating high school seniors and current undergraduate students who are residents of Kansas or Missouri. Applicants must have lost a parent due to melanoma cancer. They must be able to demonstrate academic ability and leadership qualities. Financial need is not considered in the selection process.

Financial data The stipend ranges up to $5,000.

Duration 1 year.

Number awarded 1 or more each year.

Deadline February of each year.

[897]
A.L.S. FAMILY CHARITABLE FOUNDATION SCHOLARSHIP

A.L.S. Family Charitable Foundation, Inc.
Attn: Scholarship Committee
P.O. Box 229
Buzzards Bay, MA 02532
(508) 759-9696   Fax: (508) 759-9606
E-mail: alsfamily@aol.com
Web: www.alsfamily.net/support/patient-programs

Summary To provide financial assistance to residents of the New England states who have a parent with Amyotrophic Lateral Sclerosis (A.L.S.) and are interested in attending college in any state.

Eligibility This program is open to residents of Connecticut, Maine, Massachusetts, New Hampshire, Rhode Island, and Vermont who are the child (biological/adopted/step) of an A.L.S. patient (living or deceased). Applicants must have graduated from high school with a GPA of 3.0

or higher and be enrolled full time at an accredited institution of higher education in any state. Along with their application, they must submit an essay of 500 to 1,000 words describing how A.L.S. has impacted their life and their educational and life goals.

Financial data The stipend is $3,000 per year.

Duration 1 year.

Number awarded Varies each year.

Deadline Deadline not specified.

[898]
AMERICAN BUS ASSOCIATION YELLOW RIBBON SCHOLARSHIP

American Bus Association
Attn: ABA Foundation
111 K Street, N.E., Ninth Floor
Washington, DC 20002
(202) 842-1645   Toll Free: (800) 283-2877
Fax: (202) 842-0850   E-mail: abainfo@buses.org
Web: www.buses.org

Summary To provide financial assistance for college or graduate school to people with disabilities, veterans, and children of wounded veterans who are preparing for a career in the transportation, travel, and tourism industry.

Eligibility This program is open to U.S. and Canadian citizens and permanent residents who are enrolled as an undergraduate or graduate student in a program related to the transportation, travel, and tourism industry. Applicants must 1) have a physical or sensory disability; 2) be a veteran of the U.S. or Canadian military; or 3) be a child or a wounded U.S. or Canadian military veteran. They must have a GPA of 3.0 or higher.

Financial data The stipend is $2,500.

Duration 1 or more each year.

Deadline April of each year.

[899]
AMERICAN LEGION LEGACY SCHOLARSHIPS

American Legion
Attn: Americanism and Children & Youth Division
700 North Pennsylvania Street
P.O. Box 1055
Indianapolis, IN 46206-1055
(317) 630-1212   Fax: (317) 630-1223
E-mail: scholarships@legion.org
Web: www.legion.org/scholarships/legacy

Summary To provide financial assistance for college to children of U.S. military personnel killed on active duty or disabled on or after September 11, 2001.

Eligibility This program is open to the children (including adopted children and stepchildren) of active-duty U.S. military personnel (including federalized National Guard and Reserve members) who died on active duty or became 50% or more disabled on or after September 11, 2001. Applicants must be high school seniors or graduates planning to enroll full time at an accredited institution of higher education in the United States. Selection is based on academic achievement, school and community activities, leadership skills, and financial need.

Financial data Recently, stipends averaged $1,612.
Duration 1 year; may be renewed.
Additional data This program began in 2003.
Number awarded Varies each year; recently, 31 were awarded. Since the program began, it has awarded nearly $500,000 to more than 200 students.
Deadline April of each year.

[900]
ANNE SMEDINGHOFF MEMORIAL SCHOLARSHIP

Ulman Cancer Fund for Young Adults
Attn: Scholarship Committee
921 East Fort Avenue, Suite 325
Baltimore, MD 21230
(410) 964-0202			Toll Free: (888) 393-FUND
Fax: (888) 964-0402
E-mail: scholarship@ulmanfund.org
Web: www.ulmanfund.org/scholarships

Summary To provide financial assistance for college or graduate school to students who have been diagnosed with cancer or have or have lost a family member with cancer.
Eligibility This program is open to students who 1) have been diagnosed with cancer; 2) have a parent or sibling living with cancer; or 3) have lost a parent or sibling to cancer. Applicants must be attending, or planning to attend, a college or university in any state to work on an undergraduate, graduate, or professional degree. They should demonstrate the qualities of the program's namesake-adventurous, upbeat, vivacious, and with a strong desire to make a difference in the lives of others. The first diagnosis of cancer (whether of the applicant, a parent, or sibling) must have occurred after the applicant was 15 years of age. Along with their application, they must submit a 500-word essay or 3-minute video on either 1) a letter that they would have liked to receive during their cancer experience; or 2) what they would tell the young adults who participate in the sponsor's summer-long drive to support the organization about being a young adult impacted by cancer. U.S. citizenship or permanent resident status is required.
Financial data The stipend is $2,500. Funds are paid directly to the educational institution.
Duration 1 year.
Additional data This program, which began in 2013, is funded by the 4K for Cancer, an organization of college students who ride bicycles across the country every summer and raise funds for cancer. Recipients are obligated to organize and run a bone marrow registry drive with the support of Delete Blood Cancer and There Goes My Hero.
Number awarded 1 each year.
Deadline March of each year.

[901]
ARKANSAS LAW ENFORCEMENT OFFICERS' DEPENDENTS' SCHOLARSHIPS

Arkansas Department of Higher Education
Attn: Financial Aid Division
423 Main Street, Suite 400
Little Rock, AR 72201-3801
(501) 371-2050			Toll Free: (800) 54-STUDY
Fax: (501) 371-2001		E-mail: finaid@adhe.edu
Web: scholarships.adhe.edu

Summary To provide financial assistance for undergraduate education to the dependents of deceased or disabled Arkansas law enforcement officers, firefighters, or other designated public employees.
Eligibility This program is open to the spouses and/or children (natural, adopted, or step) of Arkansas residents who were killed or permanently disabled in the line of duty as law enforcement officers, municipal and/or college or university police officers, sheriffs and deputy sheriffs, constables, state correction employees, game wardens, state park employees who are commissioned law enforcement officers or emergency response employees, full-time or volunteer firefighters, state forestry employees engaged in fighting forest fires, certain Arkansas Highway and Transportation Department employees, emergency medical technicians, or Department of Community Punishment employees. Children must be less than 23 years of age. Spouses may not have remarried. All applicants must have been Arkansas residents for at least 6 months.
Financial data The scholarship covers tuition, on-campus room charges, and fees (but not books, school supplies, food, materials, or dues for extracurricular activities) at any state-supported college or university in Arkansas.
Duration Up to 8 semesters, provided the student is working on a baccalaureate or associate degree and maintains a GPA of 2.0 or higher.
Number awarded Varies each year.
Deadline May of each year.

[902]
ARKANSAS MILITARY DEPENDENTS SCHOLARSHIP PROGRAM

Arkansas Department of Higher Education
Attn: Financial Aid Division
423 Main Street, Suite 400
Little Rock, AR 72201-3801
(501) 371-2050			Toll Free: (800) 54-STUDY
Fax: (501) 371-2001		E-mail: finaid@adhe.edu
Web: scholarships.adhe.edu

Summary To provide financial assistance for educational purposes to dependents of certain categories of Arkansas veterans.
Eligibility This program is open to the natural children, adopted children, stepchildren, and spouses of Arkansas residents who have been declared to be a prisoner of war, killed in action, missing in action, killed on ordnance delivery, or 100% totally and permanently disabled during, or as a result of, active military service. Applicants and their parent or spouse must be residents of Arkansas. They

must be working on, or planning to work on, a bachelor's degree or certificate of completion at a public college, university, or technical school in Arkansas.

Financial data The program pays for tuition, general registration fees, special course fees, activity fees, room and board (if provided in campus facilities), and other charges associated with earning a degree or certificate.

Duration 1 year; participants may obtain renewal provided they make satisfactory progress toward a baccalaureate degree.

Additional data This program began in 1973 as the Arkansas Missing in Action/Killed in Action Dependents Scholarship Program to provide assistance to the dependents of veterans killed in action, missing in action, or declared a prisoner of war. In 2005, it was amended to include dependents of disabled veterans and given its current name. Applications must be submitted to the financial aid director at an Arkansas state-supported institution of higher education or state-supported vocational/technical school.

Number awarded Varies each year; recently, 4 were awarded.

Deadline May of each year.

[903]
ATP AND WTA MEMORIAL SCHOLARSHIP

Central Indiana Community Foundation
Attn: Scholarship Program
615 North Alabama Street, Suite 119
Indianapolis, IN 46204-1498
(317) 634-2423   Fax: (317) 684-0943
E-mail: scholarships@cicf.org
Web: www.cicf.org/scholarships

Summary To provide financial assistance for college in any state to residents of Indiana who are children of members of the Association of Tennis Professionals (ATP) or Women's Tennis Association (WTA) who have been affected by cancer.

Eligibility This program is open to residents of Indiana who are high school seniors or students already enrolled at a college, university, or vocational/technical school in any state. Applicants must be a child of an ATP or WTA member who has been affected by cancer, have an unweighted GPA of 2.0 or higher, and be able to demonstrate community involvement. Financial need is considered in the selection process.

Financial data The stipend is at least $1,000.

Duration 1 year.

Number awarded 1 or more each year.

Deadline February of each year.

[904]
AVONTE OQUENDO MEMORIAL SCHOLARSHIP FOR AUTISM

The Perecman Firm, P.L.L.C.
250 West 57th Street, Suite 401
New York, NY 10107
(212) 577-9325
Web: www.perecman.com

Summary To provide financial assistance for college or graduate school to people diagnosed with autism and their families.

Eligibility This program is open students currently enrolled or accepted at an accredited college or university as an undergraduate or graduate students. Applicants or a close family member must have been diagnosed with a form of autism, including Asperger syndrome. Along with their application, they must submit an essay of 500 to 1,000 words on 1 of the following topics: 1) a time that they have had to overcome an obstacle as a person with autism that other people would not have had to face; 2) how their family member's autism has affected them and how they have adapted to help them; and 3) what they feel is the biggest obstacle holding people with autism back today. Selection is based on the essay and transcripts.

Financial data The stipend is $1,000.

Duration 1 year.

Number awarded 1 each year.

Deadline July of each year.

[905]
BEACON BRIGHTER TOMORROWS SCHOLARSHIP

Rhode Island Foundation
Attn: Donor Services Administrator
One Union Station
Providence, RI 02903
(401) 427-4028   Fax: (401) 331-8085
E-mail: kriley@rifoundation.org
Web: www.rifoundation.org

Summary To provide financial assistance for college to dependent children of workers insured by Beacon Mutual Insurance Company who were killed or permanently disabled in industrial accidents.

Eligibility This program is open to dependent children of workers insured by the company and whose parent 1) collected at least 6 months of qualifying indemnity benefits; or 2) collected for an accepted permanent total disability. Students who collected for an accepted fatal claim are also eligible. Applicants must have a GPA of 2.0 or higher and be able to demonstrate financial need. They must have been accepted into an accredited postsecondary institution on a full- or part-time basis. U.S. citizenship or permanent resident status is required.

Financial data Stipends range from $1,000 to $2,000.

Duration 1 year; may be renewed up to 3 additional years.

Number awarded 1 to 2 each year.

Deadline June of each year.

[906]
BERNICE MCNAMARA MEMORIAL SCHOLARSHIP

Ulman Cancer Fund for Young Adults
Attn: Scholarship Committee
921 East Fort Avenue, Suite 325
Baltimore, MD 21230
(410) 964-0202   Toll Free: (888) 393-FUND
Fax: (888) 964-0402
E-mail: scholarship@ulmanfund.org
Web: www.ulmanfund.org

Summary To provide financial assistance to students who have lost a parent with cancer and are interested in working on an undergraduate or graduate degree in the sciences.

Eligibility This program is open to U.S. citizens who have lost a parent or guardian to cancer. Applicants must be 25 years of age or younger and attending, or planning to attend, a 4-year college or university to work on an undergraduate or graduate degree in the sciences. The parent or guardian must have been first diagnosed with cancer when the applicant was at least 15 years of age. Along with their application, they must submit a 500-word essay or 3-minute video on either 1) a letter that they would have liked to receive during their cancer experience; or 2) what they would tell the young adults who participate in the sponsor's summer-long drive to support the organization about being a young adult impacted by cancer. Financial need is considered in the selection process. U.S. citizenship or permanent resident status is required.

Financial data The stipend is $2,500. Funds are paid directly to the educational institution.

Duration 1 year; nonrenewable.

Additional data Recipients are obligated to organize and run a bone marrow registry drive with the support of Delete Blood Cancer and There Goes My Hero.

Number awarded 1 each year.

Deadline March of each year.

[907]
BERYL V. SMITH SCHOLARSHIP

Package of Prevention
Attn: Scholarship Panel
3941 Lorado Way
Los Angeles, CA 90043
E-mail: info@packageofprevention.com
Web: www.packageofprevention.com

Summary To provide financial assistance for college to high school seniors in California who have had a parent or legal guardian diagnosed with cancer.

Eligibility This program is open to seniors graduating from high schools in California and planning to enroll full time at an accredited 2- or 4-year college or university. Applicants must have lost a parent or guardian to cancer or have a parent or guardian who is a cancer survivor. Along with their application, they must submit an essay, up to 2 pages in length, on 1 of the following topics: 1) the ways in which their parent's battle with cancer made them the person they are today; or 2) the program they would implement to get youth involved in cancer prevention. Selection is based primarily on the essay, although grades and financial need may also be considered.

Financial data The stipend is $1,000.

Duration 1 year.

Number awarded 1 each year.

Deadline April of each year.

[908]
BIORX/HEMOPHILIA OF NORTH CAROLINA EDUCATIONAL SCHOLARSHIPS

BioRx, LLC
Attn: Hemophilia Services
7167 East Kemper Road
Cincinnati, OH 45249
Toll Free: (866) 442-4679   Fax: (919) 319-0016
E-mail: cbarnes@biorx.net
Web: www.biorxhemophilia.com

Summary To provide financial assistance for college to people with hemophilia, their caregivers, and their families.

Eligibility This program is open to caregivers of children or adults affected with bleeding disorders, people who have been diagnosed with a bleeding disorder, and siblings and parents of people diagnosed with bleeding disorders. Residents of all states are eligible. Applicants must be enrolled or planning to enroll at an accredited college, university, or certified training program. Along with their application, they must submit an essay of 1 to 2 pages describing their occupational goals and objectives in life and how their or their family's experiences with bleeding disorders have affected their choices. Preference is given to applicants who are studying or planning to study a health care-related field. Selection is primarily based on merit, although financial need may be considered as well.

Financial data The stipend ranges from $500 to $3,000.

Duration 1 year.

Additional data This program, established in 2004, is sponsored by BioRx and administered by Hemophilia of North Carolina (although no preference is given to residents of North Carolina.

Number awarded 4 each year, of which at least 1 of which is reserved for an applicant studying in a health-related field.

Deadline April of each year.

[909]
BLACKHORSE SCHOLARSHIP

Blackhorse Association
c/o Bob Hatcher, Scholarship Committee Chair
426 Bentley Ridge Boulevard
Lancaster, PA 17602
(804) 621-3651 E-mail: robert.lee.hatcher@gmail.com
Web: www.blackhorse.org/scholarships.cfm

Summary To provide financial assistance for college to children of members of the Blackhorse Association who are currently serving or have served with the 11th Armored Cavalry Regiment (ACR).

Eligibility This program is open to the natural and adopted children of current or former 11th ACR solders who are also members of the association. Applicants must be attending or planning to attend college. Along with their application, they must submit a 250-word essay on their ambitions and goals; a 250-word essay on 2 persons in their chosen field who have most influenced them and why; a list of activities, training, and awards received in high school; 2 letters of recommendation; and transcripts that include SAT and/or ACT scores. In the selection process, first priority is given to children who lost a parent in service of the regiment; second priority is given to children of those incapacitated by wounds or injury while serving the regiment; third priority is given based on financial need of the applicant and family.

Financial data The stipend is $3,000 per year.

Duration 1 year; may be renewed up to 3 additional years.

Additional data The Blackhorse Association was founded in 1970 by veterans of the 11th ACR who had served in Vietnam.

Number awarded Varies each year; recently, 17 were awarded. Since this program was established, it has awarded more than $600,000 in scholarships.

Deadline March of each year.

[910]
BOBBY JONES OPEN SCHOLARSHIPS

American Syringomyelia & Chiari Alliance Project, Inc.
P.O. Box 1586
Longview, TX 75606-1586
(903) 236-7079   Toll Free: (800) ASAP-282
Fax: (903) 757-7456   E-mail: info@ASAP.org
Web: www.asap.org

Summary To provide financial assistance for college or graduate school to members of the American Syringomyelia & Chiari Alliance Project (ASAP) and their children.

Eligibility This program is open to students entering or enrolled in college or graduate school who have syringomeylia (SM) and/or Chiari Malformation (CM) or whose parent is affected by SM and/or CM. Applicants or parents must have been ASAP members for at least 6 months. They may be of any age. Along with their application, they must submit 4 essays on assigned topics related to their experience with SM and/or CM. Selection is based on those essay and financial need.

Financial data Stipends are $1,000 for full-time students or $500 for part-time students. Recipients may reapply, but they may receive only a total of $4,000 in support from this program.

Duration 1 year.

Additional data This program is funded by the Bobby Jones Open, an annual golf tournament in which participation is restricted to golfers named Bobby Jones (e.g., Robert Jones, Roberta Jones). The tournament began in 1979 and since 1990 has raised money for activities of the ASAP.

Number awarded Varies each year; a total of $5,000 is available for this program annually.

Deadline May of each year.

[911]
BRADLEY KRUEGER SCHOLARSHIP

Bleeding Disorders Alliance Illinois
Attn: Program Coordinator
210 South DesPlaines Street
Chicago, IL 60661-5500
(312) 427-1495   Fax: (312) 427-1602
E-mail: ahii@bdai.org
Web: www.bdai.org/support/assistance/scholarships

Summary To provide financial assistance for attendance at a college in any state to residents of Illinois who have a bleeding disorder and their families.

Eligibility This program is open to residents of Illinois who have a bleeding disorder and their spouses, parents, siblings, and children; people who are carriers of the disease are also eligible. Applicants must be attending or planning to attend a postsecondary institution, including a trade school, in any state. Along with their application, they must submit essays on their goals for furthering their education, the steps they have taken to meet those goals, how this scholarship will help them achieve those goals, what it means to them to live with hemophilia, and what they consider their responsibility to the bleeding disorders community. Financial need is not considered in the selection process.

Financial data Stipends range up to $5,000. Funds are paid directly to the educational institution to be used for payment of tuition, room and board, books, and supplies (including computer equipment).

Duration 1 year.

Additional data Bleeding Disorders Alliance Illinois was formerly the Hemophilia Foundation of Illinois.

Number awarded 1 or more each year.

Deadline June of each year.

[912]
BRYON RIESCH SCHOLARSHIPS

Bryon Riesch Paralysis Foundation
P.O. Box 1388
Waukesha, WI 53187-1388
(262) 547-2083   E-mail: info@brpf.org
Web: www.brpf.org/scholarship-application

Summary To provide financial assistance to undergraduate and graduate students who have a neurological disability or the children of people with such a disability.

Eligibility This program is open to students entering or enrolled at a 2- or 4-year college or university as an undergraduate or graduate student. Applicants must have a neurological disability or be the child of a person with such a disability. First priority is given to individuals suffering from a direct spinal cord injury or disease resulting in paralysis such as spinal tumors, strokes, or aneurysms affecting the spinal cord, or spina bifida. Other diseases and disorders that qualify include multiple sclerosis, traumatic brain injuries, Parkinson's, and cerebral palsy. Priority is also given to residents of Wisconsin. Applicants must have a GPA of 2.5 or higher in high school or college. Along with their application, they must submit a 200-word essay on why they deserve the scholarship, a statement of their 5- and 10-year goals, and a list of work experience. Financial need is not considered in the selection process.

Financial data   The stipend is $2,000.

Duration   1 year; may be renewed.

Number awarded   Varies each semester; recently, 7 were awarded for the fall semester and 5 for the spring semester.

Deadline   June of each year for fall semester; December of each year for spring semester.

[913]
CALIFORNIA COLLEGE FEE WAIVER PROGRAM FOR CHILDREN OF VETERANS

California Department of Veterans Affairs
Attn: Division of Veterans Services
1227 O Street, Room 105
P.O. Box 942895
Sacramento, CA 94295
(916) 653-2573   Toll Free: (800) 952-5626
Fax: (916) 653-2563   TDD: (800) 324-5966
Web: www.calvet.ca.gov

Summary   To provide financial assistance for college to the children of disabled or deceased veterans in California.

Eligibility   Eligible for this program are the children of veterans who 1) died of a service-connected disability; 2) had a service-connected disability at the time of death; or 3) currently have a service-connected disability of any level of severity. Applicants must plan to attend a community college in California, branch of the California State University system, or campus of the University of California. Their income, including the value of support received from parents, cannot exceed a specified level (recently, $12,486). The veteran is not required to have a connection to California for this program. Dependents in college who are eligible to receive federal education benefits from the U.S. Department of Veterans Affairs are not eligible for these fee waivers.

Financial data   This program provides for waiver of registration fees to students attending any publicly-supported community or state college or university in California.

Duration   1 year; may be renewed.

Number awarded   Varies each year.

Deadline   Deadline not specified.

[914]
CALIFORNIA FEE WAIVER PROGRAM FOR DEPENDENTS OF DECEASED OR DISABLED NATIONAL GUARD MEMBERS

California Department of Veterans Affairs
Attn: Division of Veterans Services
1227 O Street, Room 105
P.O. Box 942895
Sacramento, CA 94295
(916) 653-2573   Toll Free: (800) 952-5626
Fax: (916) 653-2563   TDD: (800) 324-5966
Web: www.calvet.ca.gov

Summary   To provide financial assistance for college to dependents of disabled and deceased members of the California National Guard.

Eligibility   Eligible for this program are dependents, unremarried surviving spouses, and current registered domestic partners (RDPs) of members of the California National Guard who, in the line of duty and in the active service of the state, were killed, died of a disability, or became permanently disabled. Applicants must be attending or planning to attend a community college, branch of the California State University system, or campus of the University of California.

Financial data   Full-time college students receive a waiver of tuition and registration fees at any publicly-supported community or state college or university in California.

Duration   1 year; may be renewed.

Number awarded   Varies each year.

Deadline   Deadline not specified.

[915]
CALIFORNIA FEE WAIVER PROGRAM FOR DEPENDENTS OF TOTALLY DISABLED VETERANS

California Department of Veterans Affairs
Attn: Division of Veterans Services
1227 O Street, Room 105
P.O. Box 942895
Sacramento, CA 94295
(916) 653-2573   Toll Free: (800) 952-5626
Fax: (916) 653-2563   TDD: (800) 324-5966
Web: www.calvet.ca.gov

Summary   To provide financial assistance for college to dependents of disabled and other California veterans.

Eligibility   Eligible for this program are spouses, children, and unremarried spouses or registered domestic partners (RDPs) of veterans who are currently totally service-connected disabled (or are being compensated for a service-connected disability at a rate of 100%) or who died of a service-connected cause or disability. The veteran parent must have served during a qualifying war period and must have been discharged or released from military service under honorable conditions. Children must be younger than 27 years of age (extended to 30 if the child is a veteran); there are no age restrictions for spouses, surviving spouses, or RDPs. This program does not have an income limit. Dependents in college are not eligible if they are qualified to receive educational benefits from the U.S. Department of Veterans Affairs. Applicants must be attending or planning to attend a community college, branch of the California State University system, or campus of the University of California.

Financial data Full-time college students receive a waiver of tuition and registration fees at any publicly-supported community or state college or university in California.

Duration Children of eligible veterans may receive postsecondary benefits until the needed training is completed or until the dependent reaches 27 years of age (extended to 30 if the dependent serves in the armed forces). Spouses and surviving spouses are limited to a maximum of 48 months' full-time training or the equivalent in part-time training.

Number awarded Varies each year.

Deadline Deadline not specified.

[916]
CALIFORNIA LAW ENFORCEMENT PERSONNEL DEPENDENTS GRANT PROGRAM

California Student Aid Commission
Attn: Specialized Programs Operations Branch
10811 International Drive, Suite 100
P.O. Box 419029
Rancho Cordova, CA 95741-9029
(916) 526-8276   Toll Free: (888) 224-7268
Fax: (916) 464-8240 E-mail: specialized@csac.ca.gov
Web: www.csac.ca.gov/doc.asp?id=109

Summary To provide financial assistance for college to the dependents of California law enforcement officers who have been totally disabled or killed in the line of duty.

Eligibility This program is open to the natural children, adopted children, and spouses of a California peace officer (Highway Patrol, marshal, sheriff, police officer), employee of the Department of Corrections or Youth Authority, or firefighter. The parent or spouse must have died or become totally disabled as the result of an accident or injury caused by external violence or physical force incurred in the performance of duty. Applicants must be enrolled in at least 6 units at an accredited California postsecondary institution and able to demonstrate financial need.

Financial data Stipends range from $100 to $12,192 per year, depending on the need of the recipient.

Duration 1 academic year; may be renewed for up to 5 additional years at 4-year colleges and universities or up to 3 additional years at community colleges.

Additional data If the student receives other scholarships or grants, the award may be adjusted or withdrawn, depending upon financial need. Acceptance of work-study, loans, or employment will generally not affect the amount of money offered through this program.

Number awarded Varies each year; recently, 11 students received $82,000 in assistance from this program.

Deadline Applications may be submitted at any time.

[917]
CANCER UNWRAPPED TEEN WRITING CONTEST

Cancer Pathways
1400 Broadway
Seattle, WA 98122-3809
(206) 709-1400   Fax: (866) 200-2383
E-mail: info@cancerpathways.org
Web: www.cancerpathways.org/cancer-unwrapped

Summary To recognize and reward high school students in Washington who submit outstanding essays related to their experience with cancer.

Eligibility This competition is open to students enrolled in grades 9-12 at high schools in Washington. Applicants must have been affected by cancer, either through a personal diagnosis or that of a family member or friend. They must submit an essay of 500 to 2,000 words about their experience of dealing with cancer.

Financial data The prize is $1,000.

Duration The competition is held annually.

Additional data This competition was established in 2006 by Gilda's Club Seattle. The name was "It's Always Something" Writing Contest; it offered the Guy Robichaud Prizes and the Kai Leamer Prizes. The organization adopted its current name in 2016.

Number awarded Varies each year; recently, 15 were awarded.

Deadline March of each year.

[918]
CFA INSTITUTE 11 SEPTEMBER MEMORIAL SCHOLARSHIP

CFA Institute
Attn: Research Foundation
915 East High Street
P.O. Box 2082
Charlottesville, VA 22902-2082
(434) 951-5499   Toll Free: (800) 247-8132
Fax: (434) 951-5240   E-mail: rf@cfainstitute.org
Web: www.cfainstitute.org

Summary To provide financial assistance to individuals and their families who were disabled or killed in the September 11, 2001 terrorist attacks and who wish to major in business-related fields in college.

Eligibility This program is open to residents of any state or country who either 1) were permanently disabled in the attacks of September 11, 2001; or 2) are the spouses, domestic partners, or children of anyone killed or permanently disabled in the attacks. Applicants must be working full or part time on an undergraduate degree in finance, economics, accounting, or business ethics. Selection is based on demonstrated leadership and good citizenship, academic record, and financial need.

Financial data Stipends range up to $25,000 per year, depending on the need of the recipient.

Duration 1 year; renewable up to 4 additional years.

Additional data The CFA (Chartered Financial Analyst) Institute was formerly the Association for Investment Management and Research (AIMR). It lost at least 56 of its members and CFA candidates in the terrorist attacks of 11 September. This program is managed by Scholarship Management Services, a division of Scholarship America.

Number awarded Varies each year; recently, 12 were awarded.

Deadline May of each year.

[919]
CHARLES KOSMUTZA SCHOLARSHIP FUND

Disabled American Veterans-Department of New Jersey
Attn: Scholarship Committee
135 West Hanover Street, Fourth Floor
Trenton, NJ 08618
(609) 396-2885   Fax: (609) 396-9562
Web: www.davnj.org

Summary To provide financial assistance to high school seniors who are the children or grandchildren of members of the Disabled American Veterans (DAV) in New Jersey and planning to attend college in any state.

Eligibility This program is open to seniors graduating from high schools in New Jersey and planning to attend a college, university, community college, or trade school in any state. Applicants must be the natural or adopted descendant (child, grandchild, niece, nephew, cousin) of a member of the DAV Department of New Jersey. Along with their application, they must submit a 500-word essay on a topic that changes annually; recently, students were asked to write on what they would do to make this country more secured from ISIS. Financial need is not considered in the selection process.

Financial data The stipend is $1,000.

Duration 1 year.

Number awarded 3 each year: 1 in each region (north, central, and south) of the state.

Deadline May of each year.

[920]
CHIEF MASTER SERGEANT OF THE AIR FORCE SCHOLARSHIP PROGRAM

Air Force Sergeants Association
Attn: Membership and Field Relations
5211 Auth Road
Suitland, MD 20746
(301) 899-3500   Toll Free: (800) 638-0594
Fax: (301) 899-8136   E-mail: staff@hqafsa.org
Web: www.hqafsa.org/scholarships.html

Summary To provide financial assistance for college to the dependent children of enlisted Air Force personnel.

Eligibility This program is open to the unmarried children (including stepchildren and legally adopted children) of enlisted active-duty, retired, or veteran members of the U.S. Air Force, Air National Guard, or Air Force Reserves. Applicants must be attending or planning to attend an accredited academic institution. They must have an unweighted GPA of 3.5 or higher. Along with their application, they must submit 1) a paragraph on their life objectives and what they plan to do with the education they receive; and 2) an essay on the most urgent problem fac-

ing society today. High school seniors must also submit a transcript of all high school grades and a record of their SAT or ACT scores. Selection is based on academic record, character, leadership skills, writing ability, versatility, and potential for success. Financial need is not a consideration. A unique aspect of these scholarships is that applicants may supply additional information regarding circumstances that entitle them to special consideration; examples of such circumstances include student disabilities, financial hardships, parent disabled and unable to work, parent missing in action/killed in action/prisoner of war, or other unusual extenuating circumstances.

Financial data Stipends range from $1,000 to $3,500; funds may be used for tuition, room and board, fees, books, supplies, and transportation.

Duration 1 year; may be renewed if the recipient maintains full-time enrollment.

Additional data The Air Force Sergeants Association administers this program on behalf of the Airmen Memorial Foundation. It was established in 1987 and named in honor of CMSAF Richard D. Kisling, the late third Chief Master Sergeant of the Air Force. In 1997, following the deaths of CMSAF's (Retired) Andrews and Harlow, it was given its current name. The highest-ranked applicant receives the Paul W. Airey Memorial Scholarship, sponsored by GEICO Insurance.

Number awarded Varies each year; recently, 11 worth $16,500 were awarded: 1 at $3,500, 1 at $2,500, 1 at $2,000, 1 at $1,500, and 7 at $1,000. Since this program began, it has awarded more than 270 scholarships valued at more than $383,580.

Deadline March of each year.

[921]
CHILDREN OF FALLEN SOLDIERS RELIEF FUND COLLEGE GRANTS

Children of Fallen Soldiers Relief Fund
P.O. Box 1099
Temple Hills, MD 20757
(301) 685-3421   Toll Free: (866) 96-CFSRF
Fax: (301) 685-3271 E-mail: yellowribbon7@msn.com
Web: www.cfsrf.org

Summary To provide financial assistance for college to children and spouses of military personnel killed or severely disabled during service in Iraq or Afghanistan.

Eligibility This program is open to spouses and children of military personnel killed or severely disabled as a result of service in Operation Iraqi Freedom or Operation Enduring Freedom. Applicants must be enrolled or planning to enroll at a college or university. They must have a GPA of 2.75 or higher and be able to demonstrate financial need.

Financial data The stipend is $3,500 per semester ($7,000 per year).

Duration 1 semester; may be renewed.

Additional data This organization was founded in 2003.

Number awarded Varies each year; since the organization was founded, it has awarded more than $1,900,000 in grants.

Deadline October of each year for fall; April of each year for spring.

[922]
CHILDREN OF INJURED WORKERS SCHOLARSHIPS

Children of Injured Workers, Inc.
4983 Brittonfield Parkway
East Syracuse, NY 13057
(315) 449-4306   Fax: (315) 449-4358
E-mail: info@kidschanceny.org
Web: www.kidschanceny.org

Summary To provide financial assistance to residents of New York whose parent was seriously injured or killed in a workplace accident and who are interested in attending college in any state.

Eligibility This program is open to New York residents attending or planning to attend a college or technical school in any state. Applicants must be the child of a worker who suffered injury or death in an accident that is either established or accepted under the Workers' Compensation Law of the state of New York. The injury or death must have had a demonstrable impact on the financial ability of the child to attend college.

Financial data A stipend is awarded (amount not specified).

Duration 1 year; recipients may reapply.

Number awarded Varies each year.

Deadline Deadline not specified.

[923]
COLORADO CHAPTER NHF ACADEMIC SCHOLARSHIP PROGRAM

National Hemophilia Foundation-Colorado Chapter
Attn: Academic Scholarship Program
1385 South Colorado Boulevard, Suite 610
Denver, CO 80222
(720) 545-0755   E-mail: info@cohemo.org
Web: www.cohemo.org

Summary To provide financial assistance to residents of Colorado who have a bleeding disorder or are relatives of a person with a bleeding disorder and are interested in attending college in any state.

Eligibility This program is open to residents of Colorado who are 1) persons with hemophilia or a related inherited bleeding disorder; 2) parents of a minor child with a bleeding disorder; 3) siblings of a person with a bleeding disorder; and 4) immediate family members of persons who died because of complications of a bleeding disorder. Applicants must be enrolled or planning to enroll at a college, university, or trade school in any state. Selection is based on academic merit, employment status, narrative and reference letters, impact of the bleeding disorder on educational activities, and financial need.

Financial data The stipend is $2,500. Funds must be used for tuition, room, board, and related educational expenses.

Duration 1 year; nonrenewable.

Number awarded 1 each year.

Deadline April of each year.

[924]
COLORADO DEPENDENTS TUITION ASSISTANCE PROGRAM

Colorado Commission on Higher Education
1560 Broadway, Suite 1600
Denver, CO 80202
(303) 862-3001   Fax: (303) 996-1329
E-mail: cche@state.co.us
Web: highered.colorado.gov

Summary To provide financial assistance for college to the dependents of disabled or deceased Colorado National Guardsmen, law enforcement officers, and firefighters.

Eligibility Eligible for the program are dependents of Colorado law enforcement officers, firefighters, and National Guardsmen disabled or killed in the line of duty, as well as dependents of prisoners of war or service personnel listed as missing in action. Students must be Colorado residents under 22 years of age enrolled at 1) a state-supported 2- or 4-year Colorado college or university; 2) a private college, university, or vocational school in Colorado approved by the commission; or 3) an out-of-state 4-year college. Financial need is considered in the selection process.

Financial data Eligible students receive free tuition at Colorado public institutions of higher education. If the recipient wishes to attend a private college, university, or proprietary school, the award is limited to the amount of tuition at a comparable state-supported institution. Students who have applied to live in a dormitory, but have not been accepted because there is not enough space, may be provided supplemental assistance. Students who choose to live off-campus are not eligible for room reimbursement or a meal plan. Students who attend a non-residential Colorado institution and do not live at home are eligible for a grant of $1,000 per semester to assist with living expenses. Students who attend an out-of-state institution are eligible for the amount of tuition equivalent to that at a comparable Colorado public institution, but they are not eligible for room and board.

Duration Up to 6 years or until completion of a bachelor's degree, provided the recipient maintains a GPA of 2.5 or higher.

Additional data Recipients must attend accredited postsecondary institutions in Colorado.

Number awarded Varies each year; recently, nearly $672,000 was allocated to this program.

Deadline Deadline not specified.

[925]
COUEY MEMORIAL EDUCATIONAL SCHOLARSHIP

Georgia Transplant Foundation
Attn: Scholarship Program
2201 Macy Drive
Roswell, GA 30076
(770) 457-3796   Fax: (770) 457-7916
E-mail: gtf@gatransplant.org
Web: www.gatransplant.org

Summary   To provide financial assistance to residents of Georgia who are transplant recipients or siblings of recipients and interested in attending college in any state.

Eligibility   This program is open to residents of Georgia who are entering or continuing at an accredited institution of higher learning in any state. Applicants must be an organ transplant recipient or the sibling of a recipient. Along with their application, they must submit a 3-page personal statement on their career objectives, how this scholarship will help them attain their goals, and how transplantation has affected their life. Selection is based on that statement, transcripts, high school exit examination scores, ACT/SAT scores, 3 letters of reference, and financial need.

Financial data   The stipend is $1,000 per year.

Duration   1 year; may be renewed up to 3 additional years.

Number awarded   1 each year.

Deadline   April of each year.

[926]
DALY "PERFECT MATCH" SCHOLARSHIP

Georgia Transplant Foundation
Attn: Scholarship Program
2201 Macy Drive
Roswell, GA 30076
(770) 457-3796   Fax: (770) 457-7916
E-mail: gtf@gatransplant.org
Web: www.gatransplant.org

Summary   To provide financial assistance to residents of Georgia who are transplant recipients or dependents or siblings of recipients and interested in attending college in any state.

Eligibility   This program is open to residents of Georgia who are entering or continuing at an accredited institution of higher learning in any state. Applicants must be an organ transplant recipient or the dependent or sibling of a recipient. Along with their application, they must submit a 3-page personal statement on their career objectives, how this scholarship will help them attain their goals, and how transplantation has affected their life. Selection is based on that statement, transcripts, high school exit examination scores, ACT/SAT scores, 3 letters of reference, and financial need.

Financial data   The stipend is $1,000 per year.

Duration   1 year; may be renewed up to 3 additional years.

Number awarded   1 each year.

Deadline   April of each year.

[927]
DAVID NELSON JR. MEMORIAL FUND SCHOLARSHIP

Gift of Life Donor Program
Attn: David Nelson Jr. Memorial Fund
401 North Third Street
Philadelphia, PA 19123-4101
Toll Free: (800) DONORS-1
Web: www.donors1.org/donor/nelsonmemorialfund

Summary   To provide financial assistance to the children of deceased organ and tissue donors who live in the service area of the Gift of Life Donor Program and are interested in attending high school in the region or college in any state.

Eligibility   This program is open to the children of deceased organ and tissue donors who live in eastern Pennsylvania, southern New Jersey, or Delaware. Applicants must be younger than 25 years of age and either currently enrolled at 1) a private or parochial high school in the region; or 2) a 2- or 4-year college, university, or trade/technical school in any state. Along with their application, they must submit a brief statement summarizing their academic ambitions and extracurricular and/or volunteer activities and a 500-word essay describing how donation has touched their life. Financial need is not considered in the selection process.

Financial data   The stipend is $1,000.

Duration   1 year.

Number awarded   Varies each year; recently, 4 were awarded.

Deadline   April of each year.

[928]
DEPENDENT CHILDREN SCHOLARSHIP PROGRAM OF TENNESSEE

Tennessee Student Assistance Corporation
Parkway Towers
404 James Robertson Parkway, Suite 1510
Nashville, TN 37243-0820
(615) 741-1346   Toll Free: (800) 342-1663
Fax: (615) 741-6101   E-mail: TSAC.Aidinfo@tn.gov
Web: www.tn.gov

Summary   To provide financial assistance to the dependent children of disabled or deceased Tennessee law enforcement officers, firefighters, or emergency medical service technicians who plan to attend college in the state.

Eligibility   This program is open to Tennessee residents who are the dependent children of a Tennessee law enforcement officer, firefighter, or emergency medical service technician who was killed or totally and permanently disabled in the line of duty. Applicants must be enrolled or accepted for enrollment as a full-time undergraduate student at a college or university in Tennessee.

Financial data   The award covers tuition and fees, books, supplies, and room and board, minus any other financial aid for which the student is eligible.

Duration   1 year; may be renewed for up to 3 additional years or until completion of a program of study.

Additional data   This program began in 1990.

Number awarded Varies each year; recently, 26 students received $290,000 in support from this program.
Deadline July of each year.

[929]
DIABETES, INCORPORATED COLLEGE SCHOLARSHIP

Diabetes, Incorporated
Attn: Executive Director
P.O. Box 9368
Rapid City, SD 57709-9368
(605) 341-1273   Fax: (605) 342-5887
E-mail: diabetesinc@qwestoffice.net
Web: www.diabetesincorporated.org/Scholarship.html

Summary To provide financial assistance to high school seniors and current college students who have or have a family member who has diabetes and is a member of Diabetes, Incorporated.
Eligibility This program is open to graduating high school seniors and students who are continuing their education beyond high school. Applicants must have diabetes or have a family member who has diabetes. In either case, they must have a relative who is a current member of Diabetes, Incorporated. Along with their application, they must submit a 100-word essay on how their life has been affected by diabetes. Selection is based on that essay, GPA and SAT/ACT score, honors and awards, and community contribution. Preference is given to previous participants in the sponsor's Kamp for Kids.
Financial data The stipend is $1,000 per year. Funds are paid directly to the educational institution.
Duration 1 year; recipients may reapply.
Additional data This program includes the following named awards: the Kris Sanders Scholarship, the Micah Jerde Scholarship, and the Daniel Silvernail Scholarship.
Number awarded Varies each year; recently, 11 were awarded.
Deadline April of each year.

[930]
DISABLED AMERICAN VETERANS AUXILIARY NATIONAL EDUCATION SCHOLARSHIP FUND

Disabled American Veterans Auxiliary
Attn: National Education Scholarship Fund
3725 Alexandria Pike
Cold Spring, KY 41076
(859) 441-7300   Toll Free: (877) 426-2838, ext. 4020
Fax: (859) 442-2095   E-mail: dava@davmail.org
Web: www.davauxiliary.org/membership/Programs.aspx

Summary To provide financial assistance to members of the Disabled American Veterans (DAV) Auxiliary who are interested in attending college or graduate school.
Eligibility This program is open to paid life members of the auxiliary who are attending or planning to attend a college, university, or vocational school as a full- or part-time undergraduate or graduate student. Applicants must be at least seniors in high school, but there is no maximum age limit. Selection is based on academic achievement; participation in DAV activities; participation in other activities for veterans in their school, community, or elsewhere; volunteer work; membership in clubs or organizations; honors and awards; a statement of academic goals; and financial need.
Financial data Stipends are $1,500 per year for full-time students or $750 per year for part-time students.
Duration 1 year; may be renewed for up to 4 additional years, provided the recipient maintains a GPA of 2.5 or higher.
Additional data Membership in the DAV Auxiliary is available to extended family members of veterans eligible for membership in Disabled American Veterans (i.e., any man or woman who served in the armed forces during a period of war or under conditions simulating war and was wounded, disabled to any degree, or left with long-term illness as a result of military service and was discharged or retired from military service under honorable conditions). This program was established in September 2010 as a replacement for the educational loan program that the DAV Auxiliary operated from 1931 until August 2010.
Number awarded Varies each year.
Deadline March of each year.

[931]
DKF VETERANS ASSISTANCE FOUNDATION SCHOLARSHIPS

DKF Veterans Assistance Foundation
P.O. Box 7166
San Carlos, CA 94070
(650) 595-3896   E-mail: admin@dkfveterans.com
Web: www.dkfveterans.com/apply.html

Summary To provide financial assistance for college in any state to California residents who are veterans of Operation Enduring Freedom (OEF) in Afghanistan or Operation Iraqi Freedom (OIF) or the dependents of deceased or disabled veterans of those actions.
Eligibility This program is open to 1) veterans of the U.S. armed forces (including the Coast Guard) who served in support of OEF or OIF within the central command area of responsibility; and 2) dependents of those veterans who were killed in action or incurred disabilities rated as 75% or more. Applicants must be residents of California enrolled or planning to enroll full time at a college, university, community college, or trade institution in any state. Along with their application, they must submit a cover letter introducing themselves and their educational goals.
Financial data The stipend is $5,000 per year for students at universities and state colleges or $1,500 per year for students at community colleges and trade institutions.
Duration 1 year; may be renewed up to 3 additional years, provided the recipient maintains a GPA of 3.0 or higher.
Additional data This foundation was established in 2005.
Number awarded A limited number of these scholarships are awarded each year.
Deadline Deadline not specified.

[932]
DONNA T. DARRIEN MEMORIAL SCHOLARSHIP

Donna T. Darrien Memorial Foundation for Sickle Cell,
Inc.
P.O. Box 3331
Newark, NJ 07103
(973) 282-1997   E-mail: dtdsicklecell@hotmail.com
Web: www.dtdsicklecell.org/scholarship-information

Summary To provide financial assistance to residents
of New Jersey who have or whose parents have sickle cell
disease and are interested in attending college in any
state.

Eligibility This program is open to residents of New Jersey who are able to document a diagnosis of sickle cell
disease or are the children of parents with the disease.
Applicants must be enrolled or planning to enroll at an
accredited college, university, or vocational/technical
school in any state and have a GPA of 2.0 or higher. Along
with their application, they must submit a 1,000-word
essay on how they face their challenges, their educational
plans, and their career objectives. Financial need is not
considered in the selection process.

Financial data A stipend is awarded (amount not specified).

Duration 1 year; recipients may reapply.

Additional data This program began in 2001.

Number awarded 1 or more each year.

Deadline April of each year.

[933]
DOUG HITESHEW MEMORIAL SCHOLARSHIP PROGRAM

Hemophilia Foundation of Maryland
Attn: Executive Director
13 Class Court, Suite 200
Parkville, MD 21234
(410) 661-2307   Toll Free: (800) 964-3131
Fax: (410) 661-2308 E-mail: miller8043@comcast.net
Web: www.hfmonline.webs.com/scholarship-info

Summary To provide financial assistance to residents
of Maryland and students attending college in the state
who have hemophilia or von Willebrand Disease or are
immediate family of such people.

Eligibility This program is open to students who have
hemophilia or von Willebrand Disease and their siblings,
children, or parents. Applicants must be 1) Maryland residents who are entering or attending a community college,
junior college, 4-year college, university, or vocational
school in any state; or 2) students who have attended a
Maryland school for at least 1 year. Along with their application, they must submit 1-page essays on 1) their career
goals; and 2) their previous participation with the Hemophilia Foundation of Maryland or another chapter and how
they plan to contribute to the chapter in the future. Selection is based on those essays, academic goals, transcripts
of current academic work, volunteer work, and letters of
recommendation.

Financial data Stipends are $2,500, $1,000, or $500.

Duration 1 year.

Additional data This program began in 2010.

Number awarded Varies each year; recently, 9 were
awarded: 3 at $2,500 each to students who live or attend
school in Maryland and have a bleeding disorder, 3 at
$1,000 each to siblings or children of persons who live in
Maryland and have a bleeding disorder, and 3 at $500
each to parents of children who live in Maryland and have
a bleeding disorder.

Deadline April of each year.

[934]
DUGDALE/VAN EYS SCHOLARSHIP AWARD

Tennessee Hemophilia and Bleeding Disorders
Foundation
Attn: Scholarship Committee
1819 Ward Drive, Suite 102
Murfreesboro, TN 37129
(615) 900-1486   Toll Free: (888) 703-3269
Fax: (615) 900-1487   E-mail: mail@thbdf.org
Web: www.thbdf.org

Summary To provide financial assistance for college to
students with hemophilia or their family members in Tennessee.

Eligibility This program is open to college-bound high
school seniors, college students, and technical school students who have a bleeding disorder and are receiving
treatment in Tennessee. Their children, spouses, and
guardians are also eligible. Applicants must have a GPA of
2.5 or higher and be enrolled or planning to enroll full time.
They must submit a 500-word essay on their life goals, a
resume, 3 letters of recommendation, proof of enrollment,
and documentation of community service of at least 10
hours per semester. Financial need is considered in the
selection process.

Financial data Stipends range from $500 to $2,000.

Duration 1 year; recipients may reapply.

Number awarded Varies each year; recently, 6 were
awarded: 1 at $2,000, 1 at $1,500, 1 at $1,000, and 3 at
$500.

Deadline March of each year.

[935]
DUNKERLEY FAMILY SCHOLARSHIP

Georgia Transplant Foundation
Attn: Scholarship Program
2201 Macy Drive
Roswell, GA 30076
(770) 457-3796   Fax: (770) 457-7916
E-mail: gtf@gatransplant.org
Web: www.gatransplant.org

Summary To provide financial assistance to residents
of Georgia who are dependents of transplant recipients
and interested in attending college in any state.

Eligibility This program is open to residents of Georgia
who are entering or continuing at an accredited college,
university, or vocational/technical school in any state.
Applicants must be the dependent of an organ transplant
recipient. Along with their application, they must submit a

3-page personal statement on their career objectives, how this scholarship will help them attain their goals, and how transplantation has affected their life. Selection is based on that statement, transcripts, high school exit examination scores, ACT/SAT scores, 3 letters of reference, and financial need.

Financial data The stipend is $1,000 per year.

Duration 1 year; may be renewed up to 3 additional years.

Number awarded 1 each year.

Deadline April of each year.

[936]
EAGA SCHOLARSHIP FUND

Eastern Amputee Golf Association
Attn: Lind Buck, Secretary
2015 Amherst Drive
Bethlehem, PA 18015-5606
(610) 867-9295   Fax: (610) 867-9295
E-mail: lindajean18015@aolc.om
Web: www.eagagolf.org/scholarships.html

Summary To provide financial assistance for college to members of the Eastern Amputee Golf Association (EAGA) and their families.

Eligibility This program is open to students who are residents of and/or currently enrolled or accepted for enrollment at a college or university in designated eastern states (Connecticut, Delaware, District of Columbia, Maine, Maryland, Massachusetts, New Hampshire, New Jersey, New York, Pennsylvania, Rhode Island, Vermont, Virginia, or West Virginia). Applicants must be amputee members of the association (those who have experienced the loss of 1 or more extremities at a major joint due to amputation or birth defect) or members of their families. Financial need is considered in the selection process.

Financial data The stipend is $1,000.

Duration 1 year; may be renewed if the recipient maintains a GPA of 2.0 or higher and continues to demonstrate financial need.

Additional data The EAGA was incorporated in 1987. It welcomes 2 types of members: amputee members and associate members (non-amputees who are interested in the organization and support its work but are not eligible for these scholarships). This program includes the following named scholarships: the Paul DesChamps Scholarship Award, the Tom Reed Scholarship, the Ray Froncillo Scholarship, the Howard Taylor Scholarship, the Paul Liemkuehler Memorial Scholarship, the Buffalo Amputee Golf Classic Scholarship Award, and the Lehigh Valley Amputee Support Group Scholarship Award.

Number awarded Varies each year; recently, 20 were awarded.

Deadline June of each year.

[937]
EDUCATIONAL GRATUITY OF THE PENNSYLVANIA DEPARTMENT OF MILITARY AND VETERANS AFFAIRS

Pennsylvania Department of Military and Veterans Affairs
Attn: Educational Gratuity
Building 0-47
Fort Indiantown Gap
Annville, PA 17003-5002
(717) 861-8910   Toll Free: (800) 547-2838
Fax: (717) 861-8589   E-mail: ra-eg@pa.gov
Web: www.dmva.pa.gov

Summary To provide financial assistance to residents of Pennsylvania who are the child of a deceased or disabled veteran and wish to attend college in the state.

Eligibility This program is open to students between 16 and 23 years of age who have been residents of Pennsylvania for at least 5 years. Applicants must be the child of a veteran who 1) died in service during a period of war or armed conflict; or 2) received an honorable discharge, served during established dates of war, and has a 100% permanent and total service-connected disability. They must be enrolled or planning to enroll at a college or university in Pennsylvania. Financial need is considered in the selection process.

Financial data The stipend is $500 per semester. Funds are paid directly to the educational institution.

Duration 1 semester; may be renewed up to 7 additional semesters.

Number awarded Varies each year.

Deadline Deadline not specified.

[938]
EDWARD T. AND MARY A. CONROY MEMORIAL SCHOLARSHIP PROGRAM

Maryland Higher Education Commission
Attn: Office of Student Financial Assistance
6 North Liberty Street, Ground Suite
Baltimore, MD 21201
(410) 767-3301   Toll Free: (800) 974-0203
Fax: (410) 332-0250   TDD: (800) 735-2258
E-mail: osfamail.mhec@maryland.gov
Web: www.mhec.state.md.us

Summary To provide financial assistance for college or graduate school in Maryland to children and spouses of victims of the September 11, 2001 terrorist attacks and specified categories of veterans, public safety employees, and their children or spouses.

Eligibility This program is open to entering and continuing undergraduate and graduate students in the following categories: 1) children and surviving spouses of victims of the September 11, 2001 terrorist attacks who died in the World Trade Center in New York City, in the Pentagon in Virginia, or on United Airlines Flight 93 in Pennsylvania; 2) veterans who have, as a direct result of military service, a disability of 25% or greater and have exhausted or are no longer eligible for federal veterans' educational benefits; 3) children and unremarried surviving spouses of armed forces members whose death or 100% disability was directly caused by military service; 4) POW/MIA veterans of the Vietnam Conflict and their children; 5) state or local public safety officers or volunteers who became 100% disabled in the line of duty; 6) children and unremarried surviving spouses of state or local public safety employees or volunteers who died or became 100% disabled in the line of duty. and 7) children and unremarried surviving spouses or a school employee who, as a result of an act of violence, either died in the line of duty or sustained an injury that rendered the school employee 100% disabled. The parent, spouse, veteran, POW, public safety officer or volunteer, or school employee must have been a resident of Maryland at the time of death or when declared disabled. Applicants must be planning to enroll at a 2- or 4-year Maryland college or university as a full-time or part-time degree-seeking undergraduate or graduate student or attend a private career school. Financial need is not considered.

Financial data   The amount of the award is equal to tuition and fees at a Maryland postsecondary institution, to a maximum of $10,182. The total amount of all Maryland scholarship awards from all sources may not exceed the cost of attendance or $19,000, whichever is less.

Duration   Up to 5 years of full-time study or 8 years of part-time study.

Number awarded   Varies each year.

Deadline   July of each year.

[939]
ELAINE CHAPIN FUND SCHOLARSHIPS

Elaine Chapin Fund
1440 Heritage Landing, Suite 109
St. Charles, MO 63303
E-mail: elainechapinfund@gmail.com
Web: sites.google.com/site/theelainechapinfund

Summary   To provide financial assistance for college to people who have multiple sclerosis (MS) and their families.

Eligibility   This program is open to people whose lives have been affected by MS, either directly or as a family member. Applicants must be enrolled or planning to enroll as full-time undergraduates at an accredited 2- or 4-year college, university, or vocational/technical school in the United States. They must be U.S. citizens. Along with their application, they must submit a short essay on the impact of MS on their life. Selection is based on that essay, academic standing, and financial need.

Financial data   The stipend is $1,000.

Duration   1 year.

Additional data   This program is administered through the Gateway Area Chapter of the National Multiple Sclerosis Society.

Number awarded   Varies each year; recently, 9 were awarded.

Deadline   April of each year.

[940]
ELKS NATIONAL FOUNDATION EMERGENCY EDUCATIONAL FUND GRANTS

Elks National Foundation
Attn: Scholarship Department
2750 North Lakeview Avenue
Chicago, IL 60614-2256
(773) 755-4732   Fax: (773) 755-4729
E-mail: scholarship@elks.org
Web: www.elks.org

Summary   To provide emergency financial assistance to college students who are children of deceased or disabled members of B.P.O. Elks.

Eligibility   This program is open to children of Elks who have died or are totally disabled. Applicants must be unmarried, under 23 years of age, able to demonstrate financial need, and attending a college or university in the United States as a full-time undergraduate student. The student's parent must have been a member in good standing for at least 1 year at the time of death or, if disabled, have been a member in good standing for at least 1 year before he or she became incapacitated and must continue to be an Elk in good standing when the application for assistance is submitted. Applications must give the B.P.O. Elks Lodge affiliation of the Elk parent.

Financial data   The amount of the assistance depends on the need of the applicant but normally ranges up to $4,000 per year.

Duration   1 year; may be renewed up to 3 additional years.

Number awarded   Varies each year.

Deadline   December of each year for new applications; October of each year for renewal applications.

[941]
ERIC DOSTIE MEMORIAL COLLEGE SCHOLARSHIP

NuFACTOR Specialty Pharmacy
Attn: Scholarship Administrator
41093 County Center Drive, Suite B
Temecula, CA 92591
(951) 296-2516   Toll Free: (800) 323-6832, ext. 1300
Fax: (855) 270-7347   E-mail: info@kelleycom.com
Web: www.nufactor.com

Summary   To provide financial assistance for college to students with hemophilia or members of their families.

Eligibility   This program is open to 1) students with hemophilia or a related bleeding disorder; or 2) members of their families. Applicants must be U.S. citizens and enrolled or planning to enroll full time at an accredited 2- or 4-year college or university. They must have a GPA of 2.5 or higher. Along with their application, they must submit an essay on how their education will be used to serve humankind and to encourage self-improvement and enrichment. Selection is based on academic achievement, community service, and financial need.

Financial data   The stipend is $1,000.

Duration   1 year.

Number awarded 10 each year.
Deadline February of each year.

[942]
ERIC MARTINEZ MEMORIAL SCHOLARSHIP FOR THE SIBLING OF AN INDIVIDUAL WITH DOWN SYNDROME

United Parent Support for Down Syndrome
Attn: UPS for DownS Memorial Scholarship Program
1070 South Roselle Road
Schaumburg, IL 60193
(847) 895-2100   E-mail: embarrett@upsfordowns.org
Web: www.upsfordowns.org/support/Scholarships.aspx

Summary To provide financial assistance to individuals who are working on an undergraduate or graduate degree in a disability-related field.

Eligibility This program is open to students currently enrolled at a college, university, or community college who have a sibling with Down syndrome. Applicants must be working on an undergraduate or graduate degree in any field. Along with their application, they must submit a 1-page essay that includes their relationship with the sponsoring organization and disability community, their future career plans, and how the inclusion of individuals with disabilities in the community has affected them and how it might affect them in the future. They must also submit a service activity sheet that provides information on the name or type of service activity they have performed, estimated annual activity hours, and names of organizations involved. U.S. citizenship is required.

Financial data The stipend is $2,500. Funds are sent directly to the institution.

Duration 1 year.

Number awarded 1 each year.

Deadline May of each year.

[943]
ERNST LAW GROUP BRAIN INJURY CAREGIVERS SCHOLARSHIP

Ernst Law Group
1020 Palm Street
San Luis Obispo, CA 93401
(805) 678-0272   E-mail: info@ernstlawgroup.com
Web: www.ernstlawgroup.com

Summary To provide financial assistance to college students who are or have been a caregiver of someone living with a serious brain injury.

Eligibility This program is open to students enrolled or planning to enroll at an accredited college or university. Applicants must be or have been a caregiver of a loved one living with a serious brain injury. They must have a GPA of 2.8 or higher. Along with their application, they must submit an essay of 500 to 1,000 words on 1 of the following topics: 1) a time when being the caregiver of a brain injury victim created an obstacle or special challenge and how they overcame it; 2) how being the caregiver of a brain injury victim affected their goals and dreams for the future; or 3) how they learned to accept being the caregiver of a brain injury victim and how that acceptance has changed them.

Financial data The stipend is $1,000.

Duration 1 year.

Number awarded 1 each year.

Deadline July of each year.

[944]
FAMILIES OF FREEDOM SCHOLARSHIP FUND

Scholarship America
Attn: Scholarship Management Services
One Scholarship Way
P.O. Box 297
St. Peter, MN 56082
(507) 931-1682   Toll Free: (877) 862-0136
Fax: (507) 931-9168
E-mail: info@familiesoffreedom.org
Web: www.familiesoffreedom.org

Summary To provide college scholarships to financially-needy individuals and the families of individuals who were victims of the terrorist attacks on September 11, 2001.

Eligibility This program is open to the individuals who were disabled as a result of the terrorist attacks on September 11, 2001 and to the relatives of those individuals who were killed or permanently disabled during the attacks. Primarily, the fund will benefit dependents (including spouses and children) of the following groups: airplane crew and passengers; World Trade Center workers and visitors; Pentagon workers and visitors; and rescue workers, including firefighters, emergency medical personnel, and law enforcement personnel. Applicants must be enrolled or planning to enroll in an accredited 2- or 4-year college, university, or vocational/technical school in the United States. They must be able to demonstrate financial need. In addition, all students who can demonstrate financial need are eligible.

Financial data Stipends range from $1,000 to $28,000 per year, depending upon the need of the recipient. Recently, awards averaged $14,553 per academic year. Funds are distributed annually, in 2 equal installments. Checks are made payable jointly to the student and the student's school.

Duration 1 year; may be renewed.

Additional data This program was established on September 17, 2001. The fundraising goal of $100 million was reached on September 4, 2002. The fund will operate until December 31, 2030.

Number awarded Varies each year; recently, 827 students received nearly $13 million in assistance. Since the program began, it has awarded $135 million to 3,100 students.

Deadline Full-time students must apply by May of each year; other students must submit their applications by the end of the term.

[945]
FIRST CAVALRY DIVISION ASSOCIATION SCHOLARSHIPS

First Cavalry Division Association
Attn: Foundation
302 North Main Street
Copperas Cove, TX 76522-1703
(254) 547-6537   Fax: (254) 547-8853
E-mail: firstcav@1cda.org
Web: www.1cda.org/foundation—scholarships-.html

Summary To provide financial assistance for undergraduate education to soldiers currently or formerly assigned to the First Cavalry Division and their families.

Eligibility This program is open to children of soldiers who died or have been declared totally and permanently disabled from injuries incurred while serving with the First Cavalry Division during any armed conflict; children of soldiers who died while serving in the First Cavalry Division during peacetime; and active-duty soldiers currently assigned or attached to the First Cavalry Division and their spouses and children.

Financial data The stipend is $1,200 per year. The checks are made out jointly to the student and the school and may be used for whatever the student needs, including tuition, books, and clothing.

Duration 1 year; may be renewed up to 3 additional years.

Number awarded Varies each year; since the program was established, it has awarded more than $783,000 to 488 children of disabled and deceased Cavalry members and more than $269,000 to 277 current members of the Division and their families.

Deadline July of each year.

[946]
FIRST MARINE DIVISION ASSOCIATION SCHOLARSHIPS

First Marine Division Association
P.O. Box 9000, Box 902
Oceanside, CA 92051
(760) 763-3268   E-mail: june.oldbreed@fmda.us
Web: www.1stmarinedivisionassociation.org

Summary To provide financial assistance for college to dependents of deceased or disabled veterans of the First Marine Division.

Eligibility This program is open to dependents of veterans who served in the First Marine Division or in a unit attached to that Division, are honorably discharged, and now are either totally and permanently disabled or deceased from any cause. Applicants must be attending or planning to attend an accredited college, university, or trade school as a full-time undergraduate student. Graduate students and students still in high school or prep school are not eligible.

Financial data The stipend is $1,750 per year.

Duration 1 year; may be renewed up to 3 additional years.

Additional data Award winners who marry before completing the course or who drop out for non-scholastic rea-

sons must submit a new application before benefits can be resumed.

Number awarded Varies each year; recently, 23 were awarded.

Deadline Deadline not specified.

[947]
FLEETWOOD MEMORIAL FOUNDATION EDUCATIONAL AID FOR RESIDENT DEPENDENT CHILDREN

Fleetwood Memorial Foundation
c/o North Texas Community Foundation
306 West Seventh Street, Suite 1045
Fort Worth, TX 76102
(817) 877-0702   Fax: (817) 632-8711
E-mail: rmoore@northtexascf.org
Web: www.fleetwoodmemorial.org/form.php

Summary To provide funding for educational expenses to the dependent children of deceased or disabled firefighter or peace officer personnel in Texas.

Eligibility This program is open to dependent children of certified Texas law enforcement or fire protection personnel who were killed or permanently disabled in the performance of their duties. Applicants must be enrolled or planning to enroll full time at a public junior or senior college in the state. They must have a GPA of 2.5 or higher.

Financial data These funds are intended to provide support for housing and other needs not covered by funding from the Texas Higher Education Coordinating Board.

Duration 1 year; may be renewed, provided the recipient remains enrolled full time and maintains a GPA of 2.5 or higher.

Number awarded Since its inception in 1974, the foundation has provided more than 500 grants to qualified recipients, totaling nearly $4.0 million.

Deadline Applications may be submitted at any time.

[948]
FLORIDA SCHOLARSHIPS FOR CHILDREN AND SPOUSES OF DECEASED OR DISABLED VETERANS

Florida Department of Education
Attn: Office of Student Financial Assistance
State Scholarship and Grant Programs
325 West Gaines Street, Suite 1314
Tallahassee, FL 32399-0400
(850) 410-5160   Toll Free: (888) 827-2004
Fax: (850) 487-1809   E-mail: osfa@fldoe.org
Web: www.floridastudentfinancialaid.org

Summary To provide financial assistance for college to the children and spouses of Florida veterans who are disabled, deceased, or officially classified as prisoners of war (POW) or missing in action (MIA).

Eligibility This program is open to residents of Florida who are U.S. citizens or eligible noncitizens and the dependent children or spouses of veterans or servicemembers who 1) died as a result of service-connected injuries, diseases, or disabilities sustained while on active duty during a period of war; 2) have a service-connected

100% total and permanent disability; or 3) were classified as POW or MIA by the U.S. armed forces or as civilian personnel captured while serving with the consent or authorization of the U.S. government during wartime service. The veteran or servicemember must have been a U.S. citizen or eligible noncitizens and a resident of Florida for at least 1 year before death, disability, or POW/MIA status. Children must be between 16 and 22 years of age. Spouses of deceased veterans or servicemembers must be unremarried and must apply within 5 years of their spouse's death. Spouses of disabled veterans must have been married for at least 1 year.

Financial data Students at public institutions receive full payment of tuition and fees. Students at 4-year private institutions receive $212 per semester credit hour. Students at 2-year private institutions receive $105 per semester credit hour.

Duration 1 quarter or semester; may be renewed for up to 110% of the required credit hours of an initial associate, baccalaureate, diploma, or certificate program, provided the student maintains a GPA of 2.0 or higher.

Number awarded Varies each year; recently, 214 new and 550 renewal scholarships were awarded.

Deadline March of each year.

[949]
FREE TUITION FOR NORTH DAKOTA DEPENDENTS

North Dakota University System
Attn: Financial Aid Office
State Capitol, Judicial Wing, Room 103
600 East Boulevard Avenue, Department 21
Bismarck, ND 58505-0602
(701) 328-2906   Fax: (701) 328-2979
E-mail: ndfinaid@ndus.edu
Web: www.ndus.edu

Summary To waive tuition and fees for dependents of deceased or other veterans at public institutions in North Dakota.

Eligibility Eligible for this benefit are the dependents of veterans who were North Dakota residents when they entered the armed forces and died of service-related causes, were killed in action, became totally disabled, or were declared missing in action. Applicants must be attending or planning to attend a public college or university in North Dakota.

Financial data Qualified students are entitled to a waiver of all tuition and fees (except fees charged to retire outstanding bonds) at public institutions in North Dakota.

Duration Up to 45 months.

Number awarded Varies each year.

Deadline Deadline not specified.

[950]
FREEDOM ALLIANCE SCHOLARSHIPS

Freedom Alliance
Attn: Scholarship Fund
22570 Markey Court, Suite 240
Dulles, VA 20166-6915
(703) 444-7940   Toll Free: (800) 475-6620
Fax: (703) 444-9893 E-mail: info@freedomalliance.org
Web: www.fascholarship.com

Summary To provide financial assistance for college to the children of deceased and disabled military personnel.

Eligibility This program is open to high school seniors, high school graduates, and undergraduate students under 26 years of age who are dependent children of military personnel (soldier, sailor, airman, Marine, or Guardsman). The military parent must 1) have been killed or permanently disabled as a result of an operational mission or training accident; or 2) be currently classified as a POW or MIA. For disabled parents, the disability must be permanent, service-connected, and rated at 100% by the U.S. Department of Veterans Affairs. Applicants must submit a 500-word essay on what their parent's service means to them.

Financial data Stipends range up to $6,000 per year.

Duration 1 year; may be renewed up to 3 additional years, provided the recipient remains enrolled full time with a GPA of 2.0 or higher.

Number awarded Varies each year; recently, 240 were awarded. Since the program was established, it has awarded more than $7 million in scholarships.

Deadline July of each year.

[951]
FRIENDS OF 440 SCHOLARSHIPS

Friends of 440 Scholarship Fund, Inc.
Attn: Managing Director
9100 South Dadeland Boulevard, Suite 1010
Miami, FL 33156-7800
(305) 423-8710   Fax: (305) 670-0716
E-mail: info@440scholarship.org
Web: www.440scholarship.org/portal/application

Summary To provide financial assistance to Florida residents whose parent was killed or permanently disabled in an employment-related accident and who are interested in attending college in any state.

Eligibility This program is open to students who are dependents or descendants of workers injured or killed in the course and scope of their employment and who are eligible to receive benefits under the Florida Workers' Compensation Law. Dependents and descendants of people who are primarily engaged in the administration of the Florida Workers' Compensation Law are also eligible. Applicants must be attending or planning to attend a college or university in any state. High school seniors must have a GPA of 2.7 or higher; students currently enrolled in college must have a GPA of 3.0 or higher. Selection is based on merit, financial need, and connection to the worker's compensation field.

Financial data Stipends range up to $6,000 per year. Funds may be used to cover the cost of tuition, room, board, and books.

Duration 1 year; may be renewed, provided the recipient maintains a GPA of 3.0 or higher.

Additional data This program, established in 1991, takes its name from the Florida Workers' Compensation Law, which is chapter 440 of Florida Statutes.

Number awarded Varies each year; recently, 48 of these scholarships, worth $77,000, were awarded. Since the program was established, it has awarded more than $1.4 million to more than 700 students.

Deadline February of each year.

[952]
FRIENDS OF PAM SCHOLARSHIP FUND

Healin' Wheels LLC
c/o Scholarship Management Services
One Scholarship Way
P.O. Box 297
St. Peter, MN 56082
(507) 931-1682   Toll Free: (800) 537-4180
Fax: (507) 931-9168
E-mail: ssykora@scholarshipamerica.org
Web: sms.scholarshipamerica.org/healinwheels

Summary To provide financial assistance for college to dependents of Amyotrophic Lateral Sclerosis (A.L.S.) patients.

Eligibility This program is open to dependents of a current or deceased ALS patient during the time of the patient's diagnosed illness. Primary caregivers or providers for the A.L.S. patient who resided in the same household during the illness are also eligible. Applicants must be high school seniors, high school graduates, or current undergraduates enrolled or planning to enroll full time at a 2- or 4-year college, university, or vocational/technical school. They must be U.S. citizens and have a GPA of 2.5 or higher. Selection is based on academic record, community service, and financial need.

Financial data The stipend ranges from $1,000 to $5,000 per year.

Duration 1 year; may be renewed for up to 3 additional years or completion of a bachelor's degree, whichever occurs first.

Additional data This program began in 2013.

Number awarded Up to 5 each year.

Deadline January of each year.

[953]
GENERAL HENRY H. ARNOLD EDUCATION GRANT PROGRAM

Air Force Aid Society
Attn: Education Assistance Department
241 18th Street South, Suite 202
Arlington, VA 22202-3409
(703) 972-2647   Toll Free: (866) 896-5637
Fax: (703) 972-2646   E-mail: ed@afas-hq.org
Web: www.afas.org

Summary To provide need-based financial assistance for college to dependents of active-duty, retired, disabled, or deceased Air Force personnel.

Eligibility This program is open to 1) dependent children of Air Force personnel who are active duty, Title 10 Reservists on extended active duty, Title 32 Guard performing full-time active-duty service, retired due to length of active-duty service or disability, or deceased while on active duty or in retired status; 2) spouses of active-duty Air Force members and Title 10 Reservists on extended active duty; and 3) surviving spouses of Air Force members who died while on active duty or in retired status. Applicants must be enrolled or planning to enroll as full-time undergraduate students at an accredited college, university, or trade/vocational school. Spouses must be attending school within the 48 contiguous states. Selection is based on family income and education costs.

Financial data Stipends range from $500 to $4,000.

Duration 1 year; may be renewed if the recipient maintains a GPA of 2.0 or higher.

Additional data Since this program was established in the 1988-89 academic year, it has awarded more than 100,000 grants.

Number awarded Varies each year.

Deadline March of each year.

[954]
GEORGE AND LINDA PRICE SCHOLARSHIP

Hemophilia Association of the Capital Area
8136 Old Keene Mill Road, Suite A312
Springfield, VA 22152
(703) 352-7641   Fax: (540) 427-6589
E-mail: admin@hacacares.org
Web: www.hacacares.org

Summary To provide financial assistance to individuals with bleeding disorders and their families who are members of the Hemophilia Association of the Capital Area (HACA) and interested in attending college or graduate school in any state.

Eligibility This program is open to residents of northern Virginia, Montgomery and Prince George's County in Maryland, and Washington, D.C. who have a bleeding disorder and their siblings and parents. Applicants must be members of HACA. They must be 1) high school seniors or graduates who have not yet attended college; 2) full-time freshmen, sophomores, or juniors at a college, university, or vocational/technical school in any state; or 3) college seniors planning to attend graduate school and students already enrolled at a graduate school in any state. Along with their application, they must submit a 500-word essay on what they have done to contribute to the bleeding disorders community and how they plan to contribute to that community in the future. Financial need is not considered in the selection process.

Financial data The stipend is $2,500.

Duration 1 year; recipients may reapply.

Number awarded 2 each year.

Deadline May of each year.

[955]
GEORGE BARTOL MEMORIAL SCHOLARSHIPS

George Bartol Memorial Scholarship Fund
c/o Heather M. Bartol
4863 Riverton Drive
Orlando, FL 32817
(407) 382-5982

Summary To provide financial assistance for college to children of brain tumor patients.

Eligibility This program is open to students who are enrolled full time at an accredited 2- or 4-year college or university and have a GPA of 2.5 or higher. Applicants must have a parent battling a primary brain tumor or a parent who has passed away as a result of a primary brain tumor. They must be between 18 and 23 years of age. Along with their application, they must submit 250-word essays on the following topics: 1) their parent who has lost their battle to a primary brain tumor or who is currently battling a primary brain tumor; 2) how this scholarship will affect them and their family; 3) how cancer has impacted their life; 4) their biggest adjustment since their parent's battle with brain cancer began; and 5) what they have learned from this experience and how they might help others as a result. Selection is based on the essays, grades, letters of recommendation, and financial need.

Financial data The stipend is $1,000 per semester ($3,000 per year, including summer semester). Students at schools on the quarter system may receive $750 per quarter ($3,000 per year, including summer quarter). Funds are paid directly to the financial aid office at the school the recipient is attending.

Duration 1 semester or quarter; may be renewed if the recipient maintains a GPA of 2.5 or higher.

Additional data This program began in 2004.

Number awarded Varies each year; recently, 3 were awarded.

Deadline September of each year.

[956]
GEORGIA CHAPTER OF THE INTERNATIONAL TRANSPLANT NURSES SOCIETY SCHOLARSHIP

Georgia Transplant Foundation
Attn: Scholarship Program
2201 Macy Drive
Roswell, GA 30076
(770) 457-3796   Fax: (770) 457-7916
E-mail: gtf@gatransplant.org
Web: www.gatransplant.org

Summary To provide financial assistance to residents of Georgia who are transplant recipients or their siblings or dependents and interested in attending college in any state to work on a degree in health care.

Eligibility This program is open to residents of Georgia who are entering or continuing at an accredited institution of higher learning in any state to work on a degree in health care. Applicants must be an organ transplant recipient, a dependent of a recipient, a parent of a recipient, a

living donor, or the sibling of a recipient (both the sibling and the recipient must be under 22 years of age). Along with their application, they must submit a 3-page personal statement on their career objectives, how this scholarship will help them attain their goals, and how transplantation has affected their life. Selection is based on that statement, transcripts, high school exit examination scores, ACT/SAT scores, 3 letters of reference, and financial need.

Financial data The stipend is $1,000.

Duration 1 year; nonrenewable.

Additional data This program is sponsored by the Georgia Chapter of the International Transplant Nurses Society.

Number awarded 1 each year.

Deadline April of each year.

[957]
GEORGIA PUBLIC SAFETY MEMORIAL GRANT

Georgia Student Finance Commission
Attn: Scholarships and Grants Division
2082 East Exchange Place, Suite 200
Tucker, GA 30084-5305
(770) 724-9249   Toll Free: (800) 505-GSFC
Fax: (770) 724-9089   E-mail: GAfutures@gsfc.org
Web: www.gafutures.org

Summary To provide financial assistance for college to the children of Georgia public safety officers who have been permanently disabled or killed in the line of duty.

Eligibility This program is open to dependent children of Georgia law enforcement officers, firefighters, EMT, correction officers, or prison guards who have been permanently disabled or killed in the line of duty. Applicants must be enrolled or accepted as full-time undergraduate students in a Georgia public or private college, university, or technical institution and be in compliance with the Georgia Drug-Free Postsecondary Education Act. U.S. citizenship or status as a national or permanent resident is required. Financial need is not considered in the selection process.

Financial data The award covers the cost of attendance at a public postsecondary school in Georgia, minus any other aid received, to a maximum of $18,000 per year.

Duration 1 year; may be renewed (if satisfactory progress is maintained) for up to 3 additional years.

Additional data This program, which began in 1994, is funded by the Georgia Lottery for Education.

Number awarded Varies each year; recently, 18 were awarded.

Deadline July of each year.

[958]
GEORGIA'S HERO SCHOLARSHIP PROGRAM

Georgia Student Finance Commission
Attn: Scholarships and Grants Division
2082 East Exchange Place, Suite 200
Tucker, GA 30084-5305
(770) 724-9249   Toll Free: (800) 505-GSFC
Fax: (770) 724-9089   E-mail: GAfutures@gsfc.org
Web: www.gafutures.org

Summary   To provide financial assistance for college to members of the National Guard or Reserves in Georgia and their children and spouses.

Eligibility   This program is open to Georgia residents who are active members of the Georgia National Guard or U.S. Military Reserves, were deployed outside the United States for active-duty service on or after February 1, 2003 to a location designated as a combat zone, and served in that combat zone for at least 181 consecutive days. Also eligible are 1) the children, younger than 25 years of age, of Guard and Reserve members who completed at least 1 term of service (of 181 days each) overseas on or after February 1, 2003; 2) the children, younger than 25 years of age, of Guard and Reserve members who were killed or totally disabled during service overseas on or after February 1, 2003, regardless of their length of service; and 3) the spouses of Guard and Reserve members who were killed in a combat zone, died as a result of injuries, or became 100% disabled as a result of injuries received in a combat zone during service overseas on or after February 1, 2003, regardless of their length of service. Applicants must be interested in attending a unit of the University System of Georgia, a unit of the Technical College System of Georgia, or an eligible private college or university in Georgia.

Financial data   The stipend for full-time study is $2,000 per academic year, not to exceed $8,000 during an entire program of study. The stipend for part-time study is prorated appropriately.

Duration   1 year; may be renewed (if satisfactory progress is maintained) for up to 3 additional years.

Additional data   This program, which stands for Helping Educate Reservists and their Offspring, was established in 2005.

Number awarded   Varies each year.

Deadline   June of each year.

[959]
GLOBAL FIRST RESPONDERS SCHOLARSHIP

National Law Enforcement and Firefighters Children's
   Foundation
928 Broadway, Suite 703
New York, NY 10010
(646) 822-4236   E-mail: nleafcf@ncleafcf.org
Web: www.nleafcf.org

Summary   To provide financial assistance as college freshmen to the children of law enforcement officers and firefighters who were killed or disabled in the line of duty.

Eligibility   This program is open to the dependent children (including stepchildren and adopted children) of law enforcement officers and firefighters who were killed or totally and permanently disabled in the line of duty. Applicants must be entering full-time freshmen at a college, university, or vocational/technical institute in the United States. They must be U.S. citizens or permanent residents. Preference is given to students who reside or attend school in the New York tri-state area (Connecticut, New Jersey, New York). Selection is based on academics, demonstrated leadership, outstanding performance in the arts or sports, volunteer activities benefiting the community, and financial need.

Financial data   The stipend is $5,000 per year. Funds are paid directly to the recipient's institution.

Duration   4 years, provided the recipient remains enrolled full time and maintains a GPA of 2.7 or higher.

Additional data   This program began in 2016 as a partnership with the Global Foundation for First Responders.

Number awarded   1 each year.

Deadline   June of each year.

[960]
GOLDEN CORRAL SCHOLARSHIP FUND

National Multiple Sclerosis Society-Greater Carolinas
   Chapter
3101 Industrial Drive, Suite 210
Raleigh, NC 27609
(919) 834-0678   Toll Free: (800) 344-4867
Fax: (704) 527-0406   E-mail: nct@nmss.org
Web: www.nationalmssociety.org

Summary   To provide financial assistance to high school seniors and graduates from South Carolina and North Carolina who have multiple sclerosis (MS) or have a parent with MS and who are planning to attend college in any state.

Eligibility   This program is open to graduating high school seniors, recent graduates, and GED recipients from South Carolina and North Carolina who have MS or a parent who has MS. Applicants must be planning to enroll as a first-time student at a 2- or 4-year college, university, or vocational/technical school in the United States on at least a half-time basis. Along with their application, they must submit an essay on the impact MS has had on their lives. Selection is based on that essay, academic record, leadership and participation in school or community activities, work experience, goals and aspirations, an outside appraisal, special circumstances, and financial need. U.S. citizenship or permanent resident status is required.

Financial data   Stipends range up to $3,000.

Duration   1 year.

Additional data   This program, which operates jointly with the Central North Carolina chapter, receives support from the Golden Corral Corporation.

Number awarded   Varies each year; recently, 50 were awarded.

Deadline   January of each year.

[961]
GREAT LAKES HEMOPHILIA FOUNDATION EDUCATION SCHOLARSHIPS

Great Lakes Hemophilia Foundation
Attn: Program Services Committee
638 North 18th Street, Suite 108
Milwaukee, WI 53233
(414) 937-6782   Toll Free: (888) 797-GLHF
Fax: (414) 257-1225   E-mail: kkoppen@glhf.org
Web: www.glhf.org/what-we-do/scholarships

Summary To provide financial assistance to Wisconsin residents who have a bleeding disorder (and their families) and are interested in attending college in any state.

Eligibility This program is open to members of the bleeding disorder community in Wisconsin. Applicants must be attending or planning to attend college, vocational school, technical school, or a certification program in any state. Along with their application, they must submit an essay of 500 to 750 words on their educational and career goals, what they have done to work toward achieving those goals, how the education or training program in which they are enrolled will help them meet their goals, what they consider the most significant challenges associated with living with a bleeding disorder, the opportunities or benefits have those challenges provided them, and how they plan on contributing back to the bleeding disorders community. First priority is given to people affected by bleeding disorders, then to parents of young children with bleeding disorders, and then to spouses of individuals with bleeding disorders. If sufficient funds are available, consideration may be given to siblings and other family members of individuals with a bleeding disorder. Financial need is considered in the selection process.

Financial data Stipends range up to $3,000.

Duration 1 year.

Number awarded Varies each year; recently, 3 were awarded.

Deadline April of each year.

[962]
GREEN BERET FOUNDATION AND NO GREATER SACRIFICE SCHOLARSHIP AWARD IN MEMORY OF SGM WALTER SHUMATE AND SSG ROBERT MILLER

Green Beret Foundation
14402 Blanco Road, Suite 101
San Antonio, TX 78216
(910) 787-3309   Toll Free: (844) 287-7133
E-mail: angie@greenberetfoundation.org
Web: www.greenberetfoundation.org/scholarships

Summary To provide financial assistance to children of soldiers previously assigned to Special Forces but who are currently rated as disabled.

Eligibility This program is open to children of wounded, ill, or injured U.S. Army Special Forces soldiers who are rated as 60% disabled or higher. Applicants must be enrolled or planning to enroll at a college or university. They must have a GPA of 2.5 or higher. Along with their application, they must submit transcripts that include SAT and/or ACT scores; a 1-page resume with information about their extracurricular activities, honors, employment, community service, and special skills; and an essay of 500 to 1,000 words explaining their need, intended use of the scholarship, and how their experiences or their family member's experiences in the Special Forces have affected them.

Financial data Funding for this program is based on the Post-9/11 GI Bill, which covers tuition at the rate of the highest-cost public institution in the recipient's home state.

Duration 1 year.

Additional data This program operates in partnership with the No Greater Sacrifice Foundation.

Number awarded 1 or more each year.

Deadline May.

[963]
GTF SIBLING SCHOLARSHIP

Georgia Transplant Foundation
Attn: Scholarship Program
2201 Macy Drive
Roswell, GA 30076
(770) 457-3796   Fax: (770) 457-7916
E-mail: gtf@gatransplant.org
Web: www.gatransplant.org

Summary To provide financial assistance to residents of Georgia who are siblings of transplant recipients and interested in attending college in any state.

Eligibility This program is open to residents of Georgia who are entering or continuing at an accredited institution of higher learning in any state. Applicants must be the sibling of an organ transplant recipient (both the sibling and the recipient must be under 22 years of age). Along with their application, they must submit a 3-page personal statement on their career objectives, how this scholarship will help them attain their goals, and how transplantation has affected their life. Selection is based on that statement, transcripts, high school exit examination scores, ACT/SAT scores, 3 letters of reference, and financial need.

Financial data The stipend is $1,000 per year.

Duration 1 year; may be renewed up to 3 additional years.

Number awarded 1 each year.

Deadline April of each year.

[964]
HARVEY PICKER HORIZON SCHOLARSHIPS

Maine Employers' Mutual Insurance Company
Attn: MEMIC Education Fund
261 Commercial Street
P.O. Box 11409
Portland, ME 04104
(207) 791-3300   Toll Free: (800) 660-1306
Fax: (207) 791-3336   E-mail: mbourque@memic.com
Web: www.memic.com

Summary To provide financial assistance to Maine residents whose parent or spouse was killed or permanently disabled in a work-related accident and are interested in attending college or graduate school in any state.

Eligibility This program is open to Maine residents who are the child or spouse of a worker killed or permanently disabled as the result of a work-related injury. The worker must have been insured through the sponsor at the time of the workplace injury. Applicants must be attending or planning to attend an accredited college or university in any state as an undergraduate or graduate student. Along with their application, they must submit a 500-word personal statement on their aspirations and how their educational plans relate to those. Selection is based on financial need, academic performance, community involvement, other life experiences, and future promise.

Financial data Stipends range up to $5,000, depending on the need of the recipient. Funds are paid directly to the recipient's institution.

Duration 1 year; may be renewed.

Additional data The Maine Employers' Mutual Insurance Company (MEMIC) was established in 1993 as the result of reforms in Maine's workers' compensation laws. It is currently the largest workers' compensation insurance company in the state. It established this scholarship program in 2001.

Number awarded 1 or more each year.

Deadline April of each year.

[965]
HAWKINS SPIZMAN KILGO, LLC CHILDHOOD CANCER AWARENESS SCHOLARSHIP

Hawkins Spizman Kilgo, LLC
1535 Mount Vernon Road, Suite 200
Atlanta, GA 30338
(770) 685-6400   Fax: (770) 685-6403
E-mail: info@hawkinsduilaw.com
Web: www.hawkinsduilaw.com

Summary To provide financial assistance to undergraduate and graduate students who are survivors of childhood cancer or loved ones of survivors.

Eligibility This program is open to students currently enrolled or accepted for enrollment as an undergraduate or graduate student at an accredited college or university in any state. Applicants must be a survivor or childhood cancer or a loved one who has been directly affected by childhood cancer. They must have a GPA of 2.8 or higher. Along with their application, they must submit an essay of 500 to 1,000 words on 1 of the following: 1) how childhood cancer affected them; 2) how cancer has influenced their dreams and career goals; or 3) what they would say to a young person who has just been diagnosed with cancer to help them prepare for their future.

Financial data The stipend is $1,000.

Duration 1 year.

Number awarded 1 each year.

Deadline July of each year.

[966]
HAZLEWOOD ACT FOR SPOUSE/CHILD

Texas Veterans Commission
1700 North Congress Avenue, Suite 800
P.O. Box 12277
Austin, TX 78711-2277
(512) 463-6160   Toll Free: (877) 898-3833
Fax: (512) 463-3932 E-mail: education@tvc.texas.gov
Web: www.tvc.texas.gov/Hazlewood-Act.aspx

Summary To exempt children and spouses of disabled or deceased U.S. veterans from payment of tuition at public universities in Texas.

Eligibility This program is open to residents of Texas whose parent or spouse was a resident of the state at the time of entry into the U.S. armed forces, the Texas National Guard, or the Texas Air National Guard. The veteran parent or spouse must have died as a result of service-related injuries or illness, be missing in action, or have become totally disabled as a result of service-related injury or illness. Applicants must have no remaining federal education benefits. They must be attending or planning to attend a public college or university in the state and have no available federal veterans educational benefits. Children of veterans must be 25 years of age or younger.

Financial data Eligible students are exempt from payment of tuition, dues, fees, and charges at state-supported colleges and universities in Texas.

Duration 1 year; may be renewed.

Additional data This program was previously administered by the Texas Higher Education Coordinating Board but was transferred to the Texas Veterans Commission in 2013.

Number awarded Varies each year; recently, 2,183 dependents received $12,690,827 in support and 342 spouses received $1,172,875 in support.

Deadline Deadline not specified.

[967]
HEMOPHILIA FEDERATION OF AMERICA PARENT/SIBLING/CHILD EDUCATIONAL SCHOLARSHIP

Hemophilia Federation of America
Attn: Scholarship Committee
820 First Street, N.E., Suite 720
Washington, DC 20002
(202) 675-6984   Toll Free: (800) 230-9797
Fax: (202) 675-6983
E-mail: scholarship@hemophiliafed.org
Web: www.hemophiliafed.org

Summary To provide financial assistance for college to parents, siblings, and children of students with a bleeding disorder.

Eligibility This program is open to parents, siblings, and children of students who have a blood clotting disorder. Applicants must be attending or planning to attend an accredited 2- or 4-year college, university, or trade school in any state. Along with their application, they must submit a 1-page essay on their goals and aspirations and how the bleeding community has played a part in their lives. Financial need is considered in the selection process.

Financial data The stipend is $2,000 per year.

Duration 1 year; may be renewed.

Number awarded 1 each year.

Deadline April of each year.

[968]
HEMOPHILIA FOUNDATION OF MICHIGAN ACADEMIC SCHOLARSHIPS

Hemophilia Foundation of Michigan
Attn: Outreach and Community Education Manager
1921 West Michigan Avenue
Ypsilanti, MI 48197
(734) 544-0015   Toll Free: (800) 482-3041
Fax: (734) 544-0095   E-mail: lclothier@hfmich.org
Web: www.hfmich.org/?module=Page&sID=scholarships

Summary To provide financial assistance to Michigan residents with hemophilia and their families who are interested in attending college in any state.

Eligibility This program is open to high school seniors, high school graduates, and currently-enrolled college students who are Michigan residents and have hemophilia or another bleeding disorder. Family members of people with bleeding disorders and family members of people who have died from the complications of a bleeding disorder are also eligible. Applicants must submit a 300-word statement on their educational and career goals, the role that the bleeding disorder has played in influencing those goals, and how receiving the scholarship will help them to meet those goals. Selection is based on that statement, academic merit, employment status, reference letters, financial need, and the impact of bleeding disorder on educational activities.

Financial data The stipend is $2,500.

Duration 1 year; recipients may reapply.

Number awarded 2 each year.

Deadline March of each year.

[969]
HEMOPHILIA OF IOWA SCHOLARSHIPS

Hemophilia of Iowa, Inc.
Attn: Scholarship Committee
6300 Rockwell Drive, N.E., Suite 104
Cedar Rapids, IA 52402-7220
Toll Free: (319) 393-4007
E-mail: hoi_director@hemophiliaofiowa.com
Web: www.hemophiliaofiowa.org/scholarships.html

Summary To provide financial assistance to members of Hemophilia of Iowa who are interested in attending college in any state.

Eligibility This program is open to members of the sponsoring organization who either have hemophilia (or a related bleeding disorder) or are the immediate family member (caregiver, sibling, child) of someone who has hemophilia or a related bleeding disorder. Applicants may be graduating high school seniors or students currently enrolled at an accredited college, university, or trade school in any state. Along with their application, they must

submit brief statements on 1) their short- and long-range career plans; and 2) their personal background related to the bleeding disorder community. Selection is based on personal qualities and community service. Applicants who have a record of outstanding support for the mission of Hemophilia of Iowa are considered for supplemental funding provided by the John Heisner Scholarship and the Dude Cremer Scholarship.

Financial data The stipend is $1,000 for students with a bleeding disorder or $750 for family members. Applicants selected for the supplemental funding provided by the named scholarships receive an additional $500.

Duration 1 semester; recipients may reapply.

Number awarded Varies each year; recently, 20 were awarded.

Deadline April of each year.

[970]
HEROES' LEGACY SCHOLARSHIPS

Fisher House Foundation
111 Rockville Pike, Suite 420
Rockville, MD 20850
Toll Free: (888) 294-8560
E-mail: bgawne@fisherhouse.org
Web: www.militaryscholar.org/legacy/index.html

Summary To provide financial assistance for college to the children of deceased and disabled veterans and military personnel.

Eligibility This program is open to the unmarried sons and daughters of U.S. military servicemembers (including active duty, retirees, Guard/Reserves, and survivors) who are high school seniors or full-time students at an accredited college, university, or community college and younger than 23 years of age. Applicants must have at least 1 parent who, while serving on active duty after September 11, 2001, either died or became disabled, defined as qualified for receipt of Traumatic Servicemembers Group Life Insurance (TSGLI) or rated as 100% permanently and totally disabled by the U.S. Department of Veterans Affairs. High school applicants must have a GPA of 3.0 or higher and college applicants must have a GPA of 2.5 or higher. Along with their application, they must submit a 500-word essay on a topic that changes annually; recently, students were asked to write on the greatest challenge military families face. Selection is based on that essay, academic achievement, work experience, and participation in school, community, and volunteer activities.

Financial data The stipend is $5,000 per year.

Duration 1 year; recipients may reapply.

Additional data This program began in 2010 with proceeds from the sale of the book *Of Thee I Sing: A Letter to My Daughters* by President Barack Obama.

Number awarded Varies each year, depending on the availability of funds. In its first 3 years, the program awarded 130 scholarships.

Deadline March of each year.

[971]
HOPE FOR THE WARRIORS SPOUSE/ CAREGIVER SCHOLARSHIPS

Hope for the Warriors
Attn: Spouse/Caregiver Scholarships Director
8003 Forbes Place, Suite 201
Springfield, VA 22151
Toll Free: (877) 246-7349
E-mail: scholarships@hopeforthewarriors.org
Web: www.hopeforthewarriors.org

Summary To provide financial assistance for college to the spouses and caregivers of wounded or deceased military personnel or veterans.

Eligibility This program is open to spouses and caregivers of current and former servicemembers who were wounded or killed in the line of duty while serving in support of Operation Enduring Freedom and/or Operation Iraqi Freedom. Support is available in 5 categories: 1) Honorary Scholarships, for those seeking graduate or postgraduate degrees; 2) New Beginnings Scholarships, awarded to those pursuing entry-level classes or training; 3) Restoring Family Scholarships, awarded to spouses of the fallen; 4) Restoring Hope Scholarships, awarded to master's in social work students; or 5) Restoring Self Scholarships, awarded to those seeking any undergraduate degree. Applicants in all categories must submit a 1,500-word essay on the challenges they have experienced as a spouse/caregiver and have overcome, what they have learned about themselves through the spouse/ caregiver experience, some of their future goals, and how this scholarship would impact those goals. Selection is based on that essay, academic achievement, personal goals, and letters of recommendation.

Financial data A stipend is awarded (amount not specified); funds are paid directly to the recipient's institution.

Duration 1 year; may be renewed up to 3 additional years.

Number awarded Varies each year.

Deadline May of each year.

[972]
HSC ACADEMIC SCHOLARSHIP PROGRAM

Hemophilia of South Carolina
Attn: Academic Scholarship Awards Program
439 Congaree Road, Suite 5
Greenville, SC 29607
(864) 350-9941   Fax: (864) 244-8287
E-mail: Info@hemophiliasc.org
Web: www.hemophiliasc.org/services

Summary To provide financial assistance to residents of South Carolina who are affiliated with the bleeding disorders community and interested in attending college in any state.

Eligibility This program is open to residents of South Carolina who are persons with a bleeding disorder or children, siblings, parents, or spouses of someone with a bleeding disorder. Applicants must be enrolled or planning to enroll at an accredited college, university, or vocational/ technical school in any state. Along with their application,

they must submit transcripts that include SAT scores; a summary about themselves that includes a statement of their goals for the future, volunteer work, awards, and organizations to which they belong; and an essay on the impact that hemophilia has had on them and their family. Selection is based on that essay, academic merit, leadership qualities, reference letters, and financial need.

Financial data The stipend ranges from $500 to $1,500. Funds are paid directly to the recipient's school.

Duration 1 year.

Number awarded Up to 5 each year.

Deadline May of each year.

[973]
HUEY AND ANGELINA WILSON NONTRADITIONAL SCHOLARSHIPS

Louisiana Hemophilia Foundation
Attn: Scholarship Committee
3636 South Sherwood Forest Boulevard, Suite 390
Baton Rouge, LA 70816-5211
(225) 291-1675   Toll Free: (800) 749-1680
Fax: (225) 291-1679   E-mail: contact@lahemo.org
Web: www.lahemo.org/services/scholarships

Summary To provide financial assistance for college in the state to Louisiana residents who are nontraditional students and a hemophilia patient or the parent of a patient.

Eligibility This program is open to residents of Louisiana who are a hemophilia patient or the parent of a patient. Applicants must be enrolled or planning to enroll at a Louisiana college or university as a nontraditional student. Along with their application, they must submit a 250-word essay on why they should receive this scholarship.

Financial data The stipend is $1,000 per semester.

Duration 1 semester. Recipients may reapply if they remain enrolled full time, have a GPA of 2.75 or higher, and provide 8 hours of community service to the sponsoring organization.

Number awarded Varies each semester; the foundation first awards scholarships to traditional students; if funds remain, it may award scholarships to qualified nontraditional students.

Deadline June of each year for fall semester; December of each year for spring semester.

[974]
IDAHO ARMED FORCES AND PUBLIC SAFETY OFFICER SCHOLARSHIPS

Idaho State Board of Education
Attn: Scholarships Program Manager
650 West State Street, Room 307
P.O. Box 83720
Boise, ID 83720-0037
(208) 334-2270   Fax: (208) 334-2632
E-mail: scholarshiphelp@osbe.idaho.gov
Web: www.boardofed.idaho.gov

Summary To provide financial assistance for college in Idaho to dependents of certain members of the armed forces and of disabled or deceased public safety officers.

Eligibility This program is open to spouses and children of 1) Idaho residents determined by the federal government to have been prisoners of war, missing in action, or killed in action or died of injuries or wounds sustained in any area of armed conflict to which the United States was a party; 2) any member of the armed forces stationed in Idaho and deployed from Idaho to any area of armed conflict to which the United States was a party and who has been determined by the federal government to be a prisoner of war or missing action or to have died of or become totally and permanently disabled by injuries or wounds sustained in action as a result of such deployment; or 3) full- or part-time Idaho public safety officers (peace officer, firefighter, paramedic, or EMT) employed by or volunteering for the state or a political subdivision who were killed or totally and permanently disabled in the line of duty. Applicants must be Idaho residents enrolled or planning to enroll at a public institution of higher education in the state.

Financial data Each scholarship provides a full waiver of tuition and fees at public institutions of higher education or public vocational schools within Idaho, an allowance of $500 per semester for books, on-campus housing, and a campus meal plan.

Duration Benefits are available for a maximum of 36 months (4 academic years).

Number awarded Varies each year.

Deadline Applications may be submitted at any time.

[975]
ILLINOIS CHILDREN OF VETERANS SCHOLARSHIPS

Illinois Department of Veterans' Affairs
833 South Spring Street
P.O. Box 19432
Springfield, IL 62794-9432
(217) 782-6641   Toll Free: (800) 437-9824 (within IL)
Fax: (217) 524-0344   TDD: (217) 524-4645
E-mail: webmail@dva.state.il.us
Web: www.illinois.gov

Summary To provide financial assistance for college to the children of Illinois veterans (with preference given to the children of disabled or deceased veterans).

Eligibility Each county in the state is entitled to award an honorary scholarship to the child of a veteran of World War I, World War II, the Korean Conflict, the Vietnam Conflict, or any time after August 2, 1990. Preference is given to children of disabled or deceased veterans.

Financial data Students selected for this program receive free tuition at any branch of the University of Illinois.

Duration Up to 4 years.

Number awarded Each county in Illinois is entitled to award 1 scholarship. The Board of Trustees of the university may, from time to time, add to the number of honorary scholarships (when such additions will not create an unnecessary financial burden on the university).

Deadline Deadline not specified.

[976]
ILLINOIS GRANT PROGRAM FOR DEPENDENTS OF CORRECTIONAL OFFICERS

Illinois Student Assistance Commission
Attn: Scholarship and Grant Services
1755 Lake Cook Road
Deerfield, IL 60015-5209
(847) 948-8550   Toll Free: (800) 899-ISAC
Fax: (847) 831-8549   TDD: (800) 526-0844
E-mail: isac.studentservices@isac.illinois.gov
Web: www.isac.org

Summary To provide financial assistance to the children or spouses of disabled or deceased Illinois correctional workers who plan to attend college in the state.

Eligibility This program is open to the spouses and children of Illinois correctional officers who were at least 90% disabled or killed in the line of duty. Applicants must be enrolled on at least a half-time basis as an undergraduate at an approved Illinois public or private 2- or 4-year college or university. They need not be Illinois residents at the time of application. U.S. citizenship or eligible noncitizen status is required.

Financial data The grants provide full payment of tuition and mandatory fees at approved public colleges in Illinois or an equivalent amount at private colleges.

Duration Up to 8 academic semesters or 12 academic quarters of study.

Number awarded Varies each year.

Deadline September of each year for the academic year; February of each year for spring semester or winter or spring quarter; June of each year for summer term.

[977]
ILLINOIS GRANT PROGRAM FOR DEPENDENTS OF POLICE OR FIRE OFFICERS

Illinois Student Assistance Commission
Attn: Scholarship and Grant Services
1755 Lake Cook Road
Deerfield, IL 60015-5209
(847) 948-8550   Toll Free: (800) 899-ISAC
Fax: (847) 831-8549   TDD: (800) 526-0844
E-mail: isac.studentservices@isac.illinois.gov
Web: www.isac.org

Summary To provide financial assistance to the children or spouses of disabled or deceased Illinois police or fire officers who plan to attend college or graduate school in the state.

Eligibility This program is open to the spouses and children of Illinois police and fire officers who were at least 90% disabled or killed in the line of duty. Applicants must be enrolled on at least a half-time basis in either undergraduate or graduate study at an approved Illinois public or private 2- or 4-year college, university, or hospital school. They need not be Illinois residents at the time of application. U.S. citizenship or eligible noncitizen status is required.

Financial data The grants provide full payment of tuition and mandatory fees at approved public colleges in Illinois or an equivalent amount at private colleges.

Duration Up to 8 academic semesters or 12 academic quarters of study.

Number awarded Varies each year.

Deadline September of each year for the academic year; February of each year for spring semester or winter or spring quarter; June of each year for summer term.

[978]
ILLINOIS MIA/POW SCHOLARSHIP

Illinois Department of Veterans' Affairs
833 South Spring Street
P.O. Box 19432
Springfield, IL 62794-9432
(217) 782-3564   Toll Free: (800) 437-9824 (within IL)
Fax: (217) 524-0344   TDD: (217) 524-4645
E-mail: webmail@dva.state.il.us
Web: www2.illinois.gov

Summary To provide financial assistance for 1) the undergraduate education of Illinois dependents of disabled or deceased veterans or those listed as prisoners of war or missing in action; and 2) the rehabilitation or education of disabled dependents of those veterans.

Eligibility This program is open to the spouses, natural children, legally adopted children, or stepchildren of a veteran or servicemember who 1) has been declared by the U.S. Department of Veterans Affairs to be permanently disabled from service-connected causes with 100% disability, deceased as the result of a service-connected disability, a prisoner of war, or missing in action; and 2) at the time of entering service was an Illinois resident or was an Illinois resident within 6 months of entering such service.

Financial data An eligible dependent is entitled to full payment of tuition and certain fees at any Illinois state-supported college, university, or community college. The total benefit cannot exceed the cost equivalent of 4 calendar years of full-time enrollment, including summer terms, at the University of Illinois.

Duration This scholarship may be used for a period equivalent to 4 calendar years, including summer terms. Dependents have 12 years from the initial term of study to complete the equivalent of 4 calendar years.

Number awarded Varies each year.

Deadline Deadline not specified.

[979]
INDIANA CHILDREN AND SPOUSES OF PUBLIC SAFETY OFFICERS PROGRAM

Indiana Commission for Higher Education
Attn: Financial Aid and Student Support Services
101 West Ohio Street, Suite 300
Indianapolis, IN 46204-4206
(317) 232-1023   Toll Free: (888) 528-4719 (within IN)
Fax: (317) 232-3260   E-mail: Scholars@che.in.gov
Web: www.in.gov/che/4520.htm

Summary To provide financial assistance to residents of Indiana who are the children or spouses of specified categories of deceased or disabled public safety officers and interested in attending college or graduate school in the state.

Eligibility This program is open to 1) children of public safety officers (law enforcement officers, firefighters, paramedics, and emergency medical technicians) who were killed in the line of duty when the child was younger than 24 years of age; 2) spouses of public safety officers killed in the line of duty; 3) children younger than 23 years of age of a permanently disabled state trooper; and 4) spouses of permanently disabled state troopers. Applicants must be enrolled or planning to enroll at an eligible Indiana institution (for a list, contact the sponsor). Children must be enrolled full time and working on an undergraduate or graduate degree; spouses may be enrolled part time but may only be undergraduate students.

Financial data Qualified applicants receive a 100% remission of tuition and all mandatory fees at eligible colleges and universities in Indiana. Support is not provided for such fees as room and board.

Duration Up to 8 semesters for children of deceased public safety officers or up to 124 hours of study for other categories of students.

Number awarded Varies each year.

Deadline Applications must be submitted at least 30 days before the start of the college term.

[980]
INDIANA CHILDREN OF DECEASED OR DISABLED VETERANS PROGRAM

Indiana Commission for Higher Education
Attn: Financial Aid and Student Support Services
101 West Ohio Street, Suite 300
Indianapolis, IN 46204-4206
(317) 232-1023   Toll Free: (888) 528-4719 (within IN)
Fax: (317) 232-3260   E-mail: Scholars@che.in.gov
Web: www.in.gov/che/4517.htm

Summary To provide financial assistance to residents of Indiana who are the children of deceased or disabled veterans and interested in attending college in the state.

Eligibility This program is open to residents of Indiana whose parent served in the U.S. armed forces during a war or performed duty equally hazardous that was recognized by the award of a U.S. service or campaign medal, suffered a service-connected death or disability, and received a discharge or separation other than dishonorable. Applicants must be the biological child of the veteran or legally adopted prior to their 24th birthday; stepchildren are not eligible. Parents who enlisted on or before June 30, 2011 must have resided in Indiana for at least 36 consecutive months during their lifetime. Parents who enlisted after June 30, 2011 must have designated Indiana as home of record at the time of enlistment or resided in that state at least 5 years before the child first applies for the benefit.

Financial data If the veterans parent initially enlisted on or before June 30, 2011, the child receives a 100% remission of tuition and all mandatory fees for undergraduate, graduate, or professional degrees at eligible postsecondary schools and universities in Indiana. If the veteran parent initially enlisted after June 30, 2011 and suffered a disability with a rating of 80% or more, the child receives a 100% remission of tuition and all mandatory fees for undergraduate or professional degrees at eligible postsecondary schools and universities in Indiana. If the veteran parent initially enlisted after June 30, 2011 and suffered a disability with a rating less than 80%, the rate of remission for tuition and regularly assessed fees is 20% plus the disability rating. Support is not provided for such fees as room and board.

Duration Up to 124 semester hours of study. If the veteran parent initially enlisted on or before June 30, 2011, there is no time limit to use those hours. If the veteran parent initially enlisted after June 30, 2011, the allotted 124 credit hours must be used within 8 years after the date the child first applied.

Number awarded Varies each year.

Deadline Applications must be submitted at least 30 days before the start of the college term.

[981]
INDIANA DONOR NETWORK FOUNDATION SCHOLARSHIP

Indiana Donor Network, Inc.
Attn: Foundation/Care Council
3760 Guion Road
Indianapolis, IN 46222-1618
(317) 685-0389   Toll Free: (888) 275-4676
E-mail: info@INDonorNetwork.org
Web: www.indianadonornetwork.org

Summary To provide financial assistance to residents of Indiana who have been involved in organ or tissue donation and are interested in attending college in any state.

Eligibility This program is open to family members of Indiana organ and tissue donors as well as living organ donors, transplant recipients, people waiting for organs, and their families. Applicants must be enrolled or planning to enroll full or part time at a college, university, or technical school in any state. They must have a GPA of 2.0 or higher. There are no age limitations and nontraditional students are encouraged to apply. Along with their application, they must submit a 2- to 5-page essay on their career goals, experience with organ or tissue donation and/or transplantation, and personal goals.

Financial data A stipend is awarded (amount not specified).

Duration 1 year; nonrenewable.

Number awarded Varies each year.

Deadline March of each year.

[982]
INDIANA DONOR NETWORK SCHOLARSHIPS

Indiana Donor Network
Attn: Foundation
3760 Guion Road
Indianapolis, IN 46222-1618
(317) 685-0389   Toll Free: (888) 275-4676
E-mail: info@INDonorNetwork.org
Web: www.indianadonornetwork.org

Summary To provide financial assistance for college attendance in any state to Indiana residents who are organ, tissue, or eye transplant donors, recipients, candidates, or their families.

Eligibility This program is open to Indiana residents who are organ, tissue, or eye transplant donors, recipients, candidates, or relatives (including spouses, parents, children, grandchildren, siblings, aunts, uncles, nieces, nephews, and cousins). Applicants must be high school seniors or students already attending a college or technical school in any state on a full- or part-time basis. They must have a GPA of 2.0 or higher; high school seniors must be in the top 50% of their class. Along with their application, they must submit a 1,500-word essay describing their career goals, experience with organ or tissue donation and/or transplantation, and personal goals. Financial need is considered in the selection process.

Financial data Recently, stipends were $3,000, $2,000, or $1,000.

Duration 1 year; nonrenewable.

Additional data This organization was formerly named the Indiana Organ Procurement Organization (IOPO).

Number awarded Varies each year; recently, 3 were awarded: 1 at $3,000, 1 at $2,000, and 1 at $1,000.

Deadline March of each year.

[983]
ISABELLE CHRISTENSON MEMORIAL SCHOLARSHIP

Izzie's Gifts of Hope Foundation
c/o Center for Organ Recovery and Education
204 Sigma Drive
RIDC Park
Pittsburgh, PA 15238
(724) 591-6009   E-mail: izziesgifts@gmail.com
Web: www.izziesgifts.org/scholarships.php

Summary To provide financial assistance for college to organ transplant candidates, donors, recipients, and their families.

Eligibility This program is open to organ transplant candidates, recipients, donor family members, and immediate family members of a transplant candidate or recipient. Applicants must be attending or planning to attend a college, university, or trade/technical school. Along with their application, they must submit an explanation of how donation/transplantation has influenced their life; an explanation of what they have done or what you will do to promote organ, tissue and cornea donation; a description of any community service in which they have taken part; a statement on their educational and career goals; and 2 letters of recommendation.

Financial data A stipend is awarded (amount not specified).

Duration 1 year; nonrenewable.

Additional data This program awarded its first scholarship in 2010.

Number awarded Varies each year; recently, 7 were awarded.

Deadline March of each year.

[984]
J. PARIS MOSLEY SCHOLARSHIP

Cleveland Foundation
Attn: Scholarship Processing
1422 Euclid Avenue, Suite 1300
Cleveland, OH 44115-2001
(216) 861-3810   Fax: (216) 861-1729
E-mail: TCFscholarships@clevefdn.org
Web: www.clevelandfoundation.org

Summary To provide financial assistance for college to high school seniors in any state who are deaf or whose primary caregivers are deaf.

Eligibility This program is open to high school seniors in any state who are deaf or hard of hearing or have a relative living in their household who is deaf or hard of hearing. Applicants must be planning to attend a college, university, vocational school, or other postsecondary program in any state. They must use some form of sign language, have a GPA of 2.5 or higher, and be able to demonstrate financial need. Preference is given to students of African American, Latino American, or Native American descent.

Financial data The stipend ranges from $500 to $1,000.

Duration 1 year.

Number awarded 1 or more each year.

Deadline March of each year.

[985]
JACKIE SPELLMAN SCHOLARSHIPS

Jackie Spellman Scholarship Foundation
935 Eldridge Road
Box 200
Sugar Land, TX 77478
Toll Free: (888) 553-JSSF
E-mail: jackiespellmanfoundation@gmail.com
Web: www.jackiespellmanbenefit.org/scholarship.shtml

Summary To provide financial assistance for college or graduate school to students who have or whose family member has leukemia or lymphoma.

Eligibility This program is open to high school seniors, community college and 4-year university students, and graduate students who are leukemia or lymphoma survivors, patients, and/or children, siblings, or parents of leukemia or lymphoma patients. Applicants must be U.S. citizens and enrolled or planning to enroll full time. They must have a GPA of 3.0 or higher and be able to demonstrate financial need. Along with their application, they must submit transcripts; SAT and/or ACT test scores; documentation of financial need; a letter describing any special circumstances that have impacted their academic performance, community service, or leadership activities (if relevant); and an essay of 600 to 800 words describing how leukemia or lymphoma has affected their life, their future plans and desired career path, and how this scholarship will impact them. Students majoring in health or nursing-related majors may receive priority.

Financial data Stipends range from $1,000 to $5,000.

Duration 1 year.

Number awarded Approximately 15 each year.

Deadline April of each year.

[986]
JACOB N. SHANBERGE, M.D. MEMORIAL SCHOLARSHIP

Great Lakes Hemophilia Foundation
Attn: Program Services Committee
638 North 18th Street, Suite 108
Milwaukee, WI 53233
(414) 937-6782   Toll Free: (888) 797-GLHF
Fax: (414) 257-1225   E-mail: kkoppen@glhf.org
Web: www.glhf.org/what-we-do/scholarships

Summary To provide financial assistance to Wisconsin residents who have a bleeding disorder (and their families) and are interested in attending college in any state.

Eligibility This program is open to members of the bleeding disorder community in Wisconsin. Applicants must be attending or planning to attend college, vocational school, technical school, or a certification program in any state to prepare for a career in science or medicine. Along with their application, they must submit an essay of 500 to 750 words on their educational and career goals, what they have done to work toward achieving those goals, how the education or training program in which they are enrolled will help them meet their goals, what they consider the most significant challenges associated with living with a bleeding disorder, the opportunities or benefits have those challenges provided them, and how they plan on contributing back to the bleeding disorders community. First priority is given to people affected by bleeding disorders, then to parents of young children with bleeding disorders, and then to spouses of individuals with bleeding disorders. If sufficient funds are available, consideration may be given to siblings and other family members of individuals with a bleeding disorder. Financial need is considered in the selection process.

Financial data Stipends range up to $3,000.

Duration 1 year.

Number awarded 1 each year.

Deadline April of each year.

[987]
JACQUELINE SHEARER MEMORIAL SCHOLARSHIP

Ulman Cancer Fund for Young Adults
Attn: Scholarship Committee
921 East Fort Avenue, Suite 325
Baltimore, MD 21230
(410) 964-0202   Toll Free: (888) 393-FUND
Fax: (888) 964-0402
E-mail: scholarship@ulmanfund.org
Web: www.ulmanfund.org/scholarships

Summary To provide financial assistance for college or graduate school to students from the Baltimore/Washington metropolitan area who have or have lost a parent to cancer.

Eligibility This program is open to residents of the Baltimore/Washington metropolitan area who have or have lost a parent or guardian to cancer. Applicants must be 35 years of age or younger and attending, or planning to attend, a 2- or 4-year college, university, or vocational program in any state to work on an undergraduate or graduate degree. The parent or guardian must have been first diagnosed with cancer after the applicant was 15 years of age. Along with their application, they must submit a 500-word essay or 3-minute video on either 1) a letter that they would have liked to receive during their cancer experience; or 2) what they would tell the young adults who participate in the sponsor's summer-long drive to support the organization about being a young adult impacted by cancer. Financial need is considered in the selection process. U.S. citizenship or permanent resident status is required.

Financial data The stipend is $2,500. Funds are paid directly to the educational institution.

Duration 1 year.

Additional data Recipients are obligated to organize and run a bone marrow registry drive with the support of Delete Blood Cancer and There Goes My Hero.

Number awarded 2 each year.

Deadline March of each year.

[988]
JAMES AND PATRICIA SOOD SCHOLARSHIP

Ulman Cancer Fund for Young Adults
Attn: Scholarship Committee
921 East Fort Avenue, Suite 325
Baltimore, MD 21230
(410) 964-0202   Toll Free: (888) 393-FUND
Fax: (888) 964-0402
E-mail: scholarship@ulmanfund.org
Web: www.ulmanfund.org/scholarships

Summary To provide financial assistance to students who have been diagnosed with cancer or have or have lost a family member with cancer and are interested in working on an undergraduate or graduate degree in education.

Eligibility This program is open to students who 1) have been diagnosed with cancer; 2) have a parent or sibling living with cancer; or 3) have lost a parent or sibling to cancer. Applicants must be attending, or planning to attend, a college or university in any state to work on an undergraduate or graduate degree in education. The first diagnosis of cancer (whether of the applicant, a parent, or sibling) must have occurred after the applicant was 15 years of age. Along with their application, they must submit a 500-word essay or 3-minute video on either 1) a letter that they would have liked to receive during their cancer experience; or 2) what they would tell the young adults who participate in the sponsor's summer-long drive to support the organization about being a young adult impacted by cancer. U.S. citizenship or permanent resident status is required.

Financial data The stipend is $2,500. Funds are paid directly to the educational institution.

Duration 1 year.

Additional data Recipients are obligated to organize and run a bone marrow registry drive with the support of Delete Blood Cancer and There Goes My Hero.

Number awarded 1 each year.

Deadline March of each year.

[989]
JAMES DOYLE CASE MEMORIAL SCHOLARSHIPS

Mississippi Council of the Blind
c/o Randy Thompson, Scholarship Committee
107 Chalet Strasse
Brandon, MS 39042-2082
(601) 956-7906   E-mail: bonnieg06@comcast.net
Web: www.mscounciloftheblind.org/node/3

Summary To provide financial assistance to legally blind residents of Mississippi and their children who plan to attend college or graduate school in any state.

Eligibility This program is open to residents of Mississippi who are legally blind or the children of at least 1 legally blind parent. Applicants must be enrolled full time or accepted for enrollment in an undergraduate, graduate, or vocational/technical program in any state and have a GPA of 3.0 or higher. Along with their application, they must submit a 2-page autobiographical sketch, transcripts, standardized test scores (ACT or SAT for undergraduates; GRE, MCAT, LSAT, etc. for graduate students), 2 letters of recommendation, proof of acceptance from a postsecondary school, and verification of blindness of the qualifying person (applicant or parent).

Financial data The stipend is $1,500 per year.

Duration 4 years.

Number awarded 2 each year.

Deadline February of each year.

[990]
JAMIE L. ROBERTS MEMORIAL SCHOLARSHIP

Ulman Cancer Fund for Young Adults
Attn: Scholarship Committee
921 East Fort Avenue, Suite 325
Baltimore, MD 21230
(410) 964-0202   Toll Free: (888) 393-FUND
Fax: (888) 964-0402
E-mail: scholarship@ulmanfund.org
Web: www.ulmanfund.org/scholarships

Summary To provide financial assistance for college or graduate school to students who have been diagnosed with cancer or have or have lost a family member with cancer.

Eligibility This program is open to students who 1) have been diagnosed with cancer; 2) have a parent or sibling living with cancer; or 3) have lost a parent or sibling to cancer. Applicants must be attending, or planning to attend, a college or university in any state to work on an undergraduate, graduate, or professional degree. They should demonstrate the qualities of the program's namesake-an infectious positive attitude, love of adventure, and ability to inspire others to achieve higher goals. The first diagnosis of cancer (whether of the applicant, a parent, or sibling) must have occurred after the applicant was 15 years of age. Along with their application, they must submit a 500-word essay or 3-minute video on either 1) a letter that they would have liked to receive during their cancer experience; or 2) what they would tell the young adults who participate in the sponsor's summer-long drive to support the organization about being a young adult impacted by cancer. U.S. citizenship or permanent resident status is required.

Financial data The stipend is $2,500. Funds are paid directly to the educational institution.

Duration 1 year.

Additional data This program, which began in 2014, is funded by the 4K for Cancer, an organization of college students who ride bicycles across the country every summer and raise funds for cancer. Recipients are obligated to organize and run a bone marrow registry drive with the support of Delete Blood Cancer and There Goes My Hero.

Number awarded 6 each year.

Deadline March of each year.

[991]
JEAN B. CRYOR MEMORIAL SCHOLARSHIP PROGRAM

Maryland Higher Education Commission
Attn: Office of Student Financial Assistance
6 North Liberty Street, Ground Suite
Baltimore, MD 21201
(410) 767-3301   Toll Free: (800) 974-0203
Fax: (410) 332-0250   TDD: (800) 735-2258
E-mail: osfamail.mhec@maryland.gov
Web: www.mhec.state.md.us

Summary To provide financial assistance for college or graduate school in Maryland to children and spouses of victims of the September 11, 2001 terrorist attacks and specified categories of veterans, public safety employees, and their children or spouses.

Eligibility This program is open to entering and continuing undergraduate and graduate students in the following categories: 1) children and surviving spouses of victims of the September 11, 2001 terrorist attacks who died in the World Trade Center in New York City, in the Pentagon in Virginia, or on United Airlines Flight 93 in Pennsylvania; 2) veterans who have, as a direct result of military service, a disability of 25% or greater and have exhausted or are no longer eligible for federal veterans' educational benefits; 3) children and unremarried surviving spouses of armed forces members whose death or 100% disability was directly caused by military service; 4) POW/MIA veterans of the Vietnam Conflict and their children; 5) state or local public safety officers or volunteers who became 100% disabled in the line of duty; 6) children and unremarried surviving spouses of state or local public safety employees or volunteers who died or became 100% disabled in the line of duty. and 7) children and unremarried surviving spouses or a school employee who, as a result of an act of violence, either died in the line of duty or sustained an injury that rendered the school employee 100% disabled. The parent, spouse, veteran, POW, public safety officer or volunteer, or school employee must have been a resident of Maryland at the time of death or when declared

disabled. Applicants must be planning to enroll at a 2- or 4-year Maryland college or university as a full-time or part-time degree-seeking undergraduate or graduate student or attend a private career school. Financial need is not considered.

Financial data The amount of the award is equal to tuition and fees at a Maryland postsecondary institution, to a maximum of $10,182. The total amount of all Maryland scholarship awards from all sources may not exceed the cost of attendance or $19,000, whichever is less.

Duration Up to 5 years of full-time study or 8 years of part-time study.

Number awarded Varies each year.

Deadline July of each year.

[992]
JEANNE E. BRAY MEMORIAL SCHOLARSHIP

National Rifle Association of America
Attn: Law Enforcement Activities Division
11250 Waples Mill Road
Fairfax, VA 22030-7400
Toll Free: (800) 554-9498
E-mail: jebrayscholarship@nrahq.org
Web: awards.nra.org

Summary To provide financial assistance for college to children of law enforcement officers who are members of the National Rifle Association (NRA).

Eligibility This program is open to NRA members who are the dependent children of 1) currently serving full-time commissioned peace officers who are also NRA members; 2) deceased full-time commissioned peace officers who lost their lives in the performance of assigned peace officer duties and were current members of NRA at the time of their death; 3) full-time commissioned peace officers, disabled as a result of a line-of-duty incident, who are also NRA members; or 4) retired full-time commissioned peace officers who are also NRA members. Applicants must be U.S. citizens who have a GPA of 3.0 or higher and scores of at least 730 on the SAT I or 25 on the ACT. Along with their application, they must submit an essay of 500 to 700 words in support of the rights secured by the second amendment to the constitution.

Financial data The stipend is $5,000 per year.

Duration Up to 4 years, provided the recipient maintains a GPA of 2.0 or higher.

Number awarded 1 or more each year.

Deadline November of each year.

[993]
JILL WEAVER STARKMAN SCHOLARSHIP

Ulman Cancer Fund for Young Adults
Attn: Scholarship Committee
921 East Fort Avenue, Suite 325
Baltimore, MD 21230
(410) 964-0202   Toll Free: (888) 393-FUND
Fax: (888) 964-0402
E-mail: scholarship@ulmanfund.org
Web: www.ulmanfund.org/scholarships

Summary To provide financial assistance for college or graduate school to students who have been diagnosed with cancer or have or have lost a family member with cancer.

Eligibility This program is open to students who 1) have been diagnosed with cancer; 2) have a parent or sibling living with cancer; or 3) have lost a parent or sibling to cancer. Applicants must be attending, or planning to attend, a college or university in any state to work on an undergraduate, graduate, or professional degree. They should demonstrate the qualities of the program's namesake-the spirit of adventure and compassion and skill for communicating with humans and animals alike. The first diagnosis of cancer (whether of the applicant, a parent, or sibling) must have occurred after the applicant was 15 years of age. Along with their application, they must submit a 500-word essay or 3-minute video on either 1) a letter that they would have liked to receive during their cancer experience; or 2) what they would tell the young adults who participate in the sponsor's summer-long drive to support the organization about being a young adult impacted by cancer. U.S. citizenship or permanent resident status is required.

Financial data The stipend is $2,500. Funds are paid directly to the educational institution.

Duration 1 year.

Additional data This program began in 2012. Recipients are obligated to organize and run a bone marrow registry drive with the support of Delete Blood Cancer and There Goes My Hero.

Number awarded 1 each year.

Deadline March of each year.

[994]
JIM NOLAND FOUNDATION SCHOLARSHIP

Three Rivers Community Foundation
Attn: Executive Director
1333 Columbia Park Trail, Suite 310
Richland, WA 99352
(509) 735-5559   E-mail: carrie@3rcf.org
Web: www.3rcf.org

Summary To provide financial assistance to high school seniors in Washington who have lost a parent to cancer or are dealing with cancer in the immediate family and plan to attend college in any state.

Eligibility This program is open to seniors graduating from high schools in Washington who plan to enroll full time at a 2-year community college or 4-year public university in any state. Applicants must have lost a parent to cancer or be dealing with cancer in the immediate family. They must have a GPA of 3.0 or higher and be able to demonstrate financial need. Along with their application, they must submit a 250-word essay about themselves, their educational achievements, their future career goals, and how they plan to accomplish their goals; the essay must discuss how losing a parent to cancer or having an immediate family member with cancer has affected their life.

Financial data The stipend is $1,000 per year.

Duration 1 year; may be renewed, provided the recipient maintains a GPA of 3.0 or higher.

Number awarded 1 each year.

Deadline June of each year.

[995]
JOHN DUVALL MEMORIAL SCHOLARSHIP

Ulman Cancer Fund for Young Adults
Attn: Scholarship Committee
921 East Fort Avenue, Suite 325
Baltimore, MD 21230
(410) 964-0202   Toll Free: (888) 393-FUND
Fax: (888) 964-0402
E-mail: scholarship@ulmanfund.org
Web: www.ulmanfund.org/scholarships

Summary To provide financial assistance to students who have been diagnosed with cancer or have or have lost a family member with cancer and are interested in attending designated universities.

Eligibility This program is open to students who 1) have been diagnosed with cancer; 2) have a parent or sibling living with cancer; or 3) have lost a parent or sibling to cancer. Applicants must be working on or planning to work on an undergraduate, graduate, or professional degree at the University of Maryland, Towson University, Elon University, or the Savannah College of Art and Design. They must be able to demonstrate financial need. The first diagnosis of cancer (whether of the applicant, a parent, or sibling) must have occurred after the applicant was 15 years of age. Along with their application, they must submit a 500-word essay or 3-minute video on either 1) a letter that they would have liked to receive during their cancer experience; or 2) what they would tell the young adults who participate in the sponsor's summer-long drive to support the organization about being a young adult impacted by cancer. U.S. citizenship or permanent resident status is required.

Financial data The stipend is $2,500. Funds are paid directly to the educational institution.

Duration 1 year.

Additional data Recipients are obligated to organize and run a bone marrow registry drive with the support of Delete Blood Cancer and There Goes My Hero.

Number awarded 1 each year.

Deadline March of each year.

[996]
JOHN FOY & ASSOCIATES STRONG ARM LEUKEMIA SCHOLARSHIP

John Foy & Associates
3343 Peachtree Road, Suite 350
Atlanta, GA 30326
(404) 982-4326
Web: www.johnfoy.com

Summary To provide financial assistance to undergraduate and graduate students and their loved ones who have been affected by leukemia.

Eligibility This program is open to entering college freshmen, undergraduates, and graduate students at

accredited colleges and universities in any state. Applicants or a loved one must have been affected by leukemia. Along with their application, they must submit an essay of 500 to 1,000 words on 1 of the following: 1) how living with their or their loves one's leukemia has affected their education; 2) the adjustments they have made as a student to accommodate their or a loved one's leukemia; or 3) an obstacle that people with leukemia face that they want the general public to know about.
Financial data   The stipend is $1,000.
Duration   1 year.
Number awarded   1 each year.
Deadline   December of each year.

[997]
JOHN YOUTSEY MEMORIAL SCHOLARSHIP FUND

Hemophilia of Georgia
8800 Roswell Road, Suite 170
Atlanta, GA 30350-1844
(770) 518-8272   Fax: (770) 518-3310
E-mail: mail@hog.org
Web: www.hog.org/programs/page/scholarships

Summary   To provide financial assistance to residents of Georgia who have a bleeding disorder or have lost a parent because of the disorder and are interested in attending college in any state.
Eligibility   This program is open to residents of Georgia who 1) have hemophilia, von Willebrand Disease, or other inherited bleeding disorder; or 2) are children whose parent died as a result of complications from a bleeding disorder. Applicants or their deceased parents must be or have been clients of Hemophilia of Georgia. They may be graduating high school seniors or students currently enrolled at an accredited college, university, vocational/technical school, or professional degree program in any state. Selection is based on academic record, financial need, and personal goals.
Financial data   A stipend is awarded (amount not specified).
Duration   1 year.
Additional data   Recipients must provide at least 12 hours of volunteer service with Hemophilia of Georgia.
Number awarded   Varies each year. Since this program was established, it has awarded more than 400 scholarship with a value greater than $1,000,000.
Deadline   April of each year.

[998]
JOSEPH W. MAYO ALS SCHOLARSHIP

Maine Community Foundation
Attn: Program Director
245 Main Street
Ellsworth, ME 04605
(207) 667-9735   Toll Free: (877) 700-6800
Fax: (207) 667-0447   E-mail: info@mainecf.org
Web: www.mainecf.org

Summary   To provide financial assistance to college students from Maine who have a relative with Amyotrophic Lateral Sclerosis (A.L.S.).
Eligibility   This program is open to students enrolled at a 2- or 4-year college or university who graduated from a Maine high school or GED program. Applicants must be the child, stepchild, grandchild, spouse, domestic partner, or primary caregiver of an A.L.S. patient. Along with their application, they must submit essays on their educational plans and involvement with school or community service activities, including any associated with ALS programs.
Financial data   Stipends range from $500 to $3,000.
Duration   1 year.
Additional data   This program began in 2001.
Number awarded   Varies each year; recently, 6 were awarded.
Deadline   April of each year.

[999]
JUMPSTART MS SCHOLARSHIP

National Multiple Sclerosis Society-Upper Midwest Chapter
Attn: Jumpstart MS Scholarship Program
200 12th Avenue South
Minneapolis, MN 55415
(612) 335-7937   Toll Free: (800) 582-5296
Fax: (612) 335-7997 E-mail: krista.harding@nmss.org
Web: www.nationalmssociety.org

Summary   To provide financial assistance to high school freshmen from Iowa, Minnesota, and North and South Dakota who have multiple sclerosis (MS) or have a parent with MS and are planning to attend college in any state.
Eligibility   This program is open to students currently enrolled as freshmen at high schools in Iowa, Minnesota, North Dakota, and South Dakota who have MS or a parent who has MS. Applicants must be planning to enroll at a 2- or 4-year college, university, or vocational/technical school in the United States after they graduate from high school. Along with their application, they must submit an 850-word essay on the impact MS has had on their lives. Selection is based on that essay, academic record, leadership and participation in school or community activities, goals and aspirations, and special circumstances (such as financial need).
Financial data   The stipend is $1,500.
Duration   1 year.
Additional data   This program is sponsored by Best Buy.
Number awarded   1 each year.
Deadline   February of each year.

[1000]
KATHERN F. GRUBER SCHOLARSHIPS

Blinded Veterans Association
Attn: Scholarship Coordinator
125 North West Street, Third Floor
Alexandria, VA 22314
(202) 371-8880, ext. 313   Toll Free: (800) 669-7079
Fax: (202) 371-8258   E-mail: cdumond@bva.org
Web: www.bva.org

Summary To provide financial assistance for undergraduate or graduate study to immediate family of blinded veterans and servicemembers.

Eligibility This program is open to dependent children, grandchildren, and spouses of blinded veterans and active-duty blinded servicemembers of the U.S. armed forces. The veteran or servicemember must be legally blind; the blindness may be either service-connected or nonservice-connected. Applicants must have been accepted or be currently enrolled as a full-time student in an undergraduate or graduate program at an accredited institution of higher learning. Along with their application, they must submit a 300-word essay on their career goals and aspirations. Financial need is not considered in the selection process.

Financial data The stipend is $2,000; funds are intended to be used to cover the student's expenses, including tuition, other academic fees, books, dormitory fees, and cafeteria fees. Funds are paid directly to the recipient's school.

Duration 1 year; recipients may reapply for up to 3 additional years.

Number awarded 6 each year.

Deadline April of each year.

[1001]
KATZ & PHILLIPS BEATING HEART DISEASE SCHOLARSHIP

Katz & Phillips, P.A.
509 West Colonial Drive
Orlando, FL 32804
(321) 332-6864   Fax: (321) 422-3457
Web: www.orlandocriminalteam.com/giving-back

Summary To provide financial assistance to college students who have personally faced heart disease or have seen loved ones deal with the illness.

Eligibility This program is open to students who have been accepted or are enrolled at a college or university in any state. Applicants must be suffering from heart disease, have overcome heart disease, or be providing care and support for a family member with heart disease. They must have a GPA of 2.8 or higher. Along with their application, they must submit an essay of 500-1,000 words on their choice of 3 essay topics that deal with heart disease.

Financial data The stipend is $1,000.

Duration 1 year.

Number awarded 1 each year.

Deadline July of each year.

[1002]
KELLY LYNN LUTZ MEMORIAL SCHOLARSHIP

Kelly Lynn Lutz Memorial Foundation
P.O. Box 23395
Shawnee Mission, KS 66283
E-mail: info@kllscholarshipfund.org
Web: www.kllscholarshipfund.org

Summary To provide financial assistance to high school seniors and current college students who have lost the life of at least 1 parent.

Eligibility This program is open to students who are graduating high school seniors or students currently enrolled at a 2- or 4-year institution of higher education in any state with a demonstrated interest in education, arts, environment, mathematics, or science. Applicants must have lost the life of at least 1 parent (biological or not) to cancer before the age of 22. They must be able to demonstrate financial need and a record of involvement in the community, church, school, or other non-curricular activity. U.S. citizenship is required. No residential requirement is specified, but all recipients have been residents of Kansas or Missouri.

Financial data The stipend is $2,000 per year.

Duration 1 year; may be renewed up to 3 additional years, provided the recipient maintains a GPA of 3.0 or higher.

Additional data This program began in 2008.

Number awarded Varies each year; recently, 5 were awarded.

Deadline January of each year.

[1003]
KENTUCKY DECEASED OR DISABLED LAW ENFORCEMENT OFFICER AND FIRE FIGHTER DEPENDENT TUITION WAIVER

Kentucky Community and Technical College System
Attn: Financial Aid
300 North Main Street
Versailles, KY 40383
(859) 256-3100   Toll Free: (877) 528-2748 (within KY)
Web: kctcs.edu

Summary To provide financial assistance for college to the children and spouses of Kentucky police officers or firefighters deceased or disabled in the line of duty.

Eligibility This program is open to spouses, widow(er)s, and children of Kentucky residents who became a law enforcement officer, firefighter, or volunteer firefighter and who 1) were killed while in active service or training for active service; 2) died as a result of a service-connected disability; or 3) became permanently and totally disabled as a result of active service or training for active service. Children must be between 17 and 23 years of age; spouses and widow(er)s may be of any age.

Financial data Recipients are entitled to a waiver of tuition at state-supported universities, community colleges, and technical training institutions in Kentucky.

Duration 1 year; may be renewed up to a maximum total of 36 months.

Number awarded   Varies each year; all qualified applicants are entitled to this aid.
Deadline   Deadline not specified.

[1004]
KENTUCKY VETERANS TUITION WAIVER PROGRAM

Kentucky Department of Veterans Affairs
Attn: Tuition Waiver Coordinator
321 West Main Street, Suite 390
Louisville, KY 40202
(502) 595-4447   Toll Free: (800) 928-4012 (within KY)
Fax: (502) 595-3369
Web: www.veterans.ky.gov

Summary   To provide financial assistance for college to the children, spouses, or unremarried widow(er)s of disabled or deceased Kentucky veterans.

Eligibility   This program is open to the children, stepchildren, spouses, and unremarried widow(er)s of veterans who are residents of Kentucky (or were residents at the time of their death). The qualifying veteran must meet 1 of the following conditions: 1) died on active duty (regardless of wartime service); 2) died as a result of a service-connected disability (regardless of wartime service); 3) has a 100% service-connected disability; 4) is totally disabled (nonservice-connected) with wartime service; or 5) is deceased and served during wartime. The military service may have been as a member of the U.S. armed forces, the Kentucky National Guard, or a Reserve component; service in the Guard or Reserves must have been on state active duty, active duty for training, inactive duty training, or active duty with the U.S. armed forces. Children of veterans must be under 26 years of age; no age limit applies to spouses or unremarried widow(er)s. All applicants must be attending or planning to attend a 2-year, 4-year, or vocational technical school operated and funded by the Kentucky Department of Education.

Financial data   Eligible dependents and survivors are exempt from tuition and matriculation fees at any state-supported institution of higher education in Kentucky.

Duration   Tuition is waived until the recipient completes 45 months of training, receives a college degree, or (in the case of children of veterans) reaches 26 years of age, whichever comes first. Spouses and unremarried widow(er)s are not subject to the age limitation.

Number awarded   Varies each year.
Deadline   Deadline not specified.

[1005]
KERIN KELLER MEMORIAL SCHOLARSHIP

College Planning Network
Attn: Vicki Breithaupt
43 Bentley Place
Port Townsend, WA 98368
(206) 323-0624   E-mail: Doug@collegeplan.org
Web: www.collegeplan.org

Summary   To provide financial assistance to residents of Washington who are related to a cancer patient and planning to study business or communications at a college in the state.

Eligibility   This program is open to residents of Washington who are attending or planning to attend an accredited 2- or 4-year college or university in the state. Applicants must major in business or communications; a focus in marketing, advertising, and public relations is strongly encouraged. They must be related to a victim of cancer. Along with their application, they must submit 2 letters of recommendation, a list of significant activities and honors, an official transcript from the high school or college they are currently attending, and a 1-page essay explaining their relationship to a victim of cancer and how this award will help them attain their educational goals. Financial need is considered in the selection process, but it is not the determining factor.

Financial data   The stipend is $1,000.
Duration   1 year; nonrenewable.
Additional data   This program is sponsored by Ad Club Seattle, formerly the Seattle Advertising Federation.
Number awarded   1 each year.
Deadline   March of each year.

[1006]
KIDNEY TRANSPLANT/DIALYSIS ASSOCIATION SCHOLARSHIP PROGRAM

Kidney Transplant/Dialysis Association, Inc.
Attn: Scholarship Committee
P.O. Box 51362 GMF
Boston, MA 02205-1362
(781) 641-4000   E-mail: Business@ktda.org
Web: www.ktda.org/scholarship.html

Summary   To provide financial assistance to residents of New England who are kidney patients or donors or members of their families and interested in attending college in any state.

Eligibility   This program is open to residents of New England who are kidney patients, kidney donors, or members of a patient's immediate family. Applicants must be interested in continuing their education beyond high school. Along with their application, they must submit 2 letters of recommendation, transcripts, and a 500-word essay on how kidney disease has impacted their family. Selection is based on academic merit and financial need.

Financial data   Stipends range from $500 to $1,000.
Duration   1 year.
Number awarded   Varies each year; recently, 2 were awarded.
Deadline   January of each year.

[1007]
KIDS' CHANCE OF ARIZONA SCHOLARSHIPS

Kids' Chance of Arizona
P.O. Box 36753
Phoenix, AZ 85067-6753
(602) 253-4360   Toll Free: (877) 253-4360
E-mail: execdir@azkidschance.org
Web: www.azkidschance.org

Summary To provide financial assistance to Arizona residents whose parent was killed or permanently disabled in an employment-related accident and who are interested in attending college in any state.

Eligibility This program is open to Arizona residents between 16 and 25 years of age whose parent was killed or disabled in an employment-related accident. Applicants must be attending or planning to attend a college, university, or trade school in any state. They must have a GPA of 2.5 or higher. Along with their application, they must submit high school transcripts, letters of recommendation, verification of school attendance, and a 1-page letter explaining their educational goals and need for financial assistance.

Financial data Stipends are approximately $2,000.

Duration 1 year; may be renewed.

Additional data This program began in 1997.

Number awarded Varies each year; recently, 13 were awarded. Since the program was established, it has awarded 276 scholarships worth $640,600.

Deadline Deadline not specified.

[1008]
KIDS' CHANCE OF ARKANSAS SCHOLARSHIPS

Kids' Chance of Arkansas, Inc.
Attn: Scholarship Board
P.O. Box 250249
Little Rock, AR 72225-0249
Toll Free: (866) 880-8444
E-mail: KidsChance@awcc.state.ar.us
Web: www.kidschancear.org/application.html

Summary To provide financial assistance to Arkansas residents whose parent was killed or permanently disabled in an employment-related accident and who are interested in attending college in any state.

Eligibility This program is open to children of workers who have been killed or become permanently and totally disabled from a compensable Arkansas Workers' Compensation injury or accident. Applicants must be between 16 and 22 years of age; be able to demonstrate academic achievement and aptitude; and be attending or planning to attend an accredited vocational/technical school, college, or university in any state. The injury or death of their parent must have resulted in a decrease in family earnings that creates an obstacle to the continuation of their education. Along with their application, they must submit a 2-page essay that describes 1) the circumstances of the work-related injury or death of their parent or guardian; 2) their academic and career aspirations; and 3) the biggest challenge in attending college and plans to overcome it.

Financial data Stipends are approximately $2,000.

Duration 1 year.

Additional data This program began in 2002.

Number awarded Varies each year; recently, 26 of these scholarships, with a value of $48,500, were awarded. Since the program was established, it has awarded 205 scholarships with a total value of $368,000.

Deadline May of each year.

[1009]
KIDS' CHANCE OF CALIFORNIA SCHOLARSHIPS

Kids' Chance of California, Inc.
Attn: Scholarship Committee
P.O. Box 192052
San Francisco, CA 94119-2052
(415) 609-4007
E-mail: maria.s.henderson@outlook.com
Web: www.kidschanceca.org/scholarships

Summary To provide financial assistance for college to children of workers killed or disabled in an accident that meets the criteria of the California Workers' Compensation Act.

Eligibility This program is open to students between 16 and 25 years of age who are enrolled or planning to enroll full or part time at a college, university, or technical school in any state. Applicants must have a parent who has been killed or seriously injured as a result of a work-related accident with a California employer that meets the criteria of the California Workers' Compensation Act, although neither the student nor the parent are required to be residents of California. Selection is based on academic achievement, aptitude, community service, and financial need.

Financial data Stipends range from $2,500 to $10,000 per year.

Duration 1 year; recipients may reapply.

Additional data This program began in 2013.

Number awarded Varies each year.

Deadline May of each year.

[1010]
KIDS' CHANCE OF FLORIDA SCHOLARSHIP PROGRAM

Kids' Chance of Florida
Attn: Scholarship Committee
P.O. Box 1648
Sarasota, FL 34230-1648
Fax: (866) 243-2066   E-mail: info@kidschancefl.org
Web: www.kidschancefl.org/scholarship-info

Summary To provide financial assistance to Florida residents whose parent was killed or seriously injured in an industrial accident and who are interested in attending college in the state.

Eligibility This program is open to Florida residents between 16 and 25 years of age who are the natural child, adopted child, or stepchild of a Florida worker killed or seriously injured in a claim compensable under the Florida Workers' Compensation Act, Longshore and Harbor Workers Compensation Act, or Federal Employees' Compensation Act. Applicants must be enrolled or planning to enroll at an accredited Florida college, university, community college, technical or vocational school, or state-approved proprietary school and working on an associate or bachelor's degree or vocational education and training certificate or license. They must have a GPA of 2.5 or higher and be able to demonstrate substantial financial need. Along with their application, they must submit a statement describing the nature and extent of the accident and any ongoing injuries in detail; their honors, achievements, and accomplishments; their goals and career plans; how this scholarship will help them achieve their goals; how special circumstances (death of a parent or loss of parent's livelihood) has affected the achievement of their goals; and hose they have overcome those circumstances and triumphed in their life. Selection is also based on academic achievement, aptitude, extracurricular activities, and community service.

Financial data Stipend amounts vary; recently, they averaged $3,750.

Duration 1 year; may be renewed.

Additional data This program began in 2015.

Number awarded Varies each year; recently, 4 were awarded.

Deadline August of each year.

[1011]
KIDS' CHANCE OF GEORGIA SCHOLARSHIPS

Kids' Chance of Georgia, Inc.
Attn: Operations and Scholarship Coordinator
P.O. Box 5294
Canton, GA 30114
(770) 933-7767   TDD: (770) 933-6995
E-mail: candence@kidschancega.org
Web: www.kidschancega.org/scholarships

Summary To provide financial assistance to Georgia residents whose parent was killed or permanently disabled in an employment-related accident and who are interested in attending college in any state.

Eligibility This program is open to Georgia residents between 16 and 25 years of age whose parent's work-related death or injury resulted in a substantial decline in family income. Applicants must be enrolled or planning to enroll full time at a college, university, or technical school in any state. Along with their application, they must submit an autobiography of 250 to 500 words on their educational goals and how this organization can help them achieve success.

Financial data The stipend depends on the financial need of the recipient, ranging from $1,200 to $6,500. Funds may be used for tuition, books, housing, meals, transportation, and/or as a supplement to the income of the family to compensate for money the student would earn by dropping out of school.

Duration 1 year; may be renewed up to 4 additional years, provided the recipient maintains satisfactory academic progress and a GPA of 2.0 or higher.

Additional data This program was established by the Workers' Compensation Section of the Georgia Bar in 1988. It has served as a model for comparable programs that currently operate in 29 other states.

Number awarded Approximately 35 each year.

Deadline April of each year.

[1012]
KIDS' CHANCE OF ILLINOIS SCHOLARSHIPS

Kids' Chance Inc. of Illinois
Attn: James B. Hardy, Scholarship Chair
P.O. Box 64583
Chicago, IL 60664
(312) 464-1200 E-mail: info@kidschanceofillinois.com
Web: www.kidschanceofillinois.com/scholarships

Summary To provide financial assistance to students interested in attending college in any state whose parent was killed or injured in a work-related accident in Illinois.

Eligibility This program is open to students between 16 and 25 years of age who are enrolled or planning to enroll full or part time at an accredited college, university, or technical school in any state. Applicants must have a parent who has been killed or seriously injured as a result of a work-related accident that meets the criteria of the Illinois Workers' Compensation Act, although neither the student nor the parent are required to be legal residents of Illinois. The death or injury of the parent must have resulted in demonstrated financial need.

Financial data A stipend is awarded (amount not specified).

Duration 1 year; may be renewed.

Number awarded Varies each year; recently, 4 new and 2 renewal scholarships were awarded.

Deadline April of each year.

[1013]
KIDS' CHANCE OF INDIANA SCHOLARSHIP PROGRAM

Kids' Chance of Indiana, Inc.
c/o Jenni Bolen
Objective Group
8330 Naab Road, Suite 140
Indianapolis, IN 46260
(317) 400-7030   Fax: (317) 672-4300
E-mail: ngath@fdgtlaborlaw.com
Web: www.kidschancein.org/scholarship.html

Summary To provide financial assistance to Indiana residents whose parent was killed or permanently disabled in a work-related accident and who are interested in attending college or graduate school in any state.

Eligibility This program is open to Indiana residents between 16 and 25 years of age who are the children of workers fatally or catastrophically injured as a result of a work-related accident or occupational disease. The death or injury must be compensable by the Workers' Compensation Board of the state of Indiana and must have resulted in a substantial decline in the family's income that is likely to impede the student's pursuit of his or her educational objectives. Applicants must be attending or planning to attend a trade/vocational school, industrial/commercial training institution, junior/community college, 4-year college or university, or graduate school in any state. Along with their application, they must submit an autobiography of 250 to 500 words on their educational goals and how this organization can help them achieve success. Financial need is considered in the selection process.

Financial data   Stipends range from $500 to $6,000 per year. Funds may be used for tuition and fees, books, room and board, and utilities.

Duration   1 year; may be renewed.

Number awarded   Varies each year.

Deadline   May of each year.

[1014]
KIDS' CHANCE OF KENTUCKY SCHOLARSHIPS

Kids' Chance of Kentucky
Attn: Scholarship Committee
P.O. Box 910234
Lexington, KY 40591
E-mail: info@kidschanceky.org
Web: www.kidschanceky.org/apply

Summary   To provide financial assistance to Kentucky residents whose parent was killed or seriously injured in an employment-related accident and who are interested in attending college in any state.

Eligibility   This program is open to residents of Kentucky between 16 and 25 years of age. Applicants must be the natural child, adopted child, stepchild, or full dependent of a worker killed or permanently injured in a compensable work-related accident during the course of employment with a Kentucky employer and entitled to receive benefits under the Kentucky Workers' Compensation Act. They must be attending or planning to attend college in any state. The parent's death or injury must have resulted in a substantial decline in the family income. Selection is based primarily on financial need, although academic achievement, aptitude, and community service are also considered.

Financial data   The stipend depends on the need of the recipient. Funds may be used to cover tuition, books, housing, and meals.

Duration   1 year; recipients may reapply.

Additional data   This program began in 2003.

Number awarded   Varies each year.

Deadline   April of each year for fall semester; October of each year for spring semester.

[1015]
KIDS' CHANCE OF LOUISIANA SCHOLARSHIPS

Kids' Chance of Louisiana
c/o The Louisiana Bar Foundation
1615 Poydras Street, Suite 1000
New Orleans, LA 70112
(504) 561-1046   Fax: (504) 566-1926
E-mail: dee@raisingthebar.org
Web: www.raisingthebar.org

Summary   To provide financial assistance to Louisiana residents whose parent was killed or permanently disabled in an employment-related accident and who are interested in attending college in the state.

Eligibility   This program is open to Louisiana residents between 16 and 25 years of age who are the dependent of a worker killed or permanently and totally disabled in an

accident that is compensable under a state or federal Workers' Compensation Act or law. Applicants must be working on or planning to work on a certificate, license, or associate or bachelor's degree from an accredited Louisiana university, community college, vocational/technical institute, or state-approved proprietary school. Financial need is considered in the selection process.

Financial data   Stipends range from $500 to $3,000. Funds, paid directly to the school where the child is enrolled, may be used for tuition, books, fees, room, and general living expenses.

Duration   1 year; recipients may reapply, provided they maintain a "C" average or higher.

Additional data   This program began in 2004.

Number awarded   Varies each year; recently, 20 were awarded. Since the program began, it has awarded 255 scholarships worth $533,100.

Deadline   February of each year.

[1016]
KIDS' CHANCE OF MARYLAND SCHOLARSHIPS

Kids' Chance of Maryland, Inc.
Attn: Executive Director
P.O. Box 20262
Towson, MD 21284-0262
(410) 832-4702   Fax: (410) 832-4726
E-mail: info@kidschance-md.org
Web: www.kidschance-md.org

Summary   To provide financial assistance to Maryland residents whose parent was killed or permanently disabled in an employment-related accident and who are interested in attending college in any state.

Eligibility   This program is open to Maryland residents between 16 and 25 years of age who have a parent permanently or catastrophically injured or killed in an employment-related accident compensable under the Maryland Workers' Compensation Act. The parent's death or injury must have resulted in a substantial decline in the family income. Applicants must be attending or planning to attend college or technical school in any state. Financial need is considered in the selection process.

Financial data   Stipends range from $1,000 to $5,000 per semester. Funds are intended to cover tuition and books but may also include housing and meals.

Duration   1 semester; recipients may reapply.

Number awarded   Varies each year; recently, 15 were awarded.

Deadline   Deadline not specified.

[1017]
KIDS' CHANCE OF MICHIGAN SCHOLARSHIPS

Kids' Chance of Michigan
Attn: Application Coordinator
26125 Woodward Avenue
Huntington Woods, MI 49070
(248) 205-2760   E-mail: admin@kidschanceofmi.org
Web: www.kidschanceofmi.org/scholarships.html

Summary To provide financial assistance to residents of Michigan whose parent was killed or injured in a work-related accident and who plan to attend college in the state.

Eligibility This program is open to residents of Michigan between 17 and 22 years of age who are graduating high school seniors planning to attend or students already attending a college, university, community college, or trade/vocational school in the state. Applicants' parent must have sustained a catastrophic injury or fatality in a Michigan work-related accident covered by workers' compensation. Selection is based primarily on financial need related to the parents' injury or death.

Financial data Stipends range from $2,500 to $5,000 per year. Funds are paid directly to the educational institution.

Duration 1 year; recipients may reapply.

Number awarded Varies each year; recently, 6 were awarded.

Deadline Deadline not specified.

[1018]
KIDS' CHANCE OF MISSISSIPPI SCHOLARSHIP FUND

Mississippi Bar Foundation
Attn: Administrative Law and Workers' Compensation
 Section
643 North State Street
P.O. Box 2168
Jackson, MS 39225-2168
(601) 948-4471   Fax: (601) 355-8635
E-mail: acook@msbar.org
Web: www.msbar.org

Summary To provide financial assistance to Mississippi residents whose parent was killed or disabled on the job and who are interested in attending college in any state.

Eligibility This program is open to Mississippi residents between 17 and 23 years of age who have had a parent killed or permanently and totally disabled in an accident that is compensable under the Mississippi Workers' Compensation Act. Applicants must demonstrate substantial financial need.

Financial data A stipend is awarded (amount not specified).

Duration 1 year; may be renewed.

Number awarded Varies each year.

Deadline April of each year.

[1019]
KIDS' CHANCE OF MISSOURI SCHOLARSHIPS

Kids' Chance Inc. of Missouri
Attn: Scholarship Committee
P.O. Box 410384
St. Louis, MO 63141
(314) 997-3390   Fax: (314) 432-5894
E-mail: susgroup@gmail.com
Web: www.mokidschance.org

Summary To provide financial assistance to Missouri residents whose parent was killed or permanently disabled in a work-related accident and who are interested in attending college in any state.

Eligibility This program is open to Missouri residents whose parent sustained a serious injury or fatality in a Missouri work-related accident covered by workers' compensation. Applicants must be attending or planning to attend an accredited college, university, trade school, community college, or graduate school within the United States. They must be able to demonstrate financial need.

Financial data Stipends depend on the need of the recipient, to a maximum of $2,500 per year. Funds may be used to cover tuition, books, supplies, housing, meals, and other expenses not covered by other grants and/or scholarships.

Duration 1 year; recipients may reapply.

Additional data This program began in 1996. It operates in partnership with a similar program offered by the Missouri Department of Higher Education. Students who do not receive support from the state-funded program are considered for this assistance.

Number awarded Varies each year. Recently, the program awarded nearly $200,000 in scholarships.

Deadline May of each year for academic year scholarships; October of each year for spring semester scholarships.

[1020]
KIDS' CHANCE OF NEBRASKA SCHOLARSHIPS

Kids' Chance of Nebraska
15418 Weir Street, Suite 157
Omaha, NE 68137
(402) 573-2175   E-mail: info@kidschanceofne.org
Web: www.kidschanceofne.org/scholarship-application

Summary To provide financial assistance to residents of Nebraska whose are interested in attending college or graduate school in any state and whose parent was killed or injured in an on-the-job accident.

Eligibility This program is open to Nebraska residents between 16 and 25 years of age who are graduating high school seniors, GED recipients, or students currently enrolled at a college, university, junior college, vocational/technical school, or graduate program in any state. Applicants must be the dependent of a parent who suffered an on-the-job fatality or injuries that have had a significant adverse effect on family income. Along with their application, they must submit documentation of financial need and a 2-page essay describing their parent's work-related accident, its personal economic impact on them and their family, and why this scholarship will help them attain their educational goals.

Financial data The stipend is $2,500. Funds are paid directly to the recipient's institution.

Duration 1 year; may be renewed.

Additional data This program began in 2015.

Number awarded Varies each year; recently, 5 were awarded.

Deadline April of each year.

[1021]
KIDS' CHANCE OF NEW JERSEY SCHOLARSHIPS

Kids' Chance of New Jersey
Attn: Scholarship Coordinator
P.O. Box 166
Matawan, NJ 07747
(201) 481-7519   E-mail: sherrylee36@aol.com
Web: www.kidschancenj.org/scholarships

Summary To provide financial assistance to residents of New Jersey whose parent was fatally or catastrophically injured in a work-related accident and who are interested in attending college in any state.

Eligibility This program is open to children of New Jersey workers who have been fatally, seriously, or catastrophically injured in a work-related accident that meets the criteria of the New Jersey Workers' Compensation Act. Applicants must be between 16 and 25 years of age and enrolled or planning to enroll full time at a college, university, or technical school in any state. Selection is based primarily on financial need.

Financial data The stipend is $10,000.

Duration 1 year.

Additional data This program began in 2013.

Number awarded Varies each year; recently, 10 were awarded.

Deadline May of each year.

[1022]
KIDS' CHANCE OF NEW YORK SCHOLARSHIPS

Kids' Chance of New York
c/o Bartlett, McDonough and Monighan LLP
170 Old Country Road
Mineola, NY 11501-4112
(516) 877-2900   Fax: (516) 877-0732
E-mail: admin@kcnewyork.org
Web: www.kcnewyork.org/apply

Summary To provide financial assistance for undergraduate or graduate study in any state to residents of New York whose parent was killed or disabled in a work-related accident.

Eligibility This program is open to students between 16 and 25 years of age whose parent or guardian suffered a serious or fatal accidental injury or occupational disease while working for a New York employer. Applicants must be interested in obtaining a vocational, college, or graduate education as a full- or part-time student at a college, university, or technical school in any state. Along with their application, they must submit documents filed with the New York Workers Compensation Board, academic transcripts, documentation of financial need, and a 1-page essay on how this scholarship will help them attain their educational goals.

Financial data A stipend is awarded (amount not specified). Funds are sent directly to the recipient's institution.

Duration 1 year; may be renewed.

Number awarded Varies each year.

Deadline Applications may be submitted at any time, but they must be received at least 3 months before the funds are needed.

[1023]
KIDS' CHANCE OF NORTH CAROLINA SCHOLARSHIPS

Kids' Chance of North Carolina, Inc.
Attn: Executive Director
P.O. Box 13756
Greensboro, NC 27415
(336) 404-5069   E-mail: kidschancenc@gmail.com
Web: www.kidschancenc.org/scholarship

Summary To provide financial assistance to North Carolina residents whose parent was seriously injured or killed in a workplace accident and who are interested in attending college in any state.

Eligibility This program is open to residents of North Carolina between 16 and 25 years of age who are attending or planning to attend college or vocational school in any state. Applicants must be children of employees who have been seriously injured or killed as a result of a workplace accident that is covered under the North Carolina Workers' Compensation Act. They must be able to demonstrate financial hardship caused by the death or serious injury of their parent.

Financial data Stipends range up to $5,000 per year. Funds may be used for tuition, books, meals, housing, and transportation, and/or they may be used to supplement the income of the family to compensate for money the student would earn by dropping out of school.

Duration 1 year; may be renewed if the recipient maintains an acceptable academic level.

Additional data This program began in 2004.

Number awarded Varies each year; recently, 8 were awarded.

Deadline Applications may be submitted at any time.

[1024]
KIDS' CHANCE OF OHIO SCHOLARSHIPS

Kids' Chance of Ohio
Attn: Executive Director
52 East Gay Street
P.O. Box 1008
Columbus, OH 43216-1008
(614) 464-6410   E-mail: raminor@vssp.com
Web: www.kidschanceohio.org/scholarships

Summary To provide financial assistance for undergraduate or graduate study in any state to children of Ohio employees who were killed or disabled as a result of a work-related injury or occupational disease.

Eligibility This program is open to the children between 16 and 25 years of age of employees who have been declared to be permanently and totally disabled or who were fatally injured as a result of a work-related injury or occupational disease. The death, injury, or illness must have occurred as a result of work activities performed for an Ohio employer covered by the Ohio workers' compensation law, although neither the student nor the parent is required to be an Ohio resident. The injury or death must have resulted in a decline in the family's income. Applicants must be attending or planning to attend a college, university, community college, trade/vocational school, industrial/commercial training institute, or graduate school in any state.

Financial data The stipend depends on the need of the recipient, to a maximum of $5,000 per year. Funds may be used for payment of tuition, fees, books, room, and board.

Duration 1 year; recipients may reapply.

Number awarded Varies each year.

Deadline Applications must be submitted at least 1 month prior to the beginning of the semester or quarter.

[1025]
KIDS' CHANCE OF OKLAHOMA SCHOLARSHIPS

Kids' Chance of Oklahoma, Inc.
1901 North Walnut Avenue
Oklahoma City, OK 73105
(405) 962-3245   Fax: (405) 962-3127
E-mail: kidschanceok@kidschanceok.org
Web: www.kidschanceok.org/scholarship-eligibility

Summary To provide financial assistance to residents of Oklahoma whose are interested in attending college or graduate school in any state and whose parent was killed or injured in a workplace accident.

Eligibility This program is open to Oklahoma residents between 17 and 25 years of age who are graduating high school seniors, GED recipients, or students currently enrolled full or part time at a college in any state. Applicants must be working on a bachelor's or master's degree at a 4-year college or university, an associate degree at a junior or community college, or a certificate or license at a career technical school. Along with their application, they must submit a letter explaining why this scholarship will help them attain their educational goals. They must have a GPA of 2.5 or higher and be able to demonstrate financial need. Other factors considered in the selection process include academic achievement, student government involvement, aptitude, extracurricular activities, and community service.

Financial data A stipend is awarded (amount not specified).

Duration 1 year; may be renewed.

Number awarded Varies each year.

Deadline November of each year.

[1026]
KIDS' CHANCE OF OREGON SCHOLARSHIPS

Kids' Chance of Oregon
Attn: Scholarship Committee
P.O. Box 1728
Lake Oswego, OR 97035
(503) 323-2812
E-mail: info@kidschanceoforegon.com
Web: www.kidschanceoforegon.com

Summary To provide financial assistance to undergraduate and graduate students whose parent or guardian was killed or permanently disabled as a result of an injury covered by Oregon workers' compensation.

Eligibility This program is open to high school seniors, GED participants, full- or part-time undergraduates (university or community college), trade/technical/vocational school students, apprentice program participants, and graduate students in any state who are between 16 and 25 years of age. Applicants' must be affected by the death or permanent and total disability of a parent or guardian as the result of an injury arising out of employment for an Oregon employer cover by workers' compensation. They must submit a statement of their financial need, the circumstances of need, and how a scholarship will assist.

Financial data A stipend is awarded (amount not specified).

Duration 1 year; may be renewed.

Number awarded Varies each year.

Deadline Applications may be submitted at any time, but they must be received at least 2 months before the term for which the scholarship is sought.

[1027]
KIDS' CHANCE OF PENNSYLVANIA SCHOLARSHIPS

Kids' Chance of Pennsylvania
P.O. Box 543
Pottstown, PA 19464
(610) 850-0150   E-mail: info@kidschanceofpa.org
Web: www.kidschanceofpa.org

Summary To provide financial assistance to Pennsylvania residents whose parent was killed or permanently disabled in a work-related accident and who are interested in attending college in any state.

Eligibility This program is open to Pennsylvania residents between 16 and 25 years of age who have been accepted by an accredited postsecondary educational institution anywhere in the United States. At least 1 parent must have been killed or seriously injured as a result of a work-related accident covered under the Pennsylvania Workers' Compensation Act. Financial need is considered in the selection process.

Financial data Stipends range from $500 to $5,000; recently, they averaged $3,272.

Duration 1 year; may be renewed up to 3 additional years.

Additional data This program began in 1997. Matching funding for students with remaining unmet financial need is provided by the Pennsylvania Higher Education Assistance Agency (PHEAA) in collaboration with American Education Services. Students who demonstrate exceptional academic progress and significant financial need receive funding through a grant from the ACE INA Foundation.

Number awarded Varies each year; recently, 57 of these scholarships, worth $186,500, were awarded.

Deadline April of each year.

[1028]
KIDS' CHANCE OF SOUTH CAROLINA SCHOLARSHIPS

Kids' Chance of South Carolina
P.O. Box 2957
Georgetown, SC 29442-2957
(843) 546-5837   E-mail: info@kidschancesc.org
Web: www.kidschancesc.org/index.php/scholarships

Summary To provide financial assistance to South Carolina residents whose parent was killed or permanently disabled in a work-related accident and who are interested in attending college or graduate school in any state.

Eligibility This program is open to South Carolina residents between 16 and 25 years of age who are the children of workers fatally or catastrophically injured as a result of a work-related accident or occupational disease. Applicants must be attending or planning to attend a trade school, vocational school, community or junior college, 4-year college or university, or graduate school in any state. They must have a GPA of 2.0 or higher. The work-related injury or occupational disease from which their parent suffers or died must be compensable by the Workers' Compensation Board of the state of South Carolina and must have resulted in a substantial decline in the family's income that is likely to interfere with the student's pursuit of his or her educational objectives.

Financial data Stipends range up to $3,000 per semester ($6,000 per year). Funds may be used for tuition and fees, books, room and board, and utilities.

Duration 1 semester; may be renewed up to 7 additional semesters, provided the recipient maintains a GPA of 2.5 or higher.

Number awarded Varies each year; recently, 43 of these scholarships, with a total value of $106,060 were awarded.

Deadline Applications must be submitted 1 month before the beginning of the semester, or July for the fall semester and December for the spring semester.

[1029]
KIDS' CHANCE OF SOUTH DAKOTA SCHOLARSHIPS

Kids' Chance of South Dakota
c/o Michael McKnight, President
Boyce Law Firm, L.L.P.
300 South Main Avenue
P.O. Box 5015
Sioux Falls, SD 57117-5015
(605) 336-2424   Fax: (605) 334-0618
E-mail: admin@kidschanceofsd.org
Web: www.kidschanceofsd.org/scholarship-application

Summary To provide financial assistance to residents of South Dakota whose are interested in attending college or graduate school in any state and whose parent was killed or injured in an on-the-job accident.

Eligibility This program is open to South Dakota residents between 16 and 25 years of age who are graduating high school seniors, GED recipients, or students currently enrolled at a college, university, junior college, vocational/technical school, or graduate program in any state. Applicants must be the dependent of a parent who suffered an on-the-job fatality or injuries that have had a significant adverse effect on family income. Along with their application, they must submit documentation of financial need and a 2-page essay describing their parent's work-related accident, its personal economic impact on them and their family, and why this scholarship will help them attain their educational goals.

Financial data A stipend is awarded (amount not specified). Funds are paid directly to the recipient's institution.

Duration 1 year; may be renewed.

Number awarded Varies each year.

Deadline April of each year.

[1030]
KIDS' CHANCE OF TENNESSEE SCHOLARSHIP PROGRAM

Kids' Chance of Tennessee
c/o Kathy Kirby-Smithson
809 North Hampton Cove
Franklin, TN 37064
(615) 336-1956   E-mail: kirby59@gmail.com

Summary To provide financial assistance to Tennessee residents whose parent was killed or permanently disabled in a work-related accident and who are interested in attending college in any state.

Eligibility This program is open to Tennessee residents between 16 and 22 years of age who are the children of workers who died or suffered a serious or catastrophic injury or a permanent disability as a result of an employment-related accident. The parent or deceased parent's family must be entitled to receive benefits under the Tennessee Workers' Compensation Act. The parent's death or injury must have resulted in a substantial decline in the family's income that is likely to impede the student's pursuit of his or her educational objectives. Applicants must be attending or planning to attend a college, university, or vocational/technical school in any state.

Financial data A stipend is awarded (amount not specified).

Duration 1 year.

Number awarded 1 or more each year.

Deadline Deadline not specified.

[1031]
KIDS' CHANCE OF TEXAS SCHOLARSHIPS

Kids' Chance of Texas
P.O. Box 30111
Austin, TX 78731
Toll Free: (888) 404-KCTX
E-mail: information@kidschanceoftexas.org
Web: www.kidschanceoftexas.org

Summary To provide financial assistance to residents of Texas who are interested in attending college in any state and whose parent was killed or injured in a work-related accident.

Eligibility This program is open to residents of Texas between 16 and 25 years of age who are enrolled or planning to enroll full time at a college or university in any state. Applicants must be the dependent of a parent who was seriously, catastrophically, or fatally injured in a work-related accident while working for a Texas employer. The parent's death or injury must have resulted in a substantial decline in family income. Along with their application, they must submit an autobiography of 250 to 500 words that describes their educational goals and how this scholarship can help them achieve success.

Financial data   A stipend is awarded (amount not specified).

Duration   1 year; may be renewed up to 4 additional years.

Additional data   This program began in 2015.

Number awarded   Varies each year.

Deadline   Applications must be received at least 1 month before the tuition deadline of their school.

[1032]
KIDS' CHANCE OF VERMONT SCHOLARSHIPS

Kids' Chance of Vermont
c/o Heidi Groff, Vice President
Biggam, Fox & Skinner
453 Stone Cutters Way
Montpelier, VT 05602
(802) 229-5146   Toll Free: (800) 995-4807

Summary   To provide financial assistance to residents of Vermont who are interested in attending college in any state and whose parent was killed or injured in a work-related accident.

Eligibility   This program is open to residents of Vermont between 16 and 25 years of age who are enrolled or planning to enroll full time at a college or university in any state. Applicants must be the dependent of a parent who was seriously, catastrophically, or fatally injured in a work-related accident while working for a Texas employer. The parent's death or injury must have resulted in a substantial decline in family income.

Financial data   Stipends range up to $10,000.

Duration   1 year.

Additional data   This program began in 2014.

Number awarded   1 each year.

Deadline   March of each year.

[1033]
KIDS' CHANCE OF VIRGINIA SCHOLARSHIPS

Kids' Chance of Virginia
c/o Berkley Net
12701 Marblestone Drive, Suite 250
Woodbridge, VA 22192
(703)586-6303   E-mail: info@kidschanceva.org
Web: www.kidschanceva.org/scholarship-overview

Summary   To provide financial assistance to Virginia residents whose parent was killed or disabled in a work-related accident and who are interested in attending college in any state.

Eligibility   This program is open to residents of Virginia between 16 and 25 years of age who are attending or planning to attend a college, university, or vocational/tech-

nical institute in any state. Applicants be the child of a parent whose death or disability resulted from a work-related injury that was covered by workers' compensation. That injury must have caused a significant decline in family income and circumstances.

Financial data   A stipend is awarded (amount not specified).

Duration   1 year.

Additional data   This program began in 2011.

Number awarded   1 or more each year.

Deadline   April of each year.

[1034]
KIDS' CHANCE OF WASHINGTON SCHOLARSHIPS

Kids' Chance of Washington
P.O. Box 185
Olympia, WA 98507-0185
Toll Free: (800) 572-5762   Fax: (360) 943-2333
E-mail: debbie@wscff.org
Web: www.kidschancewa.com/application

Summary   To provide financial assistance to residents of Washington whose parent or spouse was killed or seriously disabled in a workplace accident and who are interested in attending college in any state.

Eligibility   This program is open to Washington residents attending or planning to attend an accredited community college, university, college, or vocational/technical school in any state. Applicants must be the child or spouse of a Washington worker permanently or catastrophically injured or deceased while on the job. Selection is based primarily on financial need.

Financial data   A stipend is awarded (amount not specified). Funds are paid directly to the student's school to be used for tuition, books, fees, room, and general living expenses.

Duration   1 year; may be renewed.

Additional data   This program began in 2001.

Number awarded   Varies each year.

Deadline   Applications may be submitted at any time, but priority is given to those received by May of each year for fall semester or October of each year for winter or spring.

[1035]
KIDS' CHANCE OF WEST VIRGINIA SCHOLARSHIPS

Greater Kanawha Valley Foundation
Attn: Scholarship Program Officer
1600 Huntington Square
900 Lee Street East, 16th Floor
Charleston, WV 25301
(304) 346-3620   Toll Free: (800) 467-5909
Fax: (304) 346-3640   E-mail: shoover@tgkvf.org
Web: www.tgkvf.org/kids-chance-of-west-virginia-inc

Summary   To provide financial assistance for college to students whose parent was injured or killed in a West Virginia work-related accident.

Eligibility This program is open to children between 16 and 25 years of age whose parent 1) was fatally injured in a West Virginia work-related accident; or 2) is currently receiving permanent total disability benefits from the West Virginia Workers' Compensation Division. Applicants may reside in any state and be pursuing any field of study at an accredited trade or vocational school, college, or university. They must have at least a 2.5 GPA and demonstrate good moral character. Preference is given to applicants who can demonstrate financial need, academic excellence, leadership abilities, and contributions to school and community.

Financial data Recently, stipends averaged $4,000 per year.

Duration 1 year; may be renewed.

Additional data This program is sponsored by Kids' Chance of West Virginia, Inc.

Number awarded Varies each year; recently, 2 were awarded.

Deadline January of each year.

[1036]
KIDS' CHANCE OF WISCONSIN SCHOLARSHIPS

Kids' Chance of Wisconsin
P.O. Box 1546
Brookfield, WI 53008-1546
E-mail: charlie@domerlaw.com
Web: kidschanceofwi.org/?page_id=18

Summary To provide financial assistance for college to residents of Wisconsin whose parent sustained a work-related serious injury or fatality.

Eligibility This program is open to Wisconsin residents between 17 and 24 years of age who are enrolled or planning to enroll at a college or university; preference is given to students entering Wisconsin schools. Applicants must have a parent who sustained a work-related injury or serious fatality covered by the workers' compensation laws of Wisconsin. The parent's injury or death must have had a financial impact on the family. Along with their application, they must submit a 2-page narrative describing the parent's work-related accident, its personal and economic impact on them and their family, and why this scholarship will help them attain their educational goals.

Financial data Stipends range from $500 to $4,000 per year.

Duration 1 year; may be renewed, provided the recipient remains enrolled full time and maintains a GPA of 2.0 or higher.

Additional data This program began in 2013.

Number awarded Varies each year; recently, 10 were awarded.

Deadline The priority deadline is April of each year; the regular deadline is June of each year.

[1037]
KIDS' CHANCE SCHOLARSHIP FUND

Alabama Law Foundation
415 Dexter Avenue
P.O. Box 4129
Montgomery, AL 36101
(334) 387-1600
E-mail: tdaniel@alabamalawfoundation.org
Web: www.alabamalawfoundation.org

Summary To provide financial assistance to Alabama residents whose parent was killed or disabled on the job and who are interested in attending college in any state.

Eligibility This program is open to high school seniors and college students (including students at technical colleges) in Alabama whose parent was killed or permanently and totally disabled in an on-the-job accident. Applicants must be attending or planning to attend a college or technical school in any state. Financial need is considered in the selection process.

Financial data Stipends range from $500 to $2,500 per year, but they do not exceed the cost of tuition and books at the most expensive public university in Alabama.

Duration 1 year; may be renewed.

Additional data This program began in 1992 by the Workers' Compensation Section of the Alabama State Bar and is currently administered by the Alabama Law Foundation.

Number awarded Varies each year; recently, 10 scholarships were awarded. Since the program was established, it has awarded more than 200 scholarships worth $621,000.

Deadline April of each year.

[1038]
LANFORD FAMILY HIGHWAY WORKER MEMORIAL SCHOLARSHIP PROGRAM

American Road and Transportation Builders Association
Attn: Transportation Development Foundation
250 E Street, S.W., Suite 900.
Washington, DC 20024
(202) 289-4434   Fax: (202) 289-4435
E-mail: ehoulihan@artba.org
Web: www.artba.org/foundation/awards-scholarships

Summary To provide financial assistance for college to children of highway workers killed or disabled on the job.

Eligibility This program is open to the sons, daughters, and legally adopted children of highway workers who have died or become permanently disabled in roadway construction zone accidents. Applicants must be attending or planning to attend an accredited 4-year college or university, 2-year college, or vocational/technical school. Candidates for an M.B.A. degree or a master's degree in civil engineering, construction management, or another construction-related program are also eligible. Their parent must have been employed by a transportation construction firm or a transportation public agency at the time of death or disabling injury. Selection is based on academic performance (GPA of 2.5 or higher), a 200-word statement from the applicant on reasons for wanting to continue education, letters of recommendation, and financial need.

Financial data The stipend is $5,000. Funds are paid directly to the recipient's institution to be used for tuition, books, or required fees, but not for room and board.

Duration 1 year.

Additional data This program began in 1999.

Number awarded Varies each year; recently, 11 were awarded.

Deadline April of each year.

[1039]
LILLIAN JEANETTE CRAIG MEMORIAL SCHOLARSHIP

University of Idaho 4-H Youth Development
Attn: Shana Codr, 4-H Program Specialist
Forney 206
875 Perimeter Drive, MS 3015
Moscow, ID 83844-3015
(208) 885-6321   E-mail: scodr@uidaho.edu
Web: www.uidaho.edu

Summary To provide financial assistance for college to members of 4-H in Idaho who are childhood cancer survivors or the sibling of someone who has had childhood cancer.

Eligibility This program is open to residents of Idaho who have been involved with 4-H and are graduating high school seniors or current college students. Applicants must be a childhood cancer survivor or the sibling of someone who has or has had childhood cancer. If a sibling, the applicant must have lived in the same household and been between 4 and 18 years of age when the sibling was diagnosed and treated. They may be enrolled or planning to enroll at a college, university, or vocational institution in any state; preference is given to students at academic institutions in Idaho.

Financial data The stipend is $1,000.

Duration 1 year.

Number awarded 1 or more each year.

Deadline November of each year.

[1040]
LISA HIGGINS-HUSSMAN FOUNDATION SCHOLARSHIP

Ulman Cancer Fund for Young Adults
Attn: Scholarship Committee
921 East Fort Avenue, Suite 325
Baltimore, MD 21230
(410) 964-0202   Toll Free: (888) 393-FUND
Fax: (888) 964-0402
E-mail: scholarship@ulmanfund.org
Web: www.ulmanfund.org/scholarships

Summary To provide financial assistance for college or graduate school to students from Washington, D.C., Maryland, or Virginia who have been diagnosed with cancer or have or have lost a family member with cancer.

Eligibility This program is open to students who 1) have been diagnosed with cancer; 2) have a parent, sibling, or guardian living with cancer; or 3) have lost a par-

ent, sibling, or guardian to cancer. Applicants must be residents of Washington, D.C., Maryland, or Virginia. They must be between 15 and 35 years of age and attending, or planning to attend, a 2- or 4-year college, university, or vocational program in any state to work on an undergraduate or graduate degree. The first diagnosis of cancer (whether of the applicant, a parent, a sibling, or a guardian) must have occurred after the applicant was 15 years of age. Along with their application, they must submit a 500-word essay or 3-minute video on either 1) a letter that they would have liked to receive during their cancer experience; or 2) what they would tell the young adults who participate in the sponsor's summer-long drive to support the organization about being a young adult impacted by cancer. U.S. citizenship or permanent resident status is required.

Financial data The stipend is $2,500. Funds are paid directly to the educational institution.

Duration 1 year.

Additional data Recipients are obligated to organize and run a bone marrow registry drive with the support of Delete Blood Cancer and There Goes My Hero.

Number awarded 1 each year.

Deadline March of each year.

[1041]
LITTLE PEOPLE OF AMERICA SCHOLARSHIPS

Little People of America, Inc.
Attn: Vice President of Programs
250 El Camino Real, Suite 218
Tustin, CA 92780
(714) 368-3689   Toll Free: (888) LPA-2001
Fax: (714) 368-3367   E-mail: info@lpaonline.org
Web: www.lpaonline.org

Summary To provide financial assistance for college or graduate school to members of the Little People of America (LPA), to their families, and (in limited cases) to others.

Eligibility This program is open to members of LPA (limited to people who, for medical reasons, are 4 feet 10 inches or under in height). Applicants must be high school seniors or students attending college, vocational school, or graduate school. Along with their application, they must submit a 500-word personal statement that explains their reasons for applying for a scholarship, their plans for the future, how they intend to be of service to LPA after graduation, and any other relevant information about themselves, their family, their background, and their educational achievements. Financial need is also considered in the selection process. Scholarships are awarded in the following priority order: 1) members of LPA who have a medically diagnosed form of dwarfism; 2) immediate family members of dwarfs who are also paid members of LPA; and 3) people with dwarfism who are not members of LPA.

Financial data Stipends range from $250 to $1,000.

Duration 1 year; awards are limited to 2 for undergraduate study and 1 for graduate study.

Number awarded Varies; generally between 5 and 10 each year.

Deadline April of each year.

[1042]
LOUISIANA TITLE 29 DEPENDENTS' EDUCATIONAL ASSISTANCE

Louisiana Department of Veterans Affairs
Attn: Education Program
602 North Fifth Street
Baton Rouge, LA 70802
(225) 219-5000   Toll Free: (877) GEAUX-VA
Fax: (225) 219-5590   E-mail: veteran@la.gov
Web: www.vetaffairs.la.gov/benefits

Summary To provide financial assistance to children, spouses, and surviving spouses of certain disabled or deceased Louisiana veterans who plan to attend college in the state.

Eligibility This program is open to children (between 16 and 25 years of age), spouses, or surviving spouses of veterans who served during specified periods of wartime and 1) were killed in action or died in active service; 2) died of a service-connected disability; 3) are missing in action (MIA) or a prisoner of war (POW); 4) sustained a disability rated as 90% or more by the U.S. Department of Veterans Affairs; or 5) have been determined to be unemployable as a result of a service-connected disability. Deceased, MIA, and POW veterans must have resided in Louisiana for at least 12 months prior to entry into service. Living disabled veterans must have resided in Louisiana for at least 24 months prior to the child's or spouse's admission into the program.

Financial data Eligible persons accepted as full-time students at Louisiana state-supported colleges, universities, trade schools, or vocational/technical schools are admitted free and are exempt from payment of tuition, laboratory, athletic, medical, and other special fees. Free registration does not cover books, supplies, room and board, or fees assessed by the student body on themselves (such as yearbooks and weekly papers).

Duration Support is provided for a maximum of 4 school years, to be completed in not more than 5 years from date of original entry.

Additional data Attendance must be on a full-time basis. Surviving spouses must remain unremarried and must take advantage of the benefit within 10 years after eligibility is established.

Number awarded Varies each year.

Deadline Applications must be received no later than 3 months prior to the beginning of a semester.

[1043]
LT. JON C. LADDA MEMORIAL FOUNDATION SCHOLARSHIP

Lt. Jon C. Ladda Memorial Foundation
7 Gillette Way
Farmington, CT 06032
E-mail: info@jonladda.org
Web: www.jonladda.org/scholarship.htm

Summary To provide financial assistance for college to children of deceased and disabled U.S. Naval Academy graduates and members of the Navy submarine service.

Eligibility This program is open to children of U.S. Naval Academy graduates and members of the U.S. Navy submarine service. The parent must have died on active duty or been medically retired with a 100% disability. Applicants must be enrolled or accepted at a 4-year college or university, including any of the service academies. Along with their application, they must submit an essay on a topic that changes annually. Selection is based on academic achievement, financial need, and merit.

Financial data A stipend is awarded (amount not specified). Funds are disbursed directly to the recipient's institution.

Duration 1 year; may be renewed.

Number awarded 1 or more each year.

Deadline March of each year.

[1044]
LYMAN FISHER SCHOLARSHIPS

Virginia Hemophilia Foundation
410 North Ridge Road, Suite 215
Richmond, VA 23228
Toll Free: (800) 266-8438   Fax: (800) 266-8438
E-mail: info@vahemophilia.org
Web: www.vahemophilia.org

Summary To provide financial assistance to people from Virginia who have participated in activities of the Virginia Hemophilia Foundation (VHF) and are interested in attending college.

Eligibility This program is open to members of the bleeding disorder community and their families who are attending or planning to attend college. Applicants must have a record of prior participation with VHF and be a resident of Virginia or planning to attend college in Virginia. Along with their application, they must submit a brief biographical sketch of themselves that includes their interests, hobbies, vocational and educational goals, volunteer and community involvement, and work or internship experience; a description of their previous participation with VHF and how they plan to contribute to the organization and support other persons with inherited bleeding disorders; a detailed statement of financial need; a 1-page essay on their career goals; another 1-page essay on a topic of their choice; and 3 letters of recommendation.

Financial data The stipend is $2,000.

Duration 1 year.

Number awarded 2 each year.

Deadline April of each year.

[1045]
MAINE VETERANS DEPENDENTS EDUCATIONAL BENEFITS

Bureau of Veterans' Services
117 State House Station
Augusta, ME 04333-0117
(207) 430-6035   Toll Free: (800) 345-0116 (within ME)
Fax: (207) 626-4471   E-mail: mainebvs@maine.gov
Web: www.maine.gov

Summary To provide financial assistance for undergraduate or graduate education to dependents of disabled and other Maine veterans.

Eligibility Applicants for these benefits must be children (high school seniors or graduates under 22 years of age), non-divorced spouses, or unremarried widow(er)s of veterans who meet 1 or more of the following requirements: 1) living and determined to have a total permanent disability resulting from a service-connected cause; 2) killed in action; 3) died from a service-connected disability; 4) died while totally and permanently disabled due to a service-connected disability but whose death was not related to the service-connected disability; or 5) a member of the armed forces on active duty who has been listed for more than 90 days as missing in action, captured, forcibly detained, or interned in the line of duty by a foreign government or power. The veteran parent must have been a resident of Maine at the time of entry into service or a resident of Maine for 5 years preceding application for these benefits. Children may be working on an associate or bachelor's degree. Spouses, widows, and widowers may work on an associate, bachelor's, or master's degree.

Financial data Recipients are entitled to free tuition at institutions of higher education supported by the state of Maine.

Duration Children may receive up to 8 semesters of support; they have 6 years from the date of first entrance to complete those 8 semesters. Continuation in the program is based on their earning a GPA of 2.0 or higher each semester. Spouses are entitled to receive up to 120 credit hours of educational benefits and have 10 years from the date of first entrance to complete their program.

Additional data College preparatory schooling and correspondence courses are not supported under this program.

Number awarded Varies each year.

Deadline Deadline not specified.

[1046]
MALLORY SMITH LEGACY SCHOLARSHIP

Georgia Transplant Foundation
Attn: Scholarship Program
2201 Macy Drive
Roswell, GA 30076
(770) 457-3796   Fax: (770) 457-7916
E-mail: gtf@gatransplant.org
Web: www.gatransplant.org

Summary To provide financial assistance to residents of Georgia who are transplant recipients or dependents of recipients and interested in attending college in any state.

Eligibility This program is open to residents of Georgia who are entering or continuing at an accredited institution of higher learning in any state. Applicants must be an organ transplant recipient or the dependent of a recipient. Along with their application, they must submit a 3-page personal statement on their career objectives, how this scholarship will help them attain their goals, and how transplantation has affected their life. Selection is based on that statement, transcripts, high school exit examination scores, ACT/SAT scores, 3 letters of reference, and financial need.

Financial data The stipend is $1,000 per year.

Duration 1 year; may be renewed up to 3 additional years.

Number awarded 1 each year.

Deadline April of each year.

[1047]
MARILYN YETSO MEMORIAL SCHOLARSHIP

Ulman Cancer Fund for Young Adults
Attn: Scholarship Committee
921 East Fort Avenue, Suite 325
Baltimore, MD 21230
(410) 964-0202   Toll Free: (888) 393-FUND
Fax: (888) 964-0402
E-mail: scholarship@ulmanfund.org
Web: www.ulmanfund.org/scholarships

Summary To provide financial assistance for college or graduate school to students from the Baltimore/Washington metropolitan area who have or have lost a parent to cancer.

Eligibility This program is open to residents of the Baltimore/Washington metropolitan area who have or have lost a parent or guardian to cancer. Applicants must be 35 years of age or younger and attending, or planning to attend, a 2- or 4-year college, university, or vocational program in any state to work on an undergraduate or graduate degree. The parent or guardian must have been first diagnosed with cancer after the applicant was 15 years of age. Along with their application, they must submit a 500-word essay or 3-minute video on either 1) a letter that they would have liked to receive during their cancer experience; or 2) what they would tell the young adults who participate in the sponsor's summer-long drive to support the organization about being a young adult impacted by cancer. Financial need is considered in the selection process. U.S. citizenship or permanent resident status is required.

Financial data The stipend is $2,500. Funds are paid directly to the educational institution.

Duration 1 year.

Additional data This program began in 2002. Recipients are obligated to organize and run a bone marrow registry drive with the support of Delete Blood Cancer and There Goes My Hero.

Number awarded 1 each year.

Deadline March of each year.

[1048]
MARK COATS MEMORIAL SCHOLARSHIP

Matrix Health Group
Attn: Memorial Scholarship Program
2202 Brownstone Court
Champaign, IL 61822
(217) 840-1033
E-mail: maria.vetter@matrixhealthgroup.com
Web: www.factorsupportnetwork.com

Summary To provide financial assistance for college to people who have a bleeding disorder and members of their immediate family.

Eligibility This program is open to graduating male and female high school seniors and students currently enrolled full time at an accredited college, university, or technical school. Applicants must have hemophilia, von Willebrand's disease, or other bleeding disorder or be an immediate family member of a person with a bleeding disorder. Applicants must have a GPA of 2.0 or higher for their senior year in high school or their current year in college. Along with their application, they must submit transcripts, ACT or SAT test scores, 2 letters of recommendation, information on their work and school activities, and an essay of 300 to 400 words on 1 of the following topics: 1) the experiences that have influenced their decision to pursue their educational goals or career choice; 2) how they feel their life has been influenced by having a bleeding disorder or by having a bleeding disorder in their family; or 3) their biggest challenge in having a bleeding disorder and how they have or are working through it. Selection is based on that essay, academic merit, and reference letters.

Financial data The stipend is $1,000.

Duration 1 year.

Additional data This program is supported by Homecare for the Cure and administered by Matrix Health Group.

Number awarded 1 each year.

Deadline July of each year.

[1049]
MARY BARTON FREEMAN SCHOLARSHIPS

Ulman Cancer Fund for Young Adults
Attn: Scholarship Committee
921 East Fort Avenue, Suite 325
Baltimore, MD 21230
(410) 964-0202   Toll Free: (888) 393-FUND
Fax: (888) 964-0402
E-mail: scholarship@ulmanfund.org
Web: www.ulmanfund.org/scholarships

Summary To provide financial assistance for college or graduate school to students who have been diagnosed with cancer or have or have lost a family member with cancer.

Eligibility This program is open to students who 1) have been diagnosed with cancer; 2) have a parent or sibling living with cancer; or 3) have lost a parent or sibling to cancer. Applicants must be attending, or planning to attend, a college or university in any state to work on an undergraduate, graduate, or professional degree. They must be working on career or higher eduction goals. The first diagnosis of cancer (whether of the applicant, a parent, or sibling) must have occurred after the applicant was 15 years of age. Along with their application, they must submit a 500-word essay or 3-minute video on either 1) a letter that they would have liked to receive during their cancer experience; or 2) what they would tell the young adults who participate in the sponsor's summer-long drive to support the organization about being a young adult impacted by cancer. U.S. citizenship or permanent resident status is required.

Financial data The stipend is $2,500. Funds are paid directly to the educational institution.

Duration 1 year.

Additional data Recipients are obligated to organize and run a bone marrow registry drive with the support of Delete Blood Cancer and There Goes My Hero.

Number awarded 5 each year.

Deadline March of each year.

[1050]
MATTHEWS AND SWIFT EDUCATIONAL TRUST SCHOLARSHIPS

Knights of Columbus
Attn: Department of Scholarships
1 Columbus Plaza
P.O. Box 1670
New Haven, CT 06507-0901
(203) 752-4332   Fax: (203) 772-2696
E-mail: scholarships@kofc.org
Web: www.kofc.org/en/scholarships/matthews_swift.html

Summary To provide financial assistance at Catholic colleges or universities in any country to children of disabled or deceased veterans, law enforcement officers, or firemen who are/were also Knights of Columbus members.

Eligibility This program is open to children of members of the sponsoring organization who are high school seniors in any country planning to attend a 4-year Catholic college or university in their country. The parent must be a member of Knights of Columbus who 1) was serving in the military forces of their country and was killed by hostile action or wounded by hostile action, resulting within 2 years in permanent and total disability; 2) was a full-time law enforcement officer who became disabled or died as a result of criminal violence; or 3) was a firefighter who became disabled or deceased in the line of duty.

Financial data The amounts of the awards vary but are designed to cover tuition, to a maximum of $25,000 per year, at the Catholic college or university of the recipient's choice in the country of their residence. Funds are not available for room, board, books, fees, transportation, dues, computers, or supplies.

Duration 1 year; may be renewed up to 3 additional years.

Additional data This program began in 1944 to provide scholarships to the children of Knights who became totally and permanently disabled through service during World

War II. It has been modified on many occasions, most recently in 2007 to its current requirements.
Number awarded   Varies each year.
Deadline   February of each year.

[1051]
MERFELD FAMILY FOUNDATION SCHOLARSHIPS

Ventura County Community Foundation
Attn: Scholarships
4001 Mission Oaks Boulevard, Suite A
Camarillo, CA 93012
(805) 988-0196, ext. 119   Fax: (805) 484-2700
E-mail: vweber@vccf.org
Web: www.vccf.org/scholarship/merf/index.shtml

Summary   To provide financial assistance to college students who parents have been diagnosed with Amyotrophic Lateral Sclerosis (A.L.S.).
Eligibility   This program is open to students who have a parent diagnosed with A.L.S. and are either graduating high school seniors or students. Applicants may be residents of any state, but preference is given to those from Iowa and southern California (Imperial, Kern, Los Angeles, Orange, Riverside, San Bernardino, San Diego, and Ventura counties). They must have a GPA of 2.75 or higher. Along with their application, they must submit an essay on why they deserve this scholarship award and how it will help them. Financial need is not required, but may be considered in the selection process.
Financial data   The stipend is $2,500.
Duration   1 year.
Additional data   This program began in 2011.
Number awarded   Approximately 3 each year, including 1 from Iowa and 1 from southern California.
Deadline   January of each year.

[1052]
MESOTHELIOMA CANCER ALLIANCE SCHOLARSHIP

Mesothelioma Cancer Alliance
c/o Early, Lucarelli, Sweeney, Meisenkothen
360 Lexington Avenue, 20th Floor
New York, NY 10017
(212) 968-2233   Toll Free: (800) 336-0086
Fax: (212) 986-2255
Web: www.mesothelioma.com/scholarship

Summary   To provide financial assistance to undergraduate and graduate students who have had cancer or whose family member has had cancer.
Eligibility   This program is open to U.S. citizens enrolled or planning to enroll full time at a 2- or 4-year college or university as an undergraduate or graduate student. Applicants must have battled cancer at any point in their lives (not limited to mesothelioma) or have a parent, sibling, immediate family member, or close friend who has battled or is currently fighting cancer. They must have a GPA of 3.0 or higher. Along with their application, they must submit an essay of 500 to 1,500 words or a video up to 5 minutes in length on how cancer has affected their life, how

they overcame that strong adversity, how cancer has affected their outlook on their life and personal or career goals, how that adversity shaped who they are today, what the scholarship would mean to them, and why it is important. Selection is based on the positive impact they have on those around them, strength in the face of adversity, commitment to academic excellence, and financial need.
Financial data   The stipend is $4,000.
Duration   1 year.
Number awarded   2 each year: 1 in fall and 1 in spring.
Deadline   March of each year for fall semester; November of each year for spring semester.

[1053]
MICHAEL A. HUNTER MEMORIAL SCHOLARSHIP

Orange County Community Foundation
Attn: Scholarship Officer
4041 MacArthur Boulevard, Suite 510
Newport Beach, CA 92660
(949) 553-4202, ext. 246   Fax: (949) 553-4211
E-mail: mabril@oc-cf.org
Web: oc-cf.academicworks.com/opportunities/1568

Summary   To provide financial assistance for college to leukemia and lymphoma patients and the children of non-surviving leukemia and lymphoma patients.
Eligibility   This program is open to graduating high school seniors, community college students, and 4-year university students nationwide. Applicants must be leukemia or lymphoma patients and/or the children of non-surviving leukemia or lymphoma patients who are enrolled or planning to enroll full time. They must have a GPA of 3.0 or higher and be able to document financial need. Along with their application, they must submit a 600-word essay on hoe leukemia or lymphoma has affected their life.
Financial data   Stipends range from $2,000 to $3,000.
Duration   1 year.
Number awarded   2 each year.
Deadline   March of each year.

[1054]
MICHAEL CALKINS MEMORIAL SCHOLARSHIP

Georgia Transplant Foundation
Attn: Scholarship Program
2201 Macy Drive
Roswell, GA 30076
(770) 457-3796   Fax: (770) 457-7916
E-mail: gtf@gatransplant.org
Web: www.gatransplant.org

Summary   To provide financial assistance to residents of Georgia who are transplant recipients or dependents or siblings of recipients and interested in attending college in any state.
Eligibility   This program is open to residents of Georgia who are entering or continuing at an accredited institution of higher learning in any state. Applicants must be an organ transplant recipient or the dependent or sibling of a recipient. Along with their application, they must submit a

3-page personal statement on their career objectives, how this scholarship will help them attain their goals, and how transplantation has affected their life. Selection is based on that statement, transcripts, high school exit examination scores, ACT/SAT scores, 3 letters of reference, and financial need.

Financial data The stipend is $1,000 per year.

Duration 1 year; may be renewed up to 3 additional years.

Number awarded 1 each year.

Deadline April of each year.

[1055]
MICHIGAN CHILDREN OF VETERANS TUITION GRANTS

Michigan Department of Treasury
Attn: Student Scholarships and Grants
P.O. Box 30462
Lansing, MI 48909-7962
(517) 373-0457   Toll Free: (888) 4-GRANTS
Fax: (517) 241-5835
E-mail: mistudentaid@michigan.gov
Web: www.michigan.gov

Summary To provide financial assistance for college to the children of Michigan veterans who are totally disabled or deceased as a result of service-connected causes.

Eligibility This program is open to natural and adopted children of veterans who have been totally and permanently disabled as a result of a service-connected illness or injury prior to death and have now died, have died or become totally and permanently disabled as a result of a service-connected illness or injury, have been killed in action or died from another cause while serving in a war or war condition, or are listed as missing in action in a foreign country. The veteran must have been a legal resident of Michigan immediately before entering military service and did not reside outside of Michigan for more than 2 years, or must have established legal residency in Michigan after entering military service. Applicants must be between 16 and 26 years of age and must have lived in Michigan at least 12 months prior to the date of application. They must be enrolled or planning to enroll at least half time at a community college, public university, or independent degree-granting college or university in Michigan. U.S. citizenship or permanent resident status is required.

Financial data Full-time recipients are exempt from payment of the first $2,800 per year of tuition or any other fee that takes the place of tuition. Prorated exemptions apply to three-quarter time and half-time students.

Duration 1 year; may be renewed for up to 3 additional years if the recipient maintains full-time enrollment and a GPA of 2.25 or higher.

Additional data This program was formerly known as the Michigan Veterans Trust Fund Tuition Grants, administered by the Michigan Veterans Trust Fund within the Department of Military and Veterans Affairs. It was transferred to Student Scholarships and Grants in 2006.

Number awarded Varies each year; recently, 414 of these grants, worth $967,853, were awarded.

Deadline Deadline not specified.

[1056]
MID AMERICA CHAPTER MS SOCIETY SCHOLARSHIP PROGRAM

National Multiple Sclerosis Society-Mid America
  Chapter
Attn: Scholarship Program
7611 State Line Road, Suite 100
Kansas City, MO 64114
(816) 448-2180   Toll Free: (800) 344-4867
Fax: (816) 361-2369   E-mail: jean.long@nmss.org
Web: www.nationalmssociety.org

Summary To provide financial assistance to high school seniors and graduates from the Midwest region who have multiple sclerosis (MS) or have a parent with MS and are planning to attend college in any state.

Eligibility This program is open to graduating high school seniors, recent graduates, and GED recipients from Kansas, western Missouri, Nebraska, or Pottawattamie County, Iowa who have MS or a parent who has MS. Applicants must be planning to enroll as a first-time student at a 2- or 4-year college, university, or vocational/technical school in the United States on at least a half-time basis. Along with their application, they must submit an essay on the impact MS has had on their lives. Selection is based on that essay, academic record, leadership and participation in school or community activities, work experience, goals and aspirations, an outside appraisal, special circumstances, and financial need. U.S. citizenship or permanent resident status is required.

Financial data The stipend is $1,000.

Duration 1 year.

Number awarded Varies each year; recently, 7 were awarded.

Deadline January of each year.

[1057]
MIKE HYLTON SCHOLARSHIP

Matrix Health Group
Attn: Memorial Scholarship Program
2202 Brownstone Court
Champaign, IL 61822
(217) 840-1033
E-mail: maria.vetter@matrixhealthgroup.com
Web: www.factorsupportnetwork.com

Summary To provide financial assistance for college to men who have a bleeding disorder and members of their immediate family.

Eligibility This program is open to graduating male high school seniors and students currently enrolled full time at an accredited college, university, or technical school. Applicants must have hemophilia, von Willebrand's disease or other bleeding disorder or be an immediate family member of a person with a bleeding disorder. They must have a GPA of 2.0 or higher for their senior year in high school or their current year in college. Along with their application, they must submit transcripts, ACT or SAT test scores, 2 letters of recommendation, information on their work and school activities, and an essay of 300 to 400 words on 1 of the following topics: 1) the experiences that have influenced their decision to pursue their educational goals or career choice; 2) how they feel their life has been influenced by having a bleeding disorder or by having a bleeding disorder in their family; or 3) their biggest challenge in having a bleeding disorder and how they have or are working through it. Selection is based on that essay, academic merit, and reference letters.

Financial data The stipend is $1,000.
Duration 1 year.
Additional data This program is supported by Factor Support Network Pharmacy and administered by Matrix Health Group.
Number awarded 1 each year.
Deadline July of each year.

[1058]
MILLIE BROTHER SCHOLARSHIPS

Children of Deaf Adults Inc.
c/o Jennie E. Pyers, Scholarship Committee
Wellesley College
106 Central Street, SCI484A
Wellesley, MA 02481-8203
(413) 650-2632
E-mail: scholarships@coda-international.org
Web: www.coda-international.org/scholarship

Summary To provide financial assistance for college or graduate school to the children of deaf parents.
Eligibility This program is open to the hearing children of deaf parents who are high school seniors or graduates attending or planning to attend college or graduate school. Applicants must submit a 2-page essay on 1) how their experience as the child of deaf parents has shaped their life and goals; and 2) their future career aspirations. Essays are judged on organization, content, and creativity. In addition to the essay, selection is based on a high school and/or college transcript and 2 letters of recommendation.
Financial data The stipend is $3,000.
Duration 1 year; recipients may reapply.
Number awarded Normally, 2 each year.
Deadline March of each year.

[1059]
MINNESOTA G.I. BILL PROGRAM

Minnesota Department of Veterans Affairs
Attn: Programs and Services Division
20 West 12th Street, Room 206
St. Paul, MN 55155
(651) 296-2562   Toll Free: (888) LINK-VET
Fax: (651) 296-3954   TDD: (800) 627-3529
E-mail: MNGIBill@state.mn.us
Web: mn.gov

Summary To provide financial assistance for college or graduate school in the state to residents of Minnesota who

served in the military after September 11, 2001 and the families of deceased or disabled military personnel.
Eligibility This program is open to residents of Minnesota enrolled at colleges and universities in the state as undergraduate or graduate students. Applicants must be 1) a veteran who is serving or has served honorably in a branch of the U.S. armed forces at any time; 2) a non-veteran who has served honorably for a total of 5 years or more cumulatively as a member of the Minnesota National Guard or other active or Reserve component of the U.S. armed forces, and any part of that service occurred on or after September 11, 2001; or 3) a surviving child or spouse of a person who has served in the military at any time and who has died or has a total and permanent disability as a result of that military service. They may be attending college in the state or participating in an apprenticeship or on-the-job (OJT) training program. Financial need is also considered in the selection process.
Financial data The college stipend is $1,000 per semester for full-time study or $500 per semester for part-time study. The maximum award is $3,000 per academic year or $10,000 per lifetime. Apprenticeship and OJT students are eligible for up to $2,000 per fiscal year. Approved employers are eligible to receive $1,000 placement credit payable upon hiring a person under this program and another $1,000 after 12 consecutive months of employment. No more than $3,000 in aggregate benefits under this paragraph may be paid to or on behalf of an individual in one fiscal year, and not more than $9,000 over any period of time.
Duration 1 year; may be renewed, provided the recipient continues to make satisfactory academic progress.
Additional data This program was established by the Minnesota Legislature in 2007.
Number awarded Varies each year.
Deadline Deadline not specified.

[1060]
MISSISSIPPI LAW ENFORCEMENT OFFICERS AND FIREMEN SCHOLARSHIP PROGRAM

Mississippi Office of Student Financial Aid
3825 Ridgewood Road
Jackson, MS 39211-6453
(601) 432-6997   Toll Free: (800) 327-2980 (within MS)
Fax: (601) 432-6527   E-mail: sfa@ihl.state.ms.us
Web: www.riseupms.com/state-aid/mleof

Summary To provide financial assistance to the spouses and children of disabled or deceased Mississippi law enforcement officers and firefighters who are interested in attending college in the state.
Eligibility This program is open to children and spouses of law enforcement officers, full-time firefighters, and volunteer firefighters who became permanently and totally disabled or who died in the line of duty and were Mississippi residents at the time of death or injury. Applicants must be high school seniors or graduates interested in attending a state-supported postsecondary institution in Mississippi on a full-time basis. Children may be natural,

adopted, or stepchildren up to 23 years of age; spouses may be of any age.

Financial data Students in this program receive full payment of tuition fees, the average cost of campus housing, required fees, and applicable course fees at state-supported colleges and universities in Mississippi. Funds may not be used to pay for books, food, school supplies, materials, dues, or fees for extracurricular activities.

Duration Up to 8 semesters.

Number awarded Varies each year; recently, 14 of these awards, worth more than $116,000, were granted.

Deadline September of each year.

[1061]
MISSOURI KIDS' CHANCE SCHOLARSHIP PROGRAM

Missouri Department of Higher Education
Attn: Student Financial Assistance
205 Jefferson Street
P.O. Box 1469
Jefferson City, MO 65102-1469
(573) 751-2361   Toll Free: (800) 473-6757
Fax: (573) 751-6635   E-mail: info@dhe.mo.gov
Web: www.dhe.mo.gov/ppc/grants/kidschance.php

Summary To provide financial assistance to residents of Missouri whose parent was seriously injured or killed in an accident covered by Workers' Compensation.

Eligibility This program is residents of Missouri between 17 and 22 years of age whose parent was seriously injured or killed in a work-related accident or from an occupational disease and covered by Workers' Compensation. Applicants must be enrolled or planning to enroll at least half time at a college or university in the state. They must have an expected family contribution (EFC) from their FAFSA of $12,000 or less. U.S. citizenship, permanent resident status, or lawful presence in the United States is required.

Financial data Stipends are the lesser of 1) the actual tuition charged to a Missouri resident at the school where the recipient is enrolled; 2) the amount of tuition charged to a Missouri resident enrolled for the same number of hours as a student at the University of Missouri at Columbia; or 3) the maximum private scholarship amount available through Kids' Chance Inc. of Missouri (recently, $2,500).

Duration 1 year; may be renewed until the age of 22, provided the recipient continues to maintain satisfactory academic progress with a GPA of 2.5 or higher.

Additional data This program operates in partnership with the private organization Kids' Chance Inc. of Missouri. Both organizations use the same application form so the Missouri Department of Higher Education automatically forwards applications of students who do not receive these scholarships because of a lack of state funding to the private organization for its consideration.

Number awarded Varies each year.

Deadline April of each year.

[1062]
MISSOURI PUBLIC SERVICE OFFICER OR EMPLOYEE'S CHILD SURVIVOR GRANT PROGRAM

Missouri Department of Higher Education
Attn: Student Financial Assistance
205 Jefferson Street
P.O. Box 1469
Jefferson City, MO 65102-1469
(573) 751-2361   Toll Free: (800) 473-6757
Fax: (573) 751-6635   E-mail: info@dhe.mo.gov
Web: www.dhe.mo.gov

Summary To provide financial assistance to disabled public safety officers in Missouri and the spouses and children of disabled or deceased officers who are interested in attending college in the state.

Eligibility This program is open to residents of Missouri who are 1) public safety officers who were permanently and totally disabled in the line of duty; 2) spouses of public safety officers who were killed or permanently and totally disabled in the line of duty; or 3) children of Missouri public safety officers or Department of Transportation employees who were killed or permanently and totally disabled while engaged in the construction or maintenance of highways, roads, and bridges. Applicants must be Missouri residents enrolled or accepted for enrollment as a full-time undergraduate student at a participating Missouri college or university; children must be younger than 24 years of age. Students working on a degree or certificate in theology or divinity are not eligible. U.S. citizenship or permanent resident status is required.

Financial data The maximum annual grant is the lesser of 1) the actual tuition charged at the school where the recipient is enrolled; or 2) the amount of tuition charged to a Missouri undergraduate resident enrolled full time in the same class level and in the same academic major as a student at the University of Missouri at Columbia.

Duration 1 year; may be renewed.

Additional data Public safety officers include firefighters, police officers, capitol police officers, parole officers, probation officers, state correctional employees, water safety officers, conservation officers, park rangers, and highway patrolmen.

Number awarded Varies each year; recently, 11 students received $47,045 in support from this program.

Deadline There is no application deadline, but early submission of the completed application is encouraged.

[1063]
MISSOURI WARTIME VETERAN'S SURVIVOR GRANT PROGRAM

Missouri Department of Higher Education
Attn: Student Financial Assistance
205 Jefferson Street
P.O. Box 1469
Jefferson City, MO 65102-1469
(573) 751-2361   Toll Free: (800) 473-6757
Fax: (573) 751-6635   E-mail: info@dhe.mo.gov
Web: www.dhe.mo.gov

Summary To provide financial assistance to survivors of deceased or disabled Missouri post-September 11, 2001 veterans who plan to attend college in the state.

Eligibility This program is open to spouses and children of veterans whose deaths or injuries were a result of combat action or were attributed to an illness that was contracted while serving in combat action, or who became at least 80% disabled as a result of injuries or accidents sustained in combat action after September 11, 2001. The veteran must have been a Missouri resident when first entering military service or at the time of death or injury. The spouse or child must be a U.S. citizen or permanent resident or otherwise lawfully present in the United States; children of veterans must be younger than 25 years of age. All applicants must be enrolled or accepted for enrollment at least half time at participating public college or university in Missouri.

Financial data The maximum annual grant is the lesser of 1) the actual tuition charged at the school where the recipient is enrolled; or 2) the amount of tuition charged to a Missouri resident enrolled in the same number of hours at the University of Missouri at Columbia. Additional allowances provide up to $2,000 per semester for room and board and the lesser of the actual cost for books or $500.

Duration 1 year. May be renewed, provided the recipient maintains a GPA of 2.5 or higher and makes satisfactory academic progress; children of veterans are eligible until they turn 25 years of age or receive their first bachelor's degree, whichever occurs first.

Number awarded Up to 25 each year.

Deadline There is no application deadline, but early submission of the completed application is encouraged.

[1064]
MOUSE HOLE SCHOLARSHIPS

Blind Mice, Inc.
16810 Pinemoor Way
Houston, TX 77058
(713) 893-7277   E-mail: blindmicemart@att.net
Web: www.blindmicemegamall.com

Summary To provide financial assistance for college to blind students and the children of blind parents.

Eligibility This program is open to visually-impaired students and to sighted students who have visually-impaired parents. Applicants must be high school seniors or graduates who have never been enrolled in college. Along with their application, they must submit an essay, between 4 and 15 pages in length, on a topic that changes annually; recently, students were asked to imagine that they are attending their tenth high school reunion and to think back over their life since they graduated from high school. Essays are judged on originality, creativity, grammar, spelling, and the judge's overall impression of the applicant.

Financial data Stipends are $2,000 for the winner and $1,000 for the first runner-up.

Duration 1 year.

Additional data This program began in 2003. The winner receives the Antonia M. Derks Memorial Scholarship and the first runner-up receives the Kelsey Campbell Memorial Scholarship.

Number awarded 2 each year. Since the program began, it has awarded more than $28,350 in scholarships.

Deadline May of each year.

[1065]
MPPA FOUNDATION SCHOLARSHIPS

Montana Police Protective Association
Attn: MPPA Foundation, Inc.
P.O. Box 7
Butte, MT 59703
(406) 490-1947   Toll Free: (800) 565-8557
E-mail: jdwilli@bresnan.net
Web: www.mppaonline.org/foundation/scholarship.php

Summary To provide financial assistance to children of members of the Montana Police Protective Association (MPPA) who are interested in attending college in any state.

Eligibility This program is open to children of Montana police officers who are MPPA members, whether active, retired, or medical disability retired. Applicants must be enrolled or planning to enroll full time at a college, university, junior college, or vocational/technical school in any state. They must have a GPA of 2.5 or higher.

Financial data The maximum lifetime award for each recipient is $5,000 over 5 years.

Duration 1 year; may be renewed up to 4 additional years, provided the recipient maintains a GPA of 2.85 or higher.

Number awarded 1 or more each year.

Deadline April of each year.

[1066]
NAGA EDUCATIONAL SCHOLARSHIP GRANT

National Amputee Golf Association
Attn: Executive Director
701 Orkney Court
Smyrna, TN 37167-6395
(615) 967-4555   E-mail: info@nagagolf.org
Web: www.nagagolf.org

Summary To provide financial assistance for college to members of the National Amputee Golf Association (NAGA) and their dependents.

Eligibility This program is open to amputee members in good standing in the association and their dependents. Applicants must submit information on their scholastic background (GPA in high school and college, courses of study); type of amputation and cause (if applicable), a cover letter describing their plans for the future; and documentation of financial need. They need not be competitive golfers. Selection is based on academic record, financial need, involvement in extracurricular or community activities, and area of study.

Financial data The stipend for a 4-year bachelor's degree program is $1,000 per year. The stipend for a 2-year technical or associate degree is $500 per year.

Duration Up to 4 years, provided the recipient maintains at least half-time enrollment and a GPA of 3.0 or higher and continues to demonstrate financial need.

Number awarded 1 or more each year.

Deadline June of each year.

[1067]
NANCY JAYNES MEMORIAL SCHOLARSHIP AWARD

Indiana Breast Cancer Awareness Trust, Inc.
P.O. Box 8212
Evansville, IN 47716
Toll Free: (866) 724-2228   Fax: (812) 868-8773
E-mail: info@breastcancerplate.org
Web: www.breastcancerplate.org/scholarships

Summary To provide financial assistance to high school seniors in Indiana whose parent has or had breast cancer and who are planning to attend college in the state.

Eligibility This program is open to seniors graduating from high schools in Indiana who are planning to enroll full or part time at a college, university, or technical school in the state. Applicants must have lost a parent to breast cancer or have a parent who is battling breast cancer. They must have a GPA of 2.8 or higher and be U.S. citizens or permanent residents. Along with their application, they must submit a 500-word essay on how breast cancer has changed them and how they have demonstrated their support in the fight against breast cancer.

Financial data The stipend is $1,500.

Duration 1 year.

Number awarded 1 or more each year.

Deadline February of each year.

[1068]
NATE SLACK SCHOLARSHIP

HF Healthcare
Attn: Scholarship
411 North Lombard Street, Suite B
Oxnard, CA 93030
Toll Free: (866) 981-1171   Fax: (805) 981-1121
E-mail: scholarship@hfhealthcare.com
Web: www.hfhealthcare.com/scholarship

Summary To provide financial assistance for college to students who have hemophilia or a related bleeding disorder and their immediate family.

Eligibility This program is open to U.S. residents who have hemophilia or a related bleeding disorder or are the immediate family member of a person with hemophilia or a related bleeding disorder. Applicants must be enrolled or

planning to enroll at an accredited college, university, community college, or trade school. Along with their application, they must submit a 500-word essay the covers their experience living with hemophilia or a related bleeding disorder, their current educational goals, and what they plan to do after they complete those.

Financial data The stipend is $1,000.

Duration 1 year.

Number awarded 2 each year.

Deadline May of each year.

[1069]
NATIONAL COLLEGIATE CANCER FOUNDATION LEGACY SCHOLARSHIP PROGRAM

National Collegiate Cancer Foundation
Attn: Scholarship Committee
4858 Battery Lane, Suite 216
Bethesda, MD 20814
(240) 515-6262   E-mail: info@collegiatecancer.org
Web: www.collegiatecancer.org/scholarships

Summary To provide financial assistance to undergraduate and graduate students who have lost a parent or guardian to cancer.

Eligibility This program is open to students between 18 and 35 years of age who have lost a parent or guardian to cancer. Applicants must be enrolled or planning to enroll at a college or university to work on a certificate or an associate, bachelor's, master's, or doctoral degree. Along with their application, they must submit a 1,000-word essay on 1 of 4 assigned topics related to their experiences with cancer and college. Selection is based on notable accomplishments, recommendations, encouragement, and financial need. U.S. citizenship or permanent resident status is required.

Financial data The stipend is $1,000.

Duration 1 year.

Additional data This program began in 2014.

Number awarded Varies each year; recently, 21 were awarded.

Deadline May of each year.

[1070]
NATIONAL LAW ENFORCEMENT AND FIREFIGHTERS CHILDREN'S FOUNDATION GENERAL SCHOLARSHIPS

National Law Enforcement and Firefighters Children's
  Foundation
928 Broadway, Suite 703
New York, NY 10010
(646) 822-4236   E-mail: nleafcf@ncleafcf.org
Web: www.nleafcf.org/scholarships/general-scholarship

Summary To provide financial assistance for college to the children of law enforcement officers and firefighters who were killed or disabled in the line of duty.

Eligibility This program is open to the dependent children (including stepchildren and adopted children) of law enforcement officers and firefighters who were killed or totally and permanently disabled in the line of duty. Applicants must be working or planning to work full time on an associate or bachelor's degree or vocational certificate at a college, university, or vocational/technical institute in the United States. They must be U.S. citizens or permanent residents. Selection is based on academics, demonstrated leadership, outstanding performance in the arts or sports, volunteer activities benefiting the community, and financial need.

Financial data Stipends range from $500 to $5,000 per year. Funds are paid directly to the recipient's institution.

Duration 1 year; may be renewed up to 3 additional years, provided the recipient continues to make satisfactory academic progress and demonstrates financial need.

Number awarded Varies each year.

Deadline June of each year.

[1071]
NATIONAL MS SOCIETY SCHOLARSHIP PROGRAM

National Multiple Sclerosis Society
Attn: Scholarship Fund
900 South Broadway, Suite 200
Denver, CO 80209
(303) 698-6100, ext. 15259   E-mail: nmss@act.org
Web: www.nationalmssociety.org

Summary To provide financial assistance for college to students who have Multiple Sclerosis (MS) or are the children of people with MS.

Eligibility This program is open to 1) high school seniors who have MS and will be attending an accredited postsecondary school for the first time; 2) high school seniors who are the children of parents with MS and will be attending an accredited postsecondary school for the first time; 3) high school (or GED) graduates of any age who have MS and will be attending an accredited postsecondary school for the first time; and 4) high school (or GED) graduates of any age who have a parent with MS and will be attending an accredited postgraduate school for the first time. Applicants must be U.S. citizens or permanent residents who plan to enroll for at least 6 credit hours per semester in an undergraduate course of study at an accredited 2- or 4-year college, university, or vocational/technical school in the United States or its territories to work on a degree, license, or certificate. Along with their application, they must submit a 1-page personal statement on the impact MS has had on their life. Selection is based on that statement, academic record, leadership and participation in school or community activities, work experience, goals and aspirations, an outside appraisal, special circumstances, and financial need.

Financial data Stipends range from $1,000 to $3,000 per year.

Duration 1 year; may be renewed.

Additional data This program, which began in 2003, is managed by ACT Scholarship and Recognition Services.

Number awarded Varies each year; recently, 815 were awarded.

Deadline January of each year.

[1072]
NCSA ANNUAL SCHOLARSHIP AWARDS

North Carolina Sheriffs' Association
2501 Blue Ridge Road, Suite 250
P.O. Box 20049
Raleigh, NC 27619-0049
(919) 743-7433   Fax: (919) 783-5272
E-mail: ncsa@ncsheriffs.net
Web: www.ncsheriffs.org/about/scholarships

Summary To provide financial assistance to residents of North Carolina, especially children of deceased or disabled law enforcement officers, who are majoring in criminal justice at a campus of the University of North Carolina (UNC) system.

Eligibility Eligible for this program are North Carolina residents enrolled full time in a criminal justice program at any of the 12 state institutions offering that major. Interested students apply to the university they are attending. They must provide a letter of recommendation from the sheriff of their home county. First priority in selection is given to children and stepchildren of North Carolina sheriffs and deputy sheriffs; second to children and stepchildren of North Carolina law enforcement officers killed in the line of duty; third to children and stepchildren of sheriffs or deputy sheriffs who are deceased or retired (regular or disability; fourth to other resident criminal justice students meeting their institution's academic and financial need criteria.

Financial data The stipend is $2,000.

Duration 1 year; nonrenewable.

Additional data The UNC institutions offering a criminal justice major are Appalachian State University, East Carolina University, Elizabeth City State University, Fayetteville State University, North Carolina A&T State University, North Carolina Central University, North Carolina State University, the University of North Carolina at Charlotte, the University of North Carolina at Pembroke, the University of North Carolina at Wilmington, Western Carolina University, and Winston-Salem State University.

Number awarded Up to 12 each year: 1 at each of the eligible state institutions.

Deadline Each of the 12 participating universities sets its own deadline.

[1073]
NEBRASKA CHAPTER NHF POST-SECONDARY SCHOLARSHIPS

National Hemophilia Foundation-Nebraska Chapter
Attn: Scholarship Selection Committee
215 Centennial Mall South, Suite 512
Lincoln, NE 68508
(402) 742-5663   Fax: (402) 742-5677
E-mail: office@nebraskanhf.org
Web: www.nebraskanhf.org

Summary To provide financial assistance for attendance at a college in any state to high school seniors in Nebraska who have a bleeding disorder, are relatives of a person with a bleeding disorder, or are a carrier of a defective gene related to a bleeding disorder.

Eligibility This program is open to seniors graduating from high schools in Nebraska who plan to attend a college or university in any state. Applicants must have a bleeding disorder, be an immediately family member of a person with a bleeding disorder, or be the carrier of a defective gene related to a bleeding disorder. Along with their application, they must submit a brief statement on how a bleeding disorder influences their family life and a 250-word essay on their purpose and motivation for pursuing a postsecondary educational degree. Selection is based on that statement and essay, academic promise in their major field, and financial need. Preference is given to members of the Nebraska Chapter of the National Hemophilia Foundation (NHF).

Financial data The stipend ranges from $500 to $1,000 per academic term ($1,000 to $2,000 per year).

Duration 1 year.

Number awarded 1 or more each year.

Deadline June of each year.

[1074]
NEBRASKA WAIVER OF TUITION FOR VETERANS' DEPENDENTS

Department of Veterans' Affairs
State Office Building
301 Centennial Mall South, Sixth Floor
P.O. Box 95083
Lincoln, NE 68509-5083
(402) 471-2458   Fax: (402) 742-1142
E-mail: ndva@nebraska.gov
Web: www.vets.state.ne.us/benefits.html

Summary To provide financial assistance for college to dependents of deceased and disabled veterans and military personnel in Nebraska.

Eligibility Eligible are spouses, widow(er)s, and children who are residents of Nebraska and whose parent, stepparent, or spouse was a member of the U.S. armed forces and 1) died of a service-connected disability; 2) died subsequent to discharge as a result of injury or illness sustained while in service; 3) is permanently and totally disabled as a result of military service; or 4) is classified as missing in action or as a prisoner of war during armed hostilities. Applicants must be attending or planning to attend a branch of the University of Nebraska, a state college, or a community college in Nebraska.

Financial data Tuition is waived at public institutions in Nebraska.

Duration Spouses may receive support until completion of a bachelor's degree; children are eligible until the complete a bachelor's degree or reach 26 years of age.

Additional data Applications may be submitted through 1 of the recognized veterans' organizations or any county service officer.

Number awarded Varies each year; recently, 311 were awarded.

Deadline Deadline not specified.

[1075]
NEW JERSEY BANKERS EDUCATION FOUNDATION SCHOLARSHIPS

New Jersey Bankers Association
Attn: New Jersey Bankers Education Foundation, Inc.
411 North Avenue East
Cranford, NJ 07016-2436
(908) 272-8500, ext. 614   Fax: (908) 272-6626
E-mail: j.meredith@njbankers.com
Web: www.njbankers.com

Summary To provide financial assistance to dependents of deceased and disabled military personnel who have a connection to New Jersey and are interested in attending college in any state.

Eligibility This program is open to the spouses, children, stepchildren, and grandchildren of members of the armed services who died or became disabled while on active duty; it is not required that the military person died in combat. Applicants must have a high school or equivalency diploma and be attending college in any state. Adult dependents who wish to obtain a high school equivalency diploma are also eligible. Either the dependent or the servicemember must have a connection to New Jersey; the applicant's permanent address must be in New Jersey or the servicemember's last permanent address or military base must have been in the state. Financial need is considered in the selection process.

Financial data A stipend is awarded (amount not specified).

Duration 1 year; may be renewed if the recipient maintains a "C" average.

Additional data This program began in 2005.

Number awarded 1 or more each year.

Deadline June of each year.

[1076]
NEW JERSEY SHARING NETWORK SCHOLARSHIPS

New Jersey Sharing Network Foundation
Attn: Scholarship Committee
691 Central Avenue
New Providence, NJ 07974
(908) 516-5400   Toll Free: (800) 742-7365
Fax: (908) 516-5501
E-mail: info@njsharingnetwork.org
Web: www.njsharingnetwork.org/scholarship

Summary To provide financial assistance to high school seniors in New Jersey who are organ transplant recipients or donors (or their family or friends) and interested in attending college in any state.

Eligibility This program is open to seniors graduating from high schools in New Jersey and planning to attend a college or university in any state. Applicants must have been a donor awareness advocate or have been personally affected by or is a family member of someone personally affected by organ and tissue donation and transplantation (i.e., organ and/or tissue donor, living donor, transplant recipient, waiting for a transplant, or died waiting for a transplant). Along with their application, they must submit an essay on what donation has meant in their life, their knowledge of donation, and their active participation in awareness events.

Financial data The stipend is $5,000; funds are paid directly to the school.

Duration 1 year.

Additional data This program includes the Betsy Niles Scholarship and the Missy's Miracle Scholarship.

Number awarded Varies each year; recently, 4 were awarded.

Deadline April of each year.

[1077]
NEW YORK MILITARY ENHANCED RECOGNITION INCENTIVE AND TRIBUTE (MERIT) SCHOLARSHIPS

New York State Higher Education Services Corporation
Attn: Student Information
99 Washington Avenue
Albany, NY 12255
(518) 473-1574   Toll Free: (888) NYS-HESC
Fax: (518) 473-3749   TDD: (800) 445-5234
E-mail: scholarships@hesc.com
Web: www.hesc.ny.gov

Summary To provide financial assistance to disabled veterans and the family members of deceased or disabled veterans who are residents of New York and interested in attending college in the state.

Eligibility This program is open to New York residents who served in the armed forces of the United States or state organized militia at any time on or after August 2, 1990 and became severely and permanently disabled as a result of injury or illness suffered or incurred in a combat theater or combat zone or during military training operations in preparation for duty in a combat theater or combat zone of operations. Also eligible are the children, spouses, or financial dependents of members of the armed forces of the United States or state organized militia who at any time after August 2, 1990 1) died, became severely and permanently disabled as a result of injury or illness suffered or incurred, or are classified as missing in action in a combat theater or combat zone of operations; 2) died as a result of injuries incurred in those designated areas; or 3) died or became severely and permanently disabled as a result of injury or illness suffered or incurred during military training operations in preparation for duty in a combat theater or combat zone of operations. Applicants must be attending or accepted at an approved program of study as full-time undergraduates at a public college or university or private institution in New York.

Financial data At public colleges and universities, this program provides payment of actual tuition and mandatory educational fees; actual room and board charged to students living on campus or an allowance for room and board for commuter students; and allowances for books, supplies, and transportation. At private institutions, the award is equal to the amount charged at the State University of New York (SUNY) for 4-year tuition and average mandatory fees (or the student's actual tuition and fees,

whichever is less) plus allowances for room, board, books, supplies, and transportation. Recently, maximum awards were $23,045 for students living on campus or $15,125 for commuter students.

Duration This program is available for 4 years of full-time undergraduate study (or 5 years in an approved 5-year bachelor's degree program).

Additional data This program was previously known as the New York State Military Service Recognition Scholarships (MSRS).

Number awarded Varies each year; recently, 93 students received more than $1.3 million from is program.

Deadline April of each year.

[1078]
NEW YORK STATE WORLD TRADE CENTER MEMORIAL SCHOLARSHIPS

New York State Higher Education Services Corporation
Attn: Student Information
99 Washington Avenue
Albany, NY 12255
(518) 473-1574   Toll Free: (888) NYS-HESC
Fax: (518) 473-3749   TDD: (800) 445-5234
E-mail: scholarships@hesc.com
Web: www.hesc.ny.gov

Summary To provide financial assistance to undergraduates in New York who are survivors or victims of the terrorist attacks on September 11, 2001 or their relatives.

Eligibility This program is open to 1) the children, spouses, and financial dependents of deceased or severely and permanently disabled victims of the September 11, 2001 terrorist attacks or the subsequent rescue and recovery operations; and 2) survivors of the terrorist attacks who are severely and permanently disabled as a result of injuries sustained in the attacks or the subsequent rescue and recovery operations. Applicants must be attending or accepted at an approved program of study as full-time undergraduates at a public college or university or private institution in New York.

Financial data At public colleges and universities, this program provides payment of actual tuition and mandatory educational fees; actual room and board charged to students living on campus or an allowance for room and board for commuter students; and allowances for books, supplies, and transportation. At private institutions, the award is equal to the amount charged at the State University of New York (SUNY) for 4-year tuition and average mandatory fees (or the student's actual tuition and fees, whichever is less) plus allowances for room, board, books, supplies, and transportation. Recently, maximum awards were $23,045 for students living on campus or $15,125 for commuter students.

Duration This program is available for 4 years of full-time undergraduate study (or 5 years in an approved 5-year bachelor's degree program).

Number awarded Varies each year; recently, 807 students received more than $13.3 in support from this program.

Deadline April of each year.

[1079]
NO ANGEL LEFT BEHIND SCHOLARSHIP

No Angel Left Behind
c/o Aerial Construction
3062 Anderson Street
Bonita, CA 91902
(619) 990-1007   Fax: (619) 434-5374
Web: www.noangelsleftbehind.org/scholarship

Summary To provide financial assistance for to children of military personnel killed or disabled in service.

Eligibility This program is open to graduating high school seniors who plan to attend an accredited college or university in their state. Priority is given in order to applicants who have at least 1 parent who was 1) killed in active duty on foreign soil; 2) killed in active duty by friendly fire; 3) accidentally killed while serving; 4) died while in service; or 5) maimed or disabled while in the service. Applicants must be planning to study economics, education, engineering, finance, liberal arts, or science. They must have a GPA of 2.8 or higher and scores of at least 1450 on the SAT or 20 on the ACT. Financial need is considered in the selection process.

Financial data Stipends range from $1,000 to $5,000 per year.

Duration 1 year; may be renewed up to 3 additional years, provided the recipient demonstrates satisfactory academic performance and maintains a high level of community commitment and involvement.

Number awarded Varies each year.

Deadline July or December of each year.

[1080]
NO GREATER SACRIFICE SCHOLARSHIP

No Greater Sacrifice
Attn: Foundation
1101 Pennsylvania Avenue, N.W. Suite 300
Washington, DC 20004
(202) 756-1980   E-mail: info@nogreatersacrifice.org
Web: www.nogreatersacrifice.org/who-we-help

Summary To provide financial assistance for college to children of deceased and disabled veterans who served after September 11, 2001.

Eligibility This program is open to children up to 26 years of age whose parent or legal guardian has fallen or suffered from a wound, illness, or injury in the line of duty while serving in the United States military after September 11, 2001. Living parents must have a Veterans Affairs disability rating of 60% or more or active duty equivalent.

Financial data The program pays benefits up to the amount of the Post-9/11 GI Bill (recently, that was full payment of tuition and fees at public institutions in the student's home state or up to $21,970.46 at private institutions).

Duration 1 year; may be renewed for up to 36 additional months or until completion of an associate or bachelor's degree.

Number awarded Varies each year.

Deadline April of each year.

[1081]
NORTH CAROLINA BAR ASSOCIATION SCHOLARSHIPS

North Carolina Bar Association
Attn: Young Lawyers Division Scholarship Committee
8000 Weston Parkway
P.O. Box 3688
Cary, NC 27519-3688
(919) 677-0561   Toll Free: (800) 662-7407
Fax: (919) 677-0761   E-mail: jterrell@ncbar.org
Web: www.ncbar.org/members/divisions/young-lawyers

Summary To provide financial assistance for college or graduate school to the children of disabled or deceased law enforcement officers in North Carolina.

Eligibility This program is open to the natural or adopted children of North Carolina law enforcement officers who were permanently disabled or killed in the line of duty. Applicants must be younger than 27 years of age and enrolled or planning to enroll full time at an accredited institution of higher learning (including community colleges, trade schools, colleges, universities, and graduate programs) in North Carolina. Selection is based on academic performance and financial need.

Financial data A stipend is awarded (amount not specified).

Duration Up to 4 years.

Number awarded Varies each year; recently, 17 were awarded.

Deadline April of each year.

[1082]
NORTH CAROLINA LIONS EDUCATION GRANT PROGRAM

North Carolina Lions, Inc.
Attn: Executive Director
7050 Camp Dogwood Drive
P.O. Box 39
Sherrills Ford, NC 28673
(828) 478-2135, ext. 223
Toll Free: (800) 662-7401, ext. 223
Fax: (828) 478-4419   E-mail: steve@nclionsinc.org
Web: www.nclionsinc.org

Summary To provide financial assistance for college to sighted children of blind or visually impaired parents in North Carolina.

Eligibility This program is open to residents of North Carolina who are sighted children of blind or visually-impaired parents. Applicants must be working on or planning to work on an undergraduate degree or certificate. Family income may not exceed $40,000 for families with 1 dependent child, increasing by $10,000 for each additional dependent child. Selection is based on the financial need of the family and the academic record and character of the applicant.

Financial data The stipend is $1,500. Funds are paid directly to the college, community college, or trade/technical school selected by the recipient.

Duration 1 year; may be renewed up to 4 additional years, provided the recipient maintains full-time enrollment and a GPA of 2.0 or higher.

Additional data This program was formerly known as the William L. Woolard Educational Grant Program.

Number awarded 1 or more each year.

Deadline March of each year.

[1083]
NORTH CAROLINA SCHOLARSHIPS FOR CHILDREN OF WAR VETERANS

North Carolina Department of Military and Veterans
  Affairs
413 North Salisbury Street
4001 Mail Service Center
Raleigh, NC 27699-4001
(984) 204-8366   Fax: (919) 807-4260
Web: www.milvets.nc.gov

Summary To provide financial assistance to the children of disabled and other classes of North Carolina veterans who plan to attend college in the state.

Eligibility Eligible applicants come from 5 categories: Class I-A: the veteran parent died in wartime service or as a result of a service-connected condition incurred in wartime service; Class I-B: the veteran parent is rated by the U.S. Department of Veterans Affairs (VA) as 100% disabled as a result of wartime service and currently or at the time of death was drawing compensation for such disability; Class II: the veteran parent is rated by the VA as much as 20% but less than 100% disabled due to wartime service, or was awarded a Purple Heart medal for wounds received, and currently or at the time of death drawing compensation for such disability; Class III: the veteran parent is currently or was at the time of death receiving a VA pension for total and permanent disability, or the veteran parent is deceased but does not qualify under any other provisions, or the veteran parent served in a combat zone or waters adjacent to a combat zone and received a campaign badge or medal but does not qualify under any other provisions; Class IV: the veteran parent was a prisoner of war or missing in action. For all classes, applicants must 1) be under 25 years of age and have a veteran parent who was a resident of North Carolina at the time of entrance into the armed forces; or 2) be the natural child, or adopted child prior to age 15, who was born in North Carolina, has been a resident of the state continuously since birth, and is the child of a veteran whose disabilities occurred during a period of war.

Financial data Students in Classes I-A, II, III, and IV receive $4,500 per academic year if they attend a private college or junior college; if attending a public postsecondary institution, they receive free tuition, a room allowance, a board allowance, and exemption from certain mandatory fees. Students in Class I-B receive $1,500 per academic year if they attend a private college or junior college; if attending a public postsecondary institution, they receive free tuition and exemption from certain mandatory fees.

Duration 4 academic years.

Number awarded An unlimited number of awards are made under Classes I-A, I-B, and IV. Classes II and III are limited to 100 awards each year in each class.

Deadline Applications for Classes I-A, I-B, and IV may be submitted at any time; applications for Classes II and III must be submitted by February of each year.

[1084]
NORTH CAROLINA TROOPERS ASSOCIATION SCHOLARSHIPS

North Carolina Troopers Association
Attn: Scholarship Committee
3505 Vernon Woods Drive
P.O. Box 840
Summerfield, NC 27358
(336) 644-8914   Toll Free: (800) 446-7334
Fax: (336) 644-6205   E-mail: info@nctroopers.org
Web: www.nctroopers.org/membership

Summary To provide financial assistance for college to children of members of the North Carolina Troopers Association (NCTA) and of disabled and deceased North Carolina Highway Patrol troopers.

Eligibility This program is open to dependent children between 16 and 23 years of age of active or deceased members of the NCTA who have been members for at least 2 years. Applicants must be enrolled or planning to enroll full time at a university, college, community college, technical college, or trade school in North Carolina. Along with their application, they must submit an essay of 750 to 1,000 words on how the scholarship will benefit them. Special applications are accepted from the children of disabled or deceased troopers of the North Carolina State Highway Patrol.

Financial data Stipends are $1,000 for students at 4-year colleges and universities or $500 for students at community, technical, and trade colleges.

Duration 1 year; may be renewed as long as the recipient remains enrolled full time with a grade average of "C" or higher.

Additional data This program includes the Colonel Bob Barefoot Scholarship for a student at a 4-year college or university and the Captain Ivan Stroud Scholarship for a student at a community college.

Number awarded 8 each year: 5 at $1,000 to students at 4-year institutions and 3 at $500 to students at 2-year institutions.

Deadline March of each year.

[1085]
NORTH DAKOTA EDUCATIONAL ASSISTANCE FOR DEPENDENTS OF VETERANS

Department of Veterans Affairs
4201 38th Street S.W., Suite 104
P.O. Box 9003
Fargo, ND 58106-9003
(701) 239-7165   Toll Free: (866) 634-8387
Fax: (701) 239-7166
Web: www.nd.gov

Summary To provide financial assistance for college to the spouses, widow(er)s, and children of disabled and other North Dakota veterans and military personnel.

Eligibility This program is open to the spouses, widow(er)s, and dependent children of veterans who were killed in action, died from wounds or other service-connected causes, were totally disabled as a result of service-connected causes, died from service-connected disabilities, were a prisoner of war, or were declared missing in action. Veteran parents must have been born in and lived in North Dakota until entrance into the armed forces (or must have resided in the state for at least 6 months prior to entrance into military service) and must have served during wartime.

Financial data Eligible dependents receive free tuition and are exempt from fees at any state-supported institution of higher education, technical school, or vocational school in North Dakota.

Duration Up to 45 months or 10 academic semesters.

Number awarded Varies each year.

Deadline Deadline not specified.

[1086]
OHIO LEGION AUXILIARY DEPARTMENT PRESIDENT'S SCHOLARSHIP

American Legion Auxiliary
Department of Ohio
1100 Brandywine Boulevard, Suite D
P.O. Box 2760
Zanesville, OH 43702-2760
(740) 452-8245   Fax: (740) 452-2620
E-mail: ala_katie@rrohio.com
Web: www.alaohio.org/Scholarships

Summary To provide financial assistance to veterans and their descendants in Ohio who are interested in attending college in any state.

Eligibility This program is open to honorably-discharged veterans and the children, grandchildren, and great-grandchildren of living, deceased, or disabled honorably-discharged veterans who served during designated periods of wartime. Applicants must be residents of Ohio, seniors at an accredited high school, planning to enter a college in any state, and sponsored by an American Legion Auxiliary Unit. Along with their application, they must submit an original article (up to 500 words) written by the applicant on a topic that changes annually. Recently, students were asked to write on "Education and the American Dream." Selection is based on character, Americanism, leadership, scholarship, and financial need.

Financial data Stipends are $1,500 or $1,000. Funds are paid to the recipient's school.

Duration 1 year.

Number awarded 2 each year: 1 at $1,500 and 1 at $1,000.

Deadline March of each year.

[1087]
OHIO WAR ORPHANS SCHOLARSHIP

Ohio Department of Higher Education
Attn: Office of Financial Aid
25 South Front Street
Columbus, OH 43215-3414
(614) 752-9528   Toll Free: (888) 833-1133
Fax: (614) 752-5903
E-mail: rchurch@highered.ohio.gov
Web: www.ohiohighered.org/ohio-war-orphans

Summary To provide financial assistance to the children of deceased or disabled Ohio veterans who plan to attend college in the state.

Eligibility This program is open to residents of Ohio who are under 25 years of age and interested in enrolling full time at an eligible college or university in the state. Applicants must be the child of a veteran who 1) was a member of the U.S. armed forces, including the organized Reserves and Ohio National Guard, for a period of 90 days or more (or discharged because of a disability incurred after less than 90 days of service); 2) served during specified periods of wartime; 3) entered service as a resident of Ohio; and 4) as a result of that service, either was killed or became at least 60% service-connected disabled. Also eligible are children of veterans who have a permanent and total nonservice-connected disability and are receiving disability benefits from the U.S. Department of Veterans Affairs. If the veteran parent served only in the organized Reserves or Ohio National Guard, the parent must have been killed or became permanently and totally disabled while at a scheduled training assembly, field training period (of any duration or length), or active duty for training, pursuant to bona fide orders issued by a competent authority. Financial need is considered in the selection process.

Financial data At Ohio public colleges and universities, the program currently provides payment of 88% of tuition and fees. At Ohio private colleges and universities, the stipend is $5,112 per year.

Duration 1 year; may be renewed up to 4 additional years, provided the recipient maintains a GPA of 2.0 or higher.

Additional data Eligible institutions are Ohio state-assisted colleges and universities and Ohio institutions approved by the Board of Regents. This program was established in 1957.

Number awarded Varies, depending upon the funds available. If sufficient funds are available, all eligible applicants are given a scholarship. Recently, 861 students received benefits from this program.

Deadline May of each year.

[1088]
OPERATION ENDURING FREEDOM AND OPERATION IRAQI FREEDOM SCHOLARSHIP

Vermont Student Assistance Corporation
Attn: Scholarship Programs
10 East Allen Street
P.O. Box 2000
Winooski, VT 05404-2601
(802) 654-3798   Toll Free: (888) 253-4819
Fax: (802) 654-3765 TDD: (800) 281-3341 (within VT)
E-mail: info@vsac.org
Web: www.vsac.org

Summary To provide financial assistance to residents of Vermont whose parent has served or is serving in the U.S. armed forces or National Guard.

Eligibility This program is open to residents of Vermont who are children of a member of any branch of the armed forces or National Guard whose residence or home of record is in Vermont. Applicants must plan to enroll full time in a certificate, associate degree, or bachelor's degree program at an accredited postsecondary school in any state. Preference is given to applicants whose parent was killed, was wounded, or became permanently disabled as a result of their service during Operation Enduring Freedom or Operation Iraqi Freedom. Along with their application, they must submit a 250-word essay on their interest in and commitment to the career or program of study they have chosen to pursue; their short- and long-term academic, career, and/or employment goals; their financial need; the impact that their participation in community service has had on their life; and what they believe distinguishes their application from others that may be submitted. Selection is based on that essay, a letter of recommendation, and financial need.

Financial data The stipend ranges from $3,500 to $7,000 per year.

Duration 1 year; may be renewed up to 3 additional years.

Additional data This program, established in 2007, is sponsored by the Hoehl Family Foundation.

Number awarded Varies each year; recently, 10 were awarded.

Deadline March of each year.

[1089]
OREGON DECEASED OR DISABLED PUBLIC SAFETY OFFICER GRANT PROGRAM

Oregon Student Access Commission
Attn: Public Programs
1500 Valley River Drive, Suite 100
Eugene, OR 97401-2130
(541) 687-7400   Toll Free: (800) 452-8807
Fax: (541) 687-7414   TDD: (800) 735-2900
E-mail: PublicPrograms@osac.state.or.us
Web: www.oregonstudentaid.gov/ddpso-grant.aspx

Summary To provide financial assistance for college or graduate school in the state to the children of disabled or deceased Oregon public safety officers.

Eligibility This program is open to the natural, adopted, or stepchildren of Oregon public safety officers (firefighters, state fire marshals, chief deputy fire marshals, deputy state fire marshals, police chiefs, police officers, sheriffs, deputy sheriffs, county adult parole and probation officers, correction officers, and investigators of the Criminal Justice Division of the Department of Justice) who, in the line of duty, were killed or disabled. Applicants must be enrolled or planning to enroll as a full-time undergraduate student at a public or private college or university in Oregon. Children of deceased officers are also eligible for graduate study. Financial need must be demonstrated.

Financial data At a public 2- or 4-year college or university, the amount of the award is equal to the cost of tuition and fees. At an eligible private college, the award amount is equal to the cost of tuition and fees at the University of Oregon.

Duration 1 year; may be renewed for up to 3 additional years of undergraduate study, if the student maintains satisfactory academic progress and demonstrates continued financial need. Children of deceased public safety officers may also receive support for 12 quarters of graduate study.

Number awarded Varies each year.

Deadline Deadline not specified.

[1090]
OREGON LEGION AUXILIARY DEPARTMENT NURSES SCHOLARSHIP FOR DEPENDENTS OF DISABLED VETERANS

American Legion Auxiliary
Department of Oregon
30450 S.W. Parkway Avenue
P.O. Box 1730
Wilsonville, OR 97070-1730
(503) 682-3162   Fax: (503) 685-5008
E-mail: alaor@alaoregon.com
Web: www.alaoregon.org/scholarships.php

Summary To provide financial assistance for study of nursing at a school in any state to the wives and children of disabled Oregon veterans and military personnel.

Eligibility This program is open to Oregon residents who are the sons, daughters, or wives of veterans or of persons still serving in the armed forces who have a disability. Applicants must have been accepted by an accredited hospital or university school of nursing in any state. Along with their application, they must submit a 500-word essay on a topic that changes annually; recently, students were asked to write on "How Pride in country, community, school and family directs my daily life." Selection is based on ability, aptitude, character, determination, seriousness of purpose, and financial need.

Financial data The stipend is $1,500.

Duration 1 year; may be renewed.

Number awarded 1 each year.

Deadline April of each year.

[1091]
OREGON LEGION AUXILIARY DEPARTMENT SCHOLARSHIPS FOR WIVES OF DISABLED VETERANS

American Legion Auxiliary
Department of Oregon
30450 S.W. Parkway Avenue
P.O. Box 1730
Wilsonville, OR 97070-1730
(503) 682-3162   Fax: (503) 685-5008
E-mail: alaor@alaoregon.com
Web: www.alaoregon.org/scholarships.php

Summary To provide financial assistance to the wives of disabled Oregon veterans who are interested in attending college in any state.

Eligibility This program is open to Oregon residents who are wives of disabled veterans. Applicants must be interested in obtaining education beyond the high school level at a college, university, business school, vocational school, or any other accredited postsecondary school in any state. Along with their application, they must submit a 500-word essay on a topic that changes annually; recently, students were asked to write on "How Pride in country, community, school and family directs my daily life." Selection is based on ability, aptitude, character, seriousness of purpose, and financial need.

Financial data The stipend is $1,000.

Duration 1 year; nonrenewable.

Number awarded 1 or more each year.

Deadline February of each year.

[1092]
OREGON OCCUPATIONAL SAFETY AND HEALTH DIVISION WORKERS MEMORIAL SCHOLARSHIPS

Oregon Office of Student Access and Completion
Attn: Scholarship Processing Coordinator
1500 Valley River Drive, Suite 100
Eugene, OR 97401-2146
(541) 687-7422   Toll Free: (800) 452-8807, ext. 7422
Fax: (541) 687-7414   TDD: (800) 735-2900
E-mail: cheryl.a.connolly@state.or.us
Web: app.oregonstudentaid.gov/Catalog/Default.aspx

Summary To provide financial assistance to the children and spouses of disabled or deceased workers in Oregon who are interested in attending college or graduate school in any state.

Eligibility This program is open to residents of any state who are U.S. citizens or permanent residents. Applicants must be high school seniors or graduates who 1) are dependents or spouses of an Oregon worker who has suffered permanent total disability on the job; or 2) are receiving, or have received, fatality benefits as dependents or spouses of a worker fatally injured in Oregon. They may be attending a college or graduate school in any state. Along with their application, they must submit an essay of up to 500 words on how the injury or death of their parent or spouse has affected or influenced their decision to fur-

ther their education. Financial need is not required, but it is considered in the selection process.

Financial data Stipends for scholarships offered by the Oregon Office of Student Access and Completion (OSAC) range from $1,000 to $10,000 but recently averaged $4,368.

Duration 1 year.

Additional data This program, established in 1991, is sponsored by the Oregon Occupational Safety and Health Division of the Department of Consumer and Business Services.

Number awarded Varies each year; recently, 7 were awarded.

Deadline February of each year.

[1093]
OREGON STUDENT CHILD CARE GRANTS

Oregon Student Access Commission
Attn: Public Programs
1500 Valley River Drive, Suite 100
Eugene, OR 97401-2130
(541) 687-7400   Toll Free: (800) 452-8807
Fax: (541) 687-7414   TDD: (800) 735-2900
E-mail: PublicPrograms@osac.state.or.us
Web: www.oregonstudentaid.gov/child-care-grant.aspx

Summary To provide funding for child care to undergraduate students at colleges in Oregon.

Eligibility This program is open to residents of Oregon who are enrolled at colleges and universities in the state. Applicants must be able to demonstrate financial need to care for a child or legal dependent 12 years of age or younger; children older than 12 years also qualify if they satisfy the requirements of special needs. In the selection process, first priority is given to prior recipients who maintain a child care provider registered with the Oregon Department of Human Services or registered/certified with the Child Care Division of the Oregon Department of Employment; second priority is given to new applicants based on the following criteria: 1) financial need; 2) credits earned toward a certificate, associate degree, or first bachelor's degree; 3) use of registered child care providers; 4) full-time students; and 5) half-time students. Applicants must be U.S. citizens or eligible noncitizens and not in default on any federal student loan.

Financial data Grant amounts vary, depending on the need of the recipient; recently, they averaged approximately $5,200.

Duration 1 year; may be renewed, provided the student meets the first selection priority. Maximum enrollment in the program is 6 years.

Number awarded Varies each year; recently, approximately 60 students received these grants.

Deadline May of each year.

[1094]
OUR BROTHER'S KEEPER FOUNDATION SCHOLARSHIPS

Our Brother's Keeper Foundation
c/o James Wiederstein, Secretary/Treasurer
1382 East Nichols Avenue
Centennial, CO 80122
E-mail: obkf.o2@verizon.net
Web: www.ble-t.org/pr/news/pf_newsflash.asp?id=5238

Summary To provide financial assistance for college to spouses and children of railroad workers injured on the job.

Eligibility This program is open to students entering or enrolled at an accredited college, university, or trade/technical school. Applicants must be the spouse or child of a worker seriously injured in a career-ending railroad accident who was a member of the Brotherhood of Locomotive Engineers and Trainmen (BLET) at the time of the injury. Along with their application, they must submit information on the career fields that interest them the most, why they are interested in that career field, their SAT/ACT scores, their most recent work-related activities, their most recent volunteer activities, their favorite hobbies, and other scholarships they have been awarded along with an estimate of the annual cost of attending their chosen institution. Primary consideration is given to families of workers who have not yet settled their legal claims or those whose claim settlements have left the family with insufficient resources to fund educational opportunities.

Financial data The stipend is $1,000.

Duration 1 year.

Additional data This program began in 2008.

Number awarded 4 each year: 1 in each of the BLET regions.

Deadline Applications must be submitted 30 days prior to the start of the meeting of the BLET region to which the injured worker belongs; that means deadlines are normally May of each year for the Southeastern Meeting Association (SMA), June of each year for the International Western Convention (IWC), July of each year for the Eastern Union Meeting Association (EUMA), or August of each year for the Southwestern Convention Meeting (SWCM).

[1095]
PATRIOT SCHOLARSHIP OF THE UNIVERSITY INTERSCHOLASTIC LEAGUE

University Interscholastic League
Attn: Texas Interscholastic League Foundation
1701 Manor Road
P.O. Box 151027
Austin, TX 78715-1027
(512) 382-0916   Fax: (512) 382-0377
E-mail: info@tilfoundation.org
Web: www.tilfoundation.org/scholarships/list

Summary To provide financial assistance to high school seniors who participate in programs of the Texas Interscholastic League Foundation (TILF), are children of veterans, and plan to attend college in the state.

Eligibility This program is open to seniors graduating from high schools in Texas who have competed in a University Interscholastic League (UIL) academic state meet (participation in athletic or music contests does not qualify). Applicants must be the child of a veteran, rank in the top 25% of their class, and have a GPA of 2.5 or higher. They must be planning to enroll full time at a college or university in the state and major in any field. Along with their application, they must submit high school transcripts that include SAT and/or ACT scores and documentation of financial need. Preference is given to children of injured veterans.

Financial data The stipend is $2,000.

Duration 1 year; nonrenewable.

Number awarded 1 or more each year.

Deadline May of each year.

[1096]
PENNSYLVANIA NATIONAL GUARD SCHOLARSHIP FUND

Pennsylvania National Guard Associations
Attn: Pennsylvania National Guard Scholarship Fund
Biddle Hall (Building 9-109)
Fort Indiantown Gap
Annville, PA 17003-5002
(717) 865-9631   Toll Free: (800) 997-8885
Fax: (717) 861-5560   E-mail: oswalddean@aol.com
Web: www.pngas.net/news/75652

Summary To provide financial assistance to Pennsylvania National Guard members and the children of disabled or deceased members who are interested in attending college in any state.

Eligibility This program is open to active members of the Pennsylvania Army or Air National Guard. Children of members of the Guard who died or were permanently disabled while on Guard duty are also eligible. Applicants must be entering their first year of higher education as a full-time student or presently attending a college or vocational school in any state as a full-time student. Along with their application, they must submit an essay that outlines their military and civilian plans for the future. Selection is based on academic potential, military commitment, extracurricular activities, and Guard participation.

Financial data Stipends range from $400 to $1,000.

Duration 1 year.

Additional data The sponsoring organization includes the National Guard Association of Pennsylvania (NGAP) and the Pennsylvania National Guard Enlisted Association (PNGEA). This program, which began in 1977, includes the following named scholarships: the BG Richard E. Thorn Memorial Scholarship, the Murtha Memorial Scholarship, the BG Hugh S. Niles Memorial Scholarship, the PNGEA USAA Scholarship (sponsored by the USAA Insurance Corporation), and the 28th Infantry Division Scholarship.

Number awarded Varies each year; recently, 13 were awarded: 4 at $1,000, 2 at $500, and 7 at $400.

Deadline June of each year.

[1097]
PERLITA LIWANAG MEMORIAL SCHOLARSHIP

Ulman Cancer Fund for Young Adults
Attn: Scholarship Committee
921 East Fort Avenue, Suite 325
Baltimore, MD 21230
(410) 964-0202   Toll Free: (888) 393-FUND
Fax: (888) 964-0402
E-mail: scholarship@ulmanfund.org
Web: www.ulmanfund.org/scholarships

Summary To provide financial assistance for college or graduate school to students from the Washington, D.C. metropolitan area who have been diagnosed with cancer or have or have lost a family member with cancer.

Eligibility This program is open to students who 1) have been diagnosed with cancer; 2) have a parent, sibling, or guardian living with cancer; or 3) have lost a parent, sibling, or guardian to cancer. Applicants must be residents of Washington, D.C., Maryland, or northern Virginia. They must be 35 years of age or younger and attending, or planning to attend, a 2- or 4-year college, university, or vocational program in any state to work on an undergraduate or graduate degree. The first diagnosis of cancer (whether of the applicant, a parent, a sibling, or a guardian) must have occurred after the applicant was 15 years of age. Along with their application, they must submit a 500-word essay or 3-minute video on either 1) a letter that they would have liked to receive during their cancer experience; or 2) what they would tell the young adults who participate in the sponsor's summer-long drive to support the organization about being a young adult impacted by cancer. U.S. citizenship or permanent resident status is required.

Financial data The stipend is $2,500. Funds are paid directly to the educational institution.

Duration 1 year.

Additional data This program began in 2011. Recipients are obligated to organize and run a bone marrow registry drive with the support of Delete Blood Cancer and There Goes My Hero.

Number awarded 1 each year.

Deadline March of each year.

[1098]
PINK BANDANA SCHOLARSHIPS

Pink Bandana
Attn: Scholarships
P.O. Box 83282
Lincoln, NE 68501
(402) 560-1578 E-mail: scholarship@pinkbandana.org
Web: pinkbandana.org/scholarship

Summary To provide financial assistance for college in any state to high school seniors in Nebraska who have battled breast cancer or have a family member who has battled cancer.

Eligibility This program is open to seniors graduating from high schools in Nebraska and planning to enroll full time at a college, university, or community college in any state. Applicants must have battled breast cancer or have a sibling, guardian, or biological parent who has battled breast cancer within the past 10 years. Along with their application, they must submit a list of extracurricular activities, information on the member of their family who has battled breast cancer, an essay on how the battle against breast cancer has affected them and their family, and information on their financial situation.

Financial data The total stipend is $4,000, paid in increments of $1,000 per year for students at 4-year colleges and university or $2,000 per year for students at 2-year colleges.

Duration Up to 4 years for students at 4-year colleges and universities or up to students at 2-year colleges.

Number awarded 1 or more each year.

Deadline March of each year.

[1099]
PINKROSE BREAST CANCER SCHOLARSHIPS

PinkRose Foundation, Inc.
P.O. Box 4025
Dedham, MA 02027
E-mail: info@pinkrose.org
Web: www.pinkrose.org/scholarships

Summary To provide financial assistance for college to students who have lost a parent or legal guardian to breast cancer.

Eligibility This program is open to U.S. citizens and permanent residents under 25 years of age who are enrolled or planning to enroll in a college degree or certificate program. Applicants must have lost a parent or legal guardian to breast cancer. Along with their application, they must submit a 2-page essay describing the significant impact of breast cancer in their life; how their academic motivation and interests, professional and volunteer experience, and career objectives were altered; their interest in this scholarship; and how obtaining a postsecondary degree or certificate will benefit their future by helping to fulfill their goals and dreams.

Financial data The stipend is $1,000.

Duration 1 year.

Additional data This program began in 2003.

Number awarded Varies each year. Since the program began, it has awarded 87 scholarships.

Deadline July of each year.

[1100]
PINNACOL FOUNDATION SCHOLARSHIP PROGRAM

Pinnacol Foundation
Attn: Edie Sonn
7501 East Lowry Boulevard
Denver, CO 80230
(303) 361-4775   Toll Free: (800) 873-7242, ext. 4775
Fax: (303) 361-5775
E-mail: pinnacol.foundation@pinnacol.com
Web: www.pinnacol.com/foundation/apply-scholarship

Summary To provide financial assistance to Colorado residents whose parent was killed or permanently disabled in a work-related accident and who are interested in attending college in any state.

Eligibility This program is open to the natural, adopted, step, or fully dependent children of workers killed or permanently injured in a compensable work-related accident during the course and scope of employment with a Colorado-based employer and entitled to receive benefits under the Colorado Workers' Compensation Act. Applicants must be between 16 and 25 years of age and attending or planning to attend a college or technical school in any state. They must have a GPA of 2.0 or higher. Selection is based on academic achievement and aptitude, extracurricular activities, community service, and financial need.

Financial data The amount of the stipend depends on the need of the recipient; recently, the average award was approximately $3,500.

Duration 1 year; may be renewed up to 4 additional years.

Additional data Pinnacol Assurance, a workers' compensation insurance carrier, established this program in 2001. Students are eligible regardless of the insurance carrier for their parent's accident.

Number awarded Varies each year; recently, 109 of these scholarships, with a value of nearly $390,000, were awarded. Since the program was established, it has awarded more than 450 scholarships worth $4 million.

Deadline April of each year.

[1101]
PSOB EDUCATIONAL ASSISTANCE PROGRAM

Department of Justice
Attn: Bureau of Justice Assistance
Public Safety Officers' Benefits Office
810 Seventh Street, N.W., Fourth Floor
Washington, DC 20531
Toll Free: (888) 744-6513
E-mail: AskPSOB@usdoj.gov
Web: www.psob.gov/file_education_claim.html

Summary To provide financial assistance for college to the spouses and children of deceased or disabled federal, police, fire, and emergency public safety officers.

Eligibility This program is open to the spouses and children under 27 years of age of federal, police, fire, and emergency public safety officers whose death or permanent and total disability resulted from catastrophic injuries sustained in the line of duty. Applicants must be enrolled or planning to enroll full or part time at an institution of higher education. The death must have occurred on or after January 1, 1978; the effective date of disability of federal law enforcement officers is October 3, 1996; families of state and local police, fire, and emergency public safety officials are covered for line-of-duty permanent and totally disabling injuries that occurred on or after November 13, 1998.

Financial data The stipend is currently $1,021 per month for full-time students or a prorated amount for part-time students.

Duration Up to 45 months of full-time study or a proportional period of time for a part-time program.

Additional data Congress established this program for spouses and children of federal law enforcement officers killed in the line of duty in 1996 and amended it in 1998 to cover spouses and children of all police, fire, and emergency public safety officers killed or disabled in the line of duty. .

Number awarded Varies each year.

Deadline Deadline not specified.

[1102]
PVA EDUCATIONAL SCHOLARSHIP PROGRAM

Paralyzed Veterans of America
Attn: Communications and Membership Department
801 18th Street, N.W.
Washington, DC 20006-3517
(202) 416-7776   Toll Free: (800) 424-8200, ext. 776
Fax: (202) 416-1250   TDD: (202) 416-7622
E-mail: christih@pva.org
Web: www.pva.org

Summary To provide financial assistance for college to members of the Paralyzed Veterans of America (PVA) and their families.

Eligibility This program is open to PVA members, spouses of members, and unmarried dependent children of members under 24 years of age. Applicants must be attending or planning to attend an accredited U.S. college or university as a full- or part-time student. They must be U.S. citizens. Along with their application, they must submit a personal statement explaining why they wish to further their education, short- and long-term academic goals, how this will meet their career objectives, and how it will affect the PVA membership. Selection is based on that statement, academic records, letters of recommendation, and extracurricular and community activities.

Financial data The stipend is $1,000.

Duration 1 year.

Additional data This program began in 1986.

Number awarded Varies each year; recently 20 were awarded. Since this program was established, it has awarded more than $300,000 in scholarships.

Deadline June of each year.

[1103]
REDUCED TUITION FOR CHILDREN AND SPOUSES OF SOUTH DAKOTA NATIONAL GUARDSMEN DISABLED OR DECEASED IN THE LINE OF DUTY

South Dakota Board of Regents
Attn: Scholarship Committee
306 East Capitol Avenue, Suite 200
Pierre, SD 57501-3159
(605) 773-3455   Fax: (605) 773-5320
E-mail: info@sdbor.edu
Web: www.sdbor.edu

Summary To provide reduced tuition at public universities in South Dakota to the children and spouses of disabled and deceased members of the National Guard.

Eligibility This program is open to the spouses and children (24 years of age or younger) of members of the South Dakota Army or Air National Guard who died or sustained a total and permanent disability while on state active duty, federal active duty, or any authorized duty training. Applicants must be proposing to work on an undergraduate degree at a public institution of higher education in South Dakota.

Financial data Qualifying applicants are granted a 100% tuition waiver at state-supported postsecondary institutions in South Dakota. The waiver applies only to tuition, not fees.

Duration 8 semesters or 12 quarters of either full- or part-time study.

Number awarded Varies each year.

Deadline Deadline not specified.

[1104]
RENEE FELDMAN SCHOLARSHIPS

Blinded Veterans Association Auxiliary
c/o Lottie Davis, Scholarship Chair
615 South Adams Street
Arlington, VA 22204-2112
(703) 521-3745
Web: www.bvaaux.org

Summary To provide financial assistance for college to spouses and children of blinded veterans.

Eligibility This program is open to children and spouses of blinded veterans who are enrolled or planning to enroll full time at a college, university, community college, or vocational school. Grandchildren are not eligible. The veteran's blindness may be service-connected or non-service connected. The veteran is not required to be a member of the Blinded Veterans Association. Applicants must submit a 300-word essay on their career goals and aspirations. Selection is based on that essay, academic achievement, and financial need.

Financial data Stipends are $2,000 or $1,000 per year. Funds are paid directly to the recipient's school to be applied to tuition, books, and general fees.

Duration 1 year; may be renewed up to 3 additional years.

Number awarded 3 each year: 2 at $2,000 and 1 at $1,000.

Deadline April of each year.

[1105]
REOC CHARITABLE SCHOLARSHIP FUND

San Antonio Area Foundation
Attn: Scholarship Funds Program Officer
303 Pearl Parkway, Suite 114
San Antonio, TX 78215-1285
(210) 228-3759   Fax: (210) 225-1980
E-mail: buresti@ssafdn.org
Web: www.saafdn.org

Summary To provide financial assistance for college to the children of armed services members who were killed in action, lost limbs, or suffered a serious traumatic injury.

Eligibility This program is open to seniors graduating from high schools in any state who are the child of an American service man or woman who has been killed in action, lost limbs, or suffered a serious traumatic injury. Applicants must be planning to attend an accredited college, university, or vocational school in any state and major in any field. They must have a GPA of 2.5 or higher.

Financial data A stipend is awarded (amount not specified).

Duration 1 year; may be renewed.

Number awarded 1 or more each year.

Deadline February of each year.

[1106]
RIDE FOR LIFE SCHOLARSHIP

Ride for Life, Inc.
Stony Brook University
HSC, Level 2, Room 106
Stony Brook, NY 11794-8231
(631) 444-1292   Fax: (631) 444-7565
E-mail: RFLpals@aol.com
Web: www.alsrideforlife.org

Summary To provide financial assistance for college to high school seniors in New York who have a family member with Amyotrophic Lateral Sclerosis (A.L.S.).

Eligibility This program is open to seniors graduating from high schools in New York who are planning to attend an accredited college or university in any state. Applicants must have a direct family connection to A.L.S., as through a parent, stepparent, grandparent, uncle, aunt, or sibling. Along with their application, they must submit a 1-page essay describing how A.L.S. has affected their family.

Financial data The stipend is approximately $1,500.

Duration 1 year.

Number awarded Approximately 4 each year.

Deadline February of each year.

[1107]
RMHBDA EDUCATION SCHOLARSHIP

Rocky Mountain Hemophilia and Bleeding Disorder
  Association
Attn: Executive Director
1627 West Main Street, Suite 142
Bozeman, MT 59715
(406) 586-4050   Fax: (406) 586-4050
E-mail: brad.rhmbda@gmail.com
Web: www.rmhbda.org/html/financialAssistance.html

Summary To provide financial assistance to residents of Montana and Wyoming who have a bleeding disorder or are relatives of a person with a bleeding disorder and are interested in attending college in any state.

Eligibility This program is open to residents of Montana or Wyoming who have or have a family member with an inherited bleeding disorder. Applicants must be entering or attending a 2- or 4-year undergraduate institution in any state; that includes graduating high school seniors, current undergraduate students, and adults seeking undergraduate studies later in life. They must have been involved with the Rocky Mountain Hemophilia and Bleeding Disorder Association (RMHBDA) at some point and in some capacity. Selection is based on GPA, extracurricular activities, success in various activities, volunteerism in general, volunteerism in the bleeding disorder community.

Financial data The stipend is $1,000 per year. Funds are disbursed directly to the student.

Duration 1 year; recipients may reapply.

Number awarded 1 or more each year.

Deadline May of each year.

[1108]
ROADWAY WORKER MEMORIAL SCHOLARSHIPS

American Traffic Safety Services Foundation
Attn: Foundation Director
15 Riverside Parkway, Suite 100
Fredericksburg, VA 22406-1077
(540) 368-1701   Toll Free: (800) 272-8772
Fax: (540) 368-1717   E-mail: foundation@atssa.com
Web: www.atssa.com

Summary To provide financial assistance for college to children of roadway workers killed or permanently disabled in work zones.

Eligibility This program is open to students enrolled or planning to enroll at a 4-year college or university, 2-year accredited college, or vocational/technical school or training institution. Applicants must be children of roadway workers killed or permanently disabled in work zones, including mobile operations and the installation of roadway safety features. They must submit a statement, up to 200 words, explaining their reasons for wanting to continue their education and listing any volunteer activities or accomplishments. Selection is based on that statement, academic performance, 2 letters of recommendation, and financial need.

Financial data The stipend is $10,000. The Chuck Bailey Scholarship provides an additional $1,000 to recipients who demonstrate a strong commitment to volunteerism.

Duration 1 year.

Additional data This program began in 2001.

Number awarded Varies each year; recently, 4 were awarded.

Deadline February of each year.

[1109]
ROBYN'S WAY SCHOLARSHIP

Oklahoma City Community Foundation
Attn: Scholarship Coordinator
1000 North Broadway
P.O. Box 1146
Oklahoma City, OK 73101-1146
(405) 606-2907   Fax: (405) 235-5612
E-mail: w.minter@occf.org
Web: occf.academicworks.com/opportunities/2209

Summary To provide financial assistance for college in any state to high school seniors in Oklahoma who come from a single parent home or from a family impacted by cancer.

Eligibility This program is open to seniors graduating from high schools in Oklahoma who are the child of a single parent or come from a family that has been impacted by cancer. Applicants must be planning to enroll at an accredited 2- or 4-year college or university in any state. Preference is given to students who 1) have been treated for cancer; 2) are a cancer survivor; 3) have lost a parent to cancer; or 4) have volunteered or are actively volunteering for a cancer related organization and/or events. Along with their application, they must submit documentation of financial need and brief essays on how cancer has impacted and affected their education and a summary of their volunteer history with cancer related organizations and/or events.

Financial data The stipend is $2,000.

Duration 1 year; nonrenewable.

Additional data This program began in 2017.

Number awarded 1 or more each year.

Deadline February of each year.

[1110]
RON NIEDERMAN SCHOLARSHIP

Matrix Health Group
Attn: Memorial Scholarship Program
2202 Brownstone Court
Champaign, IL 61822
(217) 840-1033
E-mail: maria.vetter@matrixhealthgroup.com
Web: www.factorsupportnetwork.com

Summary To provide financial assistance for college to men who have a bleeding disorder and members of their immediate family.

Eligibility This program is open to graduating male high school seniors and students currently enrolled full time at an accredited college, university, or technical school. Applicants must have hemophilia, von Willebrand's disease or other bleeding disorder or be an immediate family member of a person with a bleeding disorder. They must have a GPA of 2.0 or higher for their senior year in high school or their current year in college. Along with their application, they must submit transcripts, ACT or SAT test scores, 2 letters of recommendation, information on their work and school activities, and an essay of 300 to 400 words on 1 of the following topics: 1) the experiences that have influenced their decision to pursue their educational goals or career choice; 2) how they feel their life has been influenced by having a bleeding disorder or by having a bleeding disorder in their family; or 3) their biggest challenge in having a bleeding disorder and how they have or are working through it. Selection is based on that essay, academic merit, and reference letters.

Financial data The stipend is $1,000.

Duration 1 year.

Additional data This program is supported by Factor Support Network Pharmacy and administered by Matrix Health Group.

Number awarded 1 each year.

Deadline July of each year.

[1111]
SAD SACKS NURSING SCHOLARSHIP

AMVETS-Department of Illinois
2200 South Sixth Street
Springfield, IL 62703
(217) 528-4713   Toll Free: (800) 638-VETS (within IL)
Fax: (217) 528-9896   E-mail: info@ilamvets.org
Web: www.ilamvets.org

Summary To provide financial assistance for nursing education to Illinois residents, especially descendants of disabled or deceased veterans.

Eligibility This program is open to seniors at high schools in Illinois who have been accepted to an approved nursing program and students already enrolled in an approved school of nursing in Illinois. Priority is given to dependents of deceased or disabled veterans. Selection is based on academic record, character, interest and activity record, and financial need. Preference is given to students in the following order: third-year students, second-year students, and first-year students.

Financial data A stipend is awarded (amount not specified).

Duration 1 year; nonrenewable.

Number awarded Varies each year; recently, 2 were awarded.

Deadline February of each year.

[1112]
SATOLA FAMILY SCHOLARSHIP

Ulman Cancer Fund for Young Adults
Attn: Scholarship Committee
921 East Fort Avenue, Suite 325
Baltimore, MD 21230
(410) 964-0202   Toll Free: (888) 393-FUND
Fax: (888) 964-0402
E-mail: scholarship@ulmanfund.org
Web: www.ulmanfund.org/scholarships

Summary To provide financial assistance for college or graduate school to students who have been diagnosed with cancer or have or have lost a family member with cancer.

Eligibility This program is open to students who 1) have been diagnosed with cancer; 2) have a parent or sibling living with cancer; or 3) have lost a parent or sibling to cancer. Applicants must be attending, or planning to attend, a college or university in any state to work on an undergraduate, graduate, or professional degree. They should be able to demonstrate courage, spirit, and determination. The first diagnosis of cancer (whether of the applicant, a parent, or sibling) must have occurred after the applicant was 15 years of age. Along with their application, they must submit a 500-word essay or 3-minute video on either 1) a letter that they would have liked to receive during their cancer experience; or 2) what they would tell the young adults who participate in the sponsor's summer-long drive to support the organization about being a young adult impacted by cancer. U.S. citizenship is required.

Financial data The stipend is $2,500. Funds are paid directly to the educational institution.

Duration 1 year.

Additional data This program began in 2009. Recipients are obligated to organize and run a bone marrow registry drive with the support of Delete Blood Cancer and There Goes My Hero.

Number awarded 1 each year.

Deadline March of each year.

[1113]
SCHOLARSHIP FOR STUDENTS WITH AN AUTISTIC SIBLING

Knapp & Roberts
850 North Second Avenue
Phoenix, AZ 85003
(480) 991-7677   E-mail: roberts@krattorneys.com
Web: www.knappandroberts.com/scholarship

Summary To provide financial assistance to high school seniors and current college students who have a sibling with autism.

Eligibility This program is open to residents of any state who are graduating high school seniors or students currently enrolled as undergraduate or graduate students at an accredited college or university. Applicants must have a sibling or siblings with a diagnosis of autism. They must submit a picture of their special needs sibling along with a letter from a physician confirming the diagnosis of autism. Selection is based primarily on a 500-word essay about their family's story, where they are going to college, the career they plan to pursue, and how they would benefit from this scholarship.

Financial data The stipend is $2,500.

Duration 1 year.

Number awarded 1 each year.

Deadline April of each year.

[1114]
SCROOGE SCHOLARSHIP FUND

Community Foundation of Utah
2257 South 1100 East, Suite 205
Salt Lake City, UT 84106
(801) 559-3005   Fax: (866) 935-2353
E-mail: scholarships@utahcf.org
Web: www.utahcf.org

Summary To provide financial assistance to students at colleges in Utah who are the parent of a child with disabilities.

Eligibility This program is open to undergraduate students entering or enrolled at a 2- or 4-year accredited college or university in Utah. Applicants must be the parent or long-term legal guardian of a child with a disability (e.g., debilitating medical illness, severe emotional disorder, on the autism spectrum, intellectual disability). They must be able to demonstrate financial need. Along with their application, they must submit an essay describing the disability of their child and how it has inspired and/or challenged them to pursue higher education.

Financial data The stipend ranges from $500 to $1,000.
Duration 1 year.
Number awarded 1 or more each year.
Deadline April of each year.

[1115]
SFM FOUNDATION SCHOLARSHIP

SFM Foundation
Attn: Scholarship Coordinator
P.O. Box 582992
Minneapolis, MN 55458-2992
Toll Free: (855) 621-2076   Fax: (952) 838-2055
E-mail: info@sfm-foundation.org
Web: www.sfmfoundation.com

Summary To provide financial assistance to residents of Iowa, Minnesota, and Wisconsin whose parent was injured or killed in a work-related accident and who are interested in attending college, preferably in those state.
Eligibility This program is open to residents of Iowa, Minnesota, and Wisconsin between 16 and 25 years of age who are high school students, GED recipients, or high school graduates. Applicants must be the natural, adopted, or stepchild of a worker injured or killed in a work-related accident during the course and scope of employment with an Iowa-, Minnesota-, or Wisconsin-based employer and entitled to receive benefits under the workers' compensation laws of their state. They must be planning to work on an associate or bachelor's degree or a certificate or license from an accredited school in any state. Financial need is considered in the selection process.
Financial data Stipends range from $1,000 to $10,000 per year. Funds are paid directly to the educational institution.
Duration 1 year; may be renewed for a total of 2 years for a 2-year program or 5 years for a bachelor's program, provided the recipient maintains a GPA of 2.0 or higher.
Additional data The SFM Foundation was established in 2008 by SFM Companies, a regional workers' compensation insurance group headquartered in Bloomington, Minnesota. It is the regional affiliate of Kids' Chance of America. The employers of students are not required to have any connection to SFM Companies.
Number awarded Varies each year; recently, 21 were awarded. Since the program began, it has awarded $1.1 million to 115 students.
Deadline March of each year.

[1116]
SOUTH CAROLINA TUITION ASSISTANCE FOR CERTAIN WAR VETERANS CHILDREN

South Carolina Division of Veterans' Affairs
c/o VA Regional Office Building
6437 Garners Ferry Road, Suite 1126
Columbia, SC 29209
(803) 647-2434   Fax: (803) 647-2312
E-mail: va@admin.sc.gov
Web: va.sc.gov/benefits.html

Summary To provide free college tuition to the children of disabled and other South Carolina veterans.
Eligibility This program is open to the children of wartime veterans who were legal residents of South Carolina both at the time of entry into military or naval service and during service, or who have been residents of South Carolina for at least 1 year. Veteran parents must 1) be permanently and totally disabled as determined by the U.S. Department of Veterans Affairs; 2) have been a prisoner of war; 3) have been killed in action; 4) have died from other causes while in service; 5) have died of a disease or disability resulting from service; 6) be currently missing in action; 7) have received the Congressional Medal of Honor; 8) have received the Purple Heart Medal from wounds received in combat; or 9) now be deceased but qualified under categories 1 or 2 above. The veteran's child must be 26 years of age or younger and working on an undergraduate degree.
Financial data Children who qualify are eligible for free tuition at any South Carolina state-supported college, university, or postsecondary technical education institution. The waiver applies to tuition only. The costs of room and board, certain fees, and books are not covered.
Duration Students are eligible to receive this support as long as they are younger than 26 years of age and working on an undergraduate degree.
Number awarded Varies each year.
Deadline Deadline not specified.

[1117]
SURVIVORS' AND DEPENDENTS' EDUCATIONAL ASSISTANCE PROGRAM

Department of Veterans Affairs
Attn: Veterans Benefits Administration
810 Vermont Avenue, N.W.
Washington, DC 20420
(202) 418-4343   Toll Free: (888) GI-BILL1
Web: www.benefits.va.gov/GIBILL/DEA.asp

Summary To provide financial assistance for undergraduate or graduate study to children and spouses of deceased and disabled veterans, MIAs, and POWs.
Eligibility Eligible for this assistance are spouses and children of 1) veterans who died or are permanently and totally disabled as the result of active service in the armed forces; 2) veterans who died from any cause while rated permanently and totally disabled from a service-connected disability; 3) servicemembers listed as missing in action or captured in the line of duty by a hostile force; 4) servicemembers listed as forcibly detained or interned by a foreign government or power; and 5) servicemembers who are hospitalized or receiving outpatient treatment for a service-connected permanent and total disability and are likely to be discharged for that disability. Children must be between 18 and 26 years of age, although extensions may be granted. Spouses and children over 14 years of age with physical or mental disabilities are also eligible.
Financial data Monthly stipends for study at an academic institution are $1,024 for full time, $767 for three-quarter time, or $510 for half-time. Other rates apply for

apprenticeship and on-the-job training, farm cooperative training, and special restorative training.

Duration Benefits are provided for up to 45 months (or the equivalent in part-time training). Some beneficiaries who qualify for more than 1 education program may be eligible for up to 81 months. Spouses must complete their training within 10 years of the date they are first found eligible. For spouses of servicemembers who died on active duty, benefits end 20 years from the date of death.

Additional data Benefits may be used to work on associate, bachelor's, or graduate degrees at colleges and universities, including independent study, cooperative training, and study abroad programs. Courses leading to a certificate or diploma from business, technical, or vocational schools may also be taken. Other eligible programs include apprenticeships, on-the-job training programs, farm cooperative courses, and correspondence courses (for spouses only). Remedial, deficiency, and refresher courses may be approved under certain circumstances.

Number awarded Varies each year.

Deadline Applications may be submitted at any time.

[1118]
TEXAS CHILDREN OF DISABLED OR DECEASED FIREMEN, PEACE OFFICERS, GAME WARDENS, AND EMPLOYEES OF CORRECTIONAL INSTITUTIONS EXEMPTION PROGRAM

Texas Higher Education Coordinating Board
Attn: Grants and Special Programs
1200 East Anderson Lane
P.O. Box 12788
Austin, TX 78711-2788
(512) 427-6340   Toll Free: (800) 242-3062
Fax: (512) 427-6420
E-mail: grantinfo@thecb.state.tx.us
Web: www.collegeforalltexans.com

Summary To provide educational assistance at public colleges in the state to the children of disabled or deceased firefighters, peace officers, game wardens, and employees of correctional institutions.

Eligibility Eligible are children of Texas paid or volunteer firefighters; paid municipal, county, or state peace officers; custodial employees of the Department of Corrections; or game wardens. The parent must have suffered an injury in the line of duty, resulting in disability or death. Applicants must be under 21 years of age.

Financial data Eligible students are exempted from the payment of all dues, fees, and tuition charges at publicly-supported colleges and universities in Texas.

Duration Support is provided for up to 120 semester credit hours of undergraduate study or until the recipient reaches 26 years of age, whichever comes first.

Number awarded Varies each year; recently, 108 students received $516,935 in support through this program.

Deadline Deadline not specified.

[1119]
TEXAS MUTUAL SCHOLARSHIP PROGRAM

Texas Mutual Insurance Company
Attn: Office of the President
6210 East Highway 290
Austin, TX 78723-1098
(512) 224-3820   Toll Free: (800) 859-5995, ext. 3820
Fax: (512) 224-3889   TDD: (800) 853-5339
E-mail: information@texasmutual.com
Web: www.texasmutual.com/workers/scholarship.shtm

Summary To provide financial assistance for college to workers and their families covered by workers' compensation insurance in Texas.

Eligibility This program is open to 1) employees who qualify for lifetime income benefits as a result of injuries suffered on the job as covered by the Texas Workers' Compensation Act; 2) unmarried children and spouses of injured workers; and 3) unmarried children and unremarried spouses of employees who died as a result of a work-related injury. The employee's company must have been a Texas Mutual Insurance Company policyholder at the time of the accident. Children must be between 16 and 25 years of age. Surviving spouses must still be eligible for workers' compensation benefits. Financial need is considered in the selection process.

Financial data Scholarships are intended to cover normal undergraduate, technical, or vocational school tuition and fees, to a maximum of $6,000 per semester. Those funds are paid directly to the college or vocational school. The cost of course-related books and fees are also reimbursed, up to a maximum of $500 per semester. Those funds are paid directly to the student.

Duration 1 year; may be renewed if the recipient remains enrolled full time and maintains a GPA of 2.5 or higher.

Number awarded Varies each year.

Deadline Applications may be submitted at any time.

[1120]
THANKSUSA SCHOLARSHIPS

ThanksUSA
1390 Chain Bridge Road, Suite 260
McLean, VA 22101
(703) 641-3767   Toll Free: (888) 849-8720
E-mail: thanksusa@scholarshipamerica.org
Web: www.thanksusa.org/scholarship-program.html

Summary To provide financial assistance for college to children and spouses of military personnel who served after September 11, 2001.

Eligibility This program is open to dependent children 24 years of age or younger and spouses of active-duty military personnel. The parent or spouse must 1) have served on active duty for at least 180 days since September 11, 2001; 2) have been killed or wounded in action since that date; 3) be a member of the military Reserves activated to full-time duty; or 4) be a member of the National Guard who have been federalized. Children and spouses of retired or discharged service personnel are eligible if the parent or spouse served 180 days after September 11, 2011. Applicants must be entering or attending an accredited 2- or 4-year college, university, vocational school, or technical school as a full-time student. Spouses may use the award for non-degree licensure or certification programs and may enroll part time. All applicants must have a GPA of 2.0 or higher. Selection is based on financial need, academic record, a statement of goals, and demonstrated leadership and participation in school and community activities. Preference is given to children or spouses of service personnel killed or injured during active duty.

Financial data The stipend is $3,000.

Duration 1 year; recipients may reapply.

Additional data This program began in 2006. Selection of recipients is made by Scholarship Management Services, a division of Scholarship America.

Number awarded Approximately 250 each year. Since the program was established, it has awarded more than 4,200 scholarships with a value of more than $13 million.

Deadline May of each year.

[1121]
THOMAS H. MILLER SCHOLARSHIP

Blinded Veterans Association
Attn: Scholarship Coordinator
125 North West Street, Third Floor
Alexandria, VA 22314
(202) 371-8880, ext. 313   Toll Free: (800) 669-7079
Fax: (202) 371-8258   E-mail: cdumond@bva.org
Web: www.bva.org

Summary To provide financial assistance for undergraduate or graduate study, especially of music or the fine arts, to immediate family of blinded veterans and servicemembers.

Eligibility This program is open to dependent children, grandchildren, and spouses of blinded veterans and active-duty blinded servicemembers of the U.S. armed forces. The veteran or servicemember must be legally blind; the blindness may be either service-connected or nonservice-connected. Applicants must have been accepted or be currently enrolled as a full-time student in an undergraduate or graduate program at an accredited institution of higher learning. Preference is given to students of music or the fine arts. Along with their application, they must submit a 300-word essay on their career goals and aspirations. Financial need is not considered in the selection process.

Financial data The stipend is $1,000; funds are intended to be used to cover the student's expenses, including tuition, other academic fees, books, dormitory fees, and cafeteria fees. Funds are paid directly to the recipient's school.

Duration 1 year; recipients may reapply for up to 3 additional years.

Number awarded 1 each year.

Deadline April of each year.

[1122]
THROUGH THE LOOKING GLASS SCHOLARSHIPS

Through the Looking Glass
3075 Adeline Street, Suite 120
Berkeley, CA 94703
(510) 848-1112   Toll Free: (800) 644-2666
Fax: (510) 848-4445   TDD: (510) 848-1005
E-mail: scholarships@lookingglass.org
Web: www.lookingglass.org

Summary To provide financial assistance for college to high school seniors who have a parent with a disability.

Eligibility This program is open to graduating high school seniors and full-time college students who are 21 years of age or younger. Applicants must have at least 1 parent who has a physical, sensory, intellectual, medical, or mental health disability. Along with their application, they must submit a 3-page essay describing the experience of growing up with a parent with a disability. Selection is based on that essay, academic performance, community service, and letters of recommendation; financial need is considered for some of the scholarships.

Financial data The stipend is $1,000.

Duration 1 year.

Additional data Funding for this program is provided by a grant from the National Institute on Disability and Rehabilitation Research (NIDRR) of the U.S. Department of Education, Office of Special Education and Rehabilitative Services.

Number awarded Varies each year; recently, 16 were awarded, of which 5 were presented to students who demonstrated extreme financial hardship.

Deadline February of each year.

[1123]
TOBY WRIGHT SCHOLARSHIP FUND

Workers' Compensation Association of New Mexico
Attn: Brock Carter
3207 Matthew Avenue, N.E., Suite A
Albuquerque, NM 87107
(505) 881-1112   Toll Free: (800) 640-0724
E-mail: brock@safetycounseling.com
Web: www.wcaofnm.com/toby-wright-scholarship

Summary To provide financial assistance for college to residents of New Mexico whose parent was permanently disabled or killed in an employment-related accident.

Eligibility This program is open to residents of New Mexico between 16 and 25 years of age who are attending or planning to attend a college, university, or trade school in the state. Applicants must have a parent who was permanently or catastrophically injured or killed in an employment-related accident that resulted in a New Mexico workers' compensation claim. The parent's death or injury must have resulted in a substantial decline in the family income.

Financial data A stipend is awarded (amount not specified). Funds may be used for tuition, books, housing, meals, and course fees.

Duration 1 semester or quarter; may be renewed if the recipient maintains a GPA of 2.5 or higher and full-time enrollment.

Additional data This program began in 2011.

Number awarded Varies each year; recently, 8 were awarded.

Deadline Deadline not specified.

[1124]
TRIO SCHOLARSHIP PROGRAM

Transplant Recipients International Organization, Inc.
Attn: Scholarship Committee
2100 M Street, N.W., Suite 170-353
Washington, DC 20037-1233
(202) 293-0980   Toll Free: (800) TRIO-386
E-mail: info@trioweb.org
Web: www.trioweb.org/resources/trio-scholarships.html

Summary To provide financial assistance for college to members of the Transplant Recipients International Organization (TRIO) and their families.

Eligibility This program is open to TRIO members and their immediate family who are solid organ or bone marrow candidates, recipients, donors, or their immediate family members. Applicants must be attending or planning to attend an accredited college, university, or trade/technical certificate program. They must have a cumulative GPA of 2.5 or higher and be able to demonstrate financial need. Along with their application, they must submit a 500-word essay on their personal history and educational and career ambitions and a statement on how transplantation has affected their life.

Financial data The stipend is $1,000.

Duration 1 year; nonrenewable.

Number awarded Varies each year; recently, 4 were awarded. Since the program was established 20 years ago, it has awarded 125 scholarships.

Deadline June of each year.

[1125]
TROY BARBOZA EDUCATIONAL FUND SCHOLARSHIP

Hawai'i Community Foundation
Attn: Scholarship Department
827 Fort Street Mall
Honolulu, HI 96813
(808) 566-5570   Toll Free: (888) 731-3863
Fax: (808) 521-6286   .
E-mail: scholarships@hcf-hawaii.org
Web: hcf.scholarships.ngwebsolutions.com

Summary To provide financial assistance to disabled public employees in Hawaii or their dependents who plan to attend college in any state.

Eligibility This program is open to 1) disabled public employees in Hawaii who were injured in the line of duty; 2) dependents or other immediate family members of public employees in Hawaii who were disabled or killed in the line of duty; and 3) private citizens in Hawaii who have performed a heroic act for the protection and welfare of others. The public employee must work or have worked in a job where lives are risked for the protection and safety of others. The injury must have left the employee incapacitated or incapable or continuing in his or her profession. For private citizens, the heroic act must have occurred after October 21, 1986. Applicants must submit a short statement describing their course of study, career goals, outstanding attributes, talents, community service, family circumstances, and any other relevant information. Financial need is considered in the selection process.

Financial data The amount awarded varies, depending upon the needs of the recipient and the funds available; recently, the average value of the scholarships awarded by the foundation was $2,800.

Duration 1 year; scholarships for employees and their dependents may be renewed; scholarships for private citizens who have performed a heroic act are nonrenewable.

Additional data This program began in 1991.

Number awarded 1 or more each year.

Deadline February of each year.

[1126]
UCB FAMILY EPILEPSY SCHOLARSHIP PROGRAM

UCB, Inc.
Family Scholarship Program
c/o Summit Medical Communications
1421 East Broad Street, Suite 340
Fuquay-Varina, NC 27526
Toll Free: (866) 825-1920   Fax: (919) 567-7591
E-mail: ucbepilepsyscholarship@summitmedcomm.
com
Web: www.ucbepilepsyscholarship.com

Summary To provide financial assistance for college or graduate school to epilepsy patients and their family members and caregivers.

Eligibility This program is open to epilepsy patients and their family members and caregivers. Applicants must be working on or planning to work on an undergraduate or graduate degree at an institution of higher education in the United States. They must be able to demonstrate academic achievement, a record of participation in activities outside of school, and service as a role model. Along with their application, they must submit a 1-page essay explaining why they should be selected for the scholarship, how epilepsy has impacted their life either as a patient or as a family member or caregiver, and how they will benefit from the scholarship. U.S. citizenship or permanent resident status is required.

Financial data The stipend is $5,000.

Duration 1 year; nonrenewable.

Additional data This program, previously known as the Keppra Family Epilepsy Scholarship Program, was established in 2004.

Number awarded 30 each year. Since this program was established, it has awarded $1,700,000 to more than 340 students.

Deadline April of each year.

[1127]
UTAH HEMOPHILIA FOUNDATION SCHOLARSHIPS

Utah Hemophilia Foundation
772 East 3300 South, Suite 210
Salt Lake City, UT 84106
(801) 484-0325   Toll Free: (877) 463-6893
Fax: (801) 746-2488
E-mail: western@hemophiliautah.org
Web: www.hemophiliautah.org/resources.php

Summary To provide financial assistance to members of the bleeding disorders community served by the Utah Hemophilia Foundation (UHF) who are interested in attending college in any state.

Eligibility This program is open to members of the bleeding disorders community served by UHF and/or the Intermountain Hemophilia and Thrombosis Center in Salt Lake City, including those who have a bleeding disorder, their spouses, siblings, children, and parents. Applicants must be enrolled or planning to enroll at a college, university, trade school, or technical program in any state. Preference is given to applicants must directly affected by a bleeding disorder, those involved with UHF activities, those without other scholarships or financial assistance, and residents of Utah.

Financial data Stipends range from $100 to $1,500.

Duration 1 year.

Additional data This program includes awards designated as Robert Price Memorial Scholarships.

Number awarded Varies each year.

Deadline May of each year.

[1128]
VERA YIP MEMORIAL SCHOLARSHIP

Ulman Cancer Fund for Young Adults
Attn: Scholarship Committee
921 East Fort Avenue, Suite 325
Baltimore, MD 21230
(410) 964-0202   Toll Free: (888) 393-FUND
Fax: (888) 964-0402
E-mail: scholarship@ulmanfund.org
Web: www.ulmanfund.org/scholarships

Summary To provide financial assistance for college or graduate school to students from any state who have been diagnosed with cancer or have or have lost a family member with cancer.

Eligibility This program is open to U.S. citizens and permanent residents between 15 and 35 years of age from any state. Applicants must 1) have been diagnosed with cancer and currently in relapse or active treatment; 2) have a parent or guardian living with cancer; or 3) have lost a parent or guardian to cancer. The student, parent, or guardian must have been first diagnosed with cancer after the applicant was 15 years of age. Along with their application, they must submit a 500-word essay or 3-minute video on either 1) a letter that they would have liked to receive during their cancer experience; or 2) what they would tell the young adults who participate in the sponsor's summer-long drive to support the organization about being a young adult impacted by cancer. U.S. citizenship or permanent resident status is required. This award is presented to the applicant who best demonstrates the qualities of Vera Yip of courage, determination, motivation, and dedication.

Financial data The stipend is $2,500. Funds are paid directly to the educational institution.

Duration 1 year; nonrenewable.

Additional data Recipients are obligated to organize and run a bone marrow registry drive with the support of Delete Blood Cancer and There Goes My Hero.

Number awarded 1 each year.

Deadline March of each year.

[1129]
VICTORIA OVIS MEMORIAL SCHOLARSHIP

National Law Enforcement and Firefighters Children's
   Foundation
928 Broadway, Suite 703
New York, NY 10010
(646) 822-4236   E-mail: nleafcf@ncleafcf.org
Web: www.nleafcf.org

Summary To provide financial assistance to the children of deceased or disabled law enforcement officers and firefighters who reside or attend college in New York state or the New York City metropolitan area.

Eligibility This program is open to the dependent children (including stepchildren and adopted children) of law enforcement officers and firefighters who were killed or totally and permanently disabled in the line of duty. Applicants must reside or attend school in the state of New York or the New York City metropolitan area. They must be U.S. citizens or permanent residents working or planning to work full time on an associate or bachelor's degree or vocational certificate at a college, university, or vocational/technical institute. Selection is based on academics, demonstrated leadership, outstanding performance in the arts or sports, volunteer activities benefiting the community, and financial need. A declared major is not required, but preference is given to applicants who are majoring in criminology or pre-law.

Financial data The stipend is $2,000. Funds are paid directly to the recipient's institution.

Duration 1 year; nonrenewable.

Number awarded 1 each year.

Deadline June of each year.

[1130]
VINCENT BENNETT, JR. MEMORIAL SCHOLARSHIP

National Law Enforcement and Firefighters Children's
   Foundation
928 Broadway, Suite 703
New York, NY 10010
(646) 822-4236   E-mail: nleafcf@ncleafcf.org
Web: www.nleafcf.org

Summary To provide financial assistance as college freshmen to the children of law enforcement officers and firefighters who were killed or disabled in the line of duty.

Eligibility This program is open to the dependent children (including stepchildren and adopted children) of law enforcement officers and firefighters who were killed or totally and permanently disabled in the line of duty. Applicants must be entering full-time freshmen at a college, university, or vocational/technical institute in the United States. They must be U.S. citizens or permanent residents. Selection is based on academics, demonstrated leadership, outstanding performance in the arts or sports, volunteer activities benefiting the community, and financial need. A declared major is not required, but preference is given to applicants who are majoring in engineering.

Financial data The stipend is $5,000 per year. Funds are paid directly to the recipient's institution.

Duration 4 years, provided the recipient remains enrolled full time and maintains a GPA of 2.7 or higher.

Number awarded 1 each year.

Deadline June of each year.

[1131]
VIRGINIA MILITARY SURVIVORS AND DEPENDENTS EDUCATION PROGRAM

Virginia Department of Veterans Services
Attn: VMSDEP Coordinator
101 North 14th Street, 17th Floor
Richmond, VA 23219
(804) 225-2083   Fax: (804) 786-0809
E-mail: vmsdep@dvs.virginia.gov
Web: www.dvs.virginia.gov

Summary To provide educational assistance to the children and spouses of disabled and other Virginia veterans or service personnel.

Eligibility This program is open to residents of Virginia whose parent or spouse served in the U.S. armed forces (including the Reserves, the Virginia National Guard, or the Virginia National Guard Reserves) during any armed conflict subsequent to December 6, 1941, as a result of a terrorist act, during military operations against terrorism, or on a peacekeeping mission. The veterans must have been killed, be missing in action, have been taken prisoner of war, or become at least 90% disabled as a result of such service. Applicants must have been accepted at a public college or university in Virginia as an undergraduate or graduate student. Children must be between 16 and 29 years of age; there are no age restrictions for spouses. The veteran must have been a resident of Virginia at the time of entry into active military service or for at least 5 consecutive years immediately prior to the date of application or death. Surviving spouses must have been residents of Virginia for at least 5 years prior to marrying the veteran or for at least 5 years immediately prior to the date on which the application was submitted.

Financial data The program provides 1) waiver of tuition and all required fees at public institutions of higher education in Virginia; and 2) a stipend to offset the costs of room, board, books, and supplies at those institutions; recently, the stipend for full-time study was $1,800 per academic year.

Duration Entitlement extends to a maximum of 36 months (4 years).

Additional data Individuals entitled to this benefit may use it to pursue any vocational, technical, undergraduate, or graduate program of instruction. Generally, programs listed in the academic catalogs of state-supported institutions are acceptable, provided they have a clearly-defined educational objective (such as a certificate, diploma, or degree). This program was formerly known as the Virginia War Orphans Education Program.

Number awarded Varies each year; recently, funding allowed for a total of 1,000 stipends.

Deadline Applications may be submitted at any time, but they must be received at least 90 days prior to the start of the term.

[1132]
VITTORIA DIANA RICARDO SCHOLARSHIP

Ulman Cancer Fund for Young Adults
Attn: Scholarship Committee
921 East Fort Avenue, Suite 325
Baltimore, MD 21230
(410) 964-0202   Toll Free: (888) 393-FUND
Fax: (888) 964-0402
E-mail: scholarship@ulmanfund.org
Web: www.ulmanfund.org/scholarships

Summary To provide financial assistance for college or graduate school to students who have been diagnosed with cancer or have or have lost a family member with cancer.

Eligibility This program is open to students who 1) have been diagnosed with cancer; 2) have a parent or sibling living with cancer; or 3) have lost a parent or sibling to cancer. Applicants must be attending, or planning to attend, a 4-year college or university in any state to work on an undergraduate, graduate, or professional degree. They must have a GPA of 3.0 or higher in high school or college and be able to demonstrate financial need. The first diagnosis of cancer (whether of the applicant, a parent, or sibling) must have occurred after the applicant was 15 years of age. Along with their application, they must submit a 500-word essay or 3-minute video on either 1) a letter that they would have liked to receive during their cancer experience; or 2) what they would tell the young adults who participate in the sponsor's summer-long drive to support the organization about being a young adult impacted by cancer. U.S. citizenship or permanent resident status is required.

Financial data The stipend is $2,500. Funds are paid directly to the educational institution.

Duration 1 year.

Additional data Recipients are obligated to organize and run a bone marrow registry drive with the support of Delete Blood Cancer and There Goes My Hero.

Number awarded 1 each year.

Deadline March of each year.

[1133]
WASHINGTON NATIONAL GUARD STATE EDUCATION ASSISTANCE PROGRAM (EAP)

Washington National Guard
Attn: Education Services Office
JFHQ-WA
41st Division Drive, Building 15
Camp Murray, WA 98430
(253) 512-8435   Toll Free: (800) 606-9843 (within WA)
Fax: (253) 512-8941
E-mail: education@washingtonguard.org
Web: mil.wa.gov/national-guard/army-guard/education

Summary To waive tuition at public colleges in Washington for veterans, members of the National Guard, and the family of deceased and disabled veterans and National Guard members.

Eligibility This program is open to 1) active military and naval veterans, Reserve military and naval veterans, and National Guard members called to active duty to serve on foreign soil or in international waters or in another location in support of those serving on foreign soil or in international waters; 2) children and spouses or domestic partners of eligible veterans or National Guard members who became totally disabled as a result of serving in active federal military or naval service; 3) children and spouses or domestic partners of eligible veterans or National Guard members who is determined by the federal government to be a prisoner of war or missing in action; and 4) children and surviving spouses or surviving domestic partners of eligible veterans or National Guard members who lost their life as a result of serving in active federal military or naval service. Applicants must be residents of Washington and enrolled or planning to enroll full or part time at a state university, regional university, Evergreen State College, or community or technical college in the state. Children must be between 17 and 26 years of age. Surviving spouses of deceased personnel have 10 years from the date of death to receive benefits.

Financial data Qualified veterans, National Guard members, children, and spouses may attend public institutions in Washington without payment of tuition or fees.

Duration 1 year; may be renewed.

Number awarded Varies each year.

Deadline Each participating institution sets its own deadline.

[1134]
WBDN EDUCATIONAL SCHOLARSHIP

Wisconsin Bleeding Disorders Network
W237S9730 Par Avenue
Big Bend, WI 53103
(608) 359-9103   E-mail: MyWBDN@gmail.com
Web: www.mywbdn.org/scholarships

Summary To provide financial assistance to residents of Wisconsin who have a connection to the bleeding community and are interested in attending college in any state.

Eligibility This program is open to residents of Wisconsin who have an inherited bleeding disorder, are the child of a parent with a bleeding disorder, or are the parent of a child with a bleeding disorder. Applicants must be attending or planning to attend a college or university in any state. They may be full-time traditional students or part-time nontraditional students.

Financial data A stipend is awarded (amount not specified).

Duration 1 year.

Number awarded Varies each year; recently, 3 were awarded.

Deadline March of each year.

[1135]
WISCONSIN G.I. BILL TUITION REMISSION PROGRAM

Wisconsin Department of Veterans Affairs
201 West Washington Avenue
P.O. Box 7843
Madison, WI 53707-7843
(608) 266-1311   Toll Free: (800) WIS-VETS
Fax: (608) 267-0403
E-mail: WDVAInfo@dva.state.wi.us
Web: www.dva.state.wi.us

Summary To provide financial assistance for college or graduate school to Wisconsin veterans and their dependents.

Eligibility This program is open to current residents of Wisconsin who 1) were residents of the state when they entered or reentered active duty in the U.S. armed forces; or 2) have moved to the state and have been residents for at least 5 consecutive years after entry or reentry into service. Applicants must have served on active duty for at least 2 continuous years or for at least 90 days during specified wartime periods. Also eligible are 1) qualifying children and unremarried surviving spouses of Wisconsin veterans who died in the line of duty or as the direct result of a service-connected disability; and 2) children and spouses of Wisconsin veterans who have a service-connected disability rated by the U.S. Department of Veterans Affairs as 30% or greater. Children must be between 17 and 25 years of age (regardless of the date of the veteran's death or initial disability rating) and be a Wisconsin resident for tuition purposes. Spouses remain eligible for 10 years following the date of the veteran's death or initial disability rating; they must be Wisconsin residents for tuition purposes but they may enroll full or part time. Students may attend any institution, center, or school within the University of Wisconsin (UW) System or the Wisconsin Technical College System (WCTS). There are no income limits, delimiting periods following military service during which the benefit must be used, or limits on the level of study (e.g., vocational, undergraduate, professional, or graduate).

Financial data Veterans who qualify as a Wisconsin resident for tuition purposes are eligible for a remission of 100% of standard academic fees and segregated fees at a UW campus or 100% of program and material fees at a WCTS institution. Veterans who qualify as a Wisconsin veteran for purposes of this program but for other reasons fail to meet the definition of a Wisconsin resident for tuition purposes at the UW system are eligible for a remission of 100% of non-resident fees. Spouses and children of deceased or disabled veterans are entitled to a remission of 100% of tuition and fees at a UW or WCTS institution.

Duration Up to 8 semesters or 128 credits, whichever is greater.

Additional data This program began in 2005 as a replacement for Wisconsin Tuition and Fee Reimbursement Grants.

Number awarded Varies each year.

Deadline Applications must be submitted within 14 days from the office start of the academic term: in October for fall, March for spring, or June for summer.

[1136]
WSI SCHOLARSHIPS

Workforce Safety & Insurance
1600 East Century Avenue, Suite 1
P.O. Box 5585
Bismarck, ND 58506-5585
Toll Free: (800) 777-5033   Fax: (888) 786-8695
TDD: (800) 366-6888   E-mail: ndwsi@nd.gov
Web: www.workforcesafety.com

Summary To provide financial assistance for college to injured workers and the families of workers who became disabled or died in work-related accidents in North Dakota.

Eligibility This program is open to 1) workers in North Dakota who have suffered an injury compensable by the state's Workforce Safety & Insurance (WSI); 2) spouses and children of catastrophically injured workers; and 3) surviving spouses and children of workers killed in a catastrophic injury. Applicants must be attending or planning to attend an accredited college, university, or technical school in any state. Injured workers must be able to demonstrate that a scholarship would be beneficial and appropriate upon successful completion of a rehabilitation program.

Financial data The maximum stipend is $10,000 per year.

Duration 1 year; may be renewed up to 4 additional years.

Additional data This program began in 1997. The sponsoring company was formerly North Dakota Workers Compensation.

Number awarded Varies each year.

Deadline Deadline not specified.

[1137]
YE NOTORIOUS KREWE OF THE PEG LEG PIRATE SCHOLARSHIPS

Ye Notorious Krewe of the Peg Leg Pirate, Inc.
P.O. Box 1854
Ruskin, LA 33575-1854
Web: www.peglegpirate.org

Summary To provide financial assistance for college or graduate school to amputees and their families.

Eligibility This program is open to amputees, families of amputees, and organizations that work with amputees.

Applicants must be attending or planning to attend an accredited college, university, community college, vocational/technical school, or graduate school. They must have a GPA of 3.5 or higher. Along with their application, they must submit 2 recommendations, transcripts, documentation of financial need, and a 300-word essay describing their future goals.

Financial data Stipends vary but recently have averaged $1,150. Funds are paid directly to the recipient's institution.

Duration 1 year.

Additional data This program began in 2008.

Number awarded Varies each year; recently 4 were awarded.

Deadline March of each year.

Graduate Students

[1138]
ALABAMA G.I. DEPENDENTS' SCHOLARSHIP PROGRAM

Alabama Department of Veterans Affairs
770 Washington Avenue, Suite 470
Montgomery, AL 36102-1509
(334) 242-5077   Fax: (334) 242-5102
Web: www.va.state.al.us/gi_dep_scholarship.aspx

Summary To provide educational benefits to the dependents of disabled, deceased, and other Alabama veterans.

Eligibility This program is open to children, spouses, and unremarried widow(er)s of veterans who are currently rated as 20% or more service-connected disabled or were so rated at time of death, were a former prisoner of war, have been declared missing in action, died as the result of a service-connected disability, or died while on active military duty in the line of duty. The veteran must have been a permanent civilian resident of Alabama for at least 1 year prior to entering active military service and served honorably for at least 90 days during wartime (or less, in case of death or service-connected disability). Veterans who were not Alabama residents at the time of entering active military service may also qualify if they have a 100% disability and were permanent residents of Alabama for at least 5 years prior to filing the application for this program or prior to death, if deceased. Children and stepchildren must be under the age of 26, but spouses and widow(er)s may be of any age. Spouses cease to be eligible if they become divorced from the qualifying veteran. Widow(er)s cease to be eligible if they remarry.

Financial data Eligible dependents may attend any state-supported Alabama institution of higher learning or enroll in a prescribed course of study at any Alabama state-supported trade school without payment of any tuition, book fees, or laboratory charges.

Duration This is an entitlement program for 5 years of full-time undergraduate or graduate study or part-time equivalent for all qualifying children and for spouses and unremarried widow(er)s who veteran spouse is or was rated 100% disabled or meets other qualifying requirements. Spouses and unremarried widow(er)s whose veteran spouse is or was rated between 20% and 90% disabled may attend only 3 standard academic years.

Additional data Benefits for children, spouses, and unremarried widow(er)s are available in addition to federal government benefits. Assistance is not provided for non-credit courses, placement testing, GED preparation, continuing educational courses, pre-technical courses, or state board examinations.

Number awarded Varies each year.

Deadline Applications may be submitted at any time.

[1139]
ALFRED CAMP MEMORIAL SCHOLARSHIP

Georgia Council of the Blind
c/o Debbie Williams, Scholarship Committee Chair
1477 Nebo Road
Dallas, GA 30157
(770) 595-1007
E-mail: williamsdebk@wmconnect.com
Web: www.georgiacounciloftheblind.org

Summary To provide financial assistance students in Georgia who plan to attend college or graduate school in any state and are either legally blind or have legally blind parents.

Eligibility This program is open to residents of Georgia who are either 1) legally blind students; or 2) sighted students financially dependent on legally blind parents. Applicants must be enrolled or accepted for enrollment at a vocational/technical school, a 2- or 4-year college, or a master's or doctoral program in any state. All fields of study are eligible. Selection is based on academic transcripts, 2 letters of recommendation, a 1-page typed statement of the applicant's educational goals, an audio cassette recording of the applicant reading the goals statement, extracurricular activities, and financial need.

Financial data Stipends up to $1,000 per year are available.

Duration 1 year; recipients may reapply.

Additional data This program began in 1988.

Number awarded 1 or more each year.

Deadline June of each year.

[1140]
AMERICAN BUS ASSOCIATION YELLOW RIBBON SCHOLARSHIP

American Bus Association
Attn: ABA Foundation
111 K Street, N.E., Ninth Floor
Washington, DC 20002
(202) 842-1645   Toll Free: (800) 283-2877
Fax: (202) 842-0850   E-mail: abainfo@buses.org
Web: www.buses.org

Summary To provide financial assistance for college or graduate school to people with disabilities, veterans, and

children of wounded veterans who are preparing for a career in the transportation, travel, and tourism industry.

Eligibility This program is open to U.S. and Canadian citizens and permanent residents who are enrolled as an undergraduate or graduate student in a program related to the transportation, travel, and tourism industry. Applicants must 1) have a physical or sensory disability; 2) be a veteran of the U.S. or Canadian military; or 3) be a child or a wounded U.S. or Canadian military veteran. They must have a GPA of 3.0 or higher.

Financial data The stipend is $2,500.

Duration 1 or more each year.

Deadline April of each year.

[1141]
ANNE SMEDINGHOFF MEMORIAL SCHOLARSHIP

Ulman Cancer Fund for Young Adults
Attn: Scholarship Committee
921 East Fort Avenue, Suite 325
Baltimore, MD 21230
(410) 964-0202   Toll Free: (888) 393-FUND
Fax: (888) 964-0402
E-mail: scholarship@ulmanfund.org
Web: www.ulmanfund.org/scholarships

Summary To provide financial assistance for college or graduate school to students who have been diagnosed with cancer or have or have lost a family member with cancer.

Eligibility This program is open to students who 1) have been diagnosed with cancer; 2) have a parent or sibling living with cancer; or 3) have lost a parent or sibling to cancer. Applicants must be attending, or planning to attend, a college or university in any state to work on an undergraduate, graduate, or professional degree. They should demonstrate the qualities of the program's namesake-adventurous, upbeat, vivacious, and with a strong desire to make a difference in the lives of others. The first diagnosis of cancer (whether of the applicant, a parent, or sibling) must have occurred after the applicant was 15 years of age. Along with their application, they must submit a 500-word essay or 3-minute video on either 1) a letter that they would have liked to receive during their cancer experience; or 2) what they would tell the young adults who participate in the sponsor's summer-long drive to support the organization about being a young adult impacted by cancer. U.S. citizenship or permanent resident status is required.

Financial data The stipend is $2,500. Funds are paid directly to the educational institution.

Duration 1 year.

Additional data This program, which began in 2013, is funded by the 4K for Cancer, an organization of college students who ride bicycles across the country every summer and raise funds for cancer. Recipients are obligated to organize and run a bone marrow registry drive with the support of Delete Blood Cancer and There Goes My Hero.

Number awarded 1 each year.

Deadline March of each year.

[1142]
AVONTE OQUENDO MEMORIAL SCHOLARSHIP FOR AUTISM

The Perecman Firm, P.L.L.C.
250 West 57th Street, Suite 401
New York, NY 10107
(212) 577-9325
Web: www.perecman.com

Summary To provide financial assistance for college or graduate school to people diagnosed with autism and their families.

Eligibility This program is open students currently enrolled or accepted at an accredited college or university as an undergraduate or graduate students. Applicants or a close family member must have been diagnosed with a form of autism, including Asperger syndrome. Along with their application, they must submit an essay of 500 to 1,000 words on 1 of the following topics: 1) a time that they have had to overcome an obstacle as a person with autism that other people would not have had to face; 2) how their family member's autism has affected them and how they have adapted to help them; and 3) what they feel is the biggest obstacle holding people with autism back today. Selection is based on the essay and transcripts.

Financial data The stipend is $1,000.

Duration 1 year.

Number awarded 1 each year.

Deadline July of each year.

[1143]
BERNICE MCNAMARA MEMORIAL SCHOLARSHIP

Ulman Cancer Fund for Young Adults
Attn: Scholarship Committee
921 East Fort Avenue, Suite 325
Baltimore, MD 21230
(410) 964-0202   Toll Free: (888) 393-FUND
Fax: (888) 964-0402
E-mail: scholarship@ulmanfund.org
Web: www.ulmanfund.org

Summary To provide financial assistance to students who have lost a parent with cancer and are interested in working on an undergraduate or graduate degree in the sciences.

Eligibility This program is open to U.S. citizens who have lost a parent or guardian to cancer. Applicants must be 25 years of age or younger and attending, or planning to attend, a 4-year college or university to work on an undergraduate or graduate degree in the sciences. The parent or guardian must have been first diagnosed with cancer when the applicant was at least 15 years of age. Along with their application, they must submit a 500-word essay or 3-minute video on either 1) a letter that they would have liked to receive during their cancer experience; or 2) what they would tell the young adults who participate in the sponsor's summer-long drive to support the organization about being a young adult impacted by cancer. Financial need is considered in the selection process. U.S. citizenship or permanent resident status is required.

Financial data The stipend is $2,500. Funds are paid directly to the educational institution.

Duration 1 year; nonrenewable.

Additional data Recipients are obligated to organize and run a bone marrow registry drive with the support of Delete Blood Cancer and There Goes My Hero.

Number awarded 1 each year.

Deadline March of each year.

[1144]
BOARD OF YOUNG ADULT ADVISORS SCHOLARSHIP

Ulman Cancer Fund for Young Adults
Attn: Scholarship Committee
921 East Fort Avenue, Suite 325
Baltimore, MD 21230
(410) 964-0202   Toll Free: (888) 393-FUND
Fax: (888) 964-0402
E-mail: scholarship@ulmanfund.org
Web: www.ulmanfund.org

Summary To provide financial assistance for graduate school to young adults from the Baltimore/Washington, D.C. area who have been diagnosed with cancer or have or have lost a family member with cancer.

Eligibility This program is open to students who 1) have been diagnosed with cancer; 2) have a parent or sibling living with cancer; or 3) have lost a parent or sibling to cancer. Applicants must be residents of the Baltimore/Washington, D.C. area. They must be 35 years of age or younger and attending, or planning to attend, a college or university in any state to work on a graduate or professional degree. The first diagnosis of cancer (whether of the applicant, a parent, or sibling) must have occurred after the applicant was 15 years of age. Along with their application, they must submit a 500-word essay or 3-minute video on either 1) a letter that they would have liked to receive during their cancer experience; or 2) what they would tell the young adults who participate in the sponsor's summer-long drive to support the organization about being a young adult impacted by cancer. U.S. citizenship or permanent resident status is required.

Financial data The stipend is $2,500. Funds are paid directly to the educational institution.

Duration 1 year.

Additional data This program began in 2012. Recipients are obligated to organize and run a bone marrow registry drive with the support of Delete Blood Cancer and There Goes My Hero.

Number awarded 1 each year.

Deadline March of each year.

[1145]
BOBBY JONES OPEN SCHOLARSHIPS

American Syringomyelia & Chiari Alliance Project, Inc.
P.O. Box 1586
Longview, TX 75606-1586
(903) 236-7079   Toll Free: (800) ASAP-282
Fax: (903) 757-7456   E-mail: info@ASAP.org
Web: www.asap.org

Summary To provide financial assistance for college or graduate school to members of the American Syringomyelia & Chiari Alliance Project (ASAP) and their children.

Eligibility This program is open to students entering or enrolled in college or graduate school who have syringomeylia (SM) and/or Chiari Malformation (CM) or whose parent is affected by SM and/or CM. Applicants or parents must have been ASAP members for at least 6 months. They may be of any age. Along with their application, they must submit 4 essays on assigned topics related to their experience with SM and/or CM. Selection is based on those essay and financial need.

Financial data Stipends are $1,000 for full-time students or $500 for part-time students. Recipients may reapply, but they may receive only a total of $4,000 in support from this program.

Duration 1 year.

Additional data This program is funded by the Bobby Jones Open, an annual golf tournament in which participation is restricted to golfers named Bobby Jones (e.g., Robert Jones, Roberta Jones). The tournament began in 1979 and since 1990 has raised money for activities of the ASAP.

Number awarded Varies each year; a total of $5,000 is available for this program annually.

Deadline May of each year.

[1146]
BRYON RIESCH SCHOLARSHIPS

Bryon Riesch Paralysis Foundation
P.O. Box 1388
Waukesha, WI 53187-1388
(262) 547-2083   E-mail: info@brpf.org
Web: www.brpf.org/scholarship-application

Summary To provide financial assistance to undergraduate and graduate students who have a neurological disability or the children of people with such a disability.

Eligibility This program is open to students entering or enrolled at a 2- or 4-year college or university as an undergraduate or graduate student. Applicants must have a neurological disability or be the child of a person with such a disability. First priority is given to individuals suffering from a direct spinal cord injury or disease resulting in paralysis such as spinal tumors, strokes, or aneurysms affecting the spinal cord, or spina bifida. Other diseases and disorders that qualify include multiple sclerosis, traumatic brain injuries, Parkinson's, and cerebral palsy. Priority is also given to residents of Wisconsin. Applicants must have a GPA of 2.5 or higher in high school or college. Along with their application, they must submit a 200-word essay on why they deserve the scholarship, a statement of their 5- and 10-year goals, and a list of work experience. Financial need is not considered in the selection process.

Financial data The stipend is $2,000.

Duration 1 year; may be renewed.

Number awarded Varies each semester; recently, 7 were awarded for the fall semester and 5 for the spring semester.

Deadline June of each year for fall semester; December of each year for spring semester.

[1147]
DISABLED AMERICAN VETERANS AUXILIARY NATIONAL EDUCATION SCHOLARSHIP FUND

Disabled American Veterans Auxiliary
Attn: National Education Scholarship Fund
3725 Alexandria Pike
Cold Spring, KY 41076
(859) 441-7300   Toll Free: (877) 426-2838, ext. 4020
Fax: (859) 442-2095   E-mail: dava@davmail.org
Web: www.davauxiliary.org/membership/Programs.aspx

Summary To provide financial assistance to members of the Disabled American Veterans (DAV) Auxiliary who are interested in attending college or graduate school.

Eligibility This program is open to paid life members of the auxiliary who are attending or planning to attend a college, university, or vocational school as a full- or part-time undergraduate or graduate student. Applicants must be at least seniors in high school, but there is no maximum age limit. Selection is based on academic achievement; participation in DAV activities; participation in other activities for veterans in their school, community, or elsewhere; volunteer work; membership in clubs or organizations; honors and awards; a statement of academic goals; and financial need.

Financial data Stipends are $1,500 per year for full-time students or $750 per year for part-time students.

Duration 1 year; may be renewed for up to 4 additional years, provided the recipient maintains a GPA of 2.5 or higher.

Additional data Membership in the DAV Auxiliary is available to extended family members of veterans eligible for membership in Disabled American Veterans (i.e., any man or woman who served in the armed forces during a period of war or under conditions simulating war and was wounded, disabled to any degree, or left with long-term illness as a result of military service and was discharged or retired from military service under honorable conditions). This program was established in September 2010 as a replacement for the educational loan program that the DAV Auxiliary operated from 1931 until August 2010.

Number awarded Varies each year.

Deadline March of each year.

[1148]
EDWARD T. AND MARY A. CONROY MEMORIAL SCHOLARSHIP PROGRAM

Maryland Higher Education Commission
Attn: Office of Student Financial Assistance
6 North Liberty Street, Ground Suite
Baltimore, MD 21201
(410) 767-3301   Toll Free: (800) 974-0203
Fax: (410) 332-0250   TDD: (800) 735-2258
E-mail: osfamail.mhec@maryland.gov
Web: www.mhec.state.md.us

Summary   To provide financial assistance for college or graduate school in Maryland to children and spouses of victims of the September 11, 2001 terrorist attacks and specified categories of veterans, public safety employees, and their children or spouses.

Eligibility   This program is open to entering and continuing undergraduate and graduate students in the following categories: 1) children and surviving spouses of victims of the September 11, 2001 terrorist attacks who died in the World Trade Center in New York City, in the Pentagon in Virginia, or on United Airlines Flight 93 in Pennsylvania; 2) veterans who have, as a direct result of military service, a disability of 25% or greater and have exhausted or are no longer eligible for federal veterans' educational benefits; 3) children and unremarried surviving spouses of armed forces members whose death or 100% disability was directly caused by military service; 4) POW/MIA veterans of the Vietnam Conflict and their children; 5) state or local public safety officers or volunteers who became 100% disabled in the line of duty; 6) children and unremarried surviving spouses of state or local public safety employees or volunteers who died or became 100% disabled in the line of duty. and 7) children and unremarried surviving spouses or a school employee who, as a result of an act of violence, either died in the line of duty or sustained an injury that rendered the school employee 100% disabled. The parent, spouse, veteran, POW, public safety officer or volunteer, or school employee must have been a resident of Maryland at the time of death or when declared disabled. Applicants must be planning to enroll at a 2- or 4-year Maryland college or university as a full-time or part-time degree-seeking undergraduate or graduate student or attend a private career school. Financial need is not considered.

Financial data   The amount of the award is equal to tuition and fees at a Maryland postsecondary institution, to a maximum of $10,182. The total amount of all Maryland scholarship awards from all sources may not exceed the cost of attendance or $19,000, whichever is less.

Duration   Up to 5 years of full-time study or 8 years of part-time study.

Number awarded   Varies each year.

Deadline   July of each year.

[1149]
ERIC MARTINEZ MEMORIAL SCHOLARSHIP FOR THE SIBLING OF AN INDIVIDUAL WITH DOWN SYNDROME

United Parent Support for Down Syndrome
Attn: UPS for DownS Memorial Scholarship Program
1070 South Roselle Road
Schaumburg, IL 60193
(847) 895-2100   E-mail: embarrett@upsfordowns.org
Web: www.upsfordowns.org/support/Scholarships.aspx

Summary   To provide financial assistance to individuals who are working on an undergraduate or graduate degree in a disability-related field.

Eligibility   This program is open to students currently enrolled at a college, university, or community college who have a sibling with Down syndrome. Applicants must be working on an undergraduate or graduate degree in any field. Along with their application, they must submit a 1-page essay that includes their relationship with the sponsoring organization and disability community, their future career plans, and how the inclusion of individuals with disabilities in the community has affected them and how it might affect them in the future. They must also submit a service activity sheet that provides information on the name or type of service activity they have performed, estimated annual activity hours, and names of organizations involved. U.S. citizenship is required.

Financial data   The stipend is $2,500. Funds are sent directly to the institution.

Duration   1 year.

Number awarded   1 each year.

Deadline   May of each year.

[1150]
GEORGE AND LINDA PRICE SCHOLARSHIP

Hemophilia Association of the Capital Area
8136 Old Keene Mill Road, Suite A312
Springfield, VA 22152
(703) 352-7641   Fax: (540) 427-6589
E-mail: admin@hacacares.org
Web: www.hacacares.org

Summary   To provide financial assistance to individuals with bleeding disorders and their families who are members of the Hemophilia Association of the Capital Area (HACA) and interested in attending college or graduate school in any state.

Eligibility   This program is open to residents of northern Virginia, Montgomery and Prince George's County in Maryland, and Washington, D.C. who have a bleeding disorder and their siblings and parents. Applicants must be members of HACA. They must be 1) high school seniors or graduates who have not yet attended college; 2) full-time freshmen, sophomores, or juniors at a college, university, or vocational/technical school in any state; or 3) college seniors planning to attend graduate school and students already enrolled at a graduate school in any state. Along with their application, they must submit a 500-word essay on what they have done to contribute to the bleeding disorders community and how they plan to contribute to that community in the future. Financial need is not considered in the selection process.

Financial data   The stipend is $2,500.

Duration   1 year; recipients may reapply.

Number awarded   2 each year.

Deadline   May of each year.

[1151]
HARVEY PICKER HORIZON SCHOLARSHIPS

Maine Employers' Mutual Insurance Company
Attn: MEMIC Education Fund
261 Commercial Street
P.O. Box 11409
Portland, ME 04104
(207) 791-3300   Toll Free: (800) 660-1306
Fax: (207) 791-3336   E-mail: mbourque@memic.com
Web: www.memic.com

Summary   To provide financial assistance to Maine residents whose parent or spouse was killed or permanently disabled in a work-related accident and are interested in attending college or graduate school in any state.

Eligibility   This program is open to Maine residents who are the child or spouse of a worker killed or permanently disabled as the result of a work-related injury. The worker must have been insured through the sponsor at the time of the workplace injury. Applicants must be attending or planning to attend an accredited college or university in any state as an undergraduate or graduate student. Along with their application, they must submit a 500-word personal statement on their aspirations and how their educational plans relate to those. Selection is based on financial need, academic performance, community involvement, other life experiences, and future promise.

Financial data   Stipends range up to $5,000, depending on the need of the recipient. Funds are paid directly to the recipient's institution.

Duration   1 year; may be renewed.

Additional data   The Maine Employers' Mutual Insurance Company (MEMIC) was established in 1993 as the result of reforms in Maine's workers' compensation laws. It is currently the largest workers' compensation insurance company in the state. It established this scholarship program in 2001.

Number awarded   1 or more each year.

Deadline   April of each year.

[1152]
HAWKINS SPIZMAN KILGO, LLC CHILDHOOD CANCER AWARENESS SCHOLARSHIP

Hawkins Spizman Kilgo, LLC
1535 Mount Vernon Road, Suite 200
Atlanta, GA 30338
(770) 685-6400   Fax: (770) 685-6403
E-mail: info@hawkinsduilaw.com
Web: www.hawkinsduilaw.com

Summary   To provide financial assistance to undergraduate and graduate students who are survivors of childhood cancer or loved ones of survivors.

Eligibility   This program is open to students currently enrolled or accepted for enrollment as an undergraduate or graduate student at an accredited college or university in any state. Applicants must be a survivor or childhood cancer or a loved one who has been directly affected by childhood cancer. They must have a GPA of 2.8 or higher. Along with their application, they must submit an essay of 500 to 1,000 words on 1 of the following: 1) how childhood cancer affected them; 2) how cancer has influenced their dreams and career goals; or 3) what they would say to a young person who has just been diagnosed with cancer to help them prepare for their future.

Financial data   The stipend is $1,000.

Duration   1 year.

Number awarded   1 each year.

Deadline   July of each year.

[1153]
HOPE FOR THE WARRIORS SPOUSE/CAREGIVER SCHOLARSHIPS

Hope for the Warriors
Attn: Spouse/Caregiver Scholarships Director
8003 Forbes Place, Suite 201
Springfield, VA 22151
Toll Free: (877) 246-7349
E-mail: scholarships@hopeforthewarriors.org
Web: www.hopeforthewarriors.org

Summary   To provide financial assistance for college to the spouses and caregivers of wounded or deceased military personnel or veterans.

Eligibility   This program is open to spouses and caregivers of current and former servicemembers who were wounded or killed in the line of duty while serving in support of Operation Enduring Freedom and/or Operation Iraqi Freedom. Support is available in 5 categories: 1) Honorary Scholarships, for those seeking graduate or postgraduate degrees; 2) New Beginnings Scholarships, awarded to those pursuing entry-level classes or training; 3) Restoring Family Scholarships, awarded to spouses of the fallen; 4) Restoring Hope Scholarships, awarded to master's in social work students; or 5) Restoring Self Scholarships, awarded to those seeking any undergraduate degree. Applicants in all categories must submit a 1,500-word essay on the challenges they have experienced as a spouse/caregiver and have overcome, what they have learned about themselves through the spouse/caregiver experience, some of their future goals, and how this scholarship would impact those goals. Selection is based on that essay, academic achievement, personal goals, and letters of recommendation.

Financial data   A stipend is awarded (amount not specified); funds are paid directly to the recipient's institution.

Duration   1 year; may be renewed up to 3 additional years.

Number awarded   Varies each year.

Deadline   May of each year.

[1154]
ILLINOIS GRANT PROGRAM FOR DEPENDENTS OF POLICE OR FIRE OFFICERS

Illinois Student Assistance Commission
Attn: Scholarship and Grant Services
1755 Lake Cook Road
Deerfield, IL 60015-5209
(847) 948-8550   Toll Free: (800) 899-ISAC
Fax: (847) 831-8549   TDD: (800) 526-0844
E-mail: isac.studentservices@isac.illinois.gov
Web: www.isac.org

Summary To provide financial assistance to the children or spouses of disabled or deceased Illinois police or fire officers who plan to attend college or graduate school in the state.

Eligibility This program is open to the spouses and children of Illinois police and fire officers who were at least 90% disabled or killed in the line of duty. Applicants must be enrolled on at least a half-time basis in either undergraduate or graduate study at an approved Illinois public or private 2- or 4-year college, university, or hospital school. They need not be Illinois residents at the time of application. U.S. citizenship or eligible noncitizen status is required.

Financial data The grants provide full payment of tuition and mandatory fees at approved public colleges in Illinois or an equivalent amount at private colleges.

Duration Up to 8 academic semesters or 12 academic quarters of study.

Number awarded Varies each year.

Deadline September of each year for the academic year; February of each year for spring semester or winter or spring quarter; June of each year for summer term.

[1155]
INDIANA CHILDREN AND SPOUSES OF PUBLIC SAFETY OFFICERS PROGRAM

Indiana Commission for Higher Education
Attn: Financial Aid and Student Support Services
101 West Ohio Street, Suite 300
Indianapolis, IN 46204-4206
(317) 232-1023   Toll Free: (888) 528-4719 (within IN)
Fax: (317) 232-3260   E-mail: Scholars@che.in.gov
Web: www.in.gov/che/4520.htm

Summary To provide financial assistance to residents of Indiana who are the children or spouses of specified categories of deceased or disabled public safety officers and interested in attending college or graduate school in the state.

Eligibility This program is open to 1) children of public safety officers (law enforcement officers, firefighters, paramedics, and emergency medical technicians) who were killed in the line of duty when the child was younger than 24 years of age; 2) spouses of public safety officers killed in the line of duty; 3) children younger than 23 years of age of a permanently disabled state trooper; and 4) spouses of permanently disabled state troopers. Applicants must be enrolled or planning to enroll at an eligible Indiana institution (for a list, contact the sponsor). Children must be

enrolled full time and working on an undergraduate or graduate degree; spouses may be enrolled part time but may only be undergraduate students.

Financial data Qualified applicants receive a 100% remission of tuition and all mandatory fees at eligible colleges and universities in Indiana. Support is not provided for such fees as room and board.

Duration Up to 8 semesters for children of deceased public safety officers or up to 124 hours of study for other categories of students.

Number awarded Varies each year.

Deadline Applications must be submitted at least 30 days before the start of the college term.

[1156]
INDIANA CHILDREN OF DECEASED OR DISABLED VETERANS PROGRAM

Indiana Commission for Higher Education
Attn: Financial Aid and Student Support Services
101 West Ohio Street, Suite 300
Indianapolis, IN 46204-4206
(317) 232-1023   Toll Free: (888) 528-4719 (within IN)
Fax: (317) 232-3260   E-mail: Scholars@che.in.gov
Web: www.in.gov/che/4517.htm

Summary To provide financial assistance to residents of Indiana who are the children of deceased or disabled veterans and interested in attending college in the state.

Eligibility This program is open to residents of Indiana whose parent served in the U.S. armed forces during a war or performed duty equally hazardous that was recognized by the award of a U.S. service or campaign medal, suffered a service-connected death or disability, and received a discharge or separation other than dishonorable. Applicants must be the biological child of the veteran or legally adopted prior to their 24th birthday; stepchildren are not eligible. Parents who enlisted on or before June 30, 2011 must have resided in Indiana for at least 36 consecutive months during their lifetime. Parents who enlisted after June 30, 2011 must have designated Indiana as home of record at the time of enlistment or resided in that state at least 5 years before the child first applies for the benefit.

Financial data If the veterans parent initially enlisted on or before June 30, 2011, the child receives a 100% remission of tuition and all mandatory fees for undergraduate, graduate, or professional degrees at eligible postsecondary schools and universities in Indiana. If the veteran parent initially enlisted after June 30, 2011 and suffered a disability with a rating of 80% or more, the child receives a 100% remission of tuition and all mandatory fees for undergraduate or professional degrees at eligible postsecondary schools and universities in Indiana. If the veteran parent initially enlisted after June 30, 2011 and suffered a disability with a rating less than 80%, the rate of remission for tuition and regularly assessed fees is 20% plus the disability rating. Support is not provided for such fees as room and board.

Duration Up to 124 semester hours of study. If the veteran parent initially enlisted on or before June 30, 2011, there is no time limit to use those hours. If the veteran parent initially enlisted after June 30, 2011, the allotted 124 credit hours must be used within 8 years after the date the child first applied.

Number awarded   Varies each year.

Deadline   Applications must be submitted at least 30 days before the start of the college term.

[1157]
JACKIE SPELLMAN SCHOLARSHIPS

Jackie Spellman Scholarship Foundation
935 Eldridge Road
Box 200
Sugar Land, TX 77478
Toll Free: (888) 553-JSSF
E-mail: jackiespellmanfoundation@gmail.com
Web: www.jackiespellmanbenefit.org/scholarship.shtml

Summary   To provide financial assistance for college or graduate school to students who have or whose family member has leukemia or lymphoma.

Eligibility   This program is open to high school seniors, community college and 4-year university students, and graduate students who are leukemia or lymphoma survivors, patients, and/or children, siblings, or parents of leukemia or lymphoma patients. Applicants must be U.S. citizens and enrolled or planning to enroll full time. They must have a GPA of 3.0 or higher and be able to demonstrate financial need. Along with their application, they must submit transcripts; SAT and/or ACT test scores; documentation of financial need; a letter describing any special circumstances that have impacted their academic performance, community service, or leadership activities (if relevant); and an essay of 600 to 800 words describing how leukemia or lymphoma has affected their life, their future plans and desired career path, and how this scholarship will impact them. Students majoring in health or nursing-related majors may receive priority.

Financial data   Stipends range from $1,000 to $5,000.

Duration   1 year.

Number awarded   Approximately 15 each year.

Deadline   April of each year.

[1158]
JACQUELINE SHEARER MEMORIAL SCHOLARSHIP

Ulman Cancer Fund for Young Adults
Attn: Scholarship Committee
921 East Fort Avenue, Suite 325
Baltimore, MD 21230
(410) 964-0202   Toll Free: (888) 393-FUND
Fax: (888) 964-0402
E-mail: scholarship@ulmanfund.org
Web: www.ulmanfund.org/scholarships

Summary   To provide financial assistance for college or graduate school to students from the Baltimore/Washington metropolitan area who have or have lost a parent to cancer.

Eligibility   This program is open to residents of the Baltimore/Washington metropolitan area who have or have

lost a parent or guardian to cancer. Applicants must be 35 years of age or younger and attending, or planning to attend, a 2- or 4-year college, university, or vocational program in any state to work on an undergraduate or graduate degree. The parent or guardian must have been first diagnosed with cancer after the applicant was 15 years of age. Along with their application, they must submit a 500-word essay or 3-minute video on either 1) a letter that they would have liked to receive during their cancer experience; or 2) what they would tell the young adults who participate in the sponsor's summer-long drive to support the organization about being a young adult impacted by cancer. Financial need is considered in the selection process. U.S. citizenship or permanent resident status is required.

Financial data   The stipend is $2,500. Funds are paid directly to the educational institution.

Duration   1 year.

Additional data   Recipients are obligated to organize and run a bone marrow registry drive with the support of Delete Blood Cancer and There Goes My Hero.

Number awarded   2 each year.

Deadline   March of each year.

[1159]
JAMES AND PATRICIA SOOD SCHOLARSHIP

Ulman Cancer Fund for Young Adults
Attn: Scholarship Committee
921 East Fort Avenue, Suite 325
Baltimore, MD 21230
(410) 964-0202   Toll Free: (888) 393-FUND
Fax: (888) 964-0402
E-mail: scholarship@ulmanfund.org
Web: www.ulmanfund.org/scholarships

Summary   To provide financial assistance to students who have been diagnosed with cancer or have or have lost a family member with cancer and are interested in working on an undergraduate or graduate degree in education.

Eligibility   This program is open to students who 1) have been diagnosed with cancer; 2) have a parent or sibling living with cancer; or 3) have lost a parent or sibling to cancer. Applicants must be attending, or planning to attend, a college or university in any state to work on an undergraduate or graduate degree in education. The first diagnosis of cancer (whether of the applicant, a parent, or sibling) must have occurred after the applicant was 15 years of age. Along with their application, they must submit a 500-word essay or 3-minute video on either 1) a letter that they would have liked to receive during their cancer experience; or 2) what they would tell the young adults who participate in the sponsor's summer-long drive to support the organization about being a young adult impacted by cancer. U.S. citizenship or permanent resident status is required.

Financial data   The stipend is $2,500. Funds are paid directly to the educational institution.

Duration   1 year.

Additional data   Recipients are obligated to organize and run a bone marrow registry drive with the support of Delete Blood Cancer and There Goes My Hero.

Number awarded 1 each year.

Deadline March of each year.

[1160]
JAMES DOYLE CASE MEMORIAL SCHOLARSHIPS

Mississippi Council of the Blind
c/o Randy Thompson, Scholarship Committee
107 Chalet Strasse
Brandon, MS 39042-2082
(601) 956-7906   E-mail: bonnieg06@comcast.net
Web: www.mscounciloftheblind.org/node/3

Summary To provide financial assistance to legally blind residents of Mississippi and their children who plan to attend college or graduate school in any state.

Eligibility This program is open to residents of Mississippi who are legally blind or the children of at least 1 legally blind parent. Applicants must be enrolled full time or accepted for enrollment in an undergraduate, graduate, or vocational/technical program in any state and have a GPA of 3.0 or higher. Along with their application, they must submit a 2-page autobiographical sketch, transcripts, standardized test scores (ACT or SAT for undergraduates; GRE, MCAT, LSAT, etc. for graduate students), 2 letters of recommendation, proof of acceptance from a postsecondary school, and verification of blindness of the qualifying person (applicant or parent).

Financial data The stipend is $1,500 per year.

Duration 4 years.

Number awarded 2 each year.

Deadline February of each year.

[1161]
JAMIE L. ROBERTS MEMORIAL SCHOLARSHIP

Ulman Cancer Fund for Young Adults
Attn: Scholarship Committee
921 East Fort Avenue, Suite 325
Baltimore, MD 21230
(410) 964-0202   Toll Free: (888) 393-FUND
Fax: (888) 964-0402
E-mail: scholarship@ulmanfund.org
Web: www.ulmanfund.org/scholarships

Summary To provide financial assistance for college or graduate school to students who have been diagnosed with cancer or have or have lost a family member with cancer.

Eligibility This program is open to students who 1) have been diagnosed with cancer; 2) have a parent or sibling living with cancer; or 3) have lost a parent or sibling to cancer. Applicants must be attending, or planning to attend, a college or university in any state to work on an undergraduate, graduate, or professional degree. They should demonstrate the qualities of the program's namesake-an infectious positive attitude, love of adventure, and ability to inspire others to achieve higher goals. The first diagnosis of cancer (whether of the applicant, a parent, or sibling) must have occurred after the applicant was 15 years of age. Along with their application, they must submit a 500-word essay or 3-minute video on either 1) a letter that they would have liked to receive during their cancer experience; or 2) what they would tell the young adults who participate in the sponsor's summer-long drive to support the organization about being a young adult impacted by cancer. U.S. citizenship or permanent resident status is required.

Financial data The stipend is $2,500. Funds are paid directly to the educational institution.

Duration 1 year.

Additional data This program, which began in 2014, is funded by the 4K for Cancer, an organization of college students who ride bicycles across the country every summer and raise funds for cancer. Recipients are obligated to organize and run a bone marrow registry drive with the support of Delete Blood Cancer and There Goes My Hero.

Number awarded 6 each year.

Deadline March of each year.

[1162]
JEAN B. CRYOR MEMORIAL SCHOLARSHIP PROGRAM

Maryland Higher Education Commission
Attn: Office of Student Financial Assistance
6 North Liberty Street, Ground Suite
Baltimore, MD 21201
(410) 767-3301   Toll Free: (800) 974-0203
Fax: (410) 332-0250   TDD: (800) 735-2258
E-mail: osfamail.mhec@maryland.gov
Web: www.mhec.state.md.us

Summary To provide financial assistance for college or graduate school in Maryland to children and spouses of victims of the September 11, 2001 terrorist attacks and specified categories of veterans, public safety employees, and their children or spouses.

Eligibility This program is open to entering and continuing undergraduate and graduate students in the following categories: 1) children and surviving spouses of victims of the September 11, 2001 terrorist attacks who died in the World Trade Center in New York City, in the Pentagon in Virginia, or on United Airlines Flight 93 in Pennsylvania; 2) veterans who have, as a direct result of military service, a disability of 25% or greater and have exhausted or are no longer eligible for federal veterans' educational benefits; 3) children and unremarried surviving spouses of armed forces members whose death or 100% disability was directly caused by military service; 4) POW/MIA veterans of the Vietnam Conflict and their children; 5) state or local public safety officers or volunteers who became 100% disabled in the line of duty; 6) children and unremarried surviving spouses of state or local public safety employees or volunteers who died or became 100% disabled in the line of duty. and 7) children and unremarried surviving spouses or a school employee who, as a result of an act of violence, either died in the line of duty or sustained an injury that rendered the school employee 100% disabled. The parent, spouse, veteran, POW, public safety officer or volunteer, or school employee must have been a resident of Maryland at the time of death or when declared disabled. Applicants must be planning to enroll at a 2- or 4-year Maryland college or university as a full-time or part-time degree-seeking undergraduate or graduate student or attend a private career school. Financial need is not considered.

Financial data The amount of the award is equal to tuition and fees at a Maryland postsecondary institution, to a maximum of $10,182. The total amount of all Maryland scholarship awards from all sources may not exceed the cost of attendance or $19,000, whichever is less.

Duration Up to 5 years of full-time study or 8 years of part-time study.

Number awarded Varies each year.

Deadline July of each year.

[1163]
JILL WEAVER STARKMAN SCHOLARSHIP

Ulman Cancer Fund for Young Adults
Attn: Scholarship Committee
921 East Fort Avenue, Suite 325
Baltimore, MD 21230
(410) 964-0202   Toll Free: (888) 393-FUND
Fax: (888) 964-0402
E-mail: scholarship@ulmanfund.org
Web: www.ulmanfund.org/scholarships

Summary To provide financial assistance for college or graduate school to students who have been diagnosed with cancer or have or have lost a family member with cancer.

Eligibility This program is open to students who 1) have been diagnosed with cancer; 2) have a parent or sibling living with cancer; or 3) have lost a parent or sibling to cancer. Applicants must be attending, or planning to attend, a college or university in any state to work on an undergraduate, graduate, or professional degree. They should demonstrate the qualities of the program's namesake-the spirit of adventure and compassion and skill for communicating with humans and animals alike. The first diagnosis of cancer (whether of the applicant, a parent, or sibling) must have occurred after the applicant was 15 years of age. Along with their application, they must submit a 500-word essay or 3-minute video on either 1) a letter that they would have liked to receive during their cancer experience; or 2) what they would tell the young adults who participate in the sponsor's summer-long drive to support the organization about being a young adult impacted by cancer. U.S. citizenship or permanent resident status is required.

Financial data The stipend is $2,500. Funds are paid directly to the educational institution.

Duration 1 year.

Additional data This program began in 2012. Recipients are obligated to organize and run a bone marrow registry drive with the support of Delete Blood Cancer and There Goes My Hero.

Number awarded 1 each year.

Deadline March of each year.

[1164]
JOHN DUVALL MEMORIAL SCHOLARSHIP

Ulman Cancer Fund for Young Adults
Attn: Scholarship Committee
921 East Fort Avenue, Suite 325
Baltimore, MD 21230
(410) 964-0202   Toll Free: (888) 393-FUND
Fax: (888) 964-0402
E-mail: scholarship@ulmanfund.org
Web: www.ulmanfund.org/scholarships

Summary To provide financial assistance to students who have been diagnosed with cancer or have or have lost a family member with cancer and are interested in attending designated universities.

Eligibility This program is open to students who 1) have been diagnosed with cancer; 2) have a parent or sibling living with cancer; or 3) have lost a parent or sibling to cancer. Applicants must be working on or planning to work on an undergraduate, graduate, or professional degree at the University of Maryland, Towson University, Elon University, or the Savannah College of Art and Design. They must be able to demonstrate financial need. The first diagnosis of cancer (whether of the applicant, a parent, or sibling) must have occurred after the applicant was 15 years of age. Along with their application, they must submit a 500-word essay or 3-minute video on either 1) a letter that they would have liked to receive during their cancer experience; or 2) what they would tell the young adults who participate in the sponsor's summer-long drive to support the organization about being a young adult impacted by cancer. U.S. citizenship or permanent resident status is required.

Financial data The stipend is $2,500. Funds are paid directly to the educational institution.

Duration 1 year.

Additional data Recipients are obligated to organize and run a bone marrow registry drive with the support of Delete Blood Cancer and There Goes My Hero.

Number awarded 1 each year.

Deadline March of each year.

[1165]
JOHN FOY & ASSOCIATES STRONG ARM LEUKEMIA SCHOLARSHIP

John Foy & Associates
3343 Peachtree Road, Suite 350
Atlanta, GA 30326
(404) 982-4326
Web: www.johnfoy.com

Summary To provide financial assistance to undergraduate and graduate students and their loved ones who have been affected by leukemia.

Eligibility This program is open to entering college freshmen, undergraduates, and graduate students at accredited colleges and universities in any state. Applicants or a loved one must have been affected by leukemia. Along with their application, they must submit an essay of 500 to 1,000 words on 1 of the following: 1) how living with their or their loves one's leukemia has affected their education; 2) the adjustments they have made as a student to accommodate their or a loved one's leukemia; or 3) an obstacle that people with leukemia face that they want the general public to know about.

Financial data The stipend is $1,000.

Duration 1 year.

Number awarded 1 each year.

Deadline December of each year.

[1166]
KATHERN F. GRUBER SCHOLARSHIPS

Blinded Veterans Association
Attn: Scholarship Coordinator
125 North West Street, Third Floor
Alexandria, VA 22314
(202) 371-8880, ext. 313   Toll Free: (800) 669-7079
Fax: (202) 371-8258   E-mail: cdumond@bva.org
Web: www.bva.org

Summary To provide financial assistance for undergraduate or graduate study to immediate family of blinded veterans and servicemembers.

Eligibility This program is open to dependent children, grandchildren, and spouses of blinded veterans and active-duty blinded servicemembers of the U.S. armed forces. The veteran or servicemember must be legally blind; the blindness may be either service-connected or nonservice-connected. Applicants must have been accepted or be currently enrolled as a full-time student in an undergraduate or graduate program at an accredited institution of higher learning. Along with their application, they must submit a 300-word essay on their career goals and aspirations. Financial need is not considered in the selection process.

Financial data The stipend is $2,000; funds are intended to be used to cover the student's expenses, including tuition, other academic fees, books, dormitory fees, and cafeteria fees. Funds are paid directly to the recipient's school.

Duration 1 year; recipients may reapply for up to 3 additional years.

Number awarded 6 each year.

Deadline April of each year.

[1167]
KIDS' CHANCE OF INDIANA SCHOLARSHIP PROGRAM

Kids' Chance of Indiana, Inc.
c/o Jenni Bolen
Objective Group
8330 Naab Road, Suite 140
Indianapolis, IN 46260
(317) 400-7030   Fax: (317) 672-4300
E-mail: ngath@fdgtlaborlaw.com
Web: www.kidschancein.org/scholarship.html

Summary To provide financial assistance to Indiana residents whose parent was killed or permanently disabled in a work-related accident and who are interested in attending college or graduate school in any state.

Eligibility This program is open to Indiana residents between 16 and 25 years of age who are the children of workers fatally or catastrophically injured as a result of a work-related accident or occupational disease. The death or injury must be compensable by the Workers' Compensation Board of the state of Indiana and must have resulted in a substantial decline in the family's income that is likely to impede the student's pursuit of his or her educational objectives. Applicants must be attending or planning to attend a trade/vocational school, industrial/commercial training institution, junior/community college, 4-year college or university, or graduate school in any state. Along with their application, they must submit an autobiography of 250 to 500 words on their educational goals and how this organization can help them achieve success. Financial need is considered in the selection process.

Financial data Stipends range from $500 to $6,000 per year. Funds may be used for tuition and fees, books, room and board, and utilities.

Duration 1 year; may be renewed.

Number awarded Varies each year.

Deadline May of each year.

[1168]
KIDS' CHANCE OF MISSOURI SCHOLARSHIPS

Kids' Chance Inc. of Missouri
Attn: Scholarship Committee
P.O. Box 410384
St. Louis, MO 63141
(314) 997-3390   Fax: (314) 432-5894
E-mail: susgroup@gmail.com
Web: www.mokidschance.org

Summary To provide financial assistance to Missouri residents whose parent was killed or permanently disabled in a work-related accident and who are interested in attending college in any state.

Eligibility This program is open to Missouri residents whose parent sustained a serious injury or fatality in a Missouri work-related accident covered by workers' compensation. Applicants must be attending or planning to attend an accredited college, university, trade school, community college, or graduate school within the United States. They must be able to demonstrate financial need.

Financial data Stipends depend on the need of the recipient, to a maximum of $2,500 per year. Funds may be used to cover tuition, books, supplies, housing, meals, and other expenses not covered by other grants and/or scholarships.

Duration 1 year; recipients may reapply.

Additional data This program began in 1996. It operates in partnership with a similar program offered by the Missouri Department of Higher Education. Students who do not receive support from the state-funded program are considered for this assistance.

Number awarded Varies each year. Recently, the program awarded nearly $200,000 in scholarships.

Deadline May of each year for academic year scholarships; October of each year for spring semester scholarships.

[1169]
KIDS' CHANCE OF NEBRASKA SCHOLARSHIPS

Kids' Chance of Nebraska
15418 Weir Street, Suite 157
Omaha, NE 68137
(402) 573-2175   E-mail: info@kidschanceofne.org
Web: www.kidschanceofne.org/scholarship-application

Summary To provide financial assistance to residents of Nebraska whose are interested in attending college or graduate school in any state and whose parent was killed or injured in an on-the-job accident.

Eligibility This program is open to Nebraska residents between 16 and 25 years of age who are graduating high school seniors, GED recipients, or students currently enrolled at a college, university, junior college, vocational/technical school, or graduate program in any state. Applicants must be the dependent of a parent who suffered an on-the-job fatality or injuries that have had a significant adverse effect on family income. Along with their application, they must submit documentation of financial need and a 2-page essay describing their parent's work-related accident, its personal economic impact on them and their family, and why this scholarship will help them attain their educational goals.

Financial data The stipend is $2,500. Funds are paid directly to the recipient's institution.

Duration 1 year; may be renewed.

Additional data This program began in 2015.

Number awarded Varies each year; recently, 5 were awarded.

Deadline April of each year.

[1170]
KIDS' CHANCE OF NEW YORK SCHOLARSHIPS

Kids' Chance of New York
c/o Bartlett, McDonough and Monighan LLP
170 Old Country Road
Mineola, NY 11501-4112
(516) 877-2900   Fax: (516) 877-0732
E-mail: admin@kcnewyork.org
Web: www.kcnewyork.org/apply

Summary To provide financial assistance for undergraduate or graduate study in any state to residents of New York whose parent was killed or disabled in a work-related accident.

Eligibility This program is open to students between 16 and 25 years of age whose parent or guardian suffered a serious or fatal accidental injury or occupational disease while working for a New York employer. Applicants must be interested in obtaining a vocational, college, or graduate education as a full- or part-time student at a college, university, or technical school in any state. Along with their application, they must submit documents filed with the New York Workers Compensation Board, academic transcripts, documentation of financial need, and a 1-page essay on how this scholarship will help them attain their educational goals.

Financial data A stipend is awarded (amount not specified). Funds are sent directly to the recipient's institution.

Duration 1 year; may be renewed.

Number awarded Varies each year.

Deadline Applications may be submitted at any time, but they must be received at least 3 months before the funds are needed.

[1171]
KIDS' CHANCE OF OHIO SCHOLARSHIPS

Kids' Chance of Ohio
Attn: Executive Director
52 East Gay Street
P.O. Box 1008
Columbus, OH 43216-1008
(614) 464-6410   E-mail: raminor@vssp.com
Web: www.kidschanceohio.org/scholarships

Summary To provide financial assistance for undergraduate or graduate study in any state to children of Ohio employees who were killed or disabled as a result of a work-related injury or occupational disease.

Eligibility This program is open to the children between 16 and 25 years of age of employees who have been declared to be permanently and totally disabled or who were fatally injured as a result of a work-related injury or occupational disease. The death, injury, or illness must have occurred as a result of work activities performed for an Ohio employer covered by the Ohio workers' compensation law, although neither the student nor the parent is required to be an Ohio resident. The injury or death must have resulted in a decline in the family's income. Applicants must be attending or planning to attend a college, university, community college, trade/vocational school, industrial/commercial training institute, or graduate school in any state.

Financial data The stipend depends on the need of the recipient, to a maximum of $5,000 per year. Funds may be used for payment of tuition, fees, books, room, and board.

Duration 1 year; recipients may reapply.

Number awarded Varies each year.

Deadline Applications must be submitted at least 1 month prior to the beginning of the semester or quarter.

[1172]
KIDS' CHANCE OF OKLAHOMA SCHOLARSHIPS

Kids' Chance of Oklahoma, Inc.
1901 North Walnut Avenue
Oklahoma City, OK 73105
(405) 962-3245   Fax: (405) 962-3127
E-mail: kidschanceok@kidschanceok.org
Web: www.kidschanceok.org/scholarship-eligibility

Summary To provide financial assistance to residents of Oklahoma whose are interested in attending college or graduate school in any state and whose parent was killed or injured in a workplace accident.

Eligibility This program is open to Oklahoma residents between 17 and 25 years of age who are graduating high school seniors, GED recipients, or students currently enrolled full or part time at a college in any state. Applicants must be working on a bachelor's or master's degree at a 4-year college or university, an associate degree at a junior or community college, or a certificate or license at a career technical school. Along with their application, they must submit a letter explaining why this scholarship will help them attain their educational goals. They must have a GPA of 2.5 or higher and be able to demonstrate financial need. Other factors considered in the selection process include academic achievement, student government involvement, aptitude, extracurricular activities, and community service.

Financial data A stipend is awarded (amount not specified).

Duration 1 year; may be renewed.

Number awarded Varies each year.

Deadline November of each year.

[1173]
KIDS' CHANCE OF OREGON SCHOLARSHIPS

Kids' Chance of Oregon
Attn: Scholarship Committee
P.O. Box 1728
Lake Oswego, OR 97035
(503) 323-2812
E-mail: info@kidschanceoforegon.com
Web: www.kidschanceoforegon.com

Summary To provide financial assistance to undergraduate and graduate students whose parent or guardian was killed or permanently disabled as a result of an injury covered by Oregon workers' compensation.

Eligibility This program is open to high school seniors, GED participants, full- or part-time undergraduates (university or community college), trade/technical/vocational school students, apprentice program participants, and graduate students in any state who are between 16 and 25 years of age. Applicants' must be affected by the death or permanent and total disability of a parent or guardian as the result of an injury arising out of employment for an Oregon employer cover by workers' compensation. They must submit a statement of their financial need, the circumstances of need, and how a scholarship will assist.

Financial data A stipend is awarded (amount not specified).

Duration 1 year; may be renewed.

Number awarded Varies each year.

Deadline Applications may be submitted at any time, but they must be received at least 2 months before the term for which the scholarship is sought.

[1174]
KIDS' CHANCE OF SOUTH CAROLINA SCHOLARSHIPS

Kids' Chance of South Carolina
P.O. Box 2957
Georgetown, SC 29442-2957
(843) 546-5837   E-mail: info@kidschancesc.org
Web: www.kidschancesc.org/index.php/scholarships

Summary To provide financial assistance to South Carolina residents whose parent was killed or permanently disabled in a work-related accident and who are interested in attending college or graduate school in any state.

Eligibility This program is open to South Carolina residents between 16 and 25 years of age who are the children of workers fatally or catastrophically injured as a result of a work-related accident or occupational disease. Applicants must be attending or planning to attend a trade school, vocational school, community or junior college, 4-year college or university, or graduate school in any state. They must have a GPA of 2.0 or higher. The work-related injury or occupational disease from which their parent suffers or died must be compensable by the Workers' Compensation Board of the state of South Carolina and must have resulted in a substantial decline in the family's income that is likely to interfere with the student's pursuit of his or her educational objectives.

Financial data Stipends range up to $3,000 per semester ($6,000 per year). Funds may be used for tuition and fees, books, room and board, and utilities.

Duration 1 semester; may be renewed up to 7 additional semesters, provided the recipient maintains a GPA of 2.5 or higher.

Number awarded Varies each year; recently, 43 of these scholarships, with a total value of $106,060 were awarded.

Deadline Applications must be submitted 1 month before the beginning of the semester, or July for the fall semester and December for the spring semester.

[1175]
KIDS' CHANCE OF SOUTH DAKOTA SCHOLARSHIPS

Kids' Chance of South Dakota
c/o Michael McKnight, President
Boyce Law Firm, L.L.P.
300 South Main Avenue
P.O. Box 5015
Sioux Falls, SD 57117-5015
(605) 336-2424   Fax: (605) 334-0618
E-mail: admin@kidschanceofsd.org
Web: www.kidschanceofsd.org/scholarship-application

Summary To provide financial assistance to residents of South Dakota whose are interested in attending college or graduate school in any state and whose parent was killed or injured in an on-the-job accident.

Eligibility This program is open to South Dakota residents between 16 and 25 years of age who are graduating high school seniors, GED recipients, or students currently enrolled at a college, university, junior college, vocational/technical school, or graduate program in any state. Applicants must be the dependent of a parent who suffered an on-the-job fatality or injuries that have had a significant adverse effect on family income. Along with their application, they must submit documentation of financial need and a 2-page essay describing their parent's work-related accident, its personal economic impact on them and their family, and why this scholarship will help them attain their educational goals.

Financial data   A stipend is awarded (amount not specified). Funds are paid directly to the recipient's institution.

Duration   1 year; may be renewed.

Number awarded   Varies each year.

Deadline   April of each year.

[1176]
LANFORD FAMILY HIGHWAY WORKER MEMORIAL SCHOLARSHIP PROGRAM

American Road and Transportation Builders
  Association
Attn: Transportation Development Foundation
250 E Street, S.W., Suite 900.
Washington, DC 20024
(202) 289-4434   Fax: (202) 289-4435
E-mail: ehoulihan@artba.org
Web: www.artba.org/foundation/awards-scholarships

Summary   To provide financial assistance for college to children of highway workers killed or disabled on the job.

Eligibility   This program is open to the sons, daughters, and legally adopted children of highway workers who have died or become permanently disabled in roadway construction zone accidents. Applicants must be attending or planning to attend an accredited 4-year college or university, 2-year college, or vocational/technical school. Candidates for an M.B.A. degree or a master's degree in civil engineering, construction management, or another construction-related program are also eligible. Their parent must have been employed by a transportation construction firm or a transportation public agency at the time of death or disabling injury. Selection is based on academic performance (GPA of 2.5 or higher), a 200-word statement from the applicant on reasons for wanting to continue education, letters of recommendation, and financial need.

Financial data   The stipend is $5,000. Funds are paid directly to the recipient's institution to be used for tuition, books, or required fees, but not for room and board.

Duration   1 year.

Additional data   This program began in 1999.

Number awarded   Varies each year; recently, 11 were awarded.

Deadline   April of each year.

[1177]
LEUKEMIA & LYMPHOMA LAW SCHOOL SCHOLARSHIP

Law Office of Renkin & Associates
Attn: Paula Renkin
320 Encinitas Boulevard
Encinitas, CA 92024
(619) 299-7100   Toll Free: (888) 837-3564
E-mail: Paula@renkinlaw.com
Web: www.renkinlaw.com

Summary   To provide financial assistance to law students whose lives have been affected by leukemia or lymphoma, either in themselves or a member of their family.

Eligibility   This program is open to U.S. citizens older than 18 years of age who are current or entering students at accredited law schools in the United States. Applicants must have been affected by or dealing with issues related to leukemia or lymphoma, either in themselves or a family member. They must have a GPA of 3.0 or higher from undergraduate or current law school work. Along with their application, they must submit an essay of 1 to 2 pages describing how their life has been impacted by leukemia or lymphoma.

Financial data   The stipend is $1,000.

Duration   1 year.

Additional data   This program began in 2015.

Number awarded   1 each year.

Deadline   July of each year.

[1178]
LISA HIGGINS-HUSSMAN FOUNDATION SCHOLARSHIP

Ulman Cancer Fund for Young Adults
Attn: Scholarship Committee
921 East Fort Avenue, Suite 325
Baltimore, MD 21230
(410) 964-0202   Toll Free: (888) 393-FUND
Fax: (888) 964-0402
E-mail: scholarship@ulmanfund.org
Web: www.ulmanfund.org/scholarships

Summary   To provide financial assistance for college or graduate school to students from Washington, D.C., Maryland, or Virginia who have been diagnosed with cancer or have or have lost a family member with cancer.

Eligibility   This program is open to students who 1) have been diagnosed with cancer; 2) have a parent, sibling, or guardian living with cancer; or 3) have lost a parent, sibling, or guardian to cancer. Applicants must be residents of Washington, D.C., Maryland, or Virginia. They must be between 15 and 35 years of age and attending, or planning to attend, a 2- or 4-year college, university, or vocational program in any state to work on an undergraduate or graduate degree. The first diagnosis of cancer (whether of the applicant, a parent, a sibling, or a guardian) must have occurred after the applicant was 15 years of age. Along with their application, they must submit a 500-word essay or 3-minute video on either 1) a letter that they would have liked to receive during their cancer experience; or 2) what they would tell the young adults who participate in the sponsor's summer-long drive to support the organization about being a young adult impacted by cancer. U.S. citizenship or permanent resident status is required.

Financial data   The stipend is $2,500. Funds are paid directly to the educational institution.

Duration   1 year.

Additional data   Recipients are obligated to organize and run a bone marrow registry drive with the support of Delete Blood Cancer and There Goes My Hero.

Number awarded   1 each year.

Deadline   March of each year.

[1179]
LITTLE PEOPLE OF AMERICA SCHOLARSHIPS

Little People of America, Inc.
Attn: Vice President of Programs
250 El Camino Real, Suite 218
Tustin, CA 92780
(714) 368-3689   Toll Free: (888) LPA-2001
Fax: (714) 368-3367   E-mail: info@lpaonline.org
Web: www.lpaonline.org

Summary To provide financial assistance for college or graduate school to members of the Little People of America (LPA), to their families, and (in limited cases) to others.

Eligibility This program is open to members of LPA (limited to people who, for medical reasons, are 4 feet 10 inches or under in height). Applicants must be high school seniors or students attending college, vocational school, or graduate school. Along with their application, they must submit a 500-word personal statement that explains their reasons for applying for a scholarship, their plans for the future, how they intend to be of service to LPA after graduation, and any other relevant information about themselves, their family, their background, and their educational achievements. Financial need is also considered in the selection process. Scholarships are awarded in the following priority order: 1) members of LPA who have a medically diagnosed form of dwarfism; 2) immediate family members of dwarfs who are also paid members of LPA; and 3) people with dwarfism who are not members of LPA.

Financial data Stipends range from $250 to $1,000.

Duration 1 year; awards are limited to 2 for undergraduate study and 1 for graduate study.

Number awarded Varies; generally between 5 and 10 each year.

Deadline April of each year.

[1180]
MAINE VETERANS DEPENDENTS EDUCATIONAL BENEFITS

Bureau of Veterans' Services
117 State House Station
Augusta, ME 04333-0117
(207) 430-6035 Toll Free: (800) 345-0116 (within ME)
Fax: (207) 626-4471   E-mail: mainebvs@maine.gov
Web: www.maine.gov

Summary To provide financial assistance for undergraduate or graduate education to dependents of disabled and other Maine veterans.

Eligibility Applicants for these benefits must be children (high school seniors or graduates under 22 years of age), non-divorced spouses, or unremarried widow(er)s of veterans who meet 1 or more of the following requirements: 1) living and determined to have a total permanent disability resulting from a service-connected cause; 2) killed in action; 3) died from a service-connected disability; 4) died while totally and permanently disabled due to a service-connected disability but whose death was not related to the service-connected disability; or 5) a member of the armed forces on active duty who has been listed for more than 90 days as missing in action, captured, forcibly detained, or interned in the line of duty by a foreign government or power. The veteran parent must have been a resident of Maine at the time of entry into service or a resident of Maine for 5 years preceding application for these benefits. Children may be working on an associate or bachelor's degree. Spouses, widows, and widowers may work on an associate, bachelor's, or master's degree.

Financial data Recipients are entitled to free tuition at institutions of higher education supported by the state of Maine.

Duration Children may receive up to 8 semesters of support; they have 6 years from the date of first entrance to complete those 8 semesters. Continuation in the program is based on their earning a GPA of 2.0 or higher each semester. Spouses are entitled to receive up to 120 credit hours of educational benefits and have 10 years from the date of first entrance to complete their program.

Additional data College preparatory schooling and correspondence courses are not supported under this program.

Number awarded Varies each year.

Deadline Deadline not specified.

[1181]
MARILYN YETSO MEMORIAL SCHOLARSHIP

Ulman Cancer Fund for Young Adults
Attn: Scholarship Committee
921 East Fort Avenue, Suite 325
Baltimore, MD 21230
(410) 964-0202   Toll Free: (888) 393-FUND
Fax: (888) 964-0402
E-mail: scholarship@ulmanfund.org
Web: www.ulmanfund.org/scholarships

Summary To provide financial assistance for college or graduate school to students from the Baltimore/Washington metropolitan area who have or have lost a parent to cancer.

Eligibility This program is open to residents of the Baltimore/Washington metropolitan area who have or have lost a parent or guardian to cancer. Applicants must be 35 years of age or younger and attending, or planning to attend, a 2- or 4-year college, university, or vocational program in any state to work on an undergraduate or graduate degree. The parent or guardian must have been first diagnosed with cancer after the applicant was 15 years of age. Along with their application, they must submit a 500-word essay or 3-minute video on either 1) a letter that they would have liked to receive during their cancer experience; or 2) what they would tell the young adults who participate in the sponsor's summer-long drive to support the organization about being a young adult impacted by cancer. Financial need is considered in the selection process. U.S. citizenship or permanent resident status is required.

Financial data The stipend is $2,500. Funds are paid directly to the educational institution.

Duration 1 year.

Additional data This program began in 2002. Recipients are obligated to organize and run a bone marrow registry drive with the support of Delete Blood Cancer and There Goes My Hero.

Number awarded   1 each year.

Deadline   March of each year.

[1182]
MARY BARTON FREEMAN SCHOLARSHIPS

Ulman Cancer Fund for Young Adults
Attn: Scholarship Committee
921 East Fort Avenue, Suite 325
Baltimore, MD 21230
(410) 964-0202   Toll Free: (888) 393-FUND
Fax: (888) 964-0402
E-mail: scholarship@ulmanfund.org
Web: www.ulmanfund.org/scholarships

Summary   To provide financial assistance for college or graduate school to students who have been diagnosed with cancer or have or have lost a family member with cancer.

Eligibility   This program is open to students who 1) have been diagnosed with cancer; 2) have a parent or sibling living with cancer; or 3) have lost a parent or sibling to cancer. Applicants must be attending, or planning to attend, a college or university in any state to work on an undergraduate, graduate, or professional degree. They must be working on career or higher eduction goals. The first diagnosis of cancer (whether of the applicant, a parent, or sibling) must have occurred after the applicant was 15 years of age. Along with their application, they must submit a 500-word essay or 3-minute video on either 1) a letter that they would have liked to receive during their cancer experience; or 2) what they would tell the young adults who participate in the sponsor's summer-long drive to support the organization about being a young adult impacted by cancer. U.S. citizenship or permanent resident status is required.

Financial data   The stipend is $2,500. Funds are paid directly to the educational institution.

Duration   1 year.

Additional data   Recipients are obligated to organize and run a bone marrow registry drive with the support of Delete Blood Cancer and There Goes My Hero.

Number awarded   5 each year.

Deadline   March of each year.

[1183]
MESOTHELIOMA CANCER ALLIANCE SCHOLARSHIP

Mesothelioma Cancer Alliance
c/o Early, Lucarelli, Sweeney, Meisenkothen
360 Lexington Avenue, 20th Floor
New York, NY 10017
(212) 968-2233   Toll Free: (800) 336-0086
Fax: (212) 986-2255
Web: www.mesothelioma.com/scholarship

Summary   To provide financial assistance to undergraduate and graduate students who have had cancer or whose family member has had cancer.

Eligibility   This program is open to U.S. citizens enrolled or planning to enroll full time at a 2- or 4-year college or university as an undergraduate or graduate student. Applicants must have battled cancer at any point in their lives (not limited to mesothelioma) or have a parent, sibling, immediate family member, or close friend who has battled or is currently fighting cancer. They must have a GPA of 3.0 or higher. Along with their application, they must submit an essay of 500 to 1,500 words or a video up to 5 minutes in length on how cancer has affected their life, how they overcame that strong adversity, how cancer has affected their outlook on their life and personal or career goals, how that adversity shaped who they are today, what the scholarship would mean to them, and why it is important. Selection is based on the positive impact they have on those around them, strength in the face of adversity, commitment to academic excellence, and financial need.

Financial data   The stipend is $4,000.

Duration   1 year.

Number awarded   2 each year: 1 in fall and 1 in spring.

Deadline   March of each year for fall semester; November of each year for spring semester.

[1184]
MILLIE BROTHER SCHOLARSHIPS

Children of Deaf Adults Inc.
c/o Jennie E. Pyers, Scholarship Committee
Wellesley College
106 Central Street, SCI484A
Wellesley, MA 02481-8203
(413) 650-2632
E-mail: scholarships@coda-international.org
Web: www.coda-international.org/scholarship

Summary   To provide financial assistance for college or graduate school to the children of deaf parents.

Eligibility   This program is open to the hearing children of deaf parents who are high school seniors or graduates attending or planning to attend college or graduate school. Applicants must submit a 2-page essay on 1) how their experience as the child of deaf parents has shaped their life and goals; and 2) their future career aspirations. Essays are judged on organization, content, and creativity. In addition to the essay, selection is based on a high school and/or college transcript and 2 letters of recommendation.

Financial data   The stipend is $3,000.

Duration   1 year; recipients may reapply.

Number awarded   Normally, 2 each year.

Deadline   March of each year.

[1185]
MINNESOTA G.I. BILL PROGRAM

Minnesota Department of Veterans Affairs
Attn: Programs and Services Division
20 West 12th Street, Room 206
St. Paul, MN 55155
(651) 296-2562   Toll Free: (888) LINK-VET
Fax: (651) 296-3954   TDD: (800) 627-3529
E-mail: MNGIBill@state.mn.us
Web: mn.gov

Summary To provide financial assistance for college or graduate school in the state to residents of Minnesota who served in the military after September 11, 2001 and the families of deceased or disabled military personnel.

Eligibility This program is open to residents of Minnesota enrolled at colleges and universities in the state as undergraduate or graduate students. Applicants must be 1) a veteran who is serving or has served honorably in a branch of the U.S. armed forces at any time; 2) a non-veteran who has served honorably for a total of 5 years or more cumulatively as a member of the Minnesota National Guard or other active or Reserve component of the U.S. armed forces, and any part of that service occurred on or after September 11, 2001; or 3) a surviving child or spouse of a person who has served in the military at any time and who has died or has a total and permanent disability as a result of that military service. They may be attending college in the state or participating in an apprenticeship or on-the-job (OJT) training program. Financial need is also considered in the selection process.

Financial data The college stipend is $1,000 per semester for full-time study or $500 per semester for part-time study. The maximum award is $3,000 per academic year or $10,000 per lifetime. Apprenticeship and OJT students are eligible for up to $2,000 per fiscal year. Approved employers are eligible to receive $1,000 placement credit payable upon hiring a person under this program and another $1,000 after 12 consecutive months of employment. No more than $3,000 in aggregate benefits under this paragraph may be paid to or on behalf of an individual in one fiscal year, and not more than $9,000 over any period of time.

Duration 1 year; may be renewed, provided the recipient continues to make satisfactory academic progress.

Additional data This program was established by the Minnesota Legislature in 2007.

Number awarded Varies each year.

Deadline Deadline not specified.

[1186]
NATIONAL COLLEGIATE CANCER FOUNDATION LEGACY SCHOLARSHIP PROGRAM

National Collegiate Cancer Foundation
Attn: Scholarship Committee
4858 Battery Lane, Suite 216
Bethesda, MD 20814
(240) 515-6262   E-mail: info@collegiatecancer.org
Web: www.collegiatecancer.org/scholarships

Summary To provide financial assistance to undergraduate and graduate students who have lost a parent or guardian to cancer.

Eligibility This program is open to students between 18 and 35 years of age who have lost a parent or guardian to cancer. Applicants must be enrolled or planning to enroll at a college or university to work on a certificate or an associate, bachelor's, master's, or doctoral degree. Along with their application, they must submit a 1,000-word essay on 1 of 4 assigned topics related to their experiences with cancer and college. Selection is based on notable accomplishments, recommendations, encouragement, and financial need. U.S. citizenship or permanent resident status is required.

Financial data The stipend is $1,000.

Duration 1 year.

Additional data This program began in 2014.

Number awarded Varies each year; recently, 21 were awarded.

Deadline May of each year.

[1187]
NORTH CAROLINA BAR ASSOCIATION SCHOLARSHIPS

North Carolina Bar Association
Attn: Young Lawyers Division Scholarship Committee
8000 Weston Parkway
P.O. Box 3688
Cary, NC 27519-3688
(919) 677-0561   Toll Free: (800) 662-7407
Fax: (919) 677-0761   E-mail: jterrell@ncbar.org
Web: www.ncbar.org/members/divisions/young-lawyers

Summary To provide financial assistance for college or graduate school to the children of disabled or deceased law enforcement officers in North Carolina.

Eligibility This program is open to the natural or adopted children of North Carolina law enforcement officers who were permanently disabled or killed in the line of duty. Applicants must be younger than 27 years of age and enrolled or planning to enroll full time at an accredited institution of higher learning (including community colleges, trade schools, colleges, universities, and graduate programs) in North Carolina. Selection is based on academic performance and financial need.

Financial data A stipend is awarded (amount not specified).

Duration Up to 4 years.

Number awarded Varies each year; recently, 17 were awarded.

Deadline April of each year.

[1188]
OREGON DECEASED OR DISABLED PUBLIC SAFETY OFFICER GRANT PROGRAM

Oregon Student Access Commission
Attn: Public Programs
1500 Valley River Drive, Suite 100
Eugene, OR 97401-2130
(541) 687-7400   Toll Free: (800) 452-8807
Fax: (541) 687-7414   TDD: (800) 735-2900
E-mail: PublicPrograms@osac.state.or.us
Web: www.oregonstudentaid.gov/ddpso-grant.aspx

Summary To provide financial assistance for college or graduate school in the state to the children of disabled or deceased Oregon public safety officers.

Eligibility This program is open to the natural, adopted, or stepchildren of Oregon public safety officers (firefighters, state fire marshals, chief deputy fire marshals, deputy state fire marshals, police chiefs, police officers, sheriffs, deputy sheriffs, county adult parole and probation officers, correction officers, and investigators of the Criminal Justice Division of the Department of Justice) who, in the line of duty, were killed or disabled. Applicants must be enrolled or planning to enroll as a full-time undergraduate student at a public or private college or university in Oregon. Children of deceased officers are also eligible for graduate study. Financial need must be demonstrated.

Financial data At a public 2- or 4-year college or university, the amount of the award is equal to the cost of tuition and fees. At an eligible private college, the award amount is equal to the cost of tuition and fees at the University of Oregon.

Duration 1 year; may be renewed for up to 3 additional years of undergraduate study, if the student maintains satisfactory academic progress and demonstrates continued financial need. Children of deceased public safety officers may also receive support for 12 quarters of graduate study.

Number awarded Varies each year.

Deadline Deadline not specified.

[1189]
OREGON OCCUPATIONAL SAFETY AND HEALTH DIVISION WORKERS MEMORIAL SCHOLARSHIPS

Oregon Office of Student Access and Completion
Attn: Scholarship Processing Coordinator
1500 Valley River Drive, Suite 100
Eugene, OR 97401-2146
(541) 687-7422   Toll Free: (800) 452-8807, ext. 7422
Fax: (541) 687-7414   TDD: (800) 735-2900
E-mail: cheryl.a.connolly@state.or.us
Web: app.oregonstudentaid.gov/Catalog/Default.aspx

Summary To provide financial assistance to the children and spouses of disabled or deceased workers in Oregon who are interested in attending college or graduate school in any state.

Eligibility This program is open to residents of any state who are U.S. citizens or permanent residents. Applicants must be high school seniors or graduates who 1) are dependents or spouses of an Oregon worker who has suffered permanent total disability on the job; or 2) are receiving, or have received, fatality benefits as dependents or spouses of a worker fatally injured in Oregon. They may be attending a college or graduate school in any state. Along with their application, they must submit an essay of up to 500 words on how the injury or death of their parent or spouse has affected or influenced their decision to further their education. Financial need is not required, but it is considered in the selection process.

Financial data Stipends for scholarships offered by the Oregon Office of Student Access and Completion (OSAC) range from $1,000 to $10,000 but recently averaged $4,368.

Duration 1 year.

Additional data This program, established in 1991, is sponsored by the Oregon Occupational Safety and Health Division of the Department of Consumer and Business Services.

Number awarded Varies each year; recently, 7 were awarded.

Deadline February of each year.

[1190]
PERLITA LIWANAG MEMORIAL SCHOLARSHIP

Ulman Cancer Fund for Young Adults
Attn: Scholarship Committee
921 East Fort Avenue, Suite 325
Baltimore, MD 21230
(410) 964-0202   Toll Free: (888) 393-FUND
Fax: (888) 964-0402
E-mail: scholarship@ulmanfund.org
Web: www.ulmanfund.org/scholarships

Summary To provide financial assistance for college or graduate school to students from the Washington, D.C. metropolitan area who have been diagnosed with cancer or have or have lost a family member with cancer.

Eligibility This program is open to students who 1) have been diagnosed with cancer; 2) have a parent, sibling, or guardian living with cancer; or 3) have lost a parent, sibling, or guardian to cancer. Applicants must be residents of Washington, D.C., Maryland, or northern Virginia. They must be 35 years of age or younger and attending, or planning to attend, a 2- or 4-year college, university, or vocational program in any state to work on an undergraduate or graduate degree. The first diagnosis of cancer (whether of the applicant, a parent, a sibling, or a guardian) must have occurred after the applicant was 15 years of age. Along with their application, they must submit a 500-word essay or 3-minute video on either 1) a letter that they would have liked to receive during their cancer experience; or 2) what they would tell the young adults who participate in the sponsor's summer-long drive to support the organization about being a young adult impacted by cancer. U.S. citizenship or permanent resident status is required.

Financial data The stipend is $2,500. Funds are paid directly to the educational institution.

Duration 1 year.

Additional data This program began in 2011. Recipients are obligated to organize and run a bone marrow registry drive with the support of Delete Blood Cancer and There Goes My Hero.

Number awarded 1 each year.

Deadline March of each year.

[1191]
SATOLA FAMILY SCHOLARSHIP

Ulman Cancer Fund for Young Adults
Attn: Scholarship Committee
921 East Fort Avenue, Suite 325
Baltimore, MD 21230
(410) 964-0202   Toll Free: (888) 393-FUND
Fax: (888) 964-0402
E-mail: scholarship@ulmanfund.org
Web: www.ulmanfund.org/scholarships

Summary To provide financial assistance for college or graduate school to students who have been diagnosed with cancer or have or have lost a family member with cancer.

Eligibility This program is open to students who 1) have been diagnosed with cancer; 2) have a parent or sibling living with cancer; or 3) have lost a parent or sibling to cancer. Applicants must be attending, or planning to attend, a college or university in any state to work on an undergraduate, graduate, or professional degree. They should be able to demonstrate courage, spirit, and determination. The first diagnosis of cancer (whether of the applicant, a parent, or sibling) must have occurred after the applicant was 15 years of age. Along with their application, they must submit a 500-word essay or 3-minute video on either 1) a letter that they would have liked to receive during their cancer experience; or 2) what they would tell the young adults who participate in the sponsor's summer-long drive to support the organization about being a young adult impacted by cancer. U.S. citizenship is required.

Financial data The stipend is $2,500. Funds are paid directly to the educational institution.

Duration 1 year.

Additional data This program began in 2009. Recipients are obligated to organize and run a bone marrow registry drive with the support of Delete Blood Cancer and There Goes My Hero.

Number awarded 1 each year.

Deadline March of each year.

[1192]
SCHOLARSHIP FOR STUDENTS WITH AN AUTISTIC SIBLING

Knapp & Roberts
850 North Second Avenue
Phoenix, AZ 85003
(480) 991-7677   E-mail: roberts@krattorneys.com
Web: www.knappandroberts.com/scholarship

Summary To provide financial assistance to high school seniors and current college students who have a sibling with autism.

Eligibility This program is open to residents of any state who are graduating high school seniors or students currently enrolled as undergraduate or graduate students at an accredited college or university. Applicants must have a sibling or siblings with a diagnosis of autism. They must submit a picture of their special needs sibling along with a letter from a physician confirming the diagnosis of autism. Selection is based primarily on a 500-word essay about their family's story, where they are going to college, the career they plan to pursue, and how they would benefit from this scholarship.

Financial data The stipend is $2,500.

Duration 1 year.

Number awarded 1 each year.

Deadline April of each year.

[1193]
SURVIVORS' AND DEPENDENTS' EDUCATIONAL ASSISTANCE PROGRAM

Department of Veterans Affairs
Attn: Veterans Benefits Administration
810 Vermont Avenue, N.W.
Washington, DC 20420
(202) 418-4343   Toll Free: (888) GI-BILL1
Web: www.benefits.va.gov/GIBILL/DEA.asp

Summary To provide financial assistance for undergraduate or graduate study to children and spouses of deceased and disabled veterans, MIAs, and POWs.

Eligibility Eligible for this assistance are spouses and children of 1) veterans who died or are permanently and totally disabled as the result of active service in the armed forces; 2) veterans who died from any cause while rated permanently and totally disabled from a service-connected disability; 3) servicemembers listed as missing in action or captured in the line of duty by a hostile force; 4) servicemembers listed as forcibly detained or interned by a foreign government or power; and 5) servicemembers who are hospitalized or receiving outpatient treatment for a service-connected permanent and total disability and are likely to be discharged for that disability. Children must be between 18 and 26 years of age, although extensions may be granted. Spouses and children over 14 years of age with physical or mental disabilities are also eligible.

Financial data Monthly stipends for study at an academic institution are $1,024 for full time, $767 for three-quarter time, or $510 for half-time. Other rates apply for apprenticeship and on-the-job training, farm cooperative training, and special restorative training.

Duration Benefits are provided for up to 45 months (or the equivalent in part-time training). Some beneficiaries who qualify for more than 1 education program may be eligible for up to 81 months. Spouses must complete their training within 10 years of the date they are first found eligible. For spouses of servicemembers who died on active duty, benefits end 20 years from the date of death.

Additional data Benefits may be used to work on associate, bachelor's, or graduate degrees at colleges and universities, including independent study, cooperative training, and study abroad programs. Courses leading to a certificate or diploma from business, technical, or vocational schools may also be taken. Other eligible programs include apprenticeships, on-the-job training programs, farm cooperative courses, and correspondence courses (for spouses only). Remedial, deficiency, and refresher courses may be approved under certain circumstances.

Number awarded Varies each year.

Deadline Applications may be submitted at any time.

[1194]
THOMAS H. MILLER SCHOLARSHIP

Blinded Veterans Association
Attn: Scholarship Coordinator
125 North West Street, Third Floor
Alexandria, VA 22314
(202) 371-8880, ext. 313   Toll Free: (800) 669-7079
Fax: (202) 371-8258   E-mail: cdumond@bva.org
Web: www.bva.org

Summary To provide financial assistance for undergraduate or graduate study, especially of music or the fine arts, to immediate family of blinded veterans and servicemembers.

Eligibility This program is open to dependent children, grandchildren, and spouses of blinded veterans and active-duty blinded servicemembers of the U.S. armed forces. The veteran or servicemember must be legally blind; the blindness may be either service-connected or nonservice-connected. Applicants must have been accepted or be currently enrolled as a full-time student in an undergraduate or graduate program at an accredited institution of higher learning. Preference is given to students of music or the fine arts. Along with their application, they must submit a 300-word essay on their career goals and aspirations. Financial need is not considered in the selection process.

Financial data The stipend is $1,000; funds are intended to be used to cover the student's expenses, including tuition, other academic fees, books, dormitory fees, and cafeteria fees. Funds are paid directly to the recipient's school.

Duration 1 year; recipients may reapply for up to 3 additional years.

Number awarded 1 each year.

Deadline April of each year.

[1195]
UCB FAMILY EPILEPSY SCHOLARSHIP PROGRAM

UCB, Inc.
Family Scholarship Program
c/o Summit Medical Communications
1421 East Broad Street, Suite 340
Fuquay-Varina, NC 27526
Toll Free: (866) 825-1920   Fax: (919) 567-7591
E-mail: ucbepilepsyscholarship@summitmedcomm.
com
Web: www.ucbepilepsyscholarship.com

Summary To provide financial assistance for college or graduate school to epilepsy patients and their family members and caregivers.

Eligibility This program is open to epilepsy patients and their family members and caregivers. Applicants must be working on or planning to work on an undergraduate or graduate degree at an institution of higher education in the United States. They must be able to demonstrate academic achievement, a record of participation in activities outside of school, and service as a role model. Along with their application, they must submit a 1-page essay explaining why they should be selected for the scholarship, how epilepsy has impacted their life either as a patient or as a family member or caregiver, and how they will benefit from the scholarship. U.S. citizenship or permanent resident status is required.

Financial data The stipend is $5,000.

Duration 1 year; nonrenewable.

Additional data This program, previously known as the Keppra Family Epilepsy Scholarship Program, was established in 2004.

Number awarded 30 each year. Since this program was established, it has awarded $1,700,000 to more than 340 students.

Deadline April of each year.

[1196]
VERA YIP MEMORIAL SCHOLARSHIP

Ulman Cancer Fund for Young Adults
Attn: Scholarship Committee
921 East Fort Avenue, Suite 325
Baltimore, MD 21230
(410) 964-0202   Toll Free: (888) 393-FUND
Fax: (888) 964-0402
E-mail: scholarship@ulmanfund.org
Web: www.ulmanfund.org/scholarships

Summary To provide financial assistance for college or graduate school to students from any state who have been diagnosed with cancer or have or have lost a family member with cancer.

Eligibility This program is open to U.S. citizens and permanent residents between 15 and 35 years of age from any state. Applicants must 1) have been diagnosed with cancer and currently in relapse or active treatment; 2) have a parent or guardian living with cancer; or 3) have lost a parent or guardian to cancer. The student, parent, or guardian must have been first diagnosed with cancer after the applicant was 15 years of age. Along with their application, they must submit a 500-word essay or 3-minute video on either 1) a letter that they would have liked to receive during their cancer experience; or 2) what they would tell the young adults who participate in the sponsor's summer-long drive to support the organization about being a young adult impacted by cancer. U.S. citizenship or permanent resident status is required. This award is presented to the applicant who best demonstrates the qualities of Vera Yip of courage, determination, motivation, and dedication.

Financial data The stipend is $2,500. Funds are paid directly to the educational institution.

Duration 1 year; nonrenewable.

Additional data Recipients are obligated to organize and run a bone marrow registry drive with the support of Delete Blood Cancer and There Goes My Hero.

Number awarded 1 each year.

Deadline March of each year.

[1197]
VIRGINIA MILITARY SURVIVORS AND DEPENDENTS EDUCATION PROGRAM

Virginia Department of Veterans Services
Attn: VMSDEP Coordinator
101 North 14th Street, 17th Floor
Richmond, VA 23219
(804) 225-2083   Fax: (804) 786-0809
E-mail: vmsdep@dvs.virginia.gov
Web: www.dvs.virginia.gov

Summary To provide educational assistance to the children and spouses of disabled and other Virginia veterans or service personnel.

Eligibility This program is open to residents of Virginia whose parent or spouse served in the U.S. armed forces (including the Reserves, the Virginia National Guard, or the Virginia National Guard Reserves) during any armed conflict subsequent to December 6, 1941, as a result of a terrorist act, during military operations against terrorism, or on a peacekeeping mission. The veterans must have been killed, be missing in action, have been taken prisoner of war, or become at least 90% disabled as a result of such service. Applicants must have been accepted at a public college or university in Virginia as an undergraduate or graduate student. Children must be between 16 and 29 years of age; there are no age restrictions for spouses. The veteran must have been a resident of Virginia at the time of entry into active military service or for at least 5 consecutive years immediately prior to the date of application or death. Surviving spouses must have been residents of Virginia for at least 5 years prior to marrying the veteran or for at least 5 years immediately prior to the date on which the application was submitted.

Financial data The program provides 1) waiver of tuition and all required fees at public institutions of higher education in Virginia; and 2) a stipend to offset the costs of room, board, books, and supplies at those institutions; recently, the stipend for full-time study was $1,800 per academic year.

Duration Entitlement extends to a maximum of 36 months (4 years).

Additional data Individuals entitled to this benefit may use it to pursue any vocational, technical, undergraduate, or graduate program of instruction. Generally, programs listed in the academic catalogs of state-supported institutions are acceptable, provided they have a clearly-defined educational objective (such as a certificate, diploma, or degree). This program was formerly known as the Virginia War Orphans Education Program.

Number awarded Varies each year; recently, funding allowed for a total of 1,000 stipends.

Deadline Applications may be submitted at any time, but they must be received at least 90 days prior to the start of the term.

[1198]
VITTORIA DIANA RICARDO SCHOLARSHIP

Ulman Cancer Fund for Young Adults
Attn: Scholarship Committee
921 East Fort Avenue, Suite 325
Baltimore, MD 21230
(410) 964-0202   Toll Free: (888) 393-FUND
Fax: (888) 964-0402
E-mail: scholarship@ulmanfund.org
Web: www.ulmanfund.org/scholarships

Summary To provide financial assistance for college or graduate school to students who have been diagnosed with cancer or have or have lost a family member with cancer.

Eligibility This program is open to students who 1) have been diagnosed with cancer; 2) have a parent or sibling living with cancer; or 3) have lost a parent or sibling to cancer. Applicants must be attending, or planning to attend, a 4-year college or university in any state to work on an undergraduate, graduate, or professional degree. They must have a GPA of 3.0 or higher in high school or college and be able to demonstrate financial need. The first diagnosis of cancer (whether of the applicant, a parent, or sibling) must have occurred after the applicant was 15 years of age. Along with their application, they must submit a 500-word essay or 3-minute video on either 1) a letter that they would have liked to receive during their cancer experience; or 2) what they would tell the young adults who participate in the sponsor's summer-long drive to support the organization about being a young adult impacted by cancer. U.S. citizenship or permanent resident status is required.

Financial data The stipend is $2,500. Funds are paid directly to the educational institution.

Duration 1 year.

Additional data Recipients are obligated to organize and run a bone marrow registry drive with the support of Delete Blood Cancer and There Goes My Hero.

Number awarded 1 each year.

Deadline March of each year.

[1199]
WASHINGTON NATIONAL GUARD STATE EDUCATION ASSISTANCE PROGRAM (EAP)

Washington National Guard
Attn: Education Services Office
JFHQ-WA
41st Division Drive, Building 15
Camp Murray, WA 98430
(253) 512-8435   Toll Free: (800) 606-9843 (within WA)
Fax: (253) 512-8941
E-mail: education@washingtonguard.org
Web: mil.wa.gov/national-guard/army-guard/education

Summary   To waive tuition at public colleges in Washington for veterans, members of the National Guard, and the family of deceased and disabled veterans and National Guard members.

Eligibility   This program is open to 1) active military and naval veterans, Reserve military and naval veterans, and National Guard members called to active duty to serve on foreign soil or in international waters or in another location in support of those serving on foreign soil or in international waters; 2) children and spouses or domestic partners of eligible veterans or National Guard members who became totally disabled as a result of serving in active federal military or naval service; 3) children and spouses or domestic partners of eligible veterans or National Guard members who is determined by the federal government to be a prisoner of war or missing in action; and 4) children and surviving spouses or surviving domestic partners of eligible veterans or National Guard members who lost their life as a result of serving in active federal military or naval service. Applicants must be residents of Washington and enrolled or planning to enroll full or part time at a state university, regional university, Evergreen State College, or community or technical college in the state. Children must be between 17 and 26 years of age. Surviving spouses of deceased personnel have 10 years from the date of death to receive benefits.

Financial data   Qualified veterans, National Guard members, children, and spouses may attend public institutions in Washington without payment of tuition or fees.

Duration   1 year; may be renewed.

Number awarded   Varies each year.

Deadline   Each participating institution sets its own deadline.

[1200]
WISCONSIN G.I. BILL TUITION REMISSION PROGRAM

Wisconsin Department of Veterans Affairs
201 West Washington Avenue
P.O. Box 7843
Madison, WI 53707-7843
(608) 266-1311   Toll Free: (800) WIS-VETS
Fax: (608) 267-0403
E-mail: WDVAInfo@dva.state.wi.us
Web: www.dva.state.wi.us

Summary   To provide financial assistance for college or graduate school to Wisconsin veterans and their dependents.

Eligibility   This program is open to current residents of Wisconsin who 1) were residents of the state when they entered or reentered active duty in the U.S. armed forces; or 2) have moved to the state and have been residents for at least 5 consecutive years after entry or reentry into service. Applicants must have served on active duty for at least 2 continuous years or for at least 90 days during specified wartime periods. Also eligible are 1) qualifying children and unremarried surviving spouses of Wisconsin veterans who died in the line of duty or as the direct result of a service-connected disability; and 2) children and spouses of Wisconsin veterans who have a service-connected disability rated by the U.S. Department of Veterans Affairs as 30% or greater. Children must be between 17 and 25 years of age (regardless of the date of the veteran's death or initial disability rating) and be a Wisconsin resident for tuition purposes. Spouses remain eligible for 10 years following the date of the veteran's death or initial disability rating; they must be Wisconsin residents for tuition purposes but they may enroll full or part time. Students may attend any institution, center, or school within the University of Wisconsin (UW) System or the Wisconsin Technical College System (WCTS). There are no income limits, delimiting periods following military service during which the benefit must be used, or limits on the level of study (e.g., vocational, undergraduate, professional, or graduate).

Financial data   Veterans who qualify as a Wisconsin resident for tuition purposes are eligible for a remission of 100% of standard academic fees and segregated fees at a UW campus or 100% of program and material fees at a WCTS institution. Veterans who qualify as a Wisconsin veteran for purposes of this program but for other reasons fail to meet the definition of a Wisconsin resident for tuition purposes at the UW system are eligible for a remission of 100% of non-resident fees. Spouses and children of deceased or disabled veterans are entitled to a remission of 100% of tuition and fees at a UW or WCTS institution.

Duration   Up to 8 semesters or 128 credits, whichever is greater.

Additional data   This program began in 2005 as a replacement for Wisconsin Tuition and Fee Reimbursement Grants.

Number awarded   Varies each year.

Deadline   Applications must be submitted within 14 days from the office start of the academic term: in October for fall, March for spring, or June for summer.

[1201]
YE NOTORIOUS KREWE OF THE PEG LEG PIRATE SCHOLARSHIPS

Ye Notorious Krewe of the Peg Leg Pirate, Inc.
P.O. Box 1854
Ruskin, LA 33575-1854
Web: www.peglegpirate.org

Summary To provide financial assistance for college or graduate school to amputees and their families.

Eligibility This program is open to amputees, families of amputees, and organizations that work with amputees. Applicants must be attending or planning to attend an accredited college, university, community college, vocational/technical school, or graduate school. They must have a GPA of 3.5 or higher. Along with their application, they must submit 2 recommendations, transcripts, documentation of financial need, and a 300-word essay describing their future goals.

Financial data Stipends vary but recently have averaged $1,150. Funds are paid directly to the recipient's institution.

Duration 1 year.

Additional data This program began in 2008.

Number awarded Varies each year; recently 4 were awarded.

Deadline March of each year.

Indexes

Program Title Index ●
Sponsoring Organization Index ●
Residency Index ●
Tenability Index ●
Subject Index ●
Calendar Index ●

Program Title Index

If you know the name of a particular funding program and want to find out where it is covered in the directory, use the Program Title Index. Here, program titles are arranged alphabetically, word by word. To assist you in your search, every program is listed by all its known names or abbreviations. In addition, we've used a two-character alphabetical code (within parentheses) to help you determine if the program falls within your scope of interest. The first character (capitalized) in the code identifies the program focus: A = Any Disability; V = Visual Disabilities; H = Hearing Disabilities; P = Physical/Orthopedic; O = Other Disabilities/Disorders; F = Families of the Disabled. The second character (lower-cased) identifies funding type: u = undergraduates; g = graduate student. Here's how the code works: if a program is followed by (H–g) 281, the program is described in the Hearing Disabilities chapter, in the graduate student section, in entry 281. If the same program title is followed by another entry number—for example, (F–u) 984—the program is also described in the Families of the Disabled chapter, in the undergraduate section, in entry 984. Remember: the numbers cited here refer to program entry numbers, not to page numbers in the book.

180 Medical Scholarships, (P–u) 471, (P–g) 531

28th Infantry Division Scholarship. *See* Pennsylvania National Guard Scholarship Fund, entry (F–u) 1096

A

A. Richard Grossman College Scholarship Fund, (O–u) 554

AAHD Frederick J. Krause Scholarship on Health and Disability, (A–u) 1, (A–g) 128

AAPA Past Presidents Scholarship, (A–u) 2, (A–g) 129

Abbene Scholarship. *See* Hydrocephalus Association Scholarships, entries (O–u) 656, (O–g) 843

AbbVie CF Scholarships, (O–u) 555, (O–g) 810

AbbVie Immunology Scholarship, (O–u) 556, (O–g) 811

ABC Medical Scholarship Program, (P–u) 472

Able Flight Career Training Scholarships, (P–u) 473

Abt Scholarships. *See* Alexander Graham Bell College Scholarship Awards Program, entries (H–u) 441, (H–g) 459

Academic Library Association of Ohio Diversity Scholarship, (A–g) 130

Academy of Special Dreams Foundation College Scholarship Fund, (A–u) 3

ACB Students Brenda Dillon Memorial Scholarship, (V–u) 250

Access Path to Psychology and Law Experience (APPLE) Program, (P–u) 474

Access Technology Scholarship, (A–u) 4, (A–g) 131

ACES Scholarship for Rare Diseases. *See* Shire ACES Scholarship for Rare Diseases, entry (O–u) 775

Achievement Scholarship for Students with a History of Chronic Illness Fund, (O–u) 557

Ackerman Memorial Scholarships. *See* Jason Ackerman Memorial Scholarships, entry (O–u) 667

Acxiom Diversity Scholarship Program, (A–u) 5, (A–g) 132

Adrienne Asch Memorial Scholarship, (V–u) 251, (V–g) 371

Advanced Study Program Graduate Student Visitor Program. *See* ASP Graduate Student Visitor Program, entry (A–g) 146

AFA Teens for Alzheimer's Awareness College Scholarship Essay Competition, (F–u) 889

AFAS Merit Scholarships, (F–u) 890

AFRL/DAGSI Ohio Student-Faculty Research Fellowship Program, (A–g) 133

Aging Research Dissertation Awards to Increase Diversity, (A–g) 134

AHIMA Foundation Diversity Scholarships, (A–u) 6, (A–g) 135

A–Any Disability   V–Visual   H–Hearing   P–Physical/Orthopedic   O–Other Disabilities   F–Families
u–undergraduates   g–graduate students

AHIMA Veterans Scholarship, (A—u) 7, (A—g) 136

Air Force Aid Society Merit Scholarships. *See* AFAS Merit Scholarships, entry (F—u) 890

Air Force Research Laboratory/Dayton Area Graduate Studies Institute Ohio Student-Faculty Research Fellowship Program. *See* AFRL/DAGSI Ohio Student-Faculty Research Fellowship Program, entry (A—g) 133

Air Line Pilots Association Scholarship Program, (F—u) 891

Airey Memorial Scholarship. *See* Chief Master Sergeant of the Air Force Scholarship Program, entries (A—u) 26, (F—u) 920

ALA Century Scholarship, (A—g) 137

Alabama G.I. Dependents' Scholarship Program, (F—u) 892, (F—g) 1138

Alabama Scholarships for Dependents of Blind Parents, (F—u) 893

Alain Roby Culinary Scholarship. *See* Chef Alain Roby Culinary Scholarship, entry (O—u) 594

Alan B., '32, and Florence B., '35, Crammatte Fellowship, (H—g) 458

Albert M. Becker Memorial Youth Scholarship, (F—u) 894

Alexander Graham Bell College Scholarship Awards Program, (H—u) 441, (H—g) 459

Alfred Camp Memorial Scholarship, (V—u) 252, (V—g) 372, (F—u) 895, (F—g) 1139

Alger National Career and Technical Scholarship Program. *See* Horatio Alger National Career and Technical Scholarship Program, entry (A—u) 48

Alger National Scholarship Program. *See* Horatio Alger National Scholarship Program, entry (A—u) 49

All in for Skin Scholarship, (F—u) 896

Allegra Ford Scholarship. *See* Allegra Ford Thomas Scholarship, entry (O—u) 558

Allegra Ford Thomas Scholarship, (O—u) 558

Allen Scholarship. *See* Charles and Betty Allen Scholarship, entry (V—u) 269

Allen-Sprinkle Memorial Gift, (V—u) 253, (V—g) 373

Allie Raney Hunt Scholarship. *See* Alexander Graham Bell College Scholarship Awards Program, entries (H—u) 441, (H—g) 459

Allstate Foundation/VHSL Achievement Awards, (A—u) 8

Alma Murphey Memorial Scholarship, (V—g) 374

Alpha Sigma Pi Fraternity Fellowship, (H—g) 460

A.L.S. Family Charitable Foundation Scholarship, (F—u) 897

Alston Memorial Scholarship. *See* Hydrocephalus Association Scholarships, entries (O—u) 656, (O—g) 843

Alyssa McCroskey Memorial Scholarship, (A—u) 9, (A—g) 138

Alzheimer's Foundation of America Teens for Alzheimer's Awareness College Scholarship Essay Competition. *See* AFA Teens for Alzheimer's Awareness College Scholarship Essay Competition, entry (F—u) 889

American Academy of Physician Assistants Past Presidents Scholarship. *See* AAPA Past Presidents Scholarship, entries (A—u) 2, (A—g) 129

American Association on Health and Disability Frederick J. Krause Scholarship on Health and Disability. *See* AAHD Frederick J. Krause Scholarship on Health and Disability, entries (A—u) 1, (A—g) 128

American Bus Association Yellow Ribbon Scholarship, (A—u) 10, (A—g) 139, (F—u) 898, (F—g) 1140

American Council of the Blind of Minnesota Scholarships, (V—u) 254, (V—g) 375

American Council of the Blind of Oregon Scholarships, (V—u) 255

American Council of the Blind of Texas Scholarships, (V—u) 256

American Council of the Blind Students Brenda Dillon Memorial Scholarship. *See* ACB Students Brenda Dillon Memorial Scholarship, entry (V—u) 250

American Epilepsy Society Predoctoral Research Fellowships, (A—g) 140

American Health Information Management Association Foundation Diversity Scholarships. *See* AHIMA Foundation Diversity Scholarships, entries (A—u) 6, (A—g) 135

American Health Information Management Association Veterans Scholarship. *See* AHIMA Veterans Scholarship, entries (A—u) 7, (A—g) 136

American Legion Legacy Scholarships, (F—u) 899

American Library Association Century Scholarship. *See* ALA Century Scholarship, entry (A—g) 137

American Meteorological Society Freshman Undergraduate Scholarships. *See* AMS Freshman Undergraduate Scholarships, entry (A—u) 11

American Meteorological Society Graduate Fellowships. *See* AMS Graduate Fellowships, entry (A—g) 143

American Meteorological Society Senior Named Scholarships. *See* AMS Senior Named Scholarships, entry (A—u) 12

American Museum of Natural History Graduate Student Fellowship Program. *See* AMNH Graduate Student Fellowship Program, entry (A—g) 142

American Psychological Association of Graduate Students Disabilities Grant Program. *See* APAGS Disabilities Grant Program, entry (A—g) 144

American Society of Safety Engineers Diversity Committee Graduate Scholarship. *See* ASSE Diversity Committee Graduate Scholarship, entry (P—g) 533

American Society of Safety Engineers Diversity Committee Undergraduate Scholarship. *See* ASSE Diversity Committee Undergraduate Scholarship, entry (P—u) 478

American Speech-Language-Hearing Foundation Scholarship for Students with a Disability, (A—g) 141

AmeriGlide Achiever Scholarship, (P—u) 475, (P—g) 532

Amitrani Scholarship. *See* Hemophilia Association of New Jersey Scholarships, entries (O—u) 646, (O—g) 840

AMNH Graduate Student Fellowship Program, (A—g) 142

A—Any Disability   V—Visual   H—Hearing   P—Physical/Orthopedic   O—Other Disabilities   F—Families

u—undergraduates   g—graduate students

AMS Freshman Undergraduate Scholarships, (A—u) 11

AMS Graduate Fellowships, (A—g) 143

AMS Senior Named Scholarships, (A—u) 12

Amy Seeherman Scholarships. See Epilepsy Foundation New England Scholarships, entries (O—u) 623, (O—g) 835

Amyotrophic Lateral Sclerosis Family Charitable Foundation Scholarship. See A.L.S. Family Charitable Foundation Scholarship, entry (F—u) 897

Anders Tjellström Scholarships, (H—u) 442

Anderson Memorial Scholarship. See R.L. Gillette, Gladys C. Anderson, and Karen D. Carsel Memorial Scholarship, entry (V—u) 349

André Sobel Award, (O—u) 559

Andrew Craig Memorial Scholarship, (O—u) 560

Andrew Mullins Courageous Achievement Award. See Allstate Foundation/VHSL Achievement Awards, entry (A—u) 8

Angel and Marie Solie Scholarship. See Salem Foundation Angel and Marie Solie Scholarship, entry (V—u) 353

Angela Woolsey Education Award. See Missy and Angela Woolsey Education Award, entry (O—u) 732

Angelina Wilson Nontraditional Scholarships. See Huey and Angelina Wilson Nontraditional Scholarships, entries (O—u) 654, (F—u) 973

Angelina Wilson Traditional Scholarships. See Huey and Angelina Wilson Traditional Scholarships, entry (O—u) 655

Anne and Matt Harbison Scholarship, (O—u) 561

Anne Ford Scholarship, (O—u) 562

Anne M. Fassett Scholarship, (P—u) 476

Anne Smedinghoff Memorial Scholarship, (O—u) 563, (O—g) 812, (F—u) 900, (F—g) 1141

Annual Breast Cancer Survivor Scholarship, (O—u) 564

Anthony Abbene Scholarship. See Hydrocephalus Association Scholarships, entries (O—u) 656, (O—g) 843

Antonia M. Derks Memorial Scholarship. See Mouse Hole Scholarships, entries (V—u) 317, (F—u) 1064

APAGS Disabilities Grant Program, (A—g) 144

Arbus Focus on Disability Scholarship. See Loreen Arbus Focus on Disability Scholarship, entries (A—u) 63, (A—g) 199

AR-CEC Exceptional Student Scholarship, (O—u) 565

Arehart Family Scholarship Award. See Ruby's Rainbow Scholarships, entry (O—u) 766

Arizona Council of the Blind Scholarship Program, (V—u) 257, (V—g) 376

Arizona Hispanic Chamber of Commerce Scholarship, (P—u) 477

Arkansas Council for Exceptional Children Exceptional Student Scholarship. See AR-CEC Exceptional Student Scholarship, entry (O—u) 565

Arkansas Council of the Blind Scholarships, (V—u) 258

Arkansas Law Enforcement Officers' Dependents' Scholarships, (F—u) 901

Arkansas Military Dependents Scholarship Program, (F—u) 902

Arkansas Missing in Action/Killed in Action Dependents Scholarship Program. See Arkansas Military Dependents Scholarship Program, entry (F—u) 902

Arnold Education Grant Program. See General Henry H. Arnold Education Grant Program, entry (F—u) 953

Arnold & Porter Kaye Scholer Diversity Scholarship, (A—g) 145

Arnold Sadler Memorial Scholarship, (V—u) 259, (V—g) 377

Arts and Sciences Awards, (H—u) 443

Asarch Elder Law and Special Needs Section Scholarship. See The Honorable Joel K. Asarch Elder Law and Special Needs Section Scholarship, entry (A—g) 241

AS&ASTAR Fellowships. See NASA Education Aeronautics Scholarship and Advanced STEM Training and Research Fellowship, entry (A—g) 207

Asch Memorial Scholarship. See Adrienne Asch Memorial Scholarship, entries (V—u) 251, (V—g) 371

Ashley K. Fritz Memorial "Humanitarian" Scholarship, (V—u) 260, (V—g) 378

Ashley Rose Honorary Diabetes Law Student Scholarship, (O—g) 813

ASP Graduate Student Visitor Program, (A—g) 146

ASSE Diversity Committee Graduate Scholarship, (P—g) 533

ASSE Diversity Committee Undergraduate Scholarship, (P—u) 478

Association of Tennis Professionals and Women's Tennis Association Memorial Scholarship. See ATP and WTA Memorial Scholarship, entry (F—u) 903

ATP and WTA Memorial Scholarship, (F—u) 903

Auger & Auger Disabled Scholar Award, (A—u) 13

Austin Board of Realtors Foundation Scholarship Award. See Ruby's Rainbow Scholarships, entry (O—u) 766

Autism Delaware Adults with Autism Scholarship, (O—u) 566

Avonte Oquendo Memorial Scholarship for Autism, (O—u) 567, (O—g) 814, (F—u) 904, (F—g) 1142

Award for Collegiate Education from Shire. See Shire ACES Scholarship for Rare Diseases, entry (O—u) 775

B

Bacon Memorial Scholarship. See Betty Bacon Memorial Scholarship, entries (A—u) 14, (A—g) 150

Baer and Janis Clay Educational Scholarship. See Elam Baer and Janis Clay Educational Scholarship, entry (O—u) 620

Baer Reintegration Scholarships, (O—u) 568, (O—g) 815

Bailey Scholarship. See Roadway Worker Memorial Scholarships, entry (F—u) 1108

Balboni Memorial Scholarships. See Jill M. Balboni Memorial Scholarships, entry (O—u) 674

Bambino Memorial Scholarship. See Cristin Ann Bambino Memorial Scholarship, entry (O—u) 599

Banner Diversity Scholarship. *See* Donald W. Banner Diversity Scholarship, entry (A—g) 166

Banner Scholarship for Law Students. *See* Mark T. Banner Scholarship for Law Students, entry (A—g) 200

Barbara E. Fohl Memorial Scholarship. *See* National Federation of the Blind of Ohio Scholarships, entries (V—u) 331, (V—g) 417

Barboza Educational Fund Scholarship. *See* Troy Barboza Educational Fund Scholarship, entries (A—u) 116, (F—u) 1125

Barefoot Scholarship. *See* North Carolina Troopers Association Scholarships, entry (F—u) 1084

Bartol Memorial Scholarships. *See* George Bartol Memorial Scholarships, entry (F—u) 955

Basic Psychological Science Research Grant, (A—g) 147

Baswell Combat Wounded Engineer Scholarship. *See* COL Carl F. Baswell Combat Wounded Engineer Scholarship, entries (P—u) 487, (P—g) 538

Baxter Scholarship Award. *See* Ruby's Rainbow Scholarships, entry (O—u) 766

Bay Area Minority Law Student Scholarships, (A—g) 148

Bay State Council of the Blind Scholarship, (V—u) 261

BB&K First Year Law Student Diversity Fellowship/ Scholarship Program, (A—g) 149

Beacon Brighter Tomorrows Scholarship, (F—u) 905

Becker Memorial Youth Scholarship. *See* Albert M. Becker Memorial Youth Scholarship, entry (F—u) 894

BEF General Academic Scholarships, (O—u) 569, (O—g) 816

Belli Memorial Endowment Fund. *See* John, Lynne, and Nicole Belli Memorial Endowment Fund, entry (O—u) 683

The Bennett Clayton Foundation Scholarship Program, (P—u) 522

Bennett, Jr. Memorial Scholarship. *See* Vincent Bennett, Jr. Memorial Scholarship, entry (F—u) 1130

Bennion Family Scholarship. *See* Alexander Graham Bell College Scholarship Awards Program, entries (H—u) 441, (H—g) 459

Berner Scholarship for Students with Epilepsy, (O—u) 570, (O—g) 817

Bernice McNamara Memorial Scholarship, (F—u) 906, (F—g) 1143

Beryl V. Smith Scholarship, (F—u) 907

Best Best & Krieger First Year Law Student Diversity Fellowship/Scholarship Program. *See* BB&K First Year Law Student Diversity Fellowship/Scholarship Program, entry (A—g) 149

Beth Carew Memorial Scholarships, (O—u) 571

Betsy Niles Scholarship. *See* New Jersey Sharing Network Scholarships, entries (O—u) 739, (F—u) 1076

Betty Allen Scholarship. *See* Charles and Betty Allen Scholarship, entry (V—u) 269

Betty Bacon Memorial Scholarship, (A—u) 14, (A—g) 150

Betty J. Niceley Memorial Scholarship, (V—u) 262

Beverly Prows Memorial Scholarship, (V—u) 263, (V—g) 379

Beyond the Cure Ambassador Scholarship Program, (O—u) 572

BG Hugh S. Niles Memorial Scholarship. *See* Pennsylvania National Guard Scholarship Fund, entry (F—u) 1096

BG Richard E. Thorn Memorial Scholarship. *See* Pennsylvania National Guard Scholarship Fund, entry (F—u) 1096

Bhaskaran (WAS) Scholarship Program. *See* Varun Bhaskaran (WAS) Scholarship Program, entries (O—u) 801, (O—g) 884

BIAWA Eastern Washington Student Scholarship, (O—u) 573

Bidstrup Scholarship Fund. *See* Peter and Bruce Bidstrup Scholarship Fund, entry (O—u) 753

Bill Tomlin Scholarship Award, (V—u) 264

BioRx/Hemophilia of North Carolina Educational Scholarships, (O—u) 574, (F—u) 908

Biunno Scholarship for Law Students with Disabilities, (A—g) 151

Blackhorse Scholarship, (F—u) 909

Blandy Experimental Farm Research Experiences for Undergraduates Program, (A—u) 15

Bleeding and Clotting Disorders Institute Scholarship Fund, (O—u) 575

Blessing Scholarship. *See* Teresa Blessing Scholarship, entry (V—u) 358

BMO Capital Markets Lime Connect Equity Through Education Scholarships for Students with Disabilities, (A—u) 16, (A—g) 152

BMW Hope Endowment Scholarship, (O—u) 576

Board of Young Adult Advisors Scholarship, (O—g) 818, (F—g) 1144

Bob Barefoot Scholarship. *See* North Carolina Troopers Association Scholarships, entry (F—u) 1084

Bobby Dodd Memorial Scholarship for Outstanding Community Service, (P—u) 479

Bobby Jones Open Scholarships, (P—u) 480, (P—g) 534, (F—u) 910, (F—g) 1145

Bolin Dissertation and Post-MFA Fellowships. *See* Gaius Charles Bolin Dissertation and Post-MFA Fellowships, entry (A—g) 172

Bonasera Scholarship. *See* Epilepsy Foundation New England Scholarships, entries (O—u) 623, (O—g) 835

Bonnie Strangio Education Scholarship, (O—u) 577, (O—g) 819

Book Coleman, Foster Dow and Irma Dow Scholarships, (O—u) 578

Boomer Esiason Foundation General Academic Scholarships. *See* BEF General Academic Scholarships, entries (O—u) 569, (O—g) 816

Boyce R. Williams, '32, Fellowship. *See* Gallaudet University Alumni Association Graduate Fellowship Fund, entry (H—g) 463

Bradley Annual Diversity Scholarship, (A—g) 153

Bradley D. Gendron Memorial Scholarship, (O—u) 579

Bradley Krueger Scholarship, (O—u) 580, (F—u) 911

Brain Injury Alliance of Washington Eastern Washington Student Scholarship. *See* BIAWA Eastern Washington Student Scholarship, entry (O—u) 573

Bray Memorial Scholarship. *See* Jeanne E. Bray Memorial Scholarship, entry (F—u) 992

Brenda Dillon Memorial Scholarship. *See* ACB Students Brenda Dillon Memorial Scholarship, entry (V—u) 250

Brennan Award. *See* Mary Brennan Award, entry (O—u) 720

Bressman Law Traumatic Brain Injury Scholarship, (O—u) 581

Brian Morden Memorial Scholarship, (O—u) 582

B.R.I.D.G.E. Endowment Fund Scholarships. *See* Building Rural Initiative for Disabled through Group Effort (B.R.I.D.G.E.) Endowment Fund Scholarships, entry (P—u) 482

Bridge to Life Survivor Scholarship. *See* Woody and Louise Reed Bridge to Life Survivor Scholarship, entries (O—u) 808, (O—g) 888

Brody and Amy Seeherman Scholarships. *See* Epilepsy Foundation New England Scholarships, entries (O—u) 623, (O—g) 835

Brother James Kearney Scholarship for the Blind, (V—u) 265, (V—g) 380

Brother Scholarships. *See* Millie Brother Scholarships, entries (F—u) 1058, (F—g) 1184

Broyles Diverse Scholars Program. *See* Deborah J. Broyles Diverse Scholars Program, entry (A—g) 161

Bruce Bidstrup Scholarship Fund. *See* Peter and Bruce Bidstrup Scholarship Fund, entry (O—u) 753

Bryant Scholarship Program. *See* Byrd Bryant Scholarship Program, entry (V—u) 266

Bryon Riesch Scholarships, (P—u) 481, (P—g) 535, (O—u) 583, (O—g) 820, (F—u) 912, (F—g) 1146

Buckfire & Buckfire Disability Scholarship, (A—u) 17

Buckley Memorial Scholarship. *See* Duane Buckley Memorial Scholarship, entry (V—u) 275

Buffalo Amputee Golf Classic Scholarship Award. *See* EAGA Scholarship Fund, entries (P—u) 489, (F—u) 936

Building Rural Initiative for Disabled through Group Effort (B.R.I.D.G.E.) Endowment Fund Scholarships, (P—u) 482

Buller Scholarship. *See* John Buller Scholarship, entries (O—u) 678, (O—g) 849

Bunch Memorial Scholarship. *See* Susan Bunch Memorial Scholarship, entries (O—u) 783, (O—g) 879

Burns Memorial Scholarships. *See* Heather Burns Memorial Scholarships, entry (O—u) 645

"Business Plan" Scholarship for Students with Disabilities, (A—u) 18, (A—g) 154

Byrd Bryant Scholarship Program, (V—u) 266

C

C. Rodney Demarest Memorial Scholarship. *See* National Federation of the Blind of Connecticut Scholarships, entries (V—u) 320, (V—g) 412

Cahill You Cannot Fail Scholarships. *See* Jerry Cahill You Cannot Fail Scholarships, entry (O—u) 672

California Association for Postsecondary Education and Disability Excellence Scholarship. *See* CAPED Excellence Scholarship, entries (A—u) 20, (A—g) 155

California Association for Postsecondary Education and Disability Memorial Scholarship. *See* CAPED Memorial Scholarship, entries (A—u) 21, (A—g) 156

California College Fee Waiver Program for Children of Veterans, (F—u) 913

California Council of the Blind Scholarships, (V—u) 267, (V—g) 381

California Fee Waiver Program for Dependents of Deceased or Disabled National Guard Members, (F—u) 914

California Fee Waiver Program for Dependents of Totally Disabled Veterans, (F—u) 915

California Law Enforcement Personnel Dependents Grant Program, (F—u) 916

California-Hawaii Elks Major Project Undergraduate Scholarship Program for Students with Disabilities, (A—u) 19

Calkins Memorial Scholarship. *See* Michael Calkins Memorial Scholarship, entries (O—u) 728, (F—u) 1054

Callward Memorial Scholarship. *See* Floyd Callward Memorial Scholarship, entries (V—u) 284, (V—g) 390

Calvin Dawson Memorial Scholarship, (O—u) 584

Camastra Scholarship Award. *See* Marco Camastra Scholarship Award, entry (O—u) 716

Camp Memorial Scholarship. *See* Alfred Camp Memorial Scholarship, entries (V—u) 252, (V—g) 372, (F—u) 895, (F—g) 1139

Campbell Memorial Scholarship. *See* Mouse Hole Scholarships, entries (V—u) 317, (F—u) 1064

Cancer for College Carolina Scholarships, (O—u) 585, (O—g) 821

Cancer for College Pacific Northwest Scholarships, (O—u) 586, (O—g) 822

Cancer for College Scholarships, (O—u) 587, (O—g) 823

Cancer Survivors' Scholarship, (O—u) 588

Cancer Unwrapped Teen Writing Contest, (O—u) 589, (F—u) 917

Candice's Sickle Cell Anemia Fund Scholarships, (O—u) 590

Cannon Memorial Scholarship. *See* Kellie Cannon Memorial Scholarship, entry (V—u) 302

CAPED Excellence Scholarship, (A—u) 20, (A—g) 155

CAPED Memorial Scholarship, (A—u) 21, (A—g) 156

Caperton Inspiration Award. *See* Kristin Caperton Inspiration Award, entry (A—u) 62

Captain Ivan Stroud Scholarship. *See* North Carolina Troopers Association Scholarships, entry (F—u) 1084

Carew Memorial Scholarships. *See* Beth Carew Memorial Scholarships, entry (O—u) 571

Cargill Scholarship. *See* Floyd R. Cargill Scholarship, entries (V—u) 286, (V—g) 392

Carl J. Megel Special Education Scholarship, (V—u) 268, (H—u) 444, (P—u) 483, (O—u) 591

Caroline Kark Award for Deaf Students, (H—u) 445

Carolyn Garrett Scholarship. *See* American Council of the Blind of Texas Scholarships, entry (V—u) 256

Carsel Memorial Scholarship. *See* R.L. Gillette, Gladys C. Anderson, and Karen D. Carsel Memorial Scholarship, entry (V—u) 349

Carver Scholars Program, (A—u) 22

Case Memorial Scholarships. *See* James Doyle Case Memorial Scholarships, entries (V—u) 295, (V—g) 397, (F—u) 989, (F—g) 1160

Catherine T. Murray Memorial Scholarship, (A—u) 23

Center on Religion and Politics Dissertation Completion Fellowship. *See* John C. Danforth Center on Religion and Politics Dissertation Completion Fellowship, entries (A—g) 191, (H—g) 468

Central Intelligence Agency Graduate Scholarship Program. *See* CIA Graduate Scholarship Program, entry (A—g) 158

Century Scholarship. *See* ALA Century Scholarship, entry (A—g) 137

CFA Institute 11 September Memorial Scholarship, (A—u) 24, (F—u) 918

CFCareForward Scholarships. *See* AbbVie CF Scholarships, entries (O—u) 555, (O—g) 810

CFSF Standard Scholarships, (O—u) 592

Chalik & Chalik Survivor's Scholarship, (O—u) 593, (O—g) 824

Chapin Fund Scholarships. *See* Elaine Chapin Fund Scholarships, entries (P—u) 492, (F—u) 939

Charles and Betty Allen Scholarship, (V—u) 269

Charles and Melva T. Owen Memorial Scholarships, (V—u) 270, (V—g) 382

Charles Kosmutza Scholarship Fund, (F—u) 919

CHASA Educational Scholarships, (P—u) 484

Chef Alain Roby Culinary Scholarship, (O—u) 594

Chesney Scholarship Fund. *See* CHASA Educational Scholarships, entry (P—u) 484

Chicago Injury Center's Annual Scholarship Fund for Disabled Veterans, (A—u) 25, (A—g) 157

Chicago Lighthouse Scholarships, (V—u) 271, (V—g) 383

Chief Master Sergeant of the Air Force Scholarship Program, (A—u) 26, (F—u) 920

Child Scholarship. *See* Kevin Child Scholarship, entries (O—u) 696, (O—g) 856

Children of Fallen Soldiers Relief Fund College Grants, (F—u) 921

Children of Injured Workers Scholarships, (F—u) 922

Children's Brittle Bone Foundation and OI Foundation Impact Grant Program, (P—u) 485, (P—g) 536

Children's Hemiplegia and Stroke Association Educational Scholarships. *See* CHASA Educational Scholarships, entry (P—u) 484

Christenson Memorial Scholarship. *See* Isabelle Christenson Memorial Scholarship, entries (O—u) 660, (F—u) 983

Christian A. Herter Memorial Scholarship, (A—u) 27

Christian Metaphysicians and Mystics Society Deshae Lott Ministries Scholarships. *See* CMMS Deshae Lott Ministries Scholarships, entries (V—g) 384, (H—g) 461, (P—g) 537

Christina Skoski, M.D., Scholarship, (P—u) 486

Christodoulou Memorial Scholarship. *See* Diane and Peter Christodoulou Memorial Scholarship, entry (O—u) 609

Chuck Bailey Scholarship. *See* Roadway Worker Memorial Scholarships, entry (F—u) 1108

CIA Graduate Scholarship Program, (A—g) 158

Clark Scholarships. *See* Graeme Clark Scholarships, entry (H—u) 447

Clay Educational Scholarship. *See* Elam Baer and Janis Clay Educational Scholarship, entry (O—u) 620

Clayton Foundation Scholarship Program. *See* The Bennett Clayton Foundation Scholarship Program, entry (P—u) 522

Cleres Memorial Scholarships. *See* Joe Cleres Memorial Scholarships, entries (A—u) 55, (A—g) 190

CMMS Deshae Lott Ministries Scholarships, (V—g) 384, (H—g) 461, (P—g) 537

CMSAF Richard D. Kisling Scholarship. *See* Chief Master Sergeant of the Air Force Scholarship Program, entries (A—u) 26, (F—u) 920

Coats Memorial Scholarship. *See* Mark Coats Memorial Scholarship, entries (O—u) 718, (F—u) 1048

Cobb Scholarship. *See* Virginia Cobb Scholarship, entries (H—u) 456, (O—u) 804

Coelho Media Scholarships. *See* NBCUniversal Tony Coelho Media Scholarships, entries (A—u) 80, (A—g) 210

COL Carl F. Baswell Combat Wounded Engineer Scholarship, (P—u) 487, (P—g) 538

Cole Fellowship. *See* Hazel D. Cole Fellowship, entry (A—g) 182

Coleman, Foster Dow and Irma Dow Scholarships. *See* Book Coleman, Foster Dow and Irma Dow Scholarships, entry (O—u) 578

Colin Lee Wozumi Scholarship. *See* Wozumi Family Scholarship, entry (O—u) 809

Collaborative Research Experiences for Undergraduates, (A—u) 28

College Access and Success Scholarship, (O—u) 595, (O—g) 825

Colodny Diversity Scholarship for Graduate Study in Historic Preservation. *See* Mildred Colodny Diversity Scholarship for Graduate Study in Historic Preservation, entry (A—g) 204

Colonel Bob Barefoot Scholarship. *See* North Carolina Troopers Association Scholarships, entry (F—u) 1084

A—Any Disability   V—Visual   H—Hearing   P—Physical/Orthopedic   O—Other Disabilities   F—Families
u—undergraduates   g—graduate students

Colorado Chapter NHF Academic Scholarship Program, (O−u) 596, (F−u) 923

Colorado Dependents Tuition Assistance Program, (F−u) 924

Comprehensive Bleeding Disorders Center Scholarship Fund, (O−u) 597

Conroy Memorial Scholarship Program. *See* Edward T. and Mary A. Conroy Memorial Scholarship Program, entries (A−u) 38, (A−g) 168, (F−u) 938, (F−g) 1148

Cooley Diversity Fellowship Program, (A−g) 159

Cooley's Anemia Foundation/ApoPharma Distinguished Scholar Award, (O−g) 826

Cordano Fellowship. *See* Gallaudet University Alumni Association Graduate Fellowship Fund, entry (H−g) 463

Corea Memorial Scholarship. *See* Michael A. Corea Memorial Scholarship, entry (O−u) 725

Corey Memorial Scholarships. *See* William G. Corey Memorial Scholarship, entries (V−u) 367, (V−g) 439

Couey Memorial Educational Scholarship, (O−u) 598, (F−u) 925

Courage Kenny Rehabilitation Institute Scholarship for People with Disabilities, (A−u) 29

Courter Hemophilia Scholarship Program. *See* Soozie Courter Hemophilia Scholarship Program, entries (O−u) 777, (O−g) 877

Craig Memorial Scholarship. *See* Andrew Craig Memorial Scholarship, entry (O−u) 560, 704, (F−u) 1039

Crammatte Fellowship. *See* Alan B., '32, and Florence B., '35, Crammatte Fellowship, entry (H−g) 458

Cremer Scholarship. *See* Hemophilia of Iowa Scholarships, entries (O−u) 652, (F−u) 969

Cristin Ann Bambino Memorial Scholarship, (O−u) 599

Cryor Memorial Scholarship Program. *See* Jean B. Cryor Memorial Scholarship Program, entries (A−u) 53, (A−g) 188, (F−u) 991, (F−g) 1162

Culpepper Exum Scholarship for People with Kidney Disease, (O−u) 600

Cummings Scholarship Award. *See* Ruby's Rainbow Scholarships, entry (O−u) 766

CURE Cancer Support Scholarship, (O−u) 601

Cynthia Ruth Russell Scholarship, (A−u) 30, (A−g) 160

D

DAGSI Ohio Student-Faculty Research Fellowship Program. *See* AFRL/DAGSI Ohio Student-Faculty Research Fellowship Program, entry (A−g) 133

Dakota Pequeno Memorial Scholarship, (O−u) 602

Dale M. Schoettler Scholarship for Visually Impaired Students, (V−u) 272, (V−g) 385

Daly "Perfect Match" Scholarship, (O−u) 603, (F−u) 926

Danforth Center on Religion and Politics Dissertation Completion Fellowship. *See* John C. Danforth Center on Religion and Politics Dissertation Completion Fellowship, entries (A−g) 191, (H−g) 468

Dangel Memorial Scholarship. *See* CFSF Standard Scholarships, entry (O−u) 592

Daniel Silvernail Scholarship. *See* Diabetes, Incorporated College Scholarship, entries (O−u) 607, (F−u) 929

Dannels Memorial Scholarship. *See* Robert A. Dannels Memorial Scholarship, entry (A−g) 225

Darrien Memorial Scholarship. *See* Donna T. Darrien Memorial Scholarship, entries (O−u) 612, (F−u) 932

David Grants for Research and International Travel in Human Reproductive Behavior and Population Studies. *See* Henry P. David Grants for Research and International Travel in Human Reproductive Behavior and Population Studies, entry (A−g) 185

David Nelson Jr. Memorial Fund Scholarship, (F−u) 927

David Newmeyer Scholarship, (V−u) 273

David Peikoff, '29 Fellowship. *See* Gallaudet University Alumni Association Graduate Fellowship Fund, entry (H−g) 463

Davies Scholarships. *See* Jim Davies Scholarships, entry (O−u) 676

Davis Scholarship Fund. *See* Larry Dean Davis Scholarship Fund, entry (O−u) 699

Dawson Memorial Scholarship. *See* Calvin Dawson Memorial Scholarship, entry (O−u) 584

Dawson Scholarship. *See* Gertrude Dawson Scholarship, entry (O−u) 639

Dayton Area Graduate Studies Institute Ohio Student-Faculty Research Fellowship Program. *See* AFRL/DAGSI Ohio Student-Faculty Research Fellowship Program, entry (A−g) 133

Deaf and Hard of Hearing Section Scholarship Fund. *See* Alexander Graham Bell College Scholarship Awards Program, entries (H−u) 441, (H−g) 459

Deanna Lynn Potts Scholarship, (O−u) 604

Dear Jack Scholarship, (O−u) 605, (O−g) 827

Debono Memorial Scholarship Fund. *See* Matthew Debono Memorial Scholarship Fund, entries (P−u) 508, (P−g) 548

Deborah J. Broyles Diverse Scholars Program, (A−g) 161

Decker, M.D., Memorial Scholarship. *See* Scott Decker, M.D., Memorial Scholarship, entry (P−u) 514

Defense Intelligence Agency Undergraduate Training Assistance Program, (A−u) 31

DeLaurentis Memorial Scholarships. *See* Susanna DeLaurentis Memorial Scholarships, entry (O−u) 784

Delgadillo Scholarship. *See* Scott Delgadillo Scholarship, entries (O−u) 773, (O−g) 875

Delson Memorial Scholarship. *See* Eric Delson Memorial Scholarship, entries (O−u) 625, (O−g) 836

Delta Gamma Foundation Florence Margaret Harvey Memorial Scholarship, (V−u) 274, (V−g) 386

DeLuca, Ricciuti & Konieczka Mental Health Scholarship, (O−u) 606, (O−g) 828

Demarest Memorial Scholarship. *See* National Federation of the Blind of Connecticut Scholarships, entries (V−u) 320, (V−g) 412

Dennis Kelly Memorial Scholarship. See Hemophilia Association of New Jersey Scholarships, entries (O—u) 646, (O—g) 840

Dependent Children Scholarship Program of Tennessee, (F—u) 928

Derks Memorial Scholarship. See Mouse Hole Scholarships, entries (V—u) 317, (F—u) 1064

DesChamps Scholarship Award. See EAGA Scholarship Fund, entries (P—u) 489, (F—u) 936

Deshae Lott Ministries Scholarships. See CMMS Deshae Lott Ministries Scholarships, entries (V—g) 384, (H—g) 461, (P—g) 537

Dexter G. Johnson Educational and Benevolent Trust Grants, (A—u) 32

Diabetes, Incorporated College Scholarship, (O—u) 607, (F—u) 929

Dialysis Scholarship Foundation, (O—u) 608, (O—g) 829

Diane and Peter Christodoulou Memorial Scholarship, (O—u) 609

Diane Donnelly Stone Award. See Novo Nordisk Donnelly Awards, entry (O—u) 743

DiCarlo Scholarship. See Alexander Graham Bell College Scholarship Awards Program, entries (H—u) 441, (H—g) 459

Dick Griffiths Memorial Scholarship, (O—u) 610, (O—g) 830

Dillman Memorial Scholarship. See Rudolph Dillman Memorial Scholarship, entries (V—u) 352, (V—g) 431

Dillon Memorial Scholarship. See ACB Students Brenda Dillon Memorial Scholarship, entry (V—u) 250

Disability Awareness Scholarship, (A—u) 33, (A—g) 162

Disabled American Veterans Auxiliary National Education Scholarship Fund, (F—u) 930, (F—g) 1147

Disabled Law Student Scholarship, (P—g) 539, (O—g) 831

Disabled Person National Scholarship Competition, (A—u) 34, (A—g) 163

Disabled Students Pursuing a Career in Law Scholarship, (A—u) 35

Distal Memorial Scholarship. See National Federation of the Blind of New York Scholarships, entries (V—u) 330, (V—g) 416

Distributed Research Experiences for Undergraduates, (A—u) 36

Diversity Bar Preparation Scholarship, (A—g) 164

Diversity in Psychology and Law Research Award, (A—u) 37, (A—g) 165

DKF Veterans Assistance Foundation Scholarships, (F—u) 931

Dodd Memorial Scholarship for Outstanding Community Service. See Bobby Dodd Memorial Scholarship for Outstanding Community Service, entry (P—u) 479

Dole Scholarship for Disabled Students. See Robert Dole Scholarship for Disabled Students, entry (A—u) 98

Dollars 4 Tic Scholars Tourette Syndrome Scholarship, (O—u) 611, (O—g) 832

Donald W. Banner Diversity Scholarship, (A—g) 166

Donna T. Darrien Memorial Scholarship, (O—u) 612, (F—u) 932

Doreen McMullan McCarthy Memorial Academic Scholarship for Women with Bleeding Disorders, (O—u) 613, (O—g) 833

Doris Ballance Orman, '25, Fellowship, (H—g) 462

Dorothy Ferrell Scholarship. See William and Dorothy Ferrell Scholarship, entries (V—u) 366, (V—g) 438

Dostie Memorial College Scholarship. See Eric Dostie Memorial College Scholarship, entries (O—u) 626, (F—u) 941

Dottie R. Walker Scholarship, (O—u) 614

Doug Hiteshew Memorial Scholarship Program, (O—u) 615, (F—u) 933

Dow Scholarships. See Book Coleman, Foster Dow and Irma Dow Scholarships, entry (O—u) 578

Dr. Leslie P. Graham Scholarship. See ICEC Dr. Leslie P. Graham Scholarship, entry (O—u) 657

Drake Family and Friends Scholarship Award. See Ruby's Rainbow Scholarships, entry (O—u) 766

Drake Memorial Scholarship. See National Federation of the Blind of California Scholarships, entries (V—u) 318, (V—g) 411

The DREAM Institute HEAP Scholar Award Scholarships, (P—u) 523, (O—u) 790

Driscoll "Dream Big" Award. See Jean Driscoll "Dream Big" Award, entries (P—u) 499, (P—g) 544

Drug Abuse Dissertation Research, (A—g) 167

Duane Buckley Memorial Scholarship, (V—u) 275

Dude Cremer Scholarship. See Hemophilia of Iowa Scholarships, entries (O—u) 652, (F—u) 969

Dugdale/van Eys Scholarship Award, (O—u) 616, (F—u) 934

Dunham-Kerley Scholarship, (P—u) 488

Dunkerley Family Scholarship, (F—u) 935

Durward K. McDaniel Scholarship. See American Council of the Blind of Texas Scholarships, entry (V—u) 256

Duvall Memorial Scholarship. See John Duvall Memorial Scholarship, entries (O—u) 679, (O—g) 850, (F—u) 995, (F—g) 1164

E

EAGA Scholarship Fund, (P—u) 489, (F—u) 936

Easter Seals South Carolina Educational Scholarships, (P—u) 490, (P—g) 540

Eastern Amputee Golf Association Scholarship Fund. See EAGA Scholarship Fund, entries (P—u) 489, (F—u) 936

Eccleston-Callahan Scholarships, (V—u) 276, (H—u) 446, (P—u) 491

Edelman Scholarship. See Max Edelman Scholarship, entry (V—u) 312

Edelstein Scholarship for the Blind. See Lillian S. Edelstein Scholarship for the Blind, entries (V—u) 309, (V—g) 407

Education Advantage Community College or Technical Scholarship, (O—u) 617

Education Advantage University Scholarship, (O—u) 618

Education Is Power Scholarships, (O—u) 619

Educational Gratuity of the Pennsylvania Department of Military and Veterans Affairs, (F—u) 937

Edward T. and Mary A. Conroy Memorial Scholarship Program, (A—u) 38, (A—g) 168, (F—u) 938, (F—g) 1148

Elaine Chapin Fund Scholarships, (P—u) 492, (F—u) 939

Elam Baer and Janis Clay Educational Scholarship, (O—u) 620

Elder Law and Special Needs Section Scholarship. *See* The Honorable Joel K. Asarch Elder Law and Special Needs Section Scholarship, entry (A—g) 241

Elizabeth Lulu Scholarship, (O—u) 621

Elizabeth Nash Foundation Scholarship Program, (O—u) 622, (O—g) 834

Elks National Foundation Emergency Educational Fund Grants, (F—u) 940

Ellen Masin Persina Scholarship. *See* National Press Club Scholarship for Journalism Diversity, entry (A—u) 76

Ellen Ruckes Scholarship. *See* Paul and Ellen Ruckes Scholarship, entries (V—u) 345, (V—g) 425

Elliott and Laurel Glass Scholarship Endowment. *See* Holly Elliott and Laurel Glass Scholarship Endowment, entries (V—g) 396, (H—g) 466

Elliott G. Heard Jr. Memorial Scholarship, (P—g) 541

Elsie M. Bell Grosvenor Scholarship Awards. *See* Alexander Graham Bell College Scholarship Awards Program, entries (H—u) 441, (H—g) 459

Emerson Foulke Memorial Scholarship, (V—u) 277

Emil A. Honka Scholarships, (V—u) 278, (V—g) 387

Emma Skogen Scholarship, (V—u) 279

Epilepsy Foundation New England Scholarships, (O—u) 623, (O—g) 835

Epilepsy Foundation of New Jersey Scholarship Program, (O—u) 624

Eric Delson Memorial Scholarship, (O—u) 625, (O—g) 836

Eric Dostie Memorial College Scholarship, (O—u) 626, (F—u) 941

Eric Marder Scholarship, (O—u) 627

Eric Martinez Memorial Scholarship for an Individual with Down Syndrome, (O—u) 628

Eric Martinez Memorial Scholarship for the Sibling of an Individual with Down Syndrome, (F—u) 942, (F—g) 1149

Erin Trujeque Memorial Scholarships, (O—u) 629

Ernst Law Group Brain Injury Caregivers Scholarship, (F—u) 943

Eschbach Scholarship. *See* National Federation of the Blind of Ohio Scholarships, entries (V—u) 331, (V—g) 417

Esiason Foundation Scholarship Program. *See* BEF General Academic Scholarships, entries (O—u) 569, (O—g) 816

Esiason Own It Scholarship. *See* Gunnar Esiason Own It Scholarship, entries (O—u) 641, (O—g) 838

Ester May Sherard Scholarship. *See* AHIMA Foundation Diversity Scholarships, entries (A—u) 6, (A—g) 135

Esther V. Taylor Scholarships, (V—u) 280

E.U. and Gene Parker Scholarship, (V—u) 281, (V—g) 388

Eunice Fiorito Memorial Scholarship, (V—u) 282, (V—g) 389

Exelon Scholarships, (A—u) 39

Exercise for Life Athletic Scholarships, (O—u) 630

Expect Miracles Foundation Scholarship, (O—u) 631

Extremity Scholarship Program, (P—u) 493, (P—g) 542

Exum Scholarship for People with Kidney Disease. *See* Culpepper Exum Scholarship for People with Kidney Disease, entry (O—u) 600

F

Faegre Baker Daniels Diversity and Inclusion Fellowships, (A—g) 169

Families of Freedom Scholarship Fund, (A—u) 40, (F—u) 944

Fassett Scholarship. *See* Anne M. Fassett Scholarship, entry (P—u) 476

Fasteau Past Presidents' Scholarship. *See* Steve Fasteau Past Presidents' Scholarship, entries (A—u) 107, (A—g) 237

FCPA High School Scholarship, (P—u) 494

Federation of Jewish Women's Organization Scholarship. *See* Alexander Graham Bell College Scholarship Awards Program, entries (H—u) 441, (H—g) 459

Feibelman, Jr. Scholarship. *See* Alexander Graham Bell College Scholarship Awards Program, entries (H—u) 441, (H—g) 459

The Feldman Law Firm Autism Scholarship, (O—u) 791

The Feldman Law Firm Disabled Veteran Scholarship, (A—u) 115

Feldman Scholarships. *See* Renee Feldman Scholarships, entry (F—u) 1104

Ferguson Memorial Scholarship of Ohio. *See* Jennica Ferguson Memorial Scholarship of Ohio, entries (V—u) 298, (V—g) 398

Ferrell Scholarship. *See* William and Dorothy Ferrell Scholarship, entries (V—u) 366, (V—g) 438

Finnegan Diversity Scholarship, (A—g) 170

Fiorito Memorial Scholarship. *See* Eunice Fiorito Memorial Scholarship, entries (V—u) 282, (V—g) 389

First Cavalry Division Association Scholarships, (F—u) 945

First Marine Division Association Scholarships, (F—u) 946

Fischer Scholarship. *See* Joann Fischer Scholarship, entry (V—g) 399

Fish & Richardson Diversity Fellowship Program, (A—g) 171

Fisher Scholarships. *See* Lyman Fisher Scholarships, entries (O—u) 712, (F—u) 1044

Fleetwood Memorial Foundation Educational Aid for Resident Dependent Children, (F—u) 947

Fleetwood Memorial Foundation Retraining for Firefighters or Peace Officers, (A—u) 41

Flicker of Hope Scholarships, (O—u) 632

Flora Marie Jenkins Memorial Disability Scholarship, (A—u) 42

Florence B., '35, Crammatte Fellowship. *See* Alan B., '32, and Florence B., '35, Crammatte Fellowship, entry (H—g) 458

Florence Margaret Harvey Memorial Scholarship. *See* Delta Gamma Foundation Florence Margaret Harvey Memorial Scholarship, entries (V—u) 274, (V—g) 386

Florida Cleft Palate-Craniofacial Association High School Scholarship. *See* FCPA High School Scholarship, entry (P—u) 494

Florida Council of Citizens with Low Vision Scholarship, (V—u) 283

Florida Scholarships for Children and Spouses of Deceased or Disabled Veterans, (F—u) 948

Floyd Callward Memorial Scholarship, (V—u) 284, (V—g) 390

Floyd Qualls Memorial Scholarships, (V—u) 285, (V—g) 391

Floyd R. Cargill Scholarship, (V—u) 286, (V—g) 392

Fohl Memorial Scholarship. *See* National Federation of the Blind of Ohio Scholarships, entries (V—u) 331, (V—g) 417

Ford Scholarship. *See* Allegra Ford Thomas Scholarship, entry (O—u) 558, 562

Foster Dow and Irma Dow Scholarships. *See* Book Coleman, Foster Dow and Irma Dow Scholarships, entry (O—u) 578

Foulke Memorial Scholarship. *See* Emerson Foulke Memorial Scholarship, entry (V—u) 277

Foy & Associates Strong Arm Leukemia Scholarship. *See* John Foy & Associates Strong Arm Leukemia Scholarship, entries (O—u) 680, (O—g) 851, (F—u) 996, (F—g) 1165

Frank Seleny Scholarships, (O—u) 633

Franke Scholarship. *See* Jay Franke Scholarship, entry (O—u) 669

Fred Scheigert Scholarships, (V—u) 287, (V—g) 393

Frederick J. Krause Scholarship on Health and Disability. *See* AAHD Frederick J. Krause Scholarship on Health and Disability, entries (A—u) 1, (A—g) 128

Free Tuition for North Dakota Dependents, (F—u) 949

Freedom Alliance Scholarships, (F—u) 950

Freeman Scholarships. *See* Mary Barton Freeman Scholarships, entries (O—u) 719, (O—g) 863, (F—u) 1049, (F—g) 1182

Friends in Art Scholarship, (V—u) 288

Friends of 440 Scholarships, (F—u) 951

Friends of Freshman Scholarship, (V—u) 289

Friends of Pam Scholarship Fund, (F—u) 952

Fritz Memorial "Humanitarian" Scholarship. *See* Ashley K. Fritz Memorial "Humanitarian" Scholarship, entries (V—u) 260, (V—g) 378

Froncillo Scholarship. *See* EAGA Scholarship Fund, entries (P—u) 489, (F—u) 936

Fudge Scholarship. *See* Hydrocephalus Association Scholarships, entries (O—u) 656, (O—g) 843

G

Gaius Charles Bolin Dissertation and Post-MFA Fellowships, (A—g) 172

Galaxy Scholarships, (O—u) 634

Gallaudet University Alumni Association Graduate Fellowship Fund, (H—g) 463

Garland Diversity Scholarship. *See* Sarasota County Bar Association Richard R. Garland Diversity Scholarship, entry (A—g) 231

Garrett Scholarship. *See* American Council of the Blind of Texas Scholarships, entry (V—u) 256

Gaspari Science Scholarship, (O—u) 635

Gayle M. Krause-Edwards Scholarship, (V—u) 290

Geddes Memorial Scholarships. *See* CFSF Standard Scholarships, entry (O—u) 592

Gemm Learning's Living With Dyslexia Scholarship, (O—u) 636

Gendron Memorial Scholarship. *See* Bradley D. Gendron Memorial Scholarship, entry (O—u) 579

Gene Parker Scholarship. *See* E.U. and Gene Parker Scholarship, entries (V—u) 281, (V—g) 388

General Henry H. Arnold Education Grant Program, (F—u) 953

Generation Google Scholarships for High School Seniors, (A—u) 43

Geography and Spatial Sciences Doctoral Dissertation Research Improvement Awards, (A—g) 173

Geological Society of America Graduate Student Research Grants, (A—g) 174

George and Linda Price Scholarship, (O—u) 637, (O—g) 837, (F—u) 954, (F—g) 1150

George Bartol Memorial Scholarships, (F—u) 955

George H. Nofer Scholarship, (H—g) 464

Georgia Chapter of the International Transplant Nurses Society Scholarship, (O—u) 638, (F—u) 956

Georgia Public Safety Memorial Grant, (F—u) 957

Georgia Transplant Foundation Sibling Scholarship. *See* GTF Sibling Scholarship, entry (F—u) 963

Georgia's Helping Educate Reservists and their Offspring Scholarship Program. *See* Georgia's HERO Scholarship Program, entry (F—u) 958

Georgia's HERO Scholarship Program, (F—u) 958

Gerald Drake Memorial Scholarship. *See* National Federation of the Blind of California Scholarships, entries (V—u) 318, (V—g) 411

Gerald Schwartz Fudge Scholarship. *See* Hydrocephalus Association Scholarships, entries (O—u) 656, (O—g) 843

Gertrude Dawson Scholarship, (O—u) 639

Gertrude G. Levy Scholarship Fund. *See* Alexander Graham Bell College Scholarship Awards Program, entries (H—u) 441, (H—g) 459

Gillette Memorial Scholarship. *See* R.L. Gillette, Gladys C. Anderson, and Karen D. Carsel Memorial Scholarship, entry (V—u) 349

A—Any Disability   V—Visual   H—Hearing   P—Physical/Orthopedic   O—Other Disabilities   F—Families
u—undergraduates   g—graduate students

Gisela Distal Memorial Scholarship. See National Federation of the Blind of New York Scholarships, entries (V—u) 330, (V—g) 416

Gittler Award. See Joseph B. Gittler Award of the American Psychological Foundation, entry (A—g) 192

Gladys C. Anderson Memorial Scholarship. See R.L. Gillette, Gladys C. Anderson, and Karen D. Carsel Memorial Scholarship, entry (V—u) 349

Glass Scholarship Endowment. See Holly Elliott and Laurel Glass Scholarship Endowment, entries (V—g) 396, (H—g) 466

Glen Parsons Memorial Scholarship. See CFSF Standard Scholarships, entry (O—u) 592

Global First Responders Scholarship, (F—u) 959

Golden Corral Scholarship Fund, (P—u) 495, (F—u) 960

Gomes Memorial Scholarship Fund. See Joshua Gomes Memorial Scholarship, entries (O—u) 688, (O—g) 853

Gonzalez Memorial Scholarships. See Millie Gonzalez Memorial Scholarships, entry (O—u) 731

Google Lime Scholarships for Students with Disabilities, (A—u) 44, (A—g) 175

Gordy Educational Scholarship. See Josh Gordy Educational Scholarship, entry (O—u) 686

Gorell Scholarship Fund. See Lillian Gorell Scholarship Fund, entries (V—u) 308, (V—g) 406

Gorman-Metz Scholarship, (A—g) 176

Governor's Coalition for Youth with Disabilities Scholarships, (A—u) 45

Graduate Fellowship in the History of Science, (A—g) 177

Graduate Research Fellowship Program of the National Science Foundation, (A—g) 178

Graduate Student Fellowships at FDA, (A—g) 179

Graeme Clark Scholarships, (H—u) 447

Graham Scholarship. See ICEC Dr. Leslie P. Graham Scholarship, entry (O—u) 657

Great Lakes Hemophilia Foundation Education Scholarships, (O—u) 640, (F—u) 961

Green Beret Foundation and No Greater Sacrifice Scholarship Award in Memory of SGM Walter Shumate and SSG Robert Miller, (F—u) 962

Greene Scholarship. See American Council of the Blind of Texas Scholarships, entry (V—u) 256

Greg Cummings Scholarship Award. See Ruby's Rainbow Scholarships, entry (O—u) 766

Gregg Foundation Grants. See Harry Gregg Foundation Grants, entry (A—u) 46

Griffiths Memorial Scholarship. See Dick Griffiths Memorial Scholarship, entries (O—u) 610, (O—g) 830

Grossman College Scholarship Fund. See A. Richard Grossman College Scholarship Fund, entry (O—u) 554

Grosvenor Scholarship Awards. See Alexander Graham Bell College Scholarship Awards Program, entries (H—u) 441, (H—g) 459

Gruber Scholarships. See Kathern F. Gruber Scholarships, entries (F—u) 1000, (F—g) 1166

Grunwald Scholarship. See National Federation of the Blind of Illinois Scholarships, entries (V—u) 322, (V—g) 413

GTF Sibling Scholarship, (F—u) 963

Gunnar Esiason Own It Scholarship, (O—u) 641, (O—g) 838

Guthrie PKU Scholarship. See Guthrie-Koch PKU Scholarship, entry (O—u) 642

Guthrie-Koch PKU Scholarship, (O—u) 642

Guy Robichaud Prizes. See Cancer Unwrapped Teen Writing Contest, entries (O—u) 589, (F—u) 917

H

Hamilton Memorial Scholarship. See James Hamilton Memorial Scholarship, entry (O—u) 665

Hank Hofstetter Opportunity Grants, (V—u) 291

Hanley Memorial Scholarship Award. See John Hanley Memorial Scholarship Award, entries (O—u) 681, (O—g) 852

Hannon Scholarship. See National Federation of the Blind of Oregon Scholarships, entries (V—u) 332, (V—g) 418

Hansen Injury Law Firm Scholarship, (P—u) 496

Hansen-Yarussi Scholarship for Western Washington. See Lisa Hansen-Yarussi Scholarship for Western Washington, entry (O—u) 706

Harbison Scholarship. See Anne and Matt Harbison Scholarship, entry (O—u) 561

Harold H. Wilke Scholarship, (A—g) 180

Harold Louie Family Foundation Scholarships. See Kim and Harold Louie Family Foundation Scholarships, entry (A—u) 61

Harry Gregg Foundation Grants, (A—u) 46

Harry Ludwig Memorial Scholarship, (V—u) 292, (V—g) 394

Harter Secrest & Emery LLP Diversity Scholarship, (A—g) 181

Harvey Memorial Scholarship. See Delta Gamma Foundation Florence Margaret Harvey Memorial Scholarship, entries (V—u) 274, (V—g) 386

Harvey Picker Horizon Scholarships, (F—u) 964, (F—g) 1151

Harvey Simon Memorial Scholarship, (O—u) 643

Hawaii Association of the Blind Scholarship, (V—u) 293

Hawkins Spizman Kilgo, LLC Childhood Cancer Awareness Scholarship, (O—u) 644, (O—g) 839, (F—u) 965, (F—g) 1152

Hazel D. Cole Fellowship, (A—g) 182

Hazel Staley Memorial Scholarship. See Robert and Hazel Staley Memorial Scholarship, entries (V—u) 350, (V—g) 428

Hazel ten Broek Memorial Scholarship, (V—u) 294, (V—g) 395

Hazlewood Act for Spouse/Child, (F—u) 966

Health Policy Research Scholars, (A—g) 183

Heard Jr. Memorial Scholarship. See Elliott G. Heard Jr. Memorial Scholarship, entry (P—g) 541

Heather Burns Memorial Scholarships, (O—u) 645

Hebner Memorial Scholarship. *See* John Hebner Memorial Scholarship, entry (V—u) 299

Heisner Scholarship. *See* Hemophilia of Iowa Scholarships, entries (O—u) 652, (F—u) 969

Helen Seitz Scholarship, (A—g) 184

Hemophilia Association of New Jersey Scholarships, (O—u) 646, (O—g) 840

Hemophilia Federation of America Educational Scholarships, (O—u) 647

Hemophilia Federation of America Medical/Healthcare Services Educational Scholarship, (O—u) 648, (O—g) 841

Hemophilia Federation of America Parent/Sibling/Child Educational Scholarship, (F—u) 967

Hemophilia Foundation of Michigan Academic Scholarships, (O—u) 649, (F—u) 968

Hemophilia Foundation of Minnesota/Dakotas Scholarships, (O—u) 650

Hemophilia of Indiana Judy Moore Memorial Scholarship, (O—u) 651, (O—g) 842

Hemophilia of Iowa Scholarships, (O—u) 652, (F—u) 969

Hemophilia of South Carolina Academic Scholarship Program. *See* HSC Academic Scholarship Program, entries (O—u) 653, (F—u) 972

Henry H. Arnold Education Grant Program. *See* General Henry H. Arnold Education Grant Program, entry (F—u) 953

Henry P. David Grants for Research and International Travel in Human Reproductive Behavior and Population Studies, (A—g) 185

Henry Streuli Scholarship. *See* Cancer for College Pacific Northwest Scholarships, entries (O—u) 586, (O—g) 822

Henry Syle Memorial Fellowship for Seminary Studies, (H—g) 465

Herbert P. Feibelman, Jr. Scholarship. *See* Alexander Graham Bell College Scholarship Awards Program, entries (H—u) 441, (H—g) 459

Heroes' Legacy Scholarships, (F—u) 970

Herter Memorial Scholarship. *See* Christian A. Herter Memorial Scholarship, entry (A—u) 27

Higgins-Hussman Foundation Memorial Scholarship. *See* Lisa Higgins-Hussman Foundation Scholarship, entries (O—u) 708, (O—g) 860, (F—u) 1040, (F—g) 1178

Hissey College Scholarships. *See* Alexander Graham Bell College Scholarship Awards Program, entries (H—u) 441, (H—g) 459

Hiteshew Memorial Scholarship Program. *See* Doug Hiteshew Memorial Scholarship Program, entries (O—u) 615, (F—u) 933

Hofstetter Opportunity Grants. *See* Hank Hofstetter Opportunity Grants, entry (V—u) 291

Holibaugh Memorial Scholarship. *See* Joe Holibaugh Memorial Scholarship, entry (O—u) 677

Holly Elliott and Laurel Glass Scholarship Endowment, (V—g) 396, (H—g) 466

Honda SWE Scholarships, (A—u) 47

Honka Scholarships. *See* Emil A. Honka Scholarships, entries (V—u) 278, (V—g) 387

The Honorable Joel K. Asarch Elder Law and Special Needs Section Scholarship, (A—g) 241

Hope for the Warriors Spouse/Caregiver Scholarships, (F—u) 971, (F—g) 1153

Horatio Alger National Career and Technical Scholarship Program, (A—u) 48

Horatio Alger National Scholarship Program, (A—u) 49

Horizon Scholarships. *See* Harvey Picker Horizon Scholarships, entries (F—u) 964, (F—g) 1151

Howard E. May Memorial Scholarship. *See* National Federation of the Blind of Connecticut Scholarships, entries (V—u) 320, (V—g) 412

Howard Taylor Scholarship. *See* EAGA Scholarship Fund, entries (P—u) 489, (F—u) 936

HSC Academic Scholarship Program, (O—u) 653, (F—u) 972

Huber Learning through Listening Awards. *See* Marion Huber Learning through Listening Awards, entry (O—u) 717

Huey and Angelina Wilson Nontraditional Scholarships, (O—u) 654, (F—u) 973

Huey and Angelina Wilson Traditional Scholarships, (O—u) 655

Hugh S. Niles Memorial Scholarship. *See* Pennsylvania National Guard Scholarship Fund, entry (F—u) 1096

Hughes, '18 Fellowship. *See* Regina Olson Hughes, '18, Fellowship, entry (H—g) 469

Hunt Scholarship. *See* Alexander Graham Bell College Scholarship Awards Program, entries (H—u) 441, (H—g) 459

Hunter Memorial Scholarship. *See* Michael A. Hunter Memorial Scholarship, entries (O—u) 726, (F—u) 1053

Hydrocephalus Association Scholarships, (O—u) 656, (O—g) 843

Hylton Scholarship. *See* Mike Hylton Scholarship, entries (O—u) 730, (F—u) 1057

I

I. King Jordan, '70 Fellowship. *See* Gallaudet University Alumni Association Graduate Fellowship Fund, entry (H—g) 463

IADES Fellowship Award, (H—g) 467

ICEC Dr. Leslie P. Graham Scholarship, (O—u) 657

Idaho Armed Forces and Public Safety Officer Scholarships, (F—u) 974

Illinois Children of Veterans Scholarships, (F—u) 975

Illinois Council for Exceptional Children Dr. Leslie P. Graham Scholarship. *See* ICEC Dr. Leslie P. Graham Scholarship, entry (O—u) 657

Illinois Grant Program for Dependents of Correctional Officers, (F—u) 976

Illinois Grant Program for Dependents of Police or Fire Officers, (F—u) 977, (F—g) 1154

Illinois MIA/POW Scholarship, (F—u) 978

Illinois Spina Bifida Association Scholarships. *See* ISBA Scholarships, entries (P—u) 498, (P—g) 543

Incight Scholarships, (A—u) 50, (A—g) 186

Indiana Children and Spouses of Public Safety Officers Program, (F—u) 979, (F—g) 1155

Indiana Children of Deceased or Disabled Veterans Program, (F—u) 980, (F—g) 1156

Indiana Donor Network Foundation Scholarship, (O—u) 658, (F—u) 981

Indiana Donor Network Scholarships, (O—u) 659, (F—u) 982

Innovation in Motion Scholarship, (P—u) 497

International Alumnae of Delta Epsilon Sorority Fellowship Award. *See* IADES Fellowship Award, entry (H—g) 467

Iowa Veterans Trust Fund Assistance, (A—u) 51

Irell & Manella Diversity Scholarship Award, (A—g) 187

Irma Dow Scholarships. *See* Book Coleman, Foster Dow and Irma Dow Scholarships, entry (O—u) 578

Isabelle Christenson Memorial Scholarship, (O—u) 660, (F—u) 983

ISBA Scholarships, (P—u) 498, (P—g) 543

"It's Always Something" Writing Contest. *See* Cancer Unwrapped Teen Writing Contest, entries (O—u) 589, (F—u) 917

Ivan Stroud Scholarship. *See* North Carolina Troopers Association Scholarships, entry (F—u) 1084

J

J. Paris Mosley Scholarship, (H—u) 448, (F—u) 984

Jabez Legacy Scholarship, (O—u) 661

Jackie Spellman Scholarships, (O—u) 662, (O—g) 844, (F—u) 985, (F—g) 1157

Jacob N. Shanberge, M.D. Memorial Scholarship, (O—u) 663, (F—u) 986

Jacqueline Shearer Memorial Scholarship, (F—u) 987, (F—g) 1158

James and Colin Lee Wozumi Scholarship. *See* Wozumi Family Scholarship, entry (O—u) 809

James and Patricia Sood Scholarship, (O—u) 664, (O—g) 845, (F—u) 988, (F—g) 1159

James Doyle Case Memorial Scholarships, (V—u) 295, (V—g) 397, (F—u) 989, (F—g) 1160

James F. Nelson, Jr. Scholarships, (V—u) 296

James Hamilton Memorial Scholarship, (O—u) 665

James Kearney Scholarship for the Blind. *See* Brother James Kearney Scholarship for the Blind, entries (V—u) 265, (V—g) 380

James N. Orman, '23, Fellowship. *See* Gallaudet University Alumni Association Graduate Fellowship Fund, entry (H—g) 463

James R. Olsen Memorial Scholarship, (V—u) 297

Jamie L. Roberts Memorial Scholarship, (O—u) 666, (O—g) 846, (F—u) 990, (F—g) 1161

Janis Clay Educational Scholarship. *See* Elam Baer and Janis Clay Educational Scholarship, entry (O—u) 620

Jason Ackerman Memorial Scholarships, (O—u) 667

Jay Cutler Athletic Scholarships, (O—u) 668

Jay Franke Scholarship, (O—u) 669

Jay Kaplan Memorial Scholarship, (A—u) 52

Jaynes Memorial Scholarship Award. *See* Nancy Jaynes Memorial Scholarship Award, entry (F—u) 1067

JC Runyon Foundation Scholarships, (O—u) 670

Jean B. Cryor Memorial Scholarship Program, (A—u) 53, (A—g) 188, (F—u) 991, (F—g) 1162

Jean Driscoll "Dream Big" Award, (P—u) 499, (P—g) 544

Jean Kelsch, '51, Cordano Fellowship. *See* Gallaudet University Alumni Association Graduate Fellowship Fund, entry (H—g) 463

Jean Kennedy Smith Playwriting Award, (A—u) 54, (A—g) 189

Jeanne E. Bray Memorial Scholarship, (F—u) 992

Jeffrey Memorial Scholarship. *See* Meg Jeffrey Memorial Scholarship, entry (O—u) 723

Jeffrey P. Meyer Memorial Scholarship, (O—u) 671, (O—g) 847

Jenkins Memorial Disability Scholarship. *See* Flora Marie Jenkins Memorial Disability Scholarship, entry (A—u) 42

Jennica Ferguson Memorial Scholarship of Ohio, (V—u) 298, (V—g) 398

Jerde Scholarship. *See* Diabetes, Incorporated College Scholarship, entries (O—u) 607, (F—u) 929

Jernigan Scholarship. *See* Kenneth Jernigan Scholarship, entries (V—u) 303, (V—g) 401

Jerry Cahill You Cannot Fail Scholarships, (O—u) 672

Jessica Beth Schwartz Memorial Scholarship, (O—u) 673

Jill M. Balboni Memorial Scholarships, (O—u) 674

Jill Weaver Starkman Scholarship, (O—u) 675, (O—g) 848, (F—u) 993, (F—g) 1163

Jim Davies Scholarships, (O—u) 676

Jim Noland Foundation Scholarship, (F—u) 994

Joann Fischer Scholarship, (V—g) 399

Joe Cleres Memorial Scholarships, (A—u) 55, (A—g) 190

Joe Holibaugh Memorial Scholarship, (O—u) 677

Joel K. Asarch Elder Law and Special Needs Section Scholarship. *See* The Honorable Joel K. Asarch Elder Law and Special Needs Section Scholarship, entry (A—g) 241

John A. Trundle, 1885, Fellowship. *See* Gallaudet University Alumni Association Graduate Fellowship Fund, entry (H—g) 463

John Buller Scholarship, (O—u) 678, (O—g) 849

John C. Danforth Center on Religion and Politics Dissertation Completion Fellowship, (A—g) 191, (H—g) 468

John Duvall Memorial Scholarship, (O—u) 679, (O—g) 850, (F—u) 995, (F—g) 1164

John E. Mayfield ABLE Scholarship, (P—u) 500

John Foy & Associates Strong Arm Leukemia Scholarship, (O—u) 680, (O—g) 851, (F—u) 996, (F—g) 1165

John Hanley Memorial Scholarship Award, (O—u) 681, (O—g) 852

John Hebner Memorial Scholarship, (V—u) 299

John Heisner Scholarship. *See* Hemophilia of Iowa Scholarships, entries (O—u) 652, (F—u) 969

John Kloss Memorial Veteran Scholarship. *See* AHIMA Veterans Scholarship, entries (A—u) 7, (A—g) 136

John Lepping Memorial Scholarship, (P—u) 501, (O—u) 682

John, Lynne, and Nicole Belli Memorial Endowment Fund, (O—u) 683

John T. McCraw Scholarships, (V—u) 300

John Youtsey Memorial Scholarship Fund, (O—u) 684, (F—u) 997

Johnson Educational and Benevolent Trust Grants. *See* Dexter G. Johnson Educational and Benevolent Trust Grants, entry (A—u) 32

Johnson Memorial Scholarship. *See* National Federation of the Blind of California Scholarships, entries (V—u) 318, (V—g) 411

Johnson Scholarship Program. *See* Theodore R. and Vivian M. Johnson Scholarship Program, entries (V—u) 360, (H—u) 455, (P—u) 525, (O—u) 793

Johnson Scholarships. *See* Roy Johnson Scholarships, entry (V—g) 430

Jon C. Ladda Memorial Foundation Scholarship. *See* Lt. Jon C. Ladda Memorial Foundation Scholarship, entry (F—u) 1043

Jonathan May Memorial Scholarship. *See* National Federation of the Blind of Connecticut Scholarships, entries (V—u) 320, (V—g) 412

Jones Memorial Scholarship. *See* Lisa Jones Memorial Scholarship, entry (P—u) 505

Jones Open Scholarships. *See* Bobby Jones Open Scholarships, entries (P—u) 480, (P—g) 534, (F—u) 910, (F—g) 1145

Jordan, '70 Fellowship. *See* Gallaudet University Alumni Association Graduate Fellowship Fund, entry (H—g) 463

Joseph B. Gittler Award of the American Psychological Foundation, (A—g) 192

Joseph James Morelli Scholarship Fund, (O—u) 685

Joseph Roeder Scholarship, (V—u) 301, (V—g) 400

Joseph W. Mayo ALS Scholarship, (F—u) 998

Josh Gordy Educational Scholarship, (O—u) 686

Josh Smith Memorial Scholarship, (O—u) 687

Joshua Gomes Memorial Scholarship, (O—u) 688, (O—g) 853

Joshua O'Neill and Zeshan Tabani Enrichment Fund. *See* O'Neill Tabani Enrichment Fund, entry (O—u) 747

Joyce Walsh Junior Disability Awards, (A—u) 56

Judy Moore Memorial Scholarship. *See* Hemophilia of Indiana Judy Moore Memorial Scholarship, entries (O—u) 651, (O—g) 842

Julie Landucci Scholarship. *See* National Federation of the Blind of California Scholarships, entries (V—u) 318, (V—g) 411

Jumpstart MS Scholarship, (P—u) 502, (F—u) 999

Juris Scholarship. *See* Patrick Juris Scholarship, entry (P—g) 549

Justin Scot Alston Memorial Scholarship. *See* Hydrocephalus Association Scholarships, entries (O—u) 656, (O—g) 843

JustNebulizers.com Respiratory Care Scholarship, (O—u) 689, (O—g) 854

JustWalkers.com Mobility Scholarship Program, (P—u) 503, (P—g) 545

K

Kai Leamer Prizes. *See* Cancer Unwrapped Teen Writing Contest, entries (O—u) 589, (F—u) 917

Kaiser Permanente Colorado Diversity Scholarship Program, (A—u) 57, (A—g) 193

Kaiser Permanente Northwest Health Care Career Scholarships, (A—u) 58

Kamehameha Schools Class of 1972 Scholarship, (A—u) 59, (A—g) 194

Kaplan Memorial Scholarship. *See* Jay Kaplan Memorial Scholarship, entry (A—u) 52

Karen D. Carsel Memorial Scholarship. *See* R.L. Gillette, Gladys C. Anderson, and Karen D. Carsel Memorial Scholarship, entry (V—u) 349

Kark Award for Deaf Students. *See* Caroline Kark Award for Deaf Students, entry (H—u) 445

Karl Pohrt Tribute Award, (O—u) 690, (O—g) 855

Karstedt Scholarship. *See* Ralph Karstedt Scholarship, entry (A—g) 220

Kathern F. Gruber Scholarships, (F—u) 1000, (F—g) 1166

Katie MacDonald Memorial Scholarships for Individuals with Down Syndrome, (O—u) 691

Katz & Phillips Beating Heart Disease Scholarship, (O—u) 692, (F—u) 1001

Kearney Scholarship for the Blind. *See* Brother James Kearney Scholarship for the Blind, entries (V—u) 265, (V—g) 380

Keker, Van Nest & Peters Diversity Scholarship, (A—g) 195

Keller Memorial Scholarship. *See* Kerin Keller Memorial Scholarship, entry (F—u) 1005

Kellie Cannon Memorial Scholarship, (V—u) 302

Kelly Law Team Autism/ASD Scholarship, (O—u) 693

Kelly Law Team Disabled Veteran Scholarship, (A—u) 60

Kelly Law Team Down Syndrome Scholarships, (O—u) 694

Kelly Lynn Lutz Memorial Scholarship, (F—u) 1002

Kelly Memorial Scholarship. *See* Hemophilia Association of New Jersey Scholarships, entries (O—u) 646, (O—g) 840

Kelsey Campbell Memorial Scholarship. *See* Mouse Hole Scholarships, entries (V—u) 317, (F—u) 1064

Kennedy Memorial Scholarship. *See* Tim Kennedy Memorial Scholarship, entry (O—u) 796

Kenneth Jernigan Scholarship, (V—u) 303, (V—g) 401

Kenneth Tiede Memorial Scholarships, (V—u) 304, (V—g) 402

A—Any Disability　　　V—Visual　　　H—Hearing　　　P—Physical/Orthopedic　　　O—Other Disabilities　　　F—Families
u—undergraduates　　　g—graduate students

Kentucky Deceased or Disabled Law Enforcement Officer and Fire Fighter Dependent Tuition Waiver, (F—u) 1003

Kentucky Veterans Tuition Waiver Program, (F—u) 1004

Keppra Family Epilepsy Scholarship Program. See UCB Family Epilepsy Scholarship Program, entries (O—u) 799, (O—g) 883, (F—u) 1126, (F—g) 1195

Kerin Keller Memorial Scholarship, (F—u) 1005

Kermit B. Nash Academic Scholarship, (O—u) 695

Kevin Child Scholarship, (O—u) 696, (O—g) 856

Kevin Tidwell Memorial Scholarship. See CFSF Standard Scholarships, entry (O—u) 592

Kidney Transplant/Dialysis Association Scholarship Program, (O—u) 697, (F—u) 1006

Kids' Chance of Arizona Scholarships, (F—u) 1007

Kids' Chance of Arkansas Scholarships, (F—u) 1008

Kids' Chance of California Scholarships, (F—u) 1009

Kids' Chance of Florida Scholarship Program, (F—u) 1010

Kids' Chance of Georgia Scholarships, (F—u) 1011

Kids' Chance of Illinois Scholarships, (F—u) 1012

Kids' Chance of Indiana Scholarship Program, (F—u) 1013, (F—g) 1167

Kids' Chance of Kentucky Scholarships, (F—u) 1014

Kids' Chance of Louisiana Scholarships, (F—u) 1015

Kids' Chance of Maryland Scholarships, (F—u) 1016

Kids' Chance of Michigan Scholarships, (F—u) 1017

Kids' Chance of Mississippi Scholarship Fund, (F—u) 1018

Kids' Chance of Missouri Scholarships, (F—u) 1019, (F—g) 1168

Kids' Chance of Nebraska Scholarships, (F—u) 1020, (F—g) 1169

Kids' Chance of New Jersey Scholarships, (F—u) 1021

Kids' Chance of New York Scholarships, (F—u) 1022, (F—g) 1170

Kids' Chance of North Carolina Scholarships, (F—u) 1023

Kids' Chance of Ohio Scholarships, (F—u) 1024, (F—g) 1171

Kids' Chance of Oklahoma Scholarships, (F—u) 1025, (F—g) 1172

Kids' Chance of Oregon Scholarships, (F—u) 1026, (F—g) 1173

Kids' Chance of Pennsylvania Scholarships, (F—u) 1027

Kids' Chance of South Carolina Scholarships, (F—u) 1028, (F—g) 1174

Kids' Chance of South Dakota Scholarships, (F—u) 1029, (F—g) 1175

Kids' Chance of Tennessee Scholarship Program, (F—u) 1030

Kids' Chance of Texas Scholarships, (F—u) 1031

Kids' Chance of Vermont Scholarships, (F—u) 1032

Kids' Chance of Virginia Scholarships, (F—u) 1033

Kids' Chance of Washington Scholarships, (F—u) 1034

Kids' Chance of West Virginia Scholarships, (F—u) 1035

Kids' Chance of Wisconsin Scholarships, (F—u) 1036

Kids' Chance Scholarship Fund, (F—u) 1037

Kim and Harold Louie Family Foundation Scholarships, (A—u) 61

King & Spalding Diversity Fellowship Program, (A—g) 196

Kirschstein National Research Service Award for Individual Predoctoral Fellows in Nursing Research. See Ruth L. Kirschstein National Research Service Award for Individual Predoctoral Fellows in Nursing Research, entry (A—g) 226

Kirschstein National Research Service Award Individual Predoctoral MD/PhD or Other Dual-Degree Fellowship. See Ruth L. Kirschstein National Research Service Award Individual Predoctoral MD/PhD or Other Dual-Degree Fellowship, entry (A—g) 227

Kirschstein National Research Service Awards for Individual Predoctoral Fellows. See Ruth L. Kirschstein National Research Service Awards for Individual Predoctoral Fellows, entry (A—g) 228

Kirschstein National Research Service Awards for Individual Predoctoral Fellowships to Promote Diversity in Health-Related Research. See Ruth L. Kirschstein National Research Service Awards for Individual Predoctoral Fellowships to Promote Diversity in Health-Related Research, entry (A—g) 229

Kirschstein National Research Service Awards (NRSA) Fellowships for Students at Institutions With NIH-Funded Institutional Predoctoral Dual-Degree Training Programs. See Ruth L. Kirschstein National Research Service Awards (NRSA) Fellowships for Students at Institutions With NIH-Funded Institutional Predoctoral Dual-Degree Training Programs, entry (A—g) 230

Kisling Scholarship. See Chief Master Sergeant of the Air Force Scholarship Program, entries (A—u) 26, (F—u) 920

K&L Gates Diversity Fellowship, (A—g) 197

Kosmutza Scholarship Fund. See Charles Kosmutza Scholarship Fund, entry (F—u) 919

Krause Scholarship on Health and Disability. See AAHD Frederick J. Krause Scholarship on Health and Disability, entries (A—u) 1, (A—g) 128

Krause-Edwards Scholarship. See Gayle M. Krause-Edwards Scholarship, entry (V—u) 290

Kreyer Scholarship. See The Rev. Virginia Kreyer Scholarship, entry (A—g) 242

Kris Sanders Scholarship. See Diabetes, Incorporated College Scholarship, entries (O—u) 607, (F—u) 929

Kristin Caperton Inspiration Award, (A—u) 62

Kristofer Robinson Scholarship, (P—u) 504, (P—g) 546

Krueger Scholarship. See Bradley Krueger Scholarship, entries (O—u) 580, (F—u) 911

Kyle R. Noble Memorial Scholarship, (O—u) 698, (O—g) 857

L

Ladda Memorial Foundation Scholarship. See Lt. Jon C. Ladda Memorial Foundation Scholarship, entry (F—u) 1043

Ladies' Auxiliary National Rural Letter Carriers Scholarship. *See* Alexander Graham Bell College Scholarship Awards Program, entries (H—u) 441, (H—g) 459

Lancaster Scholarship, (V—u) 305, (V—g) 403

Landucci Scholarship. *See* National Federation of the Blind of California Scholarships, entries (V—u) 318, (V—g) 411

Lanford Family Highway Worker Memorial Scholarship Program, (F—u) 1038, (F—g) 1176

Larry Dean Davis Scholarship Fund, (O—u) 699

Larry Smock Scholarship, (O—u) 700

Larry Streeter Memorial Scholarship, (V—u) 306, (V—g) 404

Laura Lee Scholarship Award. *See* Ruby's Rainbow Scholarships, entry (O—u) 766

Laurel Glass Scholarship Endowment. *See* Holly Elliott and Laurel Glass Scholarship Endowment, entries (V—g) 396, (H—g) 466

Lavelle Fund for the Blind Scholarships. *See* Brother James Kearney Scholarship for the Blind, entries (V—u) 265, (V—g) 380

LaVyrl "Pinky" Johnson Memorial Scholarship. *See* National Federation of the Blind of California Scholarships, entries (V—u) 318, (V—g) 411

Law and Social Sciences Doctoral Dissertation Research Improvement Grants, (A—g) 198

Lawrence "Muzzy" Marcelino Memorial Scholarship. *See* National Federation of the Blind of California Scholarships, entries (V—u) 318, (V—g) 411

LEAD Foundation Community Scholarship. *See* Dottie R. Walker Scholarship, entry (O—u) 614

Leamer Prizes. *See* Cancer Unwrapped Teen Writing Contest, entries (O—u) 589, (F—u) 917

Learning Disabilities Association of Iowa Scholarships, (O—u) 701

Learning & Education About Disabilities Foundation Community Scholarship. *See* Dottie R. Walker Scholarship, entry (O—u) 614

Lee Scholarship Award. *See* Ruby's Rainbow Scholarships, entry (O—u) 766

Lehigh Valley Amputee Support Group Scholarship Award. *See* EAGA Scholarship Fund, entries (P—u) 489, (F—u) 936

Len Hannon Scholarship. *See* National Federation of the Blind of Oregon Scholarships, entries (V—u) 332, (V—g) 418

Leonard Family Entrepreneurial Spirit Scholarship, (O—u) 702, (O—g) 858

Lepping Memorial Scholarship. *See* John Lepping Memorial Scholarship, entries (P—u) 501, (O—u) 682

Leslie G. Brody and Amy Seeherman Scholarships. *See* Epilepsy Foundation New England Scholarships, entries (O—u) 623, (O—g) 835

Leslie Londer Fund Scholarship. *See* American Speech-Language-Hearing Foundation Scholarship for Students with a Disability, entry (A—g) 141

Leslie P. Graham Scholarship. *See* ICEC Dr. Leslie P. Graham Scholarship, entry (O—u) 657

Leukemia & Lymphoma Law School Scholarship, (O—g) 859, (F—g) 1177

Levy Scholarship Fund. *See* Alexander Graham Bell College Scholarship Awards Program, entries (H—u) 441, (H—g) 459

LHF Scholarships, (O—u) 703

Liemkuehler Memorial Scholarship. *See* EAGA Scholarship Fund, entries (P—u) 489, (F—u) 936

Lighthouse Guild College-Bound Scholarships, (V—u) 307

Lighthouse Guild Graduate School Scholarship, (V—g) 405

Lillian Gorell Scholarship Fund, (V—u) 308, (V—g) 406

Lillian Jeanette Craig Memorial Scholarship, (O—u) 704, (F—u) 1039

Lillian S. Edelstein Scholarship for the Blind, (V—u) 309, (V—g) 407

Lilly Diabetes Tomorrow's Leaders Scholarships, (O—u) 705

Lilly Reintegration Scholarships. *See* Baer Reintegration Scholarships, entries (O—u) 568, (O—g) 815

Linda Price Scholarship. *See* George and Linda Price Scholarship, entries (O—u) 637, (O—g) 837, (F—u) 954, (F—g) 1150

Linwood Walker Scholarship, (V—g) 408

Lisa Hansen-Yarussi Scholarship for Western Washington, (O—u) 706

Lisa Higgins Hussman Scholarship, (O—u) 707

Lisa Higgins-Hussman Foundation Scholarship, (O—u) 708, (O—g) 860, (F—u) 1040, (F—g) 1178

Lisa Jones Memorial Scholarship, (P—u) 505

Little People of America Scholarships, (P—u) 506, (P—g) 547, (F—u) 1041, (F—g) 1179

Living Breath Foundation Scholarships, (O—u) 709, (O—g) 861

Liwanag Memorial Scholarship. *See* Perlita Liwanag Memorial Scholarship, entries (O—u) 752, (O—g) 867, (F—u) 1097, (F—g) 1190

Lois Rothschild Memorial Scholarship, (O—u) 710

Londer Fund Scholarship. *See* American Speech-Language-Hearing Foundation Scholarship for Students with a Disability, entry (A—g) 141

Loreen Arbus Focus on Disability Scholarship, (A—u) 63, (A—g) 199

Los Angeles DUI Attorney Diabetes Scholarship, (O—u) 711, (O—g) 862

Lott Ministries Scholarships. *See* CMMS Deshae Lott Ministries Scholarships, entries (V—g) 384, (H—g) 461, (P—g) 537

Louie Family Foundation Scholarships. *See* Kim and Harold Louie Family Foundation Scholarships, entry (A—u) 61

Louis DiCarlo Scholarship. *See* Alexander Graham Bell College Scholarship Awards Program, entries (H—u) 441, (H—g) 459

Louise Reed Bridge to Life Survivor Scholarship. *See* Woody and Louise Reed Bridge to Life Survivor Scholarship, entries (O—u) 808, (O—g) 888

Louise Tumarkin Zazove Scholarships, (H—u) 449

Louisiana Hemophilia Foundation Scholarships. *See* LHF Scholarships, entry (O—u) 703

Louisiana Title 29 Dependents' Educational Assistance, (F—u) 1042

Lovrin Baxter Scholarship Award. *See* Ruby's Rainbow Scholarships, entry (O—u) 766

Lozano Donate Life Scholarship Fund. *See* Marcena Lozano Donate Life Scholarship Fund, entry (O—u) 715

LPV Scholarship Award. *See* Ruby's Rainbow Scholarships, entry (O—u) 766

Lt. Jon C. Ladda Memorial Foundation Scholarship, (F—u) 1043

Lucille B. Abt Scholarships. *See* Alexander Graham Bell College Scholarship Awards Program, entries (H—u) 441, (H—g) 459

Ludwig Memorial Scholarship. *See* Harry Ludwig Memorial Scholarship, entries (V—u) 292, (V—g) 394

Lulu Scholarship. *See* Elizabeth Lulu Scholarship, entry (O—u) 621

Lutz Memorial Scholarship. *See* Kelly Lynn Lutz Memorial Scholarship, entry (F—u) 1002

Lyman Fisher Scholarships, (O—u) 712, (F—u) 1044

M

MacDonald Memorial Scholarship for the Sibling of an Individual with Down Syndrome. *See* Eric Martinez Memorial Scholarship for the Sibling of an Individual with Down Syndrome, entries (F—u) 942, (F—g) 1149

MacDonald Memorial Scholarships for Individuals with Down Syndrome. *See* Katie MacDonald Memorial Scholarships for Individuals with Down Syndrome, entry (O—u) 691

MacDonald Wood Burn Survivor Educational Scholarship Program, (O—u) 713

Maho & Prentice Scholarship, (P—u) 507

Main Memorial Scholarship. *See* National Federation of the Blind of Connecticut Scholarships, entries (V—u) 320, (V—g) 412

Maine Veterans Dependents Educational Benefits, (F—u) 1045, (F—g) 1180

Mallory Smith Legacy Scholarship, (O—u) 714, (F—u) 1046

Maltby Award. *See* Novo Nordisk Donnelly Awards, entry (O—u) 743

Marcelino Memorial Scholarship. *See* National Federation of the Blind of California Scholarships, entries (V—u) 318, (V—g) 411

Marcena Lozano Donate Life Scholarship Fund, (O—u) 715

Marchello Scholarships. *See* Stephen T. Marchello Scholarships, entry (O—u) 780

Marco Camastra Scholarship Award, (O—u) 716

Marder Scholarship. *See* Eric Marder Scholarship, entry (O—u) 627

Marie Solie Scholarship. *See* Salem Foundation Angel and Marie Solie Scholarship, entry (V—u) 353

Marilyn Yetso Memorial Scholarship, (F—u) 1047, (F—g) 1181

Marine Corps League Scholarships, (A—u) 64

Mario J. Tocco Hydrocephalus Foundation Scholarship. *See* Hydrocephalus Association Scholarships, entries (O—u) 656, (O—g) 843

Marion Huber Learning through Listening Awards, (O—u) 717

Mark Coats Memorial Scholarship, (O—u) 718, (F—u) 1048

Mark T. Banner Scholarship for Law Students, (A—g) 200

Marquart Scholarship. *See* Olivia M. Marquart Scholarship, entries (O—u) 746, (O—g) 866

Martinez Memorial Scholarship for an Individual with Down Syndrome. *See* Eric Martinez Memorial Scholarship for an Individual with Down Syndrome, entry (O—u) 628

Mary A. Conroy Memorial Scholarship Program. *See* Edward T. and Mary A. Conroy Memorial Scholarship Program, entries (A—u) 38, (A—g) 168, (F—u) 938, (F—g) 1148

Mary Barton Freeman Scholarships, (O—u) 719, (O—g) 863, (F—u) 1049, (F—g) 1182

Mary Brennan Award, (O—u) 720

Mary Main Memorial Scholarship. *See* National Federation of the Blind of Connecticut Scholarships, entries (V—u) 320, (V—g) 412

Mary P. Oenslager Scholastic Achievement Awards, (V—u) 310, (V—g) 409

Maryanne Swaton Memorial Scholarship. *See* National Federation of the Blind of New York Scholarships, entries (V—u) 330, (V—g) 416

Maryland Community College Tuition Waiver for Students with Disabilities, (A—u) 65

Massachusetts Rehabilitation Commission or Commission for the Blind Tuition Waiver Program, (A—u) 66, (V—u) 311

Mathematica Summer Fellowships, (A—g) 201

Matt Harbison Scholarship. *See* Anne and Matt Harbison Scholarship, entry (O—u) 561

Matthew Debono Memorial Scholarship Fund, (P—u) 508, (P—g) 548

Matthew Siravo Epilepsy Scholarship Award, (O—u) 721

Matthews and Swift Educational Trust Scholarships, (F—u) 1050

Maudie's Scholarship Award. *See* Ruby's Rainbow Scholarships, entry (O—u) 766

Max Edelman Scholarship, (V—u) 312

May Memorial Scholarship. *See* National Federation of the Blind of Connecticut Scholarships, entries (V—u) 320, (V—g) 412

Mayfield ABLE Scholarship. *See* John E. Mayfield ABLE Scholarship, entry (P—u) 500

Mayo ALS Scholarship. *See* Joseph W. Mayo ALS Scholarship, entry (F—u) 998

Mays Mission Scholarships, (A—u) 67

McCarthy Memorial Academic Scholarship for Women with Bleeding Disorders. *See* Doreen McMullan McCarthy Memorial Academic Scholarship for Women with Bleeding Disorders, entries (O—u) 613, (O—g) 833

McCraw Scholarships. *See* John T. McCraw Scholarships, entry (V—u) 300

McCroskey Memorial Scholarship. *See* Alyssa McCroskey Memorial Scholarship, entries (A—u) 9, (A—g) 138

McDaniel Scholarship. *See* American Council of the Blind of Texas Scholarships, entry (V—u) 256

MCEC Foundation for Exceptional Children Scholarship Program, (O—u) 722

McGowan Leadership Scholarship. *See* Michael J. McGowan Leadership Scholarship, entry (V—u) 314

McGregor Scholarship Program, (V—u) 313

McGuireWoods Diversity Scholarship Program, (A—g) 202

McNamara Memorial Scholarship. *See* Bernice McNamara Memorial Scholarship, entries (F—u) 906, (F—g) 1143

Meg Jeffrey Memorial Scholarship, (O—u) 723

Megan Chesney Scholarship Fund. *See* CHASA Educational Scholarships, entry (P—u) 484

Megel Special Education Scholarship. *See* Carl J. Megel Special Education Scholarship, entries (V—u) 268, (H—u) 444, (P—u) 483, (O—u) 591

Melva T. Owen Memorial Scholarships. *See* Charles and Melva T. Owen Memorial Scholarships, entries (V—u) 270, (V—g) 382

Memorial Veteran Scholarship. *See* AHIMA Veterans Scholarship, entries (A—u) 7, (A—g) 136

Mental Health Research Dissertation Grant to Increase Workforce Diversity, (A—g) 203

Merfeld Family Foundation Scholarships, (F—u) 1051

Mesothelioma Cancer Alliance Scholarship, (O—u) 724, (O—g) 864, (F—u) 1052, (F—g) 1183

Meyer Memorial Scholarship. *See* Jeffrey P. Meyer Memorial Scholarship, entries (O—u) 671, (O—g) 847

Micah Jerde Scholarship. *See* Diabetes, Incorporated College Scholarship, entries (O—u) 607, (F—u) 929

Michael A. Corea Memorial Scholarship, (O—u) 725

Michael A. Hunter Memorial Scholarship, (O—u) 726, (F—u) 1053

Michael Bendix Sutton Scholarships, (O—u) 727

Michael Calkins Memorial Scholarship, (O—u) 728, (F—u) 1054

Michael Geddes Memorial Scholarships. *See* CFSF Standard Scholarships, entry (O—u) 592

Michael J. McGowan Leadership Scholarship, (V—u) 314

Michael Yasick ADHD Scholarship, (O—u) 729

Michigan Children of Veterans Tuition Grants, (F—u) 1055

Michigan Council for Exceptional Children Foundation for Exceptional Children Scholarship Program. *See* MCEC Foundation for Exceptional Children Scholarship Program, entry (O—u) 722

Michigan Elks Association Gold Key Scholarship Program, (A—u) 68

Michigan Veterans Trust Fund Tuition Grants. *See* Michigan Children of Veterans Tuition Grants, entry (F—u) 1055

Microsoft DisAbility Scholarship, (A—u) 69

Mid America Chapter MS Society Scholarship Program, (P—u) 509, (F—u) 1056

Mike Hylton Scholarship, (O—u) 730, (F—u) 1057

Mildred Colodny Diversity Scholarship for Graduate Study in Historic Preservation, (A—g) 204

Miller Scholarship. *See* Thomas H. Miller Scholarship, entries (F—u) 1121, (F—g) 1194

Millie Brother Scholarships, (F—u) 1058, (F—g) 1184

Millie Gonzalez Memorial Scholarships, (O—u) 731

Minnesota G.I. Bill Program, (F—u) 1059, (F—g) 1185

Minnesota Hockey Disabled Grant Program, (A—u) 70

Minnesota Social Service Association Diversity Scholarship, (A—u) 71

Mississippi Law Enforcement Officers and Firemen Scholarship Program, (F—u) 1060

Missouri Council of the Blind Scholarships, (V—u) 315, (V—g) 410

Missouri Kids' Chance Scholarship Program, (F—u) 1061

Missouri Public Service Officer or Employee's Child Survivor Grant Program, (A—u) 72, (F—u) 1062

Missouri Rehabilitation Services for the Blind, (V—u) 316

Missouri Wartime Veteran's Survivor Grant Program, (F—u) 1063

Missy and Angela Woolsey Education Award, (O—u) 732

Missy's Miracle Scholarship. *See* New Jersey Sharing Network Scholarships, entries (O—u) 739, (F—u) 1076

Mobility Scooters Direct Scholarship Program, (A—u) 73, (A—g) 205

Montana Police Protective Association Foundation Scholarships. *See* MPPA Foundation Scholarships, entry (F—u) 1065

Moore Memorial Scholarship. *See* Hemophilia of Indiana Judy Moore Memorial Scholarship, entries (O—u) 651, (O—g) 842

Morden Memorial Scholarship. *See* Brian Morden Memorial Scholarship, entry (O—u) 582

Morelli Scholarship Fund. *See* Joseph James Morelli Scholarship Fund, entry (O—u) 685

Morris L. and Rebecca Ziskind Memorial Scholarship. *See* Hydrocephalus Association Scholarships, entries (O—u) 656, (O—g) 843

Mosley Scholarship. *See* J. Paris Mosley Scholarship, entries (H—u) 448, (F—u) 984

Moss Endowed Scholarship. *See* P. Buckley Moss Endowed Scholarship, entry (O—u) 748

Mouse Hole Scholarships, (V—u) 317, (F—u) 1064

MPPA Foundation Scholarships, (F—u) 1065

Mullins Courageous Achievement Award. *See* Allstate Foundation/VHSL Achievement Awards, entry (A—u) 8

A—Any Disability   V—Visual   H—Hearing   P—Physical/Orthopedic   O—Other Disabilities   F—Families
u—undergraduates   g—graduate students

Murphey Memorial Scholarship. *See* Alma Murphey Memorial Scholarship, entry (V—g) 374

Murray Memorial Scholarship. *See* Catherine T. Murray Memorial Scholarship, entry (A—u) 23

Murtha Memorial Scholarship. *See* Pennsylvania National Guard Scholarship Fund, entry (F—u) 1096

Musicians with Special Needs Scholarship, (A—u) 74, (A—g) 206

Muzzy Marcelino Memorial Scholarship. *See* National Federation of the Blind of California Scholarships, entries (V—u) 318, (V—g) 411

N

NAGA Educational Scholarship Grant, (P—u) 510, (F—u) 1066

Nancy Jaynes Memorial Scholarship Award, (F—u) 1067

NASA Education Aeronautics Scholarship and Advanced STEM Training and Research Fellowship, (A—g) 207

Nash Academic Scholarship. *See* Kermit B. Nash Academic Scholarship, entry (O—u) 695

Nash Foundation Scholarship Program. *See* Elizabeth Nash Foundation Scholarship Program, entries (O—u) 622, (O—g) 834

Nate Slack Scholarship, (O—u) 733, (F—u) 1068

National Aeronautics and Space Administration Education Aeronautics Scholarship and Advanced STEM Training and Research Fellowship. *See* NASA Education Aeronautics Scholarship and Advanced STEM Training and Research Fellowship, entry (A—g) 207

National Amputee Golf Association Educational Scholarship Grant. *See* NAGA Educational Scholarship Grant, entries (P—u) 510, (F—u) 1066

National Black Coalition of Federal Aviation Employees National Scholarship Program. *See* NBCFAE National Scholarship Program, entry (A—u) 79

National Collegiate Cancer Foundation Legacy Scholarship Program, (F—u) 1069, (F—g) 1186

National Collegiate Cancer Foundation Survivor Scholarship Program. *See* NCCF Survivor Scholarship Program, entries (O—u) 735, (O—g) 865

National Commission on Certification of Physician Assistants Endowed Scholarships. *See* NCCPA Endowed Scholarships, entries (A—u) 81, (A—g) 211

National Federation of the Blind of California Scholarships, (V—u) 318, (V—g) 411

National Federation of the Blind of Colorado Scholarship, (V—u) 319

National Federation of the Blind of Connecticut Scholarships, (V—u) 320, (V—g) 412

National Federation of the Blind of Connecticut-Coccomo Quarter Grants. *See* NFBCT-Coccomo Quarterly Grants, entry (V—u) 338

National Federation of the Blind of Idaho Scholarships, (V—u) 321

National Federation of the Blind of Illinois Scholarships, (V—u) 322, (V—g) 413

National Federation of the Blind of Kentucky Scholarships, (V—u) 323

National Federation of the Blind of Louisiana Scholarships, (V—u) 324

National Federation of the Blind of Massachusetts Scholarships, (V—u) 325, (V—g) 414

National Federation of the Blind of Minnesota Scholarship, (V—u) 326

National Federation of the Blind of Mississippi Scholarships, (V—u) 327

National Federation of the Blind of Nebraska Scholarship, (V—u) 328

National Federation of the Blind of New Jersey Scholarships, (V—u) 329, (V—g) 415

National Federation of the Blind of New York Scholarships, (V—u) 330, (V—g) 416

National Federation of the Blind of Ohio Scholarships, (V—u) 331, (V—g) 417

National Federation of the Blind of Oregon Scholarships, (V—u) 332, (V—g) 418

National Federation of the Blind of Pennsylvania Scholarships, (V—u) 333

National Federation of the Blind of South Carolina Scholarships, (V—u) 334

National Federation of the Blind of Texas Merit Scholarships, (V—u) 335

National Federation of the Blind Scholarships, (V—u) 336, (V—g) 419

National Hemophilia Foundation Nevada Scholarships. *See* NHF Nevada Scholarships, entry (O—u) 740

National Institutes of Health Undergraduate Scholarship Program, (A—u) 75

National Kidney Foundation of Utah and Idaho Educational Scholarship Program, (O—u) 734

National Law Enforcement and Firefighters Children's Foundation General Scholarships, (F—u) 1070

National MS Society Scholarship Program, (P—u) 511, (F—u) 1071

National Press Club Scholarship for Journalism Diversity, (A—u) 76

National Research Service Award for Individual Predoctoral Fellows in Nursing Research. *See* Ruth L. Kirschstein National Research Service Award for Individual Predoctoral Fellows in Nursing Research, entry (A—g) 226

National Research Service Award Individual Predoctoral MD/PhD or Other Dual-Degree Fellowship. *See* Ruth L. Kirschstein National Research Service Award Individual Predoctoral MD/PhD or Other Dual-Degree Fellowship, entry (A—g) 227

National Research Service Awards for Individual Predoctoral Fellows. *See* Ruth L. Kirschstein National Research Service Awards for Individual Predoctoral Fellows, entry (A—g) 228

National Research Service Awards for Individual Predoctoral Fellowships to Promote Diversity in Health-Related Research. *See* Ruth L. Kirschstein National Research Service Awards for Individual Predoctoral Fellowships to Promote Diversity in Health-Related Research, entry (A—g) 229

National Research Service Awards (NRSA) Fellowships for Students at Institutions With NIH-Funded Institutional Predoctoral Dual-Degree Training Programs. *See* Ruth L. Kirschstein National Research Service Awards (NRSA) Fellowships for Students at Institutions With NIH-Funded Institutional Predoctoral Dual-Degree Training Programs, entry (A—g) 230

National Science Foundation Graduate Research Fellowships. *See* Graduate Research Fellowship Program of the National Science Foundation, entry (A—g) 178

National Space Grant College and Fellowship Program, (A—u) 77, (A—g) 208

Navy Seal Foundation Scholarships, (A—u) 78, (A—g) 209

NBCFAE National Scholarship Program, (A—u) 79

NBCUniversal Tony Coelho Media Scholarships, (A—u) 80, (A—g) 210

NCCF Survivor Scholarship Program, (O—u) 735, (O—g) 865

NCCPA Endowed Scholarships, (A—u) 81, (A—g) 211

NCSA Annual Scholarship Awards, (F—u) 1072

Nebraska Chapter NHF Post-Secondary Scholarships, (O—u) 736, (F—u) 1073

Nebraska Waiver of Tuition for Veterans' Dependents, (F—u) 1074

Nelson Jr. Memorial Fund Scholarship. *See* David Nelson Jr. Memorial Fund Scholarship, entry (F—u) 927

Nelson, Jr. Scholarships. *See* James F. Nelson, Jr. Scholarships, entry (V—u) 296

Neuroscience Scholars Program, (A—u) 82, (A—g) 212

New Day Education and Rehabilitation Award, (O—u) 737

New Jersey Bankers Education Foundation Scholarships, (F—u) 1075

New Jersey Center for Tourette Syndrome Youth Scholarship Program. *See* NJCTS Youth Scholarship Program, entry (O—u) 742

New Jersey Commission for the Blind and Visually Impaired College Services, (V—u) 337, (V—g) 420

New Jersey Council for Exceptional Children Scholarship Program. *See* NJCEC Scholarship Program, entry (O—u) 741

New Jersey ME/CFS Association High School Scholarship, (O—u) 738

New Jersey Sharing Network Scholarships, (O—u) 739, (F—u) 1076

New Jersey State Elks Special Children's Scholarship, (A—u) 83

New Jersey Utilities Association Excellence in Diversity Scholarship. *See* NJUA Excellence in Diversity Scholarship, entry (A—u) 86

New Outlook Scholarships for Students with Disabilities. *See* Joe Cleres Memorial Scholarships, entries (A—u) 55, (A—g) 190

New York MERIT Scholarships. *See* New York Military Enhanced Recognition Incentive and Tribute (MERIT) Scholarships, entries (A—u) 84, (F—u) 1077

New York Military Enhanced Recognition Incentive and Tribute (MERIT) Scholarships, (A—u) 84, (F—u) 1077

New York State Military Service Recognition Scholarships. *See* New York Military Enhanced Recognition Incentive and Tribute (MERIT) Scholarships, entries (A—u) 84, (F—u) 1077

New York State World Trade Center Memorial Scholarships, (A—u) 85, (F—u) 1078

Newmeyer Scholarship. *See* David Newmeyer Scholarship, entry (V—u) 273

NFBCT-Coccomo Quarterly Grants, (V—u) 338

NHF Nevada Scholarships, (O—u) 740

Niceley Memorial Scholarship. *See* Betty J. Niceley Memorial Scholarship, entry (V—u) 262

Niederman Scholarship. *See* Ron Niederman Scholarship, entries (O—u) 763, (F—u) 1110

Niles Memorial Scholarship. *See* Pennsylvania National Guard Scholarship Fund, entry (F—u) 1096

Niles Scholarship. *See* New Jersey Sharing Network Scholarships, entries (O—u) 739, (F—u) 1076

NJCEC Scholarship Program, (O—u) 741

NJCTS Youth Scholarship Program, (O—u) 742

NJUA Excellence in Diversity Scholarship, (A—u) 86

No Angel Left Behind Scholarship, (F—u) 1079

No Greater Sacrifice Scholarship, (F—u) 1080

Noble Memorial Scholarship. *See* Kyle R. Noble Memorial Scholarship, entries (O—u) 698, (O—g) 857

Nofer Scholarship. *See* George H. Nofer Scholarship, entry (H—g) 464

Noland Foundation Scholarship. *See* Jim Noland Foundation Scholarship, entry (F—u) 994

Nora Webb-McKinney Scholarship, (V—u) 339, (V—g) 421

Norma Shecter Memorial Scholarship, (V—u) 340

Norman Scholarships. *See* Ralph G. Norman Scholarships, entry (O—u) 755

North Carolina Bar Association Scholarships, (F—u) 1081, (F—g) 1187

North Carolina Council of the Blind Scholarship, (V—u) 341

North Carolina Lions Education Grant Program, (F—u) 1082

North Carolina Scholarships for Children of War Veterans, (F—u) 1083

North Carolina Sheriffs' Association Annual Scholarship Awards. *See* NCSA Annual Scholarship Awards, entry (F—u) 1072

North Carolina Troopers Association Scholarships, (F—u) 1084

North Dakota Association of the Blind Scholarships, (V—u) 342, (V—g) 422

North Dakota Educational Assistance for Dependents of Veterans, (F—u) 1085

Novo Nordisk Donnelly Awards, (O—u) 743

Novo Nordisk Scholarships, (O—u) 744

NovoSecure Scholarship Program, (O—u) 745

Nuance Communications Scholarship. *See* AHIMA Veterans Scholarship, entries (A—u) 7, (A—g) 136

O

O'Daniel Memorial Scholarship. *See* Shannon O'Daniel Memorial Scholarship, entry (O—u) 774

Oenslager Scholastic Achievement Awards. *See* Mary P. Oenslager Scholastic Achievement Awards, entries (V—u) 310, (V—g) 409

Ohio Legion Auxiliary Department President's Scholarship, (F—u) 1086

Ohio War Orphans Scholarship, (F—u) 1087

Oklahoma Goodwill Industries Abilities Scholarship, (A—u) 87

Old Dominion Foundation Fellowship. *See* Gallaudet University Alumni Association Graduate Fellowship Fund, entry (H—g) 463

Olivia M. Marquart Scholarship, (O—u) 746, (O—g) 866

Olsen Memorial Scholarship. *See* James R. Olsen Memorial Scholarship, entry (V—u) 297

O'Neill and Zeshan Tabani Enrichment Fund. *See* O'Neill Tabani Enrichment Fund, entry (O—u) 747

O'Neill Tabani Enrichment Fund, (O—u) 747

Operation Enduring Freedom and Operation Iraqi Freedom Scholarship, (F—u) 1088

Optimist International Communication Contest for the Deaf and Hard of Hearing, (H—u) 450

Oquendo Memorial Scholarship for Autism. *See* Avonte Oquendo Memorial Scholarship for Autism, entries (O—u) 567, (O—g) 814, (F—u) 904, (F—g) 1142

Oracle Scholarship for Excellence in Computer Science, (V—u) 343, (V—g) 423

Oracle Scholarship for Excellence in STEM, (V—u) 344, (V—g) 424

Oregon Deceased or Disabled Public Safety Officer Grant Program, (F—u) 1089, (F—g) 1188

Oregon Legion Auxiliary Department Nurses Scholarship for Dependents of Disabled Veterans, (F—u) 1090

Oregon Legion Auxiliary Department Scholarships for Wives of Disabled Veterans, (F—u) 1091

Oregon Occupational Safety and Health Division Workers Memorial Scholarships, (F—u) 1092, (F—g) 1189

Oregon State Bar Scholarships, (A—g) 213

Oregon Student Child Care Grants, (F—u) 1093

The Orion Fund Grants, (O—u) 792, (O—g) 882

Orman, '23, Fellowship. *See* Gallaudet University Alumni Association Graduate Fellowship Fund, entry (H—g) 463

Orman, '25, Fellowship. *See* Doris Ballance Orman, '25, Fellowship, entry (H—g) 462

Otto Sussman Trust Grants, (A—u) 88, (A—g) 214

Our Brother's Keeper Foundation Scholarships, (F—u) 1094

Ovis Memorial Scholarship. *See* Victoria Ovis Memorial Scholarship, entry (F—u) 1129

Owen Memorial Scholarships. *See* Charles and Melva T. Owen Memorial Scholarships, entries (V—u) 270, (V—g) 382

P

P. Buckley Moss Endowed Scholarship, (O—u) 748

PA Foundation Scholarships, (A—u) 89, (A—g) 215

Pangere Foundation Scholarships. *See* Ross N. and Patricia Pangere Foundation Scholarships, entries (V—u) 351, (V—g) 429

Paralyzed Veterans of America Educational Scholarship Program. *See* PVA Educational Scholarship Program, entries (P—u) 512, (F—u) 1102

Parker Scholarship. *See* E.U. and Gene Parker Scholarship, entries (V—u) 281, (V—g) 388

Parsons Memorial Scholarship. *See* CFSF Standard Scholarships, entry (O—u) 592

Patient Advocate Foundation Scholarships for Survivors, (O—u) 749

Patricia Pangere Foundation Scholarships. *See* Ross N. and Patricia Pangere Foundation Scholarships, entries (V—u) 351, (V—g) 429

Patricia Sood Scholarship. *See* James and Patricia Sood Scholarship, entries (O—u) 664, (O—g) 845, (F—u) 988, (F—g) 1159

Patrick Juris Scholarship, (P—g) 549

Patriot Scholarship of the University Interscholastic League, (F—u) 1095

Paul and Ellen Ruckes Scholarship, (V—u) 345, (V—g) 425

Paul D. Amitrani Scholarship. *See* Hemophilia Association of New Jersey Scholarships, entries (O—u) 646, (O—g) 840

Paul DesChamps Scholarship Award. *See* EAGA Scholarship Fund, entries (P—u) 489, (F—u) 936

Paul Liemkuehler Memorial Scholarship. *See* EAGA Scholarship Fund, entries (P—u) 489, (F—u) 936

Paul W. Airey Memorial Scholarship. *See* Chief Master Sergeant of the Air Force Scholarship Program, entries (A—u) 26, (F—u) 920

PCMA Education Foundation Diversity Scholarship, (A—u) 90

PCSI Scholarship Award. *See* Ruby's Rainbow Scholarships, entry (O—u) 766

Peace Officers Research Association of California Scholarships. *See* PORAC Scholarships, entry (A—u) 93

Pearson Award, (V—u) 346, (V—g) 426

Pediatric Brain Tumor Foundation College Scholarship Program, (O—u) 750

Peggy Sherrell Memorial Scholarship, (O—u) 751

A—Any Disability   V—Visual   H—Hearing   P—Physical/Orthopedic   O—Other Disabilities   F—Families
u—undergraduates   g—graduate students

Peikoff, '29 Fellowship. See Gallaudet University Alumni Association Graduate Fellowship Fund, entry (H—g) 463

Pennsylvania Association of Medical Suppliers Scholarship, (A—u) 91

Pennsylvania National Guard Enlisted Association USAA Scholarship. See Pennsylvania National Guard Scholarship Fund, entry (F—u) 1096

Pennsylvania National Guard Scholarship Fund, (F—u) 1096

Pequeno Memorial Scholarship. See Dakota Pequeno Memorial Scholarship, entry (O—u) 602

Perkins Coie Diversity Student Fellowships, (A—g) 216

Perlita Liwanag Memorial Scholarship, (O—u) 752, (O—g) 867, (F—u) 1097, (F—g) 1190

Persina Scholarship. See National Press Club Scholarship for Journalism Diversity, entry (A—u) 76

Peter and Bruce Bidstrup Scholarship Fund, (O—u) 753

Peter Christodoulou Memorial Scholarship. See Diane and Peter Christodoulou Memorial Scholarship, entry (O—u) 609

Peter Grunwald Scholarship. See National Federation of the Blind of Illinois Scholarships, entries (V—u) 322, (V—g) 413

Physician Assistant Foundation Scholarships. See PA Foundation Scholarships, entries (A—u) 89, (A—g) 215

Picker Horizon Scholarships. See Harvey Picker Horizon Scholarships, entries (F—u) 964, (F—g) 1151

Pink Bandana Scholarships, (O—u) 754, (F—u) 1098

PinkRose Breast Cancer Scholarships, (F—u) 1099

Pinky Johnson Memorial Scholarship. See National Federation of the Blind of California Scholarships, entries (V—u) 318, (V—g) 411

Pinnacol Foundation Scholarship Program, (F—u) 1100

Pistilli Scholarships. See P.O. Pistilli Scholarships, entry (A—u) 92

P.O. Pistilli Scholarships, (A—u) 92

Pohrt Tribute Award. See Karl Pohrt Tribute Award, entries (O—u) 690, (O—g) 855

PORAC Scholarships, (A—u) 93

Postdoctoral Research Fellowships in Biology, (A—g) 217

Potts Scholarship. See Deanna Lynn Potts Scholarship, entry (O—u) 604

Poulson Family Scholarships, (V—u) 347, (V—g) 427

Powering Education Scholarships, (A—u) 94, (A—g) 218

Price Memorial Scholarships. See Utah Hemophilia Foundation Scholarships, entries (O—u) 800, (F—u) 1127

Price Scholarship. See George and Linda Price Scholarship, entries (O—u) 637, (O—g) 837, (F—u) 954, (F—g) 1150

Professional Convention Management Association Education Foundation Diversity Scholarship. See PCMA Education Foundation Diversity Scholarship, entry (A—u) 90

Project Red Flag Academic Scholarship for Women with Bleeding Disorders. See Doreen McMullan McCarthy Memorial Academic Scholarship for Women with Bleeding Disorders, entries (O—u) 613, (O—g) 833

Proskauer Silver Scholar Program, (A—g) 219

Prows Memorial Scholarship. See Beverly Prows Memorial Scholarship, entries (V—u) 263, (V—g) 379

PSOB Educational Assistance Program, (F—u) 1101

Public Safety Officers' Benefits Educational Assistance Program. See PSOB Educational Assistance Program, entry (F—u) 1101

PVA Educational Scholarship Program, (P—u) 512, (F—u) 1102

Q

Qualls Memorial Scholarships. See Floyd Qualls Memorial Scholarships, entries (V—u) 285, (V—g) 391

Quigley Memorial Scholarship. See Rosemary Quigley Memorial Scholarship, entries (O—u) 764, (O—g) 869

R

Ralph G. Norman Scholarships, (O—u) 755

Ralph Karstedt Scholarship, (A—g) 220

Ramsey County Bar Foundation Law Student Scholarship, (A—g) 221

Randy and Viola Greene Scholarship. See American Council of the Blind of Texas Scholarships, entry (V—u) 256

Ray Froncillo Scholarship. See EAGA Scholarship Fund, entries (P—u) 489, (F—u) 936

Reaching Out to Cancer Kids College Scholarship Program. See R.O.C.K. College Scholarship Program, entry (O—u) 762

Ready When You Are Program, (O—u) 756

Rebecca Ziskind Memorial Scholarship. See Hydrocephalus Association Scholarships, entries (O—u) 656, (O—g) 843

Red Rose Scholarship, (V—u) 348

Reduced Tuition for Children and Spouses of South Dakota National Guardsmen Disabled or Deceased in the Line of Duty, (F—u) 1103

Reed Bridge to Life Survivor Scholarship. See Woody and Louise Reed Bridge to Life Survivor Scholarship, entries (O—u) 808, (O—g) 888

Reed Scholarship. See EAGA Scholarship Fund, entries (P—u) 489, (F—u) 936

Reed Smith/BNY Mellon Diversity Fellowship Program, (A—g) 222

Reed Smith Diverse Scholars Program. See Deborah J. Broyles Diverse Scholars Program, entry (A—g) 161

Reed Smith/Kaiser Permanente 1L Diversity Fellowship Program, (A—g) 223

Reed Smith/McKesson 1L Diversity Fellowship Program, (A—g) 224

Reed Society Scholarship. See AHIMA Veterans Scholarship, entries (A—u) 7, (A—g) 136

A—Any Disability   V—Visual   H—Hearing   P—Physical/Orthopedic   O—Other Disabilities   F—Families
u—undergraduates   g—graduate students

Regina Olson Hughes, '18, Fellowship, (H—g) 469

RehabGYM Scholarship, (A—u) 95

Rehabmart.com Scholarship Fund, (A—u) 96

Renee Feldman Scholarships, (F—u) 1104

REOC Charitable Scholarship Fund, (F—u) 1105

The Rev. Virginia Kreyer Scholarship, (A—g) 242

Ricardo Scholarships. See Vittoria Diana Ricardo Scholarship, entries (O—u) 805, (O—g) 886, (F—u) 1132, (F—g) 1198

Richard Bonasera Scholarship. See Epilepsy Foundation New England Scholarships, entries (O—u) 623, (O—g) 835

Richard D. Kisling Scholarship. See Chief Master Sergeant of the Air Force Scholarship Program, entries (A—u) 26, (F—u) 920

Richard E. Thorn Memorial Scholarship. See Pennsylvania National Guard Scholarship Fund, entry (F—u) 1096

Richard R. Garland Diversity Scholarship. See Sarasota County Bar Association Richard R. Garland Diversity Scholarship, entry (A—g) 231

Ride for Life Scholarship, (F—u) 1106

Riesch Scholarships. See Bryon Riesch Scholarships, entries (P—u) 481, (P—g) 535, (O—u) 583, (O—g) 820, (F—u) 912, (F—g) 1146

Rimington Trophy Scholarship, (O—u) 757, (O—g) 868

Rise Scholarships, (O—u) 758

Ritch Dangel Memorial Scholarship. See CFSF Standard Scholarships, entry (O—u) 592

RJT Criminal Defense Autism Scholarship, (O—u) 759

RJT Criminal Defense Disabled Veteran Scholarship, (A—u) 97

R.L. Gillette, Gladys C. Anderson, and Karen D. Carsel Memorial Scholarship, (V—u) 349

RMHBDA Education Scholarship, (O—u) 760, (F—u) 1107

Roadway Worker Memorial Scholarships, (F—u) 1108

Robert A. Dannels Memorial Scholarship, (A—g) 225

Robert and Dennis Kelly Memorial Scholarship. See Hemophilia Association of New Jersey Scholarships, entries (O—u) 646, (O—g) 840

Robert and Hazel Staley Memorial Scholarship, (V—u) 350, (V—g) 428

Robert Dole Scholarship for Disabled Students, (A—u) 98

Robert Eschbach Scholarship. See National Federation of the Blind of Ohio Scholarships, entries (V—u) 331, (V—g) 417

Robert Guthrie PKU Scholarship. See Guthrie-Koch PKU Scholarship, entry (O—u) 642

Robert H. Weitbrecht Scholarship. See Alexander Graham Bell College Scholarship Awards Program, entries (H—u) 441, (H—g) 459

Robert Price Memorial Scholarships. See Utah Hemophilia Foundation Scholarships, entries (O—u) 800, (F—u) 1127

Roberts Memorial Scholarship. See Jamie L. Roberts Memorial Scholarship, entries (O—u) 666, (O—g) 846, (F—u) 990, (F—g) 1161

Robichaud Prizes. See Cancer Unwrapped Teen Writing Contest, entries (O—u) 589, (F—u) 917

Robinson Scholarship. See Kristofer Robinson Scholarship, entries (P—u) 504, (P—g) 546

Roby Culinary Scholarship. See Chef Alain Roby Culinary Scholarship, entry (O—u) 594

Robyn's Way Scholarship, (O—u) 761, (F—u) 1109

R.O.C.K. College Scholarship Program, (O—u) 762

Rocky Mountain Hemophilia and Bleeding Disorder Association Education Scholarship. See RMHBDA Education Scholarship, entries (O—u) 760, (F—u) 1107

Roeder Scholarship. See Joseph Roeder Scholarship, entries (V—u) 301, (V—g) 400

Ron Niederman Scholarship, (O—u) 763, (F—u) 1110

Rose Honorary Diabetes Law Student Scholarship. See Ashley Rose Honorary Diabetes Law Student Scholarship, entry (O—g) 813

Rosemary Quigley Memorial Scholarship, (O—u) 764, (O—g) 869

Ross N. and Patricia Pangere Foundation Scholarships, (V—u) 351, (V—g) 429

Ross Skelton Scholarship, (O—u) 765, (O—g) 870

Rothschild Memorial Scholarship. See Lois Rothschild Memorial Scholarship, entry (O—u) 710

Roy Johnson Scholarships, (V—g) 430

Ruby's Rainbow Scholarships, (O—u) 766

Ruckes Scholarship. See Paul and Ellen Ruckes Scholarship, entries (V—u) 345, (V—g) 425

Rudolph Dillman Memorial Scholarship, (V—u) 352, (V—g) 431

Runway of Dreams Scholarship, (A—u) 99

Runyon Foundation Scholarships. See JC Runyon Foundation Scholarships, entry (O—u) 670

Russell Scholarship. See Cynthia Ruth Russell Scholarship, entries (A—u) 30, (A—g) 160

Ruth L. Kirschstein National Research Service Award for Individual Predoctoral Fellows in Nursing Research, (A—g) 226

Ruth L. Kirschstein National Research Service Award Individual Predoctoral MD/PhD or Other Dual-Degree Fellowship, (A—g) 227

Ruth L. Kirschstein National Research Service Awards for Individual Predoctoral Fellows, (A—g) 228

Ruth L. Kirschstein National Research Service Awards for Individual Predoctoral Fellowships to Promote Diversity in Health-Related Research, (A—g) 229

Ruth L. Kirschstein National Research Service Awards (NRSA) Fellowships for Students at Institutions With NIH-Funded Institutional Predoctoral Dual-Degree Training Programs, (A—g) 230

S

Sacks for CF Scholarships, (O—u) 767, (O—g) 871

Sad Sacks Nursing Scholarship, (F—u) 1111

Sadler Memorial Scholarship. See Arnold Sadler Memorial Scholarship, entries (V—u) 259, (V—g) 377

Salem Foundation Angel and Marie Solie Scholarship, (V—u) 353

SAMFund Grants, (O—g) 872

Sanders Scholarship. *See* Diabetes, Incorporated College Scholarship, entries (O—u) 607, (F—u) 929

Sara Elizabeth Stubblefield Foundation Scholarship, (O—u) 768

Sarasota County Bar Association Richard R. Garland Diversity Scholarship, (A—g) 231

Satola Family Scholarship, (O—u) 769, (O—g) 873, (F—u) 1112, (F—g) 1191

Sault Tribe Special Needs Scholarships, (A—u) 100, (A—g) 232

SBWIS Educational Scholarship in Memory of Mary Ann Potts, (P—u) 513, (P—g) 550

Scheigert Scholarships. *See* Fred Scheigert Scholarships, entries (V—u) 287, (V—g) 393

Schoettler Scholarship for Visually Impaired Students. *See* Dale M. Schoettler Scholarship for Visually Impaired Students, entries (V—u) 272, (V—g) 385

Scholarship for Students with an Autistic Sibling, (F—u) 1113, (F—g) 1192

Scholarship of the Arts, (O—u) 770, (O—g) 874

Scholarship Trust for the Hearing Impaired, (H—u) 451

Scholarships for Veterans with Post-Traumatic Stress Disorder, (O—u) 771

Schwabe, Williamson & Wyatt Summer Associate Diversity Scholarship, (A—g) 233

Schwallie Family Scholarships, (O—u) 772

Schwartz Memorial Scholarship. *See* Jessica Beth Schwartz Memorial Scholarship, entry (O—u) 673

Science Graduate Student Grant Fund, (A—g) 234

Scott Decker, M.D., Memorial Scholarship, (P—u) 514

Scott Delgadillo Scholarship, (O—u) 773, (O—g) 875

Scrooge Scholarship Fund, (F—u) 1114

See the Future Fund Scholarships, (V—u) 354, (V—g) 432

Seefred Trust Scholarships. *See* Thomas J. Seefred Trust Scholarships, entry (O—u) 795

Seeherman Scholarships. *See* Epilepsy Foundation New England Scholarships, entries (O—u) 623, (O—g) 835

Seitz Scholarship. *See* Helen Seitz Scholarship, entry (A—g) 184

Seleny Scholarships. *See* Frank Seleny Scholarships, entry (O—u) 633

Sentinels of Freedom Scholarships, (A—u) 101

Sertoma Scholarships for Hard of Hearing or Deaf Students, (H—u) 452

SFM Foundation Scholarship, (F—u) 1115

Shanberge, M.D. Memorial Scholarship. *See* Jacob N. Shanberge, M.D. Memorial Scholarship, entries (O—u) 663, (F—u) 986

Shannon O'Daniel Memorial Scholarship, (O—u) 774

Shearer Memorial Scholarship. *See* Jacqueline Shearer Memorial Scholarship, entries (F—u) 987, (F—g) 1158

Shecter Memorial Scholarship. *See* Norma Shecter Memorial Scholarship, entry (V—u) 340

Sherard Scholarship. *See* AHIMA Foundation Diversity Scholarships, entries (A—u) 6, (A—g) 135

Sherrell Memorial Scholarship. *See* Peggy Sherrell Memorial Scholarship, entry (O—u) 751

Shire ACES Scholarship for Rare Diseases, (O—u) 775

Shire ADHD Scholarship Program. *See* Michael Yasick ADHD Scholarship, entry (O—u) 729

The Shoot for the Future Scholarship Fund, (P—u) 524

Sidley Diversity and Inclusion Scholarship, (A—g) 235

Silver Cross Scholarship, (P—u) 515

Silvernail Scholarship. *See* Diabetes, Incorporated College Scholarship, entries (O—u) 607, (F—u) 929

Simon Memorial Scholarship. *See* Harvey Simon Memorial Scholarship, entry (O—u) 643

Siravo Epilepsy Scholarship Award. *See* Matthew Siravo Epilepsy Scholarship Award, entry (O—u) 721

Skelton Scholarship. *See* Ross Skelton Scholarship, entries (O—u) 765, (O—g) 870

Skogen Scholarship. *See* Emma Skogen Scholarship, entry (V—u) 279

Skoski, M.D., Scholarship. *See* Christina Skoski, M.D., Scholarship, entry (P—u) 486

Slack Scholarship. *See* Nate Slack Scholarship, entries (O—u) 733, (F—u) 1068

Smedinghoff Memorial Scholarship. *See* Anne Smedinghoff Memorial Scholarship, entries (O—u) 563, (O—g) 812, (F—u) 900, (F—g) 1141

Smith, Jr. Diversity Scholarships. *See* William Reece Smith, Jr. Diversity Scholarships, entry (A—g) 247

Smith Legacy Scholarship. *See* Mallory Smith Legacy Scholarship, entries (O—u) 714, (F—u) 1046

Smith Memorial Scholarship. *See* Josh Smith Memorial Scholarship, entry (O—u) 687

Smith Playwriting Award. *See* Jean Kennedy Smith Playwriting Award, entries (A—u) 54, (A—g) 189

Smith Recipient Scholarship. *See* Thomas F. Smith Recipient Scholarship, entry (O—u) 794

Smith Scholarship. *See* Beryl V. Smith Scholarship, entry (F—u) 907

Smock Scholarship. *See* Larry Smock Scholarship, entry (O—u) 700

Snowdrop Foundation Scholarships, (O—u) 776, (O—g) 876

Sobel Award. *See* André Sobel Award, entry (O—u) 559

SolvayCARES Scholarships. *See* AbbVie CF Scholarships, entries (O—u) 555, (O—g) 810

Sonoran Spine Foundation Scholarship, (P—u) 516, (P—g) 551

Sood Scholarship. *See* James and Patricia Sood Scholarship, entries (O—u) 664, (O—g) 845, (F—u) 988, (F—g) 1159

Soozie Courter Hemophilia Scholarship Program, (O—u) 777, (O—g) 877

South Carolina Tuition Assistance for Certain War Veterans Children, (F—u) 1116

South Dakota Reduced Tuition for Veterans, (A—u) 102

South Dakota Reduced Tuition for Visual Impairment, (V—u) 355, (V—g) 433

Southwest International Dyslexia Association College Scholarship. *See* SWIDA College Scholarship, entries (O—u) 785, (O—g) 880

Special People Gifts of Love Program, (V—u) 356, (H—u) 453, (P—u) 517, (O—u) 778

Spectrum Scholarship, (O—u) 779

Spellman Scholarships. *See* Jackie Spellman Scholarships, entries (O—u) 662, (O—g) 844, (F—u) 985, (F—g) 1157

Spina Bifida Association of Alabama Advanced Education Scholarship Program, (P—u) 518, (P—g) 552

Spina Bifida Association of Connecticut Scholarship Fund, (P—u) 519

Spina Bifida Association of North Texas Scholarship, (P—u) 520

Spina Bifida Coalition of Cincinnati Postsecondary Education Scholarship, (P—u) 521

Spina Bifida Wisconsin Educational Scholarship in Memory of Mary Ann Potts. *See* SBWIS Educational Scholarship in Memory of Mary Ann Potts, entries (P—u) 513, (P—g) 550

Springboard Foundation Dow Scholarships, (A—u) 103

Springboard Foundation Scholarships, (A—u) 104

Springboard Foundation STEM Scholarships, (A—u) 105

Staley Memorial Scholarship. *See* Robert and Hazel Staley Memorial Scholarship, entries (V—u) 350, (V—g) 428

Starkman Scholarship. *See* Jill Weaver Starkman Scholarship, entries (O—u) 675, (O—g) 848, (F—u) 993, (F—g) 1163

State Vocational Rehabilitation Services Program, (A—u) 106, (A—g) 236

Stefano Scholarship Award. *See* Vincent Stefano Scholarship Award, entry (O—u) 803

Stender Scholarship. *See* U'ilani Stender Scholarship, entries (A—u) 117, (A—g) 243

Stephen T. Marchello Scholarships, (O—u) 780

Stephen's Soldiers Cancer Survivors' Scholarship, (O—u) 781

Steve Fasteau Past Presidents' Scholarship, (A—u) 107, (A—g) 237

Stoel Rives First-Year Diversity Fellowships, (A—g) 238

Stone Award. *See* Novo Nordisk Donnelly Awards, entry (O—u) 743

Strangio Education Scholarship. *See* Bonnie Strangio Education Scholarship, entries (O—u) 577, (O—g) 819

Streeter Memorial Scholarship. *See* Larry Streeter Memorial Scholarship, entries (V—u) 306, (V—g) 404

Streuli Scholarship. *See* Cancer for College Pacific Northwest Scholarships, entries (O—u) 586, (O—g) 822

Stroud Scholarship. *See* North Carolina Troopers Association Scholarships, entry (F—u) 1084

Stubblefield Foundation Scholarship. *See* Sara Elizabeth Stubblefield Foundation Scholarship, entry (O—u) 768

Students with Disabilities Endowed Scholarships Honoring Elizabeth Daley Jeffords, (A—u) 108

Sully Drake Family and Friends Scholarship Award. *See* Ruby's Rainbow Scholarships, entry (O—u) 766

Summit Disability Law Group Scholarship Program, (A—u) 109

Supreme Emblem Club of the United States of America Grant-in-Aid Awards, (A—u) 110

Survivors' and Dependents' Educational Assistance Program, (F—u) 1117, (F—g) 1193

SurvivorVision Textbook Scholarship Program, (O—u) 782, (O—g) 878

Susan Bunch Memorial Scholarship, (O—u) 783, (O—g) 879

Susanna DeLaurentis Memorial Scholarships, (O—u) 784

Susquehanna Foundation for the Blind Trustees' Scholarship. *See* VisionCorps Foundation for the Blind Trustees' Scholarship, entries (V—u) 362, (V—g) 436

Susquehanna Post-Graduate Scholarship, (V—g) 434

Sussman Trust Grants. *See* Otto Sussman Trust Grants, entries (A—u) 88, (A—g) 214

Sutton Scholarships. *See* Michael Bendix Sutton Scholarships, entry (O—u) 727

Swaton Memorial Scholarship. *See* National Federation of the Blind of New York Scholarships, entries (V—u) 330, (V—g) 416

SWIDA College Scholarship, (O—u) 785, (O—g) 880

Swift Educational Trust Scholarships. *See* Matthews and Swift Educational Trust Scholarships, entry (F—u) 1050

Swim With Mike, (A—u) 111, (A—g) 239

Syle Memorial Fellowship for Seminary Studies. *See* Henry Syle Memorial Fellowship for Seminary Studies, entry (H—g) 465

T

Tabani Enrichment Fund. *See* O'Neill Tabani Enrichment Fund, entry (O—u) 747

TAER Student with a Visual Impairment Scholarship, (V—u) 357

Taylor Scholarship. *See* EAGA Scholarship Fund, entries (P—u) 489, (F—u) 936

Taylor Scholarships. *See* Esther V. Taylor Scholarships, entry (V—u) 280

Teens Take Charge Scholarships, (O—u) 786, (O—g) 881

ten Broek Memorial Scholarship. *See* Hazel ten Broek Memorial Scholarship, entries (V—u) 294, (V—g) 395

Tennessee STEP UP Scholarships, (O—u) 787

Teresa Blessing Scholarship, (V—u) 358

Terrill Foundation Military Scholarship, (O—u) 788

Terrill Foundation Student Scholarship, (O—u) 789

Texas 4-H and Youth Development Courageous Heart Scholarships, (A—u) 112

Texas Association for Education and Rehabilitation Student with a Visual Impairment Scholarship. *See* TAER Student with a Visual Impairment Scholarship, entry (V—u) 357

Texas Blind/Deaf Student Exemption Program, (V—u) 359, (V—g) 435, (H—u) 454, (H—g) 470

Texas Children of Disabled or Deceased Firemen, Peace Officers, Game Wardens, and Employees of Correctional Institutions Exemption Program, (F—u) 1118

Texas Exemption for Peace Officers Disabled in the Line of Duty, (A—u) 113

Texas Mutual Scholarship Program, (A—u) 114, (F—u) 1119

Texas Young Lawyers Association Diversity Scholarship Program, (A—g) 240

ThanksUSA Scholarships, (F—u) 1120

Thelma C. Hissey College Scholarships. See Alexander Graham Bell College Scholarship Awards Program, entries (H—u) 441, (H—g) 459

Theodore R. and Vivian M. Johnson Scholarship Program, (V—u) 360, (H—u) 455, (P—u) 525, (O—u) 793

Thomas F. Smith Recipient Scholarship, (O—u) 794

Thomas H. Miller Scholarship, (F—u) 1121, (F—g) 1194

Thomas J. Seefred Trust Scholarships, (O—u) 795

Thomas Scholarship. See Allegra Ford Thomas Scholarship, entry (O—u) 558

Thorn Memorial Scholarship. See Pennsylvania National Guard Scholarship Fund, entry (F—u) 1096

Through the Looking Glass Scholarships, (F—u) 1122

Tidwell Memorial Scholarship. See CFSF Standard Scholarships, entry (O—u) 592

Tiede Memorial Scholarships. See Kenneth Tiede Memorial Scholarships, entries (V—u) 304, (V—g) 402

Tim and Ritch Dangel Memorial Scholarship. See CFSF Standard Scholarships, entry (O—u) 592

Tim Kennedy Memorial Scholarship, (O—u) 796

Timothy Turpin Scholarship, (V—u) 361

TIP Grants. See Wisconsin Talent Incentive Program (TIP) Grants, entry (A—u) 125

Tjellström Scholarships. See Anders Tjellström Scholarships, entry (H—u) 442

Toby Wright Scholarship Fund, (F—u) 1123

Tocco Hydrocephalus Foundation Scholarship. See Hydrocephalus Association Scholarships, entries (O—u) 656, (O—g) 843

Tom Reed Scholarship. See EAGA Scholarship Fund, entries (P—u) 489, (F—u) 936

Tomlin Scholarship Award. See Bill Tomlin Scholarship Award, entry (V—u) 264

Tony Coelho Media Scholarships. See NBCUniversal Tony Coelho Media Scholarships, entries (A—u) 80, (A—g) 210

Tracy Donnelly Maltby Award. See Novo Nordisk Donnelly Awards, entry (O—u) 743

Transplant Recipients International Organization Scholarship Program. See TRIO Scholarship Program, entries (O—u) 797, (F—u) 1124

TRIO Scholarship Program, (O—u) 797, (F—u) 1124

Troy Barboza Educational Fund Scholarship, (A—u) 116, (F—u) 1125

Trujeque Memorial Scholarships. See Erin Trujeque Memorial Scholarships, entry (O—u) 629

Trundle, 1885, Fellowship. See Gallaudet University Alumni Association Graduate Fellowship Fund, entry (H—g) 463

Tuition Waiver for Disabled Children of Kentucky Veterans, (P—u) 526

Turpin Scholarship. See Timothy Turpin Scholarship, entry (V—u) 361

Type 1 for 67 Years Scholarships, (O—u) 798

U

UCB Family Epilepsy Scholarship Program, (O—u) 799, (O—g) 883, (F—u) 1126, (F—g) 1195

U'ilani Stender Scholarship, (A—u) 117, (A—g) 243

United States Olympic Committee 2002 Olympic and Paralympic Winter Games Legacy Scholarships. See USOC 2002 Olympic and Paralympic Winter Games Legacy Scholarships, entry (P—u) 527

United States Olympic Committee Athlete Tuition Grant Program. See USOC Athlete Tuition Grant Program, entry (P—u) 528

USOC 2002 Olympic and Paralympic Winter Games Legacy Scholarships, (P—u) 527

USOC Athlete Tuition Grant Program, (P—u) 528

Utah Elks Association Special Needs Student Scholarship Award, (A—u) 118

Utah Hemophilia Foundation Scholarships, (O—u) 800, (F—u) 1127

V

V4W Academic Scholarship for Women with Bleeding Disorders. See Doreen McMullan McCarthy Memorial Academic Scholarship for Women with Bleeding Disorders, entries (O—u) 613, (O—g) 833

Valiant Scholarship, (P—u) 529

van Eys Scholarship Award. See Dugdale/van Eys Scholarship Award, entries (O—u) 616, (F—u) 934

Varun Bhaskaran (WAS) Scholarship Program, (O—u) 801, (O—g) 884

Vera Yip Memorial Scholarship, (O—u) 802, (O—g) 885, (F—u) 1128, (F—g) 1196

VHSL Achievement Awards. See Allstate Foundation/ VHSL Achievement Awards, entry (A—u) 8

Victoria Ovis Memorial Scholarship, (F—u) 1129

Victory for Women Academic Scholarship for Women with Bleeding Disorders. See Doreen McMullan McCarthy Memorial Academic Scholarship for Women with Bleeding Disorders, entries (O—u) 613, (O—g) 833

Vincent Bennett, Jr. Memorial Scholarship, (F—u) 1130

Vincent Stefano Scholarship Award, (O—u) 803

Viola Greene Scholarship. See American Council of the Blind of Texas Scholarships, entry (V—u) 256

Virgin Islands Exceptional Children Grants, (A—u) 119

Virginia Cobb Scholarship, (H—u) 456, (O—u) 804

Virginia High School League Achievement Awards. *See* Allstate Foundation/VHSL Achievement Awards, entry (A—u) 8

Virginia Kreyer Scholarship. *See* The Rev. Virginia Kreyer Scholarship, entry (A—g) 242

Virginia Military Survivors and Dependents Education Program, (F—u) 1131, (F—g) 1197

Virginia War Orphans Education Program. *See* Virginia Military Survivors and Dependents Education Program, entries (F—u) 1131, (F—g) 1197

VisionCorps Foundation for the Blind Trustees' Scholarship, (V—u) 362, (V—g) 436

Visual Aid Volunteers of Florida Scholarships, (V—u) 363

Vittoria Diana Ricardo Scholarship, (O—u) 805, (O—g) 886, (F—u) 1132, (F—g) 1198

Vivian M. Johnson Scholarship Program. *See* Theodore R. and Vivian M. Johnson Scholarship Program, entries (V—u) 360, (H—u) 455, (P—u) 525, (O—u) 793

Vocational Rehabilitation and Employment Service Program, (A—u) 120, (A—g) 244

Volkswagen Group of America Exhibition Program. *See* VSA Emerging Young Artists Program, entries (A—u) 121, (A—g) 245

Volta Scholarship Fund. *See* Alexander Graham Bell College Scholarship Awards Program, entries (H—u) 441, (H—g) 459

VSA Emerging Young Artists Program, (A—u) 121, (A—g) 245

VSA International Young Soloists Award, (A—u) 122, (A—g) 246

W

Waldo T., '49 and Jean Kelsch, '51, Cordano Fellowship. *See* Gallaudet University Alumni Association Graduate Fellowship Fund, entry (H—g) 463

Walker Scholarship. *See* Linwood Walker Scholarship, entry (V—g) 408, (O—u) 614

Walsh Junior Disability Awards. *See* Joyce Walsh Junior Disability Awards, entry (A—u) 56

Walter Reed Society Scholarship. *See* AHIMA Veterans Scholarship, entries (A—u) 7, (A—g) 136

Walter W. and Thelma C. Hissey College Scholarships. *See* Alexander Graham Bell College Scholarship Awards Program, entries (H—u) 441, (H—g) 459

Warriors for Walt Scholarship Award. *See* Ruby's Rainbow Scholarships, entry (O—u) 766

Washington Council of the Blind Scholarships, (V—u) 364, (V—g) 437

Washington National Guard State Education Assistance Program (EAP), (F—u) 1133, (F—g) 1199

Washingcton State Association for Justice Past Presidents' Scholarship. *See* WSAJ Past Presidents' Scholarship, entry (A—u) 126

Washington State Trial Lawyers Association Past Presidents' Scholarship. *See* WSAJ Past Presidents' Scholarship, entry (A—u) 126

WBDN Educational Scholarship, (O—u) 806, (F—u) 1134

WBM Disabled Veterans Scholarship, (A—u) 123

Webb-McKinney Scholarship. *See* Nora Webb-McKinney Scholarship, entries (V—u) 339, (V—g) 421

Weitbrecht Scholarship. *See* Alexander Graham Bell College Scholarship Awards Program, entries (H—u) 441, (H—g) 459

Wells Fargo Scholarship Program for People with Disabilities, (A—u) 124

White Cane Scholarship, (V—u) 365

Whitfield, Bryson & Mason Disabled Veterans Scholarship. *See* WBM Disabled Veterans Scholarship, entry (A—u) 123

Wil Can Fly Scholarship Award. *See* Ruby's Rainbow Scholarships, entry (O—u) 766

Wilke Scholarship. *See* Harold H. Wilke Scholarship, entry (A—g) 180

William and Dorothy Ferrell Scholarship, (V—u) 366, (V—g) 438

William G. Corey Memorial Scholarship, (V—u) 367, (V—g) 439

William L. Woolard Educational Grant Program. *See* North Carolina Lions Education Grant Program, entry (F—u) 1082

William Reece Smith, Jr. Diversity Scholarships, (A—g) 247

Williams, '32, Fellowship. *See* Gallaudet University Alumni Association Graduate Fellowship Fund, entry (H—g) 463

Wilson Nontraditional Scholarships. *See* Huey and Angelina Wilson Nontraditional Scholarships, entries (O—u) 654, (F—u) 973

Wilson Traditional Scholarships. *See* Huey and Angelina Wilson Traditional Scholarships, entry (O—u) 655

Winston & Strawn Diversity Scholarship Program, (A—g) 248

Winterhoff Arthritis Scholarship, (O—u) 807, (O—g) 887

Wisconsin Bleeding Disorders Network Educational Scholarship. *See* WBDN Educational Scholarship, entries (O—u) 806, (F—u) 1134

Wisconsin Council of the Blind and Visually Impaired Scholarships, (V—u) 368

Wisconsin G.I. Bill Tuition Remission Program, (F—u) 1135, (F—g) 1200

Wisconsin Hearing and Visually Handicapped Student Grant Program, (V—u) 369, (H—u) 457

Wisconsin Talent Incentive Program (TIP) Grants, (A—u) 125

Wisconsin Tuition and Fee Reimbursement Grants. *See* Wisconsin G.I. Bill Tuition Remission Program, entries (F—u) 1135, (F—g) 1200

Wood Burn Survivor Educational Scholarship Program. *See* MacDonald Wood Burn Survivor Educational Scholarship Program, entry (O—u) 713

A—Any Disability V—Visual H—Hearing P—Physical/Orthopedic O—Other Disabilities F—Families
u—undergraduates g—graduate students

Woody and Louise Reed Bridge to Life Survivor Scholarship, (O—u) 808, (O—g) 888

Woolard Educational Grant Program. *See* North Carolina Lions Education Grant Program, entry (F—u) 1082

Woolsey Education Award. *See* Missy and Angela Woolsey Education Award, entry (O—u) 732

Workforce Safety & Insurance Scholarships. *See* WSI Scholarships, entries (A—u) 127, (F—u) 1136

Wozumi Family Scholarship, (O—u) 809

Wozumi Scholarship. *See* Wozumi Family Scholarship, entry (O—u) 809

Wright Scholarship Fund. *See* Toby Wright Scholarship Fund, entry (F—u) 1123

Writing Competition to Promote Diversity in Law Schools and in the Legal Profession, (A—g) 249

WSAJ Past Presidents' Scholarship, (A—u) 126

WSI Scholarships, (A—u) 127, (F—u) 1136

WSTLA Past Presidents' Scholarship. *See* WSAJ Past Presidents' Scholarship, entry (A—u) 126

WYCB Scholarship, (V—u) 370, (V—g) 440

Wyoming Council of the Blind Scholarship. *See* WYCB Scholarship, entries (V—u) 370, (V—g) 440

Y

Yasick ADHD Scholarship. *See* Michael Yasick ADHD Scholarship, entry (O—u) 729

Ye Notorious Krewe of the Peg Leg Pirate Scholarships, (P—u) 530, (P—g) 553, (F—u) 1137, (F—g) 1201

Yetso Memorial Scholarship. *See* Marilyn Yetso Memorial Scholarship, entries (F—u) 1047, (F—g) 1181

Yip Memorial Scholarship. *See* Vera Yip Memorial Scholarship, entries (O—u) 802, (O—g) 885, (F—u) 1128, (F—g) 1196

Youth Opportunity Scholarships. *See* Achievement Scholarship for Students with a History of Chronic Illness Fund, entry (O—u) 557

Youtsey Memorial Scholarship Fund. *See* John Youtsey Memorial Scholarship Fund, entries (O—u) 684, (F—u) 997

Z

Zazove Scholarships. *See* Louise Tumarkin Zazove Scholarships, entry (H—u) 449

Zeshan Tabani Enrichment Fund. *See* O'Neill Tabani Enrichment Fund, entry (O—u) 747

Ziskind Memorial Scholarship. *See* Hydrocephalus Association Scholarships, entries (O—u) 656, (O—g) 843

Sponsoring Organization Index

The Sponsoring Organization Index makes it easy to identify agencies that offer financial aid to persons with disabilities and members of their families. In this index, sponsoring organizations are listed alphabetically, word by word. In addition, we've used a two-character alphabetical code (within parentheses) to help you identify which programs sponsored by these organizations fall within your scope of interest. The first character (capitalized) in the code identifies the program focus: A = Any Disability; V = Visual Disabilities; H = Hearing Disabilities; P = Physical/Orthopedic; O = Other Disabilities/Disorders; F = Families of the Disabled. The second character (lower-cased) identifies funding type: u = undergraduate; g = graduate student. Here's how the code works: if a program is followed by (A–g) 158, the program is described in the Any Disability chapter, in the graduate student section, in entry 158. If that sponsoring organization's name is followed by another entry number—for example, (F–u) 1028—the same or a different program sponsored by that organization is described in the Families of the Disabled chapter, in the undergraduate section, in entry 1028. Remember: the numbers cited here refer to program entry numbers, not to page numbers in the book.

180 Medical, (P—u) 471, (P—g) 531

A

Aaron Bonner Foundation, (O—u) 756
AbbVie Inc., (O—u) 555-556, (O—g) 810-811
ABC Home Medical Supply Inc., (P—u) 472
Able Flight, Inc., (P—u) 473
Academic Library Association of Ohio, (A—g) 130
Academy of Special Dreams Foundation, (A—u) 3
Academy of Television Arts & Sciences Foundation, (A—u) 63, (A—g) 199
ACE INA Foundation, (F—u) 1027
ACT Scholarship and Recognition Services, (P—u) 511, (F—u) 1071
Acxiom Corporation, (A—u) 5, (A—g) 132
Ad Club Seattle, (F—u) 1005
Air Force Aid Society, (F—u) 890, 953
Air Force Sergeants Association, (A—u) 26, (F—u) 920
Air Line Pilots Association, (F—u) 891
Airmen Memorial Foundation, (A—u) 26, (F—u) 920
Alabama Council of the Blind, (V—u) 266
Alabama Department of Rehabilitation Services, (F—u) 893

Alabama Department of Veterans Affairs, (F—u) 892, (F—g) 1138
Alabama Law Foundation, (F—u) 1037
Alabama State Bar. Workers' Compensation Section, (F—u) 1037
Alexander Graham Bell Association for the Deaf and Hard of Hearing, (H—u) 441, 443, (H—g) 459, 464
Alisa Ann Ruch Burn Foundation, (O—u) 808, (O—g) 888
Allina Health System, (A—u) 29
Allstate Foundation, (A—u) 8
Alpha One, (A—u) 94, (A—g) 218
A.L.S. Family Charitable Foundation, Inc., (F—u) 897
Alzheimer's Foundation of America, (F—u) 889
American Academy of Physician Assistants, (A—u) 2, 81, 89, (A—g) 129, 211, 215
American Action Fund for Blind Children and Adults, (V—u) 303, (V—g) 401
American Association of People with Disabilities, (A—u) 80, (A—g) 210
American Association on Health and Disability, (A—u) 1, (A—g) 128
American Bus Association, (A—u) 10, (A—g) 139, (F—u) 898, (F—g) 1140
American Cancer Society. Florida Division, (O—u) 762

A—Any Disability   V—Visual   H—Hearing   P—Physical/Orthopedic   O—Other Disabilities   F—Families
u—undergraduates   g—graduate students

American Council of the Blind, (V—u) 250, 255, 259, 261, 275, 282, 285, 297, 299, 302, 340, 351, 367, (V—g) 374, 377, 389, 391, 429, 439

American Council of the Blind of Indiana, (V—u) 291

American Council of the Blind of Minnesota, (V—u) 254, (V—g) 375

American Council of the Blind of Ohio, (V—u) 273, 289, 312, 339, (V—g) 399, 408, 421

American Council of the Blind of Oregon, (V—u) 255

American Council of the Blind of Texas, (V—u) 256

American Diabetes Association, (O—u) 743

American Education Services, (F—u) 1027

American Epilepsy Society, (A—g) 140

American Foundation for the Blind, (V—u) 274, 345, 349, 352, (V—g) 386, 425, 431

American Geophysical Union, (A—g) 177

American Health Information Management Association, (A—u) 6-7, (A—g) 135-136

American Honda Motor Company, Inc., (A—u) 47

American Legion. Americanism and Children & Youth Division, (F—u) 899

American Legion. Ohio Auxiliary, (F—u) 1086

American Legion. Oregon Auxiliary, (F—u) 1090-1091

American Library Association. Association of Specialized and Cooperative Library Agencies, (A—g) 137

American Meteorological Society, (A—u) 11-12, (A—g) 143

American Museum of Natural History, (A—g) 142

American Psychological Association. American Psychological Association of Graduate Students, (A—g) 144, 147

American Psychological Association. Division 41, (A—u) 37, (A—g) 165, (P—u) 474

American Psychological Foundation, (A—g) 185, 192

American Road and Transportation Builders Association, (F—u) 1038, (F—g) 1176

American Society of Safety Engineers, (P—u) 478, (P—g) 533

American Speech-Language-Hearing Foundation, (A—g) 141

American Syringomyelia & Chiari Alliance Project, Inc., (P—u) 480, (P—g) 534, (F—u) 910, (F—g) 1145

American Traffic Safety Services Foundation, (F—u) 1108

AmeriGlide, Inc., (P—u) 475, (P—g) 532

Amputee Coalition, (P—u) 486, 514

AMVETS. Department of Illinois, (F—u) 1111

André Sobel River of Life Foundation, (O—u) 559

Aplastic Anemia & MDS International Foundation, Inc., (P—u) 508, (P—g) 548

ApoPharma Inc., (O—g) 826

Arizona Burn Foundation, (O—u) 713

Arizona Community Foundation, (P—u) 477

Arizona Council of the Blind, (V—u) 257, (V—g) 376

Arizona Hispanic Chamber of Commerce, (P—u) 477

Arkansas Council for Exceptional Children, (O—u) 565

Arkansas Council of the Blind, (V—u) 258

Arkansas Department of Higher Education, (F—u) 901-902

Army Engineer Association, (P—u) 487, (P—g) 538

Arnold & Porter Kaye Scholer LLP, (A—g) 145

Arthritis Foundation, (O—u) 807, (O—g) 887

Association for Computing Machinery, (A—u) 92

Association for Education and Rehabilitation of the Blind and Visually Impaired, (V—u) 366, (V—g) 438

Association for Education and Rehabilitation of the Blind and Visually Impaired. Arkansas Chapter, (V—u) 264

Auger & Auger Attorneys at Law, (A—u) 13

Autism Delaware, (O—u) 566

B

Banner & Witcoff, Ltd., (A—g) 166

Bar Association of San Francisco, (A—g) 148

Baxalta Incorporated, (O—u) 617-618

Bay State Council of the Blind, (V—u) 261

Beacon Mutual Insurance Company, (F—u) 905

The Bennett Clayton Foundation, (P—u) 522

Best Best & Krieger LLP, (A—g) 149

Best Buy Children's Foundation, (P—u) 502, (F—u) 999

Billie Jean King WTT Charities, Inc., (O—u) 743

BioRx, LLC, (O—u) 574, (F—u) 908

Blackhorse Association, (F—u) 909

Bleeding and Clotting Disorders Institute, (O—u) 575

Bleeding Disorders Alliance Illinois, (O—u) 580, (F—u) 911

Blind Information Technology Specialists, Inc., (V—u) 302

Blind Mice, Inc., (V—u) 317, (F—u) 1064

Blinded Veterans Association, (F—u) 1000, 1121, (F—g) 1166, 1194

Blinded Veterans Association Auxiliary, (F—u) 1104

BMO Capital Markets, (A—u) 16, (A—g) 152

BNY Mellon, (A—g) 222

Book Industry Charitable Foundation, (O—u) 690, (O—g) 855

Boomer Esiason Foundation, (O—u) 569, 577, 630, 641, 672, 757, 764, 767, 770, (O—g) 816, 819, 838, 868-869, 871, 874

Bradley Arant Boult Cummings LLP, (A—g) 153

Braille Revival League of Missouri, (V—g) 374

The Brain Injury Alliance of Washington, (O—u) 573, 706

Bressman Law, (O—u) 581

Brian Morden Foundation, (O—u) 582

Brookhaven National Laboratory, (A—g) 176

Bryon Riesch Paralysis Foundation, (P—u) 481, (P—g) 535, (O—u) 583, (O—g) 820, (F—u) 912, (F—g) 1146

Buckfire & Buckfire, P.C., (A—u) 17

A—Any Disability　　　V—Visual　　　H—Hearing　　　P—Physical/Orthopedic　　　O—Other Disabilities　　　F—Families
u—undergraduates　　　　　　　　g—graduate students

C

California Association for Postsecondary Education and Disability, (A—u) 4, 9, 14, 20-21, 107, (A—g) 131, 138, 150, 155-156, 237, (O—u) 595, 610, 783, (O—g) 825, 830, 879

California Council of the Blind, (V—u) 267, (V—g) 381

California Department of Veterans Affairs, (F—u) 913-915

California State University. CSU Foundation, (V—u) 272, (V—g) 385

California Student Aid Commission, (F—u) 916

California-Hawaii Elks Association, (A—u) 19

Cancer for College, (O—u) 585-587, 605, 702, 765, (O—g) 821-823, 827, 858, 870

Cancer Pathways, (O—u) 589, (F—u) 917

Cancer Survivors' Fund, (O—u) 588

Candice's Sickle Cell Anemia Fund, Inc., (O—u) 590

Carlton Fields Jorden Burt, (A—g) 247

The Center for Reintegration, Inc., (O—u) 568, (O—g) 815

Central Florida Foundation, (V—u) 276, (H—u) 446, (P—u) 491

Central Indiana Community Foundation, (F—u) 903

CFA Institute, (A—u) 24, (F—u) 918

Chalik & Chalik Law Offices, (O—u) 593, (O—g) 824

The Charity League, Inc., (H—u) 456, (O—u) 804

Chicago Injury Center, (A—u) 25, (A—g) 157

Chicago Lighthouse for People Who Are Blind or Visually Impaired, (V—u) 271, (V—g) 383

Children of Deaf Adults Inc., (F—u) 1058, (F—g) 1184

Children of Fallen Soldiers Relief Fund, (F—u) 921

Children of Injured Workers, Inc., (F—u) 922

Children's Brittle Bone Foundation, (P—u) 485, (P—g) 536

Children's Cancer Fund of New Mexico, (O—u) 629

Children's Hemiplegia and Stroke Association, (P—u) 484

Cleveland Foundation, (H—u) 448, (F—u) 984

CMMS Deshae Lott Ministries Inc., (V—g) 384, (H—g) 461, (P—g) 537

Cochlear Americas, (H—u) 442, 447

Colburn-Keenan Foundation, Inc., (O—u) 571

Colgate-Palmolive Company, (A—u) 104

College Planning Network, (F—u) 1005

Colorado Commission on Higher Education, (F—u) 924

Communities Foundation of Texas, (P—u) 504, (P—g) 546

Community Foundation of Central Illinois, (O—u) 575, 597

Community Foundation of Middle Tennessee, (P—u) 500, 524

Community Foundation of Sarasota County, (A—g) 231

Community Foundation of the Ozarks, (O—u) 609

Community Foundation of Utah, (F—u) 1114

Comprehensive Bleeding Disorders Center, (O—u) 597

Computing Research Association, (A—u) 28, 36

Cooley LLP, (A—g) 159

Cooley's Anemia Foundation, Inc., (O—g) 826

Council of Citizens with Low Vision International, (V—u) 287, (V—g) 393

CURE Media Group, (O—u) 601

CVS Caremark, (O—u) 625, (O—g) 836

Cycle World Joseph C. Parkhurst Education Fund, (O—u) 750

Cystic Fibrosis Scholarship Foundation, (O—u) 592, 674

Cystinosis Foundation, (O—u) 604

D

Dayton Area Graduate Studies Institute, (A—g) 133

Delaware Community Foundation, (O—u) 557

Delta Gamma Foundation, (V—u) 274, (V—g) 386

DeLuca, Ricciuti & Konieczka, (O—u) 606, (O—g) 828

Department of Justice, (F—u) 1101

Design Automation Conference, (A—u) 92

Dexter G. Johnson Educational and Benevolent Trust, (A—u) 32

Diabetes, Incorporated, (O—u) 607, (F—u) 929

Diabetes Scholars Foundation, (O—u) 579, 594, 635, 668-669, 687, 705, 744, 798

Dialysis Scholarship Foundation, Inc., (O—u) 608, (O—g) 829

Disabled American Veterans Auxiliary, (F—u) 930, (F—g) 1147

Disabled American Veterans. Department of New Jersey, (F—u) 919

Disabled Person, Inc., (A—u) 34, (A—g) 163

DKF Veterans Assistance Foundation, (F—u) 931

Donna T. Darrien Memorial Foundation for Sickle Cell, Inc., (O—u) 612, (F—u) 932

Dow Chemical Company, (A—u) 103

Dr. Richard Grossman Community Foundation, (O—u) 554

Dr. Scholl Foundation, (P—u) 482

Dramatists Guild, Inc., (A—u) 54, (A—g) 189

Dravet Syndrome Foundation, (A—g) 140

The DREAM Institute, (P—u) 523, (O—u) 790

E

Easter Seals South Carolina, (P—u) 490, (P—g) 540

Eastern Amputee Golf Association, (P—u) 489, (F—u) 936

Elaine Chapin Fund, (P—u) 492, (F—u) 939

Elizabeth Lulu Scholarship Foundation, (O—u) 621

Elizabeth Nash Foundation, (O—u) 622, (O—g) 834

Elks National Foundation, (F—u) 940

Elliott G. Heard Jr. Memorial Scholarship Committee, (P—g) 541

Epilepsy Foundation New England, (O—u) 623, 721, (O—g) 835

Epilepsy Foundation of Greater Chicago, (O—u) 570, 676, (O—g) 817

Epilepsy Foundation of Kentuckiana, (O—u) 751, 774

Epilepsy Foundation of Michigan, (O—u) 602

A—Any Disability   V—Visual   H—Hearing   P—Physical/Orthopedic   O—Other Disabilities   F—Families
u—undergraduates   g—graduate students

Epilepsy Foundation of Minnesota, (O—u) 620
Epilepsy Foundation of New Jersey, (O—u) 624
Epsilon Sigma Alpha International, (O—u) 576
Eric Marder Scholarship Fund, (O—u) 627
Ernst Law Group, (F—u) 943
Essex County Bar Association, (A—g) 151
Exelon Corporation, (A—u) 39
Expect Miracles Foundation, (O—u) 631

F
Factor Support Network Pharmacy, (O—u) 730-731, 763, (F—u) 1057, 1110
Faegre Baker Daniels, (A—g) 169
The Feldman Law Firm, PLLC, (A—u) 115, (O—u) 791
Finnegan, Henderson, Farabow, Garrett & Dunner, LLP, (A—g) 170
First Cavalry Division Association, (F—u) 945
First Marine Division Association, (F—u) 946
Fish & Richardson P.C., (A—g) 171
Fisher House Foundation, (F—u) 970
Fit Small Business, (A—u) 18, (A—g) 154
Fleetwood Memorial Foundation, (A—u) 41, (F—u) 947
Flicker of Hope Foundation, (O—u) 632
Florida Cleft Palate-Craniofacial Association, Inc., (P—u) 494
Florida Council of Citizens with Low Vision, (V—u) 283
Florida Council of the Blind, (V—u) 290, 358, 361
Florida Department of Education, (F—u) 948
Foundation for Science and Disability, Inc., (A—g) 234
Freedom Alliance, (F—u) 950
Friedl Richardson Trial Lawyers, (A—u) 35
Friends in Art, (V—u) 288
Friends of 440 Scholarship Fund, Inc., (F—u) 951
Friends of Scott Foundation, (O—u) 773, (O—g) 875

G
Gallaudet University Alumni Association, (H—g) 458, 460, 462-463, 465, 469
GEICO Insurance, (A—u) 26, (F—u) 920
Gemm Learning, (O—u) 636
Geological Society of America, (A—g) 174
George Bartol Memorial Scholarship Fund, (F—u) 955
Georgia Council of the Blind, (V—u) 252, (V—g) 372, (F—u) 895, (F—g) 1139
Georgia District Civitan Foundation, Inc., (P—u) 479
Georgia Firefighters Burn Foundation, (O—u) 683
Georgia Student Finance Commission, (F—u) 957-958
Georgia Transplant Foundation, (O—u) 598, 603, 638, 714, 723, 728, 794, (F—u) 925-926, 935, 956, 963, 1046, 1054
Gift of Life Donor Program, (O—u) 673, (F—u) 927
Global Foundation for First Responders, (F—u) 959
Golden Corral Corporation, (P—u) 495, (F—u) 960

Google Inc., (A—u) 43-44, (A—g) 175
Governor's Coalition for Youth with Disabilities, (A—u) 45
Great Lakes Hemophilia Foundation, (O—u) 640, 663, (F—u) 961, 986
Greater Houston Community Foundation, (O—u) 678, (O—g) 849
Greater Kanawha Valley Foundation, (F—u) 1035
Greater Kansas City Community Foundation, (F—u) 896
Green Beret Foundation, (F—u) 962

H
Hansen Injury Law Firm, (P—u) 496
Harry Gregg Foundation, (A—u) 46
Harter Secrest & Emery LLP, (A—g) 181
Hawaii Association of the Blind, (V—u) 293
Hawaii Children's Cancer Foundation, (O—u) 633
Hawai'i Community Foundation, (A—u) 116, (F—u) 1125
Hawkins Spizman Kilgo, LLC, (O—u) 644, (O—g) 839, (F—u) 965, (F—g) 1152
Healin' Wheels LLC, (F—u) 952
Heather Burns Memorial Scholarship Fund, (O—u) 645
Hemophilia Association of New Jersey, (O—u) 646, (O—g) 840
Hemophilia Association of the Capital Area, (O—u) 637, (O—g) 837, (F—u) 954, (F—g) 1150
Hemophilia Federation of America, (O—u) 647-648, (O—g) 841, (F—u) 967
Hemophilia Foundation of Greater Florida, (O—u) 584
Hemophilia Foundation of Maryland, (O—u) 615, (F—u) 933
Hemophilia Foundation of Michigan, (O—u) 649, (F—u) 968
Hemophilia Foundation of Minnesota/Dakotas, (O—u) 650
Hemophilia of Georgia, (O—u) 684, (F—u) 997
Hemophilia of Indiana, (O—u) 651, (O—g) 842
Hemophilia of Iowa, Inc., (O—u) 652, (F—u) 969
Hemophilia of North Carolina, (O—u) 574, (F—u) 908
Hemophilia of South Carolina, (O—u) 653, (F—u) 972
Hermann Law Group, (P—g) 539, (O—g) 831
HF Healthcare, (O—u) 733, (F—u) 1068
Hoehl Family Foundation, (F—u) 1088
Homecare for the Cure, (O—u) 718, (F—u) 1048
Hope for the Warriors, (F—u) 971, (F—g) 1153
Horatio Alger Association of Distinguished Americans, Inc., (A—u) 48-49
Hydrocephalus Association, (O—u) 656, 786, (O—g) 843, 881

I
Idaho State Board of Education, (F—u) 974
Illinois Council for Exceptional Children, (O—u) 657
Illinois Council of the Blind, (V—u) 286, (V—g) 392

Illinois Department of Veterans' Affairs, (F—u) 975, 978

Illinois Federation of Teachers, (V—u) 268, (H—u) 444, (P—u) 483, (O—u) 591

Illinois Spina Bifida Association, (P—u) 498, 529, (P—g) 543

Illinois Student Assistance Commission, (F—u) 976-977, (F—g) 1154

Immune Deficiency Foundation, (O—u) 801, (O—g) 884

Incight Education, (A—u) 50, (A—g) 186

Indiana Breast Cancer Awareness Trust, Inc., (F—u) 1067

Indiana Commission for Higher Education, (F—u) 979-980, (F—g) 1155-1156

Indiana Donor Network, (O—u) 659, (F—u) 982

Indiana Donor Network, Inc., (O—u) 658, (F—u) 981

International Alumnae of Delta Epsilon Sorority, (H—g) 467

International Dyslexia Association. Southwest Branch, (O—u) 710, 785, (O—g) 880

International Transplant Nurses Society. Georgia Chapter, (O—u) 638, (F—u) 956

Iowa Braille School, (V—u) 313

Iowa Department of Veterans Affairs, (A—u) 51

Iowa Educational Services for the Blind and Visually Impaired, (V—u) 313

Irell & Manella LLP), (A—g) 187

Italian Catholic Federation, (V—u) 356, (H—u) 453, (P—u) 517, (O—u) 778

Izzie's Gifts of Hope Foundation, (O—u) 660, (F—u) 983

J

Jackie Spellman Scholarship Foundation, (O—u) 662, (O—g) 844, (F—u) 985, (F—g) 1157

Jason Ackerman Foundation, (O—u) 667

Jay Kaplan Retirement Education Fund, Inc., (A—u) 52

JC Runyon Foundation, (O—u) 670

John A. Coccomo, Sr. Foundation, (V—u) 320, 338, (V—g) 412

John F. Kennedy Center for the Performing Arts. American College Theater Festival, (A—u) 54, (A—g) 189

John F. Kennedy Center for the Performing Arts. Department of VSA and Accessibility, (A—u) 121-122, (A—g) 245-246

John Foy & Associates, (O—u) 680, (O—g) 851, (F—u) 996, (F—g) 1165

Joshua Gomes Memorial Scholarship Fund, (O—u) 688, (O—g) 853

Just Health Shops, (P—u) 503, (P—g) 545, (O—u) 689, (O—g) 854

K

Kaiser Permanente, (A—u) 57, (A—g) 193, 223

Kaiser Permanente Northwest, (A—u) 58

Kansas Association for the Blind and Visually Impaired, (V—u) 280

Kansas Masonic Foundation, Inc., (A—u) 30, (A—g) 160

Katz & Phillips, P.A., (O—u) 692, (O—g) 813, (F—u) 1001

Keker, Van Nest & Peters LLP, (A—g) 195

Kelly Law Team, (A—u) 60, (O—u) 693-694

Kelly Lynn Lutz Memorial Foundation, (F—u) 1002

Kelsey B. Diamantis TS Scholarship Family Foundation, Inc., (O—u) 611, (O—g) 832

Kentucky Community and Technical College System, (F—u) 1003

Kentucky Department of Veterans Affairs, (P—u) 526, (F—u) 1004

Kidney Transplant/Dialysis Association, Inc., (O—u) 697, (F—u) 1006

Kidney & Urology Foundation of America, (O—u) 737, 803

Kids' Chance Inc. of Illinois, (F—u) 1012

Kids' Chance Inc. of Missouri, (F—u) 1019, (F—g) 1168

Kids' Chance of Arizona, (F—u) 1007

Kids' Chance of Arkansas, Inc., (F—u) 1008

Kids' Chance of California, Inc., (F—u) 1009

Kids' Chance of Florida, (F—u) 1010

Kids' Chance of Georgia, Inc., (F—u) 1011

Kids' Chance of Indiana, Inc., (F—u) 1013, (F—g) 1167

Kids' Chance of Kentucky, (F—u) 1014

Kids' Chance of Louisiana, (F—u) 1015

Kids' Chance of Maryland, Inc., (F—u) 1016

Kids' Chance of Michigan, (F—u) 1017

Kids' Chance of Nebraska, (F—u) 1020, (F—g) 1169

Kids' Chance of New Jersey, (F—u) 1021

Kids' Chance of New York, (F—u) 1022, (F—g) 1170

Kids' Chance of North Carolina, Inc., (F—u) 1023

Kids' Chance of Ohio, (F—u) 1024, (F—g) 1171

Kids' Chance of Oklahoma, Inc., (F—u) 1025, (F—g) 1172

Kids' Chance of Oregon, (F—u) 1026, (F—g) 1173

Kids' Chance of Pennsylvania, (F—u) 1027

Kids' Chance of South Carolina, (F—u) 1028, (F—g) 1174

Kids' Chance of South Dakota, (F—u) 1029, (F—g) 1175

Kids' Chance of Tennessee, (F—u) 1030

Kids' Chance of Texas, (F—u) 1031

Kids' Chance of Vermont, (F—u) 1032

Kids' Chance of Virginia, (F—u) 1033

Kids' Chance of Washington, (F—u) 1034

Kids' Chance of West Virginia, Inc., (F—u) 1035

Kids' Chance of Wisconsin, (F—u) 1036

Kim and Harold Louie Family Foundation, (A—u) 61

King & Spalding, LLP, (A—g) 196

K&L Gates LLP, (A—g) 197

Knapp & Roberts, (F—u) 1113, (F—g) 1192

Knights of Columbus, (F—u) 1050

L

Lavelle Fund for the Blind, Inc., (V—u) 265, (V—g) 380

Law Office of Renkin & Associates, (O—g) 859, (F—g) 1177

A—Any Disability   V—Visual   H—Hearing   P—Physical/Orthopedic   O—Other Disabilities   F—Families
u—undergraduates   g—graduate students

Law School Admission Council, (A—g) 249

Learning Ally, (V—u) 310, (V—g) 409, (O—u) 717

Learning Disabilities Association of Arkansas, (O—u) 755

Learning Disabilities Association of Iowa, (O—u) 701

Learning Disabilities Association of North Carolina, (O—u) 716

Learning & Education About Disabilities, (O—u) 614

Lep Foundation for Youth Education, (P—u) 501, (O—u) 601, 682

LGS Foundation, (A—g) 140

Lighthouse Guild, (V—u) 307, (V—g) 405

Lilly USA, LLC, (O—u) 705

The Limb Preservation Foundation, (P—u) 493, (P—g) 542

Lime Connect, Inc., (A—u) 16, 44, (A—g) 152, 175

Lions of Michigan, (V—u) 365

Lisa Higgins Hussman Foundation, (O—u) 707

Little People of America, Inc., (P—u) 506, (P—g) 547, (F—u) 1041, (F—g) 1179

Living Breath Foundation, (O—u) 709, (O—g) 861

Loreen Arbus Foundation, (A—u) 63, (A—g) 199

Los Angeles DUI Attorney, (O—u) 711, (O—g) 862

Louise Tumarkin Zazove Foundation, (H—u) 449

Louisiana Bar Foundation, (F—u) 1015

Louisiana Department of Veterans Affairs, (F—u) 1042

Louisiana Hemophilia Foundation, (O—u) 654-655, 703, (F—u) 973

Lt. Jon C. Ladda Memorial Foundation, (F—u) 1043

Lucent Technologies, (A—u) 55, (A—g) 190

M

Maho & Prentice, LLP, (P—u) 507

Maine. Bureau of Veterans' Services, (F—u) 1045, (F—g) 1180

Maine Community Foundation, (F—u) 998

Maine Employers' Mutual Insurance Company, (F—u) 964, (F—g) 1151

Marc Whitehead & Associates, Attorneys at Law, LLP, (A—u) 42

Marcena Lozano Donate Life Scholarship Fund Committee, (O—u) 715

Marine Corps League, (A—u) 64

Maryland Higher Education Commission, (A—u) 38, 53, 65, (A—g) 168, 188, (F—u) 938, 991, (F—g) 1148, 1162

Massachusetts Office of Student Financial Assistance, (A—u) 27, 66, (V—u) 311

Mathematica Policy Research, Inc., (A—g) 201

Matrix Health Group, (O—u) 677, 718, 730-731, 763, 796, (F—u) 1048, 1057, 1110

Mays Mission for the Handicapped, Inc., (A—u) 67

McGuireWoods LLP, (A—g) 202

McKesson, (A—g) 224

MedProRx, Inc., (O—u) 619

Mesothelioma Cancer Alliance, (O—u) 724, (O—g) 864, (F—u) 1052, (F—g) 1183

Metropolitan Seattle Sickle Cell Task Force, (O—u) 639

Michael Bendix Sutton Foundation, (O—u) 727

Michigan Council for Exceptional Children, (O—u) 722

Michigan Department of Licensing and Regulatory Affairs, (V—g) 430

Michigan Department of Treasury, (F—u) 1055

Michigan Elks Association, (A—u) 68

Microsoft disAbility Employee Resource Group, (A—u) 69

Minnesota Department of Veterans Affairs, (F—u) 1059, (F—g) 1185

Minnesota Hockey, (A—u) 70

Minnesota Social Service Association, (A—u) 71

Mississippi Bar Foundation, (F—u) 1018

Mississippi Council of the Blind, (V—u) 295, (V—g) 397, (F—u) 989, (F—g) 1160

Mississippi Office of Student Financial Aid, (F—u) 1060

Missouri Council of the Blind, (V—u) 315, (V—g) 410

Missouri Department of Higher Education, (A—u) 72, (F—u) 1061-1063

Missouri Department of Social Services, (V—u) 316

Mobility Scooters Direct.com, (A—u) 73, (A—g) 205

Montana Association for the Blind, (V—u) 278, (V—g) 387

Montana Police Protective Association, (F—u) 1065

N

National Amputee Golf Association, (P—u) 510, (F—u) 1066

National Black Coalition of Federal Aviation Employees, (A—u) 79

National Center for Atmospheric Research, (A—g) 146

National Center for Learning Disabilities, (O—u) 558, 562

National Children's Cancer Society, (O—u) 572

National Collegiate Cancer Foundation, (O—u) 735, (O—g) 865, (F—u) 1069, (F—g) 1186

National Commission on Certification of Physician Assistants, (A—u) 81, (A—g) 211

National Down Syndrome Society, (O—u) 747

National Federation of Music Clubs, (A—u) 56

National Federation of the Blind, (V—u) 251, 270, 281, 303, 306, 309, 336, 343-344, 346, (V—g) 371, 382, 388, 401, 404, 407, 419, 423-424, 426

National Federation of the Blind of California, (V—u) 318, (V—g) 411

National Federation of the Blind of Colorado, (V—u) 319

National Federation of the Blind of Connecticut, (V—u) 320, 338, (V—g) 412

National Federation of the Blind of Idaho, (V—u) 321

National Federation of the Blind of Illinois, (V—u) 322, (V—g) 413

National Federation of the Blind of Kansas, (V—u) 304, (V—g) 402

National Federation of the Blind of Kentucky, (V−u) 262, 269, 277, 323

National Federation of the Blind of Louisiana, (V−u) 324

National Federation of the Blind of Maryland, (V−u) 300

National Federation of the Blind of Massachusetts, (V−u) 325, (V−g) 414

National Federation of the Blind of Minnesota, (V−u) 326

National Federation of the Blind of Mississippi, (V−u) 327

National Federation of the Blind of Nebraska, (V−u) 328

National Federation of the Blind of New Hampshire, (V−u) 284, (V−g) 390

National Federation of the Blind of New Jersey, (V−u) 329, (V−g) 415

National Federation of the Blind of New York State, Inc., (V−u) 330, (V−g) 416

National Federation of the Blind of North Carolina, (V−u) 350, (V−g) 428

National Federation of the Blind of Ohio, (V−u) 298, 331, (V−g) 398, 417

National Federation of the Blind of Oregon, (V−u) 332, (V−g) 418

National Federation of the Blind of Pennsylvania, (V−u) 333

National Federation of the Blind of South Carolina, (V−u) 334

National Federation of the Blind of Texas, (V−u) 335

National Federation of the Blind of Virginia, (V−u) 296

National Federation of the Blind of Washington, (V−u) 263, 294, (V−g) 379, 395

National Federation of the Blind of West Virginia, (V−u) 253, (V−g) 373

National FFA Organization, (P−u) 482

National Hemophilia Foundation, (O−u) 613, 686, 696, (O−g) 833, 856

National Hemophilia Foundation. Colorado Chapter, (O−u) 596, (F−u) 923

National Hemophilia Foundation. Nebraska Chapter, (O−u) 736, (F−u) 1073

National Hemophilia Foundation. Nevada Chapter, (O−u) 740

National Industries for the Blind, (V−u) 301, (V−g) 400

National Kidney Foundation of Arizona, (O−u) 753

National Kidney Foundation of Indiana, Inc., (O−u) 700

National Kidney Foundation of Michigan, Inc., (O−u) 720

National Kidney Foundation of Utah and Idaho, (O−u) 734

National Kidney Foundation Serving Western Missouri, Kansas and Oklahoma, (O−u) 600

National Law Enforcement and Firefighters Children's Foundation, (F−u) 959, 1070, 1129-1130

National Multiple Sclerosis Society, (P−u) 511, (F−u) 1071

National Multiple Sclerosis Society. Central North Carolina Chapter, (P−u) 495, (F−u) 960

National Multiple Sclerosis Society. Gateway Area Chapter, (P−u) 492, (F−u) 939

National Multiple Sclerosis Society. Greater Carolinas Chapter, (P−u) 495, (F−u) 960

National Multiple Sclerosis Society. Mid America Chapter, (P−u) 509, (F−u) 1056

National Multiple Sclerosis Society. Upper Midwest Chapter, (P−u) 502, (F−u) 999

National Organization for Albinism and Hypopigmentation, (V−u) 314

National PKU News, (O−u) 642

National Press Club, (A−u) 76

National Rifle Association of America, (F−u) 992

National Science Foundation, (A−u) 15, 28, 36, (A−g) 146

National Science Foundation. Directorate for Biological Sciences, (A−g) 217

National Science Foundation. Directorate for Computer and Information Science and Engineering, (A−g) 179

National Science Foundation. Directorate for Education and Human Resources, (A−g) 178

National Science Foundation. Directorate for Engineering, (A−g) 179

National Science Foundation. Directorate for Social, Behavioral, and Economic Sciences, (A−g) 173, 198

National Trust for Historic Preservation, (A−g) 204

Navy Seal Foundation, (A−u) 78, (A−g) 209

NBCUniversal, (A−u) 80, (A−g) 210

Nebraska Association of Blind Students, (V−u) 328

Nebraska. Department of Veterans' Affairs, (F−u) 1074

New Jersey Bankers Association, (F−u) 1075

New Jersey Center for Tourette Syndrome, Inc., (O−u) 742

New Jersey Commission for the Blind and Visually Impaired, (V−u) 337, (V−g) 420

New Jersey Council for Exceptional Children, (O−u) 741

New Jersey ME/CFS Association, Inc., (O−u) 738

New Jersey Sharing Network Foundation, (O−u) 739, (F−u) 1076

New Jersey State Elks, (A−u) 83

New Jersey Utilities Association, (A−u) 86

New Outlook Pioneers, (A−u) 55, (A−g) 190

New York American Legion Press Association, (F−u) 894

The New York Bar Foundation, (A−g) 241

New York Schools Insurance Reciprocal, (O−u) 599

New York State Bar Association. Elder Law and Special Needs Section, (A−g) 241

New York State Grange, (H−u) 445

New York State Higher Education Services Corporation, (A−u) 84-85, (F−u) 1077-1078

Nikko Cosmetic Surgery Center, (O−u) 564

No Angel Left Behind, (F−u) 1079

No Greater Sacrifice, (F−u) 962, 1080

North Carolina Bar Association, (F−u) 1081, (F−g) 1187

North Carolina Council of the Blind, (V−u) 341

North Carolina Department of Military and Veterans Affairs, (F—u) 1083

North Carolina Lions, Inc., (F—u) 1082

North Carolina Sheriffs' Association, (F—u) 1072

North Carolina Troopers Association, (F—u) 1084

North Dakota Association of the Blind, (V—u) 279, 342, (V—g) 422

North Dakota. Department of Veterans Affairs, (F—u) 1085

North Dakota University System, (F—u) 949

Novo Nordisk Inc., (O—u) 743-745

Nuance Communications, (A—u) 7, (A—g) 136

NuFACTOR Specialty Pharmacy, (O—u) 626, (F—u) 941

O

Ocean State Center for Independent Living, (A—u) 23

October, (A—u) 101

Ohio Board of Regents, (A—g) 133

Ohio Department of Higher Education, (F—u) 1087

Oklahoma City Community Foundation, (A—u) 87, (O—u) 761, (F—u) 1109

Oklahoma Goodwill Industries, (A—u) 87

The Oley Foundation, (O—u) 698, (O—g) 857

Optimist International, (H—u) 450

Oracle Corporation, (A—u) 105, (V—u) 343-344, (V—g) 423-424

Orange County Community Foundation, (O—u) 726, (F—u) 1053

Oregon Community Foundation, (V—u) 292, (V—g) 394

Oregon Department of Consumer and Business Services. Occupational Safety and Health Division, (F—u) 1092, (F—g) 1189

Oregon Office of Student Access and Completion, (V—u) 353

Oregon State Bar, (A—g) 213

Oregon Student Access Commission, (V—u) 292, (V—g) 394, (F—u) 1089, 1092-1093, (F—g) 1188-1189

Organization for Autism Research, (O—u) 707, 772

The Orion Fund, (O—u) 792, (O—g) 882

Osteogenesis Imperfecta Foundation, (P—u) 485, (P—g) 536

Oticon, Inc., (H—u) 452

Otto Sussman Trust, (A—u) 88, (A—g) 214

Our Brother's Keeper Foundation, (F—u) 1094

Outdoor Advertising Association of America, (P—u) 482

P

P. Buckley Moss Foundation for Children's Education, (O—u) 748

P. Buckley Moss Society, (O—u) 561

Package of Prevention, (F—u) 907

Paralyzed Veterans of America, (P—u) 512, (F—u) 1102

Park City Community Foundation, (O—u) 685

Patient Advocate Foundation, (O—u) 749

Pauahi Foundation, (A—u) 59, 117, (A—g) 194, 243

PCDH19 Alliance, (A—g) 140

Peace Officers Research Association of California, (A—u) 93

Pediatric Brain Tumor Foundation. Georgia Chapter, (O—u) 699

Pediatric Brain Tumor Foundation of the United States, (O—u) 634, 750

Pennsylvania Association of Medical Suppliers, (A—u) 91

Pennsylvania Cystic Fibrosis Inc., (O—u) 732

Pennsylvania Department of Military and Veterans Affairs, (F—u) 937

Pennsylvania Higher Education Assistance Agency, (F—u) 1027

Pennsylvania National Guard Associations, (F—u) 1096

The Perecman Firm, P.L.L.C., (O—u) 567, (O—g) 814, (F—u) 904, (F—g) 1142

Perkins Coie LLP, (A—g) 216

Pfizer Inc., (O—u) 777, (O—g) 877

Pink Bandana, (O—u) 754, (F—u) 1098

PinkRose Foundation, Inc., (F—u) 1099

Pinnacol Foundation, (F—u) 1100

Pittsburgh Foundation, (V—u) 308, (V—g) 406

PKU Organization of Illinois, (O—u) 560

Pride Foundation, (P—u) 488, (O—u) 661, 809

Producers Choice Network, (O—u) 781

Professional Convention Management Association, (A—u) 90

Proskauer Rose LLP, (A—g) 219

R

Ramsey County Bar Foundation, (A—g) 221

Reed Smith LLP, (A—g) 161, 222-224

Rehabmart, LLC, (A—u) 96

Rhode Island Foundation, (F—u) 905

Richard Linn American Inn of Court, (A—g) 200

Ride for Life, Inc., (F—u) 1106

Rise Scholarship Foundation, Inc., (O—u) 758

RJT Criminal Defense Attorney, (A—u) 97, (O—u) 759, 771

Robert Wood Johnson Foundation, (A—g) 183

Rocky Mountain Hemophilia and Bleeding Disorder Association, (O—u) 760, (F—u) 1107

Ross N. and Patricia Pangere Foundation, (V—u) 351, (V—g) 429

Roy J. Carver Charitable Trust, (A—u) 22

Ruby's Rainbow, (O—u) 766

Runway of Dreams Foundation, (A—u) 99

S

The SAMFund for Young Adult Survivors of Cancer, (O—g) 872

San Antonio Area Foundation, (F—u) 1105

Sangre de Oro, Inc., (O—u) 665

Sara Elizabeth Stubblefield Foundation, (O—u) 768

Sarasota County Bar Association, (A—g) 231

Sault Tribe of Chippewa Indians, (A—u) 100, (A—g) 232

Scholarship America, (A—u) 24, 40, 124, (P—u) 522, (O—u) 556, 617-618, 625, 690, (O—g) 811, 836, 855, (F—u) 918, 944, 952, 1120

Scholarship Managers Inc., (O—u) 745

Schwabe, Williamson & Wyatt, Attorneys at Law, (A—g) 233

Seattle Foundation, (A—u) 69

The See the Future Fund, (V—u) 260, 354, (V—g) 378, 432

Sertoma International, (H—u) 452

SFM Foundation, (F—u) 1115

Shire US Inc., (O—u) 729, 775

Sickle Cell Disease Association of America, (O—u) 695

Sidley Austin LLP, (A—g) 235

Sidney R. Baer, Jr. Foundation, (O—u) 568, (O—g) 815

Sigma Alpha Iota Philanthropies, Inc., (A—u) 74, (A—g) 206

Silver Cross, (P—u) 515

The Simon Cancer Foundation, (O—u) 643

Snowdrop Foundation, (O—u) 776, (O—g) 876

Society for Neuroscience, (A—u) 82, (A—g) 212

Society of Women Engineers, (A—u) 39, 47

Sonoran Spine Research and Education Foundation, (P—u) 516, (P—g) 551

South Carolina Division of Veterans' Affairs, (F—u) 1116

South Dakota Board of Regents, (A—u) 102, (V—u) 355, (V—g) 433, (F—u) 1103

Southwest Florida Community Foundation, (P—u) 476

Spectrum Scholarship Program, (O—u) 779

Spina Bifida Association of Alabama, (P—u) 518, (P—g) 552

Spina Bifida Association of Connecticut, Inc., (P—u) 519

Spina Bifida Association of Greater New England, (P—u) 499, (P—g) 544

Spina Bifida Association of Illinois, (P—g) 549

Spina Bifida Association of Indiana, (P—u) 505

Spina Bifida Association of North Texas, (P—u) 520

Spina Bifida Coalition of Cincinnati, (P—u) 521

Spina Bifida Wisconsin, Ltd., (P—u) 513, (P—g) 550

SpinLife.com LLC, (P—u) 497

Springboard Foundation, (A—u) 99, 103-105

State University System of Florida, (V—u) 360, (H—u) 455, (P—u) 525, (O—u) 793

Stephen T. Marchello Scholarship Foundation, (O—u) 780

Stephen's Soldiers Foundation, (O—u) 781

Stoel Rives LLP, (A—g) 238

Summit Disability Law Group, (A—u) 109

Supreme Emblem Club of the United States of America, (A—u) 110

SurvivorVision, (O—u) 782, (O—g) 878

Susanna DeLaurentis Charitable Foundation, (O—u) 784

T

Tennessee Hemophilia and Bleeding Disorders Foundation, (O—u) 616, (F—u) 934

Tennessee Student Assistance Corporation, (O—u) 787, (F—u) 928

Terrill Foundation, Inc., (O—u) 788-789

TESS Research Foundation, (A—g) 140

Texas 4-H and Youth Development Program, (A—u) 112

Texas Association for Education and Rehabilitation of the Blind and Visually Impaired, (V—u) 357

Texas Higher Education Coordinating Board, (A—u) 113, (V—u) 359, (V—g) 435, (H—u) 454, (H—g) 470, (F—u) 1118

Texas Mutual Insurance Company, (A—u) 114, (F—u) 1119

Texas Veterans Commission, (F—u) 966

Texas Young Lawyers Association, (A—g) 240

ThanksUSA, (F—u) 1120

Theodore R. and Vivian M. Johnson Foundation, (V—u) 360, (H—u) 455, (P—u) 525, (O—u) 793

Thomas J. Seefred Trust, (O—u) 795

Three Rivers Community Foundation, (F—u) 994

Through the Looking Glass, (F—u) 1122

Transplant Recipients International Organization. Greater Cleveland Chapter, (O—u) 725

Transplant Recipients International Organization, Inc., (O—u) 797, (F—u) 1124

Travelers Protective Association of America, (H—u) 451

TS Alliance, (A—g) 140

U

UCB, Inc., (O—u) 799, (O—g) 883, (F—u) 1126, (F—g) 1195

Ulman Cancer Fund for Young Adults, (O—u) 563, 664, 666, 671, 675, 679, 681, 708, 719, 746, 752, 769, 802, 805, (O—g) 812, 818, 845-848, 850, 852, 860, 863, 866-867, 873, 885-886, (F—u) 900, 906, 987-988, 990, 993, 995, 1040, 1047, 1049, 1097, 1112, 1128, 1132, (F—g) 1141, 1143-1144, 1158-1159, 1161, 1163-1164, 1178, 1181-1182, 1190-1191, 1196, 1198

United Cerebral Palsy Association of Greater Indiana, (O—u) 578

United Church of Christ, (A—g) 180, 242

United Methodist Foundation of Indiana, (A—g) 184, 220

United Methodist Higher Education Foundation, (V—g) 396, (H—g) 466

United Negro College Fund, (A—u) 98

United Parent Support for Down Syndrome, (O—u) 628, 691, (F—u) 942, (F—g) 1149

United States Academic Decathlon, (A—u) 62

United States Military VA Loan, (A—u) 33, (A—g) 162

United States Olympic Committee, (P—u) 527-528

A—Any Disability   V—Visual   H—Hearing   P—Physical/Orthopedic   O—Other Disabilities   F—Families
u—undergraduates   g—graduate students

University Corporation for Atmospheric Research, (A—g) 146

University Interscholastic League, (F—u) 1095

University of Idaho 4-H Youth Development, (O—u) 704, (F—u) 1039

University of Southern California. Athletic Department, (A—u) 111, (A—g) 239

University of Virginia. Blandy Experimental Farm, (A—u) 15

University of Washington. Stroum Center for Jewish Studies, (A—g) 182

U.S. Central Intelligence Agency, (A—g) 158

U.S. Defense Intelligence Agency, (A—u) 31

U.S. Department of Education. Office of Special Education and Rehabilitative Services, (A—u) 106, (A—g) 236, (F—u) 1122

U.S. Department of Veterans Affairs, (A—u) 120, (A—g) 244, (F—u) 1117, (F—g) 1193

U.S. Food and Drug Administration, (A—g) 179

U.S. National Aeronautics and Space Administration, (A—u) 77, (A—g) 207-208

U.S. National Institutes of Health, (A—g) 227-230

U.S. National Institutes of Health. National Institute of Mental Health, (A—g) 203

U.S. National Institutes of Health. National Institute of Neurological Disorders and Stroke, (A—u) 82, (A—g) 212

U.S. National Institutes of Health. National Institute of Nursing Research, (A—g) 226

U.S. National Institutes of Health. National Institute on Aging, (A—g) 134

U.S. National Institutes of Health. National Institute on Drug Abuse, (A—g) 167

U.S. National Institutes of Health. Office of Intramural Training and Education, (A—u) 75

USAA Insurance Corporation, (F—u) 1096

Utah Council of the Blind, (V—u) 347, (V—g) 427

Utah Elks Association, (A—u) 118

Utah Hemophilia Foundation, (O—u) 800, (F—u) 1127

V

Ventura County Community Foundation, (F—u) 1051

Vermont Student Assistance Corporation, (A—u) 52, 95, 108, (F—u) 1088

Virgin Islands Board of Education, (A—u) 119

Virginia Department of Veterans Services, (F—u) 1131, (F—g) 1197

Virginia Hemophilia Foundation, (O—u) 712, (F—u) 1044

Virginia High School League, (A—u) 8

VisionCorps Foundation, (V—u) 305, 348, 362, (V—g) 403, 434, 436

Visual Aid Volunteers of Florida, (V—u) 363

Volkswagen Group of America, (A—u) 121, (A—g) 245

VSA arts, (A—u) 54, (A—g) 189

W

Walter Reed Society, (A—u) 7, (A—g) 136

Washington Council of the Blind, (V—u) 364, (V—g) 437

Washington National Guard, (F—u) 1133, (F—g) 1199

Washington State Association for Justice, (A—u) 126, (A—g) 164

Washington University. John C. Danforth Center on Religion and Politics, (A—g) 191, (H—g) 468

Wells Fargo Bank, (A—u) 124

Whitfield, Bryson & Mason LLP, (A—u) 123

Williams College. Dean of the Faculty, (A—g) 172

Winston & Strawn LLP, (A—g) 248

Wisconsin Bleeding Disorders Network, (O—u) 806, (F—u) 1134

Wisconsin Council of the Blind and Visually Impaired, (V—u) 368

Wisconsin Department of Veterans Affairs, (F—u) 1135, (F—g) 1200

Wisconsin Higher Educational Aids Board, (A—u) 125, (V—u) 369, (H—u) 457

Wishes for Elliott, (A—g) 140

Workers' Compensation Association of New Mexico, (F—u) 1123

Workforce Safety & Insurance, (A—u) 127, (F—u) 1136

World Team Tennis, Inc., (O—u) 743

Wyoming Council of the Blind, (V—u) 370, (V—g) 440

Y

Ye Notorious Krewe of the Peg Leg Pirate, Inc., (P—u) 530, (P—g) 553, (F—u) 1137, (F—g) 1201

Residency Index

Some programs listed in this book are restricted to residents of a particular state or region. Others are open to applicants wherever they might live. The Residency Index will help you pinpoint programs available only to residents in your area as well as programs that have no residency restrictions at all (these are listed under the term "United States"). To use this index, look up the geographic areas that apply to you (always check the listings under "United States"), jot down the entry numbers listed after the target groups and types of funding that interest you, and use those numbers to find the program descriptions in the directory. To help you in your search, we've provided some "see also" references in the index entries. Remember: the numbers cited here refer to program entry numbers, not to page numbers in the book.

A

Alabama
Visual disabilities: **Undergraduates,** 266
Hearing disabilities: **Undergraduates,** 456
Physical/orthopedic disabilities: **Undergraduates,** 518; **Graduate students,** 552
Other disabilities/disorders: **Undergraduates,** 804
Families of the disabled: **Undergraduates,** 892-893, 1037; **Graduate students,** 1138
See also United States

Alaska
Physical/orthopedic disabilities: **Undergraduates,** 488
Other disabilities/disorders: **Undergraduates,** 809
See also United States

Arizona
Visual disabilities: **Undergraduates,** 257; **Graduate students,** 376
Physical/orthopedic disabilities: **Undergraduates,** 493, 516; **Graduate students,** 542, 551
Other disabilities/disorders: **Undergraduates,** 713, 753
Families of the disabled: **Undergraduates,** 1007
See also United States

Arkansas
Visual disabilities: **Undergraduates,** 258, 264
Other disabilities/disorders: **Undergraduates,** 565, 755
Families of the disabled: **Undergraduates,** 901-902, 1008
See also United States

C

California
Any disability: **Undergraduates,** 4, 9, 14, 19-21, 50, 93, 107; **Graduate students,** 131, 138, 150, 155-156, 186, 237
Visual disabilities: **Undergraduates,** 267, 272, 318; **Graduate students,** 381, 385, 411
Other disabilities/disorders: **Undergraduates,** 587, 595, 610, 773, 783, 808; **Graduate students,** 823, 825, 830, 875, 879, 888
Families of the disabled: **Undergraduates,** 907, 913-916, 931, 1009
See also United States

Campbellsville, Kentucky. *See* Kentucky

Canada
Any disability: **Undergraduates,** 10, 16, 43-44; **Graduate students,** 137, 139, 152, 174-175, 249
Visual disabilities: **Undergraduates,** 314
Hearing disabilities: **Undergraduates,** 443, 450
Physical/orthopedic disabilities: **Undergraduates,** 515
Families of the disabled: **Undergraduates,** 898; **Graduate students,** 1140
See also Foreign countries

Caribbean
Hearing disabilities: **Undergraduates,** 450
See also Foreign countries

Central America
Any disability: **Graduate students,** 174
See also Foreign countries

Charlotte County, Florida
Physical/orthopedic disabilities: **Undergraduates,** 476
See also Florida

Clark County, Indiana
    Other disabilities/disorders: **Undergraduates,** 751, 774
    See also Indiana
Collier County, Florida
    Physical/orthopedic disabilities: **Undergraduates,** 476
    See also Florida
Colorado
    Any disability: **Undergraduates,** 57; **Graduate
        students,** 193
    Visual disabilities: **Undergraduates,** 260, 319, 354;
        Graduate students, 378, 432
    Physical/orthopedic disabilities: **Undergraduates,**
        493; **Graduate students,** 542
    Other disabilities/disorders: **Undergraduates,** 579,
        596, 614, 780
    Families of the disabled: **Undergraduates,** 923-924,
        1100
    See also United States
Columbiana County, Ohio
    Other disabilities/disorders: **Undergraduates,** 795
    See also Ohio
Connecticut
    Any disability: **Undergraduates,** 45
    Visual disabilities: **Undergraduates,** 265, 320, 338;
        Graduate students, 380, 412
    Physical/orthopedic disabilities: **Undergraduates,**
        489, 519
    Other disabilities/disorders: **Undergraduates,** 590
    Families of the disabled: **Undergraduates,** 897, 936,
        959
    See also New England states; United States

D

Delaware
    Any disability: **Undergraduates,** 91
    Physical/orthopedic disabilities: **Undergraduates,** 489
    Other disabilities/disorders: **Undergraduates,** 557,
        566, 673
    Families of the disabled: **Undergraduates,** 927, 936
    See also United States
District of Columbia. *See* Washington, D.C.

E

El Paso, Texas
    Other disabilities/disorders: **Undergraduates,** 710,
        785; **Graduate students,** 880
    See also Texas
Essex County, New Jersey
    Any disability: **Graduate students,** 151
    See also New Jersey

F

Florida
    Visual disabilities: **Undergraduates,** 283, 290, 358,
        360-361, 363
    Hearing disabilities: **Undergraduates,** 455
    Physical/orthopedic disabilities: **Undergraduates,**
        494, 525

    Other disabilities/disorders: **Undergraduates,** 584,
        667, 762, 793
    Families of the disabled: **Undergraduates,** 948, 951,
        1010
    See also United States
Floyd County, Indiana
    Other disabilities/disorders: **Undergraduates,** 751, 774
    See also Indiana
Foreign countries
    Any disability: **Undergraduates,** 16, 24, 44, 63, 69, 92,
        122; **Graduate students,** 140, 142, 152, 161, 175,
        182, 199, 222-225, 246
    Physical/orthopedic disabilities: **Undergraduates,**
        475, 478, 497; **Graduate students,** 532-533
    Other disabilities/disorders: **Undergraduates,** 642
    Families of the disabled: **Undergraduates,** 918, 1050

G

Georgia
    Visual disabilities: **Undergraduates,** 252; **Graduate
        students,** 372
    Physical/orthopedic disabilities: **Undergraduates,** 479
    Other disabilities/disorders: **Undergraduates,** 598,
        603, 638, 683-684, 699, 714, 723, 728, 794
    Families of the disabled: **Undergraduates,** 895, 925-
        926, 935, 956-958, 963, 997, 1011, 1046, 1054;
        Graduate students, 1139
    See also United States
Glades County, Florida
    Physical/orthopedic disabilities: **Undergraduates,** 476
    See also Florida

H

Harrison County, Indiana
    Other disabilities/disorders: **Undergraduates,** 751, 774
    See also Indiana
Hawaii
    Any disability: **Undergraduates,** 19, 116
    Visual disabilities: **Undergraduates,** 293
    Other disabilities/disorders: **Undergraduates,** 633
    Families of the disabled: **Undergraduates,** 1125
    See also United States
Hendry County, Florida
    Physical/orthopedic disabilities: **Undergraduates,** 476
    See also Florida

I

Idaho
    Visual disabilities: **Undergraduates,** 321
    Physical/orthopedic disabilities: **Undergraduates,**
        488, 493; **Graduate students,** 542
    Other disabilities/disorders: **Undergraduates,** 586,
        704, 734, 809; **Graduate students,** 822
    Families of the disabled: **Undergraduates,** 974, 1039
    See also United States
Illinois
    Any disability: **Undergraduates,** 47

Visual disabilities: **Undergraduates,** 268, 271, 286, 322; **Graduate students,** 383, 392, 413
Hearing disabilities: **Undergraduates,** 444
Physical/orthopedic disabilities: **Undergraduates,** 483, 498, 529; **Graduate students,** 543, 549
Other disabilities/disorders: **Undergraduates,** 560, 570, 575, 580, 591, 594, 597, 657, 676, 768; **Graduate students,** 817
Families of the disabled: **Undergraduates,** 911, 975-978, 1012, 1111; **Graduate students,** 1154
See also United States
Imperial County, California
Families of the disabled: **Undergraduates,** 1051
See also California
Indiana
Any disability: **Undergraduates,** 47; **Graduate students,** 184, 220
Visual disabilities: **Undergraduates,** 291
Physical/orthopedic disabilities: **Undergraduates,** 505
Other disabilities/disorders: **Undergraduates,** 578, 651, 658-659, 700; **Graduate students,** 842
Families of the disabled: **Undergraduates,** 903, 979-982, 1013, 1067; **Graduate students,** 1155-1156, 1167
See also United States
Indiana, southeastern
Physical/orthopedic disabilities: **Undergraduates,** 521
See also Indiana
Iowa
Any disability: **Undergraduates,** 22, 51
Visual disabilities: **Undergraduates,** 313
Physical/orthopedic disabilities: **Undergraduates,** 502, 522
Other disabilities/disorders: **Undergraduates,** 652, 701
Families of the disabled: **Undergraduates,** 969, 999, 1051, 1115
See also United States

K

Kansas
Any disability: **Undergraduates,** 30; **Graduate students,** 160
Visual disabilities: **Undergraduates,** 280, 304; **Graduate students,** 402
Physical/orthopedic disabilities: **Undergraduates,** 493, 509; **Graduate students,** 542
Other disabilities/disorders: **Undergraduates,** 600
Families of the disabled: **Undergraduates,** 896, 1002, 1056
See also United States
Kentucky
Visual disabilities: **Undergraduates,** 262, 269, 277, 323
Physical/orthopedic disabilities: **Undergraduates,** 526
Other disabilities/disorders: **Undergraduates,** 751, 774
Families of the disabled: **Undergraduates,** 1003-1004, 1014
See also United States
Kentucky, northern
Physical/orthopedic disabilities: **Undergraduates,** 521

See also Kentucky
Kern County, California
Families of the disabled: **Undergraduates,** 1051
See also California

L

Latin America. *See* Caribbean; Central America; Mexico
Lee County, Florida
Physical/orthopedic disabilities: **Undergraduates,** 476
See also Florida
Long Island, New York
Other disabilities/disorders: **Undergraduates,** 631
See also New York
Los Angeles County, California
Families of the disabled: **Undergraduates,** 1051
See also California
Louisiana
Visual disabilities: **Undergraduates,** 324
Other disabilities/disorders: **Undergraduates,** 654-655, 703
Families of the disabled: **Undergraduates,** 973, 1015, 1042
See also United States

M

Mahoning County, Ohio
Other disabilities/disorders: **Undergraduates,** 795
See also Ohio
Maine
Any disability: **Undergraduates,** 94; **Graduate students,** 218
Physical/orthopedic disabilities: **Undergraduates,** 489
Other disabilities/disorders: **Undergraduates,** 623, 779; **Graduate students,** 835
Families of the disabled: **Undergraduates,** 897, 936, 964, 998, 1045; **Graduate students,** 1151, 1180
See also New England states; United States
Maryland
Any disability: **Undergraduates,** 38, 53, 65; **Graduate students,** 168, 188
Visual disabilities: **Undergraduates,** 300
Physical/orthopedic disabilities: **Undergraduates,** 489, 514
Other disabilities/disorders: **Undergraduates,** 615, 708, 752; **Graduate students,** 818, 860, 867
Families of the disabled: **Undergraduates,** 933, 936, 938, 987, 991, 1016, 1040, 1047, 1097; **Graduate students,** 1144, 1148, 1158, 1162, 1178, 1181, 1190
See also United States
Massachusetts
Any disability: **Undergraduates,** 27, 66
Visual disabilities: **Undergraduates,** 261, 311, 325; **Graduate students,** 414
Physical/orthopedic disabilities: **Undergraduates,** 489
Other disabilities/disorders: **Undergraduates,** 623; **Graduate students,** 835
Families of the disabled: **Undergraduates,** 897, 936
See also New England states; United States

Mexico
    Any disability: **Graduate students,** 174
    See also Foreign countries
Michigan
    Any disability: **Undergraduates,** 47, 68, 100; **Graduate
        students,** 232
    Visual disabilities: **Undergraduates,** 365
    Other disabilities/disorders: **Undergraduates,** 602,
        649, 720, 722, 781
    Families of the disabled: **Undergraduates,** 968, 1017,
        1055
    See also United States
Minnesota
    Any disability: **Undergraduates,** 29, 70
    Visual disabilities: **Undergraduates,** 254, 326;
        Graduate students, 375
    Physical/orthopedic disabilities: **Undergraduates,**
        502, 522
    Other disabilities/disorders: **Undergraduates,** 620, 650
    Families of the disabled: **Undergraduates,** 999, 1059,
        1115; **Graduate students,** 1185
    See also United States
Mississippi
    Visual disabilities: **Undergraduates,** 295, 327;
        Graduate students, 397
    Families of the disabled: **Undergraduates,** 989, 1018,
        1060; **Graduate students,** 1160
    See also United States
Missouri
    Any disability: **Undergraduates,** 72
    Visual disabilities: **Undergraduates,** 315-316;
        Graduate students, 410
    Other disabilities/disorders: **Undergraduates,** 609
    Families of the disabled: **Undergraduates,** 896, 1002,
        1019, 1061-1063; **Graduate students,** 1168
    See also United States
Missouri, western
    Physical/orthopedic disabilities: **Undergraduates,** 509
    Other disabilities/disorders: **Undergraduates,** 600
    Families of the disabled: **Undergraduates,** 1056
    See also Missouri
Montana
    Visual disabilities: **Undergraduates,** 278; **Graduate
        students,** 387
    Physical/orthopedic disabilities: **Undergraduates,**
        488, 493; **Graduate students,** 542
    Other disabilities/disorders: **Undergraduates,** 586,
        760, 780, 809; **Graduate students,** 822
    Families of the disabled: **Undergraduates,** 1065, 1107
    See also United States
Montgomery County, Maryland
    Other disabilities/disorders: **Undergraduates,** 637;
        Graduate students, 837
    Families of the disabled: **Undergraduates,** 954;
        Graduate students, 1150
    See also Maryland

N
Nebraska
    Visual disabilities: **Undergraduates,** 328
    Physical/orthopedic disabilities: **Undergraduates,**
        493, 509; **Graduate students,** 542
    Other disabilities/disorders: **Undergraduates,** 736, 754
    Families of the disabled: **Undergraduates,** 1020, 1056,
        1073-1074, 1098; **Graduate students,** 1169
    See also United States
Nevada
    Any disability: **Undergraduates,** 93
    Other disabilities/disorders: **Undergraduates,** 740
    See also United States
New England states
    Physical/orthopedic disabilities: **Undergraduates,**
        499; **Graduate students,** 544
    Other disabilities/disorders: **Undergraduates,** 631, 697
    Families of the disabled: **Undergraduates,** 1006
    See also United States
New Hampshire
    Any disability: **Undergraduates,** 46
    Visual disabilities: **Undergraduates,** 284; **Graduate
        students,** 390
    Physical/orthopedic disabilities: **Undergraduates,** 489
    Other disabilities/disorders: **Undergraduates,** 623;
        Graduate students, 835
    Families of the disabled: **Undergraduates,** 897, 936
    See also New England states; United States
New Jersey
    Any disability: **Undergraduates,** 83, 86, 88; **Graduate
        students,** 151, 214
    Visual disabilities: **Undergraduates,** 265, 329, 337;
        Graduate students, 380, 415, 420
    Physical/orthopedic disabilities: **Undergraduates,**
        489, 501
    Other disabilities/disorders: **Undergraduates,** 590,
        612, 624, 646, 682, 738-739, 741-742; **Graduate
        students,** 840
    Families of the disabled: **Undergraduates,** 919, 932,
        936, 959, 1021, 1075-1076
    See also United States
New Jersey, northern
    Other disabilities/disorders: **Undergraduates,** 631
    See also New Jersey
New Jersey, southern
    Other disabilities/disorders: **Undergraduates,** 673
    Families of the disabled: **Undergraduates,** 927
    See also New Jersey
New Mexico
    Physical/orthopedic disabilities: **Undergraduates,**
        493; **Graduate students,** 542
    Other disabilities/disorders: **Undergraduates,** 629,
        665, 710, 785; **Graduate students,** 880
    Families of the disabled: **Undergraduates,** 1123
    See also United States
New York
    Any disability: **Undergraduates,** 84-85, 88; **Graduate
        students,** 214

Visual disabilities: **Undergraduates,** 265, 330; **Graduate students,** 380, 416
Hearing disabilities: **Undergraduates,** 445
Physical/orthopedic disabilities: **Undergraduates,** 489, 501
Other disabilities/disorders: **Undergraduates,** 590, 599, 682, 715
Families of the disabled: **Undergraduates,** 894, 922, 936, 959, 1022, 1077-1078, 1106, 1129; **Graduate students,** 1170
See also United States

New York, New York
Other disabilities/disorders: **Undergraduates,** 631
Families of the disabled: **Undergraduates,** 1129
See also New York

North Carolina
Visual disabilities: **Undergraduates,** 341, 350; **Graduate students,** 428
Physical/orthopedic disabilities: **Undergraduates,** 495
Other disabilities/disorders: **Undergraduates,** 585, 716, 765; **Graduate students,** 821, 870
Families of the disabled: **Undergraduates,** 960, 1023, 1072, 1081-1084; **Graduate students,** 1187
See also United States

North Dakota
Any disability: **Undergraduates,** 127
Visual disabilities: **Undergraduates,** 279, 342; **Graduate students,** 422
Physical/orthopedic disabilities: **Undergraduates,** 502, 522
Other disabilities/disorders: **Undergraduates,** 650
Families of the disabled: **Undergraduates,** 949, 999, 1085, 1136
See also United States

North Dakota, eastern
Other disabilities/disorders: **Undergraduates,** 620
See also North Dakota

O

Ohio
Any disability: **Undergraduates,** 47; **Graduate students,** 130
Visual disabilities: **Undergraduates,** 273, 289, 298, 312, 331, 339; **Graduate students,** 398-399, 408, 417, 421
Physical/orthopedic disabilities: **Undergraduates,** 521
Other disabilities/disorders: **Undergraduates,** 687, 725, 795
Families of the disabled: **Undergraduates,** 1024, 1086-1087; **Graduate students,** 1171
See also United States

Oklahoma
Any disability: **Undergraduates,** 32, 87-88; **Graduate students,** 214
Physical/orthopedic disabilities: **Undergraduates,** 523
Other disabilities/disorders: **Undergraduates,** 645, 761, 790
Families of the disabled: **Undergraduates,** 1025, 1109; **Graduate students,** 1172

See also United States
Orange County, California
Families of the disabled: **Undergraduates,** 1051
See also California

Oregon
Any disability: **Undergraduates,** 50, 58; **Graduate students,** 186, 213
Visual disabilities: **Undergraduates,** 255, 292, 332, 353; **Graduate students,** 394, 418
Physical/orthopedic disabilities: **Undergraduates,** 488
Other disabilities/disorders: **Undergraduates,** 586, 809; **Graduate students,** 822
Families of the disabled: **Undergraduates,** 1026, 1089-1093; **Graduate students,** 1173, 1188-1189
See also United States

P

Pennsylvania
Any disability: **Undergraduates,** 47, 88, 91; **Graduate students,** 214
Visual disabilities: **Undergraduates,** 265, 305, 333, 348, 362, 367; **Graduate students,** 380, 403, 434, 436, 439
Physical/orthopedic disabilities: **Undergraduates,** 489, 501
Other disabilities/disorders: **Undergraduates,** 682, 715, 732, 746; **Graduate students,** 866
Families of the disabled: **Undergraduates,** 936-937, 1027, 1096
See also United States

Pennsylvania, eastern
Other disabilities/disorders: **Undergraduates,** 673
Families of the disabled: **Undergraduates,** 927
See also Pennsylvania

Pottawattamie County, Iowa
Physical/orthopedic disabilities: **Undergraduates,** 509
Families of the disabled: **Undergraduates,** 1056
See also Iowa

Prince George's County, Maryland
Other disabilities/disorders: **Undergraduates,** 637; **Graduate students,** 837
Families of the disabled: **Undergraduates,** 954; **Graduate students,** 1150
See also Maryland

Puerto Rico
Any disability: **Undergraduates,** 49, 77; **Graduate students,** 208
Other disabilities/disorders: **Undergraduates,** 587; **Graduate students,** 823
See also Caribbean; United States territories

R

Rhode Island
Any disability: **Undergraduates,** 23
Physical/orthopedic disabilities: **Undergraduates,** 489
Other disabilities/disorders: **Undergraduates,** 623, 721; **Graduate students,** 835
Families of the disabled: **Undergraduates,** 897, 936
See also New England states; United States

Riverside County, California
   Families of the disabled: **Undergraduates,** 1051
   See also California

S

San Bernardino County, California
   Families of the disabled: **Undergraduates,** 1051
   See also California
San Diego County, California
   Families of the disabled: **Undergraduates,** 1051
   See also California
Sarasota County, Florida
   Any disability: **Graduate students,** 231
   See also Florida
South Carolina
   Visual disabilities: **Undergraduates,** 334
   Physical/orthopedic disabilities: **Undergraduates,**
     490, 495; **Graduate students,** 540
   Other disabilities/disorders: **Undergraduates,** 585,
     653, 765; **Graduate students,** 821, 870
   Families of the disabled: **Undergraduates,** 960, 972,
     1028, 1116; **Graduate students,** 1174
   See also United States
South Dakota
   Any disability: **Undergraduates,** 102
   Visual disabilities: **Undergraduates,** 355; **Graduate
     students,** 433
   Physical/orthopedic disabilities: **Undergraduates,**
     502, 522
   Other disabilities/disorders: **Undergraduates,** 650
   Families of the disabled: **Undergraduates,** 999, 1029,
     1103; **Graduate students,** 1175
   See also United States

T

Tennessee
   Physical/orthopedic disabilities: **Undergraduates,**
     500, 524
   Other disabilities/disorders: **Undergraduates,** 616, 787
   Families of the disabled: **Undergraduates,** 928, 934,
     1030
   See also United States
Texas
   Any disability: **Undergraduates,** 41, 112-114
   Visual disabilities: **Undergraduates,** 256, 335, 357,
     359; **Graduate students,** 435
   Hearing disabilities: **Undergraduates,** 454; **Graduate
     students,** 470
   Physical/orthopedic disabilities: **Undergraduates,**
     504, 520; **Graduate students,** 546
   Other disabilities/disorders: **Undergraduates,** 678;
     Graduate students, 849
   Families of the disabled: **Undergraduates,** 947, 966,
     1031, 1095, 1118-1119
   See also United States
Trumbull County, Ohio
   Other disabilities/disorders: **Undergraduates,** 795
   See also Ohio

U

United States
   Any disability: **Undergraduates,** 1-3, 5-7, 10-13, 15-18,
     24-26, 28, 31, 33-37, 39-40, 42-44, 48-49, 54-56, 59-
     64, 67, 71, 73-82, 85, 89-90, 92, 96-99, 101, 103-106,
     109-111, 115, 117, 120-124; **Graduate students,**
     128-129, 132-137, 139-149, 152-154, 157-159, 161-
     163, 165-167, 169-183, 185, 187, 189-192, 194-212,
     215-217, 219, 221-231, 233-236, 238-249
   Visual disabilities: **Undergraduates,** 250-251, 259, 270,
     274-276, 281-282, 285, 287-288, 297, 299, 301-303,
     306-310, 314, 317, 336, 340, 343-346, 349, 351-352,
     356, 366; **Graduate students,** 371, 374, 377, 382,
     384, 386, 388-389, 391, 393, 396, 400-401, 404-407,
     409, 419, 423-426, 429-431, 438
   Hearing disabilities: **Undergraduates,** 441-443, 446-
     453; **Graduate students,** 458-469
   Physical/orthopedic disabilities: **Undergraduates,**
     471-478, 480-482, 484-487, 491-492, 496-497, 503,
     506-508, 510-512, 514-515, 517, 527-528, 530;
     Graduate students, 531-539, 541, 545, 547-548, 553
   Other disabilities/disorders: **Undergraduates,** 554-
     556, 558-559, 561-564, 567-569, 571-572, 574, 576-
     577, 581-583, 587-588, 592-593, 601, 604-608, 611,
     613, 617-619, 621-622, 625-628, 630, 632, 634-636,
     641-644, 647-648, 656, 660, 662, 664, 666, 668-672,
     674-675, 677, 679-681, 685-686, 688-696, 698, 702,
     705, 707, 709, 711, 717-719, 724, 726-727, 729-731,
     733, 735, 737, 743-745, 747-750, 756-759, 763-764,
     766-767, 769-772, 775-778, 782, 784, 786, 788-789,
     791-792, 796-799, 801-803, 805, 807; **Graduate
     students,** 810-816, 819-820, 823-824, 826-829, 831-
     834, 836, 838-839, 841, 843-848, 850-859, 861-865,
     868-869, 871-874, 876-878, 881-887
   Families of the disabled: **Undergraduates,** 889-891,
     898-900, 904-906, 908-910, 912, 918, 920-921, 929-
     930, 939-946, 950, 952-953, 955, 959, 962, 965, 967,
     970-971, 983-985, 988, 990, 992-993, 995-996, 1000-
     1001, 1038, 1041, 1043, 1048-1053, 1057-1058, 1064,
     1066, 1068-1071, 1078-1080, 1094, 1099, 1101-1102,
     1104-1105, 1108, 1110, 1112-1113, 1117, 1120-1122,
     1124, 1126, 1128, 1130, 1132, 1137; **Graduate
     students,** 1140-1143, 1145-1147, 1149, 1152-1153,
     1157, 1159, 1161, 1163-1166, 1176-1177, 1179, 1182-
     1184, 1186, 1191-1196, 1198, 1201
United States territories
   Visual disabilities: **Undergraduates,** 310; **Graduate
     students,** 409
   Physical/orthopedic disabilities: **Undergraduates,** 511
   Other disabilities/disorders: **Undergraduates,** 717
   Families of the disabled: **Undergraduates,** 1071
Utah
   Any disability: **Undergraduates,** 118
   Visual disabilities: **Undergraduates,** 347; **Graduate
     students,** 427
   Physical/orthopedic disabilities: **Undergraduates,**
     493; **Graduate students,** 542
   Other disabilities/disorders: **Undergraduates,** 734, 800
   Families of the disabled: **Undergraduates,** 1114, 1127
   See also United States

V

Ventura County, California
Families of the disabled: **Undergraduates,** 1051
See also California
Vermont
Any disability: **Undergraduates,** 52, 95, 108
Physical/orthopedic disabilities: **Undergraduates,** 489
Families of the disabled: **Undergraduates,** 897, 936, 1032, 1088
See also New England states; United States
Virgin Islands
Any disability: **Undergraduates,** 119
See also Caribbean; United States territories
Virginia
Any disability: **Undergraduates,** 8
Visual disabilities: **Undergraduates,** 296
Physical/orthopedic disabilities: **Undergraduates,** 489
Other disabilities/disorders: **Undergraduates,** 708, 712; **Graduate students,** 860
Families of the disabled: **Undergraduates,** 936, 1033, 1040, 1044, 1131; **Graduate students,** 1178, 1197
See also United States
Virginia, northern
Other disabilities/disorders: **Undergraduates,** 637, 752; **Graduate students,** 818, 837, 867
Families of the disabled: **Undergraduates,** 954, 987, 1047, 1097; **Graduate students,** 1144, 1150, 1158, 1181, 1190
See also Virginia

W

Washington
Any disability: **Undergraduates,** 50, 69, 126; **Graduate students,** 164, 186
Visual disabilities: **Undergraduates,** 263, 294, 364; **Graduate students,** 379, 395, 437
Physical/orthopedic disabilities: **Undergraduates,** 488
Other disabilities/disorders: **Undergraduates,** 573, 586, 589, 639, 661, 706, 809; **Graduate students,** 822
Families of the disabled: **Undergraduates,** 917, 994, 1005, 1034, 1133; **Graduate students,** 1199
See also United States
Washington, D.C.
Physical/orthopedic disabilities: **Undergraduates,** 489
Other disabilities/disorders: **Undergraduates,** 637, 708, 752; **Graduate students,** 818, 837, 860, 867
Families of the disabled: **Undergraduates,** 936, 954, 987, 1040, 1047, 1097; **Graduate students,** 1144, 1150, 1158, 1178, 1181, 1190
See also United States
Washington, southwestern
Any disability: **Undergraduates,** 58
See also Washington
West Virginia
Visual disabilities: **Undergraduates,** 253; **Graduate students,** 373
Physical/orthopedic disabilities: **Undergraduates,** 489
Families of the disabled: **Undergraduates,** 936, 1035
See also United States

Westchester County, New York
Other disabilities/disorders: **Undergraduates,** 631
See also New York
Wisconsin
Any disability: **Undergraduates,** 47, 125
Visual disabilities: **Undergraduates,** 368-369
Hearing disabilities: **Undergraduates,** 457
Physical/orthopedic disabilities: **Undergraduates,** 481, 513, 522; **Graduate students,** 535, 550
Other disabilities/disorders: **Undergraduates,** 583, 640, 663, 806; **Graduate students,** 820
Families of the disabled: **Undergraduates,** 912, 961, 986, 1036, 1115, 1134-1135; **Graduate students,** 1146, 1200
See also United States
Wyoming
Visual disabilities: **Undergraduates,** 370; **Graduate students,** 440
Physical/orthopedic disabilities: **Undergraduates,** 493; **Graduate students,** 542
Other disabilities/disorders: **Undergraduates,** 760
Families of the disabled: **Undergraduates,** 1107
See also United States

Tenability Index

Some programs listed in this book can be used only in specific cities, counties, states, or regions. Others may be used anywhere in the United States (or even abroad). The Tenability Index will help you locate funding that is restricted to a specific area as well as funding that has no tenability restrictions (these are listed under the term "United States"). To use this index, look up the geographic areas where you'd like to go (always check the listings under "United States"), jot down the entry numbers listed after the target group and type of funding that applies to you, and use those numbers to find the program descriptions in the directory. To help you in your search, we've provided some "see also" references in the index entries. Remember: the numbers cited here refer to program entry numbers, not to page numbers in the book.

A

Alabama
Families of the disabled: **Undergraduates,** 892-893; **Graduate students,** 1138
See also United States

Ann Arbor, Michigan
Any disability: **Graduate students,** 201
See also Michigan

Arizona
Visual disabilities: **Undergraduates,** 257; **Graduate students,** 376
Physical/orthopedic disabilities: **Undergraduates,** 477, 516; **Graduate students,** 551
Other disabilities/disorders: **Undergraduates,** 753
See also United States

Arkansas
Families of the disabled: **Undergraduates,** 901-902
See also United States

Atlanta, Georgia
Any disability: **Graduate students,** 170, 196
See also Georgia

Austin, Texas
Any disability: **Undergraduates,** 5; **Graduate students,** 132, 196
See also Texas

B

Baltimore County, Maryland
Any disability: **Undergraduates,** 39
See also Maryland

Berkeley, California
Any disability: **Graduate students,** 148, 195
See also California

Bethesda, Maryland
Any disability: **Undergraduates,** 75
See also Maryland

Birmingham, Alabama
Any disability: **Graduate students,** 153
See also Alabama

Boston, Massachusetts
Any disability: **Graduate students,** 159, 170, 235
See also Massachusetts

Boulder, Colorado
Any disability: **Graduate students,** 146, 169
See also Colorado

Bronx County, New York
Visual disabilities: **Undergraduates,** 265; **Graduate students,** 380
See also New York

Broomfield, Colorado
Any disability: **Graduate students,** 159
See also Colorado

Buffalo, New York
Visual disabilities: **Undergraduates,** 265; **Graduate students,** 380
See also New York

C

California
Any disability: **Undergraduates,** 4, 9, 14, 20-21, 107; **Graduate students,** 131, 138, 150, 155-156, 237
Visual disabilities: **Undergraduates,** 272; **Graduate students,** 385
Other disabilities/disorders: **Undergraduates,** 595, 610, 783, 792; **Graduate students,** 825, 830, 879, 882
Families of the disabled: **Undergraduates,** 913-916

See also United States

California, southern
Other disabilities/disorders: **Undergraduates,** 587; **Graduate students,** 823
See also California

Cambridge, Massachusetts
Any disability: **Graduate students,** 201
See also Massachusetts

Campbellsville, Kentucky. *See* Kentucky

Canada
Any disability: **Undergraduates,** 10, 16, 43-44; **Graduate students,** 137, 139, 152, 174-175, 249
Visual disabilities: **Undergraduates,** 314
Hearing disabilities: **Undergraduates,** 443, 450
Physical/orthopedic disabilities: **Undergraduates,** 515
Families of the disabled: **Undergraduates,** 898; **Graduate students,** 1140
See also Foreign countries

Caribbean
Hearing disabilities: **Undergraduates,** 450
See also Foreign countries

Central America
Any disability: **Graduate students,** 174
See also Foreign countries

Champaign, Illinois
Any disability: **Undergraduates,** 39
See also Illinois

Charlotte, North Carolina
Any disability: **Graduate students,** 153, 196
See also North Carolina

Chicago, Illinois
Any disability: **Undergraduates,** 39; **Graduate students,** 161, 169, 201, 216, 235
See also Illinois

Clarke County, Virginia
Any disability: **Undergraduates,** 15
See also Virginia

Cleveland, Ohio
Any disability: **Graduate students,** 207
See also Ohio

College Park, Maryland
Any disability: **Undergraduates,** 39
Other disabilities/disorders: **Undergraduates,** 679; **Graduate students,** 850
Families of the disabled: **Undergraduates,** 995; **Graduate students,** 1164
See also Maryland

Colorado
Any disability: **Undergraduates,** 57; **Graduate students,** 193
Families of the disabled: **Undergraduates,** 924
See also United States

Connecticut
Any disability: **Undergraduates,** 45
Visual disabilities: **Undergraduates,** 320, 338; **Graduate students,** 412
Physical/orthopedic disabilities: **Undergraduates,** 489
Other disabilities/disorders: **Undergraduates,** 590

Families of the disabled: **Undergraduates,** 936, 959
See also United States

Conway, Arkansas
Any disability: **Undergraduates,** 5; **Graduate students,** 132
See also Arkansas

D

Dallas, Texas
Any disability: **Graduate students,** 235
See also Texas

Davis, California
Any disability: **Graduate students,** 148
See also California

Delaware
Physical/orthopedic disabilities: **Undergraduates,** 489
Families of the disabled: **Undergraduates,** 936
See also United States

Denver, Colorado
Any disability: **Graduate students,** 169
See also Colorado

Des Moines, Iowa
Any disability: **Graduate students,** 169
See also Iowa

District of Columbia. *See* Washington, D.C.

Downers Grove, Illinois
Any disability: **Undergraduates,** 5; **Graduate students,** 132
See also Illinois

E

East Palo Alto, California
Any disability: **Graduate students,** 169
See also California

Edwards, California
Any disability: **Graduate students,** 207
See also California

Elon, North Carolina
Other disabilities/disorders: **Undergraduates,** 679; **Graduate students,** 850
Families of the disabled: **Undergraduates,** 995; **Graduate students,** 1164
See also North Carolina

F

Florida
Visual disabilities: **Undergraduates,** 276, 360
Hearing disabilities: **Undergraduates,** 446, 455
Physical/orthopedic disabilities: **Undergraduates,** 476, 491, 525
Other disabilities/disorders: **Undergraduates,** 667, 762, 793
Families of the disabled: **Undergraduates,** 948, 1010
See also United States

Foreign countries
Any disability: **Undergraduates,** 24; **Graduate students,** 178, 217, 228, 230

Other disabilities/disorders: **Undergraduates,** 642
Families of the disabled: **Undergraduates,** 918, 1050, 1117; **Graduate students,** 1193
Fort Wayne, Indiana
Any disability: **Graduate students,** 169
See also Indiana

G

Georgia
Families of the disabled: **Undergraduates,** 957-958
See also United States
Greenbelt, Maryland
Any disability: **Graduate students,** 207
See also Maryland

H

Hampton, Virginia
Any disability: **Graduate students,** 207
See also Virginia
Houston, Texas
Any disability: **Graduate students,** 153, 161, 196, 207, 235
See also Texas
Huntsville, Alabama
Any disability: **Graduate students,** 153
See also Alabama

I

Idaho
Other disabilities/disorders: **Undergraduates,** 586, 704, 734; **Graduate students,** 822
Families of the disabled: **Undergraduates,** 974, 1039
See also United States
Illinois
Any disability: **Undergraduates,** 47
Visual disabilities: **Undergraduates,** 271, 322; **Graduate students,** 383, 413
Other disabilities/disorders: **Undergraduates,** 657
Families of the disabled: **Undergraduates,** 975-978, 1111; **Graduate students,** 1154
See also United States
Indiana
Any disability: **Undergraduates,** 47
Visual disabilities: **Undergraduates,** 291
Families of the disabled: **Undergraduates,** 979-980, 1067; **Graduate students,** 1155-1156
See also United States
Iowa
Any disability: **Undergraduates,** 22, 51, 71
See also United States
Irvine, California
Any disability: **Graduate students,** 149
See also California
Ithaca, New York
Any disability: **Graduate students,** 142
See also New York

J

Jackson, Mississippi
Any disability: **Graduate students,** 153
See also Mississippi
Jamaica, New York
Visual disabilities: **Undergraduates,** 265; **Graduate students,** 380
See also New York

K

Kansas
Any disability: **Undergraduates,** 30; **Graduate students,** 160
Visual disabilities: **Undergraduates,** 304; **Graduate students,** 402
See also United States
Kennedy Space Center, Florida
Any disability: **Graduate students,** 207
See also Florida
Kentucky
Visual disabilities: **Undergraduates,** 262, 277, 323
Physical/orthopedic disabilities: **Undergraduates,** 526
Families of the disabled: **Undergraduates,** 1003-1004
See also United States

L

Latin America. *See* Caribbean; Central America; Mexico
Little Rock, Arkansas
Any disability: **Undergraduates,** 5; **Graduate students,** 132
See also Arkansas
Los Angeles, California
Any disability: **Graduate students,** 159, 161, 187, 196, 219, 235
See also California
Louisiana
Other disabilities/disorders: **Undergraduates,** 654-655
Families of the disabled: **Undergraduates,** 973, 1015, 1042
See also United States

M

Madison, Wisconsin
Any disability: **Graduate students,** 216
See also Wisconsin
Maine
Any disability: **Undergraduates,** 94; **Graduate students,** 218
Physical/orthopedic disabilities: **Undergraduates,** 489
Families of the disabled: **Undergraduates,** 936, 1045; **Graduate students,** 1180
See also United States
Marshall Space Flight Center, Alabama
Any disability: **Graduate students,** 207
See also Alabama

Maryland
    Any disability: **Undergraduates,** 38, 53, 65; **Graduate
        students,** 168, 188
    Visual disabilities: **Undergraduates,** 300
    Physical/orthopedic disabilities: **Undergraduates,** 489
    Other disabilities/disorders: **Undergraduates,** 615
    Families of the disabled: **Undergraduates,** 933, 936,
        938, 991; **Graduate students,** 1148, 1162
    See also United States
Massachusetts
    Any disability: **Undergraduates,** 66
    Visual disabilities: **Undergraduates,** 261, 311, 325;
        Graduate students, 414
    Physical/orthopedic disabilities: **Undergraduates,** 489
    Families of the disabled: **Undergraduates,** 936
    See also United States
Mexico
    Any disability: **Graduate students,** 174
    See also Foreign countries
Miami, Florida
    Any disability: **Graduate students,** 247
    See also Florida
Michigan
    Any disability: **Undergraduates,** 47, 100; **Graduate
        students,** 232
    Visual disabilities: **Graduate students,** 430
    Other disabilities/disorders: **Undergraduates,** 722
    Families of the disabled: **Undergraduates,** 1017, 1055
    See also United States
Midland, Michigan
    Any disability: **Undergraduates,** 103
    See also Michigan
Minneapolis, Minnesota
    Any disability: **Graduate students,** 169
    See also Minnesota
Minnesota
    Any disability: **Undergraduates,** 71; **Graduate
        students,** 221
    Visual disabilities: **Undergraduates,** 326
    Families of the disabled: **Undergraduates,** 1059;
        Graduate students, 1185
    See also United States
Mississippi
    Families of the disabled: **Undergraduates,** 1060
    See also United States
Missouri
    Any disability: **Undergraduates,** 72
    Visual disabilities: **Undergraduates,** 315; **Graduate
        students,** 410
    Families of the disabled: **Undergraduates,** 1061-1063
    See also United States
Moffett Field, California
    Any disability: **Graduate students,** 207
    See also California
Montana
    Other disabilities/disorders: **Undergraduates,** 586;
        Graduate students, 822
    See also United States

Montgomery, Alabama
    Any disability: **Graduate students,** 153
    See also Alabama

N
Nashville, Tennessee
    Any disability: **Undergraduates,** 5; **Graduate
        students,** 132, 153
    See also Tennessee
Nebraska
    Families of the disabled: **Undergraduates,** 1074
    See also United States
New Hampshire
    Any disability: **Undergraduates,** 46
    Visual disabilities: **Undergraduates,** 284; **Graduate
        students,** 390
    Physical/orthopedic disabilities: **Undergraduates,** 489
    Families of the disabled: **Undergraduates,** 936
    See also United States
New Jersey
    Any disability: **Undergraduates,** 86
    Visual disabilities: **Undergraduates,** 329, 337;
        Graduate students, 415, 420
    Physical/orthopedic disabilities: **Undergraduates,** 489
    Other disabilities/disorders: **Undergraduates,** 590
    Families of the disabled: **Undergraduates,** 936, 959
    See also United States
New Mexico
    Other disabilities/disorders: **Undergraduates,** 710
    Families of the disabled: **Undergraduates,** 1123
    See also United States
New York
    Any disability: **Undergraduates,** 84-85; **Graduate
        students,** 241
    Physical/orthopedic disabilities: **Undergraduates,** 489
    Other disabilities/disorders: **Undergraduates,** 590
    Families of the disabled: **Undergraduates,** 936, 959,
        1077-1078, 1129
    See also United States
New York, New York
    Any disability: **Undergraduates,** 5; **Graduate
        students,** 132, 142, 159, 161, 196, 219, 222, 235
    Visual disabilities: **Undergraduates,** 265; **Graduate
        students,** 380
    Families of the disabled: **Undergraduates,** 1129
    See also New York
Newport Beach, California
    Any disability: **Graduate students,** 187
    See also California
North Carolina
    Other disabilities/disorders: **Undergraduates,** 585,
        765; **Graduate students,** 821, 870
    Families of the disabled: **Undergraduates,** 1072, 1081,
        1083-1084; **Graduate students,** 1187
    See also United States
North Dakota
    Any disability: **Undergraduates,** 71
    Visual disabilities: **Undergraduates,** 279, 342;
        Graduate students, 422

Families of the disabled: **Undergraduates,** 949, 1085
See also United States

O

Oakland, California
Any disability: **Graduate students,** 201, 223
See also California

Ohio
Any disability: **Undergraduates,** 47; **Graduate students,** 133
Visual disabilities: **Undergraduates,** 273, 312, 339; **Graduate students,** 399, 408, 421
Families of the disabled: **Undergraduates,** 1087
See also United States

Oklahoma
Any disability: **Undergraduates,** 32
Physical/orthopedic disabilities: **Undergraduates,** 523
Other disabilities/disorders: **Undergraduates,** 790
See also United States

Ontario, California
Any disability: **Graduate students,** 149
See also California

Orangeburg, New York
Visual disabilities: **Undergraduates,** 265; **Graduate students,** 380
See also New York

Oregon
Any disability: **Graduate students,** 213
Visual disabilities: **Undergraduates,** 292, 332, 353; **Graduate students,** 394, 418
Other disabilities/disorders: **Undergraduates,** 586; **Graduate students,** 822
Families of the disabled: **Undergraduates,** 1089, 1093; **Graduate students,** 1188
See also United States

Orlando, Florida
Any disability: **Graduate students,** 247
See also Florida

P

Palo Alto, California
Any disability: **Graduate students,** 159, 170, 196, 235
See also California

Pasadena, California
Any disability: **Graduate students,** 207
See also California

Pennsylvania
Any disability: **Undergraduates,** 47
Visual disabilities: **Undergraduates,** 367; **Graduate students,** 439
Physical/orthopedic disabilities: **Undergraduates,** 489
Families of the disabled: **Undergraduates,** 936-937
See also United States

Peoria, Illinois
Any disability: **Undergraduates,** 39
See also Illinois

Philadelphia, Pennsylvania
Any disability: **Graduate students,** 161

See also Pennsylvania

Phoenix, Arizona
Any disability: **Graduate students,** 216
See also Arizona

Pittsburgh, Pennsylvania
Any disability: **Graduate students,** 161
See also Pennsylvania

Portland, Oregon
Any disability: **Graduate students,** 216, 233, 238
See also Oregon

Poughkeepsie, New York
Visual disabilities: **Undergraduates,** 265; **Graduate students,** 380
See also New York

Princeton, New Jersey
Any disability: **Graduate students,** 161, 201
See also New Jersey

Puerto Rico
Any disability: **Undergraduates,** 49, 77; **Graduate students,** 208
Other disabilities/disorders: **Undergraduates,** 587; **Graduate students,** 823
See also Caribbean; United States territories

Purchase, New York
Visual disabilities: **Undergraduates,** 265; **Graduate students,** 380
See also New York

R

Redwood City, California
Any disability: **Undergraduates,** 5; **Graduate students,** 132
See also California

Reston, Virginia
Any disability: **Graduate students,** 159, 170
See also Virginia

Rhode Island
Physical/orthopedic disabilities: **Undergraduates,** 489
Families of the disabled: **Undergraduates,** 936
See also United States

Riverside, California
Any disability: **Graduate students,** 149
See also California

Rochester, New York
Any disability: **Graduate students,** 181
See also New York

Rockville Centre, New York
Visual disabilities: **Undergraduates,** 265; **Graduate students,** 380
See also New York

S

Sacramento, California
Any disability: **Graduate students,** 148
See also California

St. Louis, Missouri
Any disability: **Graduate students,** 191

Hearing disabilities: **Graduate students,** 468
See also Missouri

Salt Lake City, Utah
Any disability: **Graduate students,** 238
See also Utah

San Diego, California
Any disability: **Graduate students,** 159
See also California

San Francisco, California
Any disability: **Graduate students,** 148, 159, 161, 195-196, 216, 223-224, 235
See also California

Santa Clara, California
Any disability: **Graduate students,** 148
See also California

Sarasota County, Florida
Any disability: **Graduate students,** 231
See also Florida

Savannah, Georgia
Other disabilities/disorders: **Undergraduates,** 679; **Graduate students,** 850
Families of the disabled: **Undergraduates,** 995; **Graduate students,** 1164
See also Georgia

Seattle, Washington
Any disability: **Graduate students,** 159, 182, 197, 216, 233, 238
See also Washington

South Bend, Indiana
Any disability: **Graduate students,** 169
See also Indiana

South Carolina
Visual disabilities: **Undergraduates,** 334
Physical/orthopedic disabilities: **Undergraduates,** 490; **Graduate students,** 540
Other disabilities/disorders: **Undergraduates,** 585, 765; **Graduate students,** 821, 870
Families of the disabled: **Undergraduates,** 1116
See also United States

South Dakota
Any disability: **Undergraduates,** 71, 102
Visual disabilities: **Undergraduates,** 355; **Graduate students,** 433
Families of the disabled: **Undergraduates,** 1103
See also United States

South Orange, New Jersey
Visual disabilities: **Undergraduates,** 265; **Graduate students,** 380
See also New Jersey

Sparkill, New York
Visual disabilities: **Undergraduates,** 265; **Graduate students,** 380
See also New York

Stanford, California
Any disability: **Graduate students,** 148, 195
See also California

Stennis Space Center, Mississippi
Any disability: **Graduate students,** 207

See also Mississippi

Stony Brook, New York
Any disability: **Graduate students,** 142
See also New York

Syracuse, New York
Visual disabilities: **Undergraduates,** 265; **Graduate students,** 380
See also New York

T

Tampa, Florida
Any disability: **Graduate students,** 153, 247
See also Florida

Tennessee
Physical/orthopedic disabilities: **Undergraduates,** 524
Other disabilities/disorders: **Undergraduates,** 616, 787
Families of the disabled: **Undergraduates,** 928, 934
See also United States

Texas
Any disability: **Undergraduates,** 41, 103, 112-113; **Graduate students,** 240
Visual disabilities: **Undergraduates,** 359; **Graduate students,** 435
Hearing disabilities: **Undergraduates,** 454; **Graduate students,** 470
Physical/orthopedic disabilities: **Undergraduates,** 504; **Graduate students,** 546
Other disabilities/disorders: **Undergraduates,** 678; **Graduate students,** 849
Families of the disabled: **Undergraduates,** 947, 966, 1095, 1118
See also United States

Towson, Maryland
Other disabilities/disorders: **Undergraduates,** 679; **Graduate students,** 850
Families of the disabled: **Undergraduates,** 995; **Graduate students,** 1164
See also Maryland

U

United States
Any disability: **Undergraduates,** 1-3, 5-8, 10-13, 16-19, 23-29, 31, 33-37, 39-40, 42-45, 47-50, 52, 54-56, 58-64, 67-70, 73-83, 87-93, 95-101, 104-106, 108-111, 114-124, 126-127; **Graduate students,** 128-130, 132, 134-137, 139-141, 143-145, 147, 149, 151-154, 157-159, 161-167, 169-171, 173-175, 177-181, 183-187, 189-190, 192, 194, 196-200, 202-212, 214-217, 219-220, 222-234, 236, 238-239, 242-249
Visual disabilities: **Undergraduates,** 250-256, 258-264, 266-271, 273-275, 277-278, 280-290, 293-310, 312-314, 316-325, 327-331, 333-336, 339-341, 343-346, 348-352, 354, 356-358, 361-367, 369-370; **Graduate students,** 371-375, 377-379, 381-384, 386-393, 395-409, 411-417, 419, 421, 423-426, 428-429, 431-432, 434, 436-440
Hearing disabilities: **Undergraduates,** 441-445, 447-453, 456-457; **Graduate students,** 458-467, 469

Physical/orthopedic disabilities: **Undergraduates,** 471-475, 478-490, 492-503, 505-515, 517-522, 524, 527-530; **Graduate students,** 531-545, 547-550, 552-553

Other disabilities/disorders: **Undergraduates,** 554-572, 574-588, 591-594, 596-609, 611-615, 617-638, 640-653, 656, 658-666, 668-677, 680-705, 707-709, 711-721, 723-733, 735-752, 754-761, 763-782, 784-786, 788-789, 791, 794-809; **Graduate students,** 810-824, 826-829, 831-848, 851-878, 880-881, 883-888

Families of the disabled: **Undergraduates,** 889-891, 894-900, 903-912, 918-923, 925-927, 929-933, 935-936, 939-946, 950-956, 959-965, 967-972, 981-990, 992-994, 996-1002, 1006-1009, 1011-1014, 1016, 1018-1035, 1037-1041, 1043-1054, 1056-1058, 1064-1066, 1068-1071, 1073, 1075-1076, 1079-1080, 1082, 1086, 1088, 1090-1092, 1094, 1096-1102, 1104-1110, 1112-1113, 1115, 1117, 1119-1122, 1124-1130, 1132, 1134, 1136-1137; **Graduate students,** 1139-1147, 1149-1153, 1157-1161, 1163, 1165-1184, 1186, 1189-1196, 1198, 1201

United States territories
Visual disabilities: **Undergraduates,** 310; **Graduate students,** 409
Physical/orthopedic disabilities: **Undergraduates,** 511
Other disabilities/disorders: **Undergraduates,** 717
Families of the disabled: **Undergraduates,** 1071

University Park, Pennsylvania
Any disability: **Undergraduates,** 39
See also Pennsylvania

Upton, New York
Any disability: **Graduate students,** 176
See also New York

Utah
Visual disabilities: **Undergraduates,** 347; **Graduate students,** 427
Physical/orthopedic disabilities: **Undergraduates,** 527
Other disabilities/disorders: **Undergraduates,** 734
Families of the disabled: **Undergraduates,** 1114
See also United States

V

Vermont
Physical/orthopedic disabilities: **Undergraduates,** 489
Families of the disabled: **Undergraduates,** 936
See also United States

Virginia
Visual disabilities: **Undergraduates,** 296
Physical/orthopedic disabilities: **Undergraduates,** 489
Other disabilities/disorders: **Undergraduates,** 712
Families of the disabled: **Undergraduates,** 936, 1044, 1131; **Graduate students,** 1197
See also United States

W

Washington
Other disabilities/disorders: **Undergraduates,** 586, 589, 639; **Graduate students,** 822

Families of the disabled: **Undergraduates,** 917, 1005, 1133; **Graduate students,** 1199
See also United States

Washington, D.C.
Any disability: **Graduate students,** 153, 158-159, 161, 169-170, 196, 201, 204, 216, 235
Physical/orthopedic disabilities: **Undergraduates,** 489
Families of the disabled: **Undergraduates,** 936
See also United States

Washington, eastern
Other disabilities/disorders: **Undergraduates,** 573
See also Washington

Washington, western
Other disabilities/disorders: **Undergraduates,** 706
See also Washington

West Lafayette, Indiana
Any disability: **Undergraduates,** 39
See also Indiana

West Palm Beach, Florida
Any disability: **Graduate students,** 247
See also Florida

West Virginia
Physical/orthopedic disabilities: **Undergraduates,** 489
Families of the disabled: **Undergraduates,** 936
See also United States

Williamstown, Massachusetts
Any disability: **Graduate students,** 172
See also Massachusetts

Wisconsin
Any disability: **Undergraduates,** 47, 71, 125
Visual disabilities: **Undergraduates,** 368-369
Hearing disabilities: **Undergraduates,** 457
Families of the disabled: **Undergraduates,** 1036, 1135; **Graduate students,** 1200
See also United States

Wyoming
Other disabilities/disorders: **Undergraduates,** 734
See also United States

Subject Index

Use the Subject Index when you want to identify the subject focus of available funding programs. There are more than 250 different subject areas indexed in this directory (each subdivided by both disability group and funding type). To help you pinpoint your search, we've also included hundreds of "see" and "see also" references. In addition to looking for terms that represent your specific subject interest, be sure to check the "General programs" entry; hundreds of programs are listed there that can be used to support study, research, or other activities in *any* subject area (although the programs may be restricted in other ways). Remember: the numbers cited in this index refer to program entry numbers, not to page numbers in the book.

A

Accounting
   Any disability: **Undergraduates,** 24
   Families of the disabled: **Undergraduates,** 918
   See also Finance; General programs

Acquired Immunodeficiency Syndrome. See AIDS

Acting. See Performing arts

Addiction. See Drug use and abuse

Administration. See Business administration; Management; Personnel administration; Public administration

Advertising
   Any disability: **Undergraduates,** 99
   Families of the disabled: **Undergraduates,** 1005
   See also Communications; General programs; Marketing; Public relations

Aeronautical engineering. See Engineering, aeronautical

Aeronautics
   Any disability: **Graduate students,** 133, 207
   See also Aviation; Engineering, aeronautical; General programs; Physical sciences

Aerospace engineering. See Engineering, aerospace

Aerospace sciences. See Space sciences

Aged and aging
   Any disability: **Graduate students,** 134
   See also General programs; Social sciences

Agriculture and agricultural sciences
   Physical/orthopedic disabilities: **Undergraduates,** 482
   See also Biological sciences; General programs

AIDS
   Other disabilities/disorders: **Undergraduates,** 809
   See also Disabilities; General programs; Medical sciences

Alzheimer's Disease
   Any disability: **Graduate students,** 134
   See also Aged and aging; Disabilities; General programs; Medical sciences

American history. See History, American

American studies
   Any disability: **Graduate students,** 191, 204
   Hearing disabilities: **Graduate students,** 468
   See also General programs; Humanities

Animation
   Any disability: **Undergraduates,** 3
   See also Filmmaking; General programs

Anthropology
   Any disability: **Graduate students,** 191
   Hearing disabilities: **Graduate students,** 468
   See also General programs; Social sciences

Aquatic sciences. See Oceanography

Architecture
   Any disability: **Graduate students,** 204
   See also Fine arts; General programs; Historical preservation

Arithmetic. See Mathematics

Art
   Any disability: **Undergraduates,** 3
   Visual disabilities: **Undergraduates,** 288
   Hearing disabilities: **Graduate students,** 462
   Other disabilities/disorders: **Undergraduates,** 669, 770; **Graduate students,** 874
   See also Fine arts; General programs; names of specific art forms

Astronomy
   Any disability: **Graduate students,** 142, 178, 207
   See also General programs; Physical sciences

Astrophysics
  Any disability: **Graduate students,** 142
  See also Astronomy; General programs
Athletic training
  Any disability: **Undergraduates,** 57; **Graduate students,** 193
  See also General programs
Atmospheric sciences
  Any disability: **Undergraduates,** 11-12; **Graduate students,** 143, 146, 207
  See also General programs; Physical sciences
Attorneys. *See* Law, general
Audiology
  Any disability: **Undergraduates,** 1, 57; **Graduate students,** 128, 193, 230
  See also General programs; Health and health care; Medical sciences
Automation. *See* Computer sciences; Technology
Automotive engineering. *See* Engineering, automotive
Aviation
  Any disability: **Undergraduates,** 79
  Physical/orthopedic disabilities: **Undergraduates,** 473
  See also General programs; Space sciences; Transportation

B
Ballet. *See* Dance
Behavioral sciences
  Any disability: **Undergraduates,** 75; **Graduate students,** 227-229
  See also General programs; Social sciences; names of special behavioral sciences
Biochemistry
  Any disability: **Graduate students,** 207
  See also Biological sciences; Chemistry; General programs
Biological sciences
  Any disability: **Undergraduates,** 15, 31; **Graduate students,** 142, 178, 207, 217
  Visual disabilities: **Undergraduates,** 345; **Graduate students,** 425
  See also General programs; Sciences; names of specific biological sciences
Biomedical engineering. *See* Engineering, biomedical
Biomedical sciences
  Any disability: **Undergraduates,** 75; **Graduate students,** 227-229
  Other disabilities/disorders: **Graduate students,** 826
  See also Biological sciences; General programs; Medical sciences
Blindness. *See* Visual impairments
Botany
  Any disability: **Undergraduates,** 15
  See also Biological sciences; General programs

Brain research. *See* Neuroscience
Business administration
  Any disability: **Undergraduates,** 16, 18, 24, 69; **Graduate students,** 152, 154
  Visual disabilities: **Undergraduates,** 301, 351; **Graduate students,** 400, 429
  Hearing disabilities: **Graduate students,** 458
  Physical/orthopedic disabilities: **Undergraduates,** 477
  Families of the disabled: **Undergraduates,** 918, 1005, 1038; **Graduate students,** 1176
  See also General programs; Management

C
Cancer
  Other disabilities/disorders: **Undergraduates,** 589
  Families of the disabled: **Undergraduates,** 917
  See also Disabilities; General programs; Health and health care; Medical sciences
Cars. *See* Engineering, automotive
Cell biology
  Any disability: **Graduate students,** 207
  See also Biological sciences; General programs
Chemical engineering. *See* Engineering, chemical
Chemistry
  Any disability: **Undergraduates,** 31; **Graduate students,** 178, 207
  See also Engineering, chemical; General programs; Physical sciences
Choruses. *See* Voice
City and regional planning. *See* Urban and regional planning
Civil engineering. *See* Engineering, civil
Classical music. *See* Music, classical
Climatology
  Any disability: **Graduate students,** 146
  See also Atmospheric sciences; General programs; Physical sciences
Clothing
  Any disability: **Undergraduates,** 99
  See also Fashion design; General programs
Commerce. *See* Business administration
Communications
  Any disability: **Undergraduates,** 80; **Graduate students,** 210
  Families of the disabled: **Undergraduates,** 894, 1005
  See also General programs; Humanities
Community services. *See* Social services
Computer engineering. *See* Engineering, computer
Computer law
  Any disability: **Undergraduates,** 69
  See also General programs; Law, general

Computer sciences
   Any disability: **Undergraduates,** 5, 28, 31, 36, 39, 43-44, 47, 69, 92; **Graduate students,** 132, 146, 175, 178, 207
   Visual disabilities: **Undergraduates,** 302, 343, 345; **Graduate students,** 423, 425
   Other disabilities/disorders: **Undergraduates,** 582
   See also General programs; Mathematics; Technology
Computers. *See* Computer sciences
Conservation. *See* Environmental sciences
Construction industry
   Families of the disabled: **Undergraduates,** 1038; **Graduate students,** 1176
   See also General programs
Cooking. *See* Culinary arts
Copyright law. *See* Intellectual property law
Counseling
   Visual disabilities: **Undergraduates,** 339; **Graduate students,** 421
   See also Behavioral sciences; General programs; Psychology
Counter-intelligence service. *See* Intelligence service
Creative writing
   Visual disabilities: **Undergraduates,** 288
   See also Fine arts; General programs
Criminal justice
   Any disability: **Undergraduates,** 93; **Graduate students,** 198
   Families of the disabled: **Undergraduates,** 1072, 1129
   See also General programs; Law, general
Criminal law
   Any disability: **Graduate students,** 198
   See also General programs; Law, general
Culinary arts
   Other disabilities/disorders: **Undergraduates,** 594
   See also Food service industry; General programs

D

Dance
   Other disabilities/disorders: **Undergraduates,** 669
   See also General programs; Performing arts
Data entry. *See* Computer sciences
Deafness. *See* Hearing impairments
Demography. *See* Population studies
Dental assisting
   Any disability: **Undergraduates,** 57; **Graduate students,** 193
   See also General programs; Health and health care
Dental hygiene
   Any disability: **Undergraduates,** 57; **Graduate students,** 193
   See also General programs; Health and health care
Dentistry
   Any disability: **Undergraduates,** 58; **Graduate students,** 230
   See also General programs; Health and health care; Medical sciences

Design
   Any disability: **Undergraduates,** 3
   See also Art; General programs
Dietetics. *See* Nutrition
Disabilities
   Any disability: **Undergraduates,** 1, 54; **Graduate students,** 128, 144, 189
   Visual disabilities: **Undergraduates,** 259, 282; **Graduate students,** 377, 389
   See also General programs; Rehabilitation; names of specific disabilities
Disabilities, hearing. *See* Hearing impairments
Disabilities, visual. *See* Visual impairments
Disability law
   Any disability: **Graduate students,** 151
   Visual disabilities: **Undergraduates,** 259, 282; **Graduate students,** 377, 389
   See also General programs; Law, general
Divinity. *See* Religion and religious activities
Documentaries. *See* Filmmaking
Drug use and abuse
   Any disability: **Graduate students,** 167
   See also General programs; Health and health care

E

Earth sciences
   Any disability: **Graduate students,** 142
   See also General programs; names of specific earth sciences
Ecology. *See* Environmental sciences
Economic planning. *See* Economics
Economics
   Any disability: **Undergraduates,** 24; **Graduate students,** 183
   Families of the disabled: **Undergraduates,** 918, 1079
   See also General programs; Social sciences
Education
   Any disability: **Graduate students,** 183
   Visual disabilities: **Graduate students,** 408
   Other disabilities/disorders: **Undergraduates,** 664, 746; **Graduate students,** 845, 866
   Families of the disabled: **Undergraduates,** 988, 1002, 1079; **Graduate students,** 1159
   See also General programs; Social sciences; names of specific types and levels of education
Education, music
   Any disability: **Undergraduates,** 74; **Graduate students,** 206
   See also Education; General programs; Music
Education, religious
   Any disability: **Graduate students,** 184
   See also Education; General programs; Religion and religious activities

Education, special
Any disability: **Undergraduates,** 1, 96; **Graduate students,** 128
Visual disabilities: **Undergraduates,** 259, 274, 282, 339, 352, 366; **Graduate students,** 377, 386, 389, 421, 431, 434, 438
See also Disabilities; Education; General programs

Elder law
Any disability: **Graduate students,** 241
See also General programs; Law, general

Electrical engineering. *See* Engineering, electrical

Electronic engineering. *See* Engineering, electronic

Emergency medical technology
Any disability: **Undergraduates,** 57; **Graduate students,** 193
See also General programs; Health and health care

Emotional disabilities. *See* Mental health

Employment
Any disability: **Undergraduates,** 120; **Graduate students,** 244
See also General programs; Occupational therapy

Engineering, aeronautical
Any disability: **Graduate students,** 133, 207
See also Aeronautics; Engineering, general; General programs

Engineering, aerospace
Any disability: **Undergraduates,** 77; **Graduate students,** 133, 207-208
See also Engineering, general; General programs; Space sciences

Engineering, automotive
Any disability: **Undergraduates,** 47
See also Engineering, general; General programs

Engineering, biomedical
Any disability: **Graduate students,** 207
See also Biomedical sciences; Engineering, general; General programs

Engineering, chemical
Any disability: **Undergraduates,** 47; **Graduate students,** 207
See also Chemistry; Engineering, general; General programs

Engineering, civil
Any disability: **Graduate students,** 207
Families of the disabled: **Undergraduates,** 1038; **Graduate students,** 1176
See also Engineering, general; General programs

Engineering, computer
Any disability: **Undergraduates,** 5, 28, 36, 39, 43-44, 92; **Graduate students,** 132, 175, 178, 207
Visual disabilities: **Undergraduates,** 343; **Graduate students,** 423
See also Computer sciences; Engineering, general; General programs

Engineering, electrical
Any disability: **Undergraduates,** 39, 47, 92; **Graduate students,** 207
See also Engineering, general; General programs

Engineering, electronic
Any disability: **Graduate students,** 207
See also Engineering, general; General programs

Engineering, environmental
Any disability: **Graduate students,** 207
Physical/orthopedic disabilities: **Undergraduates,** 478; **Graduate students,** 533
See also Engineering, general; Environmental sciences; General programs

Engineering, general
Any disability: **Undergraduates,** 16, 31, 69, 105; **Graduate students,** 146, 152, 176, 178-179, 234
Visual disabilities: **Undergraduates,** 344-345; **Graduate students,** 424-425
Other disabilities/disorders: **Undergraduates,** 685, 765; **Graduate students,** 870
Families of the disabled: **Undergraduates,** 1079, 1130
See also General programs; Physical sciences; names of specific types of engineering

Engineering, industrial
Any disability: **Graduate students,** 207
Physical/orthopedic disabilities: **Undergraduates,** 478; **Graduate students,** 533
See also Engineering, general; General programs

Engineering, manufacturing
Any disability: **Undergraduates,** 47
See also Engineering, general; General programs

Engineering, materials
Any disability: **Undergraduates,** 47; **Graduate students,** 207
See also Engineering, general; General programs; Materials sciences

Engineering, mechanical
Any disability: **Undergraduates,** 39, 47; **Graduate students,** 207
See also Engineering, general; General programs

Engineering, nuclear
Any disability: **Graduate students,** 207, 225
See also Engineering, general; General programs; Nuclear science

Engineering, ocean
Any disability: **Graduate students,** 207
See also Engineering, general; General programs; Oceanography

Engineering, optical
Any disability: **Graduate students,** 207
See also Engineering, general; General programs

Engineering, systems
Any disability: **Graduate students,** 207
See also Engineering, general; General programs

Engineering technology
Any disability: **Undergraduates,** 47
See also Engineering, general; General programs

Entomology
Any disability: **Graduate students,** 142
See also General programs

Environmental engineering. *See* Engineering, environmental

Environmental sciences
  Any disability: **Undergraduates,** 15
  Physical/orthopedic disabilities: **Undergraduates, 478; Graduate students,** 533
  Families of the disabled: **Undergraduates,** 1002
  See also General programs; Sciences

Epilepsy
  Any disability: **Graduate students,** 140
  See also Disabilities; General programs; Health and health care; Medical sciences

Ethnic studies. *See* Minority studies

Evolution
  Any disability: **Undergraduates,** 15; **Graduate students,** 142
  See also Biological sciences; General programs; Sciences

Exercise science. *See* Athletic training

Eye problems. *See* Visual impairments

F

Fabric. *See* Clothing

Farming. *See* Agriculture and agricultural sciences

Fashion design
  Any disability: **Undergraduates,** 99
  See also Clothing; Design; General programs

Feminist movement. *See* Womensstudiesandprograms'

Fiber. *See* Textiles

Filmmaking
  Any disability: **Undergraduates,** 63; **Graduate students,** 199
  See also General programs; Television

Finance
  Any disability: **Undergraduates,** 16, 24, 52; **Graduate students,** 152
  Families of the disabled: **Undergraduates,** 918, 1079
  See also Accounting; Economics; General programs

Fine arts
  Any disability: **Graduate students,** 172
  Visual disabilities: **Undergraduates,** 308; **Graduate students,** 406
  Hearing disabilities: **Undergraduates,** 443; **Graduate students,** 469
  Other disabilities/disorders: **Undergraduates,** 669
  Families of the disabled: **Undergraduates,** 1002, 1121; **Graduate students,** 1194
  See also General programs; Humanities; names of specific fine arts

Flight science. *See* Aviation

Flying. *See* Aviation

Food. *See* Culinary arts; Nutrition

Food service industry
  Any disability: **Undergraduates,** 90
  Other disabilities/disorders: **Undergraduates,** 702; **Graduate students,** 858
  See also General programs

Foreign affairs. *See* International relations

Fossils. *See* Paleontology

G

Gender. *See* Womensstudiesandprograms'

General programs
  Any disability: **Undergraduates,** 4, 8-9, 13-14, 17, 19-23, 25-27, 29-30, 32-34, 38, 40-42, 45-46, 48-51, 53, 55, 59-62, 64-68, 70, 72-73, 78, 83-88, 91, 93-98, 100-104, 106-120, 123-127; **Graduate students,** 131, 138, 150, 155-158, 160, 162-163, 168, 172, 186, 188, 190, 194, 205, 209, 214, 218, 232, 236-237, 239, 243-244
  Visual disabilities: **Undergraduates,** 250-258, 260-273, 275-276, 278-281, 283-287, 289-300, 303-307, 309-338, 340-342, 346-348, 350, 353-365, 367-370; **Graduate students,** 371-376, 378-385, 387-388, 390-395, 397-399, 401-405, 407, 409-420, 422, 426-428, 430, 432-433, 435-437, 439-440
  Hearing disabilities: **Undergraduates,** 441-442, 444-457; **Graduate students,** 459-461, 463, 467, 470
  Physical/orthopedic disabilities: **Undergraduates,** 471-472, 475-476, 479-481, 483-530; **Graduate students,** 531-532, 534-538, 540, 542-553
  Other disabilities/disorders: **Undergraduates,** 554-581, 583-588, 590-593, 595-604, 606-634, 636-637, 639-647, 649-662, 665-668, 670-684, 686-701, 703-726, 728-745, 747, 749-764, 766-769, 771-809; **Graduate students,** 810-812, 814-825, 828-830, 832-840, 842-844, 846-857, 860-865, 867-869, 871-873, 875-888
  Families of the disabled: **Undergraduates,** 889-893, 895-897, 899-905, 907-916, 919-955, 957-985, 987, 989-1001, 1003-1004, 1006-1071, 1073-1078, 1080-1089, 1091-1110, 1112-1120, 1122-1137; **Graduate students,** 1138-1139, 1141-1142, 1144-1158, 1160-1176, 1178-1193, 1195-1201

Geography
  Any disability: **Graduate students,** 173
  See also General programs; Social sciences

Geology
  Any disability: **Graduate students,** 174, 178, 207
  See also Earth sciences; General programs; Physical sciences

Geophysics
  Any disability: **Graduate students,** 174, 207
  See also General programs; Meteorology; Oceanography; Physics

Geosciences. *See* Earth sciences

Geriatrics. *See* Aged and aging

Gerontology. *See* Aged and aging

Government. *See* Political science and politics; Public administration

Graphic design
  Families of the disabled: **Undergraduates,** 894
  See also Design; General programs

Guidance. *See* Counseling

H

Handicapped. *See* Disabilities

Health and health care
   Any disability: **Undergraduates,** 1, 58, 71, 96;
      Graduate students, 128
   Visual disabilities: **Graduate students,** 408
   Other disabilities/disorders: **Undergraduates,** 574,
      638, 648, 662; **Graduate students,** 841, 844
   Families of the disabled: **Undergraduates,** 908, 956,
      985; **Graduate students,** 1157
   See also General programs; Medical sciences

Health and health care, administration
   Any disability: **Undergraduates,** 6-7; **Graduate
      students,** 135-136
   See also Business administration; General programs;
      Health and health care

Health and health care, informatics
   Any disability: **Undergraduates,** 6-7; **Graduate
      students,** 135-136
   See also General programs; Health and health care

Health information. *See* Health and health care,
   informatics

Health information administration. *See* Health and health
   care, informatics

Health policy
   Any disability: **Graduate students,** 183
   See also General programs; Health and health care;
      Public administration

Hearing impairments
   Any disability: **Graduate students,** 141
   See also Disabilities; General programs; Rehabilitation

Historical preservation
   Any disability: **Graduate students,** 204
   See also General programs; History

History
   Any disability: **Graduate students,** 204
   See also General programs; Humanities; Social
      sciences; names of specific types of history

History, American
   Any disability: **Graduate students,** 191
   Hearing disabilities: **Graduate students,** 468
   Families of the disabled: **Undergraduates,** 894
   See also American studies; General programs; History

History, natural
   Any disability: **Graduate students,** 142
   See also Sciences; names of specific aspects of natural
      history

History, science
   Any disability: **Graduate students,** 177
   See also General programs; History; Sciences

Hospitality industry. *See* Hotel and motel industry

Hospitals. *See* Health and health care

Hotel and motel industry
   Any disability: **Undergraduates,** 90
   See also General programs

Human resources. *See* Personnel administration

Human services. *See* Social services

Humanities
   Hearing disabilities: **Graduate students,** 462
   See also General programs; names of specific
      humanities

Hydrology
   Any disability: **Undergraduates,** 11; **Graduate
      students,** 143, 207
   See also Earth sciences; General programs

I

Industrial engineering. *See* Engineering, industrial

Industrial hygiene
   Physical/orthopedic disabilities: **Undergraduates,**
      478; **Graduate students,** 533
   See also General programs; Health and health care;
      Safety studies

Information systems
   Any disability: **Undergraduates,** 5; **Graduate
      students,** 132
   See also Business administration; General programs

Information technology
   Any disability: **Undergraduates,** 5, 69; **Graduate
      students,** 132, 178, 207
   See also Computer sciences; General programs

Intellectual property law
   Any disability: **Graduate students,** 166, 170, 200
   See also General programs; Law, general

Intelligence service
   Any disability: **Undergraduates,** 31
   See also General programs; International relations

International affairs. *See* International relations

International relations
   Any disability: **Undergraduates,** 31
   See also General programs; Political science and
      politics

Internet law
   Any disability: **Undergraduates,** 69
   See also General programs; Law, general

J

Jazz. *See* Music, jazz

Jewish studies
   Any disability: **Graduate students,** 182
   See also General programs; Religion and religious
      activities

Jobs. *See* Employment

Journalism
   Any disability: **Undergraduates,** 76, 80, 99; **Graduate
      students,** 210
   Families of the disabled: **Undergraduates,** 894
   See also Communications; General programs; names
      of specific types of journalism

Jurisprudence. *See* Law, general

L

Law enforcement. *See* Criminal justice

Law, general
Any disability: **Undergraduates,** 35, 37; **Graduate students,** 145, 148-149, 151, 153, 159, 161, 164-165, 169, 171, 181, 187, 196-198, 202, 213, 216, 219, 221-224, 231, 233, 235, 238, 240, 247-249
Hearing disabilities: **Graduate students,** 464
Physical/orthopedic disabilities: **Undergraduates,** 474; **Graduate students,** 539, 541
Other disabilities/disorders: **Undergraduates,** 593, 727; **Graduate students,** 813, 824, 831, 859
Families of the disabled: **Undergraduates,** 1129; **Graduate students,** 1177
See also Criminal justice; General programs; Social sciences; names of legal specialties

Lawyers. *See* Law, general

Leadership
Hearing disabilities: **Graduate students,** 462
See also General programs; Management

Legal studies and services. *See* Law, general

Librarians. *See* Library and information services, general

Library and information services, general
Any disability: **Graduate students,** 130, 137
See also General programs; Social sciences; names of specific types of librarianship

Life sciences. *See* Biological sciences

Litigation
Any disability: **Graduate students,** 195, 198
See also General programs; Law, general

M

Magazines. *See* Journalism

Management
Any disability: **Undergraduates,** 99
See also General programs; Social sciences

Management, construction
Families of the disabled: **Undergraduates,** 1038; **Graduate students,** 1176
See also Construction industry; General programs; Management

Manufacturing engineering. *See* Engineering, manufacturing

Marketing
Any disability: **Undergraduates,** 69, 99
Families of the disabled: **Undergraduates,** 1005
See also Advertising; General programs; Public relations; Sales

Mass communications. *See* Communications

Materials engineering. *See* Engineering, materials

Materials sciences
Any disability: **Undergraduates,** 47; **Graduate students,** 207
See also General programs; Physical sciences

Mathematics
Any disability: **Undergraduates,** 5, 16, 77, 105; **Graduate students,** 132, 152, 176, 178-179, 207-208, 217, 234
Visual disabilities: **Undergraduates,** 344; **Graduate students,** 424
Other disabilities/disorders: **Undergraduates,** 685
Families of the disabled: **Undergraduates,** 1002
See also Computer sciences; General programs; Physical sciences; Statistics

Mechanical engineering. *See* Engineering, mechanical

Media. *See* Communications

Media specialists. *See* Library and information services, general

Medical sciences
Any disability: **Undergraduates,** 57-58; **Graduate students,** 193, 230, 234
Other disabilities/disorders: **Undergraduates,** 582, 648, 663, 807; **Graduate students,** 826, 841, 887
Families of the disabled: **Undergraduates,** 986
See also General programs; Health and health care; Sciences; names of medical specialties; names of specific diseases

Medical technology
Any disability: **Undergraduates,** 57; **Graduate students,** 193
See also General programs; Medical sciences; Technology

Mental health
Any disability: **Graduate students,** 203
See also General programs; Health and health care

Merchandising. *See* Sales

Meteorology
Any disability: **Undergraduates,** 11; **Graduate students,** 143, 146
See also Atmospheric sciences; General programs

Microbiology
Any disability: **Undergraduates,** 31
See also Biological sciences; General programs

Microcomputers. *See* Computer sciences

Microscopy. *See* Medical technology

Minority studies
Any disability: **Graduate students,** 183
See also General programs; names of specific ethnic minority studies

Missionary work. *See* Religion and religious activities

Molecular biology
Any disability: **Graduate students,** 142
See also Biological sciences; General programs

Motel industry. *See* Hotel and motel industry

Museum studies
Any disability: **Graduate students,** 204
See also General programs; Library and information services, general

Music
  Any disability: **Undergraduates,** 56, 74, 122; **Graduate students,** 206, 246
  Visual disabilities: **Undergraduates,** 288, 349
  Other disabilities/disorders: **Undergraduates,** 582, 605, 669; **Graduate students,** 827
  Families of the disabled: **Undergraduates,** 1121; **Graduate students,** 1194
  See also Education, music; Fine arts; General programs; Humanities; Performing arts
Music, classical
  Any disability: **Undergraduates,** 122; **Graduate students,** 246
  See also General programs; Music
Music education. See Education, music
Music, jazz
  Any disability: **Undergraduates,** 122; **Graduate students,** 246
  See also General programs; Music
Music therapy
  Any disability: **Undergraduates,** 74; **Graduate students,** 206
  See also General programs; Music
Musicology
  Any disability: **Undergraduates,** 74; **Graduate students,** 206
  See also General programs; Music

N

Narcotics. See Drug use and abuse
Natural history. See History, natural
Neuroscience
  Any disability: **Undergraduates,** 82; **Graduate students,** 147, 207, 212
  See also General programs; Medical sciences
Newspapers. See Journalism; Newsroom management
Newsroom management
  Families of the disabled: **Undergraduates,** 894
  See also General programs
Nuclear engineering. See Engineering, nuclear
Nuclear science
  Any disability: **Graduate students,** 225
  See also General programs; Physical sciences
Nurses and nursing, general
  Any disability: **Undergraduates,** 57; **Graduate students,** 193, 226
  Other disabilities/disorders: **Undergraduates,** 662; **Graduate students,** 826, 844
  Families of the disabled: **Undergraduates,** 985, 1090, 1111; **Graduate students,** 1157
  See also General programs; Health and health care; Medical sciences; names of specific nursing specialties
Nurses and nursing, occupational health
  Physical/orthopedic disabilities: **Undergraduates,** 478; **Graduate students,** 533
  See also General programs; Nurses and nursing, general

Nutrition
  Any disability: **Undergraduates,** 57; **Graduate students,** 193
  See also General programs; Medical sciences

O

Occupational health nurses and nursing. See Nurses and nursing, occupational health
Occupational safety
  Physical/orthopedic disabilities: **Undergraduates,** 478; **Graduate students,** 533
  See also Employment; General programs; Health and health care
Occupational therapy
  Any disability: **Undergraduates,** 57; **Graduate students,** 193
  See also Counseling; Employment; General programs
Ocean engineering. See Engineering, ocean
Oceanography
  Any disability: **Undergraduates,** 11; **Graduate students,** 143, 207
  See also General programs
Oncology. See Cancer
Opera. See Music; Voice
Optical engineering. See Engineering, optical
Osteopathy
  Any disability: **Graduate students,** 230
  See also General programs; Medical sciences

P

Painting
  Any disability: **Undergraduates,** 3
  Other disabilities/disorders: **Undergraduates,** 770; **Graduate students,** 874
  See also Art; General programs
Paleontology
  Any disability: **Graduate students,** 142, 207
  See also General programs; Geology
Patent law. See Intellectual property law
Performing arts
  Visual disabilities: **Undergraduates,** 288
  Hearing disabilities: **Undergraduates,** 443
  Other disabilities/disorders: **Undergraduates,** 669
  See also Fine arts; General programs; names of specific performing arts
Perfusion
  Any disability: **Undergraduates,** 57; **Graduate students,** 193
  See also General programs; Medical technology
Personnel administration
  Any disability: **Undergraduates,** 31
  See also General programs; Management
Pharmaceutical sciences
  Any disability: **Undergraduates,** 31, 57; **Graduate students,** 193
  Other disabilities/disorders: **Graduate students,** 826
  See also General programs; Medical sciences

Photography
Any disability: **Undergraduates,** 3
See also Fine arts; General programs

Photojournalism
Families of the disabled: **Undergraduates,** 894
See also General programs; Journalism; Photography

Physical sciences
Any disability: **Graduate students,** 217
Visual disabilities: **Undergraduates,** 345; **Graduate students,** 425
See also General programs; Sciences; names of specific physical sciences

Physical therapy
Any disability: **Undergraduates,** 57; **Graduate students,** 193
See also Disabilities; General programs; Health and health care; Rehabilitation

Physician assistant
Any disability: **Undergraduates,** 2, 57, 81, 89; **Graduate students,** 129, 193, 211, 215
See also General programs; Health and health care; Medical sciences

Physics
Any disability: **Undergraduates,** 16, 31; **Graduate students,** 152, 178, 207
See also General programs; Mathematics; Physical sciences

Poisons. *See* Toxicology

Police science. *See* Criminal justice

Political science and politics
Any disability: **Undergraduates,** 31; **Graduate students,** 183, 191
Hearing disabilities: **Graduate students,** 468
Families of the disabled: **Undergraduates,** 894
See also General programs; Public administration; Social sciences

Population studies
Any disability: **Graduate students,** 185
See also General programs; Social sciences

Preservation, historical. *See* Historical preservation

Presidents, U.S.. *See* History, American

Press. *See* Journalism

Print journalism. *See* Journalism

Prints. *See* Art

Psychology
Any disability: **Undergraduates,** 37; **Graduate students,** 144, 147, 165, 178, 185, 192
Visual disabilities: **Undergraduates,** 277
Physical/orthopedic disabilities: **Undergraduates,** 474
See also Behavioral sciences; Counseling; General programs; Social sciences

Public administration
Any disability: **Graduate students,** 201
Visual disabilities: **Graduate students,** 408
Hearing disabilities: **Graduate students,** 464
See also General programs; Management; Political science and politics; Social sciences

Public affairs. *See* Public administration

Public health
Any disability: **Undergraduates,** 1; **Graduate students,** 128
See also General programs; Health and health care

Public interest law
Any disability: **Graduate students,** 151
See also General programs; Law, general

Public policy. *See* Public administration

Public relations
Any disability: **Undergraduates,** 99
Families of the disabled: **Undergraduates,** 894, 1005
See also General programs; Marketing

Public sector. *See* Public administration

Publicity. *See* Public relations

R

Radio
Any disability: **Undergraduates,** 80; **Graduate students,** 210
See also Communications; General programs

Radiology
Any disability: **Undergraduates,** 57; **Graduate students,** 193
See also General programs; Medical sciences

Regional planning. *See* Urban and regional planning

Rehabilitation
Visual disabilities: **Undergraduates,** 259, 274, 282, 339, 352, 366; **Graduate students,** 377, 386, 389, 421, 431, 434, 438
See also General programs; Health and health care; names of specific types of therapy

Religion and religious activities
Any disability: **Graduate students,** 180, 191, 220, 242
Visual disabilities: **Graduate students,** 396
Hearing disabilities: **Graduate students,** 465-466, 468
See also General programs; Humanities

Religious education. *See* Education, religious

Respiratory therapy
Any disability: **Undergraduates,** 57; **Graduate students,** 193
See also General programs; Health and health care

Restaurants. *See* Food service industry

Retailing. *See* Sales

S

Safety studies
Physical/orthopedic disabilities: **Undergraduates,** 478; **Graduate students,** 533
See also Engineering, general; General programs

Sales
Any disability: **Undergraduates,** 99
See also General programs; Marketing

Schools. *See* Education

Science, history. *See* History, science

Sciences
   Any disability: **Undergraduates,** 52, 79, 105; **Graduate students,** 176, 179, 234
   Visual disabilities: **Undergraduates,** 277, 344; **Graduate students,** 424
   Hearing disabilities: **Undergraduates,** 443
   Other disabilities/disorders: **Undergraduates,** 635, 663, 685
   Families of the disabled: **Undergraduates,** 906, 986, 1002, 1079; **Graduate students,** 1143
   See also General programs; names of specific sciences

Sculpture
   Any disability: **Undergraduates,** 3
   Other disabilities/disorders: **Undergraduates,** 770; **Graduate students,** 874
   See also Fine arts; General programs

Secret service. *See* Intelligence service

Sight impairments. *See* Visual impairments

Singing. *See* Voice

Social sciences
   Any disability: **Undergraduates,** 75; **Graduate students,** 178, 198, 201
   See also General programs; names of specific social sciences

Social services
   Any disability: **Undergraduates,** 71
   See also General programs; Social work

Social work
   Any disability: **Undergraduates,** 57; **Graduate students,** 183, 193
   See also General programs; Social sciences

Sociology
   Any disability: **Graduate students,** 183
   See also General programs; Social sciences

Songs. *See* Music

Space sciences
   Any disability: **Undergraduates,** 77; **Graduate students,** 207-208
   See also General programs; Physical sciences

Special education. *See* Education, special

Speech impairments
   Any disability: **Graduate students,** 141
   See also Disabilities; General programs

Sports medicine
   Any disability: **Undergraduates,** 57; **Graduate students,** 193
   See also General programs; Medical sciences

Spying. *See* Intelligence service

Stage design. *See* Performing arts

Statistics
   Any disability: **Undergraduates,** 5, 16; **Graduate students,** 132, 152
   See also General programs; Mathematics

Substance abuse. *See* Drug use and abuse

Surgery
   Any disability: **Undergraduates,** 57; **Graduate students,** 193
   See also General programs; Medical sciences

Systems engineering. *See* Engineering, systems

T

Teaching. *See* Education

Technology
   Any disability: **Undergraduates,** 77, 79, 105; **Graduate students,** 208, 234
   Visual disabilities: **Undergraduates,** 277, 344; **Graduate students,** 424
   Other disabilities/disorders: **Undergraduates,** 685
   See also Computer sciences; General programs; Sciences

Technology law. *See* Computer law; Internet law

Television
   Any disability: **Undergraduates,** 63, 80; **Graduate students,** 199, 210
   See also Communications; Filmmaking; General programs

Textiles
   Any disability: **Undergraduates,** 99
   See also General programs

Theater. *See* Performing arts

Theology. *See* Religion and religious activities

Tourism
   Any disability: **Undergraduates,** 10; **Graduate students,** 139
   Families of the disabled: **Undergraduates,** 898; **Graduate students,** 1140
   See also General programs

Toxicology
   Any disability: **Undergraduates,** 31
   See also General programs; Medical sciences

Trademarks law. *See* Intellectual property law

Transportation
   Any disability: **Undergraduates,** 10; **Graduate students,** 139
   Families of the disabled: **Undergraduates,** 898; **Graduate students,** 1140
   See also Aviation; General programs; Space sciences

Travel and tourism. *See* Tourism

TV. *See* Television

U

Unrestricted programs. *See* General programs

Urban and regional planning
   Any disability: **Graduate students,** 183, 204
   See also General programs

V

Veterinary sciences
    Any disability: **Graduate students,** 230
    See also General programs; Sciences

Video. *See* Filmmaking; Television

Visual arts
    Any disability: **Undergraduates,** 121; **Graduate students,** 245
    Other disabilities/disorders: **Undergraduates,** 669, 748
    See also General programs; Humanities; names of specific visual arts

Visual impairments
    Visual disabilities: **Undergraduates,** 274, 339, 352, 366; **Graduate students,** 386, 421, 431, 434, 438
    See also Disabilities; General programs; Health and health care

Voice
    Any disability: **Undergraduates,** 56, 122; **Graduate students,** 246
    See also General programs; Music; Performing arts

W

Weather. *See* Climatology

Welfare. *See* Social services

Women's studies and programs
    Any disability: **Graduate students,** 191
    Hearing disabilities: **Graduate students,** 468
    See also General programs

Work. *See* Employment

Calendar Index

Since most financial aid programs have specific deadline dates, some may have already closed by the time you begin to look for funding. You can use the Calendar Index to identify which programs are still open. To do that, check the type of funding sections and disability categories that apply to you, think about when you'll be able to complete your application forms, go to the appropriate months, jot down the entry numbers listed there, and use those numbers to find the program descriptions in the directory. Keep in mind that the numbers cited here refer to program entry numbers, not to page numbers in the book.

Undergraduates

Any Disability:
January: 11-12, 33, 58, 63, 92, 118, 122-124
February: 15, 27, 36, 39, 43, 47, 56-57, 59-60, 65, 76, 78, 97, 112, 116-117
March: 8, 17-19, 22-23, 26, 30, 46, 50, 52, 55, 61-62, 70, 74-75, 90, 93-95, 108, 110, 126
April: 10, 34, 42, 69, 83-86, 91, 111
May: 2, 24-25, 28-29, 39-40, 48, 71, 79, 81, 87, 89, 96, 100-101, 119
June: 46, 48, 67, 80, 82, 99, 103-105, 121
July: 13, 35, 38, 48, 53, 64, 88, 109
August: 4, 9, 14, 20-21, 107
September: 6-7, 46
October: 18, 31, 34, 49, 96, 98
November: 1, 13, 44, 54, 115
December: 5, 16, 37, 45-46, 68, 73
Any time: 3, 32, 40-41, 51, 72, 114, 120
Deadline not specified: 66, 77, 102, 106, 113, 125, 127

Visual Disabilities:
January: 284, 305, 348, 362
February: 250, 255, 259-261, 268, 275, 282, 285, 292, 295, 297, 299, 302, 327, 338, 340, 351, 353-354, 357, 367
March: 251, 258, 270-271, 278-279, 281, 283, 290, 303, 306-307, 309, 321-322, 324, 329, 336, 341-344, 346, 358, 361, 363, 366, 368, 370
April: 257, 264, 266, 274, 280, 288, 300, 308, 310, 313-315, 319, 326, 345, 347, 349, 352, 360
May: 267, 272, 293, 298, 301, 317, 331, 338
June: 252-254, 265, 276, 304, 332, 335, 350
July: 256, 262, 269, 273, 277, 286-287, 289, 312, 323, 334, 339
August: 263, 294, 333, 338, 364
September: 296, 318, 320, 328, 330
November: 293, 338
December: 325, 365
Any time: 291
Deadline not specified: 311, 316, 337, 355-356, 359, 369

Hearing Disabilities:
February: 441, 444
March: 448, 451
April: 443, 445, 452, 455
May: 449, 456
June: 446, 450-451
September: 442, 447, 451
December: 451
Deadline not specified: 453-454, 457

Physical/Orthopedic Disabilities:
January: 479, 482, 488, 495, 509, 511
February: 476, 483, 485, 502, 522
March: 472, 494, 500, 508, 520, 524, 530
April: 477, 486, 492, 501, 504-506, 514, 523, 525, 527-528
May: 471, 475, 480, 493, 499, 507, 516, 518-519
June: 481, 487, 489-491, 497-498, 503, 510, 512, 521, 529
July: 496, 528
August: 484, 513
September: 472, 493
October: 527-528
November: 474, 478
December: 481, 515
Any time: 473

Deadline not specified: 517, 526

Other Disabilities/Disorders:
January: 556, 559, 568, 576, 581, 585-587, 593, 605, 643, 661, 697, 702, 765, 767, 787, 809
February: 591, 623, 626, 642, 693, 741, 749, 758-759, 761, 775, 781, 791-792
March: 557, 561, 563, 566, 569, 572, 575, 578, 582, 588-589, 592, 597, 599, 602, 604, 609, 613-614, 616, 620, 629, 634, 649, 657-660, 664, 666, 671, 674-675, 678-679, 681, 683, 685, 690, 698, 700-701, 708-710, 716, 719, 721, 724, 726-727, 729, 740, 743, 746-748, 750, 752, 754-755, 769, 780, 785, 788-789, 795, 801-802, 805-807
April: 570-571, 574, 579, 584, 590, 594, 596, 598, 603, 607, 611-612, 615, 617-618, 621-622, 624, 627, 631, 635, 638, 640, 646-648, 652, 656, 662-663, 668-669, 672-673, 682, 684, 687, 699, 705, 707, 712, 714, 717, 720, 723, 728, 738-739, 742, 744, 762, 768, 772, 776, 779, 784, 786-787, 790, 793-794, 798-799
May: 555, 565, 600-601, 619, 628, 637, 650, 653, 667, 670, 676, 691, 695, 722, 733, 735, 737, 751, 760, 770, 774, 782, 800, 803-804
June: 554, 569, 577, 580, 583, 625, 630, 632, 636, 639, 654-655, 696, 703, 711, 736, 745, 757, 764, 797, 808
July: 567, 606, 644, 665, 677, 688, 692, 715, 718, 730-731, 763, 766, 777, 796
August: 560, 573, 595, 610, 686, 706, 773, 783, 787
September: 564, 569, 641, 645, 683, 725
October: 588, 629
November: 558, 562, 636, 665, 694, 704, 715, 724, 771
December: 569, 583, 654-655, 680, 689, 703
Any time: 713, 732
Deadline not specified: 608, 633, 651, 734, 753, 756, 778

Families of the Disabled:
January: 952, 960, 1002, 1006, 1035, 1051, 1056, 1071
February: 889, 896, 903, 941, 951, 976-977, 989, 999, 1015, 1050, 1067, 1083, 1091-1092, 1105-1106, 1108-1109, 1111, 1122, 1125
March: 890-891, 900, 906, 909, 917, 920, 930, 934, 948, 953, 968, 970, 981-984, 987-988, 990, 993, 995, 1005, 1032, 1040, 1043, 1047, 1049, 1052-1053, 1058, 1082, 1084, 1086, 1088, 1097-1098, 1112, 1115, 1128, 1132, 1134-1135, 1137
April: 894, 898-899, 907-908, 921, 923, 925-927, 929, 932-933, 935, 939, 956, 961, 963-964, 967, 969, 985-986, 997-998, 1000, 1011-1012, 1014, 1018, 1020, 1027, 1029, 1033, 1036-1038, 1041, 1044, 1046, 1054, 1061, 1065, 1076-1078, 1080-1081, 1090, 1100, 1104, 1113-1114, 1121, 1126
May: 901-902, 910, 918-919, 942, 944, 954, 962, 971-972, 1008-1009, 1013, 1019, 1021, 1034, 1064, 1068-1069, 1087, 1093-1095, 1107, 1120, 1127
June: 895, 905, 911-912, 936, 958-959, 973, 976-977, 994, 1036, 1066, 1070, 1073, 1075, 1094, 1096, 1102, 1124, 1129-1130, 1135
July: 904, 928, 938, 943, 945, 950, 957, 965, 991, 1001, 1028, 1048, 1057, 1079, 1094, 1099, 1110
August: 1010, 1094
September: 955, 976-977, 1060
October: 921, 940, 1014, 1019, 1034, 1135
November: 992, 1025, 1039, 1052
December: 912, 940, 973, 996, 1028, 1079
Any time: 892, 916, 944, 947, 974, 1022-1023, 1026, 1062, 1083, 1117, 1119, 1131
Deadline not specified: 893, 897, 913-915, 922, 924, 931, 937, 946, 949, 966, 975, 978-980, 1003-1004, 1007, 1016-1017, 1024, 1030-1031, 1042, 1045, 1055, 1059, 1063, 1072, 1074, 1085, 1089, 1101, 1103, 1116, 1118, 1123, 1133, 1136

Graduate Students

Any Disability:
January: 133, 143, 149, 159, 162, 164, 170-171, 174, 181, 191, 197-199, 216, 219, 224-225, 231, 233, 238, 246
February: 134, 137, 167, 180, 193-194, 203-204, 209, 221-222, 242-243, 247
March: 130, 145, 153-154, 160, 176, 179, 183, 186, 190, 201, 206, 213, 218, 223
April: 139, 148, 163, 195, 226-230, 239, 249
May: 129, 141, 151, 157, 184, 192, 202, 211, 215, 220, 232
June: 134, 167, 203, 207, 210, 212, 245
July: 161, 168, 188, 214
August: 131, 138, 150, 155-156, 158, 196, 219, 226-230, 237
September: 135-136, 169, 177, 187, 235, 248
October: 134, 140, 146, 154, 163, 166-167, 178, 182, 184, 203, 217, 220, 240

November: 128, 144, 147, 172, 175, 185, 189, 200, 234, 241
December: 132, 142, 152, 165, 205, 226-230
Any time: 173, 244
Deadline not specified: 208, 236

Visual Disabilities:
January: 390, 403, 434, 436
February: 374, 377-378, 389, 391, 394, 396-397, 429, 432, 439
March: 371, 382-383, 387-388, 401, 404-405, 407, 413, 415, 419, 422-424, 426, 438, 440
April: 376, 386, 406, 409-410, 425, 427, 431
May: 381, 385, 398, 400, 417, 430
June: 372-373, 375, 380, 384, 402, 418, 428
July: 392-393, 399, 408, 421
August: 379, 395, 437
September: 411-412, 416

December: 414
Deadline not specified: 420, 433, 435

Hearing Disabilities:
January: 468
February: 459, 466
April: 458, 460, 462-465, 469
June: 461
September: 467
Deadline not specified: 470

Physical/Orthopedic Disabilities:
February: 536
March: 548, 553
April: 546-547
May: 531-532, 534, 542, 544, 551-552
June: 535, 537-538, 540, 543, 545, 549
August: 539, 550
September: 542
October: 541
November: 533
December: 535

Other Disabilities/Disorders:
January: 811, 815, 821-824, 827, 858, 870-871
February: 835, 882
March: 812, 816, 818, 833, 845-850, 852, 855, 857, 860-
  861, 863-864, 866-867, 873, 880, 884-887
April: 817, 832, 834, 840-841, 843-844, 876, 881, 883
May: 810, 837, 865, 874, 878
June: 816, 819-820, 836, 856, 862, 868-869, 872, 888
July: 814, 828, 839, 853, 859, 877
August: 825, 830-831, 875, 879
September: 813, 816, 826, 838
November: 864
December: 816, 820, 851, 854
Deadline not specified: 829, 842

Families of the Disabled:
February: 1154, 1160, 1189
March: 1141, 1143-1144, 1147, 1158-1159, 1161, 1163-
  1164, 1178, 1181-1184, 1190-1191, 1196, 1198, 1200-
  1201
April: 1140, 1151, 1157, 1166, 1169, 1175-1176, 1179,
  1187, 1192, 1194-1195
May: 1145, 1149-1150, 1153, 1167-1168, 1186
June: 1139, 1146, 1154, 1200
July: 1142, 1148, 1152, 1162, 1174, 1177
September: 1154
October: 1168, 1200
November: 1172, 1183
December: 1146, 1165, 1174
Any time: 1138, 1170, 1173, 1193, 1197
Deadline not specified: 1155-1156, 1171, 1180, 1185,
  1188, 1199